Morality in Practice

Fifth Edition

Edited by
JAMES P. STERBA
University of Notre Dame

Wadsworth Publishing Company

I(T)P® An International Thomson Publishing Company

Belmont • Albany • Bonn • Boston • Cincinnati • Detroit • London • Madrid • Melbourne
Mexico City • New York • Paris • San Francisco • Singapore • Tokyo • Toronto • Washington

Philosophy Editor: Peter Adams
Assistant Editor: Clay Glad
Editorial Assistant: Greg Brueck
Print Buyer: Barbara Britton
Permissions Editor: Robert Kauser
Copy Editor: Jennifer Lindsey
Illustration, Composition, & Production: Summerlight Creative
Printer: Quebecor Fairfield, Inc.

Printed in the United States of America
   3 4 5 6 7 8 9 10

For more information, contact Wadsworth Publishing Company:

Wadsworth Publishing Company
10 Davis Drive
Belmont, California 94002, USA

International Thomson Publishing Europe
Berkshire House 168-173
High Holborn
London, WC1V 7AA, England

Thomas Nelson Australia
102 Dodds Street
South Melbourne 3205
Victoria, Australia

Nelson Canada
1120 Birchmont Road
Scarborough, Ontario
Canada M1K 5G4

International Thomson Editores
Campos Eliseos 385, Piso 7
Col. Polanco
11560 México D.F. México

International Thomson Publishing GmbH
Königswinterer Strasse 418
53227 Bonn, Germany

International Thomson Publishing Asia
221 Henderson Road
#05-10 Henderson Building
Singapore 0315

International Thomson Publishing Japan
Hirakawacho Kyowa Building, 3F
2-2-1 Hirakawacho
Chiyoda-ku, Tokyo 102, Japan

Library of Congress Cataloging-in-Publication Data
Morality in practice. / edited by James P. Sterba. — 5th ed.
       p. cm.
   Includes bibliographical references.
   ISBN 0-534-50655-0
   1. Social ethics. I. Sterba, James P.
   HM216.M667 1997
   303.3′72-dc20   97-20524

*The book is again dedicated
to Sonya, now 16,
whose sense of what are moral problems
now far exceeds my own.*

Contents

Preface

A moral problems course tends to teach itself. It takes a really bad teacher to mess one up, but it can be done in at least three different ways:

1. By presenting just one set of views on various topics. (Students appreciate the need for fair play here.)
2. By encouraging students to hold a crude relativism. (Students know that all moral stances are not equally good.)
3. By not being relevant to student concerns. (Students can reasonably expect that, at the least, an ethics course will be relevant to their lives.)

This text enables teachers to avoid (1) by presenting radically opposed selections on all topics. It enables teachers to avoid (2) by suggesting through the introductions and the ordering and selection of topics how some views turn out to be more defensible than others. It enables teachers to avoid (3) by being the only moral problems text to provide in-depth coverage of a broad range of new and standard moral problems. In fact, no other moral problems text combines such breadth and depth. In addition, it has the following to recommend it.

New Features

1. Thirty-five new readings.
2. Three new sections: hate speech, gun control, and punishment and responsibility.
3. Two sections recast and revised: affirmative action and gay and lesbian rights.
4. Revisions of all other sections.

Retained Features

1. A general introduction provides background discussion of traditional moral approaches to ethics as well as an accessible answer to the question, Why be moral?
2. Section introductions set out the framework for the discussion and criticism of the articles in each section.
3. Brief summaries at the beginning of each article enable students to test and improve their comprehension.
4. Each section concludes with one or more articles discussing specific practical applications.
5. Suggestions for further reading are found at the end of each section.

In putting together this fifth edition, I have again benefited enormously from the advice and help of many different people. Very special thanks go to Melissa Barry, who did much of the library work tracking down articles for this edition. Thanks also go to Ken Clatterbaugh of Washington University, Nicholas Capaldi of the

University of Tulsa, John Carvino of the University of Texas, Preston Covey of Carnegie-Mellon University and Hugh LaFollette of East Tennessee University, and to my wife and fellow philosopher Janet Kourany. I also thank the following reviewers whose suggestions were especially helpful: Peter Dalton, Florida State University; Mark Perlman, Arizona State University; Edward F. Becker, University of Nebraska, Lincoln; Lesley Jacobs, York University; Sally Scholz, Villanova University; and Mark Van Hook, Ohio State University.

James P. Sterba
Notre Dame, Indiana

General Introduction

Most of us like to think of ourselves as just and moral people. To be truly such, however, we need to know something about the demands of justice and how they apply in our own particular circumstances. We should be able to assess, for example, whether our society's economic and legal systems are just—that is, whether the ways income and wealth are distributed in society as well as the methods of enforcing that distribution give people what they deserve. We should also consider whether other societal institutions, such as the military defense system, the education system, and the foreign aid program, are truly just. Without investigating these systems and coming to an informed opinion, we cannot say with any certainty that we are just and moral persons rather than perpetrators or beneficiaries of injustice.

This anthology has been created to help you acquire some of the knowledge you will need to justify your belief that you are a just and moral person. For this purpose, the anthology contains a wide spectrum of readings on thirteen important, contemporary, practical problems:

1. The problem of the distribution of income and wealth. (Who should control what resources within a society?)

2. The problem of near and distant peoples. (What obligations do we have to near and distant peoples?)

3. The problem of abortion and euthanasia. (Do fetuses have a right to life, and what should we do for the dying and those requiring life-sustaining medical treatment?)

4. The problem of sex equality. (Should the sexes be treated equally, and what constitutes equal treatment?)

5. The problem of affirmative action. (What specific policies are required to remedy discrimination and prejudice?)

6. The problem of sexual harassment. (What is sexual harassment and how can it be avoided?)

7. The problem of pornography. (Should pornography be prohibited because it promotes violence against women?)

8. The problem of hate speech. (What restrictions, if any, should there be on speech in society?)

9. The problem of gay and lesbian rights. (What rights should gays and lesbians have?)

10. The problem of gun control. (What restrictions should be placed on a citizen's right to own and carry guns?)

11. The problem of animal liberation and environmental justice. (What should our policies be for the treatment of animals and the environment?)
12. The problem of punishment and responsibility. (Who should be punished and of what should their punishment consist?)
13. The problem of war and humanitarian intervention. (What are the moral limits to the international use of force?)

Before you get into these problems, however, you should know what it means to take a moral approach to these issues and how such an approach is justified.

The Essential Features of a Moral Approach to Practical Problems

To begin with, a moral approach to practical problems must be distinguished from various nonmoral approaches. Nonmoral approaches to practical problems include the *legal approach* (what the law requires with respect to this practical problem), the *group-* or *self-interest approach* (what the group- or self-interest is for the parties affected by this problem), and the *scientific approach* (how this practical problem can best be accounted for or understood). To call these approaches nonmoral, of course, does not imply that they are immoral. All that is implied is that the requirements of these approaches may or may not accord with the requirements of morality.

What, then, essentially characterizes a moral approach to practical problems? I suggest that there are two essential features to such an approach:

1. The approach is prescriptive, that is, it issues in prescriptions, such as "do this" and "don't do that."

2. The approach's prescriptions are acceptable to everyone affected by them.

The first feature distinguishes a moral approach from a scientific approach because a scientific approach is not prescriptive. The second feature distinguishes a moral approach from both a legal approach and a group- or self-interest approach because the prescriptions that accord best with the law or serve the interest of particular groups or individuals may not be acceptable to everyone affected by them.

Here the notion of "acceptable" means "ought to be accepted" or "is reasonable to accept" and not simply "is capable of being accepted." Understood in this way, certain prescriptions may be acceptable even though they are not actually accepted by everyone affected by them. For example, a particular welfare program may be acceptable even though many people oppose it because it involves an increased tax burden. Likewise, certain prescriptions may be unacceptable even though they have been accepted by everyone affected by them. For example, it may be that most women have been socialized to accept prescriptions requiring them to fill certain social roles even though these prescriptions are unacceptable because they impose second-class status on them.

Alternative Moral Approaches to Practical Problems

Using the two essential features of a moral approach to practical problems, let us consider three principal alternative moral approaches to practical problems: a *Utilitarian Approach*, an *Aristotelian Approach*, and a *Kantian Approach*.[1] The basic principle of a Utilitarian Approach is:

Do those actions that maximize the net utility or satisfaction of everyone affected by them.

A Utilitarian Approach qualifies as a moral approach because it is prescriptive and because it can be argued that its prescriptions are acceptable to everyone affected by them since they take the utility or satisfaction of all those individuals equally into account.

To illustrate, let's consider how this approach applies to the question of whether nation A should intervene in the internal affairs of nation B when nation A's choice would have the following consequences:

	Nation A's Choice	
	Intervene	*Don't Intervene*
Net utility to A	4 trillion units	8½ trillion units
Net utility to B	2 trillion units	–2 trillion units
Total utility	6 trillion units	6½ trillion units

Given that these are all the consequences that are relevant to nation A's choice, a Utilitarian Approach favors not intervening. Note that in this case, the choice favoring a Utilitarian Approach does not conflict with the group-interest of nation A, although it does conflict with the group-interest of nation B.

But are such calculations of utility possible? Admittedly, they are difficult to make. At the same time, such calculations seem to serve as a basis for public discussion. Once President Reagan, addressing a group of Black business leaders, asked whether Blacks were better off because of the Great Society programs, and although many disagreed with the answer he gave, no one found his question unanswerable.[2] Thus, faced with the exigencies of measuring utility, a Utilitarian Approach simply counsels that we do our best to determine what maximizes net utility and act on the result.

The second approach to consider is an Aristotelian Approach. Its basic principle is:

Do those actions that would further one's proper development as a human being.

This approach also qualifies as a moral approach because it is prescriptive and because it can be argued that its prescriptions are acceptable to everyone affected by them.

There are, however, different versions of this approach. According to some versions, each person can determine through the use of reason his or her proper development as a human being. Other versions disagree. For example, many religious traditions rely on revelation to guide people in their proper development as human beings. However, although an Aristotelian Approach can take these various forms, I want to focus on what is probably its philosophically most interesting form. That form specifies proper development in terms of virtuous activity and understands virtuous activity to preclude intentionally doing evil that good may come of it. In this form, an Aristotelian Approach conflicts most radically with a Utilitarian Approach, which requires intentionally doing evil whenever a *greater* good would come of it.

The third approach to be considered is a Kantian Approach. This approach has its origins in seventeenth- and eighteenth-century social contract theories, which tended to rely on actual contracts to specify moral requirements. However, actual contracts may or may not have been made, and, even if they were made, they may or may not have been moral or fair. This led Immanuel Kant and contemporary Kantian John Rawls to resort to a hypothetical contract to ground moral requirements. A difficulty with this approach is in determining under what conditions a hypothetical contract is fair and moral. Currently, the most favored Kantian Approach is specified by the following basic principle:

Do those actions that persons behind an imaginary veil of ignorance would unanimously agree should be done.[3]

This imaginary veil extends to most particular facts about oneself—anything that would bias one's choice or stand in the way of a unanimous agreement. Accordingly, the imaginary veil of ignorance would mask one's knowledge of one's social position, talents, sex, race, and religion, but not one's knowledge of such general information as would be contained in political, social, economic, and psychological theories. A Kantian Approach qualifies as a moral approach because it is prescriptive and because it can be argued that its prescriptions would be acceptable to everyone affected by them since they would be agreed to by everyone affected behind an imaginary veil of ignorance.

To illustrate the approach, let's return to the example of nation A and nation B used earlier. The choice facing nation A was the following:

Nation A's Choice

	Intervene	Don't Intervene
Net utility to A	4 trillion units	8½ trillion units
Net utility to B	2 trillion units	–2 trillion units
Total utility	6 trillion units	6½ trillion units

Given that these are all the consequences relevant to nation A's choice, a Kantian Approach favors intervention because persons behind the imaginary veil of ignorance would have to consider that they might turn out to be in nation B, and in that case, they would not want to be so disadvantaged for the greater benefit of those in nation A. This resolution conflicts with the resolution favored by a Utilitarian Approach and the group-interest of nation A, but not with the group-interest of nation B.

Assessing Alternative Moral Approaches

Needless to say, each moral approach has its strengths and weaknesses. The main strength of a Utilitarian Approach is that once the relevant utilities are determined, there is an effective decision-making procedure that can be used to resolve all practical problems. After determining the relevant utilities, all that remains is to total the net utilities and choose the alternative with the highest net utility. The basic weakness of this approach, however, is that it does not give sufficient weight to the distribution of utility among the relevant parties. For example, consider a society equally divided between the Privileged Rich and the Alienated Poor who face the following alternatives:

Nation A's Choice

	Alternative A	Alternative B
Net utility to Privileged Rich	5½ trillion units	4 trillion units
Net utility to Alienated Poor	1 trillion units	2 trillion units
Total utility	6½ trillion units	6 trillion units

Given that these are all the relevant utilities, a Utilitarian Approach favors Alternative A even though Alternative B provides a higher minimum payoff. And if the utility values for two alternatives were:

Nation A's Choice

	Alternative A	Alternative B
Net utility to Privileged Rich	4 trillion units	5 trillion units
Net utility to Alienated Poor	2 trillion units	1 trillion units
Total utility	6½ trillion units	6 trillion units

A Utilitarian Approach would be indifferent between the alternatives, even though Alternative A provides a higher minimum payoff. In this way, a Utilitarian Approach fails to take into account the distribution of utility among the relevant parties. All that matters for this approach is maximizing total utility, and the distribution of utility among the affected parties is taken into account only insofar as it contributes toward the attainment of that goal.

By contrast, the main strength of an Aristotelian Approach in the form we are considering is that it limits the means that can be chosen in pursuit of good consequences. In particular, it absolutely prohibits intentionally doing evil that good may come of it. However, although some limit on the means available for the pursuit of good consequences seems desirable, the main weakness of this version of an Aristotelian Approach is that the limit it imposes is too strong. Indeed, exceptions to this limit would seem to be justified whenever the evil to be done is:

1. Trivial (e.g., stepping on someone's foot to get out of a crowded subway).
2. Easily reparable (e.g., lying to a temporarily depressed friend to keep her from committing suicide).
3. Sufficiently outweighed by the consequences of the action (e.g., shooting one of 200 civilian hostages to prevent in the only way possible the execution of all 200).

Still another weakness of this approach is that it lacks an effective decision-making procedure for resolving practical problems. Beyond imposing limits on the means that can be employed in the pursuit of good consequences, the advocates of this approach have not agreed on criteria for selecting among the available alternatives.

The main strength of a Kantian Approach is that like an Aristotelian Approach, it seeks to limit the means available for the pursuit of good consequences. However, unlike the version of the Aristotelian Approach we considered, a Kantian Approach does not impose an absolute limit on intentionally doing evil that good may come of it. Behind the veil of ignorance, persons would surely agree that if the evil were trivial, easily reparable, or sufficiently outweighed by the con-

sequences, there would be an adequate justification for permitting it. On the other hand, the main weakness of a Kantian Approach is that although it provides an effective decision-making procedure for resolving some practical problems, such as the problem of how to distribute income and wealth and the problem of near and distant peoples, a Kantian Approach cannot be applied to all problems. For example, it will not work for the problems of animal rights and abortion unless we assume that animals and fetuses should be behind the veil of ignorance.

So far, we have seen that prescriptivity and acceptability of prescriptions by everyone affected by them are the two essential features of a moral approach to practical problems, and we have considered three principal alternative approaches that qualify as moral approaches to these problems. Let's now examine what reasons there are for giving a moral approach to practical problems precedence over any nonmoral approach with which it conflicts.

The Justification for Following a Moral Approach to Practical Problems

To begin with, the ethical egoist, by denying the priority of morality over self-interest, presents the most serious challenge to a moral approach to practical problems. Basically, that challenge takes two forms: Individual Ethical Egoism and Universal Ethical Egoism. The basic principle of Individual Ethical Egoism is:

> Everyone ought to do what is in the overall self-interest of just one particular individual.

The basic principle of Universal Ethical Egoism is:

> Everyone ought to do what is in his or her overall self-interest.

Obviously, the prescriptions deriving from these two forms of egoism would conflict significantly with prescriptions following from a moral approach to practical problems. How then can we show that a moral approach is preferable to an egoist's approach?

In Individual Ethical Egoism, all prescriptions are based on the overall interests of just one particular individual. Let's call that individual Gladys. Because in Individual Ethical Egoism Gladys's interests constitute the sole basis for determining prescriptions, there should be no problem of inconsistent prescriptions, assuming, of course, that Gladys's own particular interests are in harmony. The crucial problem for Individual Ethical Egoism, however, is justifying that only Gladys's interests count in determining prescriptions. Individual Ethical Egoism must provide at least some reason for accepting that view. Otherwise, it would be irrational to accept the theory. But what reason or reasons could serve this function? Clearly, it will not do to cite as a reason some characteristic Gladys shares with other persons because whatever justification such a characteristic would provide for favoring Gladys's interests, it would also provide for favoring the interests of those other persons. Nor will it do to cite as a reason some unique characteristic of Gladys, such as knowing all of Shakespeare's writings by heart, because such a characteristic involves a comparative element, and consequently others with similar characteristics, like knowing some or most of Shakespeare's corpus by heart, would still have some justification, although a proportionally lesser justification, for having their interests favored. But again the proposed characteristic would not justify favoring only Gladys's interests.

A similar objection could be raised if a unique relational characteristic were proposed as a reason for Gladys's special status—such as that Gladys is Seymour's wife. Because other persons would have similar but not identical relational characteristics, similar but not identical reasons would hold for them. Nor will it do to argue that the reason for Gladys's special status is not the particular unique traits that she possesses, but rather the mere fact that she has unique traits. The same would hold true of everyone else. Every individual has unique traits. If recourse to unique traits is dropped and Gladys claims that she is special simply because she is herself and wants to further her own interests, every other person could claim the same.[4]

For the Individual Ethical Egoist to argue that the same or similar reasons do *not* hold for other peoples with the same or similar characteristics to those of Gladys, she must explain *why* they do not hold. It must always be possible to understand how a characteristic serves as a reason in one case but not in another. If no explanation can be provided, and in the case of Individual Ethical Egoism none has been forthcoming, the proposed characteristic either serves as a reason in both cases or does not serve as a reason at all.

Universal Ethical Egoism

Unfortunately, these objections to Individual Ethical Egoism do not work against Universal Ethical Egoism because Universal Ethical Egoism does provide a reason why the egoist should be concerned simply about maximizing his or her own interests, which is simply that the egoist is herself and wants to further her own interests. The Individual Ethical Egoist could not recognize such a reason without giving up her view, but the Universal Ethical Egoist is willing and able to universalize her claim and recognize that everyone has a similar justification for adopting Universal Ethical Egoism.

Accordingly, the objections that typically have been raised against Universal Ethical Egoism are designed to show that the view is fundamentally inconsistent. For the purpose of evaluating these objections, let's consider the case of Gary Gyges, an otherwise normal human being who, for reasons of personal gain, has embezzled $300,000 while working at People's National Bank and is in the process of escaping to a South Sea island where he will have the good fortune to live a pleasant life protected by the local authorities and untroubled by any qualms of conscience. Suppose that Hedda Hawkeye, a fellow employee, knows that Gyges has been embezzling money from the bank and is about to escape. Suppose, further, that it is in Hawkeye's overall self-interest to prevent Gyges from escaping with the embezzled money because she will be generously rewarded for doing so by being appointed vice-president of the bank. Given that it is in Gyges's overall self-interest to escape with the embezzled money, it now appears that we can derive a contradiction from the following:

1. Gyges ought to escape with the embezzled money.
2. Hawkeye ought to prevent Gyges from escaping with the embezzled money.
3. By preventing Gyges from escaping with the embezzled money, Hawkeye is preventing Gyges from doing what he ought to do.
4. One ought never to prevent someone from doing what he ought to do.
5. Thus, Hawkeye ought not to prevent Gyges from escaping with the embezzled money.

Because premise 2 and conclusion 5 are contradictory, Universal Ethical Egoism appears to be inconsistent.

The soundness of this argument depends, however, on premise 4, and defenders of Universal Ethical Egoism believe there are grounds for rejecting this premise. For if "preventing an action" means "rendering the action impossible," it would appear that there *are* cases in which a person is justified in preventing someone else from doing what he or she ought to do. Consider, for example, the following case. Suppose Irma

and Igor are both actively competing for the same position at a prestigious law firm. If Irma accepts the position, she obviously renders it impossible for Igor to obtain the position. But surely this is *not* what we normally think of as an unacceptable form of prevention. Nor would Hawkeye's prevention of Gyges's escape appear to be unacceptable. Thus, to sustain the argument against Universal Ethical Egoism, one must distinguish between acceptable and unacceptable forms of prevention and then show that the argument succeeds even for forms of prevention that a Universal Ethical Egoist would regard as unacceptable. This requires elucidating the force of "ought" in Universal Ethical Egoism.

To illustrate the sense in which a Universal Ethical Egoist claims that other persons ought to do what is in their overall self-interest, defenders often appeal to an analogy of competitive games. For example, in football a defensive player might think that the opposing team's quarterback ought to pass on third down with five yards to go, while not wanting the quarterback to do so and planning to prevent any such attempt. Or to use Jesse Kalin's example:

> I may see how my chess opponent can put my king in check. This is how he ought to move. But believing that he ought to move his bishop and check my king does not commit me to wanting him to do that, nor to persuading him to do so. What I ought to do is sit there quietly, hoping he does not move as he ought.[5]

The point of these examples is to suggest that a Universal Ethical Egoist may, like a player in a game, judge that others ought to do what is in their overall self-interest while simultaneously attempting to prevent such actions or at least refraining from encouraging them.

The analogy of competitive games also illustrates the sense in which a Universal Ethical Egoist claims that she herself ought to do what is in her overall self-interest. For just as a player's judgment that she ought to make a particular move is followed, other things being equal, by an attempt to perform the appropriate action, so likewise when a Universal Ethical Egoist judges that she ought to do some particular action, other things being equal, an attempt to perform the appropriate action follows. In general, defenders of Universal Ethical Egoism stress that because we have little difficulty understanding the implications of the use of "ought" in competitive games, we should also have little difficulty understanding the analogous use of "ought" by the Universal Ethical Egoist.

To claim, however, that the "oughts" in competitive games are analogous to the "oughts" of Universal Ethical Egoism does not mean there are no differences between them. Most important, competitive games are governed by moral constraints such that when everyone plays the game properly, there are acceptable moral limits as to what one can do. For example, in football one cannot poison the opposing quarterback in order to win the game. By contrast, when everyone holds self-interested reasons to be supreme, the only limit to what one can do is the point beyond which one ceases to benefit. But this important difference between the "oughts" of Universal Ethical Egoism and the "oughts" found in publicly recognized activities like competitive games does not defeat the appropriateness of the analogy. That the "oughts" found in publicly recognized activities are always limited by various moral constraints (what else would get publicly recognized?) does not preclude their being a suggestive model for the unlimited action-guiding character of the "oughts" of Universal Ethical Egoism.[6]

From Rationality to Morality

Although the most promising attempts to show that Universal Ethical Egoism is inconsistent have failed, the challenge the view presents to a moral approach to practical problems can still be turned aside. It can be shown that, although consistent, the egoist acts contrary to reason in rejecting a moral approach to practical problems.

To show this, let us begin by imagining that we are members of a society deliberating over what sort of principles governing action we should accept. Let us assume that each of us is capable of entertaining and acting on both self-interested and moral reasons and that the question we are seeking to answer is what sort of principles governing action it would be rational for us to accept.[7] This question is not about what sort of principles we should publicly affirm since people will sometimes publicly affirm principles that are quite different from those they are prepared to act on, but rather it is a question of what principles it would be rational for us to accept at the deepest level—in our heart of hearts.

Of course, there are people who are incapable of acting on moral reasons. For such people, there is no question about their being required to act morally or altruistically. But the interesting philosophical question is not about such people, but about people, like ourselves, who are capable of acting self-interestedly or morally and are seeking a rational justification for following one course of action over the others.

Obviously, from a self-interested perspective the only principles we should accept are those that can be derived from the following principle of Universal Ethical Egoism:

> Each person ought to do what best serves his or her overall self-interest.

But we can no more defend egoism by simply denying the relevance of moral reasons to rational choice than we can, by simply denying the relevance of self-interested reasons to rational choice, defend the view of pure altruism that the principles we should accept are those that can be derived from the following general principle of altruism:

Each person ought to do what best serves the overall interest of others.

Consequently, in order not to beg the question against either egoism or altruism, we seem to have no other alternative but to grant the *prima facie* relevance of both self-interested and moral reasons to rational choice and then try to determine which reasons we would be rationally required to act on, all things considered.

In this regard, there are two kinds of cases that must be considered. First, there are cases in which there is a conflict between the relevant self-interested and moral reasons.[8] Second, there are cases in which there is no such conflict.

Now it seems obvious that where there is no conflict, and both reasons are conclusive reasons of their kind, both reasons should be acted on. In such contexts, we should do what is favored both by morality and by self-interest.

Consider the following example. Suppose you accepted a job marketing a baby formula in underdeveloped countries where the formula was improperly used, leading to increased infant mortality.[9] Imagine that you could just as well have accepted an equally attractive and rewarding job marketing a similar formula in developed countries, where the misuse does not occur, so that a rational weighing of the relevant self-interested reasons alone would not have favored your acceptance of one of these jobs over the other.[10] At the same time, there were obviously moral reasons that condemned your acceptance of the first job—reasons that you presumably are or were able to acquire. Moreover, by assumption in this case, the moral reasons do not clash with the relevant self-interested reasons; they simply made a recommendation where the relevant self-interested reasons are silent. Consequently, a rational weighing of all the relevant reasons in this case could not but favor acting in accord with the relevant moral reasons.[11]

Yet it might be objected that in cases of this sort there would frequently be other reasons significantly opposed to these moral reasons—other reasons that you are or were able to acquire. Such reasons would be *malevolent* reasons seeking to bring about the suffering and death of other human beings, or *benevolent* reasons concerned to promote nonhuman welfare even at the expense of human welfare, or *aesthetic* reasons concerned to produce valuable results irrespective of the effects on human or nonhuman welfare. But assuming that such malevolent reasons are ultimately rooted in some conception of what is good for oneself or others,[12] these reasons would have already been taken into account, and by assumption outweighed by the other relevant reasons in this case. And although neither benevolent reasons (concerned to promote nonhuman welfare) nor aesthetic reasons would have been taken into account, such reasons are not directly relevant to justifying morality over rational egoism.[13] Consequently, even with the presence of these three kinds of reasons, your acceptance of the first job can still be seen to be contrary to the relevant reasons in this case.

Needless to say, defenders of rational egoism cannot but be disconcerted with this result since it shows that actions that accord with rational egoism are contrary to reason at least when there are two equally good ways of pursuing one's self-interest, only one of which does not conflict with the basic requirements of morality. Notice also that in cases where there are two equally good ways of fulfilling the basic requirements of morality, only one of which does not conflict with what is in a person's overall self-interest, it is not at all disconcerting for defenders of morality to admit that we are rationally required to choose the way that does not conflict with what is in our overall self-interest. Nevertheless, exposing this defect in rational egoism for cases where moral reasons and self-interested reasons do not conflict would be but a small victory for defenders of morality if it were not also possible to show that in cases where such reasons do conflict, moral reasons have priority over self-interested reasons.

Now when we rationally assess the relevant reasons in such conflict cases, it is best to cast the conflict not as a conflict between self-interested reasons and moral reasons but instead as a conflict between self-interested reasons and altruistic reasons.[14] Viewed in this way, three solutions are possible. First, we could say that self-interested reasons always have priority over conflicting altruistic reasons. Second, we could say just the opposite, that altruistic reasons always have priority over conflicting self-interested reasons. Third, we could say that some kind of a compromise is rationally required. In this compromise, sometimes self-interested reasons would have priority over altruistic reasons and sometimes altruistic reasons would have priority over self-interested reasons.

Once the conflict is described in this manner, the third solution can be seen to be the one that is rationally required. This is because the first and second solutions give exclusive priority to one class of relevant reasons over the other, and only a completely question-begging justification can be given for such an exclusive priority. Only the third solution, by sometimes giving priority to self-interested reasons and sometimes giving priority to altruistic reasons, can avoid a completely question-begging resolution.

Consider the following example. Suppose you are in the waste disposal business and you decided to dispose of toxic wastes in a manner that was cost-efficient for you but predictably caused significant harm to future generations. Imagine that there were alternative methods available for disposing of the waste that were only slightly less cost-efficient and which did not cause any significant harm to future generations.[15] In this case, you are to weigh your self-interested reasons favoring the most cost-efficient disposal of the toxic wastes against the relevant altruistic reasons favoring the avoidance of significant harm to future generations. If we suppose that the projected loss of benefit to yourself was ever so slight and the projected harm to future generations was ever so great, then a nonarbitrary compromise between the relevant self-interested and altruistic reasons would have to favor the altruistic reasons in this case. Hence, as judged by a non–question-begging standard of rationality, your method of waste disposal was contrary to the relevant reasons.

Notice also that this standard of rationality would not support just any compromise between the relevant self-interested and altruistic reasons. The compromise must be a nonarbitrary one, for otherwise it would beg the question with respect to the opposing egoistic and altruistic views. Such a compromise would have to respect the rankings of self-interested and altruistic reasons imposed by the egoist and altruistic views, respectively. Since for each individual there is a separate ranking of that individual's relevant self-interested and altruistic reasons, we can represent these rankings from the most important reasons to the least important reasons as shown in the table below.

Individual A	
Self-Interested Reasons	*Altruistic Reasons*
1	1
2	2
3	3
⋮	⋮
N	N

Individual B	
Self-Interested Reasons	*Altruistic Reasons*
1	1
2	2
3	3
⋮	⋮
N	N

Accordingly, any nonarbitrary compromise among such reasons in seeking not to beg the question against egoism or altruism will have to give priority to those reasons that rank highest in each category. Failure to give priority to the highest-ranking altruistic or self-interested reasons would, other things being equal, be contrary to reason.

Of course, there will be cases in which the only way to avoid being required to do what is contrary to your highest-ranking reasons is by requiring someone else to do what is contrary to her highest-ranking reasons. Such cases are sometimes called "lifeboat cases." But while such cases are surely difficult to resolve (maybe only a chance mechanism can offer a reasonable resolution), they surely do not reflect the typical conflict between the relevant self-interested and altruistic reasons that we are or were able to acquire. For typically one or the other of the conflicting reasons will rank higher on its respective scale, thus permitting a clear resolution.

Now it is important to see how morality can be viewed as just such a nonarbitrary compromise between self-interested and altruistic reasons. First of all, a certain amount of self-regard is morally required or at least morally acceptable. Where this is the case, high-ranking self-interested reasons have priority over low-ranking altruistic reasons. Second, morality obviously places limits on the extent to which people should pursue their own self-interest. Where this is the case, high-ranking altruistic reasons have priority over low-ranking self-interested reasons. In this way, morality can be seen to be a nonarbitrary compromise between self-interested and altruistic reasons, and the "moral reasons" which constitute that compromise can be seen as having an absolute priority over the self-interested or altruistic reasons that conflict with them.

Of course, exactly how this compromise is to be worked out is a matter of considerable debate.

A Utilitarian Approach favors one sort of resolution, an Aristotelian Approach another, and a Kantian Approach yet another. However, irrespective of how this debate is best resolved, it is clear that some sort of a compromise view or moral solution is rationally preferable to either ethical egoism or pure altruism when judged from a non–question-begging standpoint.[16]

The Interconnectedness of Moral Solutions to Practical Problems

Given this justification for following a moral approach to practical problems, we are in a good position to begin examining the thirteen practical problems covered in this anthology. Each section contains readings defending radically opposing solutions to the problem at hand, as well as one or more readings discussing specific practical applications. Working through these readings should give you a more informed view about the demands morality places on us with respect to each of these practical problems.

Even if you do not cover all of these practical problems, you should still come to appreciate why a solution to any one of them requires solutions to the others as well. That is to say, the readings on the distribution of income and wealth (in Section I) may help you to characterize a morally defensible system for distributing income and wealth within a society, but you would still not know fully how to apply such a system in a particular society without also inquiring how just that society is with respect to the other problem areas covered by this anthology.

Or suppose justice requires us to provide for the basic nutritional needs of distant peoples as well as for people within our own society. (See the readings in Section II.) Such a requirement would at least restrict the use of nonrenewable resources to satisfy the nonbasic or luxury needs of persons within our society—a use that might otherwise be permitted by a morally defensible system for distributing income and wealth within our society.

Further moral restrictions on the satisfaction of nonbasic or luxury needs could arise from a correct determination of who has a right to life. For example, if fetuses have a right to life, many of us may be morally required to sacrifice the satisfaction of certain nonbasic or luxury needs to bring fetuses to term. If, by contrast, euthanasia can be morally justified, scarce resources that are now used to sustain human life could be freed for other purposes. (See the readings in Section III.)

Justice also may demand that we sacrifice some nonbasic or luxury needs to satisfy the requirements of sex equality and remedy past discrimination, prejudice, and harassment. For example, at the cost of considerable redistribution, we may be required to provide women with the same opportunities for self-development that are now open to men. (See the readings in Sections IV and VI.) We may also be required to turn away qualified candidates for medical schools and law schools so that other candidates who have suffered past injustices may be compensated by admission to these schools. (See the readings in Section V.) Obviously, a radical solution to the problem of pornography prohibiting its distribution would affect those who derive their income from that eight-billion-dollar-a-year industry. (See the readings in Section VII.) In addition, restrictions on who can own and carry a gun would affect those who derive their income from the sale of weapons to the civilian population. (See the readings in Section X.)

Moral restrictions on the satisfaction of nonbasic needs and even on the way basic needs are satisfied could arise from a determination of what obligations, if any, we have to animals and the environment. For example, if vegetarianism were morally required, and recognized as such, the impact on our lives would be far-reaching. (See the readings in Section XI.)

Similarly, the legitimate costs of legal enforcement must ultimately enter into any calculation of who gets to keep what in society. This will require a solution to the problem of punishment and responsibility. (See the readings in Section XII.)

A solution to the problem of punishment and responsibility, in turn, presupposes solutions to the other practical problems discussed in this anthology. Suppose that in a society with a just distribution of income and wealth, persons who put forth their best efforts receive a yearly income of at least $15,000. (If you think a just distribution of income would provide some other amount, plug that amount in and make the corresponding adjustments in subsequent figures.) Further suppose that the society in which you and I live has an unjust distribution of income and wealth because, although there are enough resources for a just distribution, many persons who put forth their best efforts receive no more than $8,000 per year, whereas others receive as much as $500,000. Let's say that your income is $500,000 and mine is only $8,000, even though I have tried every legal way to increase my income. Assume also that any resort to civil disobedience or armed revolution would be ineffectual and too costly for me personally. If I then rob you of $7,000, thus bringing my yearly income up to the just allotment of $15,000, what would a morally defensible system of punishment and responsibility do to me if I were caught? To require a punishment equal in severity to the $7,000 I took simply reinforces an unjust distribution of income and wealth. So it seems that only a fairly light punishment or no punishment at all should be required.[17] This example shows that the application of a morally defensible solution to the problem of punishment and responsibility depends on a solution to the problem of the distribution of income and wealth in a society. To know, therefore, how to apply a morally defensible system of punishment and responsibility in a particular society, you must know to what degree that society incorporates a morally defensible distribution of income and wealth.

Finally, as we in the United States are painfully aware at the present time, proposed allocations for distributing income and wealth through social welfare programs can come into conflict with proposed allocations for defense and humanitarian intervention. Many people have argued that when this happens we must sacrifice social welfare programs to meet the requirements of defense and humanitarian intervention, but many other people have disagreed. Obviously, then, to know exactly how your solutions to the other problem areas treated in this anthology should be applied in a particular society, you also need to know what are the moral limits to the international use of force. (See the readings in Section XIII.)

Many of these practical problems are also interconnected because they deal with the general question of how free people should be. Specifically, the practical problems address the following questions: Should people be free to keep for themselves all they produce? (See the readings in Sections I and II.) Should people be free to enjoy pornography? (See the readings in Section VII.) Should people be free to engage in (not be punished for) hate speech? (See the readings in Section VIII.) Should people be free from legal penalty and from moral condemnation to engage in sodomy? (See the readings in Section IX.) Should people be free to possess guns for self-defense? (See the readings in Section X.)

Put briefly, what is required (or permitted) by a morally defensible solution to the problem of the distribution of income and wealth within a society will depend on what is required (or permitted) by morally defensible solutions to the problems of near and distant peoples, abortion and euthanasia, sex equality, affirmative action, sexual harassment, pornography, hate speech, gay and lesbian rights, gun control, animal liberation and environmental justice, punishment and responsibility, and war and humanitarian intervention. This means that any solution you might devise to one of these problems is only provisional until you can determine solutions to the others as well. And even if you are unable at the moment to devise solutions to all of these practical problems (because, for example, the course you are now taking is only considering some of them), you must still acknowledge that in the final analysis your solutions to these practical problems will have to be interconnected.

Note, too, that acknowledging the interconnectedness of the solutions to these practical problems does not presuppose a commitment to any particular political or moral ideal. For example, whether you tend to be a libertarian, a welfare liberal, a socialist, or anything else, the interconnectedness of the solutions to the practical problems we are discussing still holds true. Individuals who endorse different political and moral ideals will presumably devise different solutions to these practical problems, but the solutions will still be interconnected.

Working through the readings in this anthology will not always be an easy task. Some articles will be clear on the first reading, whereas others will require closer scrutiny. You should also make sure you give each selection a fair hearing, because although some will accord with your current views, others will not. It is important that you evaluate the latter with an open mind, allowing for the possibility that after sufficient reflection you may come to view them as the most morally defensible. Indeed, to approach the selections of this anthology in any other way would surely undermine the grounds you have for thinking you are a just and moral person.

Endnotes

1. Obviously, other moral approaches to practical problems could be distinguished, but I think the three I consider reflect the range of possible approaches that are relevant to the resolution of these problems.

2. In fact, the debate as to whether Blacks are better off now because of the programs of the Great Society has taken a more scholarly turn. See Charles Murray, *Losing Ground* (New York: Basic Books, 1984), and Christopher Jencks, "How Poor Are the Poor?" *New York Review of Books,* May 9, 1985.

3. See Section II of this text and my book, *The Demands of Justice* (Notre Dame: University of Notre Dame Press, 1980), especially Chapter 2.

4. For further argument on this point, see Marcus Singer, *Generalization in Ethics* (New York: Alfred A. Knopf, 1961), Chapter 2, and Alan Gewirth, "The Non-Trivializability of Universalizability," *Australasian Journal of Philosophy* (1969), pp. 123–131.

5. Jesse Kalin, "In Defense of Egoism," in *Morality and Rational Self-Interest,* ed. David Gauthier (Englewood Cliffs, N.J.: Prentice-Hall, 1970), pp. 73–74.

6. For additional reasons why ethical egoism is a consistent view, see my article, "Ethical Egoism and Beyond," *Canadian Journal of Philosophy* (1979), pp. 91–108.

7. "Ought" presupposes "can" here. Unless the members of the society have the capacity to entertain and follow both self-interested and moral reasons for acting, it does not make any sense to ask whether they ought or ought not to do so.

8. For an account of what counts as *relevant* self-interested or moral reasons, see my *How to Make People Just* (Totowa, N.J.: Rowman and Allanheld, 1988), pp. 165–166.

9. For a discussion of the causal links involved here, see *Marketing and Promotion of Infant Formula in Development Countries.* Hearing before the Subcommittee of Interna-

tional Economic Policy and Trade of the Committee on Foreign Affairs, U.S. House of Representatives, 1980. See also Maggie McComas et al., *The Dilemma of Third World Nutrition* (1983).

10. Assume that both jobs have the same beneficial effects on the interests of others.

11. I am assuming that acting contrary to reason is an important failing with respect to the requirements of reason, and that there are many ways of not acting in (perfect) accord with reason that do not constitute acting contrary to reason.

12. Otherwise, they would really fall under the classification of aesthetic reasons.

13. Of course, such reasons would have to be taken into account at some point in a complete justification for morality, but the method of integrating such reasons into a complete justification of morality would simply parallel the method already used for integrating self-interested and altruistic reasons.

14. This is because, as I shall argue, morality itself already represents a compromise between egoism and altruism. So to ask that moral reasons be weighed against self-interested reasons is, in effect, to count self-interested reasons twice—once in the compromise between egoism and altruism and then again when moral reasons are weighed against self-interested reasons. But to count self-interested reasons twice is clearly objectionable.

15. Assume that all these methods of waste disposal have roughly the same amount of beneficial effects on the interests of others.

16. For further argument, see my article, "Justifying Morality: The Right and the Wrong Ways" (Kurt Baier Festschift) *Syntheses* (1987), vol. 1, pp. 45–70.

17. For further argument, see my article, "Is There a Rationale for Punishment?" *Philosophical Topics* (1990), pp. 105–125.

The Distribution of Income and Wealth

Introduction

Basic Concepts

The problem of the distribution of income and wealth within a society has traditionally been referred to as the problem of distributive justice. Less frequently, this problem has included the distribution of other social goods (for example, political freedoms such as speech and press) and sometimes distribution on a worldwide scale. Most philosophers, however, agree that the distribution of income and wealth within a specific society is at the heart of the problem of distributive justice.

Just as traditionally, a variety of solutions have been proposed to the problem of distributive justice. Before examining some solutions, let's observe what they all have in common.

First, even though the solutions may differ as to exactly how much income and wealth people deserve or should rightfully possess, they all purport to tell us what people deserve or have a right to possess. For example, some solutions propose that people deserve to have their needs fulfilled, whereas others state that what people deserve or should rightfully possess is what they can produce by their labor.

Second, all solutions to the problem of distributive justice distinguish between justice and charity. *Justice* is what we should do as a matter of obligation or duty, whereas *charity* is what we should do if we want to choose the morally best possible action available. Accordingly, the demands of charity go beyond duty. In addition, failure to fulfill the demands of justice is blameworthy, violates someone's rights, and can legitimately be punished. By contrast, failure to fulfill the demands of charity, although not ideal, is not blameworthy, does not violate anyone's rights, and cannot legitimately be punished. Some solutions to the problem of distributive justice give more scope to justice and less to charity, whereas others do just the opposite.

Turning from common ground to disputed territory, solutions offered to the problem of distributive justice have appealed to many political ideals. In our own time, libertarians have appealed to an ideal of liberty, socialists to an ideal of equality, and welfare liberals to an ideal of contractual fairness.

Libertarianism

Libertarians such as John Hospers (see Selection 1) take liberty as the ultimate political ideal and typically define liberty as "the state of being unconstrained by other persons from doing what one wants." This definition limits the scope of liberty in two ways. First, not all constraints, whatever the source, count as a restriction of liberty; the constraints must come from other persons. For example, people who are constrained by natural forces from getting to the top of Mount Everest do not lack liberty in this regard. Second, the constraints must run counter to people's wants. Thus, people who do not want to hear Beethoven's Fifth Symphony do not feel their liberty is restricted when other people forbid its performance, even though the proscription does in fact constrain what they are able to do.

Of course, libertarians may argue that these constraints do restrict a person's liberty because people normally want to be unconstrained by others. But other philosophers have claimed that such constraints point to a serious defect in the libertarian's definition of liberty, which can only be remedied by defining liberty more broadly as "the state of being unconstrained by other persons from doing what one is able to do." If we apply this revised definition to the previous example, we find that people's liberty to hear Beethoven's Fifth Symphony would be restricted even if they did not want to hear it (and even if, perchance, they did not want to be unconstrained by others), because other people would still be constraining them from doing what they are able to do.

Confident that problems of defining liberty can be overcome in some satisfactory manner, libertarians go on to characterize their political ideal as requiring that each person should have the greatest amount of liberty commensurate with the same liberty for all. From this ideal, libertarians claim that several more specific requirements—in particular, a right to life; a right to freedom of speech, press, and assembly; and a right to property—can be derived.

It is important to note that the libertarian's right to life is not a right to receive from others the goods and resources necessary for preserving one's life; it is simply a right not to be killed. So understood, the right to life is not a right to welfare. In fact, there are no welfare rights in the libertarian view. Accordingly, the libertarian's

understanding of the right to property is not a right to receive from others the goods and resources necessary for one's welfare, but rather a right to acquire goods and resources either by initial acquisition or by voluntary agreement.

Obviously, by defending rights such as these, libertarians can only support a limited role for government. That role is simply to prevent and punish initial acts of coercion—the only wrongful actions for libertarians.

Libertarians do not deny that it is a good thing for people to have sufficient goods and resources to meet at least their basic nutritional needs, but libertarians do deny that government has a duty to provide for such needs. Some good things, such as the provision of welfare to the needy, are requirements of charity rather than justice, libertarians claim. Accordingly, failure to make such provisions is neither blameworthy nor punishable.

A basic difficulty with the libertarian solution to the problem of distributive justice as defended by Hospers is the claim that rights to life and property (as the libertarian understands these rights) derive from an ideal of liberty. Why should we think that an ideal of liberty requires a right to life and a right to property that excludes a right to welfare? Surely a right to property might well justify a rich person's depriving a poor person of the liberty to acquire the goods and resources necessary for meeting his or her basic nutritional needs. How then could we appeal to an ideal of liberty to justify such a deprivation? In Selection 4, James P. Sterba argues that we cannot.

Socialist Justice

In contrast with libertarians, socialists take equality to be the ultimate political ideal and contend that the fundamental rights and duties in a society are determined by this ideal. More specifically, socialists defend an ideal that calls for equality of need fulfillment. As Kai Nielson contends (Selection 2), radical egalitarianism is justified because it produces the conditions for the most extensive satisfaction of everyone's needs.

At first hearing, this ideal might sound simply crazy to someone brought up in a capitalist society. The obvious problem is how to get persons to put forth their best effort if income will be distributed on the basis of individual need rather than individual contribution.

The socialist answer is to make work that must be done as enjoyable in itself as possible. Thus, people will want to do the work they are capable of doing because they find it intrinsically rewarding. For a start, socialists might try to convince workers to accept lower salaries for existing jobs that are intrinsically rewarding. For example, they might ask top executives to work for $300,000 a year rather than $600,000. Yet socialists ultimately hope to make all jobs intrinsically as rewarding as possible so that, after people no longer work primarily for external rewards when making their best contributions to society, distribution can proceed on the basis of need.

Socialists propose to implement their ideal of equality by giving workers democratic control over the workplace: If workers have more to say about how they do their work, they will find their work intrinsically more rewarding. As a consequence, they will be more motivated to work, because their work itself will be meeting their needs. Socialists believe that extending democracy to the workplace will necessarily lead to socialization of the means of production and the end of private property.

However, even with democratic control of the workplace, some jobs, such as collecting garbage or changing bedpans, probably can't be made intrinsically rewarding. What socialists propose to do with respect to such jobs is to divide them up in some equitable manner. Some people might, for example, collect garbage one day a week and then work at intrinsically rewarding jobs the rest of the week. Others would change bedpans or do some other slop job one day a week and then work at an intrinsically rewarding job the other days of the week. By making jobs intrinsically as rewarding as possible, in part through democratic control of the workplace and an equitable assignment of unrewarding tasks, socialists believe people will contribute according to their abilities even when distribution proceeds according to need.

Finally, it is important to note that the socialist ideal of equality does not accord with what existed in the Soviet Union or Eastern Europe under Communism. Judging the acceptability of the socialist ideal of equality by what took place in those countries would be as unfair as judging the acceptability of the libertarian ideal of liberty by what took place in Chile under Pinochet or South Africa under apartheid, where citizens were arrested and imprisoned without cause. By analogy, it would be like judging the merits of college football by the way Vanderbilt's or Northwestern's teams play rather than by the way Miami's or Notre Dame's teams play. Actually, a fairer comparison would be to judge the socialist ideal of equality by what takes place in countries like Sweden and to judge the libertarian ideal of liberty by what takes place in the United States. Even these comparisons, however, are not wholly appropriate because none of these countries fully conforms to those ideals.

To justify the ideal of equality, Kai Nielson argues that it is required by liberty or at least by a fair distribution of liberty. By "liberty" Nielson means both "positive liberty to receive certain goods" and "negative liberty not to be interfered with," so his argument for liberty will not have much weight with libertarians, who only value negative liberty. Rather, his argument is directed primarily at welfare liberals, who value both positive and negative liberty as well as a fair distribution of liberty.

Another basic difficulty with Nielson's socialist solution to the problem of distributive justice is the proclaimed necessity of abolishing private property and socializing the means of production. It seems possible to give workers more control over the workplace while at the same time allowing the means of production to remain privately owned. Of course, private ownership would have a somewhat different character in a society with democratic control of the workplace, but it need not cease to be private ownership. After all, private ownership would also have a somewhat different character in a society where private holdings, and hence bargaining power, were distributed more equally than is found in most capitalist societies, yet it would not cease to be private ownership. Accordingly, we could imagine a society where the means of production are privately owned but where—because ownership is so widely dispersed throughout the society (e.g., nearly everyone owns ten shares of major industrial stock and no one more than twenty shares) and because of the degree of democratic control of the workplace—many of the valid criticisms socialists make of existing capitalist societies would no longer apply.

Welfare Liberalism

In contrast with libertarians and socialists, welfare liberals, such as John Rawls (Selection 3), take contractual fairness to be the ultimate political ideal and contend that the fundamental rights and duties in a society are those that people would agree to under fair conditions.

Note that welfare liberals do not say that the fundamental rights and duties in a society are those to which people actually do agree, because these might not be fair at all. For example, people might agree to a certain system of fundamental rights and duties because they have been forced to do so or because their only alternative is starving to death. Thus, actual agreement is neither sufficient nor necessary for determining an adequate conception of justice. According to welfare liberals, what is necessary and sufficient is that people would agree to such rights and duties under fair conditions.

But what are fair conditions? According to John Rawls, fair conditions can be expressed by an "original position" in which people are concerned to advance their own interests behind a "veil of ignorance." The effect of the veil of ignorance is to deprive people in the original position of the knowledge they would need to advance their own interests in ways that are morally arbitrary.

Rawls presents the principles of justice he believes would be derived in the original position in two successive formulations. The first formulation is as follows:

I. Special conception of justice
  1. Each person is to have an equal right to the most extensive basic liberty compatible with a similar liberty for others.
  2. Social and economic inequalities are to be arranged so that they are (a) reasonably expected to be to everyone's advantage and (b) attached to positions and offices open to all.

II. General conception of justice
   All social values—liberty and opportunity, income and wealth, and the bases of self-respect—are to be distributed equally unless an unequal distribution of any or all of these values is to everyone's advantage.

Later these principles are more accurately formulated as:

I. Special conception of justice
  1. Each person is to have an equal right to the most extensive total system of equal basic liberties compatible with a similar system of liberty for all.
  2. Social and economic inequalities are to be arranged so that they are (a) to the greatest benefit of the least advantaged, consistent with the just savings principle, and (b) attached to offices and positions open to all under conditions of fair equality of opportunity.

II. General conception of justice

All social goods—liberty and opportunity, income and wealth, and the bases of self-respect—are to be distributed equally unless an unequal distribution of any or all of these goods is to the advantage of the least favored.

Under both formulations, the general conception of justice differs from the special conception of justice by allowing trade-offs between liberty and other social goods. According to Rawls, persons in the original position would want the special conception of justice to be applied in place of the general conception of justice whenever social conditions allowed all representative persons to exercise their basic liberties.

Rawls holds that these principles of justice would be chosen in the original position because persons so situated would find it reasonable to follow the conservative dictates of a "maximin strategy" and thereby secure for themselves the highest minimum payoff.

Rawls's defense of a welfare liberal conception of justice has been challenged in a variety of ways. Some critics have endorsed his contractual approach while disagreeing with him over what principles of justice would be thereby derived. These critics usually attempt to undermine the use of a maximin strategy in the original position.[1] Others, however, have found fault with the contractual approach itself. Libertarians, for example, challenge the moral adequacy of the very ideal of contractual fairness.

This second challenge to the ideal of contractual fairness is potentially more damaging because, if valid, it would force supporters to embrace some other political ideal. This challenge, however, fails if it can be shown, as James P. Sterba argues in Selection 4, that the libertarian's own ideal of liberty, when correctly interpreted, leads to a universal right to welfare usually associated with the welfare liberal's ideal of contractual fairness. But Sterba's argument also raises a problem for the welfare liberal because

he shows that recognition of this universal right to welfare leads to the equalization of resources that is characteristic of a socialist state.

Practical Applications

The application of the ideals of libertarianism, socialism, or welfare liberalism to a particular society obviously has basic and far-reaching effects. These ideals have implications for constitutional structure, the control of industry, taxing policy, social welfare programs, property law, and much more. The next two readings in this section are from important U.S. Supreme Court decisions to which our three political ideals can be usefully related.

The Supreme Court, of course, does not view itself as directly applying one or the other of these political ideals to the laws of the land. Rather the Court views itself as deciding whether particular laws accord with the provisions of the U.S. Constitution. However, most people, including Supreme Court justices, do not clearly separate their views about what are the practical applications of the political ideal they take to be the most morally defensible from their views about what sort of laws accord with the U.S. Constitution. Hence, it is frequently possible to see how commitment to a political ideal is decisive in judicial decision making.

Beyond coming to appreciate how political ideals and their presumed applications function in judicial decision making, it is important that you examine Supreme Court decisions to determine to what degree the laws of your society accord with the political ideal you take to be the most morally defensible. To have good reasons to believe that you are a just and moral person, you need to assess to what degree the laws and institutions of your society are just—in this case, to what degree they accord with the requirements of distributive justice. Examining the two U.S. Supreme Court decisions included in this section should serve this purpose well.

In the first decision *(Wyman v. James)*, the majority of the Court decided that the rights of welfare recipients are limited in various ways and in particular that recipients are not protected against mandatory visits by caseworkers. Such a decision would surely seem justified if one believed, as libertarians do, that the provision of welfare is, at best, only a requirement of charity. Welfare liberals and socialists, however, would have difficulty accepting this decision, as did the dissenting justices of the Court.

In the second decision *(Plyler v. Doe)*, the majority of the Court determined that although public education is not a right, it still cannot be denied to the children of illegal aliens because of the pivotal role of education in sustaining our political and cultural heritage. This decision has some affinity with the way welfare liberals and socialists would understand the practical requirements of their ideals; libertarians would probably find themselves persuaded by the arguments of the dissenting justices.

Notice that you can also work backward from your considered judgments about these Supreme Court cases to the political ideal you should favor. Frequently, we can only clarify our views about a morally defensible position only by considering the practical applications of alternative political ideals.

In the final reading in this section, Peter Marin (Selection 7) paints a vivid picture of the homeless in the United States and asks the relevant question, "What does a society owe its members in trouble, and how is that debt to be paid?" Surely, at least one of our three political ideals must have an adequate answer.

Notice, too, that any fully adequate solution to the problem of distributive justice within a society presupposes a solution to the other moral problems presented in this anthology. In particular, the problem of near and distant peoples, which is discussed in the following section, seems to be clearly connected with the problem of distributive justice. We cannot know for sure what resources particular persons within a society should receive unless we also know what obligations persons within that society have to distant peoples.

Endnote

1. See, for example, my article, "Distributive Justice," *American Journal of Jurisprudence* (1977), pp. 55–79, and John C. Harsanyi, *Essays on Ethics, Social Behavior, and Scientific Explanation* (Boston: D. Reidel Publishing Co., 1976), pp. 37–85.

1. *The Libertarian Manifesto*

JOHN HOSPERS

John Hospers explores various ways of understanding the basic libertarian thesis that every person is the owner of his or her own life. According to Hospers, such ownership entails rights to life, liberty, and property. Since these rights are violated by an initial use of force, the proper role of government is said to be limited to the retaliatory use of force against those who have initiated its use. All other possible roles for government, such as protecting individuals against themselves or requiring people to help one another, are regarded as illegitimate by the libertarian.

The political philosophy that is called libertarianism (from the Latin *libertas*, liberty) is the doctrine that every person is the owner of his own life, and that no one is the owner of anyone else's life—and that consequently every human being has the right to act in accordance with his own choices, unless those actions infringe on the equal liberty of other human beings to act in accordance with their choices.

There are several other ways of stating the same libertarian thesis:

1. *No one is anyone else's master, and no one is anyone else's slave.* Since I am the one to decide how my life is to be conducted just as you decide about yours, I have no right (even if I had the power) to make you my slave and be your master, nor have you the right to become the master by enslaving me. Slavery is *forced* servitude, and since no one owns the life of anyone else, no one has the right to enslave another. Political theories past and present have traditionally been concerned with who should be the master (usually the king, the dictator, or government bureaucracy) and who should be the slaves, and what the extent of the slavery should be. Libertarianism holds that no one has the right to use force to enslave the life of another, or any portion or aspect of that life.

2. *Other men's lives are not yours to dispose of.* I enjoy seeing operas; but operas are expensive to produce.

Opera-lovers often say, "The state (or the city, etc.) should subsidize opera, so that we can all see it. Also it would be for people's betterment, cultural benefit, etc." But what they are advocating is nothing more or less than legalized plunder. They can't pay for the productions themselves, and yet they want to see opera, which involves a large number of people and their labor; so what they are saying in effect is, "Get the money through legalized force. Take a little bit more out of every worker's paycheck every week to pay for the operas we want to see." But I have no right to take by force from the workers' pockets to pay for what I want.

Perhaps it would be better if he *did* go to see opera—then I should try to convince him to go voluntarily. But to take the money from him forcibly, because in my opinion it would be good for *him*, is still seizure of his earnings, which is plunder.

Besides, if I have the right to force him to help pay for my pet projects, hasn't he equally the right to force me to help pay for his? Perhaps he in turn wants the government to subsidize rock-and-roll, or his new car, or a house in the country? If I have the right to milk him, why hasn't he the right to milk me? If I can be a moral cannibal, why can't he too?

We should beware of the inventors of utopias. They would remake the world according to their vision—with the lives and fruits of the labor of *other* human beings. Is it someone's utopian vision that others should build pyramids to beautify the landscape? Very well, then other men should provide the labor; and if he is in a position of political power, and he can't get men to do it

From "What Libertarianism Is," in *The Libertarian Alternative*, edited by Tibor Machan (1974). Reprinted by permission of the author, the editor, and Nelson-Hall Inc.

voluntarily, then he must *compel* them to "cooperate"—i.e., he must enslave them.

A hundred men might gain great pleasure from beating up or killing just one insignificant human being; but other men's lives are not theirs to dispose of. "In order to achieve the worthy goals of the next five-year plan, we must forcibly collectivize the peasants . . ."; but other men's lives are not theirs to dispose of. Do you want to occupy, rent-free, the mansion that another man has worked for twenty years to buy? But other men's lives are not yours to dispose of. Do you want operas so badly that everyone is forced to work harder to pay for their subsidization through taxes? But other men's lives are not yours to dispose of. Do you want to have free medical care at the expense of other people, whether they wish to provide it or not? But this would require them to work longer for you whether they want to or not, and other men's lives are not yours to dispose of. . . .

3. *No human being should be a nonvoluntary mortgage on the life of another.* I cannot claim your life, your work, or the products of your effort as mine. The fruit of one man's labor should not be fair game for every free-loader who comes along and demands it as his own. The orchard that has been carefully grown, nurtured, and harvested by its owner should not be ripe for the plucking for any bypasser who has a yen for the ripe fruit. The wealth that some men have produced should not be fair game for looting by government, to be used for whatever purposes its representatives determine, no matter what their motives in so doing may be. The theft of your money by a robber is not justified by the fact that he used it to help his injured mother.

It will already be evident that libertarian doctrine is embedded in a view of the rights of man. Each human being has the right to live his life as he chooses, compatibly with the equal right of all other human beings to live their lives as they choose.

All men's rights are implicit in the above statement. Each man has the right to life: Any attempt by others to take it away from him, or even to injure him, violates this right, through the use of coercion against him. Each man has the right to liberty: to conduct his life in accordance with the alternatives open to him without coercive action by others. And every man has the right to property: to work to sustain his life (and

the lives of whichever others he chooses to sustain, such as his family) and to retain the fruits of his labor.

People often defend the rights of life and liberty but denigrate property rights, and yet the right to property is as basic as the other two: Indeed, without property rights no other rights are possible. Depriving you of property is depriving you of the means by which you live. . . .

I have no right to decide how *you* should spend your time or your money. I can make that decision for myself, but not for you, my neighbor. I may deplore your choice of life-style, and I may talk with you about it provided you are willing to listen to me. But I have no right to use force to change it. Nor have I the right to decide how you should spend the money you have earned. I may appeal to you to give it to the Red Cross, and you may prefer to go to prize-fights. But that is your decision, and however much I may chafe about it I do not have the right to interfere forcibly with it, for example by robbing you in order to use the money in accordance with *my* choices. (If I have the right to rob you, have you also the right to rob me?)

When I claim a right, I carve out a niche, as it were, in my life, saying in effect, "This activity I must be able to perform without interference from others. For you and everyone else, this is off limits." And so I put up a "no trespassing" sign, which marks off the area of my right. Each individual's right is his "no trespassing" sign in relation to me and others. I may not encroach upon his domain any more than he upon mine, without my consent. Every right entails a duty, true—but the duty is only that of *forbearance*—that is, of *refraining* from violating the other person's right. If you have a right to life, I have no right to take your life; if you have a right to the products of your labor (property), I have no right to take it from you without your consent. The nonviolation of these rights will not guarantee you protection against natural catastrophes such as floods and earthquakes, but it will protect you against the aggressive activities *of other men.* And rights, after all, have to do with one's relations to other human beings, not with one's relations to physical nature.

Nor were these rights created by government; governments—some governments, obviously not all—*recognize* and *protect* the rights that individuals already have. Governments regularly forbid homicide and theft; and, at a more advanced stage, protect individuals against such things as libel and breach of contract. . . .

The right to property is the most misunderstood and unappreciated of human rights, and it is one most constantly violated by governments. "Property" of course does not mean only real estate; it includes anything you can call your own—your clothing, your car, your jewelry, your books and papers.

The right of property is not the right to just *take* it from others, for this would interfere with *their* property rights. It is rather the right to work for it, to obtain noncoercively, the money or services you can present in voluntary exchange.

The right to property is consistently underplayed by intellectuals today, sometimes even frowned upon, as if we should feel guilty for upholding such a right in view of all the poverty in the world. But the right to property is absolutely basic. It is your hedge against the future. It is your assurance that what you have worked to earn will still be there and be yours, when you wish or need to use it, especially when you are too old to work any longer.

Government has always been the chief enemy of the right to property. The officials of government, wishing to increase their power, and finding an increase of wealth an effective way to bring this about, seize some or all of what a person has earned—and since government has a monopoly of physical force within the geographical area of the nation, it has the power (but not the right) to do this. When this happens, of course, every citizen of that country is insecure: He knows that no matter how hard he works the government can swoop down on him at any time and confiscate his earnings and possessions. A person sees his life savings wiped out in a moment when the tax-collectors descend to deprive him of the fruits of his work; or, an industry which has been fifty years in the making and cost millions of dollars and millions of hours of time and planning, is nationalized overnight. Or the government, via inflation, cheapens the currency, so that hard-won dollars aren't worth anything any more. The effect of such actions, of course, is that people lose hope and incentive: If no matter how hard they work the government agents can take it all away, why bother to work at all, for more than today's needs? Depriving people of property is *depriving them of the means by which they live*—the freedom of

the individual citizen to do what he wishes with his own life and to plan for the future. Indeed only if property rights are respected is there any point to planning for the future and working to achieve one's goals. *Property rights are what makes long-range planning possible*—the kind of planning which is a distinctively human endeavor, as opposed to the day-by-day activity of the lion who hunts, who depends on the supply of game tomorrow but has no real insurance against starvation in a day or a week. Without the right to property, the right to life itself amounts to little: How can you sustain your life if you cannot plan ahead? and how can you plan ahead if the fruits of your labor can at any moment be confiscated by government? . . .

Indeed, the right to property may well be considered second only to the right to life. Even the freedom of speech is limited by considerations of property. If a person visiting in your home behaves in a way undesired by you, you have every right to evict him; he can scream or agitate elsewhere if he wishes, but not in your home without your consent. Does a person have a right to shout obscenities in a cathedral? No, for the owners of the cathedral (presumably the Church) have not allowed others on their property for that purpose; one may go there to worship or to visit, but not just for any purpose one wishes. Their property right is prior to your or my wish to scream or expectorate or write graffiti on their building. Or, to take the stock example, does a person have a right to shout "Fire!" falsely in a crowded theater? No, for the theater owner has permitted others to enter and use his property only for a specific purpose, that of seeing a film or watching a stage show. If a person heckles or otherwise disturbs other members of the audience, he can be thrown out. (In fact, he can be removed for any reason the owner chooses, provided his admission money is returned.) And if he shouts "Fire!" when there is no fire, he may be endangering other lives by causing a panic or a stampede. The right to free speech doesn't give one the right to say anything anywhere; it is circumscribed by property rights.

Again, some people seem to assume that the right to free speech (including written speech) means that they can go to a newspaper publisher and demand that he print in his newspaper some propaganda or policy statement for their political party (or other group). But of course they have no right to the use of his newspaper. Ownership of the newspaper is the product of his labor, and he has a right to put into his newspaper whatever he wants, for whatever reason. If he excludes material which many readers would like to have in, perhaps they can find it in another newspaper or persuade him to print it himself (if there are enough of them, they will usually do just that). Perhaps they can even cause his newspaper to fail. But as long as he owns it, he has the right to put in it what he wishes; what would a property right be if he could not do this? They have no right to place their material in his newspaper without his consent—not for free, nor even for a fee. Perhaps other newspapers will include it, or perhaps they can start their own newspaper (in which case they have a right to put in it what they like). If not, an option open to them would be to mimeograph and distribute some handbills.

In exactly the same way, no one has a right to "free television time" unless the owner of the television station consents to give it; it is his station, he has the property rights over it, and it is for him to decide how to dispose of his time. He may not decide wisely, but it is his right to decide as he wishes. If he makes enough unwise decisions, and courts enough unpopularity with the viewing public or the sponsors, he may have to go out of business; but as he is free to make his own decisions, so is he free to face their consequences. (If the government owns the television station, then government officials will make the decisions, and there is no guarantee of *their* superior wisdom. The difference is that when "the government" owns the station, you are forced to help pay for its upkeep through your taxes, whether the bureaucrat in charge decides to give you television time or not.)

"But why have *individual* property rights? Why not have lands and houses owned by everybody together?" Yes, this involves no violation of individual rights, as long as everybody consents to this arrangement and no one is forced to join it. The parties to it may enjoy the communal living enough (at least for a time) to overcome certain inevitable problems: that some will work and some not, that some will achieve more in an hour than others can do in a day, and still they will all get the same income. The few who do the most will in the end consider themselves "workhorses" who do the work of two or three or twelve, while the others will be "freeloaders" on the efforts of

these few. But as long as they can get out of the arrangement if they no longer like it, no violation of rights is involved. They got in voluntarily, and they can get out voluntarily; no one has used force.

"But why not say that everybody owns everything? That we *all* own everything there is?"

To some this may have a pleasant ring—but let us try to analyze what it means. If everybody owns everything, then everyone has an equal right to go everywhere, do what he pleases, take what he likes, destroy if he wishes, grow crops or burn them, trample them under, and so on. Consider what it would be like in practice. Suppose you have saved money to buy a house for yourself and your family. Now suppose that the principle, "everybody owns everything," becomes adopted. Well then, why shouldn't every itinerant hippie just come in and take over, sleeping in your beds and eating in your kitchen and not bothering to replace the food supply or clean up the mess? After all, it belongs to all of us, doesn't it? So we have just as much right to it as you, the buyer, have. What happens if we *all* want to sleep in the bedroom and there's not room for all of us? Is it the strongest who wins?

What would be the result? Since no one would be responsible for anything, the property would soon be destroyed, the food used up, the facilities nonfunctional. Beginning as a house that *one* family could use, it would end up as a house that *no one* could use. And if the principle continued to be adopted, no one would build houses any more—or anything else. What for? They would only be occupied and used by others, without remuneration.

Suppose two men are cast ashore on an island, and they agree that each will cultivate half of it. The first man is industrious and grows crops and builds a shelter, making the most of the situation with which he is confronted. The second man, perhaps thinking that the warm days will last forever, lies in the sun, picks coconuts while they last, and does a minimum of work to sustain himself. At the time of harvest, the second man has nothing to harvest, nor does he assist the first man in his labors. But later when there is a dearth of food on the island, the second man comes to the first man and demands half of the harvest as his right. But of course he has no right to the product of the first man's labors. The first man may freely choose to give part of his harvest to the second out of charity rather than see him starve; but that is just what it is—charity, not the second man's right.

How can any of man's rights be violated? Ultimately, only by the use of force. I can make suggestions to you, I can reason with you, entreat you (if you are willing to listen), but I cannot *force* you without violating your rights; only by forcing you do I cut the cord between your free decisions and your actions. Voluntary relations between individuals involve no deprivation of rights, but murder, assault, and rape do, because in doing these things I make you the unwilling victim of my actions. A man's beating his wife involves no violation of rights if she *wanted* to be beaten. *Force is behavior that requires the unwilling involvement of other persons.*

Thus the use of force need not involve the use of physical violence. If I trespass on your property or dump garbage on it, I am violating your property rights, as indeed I am when I steal your watch; although this is not force in the sense of violence, it *is* a case of your being an unwilling victim of my action. Similarly, if you shout at me so that I cannot be heard when I try to speak, or blow a siren in my ear, or start a factory next door which pollutes my land, you are again violating my rights (to free speech, to property); I am, again, an unwilling victim of your actions. Similarly, if you steal a manuscript of mine and publish it as your own, you are confiscating a piece of my property and thus violating my right to keep what is the product of my labor. Of course, if I give you the manuscript with permission to sign your name to it and keep the proceeds, no violation of rights is involved—any more than if I give you permission to dump garbage on my yard.

According to libertarianism, the role of government should be limited to the retaliatory use of force against those who have initiated its use. It should not enter into any other areas, such as religion, social organization, and economics.

Government

Government is the most dangerous institution known to man. Throughout history it has violated the rights of men more than any individual or group of individuals could do: It has killed people, enslaved them, sent them to forced labor and concentration camps, and regularly robbed and pillaged them of the fruits of their expended labor. Unlike individual criminals, government has the power to arrest and try; unlike individual criminals, it can surround and encompass a person totally, dominating every aspect of one's life, so that one has no recourse from it but to leave the country (and in totalitarian nations even that is prohibited). Government throughout history has a much sorrier record than any individual, even that of a ruthless mass murderer. The signs we see on bumper stickers are chillingly accurate: "Beware: The Government Is Armed and Dangerous."

The only proper role of government, according to libertarians, is that of the protector of the citizen against aggression by other individuals. The government, of course, should never initiate aggression; its proper role is as the embodiment of the *retaliatory* use of force against anyone who initiates its use.

If each individual had constantly to defend himself against possible aggressors, he would have to spend a considerable portion of his life in target practice, karate exercises, and other means of self-defenses, and even so he would probably be helpless against groups of individuals who might try to kill, maim, or rob him. He would have little time for cultivating those qualities which are essential to civilized life, nor would improvements in science, medicine, and the arts be likely to occur. The function of government is to take this responsibility off his shoulders: The government undertakes to defend him against aggressors and to punish them if they attack him. When the government is effective in doing this, it enables the citizen to go about his business unmolested and without constant fear for his life. To do this, of course, government must have physical power—the police, to protect the citizen from aggression within its borders, and the armed forces, to protect him from aggressors outside. Beyond that, the government should not intrude upon his life, either to run his business, or adjust his daily activities, or prescribe his personal moral code.

Government, then, undertakes to be the individual's protector; but historically governments have gone far beyond this function. Since they already have the physical power, they have not hesitated to use it for purposes far beyond that which was entrusted to them in the first place. Undertaking initially to protect its citizens against aggression, it has often itself become an aggressor—a far greater aggressor, indeed, than the criminals against whom it was supposed to protect its citizens. Governments have done what no private citizen can do: arrest and imprison individuals without a trial and send them to slave labor camps. Government must have power in order to be effective—and yet the very means by which alone it can be effective make it vulnerable to the abuse of power, leading to managing the lives of individuals and even inflicting terror upon them.

What then should be the function of government? In a phrase, the *protection of human rights.*

1. *The right to life:* Libertarians support all such legislation as will protect human beings against the use of force by others, for example, laws against killing, attempting killing, maiming, beating, and all kinds of physical violence.
2. *The right to liberty:* There should be no laws compromising in any way freedom of speech, of the press, and peaceable assembly. There should be no censorship of ideas, books, films, or of anything else by government.
3. *The right to property:* Libertarians support legislation that protects the property rights of individuals against confiscation, nationalization, eminent domain, robbery, trespass, fraud and misrepresentation, patent and copyright, libel, and slander.

Someone has violently assaulted you. Should he be legally liable? Of course. He has violated one of your rights. He has knowingly injured you, and since he has initiated aggression against you he should be made to expiate.

Someone has negligently left his bicycle on the sidewalk where you trip over it in the dark and injure yourself. He didn't do it intentionally; he didn't mean you any harm. Should he be legally liable? Of course; he has, however unwittingly, injured you, and since the injury is caused by him and you are the victim, he should pay.

Someone across the street is unemployed. Should you be taxed extra to pay for his expenses? Not at all. You have not injured him, you are not responsible for the fact that he is unemployed (unless you are a senator or bureaucrat who agitated for further curtailing of business, which legislation passed, with the result that your neighbor was laid off by the curtailed business). You may voluntarily wish to help him out, or better still, try to get him a job to put him on his feet again; but since you have initiated no aggressive act against him, and neither purposely nor accidentally injured him in any way, you should not be legally penalized for the fact of his unemployment. (Actually, it is just such penalties that increase unemployment.)

One man, A, works hard for years and finally earns a high salary as a professional man. A second man, B, prefers not to work at all, and to spend wastefully what money he has (through inheritance), so that after a year or two he has nothing left. At the end of this time he has a long siege of illness and lots of medical bills to pay. He demands that the bills be paid by the government—that is, by the taxpayers of the land, including Mr. A.

But of course B has no such right. He chose to lead his life in a certain way—that was his voluntary decision. One consequence of that choice is that he must depend on charity in case of later need. Mr. A chose not to live that way. (And if everyone lived like Mr. B, on whom would he depend in case of later need?) Each has a right to live in the way he pleases, but each must live with the consequences of his own decision (which, as always, fall primarily on himself). He cannot, in time of need, claim A's beneficence as his right.

If a house-guest of yours starts to carve his initials in your walls and break up your furniture, you have a right to evict him and call the police if he makes trouble. If someone starts to destroy the machinery in a factory, the factory-owner is also entitled to evict him and call the police. In both cases, persons other than the owner are permitted on the property only under certain conditions, at the pleasure of the owner. If those conditions are violated, the owner is entitled to use force to set things straight. The case is exactly the same on a college or university campus: If a campus demonstrator starts breaking windows, occupying the president's office, and setting fire to a dean, the college authorities are certainly within their rights to evict him forcibly; one is permitted on the college grounds only under specific conditions, set by the administration: study, peaceful student activity, even political activity if those in charge choose to permit it. If they do not choose to permit peaceful political activity on campus, they may be unwise, since a campus is after all a place where all sides of every issue should get discussed, and the college that doesn't permit this may soon lose its reputation and its students. All the same, the college official who does not permit it is quite within his rights; the students do not own the campus, nor do the hired troublemakers imported from elsewhere. In the case of a privately owned college, the owners, or whoever they have delegated to administer it, have the right to make the decisions as to who shall be permitted on the campus and under what conditions. In the case of a state university or college, the ownership problem is more complex: One could say that the "government" owns the campus or that "the people" do, since they are the taxpayers who support it. But in either case, the university administration has the delegated task of keeping order, and until they are removed by the state administration or the taxpayers, it is theirs to decide who shall be permitted on campus, and what nonacademic activities will be permitted to their students on the premises.

Property rights can be violated by physical trespass, of course, or by anyone entering on your property for any reason without your consent. (If you *do* consent to having your neighbor dump garbage on your yard, there is no violation of your rights.) But the physical trespass of a person is only a special case of violation of property rights. Property rights can be violated by sound-waves, in the form of a loud noise, or the sounds of your neighbor's hi-fi set while you are trying to sleep. Such violations of property rights are of course the subject of action in the courts.

But there is another violation of property rights that has not thus far been honored by the courts; this has to do with the effects of *pollution* of the atmosphere.

> From the beginnings of modern air pollution, the courts made a conscious decision not to protect, for example, the orchards of farmers from the smoke of nearby factories or locomotives. They said, in effect, to the farmers: Yes, your private property is being invaded by this smoke, but we hold that "public policy" is more important than private property, and public policy holds factories and locomotives to be good things. These goods were allowed to

> override the defense of property rights—with our consequent headlong rush into pollution disaster. The remedy is both "radical" and crystal clear, and it has nothing to do with multibillion dollar palliative programs at the expense of the taxpayers, which do not even meet the real issue. The remedy is simply to enjoin anyone from injecting pollutants into the air, and thereby invading the rights of persons and property. Period. The argument that such an injunction prohibition would add to the costs of industrial production is as reprehensible as the pre–Civil War argument that the abolition of slavery would add to the costs of growing cotton, and therefore should not take place. For this means that the polluters are able to impose the high costs of pollution upon those whose property rights they are allowed to invade with impunity.[1]

What about automobiles, the chief polluters of the air? One can hardly sue every automobile owner. But one can sue the manufacturers of automobiles who do not install anti-smog devices on the cars which they distribute—and later (though this is more difficult), owners of individual automobiles if they discard the equipment or do not keep it functional.

The violation of rights does not apply only to air-pollution. If someone with a factory upstream on a river pollutes the river, anyone living downstream from him, finding his water polluted, should be able to sue the owner of the factory. In this way the price of adding the anti-pollutant devices will be the owner's responsibility, and will probably be added to the cost of the products which the factory produces and thus spread around among all consumers, rather than the entire cost being borne by the users of the river in the form of polluted water, with the consequent impossibility of fishing, swimming, and so on. In each case, pollution would be stopped at the source rather than having its ill effects spread around to numerous members of the population.

What about property which you do not work to earn, but which you *inherit* from someone else? Do you have a right to that? You have no right to it until someone decides to give it to you. Consider the man who willed it to you; it was his, he had the right to use and dispose of it as *he* saw fit; and if he decided to give it to you, this is a windfall for you, but it was only the exercise of *his* right. Had the property been seized by the government at the man's death, or distributed among numerous other people designated by the government, it *would* have been a violation of his rights: for he, who worked to earn and sustain it, would not have been able to dispose of it according to his own judgment. If he doesn't have the right to determine who shall have it, who does?

What about the property status of your intellectual activity, such as inventions you may devise and books you write? These, of course, are your property also; they are the products of your mind; you worked at them, you created them. Prior to that, they did not exist. If you worked five years to write a book, and someone stole it and published it as his own, receiving royalties from its sales, he would have stolen your property just as surely as if he had robbed your home. The same is true if someone used and sold without your permission an invention which was the product of your labor and ingenuity.

The role of government with respect to this issue, at least most governments of the Western world, is a proper one: Government protects the products of your labor from the moment they materialize. Copyright law protects your writings from piracy. In the United States, one's writings are protected for a period of twenty-seven years, and another twenty-seven if one applies for renewal of the copyright. In most other countries, they are protected for a period of fifty years after the author's death, permitting both himself and his surviving heirs to reap the fruits of his labor. After that they enter the "public domain"—that is, anyone may reprint them without your or your heirs' permission. Patent law protects your inventions for a limited period, which varies according to the type of invention. In no case are you forced to avail yourself of this protection; you need not apply for patent or copyright coverage if you do not wish to do so. But the protection of your intellectual property is there, in case you wish to use it.

What about the property status of the airwaves? Here the government's position is far more questionable. The government now claims ownership of the airwaves, leasing them to individuals and corporations. The government renews leases or refuses them depending on whether the programs satisfy authorities in the Federal Communications Commission. The official position is that "we all own the airwaves": But

since only one party can broadcast on a certain frequency at a certain time without causing chaos, it is simply a fact of reality that "everyone" cannot use it. In fact the government decides who shall use the airwaves and one courts its displeasure only at the price of a revoked license. One can write without government approval, but one cannot use the airwaves without the approval of government.

What policy should have been observed with regard to the airwaves? Much the same as the policy that was followed in the case of the Homestead Act, when the lands of the American West were opening up for settlement. There was a policy of "first come, first served," with the government parcelling out a certain acreage for each individual who wanted to claim the land as his own. There was no charge for the land, but if a man had not used it and built a dwelling during the first two-year period, it was assumed that he was not homesteading and the land was given to the next man in line. The airwaves too could have been given out on a "first come, first served" basis. The first man who used a given frequency would be its owner, and the government would protect him in the use of it against trespassers. If others wanted to use the same frequency, they would have to buy it from the first man, if he was willing to sell, or try to buy another, just as one now does with the land.

Laws may be classified into three types: (1) laws protecting individuals against themselves, such as laws against fornication and other sexual behavior, alcohol, and drugs; (2) laws protecting individuals against aggressions by other individuals, such as laws against murder, robbery, and fraud; (3) laws requiring people to help one another; for example, all laws which rob Peter to pay Paul, such as welfare.

Libertarians reject the first class of laws totally. Behavior which harms no one else is strictly the individual's own affair. Thus, there should be no laws against becoming intoxicated, since whether or not to become intoxicated is the individual's own decision: But there should be laws against driving while intoxicated, since the drunken driver is a threat to every other motorist on the highway (drunken driving falls into type 2). Similarly, there should be no laws against drugs (except the prohibition of sale of drugs to minors) as long as the taking of these drugs poses no threat to anyone else. Drug addiction is a psychological problem to which no present solution exists. Most of the social harm caused by addicts, other than to themselves, is the result of thefts which they perform in order to continue their habit—and then the *legal* crime is the theft, not the addiction. The actual cost of heroin is about ten cents a shot; if it were legalized, the enormous traffic in illegal sale and purchase of it would stop, as well as the accompanying proselytization to get new addicts (to make more money for the pusher) and the thefts performed by addicts who often require eighty dollars a day just to keep up the habit. Addiction would not stop, but the crimes would: It is estimated that 75 percent of the burglaries in New York City today are performed by addicts, and all these crimes could be wiped out at one stroke through the legalization of drugs. (Only when the taking of drugs could be shown to constitute a threat to *others,* should it be prohibited by law. It is only laws protecting people against *themselves* that libertarians oppose.)

Laws should be limited to the second class only: aggression by individuals against other individuals. These are laws whose function is to protect human beings against encroachment by others; and this, as we have seen, is (according to libertarianism) the sole function of government.

Libertarians also reject the third class of laws totally: No one should be forced by law to help others, not even to tell them the time of day if requested, and certainly not to give them a portion of one's weekly paycheck. Governments, in the guise of humanitarianism, have given to some by taking from others (charging a "handling fee" in the process, which, because of the government's waste and inefficiency, sometimes is several hundred percent). And in so doing they have decreased incentive, violated the rights of individuals, and lowered the standard of living of almost everyone.

All such laws constitute what libertarians call *moral cannibalism.* A cannibal in the physical sense is a person who lives off the flesh of other human beings. A *moral* cannibal is one who believes he has a right to live off the "spirit" of other human beings—who believes that he has a moral claim on the productive capacity, time, and effort expended by others.

It has become fashionable to claim virtually everything that one needs or desires as one's *right.* Thus,

many people claim that they have a right to a job, the right to free medical care, to free food and clothing, to a decent home, and so on. Now if one asks, apart from any specific context, whether it would be desirable if everyone had these things, one might well say yes. But there is a gimmick attached to each of them: *At whose expense?* Jobs, medical care, education, and so on, don't grow on trees. These are goods and services *produced only by men.* Who then is to provide them, and under what conditions?

If you have a right to a job, who is to supply it? Must an employer supply it even if he doesn't want to hire you? What if you are unemployable, or incurably lazy? (If you say "the government must supply it," does that mean that a job must be created for you which no employer needs done, and that you must be kept in it regardless of how much or little you work?) If the employer is forced to supply it at his expense even if he doesn't need you, then isn't *he* being enslaved to that extent? What ever happened to *his* right to conduct his life and his affairs in accordance with his choices? If you have a right to free medical care, then, since medical care doesn't exist in nature as wild apples do, some people will have to supply it to you for free: That is, they will have to spend their time and money and energy taking care of you whether they want to or not. What ever happened to *their* right to conduct their lives as they see fit? Or do you have a right to violate theirs? Can there be a right to violate rights?

All those who demand this or that as a "free service" are consciously or unconsciously evading the fact that there is in reality no such thing as free services. All man-made goods and services are the result of human expenditure of time and effort. There is no such thing as "something for nothing" in this world. If you demand something free, you are demanding that other men give their time and effort to you without compensation. If they voluntarily choose to do this, there is no problem; but if you demand that they be *forced* to do it, you are interfering with their right not to do it if they so choose. "Swimming in this pool ought to be free!" says the indignant passerby. What he means is that others should build a pool, others should provide the material, and still others should run it and keep it in functioning order, so that *he* can use it without fee. But what right has he to the expenditure of *their* time and effort? To expect something "for free" is to expect it *to be paid for by others* whether they choose to or not.

Many questions, particularly about economic matters, will be generated by the libertarian account of human rights and the role of government. Should government have a role in assisting the needy, in providing social security, in legislating minimum wages, in fixing prices and putting a ceiling on rents, in curbing monopolies, in erecting tariffs, in guaranteeing jobs, in managing the money supply? To these and all similar questions the libertarian answers with an unequivocal no.

"But then you'd let people go hungry!" comes the rejoinder. This, the libertarian insists, is precisely what would not happen; with the restrictions removed, the economy would flourish as never before. With the controls taken off business, existing enterprises would expand and new ones would spring into existence satisfying more and more consumer needs; millions more people would be gainfully employed instead of subsisting on welfare, and all kinds of research and production, released from the stranglehold of government, would proliferate, fulfilling man's needs and desires as never before. It has always been so whenever government has permitted men to be free traders on a free market. But *why* this is so, and how the free market is the best solution to all problems relating to the material aspect of man's life, is another and far longer story.

Endnote

1. Murray Rothbard, "The Great Ecology Issue," *The Individualist*, 2, no. 2 (February 1970): p. 5.

2. *Radical Egalitarianism*

KAI NIELSON

The fundamental requirement of radical egalitarianism is equality of basic condition for everyone. Kai Nielson justifies this requirement on the grounds that it produces the conditions for the most extensive satisfaction of everyone's needs. He also contends that radical egalitarianism is required by the moral point of view and would lead to two specific principles of justice. Finally, he defends radical egalitarianism on the grounds that it is required by liberty or at least its fair distribution.

I

I have talked of equality as a right and of equality as a goal. And I have taken, as the principal thing, to be

Abridged from *Equality and Liberty* (1985), pp. 283–292, 302–306, 309. Reprinted by permission of Rowman & Allanheld, Publishers. Notes renumbered.

able to state what goal we are seeking when we say equality is a goal. When we are in a position actually to achieve that goal, then that same equality becomes a right. The goal we are seeking is an equality of basic condition for everyone. Let me say a bit what this is: Everyone, as far as possible, should have equal life prospects, short of genetic engineering and the like and the rooting out of any form of the family and the undermining of our basic freedoms. There should, where this is possible, be an equality of access to equal resources over each person's life as a whole, though this should be qualified by people's varying needs. Where psychiatrists are in short supply only people who are in need of psychiatric help should have equal access to such help. This equal access to resources should be such that it stands as a barrier to their being the sort of differences between people that allow some to be in a position to control and to exploit others; such equal access to resources should also stand as a barrier to one adult person having power over other adult persons that does not rest on the revokable consent on the part of the persons over whom he comes to have power. Where, because of some remaining scarcity in a society of considerable productive abundance, we cannot reasonably distribute resources equally, we should first, where considerations of desert are not at issue, distribute according to stringency of need, second according to the strength of unmanipulated preferences, and third, and finally, by lottery. We should, in trying to attain equality of condition, aim at a condition of autonomy (the fuller and the more rational the better) for everyone and at a condition where everyone alike, to the fullest extent possible, has his or her needs and wants satisfied. The limitations on the satisfaction of people's wants should be only where that satisfaction is incompatible with everyone getting the same treatment. Where we have conflicting wants, such as where two persons want to marry the same person, the fair thing to do will vary with the circumstances. In the marriage case, freedom of choice is obviously the fair thing. But generally, what should be aimed at is having everyone have their wants satisfied as far as possible. To achieve equality of condition would be, as well, to achieve a condition where the necessary burdens of the society are equally shared, where to do so is reasonable, and where each person has an equal voice in deciding what these burdens shall be. Moreover, everyone, as much as possible, should be in a position—and should be equally in that position—to control his own life. The goals of egalitarianism are to achieve such equalities.

Minimally, classlessness is something we should all aim at if we are egalitarians. It is necessary for the stable achievement of equalities of the type discussed in the previous paragraph. Beyond that, we should also aim at a statusless society, though not at an undifferentiated society or a society which does not recognize merit. . . . It is only in such a classless, statusless society that the ideals of equality (the conception of equality as a very general goal to be achieved) can be realized. In aiming for a statusless society, we are aiming for a society which, while remaining a society of material abundance, is a society in which there are to be no extensive differences in life prospects between people because some have far greater income, power, authority or prestige than others. This is the *via negativia* of the egalitarian way. The *via positiva* is to produce social conditions, where there is generally material abundance, where well-being and satisfaction are not only maximized (the utilitarian thing) but, as well, a society where this condition, as far as it is achievable, is sought equally for all (the egalitarian thing). This is the underlying conception of the egalitarian commitment to equality of condition.

II

Robert Nozick asks "How do we decide how much equality is enough?"[1] In the preceding section we gestured in the direction of an answer. I should now like to be somewhat more explicit. Too much equality, as we have been at pains to point out, would be to treat everyone identically, completely ignoring their differing needs. Various forms of "barracks equality" approximating that would also be too much. Too little equality would be to limit equality of condition, as did the old egalitarianism, to achieving equal legal and political rights, equal civil liberties, to equality of opportunity, and to a redistribution of gross disparities in wealth sufficient to keep social peace; the rationale for the latter being that such gross inequalities if allowed to stand would threaten social stability. This Hobbesist stance indicates that the old egalitarianism proceeds in a very pragmatic manner. Against the old egalitarianism I would argue that we must at least aim at an equality of whole life prospects, where that is not read simply as the right to compete for scarce positions of advantage, but where there is to be brought into being the kind of equality of condition that would provide everyone equally, as far as possible, with the resources and the social conditions to satisfy their needs as fully as possible compatible with everyone else doing likewise. (Note that between people these needs will be partly the same but will still often be importantly different as well.) Ideally, as a kind of ideal limit for a society of wondrous abundance, a radical egalitarianism would go beyond that to a similar thing for wants. We should, that is, provide all people equally, as far as possible, with the resources and social conditions to satisfy their wants, as fully as possible compatible with everyone else doing likewise. (I recognize that there is a slide between wants and needs. As the wealth of a society increases and its structure changes, things that started out as wants tend to become needs, e.g., someone in the Falkland Islands might merely reasonably want an auto while someone in Los Angeles might not only want it but need it as well. But this does not collapse the distinction between wants and needs. There are things in any society people need, if they are to survive at all in anything like a commodious condition, whether they want them or not, e.g., they need food, shelter, security, companionship and the like. An egalitarian starts with basic needs, or at least with what are taken in the cultural environment in which a given person lives to be basic needs, and moves out to other needs and finally to wants as the productive power of the society increases.)

I qualified my above formulations with "as far as possible" and with "as fully as possible compatible with everyone else doing likewise." These are essential qualifications. Where, as in societies that we know, there are scarcities, even rather minimal scarcities, not everyone can have the resources or at least all the resources necessary to have their needs satisfied. Here we must first ensure that, again as far as possible, their basic needs are all satisfied and then we move on to other needs and finally to wants. But sometimes, to understate it, even in very affluent societies, everyone's needs cannot be met, or at least they cannot be equally met. In such circumstances we have to make some hard choices. I am thinking of a situation where there are not enough dialysis machines to go around so that everyone who needs one can have one. What then should we do? The thing to aim at, to try as far as possible to approximate, if only as a heuristic ideal, is the full and equal meeting of needs and wants of everyone. It is when we have that much equality that we have enough equality. But, of course, "ought implies can," and where we can't achieve it we can't

achieve it. But where we reasonably can, we ought to do it. It is something that fairness requires.

The "reasonably can" is also an essential modification: We need situations of sufficient abundance so that we do not, in going for such an equality of condition, simply spread the misery around or spread very Spartan conditions around. Before we can rightly aim for the equality of condition I mentioned, we must first have the productive capacity and resource conditions to support the institutional means that would make possible the equal satisfaction of basic needs and the equal satisfaction of other needs and wants as well.

Such achievements will often not be possible; perhaps they will never be fully possible, for, no doubt, the physically handicapped will always be with us. Consider, for example, situations where our scarcities are such that we cannot, without causing considerable misery, create the institutions and mechanisms that would work to satisfy all needs, even all basic needs. Suppose we have the technology in place to develop all sorts of complicated life-sustaining machines all of which would predictably provide people with a quality of life that they, viewing the matter clearly, would rationally choose if they were simply choosing for themselves. But suppose, if we put such technologies in place, we will then not have the wherewithal to provide basic health care in outlying regions in the country or adequate educational services in such places. We should not, under those circumstances, put those technologies in place. But we should also recognize that where it becomes possible to put these technologies in place without sacrificing other more pressing needs, we should do so. The underlying egalitarian rationale is evident enough: Produce the conditions for the most extensive satisfaction of needs for everyone. Where A's need and B's need are equally important (equally stringent) but cannot both be satisfied, satisfy A's need rather than B's if the satisfaction of A's need would be more fecund for the satisfaction of the needs of others than B's, or less undermining of the satisfaction of the needs of others than B's. (I do not mean to say that that is our only criterion of choice but it is the criterion most relevant for us here.) We should seek the satisfaction of the greatest compossible set of needs where the conditions for compossibility are (a) that everyone's needs be considered, (b) that everyone's needs be *equally* considered and where two sets of needs cannot both be satisfied, the more stringent set of needs shall first be satisfied. (Do not say we have no working criteria for what they are. If you need food to keep you from starvation or debilitating malnutrition and I need a vacation to relax after a spate of hard work, your need is plainly more stringent than mine. There would, of course, be all sorts of disputable cases, but there are also a host of perfectly determinate cases indicating that we have working criteria.) The underlying rationale is to seek compossible sets of needs so that we approach as far as possible as great a satisfaction of needs as possible for everyone.

This might, it could be said, produce a situation in which very few people got those things that they needed the most, or at least wanted the most. Remember Nozick with his need for the resources of Widner Library in an annex to his house. People, some might argue, with expensive tastes and extravagant needs, say a need for really good wine, would never, with a stress on such compossibilia, get things they are really keen about.[2] Is that the kind of world we would reflectively want? Well, *if* their not getting them is the price we have to pay for everyone having their basic needs met, then it is a price we ought to pay. I am very fond of very good wines as well as fresh ripe mangos, but if the price of my having them is that people starve or suffer malnutrition in the Sahel, or indeed anywhere else, then plainly fairness, if not just plain human decency, requires that I forego them.

In talking about how much equality is enough, I have so far talked of the benefits that equality is meant to provide. But egalitarians also speak of an equal sharing of the necessary burdens of the society as well. Fairness requires a sharing of the burdens, and for a radical egalitarian this comes to an equal sharing of the burdens where people are equally capable of sharing them. Translated into the concrete this does *not* mean that a child or an old man or a pregnant woman are to be required to work in the mines or that they be required to collect garbage, but it would involve something like requiring every able-bodied person, say from nineteen to twenty, to take his or her turn at a fair portion of the necessary unpleasant jobs in the world. In that way we all, where we are able to do it, would share equally in these burdens—in doing the things that none of us want to do but that we, if we

are at all reasonable, recognize the necessity of having done. (There are all kinds of variations and complications concerning this—what do we do with the youthful wonder at the violin? But, that notwithstanding, the general idea is clear enough.) And, where we think this is reasonably feasible, it squares with our considered judgments about fairness.

I have given you—in effect appealing to my considered judgments, but considered judgments I do not think are at all eccentric—a picture of what I would take to be enough equality, too little equality, and not enough equality. But how can we know that my proportions are right? I do not think we can avoid or should indeed try to avoid an appeal to considered judgments here. But working with them there are some arguments we can appeal to to get them in wide reflective equilibrium. Suppose we go back to the formal principle of justice, namely that we must treat like cases alike. Because it does not tell us *what* are like cases, we cannot derive substantive criteria from it. But it may, indirectly, be of some help here. We all, if we are not utterly zany, want a life in which our needs are satisfied and in which we can live as we wish and do what we want to do. Though we differ in many ways, in our abilities, capacities for pleasure, determination to keep on with a job, we do not differ about wanting our needs satisfied or being able to live as we wish. Thus, *ceterus paribus*, where questions of desert, entitlement, and the like do not enter, it is only fair that all of us should have our needs equally considered and that we should, again *ceterus paribus*, all be able to do as we wish in a way that is compatible with others doing likewise. From the formal principle of justice and a few key facts about us, we can get to the claim that *ceterus paribus* we should go for this much equality. But this is the core content of a radical egalitarianism.

However, how do we know that *ceterus* is *paribus* here? What about our entitlements and deserts? Suppose I have built my house with my own hands, from materials I have purchased, and on land that I have purchased and that I have lived in it for years and have carefully cared for it. The house is mine and I am entitled to keep it even if by dividing the house into two apartments greater and more equal satisfaction of need would obtain for everyone. Justice requires that such an entitlement be respected here. (Again, there is an implicit *ceterus paribus* clause. In extreme situations, say after a war with housing in extremely short supply, that entitlement could be rightly overridden.)

There is a response on the egalitarian's part similar to a response utilitarianism made to criticisms of a similar logical type made of utilitarians by pluralistic deontologists. One of the things that people in fact need, or at least reflectively firmly want, is to have such entitlements respected. Where they are routinely overridden to satisfy other needs or wants, we would *not* in fact have a society in which the needs of everyone are being maximally met. To the reply, but what if more needs for everyone were met by ignoring or overriding such entitlements, the radical egalitarian should respond that that is, given the way we are, a thoroughly hypothetical situation and that theories of morality cannot be expected to give guidance for all logically possible worlds but only for worlds which are reasonably like what our actual world is or plausibly could come to be. Setting this argument aside for the moment, even if it did turn out that the need satisfaction linked with having other things—things that involved the overriding of those entitlements—was sufficient to make it the case that more need satisfaction all around for *everyone* would be achieved by overriding those entitlements, then, for reasonable people who clearly saw that, these entitlements would not have the weight presently given to them. They either would not have the importance presently attached to them or the need for the additional living space would be so great that their being overridden would seem, everything considered, the lesser of two evils (as in the example of the postwar housing situation).

There are without doubt genuine entitlements and a theory of justice must take them seriously, but they are not absolute. If the need is great enough we can see the merit in overriding them, just as in law as well as morality the right of eminent domain is recognized. Finally, while I have talked of entitlements here, parallel arguments will go through for desert.

III

I want now to relate this articulation of what equality comes to to my radically egalitarian principles of justice. My articulation of justice is a certain spelling out of the

slogan proclaimed by Marx "From each according to his ability, to each according to his needs." The egalitarian conception of society argues for the desirability of bringing into existence a world, once the springs of social wealth flow freely, in which everyone's needs are as fully satisfied as possible, and in which everyone gives according to his ability. Which means, among other things, that everyone, according to his ability, shares the burdens of society. There is an equal giving and equal responsibility here according to ability. It is here, with respect to giving according to ability and with respect to receiving according to need, that a complex equality of result, i.e., equality of condition, is being advocated by the radical egalitarian. What it comes to is this: Each of us, where each is to count for one and none to count for more than one, is to give according to ability and receive according to need.

My radical egalitarian principles of justice read as follows:

(1) Each person is to have an equal right to the most extensive total system of equal basic liberties and opportunities (including equal opportunities for meaningful work, for self-determination and political and economic participation) compatible with a similar treatment of all. (This principle gives expression to a commitment to attain and/or sustain equal moral autonomy and equal self-respect.)

(2) After provisions are made for common social (community) values, for capital overhead to preserve the society's productive capacity, allowances made for differing unmanipulated needs and preferences, and due weight is given to the just entitlements of individuals, the income and wealth (the common stock of means) is to be so divided that each person will have a right to an equal share. The necessary burdens requisite to enhance human well-being are also to be equally shared, subject, of course, to limitations by differing abilities and differing situations. (Here I refer to different natural environments and the like and not to class position and the like.)

Here we are talking about equality as a right rather than about equality as a goal as has previously been the subject matter of equality in this chapter. These principles of egalitarianism spell out rights people have and duties they have under *conditions of very considerable productive abundance*. We have a right to certain basic liberties and opportunities and we have, subject to certain limitations spelled out in the second principle, a right to an equal share of the income and wealth in the world. We also have a duty, again subject to the qualifications mentioned in the principle, to do our equal share in shouldering the burdens necessary to protect us from ills and to enhance our well-being.

What is the relation between these rights and the ideal of equality of condition discussed earlier? That is a goal for which we can struggle now to bring about conditions which will some day make its achievement possible, while these rights only become rights when the goal is actually achievable. We have no such rights in slave, feudal, or capitalist societies or such duties in those societies. In that important way they are not natural rights for they depend on certain social conditions and certain social structures (socialist ones) to be realizable. What we can say is that it is always desirable that socio-economic conditions come into being which would make it possible to achieve the goal of equality of condition so that these rights and duties I speak of could obtain. But that is a far cry from saying we have such rights and duties now.

It is a corollary of this, if these radical egalitarian principles of justice are correct, that capitalist societies (even capitalist welfare state societies such as Sweden) and statist societies such as the Soviet Union or the People's Republic of China cannot be just societies or at least they must be societies, structured as they are, which are defective in justice. (This is not to say that some of these societies are not juster than others. Sweden is juster than South Africa, Canada than the United States, and Cuba and Nicaragua than Honduras and Guatemala.) But none of these statist or capitalist societies can satisfy these radical egalitarian principles of justice, for equal liberty, equal opportunity, equal wealth or equal sharing of burdens are not at all possible in societies having their social structure. So we do not have such rights now but we can take it as a goal that we bring such a society into being with a commitment to an equality of condition in which we would have these rights and duties. Here we require first the massive development of productive power.

The connection between equality as a goal and equality as a right spelled out in these principles of justice is this. The equality of condition appealed to in equality as a goal would, if it were actually to obtain, have to contain the rights and duties enunciated in those principles. There could be no equal life prospects between all people or anything approximating an equal satisfaction of needs if there were not in place something like the system of equal basic liberties referred to in the first principle. Furthermore, without the rough equality of wealth referred to in the second principle, there would be disparities in power and self-direction in society which would render impossible an equality of life prospects or the social conditions required for an equal satisfaction of needs. And plainly, without a roughly equal sharing of burdens, there cannot be a situation where everyone has equal life prospects or has the chance equally to satisfy his needs. The principles of radical egalitarian justice are implicated in its conception of an ideally adequate equality of condition.

IV

The principles of radical egalitarian justice I have articulated are meant to apply globally and not just to particular societies. But it is certainly fair to say that not a few would worry that such principles of radical egalitarian justice, if applied globally, would force the people in wealthier sections of the world to a kind of financial hari-kari. There are millions of desperately impoverished people. Indeed millions are starving or malnourished and things are not getting any better. People in the affluent societies cannot but worry about whether they face a bottomless pit. Many believe that meeting, even in the most minimal way, the needs of the impoverished is going to put an incredible burden on people—people of all classes—in the affluent societies. Indeed it will, if acted on nonevasively, bring about their impoverishment, and this is just too much to ask. Radical egalitarianism is forgetting Rawls' admonitions about "the strains of commitment"—the recognition that in any rational account of what is required of us, we must at least give a minimal healthy self-interest its due. We must construct our moral philosophy for human beings and not for saints. Human nature is less fixed than conservatives are wont to assume, but it is not so elastic that we can reasonably expect people to impoverish themselves to make the massive transfers between North and South—the industrialized world and the Third World—required to begin to approach a situation where even Rawls' principles would be in place on a global level, to say nothing of my radical egalitarian principles of justice.[3]

The first thing to say in response to this is that my radical egalitarian principles are meant actually to guide practice, to directly determine what we are to do, only in a world of extensive abundance where, as Marx put it, the springs of social wealth flow freely. If such a world cannot be attained with the undermining of capitalism and the full putting into place, stabilizing, and developing of socialist relations of production, then such radical egalitarian principles can only remain as heuristic ideals against which to measure the distance of our travel in the direction of what would be a perfectly just society.

Aside from a small capitalist class, along with those elites most directly and profitably beholden to it (together a group constituting not more than 5 percent of the world's population), there would, in taking my radical egalitarian principles as heuristic guides, be no impoverishment of people in the affluent societies, if we moved in a radically more egalitarian way to start to achieve a global fairness. There would be massive transfers of wealth between North and South, but this could be done in stages so that, for the people in the affluent societies (capitalist elites apart), there need be no undermining of the quality of their lives. Even what were once capitalist elites would not be impoverished or reduced to some kind of bleak life though they would, the incidental Spartan types aside, find their life styles altered. But their health and general well-being, including their opportunities to do significant and innovative work, would, if anything, be enhanced. And while some of the sources of their enjoyment would be a thing of the past, there would still be a considerable range of enjoyments available to them sufficient to afford anyone a rich life that could be lived with verve and zest.

A fraction of what the United States spends on defense spending would take care of immediate problems of starvation and malnutrition for most of the world. For longer range problems such as bringing conditions of life in the Third World more in line with conditions of life in Sweden and Switzerland, what is

necessary is the dismantling of the capitalist system and the creation of a socio-economic system with an underlying rationale directing it toward producing for needs—everyone's needs. With this altered productive mode, the irrationalities and waste of capitalist production would be cut. There would be no more built-in obsolescence, no more merely cosmetic changes in consumer durables, no more fashion roulette, no more useless products and the like. Moreover, the enormous expenditures that go into the war industry would be a thing of the past. There would be great transfers from North to South, but it would be from the North's capitalist fat and not from things people in the North really need. (There would, in other words, be no self-pauperization of people in the capitalist world.) . . .

V

It has been repeatedly argued that equality undermines liberty. Some would say that a society in which principles like my radical egalitarian principles were adopted, or even the liberal egalitarian principles of Rawls or Dworkin were adopted, would not be a free society. My arguments have been just the reverse. I have argued that it is only in an egalitarian society that full and extensive liberty is possible.

Perhaps the egalitarian and the anti-egalitarian are arguing at cross purposes. What we need to recognize, it has been argued, is that we have two kinds of rights, both of which are important to freedom but to rather different freedoms and which are freedoms which not infrequently conflict.[4] We have rights to *fair terms of cooperation* but we also have rights to *noninterference*. If a right of either kind is overridden our freedom is diminished. The reason why it might be thought that the egalitarian and the anti-egalitarian may be arguing at cross purposes is that the egalitarian is pointing to the fact that rights to fair terms of cooperation and their associated liberties require equality while the anti-egalitarian is pointing to the fact that rights to noninterference and their associated liberties conflict with equality. They focus on different liberties.

What I have said above may not be crystal clear, so let me explain. People have a right to fair terms of cooperation. In political terms this comes to the equal right of all to effective participation in government and, in more broadly social terms, and for a society of economic wealth, it means people having a right to a roughly equal distribution of the benefits and burdens of the basic social arrangements that affect their lives and for them to stand in such relations to each other such that no one has the power to dominate the life of another. By contrast, rights to noninterference come to the equal right of all to be left alone by the government and more broadly to live in a society in which people have a right peacefully to pursue their interests without interference.

The conflict between equality and liberty comes down to, very essentially, the conflicts we get in modern societies between rights to fair terms of cooperation and rights to noninterference. As Joseph Schumpeter saw and J. S. Mill before him, one could have a thoroughly democratic society (at least in conventional terms) in which rights to noninterference might still be extensively violated. A central anti-egalitarian claim is that we cannot have an egalitarian society in which the very precious liberties that go with the rights to noninterference would not be violated.

Socialism and egalitarianism plainly protect rights to fair terms of cooperation. Without the social (collective) ownership and control of the means of production, involving with this, in the initial stages of socialism at least, a workers' state, economic power will be concentrated in the hands of a few who will in turn, as a result, dominate effective participation in government. Some right-wing libertarians blind themselves to that reality, but it is about as evident as can be. Only an utter turning away from the facts of social life could lead to any doubts about this at all. But then this means that in a workers' state, if some people have capitalistic impulses, they would have their rights peacefully to pursue their own interests interfered with. They might wish to invest, retain, and bequeath in economic domains. In a workers' state these capitalist acts in many circumstances would have to be forbidden, but that would be a violation of an individual's right to noninterference and the fact, if it was a fact, that we by democratic vote, even with vast majorities, had made such capitalist acts illegal would still not make any difference because individuals' rights to noninterference would still be violated.

We are indeed driven, by egalitarian impulses of a perfectly understandable sort, to accept interference with laissez-faire capitalism to protect nonsubordination and nondomination of people by protecting the egalitarian right to fair terms of cooperation and the enhanced liberty that that brings. Still, as things stand, this leads inevitably to violations of the right to noninterference and this brings with it a diminution of liberty. There will be people with capitalist impulses and they will be interfered with. It is no good denying, it will be said, that egalitarianism and particularly socialism will . . . lead to interference with very precious individual liberties, namely with our right peacefully to pursue our interests without interference.[5]

The proper response to this, as should be apparent from what I have argued throughout, is that to live in any society at all, capitalist, socialist or whatever, is to live in a world in which there will be some restriction or other on our rights peacefully to pursue our interests without interference. I can't lecture in Albanian or even in French in a standard philosophy class at the University of Calgary, I can't jog naked on most beaches, borrow a book from your library without your permission, fish in your trout pond without your permission, take your dog for a walk without your say so, and the like. At least some of these things have been thought to be things which I might peacefully pursue in my own interests. Stopping me from doing them is plainly interfering with my peaceful pursuit of my own interests. And indeed it is an infringement on liberty, an interference with my doing what I may want to do.

However, for at least many of these activities, and particularly the ones having to do with property, even right-wing libertarians think that such interference is perfectly justified. But, justified or not, they still plainly constitute a restriction on our individual freedom. However, what we must also recognize is that there will always be some such restrictions on freedom in any society whatsoever, just in virtue of the fact that a normless society, without the restrictions that having norms imply, is a contradiction in terms.[6] Many restrictions are hardly felt as restrictions, as in the attitudes of many people toward seat-belt legislation, but they are, all the same, plainly restrictions on our liberty. It is just that they are thought to be unproblematically justified.

To the question would a socialism with a radical egalitarianism restrict some liberties, including some liberties rooted in rights to noninterference, the answer is that it indeed would; but so would laissez-faire capitalism, aristocratic conceptions of justice, liberal conceptions or any social formations at all, with their associated conceptions of justice. The relevant question is which of these restrictions are justified.

The restrictions on liberty proffered by radical egalitarianism and socialism, I have argued, are justified for they, of the various alternatives, give us both the most extensive and the most abundant system of liberty possible in modern conditions with their thorough protection of the right to fair terms of cooperation. Radical egalitarianism will also, and this is central for us, protect our civil liberties and these liberties are, of course, our most basic liberties. These are the liberties which are the most vital for us to protect. What it will not do is to protect our unrestricted liberties to invest, retain, and bequeath in the economic realm and it will not protect our unrestricted freedom to buy and sell. There is, however, no good reason to think that these restrictions are restrictions of anything like a basic liberty. Moreover, we are justified in restricting our freedom to buy and sell if such restrictions strengthen, rather than weaken, our total system of liberty. This is in this way justified, for only by such market restrictions can the rights of the vast majority of people to effective participation in government and an equal role in the control of their social lives be protected. I say this because if we let the market run free in this way, power will pass into the hands of a few who will control the lives of the many and determine the fundamental design of the society. The actual liberties that are curtailed in a radically egalitarian social order are inessential liberties whose restriction in contemporary circumstances enhances human well-being and indeed makes for a firmer entrenchment of basic liberties and for their greater extension globally. That is to say, we here restrict some liberty in order to attain more liberty and a more equally distributed pattern of liberty. More people will be able to do what they want and have a greater control over their own lives than in a capitalist world order with its at least implicit inegalitarian commitments.

However, some might say I still have not faced the most central objection to radical egalitarianism, namely its statism. (I would prefer to say its putative statism.) The picture is this. The egalitarian state must be in the redistribution business. It has to make, or make sure there is made, an equal relative contribution to the welfare of every citizen. But this in effect means that the socialist state or, for that matter, the welfare state, will be deeply interventionist in our personal lives. It will be in the business, as one right-winger emotively put it, of cutting one person down to size in order to bring about that person's equality with another person who was in a previously disadvantageous position.[7] That is said to be morally objectionable and it would indeed be deeply morally objectionable in many circumstances. But it isn't in the circumstances in which the radical egalitarian presses for redistribution. (I am not speaking of what might be mere equalizing upwards.) The circumstances are these: Capitalist A gets his productive property confiscated so that he could no longer dominate and control the lives of proletarians B, C, D, E, F, and G. But what is wrong with it where this "cutting down to size"—in reality the confiscation of productive property or the taxation of the capitalist—involves no violation of A's civil liberties or the harming of his actual well-being (health, ability to work, to cultivate the arts, to have fruitful personal relations, to live in comfort, and the like) and where B, C, D, E, F, and G will have their freedom and their well-being thoroughly enhanced if such confiscation or taxation occurs? Far from being morally objectionable, it is precisely the sort of state of affairs that people ought to favor. It certainly protects more liberties and more significant liberties than it undermines.

There is another familiar anti-egalitarian argument designed to establish the liberty-undermining qualities of egalitarianism. It is an argument we have touched upon in discussing meritocracy. It turns on the fact that in any society there will be both talents and handicaps. Where they exist, what do we want to do about maintaining equal distribution? Egalitarians, radical or otherwise, certainly do not want to penalize people for talent. That being so, then surely people should be allowed to retain the benefits of superior talent. But this in some circumstances will lead to significant inequalities in resources and in the meeting of needs. To sustain equality there will have to be an ongoing redistribution in the direction of the less talented and less fortunate. But this redistribution from the more to the less talented does plainly penalize the talented for their talent. That, it will be said, is something which is both unfair and an undermining of liberty.

The following, it has been argued, makes the above evident enough.[8] If people have talents they will tend to want to use them. And if they use them they are very likely to come out ahead. Must not egalitarians say they ought not to be able to come out ahead no matter how well they use their talents and no matter how considerable these talents are? But that is intolerably restrictive and unfair.

The answer to the above anti-egalitarian argument is implicit in a number of things I have already said. But here let me confront this familiar argument directly. Part of the answer comes out in probing some of the ambiguities of "coming out ahead." Note, incidentally, that (1) not all reflective, morally sensitive people will be so concerned with that, and (2) that being very concerned with that is a mentality that capitalism inculcates. Be that as it may, to turn to the ambiguities, note that some take "coming out ahead" principally to mean "being paid well for the use of those talents" where "being paid well" is being paid sufficiently well so that it creates inequalities sufficient to disturb the preferred egalitarian patterns. (Without that, being paid well would give one no relative advantage.) But, as we have seen, "coming out ahead" need not take that form at all. Talents can be recognized and acknowledged in many ways: First, in just the respect and admiration of a fine employment of talents that would naturally come from people seeing them so displayed where these people were not twisted by envy; second, by having, because of these talents, interesting and secure work that their talents fit them for and they merit in virtue of those talents. Moreover, having more money is not

going to matter much—for familiar marginal utility reasons—where what in capitalist societies would be called the welfare floors are already very high, this being made feasible by the great productive wealth of the society. Recall that in such a society of abundance everyone will be well off and secure. In such a society people are not going to be very concerned about being a little better off than someone else. The talented are in no way, in such a situation, robbed to help the untalented and handicapped or penalized for their talents. They are only prevented from amassing wealth (most particularly productive wealth), which would enable them to dominate the untalented and the handicapped and to control the social life of the world of which they are both a part. . . .

I think that the moral authority for abstract egalitarianism, for the belief that the interests of everyone matters and matters equally, comes from its being the case that it is *required by the moral point of view*.[9] What I am predicting is that a person who has a good understanding of what morality is, has a good knowledge of the facts, is not ideologically mystified, takes an impartial point of view, and has an attitude of impartial caring, would, if not conceptually confused, come to accept the abstract egalitarian thesis. I see no way of arguing someone into such an egalitarianism who does not in this general way have a love of humankind.[10] A hard-hearted Hobbesist is not reachable here. But given that a person has that love of humankind—that impartial and impersonal caring—together with the other qualities mentioned above, then I predict that that person would be an egalitarian at least to the extent of accepting the abstract egalitarian thesis. What I am claiming is that if these conditions were to obtain (if they ceased to be just counterfactuals), then there would be a consensus among moral agents about accepting the abstract egalitarian thesis. . . .

Endnotes

1. See the debate between Robert Nozick, Daniel Bell and James Tobin, "If Inequality Is Inevitable What Can Be Done About It?" *The New York Times*, January 3, 1982, p. E5. The exchange between Bell and Nozick reveals the differences between the old egalitarianism and right-wing libertarianism. It is not only that the right and left clash but sometimes right clashes with right.

2. Amartya Sen, "Equality of What?" *The Tanner Lectures on Human Values,* vol. 1 (1980), ed. Sterling M. McMurrin (Cambridge, England: Cambridge University Press, 1980), pp. 198–220.

3. Henry Shue, "The Burdens of Justice," *The Journal of Philosophy 80,* no. 10 (October 1983): 600–601; 606–608.

4. Richard W. Miller, "Marx and Morality," in *Marxism,* eds. J. R. Pennock and J. W. Chapman, Nomos 26 (New York: New York University Press, 1983), pp. 9–11.

5. Ibid., p. 10.

6. This has been argued from both the liberal center and the left. Ralf Dahrendorf, *Essays in the Theory of Society* (Stanford, Calif.: Stanford University Press, 1968), pp. 151–178; and G. A. Cohen, "Capitalism, Freedom and the Proletariat" in *The Idea of Freedom: Essays in Honour of Isaiah Berlin,* ed. Alan Ryan (Oxford: Oxford University Press, 1979).

7. The graphic language should be duly noted. Jan Narveson, "On Dworkinian Equality," *Social Philosophy and Policy 1,* no. 1 (autumn 1983): 4.

8. Ibid., 1–24.

9. Some will argue that there is no such thing as a moral point of view. My differences with him about the question of whether the amoralist can be argued into morality not withstanding, I think Kurt Baier, in a series of articles written subsequent to his *The Moral Point of View,* has clearly shown that there is something reasonably determinate that can, without ethnocentrism, be called "the moral point of view."

10. Richard Norman has impressively argued that this is an essential background assumption of the moral point of view. Richard Norman, "Critical Notice of Rodger Beehler's *Moral Life,*" *Canadian Journal of Philosophy 11,* no. 1 (March 1981): 157–183.

3. A *Social Contract Perspective*

JOHN RAWLS

John Rawls believes that principles of justice are those on which free and rational persons would agree if they were in an original position of equality. This original position is characterized as a hypothetical position in which persons are behind an imaginary veil of ignorance with respect to most particular facts about themselves. Rawls claims that persons in this original position would choose principles requiring equal political liberty and opportunity and the highest possible economic minimum because they would be committed to the maximin rule, which requires maximizing the minimum payoff.

My aim is to present a conception of justice which generalizes and carries to a higher level of abstraction the familiar theory of the social contract as found, say, in Locke, Rousseau, and Kant.[1] In order to do this we are not to think of the original contract as one to enter a particular society or to set up a particular form of government. Rather, the guiding idea is that the principles of justice for the basic structure of society are the object of the original agreement. They are the principles that free and rational persons concerned to further their own interests would accept in an initial position of equality as defining the fundamental terms of their association. These principles are to regulate all further agreements; they specify the kinds of social cooperation that can be entered into and the forms of government that can be established. This way of regarding the principles of justice I shall call justice as fairness.

Abridged from *A Theory of Justice* (1971), pp. 11–22, 60–65, 150–156, 302–303. Excerpted by permission of the publishers from *A Theory of Justice* by John Rawls. Cambridge, Mass.: The Belknap Press of Harvard University Press. Copyright © 1971 by the President and Fellows of Harvard College.

Thus we are to imagine that those who engage in social cooperation choose together, in one joint act, the principles which are to assign basic rights and duties and to determine the division of social benefits. Men are to decide in advance how they are to regulate their claims against one another and what is to be the foundation charter of their society. Just as each person must decide by rational reflection what constitutes his good—that is, the system of ends which it is rational for him to pursue—so a group of persons must decide once and for all what is to count among them as just and unjust. The choice which rational men would make in this hypothetical situation of equal liberty, assuming for the present that this choice problem has a solution, determines the principles of justice.

In justice as fairness the original position of equality corresponds to the state of nature in the traditional theory of the social contract. This original position is not, of course, thought of as an actual historical state of affairs, much less as a primitive condition of culture. It is understood as a purely hypothetical situation characterized so as to lead to a certain conception of justice.[2] Among the essential features of this situation is that no one knows his place in society, his class position or social status, nor does any one know his fortune in the distribution of natural assets and abilities, his intelligence, strength, and the like. I shall even assume that the parties do not know their conceptions of the good or their special psychological propensities. The principles of justice are chosen behind a veil of ignorance. This ensures that no one is advantaged or disadvantaged in the choice of principles by the outcome of natural chance or the contingency of social circumstances. Since all are similarly situated and no one is able to design principles to favor his particular condition, the principles of justice are the result of a fair agreement or bargain. For given the circumstances of the original position, the symmetry of everyone's relations to each other, this initial situation is fair between individuals as moral persons; that is, as rational beings with their own ends and capable, I shall assume, of a sense of justice. The original position is, one might say, the appropriate initial status quo, and thus the fundamental agreements reached in it are fair. This explains the propriety of the name "justice as fairness"; it conveys the idea that the principles of justice are agreed to in an initial situation that is fair. The name does not mean that the concepts of justice and fairness are the same, any more than the phrase "poetry as metaphor" means that the concepts of poetry and metaphor are the same.

Justice as fairness begins, as I have said, with one of the most general of all choices which persons might make together, namely, with the choice of the first principles of a conception of justice which is to regulate all subsequent criticism and reform of institutions. Then, having chosen a conception of justice, we can suppose that they are to choose a constitution and a legislature to enact laws, and so on, all in accordance with the principles of justice initially agreed upon. Our social situation is just if it is such that by this sequence of hypothetical agreements we would have contracted into the general system of rules which defines it. Moreover, assuming that the original position does determine a set of principles (that is, that a particular conception of justice would be chosen), it will then be true that whenever social institutions satisfy these principles those engaged in them can say to one another that they are cooperating on terms to which they would agree if they were free and equal persons whose relations with respect to one another were fair. They could all view their arrangements as meeting the stipulations which they would acknowledge in an initial situation that embodies widely accepted and reasonable constraints on the choice of principles. The general recognition of this fact would provide the basis for a public acceptance of the corresponding principles of justice. No society can, of course, be a scheme of cooperation which men enter voluntarily in a literal sense; each person finds himself placed at birth in some particular position in some particular society, and the nature of this position materially affects his life prospects. Yet a society satisfying the principles of justice as fairness comes as close as a society can to being a voluntary scheme, for it meets the principles which free and equal persons would assent to under circumstances that are fair. In this sense its members are autonomous and the obligations they recognize self-imposed.

One feature of justice as fairness is to think of the parties in the initial situation as rational and mutually disinterested. This does not mean that the parties are egoists; that is, individuals with only certain kinds of interests, say in wealth, prestige, and domination. But they are conceived as not taking an interest in one another's interests. They are to presume that even their spiritual aims may be opposed, in the way that the aims of those of different religions may be opposed. Moreover, the concept of rationality must be interpreted as far as possible in the narrow sense, standard in economic theory, of taking the most effective means to given ends. I shall modify this concept to some extent . . . , but one must try to avoid introducing into it any controversial ethical elements. The initial situation must be characterized by stipulations that are widely accepted.

In working out the conception of justice as fairness one main task clearly is to determine which principles of justice would be chosen in the original position. To do this we must describe this situation in some detail and formulate with care the problem of choice which it presents. It may be observed, however, that once the principles of justice are thought of as arising from an original agreement in a situation of equality, it is an open question whether the principle of utility would be acknowledged. Offhand it hardly seems likely that persons who view themselves as equals, entitled to press their claims upon one another, would agree to a principle which may require lesser life prospects for some simply for the sake of a greater sum of advantages enjoyed by others. Since each desires to protect his interests, his capacity to advance his conception of the good, no one has a reason to acquiesce in an enduring loss for himself in order to bring about a greater net balance of satisfaction. In the absence of strong and lasting benevolent impulses, a rational man would not accept a basic structure merely because it maximized the algebraic sum of advantages irrespective of its permanent effects on his own basic rights and interests. Thus it seems that the principle of utility is incompatible with the conception of social cooperation among equals for mutual advantage. It appears to be inconsistent with the idea of reciprocity implicit in the notion of a well-ordered society. Or, at any rate, so I shall argue.

I shall maintain instead that the persons in the initial situation would choose two rather different principles: The first requires equality in the assignment of basic rights and duties, while the second holds that social and economic inequalities, for example, inequalities of wealth and authority, are just only

if they result in compensating benefits for everyone, and in particular for the least advantaged members of society. These principles rule out justifying institutions on the grounds that the hardships of some are offset by a greater good in the aggregate. It may be expedient but it is not just that some should have less in order that others may prosper. But there is no injustice in the greater benefits earned by a few provided that the situation of persons not so fortunate is thereby improved. The intuitive idea is that since everyone's well-being depends upon a scheme of cooperation without which no one could have a satisfactory life, the division of advantages should be such as to draw forth the willing cooperation of everyone taking part in it, including those less well situated. Yet this can be expected only if reasonable terms are proposed. The two principles mentioned seem to be a fair agreement on the basis of which those better endowed, or more fortunate in their social position, neither of which we can be said to deserve, could expect the willing cooperation of others when some workable scheme is a necessary condition of the welfare of all.[3] Once we decide to look for a conception of justice that nullifies the accidents of natural endowment and the contingencies of social circumstance as counters in quest for political and economic advantage, we are led to these principles. They express the result of leaving aside those aspects of the social world that seem arbitrary from a moral point of view.

The problem of the choice of principles, however, is extremely difficult. I do not expect the answer I shall suggest to be convincing to everyone. It is, therefore, worth noting from the outset that justice as fairness, like other contract views, consists of two parts: (1) an interpretation of the initial situation and of the problem of choice posed there, and (2) a set of principles which, it is argued, would be agreed to. One may accept the first part of the theory (or some variant thereof), but not the other, and conversely. The concept of the initial contractual situation may seem reasonable although the particular principles proposed are rejected. To be sure, I want to maintain that the most appropriate conception of this situation does lead to principles of justice contrary to utilitarianism and perfectionism, and therefore that the contract doctrine provides an alternative to these views. Still, one may dispute this contention even though one grants that the contractarian method is a useful way of studying ethical theories and of setting forth their underlying assumptions.

Justice as fairness is an example of what I have called a contract theory. Now there may be an objection to the term *contract* and related expressions, but I think it will serve reasonably well. Many words have misleading connotations which at first are likely to confuse. The terms *utility* and *utilitarianism* are surely no exception. They too have unfortunate suggestions which hostile critics have been willing to exploit; yet they are clear enough for those prepared to study utilitarian doctrine. The same should be true of the term *contract* applied to moral theories. As I have mentioned, to understand it one has to keep in mind that it implies a certain level of abstraction. In particular, the content of the relevant agreement is not to enter a given society or to adopt a given form of government, but to accept certain moral principles. Moreover, the undertakings referred to are purely hypothetical: A contract view holds that certain principles would be accepted in a well-defined initial situation.

The merit of the contract terminology is that it conveys the idea that principles of justice may be conceived as principles that would be chosen by rational persons, and that in this way conceptions of justice may be explained and justified. The theory of justice is a part, perhaps the most significant part, of the theory of rational choice. Furthermore, principles of justice deal with conflicting claims upon the advantages won by social cooperation; they apply to the relations among several persons or groups. The word *contract* suggests this plurality as well as the condition that the appropriate division of advantages must be in accordance with principles acceptable to all parties. The condition of publicity for principles of justice is also connoted by the contract phraseology. Thus, if these principles are the outcome of an agreement, citizens have a knowledge of the principles that others follow. It is characteristic of contract theories to stress the public nature of political principles. Finally there is the long tradition of the contract doctrine. Expressing the tie with this line of thought helps to define ideas and accords with natural piety. There are then several advantages in the use of the term *contract*. With due precautions taken, it should not be misleading.

A final remark. Justice as fairness is not a complete contract theory. For it is clear that the contractarian idea can be extended to the choice of more or less an entire ethical system; that is, to a system including principles for all the virtues and not only for justice. Now for the most part I shall consider only principles of justice and others closely related to them; I make no attempt to discuss the virtues in a systematic way. Obviously if justice as fairness succeeds reasonably well, a next step would be to study the more general view suggested by the name "rightness as fairness." But even this wider theory fails to embrace all moral relationships, since it would seem to include only our relations with other persons and to leave out of account how we are to conduct ourselves toward animals and the rest of nature. I do not contend that the contract notion offers a way to approach these questions, which are certainly of the first importance; and I shall have to put them aside. We must recognize the limited scope of justice as fairness and of the general type of view that it exemplifies. How far its conclusions must be revised once these other matters are understood cannot be decided in advance.

The Original Position and Justification

I have said that the original position is the appropriate initial status quo which insures that the fundamental agreements reached in it are fair. This fact yields the name "justice as fairness." It is clear, then, that I want to say that one conception of justice is more reasonable than another, or justifiable with respect to it, if rational persons in the initial situation would choose its principles over those of the other for the role of justice. Conceptions of justice are to be ranked by their acceptability to persons so circumstanced. Understood in this way the question of justification is settled by working out a problem of deliberation: We have to ascertain which principles it would be rational to adopt given the contractual situation. This connects the theory of justice with the theory of rational choice.

If this view of the problem of justification is to succeed, we must, of course, describe in some detail the nature of this choice problem. A problem of rational decision has a definite answer only if we know the beliefs and interests of the parties, their relations with respect to one another, the alternatives between which they are to choose, the procedure whereby they make up their minds, and so on. As the circumstances are presented in different ways, correspondingly different principles are accepted. The concept of the original position, as I shall refer to it, is that of the most philosophically favored interpretation of this initial choice situation for the purposes of a theory of justice.

But how are we to decide what is the most favored interpretation? I assume, for one thing, that there is a broad measure of agreement that principles of justice should be chosen under certain conditions. To justify a particular description of the initial situation one shows that it incorporates these commonly shared presumptions. One argues from widely accepted but weak premises to more specific conclusions. Each of the presumptions should by itself be natural and plausible; some of them may seem innocuous or even trivial. The aim of the contract approach is to establish that taken together they impose significant bounds on acceptable principles of justice. The ideal outcome would be that these conditions determine a unique set of principles; but I shall be satisfied if they suffice to rank the main traditional conceptions of social justice.

One should not be misled, then, by the somewhat unusual conditions which characterize the original position. The idea here is simply to make vivid to ourselves the restrictions that it seems reasonable to impose on arguments for principles of justice, and therefore on these principles themselves. Thus it seems reasonable and generally acceptable that no one should be advantaged or disadvantaged by natural fortune or social circumstances in the choice of principles. It also seems widely agreed that it should be impossible to tailor principles to the circumstances of one's own case. We should ensure further that particular inclinations and aspirations, and persons' conceptions of their good, do not affect the principles adopted. The aim is to rule out those principles that it would be rational to propose for acceptance, however little the chance of success, only if one knew certain things that are irrelevant from the standpoint of justice. For example, if a man knew that he was wealthy, he might find it rational to advance the principle that various taxes for welfare measures be counted unjust; if he knew that he was poor, he would most likely

propose the contrary principle. To represent the desired restrictions one imagines a situation in which everyone is deprived of this sort of information. One excludes the knowledge of those contingencies which sets men at odds and allows them to be guided by their prejudices. In this manner the veil of ignorance is arrived at in a natural way. This concept should cause no difficulty if we keep in mind the constraints on arguments that it is meant to express. At any time we can enter the original position, so to speak, simply by following a certain procedure; namely, by arguing for principles of justice in accordance with these restrictions.

It seems reasonable to suppose that the parties in the original position are equal. That is, all have the same rights in the procedure for choosing principles; each can make proposals, submit reasons for their acceptance, and so on. Obviously the purpose of these conditions is to represent equality between human beings as moral persons, as creatures having a conception of their good and capable of a sense of justice. The basis of equality is taken to be similarity in these two respects. Systems of ends are not ranked in value; and each man is presumed to have the requisite ability to understand and to act upon whatever principles are adopted. Together with the veil of ignorance, these conditions define the principles of justice as those which rational persons concerned to advance their interests would consent to as equals when none are known to be advantaged or disadvantaged by social and natural contingencies.

There is, however, another side to justifying a particular description of the original position. This is to see if the principles which would be chosen match our considered convictions of justice or extend them in an acceptable way. We can note whether applying these principles would lead us to make the same judgments about the basic structure of society which we now make intuitively and in which we have the greatest confidence; or whether, in cases where our present judgments are in doubt and given with hesitation, these principles offer a resolution which we can affirm on reflection. There are questions which we feel sure must be answered in a certain way. For example, we are confident that religious intolerance and racial discrimination are unjust. We think that we have examined these things with care and have reached what we believe is an impartial judgment not likely to be distorted by an excessive attention to our own interests. These convictions are provisional fixed points which we presume any conception of justice must fit. But we have much less assurance as to what is the correct distribution of wealth and authority. Here we may be looking for a way to remove our doubts. We can check an interpretation of the initial situation, then, by the capacity of its principles to accommodate our firmest convictions and to provide guidance where guidance is needed.

In searching for the most favored description of this situation we work from both ends. We begin by describing it so that it represents generally shared and preferably weak conditions. We then see if these conditions are strong enough to yield a significant set of principles. If not, we look for further premises equally reasonable. But if so, and these principles match our considered convictions of justice, then so far well and good. But presumably there will be discrepancies. In this case we have a choice. We can either modify the account of the initial situation or we can revise our existing judgments, for even the judgments we take provisionally as fixed points are liable to revision. By going back and forth, sometimes altering the conditions of the contractual circumstances, at others withdrawing our judgments and conforming them to principle, I assume that eventually we shall find a description of the initial situation that both expresses reasonable conditions and yields principles which match our considered judgments duly pruned and adjusted. This state of affairs I refer to as reflective equilibrium.[4] It is an equilibrium because at last our principles and judgments coincide; and it is reflective since we know to what principle our judgments conform and the premises of their derivation. At the moment everything is in order. But this equilibrium is not necessarily stable. It is liable to be upset by further examination of the conditions which should be imposed on the contractual situation and by particular cases which may lead us to revise our judgments. Yet for the time being we have done what we can to render coherent and to justify our convictions of social justice. We have reached a conception of the original position.

I shall not, of course, actually work through this process. Still, we may think of the interpretation of the original position that I shall present as the result of such a hypothetical course of reflection. It represents the attempt to accommodate within one scheme both reasonable philosophical conditions on principles as well as our considered judgments of justice. In arriving at the favored interpretation of the initial situation there is no point at which an appeal is made to self-evidence in the traditional sense either of general conceptions or particular convictions. I do not claim for the principles of justice proposed that they are necessary truths or derivable from such truths. A conception of justice cannot be deduced from self-evident premises or conditions on principles; instead, its justification is a matter of the mutual support of many considerations, of everything fitting together into one coherent view.

A final comment. We shall want to say that certain principles of justice are justified because they would be agreed to in an initial situation of equality. I have emphasized that this original position is purely hypothetical. It is natural to ask why, if this agreement is never actually entered into, we should take any interest in these principles—moral or otherwise. The answer is that the conditions embodied in the description of the original position are ones that we do in fact accept. Or if we do not, then perhaps we can be persuaded to do so by philosophical reflection. Each aspect of the contractual situation can be given supporting grounds. Thus what we shall do is to collect together into one conception a number of conditions on principles that we are ready upon due consideration to recognize as reasonable. These constraints express what we are prepared to regard as limits on fair terms of social cooperation. One way to look at the idea of the original position, therefore, is to see it as an expository device which sums up the meaning of these conditions and helps us to extract their consequences. On the other hand, this conception is also an intuitive notion that suggests its own elaboration, so that led on by it we are drawn to define more clearly the standpoint from which we can best interpret moral relationships. We need a conception that enables us to envision our objective from afar: The intuitive notion of the original position is to do this for us. . . .

Two Principles of Justice

I shall now state in a provisional form the two principles of justice that I believe would be chosen in the original position. In this section I wish to make only the most general comments, and therefore the first formulation of these principles is tentative. As we go on I shall run through several formulations and approximate step by step the final statement to be given much later. I believe that doing this allows the exposition to proceed in a natural way.

The first statement of the two principles reads as follows:

> First: Each person is to have an equal right to the most extensive basic liberty compatible with a similar liberty for others.

> Second: Social and economic inequalities are to be arranged so that they are both (a) reasonably expected to be to everyone's advantage, and (b) attached to positions and offices open to all.

There are two ambiguous phrases in the second principle, namely "everyone's advantage" and "open to all." Determining their sense more exactly will lead to a second formulation of the principle. . . .

By way of general comment, these principles primarily apply, as I have said, to the basic structure of society. They are to govern the assignment of rights and duties and to regulate the distribution of social and economic advantages. As their formulation suggests, these principles presuppose that the social structure can be divided into two more or less distinct parts, the first principle applying to the one, the second to the other. They distinguish between those aspects of the social system that define and secure the equal liberties of citizenship and those that specify and establish social and economic inequalities. The basic liberties of citizens are, roughly speaking, political liberty (the right to vote and to be eligible for public office) together with freedom of speech and assembly; liberty of conscience and freedom of thought; freedom of the person along with the right to hold personal property; and freedom from arbitrary arrest and seizure as defined by the concept of the rule of law. These liberties are all required to be equal by the first principle, since citizens of a just society are to have the same basic rights.

The second principle applies, in the first approximation, to the distribution of income and wealth and to the design of organizations that make use of differences in authority and responsibility, or chains of command. While the distribution of wealth and income need not be equal, it must be to everyone's advantage, and at the same time, positions of authority and offices of command must be accessible to all. One applies the second principle by holding positions open, and then, subject to this constraint, arranges social and economic inequalities so that everyone benefits.

These principles are to be arranged in a serial order with the first principle prior to the second. This ordering means that a departure from the institutions of equal liberty required by the first principle cannot be justified by, or compensated for, by greater social and economic advantages. The distribution of wealth and income, and the hierarchies of authority, must be consistent with both the liberties of equal citizenship and equality of opportunity.

It is clear that these principles are rather specific in their content, and their acceptance rests on certain assumptions that I must eventually try to explain and justify. A theory of justice depends upon a theory of society in ways that will become evident as we proceed. For the present, it should be observed that the two principles (and this holds for all formulations) are a special case of a more general conception of justice that can be expressed as follows:

> All social values—liberty and opportunity, income and wealth, and the bases of self-respect—are to be distributed equally unless an unequal distribution of any, or all, of these values is to everyone's advantage.

Injustice, then, is simply inequalities that are not to the benefit of all. Of course, this conception is extremely vague and requires interpretation.

As a first step, suppose that the basic structure of society distributes certain primary goods, that is, things that every rational man is presumed to want. These goods normally have a use whatever a person's rational plan of life. For simplicity, assume that the chief primary goods at the disposition of society are rights and liberties, powers and opportunities, income and wealth. (Later on . . . the primary good of self-respect has a central place.) These are the social primary goods. Other primary goods such as health and vigor, intelligence and imagination, are natural goods; although their possession is influenced by the basic structure, they are not so directly under its control. Imagine, then, a hypothetical initial arrangement in which all the social primary goods are equally distributed: Everyone has similar rights and duties, and income and wealth are evenly shared. This state of affairs provides a benchmark for judging improvements. If certain inequalities of wealth and organizational powers would make everyone better off than in this hypothetical starting situation, then they accord with the general conception.

Now it is possible, at least theoretically, that by giving up some of their fundamental liberties men are sufficiently compensated by the resulting social and economic gains. The general conception of justice imposes no restrictions on what sort of inequalities are permissible; it only requires that everyone's position be improved. We need not suppose anything so drastic as consenting to a condition of slavery. Imagine instead that men forgo certain political rights when the economic returns are significant and their capacity to influence the course of policy by the exercise of these rights would be marginal in any case. It is this kind of exchange which the two principles as stated rule out; being arranged in serial order they do not permit exchanges between basic liberties and economic and social gains. The serial ordering of principles expresses an underlying preference among primary social goods. When this preference is rational so likewise is the choice of these principles in this order.

In developing justice as fairness I shall, for the most part, leave aside the general conception of justice and examine instead the special case of the two principles in serial order. The advantage of this procedure is that from the first the matter of priorities is recognized and an effort made to find principles to deal with it. One is led to attend throughout to the conditions under which the acknowledgment of the absolute weight of liberty with respect to social and economic advantages, as defined by the lexical order of the two principles, would be reasonable. Offhand, this ranking appears extreme and too special a case to be of much interest; but there is more justification for it than would appear at first sight. Or at any rate, so I shall maintain. . . . Furthermore, the distinction between fundamental rights and liberties and economic and social benefits marks a difference among primary social goods that one should try to exploit. It suggests an important division in the social system. Of course,

the distinctions drawn and the ordering proposed are bound to be at best only approximations. There are surely circumstances in which they fail. But it is essential to depict clearly the main lines of a reasonable conception of justice; and under many conditions, anyway, the two principles in serial order may serve well enough. When necessary we can fall back on the more general conception.

The fact that the two principles apply to institutions has certain consequences. Several points illustrate this. First of all, the rights and liberties referred to by these principles are those that are defined by the public rules of the basic structure. Whether men are free is determined by the rights and duties established by the major institutions of society. Liberty is a certain pattern of social forms. The first principle simply requires that certain sorts of rules, those defining basic liberties, apply to everyone equally and that they allow the most extensive liberty compatible with a like liberty for all. The only reason for circumscribing the rights defining liberty and making men's freedom less extensive than it might otherwise be is that these equal rights as institutionally defined would interfere with one another.

Another thing to bear in mind is that when principles mention persons, or require that everyone gain from an inequality, the reference is to representative persons holding the various social positions, or offices, or whatever, established by the basic structure. Thus in applying the second principle I assume that it is possible to assign an expectation of well-being to representative individuals holding these positions. This expectation indicates their life prospects as viewed from their social station. In general, the expectations of representative persons depend upon the distribution of rights and duties throughout the basic structure. When this changes, expectations change. I assume, then, that expectations are connected: By raising the prospects of the representative man in one position we presumably increase or decrease the prospects of representative men in other positions. Since it applies to institutional forms, the second principle (or rather the first part of it) refers to the expectations of representative individuals. As I shall discuss below, neither principle applies to distributions of particular goods to particular individuals who may be identified by their proper names. The situation where someone is considering how to allocate certain commodities to needy persons who are known to him is not within the scope of the principles. They are meant to regulate basic institutional arrangements. We must not assume that there is much similarity from the standpoint of justice between an administrative allotment of goods to specific persons and the appropriate design of society. Our common sense intuitions for the former may be a poor guide to the latter.

Now the second principle insists that each person benefit from permissible inequalities in the basic structure. This means that it must be reasonable for each relevant representative man defined by this structure, when he views it as a going concern, to prefer his prospects with the inequality, to his prospects without it. One is not allowed to justify differences in income or organizational powers on the ground that the disadvantages of those in one position are outweighed by the greater advantages of those in another. Much less can infringements of liberty be counterbalanced in this way. Applied to the basic structure, the principle of utility would have us maximize the sum of expectations of representative men (weighted by the number of persons they represent, on the classical view); and this would permit us to compensate for the losses of some by the gains of others. Instead, the two principles require that everyone benefit from economic and social inequalities.

The Reasoning Leading to the Two Principles of Justice

It will be recalled that the general conception of justice as fairness requires that all primary social goods be distributed equally unless an unequal distribution would be to everyone's advantage. No restrictions are placed on exchanges of these goods and therefore a lesser liberty can be compensated for by greater social and economic benefits. Now looking at the situation from the standpoint of one person selected arbitrarily, there is no way for him to win special advantages for himself. Nor, on the other hand, are there grounds for his acquiescing in special disadvantages. Since it is not reasonable for him to expect more than an equal share in the division of social goods, and since it is not

rational for him to agree to less, the sensible thing for him to do is to acknowledge as the first principle of justice one requiring an equal distribution. Indeed, this principle is so obvious that we would expect it to occur to anyone immediately.

Thus, the parties start with a principle establishing equal liberty for all, including equality of opportunity, as well as an equal distribution of income and wealth. But there is no reason why this acknowledgment should be final. If there are inequalities in the basic structure that work to make everyone better off in comparison with the benchmark of initial equality, why not permit them? The immediate gain which a greater equality might allow can be regarded as intelligently invested in view of its future return. If, for example, these inequalities set up various incentives which succeed in eliciting more productive efforts, a person in the original position may look upon them as necessary to cover the costs of training and to encourage effective performance. One might think that ideally individuals should want to serve one another. But since the parties are assumed not to take an interest in one another's interests, their acceptance of these inequalities is only the acceptance of the relations in which men stand in the circumstances of justice. They have no grounds for complaining of one another's motives. A person in the original position would, therefore, concede the justice of these inequalities. Indeed, it would be shortsighted of him not to do so. He would hesitate to agree to these regularities only if he would be dejected by the bare knowledge or perception that others were better situated; and I have assumed that the parties decide as if they are not moved by envy. In order to make the principle regulating inequalities determinate, one looks at the system from the standpoint of the least advantaged representative man. Inequalities are permissible when they maximize, or at least all contribute to, the long-term expectations of the least fortunate group in society.

Now this general conception imposes no constraints on what sorts of inequalities are allowed, whereas the special conception, by putting the two principles in serial order (with the necessary adjustments in meaning), forbids exchanges between basic liberties and economic and social benefits. I shall not try to justify this ordering here. . . . But roughly, the idea underlying this ordering is that if the parties assume that their basic liberties can be effectively exercised, they will not exchange a lesser liberty for an improvement in economic well-being. It is only when social conditions do not allow the effective establishment of these rights that one can concede their limitation; and these restrictions can be granted only to the extent that they are necessary to prepare the way for a free society. The denial of equal liberty can be defended only if it is necessary to raise the level of civilization so that in due course these freedoms can be enjoyed. Thus in adopting a serial order we are in effect making a special assumption in the original position, namely, that the parties know that the conditions of their society, whatever they are, admit the effective realization of the equal liberties. The serial ordering of the two principles of justice eventually comes to be reasonable if the general conception is consistently followed. This lexical ranking is the long-run tendency of the general view. For the most part I shall assume that the requisite circumstances for the serial order obtain.

It seems clear from these remarks that the two principles are at least a plausible conception of justice. The question, though, is how one is to argue for them more systematically. Now there are several things to do. One can work out their consequences for institutions and note their implications for fundamental social policy. In this way they are tested by a comparison with our considered judgments of justice. . . . But one can also try to find arguments in their favor that are decisive from the standpoint of the original position. In order to see how this might be done, it is useful as a heuristic device to think of the two principles as the maximin solution to the problem of social justice. There is an analogy between the two principles and the maximin rule for choice under uncertainty.[5] This is evident from the fact that the two principles are those a person would choose for the design of a society in which his enemy is to assign him his place. The maximin rule tells us to rank alternatives by their worst possible outcomes: We are to adopt the alternative the worst outcome of which is superior to the worst outcomes of the others. The persons in the original position do not, of course, assume that their initial place in society is decided by a malevolent opponent. As I note below, they should not reason from false premises. The veil of ignorance does not

violate this idea, since an absence of information is not misinformation. But that the two principles of justice would be chosen if the parties were forced to protect themselves against such a contingency explains the sense in which this conception is the maximin solution. And this analogy suggests that if the original position has been described so that it is rational for the parties to adopt the conservative attitude expressed by this rule, a conclusive argument can indeed be constructed for these principles. Clearly the maximin rule is not, in general, a suitable guide for choices under uncertainty. But it is attractive in situations marked by certain special features. My aim, then, is to show that a good case can be made for the two principles based on the fact that the original position manifests these features to the fullest possible degree, carrying them to the limit, so to speak.

Consider the gain-and-loss table in the next column. It represents the gains and losses for a situation which is not a game of strategy. There is no one playing against the person making the decision; instead he is faced with several possible circumstances which may or may not obtain. Which circumstances happen to exist does not depend upon what the person choosing decides or whether he announces his moves in advance. The numbers in the table are monetary values (in hundreds of dollars) in comparison with some initial situation. The gain (g) depends upon the individual's decision (d) and the circumstances (c). Thus $g = f(d,c)$. Assuming that there are three possible decisions and three possible circumstances, we might have this gain-and-loss table.

	Circumstances		
Decisions	c_1	c_2	c_3
d_1	-7	8	12
d_2	-8	7	14
d_3	5	6	8

The maximin rule requires that we make the third decision. For in this case the worst that can happen is that one gains five hundred dollars, which is better than the worst for the other actions. If we adopt one of these we may lose either eight or seven hundred dollars. Thus, the choice of d_3 maximizes $f(d,c)$ for that value of c which for a given d, minimizes f. The term *maximin* means the maximum minimorum; and the rule directs our attention to the worst that can happen under any proposed course of action, and to decide in the light of that.

Now there appear to be three chief features of situations that give plausibility to this unusual rule.[6] First, since the rule takes no account of the likelihoods of the possible circumstances, there must be some reason for sharply discounting estimates of these probabilities. Offhand, the most natural rule of choice would seem to be to compute the expectation of monetary gain for each decision and then to adopt the course of action with the highest prospect. (This expectation is defined as follows: Let us suppose that g_{ij} represents the numbers in the gain-and-loss table, where i is the row index and j is the column index; and let $p_i, j = 1, 2, 3$, be the likelihoods of the circumstances, with $\Sigma p_j = 1$. Then the expectation for the ith decision is equal to $\Sigma p_i g_{ij}$.) Thus it must be, for example, that the situation is one in which a knowledge of likelihoods is impossible, or at best extremely insecure. In this case it is unreasonable not to be skeptical of probabilistic calculations unless there is no other way out, particularly if the decision is a fundamental one that needs to be justified to others.

The second feature that suggests the maximin rule is the following: The person choosing has a conception of the good such that he cares very little, if anything, for what he might gain above the minimum stipend that he can, in fact, be sure of by following the maximin rule. It is not worthwhile for him to take a chance for the sake of a further advantage, especially when it may turn out that he loses much that is important to him. This last provision brings in the third feature; namely, that the rejected alternatives have outcomes that one can hardly accept. The situation involves grave risks. Of course these features work most effectively in combination. The paradigm situation for following the maximin rule is when all three features are realized to the highest degree. This rule does not, then, generally apply, nor of course is it self-evident. Rather, it is a maxim, a rule of thumb, that comes into its own in special circumstances. Its application depends upon the qualitative structure of the possible gains and losses in relation to one's conception of the good, all this against a background in which it is reasonable to discount conjectural estimates of likelihoods.

It should be noted, as the comments on the gain-and-loss table say, that the entries in the table represent monetary values and not utilities. This difference is significant since for one thing computing expectations on the basis of such objective values is not the same thing as computing expected utility and may lead to different results. The essential point, though, is that in justice as fairness the parties do not know their conception of the good and cannot estimate their utility in the ordinary sense. In any case, we want to go behind de facto preferences generated by given conditions. Therefore expectations are based upon an index of primary goods and the parties make their choice accordingly. The entries in the example are in terms of money and not utility to indicate this aspect of the contract doctrine.

Now, as I have suggested, the original position has been defined so that it is a situation in which the maximin rule applies. In order to see this, let us review briefly the nature of this situation with these three special features in mind. To begin with, the veil of ignorance excludes all but the vaguest knowledge of likelihoods. The parties have no basis for determining the probable nature of their society, or their place in it. Thus they have strong reasons for being wary of probability calculations if any other course is open to them. They must also take into account the fact that their choice of principles should seem reasonable to others, in particular their descendants, whose rights will be deeply affected by it. There are further grounds for discounting that I shall mention as we go along. For the present it suffices to note that these considerations are strengthened by the fact that the parties know very little about the gain-and-loss table. Not only are they unable to conjecture the likelihoods of the various possible circumstances, they cannot say much about what the possible circumstances are, much less enumerate them and foresee the outcome of each alternative available. Those deciding are much more in the dark than the illustration by a numerical table suggests. It is for this reason that I have spoken of an analogy with the maximin rule.

Several kinds of arguments for the two principles of justice illustrate the second feature. Thus, if we can maintain that these principles provide a workable theory of social justice, and that they are compatible with reasonable demands of efficiency, then this conception guarantees a satisfactory minimum. There may be, on reflection, little reason for trying to do better. Thus much of the argument . . . is to show, by their application to the main questions of social justice, that the two principles are a satisfactory conception. These details have a philosophical purpose. Moreover, this line of thought is practically decisive if we can establish the priority of liberty, the lexical ordering of the two principles. For this priority implies that the persons in the original position have no desire to try for greater gains at the expense of the equal liberties. The minimum assured by the two principles in lexical order is not one that the parties wish to jeopardize for the sake of greater economic and social advantages. . . .

Finally, the third feature holds if we can assume that other conceptions of justice may lead to institutions that the parties would find intolerable. For example, it has sometimes been held that under some conditions the utility principle (in either form) justifies, if not slavery or serfdom, at any rate serious infractions of liberty for the sake of greater social benefits. We need not consider here the truth of this claim, or the likelihood that the requisite conditions obtain. For the moment, this contention is only to illustrate the way in which conceptions of justice may allow for outcomes which the parties may not be able to accept. And having the ready alternative of the two principles of justice which secure a satisfactory minimum, it seems unwise, if not irrational, for them to take a chance that these outcomes are not realized.

So much, then, for a brief sketch of the features of situations in which the maximin rule comes into its own and of the way in which the arguments for the two principles of justice can be subsumed under them. . . .

The Final Formulation of the Principles of Justice

. . . I now wish to give the final statement of the two principles of justice for institutions. For the sake of completeness, I shall give a full statement including earlier formulations.

First Principle
Each person is to have an equal right to the most extensive total system of equal basic liberties compatible with a similar system of liberty for all.

Second Principle
Social and economic inequalities are to be arranged so that they are both:
(a) to the greatest benefit of the least advantaged, consistent with the just savings principle, and
(b) attached to offices and positions open to all under conditions of fair equality of opportunity.

First Priority Rule (The Priority of Liberty)
The principles of justice are to be ranked in lexical order and therefore liberty can be restricted only for the sake of liberty. There are two cases:
(a) a less extensive liberty must strengthen the total system of liberty shared by all;
(b) a less than equal liberty must be acceptable to those with the lesser liberty.

Second Priority Rule (The Priority of Justice over Efficiency and Welfare)
The second principle of justice is lexically prior to the principle of efficiency and to that of maximizing the sum of advantages; and fair opportunity is prior to the difference principle. There are two cases:
(a) an inequality of opportunity must enhance the opportunities of those with the lesser opportunity;
(b) an excessive rate of saving must on balance mitigate the burden of those bearing this hardship.

General Conception
All social primary goods—liberty and opportunity, income and wealth, and the bases of self-respect—are to be distributed equally unless an unequal distribution of any or all of these goods is to the advantage of the least favored.

By way of comment, these principles and priority rules are no doubt incomplete. Other modifications will surely have to be made, but I shall not further complicate the statement of the principles. It suffices to observe that when we come to nonideal theory, we do not fall back straightway upon the general conception of justice. The lexical ordering of the two principles, and the valuations that this ordering implies, suggest priority rules which seem to be reasonable enough in many cases. By various examples I have tried to illustrate how these rules can be used and to indicate their plausibility. Thus the ranking of the principles of justice in ideal theory reflects back and guides the application of these principles to nonideal situations. It identifies which limitations need to be dealt with first. The drawback of the general concep- tion of justice is that it lacks the definite structure of the two principles in serial order. In more extreme and tangled instances of nonideal theory there may be no alternative to it. At some point the priority of rules for nonideal cases will fail; and indeed, we may be able to find no satisfactory answer at all. But we must try to postpone the day of reckoning as long as possible, and try to arrange society so that it never comes. . . .

Endnotes

1. As the text suggests, I shall regard Locke's *Second Treatise of Government*, Rousseau's *The Social Contract*, and Kant's ethical works beginning with *The Foundations of the Metaphysics of Morals* as definitive of the contract tradition. For all of its greatness, Hobbes's *Leviathan* raises special problems. A general historical survey is provided by J. W. Gough, *The Social Contract*, 2nd ed. (Oxford, The Clarendon Press, 1957), and Otto Gierke, *Natural Law and the Theory of Society*, trans. with an intro- duction by Ernest Barker (Cambridge, The University Press, 1934). A presentation of the contract view as pri- marily an ethical theory is to be found in G. R. Grice, *The Grounds of Moral Judgment* (Cambridge, The University Press, 1967).

2. Kant is clear that the original agreement is hypo- thetical. See *The Metaphysics of Morals*, pt. I (*Rechtslehre*), especially §§ 47, 52; and pt. II of the essay "Concerning the Common Saying: This May Be True in Theory but It Does Not Apply in Practice," in *Kant's Political Writings*, ed. Hans Reiss and trans. by H. B. Nisbet (Cambridge, The University Press, 1970), pp. 73–87. See Georges Vlachos, *La pensée politique de Kant* (Paris, Presses Univer- sitaires de France, 1962), pp. 326–335; and J. G. Murphy,

Kant: The Philosophy of Right (London, Macmillan, 1970), pp. 109–112, 133–136, for a further discussion.

3. For the formulation of this intuitive idea I am in- debted to Allan Gibbard.

4. The process of mutual adjustment of principles and considered judgments is not peculiar to moral philoso- phy. See Nelson Goodman, *Fact, Fiction, and Forecast* (Cambridge, Mass., Harvard University Press, 1955), pp. 65–68, for parallel remarks concerning the justification of the principles of deductive and inductive inference.

5. An accessible discussion of this and other rules of choice under uncertainty can be found in W. J. Baumol, *Economic Theory and Operations Analysis*, 2nd ed. (Engle- wood Cliffs, N.J., Prentice-Hall, 1965), ch. 24. Baumol gives a geometric interpretation of these rules, including the diagram used . . . to illustrate the difference principle. See pp. 558–562. See also R. D. Luce and Howard Raiffa, *Games and Decisions* (New York, John Wiley and Sons, 1957), ch. XIII, for a fuller account.

6. Here I borrow from William Fellner, *Probability and Profit* (Homewood, Ill., Richard D. Irwin, 1965), pp. 140–142, where these features are noted.

4. *From Liberty to Equality*

JAMES P. STERBA

James P. Sterba argues that when a libertarian ideal of liberty is interpreted in the manner favored by libertarians as the absence of interference by other people from doing what one wants or is able to do, it leads to a universal right to welfare.

He further argues that the recognition of this universal right to welfare leads to the equalization of resources characteristic of a socialist state. He considers a number of objections to these arguments and finds them wanting.

The central contrast between libertarians and socialists is usually put this way: Libertarians take the ideal of liberty to be the ultimate political ideal from which they think it follows that only a minimal or night watchman state can be justified, whereas socialists take the ideal of equality to be the ultimate political ideal from which they think it follows that only a state that socializes the means of production can be justified. Libertarians, however, tend to agree with socialists that when the ideal of equality is interpreted in the manner favored by socialists, it would justify a socialist state. Libertarians simply contend that the socialist interpretation of the ideal of equality is morally contestable. Why not interpret the ideal in the manner favored by libertarians as equality before the law or equality of basic rights so that the ideal is at least consistent with, if not required by, the libertarian's own ideal of liberty? Why not indeed! But obviously an analogous question could be directed at libertarians. Why not interpret the ideal of liberty in the manner favored by socialists as a positive rather than a negative ideal so that it would justify the greater equality in the distribution of goods and resources that is characteristic of a socialist state?

To either of these questions, no convincing answer seems forthcoming. Both the interpretations of the ideals of liberty and equality favored by libertarians and those favored by socialists appear morally contestable. Consequently, the dispute between libertarians and socialists seems irresolvable. I wish to argue, however, that this is not the case. I will show that the dispute can be resolved, for all practical purposes, by proceeding from premises that libertarians endorse to a conclusion that socialists endorse. Specifically, I will argue that libertarians, given their ideal of liberty, must be socialists because they must endorse the equality in the distribution of goods and resources required by a socialist state.

A longer version of this article will appear as "Reconciling Liberty and Equality or Why Libertarians must be Socialists" in *Liberty and Equality,* edited by Larry May and Jonathan Schonsheck (MIT, 1996).

I

To see that this is the case, suppose we interpret the ideal of liberty as a negative ideal in the manner favored by libertarians, rather than as a positive ideal in the manner favored by socialists.[1] So understood, liberty is the absence of interference by other people from doing what one wants or is able to do. Interpreting their ideal in this way, libertarians claim to derive a number of more specific requirements, in particular, a right to life; a right to freedom of speech, press, and assembly; and a right to property. Here it is important to observe that the libertarian's right to life is not a right to receive from others the goods and resources necessary for preserving one's life; it is simply a right not to be killed unjustly. Correspondingly, the libertarian's right to property is not a right to receive from others the goods and resources necessary for one's welfare, but rather a right to acquire goods and resources either by initial acquisition or by voluntary agreement.

Of course, libertarians would allow that it would be nice of the rich to share their surplus goods and resources with the poor. Nevertheless, according to libertarians, such acts of charity should not be coercively required. For this reason, libertarians are opposed to coercively supported welfare programs. By contrast, socialists would certainly interpret their ideal of equality to require not only coercively supported welfare programs, but also considerable equality in the distribution of goods and resources as well.

In order to see why libertarians are mistaken about what their ideal requires, consider a typical conflict situation between the rich and the poor. In this situation, the rich have more than enough goods and resources to satisfy their basic needs.[2] By contrast, the poor lack the goods and resources to meet their most basic needs even though they have tried all the means available to them that libertarians regard as legitimate for acquiring such goods and resources. Under such circumstances, libertarians usually maintain that the rich should have the liberty to use their resources to satisfy their luxury needs if they so wish. Libertarians recognize that this liberty might well be enjoyed at the expense of the satisfaction of the most basic needs of the poor; they just think that liberty always has priority over other political ideals, and since they assume that the liberty of the poor is not at stake in such conflict situations, it is easy for them to conclude that the rich should not be required to sacrifice their liberty so that the basic needs of the poor may be met.

Of course, libertarians allow that it would be nice of the rich to share their surplus goods and resources with the poor. Nevertheless, according to libertarians, such acts of charity cannot be required because the liberty of the poor is not thought to be at stake in such conflict situations.

In fact, however, the liberty of the poor *is* at stake in such conflict situations. What is at stake is the liberty of the poor not to be interfered with in taking from the surplus possessions of the rich what is necessary to satisfy their basic needs.[3]

Needless to say, libertarians would want to deny that the poor have this liberty. But how could they justify such a denial? As this liberty of the poor has been specified, it is not a positive right to receive something but a negative right of noninterference. Nor will it do for libertarians to appeal to a right to life or a right to property to rule out such a liberty because on the view under consideration liberty is basic and all other rights are derived from a right to liberty.[4] Clearly, what libertarians must do is recognize the existence of such a liberty and then claim that it conflicts with other liberties of the rich. But when libertarians see that this is the case, they are often genuinely surprised—one might even say rudely awakened—for they had not previously seen the conflict between the rich and the poor as a conflict of liberties.[5]

When the conflict between the rich and the poor is viewed as a conflict of liberties, either we can say that the rich should have the liberty not to be interfered with in using their surplus goods and resources for luxury purposes, or we can say that the poor should have the liberty not to be interfered with in taking from the rich what they require to meet their basic needs. If we choose one liberty, we must reject the other. What needs to be determined, therefore, is which liberty is morally preferable: the liberty of the rich or the liberty of the poor.

Two Principles

In order to see that the liberty of the poor not to be interfered with in taking from the surplus resources of the rich what is required to meet their basic needs is morally preferable to the liberty of the rich not to be interfered with in using their surplus goods and resources for luxury purposes, we need to appeal to one of the most fundamental principles of morality, one that is common to all political perspectives. This is the "Ought" Implies "Can" Principle:

> People are not morally required to do what they lack the power to do or what would involve so great a sacrifice that it would be unreasonable to ask them to perform such an action, and/or in the case of severe conflicts of interest, unreasonable to require them to perform such an action.

For example, suppose I promised to attend a departmental meeting on Friday, but on Thursday I am involved in a serious car accident that leaves me in a coma. Surely it is no longer the case that I ought to attend the meeting, now that I lack the power to do so. Or suppose instead that on Thursday I develop a severe case of pneumonia for which I am hospitalized. Surely, I could legitimately claim that I cannot attend the meeting, on the grounds that the risk to my health involved in attending is a sacrifice that it would be unreasonable to ask me to bear. Or suppose the risk to my health from having pneumonia is not so serious that it would be unreasonable to ask me to attend the meeting (a supererogatory request), it might still be serious enough to be unreasonable to require my attendance at the meeting (a demand that is backed up by blame or coercion).

Now applying the "ought" implies "can" principle to the case at hand, it seems clear that the poor have it within their power willingly to relinquish such an important liberty as the liberty not to be interfered with in taking from the rich what they require to meet their basic needs. Nevertheless, it would be unreasonable to ask or require them to make so great a sacrifice. In the extreme case, it would involve asking or requiring the poor to sit back and starve to death. Of course, the poor may have no real alternative to relinquishing this liberty. To do anything else may involve worse consequences for themselves and their loved ones and may invite a painful death. Accordingly, we may expect that the poor would acquiesce, albeit unwillingly, to a political system that denies them the right to welfare supported by such a liberty, at the same time that we recognize that such a system imposes an unreasonable sacrifice upon the poor—a sacrifice that we cannot morally blame the poor for trying to evade.[6] Analogously, we might expect that a woman whose life was threatened would submit to a rapist's demands, at the same time that we recognize the utter unreasonableness of those demands.

By contrast, it would not be unreasonable to ask and require the rich to sacrifice the liberty to meet some of their luxury needs so that the poor can have the liberty to meet their basic needs.[7] Naturally, we might expect that the rich, for reasons of self-interest and past contribution, might be disinclined to make such a sacrifice. We might even suppose that the past contribution of the rich provides a good reason for not sacrificing their liberty to use their surplus for luxury purposes. Yet, unlike the poor, the rich could not claim that relinquishing such a liberty would involve so great a sacrifice that it would be unreasonable to ask and require them to make it; unlike the poor, the rich could be morally blameworthy for failing to make such a sacrifice.

Notice that by virtue of the "ought" implies "can" principle, this argument establishes that:

1a) Because it would be unreasonable to ask or require the poor to sacrifice the liberty not to be interfered with when taking from the surplus goods and resources of the rich what is necessary to meet their basic needs, 1b) it is not the case that the poor are morally required to make such a sacrifice.

2a) Because it would not be unreasonable to ask and require the rich to sacrifice the liberty not to be interfered when using their surplus goods and resources for luxury purposes, 2b) it may be the case that the rich are morally required to make such a sacrifice.

What the argument does not establish is that it is the case that the rich are *morally required* to sacrifice (some of) their surplus so that the basic needs of the poor can be met. To clearly establish that conclusion, we need to appeal to a principle, which is, in fact, simply the contrapositive of the "ought" implies "can" principle. It is the Conflict Resolution Principle:

What people are morally required to do is what is either reasonable to ask them to do, or in the case of severe conflicts of interest, reasonable to require them to do.

While the "ought" implies "can" principle claims that if any action is *not reasonable to ask or require* a person to do, all things considered, that action is *not morally required* for that person, all things considered [−R(A v Re) → −MRe], the conflict resolution principle claims that if any action is *morally required* for a person to do, all things considered, that action is *reasonable to ask or require* that person to do, all things considered [MRe → R(A v Re)].

This conflict resolution principle accords with the generally accepted view of morality as a system of reasons for resolving interpersonal conflicts of interest. Of course, morality is not limited to such a system of reasons. Most surely it also includes reasons of self-development. All that is being claimed by the principle is that moral resolutions of interpersonal conflicts of interest cannot be contrary to reason to ask everyone affected to accept or, in the case of severe interpersonal conflicts of interest, unreasonable to require everyone affected to accept. The reason for the distinction between the two kinds of cases is that when interpersonal conflicts of interest are not severe, moral resolutions must still be reasonable to ask everyone affected to accept but they need not be reasonable to *require* everyone affected to accept. This is because not all moral resolutions can be justifiably enforced; only moral resolutions of severe interpersonal conflicts of interest can and *should* be justifiably enforced. Furthermore, the reason moral resolutions of severe interpersonal conflicts of interest should be enforced is that if the parties are simply asked but not required to abide by a moral resolution in such cases of conflict, then it is likely that the stronger party will violate the resolution and that would be unreasonable to ask or require the weaker party to accept.

When we apply the conflict resolution principle to our example of severe conflict between the rich and the poor, there are three possible moral resolutions:

I. A moral resolution that would require the rich to sacrifice the liberty not to be interfered with when using their surplus goods and resources for luxury purposes so that the poor can have the liberty not to be interfered with when taking from the surplus resources of the rich what is necessary to meet their basic needs.

II. A moral resolution that would require the poor to sacrifice the liberty not to be interfered with when taking from the surplus goods and resources of the rich what is necessary to meet their basic needs so that the rich can have the liberty not to be interfered with when using their surplus resources for luxury purposes.

III. A moral resolution that would require the rich and the poor to accept the results of a power struggle in which both the rich and the poor are at liberty to appropriate and use the surplus goods and resources of the rich.

Applying our previous discussion of the "ought" implies "can" principle to these three possible moral resolutions, it is clear that 1a (it would be unreasonable to ask or require the poor . . .) rules out II, but 2a (it would not be unreasonable to ask and require the rich . . .) does not rule out I. But what about III? Some libertarians have contended that III is the proper resolution of severe conflicts of interest between the rich and the poor.[8] But a resolution, like III, that sanctions the results of a power struggle between the rich and the poor, is a resolution that, by and large, favors the rich over the poor. So all things considered, it would be no more reasonable to require the poor to accept III than it would be to require them to accept II. This means that only I satisfies the conflict resolution principle by being a resolution that is reasonable to require everyone affected to accept. Consequently, if we assume that, however else we specify the requirements of morality, they cannot violate the "ought" implies "can" principle or the conflict resolution principle, it follows that, despite what libertarians claim, the basic right to liberty endorsed by them, as determined by a weighing of the relevant competing liberties according to these two principles, actually favors the liberty of the poor over the liberty of the rich.[9]

Yet couldn't libertarians object to this conclusion, claiming that it would be unreasonable to require the rich to sacrifice the liberty to meet some of their luxury needs so that the poor could have the liberty to meet their basic needs? As has been pointed out, libertari-

ans don't usually see the situation as a conflict of liberties. But suppose they did. How plausible would such an objection be? Not very plausible at all.

Consider: What are libertarians going to say about the poor? Isn't it clearly unreasonable to require the poor to sacrifice the liberty to meet their basic needs so that the rich can have the liberty to meet their luxury needs? Isn't it clearly unreasonable to require the poor to sit back and starve to death? If it is, then there is no resolution of this conflict that would be reasonable to require both the rich and the poor to accept. But that would mean that libertarians could not be putting forth a moral resolution, because according to the conflict resolution principle, in cases of severe conflict of interest, a moral resolution resolves conflicts of interest in ways that it would be reasonable to require everyone affected to accept. Therefore, as long as libertarians think of themselves as putting forth a moral resolution for cases of severe conflict of interest, they cannot allow that it would be unreasonable *both* to require the rich to sacrifice the liberty to meet some of their luxury needs in order to benefit the poor and to require the poor to sacrifice the liberty to meet their basic needs in order to benefit the rich. But I submit that if one of these requirements is to be judged reasonable, then, by any neutral assessment, it must be the requirement that the rich sacrifice the liberty to meet some of their luxury needs so that the poor can have the liberty to meet their basic needs. There is no other plausible resolution if libertarians intend to be putting forth a moral resolution.

It should also be noted that this case for restricting the liberty of the rich depends upon the willingness of the poor to take advantage of whatever opportunities are available to them to engage in mutually beneficial work, so that failure of the poor to take advantage of such opportunities would normally cancel or at least significantly reduce the obligation of the rich to restrict their own liberty for the benefit of the poor.[10] In addition, the poor would be required to return the equivalent of any surplus possessions they have taken from the rich once they are able to do so and still satisfy their basic needs. Nor would the poor be required to keep the liberty to which they are entitled. They could give up part of it, or all of it, or risk losing it on the chance of gaining a greater share of liberties or other social goods.[11] Consequently, the case for restricting the liberty of the rich for the benefit of the poor is neither unconditional nor inalienable.

Of course, there will be cases in which the poor fail to satisfy their basic needs, not because of any direct restriction of liberty on the part of the rich but because the poor are in such dire need that they are unable even to attempt to take from the rich what they require to meet their basic needs. In such cases, the rich would not be performing any act of commission that would prevent the poor from taking what they require. Yet, even in such cases, the rich would normally be performing acts of commission that would prevent other persons from taking part of the rich's own surplus possessions and using it to aid the poor. And when assessed from a moral point of view, restricting the liberty of these allies or agents of the poor would not be morally justified for the very same reason that restricting the liberty of the poor to meet their own basic needs would not be morally justified: It would not be reasonable to require all of those affected to accept such a restriction of liberty.

In brief, I have argued that a libertarian ideal of liberty can be seen to support a right to welfare through an application of the "ought" implies "can" principle and the conflict resolution principle to conflicts of liberty between the rich and the poor. In this interpretation of libertarianism, these principles support a right to welfare by favoring the liberty of the poor over the liberty of the rich. In another interpretation of libertarianism (developed elsewhere), these principles support this right to welfare by favoring a conditional right to property over an unconditional right to property.[12] In either interpretation, what is crucial to the derivation of this right is the claim that it would be unreasonable to require the poor to deny their basic needs and accept anything less than this right to welfare as the condition for their willing cooperation.

Now it might be objected that the right to welfare that this argument establishes from libertarian premises are not the same as the right to welfare endorsed by socialists. This is correct. We could mark this difference by referring to the right that this argument establishes as "a negative welfare right" and by referring to the right endorsed by socialists as "a positive welfare right." The significance of this difference is that a person's negative welfare right can be violated only when other people through acts of commission interfere with its exercise, whereas a person's positive welfare right can be violated not only by such acts of commission but by acts of omission as well. Nonetheless, this difference will have little practical import. For in recognizing the legitimacy of negative welfare rights, libertarians will come to see that virtually any use of their surplus possessions is likely to violate the negative welfare rights of the poor by preventing the poor from rightfully appropriating (some part of) their surplus goods and resources. So in order to ensure that they will not be engaging in such wrongful actions, it will be incumbent on them to set up institutions guaranteeing adequate positive welfare rights for the poor. Only then will they be able to legitimately use any remaining surplus possessions to meet their own nonbasic needs. Furthermore, in the absence of adequate positive welfare rights, the poor, either acting by themselves or through their allies or agents, would have some discretion in determining when and how to exercise their negative welfare rights.[13] In order not to be subject to that discretion, libertarians will tend to favor the only morally legitimate way of preventing the exercise of such rights: They will set up institutions guaranteeing adequate positive welfare rights that will then take precedence over the exercise of negative welfare rights. For these reasons, recognizing the negative welfare rights of the poor will ultimately lead libertarians to endorse the same sort of welfare institutions favored by socialists.

II

Now it is possible that libertarians convinced to some extent by the previous argument might want to accept a right to welfare but then deny that this would lead to anything like a socialist state. After all, the fundamental rights recognized by libertarians are universal rights, that is, rights possessed by all people, not just those who live in certain places or at certain times. Of course, to claim that these rights are universal rights does not mean that they are universally recognized. Obviously, the fundamental rights that flow from the libertarian ideal have not been universally recognized. Rather, to claim that they are universal rights, despite their spotty recognition, implies only that they ought to be recognized at all times and places by people who have or could have had good reasons to recognize these rights, whether or not they actually did or do so. Nor need these universal rights be unconditional. This is particularly true in the case of the right to welfare, which, I have argued, is conditional on people doing all that they legitimately can to provide for themselves. In addition, this right is conditional on there being sufficient goods and resources available so that everyone's welfare needs can be met. So where people do not do all that they can to provide for themselves or where there are not sufficient goods and resources available, people simply do not have a right to welfare. Still, libertarians might grant that there are universal rights, even a right to welfare, that can be supported by the libertarian ideal of liberty but still deny that such rights lead to a socialist rather than a welfare state. But to see why this is not the case, consider what would be required to recognize a universal right to welfare.

Consider that at present there is probably a sufficient worldwide supply of goods and resources to meet the normal costs of satisfying the basic nutritional needs of all existing persons. According to former U.S. Secretary of Agriculture, Bob Bergland:

> For the past 20 years, if the available world food supply had been evenly divided and distributed, each person would have received more than the minimum number of calories.[14]

Other authorities have made similar assessments of the available world food supply.

Needless to say, the adoption of a policy of supporting a right to welfare for all existing persons would necessitate significant changes, especially in developed countries. For example, the large percentage of the U.S. population whose food consumption clearly exceeds even an adequately adjusted poverty index would have to substantially alter their eating habits. In particular, they would have to reduce their consumption of beef and pork in order to make more grain available for direct human consumption. (Presently the amount of grain fed to American livestock is as much as all the people of China and India eat in a year.) Thus, at least the satisfaction of some of the nonbasic needs of the more advantaged in developed countries would have to be foregone if the basic nu-

tritional needs of all existing persons in developing and underdeveloped countries are to be met. Of course, meeting the long-term basic nutritional needs of these societies will require other kinds of aid including appropriate technology and training and the removal of trade barriers favoring developed societies.[15] Furthermore, to raise the standard of living in developing and underdeveloped countries will require substantial increases in the consumption of energy and other resources. But such an increase would have to be matched by a substantial decrease in the consumption of these goods in developed countries; otherwise, global ecological disaster would result from increased global warming, ozone depletion, and acid rain, lowering virtually everyone's standard of living.[16]

In addition, once the basic nutritional needs of future generations are also taken into account, the satisfaction of the nonbasic needs of the more advantaged in developed countries would have to be further restricted in order to preserve the fertility of cropland and other food-related natural resources for the use of future generations. Obviously, the only assured way to guarantee the energy and resources necessary for the satisfaction of the basic needs of future generations is to set aside resources that would otherwise be used to satisfy the nonbasic needs of existing generations.

Once basic needs other than nutritional needs are taken into account as well, still further restrictions would be required. For example, it has been estimated that presently a North American uses fifty times more goods and resources than a person living in India. This means that in terms of resource consumption the North American continent's population is the equivalent of 12.5 billion Indians. So unless we assume that basic goods and resources—such as arable land, iron, coal, oil, and so forth—are in unlimited supply, then this unequal consumption would have to be radically altered if the basic needs of distant peoples and future generations are to be met. Accordingly, recognizing a universal right to welfare applicable both to distant peoples and to future generations would lead to an equal sharing of goods and resources over place and time. In short, socialist equality is the consequence of recognizing a universal libertarian right to welfare.

In brief, I have argued that when a libertarian ideal of liberty is correctly interpreted, it leads to a universal right to welfare, and further that the recognition of this universal right to welfare leads to the equality in the distribution of goods and resources that is charac-teristic of a socialist state. Of course, the libertarian ideal, unlike the socialist ideal, does not directly pursue the goal of (substantive) equality.[17] Nevertheless, I contend that the practical effect of both ideals is much the same.

Endnotes

I would like to thank Joan Callahan, David Duquette, Joseph Ellin, Sidney Geldin, Carol Gould, Larry May, Jan Narveson, David Phillips, Jonathan Schonsheck, and Carl Wellman for helpful comments on earlier versions of this paper.

1. See John Hospers, *Libertarianism* (Los Angeles: Nash Press, 1971).

2. Basic needs, if not satisfied, lead to significant lacks or deficiencies with respect to a standard of mental and physical well-being, Thus, a person's needs for food, shelter, medical care, protection, companionship, and self-development are, at least in part, needs of this sort. For a discussion of basic needs, see *How To Make People Just* (Totowa: Rowman and Littlefield, 1988), pp.45–48.

3. It is not being assumed here that the surplus possessions of the rich are either justifiable or unjustifiably possessed by the rich. Moreover, according to libertarians, it is an assessment of the liberties involved that determines whether the possession is justifiable or not.

4. There is another interpretation of libertarianism according to which a particular set of rights are basic and liberty is interpreted as the absence of interference with these rights. But, as I have argued elsewhere, the same sort of argument works against both forms of libertarianism. For this other interpretation, see "From Liberty to Welfare," *Ethics* (1994), and my *How To Make People Just,* Chapter 5.

5. See John Hospers, *Libertarianism* (Los Angeles: Nash Publishing, 1971), Chapter 7 and Tibor Machan, *Human Rights and Human Liberties* (Chicago: Nelson-Hall, 1975), pp. 231ff.

6. See James P. Sterba,"Is There a Rationale for Punishment?" *American Journal of Jurisprudence 29* (1984), 29–43.

7. By the liberty of the rich to meet their luxury needs I continue to mean the liberty of the rich not to be interfered with when using their surplus possessions for luxury purposes. Similarly, by the liberty of the poor to meet their basic needs I continue to mean the liberty of the poor not to be interfered with when taking what they require to meet their basic needs from the surplus possessions of the rich.

8. See, for example, Eric Mack, "Individualism, Rights and the Open Society," *The Libertarian Alternative,* edited by Tibor Machan (Chicago: Nelson-Hall, 1974).

9. Since the conflict resolution principle is the contrapositive of the "ought" implies "can" principle, whatever logically follows from the one principle logically follows from the other; nevertheless, by first appealing to the one principle and then the other, as I have here, I maintain that the conclusions that I derive can be seen to follow more clearly.

10. The employment opportunities offered to the poor must be honorable and supportive of self-respect. To do otherwise would be to offer the poor the opportunity to meet some of their basic needs at the cost of denying some of their other basic needs.

11. The poor cannot, however, give up the liberty to which their children are entitled.

12. For this other interpretation, see note #4.

13. When the poor are acting collectively in conjunction with their agents and allies to exercise their negative welfare rights, they will want, in turn, to institute adequate positive welfare rights to secure a proper distribution of the goods and resources they are acquiring.

14. Bob Bergland, "Attacking the Problem of World Hunger," *The National Forum* (1979) Vol. 69, No. 2, p. 4.

15. Henry Shue, *Basic Rights* (Princeton University Press, 1980), Chapter 7.

16. For a discussion of these causal connections, see Cheryl Silver, *One Earth One Future* (Washington, D.C.: National Academy Press, 1990); Bill McKibben, *The End of Nature* (New York: Anchor Books, 1989); Jeremy Leggett, ed., *Global Warming* (New York: Oxford University Press, 1990); Lester Brown, ed., *The World Watch Reader* (New York: Nelson, 1991).

17. Here I agree with Narveson that there are formal notions of equality, like equality before the law and equality of basic rights, that libertarians will frequently aim to achieve.

5. Wyman, Commissioner of New York Department of Social Services v. James

SUPREME COURT OF THE UNITED STATES

The issue before the Supreme Court of the United States was whether the Fourth Amendment prohibition of unreasonable searches applies to visits by welfare caseworkers to recipients of Aid to Families with Dependent Children. The majority of the Court held that the Fourth Amendment does not apply in this case because the visitation is not forced or compelled, and even if it were, the visitation serves the state's overriding interest in the welfare of dependent children. Dissenting Justices Douglas and Marshall argued that the Fourth Amendment prohibition does apply because the visitation is forced and compelled (although not normally by a threat of a criminal penalty) and because there are other ways of protecting the state's interest in this case. Justices Douglas and Marshall also argued that the decision of the majority is inconsistent with the Supreme Court's rulings with respect to the allocation of benefits in other cases.

Mr. Justice *Blackmun* delivered the opinion of the Court.

This appeal presents the issue whether a beneficiary of the program for Aid to Families with Dependent Children (AFDC) may refuse a home visit by the caseworker without risking the termination of benefits.

The New York State and City social services commissioners appeal from a judgment and decree of a divided three-judge District Court. . . .

The District Court majority held that a mother receiving AFDC relief may refuse, without forfeiting her right to that relief, the periodic home visit which the cited New York statutes and regulations prescribe as a condition for the continuance of assistance under the program. The beneficiary's thesis, and that of the District Court majority, is that home visitation is a search and, when not consented to or when not supported by a warrant based on probable cause, violates the beneficiary's Fourth and Fourteenth Amendment rights. . . .

Plaintiff Barbara James is the mother of a son, Maurice, who was born in May 1967. They reside in New York City. Mrs. James first applied for AFDC assistance shortly before Maurice's birth. A caseworker made a visit to her apartment at that time without objection. The assistance was authorized.

Two years later, on May 8, 1969, a caseworker wrote Mrs. James that she would visit her home on May 14. Upon receipt of this advice, Mrs. James telephoned the worker that, although she was willing to supply information "reasonable and relevant" to her need for public assistance, any discussion was not to take place at her home. The worker told Mrs. James that she was required by law to visit in her home and that refusal to permit the visit would result in the termination of assistance. Permission was still denied. . . .

A notice of termination [was] issued on June 2.

Thereupon, without seeking a hearing at the state level, Mrs. James, individually and on behalf of Maurice, and purporting to act on behalf of all other persons similarly situated, instituted the present civil rights suit. . . .

When a case involves a home and some type of official intrusion into that home, as this case appears to do, an immediate and natural reaction is one of concern about Fourth Amendment rights and the protection which that Amendment is intended to afford. Its emphasis indeed is upon one of the most precious aspects of personal security in the home: "The right of the people to be secure in their persons, houses, papers, and effects. . . ." This Court has characterized that right as "basic to a free society. . . ." And over the years the Court consistently has been most protective of the privacy of the dwelling. . . .

This natural and quite proper protective attitude, however, is not a factor in this case, for the seemingly obvious and simple reason that we are not concerned here with any search by the New York social service agency in the Fourth Amendment meaning of that term. It is true that the governing statute and regulations appear to make mandatory the initial home visit and the subsequent periodic "contacts" (which may include home visits) for the inception and continuance of aid. It is also true that the caseworker's posture in the home visit is perhaps, in a sense, both rehabilitative and investigative. But this latter aspect, we think, is given too broad a character and far more emphasis than it deserves if it is equated with a search in the traditional criminal law context. We note, too, that the visitation in itself is not forced or compelled, and that the beneficiary's denial of permission is not a criminal act. If consent to the visitation is withheld, no visitation takes place. The aid then never begins or merely ceases, as the case may be. There is no entry of the home and there is no search.

If, however, we were to assume that a caseworker's home visit, before or subsequent to the beneficiary's initial qualification for benefits, somehow (perhaps because the average beneficiary might feel she is in no position to refuse consent to the visit), and despite its interview nature, does possess some of the characteristics of a search in the traditional sense, we nevertheless conclude that does not fall within the Fourth Amendment's proscription. This is because it does not descend to the level of unreasonableness. It is unreasonableness which is the Fourth Amendment's standard.

There are a number of factors that compel us to conclude that the home visit proposed for Mrs. James is not unreasonable.

The public's interest in this particular segment of the area of assistance to the unfortunate is protection and aid for the dependent child whose family requires such aid for that child. . . . The dependent child's needs are paramount, and only with hesitancy would we relegate those needs, in the scale of comparative values, to a position secondary to what the mother claims as her rights.

The agency, with tax funds provided from federal as well as from state sources, is fulfilling a public trust. The State, working through its qualified welfare agency, has appropriate and paramount interest and concern in seeing and assuring that the intended and proper objects of that tax-produced assistance are the ones who benefit from the aid it dispenses. . . .

One who dispenses purely private charity naturally has an interest in and expects to know how his charitable funds are utilized and put to work. The public, when it is the provider, rightly expects the same. . . .

We therefore conclude that the home visitation as structured by the New York statutes and regulations is a reasonable administrative tool; that it serves a valid and proper administrative purpose for the dispensation of the AFDC program; that it is not an unwarranted invasion of personal privacy; and that it violates no right guaranteed by the Fourth Amendment.

Reversed and remanded with directions to enter a judgment of dismissal.

It is so ordered. . . .

Mr. Justice *Douglas,* dissenting. . . .

In 1969 roughly 127 billion dollars were spent by the federal, state, and local governments on "social welfare." To farmers alone almost four billion dollars were paid, in part for not growing certain crops. . . .

Yet almost every beneficiary whether rich or poor, rural or urban, has a "house"—one of the places protected by the Fourth Amendment against "unreasonable searches and seizures." The question in this case is whether receipt of largesse from the government makes the *home* of the beneficiary subject to access by an inspector of the agency of oversight, even though the beneficiary objects to the intrusion and even though the Fourth Amendment's procedure for access to one's *house* or *home* is not followed. The penalty here is not, of course, invasion of the privacy of Barbara James, only her loss of federal or state largesse. That, however, is merely rephrasing the problem. Whatever the semantics, the central question is whether the government by force of its largesse has the power to "buy up" rights guaranteed by the Constitution. But for the assertion of her constitutional right, Barbara James in this case would have received the welfare benefit. . . .

The applicable principle, as stated in *Camara* as "justified by history and by current experience" is that "except in certain carefully defined classes of cases, a search of private property without proper consent is 'unreasonable' unless it has been authorized by a valid search warrant."

In *See* we [decided] that the "businessman, like the occupant of a residence, has a constitutional right to go about his business free from unreasonable official entries upon his private commercial property." There is not the slightest hint in *See* that the Government could condition a business license on the "consent" of the licensee to the administrative searches we held violated the Fourth Amendment. It is a strange jurisprudence indeed which safeguards the businessman at his place of work from warrantless searches but will not do the same for a mother in her *home*.

Is a search of her home without a warrant made "reasonable" merely because she is dependent on government largesse?

Judge Skelly Wright has stated the problem succinctly:

> Welfare has long been considered the equivalent of charity and its recipients have been subjected to all kinds of dehumanizing experiences in the government's effort to police its welfare payments. In fact, over half a billion dollars are expended annually for administration and policing in connection with the Aid to Families with Dependent Children program. Why such large sums are necessary for administration and policing has never been adequately explained. No such sums are spent policing the government subsidies granted to farmers, airlines, steamship companies, and junk mail dealers, to name but a few. The truth is that in this subsidy area society has simply adopted a double standard, one for aid to business and the farmer and a different one for welfare. (Poverty, Minorities, and Respect for Law, 1970 Duke L. J. 425, 437–438.)

If the welfare recipient was not Barbara James but a prominent, affluent cotton or wheat farmer receiving benefit payments for not growing crops, would not the approach be different? Welfare in aid of dependent children, like social security and unemployment benefits, has an aura of suspicion. There doubtless are frauds in every sector of public welfare whether the recipient be a Barbara James or someone who is prominent or influential. But constitutional rights— here the privacy of the *home*—are obviously not dependent on the poverty or on the affluence of the beneficiary. It is the precincts of the *home* that the Fourth Amendment protects; and their privacy is as important to the lowly as to the mighty.

I would sustain the judgment of the three-judge court in the present case.

Mr. Justice *Marshall*, whom Mr. Justice *Brennan* joins, dissenting.

. . . The record plainly shows . . . that Mrs. James offered to furnish any information that the appellants desired and to be interviewed at any place other than her home. Appellants rejected her offers and terminated her benefits solely on the ground that she refused to permit a home visit. In addition, appellants make no contention that any sort of probable cause exists to suspect appellee of welfare fraud or child abuse.

Simply stated, the issue in this case is whether a state welfare agency can require all recipients of AFDC benefits to submit to warrantless "visitations" of their homes. In answering that question, the majority dodges between constitutional issues to reach a result clearly inconsistent with the decisions of this Court. We are told that there is no such search involved in this case; that even if there were a search, it would not be unreasonable; and that even if this were an unreasonable search, a welfare recipient waives her right to object by accepting benefits. I emphatically disagree with all three conclusions. . . .

. . . In an era of rapidly burgeoning governmental activities and their concomitant inspectors, caseworkers, and researchers, a restriction of the Fourth Amendment to "the traditional criminal law context" tramples the ancient concept that a man's home is his castle. Only last Term, we reaffirmed that this concept has lost none of its vitality. . . .

. . . [I]t is argued that the home visit is justified to protect dependent children from "abuse" and "exploitation." These are heinous crimes, but they are not confined to indigent households. Would the majority sanction, in the absence of probable cause, compulsory visits to all American homes for the purpose of discovering child abuse? Or is this Court prepared to hold as a matter of constitutional law that a mother, merely because she is poor, is substantially more likely to injure or exploit her children? Such a categorical approach to an entire class of citizens would be dangerously at odds with the tenets of our democracy. . . .

Although the Court does not agree with my conclusion that the home visit is an unreasonable search, its opinion suggests that even if the visit were unreasonable, appellee has somehow waived her right to object. Surely the majority cannot believe that valid Fourth Amendment consent can be given under the threat of the loss of one's sole means of support. . . .

In deciding that the homes of AFDC recipients are not entitled to protection from warrantless searches by welfare caseworkers, the Court declines to follow prior case law and employs a rationale that, if applied to the claims of all citizens, would threaten the validity of the Fourth Amendment. . . . Perhaps the majority has explained why a commercial warehouse deserves more protection than does this poor woman's home. I am not convinced; and, therefore, I must respectfully dissent.

6. *Plyler* v. *Doe*

SUPREME COURT OF THE UNITED STATES

The issue before the Supreme Court was whether a Texas statute that withholds from local school districts any state funds for the education of children who were not "legally admitted" into the United States and that authorizes local school districts to deny enrollment to such children violates the Equal Protection Clause of the Fourteenth Amendment. Justice Brennan, delivering the opinion of the Court, argued that the Texas statute did violate the Equal Protection Clause. He contended that although public education is not a right granted to individuals by the Constitution (Marshall dissenting), given the "pivotal role of education in sustaining our political and cultural heritage" and the economic benefits that accrue to Texas from the presence of illegal aliens, petitioners had failed to establish a legitimate state interest in denying an education to illegal aliens. In dissent, Chief Justice Burger with whom Justices White, Rehnquist, and O'Connor joined, argued that although the Texas statute is unwise and unsound, it is not unconstitutional. Burger contended that although illegal aliens are included within the category of persons protected by the Equal Protection Clause, the Texas statute does bear "a relation to a legitimate state purpose," especially in view of the fact that the federal government sees fit to exclude illegal aliens from numerous social welfare programs.

. . . In May 1975, the Texas Legislature revised its education laws to withhold from local school districts any state funds for the education of children who were not "legally admitted" into the United States. The 1975 revision also authorized local school districts to deny enrollment in their public schools to children not "legally admitted" to the country. . . . These cases involve constitutional challenges to those provisions.

[*Plyler v. Doe*] is a class action, filed in the United States District Court for the Eastern District of Texas in September 1977, on behalf of certain school-age children of Mexican origin residing in Smith County, Tex., who could not establish that they had been legally admitted into the United States. The action complained of the exclusion of plaintiff children from the public schools of the Tyler Independent School District. The Superintendent and members of the Board of Trustees of the School District were named as defendants; the State of Texas intervened as a party-defendant. After certifying a class consisting of all undocumented school-age children of Mexican origin residing in Smith County, Tex., who could not establish that they had been legally admitted into the United States. The action complained of the exclusion of plaintiff children from the public schools of the Tyler Independent School District. The Superintendent and members of the Board of Trustees of the School District were named as defendants; the State of Texas intervened as a party-defendant. After certifying a class consisting of all undocumented school-age children of Mexican origin residing within the School District, the District Court preliminarily enjoined defendants from denying a free education to members of the plaintiff class. In December 1977, the court conducted an extensive hearing on plaintiffs' motion for permanent injunctive relief. . . .

The District Court held that illegal aliens were entitled to the protection of the Equal Protection Clause of the Fourteenth Amendment, and that [this section] violated that Clause. . . .

The Court of Appeals for the Fifth Circuit upheld the District Court's injunction. . . .

The Fourteenth Amendment provides that "[n]o State shall . . . deprive any person of life, liberty, or property, without due process of law; nor deny to *any person within its jurisdiction* the equal protection of the laws." . . . [Emphasis added.] Appellants argue at the outset that undocumented aliens, because of their immigration status, are not "persons within the jurisdiction" of the State of Texas, and that they therefore have no right to the equal protection of Texas Law. We reject this argument. . . .

. . . The Equal Protection Clause was intended to work nothing less than the abolition of all caste-based and invidious class-based legislation. That objective is fundamentally at odds with the power the State asserts here to classify persons subject to its laws as nonetheless excepted from its protection.

Although the congressional debate concerning . . . the Fourteenth Amendment was limited, that debate clearly confirms the understanding that the phrase "within its jurisdiction" was intended in a broad sense to offer the guarantee of equal protection to all within a State's boundaries, and to all upon whom the State would impose the obligations of its laws. Indeed, it appears from those debates that Congress, by using the phrase "person within its jurisdiction," sought expressly to ensure that the equal protection of the

laws was provided to the alien population. Representative Bingham reported to the House the draft resolution of the Joint Committee of Fifteen on Reconstruction (H.R. 63) that was to become the Fourteenth Amendment. . . . Two days later, Bingham posed the following question in support of the resolution:

> Is it not essential to the unity of the people that the citizens of each State shall be entitled to all the privileges and immunities of citizens in the several States? Is it not essential to the unity of the Government and the unity of the people that all persons, *whether citizens or strangers, within this land,* shall have equal protection in every State in this Union in the rights of life and liberty and property?

. . . Our conclusion that the illegal aliens who are plaintiffs in these cases may claim the benefit of the Fourteenth Amendment's guarantee of equal protection only begins the inquiry. The more difficult question is whether the Equal Protection Clause has been violated by the refusal of the State of Texas to reimburse local school boards for the education of children who cannot demonstrate that their presence within the United States is lawful, or by the imposition by those school boards of the burden of tuition on those children. It is to this question that we now turn. . . .

. . . In applying the Equal Protection Clause to most forms of state action, we thus seek only the assurance that the classification at issue bears some fair relationship to a legitimate public purpose.

Of course, undocumented status is not irrelevant to any proper legislative goal. Nor is undocumented status an absolutely immutable characteristic since it is the product of conscious, indeed unlawful, action. But [this statute] is directed against children, and imposes its discriminatory burden on the basis of a legal characteristic over which children can have little control. It is thus difficult to conceive of a rational justification for penalizing these children for their presence within the United States. Yet that appears to be precisely the effect of [this statute].

Public education is not a "right" granted to individuals by the Constitution. *San Antonio Independent School Dist. v. Rodriguez* . . . (1973). But neither is it merely some governmental "benefit" indistinguishable from other forms of social welfare legislation. Both the importance of education in maintaining our basic institutions, and the lasting impact of its deprivation on the life of the child, mark the distinction. The "American people have always regarded education and [the] acquisition of knowledge as matters of supreme importance." *Meyer v. Nebraska* . . . (1923). We have recognized "the public schools as a most vital civic institution for the preservation of a democratic system of government," *Abington School District v. Schempp* . . . (1963) . . . and as the primary vehicle for transmitting "the values on which our society rests." *Ambach v. Norwick* . . . (1979). "[A]s . . . pointed out early in our history, . . . some degree of education is necessary to prepare citizens to participate effectively and intelligently in our open political system if we are to preserve freedom and independence." *Wisconsin v. Yoder* . . . (1972). And these historic "perceptions of the public schools as inculcating fundamental values necessary to the maintenance of a democratic political system have been confirmed by the observations of social scientists." *Ambach v. Norwick*. . . . In addition, education provides the basic tools by which individuals might lead economically productive lives to the benefit of us all. In sum, education has a fundamental role in maintaining the fabric of our society. We cannot ignore the significant social costs borne by our Nation when select groups are denied the means to absorb the values and skills upon which our social order rests.

In addition to the pivotal role of education in sustaining our political and cultural heritage, denial of education to some isolated group of children poses an affront to one of the goals of the Equal Protection Clause: the abolition of governmental barriers presenting unreasonable obstacles to advancement on the basis of individual merit. Paradoxically, by depriving the children of any disfavored group of an education, we foreclose the means by which that group might raise the level of esteem in which it is held by the majority. But more directly, "education prepares individuals to be self-reliant and self-sufficient participants in society." *Wisconsin v. Yoder*. . . . Illiteracy is an enduring disability. The inability to read and write will handicap the individual deprived of a basic education each and every day of his life. The inestimable toll of that deprivation on the social, economic, intellectual, and psychological well-being of the individual, and the obstacle it poses to individual achievement, make it most difficult to reconcile the cost or the principle of a status-based denial of basic education with the framework of equality embodied in the Equal Protection Clause. What we said 28 years ago in *Brown v. Board of Education*, . . . (1954), still holds true:

> Today, education is perhaps the most important function of state and local governments. Compulsory school attendance laws and the great expenditures for education both demonstrate our recognition of the importance of education to our democratic society. It is required in the performance of our most basic public responsibilities, even service in the armed forces. It is the very foundation of good citizenship. Today it is a principal instrument in awakening the child to cultural values, in preparing him for later professional training, and in helping him to adjust normally to his environment. In these days, it is doubtful that any child may reasonably be expected to succeed in life if he is denied the opportunity of an education. Such an opportunity, where the state has undertaken to provide it, is a right which must be made available to all on equal terms. . . .

. . . [A]ppellants appear to suggest that the State may seek to protect itself from an influx of illegal immigrants. While a State might have an interest in mitigating the potentially harsh economic effects of sudden shifts in population, [this statute] hardly offers an effective method of dealing with an urgent demographic or economic problem. There is no evidence in the record suggesting that illegal entrants impose any significant burden on the State's economy. To the contrary, the available evidence suggests that illegal aliens underutilize public services, while contributing their labor to the local economy and tax money to the state fisc. . . . The dominant incentive for illegal entry into the State of Texas is the availability of employment; few if any illegal immigrants come to this country, or presumably to the State of Texas, in order to avail themselves of a free education. Thus, even making the doubtful assumption that the net impact of illegal aliens on the economy of the State is negative, we think it clear that "[c]harging tuition to undocumented children constitutes a ludicrously ineffectual attempt to stem the tide of illegal immigration," at least when compared with the alternative of prohibiting the employment of illegal aliens. . . .

Accordingly, the judgment of the Court of Appeals in each of these cases is

Affirmed.

Justice *Marshall,* concurring.

While I join the Court's opinion, I do so without in any way retreating from my opinion in *San Antonio Independent School District v. Rodriguez.* . . . I continue to believe that an individual's interest in education is fundamental, and that this view is amply supported "by the unique status accorded public education by our society, and by the close relationship between education and some of our most basic constitutional values." . . . Furthermore, I believe that the facts of these cases demonstrate the wisdom of rejecting a rigidified approach to equal protection analysis, and of employing an approach that allows for varying levels of scrutiny depending upon "the constitutional and societal importance of the interest adversely affected and the recognized invidiousness of the basis upon which the particular classification is drawn." . . . It continues to be my view that a class-based denial of public education is utterly incompatible with the Equal Protection Clause of the Fourteenth Amendment.

Justice *Blackmun,* concurring.

I join the opinion and judgment of the Court.

Like Justice Powell, I believe that the children involved in this litigation "should not be left on the streets uneducated." . . . I write separately, however, because in my view the nature of the interest at stake is crucial to the proper resolution of these cases.

The "fundamental rights" aspect of the Court's equal protection analysis—the now-familiar concept that governmental classifications bearing on certain interests must be closely scrutinized—has been the subject of some controversy. . . .

[This controversy], combined with doubts about the judiciary's ability to make fine distinctions in assessing the effects of complex social policies, led the Court in *Rodriguez* to articulate a firm rule: Fundamental rights are those that "explicitly or implicitly [are] guaranteed by the Constitution." . . . It therefore squarely rejected the notion that "an ad hoc determination as to the social or economic importance" of a given interest is relevant to the level of scrutiny accorded classifications involving that interest, . . . and

made clear that "[i]t is not the province of this Court to create substantive constitutional rights in the name of guaranteeing equal protection of the laws." . . .

I joined Justice Powell's opinion for the Court in *Rodriguez,* and I continue to believe that it provides the appropriate model for resolving most equal protection disputes. Classifications infringing substantive constitutional rights necessarily will be invalid, if not by force of the Equal Protection Clause, then through operation of other provisions of the Constitution. Conversely, classifications bearing on nonconstitutional interests—even those involving "the most basic economic needs of impoverished human beings" . . . —generally are not subject to special treatment under the Equal Protection Clause, because they are not distinguishable in any relevant way from other regulations in "the area of economics and social welfare."

With all this said, however, I believe the Court's experience has demonstrated that the *Rodriguez* formulation does not settle every issue of "fundamental rights" arising under the Equal Protection Clause. Only a pedant would insist that there are *no* meaningful distinctions among the multitude of social and political interests regulated by the States, and *Rodriguez* does not stand for quite so absolute a proposition. To the contrary, *Rodriguez* implicitly acknowledged that certain interests, though not constitutionally guaranteed, must be accorded a special place in equal protection analysis. Thus, the Court's decisions long have accorded strict scrutiny to classifications bearing on the right to vote in state elections, and *Rodriguez* confirmed the "constitutional underpinnings of the right to equal treatment in the voting process." . . . Yet "the right to vote, *per se,* is not a constitutionally protected right." . . . Instead, regulation of the electoral process receives unusual scrutiny because "the right to exercise the franchise in a free and unimpaired manner is preservative of other basic civil and political rights." . . . In other words, the right to vote is accorded extraordinary treatment because it is, in equal protection terms, an extraordinary right: A citizen cannot hope to achieve any meaningful degree of individual political equality if granted an inferior right of participation in the political process. Those denied the vote are relegated, by state fiat, in a most basic way to second-class status. . . .

In my view, when the State provides an education to some and denies it to others, it immediately and inevitably creates class distinctions of a type fundamentally inconsistent with those purposes, mentioned above, of the Equal Protection Clause. Children denied an education are placed at a permanent and insurmountable competitive disadvantage, for an uneducated child is denied even the opportunity to achieve. And when those children are members of an identifiable group, that group—through the State's action—will have been converted into a discrete underclass. Other benefits provided by the State, such as housing and public assistance, are of course important; to an individual in immediate need, they may be more desirable than the right to be educated. But classifications involving the complete denial of education are in a sense unique, for they strike at the heart of equal protection values by involving the State in the creation of permanent class distinctions. . . . In a sense, then, denial of an education is the analogue of denial of the right to vote: The former relegates the individual to second-class social status; the latter places him at a permanent political disadvantage.

This conclusion is fully consistent with *Rodriguez.* The Court there reserved judgment on the constitutionality of a state system that "occasioned an absolute denial of educational opportunities to any of its children," noting that "no charge fairly could be made that the system . . . fails to provide each child with an opportunity to acquire . . . basic minimal skills." . . . And it cautioned that in a case "involv[ing] the most persistent and difficult questions of educational policy, . . . [the] Court's lack of specialized knowledge and experience counsels against premature interference with the informed judgments made at the state and local levels." . . . Thus *Rodriguez* held, and the Court now reaffirms, that "a State need not justify by compelling necessity every variation in the manner in which education is provided to its population." . . . Similarly, it is undeniable that education is not a "fundamental right" in the sense that it is constitutionally guaranteed. Here, however, the State has undertaken to provide an education to most of the children residing within its borders. And, in contrast to the situation in *Rodriguez,* it does not take an advanced degree to predict the effects of a complete denial of education upon those children targeted by the State's classifica-

tion. In such circumstances, the voting decisions suggest that the State must offer something more than a rational basis for its classification. . . .

Chief Justice *Burger,* with whom Justice *White,* Justice *Rehnquist,* and Justice *O'Connor* join, dissenting.

Were it our business to set the Nation's social policy, I would agree without hesitation that it is senseless for an enlightened society to deprive any children—including illegal aliens—of an elementary education. I fully agree that it would be folly—and wrong—to tolerate creation of a segment of society made up of illiterate persons, many having a limited or no command of our language. However, the Constitution does not constitute us as "Platonic Guardians" nor does it vest in this Court the authority to strike down laws because they do not meet our standards of desirable social policy, "wisdom," or "common sense." . . . We trespass on the assigned function of the political branches under our structure of limited and separated powers when we assume a policy-making role as the Court does today.

The Court makes no attempt to disguise that it is acting to make up for Congress's lack of "effective leadership" in dealing with the serious national problems caused by the influx of uncountable millions of illegal aliens across our borders. . . . The failure of enforcement of the immigration laws over more than a decade and the inherent difficulty and expense of sealing our vast borders have combined to create a grave socioeconomic dilemma. It is a dilemma that has not yet even been fully assessed, let alone addressed. However, it is not the function of the Judiciary to provide "effective leadership" simply because the political branches of government fail to do so.

The Court's holding today manifests the justly criticized judicial tendency to attempt speedy and wholesale formulation of "remedies" for the failures—or simply the laggard pace—of the political processes of our system of government. The Court employs, and in my view abuses, the Fourteenth Amendment in an effort to become an omnipotent and omniscient problem solver. That the motives for doing so are noble and compassionate does not alter the fact that the Court distorts our constitutional function to make amends for the defaults of others. . . .

The Court acknowledges that, except in those cases when state classifications disadvantage a "suspect class" or impinge upon a "fundamental right," the Equal Protection Clause permits a state "substantial latitude" in distinguishing between different groups of persons. . . . Moreover, the Court expressly—and correctly—rejects any suggestion that illegal aliens are a suspect class, . . . or that education is a fundamental right. . . . Yet by patching together bits and pieces of what might be termed quasi-suspect-class and quasi-fundamental-rights analysis, the Court spins out a theory custom-tailored to the facts of these cases.

In the end, we are told little more than that the level of scrutiny employed to strike down the Texas law applies only when illegal alien children are deprived of a public education. . . . If ever a court was guilty of an unabashedly result-oriented approach, this case is a prime example. . . .

Once it is conceded—as the Court does—that illegal aliens are not a suspect class, and that education is not a fundamental right, our inquiry should focus on and be limited to whether the legislative classification at issue bears a rational relationship to a legitimate state purpose. . . .

It is significant that the Federal Government has seen fit to exclude illegal aliens from numerous social welfare programs, such as the food stamp program, . . . the old-age assistance, aid to families with dependent children, aid to the blind, aid to the permanently and totally disabled, and supplemental security income programs, . . . the Medicare hospital insurance benefits program, . . . and the Medicaid hospital insurance benefits for the aged and disabled program. . . . Although these exclusions do not conclusively demonstrate the constitutionality of the State's use of the same classification for comparable purposes, at the very least they tend to support the rationality of excluding illegal alien residents of a state from such programs so as to preserve the state's finite revenues for the benefit of lawful residents. . . .

Denying a free education to illegal alien children is not a choice I would make were I a legislator. Apart from compassionate considerations, the long-range costs of excluding any children from the public schools may well outweigh the costs of educating

them. But that is not the issue; the fact that there are sound *policy* arguments against the Texas Legislature's choice does not render that choice an unconstitutional one. . . .

The Constitution does not provide a cure for every social ill, nor does it vest judges with a mandate to try to remedy every social problem. . . . Moreover, when this Court rushes in to remedy what it perceives to be the failings of the political processes, it deprives those processes of an opportunity to function. When the political institutions are not forced to exercise constitutionally allocated powers and responsibilities, those powers, like muscles not used, tend to atrophy. Today's cases, I regret to say, present yet another example of unwarranted judicial action, which in the long run tends to contribute to the weakening of our political processes.

Congress, "vested by the Constitution with the responsibility of protecting our borders and legislating with respect to aliens," . . . bears primary responsibility for addressing the problems occasioned by the millions of illegal aliens flooding across our southern border. Similarly, it is for Congress, and not this Court, to assess the "social costs borne by our Nation when select groups are denied the means to absorb the values and skills upon which our social order rests." . . . While the "specter of a permanent caste" of illegal Mexican residents of the United States is indeed a disturbing one, . . . it is but one segment of a larger problem, which is for the political branches to solve. I find it difficult to believe that Congress would long tolerate such a self-destructive result—that it would fail to deport these illegal alien families or to provide for the education of their children. Yet instead of allowing the political processes to run their course—albeit with some delay—the Court seeks to do Congress's job for it, compensating for congressional inaction. It is not unreasonable to think that this encourages the political branches to pass their problems to the Judiciary.

The solution to this seemingly intractable problem is to defer to the political processes, unpalatable as that may be to some.

7. *Homelessness*

PETER MARIN

Homelessness, in itself, is nothing more than a condition visited upon men and women (and, increasingly, children) as the final stage of a variety of problems about which the word *homelessness* tells us almost nothing. Or, to put it another way, it is a catch basin into which pour all of the people disenfranchised or marginalized or scared off by processes beyond their control, those that lie close to the heart of American life. Here are the groups packed into the single category of "the homeless":

- Veterans, mainly from the war in Vietnam. In many American cities, vets make up close to 50 percent of all homeless males.

- The mentally ill. In some parts of the country, roughly a quarter of the homeless would, a couple of decades ago, have been institutionalized.

- The physically disabled or chronically ill, who do not receive any benefits or whose benefits do not enable them to afford permanent shelter.

- The elderly on fixed incomes whose funds are no longer sufficient for their needs.

- Men, women, and whole families pauperized by the loss of a job. Some 28 percent of the homeless population is composed of families with children, and 15 percent are single women.

- Single parents, usually women, without the resources or skills to establish new lives.

From "Helping and Hating the Homeless," *This World* (January 25, 1987), pp. 7–9, 20. Copyright © 1987 by *Harper's Magazine.* All rights reserved. Reprinted from the January issue by special permission.

- Runaway children, many of whom have been abused.

- Alcoholics and those in trouble with drugs (whose troubles often begin with one of the other conditions listed here).

- Traditional tramps, hobos, and transients, who have taken to the road or the streets for a variety of reasons and who prefer to be there.

You can quickly learn two things about the homeless from this list. First, you can learn that many of the homeless, before they were homeless, were people more or less like ourselves: members of the working or middle class. And you can learn that the world of the homeless has its roots in various policies, events, and ways of life for which some of us are responsible and from which some of us actually prosper.

We decide, as a people, to go to war, we ask our children to kill and to die, and the result, years later, is grown men homeless on the street.

We change, with the best intentions, the laws pertaining to the mentally ill and then, without intention, neglect to provide them with services; and the result, in our streets, drives some of us crazy with rage.

We cut taxes and prune budgets, we modernize industry and shift the balance of trade, and the result of all these actions and errors can be read, sleeping form by sleeping form, on our city streets.

The liberals cannot blame the conservatives. The conservatives cannot blame the liberals. Homelessness is the sum total of our dreams, policies, intentions, errors, omissions, cruelties, kindnesses, all of it recorded, in flesh, in the life of the streets. The homeless can be roughly divided into two groups: those who have had homelessness forced upon them and want nothing more than to escape it; and those who have at least in part chosen it for themselves, and now accept it, or in some cases embrace it.

I understand how dangerous it is to introduce the idea of choice into a discussion of homelessness. It can all too easily be used to justify indifference or brutality toward the homeless, or to argue that they are only getting what they "deserve." And yet it seems to me that it is only by taking choice into account, in all of the intricacies of its various forms and expressions, that one can really understand certain kinds of homelessness.

The fact is, many of the homeless are not only hapless victims but voluntary exiles, "domestic refugees," people who have turned not against life itself but against us, our life, American life. Look for a moment at the vets. The price of returning to America was to forget what they had seen or learned in Vietnam, to "put it behind them." But some could not do that, and the stress of trying showed up as alcoholism, broken marriages, drug addiction, crime. And it showed up too as life on the street, which was for some vets a desperate choice made in the name of life—the best they could manage.

We must learn to accept that there may indeed be people, and not only vets, who have seen so much of our world, or seen it so clearly, that to live in it becomes impossible. Here, for example, is the story of Alice, a homeless middle-aged woman in Los Angeles, where there are perhaps 50,000 homeless people, a 50 percent increase over the previous year. It was set down last year by one of my students at the University of California at Santa Barbara, where I taught for a semester. I had encouraged them to go find the homeless and listen to their stories. And so, one day, when this student saw Alice foraging in a dumpster outside a McDonald's, he stopped and talked to her:

"She told me she had led a pretty normal life as she grew up and eventually went to college. From there she went on to Chicago to teach school. She was single and lived in a small apartment.

"One night, after she got off the train after school, a man began to follow her to her apartment building. When she got to her door she saw a knife and the man hovering behind her. She had no choice but to let him in. The man raped her.

"After that, things got steadily worse. She had a nervous breakdown. She went to a mental institution for three months, and when she went back to her apartment she found her belongings gone. The landlord had sold them to cover the rent.

"She had no place to go and no job because the school had terminated her employment. She slipped into depression. She lived with friends until she could muster enough money for a ticket to Los Angeles. She said she no longer wanted to burden her friends, and that if she had to live outside, at least Los Angeles was warmer than Chicago.

"It is as if she began back then to take on the mentality of a street person. She resolved herself to homelessness. She's been out West since 1980, without a home or job. She seems happy, with her best friend being her cat. But the scars of memories still haunt her, and she is running from them, or should I say, him."

This is, in essence, the same story one hears over and over again on the street. You begin with an ordinary life; then an event occurs—traumatic, catastrophic; smaller events follow, each one deepening the original wound; finally, homelessness becomes inevitable, or begins to seem inevitable to the person involved—the only way out of an intolerable situation.

Every government program, almost every private project, is geared as much to the needs of those giving help as it is to the needs of the homeless.

Santa Barbara is as good an example as any. There are three main shelters in the city—all of them private. Between them they provide fewer than 100 beds a night for the homeless. Two of three shelters are religious in nature: the Rescue Mission and the Salvation Army. In the mission, as in most places in the country, there are elaborate and stringent rules. Beds go first to those who have not been there for two months, and you can stay for only two nights in any two-month period. No shelter is given to those who are not sober.

Even if you go to the mission only for a meal, you are required to listen to sermons and participate in prayer, and you are regularly proselytized. There are obligatory, regimented showers. You go to bed precisely at 10: lights out, no reading, no talking. After the lights go out you will find 15 men in a room with double-decker bunks. As the night progresses the room grows stuffier and hotter. Men toss, turn, cough and moan. In the morning you are awakened precisely at 5:45. Then breakfast. At 7:30 you are back on the street.

The town's newest shelter was opened almost a year ago by a consortium of local churches. Families and those who are employed have first call on the beds—a policy that excludes the congenitally homeless. Alcohol is not simply forbidden in the shelter; those with a history of alcoholism must sign a "contract" pledging to remain sober and chemical-free. Finally, in a paroxysm of therapeutic bullying, the shelter has added a new wrinkle: If you stay more than two days you are required to fill out and then discuss with a social worker a complex form listing what you perceive as your personal failings, goals and strategies—all of this for men and women who simply want a place to lie down out of the rain.

We are moved either to "redeem" the homeless or to punish them. Perhaps there is nothing consciously hostile about it. Perhaps it is simply that as the machinery of bureaucracy cranks itself up to deal with these problems, attitudes assert themselves automatically. But whatever the case, the fact remains that almost every one of our strategies for helping the homeless is simply an attempt to rearrange the world cosmetically, in terms of how it looks and smells to us. Compassion is little more than the passion for control.

The central question emerging from all this is, What does a society owe to its members in trouble, and how is that debt to be paid? It is a question that must be answered in two parts: first, in relation to the men and women who have been marginalized against their will, and then, in a slightly different way, in relation to those who have chosen (or accept or even prize) their marginality.

Suggestions for Further Reading

Anthologies

Arthur, John, and Shaw, William. *Social and Political Philosophy*. Englewood Cliffs: Prentice-Hall, 1992.

Sterba, James P. *Social and Political Philosophy: Classical Western Texts in Feminist and Multicultural Perspectives*. Belmont: Wadsworth Publishing Co., 1994.

Sterba, James P. *Justice: Alternative Political Perspectives*. Belmont: Wadsworth Publishing Co., 2nd ed. 1992.

Basic Concepts

Plato. *The Republic*. Translated by Francis Cornford. New York: Oxford University Press, 1945.

Aristotle. *Nicomachean Ethics*. Translated by Martin Ostwald. Indianapolis: Bobbs-Merrill, 1962.

Pieper, Joseph. *Justice*. London: Faber and Faber, 1957.

Libertarianism

Hospers, John. *Libertarianism*. Los Angeles: Nash Publishing, 1971.

Nozick, Robert. *Anarchy, State and Utopia*. New York: Basic Books, 1974.

Machan, Tibor. *Individuals and Their Rights*. LaSalle: Open Court, 1989.

Welfare Liberalism

Mill, John Stuart. *On Liberty*. Indianapolis: Bobbs-Merrill Co., 1956.

Rawls, John. *Political Liberalism*. New York: Columbia University Press, 1993.

Rawls, John. *A Theory of Justice*. Cambridge: Harvard University Press, 1971.

Singer, Peter. *Practical Ethics*. Cambridge: Cambridge University Press, 1979.

Sterba, James P. *How to Make People Just*. Totowa, N.J.: Rowman and Littlefield, 1988.

Socialism

Marx, Karl. *Critique of the Gotha Program*. Edited by C. P. Dutt. New York: International Publishers, 1966.

Fisk, Milton. *Ethics and Society: A Marxist Interpretation of Value*. New York: New York University Press, 1980.

Harrington, Michael. *Socialism Past and Future*. New York: Arcade Publishing, 1989.

Schweickart, David. *Against Capitalism*. Cambridge: Cambridge University Press, 1993.

Practical Applications

Friedman, David. *The Machinery of Freedom*. 2nd edition. LaSalle: Open Court, 1989.

Haslett, D. W. *Capitalism with Morality*. Oxford: Clarendon Press, 1994.

Timmons, William. *Public Ethics and Issues*. Belmont: Wadsworth Publishing Co., 1990.

Near and Distant Peoples

Introduction

Basic Concepts

The moral problem of near and distant peoples has only recently begun to be discussed by professional philosophers. There are many reasons for this neglect, not all of them complimentary to the philosophical profession. Suffice it to say that once it became widely recognized how modern technology could significantly benefit or harm distant peoples, philosophers could no longer ignore the importance of this moral problem.

With respect to this problem, the key question that must be answered first is: Can we meaningfully speak of distant peoples as having rights against us or of our having obligations to them? Few philosophers have thought that the mere fact that people are at a distance from us precludes our having any obligations to them or their having any rights against us. Some philosophers, however, have argued that our ignorance of the specific membership of the class of distant peoples does rule out these moral relationships. Yet this cannot be right, given that in other contexts we recognize obligations to indeterminate classes of people, such as a police officer's obligation to help people in distress or the obligation of food processors not to harm those who consume their products.

What does, however, seem to be a necessary requirement before distant peoples can be said to have rights against us is that we are capable of acting across the distance that separates us. (This is simply an implication of the widely accepted philosophical principle that "ought" implies "can.") As long as this condition is met—as it typically is for people living in most technologically advanced societies—there seems to be no conceptual obstacle to claiming that distant peoples have rights against us or that we have obligations to them. Of course, showing that it is conceptually possible does not yet prove that these rights and obligations actually exist. Such proof requires a substantial moral argument.

It used to be argued that the welfare rights of distant peoples would eventually be met as a byproduct of the continued economic growth of the technologically developed societies of the world. It was believed that the transfer of investment and technology to the less developed societies of the world would eventually, if not make everyone well off, at least satisfy everyone's basic needs. Now we are not so sure. Presently more and more evidence points to the conclusion that without some substantial sacrifice on the part of the technologically developed societies of the world, many of the less developed societies will never be able to provide their members with even the basic necessities for survival.

How else are we going to meet the basic needs of the 1.2 billion people who are living today in conditions of absolute poverty without some plausible policy of redistribution? Even those, like Herman Kahn, who argue that an almost utopian world situation will obtain in the distant future, still would have to admit that unless some plausible policy of redistribution is adopted, malnutrition and starvation will continue in the less developed societies for many years to come. Thus, a recognition of the welfare rights of distant peoples would appear to have significant consequences for developed and underdeveloped societies alike.

Of course, there are various senses in which distant peoples can be said to have welfare rights and various moral grounds on which those rights can be justified. First of all, the welfare rights of distant peoples can be understood to be either negative rights or positive rights. A negative right is a right not to be interfered with in some specific manner. For example, a right to liberty is usually understood to be a negative right; it guarantees each person the right not to have her liberty interfered with provided that she does not unjustifiably interfere with the liberty of any other person. On the other hand, a positive right is a right to receive some specific goods or services. Typical positive rights are the right to have a loan repaid and the right to receive one's just earnings. Second, the welfare rights of distant peoples can be understood to be either *in personam* rights or *in rem* rights. *In personam* rights are rights that hold against some specific nameable person or persons, while *in rem* rights hold against everyone who is in a position to abide by the rights in question. A right to liberty is usually understood to be an *in rem* right while the right to have a loan repaid or the right to receive one's just earnings are typical *in personam* rights. Finally, the rights of distant peoples can be understood to be either legal rights, that is, rights that *are enforced* by coercive

sanctions, or moral rights, that is, rights that *ought to be enforced* either simply by noncoercive sanctions (for example, verbal condemnations) or by both coercive and noncoercive sanctions. Accordingly, what distinguishes the moral rights of distant peoples from the requirements of supererogation (the nonfulfillment of which is never blameworthy) is that the former but not the latter can be justifiably enforced either by noncoercive or by coercive and noncoercive sanctions.

Of the various moral grounds for justifying the welfare rights of distant peoples, quite possibly the most evident are those that appeal either to a right to life or a right to fair treatment. Libertarians interpret a person's right to life as a negative right. Welfare liberals and socialists interpret it as a positive right.

Thus, suppose we interpret a person's right to life as a positive right. So understood, the person's right to life would most plausibly be interpreted as a right to receive those goods and resources that are necessary for satisfying her basic needs. For a person's basic needs are those which must be satisfied in order not to seriously endanger her health or sanity. Thus, receiving the goods and resources that are necessary for satisfying her basic needs would preserve a person's life in the fullest sense. And if a person's positive right to life is to be universal in the sense that it is possessed by every person (as the right to life is generally understood to be) then it must be an *in rem* right. This is because an *in rem* right, unlike an *in personam* right, does not require for its possession the assumption by other persons of any special roles or contractual obligations. Interpreted as a positive *in rem* right, therefore, a person's right to life would clearly justify the welfare rights of distant peoples to have their basic needs satisfied.

Suppose, on the other hand, that we interpret a person's right to life as a negative right. Here again, if the right is to be universal in the sense that it is possessed by all persons then it must also be an *in rem* right. So understood, the right would require that everyone who is in a position to do so not interfere in certain ways with a person's attempts to meet her basic needs.

But what sort of noninterference would this right to life justify? If one's basic needs have not been met, would a person's right to life require that others not interfere with her taking the goods she needs from the surplus possessions of those who already have satisfied their own basic needs? As it is standardly interpreted, a person's negative right to life would not require such noninterference. Instead, a person's negative right to life is usually understood to be limited in such circumstances by the property rights of those who have more than enough to satisfy their own basic needs. Moreover, those who claim property rights to such surplus goods and resources are usually in a position effectively to prohibit those in need from taking what they require. For surely most underdeveloped nations of the world would be able to sponsor expeditions to the American Midwest or the Australian plains for the purpose of collecting the grain necessary to satisfy the basic needs of their citizens if they were not effectively prohibited from doing so at almost every stage of the enterprise.

But are persons with such surplus goods and resources normally justified in so prohibiting others from satisfying their basic needs? Admittedly, such persons may have contributed greatly to the value of the surplus goods and resources they possess, but why should that give them power over the life and death of those less fortunate? Even though their contribution may well justify favoring their nonbasic needs over the nonbasic needs of others, how could it justify favoring their nonbasic needs over the basic needs of others? After all, a person's negative right to life, being an *in rem* right, does not depend on the assumption by other persons of any special roles or contractual obligations. By con-

trast, property rights that are *in personam* rights require the assumption by other persons of the relevant roles and contractual obligations that constitute a particular system of acquisition and exchange, such as the role of a neighbor and the obligations of a merchant. Consequently, with respect to such property rights, it would seem that a person could not justifiably be kept from acquiring the goods and resources necessary to satisfy her basic needs by the property rights of others to surplus possessions, unless the person herself had voluntarily agreed to be so constrained by those property rights. But obviously few people would voluntarily agree to have such constraints placed upon their ability to acquire the goods and resources necessary to satisfy their basic needs. For most people their right to acquire the goods and resources necessary to satisfy their basic needs would have priority over any other person's property rights to surplus possessions, or alternatively, they would conceive of property rights such that no one could have property rights to any surplus possessions which were required to satisfy their own basic needs.

Even if some property rights could arise, as *in rem* rights by a Lockean process of mixing one's labor with previously unowned goods and resources, there would still be a need for some sort of a restriction on such appropriations. For if these *in rem* property rights are to be *moral rights* then it must be reasonable for every affected party to accept such rights, since the requirements of morality cannot be contrary to reason. Accordingly, in order to give rise to *in rem* property rights, the appropriation of previously unowned goods and resources cannot justifiably limit anyone's ability to acquire the goods and resources necessary to satisfy her basic needs, unless it would be reasonable for the person voluntarily to agree to be so constrained. But obviously it would not be reasonable for many people, particularly those whose basic needs are not being met, voluntarily to agree to be so constrained by property rights. this means that whether property rights are *in personam* rights and arise by the assumption of the relevant roles and contractual obligations or are *in rem* rights and arise by a Lockean process of mixing one's labor with previously unowned goods and resources, such rights would rarely limit a negative right to life, interpreted as an *in rem* right to noninterference with one's attempts to acquire the goods and resources necessary to satisfy one's basic needs. So interpreted, a negative right to life would clearly justify the welfare rights of distant people.

If we turn to a consideration of a person's right to fair treatment, a similar justification of the welfare rights of distant peoples emerges. To determine the requirements of fair treatment, suppose we employ a decision procedure analogous to the one John Rawls developed in *A Theory of Justice.* Suppose, that is to say, that in deciding upon the requirements of fair treatment, we were to discount the knowledge of which particular interests happen to be our own. Since we obviously know what our particular interests are, we would just not be taking that knowledge into account when selecting the requirements for fair treatment. Rather, in selecting these requirements, we would be reasoning from our knowledge of all the particular interests of everyone who would be affected by our decision but not from our knowledge of which particular interests happen to be our own. In employing this decision procedure, therefore, we (like judges who discount prejudicial information in order to reach fair decisions) would be able to give a fair hearing to everyone's particular interests. Assuming further that we are well-informed of the particular interests that would be affected by our decision and are fully capable of rationally deliberating with respect to that information, then our deliberations would culminate in a unanimous decision. This is because

each of us would be deliberating in a rationally correct manner with respect to the same information and would be using a decision procedure leading to a uniform evaluation of the alternatives. Consequently, each of us would favor the same requirements for fair treatment.

But what requirements would we select by using this decision procedure? Since by using this decision procedure we would not be using our knowledge of which particular interests happen to be our own, we would be quite concerned about the pattern according to which goods and resources would be distributed throughout the world. By using this decision procedure, we would reason as though our particular interests might be those of persons with the largest share of goods and resources as well as those of persons with the smallest share of goods and resources. Consequently, we would neither exclusively favor the interests of persons with the largest share of goods by endorsing an unlimited right to accumulate goods and resources nor exclusively favor the interests of persons with the smallest share of goods and resources by endorsing the highest possible minimum for those who are least advantaged. Rather we would compromise by endorsing a right to accumulate goods and resources that was limited by the guarantee of a minimum sufficient to provide each person with the goods and resources necessary to satisfy his or her basic needs. It seems clear, therefore, that a right to fair treatment as captured by this Rawlsian decision procedure would also justify the welfare rights of distant people.

So it would seem that the welfare rights of distant peoples can be firmly grounded either in each person's right to life or each person's right to fair treatment. As a result, it would be impossible for one to deny that distant peoples have welfare rights without also denying that each person has a right to life and a right to fair treatment, unless, that is, one drastically reinterprets the significance of a right to life and a right to fair treatment.

Alternative Views

Not surprisingly, most of the solutions to the problem of near and distant peoples that have been proposed are analogous to the solutions we discussed with regard to the problem of the distribution of income and wealth within a society. (See Section I.)

As before, there is a libertarian solution. According to this view, distant peoples have no right to receive aid from persons living in today's affluent societies, but only a right not to be harmed by them. As before, these requirements are said to be derived from a political ideal of liberty. And, as before, we can question whether such an ideal actually supports these requirements.

Garrett Hardin endorses a "no aid" view in his essay (Selection 8). However, Hardin does not support his view on libertarian grounds. Without denying that there is a general obligation to help those in need, Hardin argues that helping those who live in absolute poverty in today's world would not do any good, and *for that reason* is not required. Hardin justifies this view on empirical grounds, claiming that the giving of aid would be ineffective and even counterproductive for controlling population growth.

Peter Singer challenges the empirical grounds on which Hardin's view rests (Selection 9). Singer claims that Hardin's view accepts the certain evil of unrelieved poverty in underdeveloped countries—for instance, Bangladesh and Somalia—so as to avoid the future possibility of still greater poverty in underdeveloped countries together with deteriorating conditions in developed and developing countries. Singer argues, however, that with a serious commitment to aid from developed countries, there is a "fair chance" that underdeveloped countries will bring their population growth under control, thus avoiding the greater evil Hardin fears. Given the likelihood of this result, Singer argues that we have no moral justification for embracing, as Hardin does, the certain evil of unrelieved poverty in underdeveloped countries by denying them aid.

The positive solution to the problem of near and distant peoples defended by Singer can be characterized as a welfare liberal solution. Singer at some point would want to defend his "pro aid" view on utilitarian grounds, but he also tries to base his view on premises of a more general appeal. The fundamental premise he relies on is this: If we can prevent something bad without sacrificing anything of comparable significance, we ought to do it. Singer notes that libertarians, like Robert Nozick, would at least initially have difficulty accepting this premise. Nozick would surely claim that the requirement this premise imposes is at best only one of charity rather than justice, and that failing to abide by it is neither blameworthy nor punishable. But if a right to life interpreted as a negative right can be shown to have the same practical implications as Singer's view, then even libertarians would have to accept a "pro aid" view. (See Section I.)

Unlike Singer, Lawrence Blum supports only a "minimal aid" view grounded not on impartiality but beneficence (Selection 10). This view, Blum claims, accounts better for the role that friendships and special relationships have in our lives. In Selection 11, however, James Rachels questions whether the degree to which we tend to favor those special relations who are our children can really be morally justified. Although Rachels does not draw the same distinction between impartiality and beneficence that Blum does, he argues on grounds of what Blum would call beneficence that we have an obligation to provide basic necessities for needy children rather than provide luxuries for our own.

A socialist solution to the problem of near and distant peoples would place considerable stress on the responsibility of developed countries for the situation in underdeveloped countries.

Socialists claim that much of the poverty and unemployment found in underdeveloped countries is the result of the disruptive and exploitative influence of developed countries. For example, it is claimed that arms supplied by developed countries enable repressive regimes in underdeveloped countries to remain in power when they would otherwise be overthrown. Under these repressive regimes, small groups of landowners and capitalists are allowed to exploit the resources in underdeveloped countries for export markets in developed countries. As a result, most people in underdeveloped countries are forced off the land that their forebears have farmed for generations and are required to compete for the few, frequently low-paying jobs that have been created to serve the export markets.

Nevertheless, even if socialists are right about the responsibility of developed countries for poverty in underdeveloped countries, it is still a further question whether the socialization of the means of production and the abolition of private property are the only viable moral responses to this situation. It certainly seems possible that some form of restricted private property system that provides for the meeting of everyone's basic needs, justified either on welfare liberal grounds or on libertarian grounds, would serve as well.

Practical Application

There does not seem to be as much of a gap between the "alternative views" and the "practical applications" with respect to the problem of near and distant peoples as there is in the problem of the distribution of wealth and income. This is because most of the discussions of the alternative views have already taken up the question of practical application (e.g., Singer suggests as a practical application a 10 percent tithe on income in developed countries). The merit of Gus Speth's article, however, is that it focuses squarely on the question of practical application (Selection 12). After reviewing the world situation, Speth sketches a practical program involving conservation, sustainable growth, and equity. Because his program obviously involves substantial aid to underdeveloped and developing countries, you should not endorse such a program unless you believe that arguments such as those presented by Singer and Rachels effectively counter arguments such as those presented by Hardin and Blum.

Nevertheless, whatever solution to the problem of near and distant peoples you favor, you will still not know how goods and resources should ultimately be distributed in society unless you have a solution to the problems of abortion and euthanasia. If abortion is morally justified, perhaps we should be funding abortions so that every woman, rich or poor, can have an abortion if she wants one. And if euthanasia is morally justified, perhaps we should be reallocating resources that are now being used for the purpose of sustaining life. Appropriately, the next section of this book takes up the problem of abortion and euthanasia.

8. Lifeboat Ethics: The Case Against Helping the Poor

Garrett Hardin

Garrett Hardin argues that our first obligation is to ourselves and our posterity. For that reason, he contends, it would be foolish for rich nations to share their surplus with poor nations, whether through a World Food Bank, the exporting of technology, or unrestricted immigration. In view of the growing populations and improvident behavior of poor nations, such sharing would do no good—it would only overload the environment and lead to demands for still greater assistance in the future.

Environmentalists use the metaphor of the earth as a "spaceship" in trying to persuade countries, industries, and people to stop wasting and polluting our natural resources. Since we all share life on this planet, they argue, no single person or institution has the right to destroy, waste, or use more than a fair share of its resources.

But does everyone on earth have an equal right to an equal share of its resources? The spaceship metaphor can be dangerous when used by misguided idealists to justify suicidal policies for sharing our resources through uncontrolled immigration and foreign aid. In their enthusiastic but unrealistic generosity, they confuse the ethics of a spaceship with those of a lifeboat.

A true spaceship would have to be under the control of a captain, since no ship could possibly survive if its course were determined by committee. Spaceship Earth certainly has no captain; the United Nations is merely a toothless tiger, with little power to enforce any policy upon its bickering members.

If we divide the world crudely into rich nations and poor nations, two thirds of them are desperately poor, and only one third comparatively rich, with the United States the wealthiest of all. Metaphorically each rich nation can be seen as a lifeboat full of comparatively rich people. In the ocean outside each lifeboat swim the poor of the world, who would like to get in, or at least to share some of the wealth. What should the lifeboat passengers do?

First, we must recognize the limited capacity of any lifeboat. For example, a nation's land has a limited capacity to support a population and as the current energy crisis has shown us, in some ways we have already exceeded the carrying capacity of our land.

Adrift in a Moral Sea

So here we sit, say fifty people in our lifeboat. To be generous, let us assume it has room for ten more, making a total capacity of sixty. Suppose the fifty of us in the lifeboat see one hundred others swimming in the water outside, begging for admission to our boat or for handouts. We have several options: We may be tempted to try to live by the Christian ideal of being "our brother's keeper," or by the Marxist ideal of "to each according to his needs." Since the needs of all in the water are the same, and since they can all be seen as "our brothers," we could take them all into our boat, making a total of 150 in a boat designed for sixty. The boat swamps, everyone drowns. Complete justice, complete catastrophe.

Since the boat has an unused excess capacity of ten more passengers, we could admit just ten more to it. But which ten do we let in? How do we choose? Do we pick the best ten, the neediest ten, "first come, first served"? And what do we say to the ninety we exclude? If we do let an extra ten into our lifeboat, we will have lost our "safety factor," an engineering principle of critical importance. For example, if we don't leave room for excess capacity as a safety factor in our country's agriculture, a new plant disease or a bad change in the weather could have disastrous consequences.

Suppose we decide to preserve our small safety factor and admit no more to the lifeboat. Our survival is then possible, although we shall have to be constantly on guard against boarding parties.

While this last solution clearly offers the only means of our survival, it is morally abhorrent to many people. Some say they feel guilty about their good luck. My reply is simple: "Get out and yield your place to others." This may solve the problem of the guilt-ridden person's conscience, but it does not change the ethics of the lifeboat. The needy person to whom the guilt-ridden person yields his place will not himself feel guilty about his good luck. If he did, he would not climb aboard. The net result of conscience-stricken people giving up their unjustly held seats is the elimination of that sort of conscience from the lifeboat.

This is the basic metaphor within which we must work out our solutions. Let us now enrich the image, step by step, with substantive additions from the real world, a world that must solve real and pressing problems of overpopulation and hunger.

The harsh ethics of the lifeboat become even harsher when we consider the reproductive differences between the rich nations and the poor nations. The people inside the lifeboats are doubling in numbers every eighty-seven years; those swimming around outside are doubling, on the average, every thirty-five years, more than twice as fast as the rich. And since the world's resources are dwindling, the difference in prosperity between the rich and the poor can only increase.

As of 1973, the United States had a population of 210 million people, who were increasing by 0.8 percent per year. Outside our lifeboat, let us imagine another 210 million people (say the combined populations of Colombia, Ecuador, Venezuela, Morocco, Pakistan, Thailand, and the Philippines), who are in-

creasing at a rate of 3.3 percent per year. Put differently, the doubling time for this aggregate population is twenty-one years, compared to eighty-seven years for the United States.

Multiplying the Rich and the Poor

Now suppose the United States agreed to pool its resources with those seven countries, with everyone receiving an equal share. Initially the ratio of Americans to non-Americans in this model would be one-to-one. But consider what the ratio would be after eighty-seven years, by which time the Americans would have doubled to a population of 420 million. By then, doubling every twenty-one years, the other group would have swollen to 354 billion. Each American would have to share the available resources with more than eight people.

But, one could argue, this discussion assumes that current population trends will continue, and they may not. Quite so. Most likely the rate of population increase will decline much faster in the United States than it will in the other countries, and there does not seem to be much we can do about it. In sharing with "each according to his needs," we must recognize that needs are determined by population size, which is determined by the rate of reproduction, which at present is regarded as a sovereign right of every nation, poor or not. This being so, the philanthropic load created by the sharing ethic of the spaceship can only increase.

The Tragedy of the Commons

The fundamental error of spaceship ethics, and the sharing it requires, is that it leads to what I call "the tragedy of the commons." Under a system of private property, the men who own property recognize their responsibility to care for it, for if they don't they will eventually suffer. A farmer, for instance, will allow no more cattle in a pasture than its carrying capacity justifies. If he overloads it, erosion sets in, weeds take over, and he loses the use of the pasture.

If a pasture becomes a commons open to all, the right of each to use it may not be matched by a corresponding responsibility to protect it. Asking everyone to use it with discretion will hardly do, for the considerate herdsman who refrains from overloading the commons suffers more than a selfish one who says his needs are greater. If everyone would restrain himself, all would be well; but it takes only one less than everyone to ruin a system of voluntary restraint. In a crowded world of less than perfect human beings, mutual ruin is inevitable if there are no controls. This is the tragedy of the commons.

One of the major tasks of education today should be the creation of such an acute awareness of the dangers of the commons that people will recognize its many varieties. For example, the air and water have become polluted because they are treated as commons. Further growth in the population or per-capita conversion of natural resources into pollutants will only make the problem worse. The same holds true for the fish of the oceans. Fishing fleets have nearly disappeared in many parts of the world; technological improvements in the art of fishing are hastening the day of complete ruin. Only the replacement of the system of the commons with a responsible system of control will save the land, air, water, and oceanic fisheries.

The World Food Bank

In recent years there has been a push to create a new commons called a World Food Bank, an international depository of food reserves to which nations would contribute according to their abilities and from which they would draw according to their needs. This humanitarian proposal has received support from many liberal international groups, and from such prominent citizens as Margaret Mead, U.N. Secretary General Kurt Waldheim, and Senators Edward Kennedy and George McGovern.

A world food bank appeals powerfully to our humanitarian impulses. But before we rush ahead with such a plan, let us recognize where the greatest political push comes from, lest we be disillusioned later. Our experience with the "Food for Peace program," or Public Law 480, gives us the answer. This program moved billions of dollars worth of U.S. surplus grain to food-short, population-long countries during the past two decades. But when P.L. 480 first became law,

a headline in the business magazine *Forbes* revealed the real power behind it: "Feeding the World's Hungry Millions: How It Will Mean Billions for U.S. Business."

And indeed it did. In the years 1960 to 1970, U.S. taxpayers spent a total of $7.9 billion on the Food for Peace program. Between 1948 and 1970, they also paid an additional $50 billion for other economic-aid programs, some of which went for food and food-producing machinery and technology. Though all U.S. taxpayers were forced to contribute to the cost of P.L. 480, certain special interest groups gained handsomely under the program. Farmers did not have to contribute the grain; the Government, or rather the taxpayers, bought it from them at full market prices. The increased demand raised prices of farm products generally. The manufacturers of farm machinery, fertilizers, and pesticides benefited by the farmers' extra efforts to grow more food. Grain elevators profited from storing the surplus until it could be shipped. Railroads made money hauling it to ports, and shipping lines profited from carrying it overseas. The implementation of P.L. 480 required the creation of a vast Government bureaucracy, which then acquired its own vested interest in continuing the program regardless of its merits.

Extracting Dollars

Those who proposed and defended the Food for Peace program in public rarely mentioned its importance to any of these special interests. The public emphasis was always on its humanitarian effects. The combination of silent selfish interests and highly vocal humanitarian apologists made a powerful and successful lobby for extracting money from taxpayers. We can expect the same lobby to push now for the creation of a World Food Bank.

However great the potential benefit to selfish interests, it should not be a decisive argument against a truly humanitarian program. We must ask if such a program would actually do more good than harm, not only momentarily but also in the long run. Those who propose the food bank usually refer to a current "emergency" or "crisis" in terms of world food supply. But what is an emergency? Although they may be infrequent and sudden, everyone knows that emergencies will occur from time to time. A well-run family, company, organization, or country prepares for the likelihood of accidents and emergencies. It expects them, it budgets for them, it saves for them.

Learning the Hard Way

What happens if some organizations or countries budget for accidents and others do not? If each country is solely responsible for its own well-being, poorly managed ones will suffer. But they can learn from experience. They may mend their ways and learn to budget for infrequent but certain emergencies. For example, the weather varies from year to year, and periodic crop failures are certain. A wise and competent government saves out of the production of the good years in anticipation of bad years to come. Joseph taught this policy to Pharaoh in Egypt more than 2,000 years ago. Yet the great majority of the governments in the world today do not follow such a policy. They lack either the wisdom or the competence, or both. Should those nations that do manage to put something aside be forced to come to the rescue each time an emergency occurs among the poor nations?

"But it isn't their fault!" some kindhearted liberals argue. "How can we blame the poor people who are caught in an emergency? Why must they suffer for the sins of their governments?" The concept of blame is simply not relevant here. The real question is, what are the operational consequences of establishing a world food bank? If it is open to every country every time a need develops, slovenly rulers will not be motivated to take Joseph's advice. Someone will always come to their aid. Some countries will deposit food in the world food bank, and others will withdraw it. There will be almost no overlap. As a result of such solutions to food shortage emergencies, the poor countries will not learn to mend their ways and will suffer progressively greater emergencies as their populations grow.

0.8 percent. Only rich countries have anything in the way of food reserves set aside, and even they do not have as much as they should. Poor countries have none. If poor countries received no food from the outside, the rate of their population growth would be periodically checked by crop failures and famines. But if they can always draw on a world food bank in time of need, their population can continue to grow unchecked, and so will their "need" for aid. In the short run, a world food bank may diminish that need, but in the long run it actually increases the need without limit.

Without some system of worldwide food sharing, the proportion of people in the rich and poor nations might eventually stabilize. The overpopulated poor countries would decrease in numbers, while the rich countries that had room for more people would increase. But with a well-meaning system of sharing, such as a world food bank, the growth differential between the rich and the poor countries will not only persist, it will increase. Because of the higher rate of population growth in the poor countries of the world, 88 percent of today's children are born poor, and only 12 percent rich. Year by year the ratio becomes worse, as the fast-reproducing poor outnumber the slow-reproducing rich.

A world food bank is thus a commons in disguise. People will have more motivation to draw from it than to add to any common store. The less provident and less able will multiply at the expense of the abler and more provident, bringing eventual ruin upon all who share in the commons. Besides, any system of "sharing" that amounts to foreign aid from the rich nations to the poor nations will carry the taint of charity, which will contribute little to the world peace so devoutly desired by those who support the idea of a world food bank.

As past U.S. foreign-aid programs have amply and depressingly demonstrated, international charity frequently inspires mistrust and antagonism rather than gratitude on the part of the recipient nation.

Population Control the Crude Way

On the average, poor countries undergo a 2.5 percent increase in population each year; rich countries, about

Chinese Fish and Miracle Rice

The modern approach to foreign aid stresses the export of technology and advice, rather than money and food. As an ancient Chinese proverb goes: "Give a man a fish and he will eat for a day; teach him how to fish and he will eat for the rest of his days." Acting on this advice, the Rockefeller and Ford Foundations have financed a number of programs for improving agriculture in the hungry nations. Known as the "Green Revolution," these programs have led to the development of "miracle rice" and "miracle wheat," new strains that offer bigger harvests and greater resistance to crop damage. Norman Borlaug, the Nobel Prize–winning agronomist who, supported by the Rockefeller Foundation, developed "miracle wheat," is one of the most prominent advocates of a world food bank.

Whether or not the Green Revolution can increase food production as much as its champions claim is a debatable but possibly irrelevant point. Those who support this well-intended humanitarian effort should first consider some of the fundamentals of human ecology. Ironically, one man who did was the late Alan Gregg, a vice-president of the Rockefeller Foundation. Two decades ago he expressed strong doubts about the wisdom of such attempts to increase food production. He likened the growth and spread of humanity over the surface of the earth to the spread of cancer in the human body, remarking that "cancerous growths demand food; but, as far as I know, they have never been cured by getting it."

Overloading the Environment

Every human born constitutes a draft on all aspects of the environment: food, air, water, forests, beaches, wildlife, scenery, and solitude. Food can, perhaps, be significantly increased to meet a growing demand. But what about clean beaches, unspoiled forests, and solitude? If we satisfy a growing population's need for food, we necessarily decrease its per capita supply of the other resources needed by men.

India, for example, now has a population of 600 million, which increases by 15 million each year. This population already puts a huge load on a relatively impoverished environment. The country's forests are now only a small fraction of what they were three centuries ago, and floods and erosion continually destroy the insufficient farmland that remains. Every one of the 15 million new lives added to India's population puts an additional burden on the environment

and increases the economic and social costs of crowding. However humanitarian our intent, every Indian life saved through medical or nutritional assistance from abroad diminishes the quality of life for those who remain, and for subsequent generations. If rich countries make it possible, through foreign aid, for 600 million Indians to swell to 1.2 billion in a mere twenty-eight years, as their current growth rate threatens, will future generations of Indians thank us for hastening the destruction of their environment? Will our good intentions be sufficient excuse for the consequences of our actions?

My final example of a commons in action is one for which the public has the least desire for rational discussion—immigration. Anyone who publicly questions the wisdom of current U.S. immigration policy is promptly charged with bigotry, prejudice, ethnocentrism, chauvinism, isolationism, or selfishness. Rather than encounter such accusations, one would rather talk about other matters, leaving immigration policy to wallow in the crosscurrents of special interests that take no account of the good of the whole, or the interests of posterity.

Perhaps we still feel guilty about things we said in the past. Two generations ago the popular press frequently referred to Dagos, Wops, Polacks, Chinks, and Krauts, in articles about how America was being "overrun" by foreigners of supposedly inferior genetic stock. But because the implied inferiority of foreigners was used then as justification for keeping them out, people now assume that restrictive policies could only be based on such misguided notions. There are other grounds.

A Nation of Immigrants

Just consider the numbers involved. Our Government acknowledges a net inflow of 400,000 immigrants a year. While we have no hard data on the extent of illegal entries, educated guesses put the figure at about 600,000 a year. Since the natural increase (excess of births over deaths) of the resident population now runs about 1.7 million per year, the yearly gain from immigration amounts to at least 19 percent of the total annual increase, and may be as much as 37 percent if we include the estimate for illegal immigrants.

Considering the growing use of birth-control devices, the potential effect of educational campaigns by such organizations as Planned Parenthood Federation of America and Zero Population Growth, and the influence of inflation and the housing shortage, the fertility rate of American women may decline so much that immigration could account for all the yearly increase in population. Should we not at least ask if that is what we want?

For the sake of those who worry about whether the "quality" of the average immigrant compares favorably with the quality of the average resident, let us assume that immigrants and native-born citizens are of exactly equal quality, however one defines that term. We will focus here only on quantity; and since our conclusions will depend on nothing else, all charges of bigotry and chauvinism become irrelevant.

Immigration versus Food Supply

World food banks *move food to the people,* hastening the exhaustion of the environment of the poor countries. Unrestricted immigration, on the other hand, *moves people to the food,* thus speeding up the destruction of the environment of the rich countries. We can easily understand why poor people should want to make this latter transfer, but why should rich hosts encourage it?

As in the case of foreign-aid programs, immigration receives support from selfish interests and humanitarian impulses. The primary selfish interest in unimpeded immigration is the desire of employers for cheap labor, particularly in industries and trades that offer degrading work. In the past, one wave of foreigners after another was brought into the United States to work at wretched jobs for wretched wages. In recent years the Cubans, Puerto Ricans, and Mexicans have had this dubious honor. The interests of the employers of cheap labor mesh well with the guilty silence of the country's liberal intelligentsia. White Anglo-Saxon Protestants are particularly reluctant to call for a closing of the doors to immigration for fear of being called bigots.

But not all countries have such reluctant leadership. Most educated Hawaiians, for example, are keenly aware of the limits of their environment, particularly in terms of population growth. There is only so much

room on the islands, and the islanders know it. To Hawaiians, immigrants from the other forty-nine states present as great a threat as those from other nations. At a recent meeting of Hawaiian government officials in Honolulu, I had the ironic delight of hearing a speaker, who like most of his audience was of Japanese ancestry, ask how the country might practically and constitutionally close its doors to further immigration. One member of the audience countered: "How can we shut the doors now? We have many friends and relatives in Japan that we'd like to bring here some day so that they can enjoy Hawaii too." The Japanese-American speaker smiled sympathetically and answered: "Yes, but we have children now, and someday we'll have grandchildren too. We can bring more people here from Japan only by giving away some of the land that we hope to pass on to our grandchildren some day. What right do we have to do that?"

At this point, I can hear U.S. liberals asking: "How can you justify slamming the door once you're inside? You say that immigrants should be kept out. But aren't we all immigrants, or the descendants of immigrants? If we insist on staying, must we not admit all others?" Our craving for intellectual order leads us to seek and prefer symmetrical rules and morals: a single rule for me and everybody else; the same rule yesterday, today, and tomorrow. Justice, we feel, should not change with time and place.

We Americans of non-Indian ancestry can look upon ourselves as the descendants of thieves who are guilty morally, if not legally, of stealing this land from its Indian owners. Should we then give back the land to the now living American descendants of those Indians? However morally or logically sound this proposal may be, I, for one, am unwilling to live by it and I know no one else who is. Besides, the logical consequence would be absurd. Suppose that, intoxicated with a sense of pure justice, we should decide to turn our land over to the Indians. Since all our wealth has also been derived from the land, wouldn't we be morally obliged to give that back to the Indians too?

Pure Justice versus Reality

Clearly, the concept of pure justice produces an infinite regression to absurdity. Centuries ago, wise men invented statutes of limitations to justify the rejection of such pure justice, in the interest of preventing continual disorder. The law zealously defends property rights, but only relatively recent property rights. Drawing a line after an arbitrary time has elapsed may be unjust, but the alternatives are worse.

We are all the descendants of thieves, and the world's resources are inequitably distributed. But we must begin the journey to tomorrow from the point where we are today. We cannot remake the past. We cannot safely divide the wealth equitably among all peoples so long as people reproduce at different rates. To do so would guarantee that our grandchildren, and everyone else's grandchildren, would have only a ruined world to inhabit.

To be generous with one's own possessions is quite different from being generous with those of posterity. We should call this point to the attention of those who, from a commendable love of justice and equality, would institute a system of the commons, either in the form of a world food bank, or of unrestricted immigration. We must convince them if we wish to save at least some parts of the world from environmental ruin.

Without a true world government to control reproduction and the use of available resources, the sharing ethic of the spaceship is impossible. For the foreseeable future, our survival demands that we govern our actions by the ethics of a lifeboat, harsh though they may be. Posterity will be satisfied with nothing less.

Addendum 1989

Can anyone watch children starve on television without wanting to help? Naturally sympathetic, a normal human being thinks that he can imagine what it is like to be starving. We all want to do unto others as we would have them do unto us.

But wanting is not doing. Forty years of activity by the U.S. Agency for International Development, as well as episodic nongovernmental attempts to feed the world's starving, have produced mixed results. Before we respond to the next appeal we should ask, "Does what we call 'aid' really help?"

Some of the shortcomings of food aid can be dealt with briefly. Waste is unavoidable: Because most poor countries have wretched transportation systems, food may sit on a dock until it rots. Then there are the corrupt politicians who take donated food away from the poor and give it to their political supporters. In Somalia in the 1980s, fully 70 percent of the donated food went to the army.

We can school ourselves to accept such losses. Panicky projects are always inefficient: Waste and corruption are par for the course. But there is another kind of loss that we cannot—in fact, we should not—accept, and that is the loss caused by the boomerang effects of philanthropy. Before we jump onto the next "feed-the-starving" bandwagon we need to understand how well-intentioned efforts can be counterproductive.

Briefly put, it is a mistake to focus only on starving people while ignoring their surroundings. Where there is great starvation there is usually an impoverished environment: poor soil, scarce water, and wildly fluctuating weather. As a result, the "carrying capacity" of the environment is low. The territory simply cannot support the population that is trying to live on it. Yet if the population were much smaller, and if it would stay smaller, the people would not need to starve.

Let us look at a particular example. Nigeria, like all the central African countries, has increased greatly in population in the last quarter-century. Over many generations, Nigerians learned that their farmlands would be most productive if crop-growing alternated with "fallow years"—years in which the land was left untilled to recover its fertility.

When modern medicine reduced the death rate, the population began to grow. More food was demanded from the same land. Responding to that need, Nigerians shortened the fallow periods. The result was counterproductive. In one carefully studied village, the average fallow period was shortened from 5.3 to 1.4 years. As a result, the yearly production (averaged over both fallow and crop years) fell by 30 percent.

Are Nigerian farmers stupid? Not at all! They know perfectly well what they are doing. But a farmer whose family has grown too large for his farm has to take care of next year's need before he can provide for the future. To fallow or not to fallow translates into this choice: zero production in a fallow year or a 30 percent shortfall over the long run. Starvation cannot wait. Long-term policies have to give way to short-term ones. So the farmer plows up his overstressed fields, thus diminishing long-term productivity.

Once the carrying capacity of a territory has been transgressed, its capacity goes down, year after year. Transgression is a one-way road to ruin. Ecologists memorialize this reality with an Eleventh Commandment: "Thou shalt not transgress the carrying capacity."

Transgression takes many forms. Poor people are poor in energy resources. They need energy to cook their food. Where do they get it? Typically, from animal dung or trees and bushes. Burning dung deprives the soil of nitrogen. Cutting down trees and bushes deprives the land of protection against eroding rain. Soil-poor slopes cannot support a crop of fuel-plants. Once the soil is gone, water runs off the slopes faster and floods the valleys below. First poor people deforest their land, and then deforestation makes them poorer.

When Americans send food to a starving population that has already grown beyond the environment's carrying capacity, we become a partner in the devastation of their land. Food from the outside keeps more natives alive; these demand more food and fuel; greater demand causes the community to transgress the carrying capacity more, and transgression results in lowering the carrying capacity. The deficit grows exponentially. Gifts of food to an overpopulated country boomerang, increasing starvation over the long run. Our choice is really between letting some die this year and letting more die in the following years.

You may protest, "That's easy enough for a well-fed American to say, but do citizens of poor countries agree?" Well, wisdom is not restricted to the wealthy. The Somali novelist Nuruddin Farrah has courageously condemned foreign gifts as being not truly aid, but a poison, because (if continued) such gifts will make Africans permanently dependent on outside aid.

The ethicist Joseph Fletcher has given a simple directive to would-be philanthropists: "Give if it helps, but not if it hurts." We can grant that giving makes the donor feel good at first—but how will he feel later when he realizes that he has harmed the receiver?

Only one thing can really help a poor country: population control. Having accepted disease control the people must now accept population control.

What the philosopher-economist Kenneth Boulding has called "lovey-dovey charity" is not enough. "It is well to remember," he said, "that the symbol of Christian love is a cross and not a Teddy bear." A good Christian should obey the Eleventh Commandment, refusing to send gifts that help poor people destroy the environment that must support the next generation.

---

9. *The Famine Relief Argument*

PETER SINGER

Peter Singer argues that people in rich countries, by allowing those in poor countries to suffer and die, are actually engaged in reckless homicide. This is because people in rich countries could prevent the deaths of the poor without sacrificing anything of comparable significance. Singer considers a number of objections to his argument and finds them all wanting. Against Hardin's objection that aiding the poor now will lead to disaster in the future, Singer argues that if the right sort of aid is given conditionally, a future disaster of the sort Hardin envisions can be avoided.

Some Facts

Consider these facts: By the most cautious estimates, 400 million people lack the calories, protein, vitamins, and minerals needed for a normally healthy life. Millions are constantly hungry; others suffer from deficiency diseases and from infections they would be able to resist on a better diet. Children are worst affected. According to one estimate, 15 million children under five die every year from the combined effects of malnutrition and infection. In some areas, half the children born can be expected to die before their fifth birthday.

Nor is lack of food the only hardship of the poor. To give a broader picture, Robert McNamara, President of the World Bank, has suggested the term "absolute poverty." The poverty we are familiar with in industrialized nations is relative poverty—meaning that some citizens are poor, relative to the wealth enjoyed by their neighbours. People living in relative poverty in Australia might be quite comfortably off by comparison with old-age pensioners in Britain, and British old-age pensioners are not poor in comparison with the poverty that exists in Mali or Ethiopia. Absolute poverty, on the other hand, is poverty by any standard. In McNamara's words:

> Poverty at the absolute level . . . is life at the very margin of existence.
>
> The absolute poor are severely deprived human beings struggling to survive in a set of squalid and degraded circumstances almost beyond the power of our sophisticated imaginations and privileged circumstances to conceive.
>
> Compared to those fortunate enough to live in developed countries individuals in the poorest nations have:
>
> An infant mortality rate eight times higher
> A life expectancy one-third lower
> An adult literacy rate 60% less
> A nutritional level, for one out of every two in the population, below acceptable standards; and for millions of infants, less protein than is sufficient to permit optimum development of the brain.

From *Practical Ethics* (1979), pp. 158–181. Reprinted by permission of Cambridge University Press.

And McNamara has summed up absolute poverty as:

> a condition of life so characterized by malnutrition, illiteracy, disease, squalid surroundings, high infant mortality, and low life expectancy as to be beneath any reasonable definition of human decency.

Absolute poverty is, as McNamara has said, responsible for the loss of countless lives, especially among infants and young children. When absolute poverty does not cause death it still causes misery of a kind not often seen in the affluent nations. Malnutrition in young children stunts both physical and mental development. It has been estimated that the health, growth, and learning capacity of nearly half the young children in developing countries are affected by malnutrition. Millions of people on poor diets suffer from deficiency diseases, like goitre, or blindness caused by a lack of vitamin A. The food value of what the poor eat is further reduced by parasites such as hookworm and ringworm, which are endemic in conditions of poor sanitation and health education.

Death and disease apart, absolute poverty remains a miserable condition of life, with inadequate food, shelter, clothing, sanitation, health services, and education. According to World Bank estimates which define absolute poverty in terms of income levels insufficient to provide adequate nutrition, something like 800 million people—almost 40% of the people of developing countries—live in absolute poverty. Absolute poverty is probably the principal cause of human misery today.

This is the background situation, the situation that prevails on our planet all the time. It does not make headlines. People died from malnutrition and related diseases yesterday, and more will die tomorrow. The occasional droughts, cyclones, earthquakes, and floods that take the lives of tens of thousands in one place and at one time are more newsworthy. They add greatly to the total amount of human suffering; but it is wrong to assume that when there are no major calamities reported, all is well.

The problem is not that the world cannot produce enough to feed and shelter its people. People in the poor countries consume, on average, 400 lbs of grain a year, while North Americans average more than 2000 lbs. The difference is caused by the fact that in the rich countries we feed most of our grain to animals, converting it into meat, milk, and eggs. Because this is an inefficient process, wasting up to 95% of the food value of the animal feed, people in rich countries are responsible for the consumption of far more food than those in poor countries who eat few animal products. If we stopped feeding animals on grains, soybeans, and fishmeal the amount of food saved would—if distributed to those who need it—be more than enough to end hunger throughout the world.

These facts about animal food do not mean that we can easily solve the world food problem by cutting down on animal products, but they show that the problem is essentially one of distribution rather than production. The world does produce enough food. Moreover the poorer nations themselves could produce far more if they made more use of improved agricultural techniques.

So why are people hungry? Poor people cannot afford to buy grain grown by American farmers. Poor farmers cannot afford to buy improved seeds, or fertilizers, or the machinery needed for drilling wells and pumping water. Only by transferring some of the wealth of the developed nations to the poor of the underdeveloped nations can the situation be changed.

That this wealth exists is clear. Against the picture of absolute poverty that McNamara has painted, one might pose a picture of "absolute affluence." Those who are absolutely affluent are not necessarily affluent by comparison with their neighbours, but they are affluent by any reasonable definition of human needs. This means that they have more income than they need to provide themselves adequately with all the basic necessities of life. After buying food, shelter, clothing, necessary health services, and education, the absolutely affluent are still able to spend money on luxuries. The absolutely affluent choose their food for the pleasures of the palate, not to stop hunger; they buy new clothes to look fashionable, not to keep warm; they move house to be in a better neighbourhood or have a play room for the children, not to keep out the rain; and after all this there is still money to spend on books and records, colour television, and overseas holidays.

At this stage I am making no ethical judgments about absolute affluence, merely pointing out that it exists. Its defining characteristic is a significant amount of income above the level necessary to pro-

vide for the basic human needs of oneself and one's dependents. By this standard Western Europe, North America, Japan, Australia, New Zealand, and the oil-rich Middle Eastern states are all absolutely affluent, and so are many, if not all, of their citizens. The USSR and Eastern Europe might also be included on this list. To quote McNamara once more:

> The average citizen of a developed country enjoys wealth beyond the wildest dreams of the one billion people in countries with per capita incomes under $200. . . .

These, therefore, are the countries—and individuals—who have wealth which they could, without threatening their own basic welfare, transfer to the absolutely poor.

At present, very little is being transferred. Members of the Organization of Petroleum Exporting Countries lead the way, giving an average of 2.1% of their Gross National Product. Apart from them, only Sweden, the Netherlands, and Norway have reached the modest UN target of 0.7% of GNP. Britain gives 0.38% of its GNP in official development assistance and a small additional amount in unofficial aid from voluntary organizations. The total comes to less than £1 per month per person, and compares with 5.5% of GNP spent on alcohol, and 3% on tobacco. Other, even wealthier nations, give still less: Germany gives 0.27%, the United States 0.22%, and Japan 0.21%.

The Moral Equivalent of Murder?

If these are the facts, we cannot avoid concluding that by not giving more than we do, people in rich countries are allowing those in poor countries to suffer from absolute poverty, with consequent malnutrition, ill health, and death. This is not a conclusion which applies only to governments. It applies to each absolutely affluent individual, for each of us has the opportunity to do something about the situation; for instance, to give our time or money to voluntary organizations like Oxfam, War on Want, Freedom From Hunger, and so on. If, then, allowing someone to die is not intrinsically different from killing someone, it would seem that we are all murderers.

Is this verdict too harsh? Many will reject it as self-evidently absurd. They would sooner take it as showing that allowing to die cannot be equivalent to killing than as showing that living in an affluent style without contributing to Oxfam is ethically equivalent to going over to India and shooting a few peasants. And no doubt, put as bluntly as that, the verdict *is* too harsh.

There are several significant differences between spending money on luxuries instead of using it to save lives, and deliberately shooting people.

First, the motivation will normally be different. Those who deliberately shoot others go out of their way to kill; they presumably want their victims dead, from malice, sadism, or some equally unpleasant motive. A person who buys a colour television set presumably wants to watch television in colour—not in itself a terrible thing. At worst, spending money on luxuries instead of giving it away indicates selfishness and indifference to the sufferings of others, characteristics which may be understandable but are not comparable with actual malice or similar motives.

Second, it is not difficult for most of us to act in accordance with a rule against killing people: It is, on the other hand, very difficult to obey a rule which commands us to save all the lives we can. To live a comfortable, or even luxurious life it is not necessary to kill anyone; but it is necessary to allow some to die whom we might have saved, for the money that we need to live comfortably could have been given away. Thus the duty to avoid killing is much easier to discharge completely than the duty to save. Saving every life we could would mean cutting our standard of living down to the bare essentials needed to keep us alive.* To discharge this duty completely would require a degree of moral heroism utterly different from what is required by mere avoidance of killing.

---

*Strictly, we would need to cut down to the minimum level compatible with earning the income which, after providing for our needs, left us most to give away. Thus if my present position earns me, say, £10,000 a year, but requires me to spend £1,000 a year on dressing respectably and maintaining a car, I cannot save more people by giving away the car and clothes if that will mean taking a job which, although it does not involve me in these expenses, earns me only £5,000.

A third difference is the greater certainty of the outcome of shooting when compared with not giving aid. If I point a loaded gun at someone and pull the trigger, it is virtually certain that the person will be injured, if not killed; whereas the money that I could give might be spent on a project than turns out to be unsuccessful and helps no one.

Fourth, when people are shot there are identifiable individuals who have been harmed. We can point to them and to their grieving families. When I buy my colour television, I cannot know who my money would have saved if I had given it away. In a time of famine I may see dead bodies and grieving families on my new television, and I might not doubt that my money would have saved some of them; even then it is impossible to point to a body and say that had I not bought the set, that person would have survived.

Fifth, it might be said that the plight of the hungry is not my doing, and so I cannot be held responsible for it. The starving would have been starving if I had never existed. If I kill, however, I am responsible for my victims' deaths, for those people would not have died if I had not killed them. . . .

Do the five differences not only explain, but also justify, our attitudes? Let us consider them one by one:

1. Take the lack of an identifiable victim first. Suppose that I am a travelling salesman, selling tinned food, and I learn that a batch of tins contains a contaminant, the known effect of which when consumed is to double the risk that the consumer will die from stomach cancer. Suppose I continue to sell the tins. My decision may have no identifiable victims. Some of those who eat the food will die from cancer. The proportion of consumers dying in this way will be twice that of the community at large, but which among the consumers died because they ate what I sold, and which would have contracted the disease anyway? It is impossible to tell; but surely this impossibility makes my decision no less reprehensible than it would have been had the contaminant had more readily detectable, though equally fatal, effects.

2. The lack of certainty that by giving money I could save a life does reduce the wrongness of not giving, by comparison with deliberate killing; but it is insufficient to show that not giving is acceptable conduct.

The motorist who speeds through pedestrian crossings, heedless of anyone who might be on them, is not a murderer. She may never actually hit a pedestrian; yet what she does is very wrong indeed.

3. The notion of responsibility for acts rather than omissions is more puzzling. On the one hand we feel ourselves to be under a greater obligation to help those whose misfortunes we have caused. (It is for this reason that advocates of overseas aid often argue that Western nations have created the poverty of Third World nations, through forms of economic exploitation which go back to the colonial system.) On the other hand any consequentialist would insist that we are responsible for all the consequences of our actions, and if a consequence of my spending money on a luxury item is that someone dies, I am responsible for that death. It is true that the person would have died even if I had never existed, but what is the relevance of that? The fact is that I do exist, and the consequentialist will say that our responsibilities derive from the world as it is, not as it might have been.

One way of making sense of the nonconsequentialist view of responsibility is by basing it on a theory of rights of the kind proposed by John Locke or, more recently, Robert Nozick. If everyone has a right to life, and this right is a right *against* others who might threaten my life, but not a right *to* assistance from others when my life is in danger, then we can understand the feeling that we are responsible for acting to kill but not for omitting to save. The former violates the rights of others, the latter does not.

Should we accept such a theory of rights? If we build up our theory of rights by imagining, as Locke and Nozick do, individuals living independently from each other in a "state of nature," it may seem natural to adopt a conception of rights in which as long as each leaves the other alone, no rights are violated. I might, on this view, quite properly have maintained my independent existence if I had wished to do so. So if I do not make you any worse off than you would have been if I had had nothing at all to do with you, how can I have violated your rights? But why start from such an unhistorical, abstract, and ultimately inexplicable idea as an independent individual? We now know that our ancestors were social beings long before they were human beings, and could not have developed the abilities and capacities of human beings if they had not been social beings first. In any case we are not, now, isolated individuals. If we consider people living together in a community, it is less easy to assume that rights must be restricted to rights against interference. We might, instead, adopt the view that taking rights to life seriously is incompatible with standing by and watching people die when one could easily save them.

4. What of the difference in motivation? That a person does not positively wish for the death of another lessens the severity of the blame she deserves; but not by as much as our present attitudes to giving aid suggest. The behaviour of the speeding motorist is again comparable, for such motorists usually have no desire at all to kill anyone. They merely enjoy speeding and are indifferent to the consequences. Despite their lack of malice, those who kill with cars deserve not only blame but also severe punishment.

5. Finally, the fact that to avoid killing people is normally not difficult, whereas to save all one possibly could save is heroic, must make an important difference to our attitude to failure to do what the respective principles demand. Not to kill is a minimum standard of acceptable conduct we can require of everyone; to save all one possibly could is not something that can realistically be required, especially not in societies accustomed to giving as little as ours do. Given the generally accepted standards, people who give, say, £100 a year to Oxfam are more aptly praised for above average generosity than blamed for giving less than they might. The appropriateness of praise and blame is, however, a separate issue from the rightness or wrongness of actions. The former evaluates the agent: The latter evaluates the action. Perhaps people who give £100 really ought to give at least £1,000, but to blame them for not giving more could be counterproductive. It might make them feel that what is required is too demanding, and if one is going to be blamed anyway, one might as well not give anything at all.

(That an ethic which put saving all one possibly can on the same footing as not killing would be an ethic for saints or heroes should not lead us to assume that the alternative must be an ethic which makes it obligatory not to kill, but puts us under no obligation to save anyone. There are positions in between these extremes, as we shall soon see.)

To summarize our discussion of the five differences which normally exist between killing and allowing to die, in the context of absolute poverty and overseas aid: The lack of an identifiable victim is of no moral significance, though it may play an important role in explaining our attitudes. The idea that we are directly responsible for those we kill, but not for those we do not help, depends on a questionable notion of responsibility, and may need to be based on a controversial theory of rights. Differences in certainty and motivation are ethically significant, and show that not aiding the poor is not to be condemned as murdering them; it could, however, be on a par with killing someone as a result of reckless driving, which is serious enough. Finally the difficulty of completely discharging the duty of saving all one possibly can makes it inappropriate to blame those who fall short of this target as we blame those who kill; but this does not show that the act itself is less serious. Nor does it indicate anything about those who, far from saving all they possibly can, make no effort to save anyone.

These conclusions suggest a new approach. Instead of attempting to deal with the contrast between affluence and poverty by comparing not saving with deliberate killing, let us consider afresh whether we have an obligation to assist those whose lives are in danger, and if so, how this obligation applies to the present world situation.

The Obligation to Assist

The Argument for an Obligation to Assist

The path from the library at my university to the Humanities lecture theatre passes a shallow ornamental pond. Suppose that on my way to give a lecture I notice that a small child has fallen in and is in danger of drowning. Would anyone deny that I ought to wade in and pull the child out? This will mean getting my clothes muddy, and either cancelling my lecture or delaying it until I can find something dry to change into; but compared with the avoidable death of a child this is insignificant.

A plausible principle that would support the judgment that I ought to pull the child out is this: If it is in our power to prevent something very bad happening, without thereby sacrificing anything of comparable moral significance, we ought to do it. This principle seems uncontroversial. It will obviously win the assent of consequentialists; but nonconsequentialists should accept it too, because the injunction to prevent what is bad applies only when nothing comparably significant is at stake. Thus the principle cannot lead to the kinds of actions of which nonconsequentialists strongly disapprove—serious violations of individual rights, injustice, broken promises, and so on. If a nonconsequentialist regards any of these as comparable in moral significance to the bad thing that is to be prevented, he will automatically regard the principle as not applying in those cases in which the bad thing can only be prevented by violating rights, doing injustice, breaking promises, or whatever else is at stake. Most nonconsequentialists hold that we ought to prevent what is bad and promote what is good. Their dispute with consequentialists lies in their insistence that this is not the sole ultimate ethical principle: That it is *an* ethical principle is not denied by any plausible ethical theory.

Nevertheless the uncontroversial appearance of the principle that we ought to prevent what is bad when we can do so without sacrificing anything of comparable moral significance is deceptive. If it were taken seriously and acted upon, our lives and our world would be fundamentally changed. For the principle applies, not just to rare situations in which one can save a child from a pond, but to the everyday situation in which we can assist those living in absolute poverty. In saying this I assume that absolute poverty—with its hunger and malnutrition, lack of shelter, illiteracy, disease, high infant mortality, and low life expectancy—is a bad thing. And I assume that it is within the power of the affluent to reduce absolute poverty, without sacrificing anything of comparable moral significance. If these two assumptions and the principle we have been discussing are correct, we have an obligation to help those in absolute poverty which is no less strong than our obligation to rescue a drowning child from a pond. Not to help would be wrong, whether or not it is intrinsically equivalent to killing. Helping is not, as conventionally thought, a charitable act which it is praiseworthy to do, but not wrong to omit; it is something that everyone ought to do.

This is the argument for an obligation to assist. Set out more formally, it would look like this:

First premise:

If we can prevent something bad without sacrificing anything of comparable significance, we ought to do it.

Second premise:

Absolute poverty is bad.

Third premise:

There is some absolute poverty we can prevent without sacrificing anything of comparable moral significance.

Conclusion:

We ought to prevent some absolute poverty.

The first premise is the substantive moral premise on which the argument rests, and I have tried to show that it can be accepted by people who hold a variety of ethical positions. The second premise is unlikely to be challenged. Absolute poverty is, as McNamara put it, "beneath any reasonable definition of human decency" and it would be hard to find a plausible ethical view which did not regard it as a bad thing.

The third premise is more controversial, even though it is cautiously framed. It claims only that some absolute poverty can be prevented without the sacrifice of anything of comparable moral significance. It thus avoids the objection that any aid I can give is just "drops in the ocean" for the point is not whether my personal contribution will make any noticeable impression on world poverty as a whole (of course it won't) but whether it will prevent some poverty. This is all the argument needs to sustain its conclusion, since the second premise says that any absolute poverty is bad, and not merely the total amount of absolute poverty. If without sacrificing anything of comparable moral significance we can provide just one family with the means to raise itself out of absolute poverty, the third premise is vindicated.

I have left the notion of moral significance unexamined in order to show that the argument does not depend on any specific values or ethical principles. I think the third premise is true for most people living in industrialized nations, on any defensible view of what is morally significant. Our affluence means that we have income we can dispose of without giving up the basic necessities of life, and we can use this income to reduce absolute poverty. Just how much we will think ourselves obliged to give up will depend on what we consider to be of comparable moral significance to the poverty we could prevent: colour television, stylish clothes, expensive dinners, a sophisticated stereo system, overseas holidays, a (second?) car, a larger house, private schools for our children. . . . For a utilitarian, none of these is likely to be of comparable significance to the reduction of absolute poverty; and those who are not utilitarians surely must, if they subscribe to the principle of universalizability, accept that at least *some* of these things are of far less moral significance than the absolute poverty that could be prevented by the money they cost. So the third premise seems to be true on any plausible ethical view—although the precise amount of absolute poverty that can be prevented before anything of moral significance is sacrificed will vary according to the ethical view one accepts. . . .

Objections to the Argument
Property Rights

Do people have a right to private property, a right which contradicts the view that they are under an obligation to give some of their wealth away to those in absolute poverty? According to some theories of rights (for instance, Robert Nozick's) provided one has acquired one's property without the use of unjust means like force and fraud, one may be entitled to enormous wealth while others starve. This individualistic conception of rights is in contrast to other views, like the early Christian doctrine to be found in the works of Thomas Aquinas, which holds that since property exists for the satisfaction of human needs, "whatever a man has in superabundance is owed, of natural right, to the poor for their sustenance." A socialist would also, of course, see wealth as belonging to the community rather than the individual, while utilitarians, whether socialist or not, would be prepared to override property rights to prevent great evils.

Does the argument for an obligation to assist others therefore presuppose one of these other theories of property rights, and not an individualistic theory like Nozick's? Not necessarily. A theory of property rights can insist on our *right* to retain wealth without pronouncing on whether the rich *ought* to give to the poor. Nozick, for example, rejects the use of compulsory means like taxation to redistribute income, but suggests that we can achieve the ends we deem morally desirable by voluntary means. So Nozick would reject the claim that rich people have an "obligation" to give to the poor, insofar as this implies that the poor have a right to our aid, but might accept that giving is something we ought to do and failing to give, though within one's rights, is wrong—for rights is not all there is to ethics.

The argument for an obligation to assist can survive, with only minor modifications, even if we accept an individualistic theory of property rights. In any case, however, I do not think we should accept such a theory. It leaves too much to chance to be an acceptable ethical view. For instance, those whose forefathers happened to inhabit some sandy wastes around the Persian Gulf are now fabulously wealthy, because oil lay under those sands; while those whose forefathers settled on better land south of the Sahara live in absolute poverty, because of drought and bad harvests. Can this distribution be acceptable from an impartial point of view? If we imagine ourselves about to begin life as a citizen of either Kuwait or Chad—but we do not know which—would we accept the principle that citizens of Kuwait are under no obligation to assist people living in Chad?

Population and the Ethics of Triage

Perhaps the most serious objection to the argument that we have an obligation to assist is that since the major cause of absolute poverty is overpopulation, helping those now in poverty will only ensure that yet more people are born to live in poverty in the future.

In its most extreme form, this objection is taken to show that we should adopt a policy of "triage." The term comes from medical policies adopted in wartime. With too few doctors to cope with all the casualties, the wounded were divided into three categories: those who would probably survive without medical assistance; those who might survive if they received assistance, but otherwise probably would not; and those who even with medical assistance

probably would not survive. Only those in the middle category were given medical assistance. The idea, of course, was to use limited medical resources as effectively as possible. For those in the first category, medical treatment was not strictly necessary; for those in the third category, it was likely to be useless. It has been suggested that we should apply the same policies to countries, according to their prospects of becoming self-sustaining. We would not aid countries which even without our help will soon be able to feed their populations. We would not aid countries which, even with our help, will not be able to limit their population to a level they can feed. We would aid those countries where our help might make the difference between success and failure in bringing food and population into balance.

Advocates of this theory are understandably reluctant to give a complete list of the countries they would place into the "hopeless" category; but Bangladesh is often cited as an example. Adopting the policy of triage would, then, mean cutting off assistance to Bangladesh and allowing famine, disease, and natural disasters to reduce the population of that country (now around 80 million) to the level at which it can provide adequately for all.

In support of this view Garrett Hardin has offered a metaphor: We in the rich nations are like the occupants of a crowded lifeboat adrift in a sea full of drowning people. If we try to save the drowning by bringing them aboard, our boat will be overloaded and we shall all drown. Since it is better that some survive than none, we should leave the others to drown. In the world today, according to Hardin, "lifeboat ethics" apply. The rich should leave the poor to starve, for otherwise the poor will drag the rich down with them.

Against this view, some writers have argued that over-population is a myth. The world produces ample food to feed its population, and could, according to some estimates, feed ten times as many. People are hungry not because there are too many but because of inequitable land distribution, the manipulation of Third World economies by the developed nations, wastage of food in the West, and so on.

Putting aside the controversial issue of the extent to which food production might one day be increased, it is true, as we have already seen, that the world now produces enough to feed its inhabitants—the amount lost by being fed to animals itself being enough to meet existing grain shortages. Nevertheless population growth cannot be ignored. Bangladesh could, with land reform and using better techniques, feed its present population of 80 million; but by the year 2000, according to World Bank estimates, its population will be 146 million. The enormous effort that will have to go into feeding an extra 66 million people, all added to the population within a quarter of a century, means that Bangladesh must develop at full speed to stay where she is. Other low-income countries are in similar situations. By the end of the century, Ethiopia's population is expected to rise from 29 to 54 million, Somalia's from 3 to 7 million, India's from 620 to 958 million, Zaire's from 25 to 47 million. What will happen then? Population cannot grow indefinitely. It will be checked by a decline in birth rates or a rise in death rates. Those who advocate triage are proposing that we allow the population growth of some countries to be checked by a rise in death rates—that is, by increased malnutrition, and related diseases; by widespread famines; by increased infant mortality; and by epidemics of infectious diseases.

The consequences of triage on this scale are so horrible that we are inclined to reject it without further argument. How could we sit by our television sets, watching millions starve while we do nothing? Would not that be the end of all notions of human equality and respect for human life? Don't people have a right to our assistance, irrespective of the consequences?

Anyone whose initial reaction to triage was not one of repugnance would be an unpleasant sort of person. Yet initial reactions based on strong feelings are not always reliable guides. Advocates of triage are rightly concerned with the long-term consequences of our actions. They say that helping the poor and starving now merely ensures more poor and starving in the future. When our capacity to help is finally unable to cope—as one day it must be—the suffering will be greater than it would be if we stopped helping now. If this is correct, there is nothing we can do to prevent absolute starvation and poverty, in the long run, and so we have no obligation to assist. Nor does it seem reasonable to hold that under these circumstances people have a right to our assistance. If we do accept

such a right, irrespective of the consequences, we are saying that, in Hardin's metaphor, we would continue to haul the drowning into our lifeboat until the boat sank and we all drowned.

If triage is to be rejected it must be tackled on its own ground, within the framework of consequentialist ethics. Here it is vulnerable. Any consequentialist ethics must take probability of outcome into account. A course of action that will certainly produce some benefit is to be preferred to an alternative course that may lead to a slightly larger benefit, but is equally likely to result in no benefit at all. Only if the greater magnitude of the uncertain benefit outweighs its uncertainty should we choose it. Better one certain unit of benefit than a 10% chance of 5 units; but better a 50% chance of 3 units than a single certain unit. The same principle applies when we are trying to avoid evils.

The policy of triage involves a certain, very great evil: population control by famine and disease. Tens of millions would die slowly. Hundreds of millions would continue to live in absolute poverty, at the very margin of existence. Against this prospect, advocates of the policy place a possible evil which is greater still: The same process of famine and disease, taking place in, say, fifty years time, when the world's population may be three times its present level, and the number who will die from famine, or struggle on in absolute poverty, will be that much greater. The question is: How probable is this forecast that continued assistance now will lead to greater disasters in the future?

Forecasts of population growth are notoriously fallible, and theories about the factors which affect it remain speculative. One theory, at least as plausible as any other, is that countries pass through a "demographic transition" as their standard of living rises. When people are very poor and have no access to modern medicine their fertility is high, but population is kept in check by high death rates. The introduction of sanitation, modern medical techniques, and other improvements reduces the death rate, but initially has little effect on the birthrate. Then population grows rapidly. Most poor countries are now in this phase. If standards of living continue to rise, however, couples begin to realize that to have the same number of children surviving to maturity as in the past, they do not need to give birth to as many children as their parents did. The need for children to provide economic support in old age diminishes. Improved education and the emancipation and employment of women also reduce the birthrate, and so population growth begins to level off. Most rich nations have reached this stage, and their populations are growing only very slowly.

If this theory is right, there is an alternative to the disasters accepted as inevitable by supporters of triage. We can assist poor countries to raise the living standards of the poorest members of their population. We can encourage the governments of these countries to enact land reform measures, improve education, and liberate women from a purely childbearing role. We can also help other countries to make contraception and sterilization widely available. There is a fair chance that these measures will hasten the onset of the demographic transition and bring population growth down to a manageable level. Success cannot be guaranteed; but the evidence that improved economic security and education reduce population growth is strong enough to make triage ethically unacceptable. We cannot allow millions to die from starvation and disease when there is a reasonable probability that population can be brought under control without such horrors.

Population growth is therefore not a reason against giving overseas aid, although it should make us think about the kind of aid to give. Instead of food handouts, it may be better to give aid that hastens the demographic transition. This may mean agricultural assistance for the rural poor, or assistance with education, or the provision of contraceptive services. Whatever kind of aid proves most effective in specific circumstances, the obligation to assist is not reduced.

One awkward question remains. What should we do about a poor and already overpopulated country which, for religious or nationalistic reasons, restricts the use of contraceptives and refuses to slow its population growth? Should we nevertheless offer development assistance? Or should we make our offer conditional on effective steps being taken to reduce the birthrate? To the latter course, some would object that putting conditions on aid is an attempt to impose our own ideas on independent sovereign nations. So it is—but is this imposition unjustifiable? If the argument for an obligation to assist is sound, we have an obligation to reduce absolute poverty: But we have no

obligation to make sacrifices that, to the best of our knowledge, have no prospect of reducing poverty in the long run. Hence we have no obligation to assist countries whose governments have policies which will make our aid ineffective. This could be very harsh on poor citizens of these countries—for they may have no say in the government's policies—but we will help more people in the long run by using our resources where they are most effective. (The same principles may apply, incidentally, to countries that refuse to take other steps that could make assistance effective—like refusing to reform systems of land holding that impose intolerable burdens on poor tenant farmers.) . . .

Too High a Standard?

The final objection to the argument for an obligation to assist is that it sets a standard so high that none but a saint could attain it. How many people can we really expect to give away everything not comparable in moral significance to the poverty their donation could relieve? For most of us, with commonsense views about what is of moral significance, this would mean a life of real austerity. Might it not be counterproductive to demand so much? Might not people say: "As I can't do what is morally required anyway, I won't bother to give at all." If, however, we were to set a more realistic standard, people might make a genuine effort to reach it. Thus setting a lower standard might actually result in more aid being given.

It is important to get the status of this objection clear. Its accuracy as a prediction of human behaviour is quite compatible with the argument that we are obliged to give to the point at which by giving more we sacrifice something of comparable moral significance. What would follow from the objection is that public advocacy of this standard of giving is undesirable. It would mean that in order to do the maximum to reduce absolute poverty, we should advocate a standard lower than the amount we think people really ought to give. Of course we ourselves—those of us who accept the original argument, with its higher standard—would know that we ought to do more than we publicly propose people ought to do, and we might actually give more than we urge others to give. There is no inconsistency here, since in both our private and our public behaviour we are trying to do what will most reduce absolute poverty.

For a consequentialist, this apparent conflict between public and private morality is always a possibility, and not in itself an indication that the underlying principle is wrong. The consequences of a principle are one thing, the consequences of publicly advocating it another.

Is it true that the standard set by our argument is so high as to be counterproductive? There is not much evidence to go by, but discussions of the argument, with students and others, have led me to think it might be. On the other hand the conventionally accepted standard—a few coins in a collection tin when one is waved under your nose—is obviously far too low. What level should we advocate? Any figure will be arbitrary, but there may be something to be said for a round percentage of one's income like, say, 10 percent—

more than a token donation, yet not so high as to be beyond all but saints. (This figure has the additional advantage of being reminiscent of the ancient tithe, or tenth, which was traditionally given to the church, whose responsibilities included care of the poor in one's local community. Perhaps the idea can be revived and applied to the global community.) Some families, of course, will find 10 percent a considerable strain on their finances. Others may be able to give more without difficulty. No figure should be advocated as a rigid minimum or maximum; but it seems safe to advocate that those earning average or above average incomes in affluent societies, unless they have an unusually large number of dependents or other special needs, ought to give a tenth of their income to reducing absolute poverty. By any reasonable ethical standards this is the minimum we ought to do, and we do wrong if we do less.

---

10. *Impartiality, Beneficence, and Friendship*

LAWRENCE BLUM

Lawrence Blum argues that our duty to be impartial is limited to certain institutional roles we occupy such as that of a judge, a teacher, or a doctor. Outside of those roles, Blum argues that we may have a duty of beneficence, but not impartiality, to concern ourselves with the well-being of strangers, but this duty does not rule out special treatment for our friends.

I

I will argue . . . that impartiality is a moral requirement only in certain restricted sorts of situations. It is not a morally incumbent perspective to take up in every situation. In particular, friendship does not typically involve us in situations in which impartiality between the interests of our friends and those of others is a

From *Friendship, Altruism and Morality* (1980), Routledge. Used with the permission of the author and the publisher.

moral requirement; hence in acting beneficently towards our friends we do not typically violate a duty of impartiality.

Certainly attachments to particular persons can lead us to violate impartiality, and thus to be unfair to others. Someone in an official position to dispense jobs can use his position to get jobs for his friends and relatives, independent of their qualification for the jobs. And we may imagine a doctor who because he likes a particular patient devotes too much of his consulting time to this patient, neglecting the others who are waiting to see him.

But such situations do not point to a general conflict between helping one's friends and helping others. It is no violation of impartiality if I phone my friend to see if he is feeling better, knowing that he has been ill. Such a situation of acting from concern for a friend does not impose on me the obligation to take into account the interests of all the people whom I *might* help at that point in time, and to choose according to some impartial criterion whom to benefit. The examples so far given point to one of the primary sorts of situations in which such impartiality is demanded—namely, an official capacity within some public institution or practice.

A judge, a captain of a ship, a doctor, a nurse, a teacher, all occupy roles or positions in which a certain kind of impartiality is demanded of them regarding the interests of certain parties whom they serve or for whom they have some responsibility. This impartiality extends to persons to whom they have special attachments. The benefits or burdens dispensed by these persons are to accrue to persons not on the basis of some personal attachment of the holder of the role to them, but on the basis of some impersonal criterion, connected with need, qualification for a position, established and rational procedure, or the like.

Thus, to take the most obvious case, a judge is meant to dispense justice impartially. He is meant to make his decision on the merits of the case and not according to his attachment to one of the parties involved. A teacher is not supposed to grade a student higher because he likes him or has a special attachment to him. A nurse is supposed to help his patients according to their individual needs, not according to his own personal likings and attachments.

It is an important part of our understanding of the duties of impartiality attaching to these roles that persons who assume the roles are aware of what those duties entail; in particular, aware of how they might impinge on the interests of those to whom they are attached. Thus a doctor or nurse knows that by virtue of his position he is forbidden from attempting to secure for a friend or relative some drugs or other medical care which are properly meant for others, or which fair procedures would allot to others.

A person might refuse to (or not be allowed to) put himself in a position in which he would be required to dispense a benefit or a burden according to an impartial rule, where a friend would be one of the candidates for the benefit or burden. This could be either because he did not feel he would be capable of such impartiality, or because, if he were, he would find it too difficult or painful to be required to dispense the benefit to someone other than his friend.

For this sort of reason it is a general policy that judges not sit in cases in which they have some special connection to one of the parties (or in which they have a self-interest in the outcome). The temptations of conflict between their impersonal duties and their personal attachments would be too great and would place an extraordinary personal burden on the role-occupiers and on the friendships; so for the good of everyone such a situation is best avoided.

Institutional roles and positions are an obvious arena of life in which a certain kind of impartiality between the interests of all, including those to whom we are personally connected and attached, is demanded of us. Equally obvious is the fact that situations covered by such roles are very untypical of those in which we interact with and benefit our friends. And so the existence of such roles does not betoken a common, much less a fundamental, moral problem regarding the beneficence dispensed to our friends.

This conclusion is strengthened by the fact that even within these institutionalized roles there is a limit to the demand of impartiality, and in most cases a scope outside of that limit for benefiting those whom we choose for whatever reason (e.g., personal attachment or liking) to benefit. Thus if a doctor, having fulfilled his obligations to his patients, spends extra time on the case of a friend, this would not be a violation of impartiality, but on the contrary would be admirable behavior on his part. A teacher is permitted to give more attention to some students than to others (not merely on pedagogical grounds), as long as he gives full and adequate attention to all. The criterion here, vague though it may be, of when it is morally permissible to depart from strict impartiality, has to do with what is regarded as the duties of one's role, in contrast to what is regarded as going beyond those duties (and is in that sense supererogatory). In the latter situations, what one does for those one chooses to help is regarded as giving something of oneself, rather than as depriving others of what one owes to them by virtue of one's institutional relationship with them. The line between these is extremely difficult to draw, is not in general fixed but is subject to change (e.g., redefinition of what constitutes the responsibilities of a role), and is not applicable in all situations. But that it exists is significant for our argument. For what it shows is that even in contexts in which impartiality between the interests of one's friends and those of others is demanded, this demand is limited in its scope, and there remains an area in which we are able to express our natural care and concern for our friends, our desire to do what is good for them, outside of the constraint of impersonal considerations.

It should be noted that this argument applies not only to actual friends and personal relationships but also to people whom we like but have no substantial or developed relationship with; i.e., it applies to beneficence from personal feelings. Here too we are morally permitted to benefit them, and this benefiting is not in general required to be justified through an impartial perspective or procedure. Morality does not in most situations demand of us that we justify such beneficence with regard to the interests of others whom we could have served but did not.

II

I have claimed that institutional-role contexts are ones in which impartiality is demanded of us. What I have not yet done is to show that the demand of impartiality is limited to such institutional-role contexts. Nor, related to this, have I given a general characterization of the conditions in which such a demand is an appropriate one, from a moral point of view.

To help gain some clarity regarding the noninstitutional contexts in which impartiality is incumbent upon us, it is necessary to make an important distinction. The fact that impartiality does not demand that we constantly appraise our potential beneficence to our friends by an impartial standard does not mean that we are justified in totally disregarding the interests of others when the good of our friends is at stake, even outside contexts in which strict impartiality is demanded. To take an extreme example, suppose that I am in a train crash in which many people are injured, including my best friend (but not myself). I am certainly justified in giving my first attention to my

friend. But it seems also required for me to give some attention to others. Some weighing is evidently called for here. The point is that strict impartiality is not required or appropriate, but neither is ignoring the interests of others simply because the weal and woe of one's friend is at stake.

Suppose I pass two persons on the street digging their cars out of the snow, and one of them is my friend. Surely I am justified in choosing to help my friend in preference to helping the stranger, though it would also perhaps be the decent thing to do to attempt to help both of them. But if, say, the friend could very easily dig the car out by himself, and in fact had almost finished doing so (though there was still room for assistance from someone else), and the other person obviously could not do so without some assistance, then another factor will have been introduced which must be weighed against the desire to help the friend. Here it might be more appropriate that one help the other person. (One would imagine that the friend would agree that this was appropriate.)

We then have three different sorts of situations. In the first we are required to treat the interests of the relevant parties from a strictly impartial perspective, even if one of the parties is our friend. Personal attachments must be entirely overlooked (though only up to a certain point). In the second, we are required to give some attention to the interests of others, but are not required to regard those interests strictly impartially or as having equal weight to the interests of friends who are involved. In the third type of situation consideration to the interests of others is not at all appropriate or relevant. In such situations it is morally permissible to act solely for the benefit of one's friend.

The existence of the second category helps to define the limits of impartiality, while giving credence to our sense that in some situations the presence of friends does not or should not preclude attention to the interests of others. For we see that in some situations there is some moral constraint on us to attend to the weal and woe of others, even though the weal and woe of friends is also at stake; and yet the grounding of such moral constraint need not be located in a demand for impartiality. In the train crash example just described, I have claimed that one ought to give some help to injured persons who are not one's friends, though one's first concern is properly with one's own friend. Some might see this help as a strict duty (of beneficence) on the ground that great harm to others can be avoided with little sacrifice to myself (or to a person to whom I am attached). But even if one does not see this as an actual duty, it is possible to recognize some element of moral constraint in the consideration that my ability to help the injured persons ought to weigh with me in my actions.

Thus, that I ought to help the injured persons seems in many contexts to stem not from a general demand of impartiality between the interests of all concerned (including myself or my friends) but from something like a duty of beneficence. That this is so can be seen if we imagine the situation without the friend's being injured. There would still be moral constraint for us to help the other persons; yet this moral constraint cannot stem from a demand that we treat the interests of everyone, including those to whom we have a special attachment, impartially. What the presence of the friend does to the moral configuration of this situation is not so much to undercut this moral quasi-demand of attention to the weal and woe of others, but to bring into play another consideration against which it is to be balanced. It is still true that we ought to attend to the interests of the injured strangers, but it is entirely proper for us to attend first to our friend. It would be inappropriate for us to give our entire attention to our friend, when further attention to him would produce minimal good to him compared to the much greater good which could be produced by attention to others. But, on the other side, it is also inappropriate for us at the outset to apportion our help impartially—solely according to need—ignoring the fact that one of the persons is our friend.

It could be responded here that this argument applies only to situations where the interests of others are substantially threatened—such as in a train crash—so that attention to their interests is urgent enough to be morally incumbent upon us. The same argument would not seem to hold for the case of digging the car out of the snow (above . . .), where there would seem no demand that we attend to the interests of the person who is not our friend merely because he could use some help.

Yet it seems that whatever consideration is appropriate regarding the weal and woe of the stranger is unaffected by the presence of the friend, and so is not connected to impartiality. Though there is no *duty* to help the stranger, perhaps there is some moral deficiency or inadequacy in failing to do so, if one has nothing very important to do and could help fairly readily. Yet whatever force of "oughtness" one attributes to the consideration of the man's weal and woe (regarding digging his car out) exists independently of whether the friend is present in the situation or not.

The presence of the friend merely interjects another factor which changes the overall moral configuration of the situation. We might properly not help the other, choosing instead to help the friend (assuming we cannot do both). But we do not thereby repudiate the moral consideration of helping the other.

Thus even in cases (involving friends) in which there is nothing like a duty of beneficence, a consideration to the interests of others does not stem from a requirement of impartiality; for, first, that consideration exists even when the friendship issue does not, and second, impartiality between the interests of the friend and of the other(s) is not actually required.

III

If the argument of the previous section is right, then in noninstitutional contexts at least some of the morally appropriate regard to the interests of others can be accounted for without appeal to the principle of impartiality. This is a step towards defining the scope of the principle of impartiality in noninstitutional contexts.

I suggest that we can learn something of that scope by asking in what the nature of impartiality, justice, and fairness consists, as virtues or traits of character exhibited in one's noninstitutional (as well as institutional) life. Here the definition given by Sidgwick seems to me close to the mark:

> What then do we mean by a just man in matters where law-observance does not enter? It is natural to reply that we mean an impartial man, one who seeks with equal care to satisfy all claims which he recognizes as valid and does not let himself be unduly influenced by personal preferences.

This definition brings out that impartiality or justice has to do with overlooking personal preferences in circumstances which have to do with according burdens and benefits to persons.

For example, suppose I am helping to settle a dispute between two persons, one of whom is a friend. Both persons are looking to me for mediation in the quarrel. This is a circumstance where justice or impartiality is required, or appropriate. We are not to favor the friend simply because he is our friend. Rather we are to overlook our personal attachment and consider only the factors relevant to the dispute. Hearing the claims made on both sides, it might turn out that I feel that the nonfriend's claim has more merit, and that he is more deserving of the benefit regarding which there is a dispute.

Sidgwick's definition suggests why impartiality is not always required of us, nor required in every situation in which our actions are of a potential benefit to someone. For the application of impartiality depends on the pre-existence of claims on the part of persons involved (though the claim need not actually be made, or even recognized as existing, by the person who has it). It is only when someone has a certain claim on a benefit that it is a matter of impartiality to give due regard to his interest in that benefit. If he has no claim to it then such regard is no longer a matter relevant to impartiality. (These claims can be grounded in a person's meeting the criteria relevant for relegating a certain benefit within a certain procedure—e.g., the criteria for producing the soundest argument in a dispute, or the criteria for meeting a certain job specification.) A just person is one who can be counted on to overlook personal interest and preference, where others might tailor their views of the claims involved to their own preferences.

It is thus not impartiality regarding interest *per se* which defines impartiality, as it is impartiality regarding interests in which the parties involved have some claim, the honoring of which might require the overlooking of personal ties and preferences. This claim is not itself grounded in impartiality but is rather the grounds of it.

This is why it is not a violation of impartiality if I help my friend in preference to the other person also digging his car out of the snow. For this other person has no claim to my help. It may be good or decent of

me to help him; to do so may be something which one could expect of a decent person. But it is not a claim. It is thus not a violation of impartiality if I fail to help, preferring to help my friend.

In the train-crash case the other injured persons also have no claim on my beneficence; or, rather, if one wants to argue that a duty of beneficence exists, which is thus correlative to a right or claim on the part of the injured persons, this is not the kind of claim which demands that we overlook or abstract ourselves from our personal attachments, apportioning our attention and help purely on the basis of need. (If this is so, then not every claim can be a basis for impartiality.)

Impartiality is appropriate therefore only in certain situations. It is not a perspective which defines what it is for us to act morally, to take up a moral point of view on our actions (regarding our friends). To refer to an example from Telfer, if I choose to visit a pensioner (to help decorate his flat) rather than my friend, determining that the pensioner is in greater need of my visiting, this behavior is not in accordance with the virtues of justice or fairness; for the pensioner has no claim on my visit, which requires me to overlook my relationship with my friend and make my decision purely on the basis of which one will benefit more from my visit. Depending on other factors in the situation, my visit to the pensioner can evidence a commendable concern for a particular person to whom I have no relation; and, again depending on the situation, my friend may be able to acknowledge that it was a good thing for me to visit the pensioner rather than him. But if there is some virtue here it is not the virtue of justice or impartiality. (In other circumstances the visit to the pensioner can show an insufficient regard to the friend and to the friendship.)

The same can be said of impartiality in noninstitutional contexts as was said above about institutional ones, namely that in most cases in which we can act to benefit our friends, but in which it is also within our power to benefit someone else, there are no claims on our beneficence the honoring of which requires us to overlook our personal ties. Thus there is no general demand of impartiality.

In fact Sidgwick's definition could be taken to apply to institutional as well as noninstitutional contexts. Institutional contexts can be seen as an application of the general definition to a certain category of situation. For we can look at institutional contexts as helping to define the claims which some persons have, with regard to their interests, on other persons. For example, the claim which a patient has to be treated in a certain way by a doctor; or the student to be graded according to certain procedures by his teacher; or an applicant to be given a certain kind of consideration by the personnel officer. Part of what characterizes such institutional contexts is that they define more precisely than is often done in ordinary life what the relevant considerations are for allocating benefits to persons. This is why institutional contexts seem so appropriate for impartiality.

Finally, it should be remembered that even in contexts in which impartiality is demanded, there is almost always some room for the person of whom impartiality is demanded to benefit the friend in a way appropriate to friendship. For example, in the case of the quarrel mentioned above . . . , suppose I feel that the nonfriend's claim to benefit is greater than that of my friend. Impartiality requires me to overlook my attachment to the friend in deciding that the benefit properly goes to the nonfriend. But impartiality does not prevent me from showing special attention to my friend if he is disappointed, trying to do something to cheer him up, comforting him, etc., while not doing the same for the other person.

Thus impartiality is limited not only to certain sorts of situations. In addition, even within the situations in which it applies, it applies, so to speak, only up to a point, and generally there will be room left over for extra beneficence to be shown to the friend.

To summarize the argument so far: According to one important strain of thought within the Kantian view, a principle definitive of morality is impartiality. To take up a perspective of impartiality regarding any of one's actions which impinge on the interests of others is to take up, and act from, the moral point of view. To fail to do this is to fail to act morally. A corollary is that it is contrary to morality—because

contrary to impartiality—to favor the interests of one-self to one's friends simply as such, i.e., simply because they are one's own or one's friends.

Against this I have argued that it is not in general contrary to the demands of morality to prefer our friends' interests as such, i.e., to act for the sake of R's good simply because R is my friend, even if there are other persons whom it is in my power to help and who are in greater need than R. In fact it is entirely morally appropriate to do so. Such action does not typically violate the demands of impartiality; for that perspective is appropriate only in certain contexts, which do not include most friendship situations. There is no general demand of impartiality. Rather the demand of impartiality rests on prior claims to some benefit, the acknowledging of which requires the overlooking of personal preferences and attachments.

Thus acting morally is not always or fundamentally a matter of equality or impartiality towards all. For this is not what it is to act morally within friendship.

Thus in one sense it is actually misleading to say that we are necessarily or typically partial to our friends, if this is meant to imply a deviation from a morally requisite norm of impartiality. For such a norm is not typically in force in regard to our benefiting our friends. In another sense, however, we are partial to our friends, in that we benefit our friends without testing that benefiting against a norm of impartiality with respect to others; and we are not morally remiss for doing so.

If this argument is right, then impartiality does not define "the moral point of view." Rather, it defines a moral viewpoint appropriate in certain circumstances but not in others. When acting from friendship it is neither required nor appropriate (normally) to look to impartial or impersonal considerations to guide our actions. Impartiality, fairness, and justice are personal virtues, but they are merely some virtues among others. They are not definitive of moral virtue altogether.

11. Morality, Parents, and Children

James Rachels

James Rachels argues that the idea of morality as impartiality allows for the idea of special parental obligations particularly with regard to the day-to-day care of our own children. Nevertheless, he contends that we are not justified in providing our own children with luxuries while other children lack necessities.

The Problem

At about the same time Socrates was being put to death for corrupting the youth of Athens, the great Chinese sage Mo Tzu was also antagonizing his community. Unlike the Confucianists, who were the social conservatives of the day, Mo and his followers were sharply critical of traditional institutions and practices. One of Mo's controversial teachings was that human relationships should be governed by an "all-embracing love" that makes no distinctions between friends, family, and humanity at large. "Partiality," he said, "is to be replaced by universality." To his followers, these were the words of a moral visionary. To the Confucianists, however, they were the words of a man out of touch with moral reality. In particular, Mo's doctrine was said to subvert the family, for it recommended that one have as much regard for strangers as for one's own kin. Meng Tzu summed up the complaint when he wrote that "Mo Tzu, by preaching universal love, has repudiated the family." Mo did not deny it. Instead, he argued that universal love is a higher ideal than family loyalty, and that obligations within families can be properly understood only as particular instances of obligations to all mankind.

This ancient dispute has not disappeared. Do parents have special obligations to their own children? Or, to put the question a bit differently: Do they have obligations to their own children that they do not have

to other children, or to children in general? Our instincts are with the Confucianists. Surely, we think, parents do have a special obligation to care for their own. Parents must love and protect their children; they must feed and clothe them; they must see to their medical needs, their education, and a hundred other things. Who could deny it? At the same time, we do not believe that we have such duties toward strangers. Perhaps we do have a general duty of beneficence toward them, but that duty is not nearly so extensive or specific as the duties we have toward our own young sons and daughters. If faced with a choice between feeding our own children and sending food to orphans in a foreign country, we would prefer our own, without hesitation.

Yet the Mohist objection is still with us. The idea that morality requires us to be impartial, clearly articulated by Mo Tzu, is a recurring theme of Western moral philosophy. Perhaps the most famous expression of this idea was Bentham's formula, "Each to count for one and none for more than one." Mill's formulation was less memorable but no less emphatic: He urged that, when weighing the interests of different people, we should be "as strictly impartial as a disinterested and benevolent spectator." Utilitarianism of the kind espoused by Bentham and Mill has, of course, often been criticized for conflicting with common-sense morality, and so it will probably come as no great surprise that utilitarian notions clash with the common-sense idea of special parental obligations. However, the idea that morality requires impartiality is by no means exclusively a utilitarian doctrine. It is common ground to a considerable range of theories and thinkers.[1]

From "Morality, Parents, and Children," in *Person to Person*, ed. George Grahan and Hugh LaFollette (1989).

The problem, in its most general form, is this. As moral agents, we cannot play favorites—at least, not according to the conception of morality as impartiality. But as parents, we do play favorites. Parental love is partial through and through. And we think there is nothing wrong with this; in fact, we normally think there is something wrong with the parent who is *not* deeply partial where his own children are concerned. Therefore, it would seem, one or the other of these conceptions has to be modified or abandoned.

Of course, exactly the same is true of our relations with friends, spouses, and lovers. All these relationships, and others like them, seem to include, as part of their very nature, special obligations. Friends, spouses, and lovers are not just members of the great crowd of humanity. They are all special, at least to the one who loves them. The problem is that the conception of morality as impartiality seems to conflict with *any* kind of loving personal relationship. Mo Tzu notwithstanding, it seems to conflict with love itself. In this essay I discuss only the question of parental obligations to children, but it should be kept in mind that the deeper issue has to do with personal relationships in general.

Possible Solutions

There are three obvious approaches to solving our problem: First, we might reject the idea of morality as impartiality; second, we might reject the idea of special parental obligations; or third, we might try to find some way of understanding the two notions that would make them consistent. The first approach has recently attracted some support among philosophers, who think that although the conception of morality as impartiality seems plausible when stated abstractly, it is refuted by such counterexamples as parental obligation. Their thought is that we should reject this conception and look for a new theory of morality, one that would acknowledge from the outset that personal relationships can be the source of special obligations.

Rejecting the idea of impartiality has a certain appeal, for it is always exciting to learn that some popular philosophical view is no good and that there is interesting work to be done in formulating an alternative. However, we should not be too quick here. It is no accident that the conception of morality as impartiality has been so widely accepted. It seems to express something deeply important that we should be reluctant to give up. It is useful, for example, in explaining why egoism, racism, and sexism are morally odious, and if we abandon this conception we lose our most natural and persuasive means of combating those doctrines. (The idea of morality as impartiality is closely connected to modern thoughts about human equality. That humans are in some sense equals would never have occurred to the Confucianists, which perhaps explains why they saw nothing plausible in Mo's teaching.) Therefore, it seems desirable to retain the notion of moral impartiality in some form. The question is, can we find some way of keeping both ideas— morality as impartiality, and special parental obligations? Can we understand them in a way that makes them compatible with one another?

As it turns out, this is not a difficult task. It is fairly easy to interpret impartiality in such a way that it no longer conflicts with special parental obligations. We can say, for example, that impartiality requires us to treat people in the same way *only when there are no relevant differences between them*. This qualification is obviously needed, quite apart from any considerations about parents and children. For example, it is not a failure of impartiality to imprison a convicted criminal, while innocent citizens go free, because there is a relevant difference between them (one has committed a crime; the others have not) to which we can appeal to justify the difference in treatment. Similar examples come easily to mind. But once we have admitted the need for this qualification, we can make use of it to resolve our problem about parental obligations: We can say that there is a relevant difference between one's own children and other children that justifies treating one's own children better. The difference will have something to do with the fact that they are one's own.

We might call this the compromise view. It is appealing because it allows us to retain the plausible idea of morality as impartiality, without having to give up the equally plausible idea that we have special obligations to our own children. Having found this solution to our problem, we might be tempted to stop here. That, however, would be premature. There is a further issue that needs to be addressed, and when we do, the compromise view will begin to look less attractive.

We are not free to call just any differences between individuals relevant. Suppose a racist claimed that there is a relevant difference between blacks and whites that justifies treating whites better—the difference being that they are members of different races. We would think this mere bluster and demand to know why *that* difference should count for anything. Similarly, it is only hand-waving to say that there is a relevant difference between one's own children and others that justifies treating one's own better—the difference being that they are one's own. We need to ask why *that* difference matters.

Why Should It Matter That a Child Is One's Own?

Why should it matter, from a moral point of view, that a child is one's own? Our natural tendency is to assume that it *does* matter and to take it as a mere philosophical puzzle to figure out why. Why should anyone want to resist this tendency? The feeling that our own children have a superior natural claim on our attention is among the deepest moral instincts we have. Can it possibly be doubted? I believe there is a powerful reason for doubting that this feeling is morally legitimate—the fact that a child is one's own may *not* matter, or at least it may not matter nearly as much as we usually assume. That reason has to do with luck.

The point about luck can be brought out like this. Suppose a parent believes that, when faced with a choice between feeding his own children and feeding starving orphans, he should give preference to his own. This is natural enough. But the orphans need the food just as much, and they are no less deserving. It is only their bad luck that they were not born to affluent parents; and why should luck count, from a moral point of view? Why should we think that a moral view is correct, if it implies that some children should be fed, while others starve, for no better reason than that some were unlucky in the circumstances of their birth? This seems to me to be an extremely important matter—important enough, perhaps, that we should take seriously the possibility that a child's being one's own does not have the moral importance that we usually assume it has.

With this in mind, let us look at some of the arguments that support the Compromise View. The idea that one's own children have a superior claim to one's care might be defended in various ways. Let us consider the three arguments that seem most important.

1. The Argument from Social Roles

The first line of reasoning begins with some observations about social roles. It is not possible for an isolated individual to have anything resembling a normal human life. For that, a social setting is required. The social setting provides roles for us to fill—thus in the context of society we are able to be citizens, friends, husbands and wives, hospital patients, construction workers, scientists, teachers, customers, sports fans, and all the rest. None of us (with rare heroic exceptions) creates the roles we play; they have evolved over many centuries of human life, and we encounter them as simply the raw materials out of which we must fashion our individual lives.

These roles define, in large measure, our relations with other people. They specify how we should behave toward others. Teachers must wisely guide their students; friends must be loyal; husbands should be faithful; and so on. To the extent that you fail in these respects, you will be an inferior teacher, a bad friend, a poor husband. You can avoid these obligations by declining to enter into these roles: Not everyone will be a teacher, not everyone will marry, and some unfortunate people will not even have friends. But you can hardly avoid *all* social roles, and you cannot fill a social role without at the same time acknowledging the special responsibilities that go with it.

Now, parenthood is a social role, and like other such roles it includes special duties as part of its very nature. You can choose not to have children, or, having had a child, you may give it up for adoption. But if you *are* a parent, you are stuck with the responsibilities that go with the role. A parent who doesn't see to his children's needs is a bad parent, just as a disloyal friend is a bad friend, and an unfaithful husband is a poor husband. And that is why (according to this argument) we have obligations to our own children that we do not have to other children.

The argument from social roles is plausible; but how far should we be persuaded by it? The argument has at least four apparent weaknesses.

(i) We need to distinguish two claims: first, that our obligations to our own children *have a different basis* from our obligations to other children; and second, that our obligations to our own children *are stronger than* (take precedence over) our obligations to other children. If successful, the argument from social roles would show only that our obligations to our own children are based on different considerations than are our obligations to other children. We have a social relationship with our own children that is the basis of our obligation to them, while our obligations to other children are based on a general duty of beneficence. The argument would not show that the former obligations are *stronger*. Thus a critic of the idea of special parental obligations could continue the dispute at another level. It could be argued that, even if one's duties to one's own children have a different basis, they nevertheless are *no stronger than* one's duties to other children.

(ii) The second point is related to the first. The argument from social roles trades on the notion of what it means to be a bad father or a bad mother. Now, suppose we admit that a man who ignores the needs of his own children is a bad father. It may also be observed that a man who ignores the cries of orphans, when he could help, is a bad *man*—a man lacking a proper regard for the needs of others. While it is undesirable to be a bad father (or mother), it is also undesirable to be a bad man (or woman). So, once again, the argument from social roles does nothing to show that our obligations to other children are weaker.

(iii) Third, there is the point about luck that I have already mentioned. The system of social roles acknowledged in our society makes special provision for children lucky enough to live in homes with parents. This system favors even more those lucky enough to have affluent parents who can provide more for them than less affluent parents are able to provide. Even granting this, we can still ask: Is it a morally decent system? The system itself can be subject to criticism.

We do not have to look far to find an obvious objection to the system. The system does well enough in providing for some children; but it does miserably where others are concerned. There is no social role

comparable to the parent-child relationship that targets the interests of orphans, or the interests of children whose parents are unable or unwilling to provide for them. Thus in this system luck plays an unacceptably important part.

(iv) Finally, students of social history might find the argument from social roles rather naive. The argument draws much of its strength from the fact that contemporary American and European ideals favor families bound together by love. Anyone who is likely to read these words will have been influenced by that ideal—consider how the reader will have passed over the second paragraph of this essay, with its easy talk of parents loving and protecting their children, without a pause. Yet the cozy nuclear family, nourished by affectionate relationships, is a relatively recent development. The norm throughout most of Western history has been very different.

In his acclaimed book *The Family, Sex and Marriage in England 1500–1800*, Lawrence Stone points out that as recently as the seventeenth century affectionate relations between husbands and wives were so rare as to be virtually nonexistent, and certainly were not expected within normal marriages. Among the upper classes, husbands and wives occupied separate stations within large households and rarely saw one another in private. Children were sent away immediately after birth to be looked after by wet-nurses for 12 to 18 months; then, returning home, they would be raised largely by nurses, governesses, and tutors. Finally they would be sent away to boarding school when they were between 7 and 13, with 10 the most common age. The children of the poor were of course worse off: They would leave home at an equally early age, often to go and work in the houses of the rich. Stone writes,

> About all that can be said with confidence on the matter of emotional relations within the sixteenth-and early seventeenth-century family at all social levels is that there was a general psychological atmosphere of distance, manipulation, and deference. . . . Family relationships were characterized by interchangeability, so that substitution of another wife or another child was easy. . . . It was a structure held together not by affective bonds but by mutual economic interests.

And what of parental duties? Of course there has always been a recognition of *some* special parental duties, but in earlier times these were much more restricted and were not associated with bonds of affection. Until some time in the eighteenth century, it seems, the emphasis in European morals was almost entirely on the duties owed by children to parents, rather than the other way around. Children were commonly said to owe their parents absolute obedience, in gratitude for having been given life. The French historian Jean Flandrin notes that "In Brittany the son remained subject to the authority of his father until the age of sixty, but marriage contracted with the father's consent emancipated him." Pity the man whose father lived to a ripe old age and refused consent for marriage—his only emancipation would be to flee. Both Stone and Flandrin make it clear that, while parental *rights* is an old idea, the idea of extensive parental *obligations* is a notion of much more recent vintage. (The debate between Mo Tzu and the Confucianists was also conducted in such terms—for them, the primary issue was whether children had special duties to their fathers, not the other way around.)

These observations about social history should be approached with care. Of course they do not refute the idea of special parental obligations. However, they do go some way toward undermining our easy confidence that present-day social arrangements only institutionalize our natural duties. That is the only moral to be drawn from them, but it is an important one. In this area, as in so many others, what seems natural just depends on the conventions of one's society.

2. The Argument from Proximity

The second argument goes like this: It is reasonable to accept a social arrangement in which parents are assigned special responsibility for their own children because parents are *better situated* to look after their own. Granted, all children need help and protection. But other children are remote, and their needs are less clear, while a parent's own children live in the same house, and the parent is (or ought to be) intimately familiar with their needs. Other things being equal, it makes sense to think that A has a greater responsibility for helping B than for helping C, if A is better situated to help B. This is true in the case of helping one's own children versus helping other children; therefore, one's obligation in the first instance is greater.

This argument is plausible if we concentrate on certain kinds of aid. Children wake up sick in the middle of the night; someone must attend to them, and that someone is usually Mother or Father. The parents are in a position to do so, and (most of the time) no one else is. The complaint that you nursed your own children, but you didn't help the other children who woke up sick elsewhere in the world is obviously misguided. The same goes for countless other ways that parents assist their children, by making them take their medicine, by stopping them from playing in the roadway, by bundling them up against the cold, and so on. These are all matters of what we might call *day-to-day care.*

Day-to-day care involves a kind of personal attention that a parent *could not* provide for many others, because it is physically impossible. The importance of physical proximity is that it makes these kinds of caring behaviors possible; the impossibility of doing the same for other children is just the impossibility of being in two places at once. So if there is partiality here, it is a partiality that we need not worry about because it cannot be avoided. There is little doubt, then, that parents are normally in a better position to provide day-to-day care for their own children than for others.

This type of argument is less plausible, however, when we consider more general, fundamental needs, such as food. Is a parent in a better position to feed his own children than to provide for others? At one time this might have been the case. Before the advent of modern communications and transportation, and before the creation of efficient relief agencies, people might have been able to say that while they could feed their own, they were unable to do much about the plight of children elsewhere. But that is no longer true. Today, with relief agencies ready to take our assistance all over the world, needing only sufficient resources to do so, it is almost as easy to provide food for a child in Africa as to provide for one's own. The same goes for providing basic medical care: International relief agencies carry medical assistance around the world on the same basis.

Therefore, the argument from proximity is, at best, only partially successful. Some forms of assistance (such as getting up in the middle of the night to attend to sick children) do require proximity but others (such as providing food) do not. The argument might show that, where day-to-day care is concerned, parents have special duties. But the same cannot be said for the provision of fundamental needs.

3. The Argument from Personal Goods

The third argument hinges on the idea that loving relationships are personal goods of great importance: To love other people and be loved in return are part of what is involved in having a rich and satisfying human life. A loving relationship with one's children is, for many parents, a source of such happiness that they would sacrifice almost anything else to preserve it. But as we have already observed, love necessarily involves having a special concern for the well-being of the loved one, and so it is not impartial. An ethic that required absolute impartiality would therefore require forgoing a great personal good.

The intuitive idea behind this argument may seem plain enough. Nevertheless, it is difficult to formulate the argument with any precision. Why, exactly, is a loving relationship with another person such a great good? Part of the answer may be that pacts of mutual assistance enable all of us to fare better. If A and B have this sort of relationship, then A can count on B's assistance when it is needed, and vice versa. They are both better off. Of course, deals of this kind could be made between people who are not joined by bonds of affection, but affection makes the arrangement more dependable: People who love one another are more apt to remain faithful when the going is hard. But there is more. Bonds of affection are more than just instrumentally good. To be loved is to have one's own value affirmed; thus it is a source of self-esteem. This is important for all of us, but especially for children, who are more helpless and vulnerable than adults. Moreover, there is, at a deep level, a connection between love and the meaning of life (although I cannot go into this very deeply here). We question whether our lives have meaning when we find nothing worth valuing, when it seems to us that "all is vanity." Loving relationships provide individuals with things to value, and so give their lives this kind of meaning. That is why parents who love their children, and who strive to see that they do well, can find in this meaning for their lives.

These are important points, but they do not prove as much as they are sometimes taken to prove. In the first place, there is a lot about parental love that *is* consistent with a large measure of impartiality. Loving someone is not only a matter of preferring their interests. Love involves, among other things, intimacy and the sharing of experiences. A parent shows his love by listening to the child's jokes, by talking, by being a considerate companion, by praising, and even by scolding when that is needed. It may be objected that these kinds of behavior also show partiality, since the parent does not do these things for all children. But these are only further instances of the day-to-day care that requires proximity; again, if this is partiality, it is partiality that cannot be avoided. And there is another difference between these kinds of support and such things as providing food and medical care. The companionship, the listening, the talking, and the praising and scolding are what make personal relationships *personal*. That is why the psychic benefits that accompany such relationships are more closely associated with these matters than with such relatively impersonal things as being fed.

Moreover, it is not necessary, in order to have a loving relationship with one's children and to derive from it the benefits that the argument from personal goods envisions, to regard their interests as *always* having priority, especially when the interests in question are not comparable. One could have a loving relationship that involves all the intimacies of day-to-day care and the provision of life's necessities, while acknowledging at the same time that when it comes to choosing between luxuries for them and food for orphans, the orphans' needs should prevail. At the very least, there is nothing in the argument from personal goods that rules out such an approach.

The Moral Point of Utopian Thinking

There is another approach to our problem, favored by the Mohists, that we have not yet considered: Clinging to the ideal of impartiality, we could simply reject the idea of special parental duties. This goes against our intuitions, and it is opposed by the (partially successful) arguments we have just examined. Nevertheless, we may ask whether there is anything to be said in favor of this approach.

In fact, there is a lot that might be said in its favor. Suppose we forget, for a moment, the imperfections of actual human life, and try to imagine what it would be like if everyone behaved in a morally blameless manner. What would relations between adults and children be like in such a utopia? Here is one plausible picture of such a world. In it, children with living parents able to provide for them would be raised by their parents, who would give them all the love and care they need. Parents who through no fault of their own were unable to provide for their children would be given whatever assistance they need. Orphans would be taken in by families who would raise and love them as their own. The burdens involved in such adoptions would be shared by all.

It is fair to say that, in such a world, the ideal of impartiality is realized. In this world people do not act as if any child is more deserving than any other: One way or another, equal provision is made for the needs of all. Moreover, luck plays no part in how children will fare: The orphans' needs are satisfied too. When it is said by the Mohists that "love is universal," or by their modern counterparts, the utilitarians, that we should "promote impartially the interests of everyone alike," this might be the point: In the morally best world, we would not recognize many of the distinctions that we do recognize in the real world we inhabit.

Practical Implications

How should parents, living not in utopia but in our society, who are concerned to do what is morally best, conceive of the relation between their obligations to their own children and their obligations to other children? Here are three contrasting views; each is implausible, but for different reasons.

1. *Extreme Bias.* On this view, parents have obligations to provide for their own children, but they have *no obligations at all* to other children. Anything done for other children is at best supererogatory—good and praiseworthy if one chooses to do it, but in no way

morally mandatory. On this view, parents may provide not only necessities but also luxuries for their own children, while other children starve, and yet be immune from moral criticism.

Extreme bias is not plausible, because it makes no provision whatever for a duty of general beneficence. It is hard to believe that we do not have some obligation to be concerned with the plight of the starving, whoever they are, even if that obligation is less extensive than our obligations to our own kin.[2] Thus it will not be surprising if this view turns out to be unacceptable.

2. *Complete Equality.* The opposite view seems to be implied by the idea of morality as impartiality—the view that all children are equal and that there is no difference at all between one's moral obligations toward one's own children and one's moral obligations toward other children. This view denies that there are any good moral grounds for preferring to feed one's own child rather than an orphan in a foreign country. In our society anyone who accepted and acted on such a view would seem to his neighbors to be morally deranged, for doing so would seem to involve a rejection of one's children—a refusal to treat them with the love that is appropriate to the parent–child relationship.

3. *The Most Common View.* What, in fact, do people in our society seem to believe? Most people seem to believe that one has an obligation to provide the necessities of life for other children only after one has already provided a great range of luxuries for one's own. On this view, it is permissible to provide one's own children with virtually everything they need in order to have a good start in life—not only food and clothing, but, if possible, a good education, opportunities for travel, opportunities for enjoyable leisure, and so forth. In the United States children of affluent families often have TV sets, stereos, and now computers, all laid out in their own rooms. They drive their own cars to high school. Few people seem to think there is anything wrong with this—parents who are unable to provide their children with such luxuries nevertheless aspire to do so.

The most common view imposes *some* duty regarding other children, but not much. In practical terms, it imposes a duty only on the very rich, who have resources left over even after they have provided ample luxuries for their own children. The rest of us, who have nothing left after doing as much as we can for our own, are off the hook. It takes only a little reflection to see that this view is also implausible. How can it be right to spend money on luxuries for some children, even one's own—buying them the latest trendy toys, for example—while others do not have enough to eat?

Perhaps, when confronted with this, many people might come to doubt whether it is correct. But certainly most affluent people act as if it were correct.

Is there a better alternative? Is there a view that escapes the difficulties of extreme bias, complete equality, and the most common view, and is consistent with the various other points that have been made in our discussion? I suggest the following.

4. *Partial Bias.* We might say that, while we do have a substantial obligation to be concerned about the welfare of all children, our own nevertheless come first. This vague thought needs to be sharpened. One way of making it more precise is this: When considering similar needs, you may permissibly prefer to provide for the needs of your own children. For example, if you were faced with a choice between feeding your own children or contributing the money to provide food for other children, you could rightly choose to feed your own. But if the choice were between some relatively trivial thing for your own and necessities for other children, preference should be given to helping the others. Thus if the choice were between providing trendy toys for your own already well-fed children or feeding the starving, you should feed the starving.

This view will turn out to be more or less demanding, depending on what one counts as a "relatively trivial thing." We might agree that buying trendy toys for some children, even for one's own, while other children starve is indefensible. But what about buying them nice clothes? Or a college education? Am I justified in sending my children to an expensive college?

Clearly, the line between the trivial and the important can be drawn at different places. (One will be pushed toward a more demanding interpretation as one takes more seriously the point about the moral irrelevance of luck.) Nevertheless, the intuitive idea is plain enough. On this view, you may provide the necessities for your own children first, but you are not justified in providing them luxuries while other children lack necessities. Even in a fairly weak form, this view would still require much greater concern for others than the view that is most common in our society.

From the point of view of the various arguments we have considered, partial bias clearly stands out as the superior view. It is closer to the utopian ideal than either extreme bias or the most common view; it is morally superior in that it makes greater provision for children who have no loving parents; it is consistent with the arguments we have considered concerning the benefits to be derived from loving relationships; and it is perhaps as much as we could expect from people in the real world. It is not, in fact, very far from the utopian ideal. If we begin with Complete Equality, and then modify it in the ways suggested in our discussion of utopia, we end up with something very much like partial bias.

What would the adoption of partial bias mean for actual families? It would mean that parents could continue to provide loving day-to-day care for their own children, with all that this involves, while giving them preferential treatment in the provision of life's necessities. But it would also mean preferring to provide the necessities for needier children, rather than luxuries for their own. Children in such families would be worse off, in an obvious sense, than the children of affluent parents who continued to live according to the dictates of extreme bias or the most common view. However, we might hope that they would not regard themselves as deprived, for they might learn the moral value of giving up their luxuries so that the other children do not starve. They might even come to see their parents as morally admirable people. That hope is itself utopian enough.

Endnotes

1. "The good of any one individual is of no more importance, from the point of view (if I may say so) of the Universe, than the good of any other," says Sidgwick (1907, 382). "We [must] give equal weight in our moral deliberations to the like interests of all those affected by our actions," says Singer (1971, 197). "Moral rules must be for the good of everyone alike," says Baier (1958, 200). "A rational and impartial sympathetic spectator is a person who takes up a general perspective: He assumes a position where his own interests are not at stake and he possesses all the requisite information and powers of reasoning. So situated, he is equally responsive and sympathetic to the desires and satisfactions of everyone affected by the social system. . . . Responding to the interests of each person in the same way, an impartial spectator gives free reign to his capacity for sympathetic identification by viewing each person's situation as it affects that person," says Rawls (1971, 186). In an interesting discussion, R. M. Hare argues that virtually all the major moral theories incorporate a requirement of impartiality and adds that his own "universal prescriptivism" is no exception.

2. For arguments concerning the extensiveness of our obligations toward others, see Singer (1972) and Rachels (1979).

References

Baier, Kurt. 1958. *The Moral Point of View.* Ithaca: Cornell University Press.

Fung Yu-lan. 1960. *A Short History of Chinese Philosophy.* New York: Macmillan.

Hare, R. M. 1972. "Rules of War and Moral Reasoning." *Philosophy and Public Affairs, 1,* 166–181.

Mill, John Stuart. 1957. *Utilitarianism.* Indianapolis: Bobbs-Merrill. This work, first published in 1861, is today available in many editions.

Rachels, James. 1979. "Killing and Starving to Death." *Philosophy, 54,* 159–171.

Rawls, John. 1971. *A Theory of Justice.* Cambridge: Harvard University Press.

Rubin, Vitaly A. 1976. *Individual and State in Ancient China.* New York: Columbia University Press.

Sidgwick, Henry. 1907. *The Methods of Ethics,* 7th. ed. London: Macmillan.

Singer, Peter. 1972. "Famine, Affluence, and Morality." *Philosophy and Public Affairs, 1,* 229–243.

———. 1978. "Is Racial Discrimination Arbitrary?" *Philosophia, 8,* 185–203.

Stone, Lawrence. 1979. *The Family, Sex and Marriage in England 1500–1800.* New York: Harper & Row.

12. *Perspectives from the* Global 2000 Report

GUS SPETH

According to Gus Speth, the Global 2000 Report echoes a persistent warning sounded by many others in recent years: "Our international efforts to stem the spread of human poverty, hunger, and misery are not achieving their goals; the staggering growth of human population, coupled with ever-increasing human demands, are beginning to cause permanent damage to the planet's resource base." Speth argues that we must respond to this warning by getting serious about the conservation of resources and by pursuing a policy of sustainable economic development that is fair to the interests of the poor.

Throughout the past decade, a wide variety of disturbing studies and reports have been issued by the United Nations, the Worldwatch Institute, the World Bank, the International Union for the Conservation of Nature and Natural Resources, and other organizations. These reports have sounded a persistent warning: Our international efforts to stem the spread of human poverty, hunger, and misery are not achieving their goals; the staggering growth of human population, coupled with ever-increasing human demands, are beginning to cause permanent damage to the planet's resource base.

The most recent such warning—and the one with which I am most familiar—was issued in July of 1980 by the Council of Environmental Quality and the U.S. State Department. Called *Global 2000 Report to the President*, it is the result of a three-year effort by more than a dozen agencies of the U.S. Government to make long-term projections across the range of population, resource, and environmental concerns. Given the obvious limitations of such projections, the *Global 2000 Report* can best be seen as a reconnaissance of the future. And the results of that reconnaissance are disturbing.

I feel very strongly that the *Global 2000 Report's* findings confront the United States and other nations

From "Resources and Security: Perspectives from the *Global 2000 Report*," *World Future Society Bulletin* (1981), pp. 1–4. Reprinted by permission of *World Future Society Bulletin*.

with one of the most difficult challenges facing our planet during the next two decades—rivaling the global arms race in importance.

The Report's projections point to continued rapid population growth, with world population increasing from 4.5 billion today to more than 6 billion by 2000. More people will be added to the world's population each day in the year 2000 than were born today—about 100 million a year as compared with 75 million in 1980. Most of these additional people will live in the poorest countries, which will contain about four-fifths of the human race by the end of the century.

Unless other factors intervene, this planetary majority will see themselves growing worse off compared with those living in affluent nations. The income gap between rich and poor nations will widen, and the per capita gross national product of the less-developed countries will remain at generally low levels. In some areas—especially in parts of Latin America and East Asia—income per capita is expected to rise substantially. But gross national product in the great populous nations of South Asia—India, Bangladesh, and Pakistan—will be less than $200 per capita (in 1975 dollars) by 2000. Today, some 800 million people live in conditions of absolute poverty, their lives dominated by hunger, ill health, and the absence of hope. By 2000, if current policies remain unchanged, their number could grow by 50 percent.

While the Report projects a 90 percent increase in overall world food production in the 30 years from 1970 to 2000, a global per capita increase of less than

15 percent is projected even for the countries that are already comparatively well-fed. In South Asia, the Middle East, and the poorer countries of Africa, per capita food consumption will increase marginally at best, and in some areas may actually decline below present inadequate levels. Real prices of food are expected to double during the same 30-year period.

The pressures of population and growing human needs and expectations will place increasing strains on the Earth's natural systems and resources. The spread of desert-like conditions due to human activities now claims an area about the size of Maine each year. Croplands are lost to production as soils deteriorate because of erosion, compaction, and waterlogging and salinization, and as rural land is converted to other uses.

The increases in world food production projected by the Report are based on improvements in crop yields per acre continuing at the same rate as the record-breaking increases of the post–World War II period. These improvements depended heavily on energy-intensive technologies like fertilizer, pesticides, fuel for tractors, and power for irrigation. But the Report's projections show no relief from the world's tight energy situation. World oil production is expected to level off by the 1990s. And for the one-quarter of humanity who depend on wood for fuel, the outlook is bleak. Projected needs for wood will exceed available supplies by about 25 percent before the turn of the century.

The conversion of forested land to agricultural use and the demand for fuelwood and forest products are projected to continue to deplete the world's forests. The Report estimates that these forests are now disappearing at rates as high as 18 to 20 million hectares— an area half the size of California—each year. As much as 40 percent of the remaining forests in poor countries may be gone by 2000. Most of the loss will occur in tropical and subtropical areas.

The loss of tropical forests, along with the impact of pollution and other pressures on habitats, could cause massive destruction of the planet's genetic resource base. Between 500,000 and two million plant and animal species—15 to 20 percent of all species on Earth—could become extinct by the year 2000. One-half to two-thirds of the extinctions will result from the clearing or deterioration of tropical forests. This would be a massive loss of potentially valuable sources of food, pharmaceutical chemicals, building materials, fuel sources, and other irreplaceable resources.

Deforestation and other factors will worsen severe regional water shortages and contribute to the deterioration of water quality. Population growth alone will cause demands for water to at least double from 1971 levels in nearly half of the world.

Industrial growth is likely to worsen air quality. Air pollution in some cities in less-developed countries is already far above levels considered safe by the World Health Organization. Increased burning of fossil fuels, especially coal, may contribute to acid rain damage to lakes, plant life, and the exteriors of buildings. It also contributes to the increasing concentration of carbon dioxide in the Earth's atmosphere, which could possibly lead to climatic changes with highly disruptive effects on world agriculture. Depletion of the stratospheric ozone layer, attributed partly to chlorofluorocarbon emissions from aerosol cans and refrigeration equipment, could also have an adverse effect on food crops and human health.

Disturbing as these findings are, it is important to stress that the *Global 2000 Report*'s conclusions represent not predictions of what will occur, but projections of what could occur if we do not respond. If there was any doubt before, there should be little doubt now— the nations of the world, industrialized and less developed alike, must act urgently and in concert to alter these dangerous trends before the projections of the *Global 2000 Report* become realities.

The warnings, then, are clear. Will we heed them, and will we heed them in time? For if our response is delayed, the costs could be great.

On these matters, I am cautiously optimistic. I like to think that the human race is *not* self-destructive— that it *is* paying, or can be made to pay, attention—that as people throughout the world come to realize the full dimensions of the challenge before us, we will take the actions needed to meet it.

Our efforts to secure the future must begin with a new appreciation for, and then an application of, three fundamental concepts. They are *conservation, sustainable development,* and *equity.* I am convinced that each of them is essential to the development of the kind of long-term global resource strategy we need to deal with the problems I have been discussing.

Conservation

The first thing we must do is to get serious about the conservation of resources—renewable and nonrenewable alike. We can no longer take for granted the renewability of renewable resources. The natural systems—the air and water, the forests, the land—that yield food, shelter, and the other necessities of life are susceptible to disruption, contamination, and destruction.

Indeed, one of the most troubling of the findings of the *Global 2000 Report* is the effect that rapid population growth and poverty are already having on the productivity of renewable natural resource systems. In some areas, particularly in the less-developed countries, the ability of biological systems to support human populations is already being seriously damaged by efforts of present populations to meet desperate immediate needs, such as the needs for grazing land, firewood, and building materials.

And these stresses, while most acute in the developing countries, are not confined to them. In recent years, the United States has been losing annually about 3 million acres of rural land—a third of it prime agricultural land—due to the spread of housing developments, highways, shopping malls, and the like. We are also losing annually the rough equivalent—in terms of production capability—of another 3 million acres due to soil degradation—erosion and salinization. Other serious resource threats in the United States include those posed by toxic chemicals and other pollutants to groundwater supplies, which provide drinking water for half of the American public, and directly affect both commercial and sport fishing.

Achieving the necessary restraint in the use of renewable resources will require new ways of thinking by the peoples and governments of the world. It will require the widespread adoption of a "Conserver Society" ethic—an approach to resources and environment that, while attuned to the needs of each society, recognizes not only the importance of resources and environment to our own sustenance, well-being, and security, but also our obligation to pass this vital legacy along to future generations. Perhaps the most arrogant attitude of which the human spirit is capable is the notion that the riches of the Earth are ours to plunder or carelessly destroy . . . that the needs and the lives of those who will follow us on this tiny and fragile planet are of no concern to us. "Future generations," someone once said "What have they done for us?"

Fortunately, we are beginning to see signs that people in the United States and in other nations *are* becoming aware of the limits to our resources and the importance of conserving them. Energy problems, for example, are pointing the way to a future in which conservation is the password. As energy supplies go down and prices go up, we are learning that conserving—getting more and more out of each barrel of oil or ton of coal—is the cheapest and safest approach. Learning to conserve nonrenewable resources like oil and coal is the first step toward building a Conserver Society that values, nurtures, and protects all of its resources. Such a society appreciates economy in design and avoidance of waste. It realizes the limits to low-cost resources and to the environment's carrying capacity. It insists that market prices reflect all costs, social as well as private, so that consumers are fully aware in the most direct way of the real costs of consumption.

The Conserver Society prizes recycling over pollution, durability over obsolescence, quality over quantity, diversity over uniformity. It knows that beauty—whether natural or manmade—is too precious to be destroyed and that the Earth's wild creatures demand our conserving restraint not simply for utilitarian reasons but because, as part of the community of life that has evolved here with us, they too call this place home.

In this, the United States must take the lead. We cannot expect the rest of the world to adopt a Conserver Society ethic if we ourselves do not set a strong, successful example.

Sustainable Development

But the Conserver Society ethic, by itself, is not enough. It is unrealistic to expect people living at the margin of existence—people fighting desperately for their own survival—to think about the long-term survival of the planet. When people need to burn wood to keep from freezing, they will cut down trees.

We must find a way to break the cycle of poverty, population growth, and environmental deterioration. We must find ways to improve the social and economic conditions of the poor nations and poor people of the world—their incomes, their access to productive land, their educational and employment opportunities. It is only through sustainable economic development that real progress can be made in alleviating hunger and poverty and in erasing the conditions that contribute so dangerously to the destruction of our planet's carrying capacity.

One of the most important lessons of the *Global 2000 Report* is that the conflict between development and environmental protection is, in significant part, a myth. Only a concerted attack on the roots of extreme poverty—one that provides people with the opportunity to earn a decent livelihood in a nondestructive manner—will enable us to protect the world's natural systems. It is also clear that development and economic reforms will have no lasting success unless they are suffused with concern for ecological stability and wise management of resources. The key concept here, of course, is *sustainable* development. Economic development, if it is to be successful over the long term, must proceed in a way that enhances the natural resource base of all the developing nations, instead of exploiting those resources for short-term economic or political gain.

Unfortunately, the realities of the current North-South dialogue between the developed and the developing nations suggest that achieving steady, sustainable development will be a difficult process—one that will require great patience and understanding on all sides. For our part here in the United States, we must resist the strong temptation to turn inward—to tune out the rest of the world's problems and to focus exclusively on our own economic difficulties. We must remember that, relatively speaking, we Americans luxuriate in the Earth's abundance, while other nations can barely feed and clothe their people. Unless we act, this disparity between rich and poor will tend to grow, increasing the possibilities for anger and resentment from those on the short end of the wealth equation—the great majority of mankind. One does not have to be particularly farsighted to see that the trends discussed in *Global 2000* heighten the chances for global instability—for exploitation of fears, resent-

ments, and frustrations; for incitement to violence; for conflicts based on resources.

The *Global 2000 Report* itself discusses some of the destabilizing prospects that may be in store for us if we do not act decisively:

> The world will be more vulnerable both to natural disaster and to disruptions from human causes. . . . Most nations are likely to be still more dependent on foreign sources of energy in 2000 than they are today. Food production will be more vulnerable to disruptions of fossil fuel energy supplies and to weather fluctuations as cultivation expands to more marginal areas. The loss of diverse germ plasm in local strains and wild progenitors of food crops, together with the increase of monoculture, could lead to greater risks of massive crop failures. Larger numbers of people will be vulnerable to higher food prices or even famine when adverse weather occurs. The world will be more vulnerable to the disruptive effects of war. The tensions that could lead to war will have multiplied. The potential for conflict over fresh water alone is underscored by the fact that out of 200 of the world's major river basins, 148 are shared by two countries and 52 are shared by three to ten countries.

The 1980 Report of the Brandt Commission on International Development Issues is eloquent in its plea for action: "War is often thought of in terms of military conflict, or even annihilation. But there is a growing awareness that an equal danger might be chaos—as a result of mass hunger, economic disaster, environmental catastrophes, and terrorism, so we should not think only of reducing the traditional threats to peace, but also of the need for change from chaos to order."

Equity

The late Barbara Ward, eminent British scholar, argued that the nations of the world can learn a valuable lesson from the experience of nineteenth-century England, where the industrial revolution produced an appalling disparity in the distribution of wealth. It was a time when property owners and industrial managers reaped enormous profits while the laborers and mechanics—and their children—worked themselves into early graves.

Today, Ward observes: "The skew in world income is as great. The already developed peoples—North America, Europe, the Soviet Union, Japan—are the latter-day dukes, commanding over 70 percent of the planet's wealth for less than a quarter of the population. And in all too many developing countries the economic growth of the last two decades has been almost entirely appropriated by the wealthiest ten percent of the people. The comparisons in health, length of life, diet, literacy all work out on the old Victorian patterns of unbelievable injustice."

Ward recommends—and I heartily agree—that the developed nations of today follow the lead of men like Disraeli, who recognized the need to narrow the gap between rich and poor in nineteenth-century England and to create a new social order which allowed every citizen a share of the nation's wealth. Without perceptive leaders like Disraeli and other men of conscience who saw the need for reform, Ward argues that the growing pressure for equality and social justice would have torn British society apart. The result would have been similar to that in other nations where far-thinking leadership and compassion were lacking: "social convulsion, violent revolution and an impetus to merciless worldwide war and conquest."

The situation we face in the world today is all too similar. While the humanitarian reasons for acting generously to alleviate global poverty and injustice are compelling enough in themselves, we must also recognize the extent to which global poverty and resource problems can contribute to regional and worldwide political instability—an instability that can threaten the security of nations throughout the world.

Thus, along with conservation and sustainable development, the development of global resource strategy will require a much greater emphasis on *equity*—on a fair sharing of the means to development and the products of growth—not only among nations, but within nations as well.

Suggestions for Further Reading

Anthologies

Brown, Peter, and Shue, Henry. *Boundaries.* Totowa, N.J.: Rowman and Littlefield, 1981.

Lucas, George R., Jr., and Ogletree, Thomas W. *Lifeboat Ethics.* New York: Harper & Row, 1976.

Luper-Foy, Steven. *Problems of International Justice.* Boulder, Colo.: Westview, 1988.

Partridge, Ernest. *Responsibilities to Future Generations.* Buffalo, N.Y.: Prometheus, 1981.

Sikora, R. I., and Barry, Brian. *Obligation to Future Generations.* Philadelphia: Temple University Press, 1978.

Basic Concepts

Parfit, Derek. *Reasons and Persons.* Oxford: Oxford University Press, 1985.

Alternative Views

Amur, Samir. *Unequal Development.* New York: Monthly Review Press, 1976.

Bauer, P. T. *Equality, the Third World and Economic Delusion.* Cambridge: Harvard University Press, 1981.

Bayles, Michael D. *Morality and Population Policy.* Birmingham: University of Alabama Press, 1980.

Beitz, Charles R. *Political Theory and International Relations.* Princeton: Princeton University Press, 1979.

Elfstrom, Gerald. *Ethics for a Shrinking World.* New York: St. Martin's Press, 1990.

Hardin, Garrett. *Promethean Ethics.* Seattle: University of Washington Press, 1980.

Shue, Henry. *Basic Rights.* Princeton: Princeton University Press, 1980.

Practical Applications

Lappé, Frances Moore. *World Hunger: Twelve Myths.* New York: Grove Press, 1986.

Russett, Bruce, and Starr, Harvey. *World Politics: The Menu for Choice.* San Francisco: W. H. Freeman and Co., 1981.

Schumacher, E. F. *Small Is Beautiful.* New York: Harper & Row, 1973.

Abortion and Euthanasia

Introduction

Basic Concepts

The problem of abortion and euthanasia has been as thoroughly discussed as any contemporary moral problem. As a result, the conceptual issues have been fairly well laid out, and there have been some interesting attempts to bridge the troublesome normative and practical disagreements that remain.

First of all, almost everyone agrees that the fundamental issue in justifying abortion is the moral status of the fetus, although considerable disagreement exists as to what that status is.[1] Conservatives on the abortion question, like Don Marquis (Selection 14), contend that from conception the fetus has full moral status and hence a serious right to life. Liberals like Mary Anne Warren (Selection 15) hold that, at least until birth, the fetus has almost no moral status whatsoever and lacks a serious right to life.[2] Moderates on the question adopt some position in between these two views. And still others, like Judith Jarvis Thomson (Selection 13), adopt for the sake of argument either the conservative or the liberal view on the moral status of the fetus and then try to show that such a view does not lead to the consequences its supporters assume.[3]

Second, almost everyone agrees that the position one takes on the moral status of the fetus influences whether one considers either the distinction between killing and letting die or the doctrine of double effect to be relevant to the abortion question. For example, conservatives are quite interested in whether the killing and letting die distinction can be used to show that it is permissible to let the fetus die in certain contexts, even when it would be impermissible to kill it. However, liberals find the use of this distinction in such contexts to be completely unnecessary: They hold that the fetus has almost no moral status, so they do not object to either killing it or letting it die. Similarly, although conservatives are quite interested in whether the doctrine of double effect can be used to permit the death of the fetus as a foreseen but unintended consequence of some legitimate course of action, liberals find no use for the doctrine of double effect in such contexts.

Third, almost everyone agrees that either the killing and letting die distinction or the doctrine of double effect could prove useful in cases of euthanasia. Agreement is possible because most of the subjects of euthanasia are humans who, in everyone's view, have full moral status and hence a serious right to life. Accordingly, despite the disagreement as to where it is useful to apply the killing and letting die distinction and the doctrine of double effect, everyone agrees that both conceptual tools deserve further examination.

The distinction between killing and letting die has its advocates and its critics. Advocates maintain that, other things being equal, killing is morally worse than letting die, with the consequence that letting die is justified in cases where killing is not. The critics of this distinction maintain that, other things being equal, killing is not morally worse than letting die, with the consequence that killing is morally justified whenever letting die is. Both advocates and critics agree that other things would not be equal if the killing were justified or deserved while the letting die unwanted and undeserved. They tend to disagree, however, over whether other things would be equal if the killing were in response to a patient's request to die while the letting die involved a prolonged and excruciatingly painful death, or if the killing resulted in the death of just a few individuals while the letting die resulted in the death of many people.

Yet whatever view one adopts as to when other things are equal, it is hard to defend the moral preferability of letting die over killing when both are taken to be intentional acts. As James Rachels so graphically illustrates (Selection 17), it seems impossible to judge the act of A, who intentionally lets Z die while standing ready to finish Z off if that proves necessary, as being morally preferable to the act of B, who with similar motive and intention kills Y. But it is far from clear whether advocates of the killing and letting die distinction are claiming that the distinction holds when the killing and the letting die are both intentional acts because it is unlikely in such cases that the letting die would be morally justified when the killing is not. Rather, as Bonnie Steinbock argues (Selection 18), advocates of the distinction seem to have in mind a contrast between *intentional* killing and *unintentional* letting die, or, more fully stated, a contrast between

intentional killing and unintentional letting die when the latter is the foreseen consequence of an otherwise legitimate course of action.

Steinbock maintains that there are at least two types of cases in which letting die, distinguished in this way from killing, seems justified. In the first, a doctor ceases treatment at the patient's request, foreseeing that the patient will die or die sooner than otherwise, yet not intending that result. In the second, a doctor's intention is to avoid employing treatment that is extremely painful and has little hope of benefiting the patient, even though she foresees that this may hasten the patient's death. In addition, conservatives have argued that letting die, distinguished in this way from killing, can be justified in cases of ectopic pregnancy and cancer of the uterus because in such cases the fetus's death is the foreseen but unintended consequence of medical treatment that is necessary to preserve the basic well-being of the pregnant woman.

When the killing and letting die distinction is interpreted in this way, it has much in common with the doctrine of double effect. This doctrine places four restrictions on the permissibility of acting when some of the consequences of one's action are evil. These restrictions are as follows:

1. The act is good in itself or at least indifferent.
2. Only the good consequences of the act are intended.
3. The good consequences are not the effect of the evil.
4. The good consequences are commensurate with the evil consequences.

The basic idea of the killing and letting die distinction, as we have interpreted it, is expressed by restrictions 2 and 3.

When conservatives apply the doctrine of double effect to a case in which a pregnant woman has cancer of the uterus, the doctrine is said to justify an abortion because:

1. The act of removing the cancerous uterus is good in itself.
2. Only the removal of the cancerous uterus is intended.
3. The removal of the cancerous uterus is not a consequence of the abortion.
4. Preserving the life of the mother by removing the cancerous uterus is commensurate with the death of the fetus.

The doctrine is also said to justify unintentionally letting a person die, or "passive euthanasia," at least in the two types of cases described by Steinbock.

In recent moral philosophy, the main objection to the doctrine of double effect has been to question the necessity of its restrictions. Consider the following example. Imagine that a fat person who is leading a party of spelunkers gets herself stuck in the mouth of a cave in which flood waters are rising. The trapped party of spelunkers just happens to have a stick of dynamite with which they can blast the fat person out of the mouth of the cave; either they use the dynamite or they all drown, the fat person with them. It appears that the doctrine of double effect would *not* permit the use of the dynamite in this case because the evil consequences of the act are intended as a means to securing the good consequences in violation of restrictions 2 and 3. Yet it is plausible to argue in such a case that using the dynamite would be justified on the grounds that (a) the evil to be avoided (i.e., the evil of failing to save the party of spelunkers except for the fat person) is considerably greater than the evil resulting from the means employed (i.e., the evil of intentionally causing the death of the fat person) and/or that (b) the greater part of evil resulting from the means employed (i.e., the death of the fat person) would still occur regardless of whether those means were actually employed.

Some people might want to defend the doctrine of double effect against this line of criticism

by maintaining that the spelunkers need not intend the death of the fat person, but only that "she be blown into little pieces" or that "the mouth of the cave be suitably enlarged." But how is the use of dynamite expected to produce these results except by way of killing the fat person? Thus, the death of the fat person is part of the means employed by the spelunkers to secure their release from the cave, and thus would be impermissible according to the doctrine of double effect. If, however, we think that bringing about the death of the fat person could be morally justified in this case, because, for example, (a) and/or (b) obtain, we are left with a serious objection to the necessity of the restrictions imposed by the doctrine of double effect for acting morally.

Given these objections to the doctrine of double effect, Philippa Foot has suggested that we might more profitably deal with the moral questions at issue by distinguishing between negative and positive duties. *Negative duties* are said to be duties to refrain from doing certain sorts of actions. Typically, these are duties to avoid actions that inflict harm or injury on others. Thus, the duties not to kill or assault others are negative duties. By contrast, *positive duties* are duties to do certain actions, usually those that aid or benefit others. The duties to repay a debt and help others in need are positive duties. This distinction is used to resolve practical disputes by claiming that negative duties have priority over positive duties; accordingly, when negative and positive duties conflict, negative duties always take precedence over positive duties.

Applying this distinction, Foot claims that a doctor is justified in performing an abortion when nothing can be done to save the lives of both child and mother, but the life of the mother can be saved by killing the child. Obviously, this case is quite similar to the example of the fat person stuck in the mouth of the cave. But it is not clear how the distinction between positive and negative duties can help us in either situation. Since both the doctor and the group of spelunkers trapped by the fat person have a negative duty not to kill that takes precedence over any positive duty to help either themselves or others, it would seem that neither aborting the fetus nor blowing up the fat person could be justified on the basis of this distinction. Thus, the distinction between negative and positive duties no more justifies evil consequences in such cases than does the doctrine of double effect. Accordingly, if we want to provide such a justification, we need to find some morally acceptable way of going beyond both of these requirements.

Alternative Views

As we mentioned earlier, conservatives hold that the fetus has full moral status and hence a serious right to life. As a consequence, they oppose abortion in a wide range of cases. Hoping to undercut this antiabortion stance, Judith Jarvis Thomson adopts, for the sake of argument, the conservative position on the moral status of the fetus (Selection 13). She then tries to show that abortion is still justified in a wide range of cases. She asks us to imagine that we are kidnapped and connected to an unconscious violinist who now shares the use of our kidneys. The situation is such that if we detach ourselves from the violinist before nine months transpire, the violinist will die. Thomson thinks it obvious that we have no obligation to share our kidneys with the violinist in such a case, and hence that, in analogous cases, abortion can be justified. Thomson's view has provoked so much discussion that the authors of the four following selections feel compelled to consider her view in developing their own positions.

In his selection, Don Marquis begins by assuming what Thomson argues against—namely, that if fetuses have the same moral status as adult human beings, then the presumption that any particular abortion is immoral is exceedingly strong (Selection 14). What Marquis wants

to defend is the conservative claim that fetuses have the same moral status as adult humans. He argues that what is wrong with killing adults is that it deprives them of "all the experiences, activities, projects, and enjoyments that would otherwise have constituted (their) future." Because abortion deprives a typical fetus of a "future like ours," Marquis contends that the moral presumption against abortion is as strong as the moral presumption against killing adult human beings. But there are at least two problems with Marquis's argument. First, his argument would seem to suggest that it would be less wrong to kill an older rather than a younger person and maybe not wrong at all to kill a person who doesn't have much of a future, say only a year or two left to live. Second, Marquis tries to distinguish contraception from abortion on the grounds that only abortion deprives *something* of a "future like ours." But it is not clear why, given that abortion and contraception both prevent a "future like ours," the fact that only abortion deprives something of a "future like ours" suffices to render it morally prohibited while contraception remains morally permissible.

Like Marquis, Mary Anne Warren also distinguishes her view from Thomson's (Selection 15). In particular, she objects to Thomson's violinist example, claiming that, at most, the example justified abortion in cases of rape and hence will not provide the desired support for abortion on demand. Thomson, however, did provide additional examples and arguments in an attempt to show that abortion is justified in cases other than rape.

Like Marquis, Warren wants to build a consensus on the abortion question. To achieve this, she proposes a set of criteria for being a person with full moral status that she thinks proabortionists and antiabortionists alike could accept. The criteria are (1) consciousness; (2) developed reasoning; (3) self-motivated activity; (4) a capacity to communicate; and (5) the presence of self-concepts and self-awareness. But although most people would certainly agree that these criteria are met in paradigm cases, conservatives would still reject them as necessary requirements for being a person. But it is not clear that the concept of a person is sharp or decisive enough to bear the weight of a solution to the abortion controversy.

Those who find both the conservative and liberal views on abortion unattractive might be inclined toward the moderate view. This view attempts to draw a line—typically at implantation, or at quickening, or at viability— for the purpose of separating those who do not have full moral status from those who do. The U.S. Supreme Court in *Roe v. Wade* (1973) has frequently been understood as supporting a moderate view on abortion. In this decision, the Court, by a majority of 7 to 2, decided that the constitutional right to privacy, protected by the due process clause of the Fourteenth Amendment to the Constitution, entails that (1) no law may restrict the right of a woman to be aborted by a physician during the first three months (trimester) of her pregnancy; (2) during the second trimester abortion may be regulated by law only to the extent that the regulation is reasonably related to the preservation and protection of maternal health; and (3) when the fetus becomes viable (not before the beginning of the third trimester) a law may prohibit abortion, but only subject to an exception permitting abortion whenever necessary to protect the woman's life or health (including any aspects of her physical or mental health). But regardless of whether the Court's decision was intended to support the moderate view on abortion, some have argued that in the absence of reasonable constraints, the Court's decision has led to abortion on demand.

In Selection 16, Sally Markowitz provides what she regards as a specifically feminist argument for abortion; that is, one that is grounded on awareness of women's oppression and a commitment to a more egalitarian society. She distinguishes her view from other approaches to abortion, which focus either on the moral status of the fetus or on a woman's right to autonomy. Accordingly, Markowitz assumes for the sake of argument that the fetus has a serious right to life. She bases her defense of abortion on two principles: the Impermissible Sacrifice Principle and the Feminist Proviso. According to the Impermissible Sacrifice Principle, when one social group in a society is systematically oppressed by another, it is impermissible to require the oppressed group to make sacrifices that will exacerbate or perpetuate the oppression. According to the Feminist Proviso, women are, as a group, sexually oppressed by men, and this oppression can neither be completely understood in terms of, nor otherwise reduced to, oppressions of other sorts. From these two principles, Markowitz derives the conclusion that, because in the sexist society in which we live, women are denied the equality to which they are entitled, a right to abortion is justified. It is interesting to note, however, that Markowitz's stance on abortion might turn out to be reconciled in practice with the conservative stance on abortion, provided that those who support the conservative stance on abortion are willing to first institutionalize the feminist agenda for equality between men and women.

Although most of the contemporary discussion of abortion has focused on the moral status of the fetus, most of the discussion of euthanasia has focused on the killing and letting die distinction and the doctrine of double effect. As we noted before, advocates of the killing and letting die distinction and the doctrine of double effect tend to justify only passive euthanasia (i.e., letting a person die as a foreseen but unintended consequence of an otherwise legitimate course of action). In contrast, critics of the killing and letting die distinction and the doctrine of double effect tend also to justify active euthanasia (i.e., intentional killing) on the basis of its consequences. Rachels (Selection 17) cites the case of a person suffering from cancer of the throat who has three options: (1) with continued treatment she will have a few more days of pain and then die; (2) if treatment is stopped but nothing else is done, it will be a few more hours; or (3) with a lethal injection she will die at once. In such a case, Rachels thinks, the third option—active euthanasia—is justified on the grounds that the person would be better off dying immediately.

But euthanasia is not only passive or active, it is also voluntary or involuntary. Voluntary euthanasia has the (informed) consent of the person involved. Involuntary euthanasia lacks such consent, usually but not always because the person involved is incapable of providing it. This means that at least four different types of euthanasia are possible: voluntary passive euthanasia, involuntary passive euthanasia, voluntary active euthanasia, and involuntary active euthanasia. Of the four types, voluntary passive euthanasia seems easiest to justify, involuntary active euthanasia the most difficult. But voluntary euthanasia, both passive and active, would seem more justifiable if it could be shown that there were a fundamental moral right to be assisted in bringing about one's own death if one so desired. Even if such a right could be supported, however, it would presumably only have force when one could reasonably be judged to be better off dead.

Practical Applications

It is not at all difficult to see how the various proposed solutions to the problem of abortion and euthanasia could be applied in contemporary societies. In *Planned Parenthood v. Casey* (Selection 19), the U.S. Supreme Court reaffirmed its commitment to what they took to be the essential holding of *Roe v. Wade*, which is a woman's right to terminate her pregnancy before viability, while rejecting *Roe v. Wade*'s trimester analysis in favor of an undue burden standard, which only the spousal notification requirement of Pennsylvania's Abortion Control Act violated. In *Cruzan v. Director, Missouri Department of Health* (Selection 20) the majority of the Supreme Court held that the state of Missouri was exercising a legitimate interest in protecting and preserving human life by requiring clear and convincing evidence of an incompetent's wishes concerning the withdrawal of life-sustaining medical treatment. In Selection 21, the activities of Dr. Jack Kevorkian are described. Accordingly, if you think that different solutions to the problem of abortion and euthanasia are more morally defensible, you should favor other laws and judicial decisions.

But even as you begin to formulate the laws and social institutions, with their demands on social goods and resources, that are needed to enforce what you take to be the most morally defensible solution to the problem of abortion and euthanasia, you will still need to take into account the demands on social goods and resources that derive from solutions to other practical moral problems—such as the problem of sex equality, which is taken up in the next section.

Endnotes

1. The term "fetus" is understood to refer to any human organism from conception to birth.

2. Note that liberals on the abortion question need not be welfare liberals, although many of them are. Likewise, conservatives on the abortion question need not be libertarians or political conservatives.

3. Henceforth liberals, conservatives, and moderates on the abortion question are simply referred to as liberals, conservatives, and moderates.

13. A Defense of Abortion

JUDITH JARVIS THOMSON

Judith Jarvis Thomson begins by assuming, for the sake of argument, that the fetus is a person. Using a series of examples, she then argues that even granting this assumption, a woman has a right to abortion in cases involving rape, where her life is endangered, and when she has taken reasonable precautions to avoid becoming pregnant. In these cases, Thomson claims, the fetus's assumed right not to be killed unjustly would not be violated by abortion. Thomson further distinguishes between cases in which it would be a good thing for a woman to forego an abortion and cases in which a woman has an obligation to do so.

Most opposition to abortion relies on the premise that the fetus is a human being, a person, from the moment of conception. The premise is argued for, but, as I think, not well. Take, for example, the most common argument. We are asked to notice that the development of a human being from conception through birth into childhood is continuous; then it is said that to draw a line, to choose a point in this development and say "before this point the thing is not a person, after this point it is a person" is to make an arbitrary choice, a choice for which in the nature of things no good reason can be given. It is concluded that the fetus is, or anyway we had better say it is, a person from the moment of conception. But this conclusion does not follow. Similar things might be said about the development of an acorn into an oak tree, and it does not follow that acorns are oak trees or that we had better say they are. Arguments of this form are sometimes called "slippery slope arguments"—the phrase is perhaps self-explanatory—and it is dismaying that opponents of abortion rely on them so heavily and uncritically.

I am inclined to agree, however, that the prospects for "drawing a line" in the development of the fetus look dim. I am inclined to think also that we shall probably have to agree that the fetus has already become a human person well before birth. Indeed, it comes as a surprise when one first learns how early in its life it begins to acquire human characteristics. By the tenth week, for example, it already has a face, arms and legs, fingers and toes; it has internal organs, and brain activity is detectable.[1] On the other hand, I think that the premise is false, that the fetus is not a person from the moment of conception. A newly fertilized ovum, a newly implanted clump of cells, is no more a person than an acorn is an oak tree. But I shall not discuss any of this. For it seems to me to be of great interest to ask what happens if, for the sake of argument, we allow the premise. How, precisely, are we supposed to get from there to the conclusion that abortion is morally impermissible? Opponents of abortion commonly spend most of their time establishing that the fetus is a person, and hardly any time explaining the step from there to the impermissibility of abortion. Perhaps they think the step too simple and obvious to require much comment. Or perhaps instead they are simply being economical in argument. Many of those who defend abortion rely on the premise that the fetus is not a person, but only a bit of tissue that will become a person at birth; and why pay out more arguments than you have to? Whatever the explanation, I suggest that the step they take is neither easy nor obvious, that it calls for closer examination than it is commonly given, and that when we do give it this closer examination we shall feel inclined to reject it.

I propose, then, that we grant that the fetus is a person from the moment of conception. How does the argument go from here? Something like this, I take it.

Abridged from Judith Jarvis Thomson, "A Defense of Abortion," *Philosophy & Public Affairs 1*, no. 1 (Fall 1971). Copyright 1971 by Princeton University Press. Excerpts, pp. 47–62, 65–66, reprinted by permission of Princeton University Press.

Every person has a right to life. So the fetus has a right to life. No doubt the mother has a right to decide what shall happen in and to her body; everyone would grant that. But surely a person's right to life is stronger and more stringent than the mother's right to decide what happens in and to her body, and so outweighs it. So the fetus may not be killed; an abortion may not be performed.

It sounds plausible. But now let me ask you to imagine this. You wake up in the morning and find yourself back to back in bed with an unconscious violinist. A famous unconscious violinist. He has been found to have a fatal kidney ailment, and the Society of Music Lovers has canvassed all the available medical records and found that you alone have the right blood type to help. They have therefore kidnapped you, and last night the violinist's circulatory system was plugged into yours, so that your kidneys can be used to extract poisons from his blood as well as your own. The director of the hospital now tells you, "Look, we're sorry the Society of Music Lovers did this to you—we would never have permitted it if we had known. But still, they did it, and the violinist now is plugged into you. To unplug you would be to kill him. But never mind, it's only for nine months. By then he will have recovered from his ailment, and can safely be unplugged from you." Is it morally incumbent on you to accede to this situation? No doubt it would be very nice of you if you did, a great kindness. But do you *have* to accede to it? What if it were not nine months, but nine years? Or longer still? What if the director of the hospital says, "Tough luck, I agree, but you've now got to stay in bed, with the violinist plugged into you, for the rest of your life. Because remember this. All persons have a right to life, and violinists are persons. Granted you have a right to decide what happens in and to your body, but a person's right to life outweighs your right to decide what happens in and to your body. So you cannot ever be unplugged from him." I imagine you would regard this as outrageous, which suggests that something really is wrong with that plausible-sounding argument I mentioned a moment ago.

In this case, of course, you were kidnapped; you didn't volunteer for the operation that plugged the violinist into your kidneys. Can those who oppose abortion on the ground I mentioned make an excep-

tion for a pregnancy due to rape? Certainly. They can say that persons have a right to life only if they didn't come into existence because of rape; or they can say that all persons have a right to life, but that some have less of a right to life than others, in particular, that those who came into existence because of rape have less. But these statements have a rather unpleasant sound. Surely the question of whether you have a right to life at all, or how much of it you have, shouldn't turn on the question of whether or not you are the product of a rape. And in fact the people who oppose abortion on the ground I mentioned do not make this distinction, and hence do not make an exception in case of rape.

Nor do they make an exception for a case in which the mother has to spend the nine months of her pregnancy in bed. They would agree that would be a great pity, and hard on the mother; but all the same, all persons have a right to life, the fetus is a person, and so on. I suspect, in fact, that they would not make an exception for a case in which, miraculously enough, the pregnancy went on for nine years, or even the rest of the mother's life.

Some won't even make an exception for a case in which continuation of the pregnancy is likely to shorten the mother's life; they regard abortion as impermissible even to save the mother's life. Such cases are nowadays very rare, and many opponents of abortion do not accept this extreme view. All the same, it is a good place to begin: A number of points of interest come out in respect to it.

1. Let us call the view that abortion is impermissible even to save the mother's life "the extreme view." I want to suggest first that it does not issue from the argument I mentioned earlier without the addition of some fairly powerful premises. Suppose a woman has become pregnant, and now learns that she has a cardiac condition such that she will die if she carries the baby to term. What may be done for her? The fetus, being a person, has a right to life, but as the mother is a person too, so has she a right to life. Presumably they have an equal right to life. How is it supposed to come out that an abortion may not be performed? If mother and child have an equal right to life, shouldn't we perhaps flip a coin? Or should we add to the mother's right to life her right to decide what happens in and to her body, which everybody seems to be ready to

grant—the sum of her rights now outweighing the fetus's right to life?

The most familiar argument here is the following. We are told that performing the abortion would be directly killing[2] the child, whereas doing nothing would not be killing the mother, but only letting her die. Moreover, in killing the child, one would be killing an innocent person, for the child has committed no crime, and is not aiming at his mother's death. And then there are a variety of ways in which this might be continued. (1) But as directly killing an innocent person is always and absolutely impermissible, an abortion may not be performed. Or, (2) as directly killing an innocent person is murder, and murder is always and absolutely impermissible, an abortion may not be performed.[3] Or, (3) as one's duty to refrain from directly killing an innocent person is more stringent than one's duty to keep a person from dying, an abortion may not be performed. Or, (4) if one's only options are directly killing an innocent person or letting a person die, one must prefer letting the person die, and thus an abortion may not be performed.[4]

Some people seem to have thought that these are not further premises which must be added if the conclusion is to be reached, but that they follow from the very fact that an innocent person has a right to life.[5] But this seems to me to be a mistake, and perhaps the simplest way to show this is to bring out that while we must certainly grant that innocent persons have a right to life, the theses in (1) through (4) are all false. Take (2), for example. If directly killing an innocent person is murder, and thus is impermissible, then the mother's directly killing the innocent person inside her is murder, and thus is impermissible. But it cannot seriously be thought to be murder if the mother performs an abortion on herself to save her life. It cannot seriously be said that she *must* refrain, that she *must* sit passively by and wait for her death. Let us look again at the case of you and the violinist. There you are, in bed with the violinist, and the director of the hospital says to you, "It's all most distressing, and I deeply sympathize, but you see this is putting an additional strain on your kidneys, and you'll be dead within the month. But you *have* to stay where you are all the same. Because unplugging you would be directly killing an innocent violinist, and that's murder, and that's impermissible." If anything in the world is true, it is that you do not

commit murder, you do not do what is impermissible, if you reach around to your back and unplug yourself from that violinist to save your life.

The main focus of attention in writings on abortion has been on what a third party may or may not do in answer to a request from a woman for an abortion. This is in a way understandable. Things being as they are, there isn't much a woman can safely do to abort herself. So the question asked is what a third party may do, and what the mother may do, if it is mentioned at all, is deduced, almost as an afterthought, from what is concluded that the third parties may do. But it seems to me that to treat the matter in this way is to refuse to grant to the mother that very status of person which is so firmly insisted on for the fetus. For we cannot simply read off what a person may do from what a third party may do. Suppose you find yourself trapped in a tiny house with a growing child. I mean a very tiny house, and a rapidly growing child—you are already up against the wall of the house and in a few minutes you'll be crushed to death. The child on the other hand won't be crushed to death; if nothing is done to stop him from growing he'll be hurt, but in the end he'll simply burst open the house and walk out a free man. Now I could well understand it if a bystander were to say, "There's nothing we can do for you. We cannot choose between your life and his, we cannot be the ones to decide who is to live, we cannot intervene." But it cannot be concluded that you too can do nothing, that you cannot attack it to save your life. However innocent the child may be, you do not have to wait passively while it crushes you to death. Perhaps a pregnant woman is vaguely felt to have the status of a house, to which we don't allow the right of self-defense. But if the woman houses the child, it should be remembered that she is a person who houses it.

I should perhaps stop to say explicitly that I am not claiming that people have a right to do anything whatever to save their lives. I think, rather, that there are drastic limits to the right of self-defense. If someone threatens you with death unless you torture someone else to death, I think you have not the right, even to save your life, to do so. But the case under consideration here is very different. In our case there are only two people involved, one whose life is threatened, and one who threatens it. Both are innocent: The one who is threatened is not threatened because of any fault, the one who threatens does not threaten because of any fault. For this reason we may feel that we bystanders cannot intervene. But the person threatened can.

In sum, a woman surely can defend her life against the threat to it posed by the unborn child, even if doing so involves its death. And this shows not merely that the theses in (1) through (4) are false; it shows also that the extreme view of abortion is false, and so we need not canvass any other possible ways of arriving at it from the argument I mentioned at the outset.

2. The extreme view could of course be weakened to say that while abortion is permissible to save the mother's life, it may not be performed by a third party, but only by the mother herself. But this cannot be right either. For what we have to keep in mind is that the mother and the unborn child are not like two tenants in a small house which has, by an unfortunate mistake, been rented to both: The mother *owns* the house. The fact that she does adds to the offensiveness of deducing that the mother can do nothing from the supposition that third parties can do nothing. But it does more than this: It casts a bright light on the supposition that third parties can do nothing. Certainly it lets us see that a third party who says "I cannot choose between you" is fooling himself if he thinks this is impartiality. If Jones has found and fastened on a certain coat, which he needs to keep him from freezing, but which Smith also needs to keep him from freezing, then it is not impartiality that says "I cannot choose between you" when Smith owns the coat. Women have said again and again "This body is *my* body!" and they have reason to feel angry, reason to feel that it has been like shouting into the wind. Smith, after all, is hardly likely to bless us if we say to him, "Of course it's your coat, anybody would grant that it is. But no one may choose between you and Jones who is to have it. . . ."

3. Where the mother's life is not at stake, the argument I mentioned at the outset seems to have a much stronger pull. "Everyone has a right to life, so the unborn person has a right to life." And isn't the child's right to life weightier than anything other than the mother's own right to life, which she might put forward as ground for an abortion?

This argument treats the right to life as if it were unproblematic. It is not, and this seems to me to be precisely the source of the mistake.

For we should now, at long last, ask what it comes to, to have a right to life. In some views having a right to life includes having a right to be given at least the bare minimum one needs for continued life. But suppose that what in fact *is* the bare minimum a man needs for continued life is something he has no right at all to be given? If I am sick unto death, and the only thing that will save my life is the touch of Henry Fonda's cool hand on my fevered brow, then all the same, I have no right to be given the touch of Henry Fonda's cool hand on my fevered brow. It would be frightfully nice of him to fly in from the West Coast to provide it. It would be less nice, though no doubt well meant, if my friends flew out to the West Coast and carried Henry Fonda back with them. But I have no right at all against anybody that he should do this for me. Or again, to return to the story I told earlier, the fact that for continued life that violinist needs the continued use of your kidneys does not establish that he has a right to be given the continued use of your kidneys. He certainly has no right against you that *you* should give him continued use of your kidneys. For nobody has any right to use your kidneys unless you give him such a right; and nobody has the right against you that you shall give him this right—if you do allow him to go on using your kidneys, this is a kindness on your part, and not something he can claim from you as his due. Nor has he any right against anybody else that *they* should give him continued use of your kidneys. Certainly he had no right against the Society of Music Lovers that they should plug him into you in the first place. And if you now start to unplug yourself, having learned that you will otherwise have to spend nine years in bed with him, there is nobody in the world who must try to prevent you, in order to see to it that he is given something he has a right to be given.

Some people are rather stricter about the right to life. In their view, it does not include the right to be given anything, but amounts to, and only to, the right not to be killed by anybody. But here a related difficulty arises. If everybody is to refrain from killing that violinist, then everybody must refrain from doing a great many different sorts of things. Everybody must refrain from slitting his throat, everybody must refrain from shooting him—and everybody must refrain from unplugging you from him. But does he have a right against everybody that they shall refrain from unplugging you from him? To refrain from doing this is to allow him to continue to use your kidneys. It could be argued that he has a right against us that *we* should allow him to continue to use your kidneys. That is, while he had no right against us that we should give him the use of your kidneys, it might be argued that he anyway has a right against us that we shall not now intervene and deprive him of the use of your kidneys. I shall come back to third-party interventions later. But certainly the violinist has no right against you that *you* shall allow him to continue to use your kidneys. As I said, if you do allow him to use them, it is a kindness on your part, and not something you owe him.

The difficulty I point to here is not peculiar to the right to life. It reappears in connection with all the other natural rights; and it is something which an adequate account of rights must deal with. For present purposes it is enough just to draw attention to it. But I would stress that I am not arguing that people do not have a right to life—quite to the contrary, it seems to me that the primary control we must place on the acceptability of an account of rights is that it should turn out in that account to be a truth that all persons have a right to life. I am arguing only that having a right to life does not guarantee having either a right to be given the use of or a right to be allowed continued use of another person's body—even if one needs it for life itself. So the right to life will not serve the opponents of abortion in the very simple and clear way in which they seem to have thought it would.

4. There is another way to bring out the difficulty. In the most ordinary sort of case, to deprive someone of what he has a right to is to treat him unjustly. Suppose a boy and his small brother are jointly given a box of chocolates for Christmas. If the older boy takes the box and refuses to give his brother any of the chocolates, he is unjust to him, for the brother has been given a right to half of them. But suppose that, having learned that otherwise it means nine years in bed with that violinist, you unplug yourself from him. You surely are not being unjust to him, for you gave him no right to use your kidneys, and no one else can have given him any such right. But we have to notice that in unplugging yourself, you are killing him; and violinists, like everybody else, have a right to life, and

thus in the view we were considering just now, the right not to be killed.

So here you do what he supposedly has a right you shall not do, but you do not act unjustly to him in doing it.

The emendation which may be made at this point is this: The right to life consists not in the right not to be killed, but rather in the right not to be killed unjustly. This runs a risk of circularity, but never mind: It would enable us to square the fact that the violinist has a right to life with the fact that you do not act unjustly toward him in unplugging yourself, thereby killing him. For if you do not kill him unjustly, you do not violate his right to life, and so it is no wonder you do him no injustice. But if this emendation is accepted, the gap in the argument against abortion stares us plainly in the face: It is by no means enough to show that the fetus is a person, and to remind us that all persons have a right to life—we need to be shown also that killing the fetus violates its right to life, i.e., that abortion is unjust killing. And is it?

I suppose we may take it as a datum that in a case of pregnancy due to rape the mother has not given the unborn person a right to the use of her body for food and shelter. Indeed, in what pregnancy could it be supposed that the mother has given the unborn person such a right? It is not as if there were unborn persons drifting about the world, to whom a woman who wants a child says "I invite you in."

But it might be argued that there are other ways one can have acquired a right to the use of another person's body than by having been invited to use it by that person. Suppose a woman voluntarily indulges in intercourse, knowing of the chance it will issue in pregnancy, and then she does become pregnant; is she not in part responsible for the presence, in fact the very existence, of the unborn person inside her? No doubt she did not invite it in. But doesn't her partial responsibility for its being there itself give it a right to the use of her body? If so, then her aborting it would be more like the boy's taking away the chocolates, and less like your unplugging yourself from the violinist—doing so would be depriving it of what it does have a right to, and thus would be doing it an injustice.

Then, too, it might be asked whether she can kill it even to save her own life: If she voluntarily called it into existence, how can she now kill it, even in self-defense?

The first thing to be said about this is that it is something new. Opponents of abortion have been so concerned to make out the independence of the fetus, in order to establish that it has a right to life, just as its mother does, that they have tended to overlook the possible support they might gain from making out that the fetus is *dependent* on the mother, in order to establish that she has a special kind of responsibility for it, a responsibility that gives it rights against her which are not possessed by any independent person—such as an ailing violinist who is a stranger to her.

On the other hand, this argument would give the unborn person a right to its mother's body only if her pregnancy resulted from a voluntary act, undertaken in full knowledge of the chance a pregnancy might result from it. It would leave out entirely the unborn person whose existence is due to rape. Pending the availability of some further argument, then, we would be left with the conclusion that unborn persons whose existence is due to rape have no right to the use of their mothers' bodies, and thus that aborting them is not depriving them of anything they have a right to and hence is not unjust killing.

We should also notice that it is not at all plain that this argument really does go as far as it purports to. For there are cases and cases, and the details make a difference. If the room is stuffy, and I therefore open a window to air it, and a burglar climbs in, it would be absurd to say, "Ah, now he can stay, she's given him a right to the use of her house—for she is partially responsible for his presence there, having voluntarily done what enabled him to get in, in full knowledge that there are such things as burglars, and that burglars burgle." It would be still more absurd to say this if I had had bars installed outside my windows, precisely to prevent burglars from getting in, and a burglar got in only because of a defect in the bars. It remains equally absurd if we imagine it is not a burglar who climbs in, but an innocent person who blunders or falls in. Again, suppose it were like this: People seeds drift about in the air like pollen, and if you open your windows, one may drift in and take root in your carpets or upholstery. You don't want children, so you fix up your windows with fine mesh screens, the very best you can buy. As can happen, however, and on very, very rare occasions does happen, one of the screens is defective; a seed drifts in and takes root. Does the person-plant who now develops have a right to the use of your house?

Surely not—despite the fact that you voluntarily opened your windows, knowingly kept carpets and upholstered furniture, and knew that screens were sometimes defective. Someone may argue that you are responsible for its rooting, that it does have a right to your house, because after all you *could* have lived out your life with bare floors and furniture, or with sealed windows and doors. But this won't do—by the same token anyone can avoid a pregnancy due to rape by having a hysterectomy, or anyway by never leaving home without a (reliable!) army.

It seems to me that the argument we are looking at can establish at most that there are *some* cases in which the unborn person has a right to the use of its mother's body, and therefore *some* cases in which abortion is unjust killing. There is room for much discussion and argument as to precisely which, if any. But I think we should sidestep this issue and leave it open, for at any rate the argument certainly does not establish that all abortion is unjust killing.

5. There is room for yet another argument here, however. We surely must all grant that there may be cases in which it would be morally indecent to detach a person from your body at the cost of his life. Suppose you learn that what the violinist needs is not nine years of your life, but only one hour: All you need do to save his life is to spend one hour in that bed with him. Suppose also that letting him use your kidneys for that one hour would not affect your health in the slightest. Admittedly you were kidnapped. Admittedly you did not give anyone permission to plug him into you. Nevertheless it seems plain to me you *ought* to allow him to use your kidneys for that hour—it would be indecent to refuse.

Again, suppose pregnancy lasted only an hour, and constituted no threat to life or health. And suppose that a woman becomes pregnant as a result of rape. Admittedly she did not voluntarily do anything to bring about the existence of a child. Admittedly she did nothing at all which would give the unborn person a right to the use of her body. All the same it might well be said, as in the newly emended violinist story, that she *ought* to allow it to remain for that hour—that it would be indecent in her to refuse.

Now some people are inclined to use the term "right" in such a way that it follows from the fact that you ought to allow a person to use your body for the hour he needs, that he has a right to use your body for the hour he needs, even though he has not been given that right by any person or act. They may say that it follows also that if you refuse, you act unjustly toward him. This use of the term is perhaps so common that it cannot be called wrong; nevertheless it seems to me to be an unfortunate loosening of what we would do better to keep a tight rein on. Suppose that box of chocolates I mentioned earlier had not been given to both boys jointly, but was given only to the older boy. There he sits, stolidly eating his way through the box, his small brother watching enviously. Here we are likely to say "You ought not to be so mean. You ought to give your brother some of those chocolates." My own view is that it just does not follow from the truth of this that the brother has any right to any of the chocolates. If the boy refuses to give his brother any, he is greedy, stingy, callous—but not unjust. I suppose that the people I have in mind will say it does follow that the brother has a right to some of the chocolates, and thus that the boy does act unjustly if he refuses to give his brother any. But the effect of saying this is to obscure what we should keep distinct, namely the difference between the boy's refusal in this case and the boy's refusal in the earlier case, in which the box was given to both boys jointly, and in which the small brother thus had what was from any point of view clear title to half.

A further objection to so using the term "right" that from the fact that A ought to do a thing for B, it follows that B has a right against A that A do it for him, is that it is going to make the question of whether or not a man has a right to a thing turn on how easy it is to provide him with it; and this seems not merely unfortunate, but morally unacceptable. Take the case of Henry Fonda again. I said earlier that I had no right to the touch of his cool hand on my fevered brow, even though I needed it to save my life. I said it would be frightfully nice of him to fly in from the West Coast to provide me with it, but that I had no right against him that he should do so. But suppose he isn't on the West Coast. Suppose he has only to walk across the room, place a hand briefly on my brow—and lo, my life is saved. Then surely he ought to do it, it would be indecent to refuse. Is it to be said "Ah, well, it follows that in this case she has a right to the touch of his hand on her brow, and so it would be an injustice in him to

refuse"? So that I have a right to it when it is easy for him to provide it, though no right when it's hard? It's rather a shocking idea that anyone's rights should fade away and disappear as it gets harder and harder to accord them to him.

So my own view is that even though you ought to let the violinist use your kidneys for the one hour he needs, we should not conclude that he has a right to do so—we should say that if you refuse, you are, like the boy who owns all the chocolates and will give none away, self-centered and callous, indecent in fact, but not unjust. And similarly, that even supposing a case in which a woman pregnant due to rape ought to allow the unborn person to use her body for the hour he needs, we should not conclude that he has a right to do so; we should conclude that she is self-centered, callous, indecent, but not unjust, if she refuses. The complaints are no less grave; they are just different. However, there is no need to insist on this point. If anyone does wish to deduce "he has a right" from "you ought," then all the same he must surely grant that there are cases in which it is not morally required of you that you allow that violinist to use your kidneys, and in which he does not have a right to use them, and in which you do not do him injustice if you refuse. And so also for mother and unborn child. Except in such cases as the unborn person has a right to demand it—and we were leaving open the possibility that there may be such cases—nobody is morally *required* to make large sacrifices, of health, of all other interests and concerns, of all other duties and commitments, for nine years, or even for nine months, in order to keep another person alive....

6. My argument will be found unsatisfactory on two counts by many of those who want to regard abortion as morally permissible. First, while I do argue that abortion is not impermissible, I do not argue that it is always permissible. I am inclined to think it a merit of my account precisely that it does *not* give a general yes or a general no. It allows for and supports our sense that, for example, a sick and desperately frightened fourteen-year-old schoolgirl, pregnant due to rape, may *of course* choose abortion, and that any law which rules this out is an insane law. And it also allows for and supports our sense that in other cases resort to abortion is even positively indecent. It would be indecent in the woman to request an abor-

tion, and indecent in a doctor to perform it, if she is in her seventh month, and wants the abortion just to avoid the nuisance of postponing a trip abroad. The very fact that the arguments I have been drawing attention to treat all cases of abortion, or even all cases of abortion in which the mother's life is not at stake, as morally on a par ought to have made them suspect at the outset.

Secondly, while I am arguing for the permissibility of abortion in some cases, I am not arguing for the right to secure the death of the unborn child. It is easy to confuse these two things in that up to a certain point in the life of the fetus it is not able to survive outside the mother's body; hence removing it from her body guarantees its death. But they are importantly different. I have argued that you are not morally required to spend nine months in bed, sustaining the life of that violinist; but to say this is by no means to say that if, when you unplug yourself, there is a miracle and he survives, you then have a right to turn round and slit his throat. You may detach yourself even if this costs

him his life; you have no right to be guaranteed his death, by some other means, if unplugging yourself does not kill him. There are some people who will feel dissatisfied by this feature of my argument. A woman may be utterly devastated by the thought of a child, a bit of herself, put out for adoption and never seen or heard of again. She may therefore want not merely that the child be detached from her, but more, that it die. Some opponents of abortion are inclined to regard this as beneath contempt—thereby showing insensitivity to what is surely a powerful source of despair. All the same, I agree that the desire for the child's death is not one which anybody may gratify, should it turn out to be possible to detach the child alive.

At this place, however, it should be remembered that we have only been pretending throughout that the fetus is a human being from the moment of conception. A very early abortion is surely not the killing of a person, and so is not dealt with by anything I have said here.

Endnotes

1. Daniel Callahan, *Abortion: Law, Choice and Morality* (New York, 1970), p. 373. This book gives a fascinating survey of the available information on abortion. The Jewish tradition is surveyed in David M. Feldman, *Birth Control in Jewish Law* (New York, 1968), Part 5, the Catholic tradition in John T. Noonan, Jr., "An Almost Absolute Value in History," in *The Morality of Abortion,* ed. John T. Noonan, Jr. (Cambridge, Mass., 1970).

2. The term "direct" in the arguments I refer to is a technical one. Roughly, what is meant by "direct killing" is either killing as an end in itself, or killing as a means to some end, for example, the end of saving someone else's life. See note 5, below, for an example of its use.

3. Cf. *Encyclical Letter of Pope Pius XI on Christian Marriage,* St. Paul Editions (Boston, n.d.), p. 32: "however much we may pity the mother whose health and even life is gravely imperiled in the performance of the duty allotted to her by nature, nevertheless what could ever be a sufficient reason for excusing in any way the direct murder of the innocent? This is precisely what we are dealing with here." Noonan (*The Morality of Abortion,* p. 43) reads this as follows: "What cause can ever avail to excuse in

any way the direct killing of the innocent? For it is a question of that."

4. The thesis in (4) is in an interesting way weaker than those in (1), (2), and (3): They rule out abortion even in cases in which both mother *and* child will die if the abortion is not performed. By contrast, one who held the view expressed in (4) could consistently say that one needn't prefer letting two persons die to killing one.

5. Cf. the following passage from Pius XII, *Address to the Italian Catholic Society of Midwives:* "The baby in the maternal breast has the right to life immediately from God.—Hence there is no man, no human authority, no science, no medical, eugenic, social, economic, or moral 'indication' which can establish or grant a valid juridical ground for a direct deliberate disposition of an innocent human life, that is a disposition which looks to its destruction either as an end or as a means to another end perhaps in itself not illicit.—The baby, still not born, is a man in the same degree and for the same reason as the mother" (quoted in Noonan, *The Morality of Abortion,* p. 45).

14. *Why Abortion Is Immoral*

DON MARQUIS

Marquis argues that fetuses have the same moral status as adult human beings on the grounds that what is wrong with killing an adult human being and what is wrong with killing a fetus are the same. Both are deprived of a "future like ours." On this account, Marquis contends that the moral presumption against abortion is as strong as the moral presumption against killing adult human beings.

The view that abortion is, with rare exceptions, seriously immoral has received little support in the recent philosophical literature. No doubt most philosophers affiliated with secular institutions of higher education believe that the anti-abortion position is either a symptom of irrational religious dogma or a conclusion generated by seriously confused philosophical argument. The purpose of this essay is to undermine this general belief. This essay sets out an argument that purports to show, as well as any argument in ethics can show, that abortion is, except possibly in rare cases, seriously immoral, that it is in the same moral category as killing an innocent adult human being.

This argument is based on a major assumption: If fetuses are in the same category as adult human beings with respect to the moral value of their lives, then the *presumption* that any particular abortion is immoral is exceedingly strong. Such a presumption could be overridden only by considerations more compelling than a woman's right to privacy. The defense of this assumption is beyond the scope of this essay.[1]

Furthermore, this essay will neglect a discussion of whether there are any such compelling considerations and what they are. Plainly there are strong candidates: abortion before implantation, abortion when the life of a woman is threatened by a pregnancy, or abortion after rape. The casuistry of these hard cases will not be explored in this essay. The purpose of this essay is to develop a general argument for the claim that, subject to the assumption above, the overwhelming majority of deliberate abortions are seriously immoral. . . .

A necessary condition of resolving the abortion controversy is a . . . theoretical account of the wrongness of killing. After all, if we merely believe, but do not understand, why killing adult human beings such as ourselves is wrong, how could we conceivably show that abortion is either immoral or permissible? . . .

In order to develop such an account, we can start from the following unproblematic assumption concerning our own case: It is wrong to kill *us*. Why is it wrong? Some answers can be easily eliminated. It might be said that what makes killing us wrong is that a killing brutalizes the one who kills. But the brutalization consists of being inured to the performance of an act that is hideously immoral; hence, the brutalization does not explain the immorality. It might be said that what makes killing us wrong is the great loss others would experience due to our absence. Although such hubris is understandable, such an explanation does not account for the wrongness of killing hermits, or those whose lives are relatively independent and whose friends find it easy to make new friends.

A more obvious answer is better. What primarily makes killing wrong is neither its effect on the murderer nor its effect on the victim's friends and relatives, but its effect on the victim. The loss of one's life is one of the greatest losses one can suffer. The loss of one's life deprives one of all the experiences, activities, projects, and enjoyments that would otherwise have constituted one's future. Therefore, killing someone is wrong, primarily because the killing inflicts (one of) the greatest possible losses on the victim. To describe

Reprinted, as slightly modified by the author, with permission of the author and the publisher from the *Journal of Philosophy*, vol. 86 (April 1989).

this as the loss of life can be misleading, however. The change in my biological state does not by itself make killing me wrong. The effect of the loss of my biological life is the loss to me of all those activities, projects, experiences, and enjoyments which would otherwise have constituted my future personal life. These activities, projects, experiences, and enjoyments are either valuable for their own sakes or are means to something else that is valuable for its own sake. Some parts of my future are not valued by me now, but will come to be valued by me as I grow older and as my values and capacities change. When I am killed, I am deprived both of what I now value, which would have been part of my future personal life, but also what I would come to value. Therefore, when I die, I am deprived of all of the value of my future. Inflicting this loss on me is ultimately what makes killing me wrong. This being the case, it would seem that what makes killing *any* adult human being prima facie seriously wrong is the loss of his or her future.[2]

How should this rudimentary theory of the wrongness of killing be evaluated? It cannot be faulted for deriving an "ought" from an "is," for it does not. The analysis assumes that killing me (or you, reader) is prima facie seriously wrong. The point of the analysis is to establish which natural property ultimately explains the wrongness of the killing, given that it is wrong. A natural property will ultimately explain the wrongness of killing, only if (1) the explanation fits with our intuitions about the matter and (2) there is no other natural property that provides the basis for a better explanation of the wrongness of killing. This analysis rests on the intuition that what makes killing a particular human or animal wrong is what it does to that particular human or animal. What makes killing wrong is some natural effect or other of the killing. Some would deny this. For instance, a divine-command theorist in ethics would deny it. Surely this denial is, however, one of those features of divine-command theory which renders it so implausible.

The claim that what makes killing wrong is the loss of the victim's future is directly supported by two considerations. In the first place, this theory explains why we regard killing as one of the worst of crimes. Killing is especially wrong, because it deprives the victim of more than perhaps any other crime. In the second place, people with AIDS or cancer who know

they are dying believe, of course, that dying is a very bad thing for them. They believe that the loss of a future to them that they would otherwise have experienced is what makes their premature death a very bad thing for them. A better theory of the wrongness of killing would require a different natural property associated with killing which better fits with the attitudes of the dying. What could it be?

The view that what makes killing wrong is the loss to the victim of the value of the victim's future gains additional support when some of its implications are examined. In the first place, it is incompatible with the view that it is wrong to kill only beings who are biologically human. It is possible that there exists a different species from another planet whose members have a future like ours. Since having a future like that is what makes killing someone wrong, this theory entails that it would be wrong to kill members of such a species. Hence, this theory is opposed to the claim that only life that is biologically human has great moral worth, a claim which many anti-abortionists have seemed to adopt. This opposition, which this theory has in common with personhood theories, seems to be a merit of the theory.

In the second place, the claim that the loss of one's future is the wrong-making feature of one's being killed entails the possibility that the futures of some actual nonhuman mammals on our own planet are sufficiently like ours that it is seriously wrong to kill them also. Whether some animals do have the same right to life as human beings depends on adding to the account of the wrongness of killing some additional account of just what it is about my future or the futures of other adult human beings which makes it wrong to kill us. No such additional account will be offered in this essay. Undoubtedly, the provision of such an account would be a very difficult matter. Undoubtedly, any such account would be quite controversial. Hence, it surely should not reflect badly on this sketch of an elementary theory of the wrongness of killing that it is indeterminate with respect to some very difficult issues regarding animal rights.

In the third place, the claim that the loss of one's future is the wrong-making feature of one's being killed does not entail, as sanctity-of-human-life theories do, that active euthanasia is wrong. Persons who are severely and incurably ill, who face a future of pain and despair, and who wish to die will not have suffered a loss if they are killed. It is, strictly speaking, the value of a human's future which makes killing wrong in this theory. This being so, killing does not necessarily wrong some persons who are sick and dying. Of course, there may be other reasons for a prohibition of active euthanasia, but that is another matter. Sanctity-of-human-life theories seem to hold that active euthanasia is seriously wrong even in an individual case where there seems to be good reason for it independently of public policy considerations. This consequence is most implausible, and it is a plus for the claim that the loss of a future of value is what makes killing wrong that it does not share this consequence.

In the fourth place, the account of the wrongness of killing defended [here] does straightforwardly entail that it is prima facie seriously wrong to kill children and infants, for we do presume that they have futures of value. Since we do believe that it is wrong to kill defenseless little babies, it is important that a theory of the wrongness of killing easily account for this. Personhood theories of the wrongness of killing, on the other hand, cannot straightforwardly account for the wrongness of killing infants and young children. Hence, such theories must add special ad hoc accounts of the wrongness of killing the young. The plausibility of such ad hoc theories seems to be a function of how desperately one wants such theories to work. The claim that the primary wrong-making feature of killing is the loss to the victim of the value of its future accounts for the wrongness of killing young children and infants directly; it makes the wrongness of such acts as obvious as we actually think it is. This is a further merit of this theory. Accordingly, it seems that this value of a future-like-ours theory of the wrongness of killing shares strengths of both sanctity-of-life and personhood accounts, while avoiding weaknesses of both. In addition, it meshes with a central intuition concerning what makes killing wrong.

The claim that the primary wrong-making feature of killing is the loss to the victim of the value of its future has obvious consequences for the ethics of abortion. The future of a standard fetus includes a set of experiences, projects, activities, and such which are identical with the futures of adult human beings and are identical with the futures of young children. Since

the reason that is sufficient to explain why it is wrong to kill human beings after the time of birth is a reason that also applies to fetuses, it follows that abortion is prima facie seriously morally wrong.

This argument does not rely on the invalid inference that, since it is wrong to kill persons, it is wrong to kill potential persons also. The category that is morally central to this analysis is the category of having a valuable future like ours; it is not the category of personhood. The argument to the conclusion that abortion is prima facie seriously morally wrong proceeded independently of the notion of person or potential person or any equivalent. Someone may wish to start with this analysis in terms of the value of a human future, conclude that abortion is, except perhaps in rare circumstances, seriously morally wrong, infer that fetuses have the right to life, and then call fetuses "persons" as a result of their having the right to life. Clearly, in this case, the category of person is being used to state the *conclusion* of the analysis rather than to generate the *argument* of the analysis.

The structure of this anti-abortion argument can be both illuminated and defended by comparing it to what appears to be the best argument for the wrongness of the wanton infliction of pain on animals. This latter argument is based on the assumption that it is prima facie wrong to inflict pain on me (or you, reader). What is the natural property associated with the infliction of pain which makes such infliction wrong? The obvious answer seems to be that the infliction of pain causes suffering, and that suffering is a misfortune. The suffering caused by the infliction of pain is what makes the wanton infliction of pain on me wrong. The wanton infliction of pain on other adult humans causes suffering. The wanton infliction of pain on animals causes suffering. Since causing suffering is what makes the wanton infliction of pain wrong and since the wanton infliction of pain on animals causes suffering, it follows that the wanton infliction of pain on animals is wrong.

This argument for the wrongness of the wanton infliction of pain on animals shares a number of structural features with the argument for the serious prima facie wrongness of abortion. Both arguments start with an obvious assumption concerning what it is wrong to do to me (or you, reader). Both then look for the characteristic or the consequence of the wrong action which makes the action wrong. Both recognize that the wrong-making feature of these immoral actions is a property of actions sometimes directed at individuals other than postnatal human beings. If the structure of the argument for the wrongness of the wanton infliction of pain on animals is sound, then the structure of the argument for the prima facie serious wrongness of abortion is also sound, for the structure of the two arguments is the same. The structure common to both is the key to the explanation of how the wrongness of abortion can be demonstrated without recourse to the category of person. In neither argument is that category crucial. . . .

Of course, this value of a future-like-ours argument, if sound, shows only that abortion is prima facie wrong, not that it is wrong in any and all circumstances. Since the loss of the future to a standard fetus, if killed, is, however, at least as great a loss as the loss of the future to a standard adult human being who is killed, abortion, like ordinary killing, could be justified only by the most compelling reasons. The loss of one's life is almost the greatest misfortune that can happen to one. Presumably abortion could be justified in some circumstances, only if the loss consequent on failing to abort would be at least as great. Accordingly, morally permissible abortions will be rare indeed unless, perhaps, they occur so early in pregnancy that a fetus is not yet definitely an individual. Hence, this argument should be taken as showing that abortion is presumptively very seriously wrong, where the presumption is very strong—as strong as the presumption that killing another adult human being is wrong. . . .

In this essay, it has been argued that the correct ethic of the wrongness of killing can be extended to fetal life and used to show that there is a strong presumption that any abortion is morally impermissible. If the ethic of killing adopted here entails, however, that contraception is also seriously immoral, then there would appear to be a difficulty with the analysis of this essay.

But this analysis does not entail that contraception is wrong. Of course, contraception prevents the actualization of a possible future of value. Hence, it follows from the claim that futures of value should be maximized that contraception is prima facie immoral. This obligation to maximize does not exist, however; furthermore, nothing in the ethics of killing in this paper entails that it does. The ethics of killing in this essay would entail that contraception is wrong only if something were denied a human future of value by contraception. Nothing at all is denied such a future by contraception, however.

Candidates for a subject of harm by contraception fall into four categories: (1) some sperm or other, (2) some ovum or other, (3) a sperm and an ovum separately, and (4) a sperm and an ovum together. Assigning the harm to some sperm is utterly arbitrary, for no reason can be given for making a sperm the subject of harm rather than an ovum. Assigning the harm to some ovum is utterly arbitrary, for no reason can be given for making an ovum the subject of harm rather than a sperm. One might attempt to avoid these problems by insisting that contraception deprives both the sperm and the ovum separately of a valuable future like ours. On this alternative, too many futures are lost. Contraception was supposed to be wrong, because it deprived us of one future of value, not two. One might attempt to avoid this problem by holding that contraception deprives the combination of sperm and ovum of a valuable future like ours. But here the definite article misleads. At the time of contraception, there are hundreds of millions of sperm, one (released) ovum, and millions of possible combinations of all of these. There is no actual combination at all. Is the subject of the loss to be a merely possible combination? Which one? This alternative does not yield an actual subject of harm either. Accordingly, the immorality of contraception is not entailed by the loss of a future-like-ours argument simply because there is no nonarbitrarily identifiable subject of the loss in the case of contraception. . . .

The purpose of this essay has been to set out an argument for the serious presumptive wrongness of abortion subject to the assumption that the moral permissibility of abortion stands or falls on the moral status of the fetus. Since a fetus possesses a property, the possession of which in adult human beings is sufficient to make killing an adult human being wrong, abortion is wrong. This way of dealing with the problem of abortion seems superior to other approaches to the ethics of abortion, because it rests on an ethics of killing which is close to self-evident, because the crucial morally relevant property clearly applies to fetuses, and because the argument avoids the usual equivocations on "human life," "human being," or "person." The argument rests neither on religious claims nor on Papal dogma. It is not subject to the objection of "speciesism." Its soundness is compatible with the moral permissibility of euthanasia and contraception. It deals with our intuitions concerning young children.

Finally, this analysis can be viewed as resolving a standard problem—indeed, *the* standard problem—concerning the ethics of abortion. Clearly, it is wrong to kill adult human beings. Clearly, it is not wrong to end the life of some arbitrarily chosen single human cell. Fetuses seem to be like arbitrarily chosen human cells in some respects and like adult humans in other respects. The problem of the ethics of abortion is the problem of determining the fetal property that settles this moral controversy. The thesis of this essay is that the problem of the ethics of abortion, so understood, is solvable.

Endnotes

1. Judith Jarvis Thomson has rejected this assumption in a famous essay, "A Defense of Abortion," *Philosophy and Public Affairs 1*, 1 (1971), 47–66.
2. I have been most influenced on this matter by Jonathan Glover, *Causing Death and Saving Lives* (New York: Penguin, 1977), ch. 3; and Robert Young, "What Is So Wrong with Killing People?" *Philosophy*, LIV, 210 (1979): 515–528.

15. *On the Moral and Legal Status of Abortion*

MARY ANNE WARREN

Mary Anne Warren argues that if the fetus is assumed to be a person, there are a wide range of cases in which abortion cannot be defended. To provide such a defense, Warren sets out five criteria for being a person she feels should be acceptable to anti-abortionists and pro-abortionists alike. Appealing to these criteria, she contends that fetuses, even when their potentiality is taken into account, do not sufficiently resemble persons to have a significant right to life. In a "Postscript" to her article, Warren defends her view against the objection that it would justify infanticide. Although by her criteria newborn infants would not have a significant right to life, she claims that infanticide would still not be permissible, so long as there are people willing to care and provide for the well-being of such infants.

We will be concerned with both the moral status of abortion, which for our purposes we may define as

From "On the Moral and Legal Status of Abortion." Copyright 1973 *The Monist*, LaSalle, Illinois. Reprinted from vol. 57, no. 4, Oct. 1973 by permission; and "Postscript on Infanticide," in *Today's Moral Problems*, edited by Richard Wasserstrom (1979), pp. 135–136. Reprinted by permission of the author and editor.

the act which a woman performs in voluntarily terminating, or allowing another person to terminate, her pregnancy, and the legal status which is appropriate for this act. I will argue that, while it is not possible to produce a satisfactory defense of a woman's right to obtain an abortion without showing that a fetus is not a human being, in the morally relevant sense of that term, we ought not to conclude that the difficulties involved in determining whether or not a fetus is a human make it impossible to produce any satisfactory solution to the problem of the moral status of abortion. For it is possible to show that, on the basis of intuitions which we may expect even the opponents of abortion to share, a fetus is not a person, and hence not the sort of entity to which it is proper to ascribe full moral rights.

Of course, while some philosophers would deny the possibility of any such proof,[1] others will deny that there is any need for it, since the moral permissibility of abortion appears to them to be too obvious to require proof. But the inadequacy of this attitude should be evident from the fact that both the friends and the foes of abortion consider their position to be morally self-evident. Because pro-abortionists have never adequately come to grips with the conceptual issues surrounding abortion, most if not all of the arguments which they advance in opposition to laws restricting access to abortion fail to refute or even weaken the traditional anti-abortion argument, i.e., that a fetus is a human being, and therefore abortion is murder.

These arguments are typically of one of two sorts. Either they point to the terrible side effects of the restrictive laws, e.g., the deaths due to illegal abortions, and the fact that it is poor women who suffer the most as a result of these laws, or else they state that to deny a woman access to abortion is to deprive her of her right to control her own body. Unfortunately, however, the fact that restricting access to abortion has tragic side effects does not, in itself, show that the restrictions are unjustified, since murder is wrong regardless of the consequences of prohibiting it; and the appeal to the right to control one's body, which is generally construed as a property right, is at best a rather feeble argument for the permissibility of abortion. Mere ownership does not give me the right to kill innocent people whom I find on my property, and indeed I am apt to be held responsible if such people injure themselves while on my property. It is equally unclear that I have any moral right to expel an innocent person from my property when I know that doing so will result in his death.

Furthermore, it is probably inappropriate to describe a woman's body as her property, since it seems natural to hold that a person is something distinct from her property but not from her body. Even those who would object to the identification of a person

with his body, or with the conjunction of his body and his mind, must admit that it would be very odd to describe, say, breaking a leg, as damaging one's property, and much more appropriate to describe it as injuring one*self*. Thus it is probably a mistake to argue that the right to obtain an abortion is in any way derived from the right to own and regulate property.

But however we wish to construe the right to abortion, we cannot hope to convince those who consider abortion a form of murder of the existence of any such right unless we are able to produce a clear and convincing refutation of the traditional anti-abortion argument, and this has not, to my knowledge, been done. With respect to the two most vital issues which that argument involves, i.e., the humanity of the fetus and its implication for the moral status of abortion, confusion has prevailed on both sides of the dispute.

Thus, both pro-abortionists and anti-abortionists have tended to abstract the question of whether abortion is wrong to that of whether it is wrong to destroy a fetus, just as though the rights of another person were not necessarily involved. This mistaken abstraction has led to the almost universal assumption that if a fetus is a human being, with a right to life, then it follows immediately that abortion is wrong (except perhaps when necessary to save the woman's life), and that it ought to be prohibited. It has also been generally assumed that unless the question about the status of the fetus is answered, the moral status of abortion cannot possibly be determined. . . . John Noonan is correct in saying that "the fundamental question in the long history of abortion is, How do you determine the humanity of a being?"[2] He summarizes his own anti-abortion argument, which is a version of the official position of the Catholic Church, as follows:

> . . . it is wrong to kill humans, however poor, weak, defenseless, and lacking in opportunity to develop their potential they may be. It is therefore morally wrong to kill Biafrans. Similarly, it is morally wrong to kill embryos.[3]

Noonan bases his claim that fetuses are human on what he calls the theologians' criterion of humanity: Whoever is conceived of human beings is human. But although he argues at length for the appropriateness of this criterion, he never questions the assumption that if the fetus is human then abortion is wrong for exactly the same reason that murder is wrong.

Judith Thomson is, in fact, the only writer I am aware of who has seriously questioned this assumption; she has argued that, even if we grant the anti-abortionist his claim that a fetus is a human being, with the same right to life as any other human being, we can still demonstrate that, in at least some and perhaps most cases, a woman is under no moral obligation to complete an unwanted pregnancy.[4] Her argument is worth examining, since if it holds up it may enable us to establish the moral permissibility of abortion without becoming involved in problems about what entitles an entity to be considered human, and accorded full moral rights. To be able to do this would be a great gain in the power and simplicity of the pro-abortion position, since, although I will argue that these problems can be solved at least as decisively as can any other moral problems, we should certainly be pleased to be able to avoid having to solve them as part of the justification of abortion.

On the other hand, even if Thomson's argument does not hold up, her insight—that it requires argument to show that if fetuses are human then abortion is properly classified as murder—is extremely valuable. The assumption she attacks is particularly invidious, for it amounts to the decision that it is appropriate, in deciding the moral status of abortion, to leave the rights of the pregnant woman out of consideration entirely, except possibly when her life is threatened. Obviously, this will not do; determining what moral rights, if any, a fetus possesses is only the first step in determining the moral status of abortion. Step two, which is at least equally essential, is finding a just solution to the conflict between whatever rights the fetus may have, and the rights of the woman who is unwillingly pregnant. While the historical error has been to pay far too little attention to the second step, Ms. Thomson's suggests that if we look at the second step first we may find that a woman has a right to obtain an abortion *regardless* of what rights the fetus has.

Our own inquiry will also have two stages. In Section I, we will consider whether or not it is possible to establish that abortion is morally permissible even on the assumption that a fetus is an entity with a full-fledged right to life. I will argue that in fact this cannot be established, at least not with the conclusive-

ness which is essential to our hopes of convincing those who are skeptical about the morality of abortion, and that we therefore cannot avoid dealing with the question of whether or not a fetus really does have the same right to life as a (more fully developed) human being.

In Section II, I will propose an answer to this question, namely, that a fetus cannot be considered a member of the moral community, the set of beings with full and equal moral rights, for the simple reason that it is not a person, and that it is personhood, and not genetic humanity, i.e., humanity as defined by Noonan, which is the basis for membership in this community. I will argue that a fetus, whatever its stage of development, satisfies none of the basic criteria for personhood, and is not even enough *like* a person to be accorded even some of the same rights on the basis of this resemblance. Nor, as we will see, is a fetus's *potential* personhood a threat to the morality of abortion, since, whatever the rights of potential people may be, they are invariably overridden in any conflict with the moral rights of actual people.

═

I

We now turn to Professor Thomson's case for the claim that even if a fetus has full moral rights, abortion is still morally permissible, at least sometimes, and for some reasons other than to save the woman's life. Her argument is based upon a clever, but I think faulty, analogy. She asks us to picture ourselves waking up one day, in bed with a famous violinist. Imagine that you have been kidnapped, and your bloodstream hooked up to that of the violinist, who happens to have an ailment which will certainly kill him unless he is permitted to share your kidneys for a period of nine months. No one else can save him, since you alone have the right type of blood. He will be unconscious all that time, and you will have to stay in bed with him, but after the nine months are over he may be unplugged, completely cured; that is, provided that you have cooperated.

Now then, she continues, what are your obligations in this situation? The anti-abortionist, if he is consistent, will have to say that you are obligated to stay in bed with the violinist: for all people have a right to life, and violinists are people, and therefore it would be murder for you to disconnect yourself from him and let him die. But this is outrageous, and so there must be something wrong with the same argument when it is applied to abortion. It would certainly be commendable of you to agree to save the violinist, but it is absurd to suggest that your refusal to do so would be murder. His right to life does not obligate you to do whatever is required to keep him alive; nor does it justify anyone else in forcing you to do so. A law which required you to stay in bed with the violinist would clearly be an unjust law, since it is no proper function of the law to force unwilling people to make huge sacrifices for the sake of other people toward whom they have no such prior obligation.

Thomson concludes that, if this analogy is apt, then we can grant the anti-abortionist claim that a fetus is a human being and still hold that it is at least sometimes the case that a pregnant woman has the right to refuse to be a Good Samaritan towards the fetus, i.e., to obtain an abortion. For there is a great gap between the claim that X has a right to life, and the claim that Y is obligated to do whatever is necessary to keep X alive, let alone that he ought to be forced to do so. It is Y's duty to keep X alive only if he has somehow contracted a *special* obligation to do so; and a woman who is unwillingly pregnant, e.g, who was raped, has nothing which obligates her to make the enormous sacrifice which is necessary to preserve the conceptus.

This argument is initially quite plausible, and in the extreme case of pregnancy due to rape is probably conclusive. Difficulties arise, however, when we try to specify more exactly the range of cases in which abortion is clearly justifiable even on the assumption that the fetus is human. Professor Thomson considers it a virtue of her argument that it does not enable us to conclude that abortion is *always* permissible. It would, she says, be "indecent" for a woman in her seventh month to obtain an abortion just to avoid having to postpone a trip to Europe. On the other hand, her argument enables us to see that "a sick and desperately frightened schoolgirl pregnant due to rape may *of course* choose abortion, and that any law which rules this out is an insane law" (p. 65). So far, so good; but what are we to say about the woman who becomes pregnant not through rape but as a result of her own carelessness, or because of contraceptive failure, or

who gets pregnant intentionally and then changes her mind about wanting a child? With respect to such cases, the violinist analogy is of much less use to the defender of the woman's right to obtain an abortion.

Indeed, the choice of a pregnancy due to rape, as an example of a case in which abortion is permissible even if a fetus is considered a human being, is extremely significant; for it is only in the case of pregnancy due to rape that the woman's situation is adequately analogous to the violinist case for our intuitions about the latter to transfer convincingly. The crucial difference between a pregnancy due to rape and the *normal* case of an unwanted pregnancy is that in the normal case we cannot claim that the woman is in no way responsible for her predicament; she could have remained chaste, or taken her pills more faithfully, or abstained on dangerous days, and so on. If, on the other hand, you are kidnapped by strangers, and hooked up to a strange violinist, then you are free of any shred of responsibility for the situation, on the basis of which it could be argued that you are obligated to keep the violinist alive. Only when her pregnancy is due to rape is a woman clearly just as nonresponsible.[5]

Consequently, there is room for the anti-abortionists to argue that in the normal case of unwanted pregnancy, a woman has, by her own actions, assumed responsibility for the fetus. For if X behaves in a way which he could have avoided, and which he knows involves, let us say, a 1 percent chance of bringing into existence a human being, with a right to life, and does so knowing that if this should happen then that human being will perish unless X does certain things to keep him alive, then it is by no means clear that when it does happen X is free of any obligation to what he knew in advance would be required to keep that human being alive.

The plausibility of such an argument is enough to show that the Thomson analogy can provide a clear and persuasive defense of a woman's right to obtain an abortion only with respect to those cases in which the woman is in no way responsible for her pregnancy [e.g., rape]. In all other cases, we would almost certainly conclude that it was necessary to look carefully at the particular circumstances in order to determine the extent of the woman's responsibility, and hence the extent of her obligation. This is an extremely unsatisfactory outcome, from the viewpoint of the opponents of restrictive abortion laws, most of whom are convinced that a woman has a right to obtain an abortion regardless of how or why she got pregnant.

Of course, a supporter of the violinist analogy might point out that it is absurd to suggest that forgetting her pill one day might be sufficient to obligate a woman to complete an unwanted pregnancy. And indeed it *is* absurd to suggest this. As we will see, the moral right to obtain an abortion is not in the least dependent upon the extent to which the woman is responsible for her pregnancy. But unfortunately, once we allow the assumption that a fetus has full moral rights, we cannot avoid taking this absurd suggestion seriously. Perhaps we can make this point more clear by altering the violinist story just enough to make it more analogous to a normal unwanted pregnancy and less to a pregnancy due to rape, and then seeing whether it is still obvious that you are not obligated to stay in bed with the fellow.

Suppose, then, that violinists are peculiarly prone to the sort of illness the only cure for which is the use of someone else's bloodstream for nine months, and that because of this there has been formed a society of music lovers who agree that whenever a violinist is stricken they will draw lots and the loser will, by some means, be made the one and only person capable of saving him. Now then, would you be obligated to cooperate in curing the violinist if you had voluntarily joined this society, knowing the possible consequences, and then your name had been drawn and you had been kidnapped? Admittedly, you did not promise ahead of time that you would, but you did deliberately place yourself in a position in which it might happen that a human life would be lost if you did not. Surely this is at least a *prima facie* reason for supposing that you have an obligation to stay in bed with the violinist. Suppose you had gotten your name drawn deliberately; surely *that* would be quite a strong reason for thinking that you had such an obligation.

It might be suggested that there is one important disanalogy between the modified violinist case and the case of an unwanted pregnancy, which makes the woman's responsibility significantly less, namely, the fact that the fetus *comes into existence* as the result of the woman's actions. This fact might give her a right to refuse to keep it alive, whereas she would not have had this right had it existed previously, independently, and then as a result of her actions become dependent upon her for its survival.

My own intuition, however, is that X has no more right to bring into existence, either deliberately or as a foreseeable result of actions he could have avoided, a being with full moral rights (Y), and then refuse to do what he knew beforehand would be required to keep that being alive, than he has to enter into an agreement with an existing person, whereby he may be called upon to save that person's life, and then refuse to do so when so called upon. Thus, X's responsibility for Y's existence does not seem to lessen his obligation to keep Y alive, if he is also responsible for Y's being in a situation in which only he can save him.

Whether this intuition is entirely correct, it brings us back again to the conclusion that once we allow the assumption that a fetus has full moral rights it becomes an extremely complex and difficult question whether and when abortion is justifiable. Thus, the Thomson analogy cannot help us produce a clear and persuasive proof of the moral permissibility of abortion. Nor will the opponents of the restrictive laws thank us for anything less; for their conviction (for the most part) is that abortion is obviously *not* a morally serious and extremely unfortunate, even though sometimes justified, act comparable to killing in self-defense or to letting the violinist die, but rather is closer to being a morally neutral act like cutting one's hair.

The basis of this conviction, I believe, is the realization that a fetus is not a person, and thus does not have a full-fledged right to life. Perhaps the reason why this claim has been so inadequately defended is that it seems self-evident to those who accept it. And so it is, insofar as it follows from what I take to be perfectly obvious claims about the nature of personhood and about the proper grounds for ascribing moral rights, claims which ought, indeed, to be obvious to both the friends and foes of abortion. Nevertheless, it is worth examining these claims, and showing how they demonstrate the moral innocuousness of abortion, since this apparently has not been adequately done before.

II

The question we must answer in order to produce a

satisfactory solution to the problem of the moral status of abortion is this: How are we to define the moral community, the set of beings with full and equal moral rights, such that we can decide whether a human fetus is a member of this community or not? What sort of entity, exactly, has the inalienable rights to life, liberty, and the pursuit of happiness? Jefferson attributed these rights to all *men,* and it may or may not be fair to suggest that he intended to attribute them *only* to men. Perhaps he ought to have attributed them to all human beings. If so, then we arrive, first, at Noonan's problem of defining what makes a being human, and, second, at the equally vital question which Noonan does not consider, namely: What reason is there for identifying the moral community with the set of all human beings, in whatever way we have chosen to define that term?

1. On the Definition of "Human"

One reason why this vital second question is so frequently overlooked in the debate over the moral status of abortion is that the term *human* has two distinct, but not often distinguished, senses. This fact results in a slide of meaning, which serves to conceal the fallaciousness of the traditional argument that since (1) it is wrong to kill innocent human beings and (2) fetuses are innocent human beings, then (3) it is wrong to kill fetuses. For if *human* is used in the same sense in both (1) and (2) then, whichever of the two senses is meant, one of these premises is question-begging. And if it is used in two different senses then of course the conclusion doesn't follow.

Thus, (1) is a self-evident moral truth[6] and avoids begging the question about abortion, only if "human being" is used to mean something like " a full-fledged member of the moral community." (It may or may not also be meant to refer exclusively to members of the species *Homo sapiens.*) We may call this the *moral* sense of "human." It is not to be confused with what we will call the *genetic* sense, i.e., the sense in which *any* member of the species is a human being, and no member of any other species could be. If (1) is acceptable only if the moral sense is intended, (2) is non–question-begging only if what is intended is the genetic sense.

In "Deciding Who Is Human," Noonan argues for the classification of fetuses with human beings by pointing to the presence of the full genetic code, and the potential capacity for rational thought (p.135). It

is clear that what he needs to show, for his version of the traditional argument to be valid, is that fetuses are human in the moral sense, the sense in which it is analytically true that all human beings have full moral rights. But, in the absence of any argument showing that whatever is genetically human is also morally human, and he gives none, nothing more than genetic humanity can be demonstrated by the presence of the human genetic code. And, as we will see, the *potential* capacity for rational thought can at most show that an entity has the potential for *becoming* human in the moral sense.

2. Defining the Moral Community

Can it be established that genetic humanity is sufficient for moral humanity? I think that there are very good reasons for not defining the moral community in this way. I would like to suggest an alternative way of defining the moral community, which I will argue for only to the extent of explaining why it is, or should be, self-evident. The suggestion is simply that the moral community consists of all and only *people,* rather than all and only human beings;[7] and probably the best way of demonstrating its self-evidence is by considering the concept of personhood, to see what sorts of entity are and are not persons, and what the decision that a being is or is not a person implies about its moral rights.

What characteristics entitle an entity to be considered a person? This is obviously not the place to attempt a complete analysis of the concept of personhood, but we do not need such a fully adequate analysis just to determine whether and why a fetus is or isn't a person. All we need is a rough and approximate list of the most basic criteria of personhood, and some idea of which, or how many, of these an entity must satisfy . . . to properly be considered a person.

In searching for such criteria, it is useful to look beyond the set of people with whom we are acquainted, and ask how we would decide whether a totally alien being was a person or not. (For we have no right to assume that genetic humanity is necessary for personhood.) Imagine a space traveler who lands on an unknown planet and encounters a race of beings utterly unlike any he has ever seen or heard of. If he wants to be sure of behaving morally toward these beings, he has to somehow decide whether these are people, and hence have full moral rights, or whether they are the sort of thing which he need not feel guilty about treating as, for example, a source of food.

How should he go about making this decision? If he has some anthropological background, he might look for such things as religion, art, and the manufacturing of tools, weapons, or shelters, since these factors have been used to distinguish our human from our prehuman ancestors, in what seems to be closer to the moral than the genetic sense of "human." And no doubt he would be right to consider the presence of such factors as good evidence that the alien beings were people and morally human. It would, however, be overly anthropocentric of him to take the absence of these things as adequate evidence that they were not, since we can imagine people who have progressed beyond, or evolved without ever developing, these cultural characteristics.

I suggest that the traits which are most central to the concept of personhood, or humanity in the moral sense, are, very roughly, the following:

1. consciousness (of objects and events external and/or internal to the being), and in particular the capacity to feel pain;
2. reasoning (the *developed* capacity to solve new and relatively complex problems);
3. self-motivated activity (activity which is relatively independent of either genetic or direct external control);
4. the capacity to communicate, by whatever means, messages of an indefinite variety of types, . . . not just with an indefinite number of possible contents, but on indefinitely many possible topics;
5. the presence of self-concepts, and self-awareness, either individual or racial, or both.

Admittedly, there are apt to be a great many problems involved in formulating precise definitions of these criteria, let alone in developing universally valid behavioral criteria for deciding when they apply. But I will assume that both we and our explorer know approximately what (1)–(5) mean, and that he is also able to determine whether or not they apply. How, then, should he use his findings to decide whether . . . the alien beings are people? We needn't suppose that an entity must have *all* of these attributes to be properly considered a person; (1) and (2) alone may well

be sufficient for personhood, and quite probably (1)–(3) are sufficient. Neither do we need to insist that any one of these criteria is necessary for personhood, although once again (1) and (2) look like fairly good candidates for *necessary* conditions, as does (3), if "activity" is construed to include the activity of reasoning.

All we need to claim, to demonstrate that a fetus is not a person, is that any being which satisfies *none* of (1)–(5) is certainly not a person. I consider this claim to be so obvious that I think anyone who denied it, and claimed that a being which satisfied none of (1)–(5) was a person all the same, would thereby demonstrate that he had no notion at all of what a person is—perhaps because he had confused the concept of a person with that of genetic humanity. If the opponents of abortion were to deny the appropriateness of these five criteria, I do not know what further arguments would convince them. We would probably have to admit that our conceptual schemes were indeed irreconcilably different, and that our dispute could not be settled objectively.

I do not expect this to happen, however, since I think that the concept of a person is one which is very nearly universal (to people), and that it is common to both pro-abortionists and anti-abortionists, even though neither group has fully realized the relevance of this concept to the resolution of their dispute. Furthermore, I think that on reflection even the anti-abortionists ought to agree not only that (1)–(5) are central to the concept of personhood, but also that it is a part of this concept that all and only people have full moral rights. The concept of a person is in part a moral concept; once we have admitted that X is a person, we have recognized, even if we have not agreed to respect, X's right to be treated as a member of the moral community. It is true that the claim that X is a *human being* is more commonly voiced as part of an appeal to treat X decently than is the claim that X is a person, but this is either because "human being" is here used in the sense which implies personhood, or because the genetic and moral senses of "human" have been confused.

Now if (1)–(5) are indeed the primary criteria of personhood, then it is clear that genetic humanity is neither necessary nor sufficient for establishing that an entity is a person. Some human beings are not people, and there may well be people who are not human beings. A man or woman whose consciousness has been permanently obliterated but who remains alive is a human being which is no longer a person; defective human beings, with no appreciable mental capacity, are not and presumably never will be people; and a fetus is a human being which is not yet a person, and which therefore cannot coherently be said to have full moral rights. Citizens of the next century should be prepared to recognize highly advanced, self-aware robots or computers, should such be developed, and intelligent inhabitants of other worlds, should such be found, as people in the fullest sense, and to respect their moral rights. But to ascribe full moral rights to an entity which is not a person is as absurd as to ascribe moral obligations and responsibilities to such an entity.

3. Fetal Development and the Right to Life

Two problems arise in the application of these suggestions for the definition of the moral community to the determination of the precise moral status of a human fetus. Given that the paradigm example of a person is a normal adult human being, then (1) How like this paradigm, in particular how far advanced since conception, does a human being need to be before it begins to have a right to life by virtue, not of being fully a person as of yet, but of being *like* a person? and (2) To what extent, if any, does the fact that a fetus has the *potential* for becoming a person endow it with some of the same rights? Each of these questions requires some comment.

In answering the first question, we need not attempt a detailed consideration of the moral rights of organisms which are not developed enough, aware enough, intelligent enough, etc., to be considered people, but which resemble people in some respects. It does seem reasonable to suggest that the more like a person, in the relevant aspects, a being is, the stronger is the case for regarding it as having a right to life, and indeed the stronger its right to life is. Thus we ought to take seriously the suggestion that, insofar as "the human individual develops biologically in a continuous fashion . . . the rights of a human person might develop in the same way."[8] But we must keep in mind that the attributes which are relevant in determining whether or not an entity is enough like a person to be regarded as having some of the same moral rights are no different from those which are relevant to deter-

mining whether or not it is fully a person—i.e., are no different from (1)–(5)—and that being genetically human, or having recognizably human facial and other physical features, or detectable brain activity, or the capacity to survive outside the uterus, is simply not among those relevant attributes.

Thus it is clear that even though a seven- or eight-month fetus has features which make it apt to arouse in us almost the same powerful protective instinct as is commonly aroused by a small infant, nevertheless it is not significantly more personlike than a very small embryo. It is *somewhat* more personlike; it can apparently feel and respond to pain, and it may even have a rudimentary form of consciousness, insofar as its brain is quite active. Nevertheless, it seems safe to say that it is not fully conscious, in the way that an infant of a few months is, and that it cannot reason, or communicate messages of indefinitely many sorts, does not engage in self-motivated activity, and has no self-awareness. Thus, in the *relevant* respects, a fetus, even a fully developed one, is considerably less personlike than is the average mature mammal, indeed the average fish. And I think that a rational person must conclude that if the right to life of a fetus is to be based upon its resemblance to a person, then it cannot be said to have any more right to life than, let us say, a newborn guppy (which also seems to be capable of feeling pain), and that a right of that magnitude could never override a woman's right to obtain an abortion, at any stage of her pregnancy.

There may . . . be other arguments in favor of placing legal limits on the stage of pregnancy in which abortion may be performed. Given the relative safety of the new techniques of artificially inducing labor during the third trimester, the danger to the woman's life or health is no longer such an argument. Neither is the fact that people tend to respond to the thought of abortion in the later stages of pregnancy with emotional repulsion, since mere emotional responses cannot take the place of moral reasoning in determining what ought to be permitted. Nor, finally, is the . . . argument that legalizing abortion, especially late in the pregnancy, may erode the level of respect for human life, leading perhaps, to an increase in unjustified euthanasia and other crimes. For this threat . . . can be better met by educating people to the kinds of moral distinctions which we are making here than by limiting access to abortion (which limitation may, in its disregard for the rights of women, be just as damaging to the level of respect for human rights).

Thus, since the fact that even a fully developed fetus is not personlike enough to have any significant right to life on the basis of its personlikeness shows that no legal restrictions upon the stage of pregnancy in which an abortion may be performed can be justified on the grounds that we should protect the rights of the older fetus; and since there is no other apparent justification for such restrictions, we may conclude that they are entirely unjustified. Whether or not it would be *indecent* (whatever that means) for a woman in her seventh month to obtain an abortion just to avoid having to postpone a trip to Europe, it would not, in itself, be *immoral*, and therefore it ought to be permitted.

4. Potential Personhood and the Right to Life

We have seen that a fetus does not resemble a person in any way which can support the claim that it has even some of the same rights. But what about its *potential*, the fact that if nurtured and allowed to develop naturally it will very probably become a person? Doesn't that alone give it at least some right to life? It is hard to deny that . . . an entity is a potential person is a strong *prima facie* reason for not destroying it; but we need not conclude from this that a potential person has a right to life, by virtue of that potential. It may be that our feeling that it is better, other things being equal, not to destroy a potential person is better explained by the fact that potential people are still (felt to be) an invaluable resource, not to be lightly squandered. Surely, if every speck of dust were a potential person, we would be much less apt to conclude that every potential person has a right to become actual.

Still, we do not need to insist that a potential person has no right to life whatever. There may well be something immoral, and not just imprudent, about wantonly destroying potential people, when doing so isn't necessary to protect anyone's rights. But even if a potential person does have some prima facie right to life, such a right could not possibly outweigh the right of a woman to obtain an abortion, since the rights of any actual person invariably outweigh those of any potential person, whenever the two conflict. Since this may not be immediately obvious in the case of a human fetus, let us look at another case.

Suppose that our space explorer falls into the hands of an alien culture, whose scientists decide to create a few hundred thousand or more human beings by breaking his body into component cells and using these to create fully developed human beings with, of course, his genetic code. We may imagine that each of these newly created men will have all of the original man's abilities, skills, knowledge, and so on, and also have an individual self-concept, in short that each of them will be a bona fide (though hardly unique) person. Imagine that the whole project will take only seconds, and that its chances of success are extremely high, and that our explorer knows all of this, and also knows that these people will be treated fairly. I maintain that in such a situation he would have every right to escape if he could, and thus to deprive all of these potential people of their potential lives; for his right to life outweighs all of theirs together, in spite of the fact that they are all genetically human, all innocent, and all have a very high probability of becoming people very soon, if only he refrains from acting.

Indeed, I think he would have a right to escape even if it were not his life which the alien scientists planned to take, but only a year of his freedom, or, indeed, only a day. Nor would he be obligated to stay if he had gotten captured (thus bringing all these people potentials into existence) because of his own carelessness, or even if he had done so deliberately, knowing the consequences. Regardless of how he got captured, he is not morally obligated to remain in captivity for *any* period of time for the sake of permitting any number of potential people to come into actuality, so great is the margin by which one actual person's right to liberty outweighs whatever right to life even a hundred thousand potential people have. And it seems reasonable to conclude that the rights of a woman will outweigh by a similar margin whatever right to life a fetus may have by virtue of its potential personhood.

Thus, neither a fetus's resemblance to a person, nor its potential for becoming a person provides any basis whatever for the claim that it has any significant right to life. Consequently, a woman's right to protect her health, happiness, freedom, and even her life[9] by terminating an unwanted pregnancy, will always override whatever right to life it may be appropriate to ascribe to a fetus, even a fully developed one. And thus, in the absence of any overwhelming social need for every possible child, the laws which restrict the right to obtain an abortion, or limit the period of pregnancy during which an abortion may be performed, are a wholly unjustified violation of a woman's most basic moral and constitutional rights.[10] . . .

Postscript on Infanticide

Since the publication of this article, many people have [pointed out] that my argument appears to justify not only abortion, but also infanticide. For a newborn infant is not significantly more personlike than an advanced fetus, and consequently it would seem that if the destruction of the latter is permissible so too must be that of the former. Inasmuch as most people, regardless of how they feel about the morality of abortion, consider infanticide a form of murder, this might appear to represent a serious flaw in my argument.

Now, if I am right in holding that it is only people who have a full-fledged right to life, and who can be murdered, and if the criteria of personhood are as I have described them, then it obviously follows that killing a newborn infant isn't murder. It does *not* follow, however, that infanticide is permissible, for two reasons. In the first place, it would be wrong, at least in this country and this period of history, and other things being equal, to kill a newborn infant, because even if its parents do not want it and would not suffer from its destruction, there are other people who would like to have it and would, in all probability, be deprived of a great deal of pleasure by its destruction. Thus, infanticide is wrong for reasons analogous to those which make it wrong to wantonly destroy natural resources, or great works of art.

Second, most people, at least in this country, value infants and would much prefer that they be preserved, even if foster parents are not immediately available. Most of us would rather be taxed to support orphanages than allow unwanted infants to be destroyed. So long as there are people who want an infant preserved,

and who are willing and able to provide the means of caring for it, under reasonably humane conditions, it is, *ceteris paribus*, wrong to destroy it.

But, it might be replied, if this argument shows that infanticide is wrong, at least at this time and in this country, doesn't it also show that abortion is wrong? After all, many people value fetuses, are disturbed by their destruction, and would much prefer that they be preserved, even at some cost to themselves. Furthermore, as a potential source of pleasure to some foster family, a fetus is just as valuable as an infant. There is, however, a crucial difference between the two cases: So long as the fetus is unborn, its preservation, contrary to the wishes of the pregnant woman, violates her rights to freedom, happiness, and self-determination. Her rights override the rights of those who would like the fetus preserved, just as if someone's life or limb is threatened by a wild animal, his right to protect himself by destroying the animal overrides the rights of those who would prefer that the animal not be harmed.

The minute the infant is born, however, its preservation no longer violates any of its mother's rights, even if she wants it destroyed, because she is free to put it up for adoption. Consequently, while the moment of birth does not mark any sharp discontinuity in the degree to which an infant possesses the right to life, it does mark the end of its mother's right to determine its fate. Indeed, if abortion could be performed without killing the fetus, she would never possess the right to have the fetus destroyed, for the same reasons that she has no right to have an infant destroyed.

On the other hand, it follows from my argument that when an unwanted or defective infant is born into a society which cannot afford and/or is not willing to care for it, then its destruction is permissible. This conclusion will, no doubt, strike many people as heartless and immoral; but remember that the very existence of people who feel this way, and who are willing and able to provide care for unwanted infants, is reason enough to conclude that they should be preserved.

Endnotes

1. For example, Roger Wertheimer, who in "Understanding the Abortion Argument" (*Philosophy and Public Affairs, 1,* no. 1 [Fall, 1971], 67–95), argues that the problem of the moral status of abortion is insoluble, in that the

dispute over the status of the fetus is not a question of fact at all, but only a question of how one responds to the facts.

2. John Noonan, "Abortion and the Catholic Church: A Summary History," *Natural Law Forum, 12* (1967), 125.

3. John Noonan, "Deciding Who Is Human," *Natural Law Forum, 13* (1968), 134.

4. "A Defense of Abortion."

5. We may safely ignore the fact that she might have avoided getting raped, e.g., by carrying a gun, since by similar means you might likewise have avoided getting kidnapped, and in neither case does the victim's failure to take all possible precautions against a highly unlikely event (as opposed to reasonable precautions against a rather likely event) mean that he is morally responsible for what happens.

6. Of course, the principle that it is (always) wrong to kill innocent human beings is in need of many other modifications, e.g., that it may be permissible to do so to save a greater number of innocent human beings, but we may safely ignore these complications here.

7. From here on, we will use "human" to mean genetically human, since the moral sense seems closely connected to, and perhaps derived from, the assumption that genetic humanity is sufficient for membership in the moral community.

8. Thomas L. Hayes, "A Biological View," *Commonweal, 85* (March 17, 1967), 677–78; quoted by Daniel Callahan, in *Abortion, Law, Choice, and Morality* (London: Macmillan & Co., 1970).

9. That is, insofar as the death rate, for the woman, is higher for childbirth than for early abortion.

10. My thanks to the following people, who were kind enough to read and criticize an earlier version of this paper: Herbert Gold, Gene Glass, Anne Lauterbach, Judith Thomson, Mary Mothersill, and Timothy Binkley.

---

16. A *Feminist Defense* of Abortion

SALLY MARKOWITZ

Sally Markowitz provides what she regards as a specifically feminist argument for abortion, that is, one that is grounded on awareness of women's oppression and a commitment to a more egalitarian society. She argues that because in the sexist society in which we live women are denied the equality to which they are entitled, a right to abortion is justified until that equality is guaranteed.

In the past few decades, the issue of abortion, long of concern to women, has gained a prominent place in the platforms of politicians and a respectable, if marginal, one in the writings of moral philosophers. It is natural to speculate that the rise of and reactions to the women's liberation movement explain the feverish pitch of the recent debate, and no doubt there is much to this speculation. And yet, philosophical analyses of abortion have had surprisingly little to say directly about either women or feminism. Instead, their primary concern has been to decide whether or not the fetus is a person, with a right to life like yours or mine. That this question deserves philosophical attention becomes especially clear when we consider the frightening (if fanciful) ways it is asked and answered by those in power. Nevertheless, as many feminists and some philosophers have recognized, the way we respond to the problem of personhood will not necessarily settle the dispute over abortion once and for all. On some views, a full account must deal with the rights of pregnant women as well.

In fact, one popular defense of abortion is based on the woman's right to autonomy and avoids the per-

Reprinted from *Social Theory and Practice*, Vol. 16, No. 1 (Spring 1990) by permission.

sonhood issue altogether. The central claim of the autonomy defense is that anti-abortion policies simply interfere in an impermissible way with the pregnant woman's autonomy. In what has become the classic philosophical statement of this view, Judith Jarvis Thomson ingeniously argues that even if the fetus has a right to life, it need not also have the right to use its mother's body to stay alive. The woman's body is her own property, to dispose of as she wishes.[1] But autonomy theorists need not rest their case on the vaguely disturbing notion of the pregnant woman's property rights to her own body. For example, Jane English, in another version of the view, argues that a woman is justified in aborting if pregnancy and childbearing will prevent her from pursuing the life she wants to live, the expression of her own autonomy.[2]

Philosophers have come to call this strategy the "feminist" or "woman's liberation" approach, and some version of it seems to be favored by many feminists.[3] This is no surprise since such a view may seem to be quite an improvement over accounts that regard personhood as the only essential issue. At least it recognizes women as bearers of rights as well as of babies. In what follows, however, I suggest that this defense may fall short of the feminist mark. Then I shall offer another defense, one derived not from the right to autonomy, but from an awareness of women's oppression and a commitment to a more egalitarian society.

I will assume throughout that the fetus has a serious right to life. I do so not because I believe this to be true, but rather because a feminist defense of abortion rights should be independent of the status of the fetus. For if, as many feminists believe, the move toward a sexually egalitarian society requires women's control of their reproductive lives, and if the permissibility of this control depends ultimately upon the status of the fetus, then the future of feminism rests upon how we resolve the personhood issue. This is not acceptable to most feminists. No doubt many feminists are comforted by arguments against the fetus's personhood. But regardless of the fetus's status, more must be said.

1.

What, then, from a feminist point of view, is wrong with an autonomy defense? Feminists should be wary on three counts. First, most feminists believe not only that women in our society are oppressed, but also that our failure to face the scope and depth of this oppression does much to maintain it. This makes feminists suspicious of perspectives, often called humanist or liberal, that focus only on the individual and deemphasize the issue of gender by either refusing to acknowledge that women have less power than men or denying that this inequity is worth much attention. While liberals and humanists may try to discuss social issues, including abortion, with as little mention as possible of gender, feminists tend to search for the hidden, unexpected, and perhaps unwelcome ways in which gender is relevant. From this perspective, defenses of abortion that focus only on the personhood of the fetus are not essentially or even especially feminist ones since they completely avoid any mention of gender. Autonomy arguments, though, are not much of an improvement. They may take into account the well-being of individual women, but they manage to skirt the issue of women's status, as a group, in a sexist society.

Second, the autonomy defense incorporates a (supposedly) gender-neutral right, one that belongs to every citizen; there's nothing special about being a woman—except, of course, for the inescapable fact that only women find themselves pregnant against their wills. Some feminists have become disillusioned with this gender-neutral approach. They reject it both on principle, because it shifts attention away from gender inequality, and for practical reasons, because it often works against women in the courts.[4] Instead, feminists have come to realize that sometimes gender should be relevant in claiming rights. Some of these rights, like adequate gynecological care, may be based on women's special physiology; others may stem from the special needs experienced by female casualties of a sexist society: the impoverished, divorced, or unwed mother, the rape victim, the anorexic teen, the coed who has been convinced that she lacks (or had better lack) mathematical aptitude. A thoroughly feminist analysis, then, will not hesitate, when appropriate, to claim a right on the basis of gender, rather than in spite of it.[5] To do otherwise in the case of abortion may be not only to deny the obvious, but also to obscure the relation of reproductive practices to women's oppression.

The third problem feminists might have with an autonomy defense involves the content of the human ideal on which the right to autonomy rests. Some feminists, influenced by Marxist and socialist traditions, may reject an ideal that seems to be so ultimately connected with the individualistic ideology of capitalism. Others may suspect that this ideology is not just capitalist but male-biased. And if feminists hesitate to justify abortion by appeal to a gender-neutral right derived from a gender-neutral ideal, they are even more suspicious of an ideal that seems to be gender-neutral when really it's not. Increasingly, feminists reject the ideals of older feminists, like Simone de Beauvoir, who, in promoting for women what appeared to be an androgynous human ideal, unwittingly adopted one that was androcentric, or male-centered. Instead, feminists seek to free themselves from the misogynist perspective that sees women as incomplete men and ignores, devalues, or denies the existence of particularly female psychologies, values, and experiences. On this view, to fashion a feminist human ideal we must look to women's values and experiences—or at least we must not look only to men's.[6]

This re-evaluation has important implications for the abortion issue, since many feminists consider an overriding right to autonomy to be a characteristically male ideal, while nurturance and responsibility for others (the paradigmatic case of which is motherhood) to be characteristically female ones. Indeed, in the name of such women's values, some women who call themselves feminists have actually joined the anti-abortionist camp.[7] Most feminists, of course, don't go this far. But, paradoxically, many seem to find the ideal of autonomy less acceptable than the right to abortion it is supposed to justify. Clearly, something is awry. (I shall have more to say in section 4 about how autonomy is important to feminists.)

Feminists, therefore, need another argument. Instead of resting on an ideal many feminists reject, a feminist defense of abortion should somehow reflect an awareness of women's oppression and a commitment to ending it.

2.

Of all the philosophers, feminist and otherwise, who have discussed abortion, Alison Jaggar seems to be the only one to address the problem from this perspective. Jaggar argues that in societies where mothers bear the responsibility for pregnancy, birth, and child-rearing, women should control abortion decisions. Women who live in other, more cooperative social communities (wherever they are), where members of both sexes share such responsibilities, cannot claim a right of the same force. The strength of a woman's say about whether or not to abort, then should be relative to the amount of support (financial, emotional, physical, medical, and otherwise) she can expect from those around her.[8]

It is disheartening that the philosophical community has not paid Jaggar's paper the attention it merits in the decade and a half since its publication, but this lapse is hardly surprising. The notion of the individual's right to autonomy is so firmly entrenched that we have difficulty even entertaining other approaches. We find ourselves invoking such rights perhaps without realizing it even when we neither want nor need to. And Jaggar is no exception; despite the promising intuition with which she starts, Jaggar finally offers us another, albeit more sophisticated, version of the autonomy argument. Quite simply, her argument implies that if abortion ought to be permissible in some societies but not in others, this is only because pregnancy and motherhood create obstacles to personal autonomy in some societies but not in others.

Jaggar bases her argument for abortion rights in our society on two principles. The first, or Right to Life Principle, holds that

> the right to life, when it is claimed for a human being, means the right to a full human life and to whatever means are necessary to achieve this. . . . To be born, then, is only one of the necessary conditions for a full human life. The others presumably include nutritious food, breathable air, warm human companionship, and so on. If anyone has a right to life, she or he must be entitled to all of these.[9]

According to the second, or Personal Control Principle, "Decisions should be made by those, and only by those, who are importantly affected by them."[10] In our society, then, the state cannot legitimately set itself up as the protector of the fetus's right to life (as Jaggar has characterized it) because the mother and not the state will be expected to provide for this right, both during pregnancy and afterwards. But since, by the Personal Control Principle, only those whose lives will be importantly affected have the right to make a decision, in our society the pregnant woman should determine whether to continue her pregnancy.

Jaggar's argument incorporates both liberal and feminist perspectives, and there is a tension between them. Her argument is feminist rather than merely liberal because it does not rest exclusively on a universal right to autonomy. Instead, it takes seriously the contingent and socially variable features of reproduction and parenting, their relationship to women's position in a society, and the effect of anti-abortion policy on this position. But her argument is also a liberal one. Consider, for example, the Personal Control Principle. While Jaggar doesn't explicitly spell out its motivation, she does state that the principle "provides the fundamental justification for democracy and is accepted by most shades of political opinion."[11] Surely this wide acceptance has something to do with the belief, equally widely held, that citizens should be able to decide for themselves what courses their lives should take, especially when some courses involve sacrifices or burdens. This becomes clear when Jaggar explains that an individual or organization has no moral claim as a protector of the right to life "that would justify its insistence on just one of the many conditions necessary to a full human life, in circumstances where this would place the burden of fulfilling all the other conditions squarely on the shoulders of some other individual or organization."[12] Once again we have an appeal to a universal right to personal autonomy, indeed a right based on an ideal which not only might be unacceptable to many feminists, but may cast the net too widely even for some liberals. For example, one might claim that taxation policies designed to finance social programs interfere with personal choices about how to spend earnings, a matter that will have important consequences for one's life. Such a view also permits a range of private actions which some liberals may believe are immoral: For example, an adult grandchild may decide to stop caring for a burdensome and senile grandparent if such care places a heavy burden on the grandchild.

I shall not attempt to pass judgment here on the desirability of either redistributing income through taxation or passing laws requiring us to be Good Samaritans in our private lives. Nor do I want to beg the question, which I shall discuss later, of whether reproductive autonomy is, in all circumstances, overridingly important in a way other sorts of autonomy may not be. I can leave these matters open because a feminist defense of abortion need not depend on how we settle them. For there is a significant difference between the sacrifices required by restrictive abortion polices and those required by enforcing other sorts of Good Samaritanism: Taxes and laws against letting the aged or handicapped starve to death apply to everyone; those prohibiting abortion apply only to women. While anyone might end up with a helpless, cantankerous grandparent and most of us end up paying taxes, only women end up pregnant. So anti-abortion laws require sacrifice not of everyone, but only of women.

———

3.

This brings us to what I regard as the crucial question: When, if ever, can people be required to sacrifice for the sake of others? And how can feminists answer this question in a way that rests not on the individual right to personal autonomy, but on a view of social reality that takes seriously power relations between genders? I suggest the following principle, which I shall call the Impermissible Sacrifice Principle: *When one social group in a society is systematically oppressed by another, it is impermissible to require the oppressed group to make sacrifices that will exacerbate or perpetuate this oppression.* (Note that this principle does not exempt the members of oppressed groups from *all* sorts of sacrifices just because they are oppressed; they may be as morally responsible as anyone for rendering aid in some circumstances. Only sacrifices that will clearly perpetuate their oppression are ruled out.)

The Impermissible Sacrifice Principle focuses on power relationships between groups rather than on the rights of individuals. This approach will suit not only feminists but all who recognize and deplore other sorts of systematic social oppression as well. Indeed, if we take our opposition to oppression seriously, this approach may be necessary. Otherwise, when policy decisions are made, competing goals and commitments may distract us from the conditions we claim to deplore and encourage decisions that allow such conditions to remain. Even worse, these other goals and commitments can be used as excuses for perpetuating oppression. Testing policies against the Impermissible Sacrifice Principle keeps this from happening.

Feminists should welcome the applicability of the Impermissible Sacrifice Principle to groups other than women. Radical feminists are sometimes accused of being blind to any sort of oppression but their own. The Impermissible Sacrifice Principle, however, enables feminists to demonstrate solidarity with other oppressed groups by resting the case for abortion on the same principle that might, for example, block a policy requiring the poor rather than the rich to bear the tax burden, or workers rather than management to take a pay cut. On the other hand, feminists may worry that the Impermissible Sacrifice Principle, taken by itself, may not yield the verdict on abortion feminists seek. For if some radical feminists err by recognizing only women's oppression, some men err by not recognizing it at all. So the Impermissible Sacrifice Principle must be supplemented by what I shall call the Feminist Proviso: *Women are, as a group, sexually oppressed by men; and this oppression can neither be completely understood in terms of, nor otherwise reduced to, oppressions of other sorts.*

Feminists often understand this oppression to involve men's treating women as breeding machines, sexual or aesthetic objects, nurturers who need no nurturance. Women become alienated from their bodies, their sexuality, their work, their intellect, their emotions, their moral agency. Of course, feminists disagree about exactly how to formulate this analysis, especially since women experience oppression differently depending on their class, race, and ethnicity. But however we decide to understand women's oppression, we can be sure an anti-abortion policy will make it worse.

Adding the Feminist Proviso, then, keeps (or makes) sexism visible, ensuring that women are one of the oppressed groups to which the Principle applies. This should hardly need saying. Yet by focusing on other sorts of oppression the Principle might cover, men often trivialize or ignore feminists' demands and women's pain. For example, someone (perhaps a white male) who is more sympathetic to the claims of racial minorities or workers than to those of women

might try to trivialize or deny the sexual oppression of a white, affluent woman (perhaps his wife) by reminding her that she's richer than an unemployed black male and so should not complain. The Feminist Proviso also prevents an affluent white woman who rejects the unwelcome sexual advances of a minority or working class male from being dismissed (or dismissing herself) as a racist or classist. She may well be both. But she also lives in a world where, all things being equal, she is fair sexual game, in one way or another, for any male.[13] Finally, the Impermissible Sacrifice Principle in conjunction with the Feminist Proviso might be used to block the view that a black or Third World woman's first obligation is to bear children to swell the ranks of the revolution, regardless of the consequences of maternity within her culture. Having children for this reason may be a legitimate choice; but she also may have independent grounds to refuse.

I have added the Feminist Proviso so that the Impermissible Sacrifice Principle cannot be used to frustrate a feminist analysis. But I must also emphasize that the point is not to pit one oppressed group against another, but to make sure that the men in otherwise progressive social movements do not ignore women's oppression or, worse, find "politically correct" justifications for it. Women refuse to wait until "after the revolution" not just because they are impatient, but also because they have learned that not all revolutions are feminist ones.

The Impermissible Sacrifice Principle and the Feminist Proviso together, then, justify abortion on demand for women *because they live in a sexist society.* This approach not only gives a more explicitly feminist justification of abortion than the autonomy defense; it also gives a stronger one. For autonomy defenses are open to objections and qualifications that a feminist one avoids. Consider the ways the feminist approach handles these four challenges to the autonomy defense.

First, some philosophers have dismissed autonomy defenses by suggesting blithely that we simply compensate the pregnant woman.[14] Of what, though, will such compensation consist? Maternity leave? Tax breaks? Prenatal healthcare? Twenty points added to her civil-service exam score? Such benefits lighten one's load, no doubt. But what women suffer by being forced to continue unwanted pregnancies is not merely a matter of finances of missed opportunities; in a sexist society, there is reason to expect that an anti-abortion policy will reinforce a specifically *sexual* oppression, whatever sorts of compensation are offered. Indeed, even talk of compensation may be misguided, since it implies a prior state when things were as they should be; compensation seeks to restore the balance after a temporary upset. But in a sexist society, there is no original balance; women's oppression is the status quo. Even if individual women are compensated by money, services, or opportunities, sexual oppression may remain.

Second, an autonomy defense may seem appropriate only in cases where a woman engages in "responsible" sex: It is one thing to be a victim of rape or even contraceptive failure, one might argue; it is quite another voluntarily to have unprotected intercourse. A feminist defense suggests another approach. First, we might question the double standard that requires that women pay for "irresponsible" sex while men don't have to, even though women are oppressed by men. More importantly, if we focus on the *way* women are oppressed, we may understand many unwanted pregnancies to result from fear and paralysis rather than irresponsibility. For in a sexist society, many women simply do not believe they control the conditions under which they have sex. And, sad to say, often they may be right.[15]

Third, what about poor women's access to abortion? The sort of right the autonomy theorists invoke, after all, seems to be a right to noninterference by the state. But this negative right seems to be in tension with a demand for state-funded abortions, especially since not everyone supports abortions. At any rate, we will need another argument to justify the funding of abortion for poor women. The defense I suggest, however, is clearly committed to providing all women with access to abortion, since to allow abortions only for those who can afford them forces poor women, who are doubly oppressed, to make special sacrifices. An egalitarian society must liberate all women, not just the rich ones.

Finally, autonomy defenses allow, indeed invite, the charge that the choice to abort is selfish. Even Thomson finds abortion, while not unjust, often to be "selfish" or "indecent." Although she has deprived nothing of its rights, the woman who aborts has chosen self-interested autonomy over altruism in the same way one might choose to watch while a child starves. Of course, one is tempted to point out that the (largely male) world of commerce and politics thrives on such "morally indecent" but legal actions. But then feminists are reduced to claiming a right to be as selfish as men are. Moreover, once the specter of selfishness is raised, this defense does not allow feminists to make enough of male anti-abortionists' motives. On an autonomy defense, these motives are simply not relevant, let alone damning, and feminists who dwell on them seem to be resorting to *ad hominems*. From a feminist perspective, however, abortion is a political issue, one which essentially concerns the interests of and power relations between men and women. Thus, what women and men can expect to gain or lose from an abortion policy becomes the point rather than the subject of *ad hominem* arguments.[16]

The approach I propose does well on each of these important counts. But its real test comes when we weigh the demands of the Impermissible Sacrifice Principle against fetal rights; for we have required that a feminist analysis be independent of the status of the fetus. Indeed, we may even be tempted to regard fetuses as constituting just the sort of oppressed group to whom the principle applies, and surely a fetus about to be aborted is in worse shape than the woman who carries it.

However, it may not make sense to count fetuses as an oppressed group. A disadvantaged one, perhaps. But the Impermissible Sacrifice Principle does not prescribe that more disadvantaged groups have a right to aid from less advantaged ones; it focuses only on the particular disadvantage of social oppression. That the fetus has a serious right to life does not imply that it's the sort of being that can be oppressed, if it cannot yet enter into the sorts of social relationships that constitute oppression. I cannot argue for this here; in any case, I suspect my best argument will not convince everyone. But feminists have another, more pointed response.

Whether or not we can weigh the disadvantage of fetuses against the oppression of women, we must realize what insisting on such a comparison does to the debate. It narrows our focus, turning it back to the conflict between the rights of fetuses and of women (even if now this conflict is between the rights of groups rather than of individuals). This is certainly not to deny that fetal rights should be relevant to an abortion policy. But feminists must insist that the oppression of women should be relevant too. And it is also relevant that unless our society changes in deep and global ways, anti-abortion policies, intentionally or not, will perpetuate women's oppression by men. This, then, is where feminists must stand firm.

Does this mean that instead of overriding the fetus's right to life by women's right to autonomy, I am proposing that feminists override the fetus's right by the right of women to live in a sexually egalitarian society? This is a difficult position for feminists but not an impossible one, especially for feminists with utilitarian leanings. Many feminists, for example, see sexism as responsible for a culture of death: war, violence, child abuse, ecological disaster. Eradicate sexism, it might be argued, and we will save more lives than we will lose. Some feminists might even claim that an oppressed woman's fate can be worse than that of an aborted fetus. Although I will not argue for such claims, they may be less implausible than they seem. But feminists need not rest their case on them. Instead, they must simply insist that society

must change so that women are no longer oppressed. Such changes, of course, may require of men sacrifices unwelcome beyond their wildest dreams. But that, according to a feminist analysis, is the point.

So we should not see the choice as between liberating women and saving fetuses, but between two ways of respecting the fetus's right to life. The first requires women to sacrifice while men benefit. The second requires deep social changes that will ensure that men no longer gain and women lose through our practices of sexuality, reproduction, and parenthood. To point out how men gain from women's compulsory pregnancy is to steal the misplaced moral thunder from those male authorities—fathers, husbands, judges, congressmen, priests, philosophers—who, exhorting women to do their duty, present themselves as the benevolent, disinterested protectors of fetuses against women's selfishness. Let feminists insist that the conditions for refraining from having abortions is a sexually egalitarian society. If men do not respond, and quickly, they will have indicated that fetal life isn't so important to them after all, or at least not important enough to give up the privileges of being male in a sexist society. If this makes feminists look bad, it makes men look worse still.

Endnotes

1. Judith Jarvis Thomson, "A Defense of Abortion," *Philosophy and Public Affairs 1* (1971): 47–66.

2. Jane English, "Abortion and the Concept of a Person," in *Today's Moral Problems*, ed. by Richard A. Wasserstrom (New York: Macmillan, 1985), pp. 448–457.

3. Peter Singer, *Practical Ethics* (Cambridge: Cambridge University Press, 1979), p. 113.

4. Catherine A. MacKinnon, *Feminism Unmodified: Discourses on Life and Law* (Cambridge: Harvard University Press, 1987), pp. 35–36.

5. See, for example, Alison Jaggar, *Feminism Politics and Human Nature* (Totowa, New Jersey: Rowman & Allanheld, 1983), especially Parts 1 and 2; and Catherine A. MacKinnon, *Feminism Unmodified: Discourses on Life and Law*.

6. See Sara Ruddick, "Maternal Thinking," *Feminist Studies 6* (1980): 345–346; Nancy Chodorow, *The Reproduction of Mothering: Psychoanalysis and the Sociology of Gender* (Berkeley and Los Angeles: University of California Press, 1978); Carol Gilligan, *In a Different Voice: Psychological Theory and Women's Development* (Cambridge: Harvard University Press, 1982).

7. Sidney Callahan, "A Pro-Life Feminist Makes Her Case," *Commonweal* (April 25, 1986), quoted in the *Utne Reader 20* (1987): 104–108.

8. Alison Jaggar, "Abortion and a Woman's Right to Decide," in *Philosophy and Sex*, ed. Robert Baker and Frank Elliston (Buffalo: Prometheus Press, 1975), pp. 324–337.

9. "Abortion and a Woman's Right to Decide," p. 328.

10. "Abortion and a Woman's Right to Decide," p. 328.

11. "Abortion and a Woman's Right to Decide," p. 329.

12. For classic discussions of sexism in the civil rights movement, see Susan Brownmiller, *Against Our Will: Men, Women, and Rape* (New York: Simon and Schuster, 1975), especially pp. 210–255; and Michelle Wallace, *Black Macho and the Myth of the Superwoman* (New York: Dial Press, 1978).

13. [This reference, apparently to Jaggar, is missing in the original—Ed.]

14. Michael Tooley, "Abortion and Infanticide," in Joel Feinberg, ed., *The Problem of Abortion* (Belmont, California: Wadsworth, 1983).

15. MacKinnon, *Feminism Unmodified*, p. 95.

16. This approach also allows us to understand the deep divisions between women on this issue. For many women in traditional roles fear the immediate effects on their lives of women's liberation generally and a permissive abortion policy in particular. On this, see Kristen Luker, *Abortion and the Politics of Motherhood* (Berkeley: University of California Press, 1984), especially pp. 158–215.

---

17. *Euthanasia, Killing, and Letting Die*

JAMES RACHELS

James Rachels criticizes a policy statement of the American Medical Association on the grounds that it endorses the doctrine that there is an important moral difference between active and passive euthanasia. Rachels denies that there is any moral difference between the two. He argues that once we judge a patient would be better off dead, it should not matter much whether that patient is killed or let die. He points out that both killing and letting die can be intentional and deliberate and can proceed from the same motives; further, that when killing and letting die are similar in these and other relevant respects, our moral assessment of these acts is also similar. Rachels concludes by considering a number of counterarguments to his view and finds them all wanting. In particular, Rachels rejects the idea that the killing and letting die distinction can be supported on the grounds that our duty to refrain from harming people is much stronger than our duty to help people in need. Rather, he contends that when conditions are similar our duty to refrain from harming people and our duty to help people in need have a similar moral force.

Dr. F. J. Ingelfinger, former editor of *The New England Journal of Medicine,* observes that

> this is the heyday of the ethicist in medicine. He delineates the rights of patients, of experimental subjects, of fetuses, of mothers, of animals, and even of doctors. (And what a far cry it is from the days when medical "ethics" consisted of condemning economic improprieties such as fee splitting and advertising!) With impeccable logic—once certain basic assumptions are granted—and with graceful prose, the ethicist develops his arguments. . . .
> Yet his precepts are essentially the products of armchair exercise and remain abstract and idealistic until they have been tested in the laboratory of experience.[1]

One problem with such armchair exercises, he complains, is that in spite of the impeccable logic and the graceful prose, the result is often an absolutist ethic which is unsatisfactory when applied to particular cases, and which is therefore of little use to the practicing physician. Unlike some absolutist philosophers, "the practitioner appears to prefer the principles of individualism. As there are few atheists in fox holes, there tend to be few absolutists at the bedside."[2]

I must concede at the outset that this chapter is another exercise in "armchair ethics" in the sense that I am not a physician but a philosopher. Yet I am no absolutist; and my purpose is to examine a doctrine that is held in an absolute form by many doctors. The doctrine is that there is an important moral difference between active and passive euthanasia, such that even though the latter is sometimes permissible, the former is always forbidden. This is an absolute which doctors hold "at the bedside" as well as in the seminar room, and the "principles of individualism" make little headway against it. But I will argue that this is an irrational dogma, and that there is no sound moral basis for it.

I will not argue, simply, that active euthanasia is all right. Rather, I will be concerned with the *relation* between active euthanasia and passive euthanasia: I will argue that there is no moral difference between them. By this I mean that there is no reason to prefer one over the other as a matter of principle—the fact that one case of euthanasia is active, while another is passive, is not *itself* a reason to think one morally better than the other. If you already think that passive euthanasia is all right, and you are convinced by my arguments, then you may conclude that active euthanasia must be all right, too. On the other hand, if you believe that active euthanasia is immoral, you may want to conclude that passive euthanasia must be immoral, too. Although I prefer the former alternative, I will not argue for it here. I will only argue that the two forms of euthanasia are morally equivalent—either both are acceptable or both are unacceptable.

I am aware that this will at first seem incredible to many readers, but I hope that this impression will be dispelled as the discussion proceeds. The discussion will be guided by two methodological considerations, both of which are touched on in the editorial quoted above. The first has to do with my "basic assumptions." My arguments are intended to appeal to all reasonable people, and not merely to those who already share my philosophical preconceptions. Therefore, I will try not to rely on any assumptions that cannot be accepted by any reasonable person. None of my arguments will depend on morally eccentric premises. Second, Dr. Ingelfinger is surely correct when he says that we must be as concerned with the realities of medical practice as with the more abstract issues of moral theory. As he notes, the philosopher's precepts "remain abstract and idealistic until they are tested in the laboratory of experience." Part of my argument will be precisely that, when "tested in the laboratory of experience," the doctrine in question has terrible results. I believe that if this doctrine were to be recognized as irrational, and rejected by the medical profession, the benefit to both doctors and patients would be enormous. In this sense, my paper is not intended as an "armchair exercise" at all.

The American Medical Association Policy Statement

"Active euthanasia," as the term is used, means taking some positive action designed to kill the patient; for example, giving him a lethal injection of potassium chloride. "Passive euthanasia," on the other hand, means simply refraining from doing anything to keep the patient alive. In passive euthanasia we withhold medication or other life-sustaining therapy, or we refuse to perform surgery, etc., and let the patient die "naturally" of whatever ills already afflict him.

Many doctors and theologians prefer to use the term *euthanasia* only in connection with active euthanasia, and they use other words to refer to what I am calling "passive euthanasia"—for example, instead of "passive euthanasia" they may speak of "the right to death with dignity." One reason for this choice of terms is the emotional impact of the words: It *sounds* so much better to defend "death with dignity" than to advocate "euthanasia" of any sort. And of course if one believes that there is a great moral difference between active and passive euthanasia—as most doctors and religious writers do—then one may prefer a terminology which puts as much psychological distance as possible between them. However, I do not want to become involved in a pointless dispute about terminology, because nothing of substance depends on which label is used. I will stay with the terms *active euthanasia* and *passive euthanasia* because they are the most convenient; but if the reader prefers a different terminology he may substitute his own throughout, and my arguments will be unaffected.

The belief that there is an important moral difference between active and passive euthanasia obviously has important consequences for medical practice. It makes a difference to what doctors are willing to do. Consider, for example, the following familiar situation. A patient who is dying from incurable cancer of the throat is in terrible pain that we can no longer satisfactorily alleviate. He is certain to die within a few days, but he decides that he does not want to go on living for those days since the pain is unbearable. So he asks the doctor to end his life now; and his family joins in the request. One way that the doctor might comply with this request is simply by killing the patient with a lethal injection. Most doctors would not do that, not only because of the possible legal consequences, but because they think such a course would be immoral. And this is understandable: The idea of killing someone goes against very deep moral feelings; and besides, as we are often reminded, it is the special business of doctors to save and protect life, not to destroy it. Yet, even so, the physician may sympathize with the dying patient's request and feel that it is entirely reasonable for him to prefer death now rather than after a few more days of agony. The doctrine that we are considering tells the doctor what to do: It says that although he may not administer the lethal injection—that would be "active euthanasia," which is forbidden—he *may* withhold treatment and let the patient die sooner than he otherwise would.

It is no wonder that this simple idea is so widely accepted, for it seems to give the doctor a way out of his dilemma without having to kill the patient, and without having to prolong the patient's agony. The idea is not a new one. What *is* new is that the idea is now being incorporated into official documents of medical ethics. What was once unofficially done is now becoming official policy. The idea is expressed, for example, in a 1973 policy statement of the American Medical Association, which says (in its entirety):

> The intentional termination of the life of one human being by another—mercy killing—is contrary to that for which the medical profession stands and is contrary to the policy of the American Medical Association.
>
>   The cessation of the employment of extraordinary means to prolong the life of the body when there is irrefutable evidence that biological death is imminent is the decision of the patient and/or his immediate family. The advice and judgment of the physician should be freely available to the patient and/or his immediate family.[3]

This is a cautiously worded statement, and it is not clear *exactly* what is being affirmed. I take it, however, that at least these three propositions are intended:

1.   Killing patients is absolutely forbidden; however, it is sometimes permissible to allow patients to die.
2.   It is permissible to allow a patient to die if (a) there is irrefutable evidence that he will die soon anyway; (b) "extraordinary" measures would be

required to keep him alive; and (c) the patient and/or his immediate family requests it.
3.   Doctors should make their own advice and judgments available to the patient and/or his immediate family when the latter are deciding whether to request that the patient be allowed to die.

The first proposition expresses the doctrine which is the main subject of this paper. As for the third, it seems obvious enough, provided that 1 and 2 are accepted, so I shall say nothing further about it.

I do want to say a few things about 2. Physicians often allow patients to die; however, they do *not* always keep to the guidelines set out in 2. For example, a doctor may leave instructions that if a hopeless, comatose patient suffers cardiac arrest, nothing be done to start his heart beating again. "No-coding" is the name given to this practice, and the consent of the patient and/or his immediate family is not commonly sought. This is thought to be a medical decision (in reality, of course, it is a moral one) which is the doctor's affair. To take a different sort of example, when a Down's syndrome infant is born with an intestinal blockage, the doctor and parents may agree that there will be no operation to remove the blockage, so that the baby will die.[4] (If the same infant were born without the obstruction, it certainly would not be killed. This is a clear application of the idea that "letting die" is all right even though killing is forbidden.) But in such cases it is clear that the baby is *not* going to die soon anyway. If the surgery were performed, the baby would proceed to a "normal" infancy—normal, that is, for a mongoloid. Moreover, the treatment required to save the baby—abdominal surgery—can hardly be called "extraordinary" by today's medical standards.

Therefore, all three conditions which the AMA statement places on the decision to let die are commonly violated. It is beyond the scope of this paper to determine whether doctors are right to violate those conditions. But I firmly believe that the second requirement—2b—is not acceptable. Only a little reflection is needed to show that the distinction between ordinary and extraordinary means is not important. Even a very conservative, religiously oriented writer such as Paul Ramsey stresses this. Ramsey gives these examples:

Suppose that a diabetic patient long accustomed to self-administration of insulin falls victim to terminal cancer, or suppose that a terminal cancer patient suddenly develops diabetes. Is he in the first case obliged to continue, and in the second case obliged to begin, insulin treatment and die painfully of cancer, or in either or both cases may the patient choose rather to pass into diabetic coma and an earlier death? . . . Or an old man slowly deteriorating who from simply being inactive and recumbent gets pneumonia: Are we to use antibiotics in a likely successful attack upon this disease which from time immemorial has been called "the old man's friend"?[5]

I agree with Ramsey, and with many other writers, that in such cases treatment may be withheld even though it is not "extraordinary" by any reasonable standard. Contrary to what is implied by the AMA statement, the distinction between heroic and non-heroic means of treatment *cannot* be used to determine when treatment is or is not mandatory.

Killing and Letting Die

I return now to the distinction between active and passive euthanasia. Of course, not every doctor believes that this distinction is morally important. Over twenty years ago Dr. D. C. S. Cameron of the American Cancer Society said that "Actually the difference between euthanasia [i.e., killing] and letting the patient die by omitting life-sustaining treatment is a moral quibble."[6] I argue that Cameron was right.

The initial thought can be expressed quite simply. In any case in which euthanasia seems desirable, it is because we think that the patient would literally be better off dead—or at least, no worse off dead—than continuing the kind of life available to him. (Without this assumption, even *passive* euthanasia would be unthinkable.) But, as far as the main question of ending the patient's life is concerned, it does not matter whether the euthanasia is active or passive: *In either case,* he ends up dead sooner than he otherwise would. And if the results are the same, why should it matter so much which method is used?

Moreover, we need to remember that, in cases such as that of the terminal cancer patient, the justification for allowing him to die, rather than prolonging his life

for a few more hopeless days, is that he is in horrible pain. But if we simply withhold treatment, it may take him *longer* to die, and so he will suffer *more* than he would if we were to administer the lethal injection. This fact provides strong reason for thinking that, once we have made the initial decision not to prolong his agony, active euthanasia is actually preferable to passive euthanasia rather than the reverse. It also shows a kind of incoherence in the conventional view: To say that passive euthanasia is preferable is to endorse the option which leads to more suffering rather than less, and is contrary to the humanitarian impulse which prompts the decision not to prolong his life in the first place.

But many people are convinced that there is an important moral difference between active and passive euthanasia because they think that, in passive euthanasia, the doctor does not really *do* anything. No action whatever is taken; the doctor simply does nothing, and the patient dies of whatever ills already afflict him. In active euthanasia, however, we *do something* to bring about the patient's death. We kill him. Thus, the difference between active and passive euthanasia is thought to be the difference between doing something to bring about someone's death, and not doing anything to bring about anyone's death. And of course if we conceive the matter in *this* way, passive euthanasia seems preferable. Ramsey, who denounces the view I am defending as "extremist" and who regards the active/passive distinction as one of the "flexibly wise categories of traditional medical ethics," takes just this view of the matter. He says that the choice between active and passive euthanasia "is not a choice between directly and indirectly willing and doing something. *It is rather the important choice between doing something and doing nothing,* or (better said) ceasing to do something that was begun in order to do something that is better because now more fitting."[7]

This is a very misleading way of thinking, for it ignores the fact that in passive euthanasia the doctor *does* do one thing which is very important: Namely, he lets the patient die. We may overlook this obvious fact—or at least, we may put it out of our minds—if we concentrate only on a very restricted way of describing what happens: "The doctor does not administer medication or any other therapy; he does not instruct the nurses to administer any such medication;

he does not perform any surgery"; and so on. And of course this description of what happens is correct, as far as it goes—these are all things that the doctor does not do. But the point is that the doctor *does* let the patient die when he could save him, and this must be included in the description, too.

There is another reason why we might fall into this error. We might confuse *not saving* someone with *letting him die*. Suppose a patient is dying, and Dr. X could prolong his life. But he decides not to do so and the patient dies. Now it is true of everyone on earth that he did not save the patient. Dr. X did not save him, and neither did you, and neither did I. So we might be tempted to think that all of us are in the same moral position, reasoning that since neither you nor I are responsible for the patient's death, neither is Dr. X. None of us did anything. This, however, is a mistake, for even though it is true that none of us saved the patient, it is *not* true that we all let him die. In order to let someone die, one must be *in a position* to save him. You and I were not in a position to save the patient, so we did not let him die. Dr. X, on the other hand, was in a position to save him, and did let him die. Thus the doctor is in a special moral position which not just everyone is in.

Here we must remember some elementary points, which are so obvious that they would not be worth mentioning except for the fact that overlooking them is a source of so much confusion in this area. The act of letting someone die may be intentional and deliberate, just as the act of killing someone may be intentional and deliberate. Moreover, the doctor is *responsible* for his decision to let the patient die, just as he would be responsible for giving the patient a lethal injection. The decision to let a patient die is subject to moral appraisal in the same way that a decision to kill is subject to moral appraisal: It may be assessed as wise or unwise, compassionate or sadistic, right or wrong. If a doctor deliberately let a patient die who was suffering from a routinely curable illness, then he would be to blame for what he did, just as he would be to blame if he had needlessly killed the patient. It would be no defense at all for him to insist that, *really*, he didn't "do anything" but just stand there. We would all know that he did do something very serious indeed, for he let the patient die.

These considerations show how misleading it is to characterize the difference between active and pas-

sive euthanasia as a difference between doing something (killing), for which the doctor may be morally culpable; and doing nothing (just standing there while the patient dies), for which the doctor is not culpable. The real difference between them is, rather, the difference between *killing* and letting die, both of which are actions for which a doctor, or anyone else, will be morally responsible.

Now we can formulate our problem more precisely. If there is an important moral difference between active and passive euthanasia, it must be because *killing someone is morally worse than letting someone die.* But is it? Is killing, in itself, worse than letting die? In order to investigate this issue, we may consider two cases which are exactly alike except that one involves killing where the other involves letting someone die. Then we can ask whether this difference makes any difference to our moral assessments. It is important that the cases be *exactly* alike except for this one difference, since otherwise we cannot be confident that it is *this* difference which accounts for any variation in our assessments.

1. Smith stands to gain a large inheritance if anything should happen to his six-year-old cousin. One evening while the child is taking his bath, Smith sneaks into the bathroom and drowns the child, and then arranges things so that it will look like an accident.

2. Jones also stands to gain if anything should happen to his six-year-old cousin. Like Smith, Jones sneaks in planning to drown the child in his bath. However, just as he enters the bathroom Jones sees the child slip, hit his head, and fall face down in the water. Jones is delighted; he stands by, ready to push the child's head back under if it is necessary, but it is not necessary. With only a little thrashing about, the child drowns all by himself, "accidentally," as Jones watches and does nothing.

Now Smith killed the child, while Jones "merely" let the child die. That is the only difference between them. Did either man behave better, from a moral point of view? Is there a moral difference between them? *If the difference between killing and letting die were itself a morally important matter, then we should say that Jones's behavior was less reprehensible than Smith's.* But do we actually want to say that? I think not, for several reasons. In the first place, both men acted from the same motive, personal gain, and both had exactly the same end in view when they acted. We may infer from Smith's conduct that he is a bad man, although we may withdraw or modify that judgment if we learn certain further facts about him; for example, that he is mentally deranged. But would we not also infer the very same thing about Jones from his conduct? And would not the same further considerations also be relevant to any modification of that judgment? Moreover, suppose Jones pleaded in his defense, "After all, I didn't kill the child. I only stood there and let him die." Again, if letting die were in itself less bad than killing, this defense should have some weight. But—morally, at least—it does not. Such a "defense" can only be regarded as a grotesque perversion of moral reasoning.

Thus, it seems that when we are careful not to smuggle in any further differences which prejudice the issue, the mere difference between killing and letting die does not itself make any difference to the morality of actions concerning life and death.[8]

Now it may be pointed out, quite properly, that the cases of euthanasia with which doctors are concerned are not like this at all. They do not involve personal gain or the destruction of normal, healthy children. Doctors are concerned only with cases in which the patient's life is of no further use to him, or in which the patient's life has become or soon will become a positive burden. However, the point is the same in those cases: The difference between killing or letting die does not, *in itself*, make a difference, from the point of view of morality. If a doctor lets a patient die, for humane reasons, he is in the same moral position as if he had given the patient a lethal injection for humane reasons. If his decision was wrong—if, for example, the patient's illness was in fact curable—then the decision would be equally regrettable no matter which method was used to carry it out. And if the doctor's decision was the right one, then the method he used is not itself important.

The AMA statement isolates the crucial issue very well: "the intentional termination of the life of one human being by another." But then the statement goes on to deny that the cessation of treatment *is* the intentional termination of a life. This is where the mistake comes in, for what is the cessation of treatment, in those circumstances, if it is not "the intentional termination of the life of one human being by another"? Of course it is exactly that; if it were not, there would be no point to it.

Counterarguments

Our argument has now brought us to this point: We cannot draw any moral distinction between active and passive euthanasia on the grounds that one involves killing while the other only involves letting someone die, because that is a difference that does not make a difference, from a moral point of view. Some people will find this hard to accept. One reason, I think, is that they fail to distinguish the question of whether killing is, in itself, worse than letting die, from the very different question of whether most actual cases of killing are more reprehensible than most actual cases of letting die. Most actual cases of killing are clearly terrible—think of the murders reported in the newspapers—and we hear of such cases almost every day. On the other hand, we hardly ever hear of a case of letting die, except for the actions of doctors who are motivated by humanitarian reasons. So we learn to think of killing in a much worse light than letting die; and we conclude, invalidly, that there must be something about killing which makes it *in itself* worse than letting die. But this does not follow for it is not the bare difference between killing and letting die that makes the difference in these cases. Rather, it is the other factors—the murderer's motive of personal gain, for example, contrasted with the doctor's humanitarian motivation, or the fact that the murderer kills a healthy person while the doctor lets die a terminal patient racked with disease—that account for our different reactions to the different cases.

There are, however, some substantial arguments that may be advanced to oppose my conclusion. Here are two of them:

The first counterargument focuses specifically on the concept of *being the cause of someone's death*. If we kill someone, then we are the cause of his death. But if we merely let someone die, we are not the cause; rather, he dies of whatever condition he already has. The doctor who gives the cancer patient a lethal injection will have caused his patient's death, and will have this on his conscience; whereas if he merely ceases treatment, the cancer and not the doctor is the cause of death. This is supposed to make a moral difference. This argument has been advanced many times. Ramsey, for example, urges us to remember that "In omission no human agent causes the patient's death, directly or indirectly."[9] And, writing in the *Villanova Law Review* for 1968, Dr. J. Russell Elkinton said that what makes the active/passive distinction important is that in passive euthanasia, "the patient does not die from the act [e.g., the act of turning off the respirator] but from the underlying disease or injury."[10]

This argument will not do, for two reasons. First, just as there is a distinction to be drawn between being and not being the cause of someone's death, there is also a distinction to be drawn between letting someone die and not letting anyone die. It is certainly desirable, in general, not to be the cause of anyone's death; but it is also desirable, in general, not to let anyone die when we can save them. (Doctors act on this precept every day.) Therefore, we cannot draw any special conclusion about the relative desirability of passive euthanasia just on these grounds. Second, the reason we think it is bad to be the cause of someone's death is that we think that death is a great evil—and so it is. However, if we have decided that euthanasia, even passive euthanasia, is desirable in a given case, then we have decided that in *this* instance death is no greater an evil than the patient's continued existence. And if this is true, then the usual reason for not wanting to be the cause of someone's death simply does not apply. To put the point just a bit differently: There is nothing wrong with being the cause of someone's death if his death is, all things considered, a good thing. And if his death is *not* a good thing, then *no* form of euthanasia, active or passive, is justified. So once again we see that the two kinds of euthanasia stand or fall together.

The second counterargument appeals to a favorite idea of philosophers, namely that our duty not to harm people is generally more stringent than our duty to help them. The law affirms this when it forbids us to kill people, or steal their goods, but does not require us in general to save people's lives or give them charity. And this is said to be not merely a point about the law, but about morality as well. We do not have a strict moral duty to help some poor man in Ethiopia—although it might be kind and generous of us if we did—but we *do* have a strict moral duty to refrain from doing anything to harm him. Killing someone is a violation of our duty not to harm, whereas letting someone die is merely a failure to give help. Therefore, the former is a more serious breach of morality than the latter; and so, contrary to what was said above, there is a morally significant difference between killing and letting die.

This argument has a certain superficial plausibility, but it cannot be used to show that there is a morally important difference between active and passive euthanasia. For one thing, it only seems that our duty to help people is less stringent than our duty not to harm them when we concentrate on certain sorts of cases: cases in which the people we could help are very far away, and are strangers to us; or cases in which it would be very difficult for us to help them, or in which helping would require a substantial sacrifice on our part. Many people feel that, in *these* types of cases, it may be kind and generous of us to give help, but we are not morally required to do so. Thus it is felt that when we give money for famine relief we are being especially big-hearted, and we deserve special praise— even if it would be immodest of us to seek such praise—because we are doing more than, strictly speaking, we are required to do.[11]

However, if we think of cases in which it would be very easy for us to help someone who is close at hand and in which no great personal sacrifice is required, things look very different. Think again of the child drowning in the bathtub: *Of course* a man standing next to the tub would have a strict moral duty to help the child. Here the alleged asymmetry between the duty to help and the duty not to do harm vanishes. Since most of the cases of euthanasia with which we are concerned are of this latter type—the patient is close at hand, it is well within the professional skills of the physician to keep him alive—the alleged asymmetry has little relevance.

It should also be remembered, in considering this argument, that the duty of doctors toward their patients *is* precisely to help them; that is what doctors are supposed to do. Therefore, even if there were a general asymmetry between the duty to help and the duty not to harm—which I deny—it would not apply in the special case of the relation between doctors and their patients. Finally, it is not clear that killing such a patient *is* harming him, even though in other cases it certainly is a great harm to someone to kill him, for as I said before, we are going under the assumption that the patient would be no worse off dead than he is now; if this is so, then killing him is not harming him. For the same reason we should not classify letting such a patient die as failing to help him. Therefore, even if we grant that our duty to help people is less stringent than our duty not to harm them, nothing follows about our duties with respect to killing and letting die in the special case of euthanasia.

Practical Consequences

This is enough, I think, to show that the doctrine underlying the AMA statement is false. There is no general moral difference between active and passive euthanasia; if one is permissible, so is the other. Now if this were merely an intellectual mistake, having no significant consequences for medical practice, the whole matter would not be very important. But the opposite is true: The doctrine has terrible consequences for, as I have already mentioned—and as doctors know very well—the process of being "allowed to die" can be relatively slow and painful, while being given a lethal injection is relatively quick and painless. Dr. Anthony Shaw describes what happens when the decision has been made not to perform the surgery necessary to "save" a Down's syndrome infant:

> When surgery is denied [the doctor] must try to keep the infant from suffering while natural forces sap the baby's life away. As a surgeon whose natural inclination is to use the scalpel to fight off death, standing by and watching a salvageable baby die is the most emotionally exhausting experience I know. It is easy at a conference, in a theoretical discussion, to decide that such infants should be allowed to die. It is altogether different to stand by in the nursery and watch as dehydration and infection wither a tiny being over hours and days. This is a terrible ordeal for me and the hospital staff—much more so than for the parents who never set foot in the nursery.[12]

Why must the hospital staff "stand by in the nursery and watch as dehydration and infection wither a tiny being over hours and days"? Why must they merely "try" to reduce the infant's suffering? The doctrine that says the baby may be allowed to dehydrate and wither but not be given an injection that would end its life without suffering is not only irrational but cruel.

The same goes for the case of the man with cancer of the throat. Here there are three options: With continued treatment, he will have a few more days of pain, and then die; if treatment is stopped, but nothing else is done, it will be a few more hours; and with a lethal injection, he will die at once. Those who oppose euthanasia in all its forms say that we must take the first option, and keep the patient alive for as long as possible. This view is so patently inhumane that few defend it; nevertheless, it does have a certain kind of integrity. It is at least consistent. The third option is the one I think best. But the *middle* position—that, although the patient need not suffer for days before dying, he must nevertheless suffer for a few more hours—is a "moderate" view which incorporates the worst, and not the best, features of both extremes.

Let me mention one other practice that we would be well rid of if we stopped thinking that the distinction between active and passive euthanasia is important. About one in six hundred babies born in the United States is mongoloid. Most of these babies are otherwise healthy—that is, with only the usual pediatric care, they will proceed to a "normal" infancy. Some, however, are born with other congenital defects such as intestinal obstructions which require surgery if the baby is to live. As I have already mentioned, sometimes the surgery is withheld and the baby dies. But when there is no defect requiring surgery, the baby lives on.[13] Now surgery to remove an intestinal obstruction is not difficult; the reason it is not performed in such cases is, clearly, that the child [has Down's syndrome] and the parents and doctor judge that because of *this* it is better for the child to die.

But notice that this situation is absurd, no matter what view one takes of the lives and potentials of such babies. If you think that the life of such an infant is worth preserving, then what does it matter if it needs a simple operation? Or, if you think it better that such a baby not live on, then what difference does it make if its intestinal tract is *not* blocked? In either case, the matter of life or death is being decided on irrelevant grounds. It is the mongolism, and not the intestine, that is the issue. The matter should be decided, if at all, on *that* basis, and not be allowed to depend on the essentially irrelevant question of whether the intestinal tract is blocked.

What makes this situation possible, of course, is the idea that when there is an intestinal obstruction we can "let the baby die," but when there is no such defect there is nothing we can do, for we must not "kill" it. The fact that this idea leads to such results as deciding life or death on irrelevant grounds is another good reason it should be rejected.

Doctors may think that all of this is only of academic interest, the sort of thing which philosophers may worry about but which has no practical bearing on their own work. After all, doctors must be concerned about the legal consequences of what they do, and active euthanasia is clearly forbidden by the law. They are right to be concerned about this. There have not been many prosecutions of doctors in the United States for active euthanasia, but there have been some. Prosecutions for passive euthanasia, on the other hand, are virtually nonexistent, even though there are laws under which charges could be brought, and even though this practice is much more widespread. Passive euthanasia, unlike active euthanasia, is by and large tolerated by the law. The law may sometimes compel a doctor to take action which he might not otherwise take to keep a patient alive,[14] but of course this is very different from bringing criminal charges against him after the patient is dead.

Even so, doctors should be concerned with the fact that the law and public opinion are forcing upon them an indefensible moral position, which has a considerable effect on their practices. Of course, most doctors are not now in the position of being coerced in this matter, for they do not regard themselves as merely going along with what the law requires. Rather, in statements such as the AMA statement that I quoted, they are endorsing the doctrine as a central point of medical ethics. In that statement, active euthanasia is condemned not merely as illegal but as "contrary to that for which the medical profession stands," while passive euthanasia is approved. However, if my arguments have been sound, there really is no intrinsic moral difference between them (although there may be morally important differences in their consequences, varying from case to case); so while doctors may have to discriminate between them to satisfy the law, they should not do any *more* than that. In particular, they should not give the distinction any added authority and weight by writing it into official statements of medical ethics.

Endnotes

1. F. J. Ingelfinger, "Bedside Ethics for the Hopeless Case," *New England Journal of Medicine* 289 (25 October 1973), p. 914.

2. Ibid.

3. This statement was approved by the House of Delegates of the AMA on December 4, 1973. It is worth noting that some state medical societies have advised *patients* to take a similar attitude toward the termination of their lives. In 1973 the Connecticut State Medical Society approved a "background statement" to be signed by terminal patients which includes this sentence: "I value life and the dignity of life, so that I am not asking that my life be directly taken, but that my life not be unreasonably prolonged or the dignity of life be destroyed." Other state medical societies have followed suit.

4. A discussion of this type of case can be found in Anthony Shaw, "'Doctor, Do We Have a Choice?'" *The New York Times Magazine*, 30 January 1972, pp. 44–54. Also see Shaw's "Dilemmas of 'Informed Consent' in Children," *The New England Journal of Medicine* 289 (25 October 1973), pp. 885–990.

5. Paul Ramsey, *The Patient as Person* (New Haven, Conn.: Yale University Press, 1970), pp. 115–116.

6. D. C. S. Cameron, *The Truth About Cancer* (Englewood Cliffs, N.J.: Prentice-Hall, 1956), p. 116.

7. Ramsey, *The Patient as Person*, p. 151.

8. Judith Jarvis Thomson has argued that this line of reasoning is unsound. Consider, she says, this argument which is parallel to the one involving Smith and Jones:

Alfrieda knows that if she cuts off Alfred's head he will die, and wanting him to die, cuts it off; Bertha knows that if she punches Bert in the nose he will die—Bert is in peculiar physical condition—and, wanting him to die, punches him in the nose. But what Bertha does is surely every bit as bad as what Alfrieda does. So cutting off a man's head isn't worse than punching a man in the nose. ("Killing, Letting Die, and the Trolley Problem," *The Monist* 59 [1976], p. 204.)

She concludes that, since this absurd argument doesn't prove anything, the Smith/Jones argument doesn't prove anything either.

However, I think that the Alfrieda/Bertha argument is not absurd, as strange as it is. A little analysis shows that it is a sound argument and that its conclusion is true. We need to notice first that the reason it is wrong to chop someone's head off is, obviously, that this causes death. The act is objectionable because of its consequences. Thus, a different act with the same consequences may be equally objectionable. In Thomson's example, punching Bert in the nose has the same consequences as chopping off Alfred's head; and, indeed, the two actions are equally bad.

Now the Alfrieda/Bertha argument presupposes a distinction between the act of chopping off someone's head, and the results of this act, the victim's death. (It is stipulated that, except for the fact that Alfrieda chops off someone's head, while Bertha punches someone in the nose, the two acts are "in all other respects alike." The *other* respects include the act's consequence, the victim's death.) This is not a distinction we would normally think to make, since we cannot in fact cut off someone's head without killing him. Yet in thought the distinction can be drawn. The question raised in the argument, then, is whether, *considered apart from their consequences,* head-chopping is worse than nose-punching. And the answer to *this* strange question is No, just as the argument says it should be.

The conclusion of the argument should be construed like this: The bare fact that one act is an act of head-chopping, while another act is an act of nose-punching, is not a reason for judging the former to be worse than the latter. At the same time—and this is perfectly compatible with the argument—the fact that one act causes death, while another does not, *is* a reason for judging the former to be worse. The parallel construal of my conclusion is: The bare fact that one act is an act of killing, while another act is an act of letting die, is not a reason for judging the former to be worse than the latter. At the same time—and this is perfectly compatible with my argument—the fact that an act (of killing, for example) prevents suffering, while another act (of letting die, for example) does not, *is* a reason for preferring one over the other. So once we see exactly how the Alfrieda/Bertha argument *is* parallel to the Smith/Jones argument, we find that Thomson's argument is, surprisingly, quite all right.

9. Ramsey, *The Patient as Person,* p. 151.

10. J. Russell Elkinton, "The Dying Patient, the Doctor, and the Law," *Villanova Law Review* 13 (Summer 1968), p. 743.

11. For the purposes of this essay we do not need to consider whether this way of thinking about "charity" is justified. There are, however, strong arguments that it is morally indefensible: see Peter Singer, "Famine, Affluence, and Morality," *Philosophy and Public Affairs* 1 (Spring 1972), pp. 229–243. Also see James Rachels, "Killing and Letting People Die of Starvation," *Philosophy* 54 (1979), pp. 159–171, for a discussion of the killing/letting die distinction in the context of world hunger, as well as further arguments that the distinction is morally unimportant.

12. Shaw, "'Doctor, Do We Have a Choice?'" p. 54.

13. See the articles by Shaw cited in note 4.

14. For example, in February 1974 a Superior Court judge in Maine ordered a doctor to proceed with an operation to repair a hole in the esophagus of a baby with multiple deformities. Otherwise the operation would not have been performed. The baby died anyway a few days later. "Deformed Baby Dies Amid Controversy," *Miami Herald,* 25 February 1974, p. 4-B.

18. *The Intentional Termination of Life*

BONNIE STEINBOCK

Bonnie Steinbock defends the policy statement of the American Medical Association on euthanasia against James Rachels's critique. She argues that the statement does not rest on the belief that there is a moral difference between active and passive euthanasia. Rather, she contends that the statement rejects both active and passive euthanasia but permits "the cessation of the employment of extraordinary means," which she claims is not the same as passive euthanasia. She points out that doctors can cease to employ extraordinary means to respect the wishes of the patient or because continued treatment is painful and has little chance of success, without intending to let the patient die. She allows, however, that in some cases, ceasing to employ extraordinary means does amount to intending to let the patient die and also that in other cases, killing may even be morally preferable to letting die.

According to James Rachels[1] a common mistake in medical ethics is the belief that there is a moral difference between active and passive euthanasia. This is a mistake, [he] argues, because the rationale underlying the distinction between active and passive euthanasia is the idea that there is a significant moral difference between intentionally killing and letting die. . . . Whether the belief that there is a significant moral difference (between intentionally killing and intentionally letting die) is mistaken is not my concern here. For it is far from clear that this distinction is the basis of the doctrine of the American Medical Association which Rachels attacks. And if the killing/letting die distinction is not the basis of the AMA doctrine, then arguments showing that the distinction has no moral force do not, in themselves, reveal in the doctrine's adherents either "confused thinking" or "a moral point of view unrelated to the interests of individuals." Indeed, as we examine the AMA doctrine, I think it will become clear that it appeals to and makes use of a number of overlapping distinctions, which may have moral significance in particular cases, such as the distinction between intending and foreseeing, or between ordinary and extraordinary care. Let us then turn to the statement, from the House of Delegates of the AMA, which Rachels cites:

> The intentional termination of the life of one human being by another—mercy-killing—is contrary to that for which the medical profession stands and is contrary to the policy of the AMA.
>
> The cessation of the employment of extraordinary means to prolong the life of the body when there is irrefutable evidence that biological death is imminent is the decision of the patient and/or his immediate family. The advice and judgment of the physician should be freely available to the patient and/or his immediate family.[2]

Rachels attacks this statement because he believes that it contains a moral distinction between active and passive euthanasia. . . .

I intend to show that the AMA statement does not imply support of the active/passive euthanasia distinction. In forbidding the intentional termination of life, the statement rejects both active and passive euthanasia. It does allow for ". . . the cessation of the employment of extraordinary means . . ." to prolong life. The mistake Rachels makes is in identifying the cessation of life-prolonging treatment with passive euthanasia, or intentionally letting die. If it were right to equate the two, then the AMA statement would be self-contradictory, for it would begin by condemning, and end by allowing, the intentional termination of life. But if the cessation of life-prolonging treatment is not always or necessarily passive euthanasia, then there is no confusion and no contradiction.

Why does Rachels think that the cessation of life-prolonging treatment is the intentional termination of life? He says:

> The AMA policy statement isolates the crucial issue very well: The crucial issue is "the intentional termination of the life of one human being by another." But after identifying this issue, and forbidding "mercy-killing," the statement goes on to deny that the cessation of treatment is the intentional termination of a life. This is where the mistake comes in, for what is the cessation of treatment, in these circumstances, if it is not "the intentional termination of the life of one human being by another"? Of course it is exactly that, and if it were not, there would be no point to it.[3]

However, there *can* be a point (to the cessation of life-prolonging treatment) other than an endeavor to bring about the patient's death, and so the blanket identification of cessation of treatment with the intentional termination of a life is inaccurate. There are at least two situations in which the termination of life-prolonging treatment cannot be identified with the intentional termination of the life of one human being by another.

Reprinted with permission from *Ethics in Science and Medicine*, pp. 59–64, Bonnie Steinbock, "The Intentional Termination of Life." Copyright 1979, Pergamon Press, Ltd.

The first situation concerns the patient's right to refuse treatment. Rachels gives the example of a patient dying of an incurable disease, accompanied by unrelievable pain, who wants to end the treatment which cannot cure him but can only prolong his miserable existence. Why, they ask, may a doctor accede to the patient's request to stop treatment, but not provide a patient in a similar situation with a lethal dose? The answer lies in the patient's right to refuse treatment. In general, a competent adult has the right to refuse treatment, even where such treatment is necessary to prolong life. Indeed, the right to refuse treatment has been upheld even when the patient's reason for refusing treatment is generally agreed to be inadequate.[4] This right can be overridden (if, for example, the patient has dependent children) but, in general, no one may legally compel you to undergo treatment to which you have not consented. "Historically, surgical intrusion has always been considered a technical battery upon the person and one to be excused or justified by consent of the patient or justified by necessity created by the circumstances of the moment. . . ."[5]

At this point, it might be objected that if one has the right to refuse life-prolonging treatment, then consistency demands that one have the right to decide to end his life, and to obtain help in doing so. The idea is that the right to refuse treatment somehow implies a right to voluntary euthanasia, and we need to see why someone might think this. The right to refuse treatment has been considered by legal writers as an example of the right to privacy or, better, the right to bodily self-determination. You have the right to decide what happens to your own body, and the right to refuse treatment is an instance of that more general right. But if you have the right to determine what happens to your body, then should you not have the right to choose to end your life, and even a right to get help in doing so?

However, it is important to see that the right to refuse treatment is not the same as, nor does it entail, a right to voluntary euthanasia, even if both can be derived from the right to bodily self-determination. The right to refuse treatment is not itself a "right to die"; that one may choose to exercise this right even at the risk of death, or even *in order to die,* is irrelevant.

The purpose of the right to refuse medical treatment is not to give persons a right to decide whether to live or die, but to protect them from the unwanted interferences of others. Perhaps we ought to interpret the right to bodily self-determination more broadly so as to include a right to die: But this would be a substantial extension of our present understanding of the right to bodily self-determination, and not a consequence of it. Should we recognize a right to voluntary euthanasia, we would have to agree that people have the right not merely to be left alone, but also the right to be killed. I leave to one side that substantive moral issue. My claim is simply that there can be a reason for terminating life-prolonging treatment other than "to bring about the patient's death."

The second case in which termination of treatment cannot be identified with intentional termination of life is where continued treatment has little chance of improving the patient's condition and brings greater discomfort than relief.

The question here is what treatment is appropriate to the particular case. A cancer specialist describes it in this way:

> My general rule is to administer therapy as long as a patient responds well and has the potential for a reasonably good quality of life. But when all feasible therapies have been administered and a patient shows signs of rapid deterioration, the continuation of therapy can cause more discomfort than the cancer. From that time I recommend surgery, radiotherapy, or chemotherapy only as a means of relieving pain. But if a patient's condition should once again stabilize after the withdrawal of active therapy and if it should appear that he could still gain some good time, I would immediately reinstitute active therapy. The decision to cease anticancer treatment is never irrevocable, and often the desire to live will push a patient to try for another remission, or even a few more days of life.[6]

The decision here to cease anticancer treatment cannot be construed as a decision that the patient die, or as the intentional termination of life. It is a decision to provide the most appropriate treatment for that patient at that time. Rachels suggests that the point of the cessation of treatment is the intentional termination of life. But here the point of discontinuing treatment is not to bring about the patient's death but to avoid treatment that will cause more discomfort than the cancer and has little hope of benefiting the patient. Treatment that meets this description is often called "extraordinary."[7] The concept is flexible, and what might be considered "extraordinary" in one situation might be ordinary in another. The use of a respirator to sustain a patient through a severe bout with a respiratory disease would be considered ordinary; its use to sustain the life of a severely brain damaged person in an irreversible coma would be considered extraordinary.

Contrasted with extraordinary treatment is ordinary treatment, the care a doctor would normally be expected to provide. Failure to provide ordinary care constitutes neglect, and can even be construed as the intentional infliction of harm, where there is a legal obligation to provide care. The importance of the ordinary/extraordinary care distinction lies partly in its connection to the doctor's intention. The withholding of extraordinary care should be seen as a decision not to inflict painful treatment on a patient without reasonable hope of success. The withholding of ordinary care, by contrast, must be seen as neglect. Thus, one doctor says, "We have to draw a distinction between ordinary and extraordinary means. We never withdraw what's needed to make a baby comfortable, we would never withdraw the care a parent would provide. We never kill a baby. . . . But we may decide certain heroic intervention is not worthwhile."[8]

We should keep in mind the ordinary/extraordinary care distinction when considering an example given by Rachels to show the irrationality of the active/passive distinction with regard to infanticide. The example is this: A child is born with Down's syndrome and also has an intestinal obstruction which requires corrective surgery. If the surgery is not performed, the infant will starve to death, since it cannot take food orally. This may take days or even weeks, as dehydration and infection set in. Commenting on this situation, Rachels says:

> I can understand why some people are opposed to all euthanasia, and insist that such infants must be allowed to live. I think I can also understand why other people favor destroying these babies quickly and painlessly. But why should anyone favor letting "dehydration and infection wither a tiny being over hours and days"? The doctrine that says that a baby may be allowed to dehydrate and wither, but may

not be given an injection that would end its life without suffering, seems so patently cruel as to require no further refutation.[9]

Such a doctrine perhaps does not need further refutation; but this is not the AMA doctrine. For the AMA statement criticized by Rachels allows only for the cessation of extraordinary means to prolong life when death is imminent. Neither of these conditions is satisfied in this example. Death is not imminent in this situation, any more than it would be if a normal child had an attack of appendicitis. Neither the corrective surgery to remove the intestinal obstruction, nor the intravenous feeding required to keep the infant alive until such surgery is performed, can be regarded as extraordinary means, for neither is particularly expensive, nor does either place an overwhelming burden on the patient or others. (The continued existence of the child might be thought to place an overwhelming burden on its parents, but that has nothing to do with the characterization of the means to prolong its life as extraordinary. If it had, then *feeding* a severely defective child who required a great deal of care could be regarded as extraordinary.) The chances of success if the operation is undertaken are quite good, though there is always a risk in operating on infants. Though the Down's syndrome will not be alleviated, the child will proceed to an otherwise normal infancy.

It cannot be argued that the treatment is withheld for the infant's sake, unless one is prepared to argue that all mentally retarded babies are better off dead. This is particularly implausible in the case of Down's syndrome babies who generally do not suffer and are capable of giving and receiving love, of learning and playing, to varying degrees.

In a film on this subject entitled, "Who Should Survive?," a doctor defended a decision not to operate, saying that since the parents did not consent to the operation, the doctor's hands were tied. As we have seen, surgical intrusion requires consent, and in the case of infants, consent would normally come from the parents. But, as their legal guardians, parents are required to provide medical care for their children, and failure to do so can constitute criminal neglect or even homicide. In general, courts have been understandably reluctant to recognize a parental right to terminate life-prolonging treatment.[10] Although prosecution is unlikely, physicians who comply with invalid instructions from the parents and permit the infant's death could be liable for aiding and abetting, failure to report child neglect, or even homicide. So it is not true that, in this situation, doctors are legally bound to do as the parents wish.

To sum up, I think that Rachels is right to regard the decision not to operate in the Down's syndrome example as the intentional termination of life. But there is no reason to believe that either the law or the AMA would regard it otherwise. Certainly the decision to withhold treatment is not justified by the AMA statement. That such infants have been allowed to die cannot be denied; but this, I think, is the result of doctors misunderstanding the law and the AMA position.

Withholding treatment in this case is the intentional termination of life because the infant is deliberately allowed to die; that is the point of not operating. But there are other cases in which that is not the point. If the point is to avoid inflicting painful treatment on a patient with little or no reasonable hope of success, this is not the intentional termination of life. The permissibility of such withholding of treatment, then, would have no implications for the permissibility of euthanasia, active or passive.

The decision whether or not to operate, or to institute vigorous treatment, is particularly agonizing in the case of children born with spina bifida, an opening in the base of the spine usually accompanied by hydrocephalus and mental retardation. If left unoperated, these children usually die of meningitis or kidney failure within the first few years of life. Even if they survive, all affected children face a lifetime of illness, operations, and varying degrees of disability. The policy used to be to save as many as possible, but the trend now is toward selective treatment, based on the physician's estimate of the chances of success. If operating is not likely to improve significantly the child's condition, parents and doctors may agree not to operate. This is not the intentional termination of life, for again the purpose is not the termination of the child's life but the avoidance of painful and pointless treatment. Thus, the fact that withholding treatment is justified does not imply that killing the child would be equally justified.

Throughout the discussion, I have claimed that intentionally ceasing life-prolonging treatment is not

the intentional termination of life unless the doctor has, as his or her purpose in stopping treatment, the patient's death.

It may be objected that I have incorrectly characterized the conditions for the intentional termination of life. Perhaps it is enough that the doctor intentionally ceases treatment, foreseeing that the patient will die; perhaps the reason for ceasing treatment is irrelevant to its characterization as the intentional termination of life. I find this suggestion implausible, but am willing to consider arguments for it. Rachels has provided no such arguments: Indeed, he apparently shares my view about the intentional termination of life. For when he claims that the cessation of life-prolonging treatment *is* the intentional termination of life, his reason for making the claim is that "if it were not, there would be no point to it." Rachels believes that the point of ceasing treatment, "in these cases," is to bring about the patient's death. If that were not the point, he suggests, why would the doctor cease treatment? I have shown, however, that there can be a point to ceasing treatment which is not the death of the patient. In showing this, I have refuted Rachels's reason for identifying the cessation of life-prolonging treatment with the intentional termination of life, and thus his argument against the AMA doctrine.

Here someone might say: Even if the withholding of treatment is not the intentional termination of life, does that make a difference, morally speaking? If life-prolonging treatment may be withheld, for the sake of the child, may not an easy death be provided, for the sake of the child, as well? The unoperated child with spina bifida may take months or even years to die. Distressed by the spectacle of children "lying around waiting to die," one doctor has written, "It is time that society and medicine stopped perpetuating the fiction that withholding treatment is ethically different from terminating a life. It is time that society began to discuss mechanisms by which we can alleviate the pain and suffering for those individuals whom we cannot help."[11]

I do not deny that there may be cases in which death is in the best interests of the patient. In such cases, a quick and painless death may be the best thing. However, I do not think that, once active or vigorous treatment is stopped, a quick death is always preferable to a lingering one. We must be cautious about attributing to defective children *our* distress at seeing them linger. Waiting for them to die may be tough on parents, doctors, and nurses—it isn't necessarily tough on the child. The decision not to operate need not mean a decision to neglect, and it may be possible to make the remaining months of the child's life comfortable, pleasant, and filled with love. If this alternative is possible, surely it is more decent and humane than killing the child. In such a situation, withholding treatment, foreseeing the child's death, is not ethically equivalent to killing the child, and we cannot move from the permissibility of the former to that of the latter. I am worried that there will be a tendency to do precisely that if active euthanasia is regarded as morally equivalent to the withholding of life-prolonging treatment.

Conclusion

The AMA statement does not make the distinction Rachels wishes to attack, i.e., that between active and passive euthanasia. Instead, the statement draws a distinction between the intentional termination of life, on the one hand, and the cessation of the employment of extraordinary means to prolong life, on the other. Nothing said by Rachels shows that this distinction is confused. It may be that doctors have misinterpreted the AMA statement, and that this has led, for example, to decisions to allow defective infants slowly to starve to death. I quite agree with Rachels that the decisions to which they allude were cruel and made on irrelevant grounds. Certainly it is worth pointing out that allowing someone to die can be the intentional termination of life, and that it can be just as bad as, or worse than, killing someone. However, the withholding of life-prolonging treatment is not necessarily the intentional termination of life, so that if it is permissible to withhold life-prolonging treatment, it does not follow that, other things being equal, it is permissible to kill. Furthermore, most of the time, other things are not equal. In many of the cases in which it would be right to cease treatment, I do not think that it would also be right to kill.

Endnotes

1. James Rachels, Active and passive euthanasia. *New England Journal of Medicine*, 292, 78–80, 1975.

2. Rachels, p. 78.

3. Rachels, p. 79–80.

4. For example, *In re Yetter*, 62 Pa. D. & C. 2d 619, C.P., Northampton County Ct., 1974.

5. David W. Meyers. "Legal aspects of voluntary euthanasia." In *Dilemmas of Euthanasia* (edited by John Behnke and Sissela Bok), p. 56. Anchor Books, New York, 1975.

6. Ernest H. Rosenbaum. *Living with Cancer*, p. 27. Praeger, New York, 1975.

7. Cf. Tristam Engelhardt, Jr. "Ethical issues in aiding the death of young children." In *Beneficent Euthanasia* (edited by Marvin Kohl), Prometheus Books, Buffalo, N.Y., 1975.

8. B. D. Colen, *Karen Ann Quinlan: Living and Dying in the Age of Eternal Life*, p. 115. Nash, 1976.

9. Rachels, p. 79.

10. Cf. Norman L. Cantor. "Law and the termination of an incompetent patient's life-preserving care." *Dilemmas of Euthanasia*, op. cit., pp. 69–105.

11. John Freeman "Is there a right to die—quickly?" *Journal of Pediatrics 80*, p. 905.

19. *Planned Parenthood* v. *Casey*

SUPREME COURT OF THE UNITED STATES

The issue before the Supreme Court was whether the Pennsylvania Abortion Control Act as amended in 1988 and 1989 violated the due process clause of the U.S. Constitution by requiring informed consent, a twenty-four-hour waiting period, parental consent in the case of a minor, spousal notification, and certain reporting and record keeping by facilities that provide abortion services. While reaffirming its commitment to the essential holding of Roe v. Wade, the Court allowed that the state had a legitimate interest in imposing all of the above requirements except spousal notification.

Justices *O'Connor, Kennedy,* and *Souter* announcing the judgment of the Court in which Justices *Blackmun* and *Stevens* concurred in part:

Liberty finds no refuge in a jurisprudence of doubt. Yet nineteen years after our holding that the Constitution protects a woman's right to terminate her pregnancy in its early stages, *Roe v. Wade* . . . (1973), that definition of liberty is still questioned. . . .

At issue in these cases are five provisions of the Pennsylvania Abortion Control Act of 1982 as amended in 1988 and 1989. . . . The Act requires that a woman seeking an abortion give her informed consent prior to the abortion procedure, and specifies that she be provided with certain information at least 24 hours before the abortion is performed. . . . For a minor to obtain an abortion, the Act requires the informed consent of one of her parents, but provides for a judicial bypass option if the minor does not wish to or cannot obtain a parent's consent. . . . Another provision of the Act requires that, unless certain exceptions apply, a married woman seeking an abortion must sign a statement indicating that she has notified her husband of her intended abortion. . . . The Act exempts compliance with these three requirements in the event of a "medical emergency." . . . In addition to the above provisions regulating the performance of abortions, the Act imposes certain reporting requirements on facilities that provide abortion services. . . .

It must be stated at the outset and with clarity that *Roe*'s essential holding, the holding we reaffirm, has three parts. First is a recognition of the right of the woman to choose to have an abortion before viability and to obtain it without undue interference from the State. Before viability, the State's interests are not strong enough to support a prohibition of abortion or the imposition of a substantial obstacle to the woman's effective right to elect the procedure. Second is a confirmation of the State's power to restrict abortions after fetal viability, if the law contains exceptions for pregnancies which endanger a woman's life or health. And third is the principle that the State has legitimate interests from the outset of the pregnancy in protecting the health of the woman and the life of the fetus that may become a child. These principles do not contradict one another; and we adhere to each.

Constitutional protection of the woman's decision to terminate her pregnancy derives from the Due Process Clause of the Fourteenth Amendment. It declares that no State shall "deprive any person of life, liberty, or property, without due process of law." The controlling word in the case before us is "liberty." . . .

Men and women of good conscience can disagree . . . about the profound moral and spiritual implications of terminating a pregnancy, even in its earliest stage. Some of us as individuals find abortion offensive to our most basic principles of morality, but that cannot control our decision. Our obligation is to define the liberty of all, not to mandate our own moral code. The underlying constitutional issue is whether the State can resolve these philosophic questions in such a definitive way that a woman lacks all choice in the matter, except perhaps in those rare circumstances in which the pregnancy is itself a danger to her own life or health, or is the result of rape or incest.

It is conventional constitutional doctrine that where reasonable people disagree, the government can adopt one position or the other. . . . That theorem, however, assumes a state of affairs in which the choice does not intrude upon a protected liberty. Thus, while some people might disagree about whether or not the flag should be saluted, or disagree about the proposition that it may not be defiled, we have ruled that a State may not compel or enforce one view or the other. . . .

Our law affords constitutional protection to personal decisions relating to marriage, procreation, contraception, family relationships, child rearing, and education. . . . Our cases recognize "the right of the *individual,* married or single, to be free from unwarranted governmental intrusion into matters so fundamentally affecting a person as the decision whether to bear or beget a child." . . . Our precedents "have respected the private realm of family life which the state cannot enter." . . . These matters, involving the most intimate and personal choices a person may make in a lifetime, choices central to personal dignity and autonomy, are central to the liberty protected by the Fourteenth Amendment. At the heart of liberty is the right to define one's own concept of existence, of meaning, of the universe, and of the mystery of human life. Beliefs about these matters could not define the attributes of personhood were they formed under compulsion of the State.

These considerations begin our analysis of the woman's interest in terminating her pregnancy but cannot end it, for this reason: Though the abortion decision may originate within the zone of conscience and belief, it is more than a philosophic exercise. Abortion is a unique act. It is an act fraught with consequences for others: for the woman who must live with the implications of her decision; for the persons who perform and assist in the procedure; for the spouse, family, and society which must confront the knowledge that these procedures exist, procedures some deem nothing short of an act of violence against innocent human life; and, depending on one's beliefs, for the life or potential life that is aborted. Though abortion is conduct, it does not follow that the State is entitled to proscribe it in all instances. That is because the liberty of the woman is at stake in a sense unique to the human condition and so unique to the law. The mother who carries a child to full term is subject to anxieties, to physical constraints, to pain that only she must bear. That these sacrifices have from the beginning of the human race been endured by woman with a pride that ennobles her in the eyes of others and gives to the infant a bond of love cannot alone be grounds for the State to insist she make the sacrifice. Her suffering is too intimate and personal for the State to insist, without more, upon its own vision of the woman's role, however dominant that vision has been in the course of our history and our culture. The destiny of the woman must be shaped to a large extent on her own conception of her spiritual imperatives and her place in society.

It should be recognized, moreover, that in some critical respects the abortion decision is of the same character as the decision to use contraception, to which *Griswold v. Connecticut, Eisenstadt v. Baird,* and *Carey v. Population Services International* afford constitutional protection. We have no doubt as to the correctness of those decisions. They support the reasoning in *Roe* relating to the woman's liberty because they involve personal decisions concerning not only the meaning of procreation but also human responsibility and respect for it. As with abortion, reasonable people will have differences of opinion about these matters. One view is based on such reverence for the wonder of creation that any pregnancy ought to be welcomed and carried to full term no matter how difficult it will be to provide for the child and ensure its well-being. Another is that the inability to provide for the nurture and care of the infant is a cruelty to the child and an anguish to the parent. These are intimate views with infinite variations, and their deep, personal character underlay our decisions in *Griswold, Eisenstadt,* and *Carey.* The same concerns are present when the woman confronts the reality that, perhaps despite her attempts to avoid it, she has become pregnant.

It was this dimension of personal liberty that *Roe* sought to protect, and its holding invoked the reasoning and the tradition of the precedents we have discussed, granting protection to substantive liberties of the person. *Roe* was, of course, an extension of those cases and, as the decision itself indicated, the separate States could act in some degree to further their own legitimate interests in protecting pre-natal life. The extent to which the legislatures of the States might act to outweigh the interests of the woman in choosing to terminate her pregnancy was a subject of debate both in *Roe* itself and in decisions following it.

While we appreciate the weight of the arguments made on behalf of the State in the case before us, arguments which in their ultimate formulation conclude that *Roe* should be overruled, the reservations any of us may have in reaffirming the central holding of *Roe* are outweighed by the explication of individual liberty we have given combined with the force of *stare decisis.* We turn now to that doctrine.

The obligation to follow precedent begins with necessity, and a contrary necessity marks its outer limit. With Cardozo, we recognize that no judicial system could do society's work if it eyed each issue afresh in every case that raised it. . . . Indeed, the very concept of the rule of law underlying our own Constitution requires such continuity over time that a respect for precedent is, by definition, indispensable. . . . At the other extreme, a different necessity would make itself felt if a prior judicial ruling should come to be seen so clearly as error that its enforcement was for that very reason doomed. . . .

So in this case we may inquire whether *Roe*'s central . . . rule's limitation on state power could be removed without serious inequity to those who have relied upon it or significant damage to the stability of the society governed by the rule in question. . . .

Abortion is customarily chosen as an unplanned response to the consequence of unplanned activity or to the failure of conventional birth control, and except on the assumption that no intercourse would have occurred but for *Roe*'s holding, such behavior may appear to justify no reliance claim. Even if reliance could be claimed on that unrealistic assumption, the argument might run, any reliance interest would be *de minimis.* This argument would be premised on the hypothesis that reproductive planning could take virtually immediate account of any sudden restoration of state authority to ban abortions.

To eliminate the issue of reliance that easily, however, one would need to limit cognizable reliance to specific instances of sexual activity. But to do this would be simply to refuse to face the fact that for two decades of economic and social developments, people have organized intimate relationships and made choices that define their views of themselves and their places in society, in reliance on the availability of abortion in the event that contraception should fail. The ability of women to participate equally in the economic and social life of the nation has been facilitated by their ability to control their reproductive lives. . . .

We have seen how time has overtaken some of *Roe*'s factual assumptions: Advances in maternal health care allow for abortions safe to the mother later in pregnancy than was true in 1973. . . . But these facts go only to the scheme of time limits on the realization of competing interests, and the divergences from the factual premises of 1973 have no bearing on the validity of *Roe*'s central holding, that viability marks the earliest point at which the State's interest in fetal life is constitutionally adequate to justify a legislative ban on nontherapeutic abortions. The soundness or unsoundness of that constitutional judgment in no sense turns on whether viability occurs at approximately 28 weeks, as was usual at the time of *Roe*, at 23 to 24 weeks, as it sometimes does today, or at some moment even slightly earlier in pregnancy, as it may if fetal respiratory capacity can somehow be enhanced in the future. Whenever it may occur, the attainment of viability may continue to serve as the critical fact, just as it has done since *Roe* was decided; which is to say that no change in *Roe*'s factual underpinning has left its central holding obsolete, and none supports an argument for overruling it.

The sum of the precedential inquiry to this point shows *Roe*'s underpinnings unweakened in any way affecting its central holding. While it has engendered disapproval, it has not been unworkable. An entire generation has come of age free to assume *Roe*'s concept of liberty in defining the capacity of women to act in society, and to make reproductive decisions; no erosion of principle going to liberty or personal autonomy has left *Roe*'s central holding a doctrinal remnant; *Roe* portends no developments at odds with other precedent for the analysis of personal liberty; and no changes of fact have rendered viability more or less appropriate as the point at which the balance of interests tips. Within the bounds of normal *stare decisis* analysis, then, and subject to the considerations on which it customarily turns, the stronger argument is for affirming *Roe*'s central holding, with whatever degree of personal reluctance any of us may have, not for overruling it. . . .

From what we have said so far it follows that it is a constitutional liberty of the woman to have some freedom to terminate her pregnancy. We conclude that the basic decision in *Roe* was based on a constitutional analysis which we cannot now repudiate. The woman's liberty is not so unlimited, however, that from the outset the State cannot show its concern for the life of the unborn, and at a later point in fetal development the State's interest in life has sufficient force so that the right of the woman to terminate the pregnancy can be restricted.

That brings us, of course, to the point where much criticism has been directed at *Roe*, a criticism that always inheres when the Court draws a specific rule from what in the Constitution is but a general standard. We conclude, however, that the urgent claims of the woman to retain the ultimate control over her destiny and her body, claims implicit in the meaning of liberty, require us to perform that function. Liberty must not be extinguished for want of a line that is clear. And it falls to us to give some real substance to the woman's liberty to determine whether to carry her pregnancy to full term.

We conclude the line should be drawn at viability, so that before that time the woman has a right to choose to terminate her pregnancy. Any judicial act of line-drawing may seem somewhat arbitrary, but *Roe* was a reasoned statement, elaborated with great care. We have twice reaffirmed it in the face of great opposition. . . . The woman's right to terminate her pregnancy before viability is the most central principle of *Roe v. Wade*. It is a rule of law and a component of liberty we cannot renounce.

On the other side of the equation is the interest of the State in the protection of potential life. The *Roe* Court recognized the State's "important and legitimate interest in protecting the potentiality of human life." . . . The weight to be given this state interest, not the strength of the woman's interest, was the difficult question faced in *Roe*. We do not need to say whether each of us, had we been Members of the Court when the valuation of the State interest came before it as an original matter, would have concluded, as the *Roe* Court did, that its weight is insufficient to justify a ban on abortions prior to viability even when it is subject to certain exceptions. The matter is not before us in the first

instance, and coming as it does after nearly 20 years of litigation in *Roe*'s wake we are satisfied that the immediate question is not the soundness of *Roe*'s resolution of the issue, but the precedential force that must be accorded to its holding. And we have concluded that the essential holding of *Roe* should be reaffirmed.

Yet it must be remembered that *Roe v. Wade* speaks with clarity in establishing not only the woman's liberty but also the State's "important and legitimate interest in potential life." . . . That portion of the decision in *Roe* has been given too little acknowledgement and implementation by the Court in its subsequent cases. Those cases decided that any regulation touching upon the abortion decision must survive strict scrutiny, to be sustained only if drawn in narrow terms to further a compelling state interest. . . . Not all of the cases decided under that formulation can be reconciled with the holding in *Roe* itself that the State has legitimate interests in the health of the woman and in protecting the potential life within her. In resolving this tension, we choose to rely upon *Roe*, as against the later cases.

Roe established a trimester framework to govern abortion regulations. Under this elaborate but rigid construct, almost no regulation at all is permitted during the first trimester of pregnancy; regulations designed to protect the woman's health, but not to further the State's interest in potential life, are permitted during the second trimester; and during the third trimester, when the fetus is viable, prohibitions are permitted provided the life or health of the mother is not at stake. . . . Most of our cases since *Roe* have involved the application of rules derived from the trimester framework. . . .

The trimester framework no doubt was erected to ensure that the woman's right to choose not become so subordinate to the State's interest in promoting fetal life that her choice exists in theory but not in fact. We do not agree, however, that the trimester approach is necessary to accomplish this objective. A framework of this rigidity was unnecessary and in its later interpretation sometimes contradicted the State's permissible exercise of its powers.

Though the woman has a right to choose to terminate or continue her pregnancy before viability, it does not at all follow that the State is prohibited from taking steps to ensure that this choice is thoughtful and informed. Even in the earliest stages of pregnancy, the State may enact rules and regulations designed to encourage her to know that there are philosophic and social arguments of great weight that can be brought to bear in favor of continuing the pregnancy to full term and that there are procedures and institutions to allow adoption of unwanted children as well as a certain degree of state assistance if the mother chooses to raise the child herself. "'[T]he Constitution does not forbid a State or city, pursuant to democratic processes, from expressing a preference for normal childbirth.'" . . . It follows that States are free to enact laws to provide a reasonable framework for a woman to make a decision that has such profound and lasting meaning. This, too, we find consistent with *Roe*'s central premises, and indeed the inevitable consequence of our holding that the State has an interest in protecting the life of the unborn.

We reject the trimester framework, which we do not consider to be part of the essential holding of *Roe*. . . . Measures aimed at ensuring that a woman's choice contemplates the consequences for the fetus do not necessarily interfere with the right recognized in *Roe,* although those measures have been found to be inconsistent with the rigid trimester framework announced in that case. A logical reading of the central holding in *Roe* itself, and a necessary reconciliation of the liberty of the woman and the interest of the State in promoting prenatal life, require, in our view, that we abandon the trimester framework as a rigid prohibition on all previability regulation aimed at the protection of fetal life. The trimester framework suffers from these basic flaws: In its formulation it misconceives the nature of the pregnant woman's interest; and in practice it undervalues the State's interest in potential life, as recognized in *Roe*. . . .

The very notion that the State has a substantial interest in potential life leads to the conclusion that not all regulations must be deemed unwarranted. Not all burdens on the right to decide whether to terminate a pregnancy will be undue. In our view, the undue burden standard is the appropriate means of reconciling the State's interest with the woman's constitutionally protected liberty. . . .

An undue burden exists, and therefore a provision of law is invalid, if its purpose or effect is to place a substantial obstacle in the path of a woman seeking an abortion before the fetus attains viability. . . . The Court of Appeals applied what it believed to be the undue burden standard and upheld each of the provisions except for the husband notification requirement. We agree generally with this conclusion. . . .

Studies reveal that family violence occurs in two million families in the United States. This figure, however, is a conservative one that substantially understates (because battering is usually not reported until it reaches life-threatening proportions) the actual number of families affected by domestic violence. In fact, researchers estimate that one of every two women will be battered at some time in their life. . . .

In well-functioning marriages, spouses discuss important intimate decisions such as whether to bear a child. But there are millions of women in this country who are the victims of regular physical and psychological abuse at the hands of their husbands. Should these women become pregnant, they may have very good reasons for not wishing to inform their husbands of their decision to obtain an abortion. Many may have justifiable fears of physical abuse, but may be no less fearful of the consequences of reporting prior abuse to the Commonwealth of Pennsylvania. Many may have a reasonable fear that notifying their husbands will provoke further instances of child abuse. . . . Many may fear devastating forms of psychological abuse from their husbands, including verbal harassment, threats of future violence, the destruction of possessions, physical confinement to the home, the withdrawal of financial support, or the disclosure of the abortion to family and friends. . . . And many women who are pregnant as a result of sexual assaults by their husbands will be unable to avail themselves of the exception for spousal sexual assault . . . because the exception requires that the woman have notified law enforcement authorities within 90 days of the assault, and her husband will be notified of her report once an investigation begins. . . . If anything in this field is certain, it is that victims of spousal sexual assault are extremely reluctant to report the abuse to the government; hence, a great many spousal rape victims will not be exempt from the notification requirement. . . .

The spousal notification requirement is thus likely to prevent a significant number of women from obtaining an abortion. It does not merely make abortions a little more difficult or expensive to obtain; for many women, it will impose a substantial obstacle. We must not blind ourselves to the fact that the significant number of women who fear for their safety and the safety of their children are likely to be deterred from procuring an abortion as surely as if the Commonwealth had outlawed abortion in all cases. . . .

We recognize that a husband has a "deep and proper concern and interest . . . in his wife's pregnancy and in the growth and development of the fetus she is carrying." . . . With regard to the children he has fathered and raised, the Court has recognized his "cognizable and substantial" interest in their custody. . . . If this case concerned a State's ability to require the mother to notify the father before taking some action with respect to a living child raised by both, therefore, it would be reasonable to conclude as a general matter that the father's interest in the welfare of the child and the mother's interest are equal.

Before birth, however, the issue takes on a very different cast. It is an inescapable biological fact that state regulation with respect to the child a woman is carrying will have a far greater impact on the mother's liberty than on the father's. The effect of state regulation on a woman's protected liberty is doubly deserving of scrutiny in such a case, as the State has touched not only upon the private sphere of the family but upon the very bodily integrity of the pregnant woman. . . . The Court has held that "when the wife and the husband disagree on this decision, the view of only one of the two marriage partners can prevail. Inasmuch as it is the woman who physically bears the child and who is the more directly and immediately affected by the pregnancy, as between the two, the balance weighs in her favor." . . . This conclusion rests upon the basic nature of marriage and the nature of our Constitution: "[T]he marital couple is not an independent entity with a mind and heart of its own, but an association of two individuals each with a separate intellectual and emotional makeup. If the right of privacy means anything, it is the right of the *individual*, married or single, to be free from unwarranted governmental intrusion into matters so funda-

mentally affecting a person as the decision whether to bear or beget a child." . . . The Constitution protects individuals, men and women alike, from unjustified state interference, even when that interference is enacted into law for the benefit of their spouses. . . .

The husband's interest in the life of the child his wife is carrying does not permit the State to empower him with this troubling degree of authority over his wife. The contrary view leads to consequences reminiscent of the common law. A husband has no enforceable right to require a wife to advise him before she exercises her personal choices. If a husband's interest in the potential life of the child outweighs a wife's liberty, the State could require a married woman to notify her husband before she uses a postfertilization contraceptive. Perhaps next in line would be a statute requiring pregnant married women to notify their husbands before engaging in conduct causing risks to the fetus. After all, if the husband's interest in the fetus's safety is a sufficient predicate for state regulation, the State could reasonably conclude that pregnant wives should notify their husbands before drinking alcohol or smoking. Perhaps married women should notify their husbands before using contraceptives or before undergoing any type of surgery that may have complications affecting the husband's interest in his wife's reproductive organs. And if a husband's interest justifies notice in any of these cases, one might reasonably argue that it justifies exactly what the *Danforth* Court held it did not justify—a requirement of the husband's consent as well. A State may not give to a man the kind of dominion over his wife that parents exercise over their children. . . .

Our Constitution is a covenant running from the first generation of Americans to us and then to future generations. It is a coherent succession. Each generation must learn anew that the Constitution's written terms embody ideas and aspirations that must survive more ages than one. We accept our responsibility not to retreat from interpreting the full meaning of the covenant in light of all of our precedents. We invoke it once again to define the freedom guaranteed by the Constitution's own promise, the promise of liberty.

20. *Cruzan* v. *Director, Missouri Department of Health*

SUPREME COURT OF THE UNITED STATES

The issue before the Supreme Court was whether the state of Missouri's requirement of clear and convincing evidence of an incompetent's wishes concerning the withdrawal of life-sustaining medical treatment conflicts with the U.S. Constitution. Justice Rehnquist speaking for the majority of the Court held that the state of Missouri had a legitimate interest in protecting and preserving human life in imposing its clear and convincing evidence requirement. He further held that in imposing this requirement the state of Missouri need not make any judgment about the quality of human life.

Justice *Rehnquist* delivered the majority opinion:

Petitioner Nancy Beth Cruzan was rendered incompetent as a result of severe injuries sustained during an automobile accident. Co-petitioners Lester and Joyce Cruzan, Nancy's parents and co-guardians, sought a court order directing the withdrawal of their daughter's artificial feeding and hydration equipment after it became apparent that she had virtually no chance of recovering her cognitive faculties. The Supreme Court of Missouri held that because there was no clear and convincing evidence of Nancy's desire to have life-sustaining treatment withdrawn under such circumstances, her parents lacked authority to effectuate such a request. We . . . now affirm.

On the night of January 11, 1983, Nancy Cruzan lost control of her car as she traveled down Elm Road in Jasper County, Missouri. The vehicle overturned, and Cruzan was discovered lying face down in a ditch without detectable respiratory or cardiac function. Paramedics were able to restore her breathing and heartbeat at the accident site, and she was transported to a hospital in an unconscious state. An attending neurosurgeon diagnosed her as having sustained probable cerebral contusions compounded by significant anoxia (lack of oxygen). The Missouri trial court in this case found that permanent brain damage generally results after 6 minutes in an anoxic state; it was estimated that Cruzan was deprived of oxygen from 12 to 14 minutes. She remained in a coma for approximately three weeks and then progressed to an unconscious state in which she was able to orally ingest some nutrition. In order to ease feeding and further the recovery, surgeons implanted a gastrostomy feeding and hydration tube in Cruzan with the consent of her then husband. Subsequent rehabilitative efforts proved unavailing. She now lies in a Missouri state hospital in what is commonly referred to as a persistent vegetative state: generally, a condition in which a person exhibits motor reflexes but evinces no indications of significant cognitive function.[1] The State of Missouri is bearing the cost of her care.

After it had become apparent that Nancy Cruzan had virtually no chance of regaining her mental faculties her parents asked hospital employees to terminate the artificial nutrition and hydration procedures. All agree that such a removal would cause her death. The employees refused to honor the request without court approval. The parents then sought and received authorization from the state trial court for termination. The court found that a person in Nancy's condition had a fundamental right under the State and Federal Constitutions to refuse or direct the withdrawal of "death prolonging procedures." The court also found that Nancy's "expressed thoughts at age twenty-five in somewhat serious conversation with a housemate friend that if sick or injured she would not wish to continue her life unless she could live at least halfway normally suggests that given her present condition she would not wish to continue on with her nutrition and hydration." The Supreme Court of

Missouri reversed by a divided vote. The court recognized a right to refuse treatment embodied in the common-law doctrine of informed consent, but expressed skepticism about the application of that doctrine in the circumstances of this case. The court also declined to read a broad right of privacy into the State Constitution which would "support the right of a person to refuse medical treatment in every circumstance," and expressed doubt as to whether such a right existed under the U.S. Constitution. It then decided that the Missouri Living Will statute (1986) embodied a state policy strongly favoring the preservation of life. The court found that Cruzan's statements to her roommate regarding her desire to live or die under certain conditions were "unreliable for the purpose of determining her intent," "and thus insufficient to support the co-guardians' claim to exercise substituted judgment on Nancy's behalf." It rejected the argument that Cruzan's parents were entitled to order the termination of her medical treatment, concluding that "no person can assume that choice for an incompetent in the absence of the formalities required under Missouri's Living Will statutes or the clear and convincing, inherently reliable evidence absent here." . . .

We granted certiorari to consider the question of whether Cruzan has a right under the U.S. Constitution that would require the hospital to withdraw life-sustaining treatment from her under these circumstances.

At common law, even the touching of one person by another without consent and without legal justification was a battery. Before the turn of the century, this Court observed that "[n]o right is held more sacred, or is more carefully guarded, by the common law, than the right of every individual to the possession and control of his own person, free from all restraint or interference of others, unless by clear and unquestionable authority of law." This notion of bodily integrity has been embodied in the requirement that informed consent is generally required for medical treatment. Justice Cardozo, while on the Court of Appeals of New York, aptly described this doctrine: "Every human being of adult years and sound mind has a right to determine what shall be done with his own body; and a surgeon who performs an operation without his patient's consent commits an assault, for which he is liable in damage." The informed consent doctrine has become firmly entrenched in American tort law.

The logical corollary of the doctrine of informed consent is that the patient generally possesses the right not to consent, that is, to refuse treatment. Until about 15 years ago and the seminal decision [of the New Jersey Supreme Court] in *In re Quinlan* (1976), the number of right-to-refuse-treatment decisions were relatively few. Most of the earlier cases involved patients who refused medical treatment forbidden by their religious beliefs, thus implicating First Amendment rights as well as common law rights of self-determination. More recently, however, with the advance of medical technology capable of sustaining life well past the point where natural forces would have brought certain death in earlier times, cases involving the right to refuse life-sustaining treatment have burgeoned.

In the *Quinlan* case, young Karen Quinlan suffered severe brain damage as the result of anoxia, and entered a persistent vegetative state. Karen's father sought judicial approval to disconnect his daughter's respirator. The New Jersey Supreme Court granted the relief, holding that Karen had a right of privacy grounded in the Federal Constitution to terminate treatment. Recognizing that this right was not absolute, however, the court balanced it against asserted state interests. Noting that the State's interest "weakens and the individual's right to privacy grows as the degree of bodily invasion increases and the prognosis dims," the court concluded that the state interests had to give way in that case. The court also concluded that the "only practical way" to prevent the loss of Karen's privacy right due to her incompetence was to allow her guardian and family to decide "whether she would exercise it in these circumstances."

After *Quinlan,* however, most courts have based a right to refuse treatment either solely on the common law right to informed consent or on both the common law right and a constitutional privacy right. . . .

State courts have available to them for decision a number of sources—state constitutions, statutes, and common law—which are not available to us. In this Court, the question is simply and starkly whether the U.S. Constitution prohibits Missouri from choosing the rule of decision which it did. This is the first case in which we have been squarely presented with the issue of whether the U.S. Constitution grants what is in common parlance referred to as a "right to die." We follow the judicious counsel . . . that in deciding "a question of such magnitude and importance . . . it is the [better] part of wisdom not to attempt, by any general statement, to cover every possible phase of the subject."

The Fourteenth Amendment provides that no State shall "deprive any person of life, liberty, or property, without due process of law." The principle that a competent person has a constitutionally protected liberty interest in refusing unwanted medical treatment may be inferred from our prior decisions. In *Jacobson v. Massachusetts* (1905), for instance, the Court balanced an individual's liberty interest in declining an unwanted smallpox vaccine against the State's interest in preventing disease. . . . Just this Term, in the course of holding that a State's procedures for administering antipsychotic medication to prisoners were sufficient to satisfy due process concerns, we recognized that prisoners possess "a significant liberty interest in avoiding the unwanted administration of antipsychotic drugs under the Due Process Clause of the Fourteenth Amendment." Still other cases support the recognition of a general liberty interest in refusing medical treatment.

But determining that a person has a "liberty interest" under the Due Process Clause does not end the inquiry;[2] "whether respondent's constitutional rights have been violated must be determined by balancing his liberty interests against the relevant state interests."

Petitioners insist that under the general holdings of our cases, the forced administration of life-sustaining medical treatment, and even of artificially delivered food and water essential to life, would implicate a competent person's liberty interest. Although we think the logic of the cases [referred to] above would embrace such a liberty interest, the dramatic consequences involved in refusal of such treatment would inform the inquiry as to whether the deprivation of that interest is constitutionally permissible. But for purposes of this case, we assume that the U.S. Constitution would grant a competent person a constitutionally protected right to refuse life-saving hydration and nutrition.

Petitioners go on to assert that an incompetent person should possess the same right in this respect as is possessed by a competent person. . . . The difficulty with petitioners' claim is that in a sense it begs the question: An incompetent person is not able to make an informed and voluntary choice to exercise a hypothetical right to refuse treatment or any other right. Such a "right" must be exercised for her, if at all, by some sort of surrogate. Here, Missouri has in effect recognized that under certain circumstances a surrogate may act for the patient in electing to have hydration and nutrition withdrawn in such a way as to cause death, but it has established a procedural safeguard to assure that the action of the surrogate conforms as best it may to the wishes expressed by the patient while competent. Missouri requires that evidence of the incompetent's wishes as to the withdrawal of treatment be proved by clear and convincing evidence. The question, then, is whether the U.S. Constitution forbids the establishment of this procedural requirement by the State. We hold that it does not.

Whether or not Missouri's clear and convincing evidence requirement comports with the U.S. Constitution depends in part on what interests the State may properly seek to protect in this situation. Missouri relies on its interest in the protection and preservation of human life, and there can be no gainsaying this interest. As a general matter, the States—indeed, all civilized nations—demonstrate their commitment to life by treating homicide as serious crime. Moreover, the majority of States in this country have laws imposing criminal penalties on one who assists another to commit suicide. We do not think a State is required to remain neutral in the face of an informed and voluntary decision by a physically able adult to starve to death.

But in the context presented here, a State has more particular interests at stake. The choice between life and death is a deeply personal decision of obvious and overwhelming finality. We believe Missouri may legitimately seek to safeguard the personal element of this choice through the imposition of heightened evidentiary requirements. It cannot be disputed that the Due Process Clause protects an interest in life as well as an interest in refusing life-sustaining medical treatment. Not all incompetent patients will have loved ones available to serve as surrogate decision makers. And even where family members are present, "[t]here will, of course, be some unfortunate situations in which family members will not act to protect a patient." A State is entitled to guard against potential abuses in such situations. Similarly, a State is entitled to consider that a judicial proceeding to make a determination regarding an incompetent's wishes may very well not be an adversarial one, with the added guarantee of accurate fact finding that the adversary process brings with it. Finally, we think a State may properly decline to make judgments about the "quality" of life that a particular individual may enjoy, and simply assert an unqualified interest in the preservation of human life to be weighed against the constitutionally protected interests of the individual.

In our view, Missouri has permissibly sought to advance these interests through the adoption of a "clear and convincing" standard of proof to govern such proceedings. "The function of a standard of proof, as that concept is embodied in the Due Process Clause and in the realm of fact finding, is to 'instruct the fact finder concerning the degree of confidence our society thinks he should have in the correctness of factual conclusions for a particular type of adjudication.'" . . .

We think it self-evident that the interests at stake in the instant proceedings are more substantial, both on an individual and societal level, than those involved in a run-of-the-mill civil dispute. But not only does the standard of proof reflect the importance of a particular adjudication, it also serves as "a societal judgment about how the risk of error should be distributed between the litigants." The more stringent the burden of proof a party must bear, the more that party bears the risk of an erroneous decision. We believe that Missouri may permissibly place an increased risk of an erroneous decision on those seeking to terminate an incompetent individual's life-sustaining treatment. An erroneous decision not to terminate results in a maintenance of the status quo; the possibility of subsequent developments such as advancements in medical science, the discovery of new evidence regarding the patient's intent, changes in the law, or simply the unexpected death of the patient despite the administration of life-sustaining treatment, at least create the potential that a wrong decision will eventually be corrected or its impact mitigated. An erroneous decision to withdraw life-sustaining treatment, however, is not susceptible of correction. . . .

In sum, we conclude that a State may apply a clear and convincing evidence standard in proceedings where a guardian seeks to discontinue nutrition and hydration of a person diagnosed to be in a persistent vegetative state. . . .

The Supreme Court of Missouri held that in this case the testimony adduced at trial did not amount to clear and convincing proof of the patient's desire to have hydration and nutrition withdrawn. In so doing, it reversed a decision of the Missouri trial court which had found that the evidence "suggest[ed]" Nancy Cruzan would not have desired to continue such measures, but which had not adopted the standard of "clear and convincing evidence" enunciated by the Supreme Court. The testimony adduced at trial consisted primarily of Nancy Cruzan's statements made to a housemate about a year before her accident that she would not want to live should she face life as a "vegetable," and other observations to the same effect. The observations did not deal in terms with withdrawal of medical treatment or of hydration and nutrition. We cannot say that the Supreme Court of Missouri committed constitutional error in reaching the conclusion that it did.[3]

Petitioners alternatively contend that Missouri must accept the "substituted judgment" of close family members even in the absence of substantial proof that their views reflect the views of the patient. . . .

No doubt is engendered by anything in this record but that Nancy Cruzan's mother and father are loving and caring parents. If the State were required by the U.S. Constitution to repose a right of "substituted judgment" with anyone, the Cruzans would surely qualify. But we do not think the Due Process Clause requires the State to repose judgment on these matters with anyone but the patient herself. Close family members may have a strong feeling—a feeling not at all ignoble or unworthy, but not entirely disinterested, either—that they do not wish to witness the continuation of the life of a loved one which they regard as hopeless, meaningless, and even degrading. But there is no automatic assurance that the view of close family members will necessarily be the same as the patient's would have been had she been confronted with the prospect of her situation while competent. All of the reasons previously discussed for allowing Missouri to require clear and convincing evidence of the patient's wishes lead us to conclude that the State may choose to defer only to those wishes, rather than confide the decision to close family members.

The judgment of the Supreme Court of Missouri is *Affirmed.*

Endnotes

1. The State Supreme Court, adopting much of the trial court's findings, described Nancy Cruzan's medical condition as follows: ". . . In sum, Nancy is diagnosed as in a persistent vegetative state. She is not dead. She is not terminally ill. Medical experts testified that she could live another thirty years." . . .

2. Although many state courts have held that a right to refuse treatment is encompassed by a generalized constitutional right of privacy, we have never so held. We believe this issue is more properly analyzed in terms of a Fourteenth Amendment liberty interest. See *Bowers v. Hardwick* (1986).

3. The clear and convincing standard of proof has been variously defined in this context as "proof sufficient to persuade the trier of fact that the patient held a firm and settled commitment to the termination of life supports under the circumstances like those presented," and as evidence which "produces in the mind of the trier of fact a firm belief or conviction as to the truth of the allegations sought to be established, evidence so clear, direct, and weighty and convincing as to enable [the fact finder] to come to a clear conviction, without hesitancy, of the truth of the precise facts in issue." . . .

21. *The Case of Dr. Kevorkian*

In a campaign to allow physician-assisted suicide, Dr. Jack Kevorkian has helped a number of nonterminally ill but seriously impaired people in the state of Michigan to take their own lives. Responding to Kevorkian's actions, the state of Michigan recently outlawed assisted suicide for fifteen months to allow the issue to be studied.

A California man paralyzed from the neck down says he plans to come to Michigan in early 1993 to commit suicide with the help of Dr. Jack Kevorkian, according to a published report due out Monday.

The man, identified only as Gary, tells *Time* magazine he doesn't want to die but finds life as a quadriplegic unacceptable. He plans to end his life in Michigan before a temporary state law banning assisted suicide takes effect March 31.

"They're going to shut him down April 1, and I'm going to be one of the lifeboats off the Titanic," Gary told the magazine for its Dec. 28 issue.

"I'm thinking somewhere between January and March," he said. "It could be sooner. The luxury of having more time is gone."

Reprinted from the *South Bend Tribune*, December 20, 1992 by permission of Associated Press.

There was no answer late Saturday afternoon at Kevorkian's apartment in the Detroit suburb of Royal Oak. His attorney, Geoffrey Fieger, said there were no plans for the man to come to Michigan.

"I don't know if Jack will help him," Fieger said Saturday. "If he's announced that he's been counseling with Jack, I suppose that's true. I think Jack has been counseling him to continue to live, not to end his life."

Kevorkian has been present at the suicides of eight people, all women, since June 1990. He was present at the suicides of two suburban Detroit women last week, just hours before Gov. John Engler signed a bill outlawing assisted suicide for fifteen months while the issue is studied.

Fieger said the California man's wife wrote Kevorkian several weeks ago, saying his spirits had improved.

"The last I heard was that she for the first time had seen some glimmer of hope and . . . if that's true, and I certainly hope it is, then he should consider not coming."

Gary, 34, was left paralyzed from the neck down after being shot in the spine five years ago. "Realistically, there is no cure and this type of life is not acceptable to me," he told the magazine.

Gary said he first contacted the retired pathologist in April. Last month, Kevorkian called to ask how soon he would be ready because of impending legislative action, Gary said.

"I think his words were something to the effect, 'We have to wrap this up. How soon can you be here?' I thought for about 10 or 15 seconds and I said, 'One week,'" he said.

Gary said Kevorkian told him he could change his mind at any time.

"I look at my situation like a war," Gary said. ". . . In the final analysis I may not win this war. But I fought back hard. I don't want to die, but I don't want to live like this."

Suggestions *for* Further Reading

Anthologies

Brody, Baruch, and Engelhardt, Tristan. *Bioethics.* Englewood Cliffs, N.J.: Prentice-Hall, 1987.

Cohen, Marshall, and others. *The Rights and Wrongs of Abortion.* Princeton: Princeton University Press, 1974.

Feinberg, Joel. *The Problem of Abortion,* 2nd ed. Belmont, Calif.: Wadsworth Publishing Co., 1984.

Kohl, Marvin. *Beneficent Euthanasia.* Buffalo, N.Y.: Prometheus, 1975.

Ladd, John. *Ethical Issues Relating to Life and Death.* New York: Oxford University Press, 1979.

Munson, Ronald. *Interventions and Reflections.* Belmont, Calif.: Wadsworth Publishing Co., 1979.

Basic Concepts

Devine, Philip. *The Ethics of Homicide.* Ithaca, N.Y.: Cornell University Press, 1978.

Glover, Jonathan. *Causing Death and Saving Lives.* New York: Penguin Books, 1977.

Steinbock, Bonnie, ed. *Killing and Letting Die.* Englewood Cliffs, N.J.: Prentice-Hall, 1980.

Alternative Views

Battin, Margaret Pabst. *The Least Worst Death.* New York: Oxford University Press, 1994.

Callahan, Daniel. *Abortion: Law, Choice and Morality.* New York: Macmillan, 1970.

Crum, Gary, and McCormack, Thelma. *Abortion: Pro-Choice or Pro-Life.* Washington, D.C.: American University Press, 1992.

Grisez, Germain, and Boyle, Joseph. *Life and Death with Liberty and Justice.* Notre Dame: University of Notre Dame Press, 1979.

Luker, Kristin. *Abortion and the Politics of Motherhood.* Berkeley: University of California Press, 1984.

Nicholson, Susan. *Abortion and the Roman Catholic Church.* Knoxville: Religious Ethics, 1978.

Pojman, Louis P. *Life and Death.* Boston: Jones and Bartlett Publishers, 1992.

Rachels, James. *The End of Life.* New York: Oxford University Press, 1986.

Summer, L. W. *Abortion and Moral Theory.* Princeton: Princeton University Press, 1981.

Tribe, Lawrence. *Abortion: The Clash of Absolutes.* Norton: New York, 1990.

Practical Applications

Denes, Magda. *In Necessity and Sorrow: Life and Death in an Abortion Hospital.* New York: Penguin Books, 1977.

Law Reform Commission of Canada. *Euthanasia, Aiding Suicide and Cessation of Treatment.* Working Paper 28, 1982.

Supreme Court of Michigan, *People v. Kevorkian,* 1994.

Section IV

Sex Equality

Introduction

Basic Concepts

The problem of sex equality concerns the question of whether the sexes should be treated equally, and, if so, what constitutes equal treatment. This question was at the heart of the decade-long public debate on the Equal Rights Amendment to the Constitution (the ERA), which began in March 1972, when the Senate passed the amendment with a vote of 84 to 8, and ended in June 1982, when the extended deadline for the ERA expired—three states short of the 38 required for ratification.

The complete text of the ERA was as follows:

1. Equality of rights under the law shall not be denied or abridged by the United States or by any state on account of sex.
2. The Congress shall have the power to enforce by appropriate legislation the provisions of this article.
3. This amendment shall take effect two years after the date of ratification.

Public support for the ERA over this period, judging from opinion polls, hovered between 55 and 60 percent, but in key states anti-ERA forces were able to mount sufficient resistance to pre-

vent its passage. In the end, Alabama, Arizona, Arkansas, Florida, Georgia, Illinois, Louisiana, Mississippi, Missouri, Nevada, North Carolina, Oklahoma, Utah, and Virginia failed to ratify the amendment.

Anti-ERA forces were able to block ratification because they successfully shifted the debate from equal rights to the substantive changes the ERA might bring about. This strategy was effective because support for the amendment generally came from individuals sympathetic to the notion of "equal rights" but not necessarily committed to substantive changes in women's roles.[1] For example, in one national survey, 67 percent of the people who claimed to have heard or read about the ERA favored it, 25 percent were opposed to it, and 8 percent had no opinion. Many people in the sample, however, had quite traditional views about women's roles. Two-thirds of the respondents thought that preschool children would suffer if their mothers worked, 62 percent thought married women should not hold jobs when jobs were scarce and their husbands could support them, and 55 percent thought it was more important for a woman to advance her husband's career than to have one of her own.

But what substantive changes would the ERA have brought about if it had been ratified in 1982? The surprising answer is not many, at least in the short run.[2] In 1970, when the ERA first reached the floor of Congress, a significant number of laws and official practices denied women "equality of rights under the law." For example, in 1970, eight states treated all property that a couple bought with their earnings during marriage as "community property," and these states normally gave the husband managerial control over such property. By 1976, most of these laws had been voluntarily changed or struck down by the Supreme Court's interpretation of the equal protection clause of the Fourteenth Amendment. Of course, supporters of the ERA did attempt to argue for the amendment on the grounds that it would bring about equal pay for equal work. Lobbyists for the ERA in state capitols wore buttons that said "59¢" to remind legislators that women who worked full-time outside the home still typically earned only 59 cents for every dollar men earned—a ratio that has changed little since the federal government first began publishing such statistics in the 1950s. But the passage of the ERA would have had little immediate impact on that inequality. The ERA would have kept the federal or state governments from legally denying or abridging "equality of rights under the law." However, to help workers, the ERA would have had to do more than just make the law gender blind. It would have had to forbid wage discrimination by *private* organizations and individuals. And this it did not do.

Moreover, the ERA would have had few of the effects its opponents predicted. For example, Phyllis Schlafly frequently claimed that the ERA would require unisex public toilets and combat duty for women, but the Supreme Court would have found the first requirement an infringement of the right to privacy and the second would have run afoul of the war powers clause of the Constitution, which gives military commanders the freedom to decide how best to use their forces. Yet despite the fact that the immediate impact of the passage of the ERA would have

been largely symbolic, neither proponents nor opponents sufficiently recognized this or, if they did, were not willing to surrender their exaggerated claims about the effects the amendment would have. Leaders on both sides of this debate may have feared the difficulty of motivating their followers if these exaggerated claims were abandoned.

Alternative Views

Susan Okin argues (Selection 22) that women have not achieved equality in society. Most of the unpaid labor in the family is done by women. Most jobs assume that workers have wives at home, and traditional gender-structured families make women vulnerable in ways that men are not vulnerable. Okin points out that contemporary political philosophers have ignored all this. They have assumed without argument the justice of traditional gender-structured families. Okin contends that this is a morally unacceptable state of affairs. Families are the first school of justice, and they must be shown to be just if we are to have a just society.

In Selection 23, James P. Sterba argues that if family structures are to be just they must meet the requirements of feminist justice, which he identifies with an ideal of androgyny. This ideal of androgyny requires that traits that are truly desirable in society be equally available to both women and men, or in the case of virtues, equally expected of both women and men. He considers attempts to derive the ideal of androgyny either from a right to equal opportunity that is a central requirement of a welfare liberal conception of justice or from an equal right of self-development that is a central requirement of a socialist conception of justice. He argues that although the ideal of androgyny is compatible with the requirements of both of these two conceptions of justice, it also transcends them by requiring that all virtues be equally expected of both women and men. Sterba further argues that the ideal of androgyny would require (1) that all children irrespective of their sex must be given the same type of upbringing consistent with their native capabilities and (2) that mothers and fathers must also have the same opportunities for education and employment consistent with their native capabilities. he then considers how achieving equal opportunity for women and men requires vastly improved day-care facilities and flexible (usually part-time) work schedules for both women and men.

In Selection 24, Christina Sommers criticizes the attack by feminist philosophers, like Okin and Sterba, on traditional family structures. She distinguishes liberal feminists from radical feminists and contends that liberal feminists like herself want equal opportunity in the workplace and politics, but would leave marriage and motherhood "untouched and unimpugned." By contrast, Sommers contends that radical feminists are committed to an assimilationist or androgynous ideal that would destroy the (traditional) family and deny most women what they want. Sommers, however, never explains how it is possible to secure for women equal opportunity in the workplace and politics while rejecting androgyny in favor of traditional gender roles. For example, how could women be passive, submissive, dependent, indecisive, and weak and still enjoy the same opportunities in the workplace and politics that are enjoyed by aggressive, dominant, independent, decisive, and strong men?

Marilyn Friedman (Selection 25) does not challenge Sommers's contention that radical feminists are committed to an assimilationist or androgynous ideal. There is, however, an important distinction between these two ideals. According to an assimilationist ideal, "one's sex should be no more noticeable than one's eye color," but according to an androgynous ideal, this need not be the case, as long as all desirable traits are equally open to both women and men, and all virtues equally expected of both women and men.

Friedman does, however, question whether what Sommers supports is really what most women want. She quotes a 1983 survey which indicated that 63 percent of women preferred nontraditional family relationships, and points out that in 1977 only 16 percent of American households were traditional families consisting of a legally married heterosexual couple and their children, in which the man is the sole breadwinner and "head" of the household, and the woman does the domestic work and childcare. In responding to Friedman, Sommers explains that what she means by a traditional family is one that consists of two heterosexual parents and one or more children in which the mother plays a distinctive gender role in caring for the children.[3] This definition obviously broadens the class of families to which Sommers is referring. But in her response, Sommers goes on to renounce any attempt to be promoting even the traditional family—even as she defines it. What she claims to be promoting is simply "the right and liberty to live under the arrangement of one's choice." According to Sommers, if people want to live in nontraditional families, they should be free to do so.

Friedman further disagrees with Sommers, contending that no woman should "swoon at the sight of Rhett Butler carrying Scarlett O'Hara up the stairs to a fate undreamt of in feminist philosophy." According to Friedman, what Rhett Butler is doing in *Gone With the Wind* is raping Scarlett O'Hara. In a subsequent response to Sommers, Friedman, noting that Scarlett O'Hara, although initially unwilling, later appears to be a willing sexual partner, defines "rape" as "any very intimate sexual contact which is *initiated* forcefully or against the will of the recipient."[4] Friedman allows that others might want to define such activity as sexual domination rather than rape, but under either definition, Friedman condemns it, whereas Sommers does not. In her response, Sommers cites approvingly the following passage from *Scarlett's Women: Gone With the Wind and Its Female Fans.*

> The majority of my correspondents (and I agree) recognize the ambiguous nature of the encounter and interpret it as a scene of mutually pleasurable rough sex. . . . By far the majority of women who responded to me saw the episode as erotically exciting, emotionally stirring and profoundly memorable. Few of them referred to it as "rape."[5]

In Selection 26, Warren Farrell argues that while the various ways that women lack power in society have been noted, the various ways that men lack power have not been similarly recognized. In this selection, Farrell chronicles many of the ways that he thinks men lack power in society. For example, Farrell notes that men must fight in wars, but women do not; that the suicide rate of boys and men is much higher than that of girls and women; that 99 percent of volunteer firefighters are men; and that most men are unpaid bodyguards of the women they are with. Farrell concludes from this that there is a high degree of equality between the sexes, or as he puts it, "both sexes make themselves 'slaves' of the other sex in different ways."

While Farrell does not credit feminism for making the sexes equal, Susan Faludi (Selection 27) criticizes the view that, due to the feminist movement, women have now achieved equality with men, but that this equality has not turned out to be particularly good for women. First, Faludi denies that women have really achieved equality with men. She notes that 75 percent of full-time working women make less than $20,000 a year, which is nearly double the percentage of males in the same bracket, and that 80 percent of working women are still stuck in traditional female jobs such as secretaries, administrative "support" workers, and salesclerks. Second, Faludi notes that in national surveys 75 to 95 percent of women credit the feminist movement with actually improving their lives, not making them worse. So Faludi concludes that

while women have not yet achieved equality with men, the feminist movement has helped women to achieve the gains they have. What worries Faludi, however, is that there now exists a backlash movement to discredit the feminist movement and take back the gains that it has brought to women.

Practical Applications

Turning to practical applications, we can see that, at least in the statement of the National Organization for Women (NOW) Bill of Rights (Selection 28), there was never any confusion that the ERA would achieve all the goals of the organization. In this Bill of Rights, the ERA is one of eight goals to be achieved.

Recently, maternity leave rights in employment, another of NOW's goals, was at stake in *California Federal Savings and Loan v. the Department of Fair Employment and Housing* (Selection 29). Here the issue before the Supreme Court was whether Title VII of the Civil Rights Act of 1964 as amended by the Pregnancy Discrimination Act of 1978 (PDA) nullifies a California law that requires employers to provide leave and reinstatement to employees disabled by pregnancy. The majority of the court ruled that it did not nullify the law for two reasons. First, in passing PDA, Congress simply wanted to prohibit discrimination against pregnant women; there was no discussion of preferential treatment for pregnant women. In addition, by allowing both men and women to have families without losing their jobs, the California law did share with Title VII and PDA the goal of equal opportunity. Second, even if PDA did prohibit preferential treatment for pregnant women, an employer could avoid violating both PDA and the California statute by giving comparable benefits to all similarly disabled employees.

What is interesting is that NOW opposed the Court's decision in this case. Apparently, NOW's leaders were concerned that such preferential treatment might result in protective legislation that would be reminiscent of the nineteenth century by encouraging sexual stereotypes and restraining women from taking their rightful place in the workplace. Although this is a legitimate concern, it can be addressed by determin-ing whether each particular piece of relevant legislation advances the goal of equal opportunity. If it does, as the California law seems to do, there shouldn't be any objection to it, at least from a welfare liberal or socialist point of view.

Endnotes

1. Jane J. Mansbridge, *Why We Lost the ERA* (Chicago: University of Chicago Press, 1986), Chapter 3.

2. Ibid., Chapters 5–7.

3. Christina Sommers, "Do These Feminists Like Women?" *Journal of Social Philosophy* (1991), pp. 66–74.

4. Marilyn Friedman, "Does Sommers Like Women?" *Journal of Social Philosophy* (1991), pp. 75–90.

5. Ibid., p. 72.

22. *Justice and Gender*

SUSAN OKIN

Susan Okin points out that in the face of the radical inequality that exists between women and men in our society there is still a widespread failure of political philosophers to address gender issues in their political theories. She claims that this is true even among those philosophers who have seen the need to adopt gender-neutral language. Okin argues that no theory of justice can be adequate until it addresses these issues.

We as a society pride ourselves on our democratic values. We don't believe people should be constrained by innate differences from being able to achieve desired positions of influence to improve their well-being; equality of opportunity is our professed aim. The Preamble to our Constitution stresses the importance of justice, as well as the general welfare and the blessings of liberty. The Pledge of Allegiance asserts that our republic preserves "liberty and justice for all."

Yet substantial inequalities between the sexes still exist in our society. In economic terms, full-time work-ing women (after some very recent improvement) earn on average 71 percent of the earnings of full-time working men. One-half of poor and three-fifths of chronically poor households with dependent children are maintained by a single female parent. The poverty rate for elderly women is nearly twice that for elderly men. On the political front, two out of one hundred U.S. senators are women, one out of nine justices seems to be considered sufficient female representation on the Supreme Court, and the number of men chosen in each congressional election far exceeds the number of women elected in the entire history of the country. Underlying and intertwined with all of these inequalities is the unequal distribution of the unpaid labor of the family.

An equal sharing between the sexes of family responsibilities, especially child care, is "the great revolution that has not happened." Women, including mothers of young children, are, of course, working outside the household far more than their mothers did. And the small proportion of women who reach high-level positions in politics, business, and the professions command a vastly disproportionate amount of space in the media, compared with the millions of women who work at low-paying, dead-end jobs, the millions who do part-time work with its lack of benefits, and the millions of others who stay home performing for no pay what is frequently not even acknowledged as work. Certainly, the fact that women are doing more paid work does not imply that they are more equal. It is often said that we are living in a postfeminist era. This claim, due in part to the distorted emphasis on women who have "made it," is false, no matter which of its meanings is intended. It is certainly not true that feminism has been vanquished, and equally untrue that it is no longer needed because its aims have been fulfilled. Until there is justice within the family, women will not be able to gain equality in politics, at work, or in any other sphere.

. . . The typical current practices of family life, structured to a large extent by gender, are not just. Both the expectation and the experience of the division of labor by sex make women vulnerable. As I shall show, a cycle of power relations and decisions pervades both family and workplace, each reinforcing the inequalities between the sexes that already exist within the other. Not only women, but children of both sexes, too, are often made vulnerable by gender-structured marriage. One-quarter of children in the United States now live in families with only one parent—in almost 90 percent of cases, the mother. Contrary to common perceptions—in which the situation of never-married mothers looms largest—65 percent of single-parent families are a result of marital separation or divorce. Recent research in a number of states has shown that, in the average case, the standard of living of divorced women and the children who live with them plummets after divorce, whereas the economic situation of divorced men tends to be better than when they were married.

A central source of injustice for women these days is that the law, most noticeably in the event of divorce,

treats more or less as equals those whom custom, workplace discrimination, and the still conventional division of labor within the family have made very unequal. Central to this socially created inequality are two commonly made but inconsistent presumptions: that women are primarily responsible for the rearing of children; and that serious and committed members of the work force (regardless of class) do not have primary responsibility, or even shared responsibility, for the rearing of children. The old assumption of the workplace, still implicit, is that workers have wives at home. It is built not only into the structure and expectations of the workplace but into other crucial social institutions, such as schools, which make no attempt to take account, in their scheduled hours or vacations, of the fact that parents are likely to hold jobs.

Now, of course, many wage workers do not have wives at home. Often, they *are* wives and mothers, or single, separated, or divorced mothers of small children. But neither the family nor the workplace has taken much account of this fact. Employed wives still do by far the greatest proportion of unpaid family work, such as child care and housework. Women are far more likely to take time out of the workplace or to work part-time because of family responsibilities than are their husbands or male partners. And they are much more likely to move because of their husbands' employment needs or opportunities than their own. All these tendencies, which are due to a number of factors, including the sex segregation and discrimination of the workplace itself, tend to be cyclical in their effects: Wives advance more slowly than their husbands at work and thus gain less seniority, and the discrepancy between their wages increases over time. Then, because both the power structure of the family and what is regarded as consensual "rational" family decision-making reflect the fact that the husband usually earns more, it will become even less likely as time goes on that the unpaid work of the family will be shared between the spouses. Thus the cycle of inequality is perpetuated. Often hidden from view within a marriage, it is in the increasingly likely event of marital breakdown that the socially constructed inequality of married women is at its most visible.

This is what I mean when I say that gender-structured marriage *makes* women vulnerable. These are not matters of natural necessity, as some people would believe. Surely nothing in our natures dictates that men should not be equal participants in the rearing of their children. Nothing in the nature of work makes it impossible to adjust it to the fact that people are parents as well as workers. That these things have not happened is part of the historically, socially constructed differentiation between the sexes that feminists have come to call *gender*. We live in a society that has over the years regarded the innate characteristic of sex as one of the clearest legitimizers of different rights and restrictions, both formal and informal. While the legal sanctions that uphold male dominance have begun to be eroded in the past century, and more rapidly in the last twenty years, the heavy weight of tradition, combined with the effects of socialization, still works powerfully to reinforce sex roles that are commonly regarded as of unequal prestige and worth. The sexual division of labor has not only been a fundamental part of the marriage contract, but so deeply influences us in our formative years that feminists of both sexes who try to reject it can find themselves struggling against it with varying degrees of ambivalence. Based on this linchpin, "gender"—by which I mean *the deeply entrenched institutionalization of sexual difference*—still permeates our society.

The Construction of Gender

Due to feminism and feminist theory, gender is coming to be recognized as a social factor of major importance. Indeed, the new meaning of the word reflects the fact that so much of what has traditionally been thought of as sexual difference is now considered by many to be largely socially produced. Feminist scholars from many disciplines and with radically different points of view have contributed to the enterprise of making gender fully visible and comprehensible. At one end of the spectrum are those whose explanations of the subordination of women focus primarily on biological difference as causal in the construction of gender, and at the other end are those who argue that biological difference may not even lie at the core of the social construction that is gender; the views of the vast majority of feminists fall between these extremes. The rejection of biological determinism and the corresponding emphasis on gender as a social construction char-

acterize most current feminist scholarship. Of particular relevance is work in psychology, where scholars have investigated the importance of female primary parenting in the formation of our gendered identities, and in history and anthropology, where emphasis has been placed on the historical and cultural variability of gender. Some feminists have been criticized for developing theories of gender that do not take sufficient account of differences *among* women, especially race, class, religion, and ethnicity. While such critiques should always inform our research and improve our arguments, it would be a mistake to allow them to detract our attention from gender itself as a factor of significance. Many injustices are experienced by women *as women*, whatever the differences among them and whatever other injustices they also suffer from. The past and present gendered nature of the family, and the ideology that surrounds it, affects virtually all women, whether or not they live or ever lived in traditional families. Recognizing this is not to deny or de-emphasize the fact that gender may affect different subgroups of women to a different extent and in different ways.

The potential significance of feminist discoveries and conclusions about gender for issues of social justice cannot be overemphasized. They undermine centuries of argument that started with the notion that not only the distinct differentiation of women and men but the domination of women by men, being natural, was therefore inevitable and not even to be considered in discussions of justice. As I shall make clear . . . , despite the fact that such notions cannot stand up to rational scrutiny, they not only still survive but flourish in influential places.

During the same two decades in which feminists have been intensely thinking, researching, analyzing, disagreeing about, and rethinking the subject of gender, our political and legal institutions have been increasingly faced with issues concerning the injustices of gender and their effects. These issues are being decided within a fundamentally patriarchal system, founded in a tradition in which "individuals" were assumed to be male heads of households. Not surprisingly, the system has demonstrated a limited capacity for determining what is just, in many cases involving gender. Sex discrimination, sexual harassment, abortion, pregnancy in the workplace, parental leave, childcare, and surrogate mothering have all become major and well-publicized issues of public policy, engaging both courts and legislatures. Issues of family justice, in particular—from child custody and divorce terms to physical and sexual abuse of wives and children—have become increasingly visible and pressing, and are commanding increasing attention from the police and court systems. There is clearly a major "justice crisis" in contemporary society arising from issues of gender.

Theories of Justice and the Neglect of Gender

During these same two decades, there has been a great resurgence of theories of social justice. Political theory, which had been sparse for a period before the late 1960s except as an important branch of intellectual history, has become a flourishing field, with social justice as its central concern. Yet, remarkably, major contemporary theorists of justice have almost without exception ignored the situation just described. They have displayed little interest in or knowledge of the findings of feminism. They have largely bypassed the fact that the society to which their theories are supposed to pertain is heavily and deeply affected by gender, and faces difficult issues of justice stemming from its gendered past and present assumptions. Since theories of justice are centrally concerned with whether, how, and why persons should be treated differently from one another, this neglect seems inexplicable. These theories are *about* which initial or acquired characteristics or positions in society legitimize differential treatment of persons by social institutions, laws, and customs. They are *about* how and whether and to what extent beginnings should affect outcomes. The division of humanity into two sexes seems to provide an obvious subject for such inquiries. But, as we shall see, this does not strike most contemporary theorists of justice, and their theories suffer in both coherence and relevance because of it. This piece is . . . an attempt to rectify [this neglect], to point the way toward a more fully humanist theory of justice by confronting the question, "How just is gender?"

Why is it that when we turn to contemporary theories of justice, we do not find illuminating and positive contributions to this question? How can theo-

ries of justice that are ostensibly about people in general neglect women, gender, and all the inequalities between the sexes? One reason is that most theorists *assume*, though they do not discuss, the traditional, gender-structured family. Another is that they often employ gender-neutral language in a false, hollow way. Let us examine these two points.

The Hidden Gender-Structured Family

In the past, political theorists often used to distinguish clearly between "private" domestic life and the "public" life of politics and the marketplace, claiming explicitly that the two spheres operated in accordance with different principles. They separated out the family from what they deemed the subject matter of politics, and they made closely related, explicit claims about the nature of women and the appropriateness of excluding them from civil and political life. Men, the subjects of the theories, were able to make the transition back and forth from domestic to public life with ease, largely because of the functions performed by women in the family. When we turn to contemporary theories of justice, superficial appearances can easily lead to the impression that they are inclusive of women. In fact, they continue the same "separate spheres" tradition, by ignoring the family, its division of labor, and the related economic dependency and restricted opportunities of most women. The judgment that the family is "nonpolitical" is implicit in the fact that it is simply not discussed in most works of political theory today. In one way or another, . . . almost all current theorists continue to assume that the "individual" who is the basic subject of their theories is the male head of a fairly traditional household. Thus the application of principles of justice to relations between the sexes, or within the household, is frequently, though tacitly, ruled out from the start. In the most influential of all twentieth-century theories of justice, that of John Rawls, family life is not only assumed, but is assumed to be just—and yet the prevalent gendered division of labor within the family is neglected, along with the associated distribution of power, responsibility, and privilege. . . .

Moreover, this stance is typical of contemporary theories of justice. They persist, despite the wealth of feminist challenges to their assumptions, in their refusal even to discuss the family and its gender structure, much less to recognize the family as a political institution of primary importance. Recent theories that pay even less attention to issues of family justice than Rawls's include Bruce Ackerman's *Social Justice in the Liberal State,* Ronald Dworkin's *Taking Rights Seriously,* William Galston's *Justice and the Human Good,* Alasdair MacIntyre's *After Virtue* and *Whose Justice? Whose Rationality?,* Robert Nozick's *Anarchy, State, and Utopia,* and Roberto Unger's *Knowledge and Politics and The Critical Legal Studies Movement.* Philip Green's *Retrieving Democracy* is a welcome exception. Michael Walzer's *Spheres of Justice* is exceptional in this regard, but the conclusion that can be inferred from his discussion of the family—that its gender structure is unjust—does not sit at all easily with his emphasis on the shared understandings of a culture as the foundation of justice. For gender is one aspect of social life about which clearly, in the United States in the latter part of the twentieth century, there are no shared understandings.

What is the basis of my claim that the family, while neglected, is *assumed* by theorists of justice? One obvious indication is that they take mature, independent human beings as the subjects of their theories without any mention of how they got to be that way. We know, of course, that human beings develop and mature only as a result of a great deal of attention and hard work, by far the greater part of it done by women. But when theorists of justice talk about "work," they mean paid work performed in the marketplace. They must be assuming that women in the gender-structured family continue to do their unpaid work of nurturing and socializing the young and providing a haven of intimate relations—[or] there would be no moral subjects for them to theorize about. But these activities apparently take place outside the scope of their theories. Typically, the family itself is not examined in the light of whatever standard of justice the theorist arrives at.

The continued neglect of the family by theorists of justice flies in the face of a great deal of persuasive feminist argument. . . . Scholars have clearly revealed the interconnections between the gender structure inside and outside the family and the extent to which the personal is political. They have shown that the assignment of primary parenting to women is crucial, both in forming the gendered identities of men and women and in influencing their respective choices and opportunities in life. Yet, so far, the simultaneous assumption and neglect of the family has allowed the impact of these arguments to go unnoticed in major theories of justice.

False Gender Neutrality

Many academics . . . have become aware of the objectionable nature of using the supposedly generic male forms of nouns and pronouns. As feminist scholars have demonstrated, these words have most often *not* been used, throughout history and the history of philosophy in particular, with the intent to include women. *Man, mankind,* and *he* are going out of style as universal representations, though they have by no means disappeared. But the gender-neutral alternatives that most contemporary theorists employ are often even more misleading than the blatantly sexist use of male terms of reference. They serve to disguise the real and continuing failure of theorists to confront the fact that the human race consists of persons of two sexes. They are by this means able to ignore the fact that there are *some* socially relevant physical differences between women and men, and the even more important fact that the sexes have had very different histories, very different assigned social roles and "natures," and very different degrees of access to power and opportunity in all human societies up to and including the present.

False gender neutrality is not a new phenomenon. Aristotle, for example, used *anthropos*—"human being"—in discussions of "the human good" that turn out not only to exclude women but to depend on their subordination. Kant even wrote of "all rational beings as such" in making arguments that he did not mean to apply to women. But it was more readily apparent that such arguments or conceptions of the good were not about all of us, but only about male heads of families. For their authors usually gave at some point an explanation, no matter how inadequate, of why what they were saying did not apply to women and of the different characteristics and virtues, rights, and responsibilities they thought women ought to have. Nevertheless, their theories have often been read as though they pertain (or can easily be applied) to all of us. Feminist interpretations of the last fifteen years or so have revealed the falsity of this "add women and stir" method of reading the history of political thought.

The falseness of the gender-neutral language of contemporary political theorists is less readily apparent. Most, though not all, contemporary moral and political philosophers use "men and women," "he or she," "persons," or the increasingly ubiquitous "self." Sometimes they even get their computers to distribute masculine and feminine terms of reference randomly. Since they do not explicitly exclude or differentiate women, as most theorists in the past did, we may be tempted to read their theories as inclusive of all of us. But we cannot. Their merely terminological responses to feminist challenges, in spite of giving a superficial impression of tolerance and inclusiveness, often strain credulity and sometimes result in nonsense. They do this in two ways: by ignoring the irreducible biological differences between the sexes, and/or by ignoring their different assigned social roles and consequent power differentials, and the ideologies that have supported them. Thus gender-neutral terms frequently obscure the fact that so much of the real experience of "persons," so long as they live in gender-structured societies, *does* in fact depend on what sex they are.

False gender neutrality is by no means confined to the realm of theory. Its harmful effects can be seen in public policies that have directly affected large numbers of women adversely. It was used, for example, in the Supreme Court's 1976 decision that the exclusion of pregnancy-related disabilities from employers' disability insurance plans was "not a gender-based discrimination at all." In a now infamous phrase of its majority opinion, the Court explained that such plans did not discriminate against women because the distinction drawn by such plans was between pregnant women and "non-pregnant *persons*."

. . . I will illustrate the concept [of false gender neutrality in contemporary political theory] by citing just two examples. Ackerman's *Social Justice in the Liberal State* is a book containing scrupulously gender-neutral language. He breaks with this neutrality only, it seems, to *defy* existing sex roles; he refers to the "Commander," who plays the lead role in the theory, as "she." However, the argument of the book does not address the existing inequality or role differentiation between the sexes, though it has the potential for doing so. The full impact of Ackerman's gender-neutral language without attention to gender is revealed in his section on abortion: a two-page discussion written, with the exception of a single "she," in the completely gender-neutral language of fetuses and their "par-

ents." The impression given is that there is no relevant respect in which the relationship of the two parents to the fetus differs. Now it is, of course, possible to imagine (and in the view of many feminists, would be desirable to achieve) a society in which differences in the relation of women and men to fetuses would be so slight as to reasonably play only a minor role in the discussion of abortion. But this would have to be a society without gender—one in which sexual difference carried no social significance, the sexes were equal in power and interdependence, and "mothering" and "fathering" a child meant the same thing, so that parenting and earning responsibilities were equally shared. We certainly do not live in such a society. Neither is there any discussion of one in Ackerman's theory, in which the division of labor between the sexes is not considered a matter of social (in)justice. In such a context, a "gender-neutral" discussion of abortion is almost as misleading as the Supreme Court's "gender-neutral" discussion of pregnancy.

A second illustration of false gender neutrality comes from Derek Phillips's *Toward a Just Social Order.* Largely because of the extent of his concern—rare among theorists of justice—with how we are to *achieve and maintain* a just social order, Phillips pays an unusual amount of attention to the family. He writes about the family as the locus for the development of a sense of justice and self-esteem, of an appreciation of the meaning of reciprocity, of the ability to exercise unforced choice, and of an awareness of alternative ways of life. The problem with this otherwise admirable discussion is that, apart from a couple of brief exceptions, the family itself is presented in gender-neutral terms that bear little resemblance to actual, gender-structured life.* It is because of "parental affection," "parental nurturance," and "child rearing" that children in Phillips's families become the autonomous moral agents that his just society requires its citizens to be. The child's development of a sense of

---

*He points out the shortcomings of the "earlier ethic of sacrifice," especially for women. He also welcomes the recent lessening of women's dependence on their husbands, but at the same time blames it for tending to weaken family stability. The falseness of Phillips's gender neutrality in discussing parenting is clearly confirmed later in the book, where paid work is "men's" and it is "fathers" who bequeath wealth or poverty on their children.

identity very much depends on being raised by "parental figures who themselves have coherent and well-integrated personal identities," and we are told that such a coherent identity is "ideally one built around commitments to work and love." This all sounds very plausible. But it does not take into account the multiple inequalities of gender. In gender-structured societies—in which the child rearers are women, "parental nurturance" is largely mothering, and those who do what society regards as "meaningful work" are assumed *not* to be primary parents—women in even the best of circumstances face considerable conflicts between love (a fulfilling family life) and "meaningful work." Women in less fortunate circumstances face even greater conflicts between love (even basic care of their children) and any kind of paid work at all.

It follows from Phillips's own premises that these conflicts are very likely to affect the strength and coherence in women of that sense of identity and self-esteem, coming from love and meaningful work, that he regards as essential for being an autonomous moral agent. In turn, if they are mothers, it is also likely to affect their daughters' and sons' developing senses of their identity. Gender is clearly a major obstacle to the attainment of a social order remotely comparable to the just one Phillips aspires to—but his false gender-neutral language allows him to ignore this fact. Although he is clearly aware of how distant in some other respects his vision of a just social order is from contemporary societies, his falsely gender-neutral language leaves him quite unaware of the distance between the type of family that might be able to socialize just citizens and typical families today.

The combined effect of the omission of the family and the falsely gender-neutral language in recent political thought is that most theorists are continuing to ignore the highly political issue of gender. The language they use makes little difference to what they actually do, which is to write about men and about only those women who manage, in spite of the gendered structures and practices of the society in which they live, to adopt patterns of life that have been developed to suit the needs of men. The fact that human beings are born as helpless infants—not as the purportedly autonomous actors who populate political theories—is obscured by the implicit assumption of gendered families, operating outside the range of the theories. To a large extent, contemporary theories of justice, like those of the past, are about men with wives at home.

Gender as an Issue of Justice

For three major reasons, this state of affairs is unacceptable. The first is the obvious point that women must be fully included in any satisfactory theory of justice. The second is that equality of opportunity, not only for women but for children of both sexes, is seriously undermined by the current gender injustices of our society. And the third reason is that, as has already been suggested, the family—currently the linchpin of the gender structure—must be just if we are to have a just society, since it is within the family that we first come to have that sense of ourselves and our relations with others that is at the root of moral development.

Counting Women In

When we turn to the great tradition of Western political thought with questions about the justice of the treatment of the sexes in mind, it is to little avail. Bold feminists like Mary Astell, Mary Wollstonecraft, William Thompson, Harriet Taylor, and George Bernard Shaw have occasionally challenged the tradition, often using its own premises and arguments to overturn its explicit or implicit justification of the inequality of women. But John Stuart Mill is a rare exception to the rule that those who hold central positions in the tradition almost never question the justice of the subordination of women. This phenomenon is undoubtedly due in part to the fact that Aristotle, whose theory of justice has been so influential, relegated women to a sphere of "household justice"—populated by persons who are not fundamentally equal to the free men who participate in political justice, but inferiors whose natural function is to serve those who are more fully human. The liberal tradition, despite its supposed foundation of individual rights and human equality, is more Aristotelian in this respect than is generally acknowledged. In one way or another, almost all liberal theorists have assumed that the "individual" who is the basic subject of the theories is the male head of a patriarchal household. Thus they have not usually considered applying the principles of justice to women or to relations between the sexes.

When we turn to contemporary theories of justice, however, we expect to find more illuminating and positive contributions to the subject of gender and justice. [But as] the omission of the family and the falseness of their gender-neutral language suggest, . . . mainstream contemporary theories of justice do not address the subject any better than those of the past. Theories of justice that apply to only half of us simply won't do; the inclusiveness falsely implied by the current use of gender-neutral terms must become real. Theories of justice must apply to all of us, and to all of human life, instead of *assuming* silently that half of us take care of whole areas of life that are considered outside the scope of social justice. In a just society, the structure and practices of families must afford women the same opportunities as men to develop their capacities, to participate in political power, to influence social choices, and to be economically as well as physically secure.

Unfortunately, much feminist intellectual energy in the 1980s has gone into the claim that "justice" and "rights" are masculinist ways of thinking about morality that feminists should eschew or radically revise, advocating a morality of care. The emphasis is misplaced, I think, for several reasons. First, what is by now a vast literature on the subject shows that the evidence for differences in women's and men's ways of thinking about moral issues is not (at least yet) very clear; neither is the evidence about the source of whatever differences there might be. It may well turn out that any differences can be readily explained in terms of roles, including female primary parenting, that are socially determined and therefore alterable. There is certainly no evidence—nor could there be, in such a gender-structured society—for concluding that women are somehow naturally more inclined toward contextuality and away from universalism in their moral thinking, a false concept that unfortunately reinforces the old stereotypes that justify separate spheres. The capacity of reactionary forces to capitalize on the "different moralities" strain in feminism is particularly evident in Pope John Paul II's recent Apostolic Letter, "On the Dignity of Women," in which he refers to women's special capacity to care for others in arguing for confining them to motherhood or celibacy.

Second, . . . I think the distinction between an ethic of justice and an ethic of care has been overdrawn. The best theorizing about justice . . . has integral to it the notions of care and empathy, of thinking of the interests and well-being of others who may be very different from ourselves. It is, therefore, misleading to draw a dichotomy as though they were two contrasting ethics. The best theorizing about justice is not some abstract "view from nowhere," but results from the carefully attentive consideration of *everyone's* point of view. This means, of course, that the best theorizing about justice is not good enough if it does not, or cannot readily be adapted to, include women and their points of view as fully as men and their points of view.

Gender and Equality of Opportunity

The family is a crucial determinant of our opportunities in life, of what we "become." It has frequently been acknowledged by those concerned with real equality of opportunity that the family presents a problem. But though they have discerned a serious problem, these theorists have underestimated it because they have seen only half of it. They have seen that the disparity among families in terms of the physical and emotional environment, motivation, and material advantages they can give their children has a tremendous effect upon children's opportunities in life. We are not born as isolated, equal individuals in our society, but into family situations: some in the social middle, some poor and homeless, and some superaffluent; some to a single or soon-to-be-separated parent, some to parents whose marriage is fraught with conflict, some to parents who will stay together in love and happiness. Any claims that equal opportunity exists are therefore completely unfounded. Decades of neglect of the poor, especially of poor black and Hispanic households, accentuated by the policies of the Reagan years, have brought us farther from the principles of equal opportunity. To come close to them would require, for example, a high and uniform standard of public education and the provision of equal social services—including health care, employment training, job opportunities, drug rehabilitation, and decent housing—for all who need them. In addition to redistributive taxation, only massive reallocations of resources from the military to social services could make these things possible.

But even if all these disparities were somehow eliminated, we would still not attain equal opportunity for all. This is because what has not been recognized as an equal opportunity problem, except in feminist literature and circles, is the disparity *within* the family, the fact that its gender structure is itself a major obstacle to equality of opportunity. This is very important in itself, since one of the factors with most influence on our opportunities in life is the social significance attributed to our sex. The opportunities of girls and women are centrally affected by the structure and practices of family life, particularly by the fact that women are almost invariably primary parents. What nonfeminists who see in the family an obstacle to equal opportunity have *not* seen is that the extent to which a family is gender-structured can make the sex we belong to a relatively insignificant aspect of our identity and our life prospects or an all-pervading one. This is because so much of the social construction of gender takes place in the family, and particularly in the institution of female parenting.

Moreover, . . . with the increased rates of single motherhood, separation, and divorce, the inequalities between the sexes have *compounded* the first part of the problem. The disparity among families has grown largely because of the impoverishment of many women and children after separation or divorce. The division of labor in the typical family leaves most women far less capable than men of supporting themselves, and this disparity is accentuated by the fact that children of separated or divorced parents usually live with their mothers. The inadequacy—and frequent non-payment—of child support has become recognized as a major social problem. Thus the inequalities of gender are now directly harming many children of both sexes as well as women themselves. Enhancing equal opportunity for women, important as it is in itself, is also a crucial way of improving the opportunities of many of the most disadvantaged children.

As . . . the parts of this problem [are connected, so are] some of the solutions: Much of what needs to be done to end the inequalities of gender, and to work in the direction of ending gender itself, will also help to equalize opportunity from one family to another. Subsidized, high-quality day-care is obviously one such thing; another is the adaptation of the workplace to the needs of parents. . . .

The Family as a School of Justice

One of the things that theorists who have argued that families need not or cannot be just, or who have simply neglected them, have failed to explain is how, within a formative social environment that is *not* founded upon principles of justice, children can learn to develop that sense of justice they will require as citizens of a just society. Rather than being one among many co-equal institutions of a just society, a just family is its essential foundation.

It may seem uncontroversial, even obvious, that families must be just because of the vast influence they have on the moral development of children. But this is clearly not the case. I shall argue that unless the first and most formative example of adult interaction usually experienced by children is one of justice and reciprocity, rather than one of domination and manipulation or of unequal altruism and one-sided self-sacrifice, and unless they themselves are treated with concern and respect, they are likely to be considerably hindered in becoming people who are guided by principles of justice. Moreover, I claim, the sharing of roles by men and women, rather than the division of roles between them, would have a further positive impact because the experience of *being* a physical and psychological nurturer—whether of a child or of another adult—would increase that capacity to identify with and fully comprehend the viewpoints of others that is important to a sense of justice. In a society that minimized gender this would be more likely to be the experience of all of us.

Almost every person in our society starts life in a family of some sort or other. Fewer of these families now fit the usual, although not universal, standard of previous generations, that is, wage-working father, homemaking mother, and children. More families these days are headed by a single parent; lesbian and gay parenting is no longer so rare; many children have two wage-working parents, and receive at least some of their early care outside the home. While its forms are varied, the family in which a child is raised, especially in the earliest years, is clearly a crucial place for early moral development and for the formation of our basic attitudes to others. It is, potentially, a place where we can *learn to be just*. It is especially important for the development of a sense of justice that grows from sharing the experiences of others and becoming aware of the points of view of others who are different in some respects from ourselves, but with whom we clearly have some interests in common.

The importance of the family for the moral development of individuals was far more often recognized by political theorists of the past than it is by those of the present. Hegel, Rousseau, Tocqueville, Mill, and Dewey are obvious examples that come to mind. Rousseau, for example, shocked by Plato's proposal to abolish the family, says that it is

> as though there were no need for a natural base on which to form conventional ties; as though the love of one's nearest were not the principle of the love one owes the state; as though it were not by means of the small fatherland which is the family that the heart attaches itself to the large one.

Defenders of both autocratic and democratic regimes have recognized the political importance of different family forms for the formation of citizens. On the one hand, the nineteenth-century monarchist Louis de Bonald argued against the divorce reforms of the French Revolution, which he claimed weakened the patriarchal family, on the grounds that "in order to keep the state out of the hands of the people, it is necessary to keep the family out of the hands of women and children." Taking this same line of thought in the opposite direction, the U.S. Supreme Court decided in 1879 in *Reynolds v. Nebraska* that familial patriarchy fostered despotism and was therefore intolerable. Denying Mormon men the freedom to practice polygamy, the Court asserted that it was an offense "subversive of good order" that "leads to the patriarchal principle, . . . [and] when applied to large communities, fetters the people in stationary despotism, while that principle cannot long exist in connection with monogamy."

However, while de Bonald was consistent in his adherence to an hierarchical family structure as necessary for an undemocratic political system, the Supreme Court was by no means consistent in promoting an egalitarian family as an essential underpinning for political democracy. For in other decisions of the same period—such as *Bradwell v. Illinois*, the famous 1872 case that upheld the exclusion of women from the practice of law—the Court rejected women's claims to legal equality, in the name of a thoroughly patriar-

chal, though monogamous, family that was held to require the dependence of women and their exclusion from civil and political life. While bigamy was considered patriarchal, and as such a threat to republican, democratic government, the refusal to allow a married woman to employ her talents and to make use of her qualifications to earn an independent living was not considered patriarchal. It was so far from being a threat to the civil order, in fact, that it was deemed necessary for it, and as such was ordained by both God and nature. Clearly in both *Reynolds* and *Bradwell*, "state authorities enforced family forms preferred by those in power and justified as necessary to stability and order." The Court noticed the despotic potential of polygamy, but was blind to the despotic potential of patriarchal monogamy. This was perfectly acceptable to them as a training ground for citizens.

Most theorists of the past who stressed the importance of the family and its practices for the wider world of moral and political life by no means insisted on congruence between the structures or practices of the family and those of the outside world. Though concerned with moral development, they bifurcated public from private life to such an extent that they had no trouble reconciling inegalitarian, sometimes admittedly unjust, relations founded upon sentiment within the family with a more just, even egalitarian, social structure outside the family. Rousseau, Hegel, Tocqueville—all thought the family was centrally important for the development of morality in citizens, but all defended the hierarchy of the marital structure while spurning such a degree of hierarchy in institutions and practices outside the household. Preferring instead to rely on love, altruism, and generosity as the basis for family relations, none of these theorists argued for *just* family structures as necessary for socializing children into citizenship in a just society.

The position that justice within the family is irrelevant to the development of just citizens was not plausible even when only men were citizens. John Stuart Mill, in *The Subjection of Women*, takes an impassioned stand against it. He argues that the inequality of women within the family is deeply subversive of justice in general in the wider social world, because it subverts the moral potential of men. Mill's first answer to the question, "For whose good are all these changes in women's rights to be undertaken?" is: "the advantage of having the most universal and pervading of all human relations regulated by justice instead of injustice." Making marriage a relationship of equals, he argues, would transform this central part of daily life from "a school of despotism" into "a school of moral cultivation." He goes on to discuss, in the strongest of terms, the noxious effect of growing up in a family not regulated by justice. Consider . . . "the self-worship, the unjust self-preference," nourished in a boy growing up in a household in which "by the mere fact of being born a male he is by right the superior of all and every one of an entire half of the human race." Mill concludes that the example set by perpetuating a marital structure "contradictory to the first principles of social justice" must have such "a perverting influence" that it is hard even to imagine the good effects of changing it. All other attempts to educate people to respect and practice justice, Mill claims, will be superficial "as long as the citadel of the enemy is not attacked." Mill felt as much hope for what the family might be as he felt despair at what it was not. "The family, justly constituted, would be the real school of the virtues of freedom," primary among which was "justice, . . . grounded as before on equal, but now also on sympathetic association." Mill both saw clearly and had the courage to address what so many other political philosophers either could not see, or saw and turned away from.

Despite the strength and fervor of his advocacy of women's rights, however, Mill's idea of a just family structure falls far short of that of many feminists even of his own time, including his wife, Harriet Taylor. In spite of the fact that Mill recognized both the empowering effect of earnings on one's position in the family and the limiting effect of domestic responsibility on women's opportunities, he balked at questioning the traditional division of labor between the sexes. For him, a woman's choice of marriage was parallel to a man's choice of a profession: Unless and until she had fulfilled her obligations to her husband and children, she should not undertake anything else. But . . . however equal the legal rights of husbands and wives, this position largely undermines Mill's own insistence upon the importance of marital equality for a just society. His acceptance of the traditional division of labor, without making any provision for wives who were thereby made economically dependent on their husbands, largely undermines his insistence on family justice as the necessary foundation for social justice.

Thus even those political theorists of the past who have perceived the family as an important school of moral development have rarely acknowledged the need for congruence between the family and the wider social order, which suggests that families themselves need to be just. Even when they have, as with Mill, they have been unwilling to push hard on the traditional division of labor within the family in the name of justice or equality.

Contemporary theorists of justice, with few exceptions, have paid little or no attention to the question of moral development—of how we are to *become* just. Most seem to think, to adapt slightly Hobbes's notable phrase, that just men spring like mushrooms from the earth. Not surprisingly, then, it is far less often acknowledged in recent than in past theories that the family is important for moral development, and especially for instilling a sense of justice. As already noted, many theorists pay no attention at all to either the family or gender. In the rare case that the issue of justice within the family is given any sustained attention, the family is not viewed as a potential school of social justice. In the rare case that a theorist pays any sustained attention to the development of a sense of justice or morality, little if any attention is likely to be paid to the family. Even in the rare event that theorists pay considerable attention to the family *as* the first major locus of moral socialization, they do not refer to the fact that families are almost all still thoroughly gender-structured institutions.

Among major contemporary theorists of justice, John Rawls alone treats the family seriously as the earliest school of moral development. He argues that a just, well-ordered society will be stable only if its members continue to develop a sense of justice. And he argues that families play a fundamental role in the stages by which this sense of justice is acquired. From the parents' love for their child, which comes to be reciprocated, comes the child's "sense of his own value and the desire to become the sort of person that they are." The family, too, is the first of that series of "associations" in which we participate, from which we acquire the capacity, crucial for a sense of justice, to see things from the perspectives of others. . . . This capacity—the capacity for empathy—is essential for maintaining a sense of justice of the Rawlsian kind. For the perspective [needed to maintain] a sense of justice is not that of the egoistic or disembodied self, or of the dominant few who overdetermine "our" traditions or "shared understandings," or (to use Nagel's term) of "the view from nowhere," but rather the perspective of every person in the society for whom the principles of justice are being arrived at. . . . The problem with Rawls's rare and interesting discussion of moral development is that it rests on the unexplained *assumption* that family institutions are just. If gendered family institutions are *not* just, but are . . . a relic of caste or feudal societies in which responsibilities, roles, and resources are distributed, not in accordance with the principles of justice he arrives at or with any other commonly respected values, but in accordance with innate differences that are imbued with enormous social significance, then Rawls's theory of moral development would seem to be built on uncertain ground. This problem is exacerbated by suggestions in some of Rawls's most recent work that families are "private institutions," to which it is not appropriate to apply standards of justice. But if families are to help form just individuals and citizens, surely they must be *just families.*

In a just society, the structure and practices of families must give women the same opportunities as men to develop their capacities, to participate in political power and influence social choices, and to be economically secure. But in addition, families must be just because of the vast influence they have on the moral development of children. The family is the primary institution of formative moral development. And the structure and practices of the family must parallel those of the larger society if the sense of justice is to be fostered and maintained. [M]any theorists of justice, both past and present, appear to have denied the importance of at least one of these factors, [but] my own view is that both are absolutely crucial. A society that is committed to equal respect for all of its members, and to justice in social distributions of benefits and responsibilities, can neither neglect the family nor accept family structures and practices that violate these norms, as do current gender-based structures and practices. [C]hildren who are to develop into adults with a strong sense of justice and commitment to just institutions [must] spend their earliest and most formative years in an environment in which they are loved and nurtured, *and* in which principles of justice are abided by and respected. What is a child of either sex to learn about fairness in the average household with two full-time working parents, where the mother does, at the very least, twice as much family work as the father? What is a child to learn about the value of nurturing and domestic work in a home with a traditional division of labor in which the father either subtly or not so subtly uses the fact that he is the wage earner to "pull rank" on or to abuse his wife? What is a child to learn about responsibility for others in a family in which, after many years of arranging her life around the needs of her husband and children, a woman must provide for herself and her children but is totally ill-equipped for the task by the life she agreed to lead, has led, and expected to go on leading?

23. *Feminist Justice and the Family*

James P. Sterba

James P. Sterba sets out and defends an ideal of androgyny that he identifies with feminist justice. This ideal requires that traits that are truly desirable in society be equally available to both women and men, or in the case of virtues, equally expected in both women and men. He considers attempts to derive the ideal of androgyny either from a right to equal opportunity that is a central requirement of a welfare liberal conception of justice or from an equal right of self-development that is a central requirement of a socialist conception of justice. Sterba further argues that the ideal of androgyny would require (1) that all children irrespective of their sex must be given the same type of upbringing consistent with their native capabilities and (2) that mothers and fathers must also have the same opportunities for education and employment consistent with their native capabilities.

Contemporary feminists almost by definition seek to put an end to male domination and to secure women's liberation. To achieve these goals, many feminists support the political ideal of androgyny.* According to these feminists, all assignments of rights and duties are ultimately to be justified in terms of the ideal of androgyny. Since a conception of justice is usually thought to provide the ultimate grounds for the assignment of rights and duties in a society, I shall refer to this ideal of androgyny as "feminist justice."

The Ideal of Androgyny

But how is this ideal of androgyny to be interpreted? In a well-known article, Joyce Trebilcot distinguishes two forms of androgyny. The first form postulates the same ideal for everyone. According to this form of androgyny, the ideal person "combines characteristics usually attributed to men with characteristics usually attributed to women." Thus, we should expect both nurturance and mastery, openness and objectivity, compassion and competitiveness from each and every person who has the capacities for these traits.

By contrast, the second form of androgyny does not advocate the same ideal for everyone but rather a variety of options from "pure" femininity to "pure" masculinity. As Trebilcot points out, this form of an-

drogyny shares with the first the view that biological sex should not be the basis for determining the appropriateness of gender characterization. It differs in that it holds that "all alternatives with respect to gender should be equally available to and equally approved for everyone, regardless of sex."

It would be a mistake, however, to sharply distinguish between these two forms of androgyny. Properly understood, they are simply two different facets of a single ideal. For, as Mary Ann Warren has argued, the second form of androgyny is appropriate *only* "with respect to feminine and masculine traits which are largely matters of personal style and preference and which have little direct moral significance." However, when we consider so-called feminine and masculine *virtues,* it is the first form of androgyny that is required because, then, other things being equal, the same virtues are appropriate for everyone.

We can even formulate the ideal of androgyny more abstractly so that it is no longer specified in terms of so-called feminine and masculine traits. We can, for example, specify the ideal as requiring no more than that the traits that are truly desirable in society be equally available to both women and men, or in the case of virtues, equally expected of both women and men.

There is a problem, of course, in determining which traits of character are virtues and which traits are largely matters of personal style and preference. To make this determination, Trebilcot has suggested that we seek to bring about the second form of androgyny, where people have the option of acquiring the full range of so-called feminine and masculine traits. But surely when we already have good grounds for thinking that certain traits are virtues, such as courage and compassion, fairness and openness, there is no reason to adopt such a laissez-faire approach to moral education. Although, as Trebilcot rightly points out, proscribing certain options will involve a loss of freedom, nevertheless, we should be able to determine, at least with respect to some character traits, when a gain in virtue is worth the loss of freedom. It may even be the

---

*Someone might object that if feminist justice is worth considering, why not racial justice? In principle I have no objection to a separate consideration of racial justice although the main issues that are relevant to such a discussion have standardly been taken up in discussions of the other conceptions of justice. By contrast, feminist justice raises new issues that have usually been ignored in discussions of the other conceptions of justice (e.g., equal opportunity within the family), and for that reason, I think, this conception of justice deserves separate consideration.

From *Perspectives on the Family* (1990), edited by Robert Moffat, Joseph Grcic, and Michael Bayles. Reprinted with revisions by permission.

case that the loss of freedom suffered by an individual now will be compensated for by a gain of freedom to that same individual in the future once the relevant virtue or virtues have been acquired.

So understood, the class of virtues will turn out to be those desirable traits that can be reasonably expected of both women and men. Admittedly, this is a restrictive use of the term virtue. In normal usage, "virtue" is almost synonymous with "desirable trait." But there is good reason to focus on those desirable traits that can be justifiably inculcated in both women and men, and, for present purposes, I will refer to this class of desirable traits as virtues.

Unfortunately, many of the challenges to the ideal of androgyny fail to appreciate how the ideal can be interpreted to combine a required set of virtues with equal choice from among other desirable traits. For example, some challenges interpret the ideal as attempting to achieve "a proper balance of moderation" among opposing feminine and masculine traits and then question whether traits like feminine gullibility or masculine brutality could ever be combined with opposing gender traits to achieve such a balance. Other challenges interpret the ideal as permitting unrestricted choice of personal traits and then regard the possibility of Total Women and Hells Angels androgynes as a *reductio ad absurdum* of the ideal. But once it is recognized that the ideal of androgyny can not only be interpreted to expect of everyone a set of virtues (which need not be a mean between opposing extreme traits), but can also be interpreted to limit everyone's choice to desirable traits, then such challenges to the ideal clearly lose their force.

Actually the main challenge raised by feminists to the ideal of androgyny is that [it] is self-defeating in that it seeks to eliminate sexual stereotyping of human beings [while] it is formulated in terms of the very same stereotypical concepts it seeks to eliminate. Or as Warren has put it, "Is it not at least mildly paradoxical to urge people to cultivate both 'feminine' and 'masculine' virtues, while at the same time holding that virtues ought not to be sexually stereotyped?"

But in response to this challenge, it can be argued that to build a better society we must begin where we are now, and where we are now people still speak of feminine and masculine character traits. Consequently,

if we want to easily refer to such traits and to formulate an ideal with respect to how they should be distributed in society it is plausible to refer to them in the way that people presently refer to them, that is, as feminine or masculine traits.

Alternatively, to avoid misunderstanding altogether, the ideal could be formulated in the more abstract way I suggested earlier so that it no longer specifically refers to so-called feminine or masculine traits. So formulated, the ideal requires that the traits that are truly desirable in society be equally available to both women and men or in the case of virtues equally expected of women and men. So formulated, the ideal would, in effect, require that men and women have in the fullest sense an equal right of self-development. The ideal would require this because an equal right to self-development can only be effectively guaranteed by expecting the same virtues of both women and men and by making other desirable traits equally available to both women and men.

So characterized, the ideal of androgyny represents neither a revolt against so-called feminine virtues and traits nor their exaltation over so-called masculine virtues and traits. Accordingly, the ideal of androgyny does not view women's liberation as *simply* the freeing of women from the confines of traditional roles thus making it possible for them to develop in ways heretofore reserved for men. Nor does the ideal view women's liberation as *simply* the revaluation and glorification of so-called feminine activities like housekeeping or mothering or so-called feminine modes of thinking as reflected in an ethic of caring. The first perspective ignores or devalues genuine virtues and desirable traits traditionally associated with women while the second ignores or devalues genuine virtues and desirable traits traditionally associated with men. By contrast, the ideal of androgyny seeks a broader-based ideal for both women and men that combines virtues and desirable traits traditionally associated with women with virtues and desirable traits traditionally associated with men. Nevertheless, the ideal of androgyny will clearly reject any so-called virtues or desirable traits traditionally associated with women or men that have been supportive of discrimination or oppression against women or men.

Defenses of Androgyny

Now there are various contemporary defenses of the ideal of androgyny. Some feminists have attempted to derive the ideal from a Welfare Liberal Conception of Justice. Others have attempted to derive the ideal from a Socialist Conception of Justice. Let us briefly consider each of these defenses in turn.

In attempting to derive the ideal of androgyny from a Welfare Liberal Conception of Justice, feminists have tended to focus on the right to equal opportunity, which is a central requirement of a Welfare Liberal Conception of Justice. Of course, equal opportunity could be interpreted minimally as providing people only with the same legal rights of access to all advantaged positions in society for which they are qualified. But this is not the interpretation given the right by welfare liberals. In a Welfare Liberal Conception of Justice, equal opportunity is interpreted to require in addition the same prospects for success for all those who are relevantly similar, where relevant similarity involves more than simply present qualifications. For example, Rawls claims that persons in his original position would favor a right to "fair equality of opportunity," which means that persons who have the same natural assets and . . . willingness to use them would have the necessary resources to achieve similar life prospects. The point feminists have been making is simply that failure to achieve the ideal of androgyny translates into a failure to guarantee equal opportunity to both women and men. The present evidence for this failure to provide equal opportunity is the discrimination that exists against women in education, employment, and personal relations. Discrimination in education begins early in a child's formal educational experience as teachers and school books support different and less desirable roles for girls than for boys. Discrimination in employment has been well documented. Women continue to earn only a fraction of what men earn for the same or comparable jobs and although women make up almost half of the paid labor force in the U.S., 70 percent of them are concentrated in just twenty different job categories, only five more than in 1905. Finally, discrimination in personal relations is the most entrenched of all forms of discrimination against women. It primarily manifests itself in traditional family structures in which the woman is responsible for domestic work and childcare and the man's task is "to protect against the outside world and to show how to meet this world successfully." In none of these areas, therefore, do women have the same prospects for success as compared with men with similar natural talents and similar desires to succeed.

Now the support for the ideal of androgyny provided by a Socialist Conception of Justice appears to be much more direct than that provided by a Welfare Liberal Conception of Justice. This is because the Socialist Conception of Justice and the ideal of androgyny can be interpreted as requiring the very same equal right of self-development. What a Socialist Conception of Justice purports to add to this interpretation of the ideal of androgyny is an understanding of how the ideal is best to be realized in contemporary capitalist societies. For according to advocates of this defense of androgyny, the ideal is best achieved by socializing the means of production and satisfying people's nonbasic as well as their basic needs. Thus, the general idea behind this approach to realizing the ideal of androgyny is that a cure for capitalist exploitation will also be a cure for women's oppression.

Yet despite attempts to identify the feminist ideal of androgyny with a right to equal opportunity endorsed by a Welfare Liberal Conception of Justice or an equal right of self-development endorsed by a Socialist Conception of Justice, the ideal still transcends both of these rights by requiring not only that desirable traits be equally available to both women and men but also that the same virtues be equally expected of both women and men. Of course, part of the rationale for expecting the same virtues in both women and men is to support such rights. And if support for such rights is to be fairly allocated, the virtues needed to support such rights must be equally expected of both women and men. Nevertheless, to hold that the virtues required to support a right to equal opportunity or an equal right to self-development must be equally expected of both women and men is different from claiming, as the ideal of androgyny does, that human virtues, sans phrase, should be equally expected of both women and men. Thus, the ideal of androgyny clearly requires an inculcation of virtues beyond what is necessary to support a right to equal opportunity or . . . self-development. What additional virtues are required by the ideal obviously depends upon what other rights should be recognized. In this regard, the ideal of androgyny is somewhat open-ended. Feminists who endorse the ideal would simply have to go along with the best arguments for additional rights and corresponding virtues. In particular, I would claim that they would have to support a right to welfare that is necessary for meeting the basic needs of all legitimate claimants given the strong case that can be made for such a right from welfare liberal, socialist, and even libertarian perspectives.

Now, in order to provide all legitimate claimants with the resources necessary for meeting their basic needs, there obviously has to be a limit on the resources that will be available for each individual's self-development, and this limit will definitely have an effect upon the implementation of the ideal of androgyny. Of course, some feminists would want to pursue various possible technological transformations of human biology in order to implement their ideal. For example, they would like to make it possible for women to inseminate other women and for men to lactate and even to bring fertilized ova to term. But bringing about such possibilities would be very costly indeed. Consequently, since the means selected for meeting basic needs must be provided to all legitimate claimants including distant peoples and future generations, it is unlikely that such costly means could ever be morally justified. Rather it seems preferable radically to equalize the conventionally provided opportunities to women and men and wait for such changes to have their ultimate effect on human biology as well. Of course, if any "technological fixes" for achieving androgyny should prove to be cost-efficient as a means for meeting people's basic needs, then obviously there would be every reason to utilize them.

Unfortunately, the commitment of a Feminist Conception of Justice to a right of equal opportunity raises still another problem for the view. Some philosophers have contended that equal opportunity is ultimately an incoherent goal. As Lloyd Thomas has put the charge, "We have a problem for those who advocate competitive equality of opportunity: The prizes won in the competitions of the first generation will tend to defeat the requirements of equality of opportunity for the next." The only way to avoid this result, Thomas claims, "is by not permitting persons to be dependent for their self-development on others at all," which obviously is a completely unacceptable solution.

But this is a problem, as Thomas points out, that exists for competitive opportunities. They are opportunities for which, even when each person does her best, there are considerably more losers than winners. With respect to such opportunities, the winners may well be able to place themselves and their children in an advantageous position with respect to subsequent competitions. But under a Welfare Liberal Conception of Justice, and presumably a Feminist Conception of Justice as well, most of the opportunities people have are not competitive opportunities at all, but rather noncompetitive opportunities to acquire the resources necessary for meeting their basic needs. These are opportunities with respect to which virtually everyone who does her best can be a winner. Of course, some people who do not do their best may fail to satisfy their basic needs, and this failure may have negative consequences for their children's prospects. But under a Welfare Liberal Conception of Justice, and presumably a Feminist Conception of Justice as well, every effort is required to insure that each generation has the same opportunities to meet their basic needs, and as long as most of the opportunities that are available are of the noncompetitive sort, this goal should not be that difficult to achieve.

Now it might be objected that if all that will be accomplished under the proposed system of equal opportunity is, for the most part, the satisfaction of people's basic needs, then that would not bring about the revolutionary change in the relationship between women and men that feminists are demanding. For don't most women in technologically advanced societies already have their basic needs satisfied, despite the fact that they are not yet fully liberated?

In response, it should be emphasized that the concern of defenders of the ideal of androgyny is not just with women in technologically advanced societies. The ideal of androgyny is also applicable to women in Third World and developing societies, and in such societies it is clear that the basic needs of many women are not being met. Furthermore, it is just not the case that all the basic needs of most women in technologically advanced societies are being met. Most obviously, their basic needs for self-development are still not being met. This is because they are being denied an equal right to education, training, jobs, and a variety of social roles for which they have the native capabilities. In effect, women in technologically advanced societies are still being treated as second-class persons, no matter how well-fed, well-clothed, well-housed they happen to be. This is why there must be a radical restructuring of social institutions even in technologically advanced societies if women's basic needs for self-development are to be met.

Androgyny and the Family

Now the primary locus for the radical restructuring required by the ideal of androgyny is the family. Here two fundamental changes are needed. First, all children irrespective of their sex must be given the same type of upbringing consistent with their native capabilities. Second, mothers and fathers must also have the same opportunities for education and employment consistent with their native capabilities.

Surprisingly, however, some welfare liberals have viewed the existence of the family as imposing an acceptable limit on the right to equal opportunity. Rawls, for example, claims the principle of fair opportunity can be only imperfectly carried out, at least as long as the institution of the family exists. The extent to which natural capacities develop and reach fruition is affected by all kinds of social conditions and class attitudes. Even the willingness to make an effort, to try, and so to be deserving in the ordinary sense is itself dependent upon happy family and social circumstances. It is impossible in practice to secure equal chances of achievement and culture for those similarly endowed, and therefore we may want to adopt a principle which recognizes this fact and also mitigates the arbitrary effects of the natural lottery itself.

Thus, according to Rawls, since different families will provide different opportunities for their children, the only way to fully achieve "fair equality of opportunity" would require us to go too far and abolish or radically modify traditional family structures.

Yet others have argued that the full attainment of equal opportunity requires that we go even further

and equalize people's native as well as their social assets. For only when everyone's natural and social assets have been equalized would everyone have exactly the same chance as everyone else to attain the desirable social positions in society. Of course, feminists have no difficulty recognizing that there are moral limits to the pursuit of equal opportunity. Accordingly, feminists could grant that other than the possibility of special cases, such as sharing a surplus organ like a second kidney, it would be too much to ask people to sacrifice their native assets to achieve equal opportunity.

Rawls, however, proposes to limit the pursuit of equal opportunity still further by accepting the inequalities generated by families in any given sector of society, provided that there is still equal opportunity between the sectors or that the existing inequality of opportunity can be justified in terms of its benefit to those in the least-advantaged position. Nevertheless, what Rawls is concerned with here is simply the inequality of opportunity that exists between individuals owing to the fact that they come from different families. He fails to consider the inequality of opportunity that exists in traditional family structures, especially between adult members, in virtue of the different roles expected of women and men. When viewed from the original position, this latter inequality of opportunity clearly is sufficient to require a radical modification of traditional family structures, even if the former inequality, for the reasons Rawls suggests, does not require any such modifications.

Yet at least in the United States this need radically to modify traditional family structures to guarantee equal opportunity confronts a serious problem. Given that a significant proportion of the available jobs are at least 9 to 5, families with preschool children require day-care facilities if their adult members are to pursue their careers. Unfortunately, for many families such facilities are simply unavailable. In New York City, for example, more than 144,000 children under the age of six are competing for 46,000 full-time slots in day-care centers. In Seattle, there is licensed day-care space for 8,800 of the 23,000 children who need it. In Miami, two children, 3 and 4 years old, were left unattended at home while their mother worked. They climbed into a clothes dryer while the timer was on, closed the door and burned to death.

Moreover, even the available day-care facilities are frequently inadequate either because their staffs are poorly trained or because the child/adult ratio in such facilities is too high. At best, such facilities provide little more than custodial care; at worst, they actually retard the development of those under their care. What this suggests is that at least under present conditions if preschool children are to be adequately cared for, frequently, one of the adult members of the family will have to remain at home to provide that care. But since most jobs are at least 9 to 5, this will require that the adult members who stay at home temporarily give up pursuing a career. However, such sacrifice appears to conflict with the equal opportunity requirement of Feminist Justice.

Now families might try to meet this equal opportunity requirement by having one parent give up pursuing a career for a certain period of time and the other give up pursuing a career for a subsequent (equal) period of time. But there are problems here too. Some careers are difficult to interrupt for any significant period of time, while others never adequately reward latecomers. In addition, given the high rate of divorce and the inadequacies of most legally mandated child support, those who first sacrifice their careers may find themselves later faced with the impossible task of beginning or reviving their careers while continuing to be the primary caretaker of their children. Furthermore, there is considerable evidence that children will benefit more from equal rearing from both parents. So the option of having just one parent doing the child-rearing for any length of time is, other things being equal, not optimal.

It would seem, therefore, that to truly share child-rearing within the family, what is needed is flexible (typically part-time) work schedules that also allow both parents to be together with their children for a significant period every day. Now some flexible job schedules have already been tried by various corporations. But if equal opportunity is to be a reality in our society, the option of flexible job schedules must be guaranteed to all those with preschool children. Of course, to require employers to guarantee flexible job schedules to all those with preschool children would place a significant restriction upon the rights of employers, and it may appear to move the practical requirements of Feminist Justice closer to those of Socialist Justice. But if the case for flexible job schedules is grounded on a right to equal opportunity then at least defenders of Welfare Liberal Justice will have no reason to object. This is clearly one place where Feminist Justice with its focus on equal opportunity within the family tends to drive Welfare Liberal Justice and Socialist Justice closer together in their practical requirements.

Recently, however, Christina Hoff Sommers has criticized feminist philosophers for being "against the family." Her main objection is that feminist philosophers have criticized traditional family structures without adequately justifying what they would put in its place. In this paper, I have tried to avoid any criticism of this sort by first articulating a defensible version of the feminist ideal of androgyny which can draw upon support from both Welfare Liberal and Socialist Conceptions of Justice and then by showing what demands this ideal would impose upon family structures. Since Sommers and other critics of the feminist ideal of androgyny also support a strong requirement of equal opportunity, it is difficult to see how they can consistently do so while denying the radical implications of that requirement (and the ideal of androgyny that underlies it) for traditional family structures.

24. *Philosophers Against the Family*

CHRISTINA SOMMERS

Christina Sommers distinguishes liberal feminists from radical feminists. She contends that liberal feminists, like herself, want equal opportunity in the workplace and politics, but would leave marriage and motherhood "untouched and unimpugned." By contrast, Sommers contends that radical feminists are committed to an assimilationist or androgynous ideal that would destroy the (traditional) family and deny most women what they want.

Much of what commonly counts as personal morality is measured by how well we behave within family relationships. We live our moral lives as son or daughter to this mother and that father, as brother or sister to that sister or brother, as father or mother, grandfather, granddaughter to that boy or girl or that man or woman. These relationships and the moral duties defined by them were once popular topics of moral casuistry; but when we turn to the literature of recent moral philosophy, we find little discussion on what it means to be a good son or daughter, a good mother or father, a good husband or wife, a good brother or sister.

Modern ethical theory concentrates on more general topics. Perhaps the majority of us who do ethics accept some version of Kantianism or utilitarianism, and these mainstream doctrines are better designed for telling us about what we should do as persons in general than about our special duties as parents or children or siblings. We believe, perhaps, that these universal theories can fully account for the morality of special relations. In any case, modern ethics is singularly silent on the bread and butter issues of personal morality in daily life. But silence is only part of it. With the exception of marriage itself, the relationships in the family are biologically given. The contemporary philosopher is, on the whole, actively unsympathetic to the idea that we have *any* duties defined by relationships that we have not voluntarily entered into. We do not, after all, choose our parents or siblings, and even if we do choose to have children, this

is not the same as choosing, say, our friends. Because the special relationships that constitute the family as a social arrangement are, in this sense, not voluntarily assumed, many moralists feel bound in principle to dismiss them altogether. The practical result is that philosophers are to be found among those who are contributing to an ongoing disintegration of the traditional family. In what follows I expose some of the philosophical roots of the current hostility to family morality. My own view that the ethical theses underlying this hostility are bad philosophy is made evident throughout the discussion.

The Moral Vantage

Social criticism is a heady pastime to which philosophers are professionally addicted. One approach is Aristotelian in method and temperament. It is antiradical, though it may be liberal, and it approaches the task of needed reform with a prima facie respect for the norms of established morality. It is conservationist and cautious in its recommendations for change. It is therefore not given to such proposals as abolishing the family or abolishing private property and, indeed, does not look kindly on such proposals from other philosophers. The antiradicals I am concerned about are not those who would be called Burkean. I call them liberal but this use of the term is somewhat perverse since, in my stipulative use, a liberal is a philosopher who advocates social reform but always in a conservative spirit. My liberals share with Aristotle the conviction that the traditional arrangements have great

From "Philosophers against the Family," in *Person to Person*, George Graham and Hugh LaFollette, eds. (1989).

moral weight and that common opinion is a primary source of moral truth. A good modern example is Henry Sidgwick with his constant appeal to common sense. But philosophers like John Stuart Mill, William James, and Bertrand Russell can also be cited. On the other hand, since no radical can be called a liberal in my sense, many so-called liberals could be perversely excluded. Thus when John Rawls toys with the possibility of abolishing the family because kinship bias is a force inimical to equality of opportunity, he is no liberal.

The more exciting genre of social criticism is not liberal-Aristotelian but radical and Platonist in spirit. Its vantage is external or even supernal to the social institutions it has placed under moral scrutiny. Plato was as aware as anyone could be that what he called the cave was social reality. One reason for calling it a cave was to emphasize the need, as he saw it, for an external, objective perspective on established morality. Another point in so calling it was his conviction that common opinion was benighted, and that reform could not be accomplished except by a great deal of consciousness raising and enlightened social engineering. Plato's supernal vantage made it possible for him to look on social reality in somewhat the way the Army Corps of Engineers looks upon a river that needs to have its course changed and its waywardness tamed. In our own day much social criticism of a Marxist variety has taken this radical approach to social change. And of course much of contemporary feminist philosophy is radical. . . .

Feminism and the Family

I have said that the morality of the family has been relatively neglected. The glaring exception to this is, of course, the feminist movement. This movement is complex, but I am primarily confined to its moral philosophers, of whom the most influential is Simone de Beauvoir. For de Beauvoir, a social arrangement that does not allow all its participants the scope and liberty of a human subjectivity is to be condemned. De Beauvoir criticizes the family as an unacceptable arrangement since, for women, marriage and childbearing are essentially incompatible with their subjectivity and freedom:

The tragedy of marriage is not that it fails to assure woman the promised happiness . . . but that it mutilates her: It dooms her to repetition and routine. . . . At twenty or thereabouts mistress of a home, bound permanently to a man, a child in her arms, she stands with her life virtually finished forever (1952, 534).

For de Beauvoir the tragedy goes deeper than marriage. The loss of subjectivity is unavoidable as long as human reproduction requires the woman's womb. De Beauvoir starkly describes the pregnant woman who ought to be a "free individual" as a "stockpile of colloids, an incubator of an egg." And as recently as 1977 she compared childbearing and nurturing to slavery.

It would be a mistake to say that de Beauvoir's criticism of the family is outside the mainstream of Anglo-American philosophy. Her criterion of moral adequacy may be formulated in continental existentialist terms, but its central contention is generally accepted: Who would deny that an arrangement that systematically thwarts the freedom and autonomy of the individual is *eo ipso* defective? What is perhaps a bit odd to Anglo-American ears is that de Beauvoir makes so little appeal to ideals of fairness and equality. For her, it is the loss of autonomy that is decisive.

De Beauvoir is more pessimistic than most feminists she has influenced about the prospects for technological and social solutions. But implicit in her critique is the ideal of a society in which sexual differences are minimal or nonexistent. This ideal is shared by many contemporary feminist philosophers: . . . Richard Wasserstrom (1980), Ann Ferguson (1977), and Allison Jaggar (1977; 1983; 1986) are representative.

Wasserstrom's approach to social criticism is Platonist in its use of a hypothetical good society. The ideal society is nonsexist and "assimilationist": "In the assimilationist society in respect to sex, persons would not be socialized so as to see or understand themselves or others as essentially or significantly who they were or what their lives would be like because they were either male or female" (1980, 26). Social reality is scrutinized for its approximation to this ideal, and criticism is directed against all existing norms. Take the custom of having sexually segregated bathrooms: Whether this is right or wrong "depends on what the good society would look like in respect to sexual differentiation." The key question in evaluating any law or arrangement in which sex difference figures is: "What would the good or just society make of [it]?"

Thus the supernal light shines on the cave revealing its moral defects. *There*, in the ideal society, gender in the choice of lover or spouse would be of no more significance than eye color. *There* the family would consist of adults but not necessarily of different sexes and not necessarily in pairs. *There* we find equality ensured by a kind of affirmative action which compensates for disabilities. If women are somewhat weaker than men, or if they are subject to lunar disabilities, then this must be compensated for. (Wasserstrom compares women to persons with congenital defects for whom the good society makes special arrangements.) Male-dominated sports such as wrestling and football will . . . be eliminated, and marriage as we know it will not exist.

Other feminist philosophers are equally confident about the need for sweeping change. Ann Ferguson (1977) wants a "radical reorganization of child rearing." She recommends communal living and a deemphasis on biological parenting. In the ideal society "love relationships would be based on the meshing together of androgynous human beings." Carol Gould (1983) argues for androgyny and for abolishing legal marriage. She favors single parenting, co-parenting, and communal parenting. The only arrangement she emphatically opposes is the traditional one where the mother provides primary care for the children. Janice Raymond (1975) is an assimilationist who objects to the ideal of androgyny, preferring instead to speak of a genderless ideal free of male or female stereotypes. Allison Jaggar's ideal is described in a science-fiction story depicting a society in which "neither sex bears children, but both sexes, through hormone treatments, suckle them . . . thus [the author] envisions a society where every baby has three social 'mothers,' who may be male or female, and at least two of whom agree to breast-feed it" (1983). To those of us who find this bizarre, Jaggar replies that this shows the depth of our prejudice in favor of the natural family.

Though they differ in detail, these feminists hold to a common social ideal that is broadly assimilationist in character and inimical to the traditional family. Sometimes it seems as if the radical feminist simply takes the classical Marxist eschatology of the *Communist Manifesto* and substitutes "gender" for "class." Indeed, the feminist and the old-fashioned Marxist do have much in common. Both see their caves as politically divided into two warring factions: one oppressing, the other oppressed. Both see the need of raising the consciousness of the oppressed group to its predicament and to the possibility of removing its shackles. Both look forward to the day of a classless or genderless society. And both are zealots, paying little attention to the tragic personal costs to be paid for the revolution they wish to bring about. The feminists tell us little about that side of things. To begin with, how can the benighted myriads in the cave who do not wish to mesh together with other androgynous beings be reeducated? And how are children to be brought up in the genderless society? Plato took great pains to explain his methods. Would the new methods be as thoroughgoing? Unless these questions can be given plausible answers, the supernal attack on the family must always be irresponsible. The appeal to the just society justifies nothing until it can be shown that the radical proposals do not have monstrous consequences. That has not been shown. Indeed, given the perennially dubious state of the social sciences, it is precisely what *cannot* be shown.

Any social arrangement that falls short of the assimilationist ideal is labeled sexist. It should be noted that this characteristically feminist use of the term differs significantly from the popular or literal sense. Literally, and popularly, sexism connotes unfair discrimination. But in its extended philosophical use it connotes discrimination, period. Wasserstrom and many feminists trade on the popular pejorative connotations of sexism when they invite us to be antisexist. Most liberals are antisexist in the popular sense. But to be antisexist in the technical, radical philosophical sense is not merely to be opposed to discrimination against women; it is to be *for* what Wasserstrom calls the assimilationist ideal. The philosopher antisexist opposes any social policy that is nonandrogynous, objecting, for example, to legislation that allows for maternity leave. As Allison Jaggar remarks: "We do not, after all, elevate 'prostate leave' into a special right of men" (1977). From being liberally opposed to sexism, one may in this way insensibly be led to a radical critique of the family whose ideal is assimilationist and androgynous. For it is very clear that the realization of the androgynous ideal is incompatible with the survival of the family as we know it.

The neological extension of labels such as "sexism," "slavery," and "prostitution" is a feature of radical discourse. The liberal too will sometimes call for radical solutions to social problems. Some institutions are essentially unjust. To reform slavery or totalitarian systems of government is to eliminate them. The radical trades on these extreme practices in characterizing other practices—for example, characterizing low wages as "slave" wages and the worker who is paid them as a "slave" laborer. Taking these descriptions seriously may put one on the way to treating a system of a free labor market as a "slave system," which, in simple justice, must be overthrown and replaced by an alternative system of production.

Comparing mothers and wives to slaves is a common radical criticism of the family. Presumably most slaves do not want to be slaves. In fact, the majority of wives and mothers want to be wives and mothers. Calling these women slaves is therefore a pejorative extension of the term. To be slaves in the literal sense these women would have to be too dispirited and oppressed or too corrupt even to want freedom from slavery. Yet that is how some feminist philosophers look upon women who opt for the traditional family. It does seem fanciful and not a little condescending to see them so, but let us suppose that it is in fact a correct and profound description of the plight of married women and mothers. Would it now follow that the term "slave" literally applies to them? Not quite yet. Before we could call these women slaves, we should have to have made a further assumption. Even timorous slaves too fearful of taking any step to freedom are under no illusion that they are not slaves. Yet it is a fact that most women and mothers do not *think* of themselves as slaves, so we must assume that the majority of women have been systematically deluded into thinking they are free. And that assumption, too, is often explicitly made. Here the radical feminist will typically explain that, existentially, women, being treated by men as sex objects, are especially prone to bad faith and false consciousness. Marxist feminists will see them as part of an unawakened and oppressed economic class. Clearly we cannot call on a deluded woman to cast off her bonds before we have

made her *aware* of her bondage. So the first task of freeing the slave woman is dispelling the thrall of a false and deceptive consciousness. One must raise her consciousness to the reality of her situation. (Some feminists acknowledge that it may in fact be too late for many of the women who have fallen too far into the delusions of marriage and motherhood. But the educative process can save many from falling into the marriage and baby trap.)

In this sort of rhetorical climate nothing is what it seems. Prostitution is another term that has been subjected to a radical enlargement. Allison Jaggar believes that a feminist interpretation of the term "prostitution" is badly needed and asks for a "philosophical theory of prostitution" (1986). Observing that the average woman dresses for men, marries a man for protection, and so on, she says: "For contemporary radical feminists, prostitution is the archetypal relationship of women to men" (1986, 115).

Of course, the housewife Jaggar has in mind might be offended at the suggestion that she herself is a prostitute, albeit less well paid and less aware of it than the professional street prostitute. To this the radical feminist reply is, to quote Jaggar:

Individuals' intentions do not necessarily indicate the true nature of what is going on. Both man and woman might be outraged at the description of their candlelit dinner as prostitution, but the radical feminist argues this outrage is due simply to the participants' failure or refusal to perceive the social context in which the dinner occurs (1986, 117).

Apparently, this failure or refusal to perceive affects most women. Thus we may even suppose that the majority of women who have been treated by a man to a candlelit dinner prefer it to other dining alternatives they have experienced. To say that these preferences are misguided is a hard and condescending doctrine. It would appear that most feminist philosophers are not overly impressed with Mill's principle that there can be no appeal from a majority verdict of those who have experienced two alternatives.

The dismissive feminist attitude to the widespread preferences of women takes its human toll. Most women, for example, prefer to have children, and few of those who have them regret having them. It is no more than sensible, from a utilitarian standpoint, to take note of the widespread preference and to take it seriously in planning one's own life. But a significant number of women discount this general verdict as benighted, taking more seriously the idea that the reported joys of motherhood are exaggerated and fleeting, if not altogether illusory. These women tell themselves and others that having babies is a trap to be avoided. But for many women childlessness has become a trap of its own, somewhat lonelier than the more conventional traps of marriage and babies. Some come to find their childlessness regrettable; this sort of regret is common to those who flout Mill's reasonable maxim by putting the verdict of ideology over the verdict of human experience.

It is a serious defect of American feminism that it concentrates its zeal on impugning femininity and feminine culture at the expense of the grassroot fight against economic and social injustices to which women are subjected. As we have seen, the radical feminist attitude to the woman who enjoys her femininity is condescending or even contemptuous. Indeed, the contempt for femininity reminds one of misogynist biases in philosophers such as Kant, Rousseau, and Schopenhauer, who believed that femininity was charming but incompatible with full personhood and reasonableness. The feminists deny the charm, but they too accept the verdict that femininity is weakness. It goes without saying that an essential connection between femininity and powerlessness has not been established by *either* party.

By denigrating conventional feminine roles and holding to an assimilationist ideal in social policy, the feminist movement has lost its natural constituency. The actual concerns, beliefs, and aspirations of the majority of women are not taken seriously *except* as illustrations of bad faith, false consciousness, and successful brainwashing. What women actually want is discounted and reinterpreted as to what they have been led to *think* they want (a man, children). What most women *enjoy* (male gallantry, candlelit dinners, sexy clothes, makeup) is treated as an obscenity (prostitution).

As the British feminist Jennifer Radcliffe Richards says:

> Most women still dream about beauty, dress, weddings, dashing lovers, domesticity, and babies . . .
> but if feminists seem (as they do) to want to elimi-

nate nearly all of these things—beauty, sex conventions, families, and all—for most people that simply means the removal of everything in life which is worth living for (1980, 341–342).

Radical feminism creates a false dichotomy between sexism and assimilation, as if there were nothing in between. This is to ignore completely the middle ground in which it could be recognized that a woman can be free of oppression and nevertheless feminine in the sense abhorred by many feminists. For women are simply not waiting to be freed from the particular chains the radical feminists are trying to sunder. The average woman enjoys her femininity. She wants a man, not a roommate. She wants fair economic opportunities, and she wants children and the time to care for them. These are the goals that women actually have, and they are not easily attainable. But they will never be furthered by an elitist radical movement that views the actual aspirations of women as the product of a false consciousness. There is room for a liberal feminism that would work for reforms that would give women equal opportunity in the workplace and in politics, but would leave untouched and unimpugned the basic institutions that women want and support: marriage and motherhood. Such a feminism is already in operation in some European countries. But it has been obstructed in the United States by the ideologues who now hold the seat of power in the feminist movement (Hewlett, 1986).

In characterizing and criticizing American feminism, I have not taken into account the latest revisions and qualifications of a lively and variegated movement. There is a kind of feminism-of-the-week that one cannot hope to keep abreast of, short of giving up all other concerns. The best one can do for the present purposes is attend to central theses and arguments that bear on the feminist treatment of the family. Nevertheless, even for this limited purpose, it would be wrong to omit discussion of an important turn taken by feminism in the past few years. I have in mind the recent literature on the idea that there is a specific female ethic that is more concrete, less rule-oriented, more empathetic and caring, and more attentive to the demands of a particular context. The kind of feminism that accepts the idea that women differ from men in approaching ethical dilemmas and social problems from a care perspective is not oriented to androgyny as an ideal. Rather it seeks to develop this special female ethic andgive it greater practical scope.

The stress on context might lead one to think these feminists are more sympathetic to the family as the social arrangement that shapes the moral development of women and is the context for many of the moral dilemmas that women actually face. However, one sees as yet no attention being paid to the fact that feminism itself is a force working against the preservation of the family. Psychologists like Carol Gilligan and philosophers like Lawrence Blum concentrate their attention on the moral quality of the caring relationships, but these relationships are themselves not viewed in their concrete embeddedness in any formal social arrangement.

It should also be said that some feminists are moving away from earlier hostility to motherhood (Trebilcot, 1984). Here, too, one sees the weakening of the assimilationist ideal in the acknowledgment of a primary gender role. However, childrearing is not primarily seen within the context of the family but as a special relationship between mother and daughter or—more awkwardly—between mother and son, a relationship that effectively excludes the male parent. And the often cultist celebration of motherhood remains largely hostile to traditional familial arrangements.

It is too early to say whether a new style of nonassimilationist feminism will lead to a mitigation of the assault on the family or even on femininity. In any case, the recognition of a female ethic of care and responsibility is hardly inconsistent with a social ethic that values the family as a vital, perhaps indispensable, institution. And the recognition that women have their own moral style may well be followed by a more accepting attitude to the kind of femininity that the more assimilationist feminists reject.

References

De Beauvoir, Simone. 1952. *The Second Sex*. H. M. Parshley, trans. New York: Random House.

———. 1977. "Talking to De Beauvoir." In *Spare Rib*.

Ferguson, Ann. 1977. "Androgyny as an Ideal for Human Development." In M. Vetterling-Braggin, F. Elliston, and J. English, eds. *Feminism and Philosophy*, pp. 45–69. Totowa, N.J.: Rowman and Littlefield.

Gould, Carol. 1983. "Private Rights and Public Virtues: Woman, the Family and Democracy." In Carol Gould, ed. *Beyond Domination*, pp. 3–18. Totowa, N.J.: Rowman and Allanheld.

Hewlett, Sylvia Ann. 1986. *A Lesser Life: The Myth of Woman's Liberation in America*. New York: Morrow.

Jaggar, Allison. 1977. "On Sex Equality." In Jane English, ed. *Sex Equality*, Englewood Cliffs, N.J.: Prentice-Hall.

———. 1983. "Human Biology in Feminist Theory: Sexual Equality Reconsidered." In Gould, ed. *Beyond Domination*.

———. 1986. "Prostitution." In Marilyn Pearsell, ed. *Women and Values: Readings in Recent Feminist Philosophy*, pp. 108–121. Belmont, Calif.: Wadsworth.

Raymond, Janice. 1975. "The Illusion of Androgyny." *Quest: A Feminist Quarterly*, 2.

Richards, Jennifer Radcliffe. 1980. *The Skeptical Feminist*. Harmondsworth: Penguin.

Trebilcot, Joyce, ed. 1984. *Mothering: Essays in Feminist Theory*. Totowa, N.J.: Rowman and Allanheld.

Wasserstrom, Richard. 1980. *Philosophy and Social Issues*. Notre Dame, Ind.: University of Notre Dame Press.

25. *They Lived Happily Ever After: Sommers on Women and Marriage*

Marilyn Friedman

Marilyn Friedman questions whether what Christina Sommers supports is really what most women want. She quotes a 1983 survey which indicated that 63 percent of women preferred nontraditional family relationships. She points out that in 1977 only 16 percent of American households were traditional families. She argues that femininity as slavishly deferring to men is not good for women, and contends that no woman should "swoon at the sight of Rhett Butler carrying Scarlett O'Hara up the stairs to a fate undreamt of in feminist philosophy."

1. In a series of papers which has recently appeared in several philosophical and general academic publications,[1] Christina Sommers mounts a campaign against feminist philosophers (1989a, 85; 1989b, B2) and "American feminism" in general (1989a, 90–91). Sommers blames feminists for contributing to the current divorce rate and the breakdown of the traditional family, and she repudiates feminist critiques of traditional forms of marriage, family, and femininity. In this paper, I explore Sommers's views in some detail. My aim is not primarily to defend her feminist targets, but to ferret out Sommers's own views of traditional marriage, family, and femininity, and to see whether or not they have any philosophical merit.

2. In her writings, Sommers generally defends what she claims that feminists have challenged. Whether or not she is actually discussing the same things is often open to question since she fails to define the key terms behind which she rallies. Sommers, for example, endorses "the family," the "traditional family," and "the family as we know it" (1989a, 87–88). These are not equivalent expressions. The so-called traditional family—a nuclear family consisting of a legally married heterosexual couple and their children, in which the man is the sole breadwinner and "head" of the household, and the woman does the domestic work and childcare—comprised only 16% of all U.S. households in 1977, according to the U.S. Census Bureau.[2] Hence, the "traditional family" is no longer "*the* family" or "*the* family as we know it" (italics mine) but is only one sort of family that we know.

Sommers also rallies behind "femininity," "feminine culture," "conventional feminine roles," and "a primary gender role" (1989a, 90, 92). These expressions, as well, call for clarification; they do not necessarily refer to the same practices. In recent years, many feminists have defended various aspects of what might also be called "feminine culture." Sommers notes a few of these authors and works (Carol Gilligan, for example), but finds one reason or another for repudiating each one that she cites.[3]

3. To see what Sommers is promoting under the banner of "feminine culture," we should look to Sommers's claims about what women value, want, and enjoy.[4] First, there are wants, values, and enjoyments pertaining to men.[5] Sommers claims that women want "a man," "marriage," and "to marry good providers."[6] She asserts that "most women" enjoy "male gallantry," that the "majority of women" enjoy being "treated by a man to a candlelit dinner," and that "many women . . . swoon at the sight of Rhett Butler carrying Scarlett O'Hara up the stairs to a fate undreamt of in feminist philosophy."[7]

Second, there are wants, values, and enjoyments having to do with children. Women, Sommers tells us, want children, motherhood, "*conventional* motherhood," "family," and "the time to care for children."[8]

From "They Lived Happily Ever After: Sommers on Women and Marriage," *Journal of Social Philosophy* (1990).

In a revealing turn of phrase, Sommers also asserts that women are "willing to pay the price" for family and motherhood (1989b, B2). Sommers does not say, however, what she thinks the price is.

Third, there are wants, values, and enjoyments having to do with femininity. Women are said to enjoy their "femininity," makeup, "sexy clothes," and, even more specifically, "clothes that render them 'sex objects.'"[9] On the topic of femininity, Sommers also quotes approvingly (1989a, 90–91) the words of Janet Radcliffe Richards who wrote that, "Most women still dream about beauty, dress, weddings, dashing lovers," and "domesticity," and that, for "most people," "beauty, sex conventions, families, and all" comprise "everything in life which is worth living for."[10]

4. A very few of the wants which Sommers attributes to women do not fit into my three-part classification scheme (men, children, femininity). Sommers claims that women want "fair economic opportunities" (1989a, 91), and that they are "generally receptive to liberal feminist reforms that enhance their political and economic powers" (1989b, B2). Sommers, ironically, does not recognize that the enhanced economic and political power of women makes them less needful of traditional marriage to a "good provider," and when they are married, makes them less afraid to resort to divorce to solve marital and family problems. The economic concerns of liberal feminism directly threaten one colossal support for the "traditional family," namely, the extreme economic vulnerability of the non–income-earning woman and her concomitant material dependence on a "good provider."

Under traditional arrangements, most women not only *wanted* marriage, they *needed* it. It was by far a woman's most socially legitimate option for economic survival. Take away the need, as liberal feminism seeks to do, and at least some of the want also disappears. One otherwise very traditional aunt of mine became a wealthy widow in her late fifties when my rich uncle died. She never remarried. Now a dynamic woman of 82 who travels widely and lives well, she confesses that no man has interested her enough to make it worthwhile to give up her freedom a second time. "I'm lucky," she confides, "I don't need a meal-ticket." Even a nonfeminist can understand what she is getting at.

5. Before assessing Sommers's overall views, let us rescue Scarlett O'Hara. Sommers's remark that Scar-lett O'Hara's rape by Rhett Butler is a fate undreamt of in feminist philosophy is . . . simply stunning. (Note that Sommers does not use the word *rape* here—one of many omissions in her writings.) Even a passing knowledge of feminist philosophy reveals that rape is hardly undreamt of in it.[11] Rape, of course, is not a dream; it is a nightmare. Any form of sexual aggression can involve coercion, intimidation, degradation, physical abuse, battering, and, in extreme cases, death.

The reality of rape is rendered invisible by the many novels and films, such as *Gone With the Wind*, which romanticize and mystify it. They portray the rapist as a handsome man whose domination is pleasurable in bed, and portray women as happy to have their own sexual choices and refusals crushed by such men. In a culture in which these sorts of portrayals are routine, it is no surprise that this scene arouses the sexual desire of some women. However, the name of Richard Speck,[12] to take one example, can remind us that real rape is not the pleasurable fantasy intimated in *Gone With the Wind*. To put the point graphically: Would "many women" still swoon over Butler's rape of O'Hara if they knew that he urinated on her? When you're the victim of rape, you don't have much choice over what goes on.

6. Let us move on to femininity. Sommers never spells out exactly what she means by femininity. For guidance on this topic, we could turn to literature in social psychology which identifies the important traits of femininity and which explores the social devaluation of the feminine (Eagly, 1987). However, it might be more revealing to turn to a different sort of "expert." By a lucky coincidence, I recently acquired a gem of a cultural artifact, a 1965 book entitled, *Always Ask a Man: Arlene Dahl's Key to Femininity*, written by a rather well-known actress and model of the 1960s, Arlene Dahl. I have learned a great deal from this femininity manifesto.

As you might guess from the title, one guiding theme of the book, and of the femininity it aims to promote, is utter deference to the opinions of men. Dahl instructs the female reader: "Look at Yourself Objectively (try to see yourself through a man's eyes)" (p. 2). In Dahl's view, the "truly feminine" woman works "instinctively" at pleasing men and making men feel important. "When [a man] speaks to her, she listens with rapt attention to every word" (p. 5). Dahl believes that every woman has the capacity to measure up to men's ideals of femininity. This is because "Every woman is an actress. (Admit it!) Her first role is that of a coquette. (If you have any doubts just watch a baby girl with her father)" (p. 6).

Dahl's book is laced with quotations from male celebrities who are treated as incontrovertible authorities on what women should be like. Yul Brynner, for example, wants women to be good listeners who are not particularly logical (p. 3). Richard Burton likes women who are "faintly giggly" (p. 3). Tony Perkins thinks that a "girl should act like a girl and not like the head of a corporation—even if she is" (p. 8). The most revealing observation comes from George Hamilton: "A woman is often like a strip of film—obliterated, insignificant—until a man puts a light behind her" (pp. 5–6).

Surprisingly, some of the traits advocated for women by these male celebrities are actually valuable traits: honesty, straightforwardness, maturity, ingenuity, understanding, dignity, generosity, and humor. These traits are not distinctively feminine, however, and that may be the reason why they quickly disappear from Dahl's discussion. The twin themes that resound throughout this femininity manual are that of cultivating one's physical attractiveness and slavishly deferring to men. Instead of a chapter on honesty, a chapter on dignity, and so on, the book features chapters on every aspect of bodily grooming and adornment, including a separate chapter on each of the four basic categories of Caucasian hair color: blonde, redhead, "brownette," and brunette.

The slavish deference to men is crucial, since the whole point of the enterprise is to get a man. Thus, Dahl explains in the introduction that this book is written to counteract a tendency for women to dress to please other women, and it is also not for "women who want to be beautiful for beauty's sake. Such beauty serves no purpose, other than self-satisfaction, if that can be considered a purpose" (pp. x–xi).

The quintessential prohibition involved in femininity seems to be this: "NEVER upstage a man. Don't try to top his joke, even if you have to bite your tongue to keep from doing it. Never launch loudly into your own opinion on a subject—whether it's petunias or politics. Instead, draw out his ideas to which you can gracefully add your footnotes from time to time"

(p. 12). Dahl is less sanguine than Sommers that the role of motherhood fits comfortably into a feminine life; she advises, ". . . don't get so involved with your role of MOTHER that you forget to play WIFE" (p. 9). Once married, your own interests should never override your husband's interests, job, and even hobbies, and, "There should be nothing that takes precedence in your day's schedule over making yourself attractive and appealing for the man in your life," not even your "children's activities" (p. 175)!

Voila, femininity. Such servility shows the dubiousness of Sommers's claim that "a woman can be free of oppression and nevertheless feminine in the sense abhorred by many feminists" (1989a, 91).

7. Let us turn now to Sommers's overall philosophical defense of traditional marriage, family, and femininity. Having asserted that most women value or want all of these traditions, Sommers charges feminist views with a serious defect: They either dismiss or disparage these popular feminine wants and values.[13] Sommers herself defers to these alleged views of most women as if they were as such authoritative: Because "most women" (as she alleges) want traditional marriage and family, therefore these practices must be better than any alternatives. It is important to note that Sommers does not argue that traditional marriage and so on, on balance, promote important moral values better than any feminist alternatives.[14] No comprehensive moral comparisons appear in her writings. Her argument begins (and ends, as I will argue) with an appeal to popular opinion.

8. Is Sommers right about what "most women" think? She refers to no studies, no representative samples whatsoever to support her generalizations. Whole categories of women are patently excluded from her reference group and are invisible in her writings. This is a fitting moment to mention the "L" word—and I don't mean "liberal." Obviously, no lesbians, unless seriously closeted, are among Sommers's alleged majority of women who want "a man," conventional marriage, or a traditional family.

Even among nonlesbians, [many] women these days do not want a *traditional* marriage or a *traditional* family. Some heterosexual women simply do not want to marry or to have children at all, and many others want *nontraditional* marriages and *nontraditional* families. Surveys show that this attitude, and not the preference for tradition alleged by Sommers, is actually in the majority. In one 1983 study, 63 percent of women surveyed expressed preferences for nontraditional family arrangements (Sapiro, 1990, 355). Sommers's factual claims are, thus, debatable.

Even apart from questions of popularity, the wants, values, and enjoyments which Sommers attributes to "most women" are frankly suspicious as an ensemble. Candlelit dinners do not combine easily with babies. Dashing lovers (extramarital!) can be disastrous for a marriage. This list of wants and values seems to show a failure to separate what is idealized and mythic from what is (to put it very advisedly) authentic and genuinely possible in the daily reality of marital and family relationships over the long haul. To hear Sommers tell it, women are blandly unconcerned about wife-battering, incest, marital rape, or the profound economic vulnerability of the traditional non–income–earning wife. This is hard to believe. What is more likely is that, for many women, ". . . they got married and lived happily ever after," is only a fairy tale—especially for those who have been married for awhile. Even the most traditional of women, I am convinced, has some sense of the risks involved in traditional heterosexual relationships. As an old saying goes, "When two hearts beat as one, someone is dead."[15]

Sommers's list of women's wants and values is also woefully short. It suggests that this is *all* that "most women" want, that women's aspirations extend no farther than to being "feminine," getting a man—any man—and having babies. On the contrary, many women want meaningful and fulfilling work apart from childcare and domestic labor. Many women aspire to making a social contribution, or they have artistic impulses seeking expression, spiritual callings, deep friendships with other women, and abiding concerns for moral value and their own integrity.[16] One foundational motivation for feminism has always been the aim to overcome the *constraints* on women's genuinely wide-ranging aspirations posed by traditional marital and family arrangements.

9. What philosophical difference would it make if Sommers were right about women's wants and values in general? The popularity of an opinion is hardly an infallible measure of its empirical or moral credibility. Even popular opinions may be based on misinformation, unfounded rumor, and so on. Sommers ignores

these possibilities and recommends that we defer to popular opinion on the basis of ". . . Mill's principle that there can be no appeal from a majority verdict of those who have experienced two alternatives" (1989a, 89–90). Sommers is evidently suggesting that feminist critiques of traditional family, marriage, and femininity should be judged by whether or not they conform to the "majority verdict of those who have experienced" the relevant alternatives. Now, carefully understood, this is actually not such a bad idea. However, rather than supporting Sommers's deference to popular opinion, this principle repudiates it.

First, there are more than just "two" feminist alternatives to any of the traditions in question. Consider, for example, the traditionally married, heterosexual couple comprised of dominant, breadwinning male and domestic, childrearing female. Feminists have recommended various alternative family arrangements, including egalitarian heterosexual marriage, communal living, lesbian relationships, and single parenting when economic circumstances are favorable.[17] To decide the value of traditional marriage and family, one would have to try all the relevant alternatives—or at least *some* of them. And on Mill's view, merely experiencing alternatives is not enough; one must also be capable of "appreciating and enjoying" them (Mill, 1979, 9). If Sommers is right, however, most women want and choose traditional family, traditional marriage, and traditional femininity, and, thus, do not either experience or enjoy living according to any feminist alternatives. Women such as these are not what Mill calls "competent judges" of the value of those traditions since "they know only their own side of the question" (p. 10). And it is only from the verdict of *competent judges* that Mill believes that "there can be no appeal" (p. 11).

Second, of the "competent judges," in Mill's sense, that is, of the women who *have* experienced and enjoyed feminist alternatives to traditional marriage and family, most (I would wager) *prefer the feminist alternatives.* I am referring, among others, to women in lesbian relationships, and women in genuinely egalitarian heterosexual relationships. If I am right about this, then by Mill's principle, we must reject "popular opinion" along with traditional marriage and the rest.

10. The truth of the matter is that, in the end, Sommers does not rest her case on Mill's principle.

Apparently without realizing that she changes her argument, she ends by appealing to something less vaunted than the majority verdict of those who have experienced and enjoyed *both* traditional family, etc., and various feminist alternatives. Her final court of appeal is simply to "what most people think," "common sense," and "tradition" itself (1989a, 95, 97). Sommers urges that "A moral philosophy that does not give proper weight to the customs and opinions of the community is presumptuous in its attitude and pernicious in its consequences" (1989a, 103). She speaks warmly of the Aristotelian conviction that "traditional arrangements have great moral weight and that common opinion is a primary source of moral truth" (1989a, 83). When it comes to tradition, Sommers would do well to consider Mill again. Mill often deferred to tradition, but it was not a deference from which he thought there was "no appeal," as he amply demonstrated in the important *indictment* of nineteenth century marital traditions on which he collaborated with Harriet Taylor (Mill & Taylor, 1970). (It would be interesting to know what "pernicious . . . consequences," to use Sommers's phrase, flowed from Mill's and Taylor's critique.)

Tradition is a fickle husband. He is constantly changing his mind. On the grounds of tradition, eighty years ago, Sommers would have opposed women's suffrage. One hundred and fifty years ago, she would have opposed women speaking in public (She would have had to do so in private!), opposed the rights of married women to property in their own names, opposed the abolition of slavery, and so on. She would have supported wife-battering since it was permitted by legal tradition—so long as the rod was no bigger around than the size of the husband's thumb.

Not only is tradition ever-changing, it is also plural, both within our own society and globally. Which tradition shall we follow when there is more than one from which to choose? Islam is the world's most widely practiced religion. Shall we non-Islamic women heed the most globally numerous of our sisters' voices and don the veil, retire from public life, and allow husbands to marry up to four wives? Within our own society, marital traditions also vary. Shall we follow the traditions of orthodox Jewish and orthodox Catholic women and avoid all contraceptives? My maternal grandmother did so; she had fourteen births. At nine

months per gestation, she spent ten and a half years of her life being pregnant. Although she lingered to the age of eighty-seven, she seemed even older than her age for the final sixteen, worn-out years in which I knew her. Doubtless, that too was part of her tradition.

Why suppose that there is special merit to any of the alternative traditions that we happen to have at this historical moment in this particular geopolitical location? Why suppose that any of our current traditions are better or more deserving of loyalty and support than the traditions toward which we are evolving? And how will we ever evolve if we remain deadlocked in loyalty to all of the traditions we happen to have today?

11. Sommers allows that our traditions may need reform and even recommends "piecemeal social engineering" to deal with "imperfections" in the family (1989a, 97)—although it is noteworthy that she never specifies what these imperfections are, and, in a different passage, she inconsistently calls upon American feminism to leave marriage and motherhood simply "untouched and unimpugned" (1989a, 91).[18] Nevertheless, she insists that her arguments are directed only against those radical feminists who seek the abolition of the family and the "radical reform of preferences, values, aspirations, and prejudices" (1990, 151, 148).

A serious concern to reform imperfections in the family should lead someone to consider the views of nonradical feminist reformers who also criticize marital and family traditions. Many feminists would be content with piecemeal family reform—so long as it was genuine reform (Thorne & Yalom, 1982; Okin, 1987, 1989). Anyway, this issue is a red herring. A dispute over the pace of reform does not show that radical feminist critiques of family traditions are wrong in substance. Most important, by allowing that change is *needed* in family traditions, Sommers effectively concedes that we should not automatically defer to tradition. To admit that reform of tradition is morally permissible is to reject tradition *per se* as an incontestable moral authority. The controversy can only be decided by directly evaluating the conditions of life established by marital and family traditions—and their alternatives.

12. Sommers has one final twist to her argument which we should consider. She notes briefly—all too

briefly—that traditions "have *prima facie* moral force" so long as they are not "essentially unjust" (1989a, 97). Sommers does not explain what she means by "essential injustice." Just how much injustice makes a traditional practice "essentially unjust?"

Despite its vagueness, this concession to injustice is critically important. It makes the merit of Sommers's own appeal to tradition contingent on the essential noninjustice of the particular traditions in question. Sommers, however, provides no argument to establish that traditional marriage practices and so forth are not essentially unjust. Nor does she respond substantively to those feminist arguments which claim to locate important injustices in these traditional practices. She rejects all feminist criticisms of the traditional family because they do not coincide with "popular opinion," "common sense," or tradition. Traditional marriage and family are not essentially unjust, in Sommers's view, simply because most people allegedly do not *think* they are.

We seem to have come full circle. Sommers rejects feminist critiques of traditional marriage and so on because they are inconsistent with popular opinion, common sense, and tradition. Tradition is to be relied on, in turn, so long as it is not essentially unjust. But Sommers rejects feminist arguments to show injustices in marital and family traditions simply on the grounds that those arguments are inconsistent with popular opinion, common sense, and tradition itself. Sommers's defense of traditional marriage and family is, in the final analysis, circular and amounts to nothing more than simple *deference to tradition*—indeed, to particular traditions which are no longer so pervasive or popular as Sommers thinks.

13. One final concern: Sommers blames feminists for contributing to the growing divorce rate and the "disintegration of the traditional family."[19] However, feminism could only contribute to the divorce rate if married women ended their marriages as a result of adopting feminist ideas. If Sommers is right, however, in thinking that "most women" reject nonliberal feminist values, then nonliberal feminists could not be having a significant impact on the divorce rate. Sommers cannot have it both ways. Either feminism *is* significantly contributing to the growing divorce rate, in which case it must be in virtue of the wide appeal of feminist ideas about marriage and family, or feminist ideas do *not* have wide appeal, in which case they cannot be significantly contributing to the growing divorce rate.

14. To conclude: My overall assessment of Sommers's views on marriage, family, and femininity is grim.[20] Most important, Sommers rejects feminist views of marriage, family, and femininity ultimately on the basis of her own simple deference to (allegedly) popular opinion, common sense, and tradition. This deference is defensible only if feminist views about injustices in those traditions can be shown, on *independent* grounds, to be misguided—and Sommers never provides this independent argument.

Endnotes

1. Sommers: 1988, 1989a, 1989b, and 1990.
2. Cited in Thorne & Yalom, 1982, 5.
3. Sommers repudiates the feminist literature which explores the value of mothering (e.g., Trebilcot, 1984) on the grounds that it "remains largely hostile to traditional familial arrangements." She also claims that this literature focuses only on an abstracted mother–child relationship, especially the mother–daughter relationship—a focus that "effectively excludes the male parent" (1989a, 92). Aside from inaccurately summarizing a body of literature, this latter comment, ironically, ignores the fact that under "traditional familial arrangements," the male parent plays a *negligible role* in day-to-day, primary childcare, especially in a child's early years.

The comment also ignores the work of Dorothy Dinnerstein (1977) and, especially, of Nancy Chodorow (1978), which precisely urges *shared parenting* and a prominent role for the male parent. This work has been extremely influential and widely cited among feminists. I suspect, however, that shared parenting is not the way in which Sommers wants to include the male parent, since this arrangement is not "traditional" and it challenges the idea of a "primary gender role" that Sommers appears to support (1989a, 92). Sommers, herself, thus fails to clarify the role of the male parent in her account.

4. Sommers complains that feminist philosophers have not been entrusted by ordinary women with a mission of speaking on behalf of those ordinary women (1989b, B3).

Sommers, however, appears to think that she is thus entrusted, since she does not hesitate to make claims about what "most women . . . prefer," what "women actually want," and what "most women *enjoy*" (1989a, 90).

5. The following classification scheme is my own. The categories are not meant to be mutually exclusive.

6. Quotations are, respectively, from: 1989a, 90; 1989a, 91; and 1990, 150.

7. Quotations are, respectively, from: 1989a, 90; 1989a, 89; and 1989b, B3.

8. Quotations are, respectively, from: 1989a, 90; 1989a, 91; 1990, 150, italics mine; 1989b, B2; and 1989a, 91.

9. Quotations are, respectively, from: 1989a, 90; 1989a, 90; 1989a, 90; and 1990, 150.

10. Richards, 1980, 341–342. Quoted in Sommers, 1989a, 90–91.

11. Some important early papers are anthologized in: Vetterling-Braggin et al., 1977, Part VI. Another important, relatively early study is Brownmiller, 1976.

12. In 1966, Richard Speck stunned the city of Chicago and the nation by raping, killing, and, in some cases, mutilating the bodies of eight out of nine nursing students who shared a house together on Chicago's South Side. The nurse who survived did so by hiding under a bed until Speck left the house after having apparently lost count. That woman might well swoon over Scarlett O'Hara's rape, but it would not be a swoon of ecstasy.

13. 1989a, 88–91. Sommers writes: "It is a serious defect of American feminism that it concentrates its zeal on impugning femininity and feminine culture at the expense of the grass root fight against economic and social injustices to which women are subjected" (p. 90). American feminism has hardly neglected the fight against economic or social injustice against women. Apart from that, the *Philosopher's Index* back to 1970 contains no citations of writings by Sommers herself on "the economic and social injustices to which women are subjected." In the essays reviewed here, she does not even identify the injustices she has in mind.

14. Sommers does warn that "many women" who avoid motherhood find themselves lonely (1989a, 90), and she suggests that those who avoid or divorce themselves from the patriarchal family "often" suffer harm and "might" feel "betrayed by the ideology" which led them

to this state (1989b, B3). These faintly threatening suggestions are left unexplained and unsupported.

15. I was reminded of this old saying by an article by Janyce Katz (1990, 88) in which Dagmar Celeste, then the "First Lady of Ohio," is quoted as mentioning it.

16. Raising children involves awesome moral responsibilities, as Sommers herself emphasizes when lamenting the increasing divorce rate. These profound moral responsibilities entail that we should not casually reinforce the cultural ideology which declares that the only hope of women's fulfillment in life depends on their *having* children. Sommers complains about divorce because of the harm it inflicts on children (1989a, 98–102), but she never cautions women to consider these moral obligations before marrying or having children in the first place.

17. Cf. Hunter College Women's Studies Collective, 1983, Ch. 9.

18. My worry is that Sommers's occasional, reasonable call for piecemeal family reform disguises a hidden agenda that aims to deadlock us in certain family traditions as we know them now (or knew them three decades ago). This appearance might be dispelled if she were to identify the imperfections she recognizes in the family.

19. 1989a, 82–83, 99–102. Sommers admits that "no reliable study has yet been made comparing children of divorced parents to children from intact families who [sic] parents do not get on well together." She claims cavalierly that "any such study would be compromised by some arbitrary measures of parental incompatibility and one could probably place little reliance on them" (1989a, 101). However, she ignores her own claims of limited evidence on this issue and argues as if it were fact that children of divorced parents are invariably worse off than if their parents had remained married.

When Sommers discusses the problem of divorce, she tends to assimilate the philosophical culprits onto one model: They are all wrong for disregarding "special duties" to family members, especially to children. This latter accusation is simply irrelevant in regard to feminists; no serious feminist literature suggests that responsibilities toward children should be disregarded.

20. Overall, her presentations are marred by ambiguities, inconsistencies, dubious factual claims, misrepresentations of feminist literature, and faulty arguments.

References

Brownmiller, Susan. 1976. *Against Our Will: Men, Women and Rape*. New York: Bantam.

Chodorow, Nancy. 1978. *The Reproduction of Mothering*. Berkeley: University of California Press.

Dahl, Arlene. 1965. *Always Ask a Man: Arlene Dahl's Key to Femininity.* Englewood Cliffs, N.J.: Prentice-Hall.

Dinnerstein, Dorothy. 1977. *The Mermaid and the Minotaur: Sexual Arrangements and Human Malaise.* New York: Harper & Row.

Eagly, Alice. 1987. *Sex Differences in Social Behavior.* Hillsdale, N.J.: Erlbaum.

Hunter College Women's Studies Collective. 1983. *Women's Realities, Women's Choices.* New York: Oxford University Press.

Katz, Janyce. 1990. "Celestial Reasoning: Ohio's First Lady Talks About Love and Feminism." *Ms: The World of Women,* 1, 2 (September/October), p. 88.

Mill, John Stuart. 1979. *Utilitarianism.* George Sher, ed. Indianapolis: Hackett.

Mill, John Stuart and Harriet Taylor. 1970. *Essays on Sex Equality.* Alice S. Rossi, ed. Chicago: University of Chicago Press.

Okin, Susan Moller. 1987. "Justice and Gender." *Philosophy & Public Affairs,* 16 (Winter), pp. 42–72.

———. 1989. *Justice, Gender, and the Family.* New York: Basic Books.

Richards, Janet Radcliffe. 1980. *The Sceptical Feminist.* Harmondsworth: Penguin.

Sapiro, Virginia. 1990. *Women in American Society.* Mountain View, Calif.: Mayfield Publishing Co.

Sommers, Christina. 1988. "Should the Academy Support Academic Feminism?" *Public Affairs Quarterly,* 2, 3 (July), 97–120.

———. 1989a. "Philosophers Against the Family." In: George Graham and Hugh LaFollette, eds. *Person to Person.* Philadelphia: Temple University Press, 82–105.

———. 1989b. "Feminist Philosophers Are Oddly Unsympathetic to the Women They Claim to Represent." *Chronicle of Higher Education,* October 11, pp. B2–B3.

———. 1990. "The Feminist Revelation," *Social Philosophy and Policy Center,* 8, 1 (Autumn), 141–158.

Thorne, Barrie, with Marilyn Yalom, eds. 1982. *Rethinking the Family.* New York: Longman.

Trebilcot, Joyce, ed. 1984. *Mothering: Essays in Feminist Theory.* Totowa, N.J.: Rowman and Allanheld.

Vetterling-Braggin, Mary, Frederick A. Elliston, and Jane English, eds. 1977. *Feminism and Philosophy.* Totowa, N.J.: Littlefield, Adams & Co.

26. Is Male Power Really a Myth?

WARREN FARRELL

Warren Farrell argues that the various ways that men lack power in society have not been recognized. He chronicles many ways that he thinks men lack power in society and concludes that there is a high degree of equality between the sexes.

The weakness of men is the facade of strength; the strength of women is the facade of weakness.[1]

There are many ways in which a woman experiences a greater sense of powerlessness than her male counterpart: the fears of pregnancy, aging, rape, date rape, and being physically overpowered; less socialization to take a career that pays enough to support a husband and children; less exposure to team sports and its blend of competitiveness and cooperation that is so helpful to career preparation; greater parental pressure to marry and interrupt career for children without regard for her own wishes; not being part of an "old boys" network; having less freedom to walk into a bar without being bothered. . . .

Reprinted from *The Myth of Male Power* (1993) by permission of the author and Simon and Schuster.

Fortunately, most industrialized nations have acknowledged these female experiences. Unfortunately, they have acknowledged only the female experiences—and concluded that women *have* the problem, men *are* the problem. Men, though, have a different experience. A man who has seen his marriage become alimony payments, his home become his wife's home, and his children become child-support payments for those who have been turned against him psychologically feels he is spending his life working for people who hate him. He feels desperate for someone to love but fears another marriage might ultimately leave him with another mortgage payment, another set of children turned against him, and deeper desperation. When called "commitment phobic," he doesn't feel understood.

When a man tries to keep up with payments by working overtime and is told he is insensitive, or tries to handle the stress by drinking and is told he is a drunkard, he doesn't feel powerful, but powerless. When he fears a cry for help will be met with "stop whining," or that a plea to be heard will be met with "yes, buts," he skips past *attempting* suicide as a cry for help, and just *commits* suicide. Thus men have remained the silent sex and increasingly become the suicide sex.

A Man's Gotta Do What a Man's Gotta Do

ITEM. Imagine: Music is playing on your car radio. An announcer's voice interrupts: "We have a special bulletin from the president." (For some reason, you decide not to switch stations.) The president announces, "Since 1.2 million American men have been killed in war, as part of my new program for equality, we will draft only women until 1.2 million American women have been killed in war."

In post offices throughout the United States, Selective Service posters remind men that only they must register for the draft. If the post office had a poster saying "A Jew's Gotta Do What a Jew's Gotta Do."... Or if "A Woman's Gotta Do ..." were written across the body of a pregnant woman. . . .

The question is this: How is it that if any other group were singled out to register for the draft based merely on its characteristics at birth—be that group blacks, Jews, women, or gays—we would immediately recognize it as genocide, but when men are singled out based on their sex at birth, men call it power?

The single biggest barrier to getting men to look within is that what any other group would call powerlessness, men have been taught to call power. We don't call "male-killing" sexism; we call it "glory." We don't call the one *million* men who were killed or maimed *in one battle* in World War I (the Battle of the Somme[2]) a holocaust, we call it "serving the country." We don't call those who selected only men to die "murderers." We call them "voters."

Our slogan for women is "A Woman's Body, A Woman's Choice"; our slogan for men is "A Man's Gotta Do What a Man's Gotta Do."

The Power of Life

ITEM. In 1920 women in the United States lived *one* year longer than men.[3] Today women live *seven* years longer.[4] The male–female life-span gap increased 600 percent.

We acknowledge that blacks dying six years sooner than whites reflects the powerlessness of blacks in American society.[5] Yet men dying seven years sooner than women is rarely seen as a reflection of the powerlessness of men in American society.

Is the seven-year gap biological? If it is, it wouldn't have been just a one-year gap in 1920.

If men lived seven years *longer* than women, feminists would have helped us understand that life expectancy was the best measure of who had the power. And they would be right. Power is the ability to control one's life. Death tends to reduce control. Life expectancy is the bottom line—the ratio of our life's stresses to our life's rewards.

If power means having control over one's own life, then perhaps there is no better ranking of the impact of sex roles and racism on power over our lives than life expectancy. Here is the ranking:

Life Expectancy[6] as a Way of Seeing Who Has the Power	
Females (white)	79
Females (black)	74
Males (white)	72
Males (black)	65

The white female outlives the black male by almost fourteen years. Imagine the support for affirmative action if a 49-year-old woman were expected to die sooner than a 62-year-old man.

Suicide as Powerlessness

Just as life expectancy is [a good indicator] of power, suicide is one of the best indicators of powerlessness.

ITEM. Until boys and girls are 9, their suicide rates are identical;

- from 10 to 14, the boys' rate is twice as high as the girls';
- from 15 to 19, four times as high; and
- from 20 to 24, six times as high.[7]

ITEM. As boys experience the pressures of the male role, their suicide rate increases 25,000 percent.[8]

ITEM. The suicide rate for men over 85 is 1,350 percent higher than for women of the same age group.

Here is the breakdown:

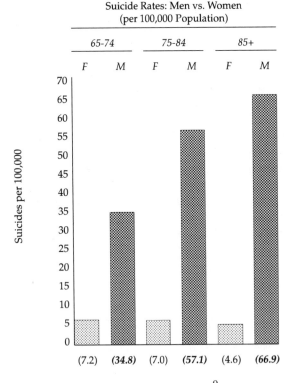

Suicide Rates: Men vs. Women
(per 100,000 Population)

65-74		75-84		85+	
F	M	F	M	F	M
(7.2)	(34.8)	(7.0)	(57.1)	(4.6)	(66.9)

Suicides per 100,000

Source: National Center for Health Statistics[9]

The Invisible Victims of Violence

ITEM. When Rodney King was beaten by police, we called it violence against blacks, not violence against men. Had *Regina* King been beaten, would no one have mentioned violence against women?

Myth. Elderly women are the most susceptible to violent crime.

Fact. Elderly women are the *least* susceptible to violent crime. The U.S. Department of Justice finds that a woman over 65 is less likely to be a victim of violent crime than anyone else in any other category. And she is less than half as vulnerable as a man her own age.[10]

Myth. Women are more likely than men to be victims of violence.

Fact. Men are almost twice as likely as women to be victims of violent crimes (even when rape is *included*).[11] Men are three times more likely to be victims of murder.[12]

When *Time* magazine ran a cover story of each of the 464 people shot in a single week, it concluded: "The victims were frequently those most vulnerable in society: the poor, the young, the abandoned, the ill, and the elderly."[13] When you read that, did you think of men? One had to count the pictures to discover that 84 percent of the faces behind the statistics were those of men and boys. In fact, the victims were mostly poor men, young men, abandoned men, ill men, and elderly men. Yet a woman—and only a woman—was featured on the cover. Men are the invisible victims of America's violence.

Net Worth Power

ITEM. The U.S. Census Bureau finds that women who are heads of households have a net worth that is 141 percent of the net worth of men who are heads of households.[14]

(The value of the net worth statistic is that it allows us to see what he and she have left when their different liabilities are subtracted from the different assets. The women's average net worth is $13,885; the men's is $9,883. This is because although male heads of households have higher gross incomes and assets, they have much higher spending obligations. They are much more likely to support wives [or ex-wives] than wives are to support them and thus their income is divided among themselves, a wife, and children—not only for food and housing but for tuition, insurance, vacations. Divorces often mean the woman receives the home the man pays for and also gets custody of the children the man pays for. A woman's obligation to spend more time with the children leaves her earning less and the man earning more but paying out more.)

ITEM. Among the wealthiest 1.6 percent of the U.S. population (those with assets of $500,000 or more), women's net worth is *more* than men's.[15]

How can so many of the wealthiest people be women when women hold none of the top corporate jobs? In part, by selecting the men who do and outliving them. And in part by having greater spending power and lower spending power obligations. . . .

Spending Power

In my own examination of large shopping malls (including men's shops and sporting goods stores) I found that seven times as much floor space is devoted to women's personal items as to men's.[16] *Both* sexes buy more for women. The key to wealth is not in what someone earns: It is in what is spent on ourselves, at our discretion—or in what is spent on us, at our hint.

Overall, women control consumer spending by a wide margin in virtually every consumer category.[17] With spending power comes other forms of power. Women's control over spending gives them control over TV programs because TV is dependent on sponsors. When this is combined with the fact that women watch more TV in every time slot,[18] shows can't afford to bite the hand that feeds them. Women are to TV what bosses are to employees. The result? Half of the 250 made-for-TV movies in 1991 depicted women as victims—subjected to "some form of physical or psychological mistreatment."[19]

The "Spending Obligation Gap"

In restaurants, men pay for women about ten times as frequently as women pay for men—the more expensive the restaurant, the more often the man pays.[20] Women often say, "Well, men earn more." But when two women go to a restaurant, they don't assume that the woman who earns more will pay the bill. The expectation on men to spend more on women creates the "Spending Obligation Gap."

I got a sense of this "Spending Obligation Gap" as soon as I thought about my first date. As a teenager, I loved babysitting. (I genuinely loved kids, but it was also the only way I could get paid for raiding a refrigerator!) But then I got to the dating age. Alas, babysitting paid only fifty cents an hour. Lawn mowing, though, paid two dollars an hour. I hated lawn mowing. (I lived in New Jersey, where bugs, humidity, and noonday sun made mowing a lawn less pleasant than raiding a refrigerator.) But as soon as I started dating, I started mowing lawns.

For boys, lawn mowing is a metaphor for the way we soon learn to take jobs we like less because they pay more. Around junior year of high school, boys begin to repress their interest in foreign languages, literature, art history, sociology, and anthropology because they know an art history major will make less than an engineer. Partially as a result of his different spending expectations (the possibility he might have to support a woman but cannot expect a woman to support him), more than 85 percent of students who take engineering as a college major are men; more than 80 percent of the art history majors are women.[21]

The difference in the earnings of the female art historian vs. the male engineer appears to be a measure of discrimination, when in fact both sexes knew ahead of time that engineering would pay more. In fact, the woman who enters engineering with the same lack of experience as the man averages $571 per year *more* than her male counterpart.[22]

In brief, the spending obligation that leads a man to choose a career he likes less that pays more is a sign of powerlessness, not power. But when he takes that job, women often assume he will pay because "after all, he earns more." Thus both sexes' expectations reinforce his powerlessness.

Influence Power

The Catholic church is often quoted as acknowledging, "Give us a child the first five years and we will shape its life." We acknowledge the influence power of the church over its youth; we often ignore the influence of a mother over her children—including her sons. But it is the mother who can make the child's bedtime earlier, take away desserts, or ground the child if it doesn't obey. It is the hand that rocks the cradle that creates the child's everyday heaven or hell.

Few men have a comparable amount of influence. While theoretically the man was "the master of the house," most men felt they were visitors in their wives' castle in the same way a woman would have felt like a visitor had she entered her husband's place of work. From a woman's perspective, a man's home is his castle; from a man's perspective, a woman's home is his mortgage.

Almost every woman had a primary role in the "female-dominated" family structure; only a small percentage of men had a primary role in the "male-dominated" governmental and religious structures. Many mothers were, in a sense, the chair of the board of a small company—their family. Even in Japan, women are in charge of the family finances—a fact that was revealed to the average American only after the Japanese stock market crashed in 1992 and thousands of women lost billions of dollars that their husbands never knew they had invested.[23] Conversely, most men were on their company's assembly line—either its physical assembly line or its psychological assembly line.

Control-Over-Life Power

Influence power, though, is not real power. If we told mothers, "The more children you have, the more power you will have," they would laugh. If we then said, "The more children you have, the more everyone will love you and respect you," the mother would feel pressured, not empowered. But when we tell men, "The more people you supervise, the more power you will have," they buy it. Real power does not come from caving in to pressure to expand obligations, it comes from controlling our own life.

Historically, a husband spent the bulk of his day under the eye of his boss—his source of income; a wife did not spend the bulk of her day under the eye of her husband—her source of income. She had more control over her work life than he had over his.

Security Power

The prohibition against divorce gave a woman security in her workplace. Nothing gave a man security in his workplace. His source of income could fire him; her source of income could not fire her. Even today, if he quits his job, he doesn't get severance pay; if she initiates divorce, she takes half the "corporate stock."

"My Body, My Choice" Power

In the 1990s, if a woman and man make love and she says she is using birth control but is not, she has the right to raise the child without his knowing he even has a child, and then to sue him for retroactive child support even ten to twenty years later (depending on the state). This forces him to take a job with more pay and more stress and therefore earlier death. Although it's his body, he has no choice. He has the option of being a slave (working for another without pay or choice) or being a criminal. *Roe v. Wade* gave women the vote over their bodies. Men still don't have the vote over theirs—whether in love or war.

The Power of Appreciation

ITEM. The Mike Tyson trial. The hotel in which the jury is sequestered goes ablaze. Two firefighters die saving its occupants.

The trial of Mike Tyson made us increasingly aware of men-as-rapists. The firefighters' deaths did not make us increasingly aware of men-as-saviors. We were more aware of one man doing harm than of two men saving; of one man threatening one woman who is still physically alive than of dozens of men saving hundreds of people and two of those men being dead. In the United States, almost one million municipal firefighters *volunteer* to risk their lives to save strangers. Ninety-nine percent of them are men.[24] In exchange they ask only for appreciation. In exchange they are ignored.

The "Work Obligation Gap"

The media popularizes studies reporting women's greater amount of time spent on housework and childcare, concluding, "Women work two jobs; men work one." But this is misleading. Women do work more hours inside the home, but men work more hours outside the home. And the average man commutes farther and spends more time doing yardwork, repairs, painting. . . . What happens when all of these are combined? The University of Michigan's study (reported in the *Journal of Economic Literature* in 1991) found the average man worked sixty-one hours per week, the average woman fifty-six.[25]

Is this just a recent change in men? No. In 1975, the largest nationwide probability sampling of households found that when all childcare, all housework, all work outside the home, commuting, and gardening were added together, husbands did 53 percent of the total work, wives 47 percent.[26]

The Unpaid Bodyguard

ITEM. Steve Petrix was a journalist who lived near me in San Diego. Every day he returned home to have lunch with his wife. Recently, as he got near his door, he heard his wife screaming. She was being attacked with a knife. Steve fought the assailant off his wife. His wife ran to call the police. The intruder killed Steve. Steve was 31.[27]

A friend of mine put it this way: "What would you pay someone who agreed that, if he was ever with you when you were attacked, he would intervene and try to get himself killed slowly enough to give you time to escape? What is the hourly wage for a bodyguard? You know that is your job as a man—every time you are with a woman . . . any woman, not just your wife."[28]

What do men as women's personal bodyguards and men as volunteer firefighters have in common besides being men? They are both unpaid. Men have not yet begun to investigate their unpaid roles. . . .

Man As "Nigger"?

In the early years of the women's movement, an article in *Psychology Today* called "Women as Nigger" quickly led to feminist activists (myself included) making parallels between the oppression of women and blacks.[29] Men were characterized as the oppressors, the "master," the "slaveholders." Black congresswoman Shirley Chisholm's statement that she faced far more discrimination as a woman than as a black was widely quoted.

The parallel allowed the hard-earned rights of the civil rights movement to be applied to women. The parallels themselves had more than a germ of truth. But what none of us realized was how each sex was the other's slave in different ways and therefore *neither* sex was the other's "nigger" ("nigger" implies a *one-sided* oppressiveness).

If "masculists" had made such a comparison, they would have had every bit as strong a case as feminists. The comparison is useful because it is not until we

understand how men were *also* women's servants that we get a clear picture of the sexual *division* of labor and therefore the fallacy of comparing either sex to "nigger." For starters . . .

Blacks were forced, via slavery, to risk their lives in cotton fields so that whites might benefit economically while blacks died prematurely. Men were forced, via the draft, to risk their lives on battlefields so that everyone else might benefit economically while men died prematurely. The disproportionate numbers of blacks and males in war increases both blacks' and males' likelihood of experiencing posttraumatic stress, of becoming killers in postwar civilian life as well, and of dying earlier. Both slaves and men died to make the world safe for freedom—someone else's.

Slaves had their own children involuntarily taken away from them; men have their own children involuntarily taken away from them. We tell women they have the right to children and tell men they have to fight for children.

Blacks were forced, via slavery, into society's most hazardous jobs; men are forced, via socialization, into society's most hazardous jobs. Both slaves and men constituted almost 100 percent of the "death professions." Men still do.

When slaves gave up their seats for whites, we called it subservience; when men give up their seats for women, we call it politeness. Similarly, we called it a symbol of subservience when slaves stood up as their master entered a room; but a symbol of politeness when men stand up as a woman enters the room. Slaves bowed before their masters; in traditional cultures, men still bow before women.[30] The slave helped the master put on his coat; the man helped the woman put on her coat. He still does. These symbols of deference and subservience are common with slaves to masters and with men to women.

Blacks are more likely than whites to be homeless; men are more likely than women to be homeless. Blacks are more likely than whites to be in prison; men are about twenty times more likely than women to be in prison. Blacks die earlier than whites; men die earlier than women. Blacks are less likely than whites to attend college or graduate from college. Men are less likely than women to attend college (46 percent versus 54 percent) and less likely to graduate from college (45 percent versus 55 percent).[31]

Apartheid forced blacks to mine diamonds for whites; socialization expected men to work in different mines to pay for diamonds for women. Nowhere in history has there been a ruling class working to afford diamonds they could give to the oppressed in hopes the oppressed would love them more.

Blacks are more likely than whites to volunteer for war in the hopes of earning money and gaining skills; men are more likely than women to volunteer for war for the same reasons. Blacks are more likely than whites to subject themselves to the child abuse of boxing and football in the hopes of earning money, respect, and love; men are more likely than women to subject themselves to the child abuse of boxing and football, with the same hopes.

Women are the only "oppressed" group to systematically grow up having their own private member of an "oppressor" class (called fathers) in the field, working for them. Traditionally, the ruling class had people in the field, working for them—called slaves.

Among slaves, the field slave was considered the second-class slave; the house slave, the first-class slave. The male role (out in the field) is akin to the field slave—or the second-class slave; the traditional female role (homemaker) is akin to the house slave—the first-class slave.

Blacks who are heads of households have a net worth much lower than heads of households who are white; men who are heads of households have a net worth much lower than heads of households who are women.[32] No oppressed group has ever had a net worth higher than the oppressor.

It would be hard to find a single example in history in which a group that cast more than 50 percent of the vote got away with calling itself the victim. Or an example of an oppressed group which chooses to vote for their "oppressors" more than it chooses to have its own members take responsibility for running. Women are the only minority group that is a majority, the only group that calls itself "oppressed" that is able to control who is elected to every office in virtually every community in the country. Power is not in who holds the office, power is in who chooses who holds the office. Blacks, Irish, and Jews never had more than 50 percent of America's vote.

Women are the only "oppressed" group to share the same parents as the "oppressor"; to be born into

the middle class and upper class as frequently as the "oppressor"; to own more of the culture's luxury items than the "oppressor"; the only "oppressed" group whose "unpaid labor" enables them to buy most of the fifty billion dollars' worth of cosmetics sold each year; the only "oppressed" group that spends more on high fashion, brand-name clothing than their "oppressors"; the only "oppressed" group that watches more TV during every time category than their "oppressors."[33]

Feminists often compare marriage to slavery—with the female as slave. It seems like an insult to women's intelligence to suggest that marriage is female slavery when we know it is 25 million American females[34] who read an average of *twenty* romance novels per *month*,[35] often with the fantasy of marriage. Are feminists suggesting that 25 million American women have "enslavement" fantasies because they fantasize marriage? Is this the reason Danielle Steele is the best-selling author in the world?

Never has there been a slave class that has spent a lot of time dreaming about being a slave and purchasing books and magazines that told them "How to Get a Slavemaster to Commit." Either marriage is something different from slavery for women or feminists are suggesting that women are not very intelligent.

The difference between slaves and males is that African-American blacks rarely thought of their slavery as "power," but men were taught to think of their slavery as "power." If men were, in fact, slavemasters, and women slaves, then why did men spend a lifetime supporting the "slaves" and the "slaves'" children? Why weren't the women supporting the men instead, the way kings were supported by their subjects? Our understanding of blacks' powerlessness has allowed us to call what we did to blacks "immoral," yet we still call what we do to males "patriotism" and "heroism" when they kill on our behalf, but "violence," "murder," and "greed" when they kill the wrong people the wrong way at the wrong time.

By understanding that what we did to blacks was immoral, we were willing to assuage our guilt via affirmative action programs and welfare. By thinking of men as the dominant oppressors who do what they do for power and greed, we feel little guilt when they die early in the process. By believing that women were an oppressed slavelike class, we extended privileges and advantages to women that had originally been designed to compensate for our immorality to blacks. For women—and only women—to take advantage of this slavery compensation was its own brand of immorality. For men to cooperate was its own brand of ignorance.

Did men do all this because they were more altruistic, loving, and less power-hungry than women? No.

Both sexes made themselves "slaves" to the other sex in different ways. Let's look at why both sexes did that; at why *neither* sex can accurately be called oppressed; at why we should be celebrating rather than blaming; and at why institutions that don't understand their new opportunities are adapting divisively because they don't understand how to adapt lovingly.

Endnotes

1. Lawrence Diggs, *Transitions,* Nov./Dec. 1990, p. 10.

2. The Battle of the Somme was in 1916. British casualties were 420,000; French were 195,000; German were 650,000. See John Laffin, *Brassey's Battles: 3,500 Years of Conflict, Campaigns, and Wars from A–Z* (London: A. Wheaton & Co., 1986), p. 399.

3. 1920 statistics from the National Center for Health Statistics, *Monthly Vital Statistics Report,* vol. 38, no. 5, supplement, September 26, 1989, p. 4. In 1920, the life expectancy for men was 53.6 years; for women, 54.6 years.

4. Ibid., vol. 39, no. 13, August 28, 1991, p. 17. In 1990, women's average length of life was 78.8 years; men's, 72.0.

5. Ibid., vol. 38, no. 5, op. cit.

6. Ibid. The exact life span difference is 6.9 years between men and women. The life span for white females is 78.9; for black females, 73.6; for white males, 72.2; and for black males, 65.2.

7. U.S. Bureau of Health and Human Services, National Center for Health Statistics (hereinafter USBH &HS/NCHS), *Vital Statistics of the United States* (Washington, D.C.: USGPO, 1991), vol. 2, part A, "Mortality," p. 51, tables 1–9, "Death Rates for 72 Selected Causes by 5-Year Age Groups, Race, and Sex: U.S., 1988." The exact rates are:

Suicide Rates by Age and Sex per 100,000 Population

Age	Male	Female
5-9	0.1	0.0
10-14	2.1	0.8
15-19	18.0	4.4
20-24	25.8	4.1

8. The 25,000 percent figure is derived by comparing the 0.1 suicides per 100,000 boys under the age of nine to the 25.8 suicides per 100,000 boys between ages 20–24 in the table in the endnote above, from ibid.

9. Latest data available as of 1992. From USBH&HS/ NCHS, *Vital Statistics of the United States,* vol. 2, "Mortality," part A, 1987.

10. Among those over the age of 65, 2.7 women per 1,000 and 6.2 men per 1,000 are victims of crimes of violence. U.S. Bureau of Justice Statistics, Office of Justice Programs, Bureau of Justice Statistics, *Criminal Victimization in the United States, 1988,* National Crime Survey Report NCJ-122024, December 1990, p. 18, table 5.

11. Ibid., *1987,* publication NCJ-115524, June, 1989, p. 16, table 3, "Personal Crimes, 1987."

12. Ibid.

13. "7 Deadly Days," *Time,* July 17, 1989, p. 31.

14. These are the latest data available (as of 1992). It is from U.S. Department of Commerce, Bureau of the Census, *Statistical Abstracts of the US, 1989,* 109th edition, p. 459, table 747—"Household Net Worth—Median Value of Holdings: 1984." Their source is U.S. Department of Commerce, Bureau of the Census, *Current Population Reports,* ser. P-70, no. 7. Since women's income has *increased* relative to men's since 1985, the gap is likely to be even greater when the next data are released. The Census Bureau defines head of household (or householder) as any person in whose name a home is owned or rented. Prior to 1980, this used to be the husband in married couple households. Now it is either the husband or wife, doubtless more often still the husband in homes where the man is earning *more.*

15. The wealthiest women's net worth averages $1.17 million; the wealthiest men's averages $1.11 million. Based on the latest data available from the Internal Revenue Service as of 1990. See the *Los Angeles Times,* August 23, 1990.

16. My examination of large shopping malls was in the San Diego area in 1985. I did a rough measurement of the approximate floor space of departments and special "boutiques" that offered male personal items (men's suits, sporting goods, etc.) vs. female personal items, on the

assumption that if women's or men's departments were not creating enough profit per foot, they would be forced to give way to general departments or those of the other sex. In addition, I found that the more valuable floor space (e.g., perfume counters immediately as we enter a department store) was devoted to women's items.

17. See Diane Crispell, "The Brave New World," *American Demographic,* January 1992, p. 38. The article concludes that women dominate consumer spending in personal items, cleaning supplies and housewares, and food. In the category of furniture/cars, it is close to even—men have only a technical dominance.

18. A. C. Nielsen ratings, 1984.

19. Harry F. Waters, "Whip Me, Beat Me, and Give Me Great Ratings," *Newsweek,* November 11, 1991.

20. This is based on my own informal discussions with waiters in restaurants around the country in cities where I speak.

21. Also, 86 percent of engineering *graduates* are men; 83 percent of art history graduates are women. Unpublished information, U.S. Department of Education, Office of Educational Research and Improvement, National Center for Education Statistics, "IPEDS Completions Study," 1989, 1990. Interview on June 1, 1992, with Norman Brandt of the U.S. Office of Education.

22. The starting salary for a female engineer exceeds that for a man by $571 per year. See the Engineering Manpower Commission's *Women in Engineering* (Washington, D.C.: American Association of Engineering Society [AAES]), EMC Bulletin no. 99, December 1989, table 5.

23. Sonni Effron, "Honey, I Shrunk the Nest Egg," *Los Angeles Times,* June 20, 1992, front page.

24. In an interview on February 11, 1992, John Oddison of the government's United States Fire Administration reported that *99 percent of volunteer municipal firefighters are men.* Of all municipal firefighters, 964,000 are volunteers and 240,000 are career.

25. F. Thomas Juster and Frank P. Stafford, "The Allocation of Time: Empirical Findings, Behavioral Models, and Problems of Measurement," *Journal of Economic Literature,* vol. 29, June 1991, p. 477. Her average hours both inside and outside the home add up to fifty-six; his, to sixty-one.

26. Martha Hill, *Patterns of Time Use in Time, Goods, and Well-Being* (Ann Arbor: Institute for Social Research, University of Michigan, 1985), ed. F. Thomas Juster and Frank

P. Stafford. See also Joseph H. Pleck, *Working Wives/Working Husbands* (Beverly Hills: Sage Publications, 1985), p. 41, table 2.3.

27. Carol J. Castañeda, *San Diego Union,* May 21, 1988.

28. Frederic Hayward, "The Male's Unpaid Role: Bodyguard and Protector," as reprinted in Francis Baumli, Ph.D., *Men Freeing Men* (Jersey City, N.J.: New Atlantis Press, 1985), p. 238.

29. Naomi Weisstein, "Women as Nigger," *Psychology Today,* vol. 3, no. 5, October, 1969, p. 20. This article is considered a classic of feminist literature. See, for example, Wendy Martin, *The American Sisterhood: Writings of the Feminist Movement from Colonial Times to the Present* (New York: Harper & Row, 1972), pp. 292–98.

30. Credit to Lawrence Diggs for some of these ideas related to symbols of deference, contained in his audiotape called "Introduction to Men's Issues" (P.O. Box 41, Roslyn, SD 57261).

31. U.S. Department of Education, National Center for Education Statistics, *Digest of Education Statistics 1991,* p. 167, table 161, "Total Enrollment in Institutions of Higher Education" shows that women are 54 percent of those enrolled in college; p. 234, table 228, "Earned Degrees Conferred by Institutions of Higher Education," shows that women are 55 percent of those receiving bachelors' degrees from college.

32. Women who are heads of households have a net worth 141 percent greater than that of men who are heads of households. This is the latest data available from the Bureau of the Census as of 1992. See U.S. Department of Commerce, Bureau of the Census, *Statistical Abstracts of the US, 1989,* op cit.

33. A. C. Nielsen ratings, 1984.

34. Interview, February 18, 1985, with John Markert, independent researcher and contributor to *Romantic Times* and author of "Marketing Love," dissertation in progress.

35. *Forbes* reports that the average romance novel buyer spent $1,200 in 1991. The average romance costs about $5 in 1991, leading to the purchase of approximately 240 books a year, or 20 books per month. For women who also read their friends' books, the number of books they read is more than 20 per month; for women who do not do this but buy some hardcovers, the figure is less than 20 per month. See Dana Wechsler Linden and Matt Rees, "I'm hungry. But not for food," *Forbes,* July 6, 1992, pp. 70–75.

27. *Blame* It *on Feminism*

SUSAN FALUDI

Susan Faludi criticizes the view that due to the feminist movement women have now achieved equality with men, but that this equality has not turned out to be particularly good for women. First, Faludi denies that women have really achieved equality with men. Second, Faludi notes that in national surveys 75 to 95 percent of women credit the feminist movement with actually improving their lives, not making them worse. So Faludi concludes that while women have not yet achieved equality with men, the feminist movement has helped women to achieve the gains they have.

To be a woman in America at the close of the twentieth century—what good fortune. That's what we keep hearing, anyway. The barricades have fallen, politicians assure us. Women have "made it," Madison Avenue cheers. Women's fight for equality has "largely been won," *Time* magazine announces. Enroll at any university, join any law firm, apply for credit at any bank. Women have so many opportunities now, corporate leaders say, that we don't really need equal opportunity policies. Women are so equal now, lawmakers say, that we no longer need an Equal Rights Amendment. Women have "so much," former President Ronald Reagan says, that the White House no longer needs to appoint them to higher office. Even American Express ads are saluting a woman's freedom to charge it. At last, women have received their full citizenship papers.

And yet. . . .

Behind this celebration of the American woman's victory, behind the news, cheerfully and endlessly repeated, that the struggle for women's rights is won, another message flashes. You may be free and equal now, it says to women, but you have never been more miserable.

This bulletin of despair is posted everywhere—at the newsstand, on the TV set, at the movies, in advertisements and doctors' offices and academic journals. Professional women are suffering "burnout" and succumbing to an "infertility epidemic." Single women

are grieving from a "man shortage." *The New York Times* reports: Childless women are "depressed and confused" and their ranks are swelling. *Newsweek* says: Unwed women are "hysterical" and crumbling under a "profound crisis of confidence." The health advice manuals inform: High-powered career women are stricken with unprecedented outbreaks of "stress-induced disorders," hair loss, bad nerves, alcoholism, and even heart attacks. The psychology books advise: Independent women's loneliness represents "a major mental health problem today." Even founding feminist Betty Friedan has been spreading the word: She warns that women now suffer from a new identity crisis and "new 'problems' that have no name.'"

How can American women be in so much trouble at the same time that they are supposed to be so blessed? If the status of women has never been higher, why is their emotional state so low? If women got what they asked for, what could possibly be the matter now?

The prevailing wisdom of the past decade has supported one, and only one, answer to this riddle: It must be all that equality that's causing all that pain. Women are unhappy precisely *because* they are free. Women are enslaved by their own liberation. They have grabbed at the gold ring of independence, only to miss the one ring that really matters. They have gained control of their fertility, only to destroy it. They have pursued their own professional dreams—and lost out on the greatest female adventure. The women's movement, as we are told time and again, has proved women's own worst enemy.

Reprinted from *Backlash* (1991) by permission of the author and Crown Publishers.

"In dispensing its spoils, women's liberation has given my generation high incomes, our own cigarette, the option of single parenthood, rape crisis centers, personal lines of credit, free love, and female gynecologists," Mona Charen, a young law student, writes in the *National Review,* in an article titled "The Feminist Mistake." "In return it has effectively robbed us of one thing upon which the happiness of most women rests—men." The *National Review* is a conservative publication, but such charges against the women's movement are not confined to its pages. "Our generation was the human sacrifice to the women's movement," *Los Angeles Times* feature writer Elizabeth Mehren contends in a *Time* cover story. Baby-boom women like her, she says, have been duped by feminism: "We believed the rhetoric." In *Newsweek,* writer Kay Ebeling dubs feminism "the Great Experiment That Failed" and asserts "women in my generation, its perpetrators, are the casualties." Even the beauty magazines are saying it: *Harper's Bazaar* accuses the women's movement of having "lost [women] ground instead of gaining it."

In the last decade, publications from the *New York Times* to *Vanity Fair* to the *Nation* have issued a steady stream of indictments against the women's movement, with such headlines as "When Feminism Failed" or "The Awful Truth About Women's Lib." They hold the campaign for women's equality responsible for nearly every woe besetting women, from mental depression to meager savings accounts, from teenage suicides to eating disorders to bad complexions. The "Today" show says women's liberation is to blame for bag ladies. A guest columnist in the *Baltimore Sun* even proposes that feminists produced the rise in slasher movies. By making the "violence" of abortion more acceptable, the author reasons, women's rights activists made it all right to show graphic murders on screen.

At the same time, other outlets of popular culture have been forging the same connection: In Hollywood films, of which *Fatal Attraction* is only the most famous, emancipated women with condominiums of their own slink wild-eyed between bare walls, paying for their liberty with an empty bed, a barren womb. "My biological clock is ticking so loud it keeps me awake at night," Sally Field cries in the film *Surrender,* as, in an all too common transformation in the cinema

of the '80s, an actress who once played scrappy working heroines is now showcased groveling for a groom. In prime-time television shows, from "ThirtySomething" to "Family Man," single, professional, and feminist women are humiliated, turned into harpies, or hit by nervous breakdowns; the wise ones recant their independent ways by the closing sequence. In popular novels, from Gail Parent's *A Sign of the Eighties* to Stephen King's *Misery,* unwed women shrink to sniveling spinsters or inflate to fire-breathing she-devils; renouncing all aspirations but marriage, they beg for wedding bands from strangers or swing sledgehammers at reluctant bachelors. We "blew it by waiting," a typically remorseful careerist sobs in Freda Bright's *Singular Women;* she and her sister professionals are "condemned to be childless forever." Even Erica Jong's high flying independent heroine literally crashes by the end of the decade, as the author supplants *Fear of Flying*'s saucy Isadora Wing, a symbol of female sexual emancipation in the '70s, with an embittered careerist-turned-recovering "co-dependent" in *Any Woman's Blues*—a book that is intended, as the narrator bluntly states, "to demonstrate what a deadend the so-called sexual revolution had become, and how desperate so-called free women were in the last few years of our decadent epoch."

Popular psychology manuals peddle the same diagnosis for contemporary female distress. "Feminism, having promised her a stronger sense of her own identity, has given her little more than an identity *crisis,*" the best-selling advice manual *Being a Woman* asserts. The authors of the era's self-help classic *Smart Women/Foolish Choices* proclaim that women's distress was "an unfortunate consequence of feminism," because "it created a myth among women that the apex of self-realization could be achieved only through autonomy, independence, and career."

In the Reagan and Bush years, government officials have needed no prompting to endorse this thesis. Reagan spokeswoman Faith Whittlesey declared feminism a "straitjacket" for women, in the White House's only policy speech on the status of the American female population—entitled "Radical Feminism in Retreat." Law enforcement officers and judges, too, have pointed a damning finger at feminism, claiming that they can chart a path from rising female independence to rising female pathology. As a California sheriff explained it to the press, "Women are enjoying a lot more freedom now, and as a result, they are committing more crimes." The U.S. Attorney General's Commission on Pornography even proposed that women's professional advancement might be responsible for rising rape rates. With more women in college and at work now, the commission members reasoned in their report, women just have more opportunities to be raped.

Some academics have signed on to the consensus, too—and they are the "experts" who have enjoyed the highest profiles on the media circuit. On network news and talk shows, they have advised millions of women that feminism has condemned them to "a lesser life." Legal scholars have railed against "the equality trap." Sociologists have claimed that "feminist-inspired" legislative reforms have stripped women of special "protections." Economists have argued that well-paid working women have created "a less stable American family." And demographers, with greatest fanfare, have legitimated the prevailing wisdom with so-called neutral data on sex ratios and fertility trends; they say they actually have the numbers to prove that equality doesn't mix with marriage and motherhood.

Finally, some "liberated" women themselves have joined the lamentations. In confessional accounts, works that invariably receive a hearty greeting from the publishing industry, "recovering Superwomen" tell all. In *The Cost of Loving: Women and the New Fear of Intimacy,* Megan Marshall, a Harvard-pedigreed writer, asserts that the feminist "Myth of Independence" has turned her generation into unloved and unhappy fast-trackers, "dehumanized" by careers and "uncertain of their gender identity." Other diaries of mad Superwomen charge that "the hard-core feminist viewpoint," as one of them puts it, has relegated educated executive achievers to solitary nights of frozen dinners and closet drinking. The triumph of equality, they report, has merely given women hives, stomach cramps, eye-twitching disorders, even comas.

But what "equality" are all these authorities talking about?

If American women are so equal, why do they represent two-thirds of all poor adults? Why are nearly 75 percent of full-time working women making less than $20,000 a year, nearly double the male rate? Why are they still far more likely than men to live in poor

housing and receive no health insurance, and twice as likely to draw no pension? Why does the average working woman's salary still lag as far behind the average man's as it did twenty years ago? Why does the average female college graduate today earn less than a man with no more than a high school diploma (just as she did in the '50s)—and why does the average female high school graduate today earn less than a male high school dropout? Why do American women, in fact, face one of the worst gender-based pay gaps in the developed world?

If women have "made it," then why are nearly 80 percent of working women still stuck in traditional "female" jobs—as secretaries, administrative "support" workers, and salesclerks? And, conversely, why are they less than 8 percent of all federal and state judges, less than 6 percent of all law partners, and less than one half of 1 percent of top corporate managers? Why are there only three female state governors, two female U.S. Senators, and two Fortune 500 chief executives? Why are only nineteen of the four thousand corporate officers and directors women—and why do more than half the boards of Fortune companies still lack even one female member?

If women "have it all," then why don't they have the most basic requirements to achieve equality in the work force? Unlike virtually all other industrialized nations, the U.S. Government still has no family-leave and childcare programs—and more than 99 percent of American private employers don't offer childcare either. Though business leaders say they are aware of and deplore sex discrimination, corporate America has yet to make an honest effort toward eradicating it. In a 1990 national poll of chief executives at Fortune 1000 companies, more than 80 percent acknowledged that discrimination impedes female employees' progress—yet, less than 1 percent of these same companies regarded *remedying* sex discrimination as a goal that their personnel departments should pursue. In fact, when the companies' human resource officers were asked to rate their department's priorities, women's advancement ranked last.

If women are so "free," why are their reproductive freedoms in greater jeopardy today than a decade earlier? Why do women who want to postpone childbearing now have fewer options than ten years ago? The availability of different forms of contraception has declined, research for new birth control has virtually halted, new laws restricting abortion—or even information about abortion—for young and poor women have been passed, and the U.S. Supreme Court has shown little ardor in defending the right it granted in 1973.

Nor is women's struggle for equal education over; as a 1989 study found, three-fourths of all high schools still violate the federal law banning sex discrimination in education. In colleges, undergraduate women receive only 70 percent of the aid undergraduate men get in grants and work-study jobs—and women's sports programs receive a pittance compared with men's. A review of state equal-education laws in the late '80s found that only thirteen states had adopted the minimum provisions required by the federal Title IX law—and only seven states had anti-discrimination regulations that covered all education levels.

Nor do women enjoy equality in their own homes, where they still shoulder 70 percent of the household duties—and the only major change in the last fifteen years is that now middle-class men *think* they do more around the house. (In fact, a national poll finds the ranks of women saying their husbands share equally in childcare shrunk to 31 percent in 1987 from 40 percent three years earlier.) Furthermore, in thirty states, it is still generally legal for husbands to rape their wives; and only ten states have laws mandating arrest for domestic violence—even though battering was the leading cause of injury of women in the late '80s. Women who have no other option but to flee find that isn't much of an alternative either. Federal funding for battered women's shelters has been withheld and one-third of the 1 million battered women who seek emergency shelter each year can find none. Blows from men contributed far more to the rising numbers of "bag ladies" than the ill effects of feminism. In the '80s, almost half of all homeless women (the fastest growing segment of the homeless) were refugees of domestic violence.

The word may be that women have been "liberated," but women themselves seem to feel otherwise. Repeatedly in national surveys, majorities of women say they are still far from equality. Nearly 70 percent of women polled by the *New York Times* in 1989 said the movement for women's rights had only just begun. Most women in the 1990 Virginia Slims opinion

poll agreed with the statement that conditions for their sex in American society had improved "a little, not a lot." In poll after poll in the decade, overwhelming majorities of women said they needed equal pay and equal job opportunities, they needed an Equal Rights Amendment, they needed the right to an abortion without government interference, they needed a federal law guaranteeing maternity leave, they needed decent childcare services. They have none of these. So how exactly have we "won" the war for women's rights?

Seen against this background, the much ballyhooed claim that feminism is responsible for making women miserable becomes absurd—and irrelevant. The afflictions ascribed to feminism are all myths. From "the man shortage" to "the infertility epidemic" to "female burnout" to "toxic day care," these so-called female crises have had their origins not in the actual conditions of women's lives but rather in a closed system that starts and ends in the media, popular culture, and advertising—an endless feedback loop that perpetuates and exaggerates its own false images of womanhood.

Women themselves don't single out the women's movement as the source of their misery. To the contrary, in national surveys 75 to 95 percent of women credit the feminist campaign with *improving* their lives, and a similar proportion say that the women's movement should keep pushing for change. Less than 8 percent think the women's movement might have actually made their lot worse.

What actually is troubling the American female population, then? If the many ponderers of the Woman Question really wanted to know, they might have asked their subjects. In public opinion surveys, women consistently rank their own *inequality*, at work and at home, among their most urgent concerns. Over and over, women complain to pollsters about a lack of economic, not marital opportunities; they protest that working men, not working women, fail to spend time in the nursery and the kitchen. The Roper Organization's survey analysts find that men's opposition to equality is "a major cause of resentment and stress" and "a major irritant for most women today." It is justice for their gender, not wedding rings and bassinets, that women believe to be in desperately short supply. When the *New York Times* polled women in 1989 about "the most important problem facing women today," job discrimination was the overwhelming winner; none of the crises the media and popular culture had so assiduously promoted even made the charts. In the 1990 Virginia Slims poll, women were most upset by their lack of money, followed by the refusal of their men to shoulder childcare and domestic duties. By contrast, when the women were asked where the quest for a husband or the desire to hold a "less pressured" job or to stay at home ranked on their list of concerns, they placed them at the bottom.

As the last decade ran its course, women's unhappiness with inequality only mounted. In national polls, the ranks of women protesting discriminatory treatment in business, political, and personal life climbed sharply. The proportion of women complaining of unequal employment opportunities jumped more than ten points from the '70s, and the number of women complaining of unequal barriers to job advancement climbed even higher. By the end of the decade, 80 percent to 95 percent of women said they suffered from job discrimination and unequal pay. Sex discrimination charges filed with the Equal Employment Opportunity Commission rose nearly 25 percent in the Reagan years, and charges of general harassment directed at working women more than doubled. In the decade, complaints of sexual harassment nearly doubled. At home, a much increased proportion of women complained to pollsters of male mistreatment, unequal relationships, and male efforts to, in the words of the Virginia Slims poll, "keep women down." The share of women in the Roper surveys who agreed that men were "basically kind, gentle, and thoughtful" fell from almost 70 percent in 1970 to 50 percent by 1990. And outside their homes, women felt more threatened, too: In the 1990 Virginia Slims poll, 72 percent said they felt "more afraid and uneasy on the streets today" than they did a few years ago. Lest this be attributed only to a general rise in criminal activity, by contrast only 49 percent of men felt this way.

While the women's movement has certainly made women more cognizant of their own inequality, the rising chorus of female protest shouldn't be written off as feminist-induced "oversensitivity." The monitors that serve to track slippage in women's status have been working overtime since the early '80s. Gov-

ernment and private surveys are showing that women's already vast representation in the lowliest occupations is rising, their tiny presence in higher-paying trade and craft jobs stalled or backsliding, their minuscule representation in upper management posts stagnant or falling, and their pay dropping in the very occupations where they have made the most "progress." The status of women lowest on the income ladder has plunged most perilously; government budget cuts in the first four years of the Reagan administration alone pushed nearly 2 million female-headed families and nearly 5 million women below the poverty line. And the prime target of government rollbacks has been one sex only: One-third of the Reagan budget cuts, for example, came out of programs that predominantly serve women—even more extraordinary when one considers that all these programs combined represent only 10 percent of the federal budget.

The alarms aren't just going off in the work force. In national politics, the already small numbers of women in both elective posts and political appointments fell during the '80s. In private life the average amount that a divorced man paid in child support fell by about 25 percent from the late '70s to the mid-1980s (to a mere $140 a month). Domestic-violence shelters recorded a more than 100 percent increase in the numbers of women taking refuge in their quarters between 1983 and 1987. And government records chronicled a spectacular rise in sexual violence against women. Reported rapes more than doubled from the early '70s—at nearly twice the rate of all other violent crimes and four times the overall crime rate in the United States. While the homicide rate declined, sex-related murders rose 160 percent between 1976 and 1984. And these murders weren't simply the random, impersonal by-product of a violent society; at least one-third of the women were killed by their husbands or boyfriends, and the majority of that group were murdered just after declaring their independence in the most intimate manner—by filing for divorce and leaving home.

By the end of the decade, women were starting to tell pollsters that they feared their sex's social status was once again beginning to slip. They believed they were facing an "erosion of respect," as the 1990 Virginia Slims poll summed up the sentiment. After years in which an increasing percentage of women had said their status had improved from a decade earlier, the proportion suddenly shrunk by 5 percent in the last half of the '80s, the Roper Organization reported. And it fell most sharply among women in their thirties—the age group most targeted by the media and advertisers—dropping about ten percentage points between 1985 and 1990.

Some women began to piece the picture together, In the 1989 *New York Times* poll, more than half of black women and one-fourth of white women put it into words. They told pollsters they believed men were now trying to retract the gains women had made in the last twenty years. "I wanted more autonomy," was how one thirty-seven-year-old nurse put it. And her estranged husband "wanted to take it away."

The truth is that the last decade has seen a powerful counterassault on women's rights, a backlash, an attempt to retract the handful of small and hard-won victories that the feminist movement did manage to win for women. This counterassault is largely insidious: In a kind of pop-culture version of the Big Lie, it stands the truth boldly on its head and proclaims that the very steps that have elevated women's position have actually led to their downfall.

The backlash is at once sophisticated and banal, deceptively "progressive," and proudly backward. It deploys both the "new" findings of "scientific research" and the dime-store moralism of yesteryear; it turns into media sound bites both the glib pronouncements of pop-psych trend-watchers and the frenzied rhetoric of New Right preachers. The backlash has succeeded in framing virtually the whole issue of women's rights in its own language. Just as Reaganism shifted political discourse far to the right and demonized liberalism, so the backlash convinced the public that women's "liberation" was the true contemporary American scourge—the source of an endless laundry list of personal, social, and economic problems.

But what has made women unhappy in the last decade is not their "equality"—which they don't yet have—but the rising pressure to halt, and even reverse, women's quest for that equality. The "man shortage" and the "infertility epidemic" are not the price of liberation; in fact, they do not even exist. But these chimeras are the chisels of a society-wide backlash. They are part of a relentless whittling-down process—much of it amounting to outright propaganda—that has served to stir women's private anxieties and break their political wills. Identifying feminism as women's enemy only furthers the ends of a backlash against women's equality, simultaneously deflecting attention from the backlash's central role and recruiting women to attack their own cause.

Some social observers may well ask whether the current pressures on women actually constitute a backlash—or just a continuation of American society's long-standing resistance to women's rights. Certainly hostility to female independence has always been with us. But if fear and loathing of feminism is a sort of perpetual viral condition in our culture, it is not always in an acute stage; its symptoms subside and resurface periodically. And it is these episodes of resurgence, such as the one we face now, that can accurately be termed "backlashes" to women's advancement. If we trace these occurrences in American history (as we will do in a later chapter), we find such flare-ups are hardly random; they have always been triggered by the perception—accurate or not—that women are making great strides. These outbreaks are backlashes because they have always arisen in reaction to women's "progress," caused not simply by a bedrock of misogyny but by the specific efforts of contemporary women to improve their status, specific efforts that have been interpreted time and again by men—especially men grappling with real threats to their economic and social well-being on other fronts—as spelling their own masculine doom.

The most recent round of backlash first surfaced in the late '70s on the fringes, among the evangelical right. By the early '80s, the fundamentalist ideology had shouldered its way into the White House. By the mid-1980s, as resistance to women's rights acquired political and social acceptability, it passed into the popular culture. And in every case, the timing coincided with signs that women were believed to be on the verge of breakthrough.

Just when women's quest for equal rights seemed closest to achieving its objectives, the backlash struck it down. Just when a "gender gap" at the voting booth surfaced in 1980, and women in politics began to talk of capitalizing on it, the Republican party elevated Ronald Reagan and both political parties began to shunt women's rights off their platforms. Just when support for feminism and the Equal Rights Amendment reached a record high in 1981, the amendment was defeated the following year. Just when women were starting to mobilize against battering and sexual assaults, the federal government stalled funding for battered-women's programs, defeated bills to fund shelters, and shut down its Office of Domestic Violence—only two years after opening it in 1979. Just when record numbers of younger women were supporting feminist goals in the mid-1980s (more of them, in fact, than older women) and a majority of all women were calling themselves feminists, the media declared the advent of a younger "postfeminist generation" that supposedly reviled the women's movement. Just when women racked up their largest percentage ever supporting the right to abortion, the U.S. Supreme Court moved toward reconsidering it.

In other words, the antifeminist backlash has been set off not by women's achievement of full equality but by the increased possibility that they might win it. It is a preemptive strike that stops women long before they reach the finish line. "A backlash may be an indication that women really have had an effect," feminist psychologist Dr. Jean Baker Miller has written, "but backlashes occur when advances have been small, before changes are sufficient to help many people. . . . It is almost as if the leaders of backlashes use the fear of change as a threat before major change has occurred." In the last decade, some women did make substantial advances before the backlash hit, but millions of others were left behind, stranded. Some women now enjoy the right to legal abortion—but not the 44 million women, from the indigent to the military work force, who depend on the federal government for their medical care. Some women can now walk into high-paying professional careers—but not the more than 19 million still in the typing pools or behind the department store sales counters. (Contrary to popular myth about the "have-it-all" baby-boom women, the largest percentage of women in this generation remain typists and clerks.)

As the backlash has gathered force, it has cut off the few from the many—and the few women who have advanced seek to prove, as a social survival tactic, that they aren't so interested in advancement after all. Some of them parade their defection from the women's movement, while their working-class peers

founder and cling to the splintered remains of the feminist cause. While a very few affluent and celebrity women who are showcased in news articles boast about having "found my niche as Mrs. Andy Mill" and going home to "bake bread," the many working-class women appeal for their economic rights—flocking to unions in record numbers, striking on their own for pay equity and establishing their own fledgling groups for working women's rights. In 1986, while 41 percent of upper-income women claimed in the Gallup poll that they were not feminists, only 26 percent of low-income women made the same claim.

Women's advances and retreats are generally described in military terms: battles won, battles lost, points and territory gained and surrendered. The metaphor of combat is not without its merits in this context and, clearly, the same sort of martial accounting and vocabulary is already surfacing here. But by imagining the conflict as two battalions neatly arrayed on either side of the line, we miss the entangled nature, the locked embrace, of a "war" between women and the male culture they inhabit. We miss the reactive nature of a backlash, which, by definition, can exist only in response to another force.

In times when feminism is at a low ebb, women assume the reactive role—privately and most often covertly struggling to assert themselves against the dominant cultural tide. But when feminism itself becomes the tide, the opposition doesn't simply go along with the reversal: It digs in its heels, brandishes its fists, builds walls and dams. And its resistance creates countercurrents and treacherous undertows.

The force and furor of the backlash churn beneath the surface, largely invisible to the public eye. On occasion in the last decade, they have burst into view. We have seen New Right politicians condemn women's independence, antiabortion protesters firebomb women's clinics, fundamentalist preachers damn feminists as "whores" and "witches." Other signs of the backlash's wrath, by their sheer brutality, can push their way into public consciousness for a time—the sharp increase in rape . . . or the rise in pornography that depicts extreme violence against women.

More subtle indicators in popular culture may receive momentary, and often bemused, media notice, then quickly slip from social awareness: A report, for instance, that the image of women on prime-time TV shows has suddenly degenerated. A survey of mystery fiction finding the numbers of female characters tortured and mutilated mysteriously multiplying. The puzzling news that, as one commentator put it, "So many hit songs have the B-word [bitch] to refer to women that some rap music seems to be veering toward rape music." The ascendancy of virulently misogynist comics like Andrew Dice Clay—who called women "pigs" and "slugs" and strutted in films in which women were beaten, tortured, and blown up— or radio hosts like Rush Limbaugh, whose broadsides against "femi-Nazi" feminists made his syndicated program the most popular radio talk show in the nation. Or word that in 1987, the American Women in Radio & Television couldn't award its annual prize for ads that feature women positively: It could find no ad that qualified.

These phenomena are all related, but that doesn't mean they are somehow coordinated. The backlash is not a conspiracy, with a council dispatching agents from some central control room, nor are the people who serve its ends often aware of their roles; some even consider themselves feminists. For the most part, its workings are encoded and internalized, diffuse and chameleonic. Not all manifestations of the backlash are of equal weight or significance either; some are mere ephemera, generated by a culture machine that always scrounges for a "fresh" angle. Taken as a whole, however, these codes, and cajolings, these whispers and threats and myths, move overwhelmingly in one direction: They try to push women back into their "acceptable" roles—whether as Daddy's girl or fluttery romantic, active nester or passive love object.

Although the backlash is not an organized movement, that doesn't make it any less destructive. In fact, the lack of orchestration, the absence of a single string-puller, only makes it harder to see—and perhaps more effective. A backlash against women's rights succeeds to the degree that it appears *not* to be political, that it appears not to be a struggle at all. It is most powerful when it goes private, when it lodges inside a woman's mind and turns her vision inward, until she imagines the pressure is all in her head, until she begins to enforce the backlash, too—on herself.

In the last decade, the backlash has moved through the culture's secret chambers, traveling through pas-

sageways of flattery and fear. Along the way, it has adopted disguises: a mask of mild derision or the painted face of deep "concern." Its lips profess pity for any woman who won't fit the mold, while it tries to clamp the mold around her ears. It pursues a divide-and-conquer strategy: single versus married women, working women versus homemakers, middle- versus working-class. It manipulates a system of rewards and punishments, elevating women who follow its rules, isolating those who don't. The backlash remarkets old myths about women as new facts and ignores all appeals to reason. Cornered, it denies its own existence, points an accusatory finger at feminism, and burrows deeper underground.

Backlash happens to be the title of a 1947 Hollywood movie in which a man frames his wife for a murder he's committed. The backlash against women's rights works in much the same way: Its rhetoric charges feminists with all the crimes it perpetrates. The backlash line blames the women's movement for the "feminization of poverty"—while the backlash's own instigators in Washington pushed through the budget cuts that helped impoverish millions of women, fought pay equity proposals, and undermined equal opportunity laws. The backlash lines claims the women's movement cares nothing for children's rights—while its own representatives in the capital and state legislatures have blocked one bill after another to improve childcare, slashed billions of dollars in federal aid for children, and relaxed state licensing standards for day-care centers. The backlash line accuses the women's movement of creating a generation of unhappy single and childless women—but its purveyors in the media are the ones guilty of making single and childless women feel like circus freaks.

To blame feminism for women's "lesser life" is to miss entirely [its point], which is to win women a wider range of experience. Feminism remains a pretty simple concept, despite repeated—and enormously effective—efforts to dress it up . . . and turn its proponents into gargoyles. As Rebecca West wrote sardonically in 1913, "I myself have never been able to find out precisely what feminism is: I only know that people call me a feminist whenever I express sentiments that differentiate me from a doormat."

The meaning of the word *feminist* has not really changed since it first appeared in a book review in the

Athenaeum of April 27, 1895, describing a woman who "has in her the capacity of fighting her way back to independence." It is the basic proposition that, as Nora put it in Ibsen's *A Doll's House* a century ago, "Before everything else I'm a human being." It is the simply worded sign hoisted by a little girl in the 1970 Women's Strike for Equality: I AM NOT A BARBIE DOLL. Feminism asks the world to recognize at long last that women aren't decorative ornaments, worthy vessels, members of a "special-interest group." They are half (in fact, now more than half) of the national population, and just as deserving of rights and opportunities, just as capable of participating in the world's events, as the other half. Feminism's agenda is basic: It asks that women not be forced to "choose" between public justice and private happiness. It asks that women be free to define themselves—instead of having their identity defined for them, time and again, by their culture and their men.

The fact that these are still such incendiary notions should tell us that American women have a way to go before they enter the promised land of equality.

---

28. *National Organization for Women (NOW) Bill of Rights*

I   Equal Rights Constitutional Amendment
II Enforce Law Banning Sex Discrimination in Employment
III Maternity Leave Rights in Employment and in Social Security Benefits
IV Tax Deduction for Home and Childcare Expenses for Working Parents
V   Childcare Centers
VI Equal and Unsegregated Education
VII Equal Job Training Opportunities and Allowances for Women in Poverty
VIII The Right of Women to Control Their Reproductive Lives

We Demand:

I That the United States Congress immediately pass the Equal Rights Amendment to the Constitution to provide that "Equality of rights under the law shall not be denied or abridged by the United States or by any State on account of sex," and that such then be immediately ratified by the several States.

II That equal employment opportunity be guaranteed to all women, as well as men, by insisting that the Equal Employment Opportunity Commission enforce the prohibitions against sex discrimination in employment under Title VII of the Civil Rights Act of 1964 with the same vigor as it enforces the prohibitions against racial discrimination.

III That women be protected by law to ensure their rights to return to their jobs within a reasonable time after childbirth without loss of seniority or other accrued benefits, and be paid maternity leave as a form of social security and/or employee benefit.

IV Immediate revision of tax laws to permit the deduction of home and childcare expenses for working parents.

V That childcare facilities be established by law on the same basis as parks, libraries, and public schools, adequate to the needs of children from the preschool years through adolescence, as a community resource to be used by all citizens from all income levels.

VI That the right of women to be educated to their full potential equally with men be secured by Federal and State Legislation, eliminating all discrimination and segregation by sex, written and unwritten, at all levels of education, including colleges, graduate and professional schools, loans and fellowships, and Federal and State training programs such as the Job Corps.

VII The right of women in poverty to secure job training, housing, and family allowances on equal terms with men, but without prejudice to a parent's right to remain at home to care for his or her children;

revision of welfare legislation and poverty programs which deny women dignity, privacy, and self-respect.

VIII The right of women to control their own reproductive lives by removing from penal codes laws limiting access to contraceptive information and devices and laws governing abortion.

29. *California Federal Savings and Loan v. Department of Fair Employment and Housing*

SUPREME COURT OF THE UNITED STATES

The issue before the Supreme Court was whether Title VII of the Civil Rights Act of 1964 as amended by the Pregnancy Discrimination Act of 1978 (PDA) nullified a California law requiring employers to provide leave and reinstatement to employees disabled by pregnancy. The majority of the Court ruled that it did not for two reasons. First, in passing PDA, Congress was concerned with prohibiting discrimination against pregnancy; preferential treatment, as found in the California law, was not discussed. Second, even if PDA did prohibit preferential treatment of pregnancy, an employer could avoid violating PDA and the California law by giving comparable benefits to all similarly disabled employees. In dissent, Justices White, Burger, and Powell argued that even though Congress did not explicitly consider the possibility of preferential treatment of pregnancy, the language of PDA ruled it out. In addition, they argued that if such preferential treatment were ruled out, those who wrote the California law could not have intended requiring comparable benefits for all similarly disabled employees.

Justice *Marshall* delivered the opinion of the Court.

The question presented is whether Title VII of the Civil Rights Act of 1964, as amended by the Pregnancy Discrimination Act of 1978, pre-empts a state statute that requires employers to provide leave and reinstatement to employees disabled by pregnancy.

California's Fair Employment and Housing Act (FEHA), Cal. Gov't Code Ann. §12900 *et seq.* . . . is a comprehensive statute that prohibits discrimination in employment and housing. In September 1978, California amended the FEHA to proscribe certain forms of employment discrimination on the basis of pregnancy. . . . Subdivision (b)(2)—the provision at issue

here—is the only portion of the statute that applies to employers subject to Title VII. . . . It requires these employers to provide female employees an unpaid pregnancy disability leave of up to four months. Respondent Fair Employment and Housing Commission, the state agency authorized to interpret the FEHA, has construed §12945(b)(2) to require California employers to reinstate an employee returning from such pregnancy leave to the job she previously held, unless it is no longer available due to business necessity. In the latter case, the employer must make a reasonable, good faith effort to place the employee in a substantially similar job. The statute does not compel employers to provide *paid* leave to pregnant employees. Accordingly, the only benefit pregnant workers actually derive from §12945(b)(2) is a qualified right to reinstatement.

Title VII of the Civil Rights Act of 1964 . . . also prohibits various forms of employment discrimination, including discrimination on the basis of sex. However, in *General Electric Co. v. Gilbert,* . . . this Court ruled that discrimination on the basis of pregnancy was not sex discrimination under Title VII. In response to the *Gilbert* decision, Congress passed the Pregnancy Discrimination Act of 1978 (PDA). . . . The PDA specifies that sex discrimination includes discrimination on the basis of pregnancy.

Petitioner California Federal Savings and Loan Association (Cal Fed) is a federally chartered savings and loan association based in Los Angeles; it is an employer covered by both Title VII and §12945(b)(2). Cal Fed has a facially neutral leave policy that permits employees who have completed three months of service to take unpaid leaves of absence for a variety of reasons, including disability and pregnancy. Although it is Cal Fed's policy to try to provide an employee taking unpaid leave with a similar position upon returning, Cal Fed expressly reserves the right to terminate an employee who has taken a leave of absence if a similar position is not available.

Lillian Garland was employed by Cal Fed as a receptionist for several years. In January 1982, she took a pregnancy disability leave. When she was able to return to work in April of that year, Garland notified Cal Fed, but was informed that her job had been filled and that there were no receptionist or similar positions available. Garland filed a complaint with respondent Department of Fair Employment and Housing, which issued an administrative accusation against Cal Fed on her behalf. Respondent charged Cal Fed with violating §12945(b)(2) of the FEHA. Prior to the scheduled hearing before respondent Fair Housing and Employment Commission, Cal Fed, joined by petitioners . . . , brought this action in the U.S. District Court for the Central District of California. They sought a declaration that §12945(b)(2) is inconsistent with and pre-empted by Title VII and an injunction against enforcement of the section. . . .

. . . To decide whether the California statute requires or permits employers to violate Title VII, as amended by the PDA, or is inconsistent with the purposes of the statute, we must determine whether the PDA prohibits the States from requiring employers to provide reinstatement to pregnant workers, regardless of their policy for disabled workers generally. . . .

Petitioners argue that the language of the federal statute itself unambiguously rejects California's "special treatment" approach to pregnancy discrimination, thus rendering any resort to the legislative history unnecessary. They contend that the second clause of the PDA forbids an employer to treat pregnant employees any differently than other disabled employees. . . .

The context in which Congress considered the issue of pregnancy discrimination supports this view of the PDA. Congress had before it extensive evidence of discrimination *against* pregnancy, particularly in disability and health insurance programs like those challenged in *Gilbert* and *Nashville Gas Co. v. Satty.* . . . The reports, debates, and hearings make abundantly clear that Congress intended the PDA to provide relief for working women and to end discrimination against pregnant workers. In contrast to the thorough account of discrimination against pregnant workers, the legislative history is devoid of any discussion of preferential treatment of pregnancy, beyond acknowledgments of the existence of state statutes providing for such preferential treatment. . . .

In support of their argument that the PDA prohibits employment practices that favor pregnant women, petitioners and several *amici* cite statements in the legislative history to the effect that the PDA does not *require* employers to extend any benefits to pregnant women that they do not already provide to other disabled employees. For example, the House Report explained that the proposed legislation "does not require employers to treat pregnant employees in any particular manner. . . ." We do not interpret these references to support petitioners' construction of the statute. On the contrary, if Congress had intended to *prohibit* preferential treatment, it would have been the height of understatement to say only that the legislation would not *require* such conduct. It is hardly conceivable that Congress would have extensively discussed only its intent not to require preferential treatment if . . . it had intended to prohibit such treatment.

We also find it significant that Congress was aware of state laws similar to California's but apparently did not consider them inconsistent with the PDA. In the debates and reports on the bill, Congress repeatedly acknowledged the existence of state antidiscrimination laws that prohibit sex discrimination on the basis of pregnancy. Two of the States mentioned then required employers to provide reasonable leave to pregnant workers. After citing these state laws, Congress failed to evince the requisite "clear and manifest purpose" to supersede them. . . . To the contrary, both the House and Senate Reports suggest that these laws would continue to have effect under the PDA.

Title VII, as amended by the PDA, and California's pregnancy disability leave statute share a common goal. The purpose of Title VII is "to achieve equality of employment opportunities and remove barriers that have operated in the past to favor an identifiable group of . . . employees over other employees." . . . Rather than limiting existing Title VII principles and objectives, the PDA extends them to cover pregnancy. As Senator Williams, a sponsor of the Act, stated: "The entire thrust . . . behind this legislation is to guarantee women the basic right to participate fully and equally in the workforce, without denying them the fundamental right to full participation in family life." . . .

Section 12945(b)(2) also promotes equal employment opportunity. By requiring employers to reinstate women after a reasonable pregnancy disability leave, §12945(b)(2) ensures that they will not lose their jobs on account of pregnancy disability. . . . By "taking pregnancy into account," California's pregnancy disability leave statute allows women, as well as men, to have families without losing their jobs.

We emphasize the limited nature of the benefits §12945(b)(2) provides. The statute is narrowly drawn to cover only the period of *actual physical disability* on account of pregnancy, childbirth, or related medical conditions. Accordingly, unlike the protective labor legislation prevalent earlier in this century, §12945(b)(2) does not reflect archaic or stereotypical notions about pregnancy and the abilities of pregnant workers. A statute based on such stereotypical assumptions would, of course, be inconsistent with Title VII's goal of equal employment opportunity. . . .

Moreover, even if we agreed with petitioners' construction of the PDA, we would nonetheless reject their argument that the California statute requires employers to violate Title VII. . . . Section 12945(b)(2) does not compel California employers to treat preg-

nant workers *better* than other disabled employees; it merely establishes benefits that employers must, at a minimum, provide to pregnant workers. Employers are free to give comparable benefits to other disabled employees, thereby treating "women affected by pregnancy" no better than "other persons not so affected but similar in their ability or inability to work." Indeed, at oral argument, petitioners conceded that compliance with both statutes "is theoretically possible." . . .

Thus, petitioners' facial challenge to §12945(b)(2) fails. The statute is not pre-empted by Title VII, as amended by the PDA, because it is not inconsistent with the purposes of the federal statute, nor does it require the doing of an act which is unlawful under Title VII.

The judgment of the Court of Appeals is *Affirmed.*

. . . Justice *White,* with whom The *Chief Justice* and Justice *Powell* join, dissenting.

I disagree with the Court that Cal. Gov't Code Ann. §12945(b)(2) . . . is not pre-empted by the Pregnancy Discrimination Act of 1978 (PDA). . . . Section 703(a) of Title VII . . . forbids discrimination in the terms of employment on the basis of race, color, religion, sex, or national origin. The PDA gave added meaning to discrimination on the basis of sex:

> The terms "because of sex" or "on the basis of sex" [in section 703(a) of this title] include, but are not limited to, because of or on the basis of pregnancy, childbirth, or related medical conditions; and women affected by pregnancy, childbirth, or related medical conditions shall be treated the same for all employment-related purposes, including receipt of benefits under fringe benefit programs, as other persons not so affected but similar in their ability or inability to work. . . .

The second clause quoted above could not be clearer: It mandates that pregnant employees "Shall be treated the same for all employment-related purposes" as nonpregnant employees similarly situated with respect to their ability or inability to work. . . .

Contrary to the mandate of the PDA, California law requires every employer to have a disability leave policy for pregnancy even if it has none for any other disability. An employer complies with California law if it has a leave policy for pregnancy but denies it for every other disability. On its face, §12945(b)(2) is in square conflict with the PDA and is therefore pre-empted. . . .

The majority nevertheless would save the California law on two grounds. First, it holds that the PDA does not require disability from pregnancy to be treated the same as other disabilities; instead, it forbids less favorable, but permits more favorable, benefits for pregnancy disability. . . .

. . . Given the evidence before Congress of the widespread discrimination against pregnant workers, it is probable that most Congresspersons did not seriously consider the possibility that someone would want to afford preferential treatment to pregnant workers. The parties and their *amici* argued vigorously to this Court the policy implications of preferential treatment of pregnant workers. In favor of preferential treatment it was urged with conviction that preferential treatment merely enables women, like men, to have children without losing their jobs. In opposition to preferential treatment it was urged with equal conviction that preferential treatment represents a resurgence of the nineteenth-century protective legislation which perpetuated sex-role stereotypes and which impeded women in their efforts to take their rightful place in the workplace. . . . It is not the place of this Court, however, to resolve this policy dispute. . . .

Congress's acknowledgment of state antidiscrimination laws does not support a contrary inference. The most extensive discussion of state laws governing pregnancy discrimination is found in the House Report. . . . The Report did not in any way set apart the Connecticut and Montana statutes, on which the majority relies, from the other state statutes. The House Report gave no indication that these statutes required anything more than equal treatment. . . .

The Court's second, and equally strange, ground is that even if the PDA does prohibit special benefits for pregnant women, an employer may still comply with both the California law and the PDA: It can adopt the specified leave policies for pregnancy and at the same time afford similar benefits for all other disabilities. This is untenable. California surely had no intent to require employers to provide general disability leave benefits. It intended to prefer pregnancy and went no farther. . . .

In sum, preferential treatment of pregnant workers is prohibited by Title VII, as amended by the PDA. Section 12945(b)(2) of the California Gov't Code, which extends preferential benefits for pregnancy, is therefore pre-empted. . . .

Suggestions for Further Reading

Anthologies

Bishop, Sharon, and Weinzweig, Marjorie. *Philosophy and Women*. Belmont, Calif.: Wadsworth Publishing Co., 1979.

Frazer, Elizabeth, Hornsby, Jennifer, and Lovibond, Sabina. *Ethics: A Feminist Reader*. Oxford: Blackwell, 1992.

Freeman, Jo. *Women: A Feminist Perspective*. 4th ed. Palo Alto: Mayfield Publishing Co., 1989.

Gould, Carol C., and Wartofsky, Marx W. *Women and Philosophy*. New York: G. P. Putnam & Sons, 1976.

Jaggar, Alison, and Struhl, Paula Rothenberg. *Feminist Frameworks* 3rd ed. New York: McGraw-Hill Co., 1993.

Kourany, Janet, Sterba, James, and Tong, Rosemarie. *Feminist Philosophies*. Englewood Cliffs N.J.: Prentice-Hall, 1992.

Basic Concepts

Jaggar, Alison M. *Feminist Politics and Human Nature*. Totowa, N.J.: Rowman & Allanheld, 1983.

Tong, Rosemarie. *Feminist Thought*. Boulder: Westview Press, 1989.

Tuana, Nancy, and Tong, Rosemarie. *Feminism and Philosophy*. Boulder: Westview, 1995.

Alternative Views

DeCrow, Karen. *Sexist Justice*. New York: Vintage, 1975.

Eisenstein, Zellah. *Feminism and Sexual Equality*. New York: Monthly Review, 1984.

Friedan, Betty. *The Feminine Mystique*. New York: W. W. Norton & Co., 1963.

Frye, Marilyn. *The Politics of Reality*. New York: The Crossing Press, 1983.

Held, Virginia. *Feminist Morality*. Chicago: University of Chicago Press, 1993.

Okin, Susan. *Justice, Gender and the Family*. New York: Basic Books, 1989.

Pateman, Carole. *The Sexual Contract*. Stanford: Stanford University Press, 1988.

Sommers, Christina Hoff. *Who Stole Feminism*. New York: Simon and Schuster, 1994.

Young, Iris. *Justice and the Politics of Difference*. Princeton: Princeton University Press, 1990.

Practical Applications

Irving, John. *The World According to Garp*. New York: Dutton, 1978.

United States Commission on Civil Rights. *Statement on the Equal Rights Amendment*. Washington, D.C.: U.S. Government Printing Office, 1978.

Affirmative Action

Introduction

Basic Concepts

Solutions to the problem of discrimination and prejudice tend to be either backward-looking or forward-looking. The former seek to rectify and compensate for past injustices caused by discrimination or prejudice. Forward-looking solutions seek to realize an ideal of a society free from discrimination and prejudice. To justify a backward-looking solution to the problem of discrimination and prejudice, it is necessary to determine (1) who has committed or benefited from a wrongful act of discrimination or prejudice and (2) who deserves compensation for that act. To justify a forward-looking solution to the problem, it is necessary to determine (1) what a society free from discrimination and prejudice would be like and (2) how such a society might be realized. Solutions of both types have been proposed to deal with racism and sexism, the dominant forms of discrimination and prejudice in our times.

One useful way of approaching the topic of discrimination and prejudice is to note what particular solutions to the problem are favored by the political ideals of libertarianism, welfare liberalism, and socialism. (See Section I.)

Libertarians, for whom liberty is the ultimate political ideal, are not likely to recognize any need to rectify acts of discrimination and prejudice. Bad as these acts may be, they usually do not—according to libertarians—violate anyone's rights, and hence do not demand rectification. In particular, because no one can demand a right to equal basic educational opportunities (a person's educational opportunities being simply a function of the property he or she controls), no one can justify affirmative action or comparable worth on the basis that such a right was previously denied.

Socialists, for whom equality is the ultimate political ideal, recognize a need to correct for discrimination and prejudice. However, the corrective measures they favor are not limited to affirmative action; socialists ultimately want to socialize the means of production and do away with private property.

Finally, affirmative action is a central requirement of the political program of welfare liberals, whose ultimate political ideal is contractual fairness.

Proposed solutions to the problem of discrimination and prejudice usually involve favoring or compensating certain qualified individuals when there has been a wrongful denial of opportunities or benefits in the past. This practice is called affirmative action, preferential treatment, or reverse discrimination when what is provided are jobs or other desirable positions. "Affirmative action" and "preferential treatment" are basically forward-looking designations employed by proponents of the practice. "Reverse discrimination" is basically a backward-looking designation employed by opponents of the practice.

Alternative Views

In Selection 30, Louis Pojman defines affirmative action as the effort to rectify the injustice of the past by special policies. He distinguishes a weak and a strong form of affirmative action. The weak form involves such measures as the elimination of segregation, widespread advertisement to underrepresented groups, and special scholarships for the disadvantaged classes. The strong form involves such actions as hiring on the basis of race or gender to reach proportionate representation. He argues that neither form of affirmative action can be justified. He begins by considering a number of arguments in favor of affirmative action such as the argument that role models are required, that stereotypes need to be broken, that compensation is required, and that diversity is needed, and he finds all these arguments wanting. He then considers a number of arguments against affirmative action, such as that affirmative action requires discrimination against the wrong people, that it perpetuates the victimization syndrome, that it encourages mediocrity and incompetence, and that it has not worked; and he finds merit in each of these arguments. He concludes that the case against affirmative action applies not only to strong affirmative action but also to weak affirmative action because the weak form slides easily into the strong form.

One problem with Pojman's account is the way he understands affirmative action. Suppose that affirmative action with respect to women and minorities were understood to be a policy of preferring qualified women and minority candidates who have been disadvantaged by past injustices over equally or more qualified white male candidates who have not been similarly disadvantaged. Suppose also that to be justified, this policy of affirmative action must favor only candidates whose qualifications are such that when their selection or appointment is combined with a suitably designed educational enhancement program, they will normally turn out, within a reasonably short time, to be as qualified or even more qualified than their peers. Now assuming that one were to understand affirmative action in this way, it is not clear that Pojman's objections to it would still apply.

Gertrude Ezorsky maintains that the ultimate goal of affirmative action for blacks is occupational integration, that is, their appropriate statistical representation in the hierarchy of employment as in the population at large (Selection 31). She argues that the success of other minorities does not show that there is no need for affirmative action. She further argues that affirmative action is not unfair to white workers given that they have gained from past racism. She also argues that the rule of hiring by competence has been subject to so many exceptions that adding an exception for affirmative action would not constitute a significant departure from current practice.

Irrespective of whether affirmative action would constitute a significant departure from current practice, Charles Murray (Selection 32) argues that it has actually worked against the interests of blacks by encouraging a new form of racism. The old racism openly held that blacks are permanently less competent than whites. The new racism holds that blacks are temporarily less competent than whites. The main problem with the new racism, according to Murray, is that it tends to perpetuate the racial inequalities it purports to remedy. However, the examples of this new racism that Murray discusses are all composites drawn from personal observations and, hence, as even he seems to realize, do not by themselves support any generalizations. At the same time, Murray wants to conclude from his discussion that there is no such thing as good racial discrimination.

In Selection 33, Stanley Fish argues that just as it would be a mistake to equate Zionism with Nazi racism, it would be a mistake to equate affirmative action with the racism that blacks have suffered in this country. To think they are the same, Fish claims, is to ignore the importance of history. He further argues that what looks like a level playing field to some (e.g., scores on SATs) is actually a tilted field favoring those who are culturally advantaged. He also cites a 1991 broadcast of *PrimeTime Live* showing how whites are favored over comparably talented and educated blacks.

Practical Applications

Assuming that we accept the need for affirmative action programs to compensate for past injustices, there remains the question of what form such programs should take. In a recent decision, *Adarand Constructors v. Pena,* the issue before the Supreme Court was whether the race-based classifications of the Small Business Act violated Adarand's right to equal protection under the Fifth and Fourteenth Amendments. After reviewing the history of the Court's decisions in this area, the majority ruled that the Act did violate Adarand's right to equal protection because it did not meet a standard of strict scrutiny with respect to racial classifications, which,

among other things, required evidence of past discrimination before affirmative action can be applied in a particular area. In so doing, the Court overturned its earlier decision in *Metro Broadcasting Inc. v. FCC* (1990), which did not require evidence of previous discrimination before assigning broadcasting rights to secure racial and ethnic diversity. Justice Stevens joined by Justice Ginsburg dissented from the Court's decision for a number of reasons. First, Stevens claims that all racial classifications are not equally suspect; affirmative action programs cannot be equated with the racial discrimination of the past. Second, Stevens argues that there is a clear difference between state action that imposes a burden and state action that provides a benefit as in *Metro Broadcasting Inc. v. FCC* (1990); the latter requires less scrutiny. Third, Stevens argues there is an important difference between federal and state programs that involve racial classifications; the Court needs to be more deferential to the actions of Congress than to actions of state and local governments. Fourth, Stevens laments that the Court's decision in this case violates the doctrine of *stare decisis* by overturning a previous Court's decision and hinting that yet another decision of the Court may have to be overturned in the future. To say the least, this recent decision of the Court raises serious questions about the legal justification for many current affirmative action programs. Nevertheless, a moral justification for such programs will still turn on a comparative evaluation of the political ideals of libertarianism, welfare liberalism, and socialism, and their practical requirements.

30. *The Moral Status of Affirmative Action*

LOUIS P. POJMAN

Louis Pojman distinguishes a weak and a strong form of affirmative action. The weak form involves such measures as the elimination of segregation, widespread advertisement to underrepresented groups, and special scholarships for the disadvantaged classes. The strong form involves such actions as hiring on the basis of race or gender to reach proportionate representation. He considers a number of arguments both for and against affirmative action and concludes that neither form of affirmative action can]be justified.

"A ruler who appoints any man to an office, when there is in his dominion another man better qualified for it, sins against God and against the State." (The Koran).

"[Affirmative action] is the meagerest recompense for centuries of unrelieved oppression." (Quoted by Shelby Steele as the justification for affirmative action.)

Hardly a week goes by but that the subject of affirmative action does not come up. Whether in the guise of reverse discrimination, preferential hiring, nontraditional casting, quotas, goals and timetables, minority scholarships, or race norming, the issue confronts us as a terribly perplexing problem. Last summer's Actor's Equity debacle over the casting of the British actor, Jonathan Pryce, as a Eurasian in Miss Saigon; Assistant Secretary of Education Michael Williams' judgment that Minority Scholarships are unconstitutional; the "Civil Rights Bill of 1991," reversing recent decisions of the Supreme Court which constrain preferential hiring practices; the demand that Harvard Law School hire a black female professor; grade stipends for black students at Pennsylvania State University and other schools; the revelations of race norming in state employment agencies; as well as debates over quotas, underutilization guidelines, and diversity in employment; all testify to the importance of this subject for contemporary society.

There is something salutary as well as terribly tragic inherent in this problem. The salutary aspect is

the fact that our society has shown itself committed to eliminating unjust discrimination. Even in the heart of Dixie there is a recognition of the injustice of racial discrimination. Both sides of the affirmative action debate have good will and appeal to moral principles. Both sides are attempting to bring about a better society, one that is color-blind, but they differ profoundly on the morally proper means to accomplish that goal.

And this is just the tragedy of the situation: Good people on both sides of the issue are ready to tear each other to pieces over a problem that has no easy or obvious solution. And so the voices become shrill and the rhetoric hyperbolic. The same spirit which divides the pro-choice movement from the right to life movement on abortion divides liberal pro–affirmative action advocates from liberal anti–affirmative action advocates. This problem, more than any other, threatens to destroy the traditional liberal consensus in our society. I have seen family members and close friends who until recently fought on the same side of the barricades against racial injustice divide in enmity over this issue. The anti-affirmative liberals ("liberals who've been mugged") have tended towards a form of neoconservatism and the pro-affirmative liberals have tended to side with the radical left to form the "politically correct ideology" movement.

In this paper I will confine myself primarily to affirmative action policies with regard to race, but much of what I say can be applied to the areas of gender and ethnic minorities.

Reprinted from *Public Affairs Quarterly* by permission of the publisher and the author.

I. Definitions

First let me define my terms:

Discrimination is simply judging one thing to differ from another on the basis of some criterion. "Discrimination" is essentially a good quality, having reference to our ability to make distinctions. As rational and moral agents we need to make proper distinctions. To be rational is to discriminate between good and bad arguments, and to think morally is to discriminate between reasons based on valid principles and those based on invalid ones. What needs to be distinguished is the difference between rational and moral discrimination on the one hand, and irrational and immoral discrimination on the other hand.

Prejudice is a discrimination based on irrelevant grounds. It may simply be an attitude which never surfaces in action, or it may cause prejudicial actions. A prejudicial discrimination in action is immoral if it denies someone a fair deal. So discrimination on the basis of race or sex where these are not relevant for job performance is unfair. Likewise, one may act prejudicially in applying a relevant criterion on insufficient grounds, as in the case where I apply the criterion of being a hard worker but then assume, on insufficient evidence, that the black man who applies for the job is not a hard worker.

There is a difference between *prejudice* and *bias*. Bias signifies a tendency towards one thing rather than another where the evidence is incomplete or based on non-moral factors. For example, you may have a bias towards blondes and I towards redheads. But prejudice is an attitude (or action) where unfairness is present—where one *should* know or do better, as in the case where I give people jobs simply because they are redheads. Bias implies ignorance or incomplete knowledge, whereas prejudice is deeper, involving a moral failure—usually a failure to pay attention to the evidence. But note that calling people racist or sexist without good evidence is also an act of prejudice. I call this form of prejudice "defamism," for it unfairly defames the victim. It is a contemporary version of McCarthyism.

Equal opportunity is offering everyone a fair chance at the best positions that society has at its disposal.

Only native aptitude and effort should be decisive in the outcome, not factors of race, sex, or special favors.

Affirmative action is the effort to rectify the injustice of the past by special policies. Put this way, it is Janus-faced or ambiguous, having both a backward-looking and a forward-looking feature. The backward-looking feature is its attempt to correct and compensate for past injustice. This aspect of affirmative action is strictly deontological. The forward-looking feature is its implicit ideal of a society free from prejudice; this is both deontological and utilitarian.

When we look at a social problem from a backward-looking perspective we need to determine who has committed or benefited from a wrongful or prejudicial act and to determine who deserves compensation for that act.

When we look at a social problem from a forward-looking perspective we need to determine what a just society (one free from prejudice) would look like and how to obtain that kind of society. The forward-looking aspect of affirmative action is paradoxically race-conscious, since it uses race to bring about a society which is not race-conscious, which is color-blind (in the morally relevant sense of this term).

It is also useful to distinguish two versions of affirmative action. *Weak affirmative action* involves such measures as the elimination of segregation (namely the idea of "separate but equal"), widespread advertisement to groups not previously represented in certain privileged positions, special scholarships for the disadvantaged classes (e.g., all the poor), using underrepresentation or a history of past discrimination as a tie breaker when candidates are relatively equal, and the like.

Strong affirmative action involves more positive steps to eliminate past injustice, such as reverse discrimination, hiring candidates on the basis of race and gender in order to reach equal or near equal results, proportionate representation in each area of society.

II. A Brief History of Affirmative Action

1. After a long legacy of egregious racial discrimination the forces of civil justice came to a head during

the decade of 1954–1964. In the 1954 U.S. Supreme Court decision, *Brown v. Board of Education,* racial segregation was declared inherently and unjustly discriminatory, a violation of the constitutional right to equal protection, and in 1964 Congress passed the Civil Rights Act which banned all forms of racial discrimination.

During this time the goal of the Civil Rights Movement was equal opportunity. The thinking was that if only we could remove the hindrances to progress, invidious segregation, discriminatory laws, and irrational prejudice against blacks, we could free our country from the evils of past injustice and usher in a just society in which the grandchildren of the slave could play together and compete with the grandchildren of the slave owner. We were after a color-blind society in which every child had an equal chance to attain the highest positions based not on his skin color but on the quality of his credentials. In the early 60s when the idea of reverse discrimination was mentioned in civil rights groups, it was usually rejected as a new racism. The Executive Director of the NAACP, Roy Wilkins, stated this position unequivocally during congressional consideration of the 1964 civil rights law. "Our association has never been in favor of a quota system. We believe the quota system is unfair whether it is used for [blacks] or against [blacks]. . . . [We] feel people ought to be hired because of their ability, irrespective of their color. . . . We want equality, equality of opportunity and employment on the basis of ability."[1]

So the Civil Rights Act of 1964 was passed outlawing discrimination on the basis of race or sex.

> Title VII, Section 703(a) Civil Rights Act of 1964: It shall be an unlawful practice for an employer (1) to fail or refuse to hire or to discharge any individual or otherwise to discriminate against any individual with respect to his compensation, terms, conditions, or privileges of employment, because of such individual's race, color, sex, or national origin; or
>
> (2) to limit, segregate, or classify his employees or applicants for employment in any way which would deprive or tend to deprive any individual of employment opportunities or otherwise adversely affect his status as an employee because of such individual's race, color, religion, sex, or national origin. [42 U.S.C.2000e-2(a)]

> . . . Nothing contained in this title shall be interpreted to require any employer to grant preferential treatment to any individual or to any group on account of an imbalance which may exist with respect to the total numbers or percentage of persons of any race . . . employed by any employer . . . in comparison with the total or percentage of persons of such race . . . in any community, State, section, or other areas, or in the available work force in any community, State, section, or other area. [42 U.S.C.2000e-2(j)]

The Civil Rights Act of 1964 espouses a meritocratic philosophy, calling for equal opportunity and prohibiting reverse discrimination as just another form of prejudice. The Voting Rights Act (1965) was passed and Jim Crow laws throughout the South were overturned. Schools were integrated and public accommodations opened to all. Branch Rickey's promotion of Jackie Robinson from the minor leagues in 1947 to play for the Brooklyn Dodgers was seen as the paradigm case of this kind of equal opportunity—the successful recruiting of a deserving person.

2. But it was soon noticed that the elimination of discriminatory laws was not producing the fully integrated society that leaders of the civil rights movement had envisioned. Eager to improve the situation, in 1965 President Johnson went beyond equal opportunity to affirmative action. He issued the famous Executive Order 11246 in which the Department of Labor was enjoined to issue government contracts with construction companies on the basis of race. That is, it would engage in reverse discrimination in order to make up for the evils of the past. He explained the act in terms of the shackled runner analogy.

> Imagine a hundred yard dash in which one of the two runners has his legs shackled together. He has progressed ten yards, while the unshackled runner has gone fifty yards. How do they rectify the situation? Do they merely remove the shackles and allow the race to proceed? Then they could say that "equal opportunity" now prevailed. But one of the runners would still be forty yards ahead of the other. Would it not be the better part of justice to allow the previously shackled runner to make up the forty-yard gap; or to start the race all over again? That would be affirmative action towards equality.

(President Lyndon Johnson, 1965, inaugurating the affirmative action policy of Executive Order 11246).

In 1967 President Johnson issued Executive Order 11375 extending affirmative action (henceforth "AA") to women. Note here that AA originates in the executive branch of government. Until the Kennedy-Hawkins Civil Rights Act of 1990, AA policy was never put to a vote or passed by Congress. Gradually, the benefits of AA were extended to Hispanics, native Americans, Asians, and handicapped people.[2]

The phrase "An Equal Opportunity / Affirmative Action Employer" ("AA/EO") began to appear as official public policy. But few noticed an ambiguity in the notion of "AA" which could lead to a contradiction in juxtaposing it with "EO," for there are two types of AA. At first AA was interpreted as, what I have called, "weak affirmative action," in line with equal opportunity, signifying wider advertisement of positions, announcements that applications from blacks would be welcomed, active recruitment and hiring blacks (and women) over *equally* qualified men. While few liberals objected to these measures, some expressed fears of an impending slippery slope towards reverse discrimination.

However, except in professional sports—including those sponsored by universities—weak affirmative action was not working, so in the late 60s and early 70s a stronger version of affirmative action was embarked upon—one aimed at equal results, quotas (or "goals"—a euphemism for "quotas"). In *Swann v. Charlotte-Mecklenburg* (1971), regarding the busing of children out of their neighborhood . . . to promote integration, the Court, led by Justice Brennan, held that affirmative action was implied in *Brown* and was consistent with the Civil Rights Act of 1964. The NAACP now began to support reverse discrimination.

Thus began the search for minimally qualified blacks in college recruitment, hiring, and the like. Competence and excellence began to recede into second place as the quest for racial, ethnic, and gender diversity became the dominant goals. The slogan "We have to become race conscious in order to eliminate race consciousness" became the paradoxical justification for reverse discrimination.

3. In 1968 the Department of Labor ordered employers to engage in utilization studies as part of its policy of eliminating discrimination in the workplace. The office of Federal Contract Compliance of the U.S. Department of Labor (Executive Order 11246) stated that employers with a history of *underutilization* of minorities and women were required to institute programs that went beyond passive nondiscrimination through deliberate efforts to identify people of "affected classes" for the purpose of advancing their employment. Many employers found it wise to adopt policies of preferential hiring in order to preempt expensive government suits.

Employers were to engage in "utilization analysis" of their present work force in order to develop "specific and result-oriented procedures" to which the employer commits *"every good-faith effort"* in order to provide "relief for members of an *'affected class,'* who by virtue of *past discrimination* continue to suffer the present effects of that discrimination." This self-analysis is supposed to discover areas in which such affected classes are underused, considering their availability and skills. *"Goals and timetables* are to be developed to guide efforts to correct deficiencies in the employment of affected classes of people in each level and segment of the work force." Affirmative action also calls for "rigorous examination" of standards and criteria for job performance, not so as to "dilute necessary standards" but in order to ensure that "arbitrary and discriminatory employment practices are eliminated" and to eliminate unnecessary criteria which "have had the effect of eliminating women and minorities" either from selection or promotion.[3]

4. In 1969 two important events occurred. (a) The Philadelphia Plan—The Department of Labor called for "goals and timetables" for recruiting minority workers. In Philadelphia area construction industries, where these companies were all-white, family-run businesses, the contractor's union took the case to court on the grounds that Title VII of the Civil Rights Act prohibits quotas. The Third Circuit Court of Appeals upheld the Labor Department, and the Supreme Court refused to hear it. This case became the basis of the EEOC's aggressive pursuit of "goals and timetables" in other business situations.

(b) In the Spring of 1969 James Forman disrupted the service of Riverside Church in New York City and issued the Black Manifesto to the American Churches, demanding that they pay blacks $500,000,000 in reparations. The argument of the Black Manifesto was that for three and a half centuries blacks in America have been "exploited and degraded, brutalized, killed and persecuted" by whites; that this was part of the persistent institutional patterns of first, legal slavery and then, legal discrimination and forced segregation; and that through slavery and discrimination whites had procured enormous wealth from black labor with little return to blacks. These facts were said to constitute grounds for reparations on a massive scale. The American churches were but the first institutions to be asked for reparations.[4]

5. The Department of Labor issued guidelines in 1970 calling for hiring representatives of *underutilized* groups. *"Nondiscrimination* requires the elimination of all existing discriminatory conditions, whether purposeful or inadvertent. . . . Affirmative action requires . . . the employer to make additional efforts to recruit, employ and promote qualified members of groups formerly excluded" (HEW Executive Order 22346, 1972). In December of 1971 Guidelines were issued to eliminate underutilization of minorities, aiming at realignment of the job force at every level of society.

6. In *Griggs v. Duke Power Company* (1971) the Supreme Court interpreted Title VII of the Civil Rights Act as forbidding use of aptitude tests and high school diplomas in hiring personnel. These tests were deemed presumptively discriminatory, employers having the burden of proving such tests relevant to performance. The notion of *sufficiency* replaced that of excellence or best qualified, as it was realized (though not explicitly stated) that the social goal of racial diversity required compromising the standards of competence.

7. In 1977, the EEOC called for and *expected* proportional representation of minorities in every area of work (including universities).

8. In 1978 the Supreme Court addressed the Bakke case. Alan Bakke had been denied admission to the University of California at Davis Medical School even though his test scores were higher than the sixteen blacks who were admitted under the affirmative action quota program. He sued the University of California and the U.S. Supreme Court ruled (*University*

of California v. Bakke, July 28, 1978) in a 5 to 4 vote that reverse discrimination and quotas are illegal except (as Justice Powell put it) when engaged in for purposes of promoting diversity (interpreted as a means to extend free speech under the First Amendment) and restoring a situation where an institution has had a history of prejudicial discrimination. The decision was greeted with applause from anti-AA quarters and dismay from pro-AA quarters. Ken Tollett lamented, "The affirmance of Bakke would mean the reversal of affirmative action; it would be an officially sanctioned signal to turn against blacks in this country. . . . Opposition to special minority admissions programs and affirmative action is anti-black."[5]

But Tollett was wrong. The Bakke case only shifted the rhetoric from "quota" language to "goals and timetables" and "diversity" language. In the '80s affirmative action was alive and well, with preferential hiring, minority scholarships, and race norming prevailing in all walks of life. No other white who has been excluded from admission to college because of his race has ever won his case. In fact only a year later, Justice Brennan was to write in *U.S. Steel v. Weber* that prohibition of racial discrimination against "any individual" in Title VII of the Civil Rights Act did not apply to discrimination against whites.[6]

9. Perhaps the last step in the drive towards equal results took place in the institutionalization of grading applicants by group-related standards, race norming. Race norming is widely practiced but most of the public is unaware of it, so let me explain it.

Imagine that four men come into a state employment office in order to apply for a job. One is black, one Hispanic, one Asian, and one white. They take the standard test (a version of the General Aptitude Test Battery or VG-GATB). All get a composite score of 300. None of them will ever see that score. Instead the numbers will be fed into a computer and the applicants' percentile ranking emerges. The scores are group-weighted. Blacks are measured against blacks, whites against whites, Hispanics against Hispanics. Since blacks characteristically do less well than other groups, the effect is to favor blacks. For example, a score of 300 as an accountant will give the black a percentile score of 87, a Hispanic a percentile score of 74 and a white or oriental a score of 47. The black will get the job as the accountant. (See the box at the bottom of this page.)

This is known as race norming. Until an anonymous governmental employee recently blew the whistle, this practice was kept a secret in several state employment services. Prof. Linda Gottfredson of the University of Delaware, one of the social scientists to expose this practice, has since had her funding cut off. In a recent letter to the *New York Times* she writes:

> One of America's best-kept open secrets is that the Employment Service of the Department of Labor has unabashedly promulgated quotas. In 1981 the service recommended that state employment agencies adopt a race-conscious battery to avoid adverse impact when referring job applicants to employers. . . . The score adjustments are not trivial. An unadjusted score that places a job applicant at the 15th percentile among whites would, after race-norming, typically place a black near the white 50th percentile. Likewise, unadjusted scores at the white 50th percentile would, after race-norming, typically place a black near the 85th percentile for white job applicants. . . . [I]ts use by 40 states in the last decade belies the claim that *Griggs* did not lead to quotas.[7]

10. In the *Ward Cove, Richmond,* and *Martin* decisions of the mid-80s the Supreme Court limited preferential hiring practices, placing a greater burden of proof on the plaintiff, now required to prove that employers have discriminated. The Kennedy-Hawkins Civil Rights Act of 1990, which was passed by Congress last year, sought to reverse these decisions by requiring employers to justify statistical imbalances not only in the employment of racial minorities but also that of ethnic and religious minorities. Wherever underrepresentation of an "identified" group exists, the employer bears the burden of proving he is innocent of prejudicial behavior. In other words, the bill would make it easier for minorities to sue employers. President Bush vetoed the bill, deeming it a subterfuge for quotas. A revised bill is now in Congressional committee.

Affirmative action in the guise of underutilized or "affected groups" now extends to American Indians and Hispanics (including Spanish nobles) but not Portuguese, Asians, the handicapped, and in some places Irish and Italians. Estimates are that 75 percent of Americans may obtain AA status as minorities: everyone except the white nonhandicapped male. It is a strange policy that affords special treatment to the children of Spanish nobles and illegal immigrants but not the children of the survivors of Russian pogroms or Nazi concentration camps.

Of course, there is nothing new about the notions of racial discrimination and preferential treatment.

Percentile Conversion Tables

Jobs are grouped into five broad families: Family I includes, for example, machinists, cabinet makers, and tool makers; Family II includes helpers in many types of agriculture, manufacturing, and so on; Family III includes professional jobs such as accountant, chemical engineer, nurse, editor; Family IV includes bus drivers, bookkeepers, carpet layers; Family V includes exterminators, butchers, file clerks. A raw score of 300 would convert to the following percentile rankings:

	I	II	III	IV	V
Black	79	59	87	83	73
Hispanic	62	41	74	67	55
Other	39	42	47	45	42

Sources: Virginia Employment Commission: U.S. Department of Labor. Employment and Training Administration, *Validity Generalization Manual* (Section A: Job Family Scoring).

The first case of racial discrimination is the fall of man, as standardly interpreted, in which the whole race is held accountable and guilty of Adam's sin. The notion of collective responsibility also goes way back in our history. The first case of preferential treatment is God's choosing Abel's sacrifice of meat and rejecting Cain's vegetarian sacrifice—which should give all Jewish-Christian vegetarians something to think about! The first case of preferential treatment in Greek mythology is that of the Achaian horse race narrated in the 23rd book of the Illiad. Achilles had two prizes to give out. First prize went to the actual winner. Antilochus, son of Nestor, came in second, but Achilles decided to give second prize to Eumelius because he was of a nobler rank, even though he had come in last. Antilochus complained, saying in effect, "If it is preordained that some other criterion than merit is to count for the award, why should we have a race at all?" Achilles was moved by this logic and gave the prize to Antilochus, offering Eumelius a treasure of his own.

Neither is affirmative action primarily an American problem. Thomas Sowell has recently written a book on the international uses of preferential treatment, *Preferential Policies: An International Perspective,* in which he analyzes government-mandated preferential policies in India, Nigeria, Malaysia, Sri Lanka, and the United States.[8] We will consider Sowell's study towards the end of this paper.

III. *Arguments for Affirmative Action*

Let us now survey the main arguments typically cited in the debate over affirmative action. I will briefly discuss seven arguments on each side of the issue.

1. *Need For Role Models*

This argument is straightforward. We all have need of role models, and it helps to know that others like us can be successful. We learn and are encouraged to strive for excellence by emulating our heroes and role models.

However, it is doubtful whether role models of one's own racial or sexual type are necessary for success. One of my heroes was Gandhi, an Indian

Hindu, another was my grade school science teacher, one Miss DeVoe, and another was Martin Luther King. More important than having role models of one's own type is having genuinely good people, of whatever race or gender, to emulate. Furthermore, even if it is of some help to people with low self-esteem to gain encouragement from seeing others of their particular kind in leadership roles, it is doubtful whether this need is a sufficient condition to justify preferential hiring or reverse discrimination. What good is a role model who is inferior to other professors or business personnel? Excellence will rise to the top in a system of fair opportunity. Natural development of role models will come more slowly and more surely. Proponents of preferential policies simply lack the patience to let history take its own course.

2. *The Need of Breaking the Stereotypes*

Society may simply need to know that there are talented blacks and women, so that it does not automatically assign them lesser respect or status. We need to have unjustified stereotype beliefs replaced with more accurate ones about the talents of blacks and women. So we need to engage in preferential hiring of qualified minorities even when they are not the most qualified.

Again, the response is that hiring the less qualified is neither fair to those better qualified who are passed over nor an effective way of removing inaccurate stereotypes. If competence is accepted as the criterion for hiring, then it is unjust to override it for purposes of social engineering. Furthermore, if blacks or women are known to hold high positions simply because of reverse discrimination, then they will still lack the respect due to those of their rank. In New York City there is a saying among doctors, "Never go to a black physician under 40," referring to the fact that AA has affected the medical system during the past fifteen years. The police use "Quota Cops" and "Welfare Sergeants" to refer to those hired without passing the standardized tests. (In 1985 180 black and Hispanic policemen, who had failed a promotion test, were promoted anyway to the rank of sergeant.) The destruction of false stereotypes will come naturally as qualified blacks rise naturally in fair competition (or if it does not—then the stereotypes may be justified). Reverse discrimination sends the message home that the stereotypes are deserved—otherwise, why do these minorities need so much extra help?

3. Equal Results Argument

Some philosophers and social scientists hold that human nature is roughly identical, so that on a fair playing field the same proportion from every race and gender and ethnic group would attain to the highest positions in every area of endeavor. It would follow that any inequality of results itself is evidence for inequality of opportunity. John Arthur, in discussing an intelligence test, Test 21, puts the case this way.

> History is important when considering governmental rules like Test 21 because low scores by blacks can be traced in large measure to the legacy of slavery and racism: Segregation, poor schooling, exclusion from trade unions, malnutrition, and poverty have all played their roles. Unless one assumes that blacks are naturally less able to pass the test, the conclusion must be that the results are themselves socially and legally constructed, not a mere given for which law and society can claim no responsibility.
>
> The conclusion seems to be that genuine equality eventually requires equal results. Obviously blacks have been treated unequally throughout U.S. history, and just as obviously the economic and psychological effects of that inequality linger to this day, showing up in lower income and poorer performance in school and on tests than whites achieve. Since we have no reason to believe that differences in performance can be explained by factors other than history, equal results are a good benchmark by which to measure progress made toward genuine equality.[9]

The result of a just society should be equal numbers in proportion to each group in the work force.

However, Arthur fails even to consider studies that suggest that there are innate differences between races, sexes, and groups. If there are genetic differences in intelligence and temperament within families, why should we not expect such differences between racial groups and the two genders? Why should the evidence for this be completely discounted?

Perhaps some race or one gender is more intelligent in one way than another. At present we have only limited knowledge about genetic differences, but what we do have suggests some difference be-

sides the obvious physiological traits.[10] The proper use of this evidence is not to promote discriminatory policies but to be *open* to the possibility that innate differences may have led to an overrepresentation of certain groups in certain areas of endeavor. It seems that on average blacks have genetic endowments favoring them in the development of skills necessary for excellence in basketball.

Furthermore, on Arthur's logic, we should take aggressive AA against Asians and Jews since they are overrepresented in science, technology, and medicine. So that each group receives its fair share, we should ensure that 12 percent of U.S. philosophers are black, reduce the percentage of Jews from an estimated 15 percent to 2 percent—firing about 1,300 Jewish philosophers. The fact that Asians are producing 50 percent of Ph.D.'s in science and math and blacks less than 1 percent clearly shows, on this reasoning, that we are providing special secret advantages to Asians.

But why does society have to enter into this results game in the first place? Why do we have to decide whether all difference is environmental or genetic? Perhaps we should simply admit that we lack sufficient evidence to pronounce on these issues with any certainty—but if so, should we not be more modest in insisting on equal results? Here is a thought experiment. Take two families of different racial groups, Green and Blue. The Greens decide to have only two children, to spend all their resources on them, to give them the best education. The two Green kids respond well and end up with achievement test scores in the 99th percentile. The Blues fail to practice family planning. They have fifteen children. They can only afford two children, but lack of ability or whatever prevents them from keeping their family down. Now they need help for their large family. Why does society have to step in and help them? Society did not force them to have fifteen children. Suppose that the achievement test scores of the fifteen children fall below the 25th percentile. They cannot compete with the Greens. But now enters AA. It says that it is society's fault that the Blue children are not as able as the Greens and that the Greens must pay extra taxes to enable the Blues to compete. No restraints are put on the Blues regarding family size. This seems unfair to the Greens. Should the Green children be made to bear responsibility for the consequences of the Blues' voluntary behavior?

My point is simply that Arthur needs to cast his net wider and recognize that demographics and child-bearing and -rearing practices are crucial factors in achievement. People have to take some responsibility for their actions. The equal results argument (or axiom) misses a greater part of the picture.

4. The Compensation Argument

The argument goes like this: Blacks have been wronged and severely harmed by whites. Therefore white society should compensate blacks for the injury caused them. Reverse discrimination in terms of preferential hiring, contracts, and scholarships is a fitting way to compensate for the past wrongs.

This argument actually involves a distorted notion of compensation. Normally, we think of compensation as owed by a specific person A to another person B whom A has wronged in a specific way C. For example, if I have stolen your car and used it for a period of time to make business profits that would have gone to you, it is not enough that I return your car. I must pay you an amount reflecting your loss and my ability to pay. If I have only made $5,000 and only have $10,000 in assets, it would not be possible for you to collect $20,000 in damages—even though that is the amount of loss you have incurred.

Sometimes compensation is extended to groups of people who have been unjustly harmed by the greater society. For example, the U.S. government has compensated Japanese-Americans who were interred during the Second World War, and the West German government has paid reparations to the survivors of Nazi concentration camps. But here a specific people have been identified who were wronged in an identifiable way by the government of the nation in question.

On the face of it the demand by blacks for compensation does not fit the usual pattern. Perhaps Southern states with Jim Crow laws could be accused of unjustly harming blacks, but it is hard to see that the U.S. government was involved in doing so. Furthermore, it is not clear that all blacks were harmed in the same way or whether some were *unjustly* harmed or harmed more than poor whites and others (e.g., short people). Finally, even if identifiable blacks were harmed by identifiable social practices, it is not clear that most forms of affirmative action are appropriate to restore the situation. The usual practice of a finan-

cial payment seems more appropriate than giving a high-level job to someone unqualified or only minimally qualified, who, speculatively, might have been better qualified had he not been subject to racial discrimination. If John is the star tailback of our college team with a promising professional future, and I accidentally (but culpably) drive my pick-up truck over his legs, and so cripple him, John may be due compensation, but he is not due the tailback spot on the football team.

Still, there may be something intuitively compelling about compensating members of an oppressed group who are minimally qualified. Suppose that the Hatfields and the McCoys are enemy clans and some youths from the Hatfields go over and steal diamonds and gold from the McCoys, distributing it within the Hatfield economy. Even though we do not know which Hatfield youths did the stealing, we would want to restore the wealth, as far as possible, to the McCoys. One way might be to tax the Hatfields, but another might be to give preferential treatment in terms of scholarships and training programs and hiring to the McCoys.[11]

This is perhaps the strongest argument for affirmative action, and it may well justify some weak versions of AA, but it is doubtful whether it is sufficient to justify strong versions with quotas and goals and timetables in skilled positions. There are at least two reasons for this. First, we have no way of knowing how many people of group G would have been at competence level L had the world been different. Secondly, the normal criterion of competence is a strong prima facie consideration when the most important positions are at stake. There are two reasons for this: (1) Society has given people expectations that if they attain certain levels of excellence they will be awarded appropriately and (2) filling the most important positions with the best qualified is the best way to insure efficiency in job-related areas and in society in general. These reasons are not absolutes. They can be overridden. But there is a strong presumption in their favor so that a burden of proof rests with those who would override them.

At this point we get into the problem of whether innocent non-blacks should have to pay a penalty in terms of preferential hiring of blacks. We turn to that argument.

5. Compensation from Those Who Innocently Benefited from Past Injustice

White males as innocent beneficiaries of unjust discrimination of blacks and women have no grounds for complaint when society seeks to rectify the tilted field. White males may be innocent of oppressing blacks and minorities (and women), but they have unjustly benefited from that oppression or discrimination. So it is perfectly proper that less qualified women and blacks be hired before them.

The operative principle is: He who knowingly and willingly benefits from a wrong must help pay for the wrong. Judith Jarvis Thomson puts it this way. "Many [white males] have been direct beneficiaries of policies which have downgraded blacks and women . . . and even those who did not directly benefit . . . had, at any rate, the advantage in the competition which comes of the confidence in one's full membership [in the community], and of one's right being recognized as a matter of course."[12] That is, white males obtain advantages in self-respect and self-confidence deriving from a racist system that denies these to blacks and women.

Objection. As I noted in the previous section, compensation is normally individual and specific. If A harms B regarding *x*, B has a right to compensation from A in regards to *x*. If A steals B's car and wrecks it, A has an obligation to compensate B for the stolen car, but A's son has no obligation to compensate B. Furthermore, if A dies or disappears B has no moral right to claim that society compensate him for the stolen car—though if he has insurance, he can make such a claim to the insurance company. Sometimes a wrong cannot be compensated, and we just have to make the best of an imperfect world.

Suppose my parents, divining that I would grow up to have an unsurpassable desire to be a basketball player, bought an expensive growth hormone for me. Unfortunately, a neighbor stole it and gave it to little Lew Alcindor, who gained the extra 18 inches—my 18 inches—and shot up to an enviable 7 feet 2 inches. Alias Kareem Abdul Jabbar, he excelled in basketball, as I would have done had I had my proper dose.

Do I have a right to the millions of dollars that Jabbar made as a professional basketball player—the unjustly innocent beneficiary of my growth hormone? I have a right to something from the neighbor who

stole the hormone, and it might be kind of Jabbar to give me free tickets to the Laker basketball games, and perhaps I should be remembered in his will. As far as I can see, however, he does not *owe* me anything, either legally or morally.

Suppose further that Lew Alcindor and I are in high school together and we are both qualified to play basketball, only he is far better than I. Do I deserve to start in his position because I would have been as good as he is had someone not cheated me as a child? Again, I think not. But if being the lucky beneficiary of wrongdoing does not entail that Alcindor (or the coach) owes me anything in regards to basketball, why should it be a reason to engage in preferential hiring in academic positions or highly coveted jobs? If minimal qualifications are not adequate to override excellence in basketball, even when the minimality is a consequence of wrongdoing, why should they be adequate in other areas?

6. The Diversity Argument

It is important that we learn to live in a pluralistic world, learning to get along with other races and cultures, so we should have fully integrated schools and employment situations. Diversity is an important symbol and educative device. Thus preferential treatment is warranted to perform this role in society.

But, again, while we can admit the value of diversity, it hardly seems adequate to override considerations of merit and efficiency. Diversity for diversity's sake is moral promiscuity, since it obfuscates rational distinctions, and unless those hired are highly qualified the diversity factor threatens to become a fetish. At least at the higher levels of business and the professions, competence far outweighs considerations of diversity. I do not care whether the group of surgeons operating on me reflect racial or gender balance, but I do care that they are highly qualified. And likewise with airplane pilots, military leaders, business executives, and, may I say it, teachers and professors. Moreover, there are other ways of learning about other cultures besides engaging in reverse discrimination.

7. Anti-Meritocratic (Desert) Argument to Justify Reverse Discrimination: "No One Deserves His Talents"

According to this argument, the competent do not

deserve their intelligence, their superior character, their industriousness, or their discipline; thus they have no right to the best positions in society; therefore society is not unjust in giving these positions to less (but still minimally) qualified blacks and women. In one form this argument holds that since no one deserves anything, society may use any criteria it pleases to distribute goods. The criterion most often designated is social utility. Versions of this argument are found in the writings of John Arthur, John Rawls, Bernard Boxill, Michael Kinsley, Ronald Dworkin, and Richard Wasserstrom. Rawls writes, "No one deserves his place in the distribution of native endowments, any more than one deserves one's initial starting place in society. The assertion that a man deserves the superior character that enables him to make the effort to cultivate his abilities is equally problematic; for his character depends in large part upon fortunate family and social circumstances for which he can claim no credit. The notion of desert seems not to apply to these cases."[13] Michael Kinsley is even more adamant:

> Opponents of affirmative action are hung up on a distinction that seems more profoundly irrelevant: treating individuals versus treating groups. What is the moral difference between dispensing favors to people on their "merits" as individuals and passing out society's benefits on the basis of group identification?
>
> Group identifications like race and sex are, of course, immutable. They have nothing to do with a person's moral worth. But the same is true of most of what comes under the label "merit." The tools you need for getting ahead in a meritocratic society—not all of them but most: talent, education, instilled cultural values such as ambition—are distributed just as arbitrarily as skin color. They are fate. The notion that people somehow "deserve" the advantages of these characteristics in a way they don't "deserve" the advantage of their race is powerful, but illogical.[14]

It will help to put the argument in outline form.

1. Society may award jobs and positions as it sees fit as long as individuals have no claim to these positions.
2. To have a claim to something means that one has earned it or deserves it.

3. But no one has earned or deserves his intelligence, talent, education or cultural values which produce superior qualifications.
4. If a person does not deserve what produces something, he does not deserve its products.
5. Therefore better qualified people do not deserve their qualifications.
6. Therefore, society may override their qualifications in awarding jobs and positions as it sees fit (for social utility or to compensate for previous wrongs).

So it is permissible if a minimally qualified black or woman is admitted to law or medical school ahead of a white male with excellent credentials or if a less qualified person from an "underutilized" group gets a professorship ahead of a far better qualified white male. Sufficiency and underutilization together outweigh excellence.

Objection. Premise 4 is false. To see this, reflect that just because I do not deserve the money that I have been given as a gift (for instance) does not mean that I am not entitled to what I get with that money. If you and I both get a gift of $100 and I bury mine in the sand for five years while you invest yours wisely and double its value at the end of five years, I cannot complain that you should split the increase 50/50 since neither of us deserved the original gift. If we accept the notion of responsibility at all, we must hold that persons deserve the fruits of their labor and conscious choices. Of course, we might want to distinguish moral from legal desert and argue that, morally speaking, effort is more important than outcome, whereas, legally speaking, outcome may be more important. Nevertheless, there are good reasons in terms of efficiency, motivation, and rough justice for holding a strong prima facie principle of giving scarce high positions to those most competent.

The attack on moral desert is perhaps the most radical move that egalitarians like Rawls and company have made against meritocracy, but the ramifications of their attack are far-reaching. The following are some of its implications. Since I do not deserve my two good eyes or two good kidneys, the social engineers may take one of each from me to give to those needing an eye or a kidney—even if they have damaged their organs by their own voluntary actions.

Since no one deserves anything, we do not deserve pay for our labors or praise for a job well done or first prize in the race we win. The notion of moral responsibility vanishes in a system of levelling.

But there is no good reason to accept the argument against desert. We do act freely and, as such, we are responsible for our actions. We deserve the fruits of our labor, reward for our noble feats and punishment for our misbehavior.

We have considered seven arguments for affirmative action and have found no compelling case for strong AA and only one plausible argument (a version of the compensation argument) for weak AA. We must now turn to the arguments against affirmative action to see whether they fare any better.[15]

IV. Arguments Against Affirmative Action

1. Affirmative Action Requires Discrimination Against a Different Group

Weak affirmative action weakly discriminates against new minorities, mostly innocent young white males, and strong affirmative action strongly discriminates against these new minorities. As I argued in III.5, this discrimination is unwarranted, since, even if some compensation to blacks were indicated, it would be unfair to make innocent white males bear the whole brunt of the payments. In fact, it is poor white youth who become the new pariahs on the job market. The children of the wealthy have no trouble getting into the best private grammar schools and, on the basis of superior early education, into the best universities, graduate schools, managerial and professional positions. Affirmative action simply shifts injustice, setting blacks and women against young white males, especially ethnic and poor white males. It does little to rectify the goal of providing equal opportunity to all. If the goal is a society where everyone has a fair chance, then it would be better to concentrate on support for families and early education and decide the matter of university admissions and job hiring on the basis of traditional standards of competence.

2. Affirmative Action Perpetuates the Victimization Syndrome

Shelby Steele admits that affirmative action may seem "the meagerest recompense for centuries of unrelieved oppression" and that it helps promote diversity. At the same time, though, notes Steele, affirmative action reinforces the spirit of victimization by telling blacks that they can gain more by emphasizing their suffering, degradation, and helplessness than by discipline and work. This message holds the danger of blacks becoming permanently handicapped by a need for special treatment. It also sends to society at large the message that blacks cannot make it on their own.

Leon Wieseltier sums up the problem this way.

> The memory of oppression is a pillar and a strut of the identity of every people oppressed. It is no ordinary marker of difference. It is unusually stiffening. It instructs the individual and the group about what to expect of the world, imparts an isolating sense of aptness. . . . Don't be fooled, it teaches, there is only repetition. For that reason, the collective memory of an oppressed people is not only a treasure but a trap.
>
> In the memory of oppression, oppression outlives itself. The scar does the work of the wound. That is the real tragedy: that injustice obtains the power to distort long after it has ceased to be real. It is a posthumous victory for the oppressors, when pain becomes a tradition. And yet the atrocities of the past must never be forgotten. This is the unfairly difficult dilemma of the newly emancipated and the newly enfranchised: An honorable life is not possible if they remember too little and a normal life is not possible if they remember too much.[16]

With the eye of recollection, which does not "remember too much," Steele recommends a policy that offers "educational and economic development of disadvantaged people regardless of race and the eradication from our society—through close monitoring and severe sanctions—of racial and gender discrimination."[17]

3. Affirmative Action Encourages Mediocrity and Incompetence

Last spring Jesse Jackson joined protesters at Harvard Law School in demanding that the Law School faculty hire black women. Jackson dismissed Dean of the Law School Robert C. Clark's standard of choosing the best qualified person for the job as "cultural anemia." "We cannot just define who is qualified in the most narrow vertical, academic terms," he said. "Most people in the world are yellow, brown, black, poor, non-Christian and don't speak English, and they can't wait for some white males with archaic rules to appraise them."[18] It might be noted that if Jackson is correct about the depth of cultural decadence at Harvard, blacks might be well advised to form and support their own more vital law schools and leave places like Harvard to their archaism.

At several universities, the administrations have forced departments to hire members of minorities even when far superior candidates were available. Shortly after obtaining my Ph.D. in the late 70s I was mistakenly identified as a black philosopher (I had a civil rights record and was once a black studies major) and was flown to a major university, only to be rejected for a more qualified candidate when it [was] discovered that I was white.

Stories of the bad effects of affirmative action abound. The philosopher Sidney Hook writes that "At one Ivy League university, representatives of the Regional HEW demanded an explanation of why there were no women or minority students in the Graduate Department of Religious Studies. They were told that a reading knowledge of Hebrew and Greek was presupposed. Whereupon the representatives of HEW advised orally: 'Then end those old-fashioned programs that require irrelevant languages. And start up programs on relevant things which minority group students can study without learning languages.'"[19]

Nicholas Capaldi notes that the staff of HEW itself was one-half women, three-fifths members of minorities, and one-half black—a clear case of racial overrepresentation.

In 1972 officials at Stanford University discovered a proposal for the government to monitor curriculum in higher education: the "Summary Statement . . . Sex Discrimination Proposed HEW Regulation to Effectuate Title IX of the Education Amendment of 1972" to "establish and use internal procedure for reviewing curricula, designed both to ensure that they do not reflect discrimination on the basis of sex and to resolve complaints concerning allegations of such discrimi-

nation, pursuant to procedural standards to be prescribed by the Director of the office of Civil Rights." Fortunately, Secretary of HEW Caspar Weinberger, when alerted to the intrusion, assured Stanford University that he would never approve of it.[20]

Government programs of enforced preferential treatment tend to appeal to the lowest possible common denominator. Witness the 1974 HEW Revised Order No. 14 on Affirmative Action expectations for preferential hiring: "Neither minorities nor female employees should be required to possess higher qualifications than those of the lowest qualified incumbents."

Furthermore, no tests may be given to candidates unless it is *proved* to be relevant to the job.

> No standard or criteria which have, by intent or effect, worked to exclude women or minorities as a class can be utilized, unless the institution can demonstrate the necessity of such standard to the performance of the job in question.
>
> Whenever a validity study is called for . . . the user should include . . . an investigation of suitable alternative selection procedures and suitable alternative methods of using the selection procedure which have as little adverse impact as possible. . . . Whenever the user is shown an alternative selection procedure with evidence of less adverse impact and substantial evidence of validity for the same job in similar circumstances, the user should investigate it to determine the appropriateness of using or validating it in accord with these guidelines.[21]

At the same time Americans are wondering why standards in our country are falling and the Japanese are getting ahead. Affirmative action with its twin idols, Sufficiency and Diversity, is the enemy of excellence. I will develop this thought below (IV.6).

4. Affirmative Action Policies Unjustly Shift the Burden of Proof

Affirmative action legislation tends to place the burden of proof on the employer who does not have an "adequate" representation of "underutilized" groups in his work force. He is guilty until proven innocent. I have already recounted how in the mid-80s the Supreme Court shifted the burden of proof back onto the plaintiff, while Congress is now attempting to shift the burden back to the employer. Those in favor of deeming disproportional representation "guilty until proven innocent" argue that it is easy for employers to discriminate against minorities by various subterfuges, and I agree that steps should be taken to monitor against prejudicial treatment. But being prejudiced against employers is not the way to attain a just solution to discrimination. The principle: Innocent until proven guilty applies to employers as well as criminals. Indeed, it is clearly special pleading to reject this basic principle of Anglo-American law in this case of discrimination while adhering to it everywhere else.

5. An Argument from Merit

Traditionally, we have believed that the highest positions in society should be awarded to those who are best qualified—as the Koran states in the quotation at the beginning of this paper. Rewarding excellence both seems just to the individuals in the competition and makes for efficiency. Note that one of the most successful acts of integration, the recruitment of Jackie Robinson in the late 40s, was done in just this way, according to merit. If Robinson had been brought into the major league as a mediocre player or had batted .200 he would have been scorned and sent back to the minors where he belonged.

Merit is not an absolute value. There are times when it may be overridden for social goals, but there is a strong prima facie reason for awarding positions on its basis, and it should enjoy a weighty presumption in our social practices.

In a celebrated article Ronald Dworkin says that "Bakke had no case" because society did not owe Bakke anything. That may be, but then why does it owe anyone anything? Dworkin puts the matter in Utility terms, but if that is the case, society may owe Bakke a place at the University of California at Davis, for it seems a reasonable rule-utilitarian principle that achievement should be rewarded in society. We generally want the best to have the best positions, the best qualified candidate to win the political office, the most brilliant and competent scientist to be chosen for the most challenging research project, the best qualified pilots to become commercial pilots, only the best soldiers to become generals. Only when little is at stake do we weaken the standards and content ourselves with sufficiency (rather than excellence)—there are plenty of jobs where "sufficiency" rather than excel-

lence is required. Perhaps we now feel that medicine or law or university professorships are so routine that they can be performed by minimally qualified people—in which case AA has a place.

But note, no one is calling for quotas or proportional representation of *underutilized* groups in the National Basketball Association where blacks make up 80 percent of the players. But if merit and merit alone reigns in sports, should it not be valued at least as much in education and industry?

6. The Slippery Slope

Even if strong AA or reverse discrimination could meet the other objections, it would face a tough question: Once you embark on this project, how do you limit it? Who should be excluded from reverse discrimination? Asians and Jews are over-represented, so if we give blacks positive quotas, should we place negative quotas on these other groups? Since white males, "WMs," are a minority which is suffering from reverse discrimination, will we need a new affirmative action policy in the twenty-first century to compensate for the discrimination against WMs in the late twentieth century?

Furthermore, affirmative action has stigmatized the *young* white male. Assuming that we accept reverse discrimination, the fair way to make sacrifices would be to retire *older* white males who are more likely to have benefited from a favored status. Probably the least guilty of any harm to minority groups is the young white male—usually a liberal who has been required to bear the brunt of ages of past injustice. Justice Brennan's announcement that the Civil Rights Act did not apply to discrimination against whites shows how the clearest language can be bent to serve the ideology of the moment.[22]

7. The Mounting Evidence Against the Success of Affirmative Action

Thomas Sowell of the Hoover Institute has shown in his book *Preferential Policies: An International Perspective* that preferential hiring almost never solves social problems. It generally builds in mediocrity or incompetence and causes deep resentment. It is a short-term solution which lacks serious grounding in social realities.

For instance, Sowell cites some disturbing statistics on education. Although twice as many blacks as Asian students took the nationwide Scholastic Aptitude Test in 1983, approximately fifteen times as many Asian students scored above 700 (out of a possible 800) on the mathematics half of the SAT. The percentage of Asians who scored above 700 in math was also more than six times higher than the percentage of American Indians and more than ten times higher than that of Mexican Americans—as well as more than double the percentage of whites. As Sowell points out, in all countries studied, "intergroup performance disparities are huge" (108).

> There are dozens of American colleges and universities where the median combined verbal SAT score and mathematics SAT score total 1200 or above. As of 1983 there were fewer than 600 black students in the entire US with combined SAT scores of 1200. This meant that, despite widespread attempts to get a black student "representation" comparable to the black percentage of the population (about 11 percent), there were not enough black students in the entire country for the Ivy League alone to have such a "representation" without going beyond this pool— even if the entire pool went to the eight Ivy League colleges.[23]

Often it is claimed that a cultural bias is the cause of the poor performance of blacks on SATs (or IQ tests), but Sowell shows that these test scores are actually a better predictor of college performance for blacks than for Asians and whites. He also shows the harmfulness of the effect on blacks of preferential acceptance. At the University of California, Berkeley, where the freshman class closely reflects the actual ethnic distribution of California high school students, more than 70 percent of blacks fail to graduate. All 312 black students entering Berkeley in 1987 were admitted under "affirmative action" criteria rather than by meeting standard academic criteria. So were 480 out of 507 Hispanic students. In 1986 the median SAT score for blacks at Berkeley was 952, for Mexican Americans 1,014, for American Indians 1,082 and for Asian Americans 1,254. (The average SAT for all students was 1,181.)

The result of this mismatching is that blacks who might do well if they went to a second-tier or third-tier school where their test scores would indicate they belong, actually are harmed by preferential treatment. They cannot compete in the institutions where high abilities are necessary.

Sowell also points out that affirmative action policies have mainly assisted middle-class blacks, those who have suffered least from discrimination. "Black couples in which both husband and wife are college-educated overtook white couples of the same description back in the early 1970s and continued to at least hold their own in the 1980s" (115).

Sowell's conclusion is that similar patterns of results obtained from India to the United States wherever preferential policies exist. "In education, preferential admissions policies have led to high attrition rates and substandard performances for those preferred students . . . who survived to graduate." In all countries the preferred tended to concentrate in less difficult subjects which lead to less remunerative careers. "In the employment market, both blacks and untouchables at the higher levels have advanced substantially while those at the lower levels show no such advancement and even some signs of retrogression. These patterns are also broadly consistent with patterns found in countries in which majorities have created preferences for themselves. . . " (116).

The tendency has been to focus at the high-level end of education and employment rather than on the lower level of family structure and early education. But if we really want to help the worst off improve, we need to concentrate on the family and early education. It is foolish to expect equal results when we begin with grossly unequal starting points—and discriminating against young white males is no more just than discriminating against women, blacks or anyone else.

Conclusion

Let me sum up. The goal of the Civil Rights movement and of moral people everywhere has been equal opportunity. The question is: How best to get there? Civil Rights legislation removed the legal barriers to equal opportunity, but did not tackle the deeper causes that produced differential results. Weak affirmative action aims at encouraging minorities in striving for the highest positions without unduly jeopardizing the rights of majorities, but the problem of weak affirmative action is that it easily slides into strong affirmative action where quotas, "goals," and equal results are forced into groups, thus promoting mediocrity, inefficiency, and resentment. Furthermore, affirmative action aims at the higher levels of society—universities and skilled jobs—yet if we want to improve our society, the best way to do it is to concentrate on families, children, early education, and the like. Affirmative action is, on the one hand, too much, too soon and on the other hand, too little, too late.

Martin Luther said that humanity is like a man mounting a horse who always tends to fall off on the other side of the horse. This seems to be the case with affirmative action. Attempting to redress the discriminatory iniquities of our history, our well-intentioned social engineers engage in new forms of discriminatory iniquity and thereby think that they have successfully mounted the horse of racial harmony. They have only fallen off on the other side of the issue.[24]

Endnotes

1. Quoted in William Bradford Reynolds, "Affirmative Action is Unjust" in D. Bender and B. Leone (eds.), *Social Justice* (St. Paul, MN, 1984), p. 23.

2. Some of the material in this section is based on Nicholas Capaldi's *Out of Order: Affirmative Action and the Crisis of Doctrinaire Liberalism* (Buffalo, NY, 1985), chapters 1 and 2. Capaldi, using the shackled runner analogy, divides the history into three stages: a *platitude stage* "in which it is reaffirmed that the race is to be fair, and a fair race is one in which no one has either special disadvantages or special advantages (equal opportunity)"; a *remedial stage* in which victims of past discrimination are to be given special help in overcoming their disadvantages; and a *realignment stage* "in which all runners will be reassigned to those positions on the course that they would have had if the race had been fair from the beginning" (p. 18f).

3. Wanda Warren Berry, "Affirmative Action is Just" in D. Bender, *op. cit.,* p. 18.

4. Robert Fullinwider, *The Reverse Discrimination Controversy* (Totowa, NJ, 1970), p. 25.

5. Quoted in Fullinwider, *op. cit.,* p. 4f.

6. See Lino A. Graglia, "'Affirmative Action,' the Constitution, and the 1964 Civil Rights Act," *Measure,* no. 92 (1991).

7. Linda Gottfredson, "Letters to the Editor," *New York Times,* Aug. 1, 1990 issue. Gender-norming is also a feature of the proponents of affirmative action. Michael Levin begins his book *Feminism and Freedom* (New Brunswick, 1987) with federal court case *Beckman v. NYFD* in which 88 women who failed the New York City Fire Department's entrance exam in 1977 filed a class-action sex discrimination suit. The court found that the physical strength component of the test was not job-related, and thus a violation of Title VII of the Civil Rights Act, and

ordered the city to hire forty-nine of the women. It further ordered the fire department to devise a special, less-demanding physical strength exam for women. Following EEOC guidelines, if the passing rate for women is less than 80 percent that of the passing rate of men, the test is presumed invalid.

8. Thomas Sowell, *Preferential Policies: An International Perspective* (New York. I 990).

9. John Arthur, *The Unfinished Constitution* (Belmont, CA, 1990), p. 238.

10. See Phillip E. Vernon's excellent summary of the literature in *Intelligence: Heredity and Environment* (New York, 1979) and Yves Christen "Sex Differences in the Human Brain" in Nicholas Davidson (ed.), *Gender Sanity* (Lanham, 1989) and T. Bouchard et al., "Sources of Human Psychological Differences: The Minnesota Studies of Twins Reared Apart," *Science,* vol. 250 (1990).

11. See Michael Levin, "Is Racial Discrimination Special?" *Policy Review,* Fall issue (1982).

12. Judith Jarvis Thomson, "Preferential Hiring" in Marshall Cohen, Thomas Nagel and Thomas Scanlon (eds.), *Equality and Preferential Treatment* (Princeton, 1977).

13. John Rawls, *A Theory of Justice* (Cambridge, 1971), p. 104; See Richard Wasserstrom "A Defense of Programs of Preferential Treatment," *National Forum* (Phi Kappa Phi Journal), vol. 58 (1978). See also Bernard Boxill, "The Morality of Preferential Hiring," *Philosophy and Public Affairs,* vol. 7 (1978).

14. Michael Kinsley, "Equal Lack of Opportunity," *Harper's,* June issue (1983).

15. There is one other argument which I have omitted. It is one from precedence and has been stated by Judith Jarvis Thomson in the article cited earlier:

"Suppose two candidates for a civil service job have equally good test scores, but only one job is available. We could decide between them by coin-tossing. But in fact we do allow for declaring for *A* straightaway, where *A* is a veteran, and *B* is not. It may be that *B* is a non-veteran through no fault of his own. . . . Yet the fact is that *B* is not a veteran and *A* is. On the assumption that the veteran has served his country, the country owes him something. And it is plain that giving him preference is not an unjust way in which part of that debt of gratitude can be paid" (p. 379f).

The two forms of preferential hiring are analogous. Veteran's preference is justified as a way of paying a debt of gratitude; preferential hiring is a way of paying a debt of compensation. In both cases innocent parties bear the burden of the community's debt, but it is justified.

My response to this argument is that veterans should not be hired in place of better qualified candidates, but that benefits like the GI scholarships are part of the contract with veterans who serve their country in the armed services. The notion of compensation only applies to individuals who have been injured by identifiable entities. So the analogy between veterans and minority groups seems weak.

16. Quoted in Jim Sleeper, *The Closest of Strangers* (New York, 1990), p. 209.

17. Shelby Steele, "A Negative Vote on Affirmative Action," *New York Times,* May 13, 1990 issue.

18. *New York Times,* May 10, 1990 issue.

19. Nicholas Capaldi, *op. cit.,* p. 85.

20. Cited in Capaldi, *op. cit.,* p. 95.

21. *Ibid.*

22. The extreme form of this New Speak is incarnate in the Politically Correct Movement ("PC" ideology) where a new orthodoxy has emerged, condemning white, European culture and seeing African culture as the new savior of us all. Perhaps the clearest example of this is Paula Rothenberg's book *Racism and Sexism* (New York, 1987) which asserts that there is no such thing as black racism; only whites are capable of racism (p. 6). Ms. Rothenberg's book has been scheduled as required reading for all freshmen at the University of Texas. See Joseph Salemi, "Lone Star Academic Politics," no. 87 (1990).

23. Thomas Sowell, *op. cit.,* p. 108.

24. I am indebted to Jim Landesman, Michael Levin, and Abigail Rosenthal for comments on a previous draft of this paper. I am also indebted to Nicholas Capaldi's *Out of Order* for first making me aware of the extent of the problem of affirmative action.

31. *Racism and Justice*

GERTRUDE EZORSKY

Gertrude Ezorsky argues that affirmative action is not unfair to white workers because they have gained from past racism and because the success of other minorities does not show that there is no need for affirmative action. She further argues that the rule of hiring by competence has been subject to so many exceptions that adding an exception for affirmative action would not constitute a significant departure from current practice.

The ultimate goal of AA for blacks is occupational integration, that is, their approximate statistical representation in the hierarchy of employment as in the population at large. That goal was criticized by sociologists Daniel Bell and Nathan Glazer.

Reprinted by permission of Cornell University Press and the author.

According to Bell, the logic of the claim for such racial representation implies that all groups—political conservatives, for example—should have balanced representation throughout employment.[1]

Not so. Suppose both political conservatives and blacks are "underrepresented" on a university faculty. Surely the context of underrepresentation for each group is relevantly different. Because of the devastating impact of overt and institutional racism, blacks are disproportionately excluded from desirable employment and positions of power *throughout* society. No relevantly similar context exists for political conservatives. Hence while conservatives may be "underrepresented" in some pocket of employment, their situation is not analogous to the situation of blacks. I conclude that an AA commitment to parity in employment for blacks does not imply the same commitment for all groups.

Glazer claims that the goal of statistical representation of minorities in employment ignores "certain realities of community":

> Racial and ethnic communities have expressed themselves in occupations and work groups. Distinctive histories have channelled ethnic and racial groups into one kind of work or another, and this is the origin of many of the "unrepresentative" work distributions we see. These distributions have been maintained by an occupational tradition linked to an ethnic community which makes it easier for the Irish to become policemen, the Italians fruit dealers, Jews businessmen, and so on.[2]

It is true that tradition has channeled some groups into certain types of work. But while Glazer reminds us that because of historic tradition the Irish have become policemen, he fails to mention the "distinctive history" that has "channeled" blacks into the most miserable work, the distinctive history of two centuries of slavery and the murderous racism of the post-Reconstruction century. I suggest that black persons have not expressed themselves in such labor. Indeed, when offered opportunities by affirmative action programs, they were perfectly ready to express themselves in better jobs.

The Success of Other Minorities

Other minorities in the United States—European immigrants, for example—who have been victimized by discrimination moved up in American society without the assistance of AA measures. The success of other persecuted groups, such as the Jews, has suggested to some individuals that fault for the depressed status of blacks may lie not in racism but in them-

selves.[3] If this view is correct, the justification for AA appears questionable.

The situations of yesterday's European white immigrants and blacks are not analogous, however. Ethnic prejudice was not as virulent or pervasive as racism. White immigrants could assimilate while blacks were forced, in many states by law and the threat of lynching and in other states by unwritten law, to remain segregated from white society. Indeed, overt racism contributed to the occupational ascent of newly arrived whites. For many such whites eviction of a black worker from a job was the beginning of upward mobility. Thus white immigrants drove black employees out of railroads, streetcars, construction, and shipbuilding. The influx of whites into Birmingham's mills destroyed the concentration of blacks in a number of trades. When New York City's European immigrant population reached 76 percent of the total population, eviction of blacks was intensified. They were steadily pushed out of their jobs as wagon and coach drivers, house painters, tailors, longshore workers, brick layers, and waiters.[4]

According to sociologist Robert Blauner, Jewish, Irish, Italian, and German immigrants benefited from racism. For example, decent jobs were usurped from northern blacks by incoming Germans, Irish, and Italians, and as a consequence these black workers were driven into the marginal reaches of the economy. He concludes: "Without such a combination of immigration and white racism, the Harlems and the South Chicagos might have become solid working class and middle-class communities with the economic and social resources to absorb and aid the incoming masses of [black] Southerners, much as the European ethnic groups have been able to do for their newcomers."[5]

Also, the attitude of trade unions toward white immigrants and blacks differed sharply. In the early twentieth century, trade unions contributed to the impoverishment of black people by excluding them, as did the craft unions, or, like the powerful International Ladies' Garment Workers Union, by cooperating in their segregation into the lowest-paid employment. On the other hand, European immigrants established an "ethnic lock" on types of employment or on craft-union jurisdiction. Thus in New York there was a Greek furriers' local, an Italian dressmakers' union, a Jewish waiters' organization, and so forth.[6]

Thomas Sowell claims that recent immigrants who became racial minorities in the United States—such as the Asians and West Indians—are significantly more successful than native blacks and rival whites in achievements.[7] However, many of these recent arrivals have an initial advantage over native blacks. International migration from third-world countries to the United States is highly selective, bringing in skilled, educated persons, among whom are scientists, engineers, doctors, and academics. Such selectivity has created an international "brain drain."[8] Such immigrants are likely to set high economic goals for themselves because they arrive with economic and social-class advantages, such as substantial capital, as well as occupational and business experience.[9] According to a study of Koreans in New York City, the advantage of class resources attained in their homeland—higher education, professional experience, economic motivation, and money—provided "decisive" support for their success in small business. The Korean case is only one example of the importance of social-class origins for such success.[10]

Although Asian immigrants have been drawn disproportionately from occupational elites, the more recent immigrants among them include a large number of unskilled and uneducated workers, whose lives provide a sharp contrast to the Asian success story. In Chinatown, they labor long hours in restaurants and sweatshops for miserable wages, without hope of advancement. For these "Downtown Chinese," crime—break-ins, drug trafficking, and street shootouts by armed teenagers—ranks as one of their most serious problems.[11]

It is true that West Indian black immigrants have been more successful occupationally than African Americans. The virtual absence of a white working class in the West Indian homeland, where blacks held majority status, facilitated their acquisition of skilled trades. According to a study of U.S. immigration records in the 1920s, West Indians had advantages in literacy and skills, advantages that are conducive to an achievement orientation and that would tend to be replicated in their children. Although later West Indian migrants were more occupationally diverse, they benefited from this preexisting community, which provided patronage for West Indian professionals and entrepreneurs.[12]

Such advantages have contributed to the greater ability of West Indians, by comparison with African Americans, to meet the race-neutral qualification standards of employers and to ascend the occupational ladder. An analysis of the Census of 1980, however, does not corroborate the view that West Indian economic achievement rivals that of whites. According to that analysis, family income and male earnings of blacks of West Indian ancestry are significantly inferior to whites. In New York City a native white male college graduate can expect to earn 50 percent more than an equally educated black male of West Indian ancestry. In the South a native white male high-school graduate can expect to earn 60 percent more than an equally educated black of West Indian descent.[13]

In her introduction to a collection of 1987 studies of black immigrants in New York City, Nancy Foner points out that West Indians are "stigmatized as blacks." "Used to societies where blacks were a majority and where education, income and culture partially 'erased' one's blackness, West Indians find that their skin color now brands them as inferior to the white majority and that they face racial discrimination in housing, employment and innumerable personal encounters."[14]

The Rights of Employers

According to libertarian philosophers, laws that require any type of AA in the workplace—indeed, those merely requiring passive nondiscrimination—violate the rights of private employers. The philosopher Robert Nozick suggests that the right of employers to hire is relevantly similar to the right of individuals to marry.[15] Just as individuals should be free to marry whomever they please, so private entrepreneurs should be free to employ whomever they please, and government should not interfere with employers in their hiring decisions.

But surely the freedom to choose one's spouse and the freedom to select one's employees are relevantly different. Individuals denied such freedom of choice in marriage are forced to give their bodies to their spouses. They are subject to rape—a destructive, brutal, and degrading intrusion. Marital choices belong to the deeply personal sphere where indeed government should keep out. State intervention in employment is another matter. To require that an auto plant hire some black machinists falls outside the sphere of the deeply personal; it is not, like rape, a destructive, brutal, and degrading personal intrusion. I conclude that the analogy between freedom to marry and freedom to hire fails.[16]

The Rights of White Candidates

According to some philosophers, while the social goal of preferential treatment may be desirable, the moral cost is too high. The burden it imposes on adversely affected whites violates their right to equal treatment. They are unfairly singled out for sacrifice. Thomas Nagel states that "the most important argument against preferential treatment is that it subordinates the individual's right to equal treatment to broader social aims."[17]

Some proponents of preferential treatment reject the charge of unfairness because, as they see the matter, whites have either been responsible for immoral racist practices or have gained from them. According to this claim, all whites *deserve* to pay the cost of preferential treatment (hereafter, the desert claim).[18] I do not accept the desert claim; indeed, I suggest that the criticism of racial preference as unfair to adversely affected whites is not without merit. The relevant point is not that such preference be abandoned but rather that it be implemented differently.

According to the desert claim, whites have either been responsible for racism or passively benefited from it. Let us examine the responsibility claim first.

Certainly no one has demonstrated that all whites, or even a majority, are responsible for racism. How then shall the culpable whites be identified? Many employers and unions have certainly engaged in either overt racism or avoidable neutral practices that obviously excluded blacks. Perhaps they should pay the cost of discrimination remedies by, for example, continuing to pay blacks laid off by race-neutral seniority? But, on the other hand, some employers and union officials were not responsible for racist injury to blacks, and they do not deserve to pay the cost of a remedy for racism.

Similar problems arise when we attempt to identify those who passively benefited from racist practices. Let us assume that such beneficiaries do bear a measure of culpability for racism. How can we mark them out?

The salient fact is that white workers have *both* gained and lost from racism. On the one hand, the benefits to white workers from racism—overt and institutional—are undeniable. As a group, they have been first in line for hiring, training, promotion, and desirable job assignment, but last in line for seniority-based layoff. As white, they have also benefited from housing discrimination in areas where jobs could be had and from the racist impact of selection based on personal connections, seniority, and qualifications. Indeed many white candidates fail to realize that their superior qualifications may be due to their having attended predominantly white schools.

On the other hand, white workers have also lost because of racism. As a divisive force, racism harms labor, both black and white. Since blacks have more reason to fear management reprisal, they are less unwilling to work under excessive strain or for lower wages. This attitude, although quite understandable, makes it more difficult for labor, white as well as black, to attain better working conditions. I give two illustrations:

In the early 1970s a speedup was established in an auto factory whereby jobs performed by a unit of whites were assigned to a smaller group of blacks. The heavier work load then became the norm for everyone. White workers who complained were told that if they couldn't do the job, there were people who would.[19]

In 1969, an AT&T vice-president informed the assembled presidents of all Bell companies: "We must have access to an ample supply of people who will work at comparatively low rates of pay.... That means lots of black people." He explained that, of the persons available to work for "as little as four to five thousand a year," two-thirds were blacks.[20]

The willingness of blacks to accept lower wages and adverse working conditions reduces labor's bargaining power generally with management.

Racism also has inhibited the formation of trade unions. In the South, racism, because it impedes union organization, contributed to the low wage level of both white and black workers. Also some northern employers, attracted by cheaper labor costs, moved their plants—with their jobs—to the South. A labor historian summed up the divisive effect of racism: "Hiring black laborers . . . fit[s] conveniently into the anti-union efforts of many industrialists. . . . A labor force divided along ethnic and racial lines poses great difficulties for union organizers; by importing blacks, a cheap work force could be gained and unionization efforts weakened at the same time.[21]

On the whole, some white workers have lost and some have gained from racism. But to disentangle the two groups is a practical impossibility; the blameworthy cannot be marked off from the innocent.

Meritocratic Critics

Some AA critics, whom I shall call meritocrats, believe that justice in the workplace is exemplified by selection according to merit standards. Hence they claim that racial preference violates the rights of more qualified white candidates. Note the difference between the meritocratic argument and the singling-out criticism. . . . The meritocratic claim implies that the rights of rejected, more qualified whites are violated only because they are better qualified. Hence the meritocratic argument, unlike the singling-out criticism, has no bearing on racial preference in seniority-based selection.

Before we appraise the meritocratic criticism, a digression from the issue of preferential treatment will be useful. The meritocratic view conflicts with AA only when operative standards of competence are reduced by AA preference; however, there is a widespread perception that (seniority aside), all AA measures conflict with merit criteria. Hence I will show at the outset that certain types of AA, including some apparently preferential measures, actually raise the level of performance. I will then appraise the meritocratic criticism where it does apply, that is, to cases where preferential treatment would reduce competence on the job.

As indicated earlier, according to the employment guidelines upheld in *Griggs* (but now weakened), qualification requirements having exclusionary racial impact must pinpoint abilities needed for job per-

formance. When enforced, these guidelines created increased interest in ensuring that such job requirements really measure ability to do the job. Thus one of the most compelling reasons for concern that licensing examinations be effective competence measures has been enforcement of these guidelines. According to a survey reported in the *New York Times*, such enforcement has contributed to a "concerted effort" by "occupational and professional groups" to ensure that their certification tests are "job relevant."[22] In 1986 the executive officer of the American Psychological Association stated: "On the specific issues addressed in the Guidelines, . . . psychologists generally agree that the caliber of employment practices in organizations has improved dramatically since [their 1978] publication."[23]

As a consequence of AA programs, black children see more black persons as teachers, administrators, and professionals. Having such role models tends to improve the self-image, vocational aspirations, and learning ability of black students, thereby increasing the pool of qualified candidates available for training and employment, a development that is likely to raise merit standards.

Some AA measures, then, such as permitting only job-related testing, improve job-selection processes. But what, generally speaking, has been the effect of AA on work performance? According to economist Jonathan S. Leonard, while productivity estimates based on direct tests are too imprecise for a compelling conclusion either way, such tests of the effect of AA in increasing employment opportunities for blacks show no significant evidence of a productivity decline.[24]

Let us return now to a consideration of the meritocratic critique that focuses solely on preferential treatment. Whatever the effect of AA measures in their entirety, it is true that racial preference for a less qualified black can, in specific situations, reduce effective job performance. According to meritocrats, such selection violates the rights of adversely affected white candidates. Thus the philosopher Alan Goldman states:

Unless reverse discrimination violates some *presently accepted rule for hiring* it will not be seriously unjust in the current social context. . . . The *currently accepted* rule which I believe to be just is that of *hir-*

ing by competence. . . . In addition to its vast utility, competence is some barometer of prior effort. Thus society, it seems, does have a right in the name of welfare and equal opportunity to impose a rule for hiring, and the general rule ought to be hiring the most competent. This means that those individuals who attain maximal competence for various positions acquire rights through their efforts to those positions. (emphases added)[25]

Let us assume that insofar as maximally qualified candidates have exerted effort to attain positions under an accepted and just rule, they have a prima facie right to such positions. But the fact is that, contrary to Goldman, hiring the most competent candidate is not the "currently accepted" rule in employment. Being the most qualified candidate is indeed one way to get the job, but employers' ignoring of merit standards and their explicit preference for specific groups are widespread. Merit criteria are either ignored or undermined in several ways.

In accordance with a traditional legal principle—employment "at will"—private U.S. employers have had the right to discharge their workers without a reasonable cause based on work performance. This principle gives employers the legal right to dismiss qualified employees merely for refusing to support political candidates of the employer's choice or for expressing unpopular views on the job or even in the privacy of their own homes. An employer's right to arbitrary discharge without reasonable cause is hardly compatible with a merit system. Although the employer's right to discharge is now restricted by specific exceptions identified in union contracts and in federal and state laws (e.g., prohibiting race and sex discrimination), employment at will is still a significant legal principle in U.S. courts.[26]

Competent job performance has also been undermined by the widespread use of unvalidated employment tests and irrelevant subjective standards for hiring and promotion.

As I described earlier, federal and state governments have continuously given employment preference to veterans, thereby excluding large numbers of more qualified nonveterans.

Many employees obtain their vocational qualifications in colleges and professional schools. In some such institutions preference for admission has been extended to children of alumni. After Allan Bakke sued the University of California medical school, it was revealed that the dean had been permitted to select some admittees without reference to the usual screening process. As one writer noted, "The dean's 'special admissions program' was evidently devoted to the *realpolitik* of sustaining influential support for the school."[27]

Seniority-based selection for training, promotion, and retention in layoff is commonly practiced in both the private and public sector of the economy. Such selection is based on years of service, not evaluation of job performance. Adherence to meritocratic principles would in some situations require the abolition of seniority criteria for reward.

As emphasized earlier, reliance on personal connections is probably the most widely used recruitment method in American employment, a practice that often works against a merit system. An incumbent's graduate-school friend, the boss's nephew, or a political-patronage appointee is frequently not the most qualified person available for the job.

Note too that gaining promotion through social networks within the firm may have a corrupting effect on job performance as well as on moral character. The employee may see pandering to the right people as the best route to success.

Because traditionally accepted preference is so widespread, some blacks selected by AA preference may in fact replace less qualified whites who would have been chosen by such traditional preference.

I conclude that merit selection is not, as Goldman claims, the currently accepted rule. Goldman states, however, that unless preferential treatment violates a currently accepted rule it is not "seriously unjust."[28] In that case, preferential treatment is not seriously unjust.

A different version of the meritocratic claim might be that although hiring the best candidate is not the currently accepted rule and because (as Goldman says) merit selection has social utility, such selection *ought* to be the rule, and thus preferential treatment should not be extended to blacks. According to this meritocratic claim, all practices that often conflict with merit standards, such as selection by seniority ranking, veteran status, and powerful personal connections, should be eliminated. In that case, why not begin the struggle for merit in American employment by calling for an end to these practices? Why start by excluding members of a largely poor and powerless group, such as black people?

Let us focus on the consequences simply of denying preference to basically qualified blacks. Let us assume that this denial would produce some gain in social utility—that is, efficiency. That benefit would, I suggest, weigh very little in the moral balance against the double accomplishment of preferential treatment: compensation to blacks for past wrongs against them and achieving what this nation has never known—occupational integration, racial justice in the workplace.

Endnotes

1. Daniel Bell, "On Meritocracy and Equality," *Public Interest*, February 1972: 37–38.

2. Nathan Glazer, *Affirmative Discrimination* (New York: Basic Books, 1975), p. 203.

3. "Jews have moved up in American life by utilizing middle-class skills—reason, orderliness, conservation of capital, and a high valuation and use of education. . . . Finding that playing by 'the rules of the game'—reward based on merit, training and seniority—has worked for them, many Jews wonder why Negroes do not utilize the same methods for getting ahead." Murray Friedman describes this view without endorsing it in "The Jews," in *Through Different Eyes,* ed. Peter I. Rose et al. (New York: Oxford University Press, 1973), pp. 52–53.

4. Herbert Hill, "Race, Ethnicity, and Organized Labor: The Opposition to Affirmative Action," *New Politics I,* n.s. (1987): 45–52.

5. Robert Blauner, *Racial Oppression in America* (New York: Harper and Row, 1972), p. 64.

6. Hill, pp. 51–52.

7. Thomas Sowell, *Civil Rights: Rhetoric or Reality?* (New York: Quill, William Morrow, 1984), esp. pp. 77, 130–131.

8. Thomas D. Boston, *Race, Class, and Conservatism* (Boston: Unwin Hyman, 1988), p. 88.

9. Nancy Foner, "New Immigrants and Changing Patterns in New York City," in *New Immigrants in New York,* ed. Nancy Foner (New York: Columbia University Press, 1987), pp. 14–15.

10. Foner, pp. 14–15.

11. Peter Kwong, *The New Chinatown* (New York: Noonday Press, Farrar, Straus, and Giroux, 1987), pp. 5–7, 120–124.

12. Stephen Steinberg, *The Ethnic Myth: Race, Ethnicity, and Class in America*, updated and expanded ed. (Boston: Beacon Press, 1989), pp. 275–279.

13. Reynolds Farley, "West Indian Success: Myth or Fact?" (unpublished manuscript, Ann Arbor, Mich.: Population Studies Center, University of Michigan, 1987).

14. Foner, "New Immigrants," p. 11.

15. "If the woman who later became my wife rejected another suitor . . . would the rejected less intelligent and less handsome suitor have a legitimate complaint about unfairness . . . (Against whom would the rejected suitor have a legitimate complaint? Against what?). . . . The major objection to speaking of everyone's having a right to various things such as *equality of opportunity,* life and so on, and enforcing this right, is that these 'rights' require a substructure of things and materials and actions; and *other* people may have rights and entitlements over these" (Robert Nozick, *Anarchy, State, and Utopia* [New York: Basic Books, 1974], pp. 237–238; first and third emphases in original; second added).

16. Libertarians deny the right of government to interfere with private employers not only in hiring but also in determining working conditions, as by enacting minimum-wage laws and so forth. Libertarians such as Robert Nozick, however, could consistently claim such employer entitlement only for those employers who have either acquired their enterprises through efforts that satisfy an acceptable principle of justice or who received them (e.g., by inheritance) from individuals whose original acquisition and transfer satisfy these principles. But I know of no plausible historical evidence to show that, generally speaking, American private enterprises have been acquired and transferred in accordance with such moral principles. Absent such evidence, a libertarian endorsement of any general moral entitlement by private entrepreneurs today, over employment conditions in their firms, lacks a libertarian justification.

17. Thomas Nagel, *Introduction to Equality and Preferential Treatment,* ed. Marshall Cohen, Thomas Nagel, and

Thomas Scanlon (Princeton, N.J.: Princeton University Press, 1977), p. viii.

18. Steven S. Schwarzschild, "American History, Marked by Racism," *New Politics I* (1987): 56–58.

19. Victor Perlo, *Economics of Racism U.S.A.* (New York: International Publishers, 1975), p. 172.

20. *"A Unique Competence": A Study of Equal Employment Opportunity in the Bell System,* prepared by the Equal Employment Opportunity Commission, 1972.

21. Clement T. Imhoff, "The Recruiter," in *Working Lives,* ed. Mark S. Miller (New York: Pantheon, 1974), p. 56. For a comprehensive analysis of Marxian views of racial antagonisms within the working class, see Boxill, chap 3.

22. Nancy Rubin, "Consumer and Government Forces Pushing for Job Competency Tests," *New York Times,* November 11, 1979.

23. *Oversight Hearings on EEOC's Proposed Modification of Enforcement Regulations, Including Uniform Guidelines on Employee Selection Procedures,* Hearings before the Subcommittee on Employment Opportunities of the Committee on Education and Labor, House of Representatives (Washington, D.C.: U.S. Government Printing Office 1986), p. 211. Ronald Dworkin, a legal philosopher writing on the *Bakke* case, makes a similar point about racially preferential admissions to medical school. "If [merit] . . . means . . . that a medical school should choose candidates that it supposes will make the most useful doctors, then everything turns on the judgement of what factors make different doctors useful. . . . Black skin may be a socially useful trait in particular circumstances" ("Why Bakke Has No Case," *New York Review of Books,* November 10, 1977: 13–14).

24. Jonathan S. Leonard, "The Impact of Affirmative Action Regulation and Equal Employment Law on Black Employment," *Journal of Economic Perspectives* 4 (1990): 61–62.

25. Alan Goldman, "Limits to the Justification of Reverse Discrimination," *Social Theory and Practice 3* (1975): 289–291.

26. *Coppage v. Kansas,* 236 U.S. 441 (1914); Burton Hall, "Collective Bargaining and Workers' Liberty," in *Moral Rights in the Workplace,* ed. Gertrude Ezorsky (New York: State University of New York Press, 1987), pp. 161–165.

27. Allan P. Sindler, *Bakke, DeFunis, and Minority Admissions* (New York: Longman, 1978), p. 69n. This practice was ended in 1977.

28. See Goldman.

32. *Affirmative Racism*

CHARLES MURRAY

Charles Murray argues that preferential treatment for blacks has actually worked against their interest by encouraging a new form of racism that tacitly accepts the view that blacks are temporarily less competent than whites. The problem with this new form of racism, Murray claims, is that it perpetuates the race-based inequality it seeks to eliminate.

A few years ago, I got into an argument with a lawyer friend who is a partner in a New York firm. I was being the conservative, arguing that preferential treatment of blacks was immoral; he was being the liberal, urging that it was the only way to bring blacks to full equality. In the middle of all this he abruptly said, "But you know, let's face it. We must have hired at least ten blacks in the last few years, and none of them has really worked out." He then returned to his case for still stronger affirmative action, while I wondered what it had been like for those ten blacks. And if he could make a remark like that so casually, what remarks would he be able to make some years down the

From *The New Republic* (December 31, 1984). Reprinted by permission of *The New Republic* 1984, The New Republic, Inc.

road, if by that time it had been fifty blacks who hadn't "really worked out"?

My friend's comment was an outcropping of a new racism that is emerging to take its place alongside the old. It grows out of preferential treatment for blacks, and it is not just the much-publicized reactions, for example, of the white policemen or firemen who are passed over for promotion because of an affirmative action court order. The new racism that is potentially most damaging is located among the white elites—educated, affluent, and occupying the positions in education, business, and government from which this country is run. It currently focuses on blacks; whether it will eventually extend to include Hispanics and other minorities remains to be seen.

The new racists do not think blacks are inferior. They are typically longtime supporters of civil rights. But they exhibit the classic behavioral symptom of racism: They treat blacks differently from whites, because of their race. The results can be as concretely bad and unjust as any that the old racism produces. Sometimes the effect is that blacks are refused an education they otherwise could have gotten. Sometimes blacks are shunted into dead-end jobs. Always, blacks are denied the right to compete as equals.

The new racists also exhibit another characteristic of racism: They *think* about blacks differently from the way they think about whites. Their global view of blacks and civil rights is impeccable. Blacks must be enabled to achieve full equality. They are still unequal, through no fault of their own (it is the fault of racism, the fault of inadequate opportunity, the legacy of history). But the new racists' local view is that the blacks they run across professionally are not, on the average, up to the white standard. Among the new racists, lawyers have gotten used to the idea that the brief a black colleague turns in will be less rehearsed and argued than the one they would have done. Businessmen expect that a black colleague will not read a balance sheet as subtly as they do. Teachers expect black students to wind up at the bottom of the class.

The new racists also tend to think of blacks as a commodity. The office must have a sufficient supply of blacks, who must be treated with special delicacy. The personnel problems this creates are more difficult than most because whites barely admit to themselves what's going on.

What follows is a foray into very poorly mapped territory. I will present a few numbers that explain much about how the process gets started. But the ways that the numbers get translated into behavior are even more important. The cases I present are composites constructed from my own observations and taken from firsthand accounts. All are based on real events and real people, stripped of their particularities. But the individual cases are not intended as evidence, because I cannot tell you how often they happen. They have not been the kind of thing that social scientists or journalists have wanted to count. I am writing this because so many people, both white and black, to whom I tell such stories know immediately what I am talking about. It is apparent that a problem exists. How significant is it? What follows is as much an attempt to elicit evidence as to present it.

As in so many of the crusades of the 1960s, the nation began with a good idea. It was called "affirmative action," initiated by Lyndon Johnson through Executive Order 11246 in September 1965. It was an attractive label and a natural corrective to past racism: actively seek out black candidates for jobs, college, or promotions, without treating them differently in the actual decision to hire, admit, or promote. The term originally evoked both the letter and the spirit of the order.

Then, gradually, affirmative action came to mean something quite different. In 1970 a federal court established the legitimacy of quotas as a means of implementing Johnson's executive order. In 1971 the Supreme Court ruled that an employer could not use minimum credentials as a prerequisite for hiring if the credentials acted as a "built-in headwind" for minority groups—even when there was no discriminatory intent and even when the hiring procedures were "fair in form." In 1972 the Equal Employment Opportunity Commission acquired broad, independent enforcement powers.

Thus by the early 1970s it had become generally recognized that a good-faith effort to recruit qualified blacks was not enough—especially if one's school depended on federal grants or one's business depended on federal contracts. Even for businesses and schools not directly dependent on the government, the simplest way to withstand an accusation of violating Title VII of the Civil Rights Act of 1964 was to make sure not that they had not just interviewed enough minority candidates, but that they had actually hired or admitted enough of them. Employers and admissions committees arrived at a rule of thumb: If the blacks who are available happen to be the best candidates, fine; if not, the best available black candidates will be given some sort of edge in the selection process. Sometimes the edge will be small; sometimes it will be predetermined that a black candidate is essential, and the edge will be very large.

Perhaps the first crucial place where the edge applies is in admission to college. Consider the cases of the following three students: John, William, and Carol, 17 years old and applying to college, are all equal on paper. Each has a score of 520 in the mathematics section of the Scholastic Aptitude Test, which puts them in the top third—at the 67th percentile—of all students who took the test. (Figures are based on 1983 data.)

John is white. A score of 520 gets him into the state university. Against the advice of his high school counselor, he applies to a prestigious school, Ivy U., where his application is rejected in the first cut—its average white applicant has math scores in the high 600s.

William is black, from a middle-class family who sent him to good schools. His score of 520 puts him at the 95th percentile of all blacks who took the test. William's high school counselor points out that he could probably get into Ivy U. William applies and is admitted—Ivy U. uses separate standards for admission of whites and blacks, and William is among the top blacks who applied.

Carol is black, educated at an inner city school, and her score of 520 represents an extraordinary achievement in the face of terrible schooling. An alumnus of Ivy U. who regularly looks for promising inner city candidates finds her, recruits her, and sends her off with a full scholarship to Ivy U.

When American universities embarked on policies of preferential admissions by race, they had the Carols in mind. They had good reason to be optimistic that preferential treatment would work—for many years, the best universities had been weighting the test scores of applicants from small-town public schools when they were compared against those of applicants from the top private schools, and had been giving special breaks to students from distant states to ensure geographic distribution. The differences in preparation tended to even out after the first year or so. Blacks were being brought into a long-standing and successful tradition of preferential treatment.

In the case of blacks, however, preferential treatment ran up against a large black-white gap in academic performance combined with ambitious goals for proportional representation. This gap has been the hardest for whites to confront. But though it is not necessary or even plausible to believe that such differences are innate, it is necessary to recognize openly that the differences exist. By pretending they don't, we begin the process whereby both the real differences and the racial factor are exaggerated.

The black-white gap that applies most directly to this discussion is the one that separates blacks and whites who go to college. In 1983, for example, the mean Scholastic Aptitude Test score for all blacks who took the examination was more than 100 points below the white score on both the verbal and the math sections. Statistically, it is an extremely wide gap. To convert the gap into more concrete terms, think of it this way: In 1983, the same Scholastic Aptitude Test math score that put a black at the 50th percentile of all blacks who took the test put him at the 16th percentile of all whites who took the test.

These results clearly mean we ought to be making an all-out effort to improve elementary and secondary education for blacks. But that doesn't help much now, when an academic discrepancy of this magnitude is fed into a preferential admissions process. As universities scramble to make sure they are admitting enough blacks, the results feed the new racism. Here's how it works:

In 1983, only 66 black students nationwide scored above 700 in the verbal section of the Scholastic Aptitude Test, and only 205 scored above 700 in the mathematics section. This handful of students cannot begin to meet the demand for blacks with such scores. For example, Harvard, Yale, and Princeton have in recent years been bringing an aggregate of about 270 blacks into each entering class. If the black students entering these schools had the same distribution of scores as that of the freshman class as a whole, then every black student in the nation with a verbal score in the 700s, and roughly 70 percent of the ones with a math score in the 700s, would be in their freshman classes.

The main problem is not that a few schools monop-olize the very top black applicants, but that these same schools have much larger implicit quotas than they can fill with those applicants. They fill out the rest with the next students in line—students who would not have gotten into these schools if they were not black, who otherwise would have been showing up in the classrooms of the nation's less glamorous col-leges and universities. But the size of the black pool does not expand appreciably at the next levels. The number of blacks scoring in the 600s on the math section in 1983, for example, was 1,531. Meanwhile, 31,704 nonblack students in 1983 scored in the 700s on the math section and 121,640 scored in the 600s. The prestige schools cannot begin to absorb these num-bers of other highly qualified freshmen, and they are perforce spread widely throughout the system.

At schools that draw most broadly from the stu-dent population, such as the large state universities, the effects of this skimming produce a situation that confirms the old racists in everything they want most to believe. There are plenty of outstanding students in such student bodies (at the University of Colorado, for example, 6 percent of the freshmen in 1981 had math scores in the 700s and 28 percent had scores in the 600s), but the skimming process combined with the very small raw numbers means that almost none of them are black. What students and instructors see in their day-to-day experience in the classroom is a disproportionate number of blacks who are below the white average, relatively few blacks who are at the first rank. The image that the white student carries away is that blacks are less able than whites.

I am not exalting the SAT as an infallible measure of academic ability, or pointing to test scores to try to convince anyone that blacks are performing below the level of whites. I am simply using them to explain what instructors and students already notice, and talk about, among themselves.

They do not talk openly about such matters. One characteristic of the new racism is that whites deny in public but acknowledge in private that there are sig-nificant differences in black and white academic per-formance. Another is that they dismiss the importance of tests when black scores are at issue, blaming cul-tural bias and saying that test scores are not good predictors of college performance. At the same time,

they watch anxiously over their own children's test scores.

The differences in academic performance do not disappear by the end of college. Far from narrowing, the gap separating black and white academic achieve-ment appears to get larger. Various studies, most re-cently at Harvard, have found that during the 1970s blacks did worse in college (as measured by grade point average) than their test scores would have pre-dicted. Moreover, the black-white gap in the Graduate Record Examination is larger than the gap in the Scholastic Aptitude Test. The gap between black and white freshmen is a bit less than one standard devia-tion (the technical measure for comparing scores). Black and white seniors who take the Graduate Rec-ord Examination reveal a gap of about one and a quarter standard deviations.

Why should the gap grow wider? Perhaps it is an illusion—for example, perhaps a disproportionate number of the best black students never take the examination. But there are also reasons for suspecting that in fact blacks get a worse education in college than whites do. Here are a few of the hypotheses that deserve full exploration.

Take the situation of William—a slightly above-average student who, because he is black, gets into a highly competitive school. William studies very hard during the first year. He nonetheless gets mediocre grades. He has a choice. He can continue to study hard and continue to get mediocre grades, and be seen by his classmates as a black who cannot do very well. Or he can explicitly refuse to engage in the academic game. He decides to opt out, and his performance gets worse as time goes on. He emerges from college with a poor education and is further behind the whites than he was as a freshman.

If large numbers of other black students at the institution are in the same situation as William, the result can be group pressure not to compete academi-cally. (At Harvard, it is said, the current term among black students for a black who studies like a white is "incognegro.") The response is not hard to under-stand. If one subpopulation of students is conspicu-ously behind another population and is visibly iden-tifiable, then the population that is behind must come up with a good excuse for doing poorly. "Not wanting to do better" is as good as any.

But there is another crucial reason why blacks might not close the gap with whites during college: They are not taught as well as whites are. Racist teachers impeding the progress of students? Perhaps, but most college faculty members I know tend to bend over backward to be "fair" to black students—and that may be the problem. I suggest that inferior instruction is more likely to be a manifestation of the new racism than the old.

Consider the case of Carol, with outstanding abilities but deprived of decent prior schooling: She struggles the first year, but she gets by. Her academic skills still show the aftereffects of her inferior preparation. Her instructors diplomatically point out the more flagrant mistakes, but they ignore minor lapses, and never push her in the aggressive way they push white students who have her intellectual capacity. Some of them are being patronizing (she is doing quite well, considering). Others are being prudent: Teachers who criticize black students can find themselves being called racists in the classroom, in the campus newspaper, or in complaints to the administration.

The same process continues in graduate school. Indeed, because there are even fewer blacks in graduate schools than in undergraduate schools, the pressure to get black students through to the degree, no matter what, can be still greater. But apart from differences in preparation and ability that have accumulated by the end of schooling, the process whereby we foster the appearance of black inferiority continues. Let's assume that William did not give up during college. He goes to business school, where he gets his Masters degree. He signs up for interviews with the corporate recruiters. There are one hundred persons in his class, and William is ranked near the middle. But of the five blacks in his class, he ranks first (remember that he was at the 95th percentile of blacks taking the Scholastic Aptitude Test). He is hired on his first interview by his first-choice company, which also attracted the very best of the white students. He is hired alongside five of the top-ranking white members of the class.

William's situation as one of five blacks in a class of one hundred illustrates the proportions that prevail in business schools, and business schools are by no means one of the more extreme examples. The pool of black candidates for any given profession is a small fraction of the white pool. This works out to a 20-to-1 edge in business; it is even greater in most of the other professions. The result, when many hiring institutions are competing, is that a major gap between the abilities of new black and white employees in any given workplace is highly likely. Everyone needs to hire a few blacks, and the edge that "being black" confers in the hiring decision warps the sequence of hiring in such a way that a scarce resource (the blacks with a given set of qualifications) is exhausted at an artificially high rate, producing a widening gap in comparison with the remaining whites from which an employer can choose.

The more aggressively affirmative action is enforced, the greater the imbalance. In general, the first companies to hire can pursue strategies that minimize or even eliminate the difference in ability between the new black and white employees. IBM and Park Avenue law firms can do very well, just as Harvard does quite well in attracting the top black students. But the more effectively they pursue these strategies, the more quickly they strip the population of the best black candidates.

To this point I have been discussing problems that are more or less driven by realities we have very little hope of manipulating in the short term except by discarding the laws regarding preferential treatment. People do differ in acquiring abilities. Currently, acquired abilities in the white and black populations are distributed differently. Schools and firms do form a rough hierarchy when they draw from these distributions. The results follow ineluctably. The dangers they represent are not a matter of statistical probabilities, but of day-to-day human reactions we see around us.

The damage caused by these mechanistic forces should be much less in the world of work than in the schools, however. Schools deal in a relatively narrow domain of skills, and "talent" tends to be assigned specific meanings and specific measures. Workplaces deal in highly complex sets of skills, and "talent" consists of all sorts of combinations of qualities. A successful career depends in large part upon finding jobs that elicit and develop one's strengths.

At this point the young black professional must sidestep a new series of traps laid by whites who need to be ostentatiously nonracist. Let's say that William goes to work for the XYZ Corporation, where he is assigned with another management trainee (white) to a department where much of the time is spent preparing proposals for government contracts. The white trainee is assigned a variety of scut work— proofreading drafts, calculating the costs of minor items in the bid, making photocopies, taking notes at conferences. William gets more dignified work. He is assigned portions of the draft to write (which are later rewritten by more experienced staff), sits in on planning sessions, and even goes to Washington as a highly visible part of the team to present the bid. As time goes on, the white trainee learns a great deal about how the company operates, and is seen as a go-getting young member of the team. William is perceived to be a bright enough fellow, but not much of a detail man and not really much of a self-starter.

Even if a black is hired under terms that put him on a par with his white peers, the subtler forms of differential treatment work against him. Particularly for any corporation that does business with the government, the new employee has a specific, immediate value purely because he is black. There are a variety of requirements to be met and rituals to be observed for which a black face is helpful. These have very little to do with the long-term career interests of the new employee; on the contrary, they often lead to a dead end as head of the minority-relations section of the personnel department.

Added to this is another problem that has nothing to do with the government. When the old racism was at fault (as it often still is), the newly hired black employee was excluded from the socialization process because the whites did not want him to become part of the group. When the new racism is at fault, it is because many whites are embarrassed to treat black employees as badly as they are willing to treat whites. Hence another reason that whites get on-the-job training that blacks do not: Much of the early training of an employee is intertwined with menial assignments and mild hazing. Blacks who are put through these routines often see themselves as racially abused (and when a black is involved, old-racist responses may well have crept in). But even if the black is not unhappy about the process, the whites are afraid that he is, and so protect him from it. There are many variations, all having the same effect: The black is denied an apprenticeship that the white has no way of escap-

ing. Without serving the apprenticeship, there is no way of becoming part of the team.

Carol suffers a slightly different fate. She and a white woman are hired as reporters by a major newspaper. They both work hard, but after a few months there is no denying it: Neither one of them can write. The white woman is let go. Carol is kept on, because the paper cannot afford to have any fewer blacks than it already has. She is kept busy with reportorial work, even though they have to work around the writing problem. She is told not to worry—there's lots more to being a journalist than writing.

It is the mascot syndrome. A white performing at a comparable level would be fired. The black is kept on, perhaps to avoid complications with the Equal Employment Opportunity Commission (it can be very expensive to fire a black), perhaps out of a more diffuse wish not to appear discriminatory. Everybody pretends that nothing is wrong—but the black's career is at a dead end. The irony, of course, is that the white who gets fired and has to try something else has been forced into accepting a chance of making a success in some other line of work whereas the black is seduced into *not* taking the same chance.

Sometimes differential treatment takes an even more pernicious form: the conspiracy to promote a problem out of existence. As part of keeping Carol busy, the newspaper gives her some administrative responsibilities. They do not amount to much. But she has an impressive title on a prominent newspaper and she is black—a potent combination. She gets an offer from a lesser paper in another part of the country to take a senior editorial post. Her current employer is happy to be rid of an awkward situation and sends along glowing references. She gets a job that she is unequipped to handle—only this time, she is in a highly visible position, and within a few weeks the deficiencies that were covered up at the old job have become the subject of jokes all over the office. Most of the jokes are openly racist.

It is important to pause and remember who Carol is: an extremely bright young woman, not (in other circumstances) a likely object of condescension. But being bright is no protection. Whites can usually count on the market to help us recognize egregious career mistakes and to prevent us from being promoted too far from a career line that fits our strengths, and too far above our level of readiness. One of the most prevalent characteristics of white differential treatment of blacks has been to exempt blacks from these market considerations, substituting for them a market premium attached to race.

The most obvious consequence of preferential treatment is that every black professional, no matter how able, is tainted. Every black who is hired by a white-run organization that hires blacks preferentially has to put up with the knowledge that many of his coworkers believe he was hired because of his race; and he has to put up with the suspicion in his own mind that they might be right.

Whites are curiously reluctant to consider this a real problem—it is an abstraction, I am told, much less important than the problem that blacks face in getting a job in the first place. But black professionals talk about it, and they tell stories of mental breakdowns; of people who had to leave the job altogether; of long-term professional paralysis. What white would want to be put in such a situation? Of course it would be a constant humiliation to be resented by some of your coworkers and condescended to by others. Of course it would affect your perceptions of yourself and your self-confidence. No system that produces such side effects—as preferential treatment *must* do—can be defended unless it is producing some extremely important benefits.

And that brings us to the decisive question. If the alternative were no job at all, as it was for so many blacks for so long, the resentment and condescension are part of the price of getting blacks into the positions they deserve. But is that the alternative today? If the institutions of this country were left to their own devices now, to what extent would they refuse to admit, hire, and promote people because they were black? To what extent are American institutions kept from being racist by the government's intervention?

It is another one of those questions that are seldom investigated aggressively, and I have no evidence. Let me suggest a hypothesis that bears looking into: that the signal event in the struggle for black equality during the last thirty years, the one with real impact, was not the Civil Rights Act of 1964 or Executive Order 11246 or any other governmental act. It was the civil rights movement itself. It raised to a pitch of acute and lasting discomfort the racial consciousness of the

generations of white Americans who are now running the country. I will not argue that the old racism is dead at any level of society. I will argue, however, that in the typical corporation or in the typical admissions office, there is an abiding desire to be not-racist. This need not be construed as brotherly love. Guilt will do as well. But the civil rights movement did its job. I suggest that the laws and the court decisions and the continuing intellectual respectability behind preferential treatment are not holding many doors open to qualified blacks that would otherwise be closed.

Suppose for a moment that I am right. Suppose that, for practical purposes, racism would not get in the way of blacks if preferential treatment were abandoned. How, in my most optimistic view, would the world look different?

There would be fewer blacks at Harvard and Yale; but they would all be fully competitive with the whites who were there. White students at the state university would encounter a cross-section of blacks who span the full range of ability, including the top levels, just as whites do. College remedial courses would no longer be disproportionately black. Whites rejected by the school they wanted would quit assuming they were kept out because a less-qualified black was admitted in their place. Blacks in big corporations would no longer be shunted off to personnel-relations positions, but would be left on the mainline tracks toward becoming comptrollers and sales managers and chief executive officers. Whites would quit assuming that black colleagues had been hired because they were black. Blacks would quit worrying that they had been hired because they were black.

Would blacks still lag behind? As a population, yes, for a time, and the nation should be mounting a far more effective program to improve elementary and secondary education for blacks than it has mounted in the last few decades. But in years past virtually every ethnic group in America has at one time or another lagged behind as a population, and has eventually caught up. In the process of catching up, the ones who breached the barriers were evidence of the success of that group. Now blacks who breach the barriers tend to be seen as evidence of the inferiority of that group.

And that is the evil of preferential treatment. It perpetuates an impression of inferiority. The system segments whites and blacks who come in contact with each other so as to maximize the likelihood that whites have the advantage in experience and ability. The system then encourages both whites and blacks to behave in ways that create self-fulfilling prophecies even when no real differences exist.

It is here that the new racism links up with the old. The old racism has always openly held that blacks are permanently less competent than whites. The new racism tacitly accepts that, in the course of overcoming the legacy of the old racism, blacks are temporarily less competent than whites. It is an extremely fine distinction. As time goes on, fine distinctions tend to be lost. Preferential treatment is providing persuasive evidence for the old racists, and we can already hear it *sotto voce*: "We gave you your chance, we let you educate them and push them into jobs they couldn't have gotten on their own and coddle them every way you could. And see: They still aren't as good as whites,

and you are beginning to admit it yourselves." Sooner or later this message will be heard by a white elite that needs to excuse its failure to achieve black equality.

The only happy aspect of the new racism is that the corrective—to get rid of the policies encouraging preferential treatment—is so natural. Deliberate preferential treatment by race has sat as uneasily with America's equal-opportunity ideal [since 1965] as it did during the days of legalized segregation. We had to construct tortuous rationalizations when we permitted blacks to be kept on the back of the bus—and the rationalizations to justify sending blacks to the head of the line have been just as tortuous. Both kinds of rationalization say that sometimes it is all right to treat people of different races in different ways. For years, we have instinctively sensed this was wrong in principle but intellectualized our support for it as an expedient. I submit that our instincts were right. There is no such thing as good racial discrimination.

---

33. *Reverse Racism*

STANLEY FISH

Stanley Fish argues that just as it would be a mistake to equate Zionism with Nazi racism, it would be a mistake to equate affirmative action with the racism that blacks have suffered in this country. He further argues that what looks like a level playing field to some is actually a tilted field favoring those who are culturally advantaged.

I take my text from George Bush, who, in an address to the United Nations on September 23, 1991, said this of the UN resolution equating Zionism with racism: "Zionism . . . is the idea that led to the creation of a home for the Jewish people. . . . And to equate Zionism with the intolerable sin of racism is to twist history and forget the terrible plight of Jews in World War II and indeed throughout history." What happened in

Reprinted by the permission of the *Atlantic Monthly* and the author.

the Second World War was that six million Jews were exterminated by people who regarded them as racially inferior and a danger to Aryan purity. What happened after the Second World War was that the survivors of that Holocaust established a Jewish state—that is, a state centered on Jewish history, Jewish values, and Jewish traditions: in short, a Jewocentric state. What President Bush objected to was the logical sleight of hand by which these two actions were declared equivalent because they were both expressions of racial exclusiveness. Ignored, as Bush said, was the *historical* difference between them—the difference between a program of genocide and the determination of those who escaped it to establish a community in which they would be the makers, not the victims, of the laws.

Only if racism is thought of as something that occurs principally in the mind, a falling-away from proper notions of universal equality, can the desire of a victimized and terrorized people to band together be declared morally identical to the actions of their would-be executioners. Only when the actions of the two groups are detached from the historical conditions of their emergence and given a purely abstract description can they be made interchangeable. Bush was saying to the United Nations, "Look, the Nazis' conviction of racial superiority generated a policy of systematic genocide; the Jews' experience of centuries of persecution in almost every country on earth generated a desire for a homeland of their own. If you manage somehow to convince yourself that these are the same, it is you, not the Zionists, who are morally confused, and the reason you are morally confused is that you have forgotten history."

A Key Distinction

What I want to say, following Bush's reasoning, is that a similar forgetting of history has in recent years allowed some people to argue, and argue persuasively, that affirmative action is reverse racism. The very phrase "reverse racism" contains the argument in exactly the form to which Bush objected: In this country whites once set themselves apart from blacks and claimed privileges for themselves while denying them to others. Now, on the basis of race, blacks are claiming special status and reserving for themselves privileges they deny to others. Isn't one as bad as the other? The answer is no. One can see why by imagining that it is not 1993 but 1955, and that we are in a town in the South with two more or less distinct communities, one white and one black. No doubt each community would have a ready store of dismissive epithets, ridiculing stories, self-serving folk myths, and expressions of plain hatred, all directed at the other community, and all based in racial hostility. Yet to regard their respective racisms—if that is the

word—as equivalent would be bizarre, for the hostility of one group stems not from any wrong done to it but from its wish to protect its ability to deprive citizens of their voting rights, to limit access to educational institutions, to prevent entry into the economy except at the lowest and most menial levels, and to force members of the stigmatized group to ride in the back of the bus. The hostility of the other group is the result of these actions, and whereas hostility and racial anger are unhappy facts wherever they are found, a distinction must surely be made between the ideological hostility of the oppressors and the experience-based hostility of those who have been oppressed.

Not to make that distinction is, adapting George Bush's words, to twist history and forget the terrible plight of African-Americans in the more than 200 years of this country's existence. Moreover, to equate the efforts to remedy that plight with the actions that produced it is to twist history even further. Those efforts, designed to redress the imbalances caused by long-standing discrimination, are called affirmative action; to argue that affirmative action, which gives preferential treatment to disadvantaged minorities as part of a plan to achieve social equality, is no different from the policies that created the disadvantages in the first place is a travesty of reasoning. "Reverse racism" is a cogent description of affirmative action only if one considers the cancer of racism to be morally and medically indistinguishable from the therapy we apply to it. A cancer is an invasion of the body's equilibrium, and so is chemotherapy; but we do not decline to fight the disease because the medicine we employ is also disruptive of normal functioning. Strong illness, strong remedy: The formula is as appropriate to the health of the body politic as it is to that of the body proper.

At this point someone will always say, "But two wrongs don't make a right; if it was wrong to treat blacks unfairly, it is wrong to give blacks preference and thereby treat whites unfairly." This objection is just another version of the forgetting and rewriting of history. The work is done by the adverb "unfairly," which suggests two more or less equal parties, one of whom has been unjustly penalized by an incompetent umpire. But blacks have not simply been treated unfairly; they have been subjected first to decades of slavery, and then to decades of second-class citizenship, widespread legalized discrimination, economic persecution, educational deprivation, and cultural stigmatization. They have been bought, sold, killed, beaten, raped, excluded, exploited, shamed, and scorned for a very long time. The word "unfair" is hardly an adequate description of their experience, and the belated gift of "fairness" in the form of a resolution no longer to discriminate against them legally is hardly an adequate remedy for the deep disadvantages that the prior discrimination has produced. When the deck is stacked against you in more ways than you can even count, it is small consolation to hear that you are now free to enter the game and take your chances.

A Tilted Field

The same insincerity and hollowness of promise infect another formula that is popular with the anti–affirmative-action crowd: the formula of the level playing field. Here the argument usually takes the form of saying "It is undemocratic to give one class of citizens advantages at the expense of other citizens; the truly democratic way is to have a level playing field to which everyone has access and where everyone has a fair and equal chance to succeed on the basis of his or her merit." Fine words—but they conceal the facts of the situation as it has been given to us by history: The playing field is already tilted in favor of those by whom and for whom it was constructed in the first place. If mastery of the requirements for entry depends upon immersion in the cultural experiences of the mainstream majority, if the skills that make for success are nurtured by institutions and cultural practices from which the disadvantaged minority has been systematically excluded, if the language and ways of comporting oneself that identify a player as "one of us" are alien to the lives minorities are forced to live, then words like "fair" and "equal" are cruel jokes, for what they promote and celebrate is an institutionalized unfairness and a perpetuated inequality. The playing field is already tilted, and the resistance to altering it by the mechanisms of affirmative action is in fact a determination to make sure that the present imbalances persist as long as possible.

One way of tilting the field is the Scholastic Aptitude Test. This test figures prominently in Dinesh

D'Souza's book *Illiberal Education* (1991), in which one finds many examples of white or Asian students denied admission to colleges and universities even though their SAT scores were higher than the scores of some others—often African-Americans—who were admitted to the same institution. This, D'Souza says, is evidence that as a result of affirmative action policies colleges and universities tend "to depreciate the importance of merit criteria in admissions." D'Souza's assumption—and it is one that many would share—is that the test does in fact measure *merit*, with merit understood as a quality objectively determined in the same way that body temperature can be objectively determined.

In fact, however, the test is nothing of the kind. Statistical studies have suggested that test scores reflect income and socioeconomic status. It has been demonstrated again and again that scores vary in relation to cultural background; the test's questions assume a certain uniformity in educational experience and lifestyle and penalize those who, for whatever reason, have had a different experience and lived different kinds of lives. In short, what is being measured by the SAT is not absolutes like native ability and merit but accidents like birth, social position, access to libraries, and the opportunity to take vacations or to take SAT prep courses.

Furthermore, as David Owen notes in *None of the Above: Behind the Myth of Scholastic Aptitude* (1985), the "correlation between SAT scores and college grades . . . is lower than the correlation between weight and height; in other words you would have a better chance of predicting a person's height by looking at his weight than you would of predicting his freshman grades by looking only at his SAT scores." Everywhere you look in the SAT story, the claims of fairness, objectivity, and neutrality fall away, to be replaced by suspicions of specialized measures and unfair advantages.

Against this background a point that in isolation might have a questionable force takes on a special and even explanatory resonance: The principal deviser of the test was an out-and-out racist. In 1923 Carl Campbell Brigham published a book called *A Study of American Intelligence*, in which, as Owen notes, he declared, among other things, that we faced in America "a possibility of racial admixture . . . infinitely worse than that faced by any European country today, for we are incorporating the Negro into our racial stock, while all of Europe is comparatively free of this taint." Brigham had earlier analyzed the Army Mental Tests using classifications drawn from another racist text, Madison Grant's *The Passing of the Great Race,* which divided American society into four distinct racial strains, with Nordic, blue-eyed, blond people at the pinnacle and the American Negro at the bottom. Nevertheless, in 1925 Brigham became a director of testing for the College Board, and developed the SAT. So here is the great SAT test, devised by a racist in order to confirm racist assumptions, measuring not native ability but cultural advantage, an uncertain indicator of performance, an indicator of very little except what money and social privilege can buy. And it is in the name of this mechanism that we are asked to reject affirmative action and reaffirm "the importance of merit criteria in admissions."

The Reality of Discrimination

Nevertheless, there is at least one more card to play against affirmative action, and it is a strong one. Granted that the playing field is not level and that access to it is reserved for an already advantaged elite, the disadvantages suffered by others are less racial—at least in 1993—than socioeconomic. Therefore shouldn't, as D'Souza urges, "universities . . . retain their policies of preferential treatment, but alter their criteria of application from race to socioeconomic disadvantage," and thus avoid the unfairness of current policies that reward middle-class or affluent blacks at the expense of poor whites? One answer to this question is given by D'Souza himself when he acknowledges that the overlap between minority groups and the poor is very large—a point underscored by the former Secretary of Education Lamar Alexander, who said, in response to a question about funds targeted for black students, "Ninety-eight percent of race-specific scholarships do not involve constitutional problems." He meant, I take it, that 98 percent of race-specific scholarships were also scholarships to the economically disadvantaged.

Still, the other two percent—nonpoor, middle-class, economically favored blacks—are receiving special attention on the basis of disadvantages they do not experience. What about them? The force of the question depends on the assumption that in this day and age race could not possibly be a serious disadvantage to those who are otherwise well positioned in the society. But the lie was given dramatically to this assumption in a 1991 broadcast of the ABC program *PrimeTime Live.* In a stunning fifteen-minute segment reporters and a camera crew followed two young men of equal education, cultural sophistication, level of apparent affluence, and so forth around St. Louis, a city where neither was known. The two differed in only a single respect: One was white, the other black. But that small difference turned out to mean everything. In a series of encounters with shoe salesmen, record-store employees, rental agents, landlords, employment agencies, taxicab drivers, and ordinary citizens, the black member of the pair was either ignored or given a special and suspicious attention. He was asked to pay more for the same goods or come up with a larger down payment for the same car, was turned away as a prospective tenant, was rejected as a prospective taxicab fare, was treated with contempt and irritation by clerks and bureaucrats, and in every way possible was made to feel inferior and unwanted.

The inescapable conclusion was that alike though they may have been in most respects, one of these young men, because he was black, would lead a significantly lesser life than his white counterpart: He would be housed less well and at greater expense; he would pay more for services and products when and if he was given the opportunity to buy them; he would have difficulty establishing credit; the first emotions he would inspire on the part of many people he met would be distrust and fear; his abilities would be discounted even before he had a chance to display them; and, above all, the treatment he received from minute to minute would chip away at his self-esteem and self-confidence with consequences that most of us could not even imagine. As the young man in question said at the conclusion of the broadcast, "You walk down the street with a suit and tie and it doesn't matter. Someone will make determinations about you . . . that affect the quality of your life."

Of course, the same determinations are being made quite early on by kindergarten teachers, grade school principals, high school guidance counselors, and the like, with results that cut across socioeconomic lines and place young black men and women in the ranks of the disadvantaged no matter what the bank accounts of their parents happen to show. Racism is a cultural fact, and although its effects may . . . be diminished by socioeconomic variables, those effects will still be sufficiently great to warrant the nation's attention and thus the continuation of affirmative action policies. This is true even of the field thought to be dominated by blacks and often cited as evidence of the equal opportunities society now affords them. I refer, of course, to professional athletics. But national self-congratulation on this score might pause in the face of a few facts: A minuscule number of African-Americans ever receive a paycheck from a professional team. Even though nearly 1,600 daily newspapers report on the exploits of black athletes, they employ only seven full-time black sports columnists. Despite repeated pledges and resolutions, major-league teams have managed to put only a handful of blacks and Hispanics in executive positions.

Why Me?

When all is said and done, however, one objection to affirmative action is unanswerable on its own terms, and that is the objection of the individual who says, "Why me? Sure, discrimination has persisted for many years, and I acknowledge that the damage done has not been removed by changes in the law. But why me? I didn't own slaves; I didn't vote to keep people on the back of the bus; I didn't turn water hoses on civil-rights marchers. Why, then, should I be the one who doesn't get the job or who doesn't get the scholarship or who gets bumped back to the waiting list?"

I sympathize with this feeling, if only because in a small way I have had the experience that produces it. I was recently nominated for an administrative post at a large university. Early signs were encouraging, but . . . I received official notice that I would not be included at the next level of consideration, and . . . was told unofficially that at some point a decision had been made to look only in the direction of women and minorities. Although I was disappointed, I did not conclude that the situation was "unfair," because the policy was obviously not directed at me—at no point

in the proceedings did someone say, "Let's find a way to rule out Stanley Fish." Nor was it directed even at persons of my race and sex—the policy was not intended to disenfranchise white males. Rather, the policy was driven by other considerations, and it was only as a by-product of those considerations—not as the main goal—that white males like me were rejected. Given that the institution in question has a high percentage of minority students, a very low percentage of minority faculty, and an even lower percentage of minority administrators, it made perfect sense to focus on women and minority candidates, and within that sense, not as the result of prejudice, my whiteness and maleness became disqualifications.

I can hear the objection in advance: "What's the difference? Unfair is unfair: You didn't get the job; you didn't even get on the short list." The difference is not in the outcome but in the ways of thinking that led up to the outcome. It is the difference between an unfairness that befalls one as the unintended effect of a policy rationally conceived and an unfairness that is pursued as an end in itself. It is the difference between the awful unfairness of Nazi extermination camps and the unfairness to Palestinian Arabs that arose from, but was not the chief purpose of, the founding of a Jewish state.

The New Bigotry

The point is not a difficult one, but it is difficult to see when the unfairness scenarios are presented as simple contrasts between two decontextualized persons who emerge from nowhere to contend for a job or a place in a freshman class. Here is student A; he has a board score of 1,300. And here is student B; her board score is only 1,200, yet she is admitted and A is rejected. Is that fair? Given the minimal information provided, the answer is of course no. But if we expand our horizons and consider fairness in relation to the cultural and institutional histories that have brought the two students to this point, histories that weigh on them even if they are not the histories' authors, then both the question and the answer suddenly grow more complicated.

The sleight-of-hand logic that first abstracts events from history and then assesses them from behind a veil of willed ignorance gains some of its plausibility from another key word in the anti–affirmative action lexicon. That word is "individual," as in "The American way is to focus on the rights of individuals rather than groups." Now, "individual" and "individualism" have been honorable words in the American political vocabulary, and they have often been well employed in the fight against various tyrannies. But like any other word or concept, individualism can be perverted to serve ends the opposite of those it originally served, and this is what has happened when in the name of individual rights, millions of individuals are enjoined from redressing historically documented wrongs. How is this managed? Largely in the same way that the invocation of fairness is used to legitimize an institutionalized inequality. First one says, in the most solemn of tones, that the protection of individual rights is the chief obligation of society. Then one defines individuals as souls sent into the world with equal entitlements as guaranteed either by their Creator or by the Constitution. Then one pretends that nothing has happened to them since they stepped onto the world's stage. And then one says of these carefully denatured souls that they will all be treated in the same way, irrespective of any of the differences that history has produced. Bizarre as it may seem, individualism in this argument turns out to mean that everyone is or should be the *same*. This dismissal of individual difference in the name of the individual would be funny were its consequences not so serious: It is the mechanism by which imbalances and inequities suffered by millions of people through no fault of their own can be sanitized and even celebrated as the natural workings of unfettered democracy.

"Individualism," "fairness," "merit"—these three words are continually misappropriated by bigots who have learned that they need not put on a white hood or bar access to the ballot box in order to secure their ends. Rather, they need only clothe themselves in a vocabulary plucked from its historical context and made into the justification for attitudes and policies they would not acknowledge if frankly named.

34. *Adarand Constructors* v. *Pena*

THE SUPREME COURT OF THE UNITED STATES

In Adarand Constructors, v. Pena, the issue before the Supreme Court was whether the race-based classifications of the Small Business Act violated Adarand's right to equal protection under the Fifth and Fourteenth Amendments. The majority ruled that the Act did violate Adarand's right to equal protection because it did not meet a standard of strict scrutiny with respect to racial classifications. Justice Stevens, joined by Justice Ginsburg, dissented from the Court's decision.

I.

In 1989, the Central Federal Lands Highway Division (CFLHD), which is part of the United States Department of Transportation, awarded the prime contract for a highway construction project in Colorado to Mountain Gravel & Construction Company. Mountain Gravel then solicited bids from subcontractors for the guardrail portion of the contract. Adarand, a Colorado-based construction company specializing in guardrail work, submitted the low bid. Gonzales Construction Company also submitted a bid.

The prime contract's terms provide that Mountain Gravel would receive additional compensation if it hired subcontractors certified as small businesses controlled by "socially and economically disadvantaged individuals." Gonzales is certified as such a business; Adarand is not. Mountain Gravel awarded the subcontract to Gonzales, despite Adarand's low bid, and Mountain Gravel's Chief Estimator has submitted an affidavit stating that Mountain Gravel would have accepted Adarand's bid, had it not been for the additional payment it received by hiring Gonzales instead. Federal law requires that a subcontracting clause similar to the one used here must appear in most federal agency contracts, and it also requires the clause to state that "[t]he contractor shall presume that socially and economically disadvantaged individuals include Black Americans, Hispanic Americans, Native Americans, Asian Pacific Americans, and other minorities, or any other individual found to be disadvantaged by the [Small Business] Administration pursuant to section 8(a) of the Small Business Act." Adarand claims that the presumption set forth in that statute discriminates on the basis of race in violation of the Federal Government's Fifth Amendment obligation not to deny anyone equal protection of the laws.

These fairly straightforward facts implicate a complex scheme of federal statutes and regulations, to which we now turn. The Small Business Act, as amended, declares it to be "the policy of the United States that small business concerns, [and] small business concerns owned and controlled by socially and economically disadvantaged individuals . . . shall have the maximum practicable opportunity to participate in the performance of contracts let by any Federal agency." The Act defines "socially disadvantaged individuals" as "those who have been subjected to racial or ethnic prejudice or cultural bias because of their identity as a member of a group without regard to their individual qualities," and it defines "economically disadvantaged individuals" as "those socially disadvantaged individuals whose ability to compete in the free-enterprise system has been impaired due to diminished capital and credit opportunities as compared to others in the same business area who are not socially disadvantaged."

. . . The Act establishes "[t]he Government-wide goal for participation by small business concerns owned and controlled by socially and economically disadvantaged individuals" at "not less than 5 percent of the total value of all prime contract and subcontract

awards for each fiscal year." It also requires the head of each Federal agency to set agency-specific goals for participation by businesses controlled by socially and economically disadvantaged individuals.

The Small Business Administration (SBA) has implemented these statutory directives in a variety of ways, two of which are relevant here. One is the "8(a) program," which is available to small businesses controlled by socially and economically disadvantaged individuals as the SBA has defined those terms. The 8(a) program confers a wide range of benefits on participating businesses, one of which is automatic eligibility for subcontractor compensation provisions of the kind at issue in this case (conferring presumptive eligibility on anyone "found to be disadvantaged . . . pursuant to section 8(a) of the Small Business Act"). To participate in the 8(a) program, a business must be 51 percent owned by individuals who qualify as "socially and economically disadvantaged." The SBA presumes that Black, Hispanic, Asian Pacific, Subcontinent Asian, and Native Americans, as well as "members of other groups designated from time to time by SBA," are "socially disadvantaged." It also allows any individual not a member of a listed group to prove social disadvantage "on the basis of clear and convincing evidence." Social disadvantage is not enough to establish eligibility, however; SBA also requires each 8(a) program participant to prove "economic disadvantage." . . .

The other SBA program relevant to this case is the "8(d) subcontracting program," which unlike the 8(a) program is limited to eligibility for subcontracting provisions like the one at issue here. In determining eligibility, the SBA presumes social disadvantage based on membership in certain minority groups, just as in the 8(a) program, and again appears to require an individualized, although "less restrictive," showing of economic disadvantage. A different set of regulations, however, says that members of minority groups wishing to participate in the 8(d) subcontracting program are entitled to a race-based presumption of social *and* economic disadvantage. We are left with some uncertainty as to whether participation in the 8(d) subcontracting program requires an individualized showing of economic disadvantage. . . . In both the 8(a) and the 8(d) programs, the presumptions of disadvantage are rebuttable if a third party comes forward with evidence suggesting that the participant is not, in fact, either economically or socially disadvantaged. . . .

After losing the guardrail subcontract to Gonzales, Adarand filed suit against various federal officials in the United States District Court for the District of Colorado, claiming that the race-based presumptions involved in the use of subcontracting compensation clauses violate Adarand's right to equal protection. The District Court granted the Government's motion for summary judgment. The Court of Appeals for the Tenth Circuit affirmed. It understood our decision in *Fullilove v. Klutznick* (1980) to have adopted "a lenient standard, resembling intermediate scrutiny, in assessing" the constitutionality of federal race-based action. Applying that "lenient standard," as further developed in *Metro Broadcasting, Inc. v. FCC* (1990), the Court of Appeals upheld the use of subcontractor compensation clauses. We granted certiorari. . . .

II.

. . . In 1978, the Court confronted the question whether race-based governmental action designed to benefit such groups should also be subject to "the most rigid scrutiny." *Regents of University of California v. Bakke* involved an equal protection challenge to a state-run medical school's practice of reserving a number of spaces in its entering class for minority students. The petitioners argued that "strict scrutiny" should apply only to "classifications that disadvantage 'discrete and insular minorities.'" *Bakke* did not produce an opinion for the Court, but Justice Powell's opinion announcing the Court's judgment rejected the argument. In a passage joined by Justice White, Justice Powell wrote that "[t]he guarantee of equal protection cannot mean one thing when applied to one individual and something else when applied to a person of another color." He concluded that "[r]acial and ethnic distinctions of any sort are inherently suspect and thus call for the most exacting judicial examination." . . .

Two years after *Bakke*, the Court faced another challenge to remedial race-based action, this time involving action undertaken by the Federal Government. In *Fullilove v. Klutznick* (1980), the Court upheld Congress' inclusion of a 10 percent set-aside for minority-owned businesses in the Public Works Em-

ployment Act of 1977. As in *Bakke*, there was no opinion for the Court. Chief Justice Burger, in an opinion joined by Justices White and Powell, observed that "[a]ny preference based on racial or ethnic criteria must necessarily receive a most searching examination to make sure that it does not conflict with constitutional guarantees." . . .

. . . Justice Powell wrote separately to express his view that the plurality opinion had essentially applied "strict scrutiny" as described in his *Bakke* opinion—*i.e.*, it had determined that the set-aside was "a necessary means of advancing a compelling governmental interest"—and had done so correctly. . . .

In *Wygant v. Jackson Board of Ed.* (1986), the Court considered a Fourteenth Amendment challenge to another form of remedial racial classification. The issue in *Wygant* was whether a school board could adopt race-based preferences in determining which teachers to lay off. Justice Powell's plurality opinion observed that "the level of scrutiny does not change merely because the challenged classification operates against a group that historically has not been subject to governmental discrimination," and stated the two-part inquiry as "whether the layoff provision is supported by a compelling state purpose and whether the means chosen to accomplish that purpose are narrowly tailored." In other words, "racial classifications of any sort must be subjected to 'strict scrutiny.'" The plurality then concluded that the school board's interest in "providing minority role models for its minority students, as an attempt to alleviate the effects of societal discrimination," was not a compelling interest that could justify the use of a racial classification. It added that "[s]ocietal discrimination, without more, is too amorphous a basis for imposing a racially classified remedy," and insisted instead that "a public employer . . . must ensure that, before it embarks on an affirmative action program, it has convincing evidence that remedial action is warranted. That is, it must have sufficient evidence to justify the conclusion that there has been prior discrimination." . . .

The Court's failure to produce a majority opinion in *Bakke*, *Fullilove*, and *Wygant* left unresolved the proper analysis for remedial race-based governmental action. . . .The Court [partly] resolved the issue . . . in 1989. *Richmond v. J.A. Croson Co.* concerned a city's determination that 30 percent of contracting work should go to minority-owned businesses. A majority . . . held that "the standard of review under the Equal Protection Clause is not dependent on the race of those burdened or benefited by a particular classification," and that the single standard of review for racial classifications should be "strict scrutiny." . . .

Despite lingering uncertainty in the details, however, the Court's cases through *Croson* had established three general propositions with respect to governmental racial classifications. First, skepticism: "'Any preference based on racial or ethnic criteria must necessarily receive a most searching examination.'" Second, consistency: "The standard of review under the Equal Protection Clause is not dependent on the race of those burdened or benefited by a particular classification." And third, congruence: "Equal protection analysis in the Fifth Amendment area is the same as that under the Fourteenth Amendment." Taken together, these three propositions lead to the conclusion that any person, of whatever race, has the right to demand that any governmental actor subject to the Constitution justify any racial classification subjecting that person to unequal treatment under the strictest judicial scrutiny. Justice Powell's defense of this conclusion bears repeating here:

> If it is the individual who is entitled to judicial protection against classifications based upon his racial or ethnic background because such distinctions impinge upon personal rights, rather than the individual only because of his membership in a particular group, then constitutional standards may be applied consistently. Political judgments regarding the necessity for the particular classification may be weighed in the constitutional balance, but the standard of justification will remain constant. This is as it should be, since those political judgments are the product of rough compromise struck by contending groups within the democratic process. When they touch upon an individual's race or ethnic background, he is entitled to a judicial determination that the burden he is asked to bear on that basis is precisely tailored to serve a compelling governmental interest. The Constitution guarantees that right to every person regardless of his background.

A year later, however, the Court took a surprising turn. *Metro Broadcasting, Inc. v. FCC* (1990) involved a Fifth Amendment challenge to two race-based policies of the Federal Communications Commission. In *Metro Broadcasting*, the Court repudiated the long-held notion that "it would be unthinkable that the same Constitution would impose a lesser duty on the Federal Government" than it does on a State to afford equal protection of the laws. It did so by holding that "benign" federal racial classifications need only satisfy intermediate scrutiny, . . . even though *Croson* had recently concluded that such classifications enacted by a State must satisfy strict scrutiny. "[B]enign" federal racial classifications, the Court said, "—even if those measures are not 'remedial' in the sense of being designed to compensate victims of past governmental or societal discrimination—are constitutionally permissible to the extent that they serve *important* governmental objectives within the power of Congress and are *substantially related* to achievement of those objectives."

Applying this test, the Court first noted that the FCC policies at issue did not serve as a remedy for past discrimination. Proceeding on the assumption that the policies were nonetheless "benign," it concluded that they served the "important governmental objective" of "enhancing broadcast diversity." It therefore upheld the policies.

By adopting intermediate scrutiny as the standard of review for congressionally mandated "benign" racial classifications, *Metro Broadcasting* departed from prior cases in two significant respects. First, it turned its back on *Croson*'s explanation of why strict scrutiny of all governmental racial classifications is essential:

> Absent searching judicial inquiry into the justification for such race-based measures, there is simply no way of determining what classifications are benign or remedial and what classifications are in fact motivated by illegitimate notions of racial inferiority or simple racial politics. Indeed, the purpose of strict scrutiny is to smoke out illegitimate uses of race by assuring that the legislative body is pursuing a goal important enough to warrant use of a highly suspect tool. The test also ensures that the means chosen fit this compelling goal so closely that there is little or no possibility that the motive for the classification was illegitimate racial prejudice or stereotype.

We adhere to that view today, despite the surface appeal of holding "benign" racial classifications to a lower standard, because "it may not always be clear that a so-called preference is in fact benign."

Second, *Metro Broadcasting* squarely rejected one of the three propositions established by the Court's earlier equal protection cases, namely, congruence between the standards applicable to federal and state racial classifications, and in so doing also undermined the other two—skepticism of all racial classifications, and consistency of treatment irrespective of the race of the burdened or benefited group. Under *Metro Broadcasting*, certain racial classifications ("benign" ones enacted by the Federal Government) should be treated less skeptically than others; and the race of the benefited group is critical to the determination of which standard of review to apply. *Metro Broadcasting* was thus a significant departure from much of what had come before it.

The three propositions undermined by *Metro Broadcasting* all derive from the basic principle that the Fifth and Fourteenth Amendments to the Constitution protect *persons*, not *groups*. It follows from that principle that all governmental action based on race—a *group* classification long recognized as "in most circumstances irrelevant and therefore prohibited"—should be subjected to detailed judicial inquiry to ensure that the *personal* right to equal protection of the laws has not been infringed. These ideas have long been central to this Court's understanding of equal protection, and holding "benign" state and federal racial classifications to different standards does not square with them. "[A] free people whose institutions are founded upon the doctrine of equality" should tolerate no retreat from the principle that government may treat people differently because of their race only for the most compelling reasons. Accordingly, we hold today that all racial classifications, imposed by whatever federal, state, or local governmental actor, must be analyzed by a reviewing court under strict scrutiny. In other words, such classifications are constitutional only if they are narrowly tailored measures that further compelling governmental interests. To the extent that *Metro Broadcasting* is inconsistent with that holding, it is overruled. . . .

Justice *Stevens*, with whom Justice *Ginsburg* joins, dissenting.

Instead of deciding this case in accordance with controlling precedent, the Court today delivers a dis-

concerting lecture about the evils of governmental racial classifications. For its text the Court has selected three propositions, represented by the bywords *skepticism, consistency,* and *congruence*. I shall comment on each of these propositions, then add a few words about *stare decisis,* and finally explain why I believe this Court has a duty to affirm the judgment of the Court of Appeals.

III.

The Court's concept of skepticism is, at least in principle, a good statement of law and of common sense. Undoubtedly, a court should be wary of a governmental decision that relies upon a racial classification. "Because racial characteristics so seldom provide a relevant basis for disparate treatment, and because classifications based on race are potentially so harmful to the entire body politic," a reviewing court must satisfy itself that the reasons for any such classification are "clearly identified and unquestionably legitimate." . . . I welcome its renewed endorsement by the Court today. But, as the opinions in *Fullilove* demonstrate, substantial agreement on the standard to be applied in deciding difficult cases does not necessarily lead to agreement on how those cases actually should or will be resolved. In my judgment, because uniform standards are often anything but uniform, we should evaluate the Court's comments on *consistency, congruence,* and *stare decisis* with the same type of skepticism that the Court advocates for the underlying issue.

IV.

The Court's concept of "consistency" assumes that there is no significant difference between a decision by the majority to impose a special burden on the members of a minority race and a decision by the majority to provide a benefit to certain members of that minority notwithstanding its incidental burden on some members of the majority. In my opinion that assumption is untenable. There is no moral or constitutional equivalence between a policy that is designed to perpetuate a caste system and one that seeks to eradicate racial subordination. Invidious discrimination is an engine of oppression, subjugating a disfavored group to enhance or maintain the power of the majority. Remedial race-based preferences reflect the opposite impulse: a desire to foster equality in society. No sensible conception of the Government's constitutional obligation to "govern impartially" should ignore this distinction.

To illustrate the point, consider our cases addressing the Federal Government's discrimination against Japanese Americans during World War II, *Hirabayashi v. United States* (1943) and *Korematsu v. United States* (1944). The discrimination at issue in those cases was invidious because the Government imposed special burdens—a curfew and exclusion from certain areas on the West Coast—on the members of a minority class defined by racial and ethnic characteristics. Members of the same racially defined class exhibited exceptional heroism in the service of our country during that War. Now suppose Congress decided to reward that service with a federal program that gave all Japanese–American veterans an extraordinary preference in Government employment. If Congress had done so, the same racial characteristics that motivated the discriminatory burdens in *Hirabayashi* and *Korematsu* would have defined the preferred class of veterans. Nevertheless, "consistency" surely would not require us to describe the incidental burden on everyone else in the country as "odious" or "invidious" as those terms were used in those cases. We should reject a concept of "consistency" that would view the special preferences that the National Government has provided to Native Americans since 1834 as comparable to the official discrimination against African Americans that was prevalent for much of our history.

The consistency that the Court espouses would disregard the difference between a "No Trespassing" sign and a welcome mat. It would treat a Dixiecrat Senator's decision to vote against Thurgood Marshall's confirmation in order to keep African Americans off the Supreme Court as on a par with President Johnson's evaluation of his nominee's race as a positive factor. It would equate a law that made black citizens ineligible for military service with a program aimed at recruiting black soldiers. An attempt by the majority to exclude members of a minority race from a regulated market is fundamentally different from a subsidy that enables a relatively small group of newcomers to enter that market. An interest in "consistency" does not justify treating differences as though they were similarities.

The Court's explanation for treating dissimilar race-based decisions as though they were equally objectionable is a supposed inability to differentiate between "invidious" and "benign" discrimination. But the term "affirmative action" is common and well understood. Its presence in everyday parlance shows that people understand the difference between good intentions and bad. As with any legal concept, some cases may be difficult to classify, but our equal protection jurisprudence has identified a critical difference between state action that imposes burdens on a disfavored few and state action that benefits the few "in spite of" its adverse effects on the many. . . .

Moreover, the Court may find that its new "consistency" approach to race-based classifications is difficult to square with its insistence upon rigidly separate categories for discrimination against different classes of individuals. For example, as the law currently stands, the Court will apply "intermediate scrutiny" to cases of invidious gender discrimination and "strict scrutiny" to cases of invidious race discrimination, while applying the same standard for benign classifications as for invidious ones. If this remains the law, then today's lecture about "consistency" will produce the anomalous result that the Government can more easily enact affirmative-action programs to remedy discrimination against women than it can enact affirmative-action programs to remedy discrimination against African Americans—even though the primary purpose of the Equal Protection Clause was to end discrimination against the former slaves. When a court becomes preoccupied with abstract standards, it risks sacrificing common sense at the altar of formal consistency. . . .

The Court's concept of "congruence" assumes that there is no significant difference between a decision by the Congress of the United States to adopt an affirmative-action program and such a decision by a State or a municipality. In my opinion that assumption is untenable. It ignores important practical and legal differences between federal and state or local decision makers.

These differences have been identified repeatedly and consistently both in opinions of the Court and in separate opinions authored by members of today's majority. Thus, in *Metro Broadcasting, Inc. v. FCC* (1990), in which we upheld a federal program designed to foster racial diversity in broadcasting, we identified the special "institutional competence" of our National Legislature. "It is of overriding significance in these cases," we were careful to emphasize, "that the FCC's minority ownership programs have been specifically approved—indeed, mandated—by Congress." We recalled the several opinions in *Fullilove* that admonished this Court to "approach our task with appropriate deference to the Congress, a co-equal branch charged by the Constitution with the power to provide for the . . . general Welfare of the United States" and "to enforce, by appropriate legislation," the equal protection guarantees of the Fourteenth Amendment." We recalled that the opinions of Chief Justice *Burger* and Justice *Powell* in *Fullilove* had "explained that deference was appropriate in light of Congress' institutional competence as the National Legislature, as well as Congress' powers under the Commerce Clause, the Spending Clause, and the Civil War Amendments."

The majority in *Metro Broadcasting* and the plurality in *Fullilove* were not alone in relying upon a critical distinction between federal and state programs. In his separate opinion in *Richmond v. J.A. Croson Co.* (1989), Justice *Scalia* discussed the basis for this distinction. He observed that "it is one thing to permit racially based conduct by the Federal Government—whose legislative powers concerning matters of race were explicitly enhanced by the Fourteenth Amendment, and quite another to permit it by the precise entities against whose conduct in matters of race that Amendment was specifically directed." . . .

In my judgment, the Court's novel doctrine of "congruence" is seriously misguided. Congressional deliberations about a matter as important as affirmative action should be accorded far greater deference than those of a State or municipality.

The Court's concept of *stare decisis* treats some of the language . . . used in explaining our decisions as though it were more important than our actual holdings. In my opinion that treatment is incorrect.

This is the third time in the Court's entire history that it has considered the constitutionality of a federal affirmative-action program. On each of the two prior occasions, the first in 1980, *Fullilove v. Klutznick,* and the second in 1990, *Metro Broadcasting, Inc. v. FCC,* the Court upheld the program. Today the Court explicitly overrules *Metro Broadcasting* (at least in part), *ante,* at 2112–2113, and undermines *Fullilove* by recasting the standard on which it rested and by calling even its holding into question, *ante,* at 2117. By way of explanation, Justice *O'Connor* advises the federal agencies and private parties that have made countless decisions in reliance on those cases that "we do not depart from the fabric of the law; we restore it." A skeptical observer might ask whether this pronouncement is a faithful application of the doctrine of *stare decisis.* A brief comment on each of the two ailing cases may provide the answer.

In the Court's view, our decision in *Metro Broadcasting* was inconsistent with the rule . . . in *Richmond v. J.A. Croson Co.* (1989). But two decisive distinctions separate those two cases. First, *Metro Broadcasting* involved a federal program, whereas *Croson* involved a city ordinance. *Metro Broadcasting* thus drew primary support from *Fullilove,* which predated *Croson* and which *Croson* distinguished on the grounds of the federal-state dichotomy that the majority today discredits. Although members of today's majority trumpeted the importance of that distinction in *Croson,* they now reject it in the name of "congruence." It is therefore quite wrong for the Court to suggest today that overruling *Metro Broadcasting* merely restores the *status quo ante,* for the law at the time of that decision was entirely open to the result the Court reached. *Today's* decision is an unjustified departure from settled law.

Second, *Metro Broadcasting's* holding rested on more than its application of "intermediate scrutiny." Indeed, I have always believed that, labels notwithstanding, the FCC program we upheld in that case would have satisfied any of our various standards in affirmative-action cases—including the one the majority fashions today. What truly distinguishes *Metro Broadcasting* from our other affirmative-action precedents is the distinctive goal of the federal program in that case. Instead of merely seeking to "remedy" past discrimination, the FCC program was intended to achieve future benefits in the form of broadcast diversity. Reliance on race as a legitimate means of achieving diversity was first endorsed by Justice Powell in

Bakke (1978). Later, in *Wygant v. Jackson Board of Education* (1986), I also argued that race is not always irrelevant to governmental decision making; in response, Justice *O'Connor* correctly noted that, although the School Board had relied on an interest in providing black teachers to serve as role models for black students, that interest "should not be confused with the very different goal of promoting racial diversity among the faculty." She then added that because the school board had not relied on an interest in diversity, it was not "necessary to discuss the magnitude of that interest or its applicability in this case."

Thus, prior to *Metro Broadcasting*, the interest in diversity had been mentioned in a few opinions, but it is perfectly clear that the Court had not yet decided whether that interest had sufficient magnitude to justify a racial classification. *Metro Broadcasting*, of course, answered that question in the affirmative. The majority today overrules *Metro Broadcasting* only insofar as it is "inconsistent with [the] holding" that strict scrutiny applies to "benign" racial classifica-

tions promulgated by the Federal Government. The proposition that fostering diversity may provide a sufficient interest to justify such a program is *not* inconsistent with the Court's holding today—indeed, the question is not remotely presented in this case— and I do not take the Court's opinion to diminish that aspect of our decision in *Metro Broadcasting*.

The Court's suggestion that it may be necessary in the future to overrule *Fullilove* in order to restore the fabric of the law is even more disingenuous than its treatment of *Metro Broadcasting*. For the Court endorses the "strict scrutiny" standard that Justice Powell applied in *Bakke*, and acknowledges that he applied that standard in *Fullilove* as well. Moreover, Chief Justice *Burger* also expressly concluded that the program we considered in *Fullilove* was valid under any of the tests articulated in *Bakke*, which of course included Justice *Powell*'s. The Court thus adopts a standard applied in *Fullilove* at the same time it questions that case's continued vitality and accuses it of departing from prior law. . . .

Suggestions for Further Reading

Anthologies

Cahn, Steven. *Affirmative Action and the University*. Philadelphia: Temple University Press. 1993.

Cohen, M., Nagel, T., and Scanlon, T. *Equality and Preferential Treatment*. Princeton, N.J.: Princeton University Press, 1977.

Gould, C. C., and Wartofsky, M. W. *Women and Philosophy*. New York: G. P. Putnam & Sons, 1976.

Gross, B. *Reverse Discrimination*. Buffalo, N.Y.: Prometheus, 1976.

Alternative Views

Bergman, Barbara. *The Economic Emergence of Women*. New York: Basic Books, 1986.

Capaldi, Nicholas. *Out of Order: Affirmative Action and the Crisis of Doctrinaire Liberalism*. Buffalo, N.Y.: Prometheus Press, 1985.

Ezorsky, Gertrude. *Racism and Justice: The Case for Affirmative Action*. Ithaca: Cornell University Press, 1991.

Fullinwider, R. *The Reverse Discrimination Controversy*. Totowa, N.J.: Rowman and Littlefield, 1980.

Goldman, A. *Justice and Reverse Discrimination*. Princeton, N.J.: Princeton University Press, 1979.

Nieli, Russell. *Racial Preference and Racial Justice*. Washington, D.C.: Ethics and Public Policy Center, 1991.

Rosenfeld, Michel. *Affirmative Action and Justice*. New Haven, Conn.: Yale University Press, 1991.

Sowell, T. *Markets and Minorities*. New York: Basic Books, 1981.

Practical Applications

United States Commission on Civil Rights. *Toward an Understanding of Bakke*. Washington, D.C.: U.S. Government Printing Office, 1979.

Section VI

Sexual Harassment

Introduction

Basic Concepts

The moral problem of sexual harassment is the problem of determining the nature of sexual harassment and how to avoid it. Actually, sexual harassment was not recognized by U.S. trial courts as an offense until the late 1970s, and it was only affirmed by the U.S. Supreme Court as an offense in the 1980s. The term *sexual harassment* itself was not even coined until the 1970s. So the moral problem of sexual harassment is one that many people have only recently come to recognize. Obviously, the Senate Judiciary Committee hearings on Anita Hill's charge that Clarence Thomas had sexually harassed her heightened people's awareness of this problem.

In 1980, the Equal Employment Opportunity Commission issued guidelines finding harassment on the basis of sex to be a violation of Title VII of the Civil Rights Act of 1964, labeling sexual harassment "unwelcome sexual advances, requests for sexual favors, and other verbal or physical conduct of a sexual nature" when such behavior occurred in any of three circumstances:

1. Where submission to such conduct is made either explicitly or implicitly a term or condition of an individual's employment.

2. Where submission to or rejection of such conduct by an individual is used as the basis for employment decisions affecting such an individual.

3. Where such conduct has the purpose or effect of unreasonably interfering with an individual's work performance or creating an intimidating, hostile, or offensive working environment.

In 1986, the U.S. Supreme Court in *Meritor Savings Bank v. Vinson* agreed with the EEOC, ruling that there could be two types of sexual harassment: harassment that conditions concrete employment benefits on granting sexual favors (often called the *quid pro quo* type) and harassment that creates a hostile or offensive work environment without affecting economic benefits (the hostile environment type). Nevertheless, the court made it quite difficult for a plaintiff to establish that either of these types of sexual harassment had occurred. For example, a polite verbal "no" does not suffice to show that sexual advances are unwelcome; a woman's entire conduct both in and outside the workplace is subject to appraisal determining whether or not she welcomed the advances. But isn't it odd that a woman should have to prove that an offer "If you don't sleep with me you will be fired" is unwelcomed? Moreover, if a woman rejects such an offer and is fired, unless she is a perfect employee, she will have difficulty proving that she was fired because she rejected the offer. Actually, in such a case, what the Supreme Court should have required is that the employer be able to show that a woman who rejects a sexual advance would still have been fired even if she had said yes.

U.S. courts have also made it difficult to classify work environments as hostile to women. In *Christoforou v. Ryder Truck Rental, Inc.,* a supervisor's actions of fondling a plaintiff's rear end and breasts, propositioning her and trying to force a kiss at a Christmas party were considered "too sporadic and innocuous" to support a finding of a hostile work environment. In *Rabidue v. Osceola Refining Co.,* a workplace where pictures of nude and scantily clad women abounded, including one, which hung on a wall for eight years, of a woman with a golf ball on her breasts and a man with his golf club, standing over her and yelling "fore," and where a co-worker, never disciplined despite repeated complaints, routinely referred to women as "whores," "cunts," and "pussy" was judged not sufficiently hostile an environment to constitute sexual harassment. At times, the courts seem to be appealing to the pervasiveness of certain forms of harassment as grounds for tolerating them. As though we should only prohibit wrongful acts if most people aren't doing them. At other times, the courts appear to be judging sexual harassment to be what men, but not women, say it is. What this shows is that the problem of avoiding sexual harassment is intimately tied to its definition, and women and men seem to disagree radically about what constitutes sexual harassment.

Alternative Views

In Selection 35, Barbara A. Gutek surveys the research that has been done on defining sexual harassment and determining how frequently it occurs. Gutek notes that a number of factors influence whether some behavior is classified as sexual harassment:

1. How intrusive and persistent the behavior is. (The more physically intrusive and persistent the behavior is, the more likely that it will be defined as sexual harassment.)
2. The nature of the relationship between the actors. (The better the actors know each other, the less likely the behavior will be labeled sexual harassment.)
3. The characteristics of the observer. (Men and people in authority are less likely to label behavior as sexual harassment.)
4. The inequality in the relationship. (The greater the inequality, the more likely the behavior will be labeled sexual harassment.)

Gutek contends that the frequency of sexual harassment in the workplace is relatively high. For example, the U.S. Merit System Protection Board found that 42 percent of the women responding to its study reported experiencing sexual harassment on the job within the previous two years. She seeks to explain this frequency as due to the fact that women are stereotypically identified as sexual objects in ways that men are not. She notes that women are stereotypically characterized as sexy, affectionate, and attractive, whereas men are stereotypically characterized as competent and active. These stereotypes, Gutek claims, spill over into the workplace, making it difficult for women to be perceived as fellow workers rather than sex objects, and these perceptions foster sexual harassment. It would seem, therefore, that eliminating the problem of sexual harassment from our society will require breaking down these stereotypes.

Unlike Gutek, Ellen Frankel Paul (Selection 36) argues that the problem of sexual harassment is overblown. She thinks sexual harassment has been exaggerated to include everything from rape to "looks." Paul argues that the extortion of sexual favors by a supervisor from a subordinate by threatening to penalize, fire, or fail to reward is sexual harassment, but she argues that a hostile working environment should be regarded as sexual harassment only when the "reasonable man" of tort law would find the working environment offensive. However, as one of Gutek's studies shows, reasonable men and reasonable women can disagree over what constitutes sexual harassment in the workplace. In this study, 67.2 percent of men as compared to 16.8 percent of women would be flattered if asked to have sex, while 15 percent of the men and 62.8 percent of the women said they would be insulted by such an offer. So the crucial question is: Whose perspective should be determinative?

In Selection 37, Nancy Davis notes that between 25 and 40 percent of female college students report they have been subjected to some sort of harassment from their instructors. She maintains that the frequency and seriousness of sexual harassment in the university are widely underestimated because of such factors as the unequal power between students and professors, traditional gender roles and expectations, popular academic fiction that portrays "co-eds" as lusty seducers of respectable male professors, and the reluctance of educators to "break ranks" with their colleagues. She also claims that when many women are faced with sexual harassment at the university, they tend to deal with the problem by dropping the course, not coming to office hours, changing their major, or even dropping out of school altogether—all with unfortunate consequences.

Practical Application

In *Harris v. Forklift Systems Inc.* (Selection 38), the Supreme Court took an important step toward a more reasonable stance on sexual harassment. In this case, Teresa Harris worked as a rental manager at Forklift Systems. Charles Hardy, Forklift's president, told Harris on several occasions, in the presence of other employees, "You're a woman, what do you know?" and "We need a man as the rental manager." Again in front of others, he suggested that the two of them "go to the Holiday Inn to negotiate (Harris's) raise." Hardy occasionally asked Harris and other female employees to get coins from his front pants pockets. On other occasions, he threw objects on the ground in front of Harris and other women, and asked them to pick the objects up. He made sexual innuendos about Harris's and other women's clothing. On one occasion, while Harris was arranging a deal with one of Forklift's customers, Hardy asked Harris in front of other employees, "What did you do, promise some (sex) Saturday night?" Soon after, Harris quit her job at Forklift.

In this case, the Supreme Court struck down the district court's requirement that in order for sexual harassment to be established, Harris needed to show that Hardy's conduct had "seriously affected her psychological well-being." This was an important decision, but obviously it does not go far enough in specifying a reasonable standard for sexual harassment.

35. *Understanding Sexual Harassment at Work*

Barbara A. Gutek

Barbara A. Gutek surveys the research that has been done on defining sexual harassment and determining how frequently it occurs. She notes that several factors influence whether a behavior is classified as sexual harassment: (1) How intrusive and persistent the behavior is; (2) the nature of relationship between the actors; (3) the characteristics of the observer; and (4) the inequality in the relationship. Gutek contends that the frequency of sexual harassment in the workplace is relatively high. For example, the U.S. Merit System Protection Board found that 42 percent of the women responding to its study reported experiencing sexual harassment on the job within the previous two years. Gutek seeks to explain this frequency as due to the fact that women are stereotypically identified as sexual objects in ways that men are not.

I. *Introduction*

The topic of sexual harassment at work was virtually unstudied until the concern of feminists brought the issue to the attention of the public and researchers. Much of the research on sexual harassment addresses two complementary questions. (1) How do people define sexual harassment? (2) How common is it? Research on these issues provides useful background information for lawyers and policy makers interested in seeking legal redress for harassment victims, and ultimately in eradicating sexual harassment. . . .

The first issue, people's definitions of sexual harassment, shows the extent to which laws and regulations reflect broad public consensus. Knowing the frequency of sexual harassment—a workplace problem that had no name until the mid-1970s—is important for those seeking to establish laws and procedures to remedy the problem. Further, frequency or prevalence deserves study because sexual harassment has negative consequences for women workers and organizations. These two areas—definition and prevalence—are often studied independently, using different research subjects, research designs, and methods of data collection.

From "Understanding Sexual Harassment at Work," *Notre Dame Journal of Law, Ethics and Public Policy* (1992). Reprinted by permission.

This article traces the development of research on sexual behavior in the workplace from its early emphasis on defining and documenting sexual harassment through other findings on sexual nonharassment. To understand sex at work, several frameworks or theories are discussed, with special emphasis on the concept of sex-role spillover.

The term *sexual behavior* will be used throughout this article to encompass the range of sexual behaviors, such as nonwork-related behavior with sexual content or overtones, found within the workplace and included in many research studies. Few studies attempt to limit themselves to legally liable sexual harassment. Thus, the term "sexual behavior" consists of behavior that is legally considered sexual harassment as well as nonharassing sexual behavior.

Finally, it should be noted that this article is not a review of the status of sexual harassment laws or legal practices. It is limited to the social science research which addresses issues relevant to sexual harassment policy and lawsuits.

II. *The Discovery of Sexual Harassment*

In the mid-1970s, sexuality in the workplace suddenly received considerable attention through the discovery of sexual harassment, which appeared to be relatively widespread and to have long-lasting, harmful effects on a significant number of working women. This "discovery" was somewhat counterintuitive, since some women were believed to benefit from seductive behavior and sexual behaviors at work, gaining unfair advantage and acquiring perks and privileges from their flirtatious and seductive behavior. The first accounts of sexual harassment were journalistic reports and case studies. Soon the topic was catapulted into public awareness through the publication of two important books. Lin Farley's book, *Sexual Shakedown: The Sexual Harassment of Women on the Job,* aimed to bring sexual harassment to public attention, create a household word, and make people aware of harassment as a social problem. Catharine MacKinnon's book, *Sexual Harassment of Working Women,* sought a legal mechanism for handling sexual harassment and compensating its victims. In a strong and compelling argument, MacKinnon contended that sexual harassment was primarily a problem for women, that it rarely happened to men, and therefore that it should be viewed as a form of sex discrimination. Viewing sexual harassment as a form of sex discrimination would make available to victims the same legal protection available to victims of sex discrimination. In 1980, the Equal Employment Opportunity Commission (EEOC) established guidelines consistent with MacKinnon's position and defined sexual harassment under Title VII of the 1964 Civil Rights Act as a form of unlawful sex-based discrimination. Several states have passed their own increasingly strong laws aimed at eliminating sexual harassment and legal scholars have sought additional avenues to recover damages incurred from sexual harassment. Various public and private agencies as well as the courts have seen a steady if uneven increase in sexual harassment complaints since the early 1980s.

The various guidelines and regulations define sexual harassment broadly. For example, the updated EEOC guidelines state that

> [u]nwelcome sexual advances, requests for sexual favors, and other verbal or physical conduct of a sexual nature constitute sexual harassment when (1) submission to such conduct is made either explicitly or implicitly a term or condition of an individual's employment or academic advancement, (2) submission to or rejection of such conduct by an individual is used as the basis for employment

decisions or academic decisions affecting such individual, or (3) such conduct has the purpose or effect of reasonably interfering with an individual's work or academic performance or creating an intimidating, hostile, or offensive working or academic environment.

Researchers began serious study of sex at work only after Farley's and MacKinnon's books and two compendia of information on sexual harassment were in progress and generally after the EEOC had established guidelines in 1980. Not surprisingly, researchers were heavily influenced by these important developments in policy and law. These developments focused the concerns of researchers on the two specific issues mentioned above: definition of harassment and frequency of occurrence.

III. *Defining Sexual Harassment*

The first issue can be succinctly stated: "What constitutes sexual harassment?" For lawyers, the courts, personnel managers, ombudspersons, and others, this is perhaps the most important issue that they must face. If "it" is harassment, it is illegal; otherwise it is not. Researchers, aware of the problems in defining harassment and perhaps eager to contribute to the developments in law and policy, began to supply a spate of studies.

Studies concerned with the definition of sexual harassment come in two types. First are surveys of various populations of people who are asked to tell whether various acts constitute sexual harassment. Second are experimental studies in which students, employees, or managers are asked to rate one or more hypothetical situations in which aspects of the situation are varied along important dimensions. These experimental studies using a hypothetical situation, also known as the "paper people paradigm," come in two variants. In the first variant, subjects are asked to determine whether a particular scenario depicts an instance of sexual harassment. In the second variant, researchers examine the attributions of subjects to understand how subjects' interpretations of a scenario affect their use of the label, sexual harassment.

The strengths of the experimental research design—random assignment to conditions and manipulation of causal variables—allow researchers to make causal statements about what affects how people define sexual harassment. The weakness of the design is that the situation is invariably insufficiently "real": Subjects who have limited information and little appreciation of, or experience with, the subject matter may not respond the way people would in a real (rather than hypothetical) situation.

The survey studies show that sexual activity as a requirement of the job is defined as sexual harassment by about 81 percent to 98 percent of working adults, and similar results have been reported with students as subjects. Lesser forms of harassment such as sexual touching are not as consistently viewed as sexual harassment. For example, I found that 59 percent of men but 84 percent of women asserted that sexual touching at work is sexual harassment. A sizable minority (22 percent of men and 33 percent of women) considered sexual comments at work meant to be complimentary to be sexual harassment.

In contrast to the survey studies which often ask respondents to specify which of a set of actions constitutes harassment, in experimental studies, subjects are usually asked to rate how harassing some incident is, on a five-point or seven-point scale. Such a method makes it impossible to say what percentage of people consider any particular act or event harassment and results are usually reported as mean scores (on, say, a three-, five-, or seven-point scale). It should be noted that experimental studies are generally not concerned with the percentage of their subjects, usually students, who consider behavior X to be harassment, but instead address the factors or variables which affect whether or not some specified incident or act is labeled harassment.

The experimental studies show that except for the most outrageous and clearly inappropriate behavior, whether or not an incident is labeled harassment varies with several characteristics of the incident and the people involved. In these studies, the following variables make a difference: (1) the behavior in question, (2) the relationship between harasser and victim, (3) the sex of the harasser, (4) the sex and age of the victim, (5) the sex of the rater, and (6) the occupation of the person doing the rating. Another way of categorizing these factors is shown below: Characteristics of the behavior, nature of the relationship between the actors, characteristics of the observer/rater, and context factors all affect whether or not a particular act or event is considered sexual harassment.

Factors Affecting the Definition of Sexual Harassment

1. *Characteristics of the behavior.* The more physically intrusive and persistent the behavior, the more likely it is to be defined as sexual harassment by an observer.
2. *The nature of the relationship between actors.* The better the two actors know each other (friends, spouses, long-time co-workers) the less likely the behavior will be labeled sexual harassment by an observer.
3. *Characteristics of the observer.* Men and people in authority (e.g., senior faculty, senior managers) are less likely than others to label a behavior sexual harassment.
4. *Context factors.* The greater the inequality (in position, occupation, age), the more likely the behavior will be labeled sexual harassment by an observer. When the "recipient" of the behavior is low status or relatively powerless (female, young, poor), the behavior is more likely to be judged harassment than when the "recipient" is high status or relatively powerful.

The most important factor determining judgment of sexual harassment is the behavior involved. The experimental studies and survey studies yield the same pattern of findings: Explicitly sexual behavior and behavior involving implied or explicit threats are more likely to be perceived as harassment than other, less threatening or potentially complimentary behavior. Touching is also more likely to be rated as sexual harassment than comments, looks, or gestures. In addition, Weber-Burdin and Rossi concluded that the initiator's behavior is much more important than the recipient's behavior, although if a female recipient behaved seductively, college student raters may reduce the ratings of harassment.

The relationship between the two people is also important. The situation is considered more serious harassment when the initiator is a supervisor of the recipient rather than an equal or a subordinate or more serious if the person previously declined to date the harasser than if the two people had a prior dating relationship. The incident is more likely to be viewed as sexual harassment when a man is the harasser, a woman is the victim and when the female victim is young.

The person doing the rating makes a difference. The most important characteristic . . . is gender. When women are doing the rating, they define a wide variety of sexual behavior at work as sexual harassment, while men tend to rate only the more extreme behaviors as harassment. Similarly, on a scale of Tolerance for Sexual Harassment (TSHI), college men reported more tolerance than women, that is, men objected less than women to sexual harassing behavior. In short, the finding that women apply a broader definition of sexual harassment than men is pervasive and widely replicated although not universally found. It is worth noting that at least one factor strongly associated with gender, sex-role identity, did not make much of a difference in people's judgments of sexual harassment. Powell, using a student sample, found that sex-role identity generally did not affect definition of sexual harassment although highly feminine subjects were somewhat more likely than others to label some behaviors sexual harassment and highly masculine male students were somewhat less likely than others to label insulting sexual remarks sexual harassment. In addition, organizational status seems to have an effect. Higher-level managers rating an incident are less likely to see it as serious harassment than middle-level or lower-level managers. In one study, faculty tended to view an incident as less serious than students whereas in another, there were no substantial differences in the ratings of faculty and students.

The experimental studies using attribution analysis probe an evaluator's thought processes as he or she makes a determination whether or not a particular scenario constitutes harassment. Pryor suggested that people are more likely to judge a man's behavior [to be] sexual harassment if his behavior is attributed to his enduring negative intentions toward the target woman. Such negative intentions can either reflect hostility or insensitivity to women. Pryor and Day found that the perspective people take in interpreting a social-sexual encounter affects their judgments of sexual harassment. This may help explain why men and women tend to differ in their judgments of sexual harassment, that is, men may take the man's (usually the initiator's) point of view whereas women are more likely to take the woman's (the victim in many experi-

mental studies) point of view. In support of this view, Konrad and Gutek found that women's greater experience with sexual harassment helps to explain the sex differences in defining sexual harassment. In a similar vein, Kenig and Ryan came to the conclusion that men's and women's perceptions of sexual harassment reflect their self-interest. It is in men's self-interest to see relatively little sexual harassment because men are most often the offenders whereas it is in women's self-interest to see relatively more sexual harassment because women tend to be the victims in sexual harassment encounters.

Cohen and Gutek's analyses suggest that people may make different attributions depending on whether they view the initiator and recipient as friends. More specifically, they found that when student subjects were asked to evaluate an ambiguous, potentially mildly sexually harassing encounter, they tended to assume that the two participants were friends, perhaps dating partners, and that the behavior was welcome and complimentary rather than harassing. Similarly, student subjects were less likely to rate a behavior harassment if they knew that the parties [had] dated and were more likely to rate a behavior harassment if the woman recipient had . . . refused to date the male initiator. In the latter case, subjects may attribute the man's overture to his "enduring negative intentions" toward the woman since her prior refusal of a date presumably eliminates the explanation that he was unsure how she felt about him.

IV. *Frequency of Sexual Harassment at Work*

The other area of research that developed in response to legal and policy development was a documentation of the forms and prevalence of harassment experienced. In 1979, MacKinnon wrote: "The unnamed should not be taken for the nonexistent." Thus, providing a label and then a definition for sexual harassment was an important step in developing ways to measure the prevalence of sexual harassment.

The research on frequency of harassment focuses heavily but not exclusively on heterosexual encounters. It is often studied separate from the research on definition and employs a different research design and different subjects. Research aiming to establish rates of harassment in a population must be concerned with drawing a representative sample from a known population in order to generalize results in that population.

The research on prevalence shows a broad range of rates, depending in part on the time frame used. The U.S. Merit System Protection Board's study found that 42 percent of the women respondents reported experiencing sexual harassment on the job within the previous two years. When the study was repeated several years later, the figure remained the same. In a Seattle, Washington, study of city employees, more than one-third of all respondents reported sexual harassment in the previous twenty-four months of employment. Dunwoody-Miller and Gutek found that 20 percent of California state civil service employees reported being sexually harassed at work in the previous five years. Reviewing the results from several different measures of prevalence ..., Gutek suggested that up to 53 percent of women had been harassed sometime in their working life. The figures are higher in the military; two-thirds of women surveyed in a 1990 study said they had been sexually harassed.

Other studies using purposive or convenience samples generally show higher rates of harassment. In a study by the Working Women's Institute, 70 percent of the employed women respondents said they had experienced sexual harassment .... An early study of the readers of *Redbook* magazine found that 88 percent of those mailing in questionnaires had experienced sexual harassment. Schneider reported that more than two-thirds of her matched sample of lesbian and heterosexual working women had experienced unwelcome sexual advances within the previous year.

Because respondents in purposive or convenience samples can choose whether or not to respond, and participating in the study may require some expenditure of effort, researchers assume that people who have been harassed may be more motivated to participate. Thus, the incidence rates are likely to be somewhat inflated.

Although women of all ages, races, occupations, income levels, and marital statuses experience harassment, research suggests that young and unmarried women are especially vulnerable. Not surprisingly, most women are harassed by men, not by women. In addition, women in nontraditional jobs (e.g., truck driver, neurosurgeon, engineer, roofer) and in nontraditional industries such as the military and mining are more likely to experience harassment than other women. These higher rates are over and above what is expected by their high amount of work contact with men. On the basis of the set of studies done so far, it seems likely that overall, from one-third to one-half of all women have been sexually harassed at some time in their working lives, although frequency rates in some types of work may be higher.

Sexual harassment at work has also been reported by men in several studies. The U.S. Merit System Protection Board's study found 15 percent of the men to be harassed by males or females at work. On the basis of men's reports of specific behavior, Gutek suggested that up to 9 percent of men could have been harassed by women sometime in their working lives. After a careful analysis of men's accounts of harassment, however, Gutek concluded that few of the reported incidents were sexual harassment as legally defined, and some of the incidents may not have even been considered sexual if the same behavior had been initiated by a man or by another woman who was considered a less desirable sexual partner by the man.

V. *Frequency of Sexual Nonharassment*

Several studies have also examined other kinds of sexual behavior at work, behavior that most people do not consider harassment, including comments or whistles intended to be compliments, quasi-sexual touching such as hugging or an arm around the shoulder, requests for a date or sexual activity often in a joking manner, and sexual jokes or comments that are not directed to a particular person. These other "nonharassing," less serious, and presumably nonproblematic behaviors are considerably more common than harassment. For example, Gutek found that 61 percent of men and 68 percent of women said that they had received at least one sexual comment that was meant to be complimentary sometime in their working lives. In addition, 56 percent of men and 67 percent of women reported that they had been the recipient of at least one sexual look or gesture that was intended to be complimentary. About eight out of every ten workers have been recipients of some kind of sexual overture that was intended [as] a compliment. Schneider found that 55 percent of a sample of heterosexual working women and 67 percent of a sample of lesbian working women reported that within the last year at work, someone had joked with them about their body or appearance. Other studies show similar findings. Dunwoody-Miller and Gutek reported that 76 percent of women and 55 percent of men indicated that as California state civil service employees, they had received complimentary comments of a sexual nature. Looks and gestures of a sexual nature that were meant as compliments were also common (reported by 67 percent of women and 47 percent of men).

Although men [are rarely] harassed, the amount of sexual behavior reported by them at work remains substantial. For example, Gutek found that men were more likely than women to say that they were sexually touched by an opposite-sex person on their job. According to Abbey, Davies, and Gottfried and Fasenfest, men are more likely than women to perceive the world in sexual terms. Also, men are more likely than women to mistake friendliness for seduction and find the office . . . a little too exciting with women around. This seems consistent with the common stimulus-response view that women's presence elicits sexual behavior from men. Reports from men, however, suggest that sex is present in male-dominated workplaces, whether or not women are actually present. This "floating sex" takes the form of posters, jokes, sexual metaphors for work, comments, obscene language, and the like. The relationship seems to be quite straightforward: the more men, the more sexualized the workplace. [That much] of this sexualization . . . is degrading . . . as well as sexual is what creates the "hostile" environment that government regulations aim to eliminate.

[Altogether,] the research on harassment and "nonharassment" shows that sexual behavior is so common at work that one might say that sex permeates work. An equally important conclusion . . . is that the legal behavior is considerably more common than the illegal sexual harassment. This finding is not surprising, but it is important; when some people first hear about sexual harassment, they may confuse it with the more common legal behavior at work which they, themselves, have seen and experienced. This confusion of nonthreatening legal behavior with sexual harassment can lead some to incorrectly denigrate women's complaints as prudish or overly sensitive.

VI. *Impacts of Sexual Behavior at Work*

Any behavior as common as sexual harassment and nonharassment at work is likely to have a wide variety of ramifications for the individuals involved. So far researchers have concentrated on identifying negative effects of sexual harassment to call attention to harassment as a social and workplace problem. But only scattered attempts have been made [to study] the impacts of other types of sexual behavior at work.

Sexual harassment has a variety of negative consequences for women. . . . In addition to the discomfort associated with the sexually harassing experiences and violation of physical privacy, women often find that their careers are interrupted. Up to 10 percent of women have quit a job because of sexual harassment. Others fear becoming victims of retaliation if they complain about the harassment, and some are asked to leave. For example, Coles found that among eighty-one cases filed with the California Department of Fair Employment and Housing between 1979 and 1983, almost half of the complainants were fired and another quarter quit out of fear or frustration.

Women may also experience lower productivity, less job satisfaction, reduced self-confidence, and a loss of motivation and commitment to their work and their employer. They may avoid men who are known harassers, even though contact with those men is important for their work. Thus, harassment constrains the potential for forming friendships or work alliances with male workers. Furthermore, women are likely to feel anger and resentment and even exhibit self-blame, which leads to additional stress. Crull and Cohen also stated that, while the implicit/overt types of harassment may not have the same direct repercussions as those of the explicit/overt types, all types of sexual harassment at work create high stress levels and serve as a hidden occupational hazard. Finally, sexual harassment helps to maintain the sex segregation of work when it is used to coerce women out of nontraditional jobs.

Besides affecting their work, sexual harassment affects women's personal lives in the form of physical and emotional illness and disruption of marriage or other relationships. . . . For example, Tangri, Burt, and Johnson reported that 33 percent of women said their emotional or physical condition became worse, and Gutek found that 15 percent of women victims . . . said their health was affected and another 15 percent said it damaged their relationships with men.

[Even] more intriguing . . . nonharassing sexual behavior also has negative work-related consequences for women workers, although even they are not always aware of them. For example, Gutek found that the experience of all kinds of sexual behavior, including remarks intended to be complimentary, was associated with lower job satisfaction among women. . . . In addition, women reported that they are not flattered, and in fact are insulted, by sexual overtures of all kinds from men. In one study, 62 percent of women said they would be insulted by a sexual proposition from a man at work. Another example, the office "affair," can have serious detrimental effects on a woman's credibility as well as her career, especially if the relationship is with a supervisor.

Men seem to suffer virtually no work-related consequences of sexual behavior at work. Less than 1 percent of men reported that they quit a job because of sexual harassment, and, in the course of discussing sexual incidents, not one man said he lost a job as a consequence of a sexual overture or request from a woman at work. In the same study, 67 percent of men said they would be flattered by sexual overtures from women. In addition, many men view a certain amount of sexual behavior as appropriate to the work setting, and, as noted above, are less likely to consider any given behavior as sexual harassment. In one study, 51 percent of the men who received overtures from women said they themselves were at least somewhat responsible for the incident. That men experience so few work-related consequences of sex at work is especially odd, since they report so much sexual behavior both that is directed at them by women and that seems to float throughout the workplace.

When men do report "consequences," they are personal rather than work-related, and again, they are viewed in a positive manner. Most often, they report dating relationships or affairs that they find enjoy-able; for instance, "There was this little blonde who had the hots for me" or "I think she liked me. I was young and she was married. She wasn't very happy with her husband."

VII. Understanding Sexual Behavior at Work

[M]ost studies of sexual behavior at work have been in response to the discovery of sexual harassment and policies developed to address harassment. Much of the research is descriptive and diverse, providing interesting information about sexual behavior at work, and useful information for policy makers and lawyers. Some researchers have begun to develop frameworks for studying sexual behavior at work.

One framework sometimes used to study harassment is the power perspective: that is, sexual harassment is an expression of power relationships, and women constitute a threat to men's economic and social standing. With that perspective, Lipman-Blumen viewed the women's "seductive" behavior as micro-manipulation, as a response to male control of social institutions—including the workplace and the academy—which she labeled macro-manipulation. Other researchers explicitly borrowed from the literature on rape. They contend that sexual harassment is analogous to rape: Power, not sexual drive, is the dominant motivation. They further contend that victims of rape and harassment experience similar effects.

In an attempt to explain their own findings on sexual harassment, Tangri, Burt, and Johnson developed three models: the natural/biological model, the organizational model, and the sociocultural model. The natural/biological model assumes that sexual harassment and other forms of sexual expression at work are simply manifestations of natural attraction between two people. According to Tangri, Burt, and Johnson, one version of this model suggests that because men have a stronger sex drive, they more often initiate sexual overtures at work [and] in other settings. The organizational model assumes that sexual harassment is the result of certain opportunity structures within . . . hierarchies. People in higher positions can use their authority (their legitimate power) and their status to coerce lower-status people into accepting a role of sex object or engaging in sexual interactions. The third model, the sociocultural model, "argues that sexual harassment reflects the larger society's differential distribution of power and status between the sexes." Harassment is viewed as a mechanism for maintaining male dominance over women. . . . Male dominance is maintained by patterns of male–female interaction as well as by male domination of economic and political matters. Tangri, Burt, and Johnson's analysis revealed that none of the three models could by itself offer an adequate explanation of their data on sexual harassment. Another model, emphasizing the effects of sex-role expectations in an organizational context, is called sex-role spillover. The following analysis builds on earlier research on this concept.

VIII. *Sex-Role Spillover* .

Sex-role spillover denotes the carryover of gender-based expectations into the workplace. Among the characteristics assumed by many to be associated with femaleness (such as passivity, loyalty, emotionality, nurturance) is being a sex object. Women are assumed to be sexual and to elicit sexual overtures from men rather naturally. In a thirty-nation study of sex stereotypes, the characteristics of sexy, affectionate, and attractive were associated with femaleness. This aspect of sex-role spillover, the sex-object aspect, is most relevant to the study of sex at work.

Sex-role spillover occurs when women, more than men in the same work roles, are expected to be sex objects or are expected to project sexuality through their behavior, appearance, or dress. What is equally important is the fact that there is no strongly held comparable belief about men. For example, of the forty-nine items that were associated with maleness in at least nineteen of the twenty-five countries studied by Williams and Best, none was directly or indirectly related to sexuality. While it is generally assumed that men are more sexually active than women and men are the initiators in sexual encounters, the cluster of characteristics that are usually associated with the male personality do not include a sexual component. Rather the stereotype of men revolves around the dimension of competence and activity. It includes the belief that men are rational, analytic, assertive, tough, good at math and science, competi-

tive, and make good leaders. The stereotype of men—the common view of the male personality—is the perfect picture of asexuality. Sex-role spillover thus introduces the view of women as sexual beings in the workplace, but it simply reinforces the view of men as organizational beings—"active, work-oriented." [Note also] these stereotypes of female characteristics and male characteristics have remained quite stable through the 1970s and into the 1980s.

The spillover of the female sex-role, including the sexual aspect, occurs at work for at least four reasons. First, gender is the most noticeable social characteristic: People immediately notice whether a person is a man or a woman. Second, men may feel more comfortable reacting to women at work in the same manner that they react to other women in their lives, and unless a woman is too young, old, or unattractive, that includes viewing her as a potential sexual partner. Third, women may feel comfortable reacting to men in a manner expected by the men—that is, conforming to the men's stereotype. Fourth, characteristics of work and sex roles may facilitate the carryover of sex role into work role. Sex roles remain relatively stable throughout our lives and permeate all domains of life. On the other hand, the work role may change many times and is specific to only one domain of life. Sex roles are also learned much earlier than are work roles, and they entail a wide variety of diffuse skills and abilities. Work roles, on the other hand, call for more specific skills and abilities.

The important point here is that being sexual and being a sex object are aspects of the female sex role that frequently are carried over to the workplace by both men and women. A variety of subtle pressures may encourage women to behave in a sexual manner at work, and this then confirms their supposedly essential sexual nature. Because it is expected, people notice female sexuality, and they believe it is normal, natural, an outgrowth of being female.

Unfortunately, women do not seem to be able to be sex objects and analytical, rational, competitive, and assertive at the same time because femaleness is viewed as "not-maleness," and it is the men who are viewed as analytic, logical, and assertive. [Even though] the model of male and female as polar opposites has been severely criticized on several grounds, a dichotomy is used by researchers and laypersons alike (for example, we speak of the "opposite" sex). This is an important part of sex-role spillover. [The] sexual aspects of the female role [not only are] carried over to work, but also swamp or overwhelm a view of women as capable, committed workers. This is especially true in an environment where sexual jokes, innuendos, posters, and small talk are common. A recent study by Mohr and Zanna showed that sex-role traditional men exposed to sexually explicit material behaved in a significantly more sexual and obtrusive manner toward women than men who did not see sexually explicit material. As Kanter noted, a woman's perceived sexuality can "blot out" all other characteristics, particularly in a sexualized work environment. Thus, sex role interferes with and takes precedence over work role.

What is doubly troublesome about this inability to be sexual and a worker at the same time is that women are not the ones who usually choose between the two. A female employee might decide to be a sex object at work, especially if her career or job is not very important to her. More often, however, the working woman chooses not to be a sex object but may be so defined by male colleagues or supervisors anyway, regardless of her own actions. A woman's sexual behavior is noticed and labeled sexual even if it is not intended as such. To avoid being cast into the role of sex object, a woman may have to act completely asexual. Then she is subject to the charge of being a "prude," an "old maid," or "frigid," and in her attempt to avoid being a sex object, she is still stereotyped by her sexuality, or more accurately, by her perceived lack of sexuality.

The situation for men is entirely different. Benefiting from the stereotype of men as natural inhabitants of organizations—goal-oriented, rational, analytic, competitive, assertive, strong, or, . . . "active, work-oriented"—men may be able to behave in a blatantly sexual manner, seemingly with impunity. Even when a man goes so far as to say that he encourages overtures from women by unzipping his pants at work, he may escape being viewed as sexual or more interested in sex than work by supervisors and colleagues. While the image of women acting in a seductive manner and distracting men from work is viewed as a detriment to the organization, many executives know of men who are "playboys" and harassers, yet they may not see them as detriments to the organization. These men may hire the wrong women for the wrong reasons,

make poor use of female human resources in the organization, squander the organization's resources in their quests for new sexual partners, and make elaborate attempts to impress potential sexual partners—all of this may escape the notice of employers. In short, men's sexual behavior at work often goes unnoticed [for at least two reasons]. First, . . . there is no strongly recognized sexual component of the male sex role. Thus, men's sexual behavior is neither salient nor noticed. Second, perhaps sexual pursuits and conquests, jokes, and innuendos can be subsumed under the stereotype of the organizational man—goal-oriented, rational, competitive, and assertive—which are expected and recognized as male traits. Men may make sexual overtures in an assertive, competitive manner. Likewise, sexual jokes, metaphors, and innuendos may be seen as part of competitive male horseplay. Thus the traits of competitiveness, assertiveness, and goal orientation are noticed, while the sexual component is not. . . .

IX. *The Spillover Perspective: Behaviors, Impacts, and Beliefs Concerning Sex at Work*

How does the sex-role spillover perspective enrich our understanding of sex at work or integrate the diverse findings about sexual harassment? This perspective leads to an examination of both men's and women's behavior at work and stereotypes or beliefs about how men and women behave. . . . It helps to explain the apparent paradox that women are perceived as using sex to their advantage, while, in practice, they are hurt by sex at work. On the other hand, while men are not perceived as sexual at work, they may display [and benefit from] more sexual behavior.

Sex-role spillover is also useful in explaining why sexual harassment remained invisible for so long. In the absence of data on the subject, women were labeled as sexy, men as asexual. Sexual overtures including harassment were elicited by the sexy women; men who are normally active and work-oriented, "all-business," could be distracted by seductively behaving women, but these distractions were considered a trivial part of men's overall work behavior. If the woman felt uncomfortable with the situation, it was her problem. If she could not handle [it] and complained . . . , it was at least partially her fault. Men and women, including women victims, shared this belief. Thus a woman who complained might be labeled a troublemaker and be asked to leave. . . .

[Although] the spillover perspective is not incompatible with a power perspective, it falls short in accounting for hostile sexual coercion at work. To take an extreme (but not unknown) case, rape in the office [could hardly be considered] a spillover from externally imposed sex roles. Rather, it is best construed as aggression or power, and a power perspective of sexual harassment may be a better explanatory model.

X. *Closing Remarks*

Much of the research on sexual harassment was inspired by innovations and developments in law and policy, and . . . so far has focused primarily on two issues, definition and prevalence, although topics such as consequences to victims and conditions under which harassment occurs have also been studied.

Recently, Terpstra and his colleagues have engaged in . . . research in a new area: the factors that affect the outcome of decisions in sexual harassment cases. Terpstra and Baker studied Illinois state EEOC cases and examined the factors associated with the outcomes of sexual harassment charges; only 31 percent of formal charges (twenty of sixty-five cases) resulted in a settlement favorable to the complainant. Using the same set of EEOC cases, Terpstra and Cook found that employment-related consequences experienced by the complainant were the most critical factor in filing a charge. Other research, for example, on men who harass and the way men respond to women when sexually explicit material is or is not available, represent other new and important areas of research.

Overall, the research on sexual harassment and sex at work has provided data showing that many of the common beliefs about sexual behavior at work are false. The contribution of research toward understanding and explaining sex at work has been valuable. A domain of human behavior that was largely invisible a decade ago is now visible, numerous misconceptions have been uncovered, and some facts have been exposed as myths by researchers.

36. *Exaggerating the Extent of Sexual Harassment*

ELLEN FRANKEL PAUL

Ellen Frankel Paul argues that sexual harassment has been exaggerated to include everything from rape to "looks." She argues that the extortion of sexual favors by a supervisor from a subordinate by threatening to penalize, fire, or fail to reward is sexual harassment. But she argues that a hostile working environment should be regarded as sexual harassment only when the "reasonable man" of tort law would find the working environment offensive. She contends that given this understanding of sexual harassment, scatological jokes, leers, unwanted offers of dates, and other sexual annoyances would no longer have their day in court.

From "Bared Buttocks and Federal Cases," *Society* (1991). Reprinted by permission.

Women in American society are victims of sexual harassment in alarming proportions. Sexual harassment is an inevitable corollary to class exploitation; as capitalists exploit workers, so do males in positions of authority exploit their female subordinates. Male professors, supervisors, and apartment managers in ever increasing numbers take advantage of the financial dependence and vulnerability of women to extract sexual concessions.

Valid Assertions?

These are the assertions that commonly begin discussions of sexual harassment. For reasons that will be adumbrated below, dissent from the prevailing view is long overdue. Three recent episodes will serve to frame this disagreement.

Valerie Craig, an employee of Y & Y Snacks, Inc., joined several co-workers and her supervisor for drinks after work one day in July 1978. Her supervisor drove her home and proposed that they become more intimately acquainted. She refused his invitation for sexual relations, whereupon he said that he would "get even" with her. Ten days [later] she was fired from her job. She soon filed a complaint of sexual harassment with the Equal Employment Opportunity Commission (EEOC), and the case wound its way through the courts. Craig prevailed, the company was held liable for damages, and she received back pay, reinstatement, and an order prohibiting Y & Y from taking reprisals against her in the future.

Carol Zabowicz, one of only two female forklift operators in a West Bend Co. warehouse, charged that her co-workers . . . from 1978 to 1982 sexually harassed her by such acts as: asking her whether she was wearing a bra; two of the men exposing their buttocks between ten and twenty times; a male co-worker grabbing his crotch and making obscene suggestions or growling; subjecting her to offensive and abusive language; and exhibiting obscene drawings with her initials on them. Zabowicz began to show symptoms of physical and psychological stress, necessitating several medical leaves, and she filed a sexual harassment complaint with the EEOC. The district court judge remarked that "the sustained, malicious, and brutal harassment meted out . . . was more than merely unreasonable; it was malevolent and outrageous." The company knew of the harassment and took corrective action only after the employee filed an EEOC complaint. The company was thus held liable, and Zabowicz was awarded back pay for the period of her medical absence, and a judgment that her rights were violated under the Civil Rights Act of 1964.

On September 17, 1990, Lisa Olson, a sports reporter for the *Boston Herald,* charged five football players of the just-defeated New England Patriots with sexual harassment for making sexually suggestive and offensive remarks to her when she entered their locker room to conduct a post-game interview. The incident amounted to nothing short of "mind rape," according to Olson. After vociferous lamentations in the media, the National Football League fined the team and its players $25,000 each. The National Organization of Women called for a boycott of Remington electric shavers because the owner of the company, Victor Kiam, also owns the Patriots and . . . allegedly displayed insufficient sensitivity at the time . . . the episode occurred.

Utopian Treatment for Women

All these incidents are indisputably disturbing. In an ideal world—one far different from the one that we inhabit or are ever likely to inhabit— women would not be subjected to such treatment in the course of their work. Women (and men) would be accorded respect by co-workers and supervisors, their feelings would be taken into account, and their dignity would be left intact. For women to expect reverential treatment in the workplace is utopian, yet they should not have to tolerate outrageous, offensive sexual overtures and threats as they go about earning a living.

One question that needs to be pondered is: What kinds of undesired sexual behavior should women be protected against by law? That is, what kind of actions are deemed so outrageous and violate a woman's rights to such extent that the law should intervene, and what actions should be considered inconveniences of life, to be morally condemned but not adjudicated? A subsidiary question concerns the type of legal remedy appropriate for the wrongs that do require redress. Before directly addressing these questions, it might be useful to diffuse some of the hyperbole adhering to the sexual harassment issue.

Harassment Surveys

Surveys are one source of this hyperbole. If their results are accepted at face value, they lead to the conclusion that women are disproportionately victims of legions of sexual harassers. A poll by the Albuquerque *Tribune* found that nearly 80 percent of the respondents reported that they or someone they knew had been victims of sexual harassment. The Merit System Protection Board determined that 42 percent of the women (and 14 percent of men) working for the federal government had experienced some form of unwanted sexual attention between 1985 and 1987, with unwanted "sexual teasing" identified as the most prevalent form. A Defense Department survey found that 64 percent of women in the military (and 17 percent of the men) suffered "uninvited and unwanted sexual attention" within the previous year. The United Methodist Church established that 77 percent of its clergywomen experienced incidents of sexual harassment, with 41 percent of these naming a pastor or colleague as the perpetrator, and 31 percent mentioning church social functions as the setting.

A few caveats about polls in general, and these in particular. . . . Pollsters looking for a particular social ill tend to find it, usually in gargantuan proportions. (What fate would lie in store for a pollster who concluded that child abuse, or wife beating, or mistreatment of the elderly had dwindled to the point of negligibility!) Sexual harassment is a notoriously ill-defined and almost infinitely expandable concept, including everything from rape to unwelcome neck massage, discomfiture on witnessing sexual overtures directed at others, yelling at and blowing smoke in the ears of female subordinates, and displaying pornographic pictures in the workplace. Defining sexual harassment, as the United Methodists did, as "any sexually related behavior that is unwelcome, offensive, or . . . fails to respect the rights of others," [makes] the concept broad enough to include everything from "unsolicited suggestive looks or leers [or] pressures for dates" to "actual sexual assaults or rapes." Categorizing everything from rape to "looks" as sexual harassment makes us all victims, a state of affairs satisfying to radical feminists, but not very useful for distinguishing serious injuries from the merely trivial.

Yet even if the surveys exaggerate the extent of sexual harassment, however defined, what they do reflect is a great deal of tension between the sexes. As women in ever-increasing numbers entered the workplace in the last two decades, as the women's movement challenged alleged male hegemony and exploitation with ever greater intemperance, and as women entered previously all-male preserves from the board rooms to the coal pits, it is lamentable, but should not be surprising, that this tension sometimes takes sexual form. Not that sexual harassment on the job, in the university, and in other settings is a trivial or insignificant matter, but a sense of proportion needs to be restored and, even more important, distinctions need to be made. In other words, sexual harassment must be de-ideologized. Statements that paint nearly all women as victims and all men and their patriarchal, capitalist system as perpetrators, are ideological fantasy. Ideology blurs the distinction between being injured—being a genuine victim—and merely being offended. An example is this statement by Catharine A. MacKinnon, a law professor and feminist activist:

> Sexual harassment perpetuates the interlocked structure by which women have been kept sexually in thrall to men and at the bottom of the labor market. Two forces of American society converge: men's control over women's sexuality and capital's control over employees' work lives. Women historically have been required to exchange sexual services for material survival, in one form or another. Prostitution and marriage as well as sexual harassment in different ways institutionalize this arrangement.

Such hyperbole needs to be diffused, and distinctions need to be drawn. Rape, a nonconsensual invasion of a person's body, is a crime clear and simple, a violation of the right to the physical integrity of the body (the right to life, as John Locke or Thomas Jefferson would have put it). Criminal law should and does prohibit rape. Whether it is useful to call rape "sexual harassment" is doubtful, for it makes the latter concept overly broad while trivializing the former.

Extortion of Sexual Favors

Intimidation in the workplace of the kind that befell Valerie Craig—that is, extortion of sexual favors by a supervisor from a subordinate by threatening to penalize, fire, or fail to reward—is what the courts term *quid pro quo* sexual harassment. Since the mid-1970s, the federal courts have treated this type of sexual harassment as a form of sex discrimination in employment proscribed under Title VII of the Civil Rights Act of 1964. A plaintiff who prevails against an employer may receive such equitable remedies as reinstatement and back pay, and the court can order the company to prepare and disseminate a policy against sexual harassment. Current law places principal liability on the company, not the harassing supervisor, even when higher management is unaware of the harassment and thus cannot take any steps to prevent it.

Quid pro quo sexual harassment is morally objectionable and analogous to extortion: The harasser extorts property (use of the woman's body) through the leverage of fear for her job. The victim of such behavior should have legal recourse, but serious reservations can be held about rectifying these injustices through the blunt instrument of Title VII. In egregious cases the victim is left less than whole (back pay will not compensate her for ancillary losses), and no prospect for punitive damages are offered to deter would-be harassers. Even more distressing about Title VII is that the primary target of litigation is not the actual harasser, but the employer. This places a double burden on a company. The employer is swindled by the supervisor because he spent his time pursuing sexual gratification and thereby impairing the efficiency of the workplace by mismanaging his subordinates, and the employer must endure lengthy and expensive litigation, pay damages, and suffer loss to its reputation. It would be fairer to both the company and the victim to treat sexual harassment as a tort—that is, as a private wrong or injury for which the court can assess damages. Employers should be held vicariously liable only when they know of an employee's behavior and do not try to redress it.

Defining Harassment Is Difficult

As for the workplace harassment endured by Carol Zabowicz—bared buttocks, obscene portraits, etc.—that too should be legally redressable. Presently, such

incidents also fall under the umbrella of Title VII, and are termed hostile environment sexual harassment, a category accepted later than *quid pro quo* and with some judicial reluctance. The main problem with this category is that it has proven too elastic: Cases have reached the courts based on everything from off-color jokes to unwanted, persistent sexual advances by co-workers. A new tort of sexual harassment would handle these cases better. Only instances above a certain threshold of egregiousness or outrageousness would be actionable. In other words, the behavior that the plaintiff found offensive would also have to be offensive to the proverbial "reasonable man" of the tort law. That is, the behavior would have to be objectively injurious rather than merely subjectively offensive. The defendant would be the actual harasser, not the company, unless it knew about the problem and failed to act. Victims of scatological jokes, leers, unwanted offers of dates, and other sexual annoyances would no longer have their day in court.

A distinction must be restored between morally offensive behavior and behavior that causes serious harm. Only the latter should fall under the jurisdiction of criminal or tort law. Do we really want legislators and judges delving into our most intimate private lives, deciding when a look is a leer, and when a leer is a Civil Rights Act offense? Do we really want courts deciding, as one recently did, whether a school principal's disparaging remarks about a female school district administrator was sexual harassment and, hence, a breach of Title VII, or merely the act of a spurned and vengeful lover? Do we want judges settling disputes such as the one that arose at a car dealership after a female employee turned down a male co-worker's offer of a date and his colleagues retaliated by calling her offensive names and embarrassing her in front of customers? Or another case in which a female shipyard worker complained of an "offensive working environment" because of the prevalence of pornographic material on the docks? Do we want the state to prevent or compensate us for any behavior that someone might find offensive? Should people have a legally enforceable right not to be offended by others? At some point, the price for such protection is the loss of both liberty and privacy rights.

No Perfect Working Environment Exists

Workplaces are breeding grounds of envy, personal grudges, infatuation, and jilted loves, and beneath a fairly high threshold of outrageousness, these travails should be either suffered in silence, complained of to higher management, or left behind as one seeks other employment. No one, female or male, can expect to enjoy a working environment that is perfectly stress-free, or to be treated always and by everyone with kindness and respect. To the extent that sympathetic judges have encouraged women to seek monetary compensation for slights and annoyances, they have not done them a great service. Women need to develop a thick skin in order to survive and prosper in the work force. It is patronizing to think that they need to be recompensed by male judges for seeing a few pornographic pictures on a wall. By their efforts to extend sexual harassment charges to even the most trivial behavior, the radical feminists send a message that women are not resilient enough to ignore the run-of-the-mill, churlish provocation from male co-workers. It is difficult to imagine a suit by a longshoreman complaining of mental stress due to the display of nude male centerfolds by female co-workers. Women cannot expect to have it both ways: equality where convenient, but special dispensations when the going gets rough. Equality has its price and that price may include unwelcome sexual advances, irritating and even intimidating sexual jests, and lewd and obnoxious colleagues.

Egregious acts—sexual harassment per se—must be legally redressable. Lesser but not trivial offenses, whether at the workplace or in other more social settings, should be considered moral lapses for which the offending party receives opprobrium, disciplinary warnings, or penalties, depending on the setting and the severity. Trivial offenses, dirty jokes, sexual overtures, and sexual innuendoes do make many women feel intensely discomfited, but, unless they become outrageous through persistence or content, these too should be taken as part of life's annoyances. The perpetrators should be either endured, ignored, rebuked, or avoided, as circumstances and personal inclination dictate. Whether Lisa Olson's experience in the locker room of the Boston Patriots falls into the second or third category is debatable. The media circus triggered by the incident was certainly out of proportion to the event.

As the presence of women on road gangs, construction crews, and oil rigs becomes a fact of life, the animosities and tensions of this transition period are likely to abate gradually. Meanwhile, women should "lighten up," and even dispense a few risqué barbs of their own, a sure way of taking the fun out of it for offensive male bores.

37. Sexual Harassment in the University

NANCY ("ANN") DAVIS

Nancy Davis notes that between 25 and 40 percent of female college students report they have been subjected to some sort of harassment from their instructors. She maintains that the frequency and seriousness of sexual harassment in the university are widely underestimated. She also claims that when many women are faced with sexual harassment at the university, they tend to deal with the problem in ways that have unfortunate consequences for themselves.

The notion of sexual harassment entered public consciousness in the United States with the publication of a survey on sexual harassment in the workplace conducted by *Redbook* in 1976. More than 9,000 women responded to the survey, and almost nine out of ten reported experiencing some sort of sexual harassment on the job.[1] Unsurprisingly, these revelations stimulated a lot of discussion in the news media, the popular press, and academic journals.[2] At about the same time, sexual harassment was found by the courts to constitute a form of sex discrimination and thus to be illegal under the terms of Title VII of the 1964 Civil Rights Act, which prohibits discrimination on the basis of race, sex, religion, or national origin.[3] Shortly thereafter, the same sorts of protections were held to extend to the educational sphere.[4] Title IX of the Education Amendments Act of 1972 forbids sex discrimination in all public and private institutions that receive federal money from grants, loans, or contracts.

Though sexual harassment in the university began to receive attention in the media in the late 1970s, not until 1986 did educational institutions themselves really begin to sit up and take notice. In that year, in *Meritor Savings Bank FSB v. Vinson*, the courts held that it was possible for an employer to be found guilty under Title VII if an employee's harassing conduct created a "hostile environment" for the harassed employee, and it allowed individuals who were the victims of sexual harassment to sue employers that did not have a policy that clearly prohibited sexual harassment.[5] These findings have been held to be applicable to educational institutions, and though many institutions had initially been slow to react, most were not slow to draw the obvious moral, namely, that it was not just an individual harassing instructor who might be liable to prosecution but the university that employed that instructor as well.[6] Most educational institutions have formulated or are in the process of formulating policies concerning sexual harassment.

In addition to being illegal and in opposition to expressed policies of many (if not most) educational institutions, sexual harassment is condemned as unethical by the American Association of University Professors, and by many of the myriad professional organizations that most faculty members are associated with.[7] It is difficult to produce a comprehensive, uncontroversial definition of sexual harassment,[8] or

Reprinted from Steven Cahn, ed., *Moral Responsibility and the University*, by permission of Temple University Press and the author.

a philosophically watertight account that explains just what it is about the different kinds of behavior that have been described as sexual harassment that makes them all of a piece unethical. Although, as we shall see, these difficulties pose problems for attempts to formulate fair and effective policies about sexual harassment, they pose no serious impediment to the achievement of consensus about the more blatant forms of sexual harassment. In the classic *quid pro quo* case in which an instructor puts unwelcome sexual pressure on a student and makes it clear that . . . academic evaluation or professional advancement [depends] on her yielding to that pressure, what the instructor does is obviously coercive, unjust, disrespectful, and discriminatory.[9] It is an abuse of power, a betrayal of trust, and inimical to the existence of a healthy educational environment in several ways.

Yet surveys conducted at college campuses around the nation reveal that a sizable proportion of female college students—somewhere between 25 percent and 40 percent—report they have been subjected to some sort of sexual harassment on the part of their instructors,[10] and anecdotal evidence provided by female students, faculty members, and administrators corroborates those findings. Surveys may be difficult to interpret and compare, for they do not all employ the same definition of sexual harassment, and anecdotal evidence must always be treated with caution, but it is clear that sexual harassment and other forms of sexually inappropriate behavior are no rarity in the university.[11] Any serious participant in higher education must be puzzled and distressed by this fact.

Commentators have identified many different . . . factors contributing to the prevalence of sexual harassment in the university. Some have emphasized that the university was and remains a male-dominated institution whose ground rules and procedures were fashioned by men. Traditionally, the influential teaching and administrative jobs in the university have been occupied by men, and it is men who have made the policies and interpreted the rules of university governance. Though things have changed considerably in the past decade or so, most of the senior faculty and administrative positions are still occupied by men. And women remain significantly in the minority in most, if not all, academic fields. This situation is thought, in itself, to be a problem. It is women, not men, who are almost always the victims of sexual harassment and men, not women, who are almost always the harassers.[12] And men are likely to both operate with a narrower notion of sexual harassment and have lower estimates of the incidence of sexual harassment on campus than women. They are also likelier to view the incidents of sexual harassment they acknowledge do occur as isolated personal incidents rather than as expressions of an institutional (or broader) problem. Commentators thus often cite the dearth of senior women and the associated inexperience and insensitivity of academic men as among the principal factors contributing to sexual harassment on campus. If women were less of a minority on campus or if they occupied positions of power that enabled them to have greater influence on rules, practices, and policies, then (it is thought) the incidence of sexual harassment on campus would decrease.

The women's movement and other associated movements have led many women—and many men—to question received gender stereotypes. But it is clear, nevertheless, that those stereotypes continue to exert a powerful influence on people's views about the relations between male professors and female students. Although it is a truism that social attitudes about status, gender, and sexuality frame people's expectations about "proper" relations between the sexes, most of us are blind to many of the effects of those attitudes, and implications of those expectations often go unnoticed.[13] Though fewer people may now regard liaisons between experienced and influential older men and inexperienced, comparatively powerless younger women as the ideal sort of relationship, such liaisons are still widely thought to be acceptable (if not simply normal). And the persistence of romanticized Pygmalionesque views of the educational process appears to legitimate such relations between male professors and female students. It is clear that gender stereotypes and associated differential social expectations contribute in a number of ways to the incidence of sexual harassment on campus.

Until we have a better understanding of why there has been so much sexual harassment in the university, we are not likely to be able to arrive at a solid understanding of what can or should be done to curtail it: The formulation of a cogent and successful sexual harassment policy thus requires more reflection on the factors that have contributed to the existence—or persistence—of sexual harassment in the university. Commentators are correct, I believe, in citing both the dearth of senior women in the university and the persistence of conventional gender expectations as significant contributing factors. . . .

It is clear that both the frequency and the seriousness of sexual harassment in the university are widely underestimated (even when sexual harassment is given its narrow interpretation and taken to refer only to such things as *quid pro quo* threats and actual sexual assault). There are a number of reasons why this is so. Personal, institutional, ideological, and societal factors all conspire to deter students from reporting incidents of sexual harassment and from taking concerted action to follow through with the reports of sexual harassment that they do make. If the data on sexual harassment are correct, it is clear that very few of the victims of sexual harassment in the workplace or in the university report it at all.[14] It is worth making clear what in the university context specifically discourages students from reporting sexual harassment.

Students and professors possess unequal power, influence, confidence, experience, and social standing.[15] And this inequality contributes to students' fears of being ridiculed, disbelieved, punished, or thought incompetent if they come forward with reports of sexually inappropriate conduct on the part of their instructors. Fear of the humiliations that befall many of the women who report rape and other forms of sexual assault evidently makes many women wary of reporting sexual offenses, especially when—as is evidently true in cases of sexual harassment—the attacker is someone who is known to the accuser. The student who has been sexually harassed by her professor is in a particularly vulnerable position, especially if she is known to have had an ongoing personal association with him or has previously submitted to his coercion. The stereotype of the professor as brilliant, principled, and passionately dedicated to his work and to the educational growth of his students leads students to doubt that their allegations would be believed. After all, professors are widely regarded as respectable members of the community. Often enough, students lose confidence in their perceptions of their own actions: If they hadn't done something wrong, then why would this respectable citizen behave so bizarrely?[16] "Blame the victim" sensibilities pervade our society, and so it is not too hard to understand why a confused and distressed victim of sexual harassment would shoulder the blame herself, rather than attribute it to the distinguished, respectable, and (formerly) much-admired professor who was (or appeared to be) so generous with his time and concern.

There are also other factors that erode a woman's confidence, and make her fear that the instructor's harassing behavior must somehow be her fault.[17] Late adolescence and early adulthood are vulnerable and psychologically chaotic times. Among the many difficulties that college-age students face is the struggle to come to terms with their sexuality, and it is easy for them to be insecure in the midst of that process, unclear about their own desires and unsure about how to interpret (and deal with) the many conflicting and ambivalent desires that they have. Though both men and women undoubtedly undergo personal upheaval, their behavior does not meet with the same social interpretation or response, nor are men and women supposed to handle their ambivalences the same way. Men are expected to become more confident and hence more persistent in their pursuit of sexual relationships as they mature. The myth endures that women enjoy being the object of persistent male attentions and invitations but like to play "hard to get" and thus refuse invitations they really wish to accept: When a woman says "no," what she really means is "maybe" or "ask me again later." Since, moreover, women are taught to be polite and nonconfrontational, the woman who tries to act "decently" when confronted with an unwelcome sexual invitation/offer/threat may be seen as thereby expressing ambivalence, which, according to the foregoing myth, may be construed as an expression of interest. If the woman actually does feel ambivalent—she wants to refuse the invitation, but she feels some attraction to the man who has issued it—then she may guiltily believe that she "led him on" even when she said no. And so she may regard the instructor's sexually inappropriate behavior as her fault.[18]

Gender roles and social expectations affect perceptions in other ways as well. Traditionally, women have been judged by their appearance, and they have thus been obliged to devote considerable energy to the attempt to look "attractive," for except among the most wealthy, it was a woman's appearance and good (compliant) manners that were the principal determinant of whether or not she would attract a man and marry, which was essential for her economic security. Though economics have changed, the traditional view continues to exert an influence on people's thinking, and women still feel pressure to dress attractively and act politely. Yet a woman who is attractive is seen as open to, and perhaps as actually inviting, sexual responses from men. This perception, plus the myth that men's sexual self-control is so fragile that it can be overwhelmed by the presence of an attractive woman, contributes to the view that the women who are sexually harassed are those who "asked for it" (by being physically attractive, or attractively dressed).

Surveys make it clear that there is no correlation between a woman's being attractive (or "sexily" dressed) and her being sexually harassed. Sexual harassment, like rape, is primarily an issue of power, not sex. But the myth persists that it is a female student's appearance that is the cause of her instructor's sexually inappropriate behavior toward her. This myth influences female students' perceptions of both their own and their professors' conduct. And if, as she may well suppose, she bears responsibility for the instructor's behaving as he does, she is likely not to think of his conduct as being sexual harassment.[19]

Popular academic fiction has done a lot to perpetuate these myths, and a lot to reinforce unfortunate gender stereotypes. "Co-eds" are portrayed as lusty seducers of respectable male professors, who are often portrayed as hapless victims of those feminine wiles. One can conjecture that most college-age women have read a few of the standard academic novels and that those novels provide some of the background for their interpretation of their professors' conduct.[20]

Believing that her experience of sexual harassment is rare, believing, perhaps, the various myths surrounding the mechanics of male and female attraction, and being influenced by the myth-supporting academic fiction she reads in English courses, the sexually harassed student may believe that the whole thing is her fault. It is not something that she should report but something she should be ashamed of. And so her energies are likely to be spent trying to cope with or "manage" the incident, not reporting it or attempting to bring the sexual harasser to justice.[21]

The asymmetrical power and influence of students and professors not only affect the student's perception of whether or not her claims of sexual harassment would be believed, they also affect her perception of the risks involved in making such a report (even when she does not fear being disbelieved). The professor holds the power of evaluation, and often enough, the student sees him as gatekeeper to her desired career. If she displeases him, then—whether it is through the mechanism of letters of reference or the more informal workings of the "old boy network"—he may, she fears, ruin her career prospects.[22]

The structural organization of the university also serves to deter victims from reporting sexually inappropriate behavior. The myriad of departments, programs, divisions, and colleges may be quite daunting to an undergraduate, who may not understand the relations between them or be able easily to determine who has authority with respect to what.[23] Nor does it help that some of those people to whom a student might turn appear as confused and powerless as the student herself—or altogether uninterested. A student may summon up her courage to report an incident of sexual misconduct to a professor whom she feels she can trust, only to be told to report it to the department chair, whom she may not know at all. If the department chair has not been through this before or if the chair is overworked or less than sympathetic to her plight, then the student may be met with (what she interprets as) annoyance and indifference ("Well, what do you want me to do about it?") or referred to a dean, who may seem to the student a distant, busy, and daunting individual. The organization of the university, with its convoluted procedures and divisions of responsibility, is quotidian to experienced faculty members who understand the hierarchy and the system. But they may be intimidating to someone who does not understand them and who is already traumatized and alienated.

The attitudes of academics toward their colleagues and students and their views about their own intellectual mission and personal responsibilities may also serve to discourage students from reporting sexual harassment. What is perhaps more important, however, is that those attitudes clearly serve to deter faculty members who learn of a colleague's sexually inappropriate behavior from taking action on it.

"Educators see themselves as a community of scholars bound together by common interests and goals."[24] They are reluctant to "break ranks," to do things that they perceive as disloyal or damaging to a colleague. In some cases this reluctance may be an expression of a long-standing liberal commitment to tolerance of difference or a manifestation of the desire to uphold academic freedom or respect the autonomy of one's colleagues.[25] In other cases, and less (ostensibly) nobly, it may be thought to stem from academics' desire to be left alone to get on with their own work, protect their own interests, or stay out of academic politics. But whatever the precise blend of factors (what might be called) the ideology of the faculty tends to support the stance of uninvolvement.

Untenured and nontenure-track faculty are in an especially precarious position. The accused senior colleague may wield a good deal of power in the university and in his particular academic field. If displeased or moved to seek retaliation, he may do things that place the untenured faculty member's job at risk. Female faculty members—who are statistically more likely to be untenured or not tenure-track and very much in the minority in their profession—may be particularly vulnerable. Both their professional success thus far and their professional future may well depend upon their being perceived as "good colleagues," people who happen to be female in a largely male context and profession and "don't make a fuss about it." Becoming involved with a sexual harassment case may call attention to a female instructor's gender in ways that make her uncomfortable and may place her in double jeopardy, for she may feel that she is being obliged to risk her own credibility, her good relations with her colleagues, and her own professional connections. And oddly enough, though there is no shortage of good motivations for helping a student who reports an incident of sexual misconduct—a desire to help and protect a student who is hurt and frightened and feels she has nowhere else to turn, the desire to uphold the express and tacit values of the institution, the perception of the need to show students that female faculty members can act with strength and integrity—the female instructor who is willing to assist a student who complains of sexual harassment may find her own motives impugned by resentful male colleagues. As an older woman (and therefore, as convention has it, a less-attractive woman) she may be accused of projecting her unfulfilled desires for male sexual attention onto the student, of being a harridan, or a lesbian who wants to get even with men, of being bitter about her own lack of academic success (which she wrongly and wrongfully attributes to being a woman), and so on.[26]

It is clear that both students' reluctance to come forward with complaints of sexual harassment and faculty members' disinclination to get involved when students do come forward contribute to an underestimation of the scope of the problem of sexual harassment in academia. It is not only the frequency with which sexually inappropriate behavior occurs that is underestimated, however, but the extent of the damage it causes as well. The explanation of why this is so is both complex and multifaceted.

Part of the explanation lies in the invisibility of much of the damage in question. It is easy to see the harm in an instructor's following through on a threat to take reprisals against a student who rejects his demands or in an instructor's tendering an unduly (though perhaps not deliberately or even consciously) harsh evaluation of the student who does not respond favorably to his sexual overtures. Those students are the victims of unfair academic evaluations, and both the professor's integrity and the integrity of the institution's grading practices are severely compromised by such behavior. But other harms—to the individual student, to other students, to the educational institution, and to the society at large—are less obvious.

Many of the students who find themselves the recipients of unwelcome sexual overtures, remarks, or questions deal with the problem by "managing" it, and the most common form of management is avoidance: The student drops the course, ceases to attend the class, withdraws the application to be a lab assistant, quits coming to office hours, changes her major, or, in the most extreme cases, drops out of school altogether.[27] Though these avoidance tactics may effectively remove the opportunity for an instructor to engage in harassing behavior, they do so at a cost. The student who thinks she can avoid being sexually harassed by simply avoiding the professor in question may thereby be deprived of valuable academic and professional opportunities, and the pool of motivated and intelligent aspirants to the relevant profession is

thus reduced. Though, on such a scenario, both the damage to the individual and the loss to society are real, they are largely undetectable. If the number of women in the profession is already low, then the temptation may be to suppose, for example, that "women just aren't interested in engineering" or that "most women just aren't able to do the sort of abstract thinking required for graduate-level physics," adding the insult of misdiagnosis to the injury of sexual harassment. Women who were in fact driven out of the profession by being robbed of the opportunity to pursue their studies in peace are deemed uninterested or incapable. And viewing these women as uninterested or incapable obviously has implications for how other female aspirants to such careers are likely to be viewed, and to view themselves.

Nor does the damage stop there. When a student is given grounds for wondering whether her instructor's academic interest and encouragement were motivated by his sexual interest in her, she may well come to doubt the legitimacy of her previous accomplishments: Perhaps her success thus far has owed more to sexual attributes that instructors found attractive than to her own hard work and ability. A good, serious, hardworking student may thus lose the sort of self-confidence that anyone needs to succeed in a competitive field, and that women especially need if they are to succeed in traditionally male professions that remain statistically (if not ideologically) male dominated. If, in addition, other students and instructors attribute the harassed student's academic success to sexual involvement with, or manipulation of, her instructors, then relationships with her peers and her other instructors (and with her own students, if she is a teaching assistant) may well be harmed, and suspicion may be cast on the success of other women. More subtly, both students and instructors may be drawn into a familiar form of overgeneralization and thus may come to harbor the suspicion that women's successes in the academic and professional fields in which they are a significant minority owe more to the women's skills at sexually manipulating those in power than to their hard work and ability. Generalized resentment of women or the unspoken background belief that women do not play fair or cannot "pull their own weight" may result, and this consequence may silently lead instructors to interact differently with male and female students and to approach them with different expectations. Given the insidious working of socialization, neither the students nor the instructors may be aware of the existence of such differential treatment; yet it may well be prejudicial and, ultimately, extremely detrimental. Again, both the existence of the harm and its causation are difficult to pin down in such cases and difficult to distinguish from the apparently statistically supported view that "women just aren't good at (or interested in) physics."

It should be clear from this discussion that sexual harassment (or, more broadly, sexually inappropriate behavior) can cause significant damage to the individuals who are its direct victims, to other women, and to the society at large. But it is hard to make the estimation of that damage more precise, for attempts to arrive at a more precise measure of the damage are complicated by the many other factors that make academic and professional success more difficult for women. It is not likely, after all, that a woman's first or only experience of sex discrimination will occur in a college lecture hall or in a professor's office, and it is plausible to suppose that a woman's prior experiences will influence how much damage will be done to her by an instructor's sexual harassment or other

sexually inappropriate behavior. Prior experiences may both magnify the harm that is done to her by sexual harassment and, at the same time, diminish the possibility of perceiving that behavior as the cause of the harm. If women have routinely been victims of sex discrimination or societal sexist attitudes, then how can one say that it is the experience of sexual harassment in the university that is the cause of a woman's subsequent distress or the explanation of her decision to enter a "traditionally female" job or profession?[28]

Reflection on this problem suggests a connection between widespread ignorance about the extent of sexually inappropriate behavior in the university and the seriousness of the damage it may cause, and the difficulties involved in attempting to come up with a widely acceptable definition of sexual harassment. In a society that many people would characterize as pervaded by sexist attitudes (if not actual sex discrimination) and in one in which there is disagreement about what constitutes (objectionable) sexism and what is merely a response to differences between men and women, it may be difficult, if not impossible, to reach a consensus about what constitutes sexual harassment. Any university policy that hopes to do any good must take note of this fact.

Endnotes

Acknowledgment: I wish to thank Susan Hobson-Panico, Thomas A. Stermitz, and S. Mickie Grover for their helpful discussion of some of the issues addressed in this essay.

1. Claire Saffran, "What Men Do to Women on the Job," *Redbook* (November 1976), pp. 149, 217–223; see p. 217: "In fact, nearly 9 out of 10 report that they have experienced one or more forms of unwanted attentions on the job. This can be visual (leering and ogling) or verbal (sexual remarks and teasing). It can escalate to pinching, grabbing and touching, to subtle hints and pressures, to overt requests for dates and sexual favors—with the implied threat that it will go against the woman if she refuses."

2. See, e.g., Karen Lindsay, "Sexual Harassment on the Job and How to Stop It," *Ms.* (November 1977), pp. 47–48, 50–51, 74–75, 78; Margaret Mead, "A Proposal: We Need Taboos on Sex at Work," *Redbook* (April 1978), pp. 31, 33, 38; Caryl Rivers, "Sexual Harassment: The Executive's Alternative to Rape," *Mother Jones* (June 1978), pp. 21–24,

28; Claire Saffran, "Sexual Harassment: The View From the Top," *Redbook* (March 1981), pp. 45–51. See also Constance Backhouse and Leah Cohen, *Sexual Harassment on the Job* (Englewood Cliffs, N.J.: Prentice-Hall, 1981), originally published in 1978 as *The Secret Oppression;* and Catherine A. MacKinnon, *Sexual Harassment of Working Women* (New Haven: Yale University Press, 1979).

Popular discussions of sexual harassment in academia include Adrienne Munich, "Seduction in Academe," *Psychology Today* (February 1978), pp. 82–84, 108; Anne Nelson, "Sexual Harassment at Yale," *Nation*, January 14, 1978, pp. 7–10; Lorenzo Middleton, "Sexual Harassment by Professors: An 'Increasingly Visible' Problem," *Chronicle of Higher Education*, September 15, 1980, pp. 1, 4–5; Noel Epstein, "When Professors Swap Good Grades for Sex," *Washington Post*, September 6, 1981, pp. C1, C4; Anne Field, "Harassment on Campus: Sex in a Tenured Position?" *Ms.* (September 1981), pp. 68, 70, 73, 100–102; Suzanne Perry, "Sexual Harassment on the Campuses:

Deciding Where to Draw the Line," *Chronicle of Higher Education,* March 23, 1983, pp. 21–22.

3. In *Barnes v. Castle,* 561 F2d 983 (D.C. Cir. 1977), which held that sexual harassment is actionable as sex-based discrimination under Title VII and also extended some liability to an employer for the discriminatory acts of its supervisors.

4. *Alexander v. Yale University,* 549 F. Supp. 1 (D. Conn 1977), established sexual harassment as sex discrimination under Title IX.

5. *Meritor Savings Bank FSB v. Vinson,* 1206 S. Ct. 2399 (1986).

6. Thus both Title VII and Title IX apply when a student is sexually harassed by an instructor. Under Title IX, a student may have a cause of action against the individual instructor who sexually harassed her, and under Title VII, a cause of action against the university that employed that instructor. For relevant discussion, see Annette Gibbs and Robin B. Balthorpe, "Sexual Harassment in the Workplace and Its Ramifications for Academia," *Journal of College Student Personnel* 23 (1982), 158–162.

7. See, for example, "Statement on Professional Ethics," adopted in 1966 (pp. 133–134 of the *AAUP Policy Documents and Reports,* Washington, D.C.: AAUP, 1984), which condemns "any exploitation for [a teacher's] private advantage" (p. 133); "A Statement of the Association's Council: Freedom and Responsibility," (pp. 135–136), adopted in 1970, which declares that "students are entitled to an atmosphere conductive to learning and to even-handed treatment in all aspects of the teacher–student relationship" (p. 135); and "Sexual Harassment: Suggested Policy and Procedures for Handling Complaints," (pp. 98–100), adopted in 1984, which states, "it is the policy of this institution that no member of the academic community may sexually harass another" (p. 99).

8. See, e.g., Eliza G. C. Collins and Timothy B. Blodgett, "Sexual Harassment . . . Some See It . . . Some Won't," *Harvard Business Review* 59 (1981), 76–95; Phyllis L. Crocker, "An Analysis of University Definitions of Sexual Harassment," *Signs* 8 (1983), 696–707; John Hughes and Larry May, "Sexual Harassment," *Social Theory and Practice* 6 (1980), 249–280; Catherine A. MacKinnon, "Sexual Harassment: Its First Decade in Court," in her *Feminism Unmodified* (Cambridge: Harvard University Press, 1987), pp. 103–116, 251–256; Rosemary Tong, "Sexual Harassment," in her *Women, Sex, and the Law* (Totowa, N.J.: Rowman and Littlefield, 1983).

9. There is some disagreement as to whether it is sex discrimination, but there can be no serious doubt that it is wrongful discrimination. Whether he follows through on the threat and whether or not she submits to it are irrelevant. See, e.g., Crocker, "Analysis of University Definitions," p. 704: "Once a student is propositioned, all her future interactions with, and evaluations by, the professor are tainted and suspect, whether a promise or threat was ever made or carried out."

10. See Phyllis L. Crocker, "Annotated Bibliography on Sexual Harassment in Education," *Women's Rights Law Reporter* 7 (1982), 91–106. And see *Symposium on Sexual Harassment* in *Thought & Action* 5 (1989): 17–52, especially the essay by Anne Traux, "Sexual Harassment in Higher Education: What We've Learned," pp. 25–38, for an overview of surveys and results. Though a good deal of the sexual harassment on campus involves faculty members and administrators as victims, and some involves students as harassers, considerations of space and focus require that I confine this essay to the discussion of sexual harassment that involves students as victims and instructors as harassers. Discussion will also be confined to cases in which it is male instructors who are the harassers and female students who are the victims. As many commentators have observed, the cases in which a female instructor harasses a male student or a male instructor harasses a male student are few and far between. According to Traux, p. 25: "Nationally, about 95 percent of all sexual harassment reports involve men harassing females." See also Gibbs and Balthorpe, "Sexual Harassment in the Workplace"; MacKinnon, "Sexual Harassment: Its First Decade"; Tong, "Sexual Harassment"; Donna J. Benson and Gregg E. Thomson, "Sexual Harassment on a University Campus: The Confluence of Authority Relations, Sexual Interest, and Gender Stratification," *Social Problems* 29 (1982), 236–251; Bernice Lott, Mary Ellen Reilly, and Dale R. Howard, "Sexual Assault and Harassment: A Campus Community Case Study," *Signs* 8 (1982), 296–319.

11. Because . . . there is so much disagreement about what sorts of conduct constitute actual sexual harassment, and because *sexual harassment* is a legal term that is used to describe certain forms of legally proscribed sex discrimination, I prefer to use the broader (and vaguer) terms *sexually inappropriate behavior* and *sexual misconduct* whenever context and expression permit. If, as I shall argue, there are different kinds of sexually inappropriate behavior that may be wrong but are not (for various reasons) happily classified with the sorts of wrongful behavior that constitute blatant sexual harassment, then it may be misleading to use *sexual harassment* as omnivorously as many commentators—and the Equal Opportunity Commission—have done.

12. It is, of course, possible for a female professor to harass a male student or for a professor of one sex to harass a student of the same sex. But it is clear that the

vast majority of harassers are men, and the vast majority of victims are women, and surveys suggest that the incidence of sexual harassment of male students by female instructors is indeed very small. It is of course possible for a female instructor to make a *quid pro quo* offer/threat to a male student. But the fact that women are a minority, both in the upper echelons of the teaching and administrative staff and in most departments, together with the familiar facts about gender expectations and status, suggests that such harassment will be rare. And subtler forms of sexually inappropriate behavior, which the perpetrator does not perceive as unwelcome or coercive, will probably be even rarer.

Involvements between older, established men and young women are accepted as normal, while those between older, established women and young, unestablished men clearly are not. Women who are involved in relationships with young, less-established men are generally the object of criticism, not admiration or even tolerance. In addition, since the determination of a woman's social status is held to depend heavily on the status of the male she is associated with, the attractions of such a relationship are likely not to be great: Whereas a female student may gain status by involvement with a male professor, a female professor forfeits status by involvement with a male student. If, as most commentators point out, sexual harassment is primarily an issue of power, not sex, there is considerably less incentive for a female faculty member to seek involvement with a male student, and considerably more disincentive. Finally, one can reasonably suppose that because women have long been in the minority in academia and have long been subject to various forms of sex discrimination and disparagement, they are likely to be more sensitive to the risks and problems that even well-intentioned relationships between persons of unequal power create. Whether it is accurate to say that gender is itself a form of hierarchy in a society that has been and continues to be so male-dominated (see MacKinnon, "Sexual Harassment: Its First Decade"), there are good reasons to recognize that, as things now stand, the problem of sexual harassment is almost always one of men harassing women. Though, in the abstract, the issue of sexual harassment—the exploitative use of power—is sex-neutral, if not sex-blind, in circumstances in which it is men who (by and large) possess the power, it is women who will (by and large) be the victims.

That both males and females can be the victims of sexually inappropriate behavior has sometimes—mistakenly—been thought to undercut the claim that sexual harassment is a form of sex discrimination. But the existence of cases in which a male student is victimized by a female instructor does nothing to undercut such a claim, for the effects of being so victimized may be different for men and women, and the background of long-standing and ongoing discrimination against women makes it plausible to suppose that the effects would indeed be different. People suppose that because wrongs are committed both in the case in which a male professor harasses a female student and in the case in which a female professor harasses a male student, they must be the same wrong. But this is not obviously a correct assumption. In both cases there is a wrongful abuse of power and authority, but in one case . . . there is also—because of the long-standing and ongoing discrimination against women—another wrong, namely, that of sex discrimination.

Nor does the existence of cases of single-sex harassment undercut the claim that sexual harassment is sex discrimination, unless one regards the obvious and widespread discrimination against homosexuals as some form of discrimination other than sex discrimination or construes sex discrimination so narrowly that conventional gender identity is seen as defining one's sex. Neither of these assumptions is plausible.

There are reasons for being uneasy at the characterization of sexual harassment as a form of sex discrimination. In some cases of sexually inappropriate behavior (which the Equal Opportunity Commission Guidelines would classify as sexual harassment), it is primarily an instructor's obvious disrespect, rather than the sexual cast of that disrespect, that seems more perspicuously identified as the thing that makes his actions wrong.

But the best reasons for uneasiness are probably pragmatic ones. Recent Supreme Court decisions have significantly weakened the scope of protections against racial discrimination (from Title VII and elsewhere); there is reason to suspect that sex discrimination protections will fare no better. They may even fare worse, for there is good reason to insist that there are no important ineliminable differences between persons of different races, but there are obviously differences between the sexes.

13. One has only to look at advertising or television sitcoms, or—as Billie Wright Dziech and Linda Weiner point out in *The Lecherous Professor* (Boston: Beacon Press, 1984)—watch teenagers interact in a shopping mall to be reminded how powerful and pervasive gender expectations are. See Benson and Thomson, "Sexual Harassment on a University Campus"; MacKinnon, *Sexual Harassment of Working Women*; MacKinnon, "Sexual Harassment: Its First Decade."

14. According to Traux, "Sexual Harassment in Higher Education," p. 26, "Of those harassed, not more than one in 10 actually report the harassment."

15. And as many would point out, women and men are not peers in these areas either.

16. To some degree, what medical ethicists have called "the fallacy of the generalization of expertise" is at work here. People who are thought to be successful or expert in one area are frequently—and unreasonably—thought to be successful or expert in others. Thus some people wrongly suppose that physicians are knowledgeable in matters of medical ethics (simply) because they are knowledgeable in medical matters, and others suppose that the good scholar of history (e.g.) must also be a good and decent person.

17. See Robert Shrank, "Two Women, Three Men on a Raft," *Harvard Business Review* 55 (1977), 100–109 for an interesting discussion of how men may unreflectively work to undermine women's self-confidence.

18. Or she may think that she should "be complimented, not incensed, if confronted with male sexual interest" (see Benson and Thomson, "Sexual Harassment on a Campus," p. 237) and thus feel that she has no right to complain.

19. One woman interviewed by Collins and Blodgett ("Sexual Harassment," p. 93) said: "A lot of women hesitate to report sexual harassment because women: (1) don't think they'll be believed; (2) will be punished by smaller raises or cruddy jobs [the analogue in the university context: will be punished by lower grades or undeservedly harsh evaluations]; (3) will be ostracized by male and female employees [students and other instructors]; (4) will be accused of inviting the advance; (5) have guilt feelings that perhaps it was invited subconsciously; (6) fear publicity; (7) are unsure exactly what is harassment and what is just interaction of people."

20. Some of the novels that come to mind here are Joyce Carol Oates, *Them*; John Barth, *The End of the Road*; and Bernard Malamud, *Dubin's Lives*. See Dziech and Weiner, *The Lecherous Professor*, pp. 62–63, 68, 118.

21. See especially Benson and Thomson, "Sexual Harassment on Campus"; and Dziech and Weiner, *The Lecherous Professor*, chap. 4. Also relevant is Judith Berman Brandenburg, "Sexual Harassment in the University:

Guidelines for Establishing a Grievance Procedure," *Signs* 8 (1982), 321–336. See Mary P. Rowe, "Dealing with Sexual Harassment," *Harvard Business Review* 59 (1981), 42–47, for a detailed set of proposed procedures for harassed employees that places more emphasis on "management" of sexual harassment in the workplace than on prevention or redress.

22. A quotation from Dziech and Weiner, *The Lecherous Professor*, p. 83, drives this point home. One pre-med student said: It's easy for someone else to say that I should do something about Dr. —, but how can I? He was the first person at — to take my work seriously. At least I think it's my work that made him notice me. He's the one who's pushing for me to get into med school. If I refuse him, then I ruin my whole life.

23. Material in this and the succeeding paragraph benefited from the discussion in chap. 2 of Dziech and Weiner, *The Lecherous Professor*.

24. Ibid., p. 49.

25. I do not mean to suggest that respect for academic freedom or one's colleagues' autonomy requires (or even permits) a faculty member who learns of an incident of sexual harassment to ignore the student who reports it or otherwise discourage her from pressing her complaint. Neither academic freedom nor professional autonomy is absolute, and it is difficult to see what intellectually respectable academic purpose *is* served by the tolerance of sexual harassment. Of course, a faculty member who believes that some respectable academic purpose is served by tolerating a colleague's sexually inappropriate behavior should be given the opportunity to explain his or her views. But such an opportunity can arise only if students are listened to and encouraged, not dissuaded from bringing their sexual harassment complaints forward in the first place.

26. See Dziech and Weiner, *The Lecherous Professor*, chap. 6.

27. See note 21.

28. The old adage that "defendants must take plaintiffs as they find them" is of some help here, but not much.

38. *Harris* v. *Forklift Systems, Inc.*

SUPREME COURT OF THE UNITED STATES

The issue before the Supreme Court was whether a hostile work environment under Title VII of the Civil Rights Act of 1964 must cause serious harm to a reasonable person's psychological well-being. The Court unanimously ruled that behavior that fell short of seriously harming a reasonable person's psychological well-being could still be sexual harassment if in other ways it unreasonably interfered with a person's work environment.

. . . . In this case we consider the definition of a discriminatorily "abusive work environment" (also known as a "hostile work environment") under Title VII of the Civil Rights Act of 1964.

Teresa Harris worked as a manager at Forklift Systems, Inc., an equipment rental company, from April 1985 until October 1987. Charles Hardy was Forklift's president.

The magistrate found that, throughout Harris's time at forklift, Hardy often insulted her because of her gender and often made her the target of unwanted sexual innuendos. Hardy told Harris on several occasions, in the presence of other employees, "You're a woman, what do you know" and "We need a man as the rental manager"; at least once, he told her she was "a dumb ass woman." Again in front of others, he suggested that the two of them "go to the Holiday Inn to negotiate [Harris's] raise." Hardy occasionally asked Harris and other female employees to get coins from his front pants pocket. He threw objects on the ground in front of Harris and other women, and asked them to pick the objects up. He made sexual innuendos about Harris' and other women's clothing.

In mid-August 1987, Harris complained to Hardy about his conduct. Hardy said he was surprised that Harris was offended, claimed he was only joking, and apologized. He also promised he would stop, and based on this assurance Harris stayed on the job. But in early September, Hardy began anew: While Harris was arranging a deal with one of Forklift's customers, he asked her, again in front of other employees, "What did you do, promise the guy . . . some [sex] Saturday

night?" On October 1, Harris collected her paycheck and quit.

Harris then sued Forklift, claiming that Hardy's conduct had created an abusive work environment for her because of her gender. The United States District court for the Middle District of Tennessee, adopting the report and recommendation of the Magistrate, found this to be "a close case," but held that Hardy's conduct did not create an abusive environment. The court found that some of Hardy's comments "offended [Harris], and would offend the reasonable woman," but that they were not

> so severe as to be expected to seriously affect [Harris'] psychological well-being. A reasonable woman manager under like circumstances would have been offended by Hardy, but his conduct would not have risen to the level of interfering with that person's work performance.
>
> Neither do I believe that [Harris] was subjectively so offended that she suffered injury. . . . Although Hardy may at times have genuinely offended [Harris], I do not believe that he created a working environment so poisoned as to be intimidating or abusive to [Harris].

In focusing on the employee's psychological well-being, the District court was following Circuit precedent.

We granted certiorari to resolve a conflict among the Circuits on whether conduct, to be actionable as "abusive work environment" harassment (no *quid pro quo* harassment issue is present here), must "seriously affect [an employee's] psychological well-being" or lead the plaintiff to "suffe[r] injury."

Title VII of the Civil Rights Act of 1964 makes it "an unlawful employment practice for an employer . . . to discriminate against any individual with respect to his compensation, terms, conditions, or privileges of employment, because of such individual's race, color, religion, sex, or national origin." As we made clear in *Meritor Savings Bank v. Vinson* (1986), this language "is not limited to 'economic' or 'tangible' discrimination. The phrase 'terms, conditions, or privileges of employment' evinces a congressional intent 'to strike at the entire spectrum of disparate treatment of men and women' in employment," which includes requiring people to work in a discriminatorily hostile or abusive environment. When the workplace is permeated with "discriminatory intimidation, ridicule, and insult," that is "sufficiently severe or pervasive to alter the conditions of the victim's employment and create an abusive working environment," Title VII is violated.

This standard, which we reaffirm today, takes a middle path between making actionable any conduct that is merely offensive and requiring the conduct to cause a tangible psychological injury. As we pointed out in *Meritor,* "mere utterance of an . . . epithet which engenders offensive feelings in a employee" does not sufficiently affect the conditions of employment to implicate Title VII. Conduct that is not severe or pervasive enough to create an objectively hostile or abusive work environment—an environment that a reasonable person would find hostile or abusive—is beyond Title VII's purview. Likewise, if the victim does not subjectively perceive the environment to be abusive, the conduct has not actually altered the conditions of the victim's employment, and there is no Title VII violation.

But Title VII comes into play before the harassing conduct leads to a nervous breakdown. A discriminatorily abusive work environment, even one that does not seriously affect employees' psychological well-being, can and often will detract from employees' job performance, discourage employees from remaining on the job, or keep them from advancing in their careers. Moreover, even without regard to these tangible effects, the very fact that the discriminatory conduct was so severe or pervasive that it created a work environment abusive to employees because of

their race, gender, religion, or national origin offends Title VII's broad rule of workplace equality. The appalling conduct alleged in *Meritor*, and the reference in that case to environments "'so heavily polluted with discrimination as to destroy completely the emotional and psychological stability of minority group workers,'" merely present some especially egregious examples of harassment. They do not mark the boundary of what is actionable.

We therefore believe the District Court erred in relying on whether the conduct "seriously affect[ed] plaintiff's psychological well-being" or led her to "suffe[r] injury." Such an inquiry may needlessly focus the fact finder's attention on concrete psychological harm, an element Title VII does not require. Certainly Title VII bars conduct that would seriously affect a reasonable person's psychological well-being, but the statute is not limited to such conduct. So long as the environment would reasonably be perceived, and is perceived, as hostile or abusive, there is no need for it also to be psychologically injurious.

This is not, and by its nature cannot be, a mathematically precise test. We need not answer today all the potential questions it raises, nor specifically address the EEOC's new regulations on this subject. But we can say that whether an environment is "hostile" or "abusive" can be determined only by looking at all the circumstances. These may include the frequency of the discriminatory conduct; its severity; whether it is physically threatening or humiliating, or a mere offensive utterance; and whether it unreasonably interferes with an employee's work performance. The effect on the employee's psychological well-being is, of course, relevant to determining whether the plaintiff actually found the environment abusive. But while psychological harm, like any other relevant factor, may be taken into account, no single factor is required.

Forklift, while conceding that a requirement that the conduct seriously affect psychological well-being is unfounded, argues that the District Court nonetheless correctly applied the *Meritor* standard. We disagree. Though the District Court did conclude that the work environment was not "intimidating or abusive to [Harris]," it did so only after finding that the conduct was not "so severe as to be expected to seriously affect plaintiff's psychological well-being," and that Harris was not "subjectively so offended that she suffered injury." The District Court's application of these incorrect standards may well have influenced its ultimate conclusion, especially given that the court found this to be a "close case."

We therefore reverse the judgment of the Court of Appeals, and remand the case for further proceedings consistent with this opinion.

Suggestions for Further Reading

Bravo, Ellen, and Casedy, Ellen. *The 9 to 5 Guide to Combating Sexual Harassment.* New York: Wiley, 1992.

Copeland, Lois, and Wolfe, Leslie R. *Violence Against Women as Bias Motivated Hate Crime: Defining the Issues.* Washington, D.C.: Center for Women Policy Studies, 1991.

Dziech, Billie Wright, and Weiner, Linda. *The Lecherous Professor: Sexual Harassment on Campus.* Champaign: University of Illinois Press, 1992.

Hooks, Bell. "A Feminist Challenge: Must We Call All Women Sister?" *Z Magazine,* February 1992.

Larkin, June. *Sexual Harassment: High School Girls Speak Out.* Toronto: Second Story Press, 1994.

McKenzie, Richard B. "The Thomas/Hill Hearings: A New Legal Harassment." *The Freeman,* January 1992. Available from the Foundation for Economic Education, Irvington-on-Hudson, N.Y. 10533

MacKinnon, Catharine A. *Sexual Harassment of Working Women: A Case of Sex Discrimination.* New Haven: Yale University Press, 1979.

Marin, Richard. "It's Not Just a Woman Thing: Many Men Do Understand." *The Washington Post National Weekly Edition,* October 14–20, 1991.

Morgenson, Gretchen. "Watch That Leer, Stifle That Joke," *Forbes,* May 15, 1989.

Morris, Celia. *Bearing Witness: Sexual Harassment, Citizenship, Government.* New York: Little, Brown, 1994.

Niven, David. "The Case of the Hidden Harassment." *Harvard Business Review,* March–April 1992.

Paludi, Michele, ed. *Working 9 to 5: Women, Men, Sex, and Power.* Albany: State University of New York Press, 1991.

Phelps, Timothy M., and Winternitz, Helen. *Capital Games: Clarence Thomas, Anita Hill, and the Story of a Supreme Court Nomination.* Westport, Conn.: Hyperion, 1992.

Repa, Barbara Kate, and Petrocelli, William. *Sexual Harassment on the Job.* Berkeley, Calif.: Nolo Press, 1992.

Riggs, Robert, Murrell, Patricia, and Cutting, JoAnn. *Sexual Harassment in Higher Education.* Washington: George Washington University Press, 1993.

Sunrall, Amber Coverdale. *Sexual Harassment: Women Speak Out.* Freedom, Calif.: The Crossing Press, 1992.

Webb, Susan L. *Step Forward: Sexual Harassment in the Workplace.* New York: Mastermedia, 1991.

Pornography

Introduction

Basic Concepts

The problem of pornography, as Catharine MacKinnon formulates it in Selection 39, is whether pornography should be prohibited for promoting discrimination and violence against women. But this has not been how the problem has been traditionally understood. In the Anglo-American legal tradition, pornography has always been identified with obscenity.[1] The test for obscenity set forth by the U.S. Supreme Court in *Roth v. United States* (1957) is "whether to the average person, applying contemporary community standards, the dominant theme of the material taken as a whole appeals to prurient interest." This test itself was an attempt to improve upon an 1868 test of obscenity that was taken over from English law. According to this earlier test, obscene materials are such that they have the tendency "to deprave and corrupt those whose minds are open to such immoral influences, and into whose hands a publication of this sort may fall." In *Roth v. United States,* the U.S. Supreme Court sought to remedy three defects in this 1868 test. First, the 1868 test permitted books to be judged obscene on the basis of isolated passages read out of context. In contrast,

the Roth test requires that material be judged as obscene only if "the dominant theme of the material taken as a whole" is so judged. Second, the 1868 test allowed the obscenity of a work to be determined by its likely effects on unusually susceptible persons. By contrast, the Roth test judges material to be obscene on the basis of its likely effect on the "average person." Third, the 1868 test posited standards of obscenity fixed for all time. By contrast, the Roth test only appeals to "contemporary community standards."

Yet despite these advantages of the Roth test, problems remained. First, who was the average person to whose prurience the obscene materials has to appeal? In *Miskin v. New York* (1966), the Supreme Court needed to apply its Roth test to books that described sadomasochistic sexual acts, fetishism, lesbianism, and male homosexuality. Since these works did not appeal to the prurient interest of the average person in the population at large, the Supreme Court reformulated its Roth test so that when "material is designed for and primarily disseminated to a clearly defined deviant sexual group, . . . the prurient-appeal requirement of the Roth test is satisfied if the dominant theme of the material taken as a whole appeals to the prurient interest in sex of the members of that group." Second, how was the Supreme Court to avoid the task of having to determine what are community standards for an endless number of obscenity cases? In *Miller v. California* (1973), the Supreme Court dealt with the problem by delegating and relativizing the task of determining contemporary community standards to local communities. Henceforth, the application of local community standards determines whether material appeals to prurient interest. Obviously, this puts a severe burden on national publishers who now have to take into account local community standards for any work they distribute. For example, when Larry C. Flynt routinely mailed a copy of his publication *Hustler* to a person who had ordered it by mail from a town in Ohio, he was subsequently tried for a violation of the Ohio obscenity statutes and sentenced to seven to twenty-five years in prison. So even with these improvements in the Supreme Court's test for obscenity, problems still remain.

Alternative Views

In Selection 39, Catharine MacKinnon takes an entirely new approach to pornography and obscenity. She sees pornography as a practice of sex discrimination, a violation of women's civil rights. She defines pornography "as the graphic sexually explicit subordination of women through pictures or words that also includes women dehumanized as sexual objects, things or commodities; enjoying pain or humiliation or rape; being tied up, cut up, mutilated, bruised, or physically hurt; in postures of sexual submission or servility or display; reduced to body parts, penetrated by objects or animals, or presented in scenarios of degradation, injury, torture; shown as filthy or inferior; bleeding, bruised or hurt in a context that makes these conditions sexual." By contrast, she defines erotica "as sexually explicit materials premised on equality." She argues that pornography is a harmful form of gender inequality that outweighs any social interest in its protection by recognized First Amend-

ment standards. She points to recent experimental research that shows that pornography causes harm to women through increasing men's attitudes and behavior of discrimination in both violent and nonviolent forms.

In Selection 40, Wendy Kaminer surveys the history of the feminist antiporn movement in North America from the late 1970s to the present. She notes how the movement became politically allied with the New Right in the 1980s; how it succeeded in passing antiporn legislation in Indianapolis in 1984, which was later declared unconstitutional by a federal appeals court; and how, most recently, it has mounted new legislative endeavors in the United States and Canada both at the state and national levels. Kaminer points out that the feminist case against pornography is based on a presumed link between pornography and sexual violence, but she questions how direct that link is and whether it depends on a blurring of the distinction between speech and conduct. She also suggests that alcohol and other substance abuse may have a more direct role in causing sexual violence. Accordingly, she argues that legislative endeavors other than banning pornography would be more likely to reduce sexual violence, and that the most likely legislative result of the feminist antiporn movement, given its political allegiance with the New Right, would be a broader censorship that would not serve feminist interests.

Kaminer further notes that the first application of the Supreme Court ruling in Canada against pornography was to prohibit the distribution of a small lesbian magazine. But Catharine MacKinnon has argued that this action by the Canadian custom authority was not, in fact, based on Canada's recent Supreme Court decision, but rather on a more long-standing practice of the custom authority that should have been disallowed in light of the Court's recent decision.[2] Moreover, if enforcement of the Canadian Court's recent antiporn decision were actually to result in, say, a 25 percent drop in crimes of sexual violence in Canada, then, despite Kaminer's objections, it is difficult to see how this would not constitute sufficient justification for comparable judicial decisions in the United States.

Some opponents of any legal prohibition on pornography point to the Danish experience, where the legalization of pornography has not led to any increase in reported incidents of sexual assault against women. But even here the evidence is mixed because, for example, although the number of rapes reported to authorities has decreased over the years, it is estimated that the number of actual rapes has increased.

Practical Application

In *American Booksellers v. Hudnutt* (Selection 41), the federal judiciary ruled against an Indianapolis ordinance, contending that pornography which qualified as constitutionally protected speech could not be prohibited on the grounds that it caused harm to women. At the same time, the Court seemed to regard the issue of harm to women to be relevant when it argued that pornography did not harm those women who cooperated in the production of pornography because they "generally have the capacity to protect themselves from participating in and being personally victimized by pornography." By contrast, the Supreme Court of Canada judged that preventing harm to women is an acceptable grounds for restricting pornography, and that, moreover, restricting pornography would in fact prevent harm to women.

One explanation for the difference between the rules of the U.S. and Canadian Courts is that, as MacKinnon points out, in sexist societies, it is difficult to recognize the harm that pornography causes women. Yet if MacKinnon is right, treating women equally in this regard will require a radical transformation of our society that will also affect the solutions to the other moral problems discussed in this anthology. Moreover, this radical transformation would be the kind that libertarians would be expected to champion since they are so concerned with preventing harm to others.

Endnotes

1. In ordinary usage, to call something obscene is to condemn that thing as blatantly disgusting, whereas to call something pornographic is simply to characterize it as sexually explicit. So in ordinary usage, unlike the law, it is an open question whether the pornographic is also obscene.

2. Catharine MacKinnon, "The First Amendment Under Fire From the Left," in *Debating Sexual Correctness*, ed. Adele Stan, pp. 116–117.

39. *Pornography, Civil Rights, and Speech*

CATHARINE MACKINNON

Catharine MacKinnon argues that pornography is a practice of sex discrimination and, hence, a violation of women's civil rights. According to MacKinnon, pornography celebrates and legitimizes rape, battery, sexual harassment, and the sexual abuse of children. More generally, it eroticizes the dominance and submission that is the dynamic common to them all. She argues for the constitutionality of city ordinances, which she has helped design, that prohibit pornography.

. . . There is a belief that this is a society in which women and men are basically equals. Room for marginal corrections is conceded, flaws are known to exist, attempts are made to correct what are conceived as occasional lapses from the basic condition of sex equality. Sex discrimination law has concentrated most of its focus on these occasional lapses. It is difficult to overestimate the extent to which this belief in equality is an article of faith for most people, including most women, who wish to live in self-respect in an internal universe, even (perhaps especially) if not in the world. It is also partly an expression of natural law thinking: If we are inalienably equal, we can't "really" be degraded.

This is a world in which it is worth trying. In this world of presumptive equality, people make money based on their training or abilities or diligence or qualifications. They are employed and advanced on the basis of merit. In this world of just deserts, if someone is abused, it is thought to violate the basic rules of the community. If it doesn't, victims are seen to have done something they could have chosen to do differently, by exercise of will or better judgment. Maybe such people have placed themselves in a situation of vulnerability to physical abuse. Maybe they have done something provocative. Or maybe they were just unusually unlucky. In such a world, if such

a person has an experience, there are words for it. When they speak and say it, they are listened to. If they write about it, they will be published. If certain experiences are never spoken about, if certain people or issues are seldom heard from, it is supposed that silence has been chosen. The law, including much of the law of sex discrimination and the First Amendment, operates largely within the realm of these beliefs.

Feminism is the discovery that women do not live in this world, that the person occupying this realm is a man, so much more a man if he is white and wealthy. This world of potential credibility, authority, security, and just rewards, recognition of one's identity and capacity, is a world that some people do inhabit as a condition of birth, with variations among them. It is not a basic condition accorded humanity in this society, but a prerogative of status, a privilege, among other things, of gender.

I call this a discovery because it has not been an assumption. Feminism is the first theory, the first practice, the first movement, to take seriously the situation of all women from the point of view of all women, both on our situation and on social life as a whole. The discovery has therefore been made that the implicit social content of humanism, as well as the standpoint from which legal method has been designed and injuries have been defined, has not been women's standpoint. Defining feminism in a way that connects epistemology with power as the politics of women's point of view, this discovery can be summed up by saying that women live in another world: specifically, a world of *not* equality, a world of inequality.

Looking at the world from this point of view, a whole shadow world of previously invisible silent abuse has been discerned. Rape, battery, sexual harassment, forced prostitution, and the sexual abuse of children emerge as common and systematic. We find that rape happens to women in all contexts, from the family, including rape of girls and babies, to students and women in the workplace, on the streets, at home, in their own bedrooms by men they do not know and by men they do know, by men they are married to, men they have had a social conversation with, and, least often, men they have never seen before. Overwhelmingly, rape is something that men do or attempt to do to women (44 percent of American women according to a recent study) at some point in our lives. Sexual harassment of women by men is common in workplaces and educational institutions. Based on reports in one study of the federal workforce, up to 85 percent of women will experience it, many in physical forms. Between a quarter and a third of women are battered in their homes by men. Thirty-eight percent of little girls are sexually molested inside or outside the family. Until women listened to women, this world of sexual abuse was *not spoken* of. It was the unspeakable. What I am saying is, if you *are* the tree falling in the epistemological forest, your demise doesn't make a sound if no one is listening. Women did not "report" these events, and overwhelmingly do not today, because no one is listening, because no one believes us. This silence does not mean nothing happened, and it does not mean consent. It is the silence of women of which Adrienne Rich has written, "Do not confuse it with any kind of absence."

Believing women who say we are sexually violated has been a radical departure, both methodologically and legally. The extent and nature of rape, marital rape, and sexual harassment itself, were discovered in this way. Domestic battery as a syndrome, almost a habit, was discovered through refusing to believe that when a woman is assaulted by a man to whom she is connected, that it is not an assault. The sexual abuse of children was uncovered, Freud notwithstanding, by believing that children were not making up all this sexual abuse. Now what is striking is that when each discovery is made, and somehow made real in the

world, the response has been: It happens to men too. If women are hurt, men are hurt. If women are raped, men are raped. If women are sexually harassed, men are sexually harassed. If women are battered, men are battered. Symmetry must be reasserted. Neutrality must be reclaimed. Equality must be reestablished.

The only areas where the available evidence supports this, where anything like what happens to women also happens to men, involve children—little boys are sexually abused—and prison. The liberty of prisoners is restricted, their freedom restrained, their humanity systematically diminished, their bodies and emotions confined, defined, and regulated. If paid at all, they are paid starvation wages. They can be tortured at will, and it is passed off as discipline or as means to a just end. They become compliant. They can be raped at will, at any moment, and nothing will be done about it. When they scream, nobody hears. To be a prisoner means to be defined as a member of a group for whom the rules of what can be done to you, of what is seen as abuse of you, are reduced as part of the definition of your status. To be a woman is that kind of definition and has that kind of meaning.

Men *are* damaged by sexism. (By men I mean the status of masculinity that is accorded to males on the basis of their biology but is not itself biological.) But whatever the damage of sexism to men, the condition of being a man is not defined as subordinate to women by force. Looking at the facts of the abuses of women all at once, you see that a woman is socially defined as a person who, whether or not she is or has been, can be treated in these ways by men at any time, and little, if anything, will be done about it. This is what it means when feminists say that maleness is a form of power and femaleness is a form of powerlessness.

In this context, all of this "men too" stuff means that people don't really believe the things I have just said are true, though there really is little question about their empirical accuracy. The data are extremely simple, like women's pay figure of fifty-nine cents on the dollar. People don't really seem to believe that either. Yet there is no question of its empirical validity. This is the workplace story: What women do is seen as not worth much, or what is not worth much is seen as something for women to do. *Women* are seen as not worth much. . . . Now why are these basic realities of the subordination of women to men, for example, that only 7.8 percent of women have never been sexually assaulted, not effectively believed, not perceived as real in the face of all this evidence? Why don't *women* believe our own experiences? In the face of all this evidence, especially of systematic sexual abuse—subjection to violence with impunity is one extreme expression, although not the only one, of a degraded status—the view that basically the sexes are equal in this society remains unchallenged and unchanged. The day I got this was the day I understood its real message, its real coherence: *This is equality for us.*

I could describe this, but I couldn't explain it until I started studying a lot of pornography. In pornography, there it is, in one place, all of the abuses that women had to struggle so long even to begin to articulate, all the *unspeakable* abuse: the rape, the battery, the sexual harassment, the prostitution, and the sexual abuse of children. Only in pornography it is called something else: sex, sex, sex, sex, and sex, respectively. Pornography sexualizes rape, battery, sexual harassment, prostitution, and child sexual abuse; it thereby celebrates, promotes, authorizes, and legitimizes them. More generally, it eroticizes the dominance and submission that is the [common] dynamic. It makes hierarchy sexy and calls that "the truth about sex" or just a mirror of reality. Through this process pornography constructs what a woman is as what men want from sex. This is what pornography means.

Pornography constructs what a woman is in terms of its view of what men want sexually, such that acts of rape, battery, sexual harassment, prostitution, and sexual abuse of children become acts of sexual equality. Pornography's world of equality is a harmonious and balanced place. Men and women are perfectly complementary and perfectly bipolar. Women's desire to be fucked by men is equal to men's desire to fuck women. All the ways men love to take and violate women, women love to be taken and violated. The women who most love this are most men's equals, the most liberated; the most participatory child is the most grown-up, the most equal to an adult. Their consent merely expresses or ratifies these preexisting facts.

The content of pornography is one thing. There, women substantively desire dispossession and cruelty. We desperately want to be bound, battered, tortured, humiliated, and killed. Or, to be fair to the soft core, merely taken and used. This is erotic to the male

point of view. Subjection itself, with self-determination ecstatically relinquished, is the content of women's sexual desire and desirability. Women are there to be violated and possessed, men to violate and possess us, either on screen or by camera or pen on behalf of the consumer. On a simple descriptive level, the inequality of hierarchy, of which gender is the primary one, seems necessary for sexual arousal to work. Other added inequalities identify various pornographic genres or subthemes, although they are always added through gender: age, disability, homosexuality, animals, objects, race (including anti-Semitism), and so on. Gender is never irrelevant.

What pornography *does* goes beyond its content: It eroticizes hierarchy, it sexualizes inequality. It makes dominance and submission into sex. Inequality is its central dynamic; the illusion of freedom coming together with the reality of force is central to its working. Perhaps because this is a bourgeois culture, the victim must look free, appear to be freely acting. Choice is how she got there. Willing is what she is when she is being equal. It seems equally important that then and there she actually be forced and that forcing be communicated on some level, even if only through still photos of her in postures of receptivity and access, available for penetration. Pornography in this view is a form of forced sex, a practice of sexual politics, an institution of gender inequality.

From this perspective, pornography is neither harmless fantasy nor a corrupt and confused misrepresentation of an otherwise natural and healthy sexual situation. It institutionalizes the sexuality of male supremacy, fusing the erotization of dominance and submission with the social construction of male and female. To the extent that gender is sexual, pornography is part of constituting the meaning of that sexuality. Men treat women as who they see women as being. Pornography constructs who that is. Men's power over women means that the way men see women defines who women can be. Pornography is that way. Pornography is not imagery in some relation to a reality elsewhere constructed. It is not a distortion, reflection, projection, expression, fantasy, representation, or symbol either. It is a sexual reality.

In Andrea Dworkin's definitive work, *Pornography: Men Possessing Women*, sexuality itself is a social construct gendered to the ground. Male dominance here is not an artificial overlay upon an underlying inalterable substratum of uncorrupted essential sexual being. Dworkin presents a sexual theory of gender inequality of which pornography is a constitutive practice. The way pornography produces its meaning constructs and defines men and women as such. Gender has no basis in anything other than the social reality its hegemony constructs. Gender is what gender means. The process that gives sexuality its male supremacist meaning is the same process through which gender inequality becomes socially real.

In this approach, the experience of the (overwhelmingly) male audiences who consume pornography is therefore not fantasy or simulation or catharsis but sexual reality, the level of reality on which sex itself largely operates. Understanding this dimension of the problem does not require noticing that pornography models are real women to whom, in most cases, something real is being done; nor does it even require inquiring into the systematic infliction of pornography and its sexuality upon women, although it helps. What matters is the way in which the pornography itself provides what those who consume it want. Pornography *participates* in its audience's eroticism by creating an accessible sexual object, the possession and consumption of which *is* male sexuality, as socially constructed; to be consumed and possessed as which, *is* female sexuality, as socially constructed; pornography is a process that constructs it that way.

The object world is constructed according to how it looks with respect to its possible uses. Pornography defines women by how we look according to how we can be sexually used. Pornography codes how to look at women, so you know what you can do with one when you see one. Gender is an assignment made visually, both originally and in everyday life. A sex object is defined on the basis of its looks, in terms of its usability for sexual pleasure, such that both the looking—the quality of the gaze, including its point of view—and the definition according to use become eroticized as part of the sex itself. This is what the feminist concept "sex object" means. In this sense, sex in life is no less mediated than in art. Men have sex with their image of a woman. It is not that life and art imitate each other; in this sexuality, they *are* each other.

To give a set of rough epistemological translations, to defend pornography as consistent with the equality of the sexes is to defend the subordination of women to men as sexual equality. What in the pornographic view is love and romance looks a great deal like hatred and torture to the feminist. Pleasure and eroticism become violation. Desire appears as lust for dominance and submission. The vulnerability of women's projected sexual availability, that acting we are allowed (that is, asking to be acted upon), is victimization. Play conforms to scripted roles. Fantasy expresses ideology, is not exempt from it. Admiration of natural physical beauty becomes objectification. Harmlessness becomes harm. Pornography is a harm of male supremacy made difficult to see because of its pervasiveness, potency, and, principally, because of its success in making the world a pornographic place. Specifically, its harm cannot be discerned, and will not be addressed, if viewed and approached neutrally, because it *is* so much of "what is." In other words, to the extent pornography succeeds in constructing social reality, it becomes invisible as harm. If we live in a world that pornography creates through the power of men in a male-dominated situation, the issue is not what the harm of pornography is, but how that harm is to become visible.

Obscenity law provides a very different analysis and conception of the problem of pornography. In 1973 the legal definition of obscenity became that which the average person, applying contemporary community standards, would find that, taken as a whole, appeals to the prurient interest; that which depicts or describes in a patently offensive way—you feel like you're a cop reading someone's *Miranda* rights—sexual conduct specifically defined by the applicable state law; and that which, taken as a whole, lacks serious literary, artistic, political, or scientific value. Feminism doubts whether the average person gender-neutral exists; has more questions about the content and process of defining what community standards are than it does about deviations from them; wonders why prurience counts but powerlessness does not and why sensibilities are better protected from offense than women are from exploitation; defines sexuality, and thus its violation and expropriation, more broadly than does state law; and questions why a body of law that has not in practice been able to tell rape from intercourse should, without further guidance, be entrusted with telling pornography from anything less. Taking the work "as a whole" ignores that which the victims of pornography have long known: Legitimate settings diminish the perception of injury done to those whose trivialization and objectification they contextualize. Besides, and this is a heavy one, if a woman is subjected, why should it matter that the work has other value? Maybe what redeems the work's value is what enhances its injury to women, not to mention that existing standards of literature, art, science, and politics, examined in a feminist light, are remarkably consonant with pornography's mode, meaning, and message. And finally—first and foremost, actually—although the subject of these materials is overwhelmingly women, their contents almost entirely made up of women's bodies, our invisibility has been such, our equation as a sex *with* sex has been such, that the law of obscenity has never even considered pornography a women's issue.

Obscenity, in this light, is a moral idea, an idea about judgments of good and bad. Pornography, by contrast, is a political practice, a practice of power and powerlessness. Obscenity is ideational and abstract; pornography is concrete and substantive. The two concepts represent two entirely different things. Nudity, excess of candor, arousal or excitement, prurient appeal, illegality of the acts depicted, and unnaturalness or perversion are all qualities that bother obscenity law when sex is depicted or portrayed. Sex forced on real women so that it can be sold at a profit and forced on other real women; women's bodies trussed and maimed and raped and made into things to be hurt and obtained and accessed, and this presented as the nature of women in a way that is acted on and acted out, over and over; the coercion that is visible and the coercion that has become invisible—this and more bothers feminists about pornography. Obscenity as such probably does little harm. Pornography is integral to attitudes and behaviors of violence and discrimination that define the treatment and status of half the population.

At the request of the city of Minneapolis, Andrea Dworkin and I conceived and designed a local human rights ordinance in accordance with our approach to the pornography issue. We define pornography as a practice of sex discrimination, a violation of women's

civil rights, the opposite of sexual equality. Its point is to hold those who profit from and benefit from that injury accountable to those who are injured. It means that women's injury—our damage, our pain, our enforced inferiority—should outweigh their pleasure and their profits, or sex equality is meaningless.

We define pornography as the graphic sexually explicit subordination of women through pictures or words that also includes women dehumanized as sexual objects, things, or commodities; enjoying pain or humiliation or rape; being tied up, cut up, mutilated, bruised, or physically hurt; in postures of sexual submission or servility or display; reduced to body parts, penetrated by objects or animals, or presented in scenarios of degradation, injury, torture; shown as filthy or inferior; bleeding, bruised, or hurt in a context that makes these conditions sexual. Erotica, defined by distinction as not this, might be sexually explicit materials premised on equality. We also provide that the use of men, children, or transsexuals in the place of women is pornography. The definition is substantive in that it is sex-specific, but it covers everyone in a sex-specific way, so is gender neutral in overall design. . . .

This law aspires to guarantee women's rights consistent with the First Amendment by making visible a conflict of rights between the equality guaranteed to all women and what, in some legal sense, is now the freedom of the pornographers to make and sell, and their consumers to have access to, the materials this ordinance defines. Judicial resolution of this conflict, if the judges do for women what they have done for others, is likely to entail a balancing of the rights of women arguing that our lives and opportunities, including our freedom of speech and action, are constrained by—and in many cases flatly precluded by, in, and through—pornography, against those who argue that the pornography is harmless, or harmful only in part but not in the whole of the definition; or that it is more important to preserve the pornography than it is to prevent or remedy whatever harm it does.

In predicting how a court would balance these interests, it is important to understand that this ordinance cannot now be said to be either conclusively legal or illegal under existing law or precedent, although I think the weight of authority is on our side. This ordinance enunciates a new form of the previously recognized governmental interest in sex equality. Many laws make sex equality a governmental interest. Our law is designed to further the equality of the sexes, to help make sex equality real. Pornography is a practice of discrimination on the basis of sex, on one level because of its role in creating and maintaining sex as a basis for discrimination. It harms many women one at a time and helps keep all women in an inferior status by defining our subordination as our sexuality and equating that with our gender. It is also sex discrimination because its victims, including men, are selected for victimization on the basis of their gender. But for their sex, they would not be so treated.

The harm of pornography, broadly speaking, is the harm of the civil inequality of the sexes made invisible as harm because it has become accepted as the sex difference. Consider this analogy with race: If you see Black people as different, there is no harm to segregation; it is merely a recognition of that difference. To neutral principles, separate but equal was equal. The injury of racial separation to Blacks arises "solely because [they] choose to put that construction upon it." Epistemologically translated: How you see it is not the way it is. Similarly, if you see women as just different, even or especially if you don't know that you do, subordination will not look like subordination at all, much less like harm. It will merely look like an appropriate recognition of the sex difference.

Pornography does treat the sexes differently, so the case for sex differentiation can be made here. But men as a group do not tend to be (although some individuals may be) treated the way women are treated in pornography. As a social group, men are not hurt by pornography the way women as a social group are. Their social status is not defined as *less* by it. So the major argument does not turn on mistaken differentiation, particularly since the treatment of women according to pornography's dictates makes it all too often accurate. The salient quality of a distinction between the top and the bottom in a hierarchy is not difference, although top is certainly different from bottom; it is power. So the major argument is: Subordinate but equal is not equal.

Particularly since this is a new legal theory, a new law, and "new" facts, perhaps the situation of women it newly exposes deserves to be considered on its own terms. Why do the problems of 53 percent of the population have to look like somebody else's problems before they can be recognized as existing? Then, too, they can't be addressed if they do look like other people's problems, about which something might have to be done if something is done about these. This construction of the situation truly deserves inquiry. Limiting the justification for this law to the situation of the sexes would serve to limit the precedential value of a favorable ruling.

Its particularity aside, the *approach* to the injury is supported by a whole array of prior decisions that have justified exceptions to First Amendment guarantees when something that matters is seen to be directly at stake. What unites many cases in which speech interests are raised and implicated but not, on balance, protected, is harm, harm that counts. In some existing exceptions, the definitions are much more open-ended than ours. In some the sanctions are more severe, or potentially more so. For instance, ours is a civil law; most others, although not all, are criminal. Almost no other exceptions show as many people directly affected. Evidence of harm in other cases tends to be vastly less concrete and more conjectural, which is not to say that there is necessarily less of it. None of the previous cases addresses a problem of this scope or magnitude—for instance, an eight-billion-dollar-a-year industry. Nor do other cases address an abuse that has such widespread legitimacy. Courts have seen harm in other cases. The question is, will they see it here, especially given that the pornographers got there first. I will confine myself here to arguing from cases on harm to people, on the supposition that, pornographers notwithstanding, women are not flags. . . .

To reach the magnitude of this problem on the scale it exists, our law makes trafficking in pornography—production, sale, exhibition, or distribution—actionable. Under the obscenity rubric, much legal and psychological scholarship has centered on a search for the elusive link between harm and pornography defined as obscenity. Although they were not very clear on what obscenity was, it was its harm they truly could not find. They looked high and low—in the mind of the male consumer, in society or in its "moral fabric," in correlations between variations in levels of antisocial acts and liberalization of obscenity laws. The only harm they have found has been harm to "the social interest in order and morality." Until recently, no one looked very persistently for harm to women, particularly harm to women through men. The rather obvious fact that the sexes *relate* has been overlooked in the inquiry into the male consumer and his mind. The pornography doesn't just drop out of the sky, go into his head, and stop there. Specifically, men rape, batter, prostitute, molest, and sexually harass women. Under conditions of inequality, they also hire, fire, promote, and grade women, decide how much or whether we are worth paying and for what, define and approve and disapprove of women in ways that count, that determine our lives.

If women are not just born to be sexually used, the fact that we are seen and treated as though that is what we are born for becomes something in need of explanation. If we see that men relate to women in a pattern of who they see women as being, and that forms a pattern of inequality, it becomes important to ask where that view came from or, minimally, how it is perpetuated or escalated. Asking this requires asking different questions about pornography than the ones obscenity law made salient.

Now I'm going to talk about causality in its narrowest sense. Recent experimental research on pornography shows that the materials covered by our definition cause measurable harm to women through increasing men's attitudes and behaviors of discrimination in both violent and nonviolent forms. Exposure to some of the pornography in our definition increases the immediately subsequent willingness of normal men to aggress against women under laboratory conditions. It makes normal men more closely resemble convicted rapists attitudinally, although as a group they don't look all that different from them to start with. Exposure to pornography also significantly increases attitudinal measures known to correlate with rape and self-reports of aggressive acts, measures such as hostility toward women, propensity to rape, condoning rape, and predicting that one would rape or force sex on a woman if one knew one would not get caught. On this latter measure, by the way, about a third of all men predict that they would rape, and half would force sex on a woman.

As to that pornography covered by our definition in which normal research subjects seldom perceive

violence, long-term exposure still makes them see women as more worthless, trivial, nonhuman, and objectlike, that is, the way those who are discriminated against are seen by those who discriminate against them. Crucially, all pornography by our definition acts dynamically over time to diminish the consumer's ability to distinguish sex from violence. The materials work behaviorally to diminish the capacity of men (but not women) to perceive that an account of a rape is an account of a rape. The so-called sex-only materials, those in which subjects perceive no force, also increase perceptions that a rape victim is worthless and decrease the perception that she was harmed. The overall direction of current research suggests that the more expressly violent materials accomplish with less exposure what the less overtly violent—that is, the so-called sex-only materials—accomplish over the longer term. Women are rendered fit for use and targeted for abuse. The only thing that the research cannot document is which individual women will be next on the list. (This cannot be documented experimentally because of ethics constraints on the researchers—constraints that do not operate in life.) Although the targeting is systematic on the basis of sex, for individuals it is random. They are selected on a roulette basis. Pornography can no longer be said to be just a mirror. It does not just reflect the world or some people's perceptions. It *moves* them. It increases attitudes that are lived out, circumscribing the status of half the population.

What the experimental data predict will happen actually does happen in women's real lives. It's fairly frustrating that women have known for some time that these things do happen. As Ed Donnerstein, an experimental researcher in this area, often puts it, "We just quantify the obvious." It is women, primarily, to whom the research results have been the obvious, because we live them. But not until a laboratory study predicts that these things *will* happen do people begin to believe you when you say they *did* happen to you. There is no—*not any*—inconsistency between the patterns the laboratory studies predict and the data on what actually happens to real women. Show me an abuse of women in society, I'll show it to you made sex in the pornography. If you want to know who is being hurt in this society, go see what is being done and to whom in pornography and then go look for them in other places in the world. You will find them being hurt in just that way. We did in our hearings.

In our hearings women spoke, to my knowledge for the first time in history in public, about the damage pornography does to them. We learned that pornography is used to break women, to train women to sexual submission, to season women, to terrorize women, and to silence their dissent. It is this that has previously been termed "having no effect." The way men inflict on women the sex they experience through the pornography gives women no choice about seeing the pornography or doing the sex. Asked if anyone ever tried to inflict unwanted sex acts on them that they knew came from pornography, 10 percent of women in a recent random study said yes. Among married women, 24 percent said yes. That is a lot of women. A lot more don't know. Some [who do know] testified in Minneapolis. One wife said of her ex-husband, "He would read from the pornography like a textbook, like a journal. In fact when he asked me to be bound, when he finally convinced me to do it, he read in the magazine how to tie the knots." Another woman said of her boyfriend, "[H]e went to this party, saw pornography, got an erection, got me . . . to inflict his erection on. . . . There is a direct causal relationship there." One woman, who said her husband had rape and bondage magazines all over the house, discovered two suitcases full of Barbie dolls with rope tied on their arms and legs and with tape across their mouths. Now think about the silence of women. She said, "He used to tie me up and he tried those things on me." A therapist in private practice reported:

> Presently or recently I have worked with clients who have been sodomized by broom handles, forced to have sex with over 20 dogs in the back seat of their car, tied up and then electrocuted on their genitals. These are children, [all] in the ages of 14 to 18, all of whom [have been directly affected by pornography,] [e]ither where the perpetrator has read the manuals and manuscripts at night and used these as recipe books by day or had the pornography present at the time of the sexual violence.

One woman, testifying that all the women in a group of ex-prostitutes were brought into prostitution as children through pornography, characterized their collective experience: "[I]n my experience there was not one situation where a client was not using pornography while he was using me or that he had not just watched pornography or that it was verbally referred to and directed me to pornography." "Men," she continued, "witness the abuse of women in pornography constantly and if they can't engage in that behavior with their wives, girlfriends or children, they force a whore to do it."

Men also testified about how pornography hurts them. One young gay man who had seen *Playboy* and *Penthouse* as a child said of such heterosexual pornography: "It was one of the places I learned about sex and it showed me that sex was violence. What I saw there was a specific relationship between men and women. . . . [T]he woman was to be used, objectified, humiliated, and hurt; the man was in a superior position, a position to be violent. In pornography I learned that what it meant to be sexual with a man or to be loved by a man was to accept his violence." For this reason, when he was battered by his first lover, which he described as "one of the most profoundly destructive experiences of my life," he accepted it.

Pornography also hurts men's capacity to relate to women. One young man spoke about this in a way that connects pornography—not the prohibition on pornography—with fascism. He spoke of his struggle to repudiate the thrill of dominance, of his difficulty finding connection with a woman to whom he is close. He said: "My point is that if women in a society filled by pornography must be wary for their physical selves, a man, even a man of good intentions, must be wary for his mind. . . . I do not want to be a mechanical, goose-stepping follower of the Playboy bunny, because that is what I think it is. . . . [T]hese are the experiments a master race perpetuates on those slated for extinction." The woman he lives with is Jewish. There was a very brutal rape near their house. She was afraid; she tried to joke. It didn't work. "She was still afraid. And just as a well-meaning German was afraid in 1933, I am also very much afraid."

Pornography stimulates and reinforces, it does not cathect or mirror, the connection between one-sided freely available sexual access to women and masculine sexual excitement and sexual satisfaction. The catharsis hypothesis is fantasy. The fantasy theory is fantasy. Reality is: Pornography conditions male orgasm to female subordination. It tells men what sex means, what a real woman is, and codes them together in a way that is behaviorally reinforcing. This is a real five-dollar sentence, but I'm going to say it anyway: Pornography is a set of hermeneutical equivalences that work on the epistemological level. Substantively, pornography defines the meaning of what a woman is seen to be by connecting access to her sexuality with masculinity through orgasm. What pornography means *is* what it does.

So far, opposition to our ordinance centers on the trafficking provision. This means not only that it is difficult to comprehend a group injury in a liberal culture—that what it *means* to be a woman is defined by this and that it is an injury for all women, even if not for all women equally. It is not only that the pornography has got to be accessible, which is the bottom line of virtually every objection to this law. It is also that power, as I said, is when you say something, it is taken for reality. If you talk about rape, it will be agreed that rape is awful. But rape is a conclusion. If a victim describes the facts of a rape, maybe she was asking for it or enjoyed it or at least consented to it, or the man might have thought she did, or maybe she had had sex before. It is now agreed that there is something wrong with sexual harassment. But describe what happened to you, and it may be trivial or personal or paranoid, or maybe you should have worn a bra that day. People are against discrimination. But describe the situation of a real woman, and they are not so sure she wasn't just unqualified. In law, all these disjunctions between women's perspective on our injuries and the standards we have to meet go under dignified legal rubrics like burden of proof, credibility, defenses, elements of the crime, and so on. These standards all contain a definition of what a woman is in terms of what sex is and the low value placed on us through it. They reduce injuries done to us to authentic expressions of who we are. Our silence is written all over them. So is the pornography.

We have as yet encountered comparatively little objection to the coercion, force, or assault provisions of our ordinance. I think that's partly because the people who make and approve laws may not yet see what they do as that. They *know* they use the pornog-

raphy as we have described it in this law, and our law defines that, the reality of pornography, as a harm to women. If they suspect that they might on occasion engage in or benefit from coercion or force or assault, they may think that the victims won't be able to prove it—and they're right. Women who charge men with sexual abuse are not believed. The pornographic view of them is: They want it; they all want it. When women bring charges of sexual assault, motives such as veniality or sexual repression must be invented, because we cannot really have been hurt. Under the trafficking provision, women's lack of credibility cannot be relied on to negate the harm. There's no woman's story to destroy, no credibility-based decision on what happened. The hearings establish the harm. The definition sets the standard. The grounds of reality definition are authoritatively shifted. Pornography is bigotry, *period*. We are now—in the world pornography has decisively defined—having to meet the burden of proving, once and for all, for all of the rape and torture and battery, all of the sexual harassment, all of the child sexual abuse, all of the forced prostitution, *all* of it that the pornography is part of and that is part of the pornography, that the harm *does happen* and that when it happens it looks like this. Which may be why all this evidence never seems to be enough.

It is worth considering what evidence has been enough when other harms involving other purported speech interests have been allowed to be legislated against. By comparison to our trafficking provision, analytically similar restrictions have been allowed under the First Amendment, with a legislative basis far less massive, detailed, concrete, and conclusive. Our statutory language is more ordinary, objective, and precise and covers a harm far narrower than the legislative record substantiates. Under *Miller*, obscenity was allowed to be made criminal in the name of the "danger of offending the sensibilities of unwilling recipients, or exposure to juveniles." Under our law, we have direct evidence of harm, not just a conjectural danger, that unwilling women in considerable numbers are not simply offended in their sensibilities, but are violated in their persons and restricted in their options. Obscenity law also suggests that the applicable standard for legal adequacy in measuring such connections may not be statistical certainty. The Supreme Court has said that it is not their job to resolve empirical uncertainties that underlie state obscenity legislation. Rather, it is for them to determine whether a legislature could reasonably have determined that a connection might exist between the prohibited material and harm of a kind in which the state has legitimate interest. Equality should be such an area. The Supreme Court recently recognized that prevention of sexual exploitation and abuse of children is, in its words, "a governmental objective of surpassing importance." This might also be the case for sexual exploitation and abuse of women, although I think a civil remedy is initially more appropriate to the goal of empowering adult women than a criminal prohibition would be.

Other rubrics provide further support for the argument that this law is narrowly tailored to further a legitimate governmental interest consistent with the goals underlying the First Amendment. Exceptions to the First Amendment—you may have gathered from this—exist. The reason they exist is that the harm done by some speech outweighs its expressive value, if any. In our law a legislature recognizes that pornography, as defined and made actionable, undermines sex equality. One can say—and I have—that pornography is a causal factor in violations of women; one can also say that women will be violated so long as pornography exists; but one can also say simply that pornography violates women. Perhaps this is what the woman had in mind who testified at our hearings that for her the question is not just whether pornography causes violent acts to be perpetrated against some women. "Porn is already a violent act against women. It is our mothers, our daughters, our sisters, and our wives that are for sale for pocket change at the newsstands in this country." *Chaplinsky v. New Hampshire* recognized the ability to restrict as "fighting words" speech which, "by [its] very utterance inflicts injury." Perhaps the only reason that pornography has not been "fighting words"—in the sense of words that by their utterance tend to incite immediate breach of the peace—is that women have seldom fought back, yet.

Some concerns that are close to those of this ordinance underlie group libel laws, although the differences are equally important. In group libel law, as Justice Frankfurter's opinion in *Beauharnais* illustrates, it has been understood that an individual's treatment and alternatives in life may depend as much on the reputation of the group to which that person belongs as on their own merit. Not even a partial analogy can be made to group libel doctrine without examining the point made by Justice Brandeis and recently underlined by Larry Tribe: Would more speech, rather than less, remedy the harm? In the end, the answer may be yes, but not under the abstract system of free speech, which only enhances the power of the pornographers while doing nothing substantively to guarantee the free speech of women, for which we need civil equality. The situation in which women presently find ourselves with respect to the pornography is one in which more *pornography* is inconsistent with rectifying or even counterbalancing its damage through speech, because so long as the pornography exists in the way it does there *will not be more speech by women*. Pornography strips and devastates women of credibility, from our accounts of sexual assault to our everyday reality of sexual subordination. We are stripped of authority and reduced and devalidated and silenced. Silenced here means that the purposes of the First Amendment, premised upon conditions presumed and promoted by protecting free speech, do not pertain to women because they are not our conditions. Consider them: Individual self-fulfillment— how does pornography promote our individual self-fulfillment? How does sexual inequality even permit it? Even if she can form words, who listens to a woman with a penis in her mouth? Facilitating consensus—to the extent pornography does so, it does so one-sidedly by silencing protest over the injustice of sexual subordination. Participation in civic life—central to Professor Meiklejohn's theory—how does pornography enhance women's participation in civic life? Anyone who cannot walk down the street or even lie down in her own bed without keeping her eyes cast down and her body clenched against assault is unlikely to have much to say about the issues of the day, still less will she become Tolstoy. Facilitating change—*this law* facilitates the change that existing First Amendment theory had been used to throttle. Any system of freedom of expression that does not address a problem where the free speech of men silences the free speech of women, a real conflict between speech interests as well as between people, is not serious about securing freedom of expression in this country.

For those of you who still think pornography is only an idea, consider the possibility that obscenity law got one thing right. Pornography is more actlike than thoughtlike. That pornography, in a feminist view, furthers the idea of the sexual inferiority of women, which is a political idea, doesn't make the pornography itself a political idea. One can express the idea a practice embodies. That does not make that practice an idea. Segregation expresses the idea of the inferiority of one group to another on the basis of race. That does not make segregation an idea. A sign that says "Whites Only" is only words. Is it therefore protected by the First Amendment? Is it not an act, a practice, of segregation because what it means is inseparable from what it does? *Law* is only words.

The issue here is whether the fact that words and pictures are the central link in the cycle of abuse will immunize that entire cycle, about which we cannot do anything without doing something about the pornography. As Justice Stewart said in *Ginsburg*, "When expression occurs in a setting where the capacity to make a choice is absent, government regulation of that expression may coexist with and *even implement* First Amendment guarantees." I would even go so far as to say that the pattern of evidence we have closely approaches Justice Douglas's requirement that "freedom of expression can be suppressed if, and to the extent that, it is so closely brigaded with illegal action as to be an inseparable part of it." Those who have been trying to separate the acts from the speech—that's an act, that's an act, there's a law against that act, regulate that act, don't touch the speech—notice here that the illegality of the acts involved doesn't mean that the speech that is "brigaded with" it *cannot* be regulated. This is when it *can* be.

I take one of two penultimate points from Andrea Dworkin, who has often said that pornography is not speech for women, it is the silence of women. Remember the mouth taped, the woman gagged, "Smile, I can get a lot of money for that." The smile is not her expression, it is her silence. It is not her expression not because it didn't happen, but because it *did* happen. The screams of the women in pornography are si-

lence, like the screams of Kitty Genovese, whose plight was misinterpreted by some onlookers as a lovers' quarrel. The flat expressionless voice of the woman in the New Bedford gang rape, testifying, is silence. She was raped as men cheered and watched, as they do in and with the pornography. When women resist and men say, "Like this, you stupid bitch, here is how to do it" and shove their faces into the pornography, this "truth of sex" is the silence of women. When they say, "If you love me, you'll try," the enjoyment we fake, the enjoyment we learn is silence. Women who submit because there is more dignity in it than in losing the fight over and over live in silence. Having to sleep with your publisher or director to get access to what men call speech is silence. Being humiliated on the basis of your appearance, whether by approval or disapproval, because you have to look a certain way for a certain job, whether you get the job or not, is silence. The absence of a woman's voice, everywhere that it cannot be heard, is silence. And anyone who thinks that what women say in pornography is women's speech—the "Fuck me, do it to me, harder," all of that—has never heard the sound of a woman's voice.

The most basic assumption underlying First Amendment adjudication is that, socially, speech is free. The First Amendment says Congress shall not abridge the freedom of speech. Free speech, get it, *exists*. Those who wrote the First Amendment *had* speech—they wrote the Constitution. *Their* problem was to keep it free from the only power that realistically threatened it: the federal government. They designed the First Amendment to prevent government from constraining that which, if unconstrained by government, was free, meaning *accessible to them*. At the same time, we can't tell much about the intent of the framers with regard to the question of women's speech, because I don't think we crossed their minds. It is consistent with this analysis that their posture toward freedom of speech tends to presuppose that whole segments of the population are not systematically silenced socially, prior to government action. If everyone's power were equal to theirs, if this were a nonhierarchical society, that might make sense. But the place of pornography in the inequality of the sexes makes the assumption of equal power untrue.

This is a hard question. It involves risks. Classically, opposition to censorship has involved keeping government off the backs of people. Our law is about getting some people off the backs of other people. The risks that it will be misused have to be measured against the risks of the status quo. Women will never have that dignity, security, compensation that is the promise of equality so long as the pornography exists as it does now. The situation of women suggests that the urgent issue of our freedom of speech is not primarily the avoidance of state intervention as such, but getting affirmative access to speech for those to whom it has been denied.

40. *Feminists Against the First Amendment*

WENDY KAMINER

Wendy Kaminer surveys the history of the feminist antiporn movement in North America from the late 1970s to the present. She points out that the feminist case against pornography is based on a presumed link between pornography and sexual violence, but she questions how direct that link is and whether it depends on a blurring of the distinction between speech and conduct. She also suggests that alcohol and other substance abuse may have a more direct role in causing sexual violence, and argues that the most likely legislative result of the feminist antiporn movement, given its political allegiance with the New Right, would be a broader censorship that would not serve feminist interests.

Despite efforts to redevelop it, New York's 42nd Street retains its underground appeal, especially for consumers of pornography. What city officials call "sex-related uses"—triple-X video (formerly book) stores, peep shows, and topless bars—have declined in number since their heyday in the 1970s, and much of the block between Seventh and Eighth avenues is boarded up, a hostage to development. New sex businesses—yuppie topless bars and downscale lap-dancing joints (don't ask)—are prospering elsewhere in Manhattan. But Peepland (MULTI-VIDEO BOOTHS! NUDE DANCING GIRLS!) still reigns, and Show World, a glitzy sex emporium, still anchors the west end of the block, right around the corner from *The New York Times*.

In the late 1970s I led groups of suburban women on tours through Show World and other 42nd Street hot spots, exposing them, in the interests of consciousness-raising, to pornography's various genres: Nazi porn, nurse porn, lesbian porn, bondage porn—none of it terribly imaginative. The women didn't exactly hold hands as they ventured down the street with me, but they did stick close together; traveling en masse, they were not so conspicuous as individuals. With only a little less discomfort than resolve, they dutifully viewed the pornography.

Reprinted from *The Atlantic Monthly,* November 1992, by permission of the publisher and the author.

This was in the early days of the feminist antiporn movement, when legislative strategies against pornography were mere gleams in the eye of the feminist writer Andrea Dworkin, when it seemed possible to raise consciousness about pornography without arousing demands for censorship. That period of innocence did not last long. By 1981 the New Right had mounted a nationwide censorship campaign to purge schools and public libraries of sex education and other secular-humanist forms of "pornography." Sex education was "filth and perversion," Jerry Falwell announced in a fundraising letter that included, under the label "Adults Only. Sexually Explicit Material," excerpts from a college health text. By the mid-1980s right-wing advocates of traditional family values had co-opted feminist antiporn protests—or, at least, they'd co-opted feminist rhetoric. The feminist attorney and law professor Catharine MacKinnon characterized pornography as the active subordination of women, and Phyllis Schlafly wrote, "Pornography really should be defined as the degradation of women.

Pornography as Sex Discrimination

Of course, while feminists blamed patriarchy for pornography, moral majoritarians blamed feminism and other humanist rebellions. The alliance between feminists and the far right was not ideological but political. In 1984 antiporn legislation devised by Andrea Dwor-kin and Catharine MacKinnon, defining pornography as a violation of women's civil rights, was introduced in the Indianapolis city council by an anti-ERA activist, passed with the support of the right, and signed into law by the Republican mayor, William Hudnutt.

With the introduction of this bill, a new legislative front opened in the war against pornography, alienating civil-libertarian feminists from their more censorious sisters, while appealing to populist concerns about declining moral values. By calling for the cen-sorship of pornography, some radical feminists found their way into the cultural mainstream—and onto the margins of First Amendment law.

The legislation adopted in Indianapolis offered a novel approach to prohibiting pornography that had all the force of a semantic distinction: Pornography was not simply speech, Catharine MacKinnon suggested, but active sex discrimination, and thus was not protected by the First Amendment. (In her 1989 book *Toward a Feminist Theory of the State*, MacKinnon characterized pornography as "a form of forced sex.") Regarding pornography as action, defining it broadly as any verbal or visual sexually explicit material (violent or not) that subordinates women, presuming that the mere existence of pornography oppresses women, the Indianapolis ordinance gave any woman offended by any arguably pornographic material the right to seek an order prohibiting it, along with damages for the harm it presumably caused. In other words, any woman customer browsing in a bookstore or patrolling one, glancing at a newsstand or a triple-X video store, was a potential plaintiff in a sex-discrimination suit. Given all the literature, films, and videos on the mass market that could be said to subordinate women, this ordinance would have created lots of new business for lawyers—but it did not stand. Within a year of its enactment, [Dworkin and MacKinnon's] law was declared unconstitutional by a federal appeals court in a decision affirmed by the U.S. Supreme Court.

The feminist antiporn movement retreated from the legislative arena and passed out of public view in the late 1980s, only to re-emerge with renewed strength on college campuses. College professors following fashions in poststructuralism asserted that legal principles, like those protecting speech, were mere rhetorical power plays: Without any objective, universal merit, prevailing legal ideals were simply those privileged by the mostly white male ruling class. The dominant poststructural dogma of the late 1980s denied the First Amendment the transcendent value that the liberal belief in a marketplace of ideas has always awarded it.

Massachusetts Mischief

This unlikely convergence of First Amendment critiques from multiculturalists, poststructuralists, and advocates of traditional family values, recently combined with high-profile rape and harassment cases and women's abiding concern with sexual violence, buoyed the feminist antiporn movement. This year it re-emerged on the national and local scene with renewed legislative clout. The presumption that pornography oppresses women and is a direct cause of sexual violence is the basis for bills introduced in the U.S. Senate and the Massachusetts legislature. Last June the Senate Judiciary Committee passed the Pornography Victims' Compensation Act, which would make producers, distributors, exhibitors, and retailers convicted of disseminating material adjudged obscene liable for damages to victims of crimes who could claim that the material caused their victimization. The Massachusetts legislature held hearings on a much broader antiporn bill, closely modeled on the Indianapolis ordinance. Disarmingly titled "An Act to Protect the Civil Rights of Women and Children," the Massachusetts bill would not only make purveyors of pornography liable for crimes committed by their customers; it would also allow any woman, whether or not she has been the victim of a crime, to sue the producers, distributors, exhibitors, or retailers of any sexually explicit visual material that subordinates women. (The exclusion of verbal "pornography" from the antitrafficking provision would protect the likes of Norman Mailer, whom many feminists consider a pornographer, so long as his works are not adapted for the screen.) What this bill envisions is that the First Amendment would protect only that speech considered sexually correct.

The feminist case against pornography is based on the presumption that the link between pornography and sexual violence is clear, simple, and inexorable. The argument is familiar: Censorship campaigns always blame unwanted speech for unwanted behavior; Jerry Falwell once claimed that sex education causes teenage pregnancy, just as feminists claim that pornography causes rape. One objection to this assertion is that it gives rapists and batterers an excuse for their crimes, and perhaps even a "pornography made me do it" defense.

The claim that pornography causes rape greatly oversimplifies the problem of sexual violence. We can hardly say that were it not for pornography, there would be no rape or battering. As feminists opposed to antiporn legislation have pointed out, countries in which commercial pornography is illegal—Saudi Arabia, for example—are hardly safe havens for women.

This is not to deny that there probably is some link between violence in the media and violence in real life, but it is complicated, variable, and difficult to measure. Not all hate speech is an incantation; not all men are held spellbound by pornography. Poststructural feminists who celebrate subjectivism should be among the first to admit that different people respond to the same images differently. All we can confidently claim is that the way women are imagined is likely to have a cumulative effect on the way they're treated, but that does not mean any single image is the clear and simple cause of any single act.

The Dworkin-MacKinnon bill, however, did more than assume that pornography causes sex discrimination and other crimes against women. It said that pornography *is* violence and discrimination: the active subordination of women (and it assumed that we can all agree on what constitutes subordination). MacKinnon and her followers deny that prohibiting pornography is censorship, because they effectively deny that pornography is speech—and that is simply Orwellian. The line between speech and behavior is sometimes blurred: Dancing nude down a public street is one way of expressing yourself which may also be a form of disorderly conduct. But if pornography is sex discrimination, then an editorial criticizing the president is treason.

Most feminists concerned about pornography are probably not intent on suppressing political speech, but the legislation they support, like the Massachusetts antiporn bill, is so broad, and its definition of pornography so subjective, that it would be likely to jeopardize sex educators and artists more than it would hardcore pornographers, who are used to operating outside the law. Feminist legislation makes no exception for "pornography" in which some might find redeeming social value; it could, for example, apply in the case of a woman disfigured by a man who had seen too many paintings by Willem de Kooning. "If a woman is subjected," Catharine MacKinnon writes, "why should it matter that the work has other value?"

With this exclusive focus on prohibiting material that reflects incorrect attitudes toward women, antiporn feminists don't deny the chilling effect of censorship; they embrace it. Any speech that subordinates women—any pornography—is yelling "Fire!" in a crowded theater, they say, falling back on a legal canard. But that's true only if, just as all crowds are deemed potential mobs, all men are deemed potential abusers whose violent impulses are bound to be sparked by pornography. It needs to be said, by feminists, that efforts to censor pornography reflect a profound disdain for men. Catharine MacKinnon has written that "pornography works as a behavioral conditioner, reinforcer and stimulus, not as idea or advocacy. It is more like saying 'kill' to a trained guard dog—and also the training process itself." That's more a theory of sexuality than of speech: Pornography is action because all men are dogs on short leashes.

This bleak view of male sexuality condemns heterosexuality for women as an exercise in wish fulfillment (if only men weren't all dogs) or false consciousness (such as male-identified thinking). True feminism, according to MacKinnon, unlike liberal feminism, "sees sexuality as a social sphere of male power of which forced sex is paradigmatic." With varying degrees of clarity, MacKinnon and Dworkin suggest that in a context of pervasive, institutionalized inequality, there can be no consensual sex between men and women: We can never honestly distinguish rape from intercourse.

An Esoteric Debate

A modified version of this message may well have particular appeal to some college women today, who make up an important constituency for the antiporn movement. In their late teens and early twenties, these women are still learning to cope with sexuality, in a violent and unquestionably misogynistic world. Feminism on campus tends to focus on issues of sexuality, not of economic equity. Anxiety about date rape is

intense, along with anxiety about harassment and hate speech. Understanding and appreciating the First Amendment is a lot less evident, and concern about employment discrimination seems somewhat remote. It's not hard to understand why: College women in general haven't experienced overt repression of opinions and ideas or many problems in the workplace, but from childhood they've known what it is to fear rape. In the age of AIDS, the fear can be crippling.

Off campus the antiporn feminist critique of male sexuality and heterosexuality for women has little appeal, but it is not widely known. MacKinnon's theoretical writings are impenetrable to readers who lack familiarity with poststructural jargon and the patience to decode sentences like this: "If objectivity is the epistemological stance of which women's sexual objectification is the social process, its imposition the paradigm of power in the male form, then the state will appear most relentless in imposing the male point of view, when it comes closest to achieving its highest formal criterion of distanced aperspectivity." Dworkin is a much more accessible polemicist, but she is also much less visible outside feminist circles. Tailored, with an air of middle-class respectability and the authority of a law professor, MacKinnon looks far less scary to mainstream Americans than her theories about sexuality, which drive the antiporn movement, might sound.

If antipornography crusades on the right reflect grassroots concern about changing sexual mores and the decline of the traditional family, antipornography crusades on the feminist left reflect the concerns and perceptions of an educated elite. In the battle for the moral high ground, antiporn feminists claim to represent the interests of a racially diverse mixture of poor and working class women who work in the pornography industry—and they probably do represent a few. But many sex-industry workers actively oppose antiporn legislation (some feminists would say they have been brainwashed by patriarchy or actually coerced), and it's not at all clear that women who are abused in the making of pornography would be helped by forcing it deeper underground; working conditions in an illegal business are virtually impossible to police. It's hard to know how many other alleged victims of pornography feel represented by the antiporn movement, and I know of no demographic study of the movement's active members.

Leaders of the feminist antiporn movement, however, do seem more likely to emerge from academia and the professions than from the streets or battered-women's shelters. Debra Robbin, a former director of the New Bedford Women's Center, one of the first shelters in Massachusetts, doesn't believe that "women on the front lines," working with victims of sexual violence, will "put much energy into a fight against pornography." Activists don't have time: "They can barely leave their communities to go to the statehouses to fight for more funding." The poor and working-class women they serve would say, "Yeah, pornography is terrible, but I don't have food on my table." Carolin Ramsey, the executive director of the Massachusetts Coalition of Battered Women Service Groups, says that the pornography debate "doesn't have a lot to do with everyday life for me and the women I'm serving." She explains, "Violence in the home and the streets that directly threatens our lives and our families is more pressing than a movie. Keeping my kids away from drugs is more important than keeping them away from literature."

Ramsey is sympathetic to antiporn feminists ("there's room in the movement for all of us"), and she believes that "violence in the media contributes to violence in real life." Still, she considers the pornography debate "esoteric" and "intellectual" and feels under no particular pressure from her constituents to take a stand against pornography.

If censoring pornography is the central feminist issue for Catharine MacKinnon, it is a peripheral issue for activists like Robbin and Ramsey. Robbin in particular does not believe that eliminating pornography would appreciably lessen the incidence of sexual abuse. David Adams, a co-founder and the executive director of Emerge, a Boston counseling center for male batterers believes that only a minority of his clients (perhaps 10 to 20 percent) use hard-core pornography. He estimates that half may have substance-abuse problems, and adds that alcohol seems more directly involved in abuse than pornography. Adams agrees with feminists that pornography is degrading to women but does not support legislation regulating it, because "the legislation couldn't work and would only open the door to censorship."

What might work instead? Emerge conducts programs in Boston and Cambridge public schools on violence, aimed at both victims and perpetrators. "There's a lot of violence in teen relationships," Adams observes. Debra Robbin wishes that women in the antiporn movement would "channel their energies into funding battered women's shelters and rape-crisis centers."

Reforming the criminal-justice system is also a priority for many women concerned about sexual violence. Antistalking laws could protect many more women than raids on pornographic video stores are ever likely to; so could the efficient processing of cases against men who abuse women.

Sensationalism as an Organizing Tool

Why do some women channel their energies into a fight against pornography? Antiporn legislation has the appeal of a quick fix, as Robbin notes. And, she adds, "there's notoriety to be gained from protesting pornography." The "harder work"—promoting awareness and understanding of sexual violence, changing the way children are socialized, and helping women victims of violence—is less sensationalist and less visible.

Sensationalism, however, is an organizing tool for antiporn feminists. If questions about the effects of pornography seem intellectual to some women involved in social-service work, the popular campaign against pornography is aggressively anti-intellectual. Although advocates of First Amendment freedoms are stuck with intellectual defenses of the marketplace of ideas, antiporn feminists whip up support for their cause with pornographic slide shows comprising hard-core pictures of women being tortured, raped, and generally degraded. Many feminists are equally critical of the soft-core porn movies available at local video stores and on cable TV, arguing that the violence in pornography is often covert (and they include mainstream advertising images in their slide shows). But hard-core violence is what works on the crowd. Feminist rhetoric often plays on women's worst fears about men: "Pornography tells us that there but for the grace of God go us," Gail Dines, a sociology professor at Wheelock College, exclaimed during her recent slide show at Harvard, as she presented photographs of women being brutalized.

Dines's porn show was SRO, its audience some 300 undergraduates who winced and gasped at the awful slides and cheered when Dines pointed to a pornographic picture of a woman and said, "When I walk down the street, what they know about me is what they know about her!" She warned her mostly female audience that pornographers have "aggressively targeted college men." She seemed preoccupied with masturbation. Part of the problem of pornography, she suggested, is that men use it to masturbate, and "women weren't put on this world to facilitate masturbation." She advised a student concerned about the presence of *Playboy* in the college library that library collections of pornography aren't particularly worrisome, because men are not likely to masturbate in libraries.

In addition to condemnations of male sexuality, Dines offered questionable horror stories about pornography's atrocities, like this: Rape vans are roaming the streets of New York. Women are dragged into the vans and raped on camera; when their attackers sell the rape videos in commercial outlets, the women have no legal recourse.

A story like this is impossible to disprove (how do you prove a negative?), but it should probably not be taken at face value, as many students in Dines's audience seemed to take it. William Daly, the director of New York City's Office of Midtown Enforcement, which is responsible for monitoring the sex industry in New York, has never heard of rape vans; almost anything is possible on 42nd Street, but he is skeptical that rape vans are a problem. Part of Dines's story, however, is simply untrue: Under New York State privacy law, says Nan Hunter, a professor of law at Brooklyn Law School, women could seek damages for the sale of the rape videos, and also an injunction against their distribution.

It would be difficult even to raise questions about the accuracy of the rape-van story, however, in the highly emotional atmosphere of a slide show; you'd be accused of not believing the women. Just as slides of bloody fetuses pre-empt rational debate about abortion, pornographic slide shows pre-empt argumentative questions and rational consideration of First Amendment freedoms, the probable effect of efforts to censor pornography, and the actual relationship between pornography and violence.

A Pornographic Culture?

Does pornography cause violence against women, as some feminists claim? Maybe, in some cases, under some circumstances involving explicitly violent material. Readers interested in the social-science debate should see both the report of the Attorney General's Commission on Pornography, which found a link between pornography and violence against women, and the feminist writer Marcia Pally's "Sense and Censorship," published by Americans for Constitutional Freedom and the Freedom to Read Foundation. In addition to the equivocal social-science data, however, we have the testimony of women who claim to have been brutalized by male consumers of pornography. Antiporn feminists generally characterize pornography as a "how to" literature on abusing women, which men are apparently helpless to resist. But evidence is mainly anecdotal: At a hearing . . . on the antiporn bill in the Massachusetts legislature, several women told awful, lurid tales of sexual abuse, said to have been inspired by pornography. Like a TV talk show, the Attorney General's commission presented testimony from pornography's alleged victims, which may or may not have been true. It's difficult to cross-examine a sobbing self-proclaimed victim; you either take her testimony at face value or you don't.

Still, many people don't need reliable, empirical evidence about a link between pornography and behavior to believe that one exists. When feminists talk about pornography, after all, they mean a wide range of mainstream media images—Calvin Klein ads, Brian De Palma films, and the endless stream of TV shows about serial rapist stranglers and housewives who moonlight as hookers. How could we not be affected by the routine barrage of images linking sex and violence and lingerie? The more broadly pornography is defined, the more compelling are assertions about its inevitable effect on behavior, but the harder it is to control. How do we isolate the effects of any particular piece of pornography if we live in a pornographic culture?

Narrowly drawn antiporn legislation, which legislators are most likely to pass and judges most likely to uphold, could not begin to address the larger cultural problem of pornography. Feminists themselves usually claim publicly that they intend to prohibit only hard-core pornography, although on its face their legislation applies to a much broader range of material. But if you accept the feminist critique of sexism in the media, hard-core porn plays a relatively minor role in shaping attitudes and behavior. If feminists are right about pornography, it is a broad social problem, not a discrete legal one: [It] is not a problem the law can readily solve, unless perhaps we suspend the First Amendment entirely and give feminists the power to police mainstream media, the workplace, and schools.

The likelihood that feminists would not be the ones to police 42nd Street should antiporn legislation pass is one reason that many feminists oppose the antiporn campaign. If society is as sexist as Andrea Dworkin and Catharine MacKinnon claim, it is not about to adopt a feminist agenda when it sets out to censor pornography. The history of antiporn campaigns in this country is partly a history of campaigns against reproductive choice and changing roles for men and women. The first federal obscenity legislation, known as the Comstock Law, passed in 1873, prohibited the mailing of not only dirty pictures but also contraceptives and information about abortion. Early in this century Margaret Sanger and the sex educator Mary Ware Dennett were prosecuted for obscenity violations. Recently the New Right campaign against socially undesirable literature has focused on sex education in public schools. Antiporn activists on the right consider feminism and homosexuality (which they link) to be threats to traditional family life (which, in fact, they are). In Canada a landmark Supreme Court ruling . . . [that] adopted a feminist argument against pornography was first used to prohibit distribution of a small lesbian magazine, which a politically correct feminist would be careful to label erotica.

Gay and lesbian groups, as well as advocates of sex education and the usual array of feminists and nonfeminist civil libertarians, actively oppose antipornography legislation. Some state National Organization for Women chapters—New York, California, and Vermont—have taken strong anticensorship stands, but at the national level NOW has not taken a position in the pornography debate. President Patricia Ireland, would like to see pornography become socially unacceptable, "like smoking," but is wary of taking legal action against it, partly because she's wary of "giving people like Jesse Helms the power to decide what we read and see." But for major, national feminist organizations, like NOW and the NOW Legal Defense and Education Fund, the pornography debate is a minefield to be carefully avoided. Pornography is probably the most divisive issue feminists have faced since the first advocates of the ERA, in the 1920s, squared off against advocates of protective labor legislation for women. Feminists for and against antiporn legislation are almost as bitterly divided as pro-choice activists and members of Operation Rescue.

Renewed concern about abortion rights may drain energy from the antiporn movement. Feminists may awaken to the danger that antipornography laws will be used against sex educators and advocates of choice. (A gag rule on family-planning clinics may have made some feminists more protective of the First Amendment.) Politicians courting women voters may find that antiporn legislation alienates more feminists than it pleases. Still, censorship campaigns will always have considerable appeal. Like campaigns to reinstate the death penalty, they promise panaceas for profound social pathologies. They make their case by exploiting the wrenching anecdotal testimony of victims: Politicians pushing for the death penalty hold press conferences flanked by mothers of murdered children, just as feminists against pornography spotlight raped and battered women.

Rational argument is no match for highly emotional testimony. But it may be wishful thinking to believe that penalizing the production and distribution of hard-core pornography would have much effect on sexual violence. It would probably have little effect even on pornography, given the black market. It would, however, complicate campaigns to distribute information about AIDS, let alone condoms, in the public schools. It would distract us from the harder, less popular work of reforming sexual stereotypes and roles, and addressing actual instead of metaphorical instruments of violence. The promise of the antiporn movement is the promise of a world in which almost no one can buy pornography and almost anyone can buy a gun.

41. *American Booksellers* v. *Hudnutt*

UNITED STATES DISTRICT COURT
AND COURT OF APPEALS

The issue before the federal judiciary was whether the Indianapolis ordinance that sought to prohibit pornography as a practice that discriminated against women was restricting speech rather than conduct, and if it was restricting speech whether it was restricting speech that was protected by the First Amendment to the U.S. Constitution. The federal judiciary ruled that the ordinance was indeed restricting speech protected by the First Amendment rather than conduct .

Indianapolis enacted an ordinance defining "pornography" as a practice that discriminates against women. "Pornography" is to be redressed through the administrative and judicial methods used for other discrimination. . . .

> "Pornography" under the ordinance is "the graphic sexually explicit subordination of women, whether in pictures or in words, that also includes one or more of the following:
> 1. Women are presented as sexual objects who enjoy pain or humiliation; or
> 2. Women are presented as sexual objects who experience sexual pleasure in being raped; or
> 3. Women are presented as sexual objects tied up or cut up or mutilated or bruised or physically hurt, or as dismembered or truncated or fragmented or severed into body parts; or
> 4. Women are presented as being penetrated by objects or animals; or
> 5. Women are presented in scenarios of degradation, injury, abasement, torture, shown as filthy or inferior, bleeding, bruised, or hurt in a context that makes these conditions sexual; or
> 6. Women are presented as sexual objects for domination, conquest, violation, exploitation, possession, or use, or through postures or positions of servility or submission or display." . . .

First Amendment Requirements

This Ordinance cannot be analyzed adequately without first recognizing this: The drafters of the Ordinance have used what appears to be a legal term of art, "pornography," but have in fact given the term a specialized meaning which differs from the meanings ordinarily assigned to that word in both legal and common parlance. In Section 16-3(v) (page 6), the Ordinance states:

> Pornography shall mean the sexually explicit subordination of women, graphically depicted, whether in pictures or in words, that includes one or more of the following: . . . .

There follows . . . a listing of five specific presentations of women in various settings which serve as examples of "pornography" and as such further define and describe that term under the Ordinance.

As is generally recognized, the word "pornography" is usually associated, and sometimes synonymous, with the word, "obscenity." "Obscenity" not only has its own separate and specialized meaning in the law, but in laymen's use also, and it is a much broader meaning than the definition given the word "pornography" in the Ordinance which is at issue in this action. There is thus a considerable risk of confusion in analyzing this Ordinance unless care and precision are used in that process.

The Constitutional analysis of this Ordinance requires a determination of several underlying issues: First, the Court must determine whether the Ordinance imposes restraints on speech or behavior (content versus conduct); if the Ordinance is found to regulate speech, the Court must next determine whether the subject speech is protected or not protected under the First Amendment; if the speech . . . regulated by this Ordinance is protected speech under the Constitution, the Court must then decide whether the regulation is constitutionally permissible . . . based on a compelling state interest justifying the removal of such speech from First Amendment protections.

Do the Ordinances Regulate Speech or Behavior (Content or Conduct)?

It appears to be central to the defense of the Ordinance by defendants that the Court accept their premise that the City-County Council has not attempted to regulate speech, let alone protected speech. Defendants repeat throughout their briefs the incantation that their Ordinance regulates conduct, not speech. They contend (one senses with a certain sleight of hand) that the production, dissemination, and use of sexually explicit words and pictures is the actual subordination of women and not an expression of ideas deserving of First Amendment protection. . . .

Defendants claim support for their theory by analogy, arguing that it is an accepted and established legal distinction that has allowed other courts to find that advocacy of a racially "separate but equal" doctrine in a civil rights context is protected speech under the First Amendment though "segregation" is not constitutionally protected behavior. Accordingly, defendants characterize their Ordinance here as a civil rights measure, through which they seek to prevent the distribution, sale, and exhibition of "pornography," as defined in the Ordinance, in order to regulate and control the underlying unacceptable conduct.

The content-versus-conduct approach espoused by defendants is not persuasive, however, and is contrary to accepted First Amendment principles. Accepting as true the City-County Council's finding that pornography conditions society to subordinate women, the means by which the Ordinance attempts to combat this sex discrimination is nonetheless through the regulation of speech.

For instance, the definition of pornography, the control of which is the whole thrust . . . , states that it is "the sexually explicit subordination of women, graphically *depicted,* whether in *pictures* or in *words,* that includes one or more of the following:" (emphasis supplied) and the following five descriptive subparagraphs begin with . . . , "Women are *presented.* . . ."

The unlawful acts and discriminatory practices under the Ordinance are set out in Section 16-3(g):

(4) Trafficking in pornography: the production, sale, exhibition, or distribution of pornography. . . .
(5) Coercion into pornographic performance: coercing, intimidating or fraudulently inducing any person . . . into performing for pornography. . . .
(6) Forcing pornography on a person: . . . .
(7) Assault or physical attack due to pornography: the assault, physical attack, or injury of any woman, man, child or transsexual in a way that is directly caused by specific pornography. . . .

Section (7), *supra,* goes on to provide a cause of action in damages against the perpetrators, makers, distributors, sellers, and exhibitors of pornography and injunctive relief against the further exhibition, distribution or sale of pornography.

In summary, therefore, the Ordinance establishes through the legislative findings that pornography causes a tendency to commit these various harmful acts, and outlaws the pornography (that is, the "depictions"), the activities involved in the production of pornography, and the behavior caused by or resulting from pornography.

Thus, though the purpose of the Ordinance is cast in civil rights terminology—"to prevent and prohibit all discriminatory practices of sexual subordination or inequality through pornography" . . . —it is clearly aimed at controlling the content of the speech and ideas that the City-County Council has found harmful and offensive. Those words and pictures which depict women in sexually subordinate roles are banned by the Ordinance. Despite defendants' attempt to redefine offensive speech as harmful action, the clear wording of the Ordinance discloses that they seek to control speech, and those restrictions must be analyzed in light of applicable constitutional requirements and standards.

Is the Speech Regulated by the Ordinance Protected or Unprotected Speech Under the First Amendment?

The First Amendment provides that government shall make no law abridging the freedom of speech. However, "the First and Fourteenth Amendments have never been thought to give absolute protection to every individual to speak whenever or wherever he pleases or to use any form of address in any circumstances that he chooses." *Cohen v. California* (1971). Courts have recognized only a "relatively few categories of instances," . . . where the government may regulate certain forms of individual expression. The traditional categories of speech subject to permissible government regulation include "the lewd and obscene, the profane, the libelous, and the insulting or 'fighting' words—those which by their very utterance inflict injury or tend to incite an immediate breach of the peace." *Chaplinsky v. State of New Hampshire* (1942). In addition, the Supreme Court has recently upheld legislation prohibiting the dissemination of material depicting children engaged in sexual conduct. *New York v. Ferber* (1982).

Having found that the Ordinance at issue here seeks to regulate speech (and not conduct), the next question before the Court is whether the Ordinance, which seeks to restrict the distribution, sale, and exhibition of "pornography" as a form of sex discrimination against women, falls within one of the established categories of speech subject to permissible government regulation, that is, speech deemed to be unprotected by the First Amendment.

It is clear that this case does not present issues relating to profanity, libel, or "fighting words." In searching for an analytical "peg," the plaintiffs argue that the Ordinance most closely resembles obscenity, and is, therefore, subject to the requirements set forth in *Miller v. California* (1973). . . . But the defendants admit that the scope of the Ordinance is not limited to the regulation of legally obscene material as defined in *Miller.* . . . In fact, defendants concede that the "pornography" they seek to control goes beyond obscenity, as defined by the Supreme Court and excepted from First Amendment protections. Accordingly, the parties agree that the materials . . . in the restrictions set out in the Ordinance include to some extent what have traditionally been protected materials.

The test under *Miller* for determining whether material is legal obscenity is:

> (a) whether "the average person, applying contemporary community standards" would find that the work, taken as a whole, appeals to the prurient interest, . . . ; (b) whether the work depicts or describes, in a patently offensive way, sexual conduct specifically defined by the applicable state law; and (c) whether the work, taken as a whole, lacks serious literary, artistic, political, or scientific value. . . .

It is obvious that this three-step test is not directly applicable to the present case, because, as has been noted, the Ordinance goes beyond legally obscene material in imposing its controls. The restrictions in the Indianapolis ordinance reach what has otherwise traditionally been regarded as protected speech under the *Miller* test. Beyond that, the Ordinance does not speak in terms of a "community standard" or attempt to restrict the dissemination of material that appeals to the "prurient interest." Nor has the Ordinance been drafted in a way to limit only distributions of "patently offensive" materials. Neither does it provide for the dissemination of works which, though "pornographic," may have "serious literary, artistic, political or scientific value." Finally, the Ordinance does not limit its reach to "hard-core sexual conduct," though conceivably "hard-core" materials may be included in its proscriptions.

Because the Ordinance spans so much more . . . in its regulatory scope than merely "hard-core" obscenity by limiting the distribution of "pornography," the proscriptions in the Ordinance intrude with defendants' explicit approval into areas of otherwise protected speech. Under ordinary constitutional analysis, that would be sufficient grounds to overturn the Ordinance, but defendants argue that this case is not governed by any direct precedent, that it raises a new issue for the Court and even though the Ordinance regulates protected speech, it does so in a constitutionally permissible fashion.

Does Established First Amendment Law Permit the Regulation Provided for in the Ordinance of Otherwise Protected Speech?

In conceding that the scope of this Ordinance extends beyond constitutional limits, it becomes clear that what defendants actually seek by enacting this legislation is a newly defined class of constitutionally unprotected speech, labeled "pornography" and characterized as sexually discriminatory.

Defendants vigorously argue that *Miller* is not the "'constitutional divide' separating protected from unprotected expression in this area." . . . Defendants point to three cases which allegedly support their proposition that *Miller* is not the exclusive guideline for disposing of pornography/obscenity cases, and that the traditional obscenity test should not be applied in the present case. . . .

Defendants first argue that the Court must use the same reasoning applied by the Supreme Court in *New York v. Ferber,* . . . which upheld a New York statute prohibiting persons from promoting child pornography by distributing material which depicted such activity, and carve out another similar exception to protected speech under the First Amendment.

Defendants can properly claim some support for their position in *Ferber.* There the Supreme Court allowed the states "greater leeway" in their regulation of pornographic depictions of children in light of the State's compelling interest in protecting children who, without such protections, are extraordinarily vulnerable to exploitation and harm. The court stated in upholding the New York statute:

> The prevention of sexual exploitation and abuse of children constitutes a government objective of surpassing importance. The legislative findings accompanying passage of the New York laws reflect this concern: . . . .

The Supreme Court continued in *Ferber* by noting that the *Miller* standard for legal obscenity does not satisfy the unique concerns and issues posed by child pornography where children are involved; it is irrelevant, for instance, that the materials sought to be regulated contain serious literary, artistic, political, or scientific value. In finding that some speech, such as that represented in depictions of child pornography, is outside First Amendment protections, the *Ferber* court stated:

> When a definable class of material . . . bears so heavily and pervasively on the welfare of children engaged in its production, we think the balance of competing interests is clearly struck and that it is permissible to consider these materials as without the protection of the First Amendment.

Defendants, in the case at bar, argue that the interests of protecting women from sex-based discrimination are analogous to and every bit as compelling and fundamental as those which the Supreme Court upheld in *Ferber* for the benefit of children. But *Ferber* appears clearly distinguishable from the instant case on both the facts and law.

As has already been shown, the rationale applied by the Supreme Court in *Ferber* appears intended to apply solely to child pornography cases. In *Ferber,* the court recognized "that a state's interest in 'safeguarding the physical and psychological well-being of a minor' is 'compelling.'" . . . Also, the obscenity standard in *Miller* is appropriately abandoned in child pornography cases because it "[does] not reflect the State's particular and more compelling interest in prosecuting those who promote the sexual exploitations of children." . . . Since a state's compelling interest in preventing child pornography outweighs an individual's First Amendment rights, the Supreme Court held that "the states are entitled to greater leeway in the regulation of pornographic depictions of children." . . .

In contrast, the case at bar presents issues more far reaching than those in *Ferber.* Here, the City-County Council found that the distribution, sale, and exhibition of words and pictures depicting the subordination of women is a form of sex discrimination and as such is appropriate for governmental regulation. The state has a well-recognized interest in preventing sex discrimination, and, defendants argue, it can regulate speech to accomplish that end.

But the First Amendment gives primacy to free speech and any other state interest (such as the interest of sex-based equality under law) must be so compelling as to be fundamental; only then can it be deemed to outweigh the interest of free speech. This Court finds no legal authority or public policy argument which justifies so broad an incursion into First Amendment freedoms as to allow that which defendants attempt to advance here. *Ferber* does not open the door to allow the regulation contained in the Ordinance for the reason that adult women as a group do not, as a matter of public policy or applicable law, stand in need of the same type of protection which has long been afforded children. This is true even of women who are subject to the sort of inhuman treatment defendants have described and documented to the Court in support of this Ordinance. The Supreme Court's finding in *Ferber* of the uncontroverted state interest in "safeguarding the physical and psychological well-being of a minor" and its resultant characterization of that interest as "compelling," . . . is an interest that inheres to children and is not an interest which is readily transferrable to adult women as a class. Adult women generally have the capacity to protect themselves from participating in and being personally victimized by pornography, which makes the State's interest in safeguarding the physical and psychological well-being of women by prohibiting "the sexually explicit subordination of women, graphically depicted, whether in pictures or in words" not so compelling as to sacrifice the guarantees of the First Amendment. In any case, whether a state interest is so compelling as to be a fundamental interest sufficient to warrant an exception from constitutional protections, therefore, surely must turn on something other than mere legislative dictate, which issue is discussed more fully further on in this Opinion. . . .

The second case relied upon by defendants to support their contention that *Miller* is not controlling in the present case is *FCC v. Pacifica Foundation* . . . (1978). According to defendants, *Pacifica* exemplifies the Supreme Court's refusal to make obscenity the sole legal basis for regulating sexually explicit conduct.

In *Pacifica*, the Supreme Court was faced with the question of whether a broadcast of patently offensive words dealing with sex and excretion may be regulated on the basis of their content. . . . The Court held that this type of speech was not entitled to absolute constitutional protection in every context. . . . Since the context of the speech in *Pacifica* was broadcasting, it was determined only to be due "the most limited First Amendment protection." . . . The reason for such treatment was two-fold:

> First, the broadcast media have established a uniquely pervasive presence in all the lives of all Americans. Patently offensive, indecent material presented over the airwaves confronts the citizen, not only in public, but also in the privacy of the home, where the individual's right to be left alone plainly outweighs the First Amendment rights of an intruder.
>
> Second, broadcasting is uniquely accessible to children, even those too young to read. . . .

Although the defendants correctly point out that the Supreme Court did not use the traditional obscenity test in *Pacifica*, this Court is not persuaded that the rule enunciated there is applicable to the facts of the present case. The Ordinance does not attempt to regulate the airwaves; in terms of its restrictions, it is not even remotely concerned with the broadcast media. The reasons for the rule in *Pacifica*, that speech in certain contexts should be afforded minimal First Amendment protection, are not present here, since we are not dealing with a medium that "invades" the privacy of the home. In contrast, if an individual is offended by "pornography," as defined in the Ordinance, the logical thing to do is avoid it, an option frequently not available to the public with material disseminated through broadcasting.

In addition, the Ordinance is not written to protect children from the distribution of pornography, in contrast to the challenged FCC regulation in *Pacifica*. Therefore, the peculiar state interest in protecting the "well-being of its youth," . . . does not underlie this Ordinance and cannot be called upon to justify a decision by this Court to uphold the Ordinance.

The third case cited by defendants in support of their proposition that the traditional obscenity standard in *Miller* should not be used to overrule the Ordinance is *Young v. American Mini Theatres, Inc.* . . . (1976). In *Young* the Supreme Court upheld a city ordinance that restricted the location of movie theatres featuring erotic films. The Court, in a plurality opinion, stated that "[e]ven though the First Amendment protects communication in this area from total suppression, we hold that the State may legitimately use the content of these materials as the basis for placing them in a different classification from other motion pictures." . . . The Court concluded that the city's interest in preserving the character of its neighborhoods justified the ordinance which required that adult theatres be separated, rather than concentrated, in the same areas as it is permissible for other theaters to do without limitation. . . .

Young is distinguishable from the present case because we are not here dealing with an attempt by the City-County Council to restrict the time, place, and manner in which "pornography" may be distributed. Instead, the Ordinance prohibits completely the sale, distribution, or exhibition of material depicting women in a sexually subordinate role, at all times, in all places and in every manner.

The Ordinance's attempt to regulate speech beyond one of the well-defined exceptions to protected speech under the First Amendment is not supported by other Supreme Court precedents. The Court must, therefore, examine the underlying premise of the Ordinance: That the State has so compelling an interest in regulating the sort of sex discrimination imposed and perpetuated through "pornography" that it warrants an exception to free speech.

Is Sex Discrimination a Compelling State Interest Justifying an Exception to First Amendment Protections?

It is significant to note that the premise of the Ordinance is the sociological harm, *i.e.*, the discrimination, which results from "pornography" to degrade women as a class. The Ordinance does not presume or require specifically defined, identifiable victims for most of its proscriptions. The Ordinance seeks to protect adult women, as a group, from the diminution of their legal and sociological status as women, that is, from the discriminatory stigma which befalls women *as women* as a result of "pornography." On page one of the introduction to defendants' *Amicus Brief*, counsel explicitly argues that the harm which underlies this legislation is the "harm to the treatment and *status* of women . . . on the basis of sex." . . .

This is a novel theory advanced by the defendants, an issue of first impression in the courts. If this Court were to accept defendants' argument—that the State's interest in protecting women from the humiliation and degradation which comes from being depicted in a sexually subordinate context is so compelling as to warrant the regulation of otherwise free speech to accomplish that end—one wonders what would prevent the City-County Council (or any other legislative body) from enacting protections for other equally compelling claims against exploitation and discrimination as are presented here. Legislative bodies, finding support here, could also enact legislation prohibiting other unfair expression—the publication and distribution of racist material, for instance, on the grounds that it causes racial discrimination,* or legislation prohibiting ethnic or religious slurs on the grounds that they cause discrimination against particular ethnic or religious groups, or legislation barring literary depictions which are uncomplimentary

or oppressive to handicapped persons on the grounds that they cause discrimination against that group of people, and so on. If this Court were to extend to this case the rationale in *Ferber* to uphold the Amendment, it would signal so great a potential encroachment upon First Amendment freedoms that the precious liberties reposed within those guarantees would not survive. The compelling state interest, which defendants claim gives constitutional life to their Ordinance, though important and valid as that interest may be in other contexts, is not so fundamental an interest as to warrant a broad intrusion into otherwise free expression.

Defendants contend that pornography is not deserving of constitutional protection because its harms victimize all women. It is argued that "pornography" not only negatively affects women who risk and suffer the direct abuse of its production, but also, those on whom violent pornography is forced through such acts as compelled performances of "dangerous acts such as being hoisted upside down by ropes, bound by ropes and chains, hung from trees and scaffolds or having sex with animals. . . ." It is also alleged that exposure to pornography produces a negative impact on its viewers, causing in them an increased willingness to aggress toward women, *ibid.* . . . , and experience self-generated rape fantasies, increases in sexual arousal and a rise in the self-reported possibility of raping. . . . In addition, it causes discriminatory attitudes and behavior toward all women. . . . The City-County Council, after considering testimony and social research studies, enacted the Ordinance in order

---

*In *Beauharnais v. Illinois* . . . (1952), the Supreme Court upheld an Illinois libel statute prohibiting the dissemination of materials promoting racial or religious hatred and which tended to produce a breach of the peace and riots. It has been recognized that "the rationale of that decision turns quite plainly on the strong tendency of the prohibited utterances to cause violence and disorder." *Collin v. Smith* (7th Cir. 1978). The Supreme Court has recognized breach of the peace as the traditional justification for upholding a criminal libel statute. *Beauharnais* . . . Therefore, a law preventing the distribution of material that causes racial discrimination, an attitude, would be upheld under this analysis. Further, the underlying reasoning of the *Beauharnais* opinion, that the punishment of libel raises no constitutional problems, has been questioned in many recent cases. . . .

to "combat" pornography's "concrete and tangible harms to women." . . .

Defendants rely on *Paris Adult Theatre I v. Slaton* . . . (1973) to justify their regulation of "pornography." In that case the Supreme Court held "there are legitimate state interests at stake in stemming the tide of commercialized obscenity . . . [that] include the interest of the public in the quality of life and the total community environment, the tone of commerce in the great city centers, and, possibly, . . . public safety itself." . . .

The Georgia Legislature had determined that in that case exposure to obscene material adversely affected men and women, that is to say, society as a whole. Although the petitioners argued in that case that there was no scientific data to conclusively prove that proposition, the Court said, "[i]t is not for us to resolve empirical uncertainties underlying state legislation, save in the exceptional case where that legislation plainly impinges upon rights protected by the constitution itself." . . .

Based on this reasoning, defendants argue that there is more than enough "empirical" evidence in the case at bar to support the City-County Council's conclusion that "pornography" harms women in the same way obscenity harms people, and, therefore, this Court should not question the legislative finding. As has already been acknowledged, it is not the Court's function to question the City-County Council's legislative finding. The Court's solitary duty is to ensure that the Ordinance accomplishes its purpose without violating constitutional standards or impinging upon constitutionally protected rights. In applying those tests, the Court finds that the Ordinance cannot withstand constitutional scrutiny.

It has already been noted that the Ordinance does not purport to regulate legal obscenity, as defined in *Miller*. Thus, although the City-County Council determined that "pornography" harms women, this Court must and does declare the Ordinance invalid without being bound by the legislative findings because "pornography," as defined and regulated in the Ordinance, is constitutionally protected speech under the First Amendment and such an exception to [its] protections is constitutionally unwarranted. This Court cannot legitimately embark on judicial policy making, carving out a new exception to the First Amendment simply to uphold the Ordinance, even when there may be many good reasons to support legislative action. To permit every interest group, especially those who claim to be victimized by unfair expression, their own legislative exceptions to the First Amendment so long as they succeed in obtaining a majority of legislative votes in their favor demonstrates the potentially predatory nature of what defendants seek through this Ordinance and defend in this lawsuit.

It ought to be remembered by defendants and all others who would support such a legislative initiative that, in terms of altering sociological patterns, much as alteration may be necessary and desirable, free speech, rather than being the enemy, is a long-tested and worthy ally. To deny free speech in order to engineer social change in the name of accomplishing a greater good for one sector of our society erodes the freedoms of all and, as such, threatens tyranny and injustice for those subjected to the rule of such laws. The First Amendment protections presuppose the evil of such tyranny and prevent a finding by this Court upholding the Ordinance. . . .

42. *Donald Victor Butler v. Her Majesty the Queen*

THE SUPREME COURT OF CANADA

The issue before the Supreme Court of Canada was that of determining whether and to what extent Parliament may legitimately criminalize obscenity. The Court ruled that the criminalization of obscenity accorded with the Canadian Charter of Rights and Freedom. In particular, the material to be suppressed depicted women "as sexual playthings, hysterically and instantly responsive to male sexual demands" and was produced simply for economic profit. The Court ruled that just as in the case of hate propaganda, it need not require conclusive social science evidence of harm to women before justifying prohibition. The Court judged that "a reasonable apprehension of harm" sufficed. The Court further judged that less intrusive legislation would not be as effective in preventing harm to women.

This appeal [challenges] the constitutionality of the obscenity provisions of the *Criminal Code,* . . . s. 163. They are attacked on the ground that they contravene . . . the *Canadian Charter of Rights and Freedoms.* The case requires the Court to address one of the most difficult and controversial of contemporary issues, . . . determining whether, and to what extent, Parliament may legitimately criminalize obscenity. [We] begin with a review of the facts that gave rise to this appeal, as well as of the proceedings in the lower courts.

Facts and Proceedings

In August 1987, the appellant, Donald Victor Butler, opened the Avenue Video Boutique located in Winnipeg, Manitoba. The shop sells and rents "hard-core" videotapes and magazines as well as sexual paraphernalia. Outside the store is a sign that reads:

> Avenue Video Boutique; a private members only adult video/visual club. Notice: If sex-oriented material offends you, please do not enter. No admittance to persons under 18 years.

On August 21, 1987, the City of Winnipeg Police entered the appellant's store with a search warrant and seized [its] inventory. The appellant was charged with 173 counts in the first indictment: 3 counts of selling obscene material, . . . 41 counts of possessing

obscene material for the purpose of distribution, . . . 128 counts of possessing obscene material for the purpose of sale . . . and 1 count of exposing obscene material to public view. . . .

On October 19, 1987, the appellant reopened the store at the same location. As a result of a police operation a search warrant was executed on October 29, 1987, resulting in the arrest of an employee, Norma McCord. The appellant was arrested at a later date.

A joint indictment was laid against the appellant doing business as Avenue Video Boutique and Norma McCord. The joint indictment contains 77 counts: . . . 2 counts of selling obscene material, . . . 73 counts of possessing obscene material for the purpose of distribution, . . . 1 count of possessing obscene material for the purpose of sale . . . and 1 count of exposing obscene material to public view. . . .

The trial judge convicted the appellant on eight counts relating to eight films. Convictions were entered against the co-accused McCord with respect to two counts relating to two of the films. Fines of $1,000 per offence were imposed on the appellant. Acquittals were entered on the remaining charges.

The Crown appealed the 242 acquittals with respect to the appellant and the appellant cross-appealed the convictions. The majority of the Manitoba Court of Appeal allowed the appeal of the Crown and entered convictions for the appellant with respect to all of the counts, Twaddle and Helper J. J. A. dissenting. . . .

In reaching the conclusion that legislation proscribing obscenity is a valid objective that justifies some encroachment of the right to freedom of expression, I am persuaded in part that such legislation may be found in most free and democratic societies. As Nemetz C. J. B. C. aptly pointed out in *R. v. Red Hot Video*, . . . for centuries democratic societies have set certain limits to freedom of expression. He cited . . . the following passage of Dickson J. A. . . . in *R. v. Great West News Ltd.*:

> All organized societies have sought in one manner or another to suppress obscenity. The right of the state to legislate to protect its moral fibre and well-being has long been recognized, with roots deep in history. It is within this frame that the Courts and Judges must work.

The advent of the *Charter* did not have the effect of dramatically depriving Parliament of a power that it has historically enjoyed. It is also noteworthy that the criminalization of obscenity was considered to be compatible with the *Canadian Bill of Rights*. As Dickson J. A. stated in *R. v. Prairie Schooner News Ltd.* . . . :

> Freedom of speech is not unfettered either in criminal law or civil law. The *Canadian Bill of Rights* was intended to protect, and does protect, basic freedoms of vital importance to all Canadians. It does not serve as a shield behind which obscene matter may be disseminated without concern for criminal consequences. The interdiction of the publications which are the subject of the present charges in no way trenches upon the freedom of expression which the *Canadian Bill of Rights* assures.

. . . Finally, . . . the burgeoning pornography industry renders the concern even more pressing and substantial than when the impugned provisions were first enacted. [Therefore,] the objective of avoiding the harm associated with the dissemination of pornography in this case is sufficiently pressing and substantial to warrant some restriction on full exercise of the right to freedom of expression. The analysis of whether the measure is proportional to the objective must . . . be undertaken in light of the conclusion that the objective of the impugned section is valid only insofar as it relates to the harm to society associated with obscene materials. Indeed, the section as interpreted in previous decisions and in these reasons is fully consistent with that objective. The objective of maintaining conventional standards of propriety, independently of any harm to society, is no longer justified in light of the values of individual liberty that underlie the *Charter*. This, then, being the objective of s. 163, which [is] pressing and substantial, I must now determine whether the section is rationally connected and proportional to this objective. As outlined above, s. 163 criminalizes the exploitation of sex and sex and violence, when, on the basis of the community test, it is undue. The determination of when such exploitation is undue is directly related to the immediacy of a risk of harm to society that is reasonably perceived as arising from its dissemination. . . .

The proportionality requirement has three aspects:

1. the existence of a rational connection between the impugned measures and the objective;
2. minimal impairment of the right or freedom; and
3. a proper balance between the effects of the limiting measures and the legislative objective.

In assessing whether the proportionality test is met, . . . keep in mind the nature of expression that has been infringed. In the *Prostitution Reference*, . . . Dickson C. J. wrote:

> When a *Charter* freedom has been infringed by state action that takes the form of criminalization, the Crown bears the heavy burden of justifying that infringement. Yet the expressive activity, as with any infringed *Charter* right, should also be analysed in the particular context of the case. Here, the activity to which the impugned legislation is directed is expression with an economic purpose. It can hardly be said that communications regarding an economic transaction of sex for money lie at, or even near, the core of the guarantee of freedom of expression.

The values that underlie the protection of freedom of expression relate to the search for truth, participation in the political process, and individual self-fulfillment. The Attorney General for Ontario argues that, of these, only "individual self-fulfillment," and only in its most base aspect, that of physical arousal, is engaged by pornography. . . . [C]ivil liberties groups argue that pornography forces us to question conventional notions of sexuality and thus launches us into an inherently political discourse. In their factum, the B. C. Civil Liberties Association adopts a passage from

R. West, "The Feminist-Conservative Anti-Pornography Alliance and the 1986 Attorney General's Commission on Pornography Report." . . . :

> Good pornography has value because it validates women's will to pleasure. It celebrates female nature. It validates a range of female sexuality that is wider and truer than that legitimated by the non-pornographic culture. Pornography when it is good celebrates both female pleasure and male rationality.

A proper application of the test should not suppress what West refers to as "good pornography." The objective of the impugned provision is not to inhibit the celebration of human sexuality. However, it cannot be ignored that the realities of the pornography industry are far from the picture which the B. C. Civil Liberties Association would have us paint. Shannon J., in *R. v. Wagner* . . . , describes the materials more accurately when he observed:

> Women, particularly, are deprived of unique human character or identity and are depicted as sexual playthings, hysterically and instantly responsive to male sexual demands. They worship male genitals and their own value depends upon the quality of their genitals and breasts.

In my view, the kind of expression that is sought to be advanced does not stand on equal footing with other kinds of expression that directly engage the "core" of the freedom of expression values. This conclusion is further buttressed by the fact that the targeted material is expression that is motivated, in the overwhelming majority of cases, by economic profit. This Court held in *Rocket v. Royal College of Dental Surgeons of Ontario* . . . that an economic motive for expression means that restrictions on the expression might "be easier to justify than other infringements."

I will now turn to an examination of the three basic aspects of the proportionality test.

Rational Connection

The message of obscenity that degrades and dehumanizes is analogous to that of hate propaganda. As the Attorney General of Ontario has argued . . . , obscenity wields the power to wreak social damage in that a significant portion of the population is humiliated by its gross misrepresentations.

Accordingly, the rational link between s. 163 and the objective of Parliament relates to the actual causal relationship between obscenity and the risk of harm to society at large. On this point, it is clear that the literature of the social sciences remains subject to controversy. In *Fringe Product Inc.,* . . . Charron Dist. Ct. J. considered numerous written reports and works and heard six days of testimony from experts who endeavoured to describe the status of the social sciences with respect to the study of the effects of pornography. Charron Dist. Ct. J. reached the conclusion that the relationship between pornography and harm was sufficient to justify Parliament's intervention. This conclusion is not supported unanimously.

The recent conclusions of the Fraser Report . . . could not postulate any causal relationship between pornography and the commission of violent crimes, the sexual abuse of children, or the disintegration of communities and society. . . .

While a direct link between obscenity and harm to society may be difficult, if not impossible, to establish, it is reasonable to presume that exposure to images bears a causal relationship to changes in attitudes and beliefs. The Meese Commission Report . . . concluded in respect of sexually violent material:

> The available evidence strongly supports the hypothesis that substantial exposure to sexually violent materials . . . bears a causal relationship to antisocial acts of sexual violence and, for some subgroups, possibly to unlawful acts of sexual violence.
>
> Although we rely for this conclusion on significant scientific empirical evidence, we feel it worthwhile to note the underlying logic of the conclusion. The evidence says simply that the images that people are exposed to bear a causal relationship to their behavior. This is hardly surprising. What would be surprising would be to find otherwise, and we have not so found. We have not, of course, found that the images people are exposed to are a greater cause of sexual violence than all or even many other possible causes. . . . Nevertheless, it would be strange indeed if graphic representations of a form of behavior, especially in a form that almost exclusively portrays such behavior as desirable, did not have at least some effect on patterns of behavior.

In the face of inconclusive social science evidence, the approach adopted . . . in *Irwin Toy* is instructive. In that case, the basis for the legislation was that television advertising directed at young children is *per se* manipulative. The Court made it clear that in choosing its mode of intervention, it is sufficient that Parliament had a *reasonable basis:*

> In the instant case, the Court is called on to assess competing social science evidence respecting the appropriate means for addressing the problem of children's advertising. The question is whether the government had a reasonable basis, on the evidence tendered, for concluding that the ban on all advertising directed at children impaired freedom of expression as little as possible given the government's pressing and substantial objective.
>
> . . . The Court also recognized that the government was afforded a margin of appreciation to form legitimate objectives based on somewhat inconclusive social science evidence.

Similarly, . . . the absence of proof of a causative link between hate propaganda and hatred of an identifiable group was discounted as a determinative factor in assessing the constitutionality of the hate literature provisions of the *Criminal Code.* Dickson C. J. stated:

> First, to predicate the limitation of free expression upon proof of actual hatred gives insufficient attention to the severe psychological trauma suffered by members of those identifiable groups targeted by hate propaganda. Second, it is clearly difficult to prove a causative link between a specific statement and hatred of an identifiable group.

McLachlin J. (dissenting) expressed it as follows:

> To view hate propaganda as "victimless" in the absence of any proof that it moved its listeners to hatred is to discount the wrenching impact it may have on members of the target group. . . . Moreover, it is simply not possible to assess [precisely] the effects that expression of a particular message will have on all those who are ultimately exposed to it.

The American approach on the necessity of a causal link between obscenity and harm to society was set out by Burger C. J. in *Paris Adult Theatre* . . . :

> Although there is no conclusive proof of a connection between antisocial behavior and obscene material, the legislature . . . could quite reasonably determine that such a connection does or might exist. . . .

I am in agreement with Twaddle J. A. who expressed the view that Parliament was entitled to have a "reasoned apprehension of harm" resulting from the desensitization of individuals exposed to materials that depict violence, cruelty, and dehumanization in sexual relations.

Accordingly, . . . there is a sufficiently rational link between the criminal sanction, which demonstrates our community's disapproval of the dissemination of materials that potentially victimize women and restricts the negative influence that such materials have on changes in attitudes and behaviour, . . .

Minimal Impairment

In determining whether less intrusive legislation may be imagined, this Court stressed in the *Prostitution Reference* . . . that it is not necessary that the legislative scheme be the "perfect" scheme, but that it be appropriately tailored *in the context of the infringed right.* . . . Furthermore, in *Irwin Toy,* Dickson C. J., Lamer and Wilson J. J. stated:

> While evidence exists that other less intrusive options reflecting more modest objectives were available to the government, there is evidence establishing the necessity of a ban to meet the objectives the government had reasonably set. This Court will not, in the name of minimal impairment, take a restrictive approach to social science evidence and require legislatures to choose the least ambitious means to protect vulnerable groups. . . .

There are several factors that contribute to the finding that the provision minimally impairs the freedom which is infringed.

First, the impugned provision does not proscribe sexually explicit erotica without violence that is not degrading or dehumanizing. It is designed to catch material that creates a risk of harm to society. It might be suggested that proof of actual harm should be required. It is apparent from [that] above that it is sufficient . . . for Parliament to have a reasonable basis for concluding that harm will result and this requirement does not demand actual proof of harm.

Second, materials [with] scientific, artistic or literary merit are not captured by the provision. As discussed above, the Court must be generous in [applying] the "artistic defence." For example, in certain cases, materials such as photographs, prints, books and films that may undoubtedly be produced with some motive for economic profit may nonetheless claim the protection of the *Charter* insofar as their defining characteristic is . . . aesthetic expression and thus represent the artist's attempt at individual fulfillment. The existence of an accompanying economic motive does not of itself deprive a work of significance as an example of individual artistic or self-fulfillment.

Third, in considering whether the provision minimally impairs the freedom in question, it is legitimate for the Court to take into account Parliament's past abortive attempts to replace the definition with one that is more explicit. In *Irwin Toy*, our Court recognized that it is legitimate to [consider] the fact that earlier laws and proposed alternatives were thought to be less effective than the legislation [now] being challenged. The attempt to provide exhaustive instances of obscenity has been shown to be destined to fail. . . . [The] only practicable alternative is to strive toward a more abstract definition of obscenity that is contextually sensitive and responsive to progress in the knowledge and understanding of the phenomenon to which the legislation is directed. . . . [The] standard of "undue exploitation" is therefore appropriate. The intractable nature of the problem and the impossibility of precisely defining a notion that is inherently elusive makes the possibility of a more explicit provision remote. In this light, it is appropriate to question whether, and at what cost, greater legislative precision can be demanded.

Fourth, while the discussion in this appeal has been limited to the definition portion of s. 163, I would note that the impugned section, . . . has been held by this Court not to extend its reach to the private use or viewing of obscene materials. *R. v. Rioux* . . . unanimously upheld the finding of the Quebec Court of Appeal that s. 163 . . . does not include the private viewing of obscene materials. Hall J. affirmed the finding of Pratte J.:

. . . I would therefore say that showing obscene pictures to a friend or projecting an obscene film in

one's own home is not in itself a crime nor is it enough to establish intention of circulating them nor help to prove such an intention. . . .

This Court also cited with approval the words of Hyde J.:

Before I am prepared to hold that private use of written matter or pictures within an individual's residence may constitute a criminal offence, I require a much more specific text of law than we are now dealing with. It would have been very simple for Parliament to have included the word "exhibit" in this section if it had wished to cover this situation. . . .

Accordingly, it is only the public distribution and exhibition of obscene materials which is in issue here.

Finally, I wish to address the arguments of the interveners, Canadian Civil Liberties Association and Manitoba Association for Rights and Liberties, that the objectives of this kind of legislation may be met by alternative, less intrusive measures. First, it is submitted that reasonable time, manner and place restrictions would be preferable to outright prohibition. I am of the view that this argument should be rejected. Once it has been established that the objective is the avoidance of harm caused by the degradation which many women feel as "victims" of the message of obscenity, and of the negative impact exposure to such material has on perceptions and attitudes towards women, it is untenable to argue that these harms could be avoided by placing restrictions on access to such material. Making the materials more difficult to obtain by increasing their cost and reducing their availability does not achieve the same objective. Once Parliament has reasonably concluded that certain acts are harmful to certain groups in society and to society in general, it would be inconsistent, if not hypocritical, to argue that such acts could be committed in more restrictive conditions. The harm sought to be avoided would remain the same in either case.

It is also submitted that there are more effective techniques to promote the objectives of Parliament. For example, if pornography is seen as encouraging violence against women, there are certain activities which discourage it—counselling rape victims to charge their assailants, provision of shelter and assistance for battered women, campaigns for laws against discrimination on the grounds of sex, education to increase the sensitivity of law enforcement agencies and other governmental authorities. In addition, it is submitted that education is an under-used response.

It is noteworthy that many of the above suggested alternatives are in the form of *responses* to the harm engendered by negative attitudes against women. The role of the impugned provision is to control the dissemination of the very images that contribute to such attitudes. Moreover, it is true that there are additional measures which could alleviate the problem of violence against women. However, given the gravity of the harm, and the threat to the values at stake, I do not believe that the measure chosen by Parliament is equalled by the alternatives which have been suggested. Education, too, may offer a means of combating negative attitudes to women, just as it is currently used as a means of addressing other problems dealt with in the *Code*. However, there is no reason to rely on education alone. It should be emphasized that this is in no way intended to deny the value of other educational and counselling measures to deal with the roots and effects of negative attitudes. Rather, it is only to stress the arbitrariness and unacceptability of the claim that such measures represent the sole legitimate means of addressing the phenomenon. Serious social problems such as violence against women require multipronged approaches by government. Education and legislation are not alternatives but complements in addressing such problems. There is nothing in the *Charter* which requires Parliament to choose between such complementary measures.

Balance Between Effects of Limiting Measures and Legislative Objective

The final question to be answered in the proportionality test is whether the [law's] effects so severely trench on a protected right that the legislative objective is outweighed by the infringement. The infringement on freedom of expression is confined to a measure designed to prohibit the distribution of sexually explicit materials accompanied by violence and those without violence that are degrading or dehumanizing. As . . . already concluded, this kind of expression lies far from the core of the guarantee of freedom of expression. It appeals only to the most base aspect of individual fulfillment and is primarily economically motivated.

The objective of the legislation, on the other hand, is of fundamental importance in a free and democratic society. It is aimed at avoiding harm, which Parliament has reasonably concluded will be caused directly or indirectly, to individuals, groups such as women and children, and . . . to society as a whole, by the distribution of these materials. It thus seeks to enhance respect for all members of society, and nonviolence and equality in their relations with each other.

I therefore conclude that the restriction on freedom of expression does not outweigh the importance of the legislative objective.

Suggestions for Further Reading

Anthologies

Copp, D., and Wendell, S. *Pornography and Censorship.* Buffalo: Prometheus Press, 1983.

Donnerstein, E., Linz, D., and Pernod S. *The Question of Pornography.* New York: Free Press, 1987.

Dwyer, S. *The Problem of Pornography.* Belmont: Wadsworth Publishing, 1995.

Alternative Views

Dworkin, A. *Pornography: Men Possessing Women.* New York: Perigee, 1981.

Griffin, S. *Pornography and Silence.* New York: Harper & Row, 1981.

Lovelace, L., and McGrady, M. *Ordeal.* New York: Berkeley Books, 1980.

MacKinnon, C. *Only Words.* Cambridge: Harvard University Press, 1993.

Soble, A. *Pornography.* New Haven: Yale University Press, 1986.

Practical Applications

Report of the Attorney General's Commission on Pornography. Washington, D.C.: Government Printing Office, 1986.

Hate Speech

Introduction

Basic Concepts

Hate speech is any form of expression that is racist, sexist, heterosexist, or otherwise denigrating and offensive to someone or some group of people. The moral problem of hate speech concerns whether such expression should be prohibited in whole or in part. In recent years, there has been an increase in the reported incidents of hate speech on college and university campuses across the United States. At the University of Michigan, racist leaflets were distributed in dorms, and white students painted themselves black and placed rings in their noses at "jungle parties." Also at Michigan, a student walked into a classroom and saw written on the blackboard: "A mind is a terrible thing to waste—especially on a nigger." At Purdue University, a counselor found "Death Nigger" scratched on her door. At Dartmouth College, a black professor was called "a cross between a welfare queen and a bathroom attendant" and the *Dartmouth Review* purported to quote a black student, "Dese boys be sayin' that we be comin' here to Dartmut an' not takin' the classics. . . ." At Brown University, an African student found a note under her door saying, "This room is for coloreds only." At the University of Wisconsin, white male students

trailed African-American female students shouting, "I've never tried a nigger before." At Northwest Missouri State University, white supremacists distributed flyers stating, "The Knights of the Ku Klux Klan are Watching You." Responding to such incidents, colleges and universities across the country have taken steps to prohibit hate speech. At Stanford University, the following speech code was adopted:

---

1. Stanford is committed to the principles of free inquiry and free expression. Students have the right to hold and vigorously defend and promote their opinions, thus entering them into the life of the University, there to flourish or wither according to their merits. Respect for this right requires that students tolerate even expression of opinions which they find abhorrent. Intimidation of students by other students in their exercise of this right, by violence or threat of violence, is therefore considered to be a violation of the Fundamental Standard.

2. Stanford is also committed to principles of equal opportunity and nondiscrimination. Each student has the right to equal access to a Stanford education, without discrimination on the basis of sex, race, color, handicap, religion, sexual orientation, or national and ethnic origin. Harassment of students on the basis of any of these characteristics tends to create a hostile environment that makes access to education for those subjected to it less

than equal. Such discriminatory harassment is therefore considered to be a violation of the Fundamental Standard.

3. This interpretation of the Fundamental Standard is intended to clarify the point at which protected free expression ends and prohibited discriminatory harassment begins. Prohibited harassment includes discriminatory intimidation by threats of violence, and also includes personal vilification of students on the basis of their sex, race, color, handicap, religion, sexual orientation, or national and ethnic origin.

4. Speech or other expression constitutes harassment by vilification if it:
   a. is intended to insult or stigmatize an individual or a small number of individuals on the basis of their sex, race, color, handicap, religion, sexual orientation, or national and ethnic origin; and
   b. is addressed directly to the individual or individuals whom it insults or stigmatizes; and
   c. makes use of "fighting" words or nonverbal symbols. In the context of discriminatory harassment, "fighting" words or nonverbal symbols are words, pictures, or symbols that, by virtue of their form, are commonly understood to convey direct and visceral hatred or contempt for human beings on the basis of their sex, race, color, handicap, religion, sexual orientation, and national and ethnic origin.

The Stanford speech code was more limited in scope than either the University of Michigan or the University of Wisconsin speech codes, both of which were declared unconstitutional in 1989 and 1991, respectively. But in 1995 the Stanford speech code was itself declared unconstitutional by Justice Peter Stone of the California Superior Court (see Selection 47). However, this hardly settles the matter from either a legal or a moral perspective. From a legal perspective, the unwillingness of the U.S. judiciary to balance free speech concerns against concerns for equality or equal opportunity sets it apart from all other liberal democracies. So it may be that the U.S. legal system is out of touch here with its own liberal democratic traditions. And from a moral perspective, what is important is not what this or that court has decided with respect to prohibiting hate speech, but whether good moral arguments can be given for or against such a prohibition—hence, the importance of the readings in this section, which take up both the legal and moral arguments for and against prohibiting hate speech.

Alternative Views

In Selection 43, Gerald Gunther argues against Stanford's speech code and other similar university codes. He contends that university campuses should exhibit greater, not less, freedom of expression than prevails in society at large. He further argues that the "fighting words" exception to the First Amendment protection of freedom of speech is not broad enough to justify Stanford's speech code. In fact, some legal scholars have argued that the Supreme Court's fighting words exception has been so qualified over the years that it no longer restricts free speech at all.[1] In agreement with Gunther, Alan Dershowitz argues that the use of speech codes may also turn out to be counterproductive and end up restricting the freedom of expression of those who now support the speech codes. Nadine Strossen points out that this frequently has been the case in the past. For example, the British Race Relations Act of 1965, which was supposed to restrict racist speech, was later used to prosecute black power leaders.[2]

In support of such codes, Charles Lawrence III argues that the landmark *Brown v. Board of Education* Supreme Court decision disestablished racial desegregation by regulating speech as well as conduct. He further questions whether the Fourteenth Amendment's equal protection clause, on which the Brown decisions relied, prohibits only governmental and not private discrimination, and he illustrates the considerable harm racial hate speech can cause by its connection to continuing patterns of racism. By analogy with the Brown decisions, Lawrence concludes that Stanford's and other similar speech codes are justified. According to Lawrence, we cannot accept the Brown decisions as most people do and also reject limited speech codes like Stanford's.

In Selection 46, Katharine Bartlett and Jean O'Barr argue that the hate speech debate has tended to focus on the most visible forms of racism while ignoring other more subtle discriminatory practices that pervade college campuses. For example, Bartlett and O'Barr contrast the different standards of behavior that are appropriate for men and women students. Thus, for men but not for women, it is appropriate to pass gas, belch in public, spit loudly on the ground, consume particularly large quantities, and sit in undignified positions with legs apart. By contrast, it is appropriate for women to use submissive gestures such as inappropriate smiling when making a serious statement or asking a question, or averting one's eyes, especially when dealing with men, and to laugh prettily and convincingly at the male behaviors that are inappropriate for women if they want to be one of the guys. Although these more subtle forms of discrimination are not as egregious as those in discussions of hate speech, Bartlett and O'Barr contend that they may play an even larger role in establishing the subordination of members of certain groups on college campuses.

Practical Applications

The issue before the Superior Court of California was whether Stanford University's Speech Code violated the First Amendment of the U.S. Constitution. Judge Stone found that it did, in fact, violate the First Amendment because it was overbroad and restricted speech beyond fighting words. In addition, Stone found the defendant's claim that they were proscribing conduct, not speech, to be without merit. The judge further found that although the First Amendment protection of speech does not, in general, apply to private institutions, it does in California because of a 1992 law called Leonard's Law. In arguing for the appropriateness of applying the First Amendment protection of speech at Stanford University, Stone contended that the university, with all its resources, should be able to fight hate speech with more speech of its own. Although it may be true that Stanford as a whole may have resources to fight hate speech, individual victims of hate speech may lack the necessary resources and so may be deprived of the chance to benefit from the educational opportunities at Stanford as long as hate speech is protected. In Selection 48, the ACLU proposes a course of action for reconciling free speech with equal opportunity.

Obviously, the moral problem of hate speech is connected to the other moral problems discussed in this anthology (see Sections VII, IX, and X) that address different aspects of the general question of how free people should be. So it should be helpful in determining your position with respect to the problem of hate speech to see how it relates to acceptable solutions to these other moral problems.

Endnotes

1. Nadine Strossen, "Regulating Racist Speech: A Modest Proposal?" *Duke University Law Review* (1990), pp. 508–514.

2. Strossen, p. 556.

43. No *Speech* Code

GERALD GUNTHER

Gerald Gunther argues against Stanford's speech code and other similar university codes. He contends that university campuses should exhibit greater, not less, freedom of expression than prevails in society at large. He further argues that the fighting words exception to the First Amendment protection of freedom of speech is not broad enough to justify Stanford's speech code.

I am deeply troubled by current efforts—however well-intentioned—to place new limits on freedom of expression at this and other campuses. Such limits are not only incompatible with the mission and meaning of a university; they also send exactly the wrong message from academia to society as a whole. University campuses should exhibit greater, not less, freedom of expression than prevails in society at large.

Proponents of new limits argue that historic First Amendment rights must be balanced against "Stanford's commitment to the diversity of ideas and persons." Clearly, there is ample room and need for vigorous University action to combat racial and other discrimination. But curbing freedom of speech is the wrong way to do so. The proper answer to bad speech is usually more and better speech—not new laws, litigation, and repression.

Lest it be thought that I am insensitive to the pain imposed by expressions of racial or religious hatred, let me say that I have suffered that pain and empathize with others under similar verbal assault. My deep belief in the principles of the First Amendment arises in part from my own experiences.

I received my elementary education in a public school in a very small town in Nazi Germany. There I was subjected to vehement anti-Semitic remarks from my teacher, classmates and others—"Judensau," Jew

pig, was far from the harshest. I can assure you that they hurt. More generally, I lived in a country where ideological orthodoxy reigned and where the opportunity for dissent was severely limited.

The lesson . . . drawn from my childhood in Nazi Germany and my happier adult life in this country is the need to walk the sometimes difficult path of denouncing the bigots' hateful ideas with all my power, yet at the same time challenging any community's attempt to suppress hateful ideas by force of law.

Obviously, given my own experience, I do *not* quarrel with the claim that words *can* do harm. But I firmly deny that a showing of harm suffices to deny First Amendment protection, and I insist on the elementary First Amendment principle that our Constitution usually protects even offensive, harmful expression.

That is why—at the risk of being thought callous or doctrinaire—I feel compelled to speak out against the attempt by some members of the Stanford community to enlarge the area of forbidden speech under the Fundamental Standard. Such proposals, in my view, seriously undervalue the First Amendment and far too readily endanger its precious content. Limitations on free expression beyond those established by law should be eschewed in an institution committed to diversity and the First Amendment.[1]

In explaining my position, I will avoid extensive legal arguments. Instead, I want to speak from the heart, on the basis of my own background and of my understanding of First Amendment Principles—principles supported by an even larger number of scholars and Supreme Court justices, especially since the days of the Warren Court.

Reprinted by permission of *Stanford Lawyer* and the author. Adapted from two letters to the chair of the Student Conduct Legislative Council, dated March 10 and May 1, 1989, and published in *Stanford University Campus Report* on March 15 and May 3, respectively.

Among the core principles is that any official effort to suppress expression must be viewed with the greatest skepticism and suspicion. Only in very narrow, urgent circumstances should government or similar institutions be permitted to inhibit speech. True, there are certain categories of speech that may be prohibited; but the number and scope of these categories has steadily shrunk over the last fifty years. Face-to-face insults are one such category; incitement to immediate illegal action is another. But opinions expressed in debates and arguments about a wide range of political and social issues should not be suppressed simply because of disagreement with those views, with the content of the expression.

Similarly, speech should not and cannot be banned simply because it is "offensive" to substantial parts or a majority of a community. The refusal to suppress offensive speech is one of the most difficult obligations the free speech principle imposes upon all of us; yet it is also one of the First Amendment's greatest glories—indeed it is a central test of a community's commitment to free speech.

The Supreme Court's 1989 decision to allow flag-burning as a form of political protest, in *Texas v. Johnson,* warrants careful pondering by all those who continue to advocate campus restraints on "racist speech." As Justice Brennan's majority opinion in *Johnson* reminded, "If there is a bedrock principle underlying the First Amendment, it is that the Government may not prohibit the expression of an idea simply because society finds the idea itself offensive or disagreeable." In refusing to place flag-burning outside the First Amendment, moreover, the *Johnson* majority insisted (in words especially apt for the "racist speech" debate): "The First Amendment does not guarantee that other concepts virtually sacred to our Nation as a whole—such as the principle that discrimination on the basis of race is odious and destructive—will go unquestioned in the marketplace of ideas. We decline, therefore, to create for the flag an exception to the joust of principles protected by the First Amendment."

Campus proponents of restricting offensive speech are currently relying for justification on the Supreme Court's allegedly repeated reiteration that "fighting words" constitute an exception to the First Amendment. Such an exception has indeed been recognized in a number of lower court cases. However, there has only been *one* case in the history of the Supreme Court in which a majority of the Justices has ever found a statement to be a punishable resort to "fighting words." That was *Chaplinsky v. New Hampshire,* a nearly fifty-year-old case involving words that would very likely not be found punishable today.

More significant is what has happened in the nearly half-century since: Despite repeated appeals to the Supreme Court to recognize the applicability of the "fighting words" exception by affirming challenged convictions, the Court has in every instance refused. One must wonder about the strength of an exception that, while theoretically recognized, has for so long not been found apt in practice. Moreover, the proposed Stanford rules are *not* limited to face-to-face insults to an addressee, and thus go well beyond the traditional, albeit fragile, "fighting words" exception.

The phenomenon of racist and other offensive speech that Stanford now faces is not a new one in the history of the First Amendment. In recent decades, for example, well-meaning but in my view misguided majorities have sought to suppress not only racist speech but also antiwar and antidraft speech, civil rights demonstrators, the Nazis and the Ku Klux Klan, and left-wing groups.

Typically, it is people on the extremes of the political spectrum (including those who advocate overthrow of our constitutional system and those who would not protect their opponents' right to dissent were they the majority) who feel the brunt of repression and have found protection in the First Amendment; typically, it is well-meaning people in the majority who believe that their "community standards," their sensibilities, their sense of outrage, justify restraints.

Those in power in a community recurrently seek to repress speech they find abhorrent; and their efforts are understandable human impulses. Yet freedom of expression—and especially the protection of dissident speech, the most important function of the First Amendment—is an antimajoritarian principle. Is it too much to hope that, especially on a university campus, a majority can be persuaded of the value of freedom of expression and of the resultant need to curb our impulses to repress dissident views?

The principles to which I appeal are not new. They have been expressed, for example, by the most distinguished Supreme Court justices ever since the beginning of the Court's confrontations with First Amendment issues nearly seventy years ago. These principles are reflected in the words of so imperfect a First Amendment defender as Justice Oliver Wendell Holmes: "If there is any principle of the Constitution that more imperatively calls for attachment than any other, it is the principle of free thought—not free thought for those who agree with us but freedom for the thought that we hate."

This is the principle most elaborately and eloquently addressed by Justice Louis D. Branders, who reminded us that the First Amendment rests on a belief "in the power of reason as applied through public discussion" and therefore bars "silence coerced by law—the argument of force in its worst form."

This theme, first articulated in dissents, has repeatedly been voiced in majority opinions in more recent decades. It underlies Justice Douglas's remark in striking down a conviction under a law banning speech that "stirs the public to anger": "A function of free speech [is] to invite dispute. . . . Speech is often provocative and challenging. That is why freedom of speech [is ordinarily] protected against censorship or punishment."

It also underlies Justice William J. Brennan's comment about our "profound national commitment to the principle that debate on public issues should be uninhibited, robust, and wide-open, and that it may well include vehement, caustic, and sometimes unpleasantly sharp attacks"—a comment he followed with a reminder that constitutional protection "does not turn upon the truth, popularity, or social utility of the ideas and beliefs which are offered."

These principles underlie as well the repeated insistence by Justice John Marshall Harlan, again in majority opinions, that the mere "inutility or immorality" of a message cannot justify its repression, and that the state may not punish because of "the under-lying content of the message." Moreover, Justice Harlan, in one of the finest First Amendment opinions on the books, noted, in words that Stanford would ignore at its peril at this time:

"The constitutional right of free expression is powerful medicine in a society as diverse and populous as ours. To many, the immediate consequence of this freedom may often appear to be only verbal tumult, discord and even offensive utterance. These are, however, within established limits, in truth necessary side effects of the broader enduring values which the process of open debate permits us to achieve. That the air may at times seem filled with verbal cacophony is, in this sense, not a sign of weakness but of strength."

In this same passage, Justice Harlan warned that a power to ban speech merely because it is offensive is an "inherently boundless" notion, and added that "we think it is largely because the governmental officials cannot make principled distinctions in this area that the Constitution leaves the matters of taste and style so largely to the individual." The Justice made these comments while overturning the conviction of an antiwar protestor for "offensive conduct." The defendant has worn, in a courthouse corridor, a jacket bearing the words "Fuck the Draft." It bears noting, in light of the ongoing campus debate, that Justice Harlan's majority opinion also warned that "we cannot indulge in the facile assumption that one can forbid particular words without also running the substantial risk of suppressing ideas in the process."

I restate these principles and repeat these words for reasons going far beyond the fact that they are familiar to me as a First Amendment scholar. I believe—in my heart as well as my mind—that these principles and ideals are not only established but right. I hope that the entire Stanford community will seriously reflect upon the risks to free expression, lest we weaken hard-won liberties at Stanford and, by example, in this nation.

Endnote

1. These comments were directed at a proposal later withdrawn in the face of criticism to prohibit not only "personal abuse" but also "defamation of groups"—expression "that by accepted community standards . . . pejoratively characterizes persons or groups on the basis of personal or cultural differences."

44. *Speech Codes and Diversity*

ALAN DERSHOWITZ

Alan Dershowitz argues that the use of speech codes may turn out to be counterproductive and end up restricting the freedom of expression of those who now support speech codes.

There is now a debate among pundits over whether the "political correctness" movement on college and university campuses constitutes a real threat to intellectual freedom or merely provides conservatives with a highly publicized opportunity to bash the left for the kind of intolerance of which the right has often been accused.

My own sense, as a civil libertarian whose views lean to the left, is that the "P.C." movement is dangerous and that it is also being exploited by hypocritical right wingers.

In addition to being intellectually stifling, the P.C. movement is often internally inconsistent. Among its most basic tenets are (1) the demand for greater "diversity" among students and faculty members; and (2) the need for "speech codes," so that racist, sexist, and homophobic ideas, attitudes, and language do not "offend" sensitive students.

Is it really possible that the bright, well-intentioned students (and faculty) who are pressing the "politically correct" agenda do not realize how inherently self-contradictory these two basic tenets really are? Can they be blind to the . . . reality that true diversity of viewpoints is incompatible with speech codes that limit certain diverse expressions and attitudes?

I wonder if most of those who are pressing for diversity really want it. What many on the extreme left seem to want is simply more of their own: more students and faculty who think like they do, vote like they do, and speak like they do. The last thing they want is a truly diverse campus community with views that are broadly reflective of the multiplicity

of attitudes in the big, bad world outside of the ivory towers.

How many politically correct students are demanding—in the name of diversity—an increase in the number of Evangelical Christians, National Rifle Association members, and Right to Life advocates? Where is the call for more anticommunist refugees from the Soviet Union, [more] Afro-Americans who oppose race-specific quotas, and [more] women who are antifeminist?

Let's be honest: The demand for diversity is at least in part a cover for a political power grab by the left. Most of those who are recruited to provide politically correct diversity—Afro-Americans, women, gays—are thought to be supporters of the left. And historically, the left—like the right—has not been a bastion of diversity.

Now the left—certainly the extreme left that has been pushing hardest for political correctness—is behind the demands for speech codes. And if they were to get their way, these codes would not be limited to racist, sexist, or homophobic *epithets*. They would apply as well to politically incorrect *ideas* that are deemed offensive by those who would enforce the codes. Such ideas would include criticism of affirmative action programs, opposition to rape-shield laws, advocacy of the criminalization of homosexuality, and defense of pornography.

I have heard students argue that the expression of such ideas—both in and out of class, both by students and professors—contributes to an atmosphere of bigotry, harassment, and intolerance, and that it makes it difficult for them to learn.

The same students who insist that they be treated as adults when it comes to their sexuality, drinking,

---

Reprinted by permission of *Harvard Law Record* and the author.

and school work beg to be treated like children when it comes to politics, speech, and controversy. They whine to Big Father and Mother—the president or provost of the university—to "protect" them from offensive speech, instead of themselves trying to combat it in the marketplace of ideas.

Does this movement for political correctness—this intolerance of verbal and intellectual diversity—really affect college and university students today? Or is it, as some argue, merely a passing fad, exaggerated by the political right and the media?

It has certainly given the political right—not known for its great tolerance of different ideas—a hay day. Many hypocrites of the right, who would gladly impose their own speech codes if *they* had the power to enforce *their* way, are selectively wrapping themselves in the same First Amendment they willingly trash when it serves their political interest to do so.

But hypocrisy aside—since there is more than enough on both sides—the media is not exaggerating the problem of political correctness. It is a serious issue on college and university campuses. As a teacher, I can feel a palpable reluctance on the part of many students—particularly those with views in neither extreme and those who are anxious for peer acceptance—to experiment with unorthodox ideas, to make playful comments on serious subjects, to challenge politically correct views, and to disagree with minority, feminist, or gay perspectives.

I feel this problem quite personally, since I happen to agree—as a matter of substance—with most "politically correct" positions. But I am appalled at the intolerance of many who share my substantive views. And I worry about the impact of politically correct intolerance on the generation of leaders we are currently educating.

---

45. *Regulating Racist Speech on Campus*

CHARLES R. LAWRENCE III

In support of speech codes, Charles Lawrence argues that the landmark Brown v. Board of Education Supreme Court decisions disestablished racial desegregation by regulating speech as well as conduct. He further questions whether the equal protection clause of the Fourteenth Amendment on which the Brown decisions relied prohibits only governmental and not private discrimination, and he illustrates the considerable harm racial hate speech can cause through its connection to continuing patterns of racism. By analogy with the Brown decisions, Lawrence concludes that Stanford's and other similar speech codes are justified.

Racist incidents occur at the University of Michigan, University of Massachusetts-Amherst, University of Wisconsin, University of New Mexico, Columbia University, Wellesley College, Duke University, and University of California-Los Angeles. (*Ms.* Magazine, October 1987)

Reprinted by permission of *Duke University Law Review* and the author.

The campus ought to be the last place to legislate tampering with the edges of First Amendment protections.

University of Michigan:

"Greek Rites of Exclusion": Racist leaflets distributed in dorms; white students paint themselves black and place rings in their noses at "jungle parties." (*The Nation*, July 1987)

Silencing a few creeps is no victory if the price is an abrogation of free speech. Remember, censorship *is an ugly word too.*

Northwest Missouri State University:
White Supremacists distribute flyers stating: "The Knights of the Ku Klux Klan are Watching You." (Klanwatch Intelligence Report No. 42, February 1988 [*Klanwatch*])

Kansas University:
KKK members speak. *(Klanwatch)*

Temple University:
White Student Union formed. *(Klanwatch)*

Stanford University:
Aryan Resistance literature distributed. *(Klanwatch)*

Stockton State College (New Jersey):
Invisible Empire literature distributed. *(Klanwatch)*

Memphis State University:
Bomb threats at Jewish Student Union. *(Klanwatch)*

Arizona State University:
Shot fired at Hillel Foundation building. *(Klanwatch)*

The harm that censors allege will result unless speech is forbidden rarely occurs.

Dartmouth College:
Black professor called "a cross between a welfare queen and a bathroom attendant" and the *Dartmouth Review* purported to quote a Black student, "Dese boys be sayin' that we be comin' here to Dartmut an' not takin' the classics." (*The Nation*, February 27, 1989)

Yes, speech is sometimes painful. Sometimes it is abusive. That is one of the prices of a free society.

Purdue University:
Counselor finds "Death Nigger" scratched on her door. (*The Nation*, February 27, 1989)

More speech, not less, is the proper cure for offensive speech.

Smith College:
African student finds message slipped under her door that reads, "African Nigger do you want some bananas? Go back to the Jungle." (*New York Times*, October 19, 1988)

Speech cannot be banned simply because it is offensive.

University of Michigan:
Campus radio station broadcasts a call from a student who "joked": "Who are the most famous black women in history? Aunt Jemima and Mother Fucker." (*The Nation*, February 27, 1989)

Those who don't like what they are hearing or seeing should try to change the atmosphere through education. That is what they will have to do in the real world after they graduate.

University of Michigan:
A student walks into class and sees this written on the blackboard: "A mind is a terrible thing to waste—especially on a nigger." (*Chicago Tribune*, April 23, 1989)

People of color, women, and gays and lesbians owe their vibrant political movements in large measure to their freedom to communicate. If speech can be banned because it offends someone, how long will it be before the messages of these groups are themselves found offensive?

Stanford University:
"President Donald Kennedy refused yesterday to consider amnesty for students who took over his office last week. . . . Kennedy insisted that the probe of violations of the Stanford behavior code go forward. The students [who were demanding more minority faculty and ethnic studies reforms] consider the prospect of disciplinary action unfair in view of Stanford's decision earlier this year not to punish two white students who defaced a poster of 19th century composer Ludwig von Beethoven to portray a stereotypical black face, then tacked it up in a predominantly black dormitory. The two incidents differ sharply, Kennedy said. The poster was admittedly racially offensive. But its defacement probably was protected by constitutional freedoms. However, the office takeover was clearly a violation of Stanford's policy against campus disruption." (*San Francisco Chronicle*, May 25, 1989)

Now it's the left that is trying to restrict free speech. Though the political labels have shifted, the rationale is the same: Our adversaries are dangerous and therefore should not be allowed to speak.

In recent years, university campuses have seen a resurgence of racial violence and a corresponding rise in the incidence of verbal and symbolic assault and harassment to which Blacks and other traditionally subjugated groups are subjected. The events listed above were gathered from newspaper and magazine reports of racist incidents on campuses. The accompanying italicized statements criticizing proposals to regulate racism on campus were garnered from conversations, debates, and panel discussions at which I was present. Some were recorded verbatim and are exact quotes; others paraphrase the sentiment expressed. I have heard some version of each of these arguments many times over. These incidents are but a small sampling of the hate speech to which minorities are subjected on a daily basis on our nation's college campuses. There is a heated debate in the civil liberties community concerning the proper response to incidents of racist speech on campus. Strong disagreements have arisen between those individuals who believe that racist speech such as that described above should be regulated by the university or some public body and those individuals who believe that racist expression should be protected from all public regulation. At the center of the controversy is a tension between the constitutional values of free speech and equality. Like the debate over affirmative action in university admissions, this issue has divided old allies and revealed unrecognized or unacknowledged differences in the experience, perceptions, and values of members of long-standing alliances. It also has caused considerable soul searching by individuals with long-time commitments to both the cause of political expression and the cause of racial equality.

I write this chapter from within the cauldron of this controversy. I make no pretense of dispassion or objectivity, but I do .claim a deep commitment to the values that motivate both sides of the debate. I have spent the better part of my life as a dissenter. As a high school student I was threatened with suspension for my refusal to participate in a civil defense drill, and I have been a conspicuous consumer of . . . First Amendment liberties ever since. I also have experienced the injury of the historical, ubiquitous, and continuous defamation of American racism. I grew up with Little Black Sambo and Amos and Andy, and I continue to receive racist tracts in the mail and shoved under my door. As I struggle with the tension between these constitutional values, I particularly appreciate the ex-

perience of both belonging and not belonging that gives to African Americans and other outsider groups a sense of duality. W.E.B. DuBois—scholar and founder of the National Association for the Advancement of Colored People (NAACP)—called the gift and burden inherent in the dual, conflicting heritage of all African Americans their "second-sight."[1]

The double consciousness of groups outside the ethnic mainstream is particularly apparent in the context of this controversy. Blacks know and value the protection the First Amendment affords those of us who must rely on our voices to petition both government and our neighbors for redress of grievances. Our political tradition has looked to "the word,"[2] to the moral power of ideas, to change the system when neither the power of the vote nor that of the gun were available. This part of us has known the experience of belonging and recognizes our common and inseparable interest in preserving the right of free speech for all. But we also know the experience of the outsider. The framers excluded us from the protection of the First Amendment. The same Constitution that established rights for others endorsed a story that proclaimed our inferiority. It is a story that remains deeply ingrained in the American psyche. We see a different world than that seen by Americans who do not share this historical experience. We often hear racist speech when our white neighbors are not aware of its presence.

It is not my purpose to belittle or trivialize the importance of defending unpopular speech against the tyranny of the majority. There are very strong reasons for protecting even racist speech. Perhaps the most important reasons are that it reinforces our society's commitment to the value of tolerance, and that by shielding racist speech from government regulation, we are forced to combat it as a community. These reasons for protecting racist speech should not be set aside hastily, and I will not argue that we should be less vigilant in protecting the speech and associational rights of speakers with whom most of us would disagree.

But I am deeply concerned about the role that many civil libertarians have played, or the roles we have failed to play, in the continuing, real-life struggle through which we define the community in which we live. I fear that by framing the debate as we have—as one in which the liberty of free speech is in conflict with the elimination of racism—we have advanced the cause of racial oppression and placed the bigot on the moral high ground, fanning the rising flames of racism. Above all, I am troubled that we have not listened to the real victims, that we have shown so little empathy or understanding for their injury, and that we have abandoned those individuals whose race, gender, or sexual orientation provokes others to regard them as second-class citizens. These individuals' civil liberties are most directly at stake in the debate. In this chapter I focus on racism. Although I will not address violent pornography and homophobic hate speech directly, I will draw on the experience of women and gays as victims of hate speech where they operate as instructive analogues.

I have set two goals in constructing this chapter. The first goal is limited and perhaps overly modest, but it is nonetheless extremely important: I will demonstrate that much of the argument for protecting racist speech is based on the distinction that many civil libertarians draw between direct, face-to-face racial insults, which they think deserve First Amendment protection, and all other fighting words, which they find unprotected by the First Amendment. I argue that the distinction is false, that it advances none of the purposes of the First Amendment, and that the time has come to put an end to the ringing rhetoric that condemns all efforts to regulate racist speech, even narrowly drafted provisions aimed at racist speech that results in direct, immediate, and substantial injury.

I also urge the regulation of racial epithets and vilification that do not involve face-to-face encounters—situations in which the victim is part of a captive audience and the injury is experienced by all members of a racial group who are forced to hear or see these words. In such cases, the insulting words are aimed at an entire group with the effect of causing significant harm to individual group members.

My second goal is more ambitious and more indeterminate. I propose several ways in which the traditional civil liberties position on free speech does not take into account important values expressed elsewhere in the Constitution. Further, I argue that even those values the First Amendment itself is intended to promote are frustrated by an interpretation that is acontextual and idealized, by presupposing a world

characterized by equal opportunity and the absence of societally created and culturally ingrained racism.

Brown v. Board of Education: A Case About Regulating Racist Speech

The landmark case of *Brown v. Board of Education* is not one we normally think of as concerning speech. As read most narrowly, the case is about the rights of Black children to equal educational opportunity. But *Brown* can also be read more broadly to articulate a principle central to any substantive understanding of the equal protection clause, the foundation on which all antidiscrimination law rests. This is the principle of equal citizenship. Under that principle, "Every individual is presumptively entitled to be treated by the organized society as a respected, responsible, and participating member."[3] The principle further requires the affirmative disestablishment of societal practices that treat people as members of an inferior or dependent caste, as unworthy to participate in the larger community. The holding in *Brown*—that racially segregated schools violate the equal protection clause—reflects the fact that segregation amounts to a demeaning, caste-creating practice. The prevention of stigma was at the core of the Supreme Court's unanimous decision in *Brown* that segregated public schools are inherently unequal. Observing that the segregation of Black pupils "generates a feeling of inferiority as to their status in the community,"[4] Chief Justice Earl Warren recognized what a majority of the Court had ignored almost sixty years earlier in *Plessy v. Ferguson*.[5] The social meaning of racial segregation in the United States is the designation of a superior and an inferior caste, and segregation proceeds "on the ground that colored citizens are . . . inferior and degraded."[6]

The key to this understanding of *Brown* is that the practice of segregation, the practice the Court held inherently unconstitutional, was *speech*. *Brown* held that segregation is unconstitutional not simply because the physical separation of Black and white children is bad or because resources were distributed unequally among Black and white schools. *Brown* held that segregated schools were unconstitutional primarily because of the *message* segregation conveys—the message that Black children are an untouchable caste, unfit to be educated with white children. Segregation serves its purpose by conveying an idea. It stamps a badge of inferiority upon Blacks, and this badge communicates a message to others in the community, as well as to Blacks wearing the badge, that is injurious to Blacks. Therefore, *Brown* may be read as regulating the content of racist speech. As a regulation of racist speech, the decision is an exception to the usual rule that regulation of speech content is presumed unconstitutional.

The Conduct/Speech Distinction

Some civil libertarians argue that my analysis of *Brown* conflates speech and conduct. They maintain that the segregation outlawed in *Brown* was discriminatory conduct, not speech, and the defamatory message conveyed by segregation simply was an incidental by-product of that conduct. This position is often stated as follows: "Of course segregation conveys a message, but this could be said of almost all conduct. To take an extreme example, a murderer conveys a message of hatred for his victim. But we would not argue that we cannot punish the murder—the primary conduct—merely because of this message, which is its secondary by-product."[7] The Court has been reluctant to concede that the First Amendment has any relevance whatsoever in examples like this one, because the law would not be directed at anything resembling speech or at the views expressed. In such a case the regulation of speech is truly incidental to the regulation of the conduct.

These same civil libertarians assert that I suggest that all conduct with an expressive component should be treated alike—namely, as unprotected speech. This reading of my position clearly misperceives the central point of my argument. I do not contend that *all* conduct with an expressive component should be treated as unprotected speech. To the contrary, my suggestion that *racist* conduct amounts to speech is premised upon a unique characteristic of racism—namely its reliance upon the defamatory message of white supremacy to achieve its injurious purpose. I have not ignored the distinction between the speech and conduct elements of segregation, although, as the constitutional scholar Lawrence Tribe explained, "Any

particular course of conduct may be hung almost randomly on the 'speech' peg or the 'conduct' peg as one sees fit."[8] Rather, my analysis turns on that distinction; I ask the question of whether there is a purpose to outlawing segregation that is unrelated to its message and conclude that the answer is no.

If, for example, John W. Davis, counsel for the Board of Education of Topeka, Kansas, had been asked during oral argument in *Brown* to state the board's purpose in educating Black and white children in separate schools, he would have been hard pressed to answer in a way unrelated to the purpose of designating Black children as inferior. If segregation's primary goal is to convey the message of white supremacy, then *Brown*'s declaration that segregation is unconstitutional amounts to a regulation of the message of white supremacy. Properly understood, *Brown* and its progeny require that the systematic group defamation of segregation be disestablished. Although the exclusion of Black children from white schools and the denial of educational resources and association that accompany exclusion can be characterized as conduct, these particular instances of conduct are concerned primarily with communicating the idea of white supremacy. The nonspeech elements are by-products of the main message rather than the message being simply a by-product of unlawful conduct.

The public accommodations provisions of the Civil Rights Act of 1964[9] illuminate why laws against discrimination also regulate racist speech. The legislative history and the Supreme Court's opinions upholding the act establish that Congress was concerned that Blacks have access to public accommodations to eliminate impediments to the free flow of interstate commerce, but this purpose could have been achieved through a regime of separate but equal accommodations. Title II of the Civil Rights Act goes farther; it incorporates the principle of the inherent inequality of segregation and prohibits restaurant owners from providing separate places at the lunch counter for "whites" and "coloreds." Even if the same food and the same service are provided, separate but equal facilities are unlawful. If the signs indicating separate facilities remain in place, then the statute is violated despite proof that restaurant patrons are free to disregard the signs. Outlawing these signs graphically illustrates my point that antidiscrimination laws are primarily regulations of the content of racist speech.

In the summer of 1966, Robert Cover and I were working as summer interns with C. B. King in Albany, Georgia. One day we stopped for lunch at a take-out chicken joint. The establishment was housed in a long diner-like structure with an awning extending from each of two doors in the side of the building. A sign was painted at the end of each awning. One said White, the other Colored. Bob and I entered the "white" side together, knowing we were not welcome to do so. When the proprietor took my order, I asked if he knew the signs on his awnings were illegal under Title II of the Civil Rights Act of 1964. He responded, "People can come in this place through any door they want to." What this story makes apparent is that the signs themselves violate the antidiscrimination principle even when the conduct of denial of access is not present.

Another way to understand the inseparability of racist speech and discriminatory conduct is to view individual racist acts as part of a totality. When viewed in this manner, white supremacists' conduct or speech is forbidden by the equal protection clause. The goal of white supremacy is not achieved by individual acts or even by the cumulative acts of a group, but rather it is achieved by the institutionalization of the ideas of white supremacy. The institutionalization of white supremacy within our culture has created conduct on the societal level that is greater than the sum of individual racist acts. The racist acts of millions of individuals are mutually reinforcing and cumulative because the status quo of institutionalized white supremacy remains long after deliberate racist actions subside.

Professor Kendall Thomas describes the way in which racism is simultaneously speech (a socially constructed meaning or idea) and conduct by asking us to consider the concept of "race" not as a noun but as a verb. He notes that race is a social construction. The meaning of "Black" or "white" is derived through a history of acted-upon ideology. Moreover, the cultural meaning of race is promulgated through millions of ongoing contemporaneous speech/acts. Thus, he says, "We are raced." The social construction of race is an ongoing process.[10]

It is difficult to recognize the institutional significance of white supremacy or how it *acts* to harm, partially because of its ubiquity. We simply do not see most racist conduct because we experience a world in which whites are supreme as simply "the world." Much racist conduct is considered unrelated to race or regarded as neutral because racist conduct maintains the status quo . . . of the world as we have known it. Catharine MacKinnon has observed that "To the extent that pornography succeeds in constructing social reality, it becomes invisible as harm." Thus, pornography "is more act-like than thought-like."[11] This truth about gender discrimination is equally true of racism.

Just because one can express the idea or message embodied by a practice such a white supremacy does not necessarily equate that practice with the idea. Slavery was an idea as well as a practice, but the Supreme Court recognized the inseparability of idea and practice in the institution of slavery when it held the enabling clause of the Thirteenth Amendment [gave] Congress . . . the power to pass "all laws necessary and proper for abolishing all badges and incidents of slavery in the United States."[12] This understanding also informs the regulation of speech/conduct in the public accommodations provisions of the Civil Rights Act of 1964 discussed above. When the racist restaurant or hotel owner puts a Whites Only sign in his window, his sign is more than speech. Putting up the sign is more than an act excluding Black patrons who see the sign. The sign is part of the larger practice of segregation and white supremacy that constructs and maintains a culture in which nonwhites are excluded from full citizenship. The inseparability of the idea and practice of racism is central to *Brown's* holding that segregation is inherently unconstitutional.

Racism is both 100 percent speech and 100 percent conduct. Discriminatory conduct is not racist unless it also conveys the message of white supremacy— unless it is interpreted within the culture to advance the structure and ideology of white supremacy. Likewise, all racist speech constructs the social reality that constrains the liberty of nonwhites because of their race. By limiting the life opportunities of others, this act of constructing meaning also makes racist speech conduct.

The Public/Private Distinction

There are critics who would contend that *Brown* is inapposite because the equal protection clause only restricts government behavior, while the First Amendment protects the speech of private persons. They say, "Of course we want to prevent the state from defaming Blacks, but we must continue to be vigilant about protecting speech rights, even of racist individuals, from the government. In both cases our concern must be protecting the individual from the unjust power of the state."

At first blush, this position seems persuasive, but its persuasiveness relies upon the mystifying properties of constitutional ideology. In particular, I refer to the state action doctrine. Roughly stated,

> The [state action] doctrine holds that although someone may have suffered harmful treatment of a kind that one might ordinarily describe as a deprivation of liberty or a denial of equal protection of the laws, that occurrence excites no constitutional concern unless the proximate active perpetrators of the harm include persons exercising the special authority or power of the government of a state.[13]

By restricting the Fourteenth Amendment's application to discrimination implicating the government, the state action rule immunizes private discriminators from constitutional scrutiny. In so doing, it leaves untouched the largest part of the vast system of segregation in the United States. The *Civil Rights Cases*[14] in which this doctrine was firmly established stands as a monument preserving American racial discrimination. Although the origin of state action is textual, countervailing values of privacy, freedom of association, and free speech all have been used to justify the rule's exculpation of private racism.

For example, it is argued that a white family's decision to send its children to private school or to move to a racially exclusive suburb should be accorded respect in spite of the Fourteenth Amendment's requirement of nondiscrimination because these decisions are part of the right to individual familial autonomy. In this way, the state action rule's rather arbitrary limit on the scope of the antidiscrimination principle is transformed into a right of privacy—which is presented as the constitutional embodiment of an affirmative, neutral, and universally shared value. A new and positive image emerges—an image that has been abstracted from its original context.

In the abstract, the right to make decisions about how we will educate our children or with whom we will associate is an important value in American society. But when we decontextualize by viewing this privacy value in the abstract, we ignore the way it operates in the real world. We do not ask ourselves, for example, whether it is a value to which all people have equal access. And we do not inquire about who has the resources to send their children to private school or move to an exclusive suburb. The privacy value, when presented as an ideal, seems an appropriate limitation on racial justice because we naively believe that everyone has an equal stake in this value.

I do not mean to suggest that privacy or autonomy has no normative value; there is some point at which the balance ought to be struck in its favor *after full consideration of the inequities that might accompany that choice.* What is objectionable about the privacy language that I am discussing here is that it ignores inequities and assumes we all share equally in the value being promoted.

The Supreme Court's treatment of the abortion controversy provides the most striking example of the fact that the right of autonomous choice is not shared by rich and poor alike. In *Roe v. Wade,* the Court declared in no uncertain terms that the right of privacy "is broad enough to encompass a woman's decision whether or not to terminate her pregnancy."[15] Yet, in *Harris v. McRae,* the Court with equal certainty asserted, "It simply does not follow that a woman's freedom of choice carries with it a constitutional entitlement to the financial resources to avail herself of the full range of protected choices."[16]

The argument that distinguishes private racist speech from the government speech outlawed by *Brown* suffers from the same decontextualizing ideology. If the government is involved in a joint venture with private contractors to engage in the business of defaming Blacks, should it be able to escape the constitutional mandate that makes that business illegal simply by handing over the copyright and the printing presses to its partners in crime? I think not. And yet this is the essence of the position that espouses First Amendment protection for those partners.

In an insightful article considering the constitutional implications of government regulation of pornography, legal scholar Frank Michelman observed that the idea of state action plays a crucial if unspoken role for judges and civil libertarians who favor an absolute rule against government regulation of private pornographic publications (or racist speech), even when that expression causes "effects fairly describable . . . as deprivations of liberty and denials of equal protection of the laws."[17] He noted that judges and civil libertarians would not balance the evils of private subversions of liberty and equal protection against the evils of government censorship because "the Constitution, through the state action doctrine, in effect tells them not to." Michelman suggests that [this] doctrine, by directing us to the text of the Fourteenth Amendment, diverts our attention from the underlying issue—whether we should balance the evils of private deprivations of liberty against the government deprivations of liberty that may arise out of state regulations designed to avert . . . private deprivations.

A person who responds to the argument that *Brown* mandates the abolition of racist speech by reciting the state action doctrine fails to consider that the alternative to regulating racist speech is infringement of the claims of Blacks to liberty and equal protection. The best way to constitutionally protect these competing interests is to balance them directly. To invoke the state action doctrine is to circumvent our value judgment as to how these competing interests should be balanced.

The deference usually given to the First Amendment values in this balance is justified using the argument that racist speech is unpopular speech, that like the speech of civil rights activists, pacifists, and religious and political dissenters, it is in need of special protection from majoritarian censorship. But for over three hundred years, racist speech has been the liturgy of the leading established religion of the United States, the religion of racism. Racist speech remains a vital and regrettably popular characteristic of the U.S. vernacular. It must be noted that there has not yet been satisfactory retraction of the government-sponsored defamation in the slavery clauses,[18] the *Dred Scott* decision,[19] the Black codes, the segregation statutes, and countless other group libels. The injury to Blacks is hardly redressed by deciding the government must no longer injure our reputation if one then invokes the First Amendment to ensure that racist speech continues to thrive in an unregulated private market.

Consider, for example, the case of *McLaurin v. Oklahoma State Regents*,[20] in which the University of Oklahoma graduate school, under order by a federal court to admit McLaurin, a Black student, designated a special seat, roped off from other seats, in each classroom, the library, and the cafeteria. The Supreme Court held that this arrangement was unconstitutional because McLaurin could not have had an equal opportunity to learn and participate if he was humiliated and symbolically stigmatized as an untouchable. Would it be any less injurious if all McLaurin's classmates had shown up at class wearing blackface? Should this symbolic speech be protected by the Constitution? Yet, according to a *Time* magazine report, in the fall of 1988 at the University of Wisconsin, "Members of the Zeta Beta Tau fraternity staged a mock slave auction, complete with some pledges in blackface."[21] More recently, at the same university, white male students trailed Black female students shouting, "I've never tried a nigger before."[22] These young women were no less severely injured than was McLaurin simply because the university did not directly sponsor their assault. If the university fails to protect them in their right to pursue their education free from this kind of degradation and humiliation, then surely there are constitutional values at stake.

It is a very sad irony that the first instinct of many civil libertarians is to express concern for possible infringement of the assailants' liberties while barely noticing the constitutional rights of the assailed. Shortly after *Brown*, many Southern communities tried to escape the mandate of desegregation by closing public schools and opening private (white) academies. These attempts to avoid the Fourteenth Amendment through the privatization of discrimination consistently were invalidated by the courts. In essence, the Supreme Court held that the defamatory message of segregation would not be insulated from constitutional proscription simply because the speaker was a nongovernment entity.

The Supreme Court also has indicated that Congress may enact legislation regulating private racist speech. In upholding the public accommodations provisions of Title II of the Civil Rights Act of 1964 in *Heart of Atlanta Motel v. United States*,[23] the Court implicitly rejected the argument that the absence of state action meant that private discriminators were protected by

First Amendment free speech and associational rights. Likewise in *Bob Jones University v. United States*,[24] the Court sustained the Internal Revenue Service decision to discontinue tax-exempt status for a college with a policy against interracial dating and marriage. The college framed its objection in terms of the free exercise of religion, arguing its policy was religiously motivated, but the Court found that the government had "a fundamental, overriding interest in eradicating racial discrimination in education" that "substantially outweighs whatever burden denial of tax benefits" placed on the college's exercise of its religious beliefs.[25] It is difficult to believe that the university would have fared any better under free speech analysis or if the policy had been merely a statement of principle rather than an enforceable disciplinary regulation. Regulation of private racist speech also has been held constitutional in the context of prohibition of race-designated advertisements for employees, home sales, and rentals.

Thus *Brown* and the antidiscrimination law it spawned provide precedent for my position that the content regulation of racist speech is not only permissible but may be required by the Constitution in certain circumstances. This precedent may not mean that we should advocate the government regulation of all racist speech, but it should give us pause in assuming absolutist positions about regulations aimed at the message or idea such speech conveys. If we understand *Brown*—the cornerstone of the civil rights movement and equal protection doctrine—correctly, and if we understand the necessity of disestablishing the system of signs and symbols that signal Blacks' inferiority, then we should not proclaim that all racist speech that stops short of physical violence must be defended.

Racist Speech as the Functional Equivalent of Fighting Words

Much recent debate over the efficacy of regulating racist speech has focused on the efforts by colleges and universities to respond to the burgeoning incidents of racial harassment on their campuses. At Stanford, where I teach, there has been considerable controversy over whether racist and other discriminatory verbal harassment should be regulated and what form any regulation should take. Proponents of regu-

lation have been sensitive to the danger of inhibiting expression, and the current regulation (which was drafted by my colleague Tom Grey) manifests that sensitivity. It is drafted somewhat more narrowly than I would have preferred, leaving unregulated hate speech that occurs in settings where there is a captive audience, but I largely agree with this regulation's substance and approach. I include it here as one example of a regulation of racist speech that I would argue violates neither First Amendment precedent nor principle. The regulation reads as follows:

Fundamental Standard Interpretation: Free Expression and Discriminatory Harassment

1. Stanford is committed to the principles of free inquiry and free expression. Students have the right to hold and vigorously defend and promote their opinions, thus entering them into the life of the University, there to flourish or wither according to their merits. Respect for this right requires that students tolerate even expression of opinions that they find abhorrent. Intimidation of students by other students in their exercise of this right, by violence or threat of violence, is therefore considered . . . a violation of the Fundamental Standard.

2. Stanford is also committed to principles of equal opportunity and nondiscrimination. Each student has the right to equal access to a Stanford education, without discrimination on the basis of sex, race, color, handicap, religion, sexual orientation, or national and ethnic origin. Harassment of students on the basis of any of these characteristics tends to create a hostile environment that makes access to education for those subjected to it less than equal. Such discriminatory harassment is therefore considered to be a violation of the Fundamental Standard.

3. This interpretation of the Fundamental Standard is intended to clarify the point at which protected free expression ends and prohibited discriminatory harassment begins. Prohibited harassment includes discriminatory intimidation by threats of violence, and also includes personal vilification of students on the basis of their sex, race, color, handicap, religion, sexual orientation, or national and ethnic origin.

4. Speech or other expression constitutes harassment by vilification if it:
   a. is intended to insult or stigmatize an individual or a small number of individuals on the basis of their sex, race, color, handicap, religion, sexual orientation, or national and ethnic origin; and
   b. is addressed directly to the individual or individuals whom it insults or stigmatizes; and
   c. makes use of "fighting" words or nonverbal symbols.

In the context of discriminatory harassment, "fighting" words or nonverbal symbols are words, pictures, or symbols that, by virtue of their form, are commonly understood to convey direct and visceral hatred or contempt for human beings on the basis of their sex, race, color, handicap, religion, sexual orientation, and national and ethnic origin.[26]

This regulation and others like it have been characterized in the press as the work of "thought police," but the rule does nothing more than prohibit intentional face-to-face insults, a form of speech that is unprotected by the First Amendment. When racist speech takes the form of face-to-face insults, catcalls, or other assaultive speech aimed at an individual or a small group of persons, then it falls within the "fighting words" exception to First Amendment protection. The Supreme Court has held that words that "by their very utterance inflict injury or tend to incite an immediate breach of the peace"[27] are not constitutionally protected.

Face-to-face racial insults, like fighting words, are undeserving of First Amendment protection for two reasons. The first reason is the immediacy of the injurious impact of racial insults. The experience of being called "nigger," "spic," "Jap," or "kike" is like receiving a slap in the face. The injury is instantaneous. There is neither an opportunity for intermediary reflection on the idea conveyed nor an opportunity for responsive speech. The harm to be avoided is both clear and present. The second reason that racial insults should not fall under protected speech relates to the purpose underlying the First Amendment. The purpose of the First Amendment is to foster the greatest amount of speech. Racial insults disserve that pur-

pose. Assaultive racist speech functions as a preemptive strike. The racial invective is experienced as a blow, not a proffered idea, and once the blow is struck, it is unlikely that dialogue will follow. Racial insults are undeserving of First Amendment protection because the perpetrator's intention is not to discover truth or initiate dialogue, but to injure the victim.

The fighting words doctrine anticipates that the verbal slap in the face of insulting words will provoke a violent response, resulting in a breach of the peace. When racial insults are hurled at minorities, the response may be silence or flight rather than a fight, but the preemptive effect on further speech is the same. Women and minorities often report that they find themselves speechless in the face of discriminatory verbal attacks. This inability to respond is not the result of oversensitivity among these groups, as some individuals who oppose protective regulation have argued. Rather it is the produce of several factors, all of which evidence the nonspeech character of the initial preemptive verbal assault. The first factor is that the visceral emotional response to personal attack precludes speech. Attack produces an instinctive, defensive psychological reaction. Fear, rage, shock, and flight all interfere with any reasoned response. Words like "nigger," "kike," and "faggot" produce physical symptoms that temporarily disable the victim, and the perpetrators often use these words with the intention of producing this effect. Many victims do not find words of response until well after the assault, when the cowardly assaulter has departed.

A second factor that distinguishes racial insults from protected speech is the preemptive nature of such insults—words of response to such verbal attacks may never be forthcoming because speech is usually an inadequate response. When one is personally attacked with words that denote one's subhuman status and untouchability, there is little, if anything, that can be said to redress either the emotional or reputational injury. This is particularly true when the message and meaning of the epithet resonates with beliefs widely held in society. This preservation of widespread beliefs is what makes the face-to-face racial attack more likely to preempt speech than other fighting words do. The racist name caller is accompanied by a cultural chorus of equally demeaning speech and symbols. Segregation and other forms of racist speech injure victims because of their dehumanizing and excluding message. Each individual message gains its power because of the cumulative and reinforcing effect of countless similar messages that are conveyed in a society where racism is ubiquitous.

The subordinated victims of fighting words also are silenced by their relatively powerless position in society. Because of the significance of power and position, the categorization of racial epithets as fighting words provides an inadequate paradigm; instead one must speak of their functional equivalent. The fighting words doctrine presupposes an encounter between two persons of relatively equal power who have been acculturated to respond to face-to-face insults with violence: The fighting words doctrine is a paradigm based on a white male point of view. It captures the "macho" quality of male discourse. It is accepted, justifiable, and even praiseworthy when "real men" respond to personal insult with violence. (Presidential candidate George Bush effectively emulated the most macho—and not coincidentally most violent—of movie stars, Clint Eastwood, when he repeatedly used the phrase, "Read my lips!" Any teenage boy will tell you the subtext of this message: "I've got nothing else to say about this and if you don't like what I'm saying we can step outside.") The fighting words doctrine's responsiveness to this male stance in the world and its blindness to he cultural experience of women is another example of how neutral principles of law reflect the values of those who are dominant.

Black men also are well aware of the double standard that our culture applies in responding to insult. Part of the culture of racial domination through violence—a culture of dominance manifested historically in thousands of lynchings in the South and more recently in the racial violence at Howard Beach and Bensonhurst—is the paradoxical expectation on the part of whites that Black males will accept insult from whites without protest, yet will become violent without provocation. These expectations combine two assumptions: First, that Blacks as a group—and especially Black men—are more violent; and second, that as inferior persons, Blacks have no right to feel insulted. One can imagine the response of universities if Black men started to respond to racist fighting words by beating up white students.

In most situations, minorities correctly perceive that a violent response to fighting words will result in a risk to their own life and limb. This risk forces targets to remain silent and submissive. This response is most obvious when women submit to sexually assaultive speech or when the racist name caller is in a more powerful position—the boss on the job or a member of a violent racist group. Certainly, we do not expect the Black woman crossing the Wisconsin campus to turn on her tormentors and pummel them. Less obvious, but just as significant, is the effect of pervasive racial and sexual violence and coercion on individual members of subordinated groups, who must learn the survival techniques of suppressing and disguising rage and anger at an early age.

One of my students, a white gay male, related an experience that is quite instructive in understanding the fighting words doctrine. In response to my request that students describe how they experienced the injury of racist speech, Michael told a story of being called "faggot" by a man on a subway. His description included all of the speech-inhibiting elements I have noted. . . . He found himself in a state of semishock, nauseous, dizzy, unable to muster the witty, sarcastic, articulate rejoinder he was accustomed to making. He was instantly aware of the recent spate of gay bashing in San Francisco and that many of these incidents had escalated from verbal encounters. Even hours later when the shock subsided and his facility with words returned, he realized that any response was inadequate to counter the hundreds of years of societal defamation that one word—*faggot*—carried with it. Like the word *nigger* and unlike the word *liar*, it is not sufficient to deny the truth of the word's application, to say, "I am not a faggot." One must deny the truth of the word's meaning, a meaning shouted from the rooftops by the rest of the world a million times a day. The complex response "Yes, I am a member of the group you despise and [I reject] the degraded meaning of the word you use . . . " is not effective in a subway encounter. Although many of us constantly and in myriad ways seek to counter the lie spoken in the meaning of hateful words like *nigger* and *faggot*, it is a nearly impossible burden to bear when one is ambushed by a sudden, face-to-face hate speech assault.

But there was another part of my discussion with Michael that is equally instructive. I asked if he could remember a situation when he had been verbally attacked with reference to his being a white male. Had he ever been called a "honkey," a "chauvinist pig," or "mick"? (Michael is from a working-class Irish family in Boston.) He said that he had been called some version of all three and that although he found the last one more offensive than the first two, he had not experienced—even in that subordinated role—the same disorienting powerlessness he had experienced when attacked for his membership in the gay community. The question of power, of the context of the power relationships within which speech takes place, and the connection to violence must be considered as we decide how best to foster the freest and fullest dialogue within our communities. Regulation of face-to-face verbal assault in the manner contemplated by the proposed Stanford provision will make room for more speech than it chills. The provision is clearly within the spirit, if not the letter, of existing First Amendment doctrine.

The proposed Stanford regulation, and indeed regulations with considerably broader reach, can be justified as necessary to protect a captive audience from offensive or injurious speech. Courts have held that offensive speech may not be regulated in public forums such as streets and parks where listeners may avoid the speech by moving on or averting their eyes,[28] but the regulation of otherwise protected speech has been permitted when the speech invades the privacy of unwilling listeners' homes or when unwilling listeners cannot avoid the speech.[29] Racist posters, flyers, and graffiti in dorms, classrooms, bathrooms, and other common living spaces would fall within the reasoning of these cases. Minority students should not be required to remain in their rooms to avoid racial assault. Minimally, they should find a safe haven in their dorms and other common rooms that are a part of their daily routine. I would argue that the university's responsibility for ensuring these students receive an equal educational opportunity provides a compelling justification for regulations that ensure them safe passage in all common areas. Black, Latino, Asian, or Native American students should not have to risk being the target of racially assaulting speech every time they choose to walk across campus. The regulation of vilifying speech that cannot be anticipated or avoided would not preclude

announced speeches and rallies where minorities and their allies would have an opportunity to organize counterdemonstrations or avoid the speech altogether.

Knowing the Injury and Striking the Balance: Understanding What Is at Stake in Racist Speech Cases

I argued in the last section that narrowly drafted regulations of racist speech that prohibit face-to-face vilification and protect captive audiences from verbal and written harassment can be defended within the confines of existing First Amendment doctrine. Here I argue that many civil libertarians who urge that the First Amendment prohibits any regulation of racist speech have given inadequate attention to the testimony of individuals who have experienced injury from such speech. These civil libertarians fail to comprehend both the nature and extent of the injury inflicted by racist speech. I further urge that understanding the injury requires reconsideration of the balance that must be struck between our concerns for racial equality and freedom of expression.

The arguments most commonly advanced against the regulation of racist speech go something like this: We recognize that minority groups suffer pain and injury as the result of racist speech, but we must allow this hate mongering for the benefit of society as a whole. Freedom of speech is the lifeblood of our democratic system. It is a freedom that enables us to persuade others to our point of view. Free speech is especially important for minorities because often it is the only vehicle for rallying support for redress of their grievances. Even though we do not wish anyone to be persuaded that racist lies are true, we cannot allow the public regulation of racist invective and vilification because any prohibition broad enough to prevent racist speech would catch in the same net forms of speech that are central to a democratic society.

Whenever we argue that racist epithets and vilification must be allowed, not because we would condone them ourselves but because of the potential danger the precedent of regulation would pose for the speech of all dissenters, we are balancing our concern for the free flow of ideas and the democratic process with our desire for equality. This kind of categorical balance is struck whenever we frame any rule—even an absolute rule. [We must] be conscious of the nature and extent of injury to both concerns when we engage in this kind of balancing. In this case, we must place on one side of the balance the nature and extent of the injury caused by racism. We must also consider whether the racist speech we propose to regulate is advancing or retarding the values of the First Amendment.

Understanding the Injury Inflicted by Racist Speech

There can be no meaningful discussion about how to reconcile our commitment to equality and our commitment to free speech until we acknowledge that racist speech inflicts real harm and that this harm is far from trivial. I should state that more strongly: To engage in a debate about the First Amendment and racist speech without a full understanding of the nature and extent of the harm of racist speech risks making the First Amendment an instrument of domination rather than a vehicle of liberation. Not everyone has known the experience of being victimized by racist, misogynist, or homophobic speech, and we do not share equally the burden of the societal harm it inflicts. Often we are too quick to say we have heard the victims' cries when we have not; we are too eager to assure ourselves we have experienced the same injury and therefore can make the constitutional balance without danger of mismeasurement. For many of us who have fought for the rights of oppressed minorities, it is difficult to accept that by underestimating the injury from racist speech we too might be implicated in the vicious words we would never utter. Until we have eradicated racism and sexism and no longer share in the fruits of those forms of domination, we cannot legitimately strike the balance without hearing the protest of those who are dominated. My plea is simply that we listen to the victims.

Members of my own family were involved in a recent incident at a private school in Wilmington, Delaware, that taught me much about both the nature of the injury racist speech inflicts and the lack of understanding many whites have of that injury.

A good Quaker school dedicated to a deep commitment to and loving concern for all the members of its community, Wilmington Friends School also became a haven for white families fleeing the court-ordered desegregation of the Wilmington public schools. In recent years, the school strove to meet its commitment to human equality by enrolling a small (but significant) group of minority students and hiring an even smaller number of Black faculty and staff. My sister Paula, a gifted, passionate, and dedicated teacher, was the principal of the lower school. Her sons attended the high school. My brother-in-law, John, teaches geology at the University of Delaware. He is a strong, quiet, loving man, and he is white. My sister's family had moved to Wilmington, shouldering the extra burdens and anxieties borne by an interracial family moving to a town where, not long ago, the defamatory message of segregation graced the doors of bathrooms and restaurants. Within a year they had made a place as well-loved and respected members of the community, particularly the school community, where Paula was viewed as a godsend and my nephews made many good friends.

In May of their second year in Wilmington, an incident occurred that shook the entire school community but was particularly painful to my sister's family and others who [were] the objects of hateful speech. In a letter to the school community explaining a decision to expel four students, the school's headmistress described the incident as follows:

> On Sunday evening, May 1, four students in the senior class met by prearrangement to paint the soccer kickboard, a flat rectangular structure, approximately 8 ft. by 25 ft., standing in the midst of the Wilmington Friends School playing fields. They worked for approximately one hour under bright moonlight and then went home.
>
> What confronted students and staff the following morning, depicted on the kickboard, were racist and anti-Semitic slogans and, most disturbing of all, threats of violent assault against one clearly identified member of the senior class. The slogans written on the kickboard included "Save the land, join the Klan," and "Down with Jews"; among the drawings were at least twelve hooded Ku Klux Klansmen, Nazi swastikas, and a burning cross. The most frightening and disturbing depictions, however, were those that threatened violence against one of our senior Black students. He was drawn, in a car-

toon figure, identified by his name, and his initials, and by the name of his mother. Directly to the right of his head was a bullet, and farther to the right was a gun with its barrel directed toward the head. Under the drawing of the student, three Ku Klux Klansmen were depicted, one of whom was saying that the student "dies." Next to the gun was a drawing of a burning cross under which was written "Kill the Tarbaby."[30]

When I visited my sister's family a few days after this incident, the injury they had suffered was evident. The wounds were fresh. My sister, a care giver by nature and vocation, was clearly in need of care. My nephews were quiet. Their faces betrayed the aftershock of a recently inflicted blow and a newly discovered vulnerability. I knew the pain and scars were no less enduring because the injury had not been physical. And when I talked to my sister, I realized the greatest part of her pain came not from the incident itself, but rather from the reaction of white parents who had come to the school in unprecedented numbers to protest the offending students' expulsion. "It was only a prank." "No one was physically attacked." "How can you punish these kids for mere words, mere drawings." Paula's pain was compounded by the failure of these people with whom she lived and worked to recognize that she had been hurt, to understand in even the most limited way the reality of her pain and that of her family.

Many people called the incident "isolated." But Black folks know that no racial incident is "isolated" in the United States. That is what makes the incidents so horrible, so scary. It is the knowledge that they are *not* the isolated unpopular speech of a dissident few that makes them so frightening. These incidents are manifestations of an ubiquitous and deeply ingrained cultural belief system, an American way of life. Too often in recent months, as I have debated this issue with friends and colleagues, I have heard people speak of the need to protect "offensive" speech. The word offensive is used as if we were speaking of a difference in taste, as if I should learn to be less sensitive to words that "offend" me. I cannot help but believe that those people who speak of offense—those who argue that this speech must go unchecked—do not understand the great difference between offense and injury. They have not known the injury my sister

experienced, have not known the fear, vulnerability, and shame experienced by the Wisconsin students described at the beginning of this chapter. There is a great difference between the offensiveness of words that you would rather not hear because they are labeled dirty, impolite, or personally demeaning and the *injury* inflicted by words that remind the world that you are fair game for physical attack, that evoke in you all of the millions of cultural lessons regarding your inferiority that you have so painstakingly repressed, and that imprint upon you a badge of servitude and subservience for all the world to see. It is instructive that the chief proponents of restricting people who inflict these injuries are women and people of color, and there are few among these groups who take the absolutist position that any regulation of this speech is too much.

Again, *Brown v. Board of Education* is a useful case for our analysis. *Brown* is helpful because it articulates the nature of the injury inflicted by the racist message of segregation. When one considers the injuries identified in the *Brown* decision, it is clear that racist speech causes tangible injury, and it is the kind of injury for which the law commonly provides, and even requires, redress.

Psychic injury is no less an injury than being struck in the face, and it often is far more severe. *Brown* speaks directly to the psychic injury inflicted by racist speech in noting that the symbolic message of segregation affected "the hearts and minds" of Negro children "in a way unlikely ever to be undone."[31] Racial epithets and harassment often cause deep emotional scarring and feelings of anxiety and fear that pervade every aspect of a victim's life. Many victims of hate propaganda have experienced physiological and emotional symptoms, such as rapid pulse rate and difficulty in breathing.

A second injury identified in *Brown,* and present in my example, is reputational injury. As Professor Tribe has noted, "Libelous speech was long regarded as a form of personal assault . . . that government could vindicate . . . without running afoul of the constitution."[32] Although *New York Times v. Sullivan* and its progeny have subjected much defamatory speech to constitutional scrutiny—on the reasoning that "debate on public issues should be uninhibited, robust and wide-open"[33] and should not be "chilled" by the possibility of libel suits—these cases also demonstrate a concern for balancing the public's interest in being fully informed with the competing interest of defamed persons in vindicating their reputation.

The interest of defamed persons is even stronger in racial defamation cases than in the *Sullivan* line of cases. The *Sullivan* rule protects statements of fact that are later proven erroneous. But persons who defame a racial group with racial epithets and stereotyped caricatures are not concerned that they may have "guessed wrong" in attempting to ascertain the truth. The racial epithet is the expression of a widely held belief. It is invoked as an assault, not as a statement of fact that may be proven true or false. Moreover, if the *Sullivan* rule protects erroneous speech because of an ultimate concern for the discovery of truth, then the rule's application to racial epithets must be based on an acceptance of the possible "truth" of racism, a position that, happily, most First Amendment absolutists are reluctant to embrace. Furthermore, the rationale of *Sullivan* and its progeny is that public issues should be vigorously debated and that, as the Supreme Court held in *Gertz v. Robert Welch, Inc.*, there is "no such thing as a false idea."[34] But are racial insults ideas? Do they encourage wide-open debate?

Brown is a case about group defamation. The message of segregation was stigmatizing to Black children. To be labeled unfit to attend school with white children injured the reputation of Black children, thus foreclosing employment opportunities and the right to be regarded as respected members of the body politic. An extensive discussion on the constitutionality or efficacy of group libel laws is beyond the scope of this chapter, and it must suffice to note that although *Beauharnais v. Illinois*,[35] which upheld an Illinois group libel statute, has fallen into disfavor with some commentators, *Brown* remains an instructive case. By identifying the inseparability of discriminatory speech and action in the case of segregation, where the injury is inflicted by the meaning of the segregation, *Brown* limits the scope of *Sullivan*. *Brown* reflects the understanding that racism is a form of subordination that achieves its purposes through group defamation.

The third injury identified in *Brown* is the denial of equal educational opportunity. *Brown* recognized that even where segregated facilities are materially equal,

Black children did not have an equal opportunity to learn and participate in the school community if they bore the additional burden of being subjected to the humiliation and psychic assault that accompanies the message of segregation. University students bear an analogous burden when they are forced to live and work in an environment where at any moment they may be subjected to denigrating verbal harassment and assault. The testimony of nonwhite students about the detrimental effect of racial harassment on their academic performance and social integration in the college community is overwhelming. A similar injury is recognized and addressed in the requirement of Title VII of the Civil Rights Act that employers maintain a nondiscriminatory, nonhostile work environment and in federal and state regulations prohibiting sexual harassment on campuses as well as in the workplace.

All three of these very tangible, continuing, and often irreparable forms of injury—psychic, reputational, and the denial of equal educational opportunity—must be recognized, accounted for, and balanced against the claim that a regulation aimed at the prevention of these injuries may lead to restrictions on important First Amendment liberties.

The Other Side of the Balance: Does the Suppression of Racial Epithets Weigh for or Against Speech?

In striking a balance, we also must think about what we are weighing on the side of speech. Most Blacks— unlike many white civil libertarians—do not have faith in free speech as the most important vehicle for liberation. The First Amendment coexisted with slavery, and we still are not sure it will protect us to the same extent that it protects whites. It often is argued that minorities have benefited greatly from First Amendment protection and therefore should guard it jealously. We are aware that the struggle for racial equality has relied heavily on the persuasion of peaceful protest protected by the First Amendment, but experience also teaches us that our petitions often go unanswered until protests disrupt business as usual and require the self-interested attention of those persons in power.

Paradoxically, the disruption that renders protest speech effective usually causes it to be considered undeserving of First Amendment protection. Note the cruel irony in the news story cited at the beginning of this chapter that describes the Stanford president's justification for prosecuting students engaged in a peaceful sit-in for violation of the university's Fundamental Standard: The protesting students were punished, but the racist behavior the students were protesting went unpunished. This lack of symmetry was justified on the grounds that punishment might violate the bigots' First Amendment rights—a particularly ironic result given Professor Derrick Bell's observation that it was Black students' civil rights protests that underlay the precedents on which white students . . . established their First Amendment rights in school and university settings. As in so many other areas, a policy that Blacks paid the price for is used against them and on behalf of whites. Once one begins to doubt the existence of a symmetry between official reactions to racism and official reactions to protests against racism, the absolutist position loses credence: It becomes difficult . . . to believe that fighting to protect speech rights for racists will ensure our own speech rights. Our experience is that the American system of justice has never been symmetrical where race is concerned. No wonder we see equality as a precondition of free speech and place more weight on that side of the balance aimed at the removal of the badges and incidents of slavery that continue to flourish in our culture.

Blacks and other people of color are equally skeptical about the absolutist argument that even the most injurious speech must remain unregulated because in an unregulated marketplace of ideas the best ideas will rise to the top and gain acceptance. Our experience tells us the opposite. We have seen too many demagogues elected by appealing to U.S. racism. We have seen too many good, liberal politicians shy away from the issues that might brand them as too closely allied with us. The American marketplace of ideas was founded with the idea of the racial inferiority of nonwhites as one of its chief commodities, and ever since the market opened, racism has remained its most active item in trade.

But it is not just the prevalence and strength of the idea of racism that make the unregulated marketplace of ideas an untenable paradigm for those individuals who seek full and equal personhood for all. The real problem is that the idea of the racial inferiority of nonwhites infects, skews, and disables the operation of a market (like a computer virus, sick cattle, or diseased wheat). It trumps good ideas that contend with it in the market. It is an epidemic that distorts the marketplace of ideas and renders it dysfunctional.

Racism is irrational. Individuals do not embrace or reject racist beliefs as the result of reasoned deliberation. For the most part, we do not even recognize the myriad ways in which the racism that pervades our history and culture influences our beliefs. But racism is ubiquitous. We are all racists. Often we fail to see it because racism is so woven into our culture that it seems normal. In other words, most of our racism is unconscious. So it must have been with the middle-aged, white, male lawyer who thought he was complimenting a Mexican-American law student of mine who had applied for a job with his firm. "You speak very good English," he said. But she was a fourth-generation Californian, not the stereotypical poor immigrant he unconsciously imagined she must be.

The disruptive and disabling effect on the market of an idea that is ubiquitous and irrational, but seldom seen or acknowledged, should be apparent. If the community is considering competing ideas about providing food for children, shelter for the homeless, or abortions for pregnant women, and the choices made among the proposed solutions are influenced by the idea that some children, families, or women are less deserving of our sympathy because they are racially inferior, then the market is not functioning as either John Stuart Mill or Oliver Wendell Holmes envisioned it. In the term used by constitutional theorist John Ely, there is a "process defect."[36]

Professor Ely coined the term *process defect* in the context of developing a theory to identify instances in which legislative action should be subjected to heightened judicial scrutiny under the equal protection clause. Ely argued that the courts should interfere with the normal majoritarian political process when the defect of prejudice bars groups subject to widespread vilification from participation in the political process and causes governmental decision makers to misapprehend the costs and benefits of their actions. This same process defect that excludes vilified groups and misdirects the government operates in the marketplace of ideas. Mill's vision of truth emerging through competition in the marketplace of ideas relies on the ability of members of the body politic to recognize "truth" as serving their interest and to act on that recognition.[37] As such, this vision depends on the same process that James Madison referred to when he described his vision of a democracy in which the numerous minorities within society would form coalitions to create majorities with overlapping interests through pluralist wheeling and dealing.[38] Just as the defect of prejudice blinds white voters to interests that overlap with those of vilified minorities, it also blinds them to the "truth" of an idea or the efficacy of solutions associated with that vilified group. And just as prejudice causes governmental decision makers to misapprehend the costs and benefits of their actions, it also causes all of us to misapprehend the value of ideas in the market.

Prejudice that is unconscious or unacknowledged causes the most significant distortions in the market. When racism operates at a conscious level, opposing ideas may prevail in open competition for the rational or moral sensibilities of the market participant. But when individuals are unaware of their prejudice, neither reason nor moral persuasion will likely succeed.

Racist speech also distorts the marketplace of ideas by muting or devaluing the speech of Blacks and other despised minorities. Regardless of intrinsic value, their words and ideas become less salable in the marketplace of ideas. An idea that would be embraced by large numbers of individuals if it were offered by a white individual will be rejected or given less credence if its author belongs to a group demeaned and stigmatized by racist beliefs.

An obvious example of this type of devaluation is the Black political candidate whose ideas go unheard or are rejected by white voters, although voters would embrace the same ideas if they were championed by a white candidate. Once again, the experience of one of my gay students provides a paradigmatic example of how ideas are less acceptable when their authors are members of a group that has been victimized by hatred and vilification. Bob had not "come out" when he first came to law school. During his first year, when issues relating to heterosexism came up in class or in discussions with other students, he spoke to these issues as a sympathetic "straight" white male student. His arguments were listened to and taken seriously. In his second year, when he had come out and his classmates knew that he was gay, he found that he was

not nearly as persuasive an advocate for his position as when he was identified as straight. He was the same person saying the same things, but his identity gave him less authority. Similarly, Catharine MacKinnon argues that pornography causes women to be taken less seriously as they enter the public arena.[39] Racial minorities have the same experiences on a daily basis as they endure the microaggression of having their words doubted, or misinterpreted, or assumed to be without evidentiary support, or when their insights are ignored and then appropriated by whites who are assumed to have been the original authority.

Finally, racist speech decreases the total amount of speech that reaches the market by coercively silencing members of those groups who are its targets. I noted earlier in this chapter the ways in which racist speech is inextricably linked with racist conduct. The primary purpose and effect of the speech/conduct that constitutes white supremacy is the exclusion of nonwhites from full participation in the body politic. Sometimes the speech/conduct of racism is direct and obvious. When the Klan burns a cross on the lawn of a Black person who joined the NAACP or exercised the right to move to a formerly all-white neighborhood, the effect of this speech does not result from the persuasive power of an idea operating freely in the market. It is a threat; a threat made in the context of a history of lynchings, beatings, and economic reprisals that made good on earlier threats; a threat that silences a potential speaker. Such a threat may be difficult to recognize because the tie between the speech and the threatened act is unstated. The tie does not need to be explicit because the promised violence is systemic. The threat is effective because racially motivated violence is a well-known historical and contemporary reality. The threat may be even more effective than a phone call that takes responsibility for a terrorist bomb attack and promises another, a situation in which we easily recognize the inextricable link between the speech and the threatened act. The Black student who is subjected to racial epithets, like the Black person on whose lawn the Klan has burned a cross, is threatened and silenced by a credible connection between racist hate speech and racist violence. Certainly the recipients of hate speech may be uncommonly brave or foolhardy and ignore the system of violence in which this abusive speech is only a bit player. But it is more likely that we, as a community, will be denied the benefit of many of their thoughts and ideas.

Again MacKinnon's analysis of how First Amendment law misconstrues pornography is instructive. She notes that in concerning themselves only with government censorship, First Amendment absolutists fail to recognize that whole segments of the population are systematically silenced by powerful private actors. "As a result, [they] cannot grasp that the speech of some silences the speech of others in a way that is not simply a matter of competition for airtime."[40]

. . . . We must embark upon the development of a First Amendment jurisprudence that is grounded in the reality of our history and contemporary experience, particularly the experiences of the victims of oppression. We must eschew abstractions of First Amendment theory that proceed without attention to the dysfunction in the marketplace of ideas created by racism and unequal access to that market. We must think hard about how best to launch legal attacks against the most assaultive and indefensible forms of hate speech. Good lawyers can create exceptions and narrow interpretations limiting the harm of hate speech without opening the floodgates of censorship. We must weigh carefully and critically the competing constitutional values expressed in the First and Fourteenth Amendments.

A concrete step in this direction is the abandonment of overstated rhetorical and legal attacks on individuals who conscientiously seek to frame a public response to racism that preserves our First Amendment liberties. I have ventured a second step . . . by suggesting that the regulation of certain face-to-face racial vilification on university campuses may be justified under current First Amendment doctrine as an analogy to the protection of certain classes of captive audiences. Most important, we must continue this discussion—one in which victims of racist speech are heard. We must be as attentive to the achievement of the constitutional ideal of equality as we are to the ideal of untrammeled expression. There can be no true free speech where there are still masters and slaves.

Epilogue

"Eeny, meeny, miney, mo."

It is recess time at the South Main Street School. It is 1952, and I am nine. Eddie Becker, Muck Makowski, John Thomas, Terry Flynn, Howie Martin, and I are standing in a circle, each with our right foot thrust forward. The toes of our black, high-top Keds sneakers touch, forming a tight hub of white rubber at the center, our skinny blue-jeaned legs extending like spokes from the hub. Heads bowed, we are intently watching Muck, who is hunkered down on one knee so that he can touch our toes as he calls out the rhyme. We are enthralled and entranced by the drama of this boyhood ritual, this customary pregame incantation. It is no less important than the game itself.

But my mind is not on the ritual. I have lost track of the count that will determine whose foot must be removed from the hub, who will no longer have a chance to be a captain in this game. I hardly feel Muck's index finger as it presses through the rubber to my toes. My mind is on the rhyme. I am the only Black boy in this circle of towheaded prepubescent males. Time stands still for me. My palms are sweaty and I feel a prickly heat at the back of my neck. I know that Muck will not say the word.

"Catch a tiger by the toe."

The heads stay down. No one looks at me. But I know that none of them is picturing the capture of a large striped animal. They are thinking of me, imagining my toe beneath the white rubber of my Keds sneaker—my toe attached to a large, dark, thick-lipped, burr-headed American fantasy/nightmare.

"If he hollers let him go."

Tigers don't holler. I wish I could right now.

My parents have told me to ignore this word that is ringing unuttered in my ears. "You must not allow those who speak it to make you feel small or ugly," they say. They are proud, Mississippi-bred Black professionals and longtime political activists; oft-wounded veterans of the war against the racist speech/conduct of Jim Crow and his many relations, they have, on countless occasions, answered the bad speech/conduct of racism with the good speech/conduct of their lives—representing the race; being smarter, cleaner, and more morally upright than white folk to prove that Black folk are equal, are fully human—refuting the lies of the cultural myth that is American racism. "You must know that it is their smallness, their ugliness of which this word speaks," they say.

I am struggling to heed their words, to follow their example, but I feel powerless before this word and its minions. In a moment's time it has made me an other. In an instant it has rebuilt the wall between my friends' humanity and my own, the wall that I have so painstakingly disassembled.

I was good at games, not just a good athlete, but a strategist, a leader. I knew how to make my teammates feel good about themselves so that they played better. It just came naturally to me. I could choose up a team and make the members feel like family. When

other folks felt good, I felt good too. Being good at games was the main tool I used to knock down the wall I'd found when I came to this white school in this white town. I looked forward to recess because that was when I could do the most damage to the wall. But now this rhyme, this word, had undone all my labors.

"Eeny, meeny, miney, mo."

I have no memory of who got to be captain that day or what game we played. I just wished Muck had used "One potato, two potato. . . ." We always used that at home.

Endnotes

1. W.E.B. DuBois, *The Souls of Black Folk,* 16–17 (1953).

2. V. Harding, *There Is a River,* 82 (1981).

3. Karst, "Citizenship, Race and Marginality," 30 *Wm. & Mary L. Rev. 1,* 1 (1988).

4. 347 U.S. at 494.

5. 163 U.S. 537 (1896).

6. Id. at 560 (J. Harlan, dissenting).

7. See, e.g., Strossen, "Regulating Racist Speech on Campus: A Modest Proposal?" *Duke L. J.* 484 at 541–543 (1990).

8. L. Tribe, *American Constitutional Law* §12-7 at 827 (2d ed. 1988).

9. 42 U.S.C. §2000A (1982).

10. K. Thomas, comments at Frontiers of Legal Thought Conference, Duke Law School (Jan. 26, 1990).

11. C. MacKinnon, *Toward a Feminist Theory of the State,* 204 (1989).

12. *Jones v. Alfred H. Mayer Co.,* 392 U.S. 409, 439 (1968) (upholding Congress's use of the "badge of servitude" idea to justify federal legislation prohibiting racially discriminatory practices by private persons).

13. Michelman, "Conceptions of Democracy in American Constitutional Argument: The Case of Pornography Regulation," 56 *Tenn. L. Rev.* 291, 306 (1989).

14. 109 U.S. 3 (1883).

15. 410 U.S. 113 (1973).

16. 448 U.S. 297, 316 (1980).

17. See Michelman, *supra* note 14, at 306–307.

18. U.S. Const. Art. I, §2, cl. 3 and §9, cl. 1; art. IV, §2, cl. 3.

19. *Dred Scott v. Sanford,* 60 U.S. (19 How.) 393 (1857).

20. 339 U.S. 637 (1950).

21. "A Step Toward Civility," *Time,* May 1, 1989, at 43.

22. Id.

23. *Heart of Atlanta Motel, Inc. v. United States,* 379 U.S. 241, 258 (1964); see also *Roberts v. United States Jaycees,* 468 U.S. 609, 624 (1984) (Court upheld the public accommodations provision of the Minnesota Human Rights Act).

24. 461 U.S. 574, 595 (1983).

25. 461 U.S. At 604.

26. Interpretation of the Fundamental Standard defining when verbal or nonverbal abuse violates the student conduct code adopted by the Stanford University Student Conduct Legislative Council, March 14, 1990. "SCLC Offers Revised Reading of Standard," *Stanford Daily,* Apr. 4, 1990, §1, col. 4.

It is important to recognize that this regulation is not content-neutral. It prohibits "discriminatory harassment" rather than just plain harassment, and it regulates only discriminatory harassment based on "sex, race, color, handicap, religion, sexual orientation, and national and ethnic origin." It is arguably viewpoint neutral with respect to these categories, although its reference to "words . . . that, by virtue of their form, are commonly understood to convey direct and visceral hatred or contempt" probably means that there will be many more epithets that refer to subordinated groups than words that refer to superordinate groups covered by the regulation.

27. *Chaplinsky v. New Hampshire,* 315 U.S. 568, 572 (1942).

28. See *Cohen v. California,* 403 U.S. 15, 21 (1971) (holding that the state could not excise, as offensive conduct, particular epithets from public discourse); *Erznoznik v. City of Jacksonville,* 433 U.S. 205, 209 (1975) (overturning a city ordinance that deterred drive-in theaters from showing movies containing nudity).

29. See *Kovacks v. Cooper,* 336 U.S. 77, 86 (1949) (right to free speech not abridged by city ordinance outlawing use of sound trucks on city streets); *Federal Communications Comm'n. v. Pacifica Found.,* 438 U.S. 726, 748 (1978) (limited First Amendment protection of broadcasting that

extends into privacy of home); *Rowan v. United States Post Office Dep't*, 397 U.S. 728, 736 (1790) (unwilling recipient of sexually arousing material had right to instruct Postmaster General to cease mailings to protect recipient from unwanted communication of "ideas").

30. Letter from Dulany O. Bennett to parents, alumni, and friends of the Wilmington Friends School (May 17, 1988).

31. 347 U.S. at 494.

32. L. Tribe, *supra* note 9, at 861.

33. 376 U.S. 254, 270.

34. 418 U.S. 323, 339 (1974).

35. 343 U.S. 250 (1952).

36. J. Ely, *Democracy and Distrust,* 103–104, 135–179 (1980).

37. J.S. Mill, *On Liberty*, ch. 2 (1859).

38. J. Madison, *The Federalist No. 51*, at 323–324 (C. Rossiter ed. 1961).

39. MacKinnon, "Not a Moral Issue," 2 *Yale L. & Pol'y Rev.* 321, 325–326, 335 (1984).

40. C. McKinnon, *supra* note 12, at 206.

46. The Chilly Climate on College Campuses: An Expansion of the Hate Speech Debate

Katharine T. Bartlett and Jean O'Barr

Katharine Bartlett and Jean O'Barr argue that the hate speech debate has focused on the most visible forms of racism while ignoring other, more subtle, discriminatory practices that pervade college campuses. Although these more subtle forms of discrimination are not as egregious as those usually focused on in discussions of hate speech, Bartlett and O'Barr contend that they may play an even larger role in establishing the subordination of members of certain groups on college campuses.

Reports of the kind of outrageous, blatantly racist, sexist, or heterosexist events which are the subject of the powerful debate about "hate speech" regulations[1] have become increasingly frequent in the late 1980s and early 1990s. Few colleges can claim to have remained free of such events, which include verbal assaults in various public and "private" settings, defacement of posters and walls with swastikas, nude caricatures, and "KKK" signatures, and other sorts of repeated harassment based on the sex, race, or sexual lifestyle of particular individuals or groups.

In addition to these very visible incidents of blatant racial, sexual, and homophobic vilification, however, there are even more common, everyday types of behaviors that also disempower members of subordinated groups. These behaviors are so ordinary, so numerous, and so pervasive as to be taken almost entirely for granted by victims and victimizers alike. The hate speech debate focuses only on the most visible forms of racism and thus misses these more subtle discriminatory practices that pervade our current cultural milieu. In this comment, we show, through an exploration of sexism on college campuses, how the hate speech debate is incomplete, and how its terms may even stymie a full analysis of the wider range of subordinating behaviors that characterize racism, sexism, and heterosexism on college campuses in this country. Based upon this analysis, we argue in favor of branching out from a focus on

Reprinted by permission of *Duke University Law Review* and the authors.

the regulation of blatant forms of racist, sexist, and heterosexist harassment, toward a more multifaceted set of campus strategies.

Everyday Oppressions

In an effort to bring the everyday oppression of campus sexism into question, Roberta Hall and Bernice Sandler of the Project on the Status and Education of Women of the Association of American Colleges have catalogued more than thirty-five of these behaviors in two reports, *The Classroom Climate: A Chilly One for Women?* and *Out of the Classroom: A Chilly Campus Climate for Women?*[2] Examples of some of these behaviors convey a sense of how common and potentially devastating they are:

- When faculty members ask questions in class, "they mak[e] eye contact with men more often than with women, so that individual men students are more likely to feel recognized and encouraged to participate in class";[3]
- Faculty members use tones that communicate interest, and "assum[e] a posture of attentiveness (for example, leaning forward) when men speak," but a patronizing or impatient tone and inattentive posture (such as looking at the clock) when talking with women;[4]
- Faculty members call directly on men students more often than on women students, and are more likely to probe a male student's response to help the student work toward a fuller answer or explanation;[5]
- Faculty members call men students by name more often than women students, and credit comments and ideas to men but not to women;[6]
- Faculty members "wait longer for men than for women to answer a question before going on to another student," and are more likely to interrupt a woman student;[7]
- Faculty members "ask women students questions that require factual answers . . . while asking men ['higher order'] questions that demand personal evaluation and critical thinking";[8]
- Faculty members give longer and more complete responses to the questions of men students than to those of women students;[9]

- Faculty members "spontaneously offer to write letters of reference for men students but not for equally competent women students," and invite men, but not women, students to share authorships, accompany them on professional trips, and meet recognized scholars outside the department;[10]
- Female athletes' accomplishments go relatively unnoticed, as compared to men's sports, which are the focus of discussion and praise;[11]
- "Women are expected to perform stereotypically 'feminine' roles in conjunction with social events and cooperative housing arrangements—such as preparing food and cleaning up—while men make tapes, provide entertainment or do maintenance work";[12]
- Women are asked questions by faculty members, admissions staff and financial aid officers that question their seriousness of purpose, their need for educational credentials, and their actual or potential marital or parental status, that men are not asked.[13]

Not surprisingly, women minority students, older women students, lesbians, and disabled women are especially affected by these forms of behavior that devalue them both as women and as members of another outsider group. Moreover, the combination of sex and race, age, sexual preference, or disability may inspire additional forms of prejudice and subordination. Thus, for example, the silence of an African American woman may be perceived as "sullenness," whereas the silence of an Asian, Hispanic, or Native American woman may be perceived as "passivity."[14] Older women are viewed as bored, economically dependent spouses who have nothing better to do with their time and are often patronized by faculty members and other students.[15] Disabled women students are often overlooked, excluded, or dismissed; concepts are over-explained, or delivered in an overtly loud or patronizing tone.[16] Disabled women are presumed to be asexual beings, who do not date and who will never assume marital or family roles.[17]

The harm caused by these behaviors, like the harm caused by more blatant forms of sexist expression, is very real. Researchers on sex difference in language have identified patterns of women's speech that appear to correspond to the devaluation that women experience in relation to their male peers. Robin Lakoff was one of the first to identify a number of "hedges" common to women's speech that tend to convert declarative sentences into ambiguous, uncertain statements.[18] These hedges include hesitations and false starts ("I think . . . I was wondering . . ."); high pitch; "tag" questions ("This is really important, don't you think?"); a questioning intonation in making a statement; excessive use of qualifiers ("Don't you think that maybe sometimes . . . "); and other speech forms that are excessively polite and deferential ("This is probably not important, but . . .").[19] Women also tend to use more submissive gestures, such as inappropriate smiling when making a serous statement or asking a question, or averting their eyes, especially when dealing with men.[20]

These responses reflect the lower status and power that many women feel as a result of the behaviors described above.[21] They are also self-perpetuating, for they put women at a disadvantage in a classroom environment where assertion, clarity, and confidence are rewarded, and thus reinforce the attitudes of faculty and peers that women need not be taken seriously.[22]

The gendered nature of women's responses is apparent from the fact that they are more likely to be construed as signs of weakness or lack of proficiency than arguably analogous behaviors by men.

> For example, a woman student who "breaks down and cries" because of academic pressure is likely to be seen as "unstable," whereas a male student who, for the same reason, "goes out and gets drunk" is simply "blowing off steam." The man is welcomed back as "one of the guys," the woman—avoided— or advised to "get out of the kitchen if she can't take the heat."[23]

Other forms of sexism also take forms that are not widely understood as sexism. Take, for example, "red light district" (or "Bourbon Street") parties historically given by some fraternities at Duke University and elsewhere. Women attend the parties dressed as prostitutes in scanty clothing, allegedly to be "picked up" by men. These parties are understood as "just good, clean fun." They are sexy, provocative fantasies that release "normal" male energies "without harm." Everyone can have a good time. In fact, of course, such events eroticize the objectification of women. Women existing to serve men comes to stand for "good, clean fun." In such an example, injury based upon gender derives not from overt attacks and explicit messages of hate. Injury derives, instead, from eroticizing women's subordination to men. This process of definition implicates basic social patterns and explanatory frameworks—indeed, matters of fundamental identity for both women and men. For this reason, efforts by women's groups to eliminate these parties have been long, tedious, and contentious.

The difficulty of identifying, and communicating about, these issues can be seen in another Duke example. At a recent discussion in a dormitory unit, attended by women and men, the topic was acquaintance rape. The group asked a Women's Studies teacher to attend as a resource person. One of the men, whose previous comments indicated that he was sympathetic to changing the practices surrounding date rape at fraternity functions, offered this explanation for why such rapes occur. It is, he said, like driving home when you are drunk at 2 a.m. You come to a red light. You don't want anyone to think you're a softie, so you just go through it. All the guys do. The men and women listening to his account agreed with him—he had found a good image. Both the gendered nature of the image—woman/red light, hard/soft, the role of alcohol, the salience of peer pressure, ignoring established laws and conventions, the equating of woman and object, to name but a few—and its harmful implications, escaped all present. When cognitive systems about sexuality are operating in this way, getting outside them to expose their sexism—their inherent inequality—proves a formidable task.

Sexual harassment provides yet another set of examples. Although many campuses, in compliance with the law, now have student-faculty committees to hear sexual harassment cases, most committees are underutilized, in part because the victims of sexual harassment are conditioned to experience their harassment as "normal"—the way things are and will always be. Indeed, when a professor, or a graduate student in a position of authority, "comes on" to a female student or a female staff member or a female professor, she is supposed to be flattered. Her femininity is being affirmed; she is considered attractive by someone who counts. She is desirable. Such advances are dismissed, at worst, as trivial, something that women with a good sense of humor take in stride—certainly not a sign of deep sexism. The sexism, of course, is that the woman is affirmed only as an object of someone else's pleasure. She is expected 'o be pleased, grateful, and giving. The professional penalty for failing these expectations is sometimes high.

It is even more difficult to recognize the sexism of less overt forms of harassment. A recent classroom exercise in the introductory Women's Studies class at Duke enabled some students to do so. In this class, students were asked to commit gender role violations—to do something they considered inappropriate for themselves and then to analyze how they and their observers felt and explain why. Here are excerpts from a student report of violations and the reactions:

I am on a varsity team, so I spend a considerable amount of time in and around the gym every day. I therefore come into contact with more sweaty guys than anyone could ever want to. One thing, or two things, actually, that I notice many of them seem to do, *very publicly,* is scratch their crotches and spit loudly on the ground. It never seems to bother them how many people are around, or if a passer-by has to step out of their way to avoid a stream of spit. Personally, I'm not very fond of these two common traits, but even if disgusting, what upsets me most is that they are perfectly acceptable behavior for athletic men, but not women.[24]

Most of my friends are men and while I adore them and appreciate my privileged status as one of the guys, I am often amazed and frequently disgusted by the activities I observe in their presence. Furthermore, I realize that I'm only one of the guys as long as I laugh (prettily and convincingly) at their antics, but should I repeat them myself, I immediately become a girl who has overstepped her bounds. Specifically, I am referring to that boundary between men's bodies, which make noises, have needs and drives, and women's bodies, which are not allowed any of these things. Of the many functions available, I chose those three that were either the most uncommon to women, the most offensive to me/uncomfortable for me to do, or the most obvious violation of gender roles: spitting, passing gas, and consuming particularly large quantities of food.[25]

Their shock and difficulty in dealing with my crudeness was expected, as not only were they disgusted, but I was as well. I was embarrassed and confused that I had so rudely followed my instinct and belched in public. My embarrassment stemmed from the values and manners which had been so deeply ingrained in my character. These values caused me to react by apologizing for my actions. However it was actually my apology which caused me to be confused. I could not understand why I was apologizing for something which guys praise one another for doing publicly.[26]

The particular gender norm that I violated seems to come from the fact that it is acceptable for men to do "whatever" they want. . . . [M]en are allowed the luxury of sitting in undignified positions, sitting with their legs apart, or slouched down, and cursing, and other like behavior, whereas women are not. Partially this must come from the fact that our society is ingrained with the idea that whatever men do is of course "right" or "correct."[27]

If a person can be made to control their own body by an external force (even if this external force acts through internal restraints) then has not this control actually been removed from the individual? Furthermore, this process of suppression has insidious implications for the position of women in our society, for once a person's body can be controlled, how difficult is it to prevent the expression of their mind, and then their social and political needs?[28]

I've noticed that men tend to re-arrange themselves directly as an assertion of their superiority; in debates, when they cannot think of a good response (as if to say "yeah, but do you have one of these?") or in the midst of bragging (as if such an acknowledgement is corroborating evidence that his story is true).[29]

Formal definitions of harassment don't cover behaviors like these; it is hard to imagine how they could, without instituting a kind of Orwellian nightmare. It is *these ordinary, everyday* types of behaviors, however, that condition women to accept the limits placed on their social and cultural possibilities on an ordinary, everyday basis.

The Problem of Deniability

An important part of the problem we are describing is that the forms of more subtle, sexist degradation that women experience on college campuses are easily, and often, denied. This deniability is one very important reason why sexism remains an elusive target. There is a widespread belief that women in America—at least white women—have "made it." Sure, sexism used to exist, the story goes: Opportunities for women used to be limited, and there are still some old fogeys around who continue to think of women in old-fashioned, stereotypical ways. But the legal barriers have been removed, allowing full participation in society achieved by women. Equal rights have been won. Any failures that women now experience are failures of the individual, or private choices not to pursue one's full potential.[30] The institutions are clean.

The possibility exists, of course, that the very advances women have made in legal terms are countered culturally by a rise in misogyny at the individual level. In other words, the eradication of formal, visible, undesirable forms of sexism might cause a rise in the incidence and intensity of the informal, invisible, and deniable behaviors which undermine women's sense of self-value and women's opportunities.

Whether the incidence of everyday oppression is growing, the everyday behaviors we have discussed are easy to ignore. Because of their very ordinariness, these behaviors are less precise and more difficult to describe than the more extreme forms of abuse. In addition, these behaviors take enormously varied forms, which we are only now beginning to specify in any comprehensive way. They are subject to endless mutation; as one behavior is recognized as sexist, racist, or heterosexist, it may be suppressed, only to take a different, less recognizable form.[31] Moreover, these behaviors tend to be subtle and unconscious,[32] not openly hostile or mean-minded, and are sometimes [taken up] by members of the victimized groups themselves. For these reasons, even apart from whatever free speech issues might be implicated, few would argue that these behaviors can be the subject of effective, formal regulation. At most, critics argue that their identification and education about them can lead to self-regulation and eventual voluntary modification.

A focus on verbal and symbolic abuse has the unintended consequence of further reinforcing the invisibility of these everyday forms of oppression. First, by comparison, these behaviors seem so trivial, so harmless, so ordinary. How can white women, or blacks, complain of "insensitive," offhand classroom remarks or petty slights, in a world where skinheads shout "nigger" at a black man waiting to use a public telephone, or posters go up celebrating the massacre of Montreal feminists?

Second, this focus on regulation reinforces a conceptualization of racism, sexism, and heterosexism as blatant and intentional with specific perpetrators and specific victims. This conceptualization, while accurate with respect to some forms of verbal or symbolic assault, makes it more difficult to recognize and respond to the kind of racist, sexist, or heterosexist behaviors that are subtle, unknowing, and without a single clear perpetrator or intended victim. Where this conceptualization prevails, a remark which is not meant as insulting or derogating is seen as harmless, or worse, trivial.[33] The victim comes to be viewed as the problem. The question shifts from "How do we eradicate racist, sexist, and heterosexist behaviors?" to "Why do some people have to be so sensitive?"

A focus on blatant, intentional acts of verbal or symbolic abuse also enhances the likelihood that those holding such unconscious prejudices will respond with resentment and annoyance to calls to improve the campus atmosphere for members of subordinated groups.[34] The cry becomes: "We do not do *these awful things* at this university: We are civilized people. *I* certainly am not a racist; *I* would not do these things. And I don't know anyone else who would. What's the big deal all about?"

In this way, everyday behaviors are legitimated by their separation from the more blatantly assaultive behaviors that have become the rallying point for regulatory action. Defining the readily definable—trading grades for sexual favors is sexual harassment; shouting "cunts" at a group of women protesting for greater campus security against rape demeans and defames women; and so on—leaves untouched, even sanitizes, the remaining activities.[35] As a result, the pervasive behaviors that devalue individuals based upon their race, sex, and sexual lifestyle implicitly are disassociated from more blatant behaviors, and the nonregulatory alternatives that might be effective against these multiple forms of oppression remain unexplored.

Many forms of regulation, of course, necessarily leave some set of undesirable practices untouched and thus, in some sense, affirmed. The effect of not regulating the overt behaviors condones *these* behaviors, as well as the covert ones.[36] One might argue that in this area, as in others, the best way to attack many problems is "one step at a time." Distinctions between what the law forbids and what it does not, however, usually turn on the extent of the harm caused. It seems at least plausible that subtle, everyday forms of sexist oppression on college campuses are every bit as harmful as those caused by more blatant forms of oppression.[37] Indeed, the invisibility of these everyday behaviors and these everyday harms may make them all the more insidious. For this reason, it is crucial that any attempt to eradicate the more blatant examples of racism, sexism, and heterosexism simultaneously combats the validation of the remainder.

If there is a silver lining to the blatant, egregious forms of hateful harassment, it is that they help to make the underlying forms of prejudice undeniable. Incidents directed specifically against women, although fewer in number, serve the same purpose with respect to sexism. The problem is that we are in danger of getting stuck on these more dramatic examples and thereby failing to deal with the more subtle, daily forms of oppression that may play an even larger role in establishing the subordination of members of certain groups on college campuses. Recognizing that the everyday may be as oppressive as the extraordinary is essential to any meaningful transformation of the campus climate.

How might colleges and universities stimulate awareness of all those behaviors that denigrate members of subordinated groups? The simple fact that we know less about the ordinary daily forms of discrimination means that we have fewer intellectual and political tools to bring to bear on the very discussion of them. Strategies, however, are urgently needed and these strategies must be sufficiently diverse that no one single variety of degrading practices is taken for the whole problem. To take just a few examples, many universities have widely disseminated the contents of the reports upon which we have relied heavily in this comment.[38] Others have designed workshops for faculty, administrators, and students to generate awareness of these issues.[39] At least two universities have used these materials as part of classroom curricula.[40] Still other universities have initiated their own research on the campus environment at their own institutions.[41]

One recent example of a productive campus program was a mock date rape trial staged at Duke University on April 12, 1990.[42] Date rape is one of those events which is "everyday," in comparison to the more dramatic and less common instances of stranger rape that occur on college campuses. Like other more common forms of sexual oppression, its boundaries are blurred, its harm unappreciated, and its dimensions misunderstood. At the mock trial, not only students but also college faculty and administrators played roles, lending support to the message that date rape is a problem to be taken seriously on campus. A local prosecutor and well-known defense attorney played the parts of counsel. A balanced script made it clear that date rape is a complicated phenomenon, with two points of view representing conflicting, and overlapping, social norms. The event was promoted by clever advertisements in the student newspaper, that sketched out chronologically the (all-too-familiar) alternative accounts of what led to the eventual charge of rape. After the trial—attended by over 250 students—the audience divided up into six groups to deliberate as juries about the guilt or innocence of the defendant. Such events, legitimized by the support and participation of well-placed university administrators and student groups, bring hidden everyday dilemmas involving sexual oppression out into the open, where they can be revealed, taken seriously, and debated in a setting which is both real and yet controlled. They not only educate the university population about a pervasive campus problem, but also inform many women that their concerns and perspectives are important to the university.

Most of all, universities must be pressed to throw their moral weight around. Since universities cannot be neutral, they must attend to how their actions affirm some perspectives as "regular" and marginalize others as "special."[43] Curricular reforms must reflect a commitment to diverse cultural and racial experiences. Universities must support student organizations and facilitate cultural events and other campus programs to help eliminate the alien environment in which many students find themselves. Moreover, university administrators should publicly identify and condemn specific, objectionable behaviors—those that are subtle and unintentional as well as blatant and egregious, and those that cannot be legally regulated as well as those that can. This public practice must be continual and ongoing, not sporadic or only in response to the most overt and repulsive events. Moreover, strategies for change must be sensitive to the range of individuals whose attitudes and behaviors require attention. Strategies that generate only guilt will impede constructive communication, as will strategies that generate backlash by those who feel no guilt.[44] We all are implicated by the racism, sexism, and homophobia in our universities. Only strategies that produce greater self-awareness by *all* members of the university community will enable climate changes conducive to genuine understanding between individuals whose diversity we are both required, and privileged, to respect.

Endnotes

1. See Charles Lawrence, "If He Hollers, Let Him Go: Regulating Racist Speech on Campus," 1990 *Duke L.J.* 431; Nadine Strossen, "Regulating Racist Speech: A Modest Proposal?" 1990 *Duke L.J.* 484; see also Mari J. Matsuda, "Public Response to Racist Speech: Considering the Victim's Story," 87 *Mich. L. Rev.* 2320 (1989).

2. See Roberta M. Hall and Bernice R. Sandler, "The Classroom Climate: A Chilly One for Women?" (Project on the Status and Education of Women 1982) [hereinafter R. Hall and B. Sandler, "Classroom Climate"]; Roberta M. Hall and Bernice R. Sandler, "Out of the Classroom: A Chilly Campus Climate for Women?" (Project on the Status and Education of Women 1984) [hereinafter R. Hall and B. Sandler, "Out of the Classroom"].

3. R. Hall and B. Sandler, Classroom Climate, supra note 2, at 7. This, and other behaviors, have been documented even at women's colleges that have recently become co-educational. See Edward B. Fiske, "Lessons," *N.Y. Times,* Apr. 11, 1990, at B8, col. 1 (reporting experiences at Wheaton College).

4. R. Hall and B. Sandler, "Classroom Climate," supra note 2, at 7.

5. Id. at 8.

6. Id.

7. Id. at 8–9.

8. Id. at 9.

9. Id.

10. Id. at 11.

11. R. Hall and B. Sandler, "Out of the Classroom," supra note 2, at 10.

12. Id.

13. Id. at 6–7.

14. Id. at 12.

15. Id.

16. Id.

17. Id. at 13. By this criticism, we do not mean to endorse dating, or the assumption of marital or family roles, as the female norm. The point is, rather, that a particular norm is assumed with respect to disabled women that is restrictive for many of them.

18. Robin Lakoff, *Language and Woman's Place* 53 (1975). For a comprehensive, annotated bibliography of the wealth of research in this area, see Cheris Kramarae, Barrie Thorne, and Nancy Henley, "Sex Similarities and Differences in Language, Speech, and Nonverbal Communication: An Annotated Bibliography," in *Language, Gender, and Society* 151 (Barrie Thorne, Cheris Kramarae, and Nancy Henley eds. 1983).

19. R. Lakoff, supra note 18, at 53; see also R. Hall and B. Sandler, "Classroom Climate," supra note 2, at 9–10; John Conley, William O'Barr, and E. Allen Lind, "The Power of Language: Presentational Style in the Courtroom," 1978 *Duke L.J.* 1375, 1379–80 (poor and uneducated most likely to use speech that conveys a lack of forcefulness). For a riveting narrative illustrating the use of subordinate speech patterns by a welfare recipient client in an administrative hearing concerning charges of welfare fraud, see Lucie White, "Subordination, Rhetorical Survival Skills, and Sunday Shoes: Notes on the Hearing of Mrs. G.," 38 *Buffalo L. Rev.* 1, 21–32 (1990).

20. R. Hall and B. Sandler, "Classroom Climate," supra note 2, at 9–10.

21. William O'Barr and Bowman Atkins, "'Women's Language' or 'Powerless Language'?" in *Women and Language in Literature and Society* 93, 102–104 (Sally McConnell-Ginet, Ruth Borker, and Nelly Furman eds. 1980) (finding greater correlation between use of "women's language" and lower social status than with gender per se).

22. These values are perhaps most evident in law school classrooms, which are seen as the training ground for a

profession in which assertiveness and confidence are critically important. A survey of 765 law students from five different law schools revealed that male students volunteer in class significantly more often than female students, that the rate of women's participation decreases over time while the rate of men's participation remains constant, and that women students feel more insecure than male students. See Taunya Lovell Banks, "Gender Bias in the Classroom," 38 *J. Legal Educ.* 137, 141–142 (1988). A study of 667 Boalt Hall students, which corroborated these findings, also concluded that women law students with comparable entrance qualifications attained lower grades than their male peers, and had much lower self-esteem. See Suzanne Homer and Lois Schwartz, "Admitted but Not Accepted: Outsiders Take an Inside Look at Law School," 5 *Berkeley Women's L.J.* 1, 28–31, 33–34, 37–44 (1989–90). Virtually all of the work in this area has reached consistent conclusions. See Stephanie M. Wildman, "The Question of Silence: Techniques to Ensure Full Class Participation," 38 *J. Legal Educ.* 147 (1988); "Gender, Legal Education, and the Legal Profession: An Empirical Study of Stanford Law Students and Graduates," 40 *Stan. L. Rev.* 1209, 1239 (1988) (showing men law students at Stanford more likely than women to ask questions and volunteer answers in class); see also Catherine Weiss and Louise Melling, "The Legal Education of Twenty Women," 40 *Stan. L. Rev.* 1299, 1333–45 (1988) (describing experiences of twenty women law students at Yale Law School, including their disproportionate silencing in the classroom and their alienation from the classroom).

23. R. Hall and B. Sandler, "Out of the Classroom," supra note 2, at 3.

24. Comment by Kerry Dolan.

25. Comment by Janice Jensen.

26. Name withheld upon request.

27. Comment by Kerry Dolan.

28. Comment by Janice Jensen.

29. Comment by Lucy Mochman.

30. Elinor Lenz and Barbara Myerhoff express this point of view in their best-seller, *The Feminization of America: How Women's Values Are Changing Our Public and Private Lives* 248–49 (1985) ("The process of feminization has shown us the way to achieve a balanced and humane society . . . [whether we achieve such a society] will be determined by our response to this unprecedented opportunity for individual and social change."). In a powerful critique of this book, Catharine Hantzis both challenges the claim that gender justice is a completed agenda, and examines how the premature celebration of women's equality leads women to adapt to rather than

resist their oppression. See Catharine Hantzis, "Is Gender Justice a Completed Agenda?" 100 *Harv. L. Rev.* 690 (1987).

31. This phenomenon is captured by what Richard Delgado, in the context of racism, calls the "Law of Racial Thermodynamics: Racism is neither created nor destroyed." Richard Delgado, "When a Story is Just a Story: Does Voice Really Matter?" 76 *Va. L. Rev.* 95, 106 (1990). Although this phenomenon, to the best of our knowledge, has not yet been scientifically documented, it rings true to many members of "outsider" groups, who find that the identification and suppression of one form of oppression leads to the emergence and growth of another.

32. Professor Lawrence, himself, has contributed some of the most sophisticated scholarship about the unconscious aspects of racism. See Charles Lawrence, "The Id, the Ego, and Equal Protection: Reckoning With Unconscious Racism," 39 *Stan. L. Rev.* 317 (1987); see also Lawrence, supra note 1, at 468–470. Regulation seems a particularly ineffective weapon against verbal and symbolic acts driven by unconscious hate and prejudice.

33. Darryl Brown in an excellent student note on racism in the university has demonstrated the extent to which this "perpetrator perspective" is reflected in the law of race discrimination. See Note, "Racism and Race Relations in the University," 76 *Va. L. Rev.* 295, 309 (1990). Brown argues that this perspective "conceptualizes racism as a discrete and specific act, an act committed by one individual, group, or institution against another whose injury can be identified," and thus "ignores the possibility that 'race' is structural and interstitial, that it can be the root of injury even when not traceable to a specific intention or action." Id. at 309–310.

34. See Id. at 310. Brown writes:

> [A]n understanding of racism limited to the perpetrator perspective, helps to explain vocal resentment of whites to charges of racism and provides insight into allegations that the term "racism" has been so misused and overused that it has lost its meaning. When whites conceive of "racism" as requiring an intentional racist motive for which they deserve personal blame for a personal fault, they get angry because they know they had no racist intent. They plead that they were misunderstood, or that blacks are "oversensitive."

Id. at 310–311 (footnote omitted). The following line in a Letter to the Editor of the Duke student newspaper illustrates this infuriated (and infuriating) attitude: "I am sick of a bunch of whining women who place blame for social evils on the nearest scapegoat, and I am tired of these women pointing their fingers at me and all other males." Tony Leung, "Don't Assign Blame for Rape So Quickly," *Chronicle*, Mar. 28, 1990, at 8, col. 3–4.

35. A similar criticism has been made by feminists in relation to pornography and rape. See e.g., Catharine A. MacKinnon, *Feminism Unmodified: Discourses on Life and Law* 162 (1987) (in carving out and prohibiting a limited number of types of pornography, obscenity law authorizes and legitimizes the rest); Katharine T. Bartlett, "Porno-Symbolism: A Response to Professor McConahay," *Law and Contemp. Probs.*, Winter 1988, at 71, 73 (by "rendering unacceptable the most extreme forms of pornography, [society] legitimizes the remainder"); Frances Olsen, "Statutory Rape: A Feminist Critique of Rights Analysis," 63 *Tex. L. Rev.* 387, 427 (1984) ("Censuring the most blatant and oppressive manifestations of sexual aggression may make its more subtle, everyday forms actually seem more acceptable.")

36. We thank Professor Tom Grey for this point.

37. See Note, supra note 33, at 323.

38. See "Selected Activities Using 'The Classroom Climate: A Chilly One for Women?'" (Project on the Status and Education of Women 1984) (reporting dissemination strategies at the University of Delaware, Michigan State University, Pennsylvania State University, California State University at Northridge, Harvard University, and Rutgers University).

39. Id. at 2–3 (describing programs and workshops at the University of Maine at Orono, Bangor Community College, American University, Northeastern Illinois University, and the University of Nebraska, Lincoln).

40. The University of Texas at El Paso, for example, used "The Classroom Climate," supra note 2, in an upper division course, "Women, Power and Politics," both to "sensitize students to campus climate issues and to teach research [methods and] design." Id. at 3. At Denison University, these materials were used to generate discussion and paper assignments based upon the student's own experiences. Id.

41. These universities include Bowling Green State University, the University of Delaware, Rhode Island College, Massachusetts Institute of Technology, and the University of Maryland. Id. at 3–4.

42. The mock trial was based upon an original play written by Rebecca Patton, Duke Law School Class of 1991, and presented by the Duke Rape and Sexual Assault Task Force and the Interfraternity Council.

43. See Lawrence, supra note 1, at 473–475.

44. Darryl Brown makes this point specifically with respect to strategies toward ending campus racism. Note, supra note 33, at 333–334.

---

47. *Corry* v. *Stanford University*

THE SUPERIOR COURT OF CALIFORNIA

The issue before the Superior Court of California was whether Stanford University's speech code violated the First Amendment of the U.S. Constitution. Judge Stone found that it did, in fact, violate the First Amendment because it was overbroad and restricted speech beyond "fighting words." In addition, Judge Stone found the defendant's claim that they were proscribing conduct, not speech, to be without merit. The judge further found that although the First Amendment protection of speech does not, in general, apply to private institutions, it does in California because of a law passed in 1992.

To summarize the parties' arguments, defendants in this case maintain that the type of speech that the speech code proscribes is not protected under the Constitution. Defendants argue that the speech code only proscribes "fighting words," which are constitu-tionally permissible under the case of *Chaplinsky v. New Hampshire* (1942).

Plaintiffs, on the other hand, maintain that this speech code is a violation of their First Amendment rights to free speech under the U.S. Constitution.

Relying on the case of *R.A.V. v. City of St. Paul* (1992), plaintiffs argue that defendants' speech code seeks to prohibit speech on the basis of its content and therefore is constitutionally impermissible.

It must be noted, however, that the "First and Fourteenth Amendments safeguard the rights of free speech and assembly by limitations on state action, not on action by the owner of private property. . . ." The protections of the First Amendment prevent abridgment of speech by state actors only. In this case, however, defendants are private parties. The Supreme Court has declined to characterize private universities as state actors even though the "universities were publicly funded, publicly regulated, and performed a public function, and even though other nexus existed between the state and the university." Accordingly, defendants argue that since they are private parties, the First Amendment protects their speech rights, and does not prohibit them from doing anything at all.

In response, however, plaintiffs maintain that California Education Code §94367 (hereinafter, "the Leonard Law") allows a private university student to have the same right to exercise his or her right to free speech on campus as he or she enjoys off campus. This code section specifically allows a private student to commence a civil action for any violations thereof. It is plaintiffs' position that this code section enables them to take action against defendants' speech code, despite the fact that Stanford is a private party.

However, defendants maintain that even if the speech code infringes upon plaintiffs' protected speech off campus, the Leonard Law's command that Stanford must tolerate such speech on its campus would violate Stanford's First Amendment right to be free of State regulation with respect to its speech. Accordingly, it is defendants' position that the Leonard Law would be unconstitutional as applied to defendants' speech code in a number of ways.

In summarizing the parties' arguments, therefore, a two-part analysis is necessary for a proper determination of this motion. The first issue involves the constitutionality of defendants' speech code. The Court must first decide whether the speech code abridges speech which the U.S. Constitution seeks to protect outside of campus. If the answer is "no," then the analysis ends and plaintiffs' motion for a preliminary injunction should be denied. On the other hand,

if it is determined that the speech code is unconstitutional, then the second step of the analysis must be discussed: the constitutionality of the Leonard Law. This Court must then decide whether this code section violates defendants' constitutional rights. If so, then this code section would be unconstitutional and inapplicable to the defendants. If, on the other hand, the Court finds that the code section is constitutional and applicable to the defendants, then this section would give the Court access to Stanford even though it is a private party and plaintiffs' motion for a preliminary injunction should be granted.

This Court will address the two-part analysis separately below.

I. The Constitutionality of Defendants' Speech Code

A. Constitutionality Under Chaplinsky and Later Line of Cases

Defendants argue that the speech code proscribes only gutter epithets that are fighting words, and that under *Chaplinsky v. New Hampshire* (1942) such words are not subject to constitutional protection. In *Chaplinsky*, the Supreme Court upheld a conviction under New Hampshire speech statute which prohibited offensive or annoying words on public streets. The Court, basing its decision on the state court's narrow interpretation of the statute, held that "fighting words," those words "which by their very utterance inflict injury or tend to incite an immediate breach of the peace," did not enjoy First Amendment protection.

The court reasoned that the statute had been appropriately applied to Mr. Chaplinsky, who had called a city official a "God-damned racketeer" and a "damned Fascist," since his words would have "likely provoked the average person to retaliate, and thereby cause a breach of the peace." In this case, defendants argue that their speech code comports with the standard set forth in *Chaplinsky*, since the speech code explicitly sets out the fighting words test in its regulations.

Defendants further argue that this speech code is "meant to insure that no idea as such is proscribed, and accordingly it does not prohibit the expression of any view, however racist, sexist, homophobic, or blasphemous in content." Rather, defendants state that the speech code "draws the line at fighting words. . . ." Such an argument is persuasive since vilifying a student with racial epithets, for example, would clearly have the effect of likely provoking the average person to retaliate and of inflicting injury by their very utterance. If phrases such as "God damned racketeer" and "damned Fascist" are "no essential part of any exposition of ideas . . . ," then certainly words which the defendants seek to proscribe (such as "damned nigger," etc.) should not enjoy constitutional protection.

Plaintiffs' gravamen, however, does not lie with any desire to vilify another student with "gutter epithets." Instead, it appears that plaintiffs' complaint rests on the argument that defendants' speech code, as drawn, goes beyond fighting words and, in effect, proscribes the expression of particular ideas and constitutionally protected speech. Plaintiffs partly base this claim on the rationale that the *Chaplinsky* holding has now been significantly narrowed to apply to only fighting words whose "utterance is likely to lead to immediate violence." Such a claim, if valid, would undermine the constitutionality of the speech code since, as plaintiffs argue, it prohibits "insults" and "offensive speech," not just "words that make people fight."

Plaintiffs' argument has merit. A review of authority reveals that there has been an apparent narrowing of the *Chaplinsky* doctrine. For example, in *Terminiello v. Chicago* (1949), the Supreme Court reversed petitioner's conviction under a breach of the peace ordinance which the trial court had interpreted to include speech which "stirs the public anger [or] invites dispute," as well as speech which creates a disturbance. Although the petitioner's criticism of political and racial groups had caused several disturbances among spectators, the court found that such words, "unless shown likely to produce a clear and present danger of serious substantive evil that rises far above public inconvenience, annoyance, or unrest," could not be proscribed.

In *Terminiello*, the Supreme Court reasoned that speech which "stirs the audience to anger" or "invites dispute" is protected under the First Amendment.

Additionally, in the case of *Gooding v. Wilson* (1972), the Supreme Court reversed petitioner's conviction under a Georgia abusive language statute after he had threatened and insulted two police officers. The Su-

preme Court found that even though the statute regulated only language which inflicts injury or affects the "sensibilities" of the hearer, it did not meet the requirements of the fighting words doctrine because it was not limited to words that "tend to cause an immediate breach of the peace." The Court found the statute was not limited to words that would have a direct tendency to cause acts of violence by the person to whom, individually, the remark was addressed.

Thereafter, in *Lewis v. City of New Orleans* (1974), the Supreme Court remanded a conviction under a Louisiana statute that banned the use of obscene language toward any police officer in the line of duty. Even though the state court held that the law prohibited only "fighting words," the Supreme Court found that, in light of *Gooding*, the statute was unconstitutionally overbroad since "obscene" and "opprobrious" words regulated under the statute "may well have conveyed anger and frustration without provoking a violent reaction from an officer."

More recently, in the case of *UWM Post v. Board of Regents of U. of Wisconsin* (1991), the Court stated that "since *Chaplinsky*, the Supreme Court has narrowed and clarified the scope of the fighting words doctrine . . . to include only words which tend to incite an immediate breach of the peace."[1] In addition to limiting the scope of the fighting words to words which tend to incite an immediate breach of the peace, it appears that a more stringent definition of "breach of the peace" has been set forth. Referring to the *Gooding* case, the Supreme Court stated that "in order to constitute fighting words, speech must not only breach decorum but also must tend to bring the addressee to fisticuffs." Consequently, in *UWM Post*, the Court found that since the elements of the *UWM* Rule did not require that "the regulated speech, by its very utterance, tend to incite violent reaction, the rule [went] beyond the . . . scope of the fighting words doctrine."

In sum, therefore, based upon the line of cases following *Chaplinsky*, it appears that the Court has, in effect, narrowed the *Chaplinsky* definition of fighting words to eliminate the "inflict injury" prong of the test. As such, under this narrowed version of *Chaplinsky*, defendants' speech code presumably proscribes more than "fighting words" as defined in subsequent case law. On its face, the speech code prohibits words which will not only cause people to react violently, but also cause them to feel insulted or stigmatized. As discussed above, however, defendants cannot proscribe speech that merely hurts the feelings of those who hear it.

The speech code also punishes words that "are commonly understood to convey" hatred and contempt on the basis of race, religion, etc. Clearly, this focuses upon the content of the words. All that is required under the speech code is that the words convey a message of hatred and contempt, not that they will likely cause an imminent breach of the peace. By proscribing certain words, without even considering their context, i.e., whether under a given situation there will be a breach of the peace, defendants' speech code fails to meet the "fighting words" standard as set forth under *Chaplinsky* and the later line of cases. As written, the speech code clearly punishes students for words which may not cause an imminent breach of the peace, but instead merely "conveys a message of hatred and contempt." To this extent, the speech code is overbroad since it is conceivable that a student could be punished for speech that did not (and would not) result in immediate violence. As a result, due to its overbreadth, defendants' speech code cannot pass constitutional scrutiny.

B. Constitutionality Under R.A.V. v. City of St. Paul

1. The Claims of the Parties

Even assuming, arguendo, that all the expressions under the speech code are proscribable under the "fighting words" doctrine, under *R.A.V. v. City of St. Paul* (1992), the speech code would still be unconstitutional if it proscribes speech on the basis of the content the speech addresses.

Plaintiffs claim this is exactly what defendants' speech code does. Plaintiffs argue that the speech code, similar to the ordinance in *R.A.V.*, is an impermissible content-based regulation, since it does not proscribe all fighting words, but only those that are based on sex, race, color, and the like. Plaintiffs state that such "hostility" or "favoritism" toward the underlying message . . . is unconstitutional. "The First Amendment forbids such selective incorporation."

Defendants, on the other hand, argue that *R.A.V.*, is not applicable here since, unlike the ordinance in

R.A.V., defendants' speech code is directed toward conduct (discriminatory harassment), not speech. Discriminatory harassment, defendants assert, includes personal vilification by means of fighting words/gutter epithets. Defendants, citing *R.A.V.* and *Wisconsin v. Mitchell* (1993), contend that where a regulation is directed toward conduct, the expression can be "swept up incidentally" without violating First Amendment rights.

2. The Case of *R.A.V.*

In *R.A.V.*, the Supreme Court struck down a St. Paul "bias motivated hate crime" ordinance which made it a misdemeanor to place on private or public property a symbol which one knows, or has reasonable grounds to know, arouses anger in others on the basis of race, color, creed, religion or gender.

The majority accepted the Minnesota Supreme Court's construction of the ordinance as only applying to fighting words, an area of speech traditionally unprotected. Nevertheless, the Court found the ordinance unconstitutional since it did not proscribe all fighting words, but only those based on the categories listed in the ordinance.

The Court reasoned that such selectivity created the very real possibility that "the city was seeking to handicap the expression of particular ideas," and not fighting words in general. The Court did hold that the government could still prohibit fighting words so long as the proscription was unrelated to the distinct message contained in the expression. Thus, as the majority noted, libel could be proscribed, but not libel only critical of the government.

In the case at hand, a close examination of defendants' speech code reveals that plaintiffs' position is compelling. Similar to the ordinance in *R.A.V.*, defendants' speech code only proscribes a select class of fighting words: insults aimed at sex, race, color, handicap, sexual orientation, national or ethnic origin. Here, the same dangers the majority warned against exist. Defendants' speech code singles out a limited type of proscribable expression for a broad range of proscribable expression. Fighting words directed toward race and the like are punishable, yet those directed toward political affiliation, for example, are not. As plaintiffs note, "Insults, no matter how vicious or severe, are permissible unless they are addressed to one of the specified disfavored groups." Defendants, it would appear, have prohibited certain expression based on the underlying message. This is the type of content-based regulation the Court in *R.A.V.* found impermissible under the First Amendment.

3. Whether Defendants' Speech Code Falls Under an Exception . . . Whether Defendants' Speech Code Is Directed Toward Conduct

Although conceptually similar to the fourth exception enumerated in *R.A.V.*, a brief discussion is warranted since defendants raise this point separately. Defendants, as mentioned earlier, claim that their speech code is directed at prohibiting discriminatory harassment and not speech per se.

The Court in *R.A.V.* stated that its holding did not preclude regulation of subcategories of proscribable speech when such regulations are aimed at conduct. Thus, as the Court noted, sexual derogatory fighting words can be banned from the workplace because it would produce a violation of Title VII's general prohibition against sexual discrimination, a particular type of conduct. In essence, such words would be "swept up incidentally within the reach of a statute aimed at conduct rather than speech."

As it can be discerned from the above analysis, the Court, however, found the St. Paul ordinance was not directed toward conduct, but sought to prohibit certain fighting words. Similarly, as plaintiffs note, there is little evidence in the record which indicates defendants' speech code is aimed at conduct. Examination of the speech code reveals no mention of conduct or harassment as being proscribed. Rather, what is addressed is the prohibition of a certain category of expression which may result in a breach of the peace. Speech, in this respect, is not swept up incidentally, but is the aim of the proscription. It appears, therefore, that defendants' claim is without merit.

C. Conclusion

In conclusion, defendants' speech code cannot withstand the analysis and the holding in *R.A.V.* The speech code prohibits speech based on the content of the underlying expression and is not directed at conduct. It punishes those who express views on the disfavored subjects of race, gender, and the like, yet permits fighting words which do not address these

topics. For these reasons, therefore, defendants' speech code appears to be in violation of the principles of the First Amendment.

II. *The Applicability and Constitutionality of Education Code §94367 ("The Leonard Law")*

The next step in the analysis is a determination of whether the Court has standing to take action against Stanford, who is a private party. The protections of the First Amendment prevent abridgement of speech by state actors. Defendants state that as private parties, the First Amendment protects their speech rights and does not prohibit them from doing anything at all. The "First and Fourteenth Amendments safeguard the rights of free speech and assembly by limitation on state action, not on action by the owner of private property. . . ."

In response, however, plaintiffs argue that the courts have standing to take action against defendants through the enforcement of the Leonard Law. Specifically, this code section states as follows:

> (a) No private postsecondary educational institution shall make or enforce any rule subjecting any student to disciplinary sanctions solely on the basis of conduct that is speech or other communication that, when engaged in outside the campus or facility of a private postsecondary institution, is protected from governmental restriction by the First Amendment to the United States Constitution or Section 2 of Article 1 of the California Constitution.
> (b) Any student enrolled in a private postsecondary institution that has made or enforced any rule in violation of subdivision (a) may commence a civil action to obtain appropriate injunctive and declaratory relief as determined by the court. Upon motion, a court may award attorney's fees to a prevailing plaintiff in a civil action pursuant to this section.

Pursuant to this statute, a private university student has the same right to exercise his or her right to free speech on campus as he or she enjoys off campus. The Leonard Law specifically allows a private student to commence a civil action for any violation of this code section. As such, it is plaintiffs' position that the court has standing to take action against defendants in this case through the application of §94367.

Since it has been determined in Section I that the speech code is unconstitutional, the next step in the analysis is the applicability and constitutionality of Education Code §94367. It is defendants' position that even assuming that plaintiffs' fighting words are protected speech off campus, with the effect that §94367 requires Stanford to permit them on campus, Education Code §94367 would be unconstitutional as applied to defendants' speech code.

Defendant Stanford's Rights of Association

The First Amendment protects the freedom of association. Case law indicates that the State offends the right of free association by preventing an association from effectuating "its basic goals" of "high ethical standards" by preventing an association from "excluding individuals with ideologies or philosophies different from those of its existing members," or by preventing an association from "protecting [itself] 'from intrusion by those with adverse political principles.'" Indeed, there "can be no clearer example of an intrusion into the inherent structure or affairs of an association than a regulation that forces the group to accept members it does not desire." Defendants maintain that this is particularly true when the association is a university: "The freedom of a university to make its own judgments as to education includes the selection of its student body."

Defendants argue that to the extent that the Leonard Law prohibits Stanford from implementing its speech code by proscribing fighting words/gutter epithets on its campus, and from disciplining or excluding students who vilify others, the Leonard Law offends Stanford's right of freedom of association.

Expressive associational rights derive from the Court's recognition that the ability to associate with others is crucial to effective advocacy. "By collective efforts individuals can make their views known, when, individually, their voices would be faint or lost." In determining whether to extend First Amendment expressive association rights to organizations, the crucial inquiry for the Court has been whether enforcement of the legislation in question would sub-

stantially alter a group's activities. That is, the organization must be able to prove that its ability to advocate effectively the specific expressive viewpoints of the organization will be compromised. "The Court thus looks at the connection between the membership and the message." As such, a court will refuse to protect an association's expressive rights unless the association is "organized for specific expressive purposes," but there must also exist a logical nexus between the discriminatory practices of the group and its purpose or message.

With respect to the expressive associational rights of defendants, this Court must first determine the "specific expressive purpose" for which the University was founded. Plaintiffs submit that the mission of the University is to provide its students with a comprehensive liberal arts education in which controversial ideas and presuppositions are subject to academic scrutiny, challenged by others in an effort to expand the critical reasoning skill of its students. Stanford is committed to the principles of free inquiry and free expression. Students have a "right to hold and vigorously defend and promote their opinions . . . . Respect for this right requires that students tolerate even expression of opinions which they find abhorrent."

Plaintiffs' position is that the defendants have not exhibited any logical nexus between their express purposes and the unconstitutional and illegal practices— the denial of First Amendment protected speech—in which they engage. Plaintiffs argue that not only is the enforcement of the speech code inconsistent with the specific express purposes of the University, but defendants have failed to proffer any arguments that the application of the Leonard Law will compromise the ability of the University to express its alleged concern with the "principles of equal opportunity and nondiscrimination." The membership of the University is not co-extensive with the message it may wish to promulgate. Where "allowing Blacks to March with the KKK would change the primary message which the KKK advocates," allowing students who may disagree with University dogma will not extinguish the message of the University. Unlike the Ku Klux Klan, defendant Stanford is an organization where the membership and message are not co-extensive.

It appears that in cases such as this, where a party claims that it is being forced to accept members that it does not desire, the pertinent question is whether admitting the undesired members will affect the ability of the original members to express the views on which the organization was founded. For example, in *Board of Directors of Rotary Int'l v. Rotary Club* (1987), the Court held that California could force Rotary Clubs to admit women because the Court did not find enough evidence "to demonstrate that admitting women . . . will affect in any significant way the existing members' ability to carry out their various purposes."

Similarly, in this case, it does not appear that defendants' ability to express their views will be significantly impaired by the application of Education Code §94367. As plaintiffs point out, defendant Stanford is a major international institution, well funded, with access to numerous alternative means of conveying its views that the speech prohibited by the speech code is offensive and intolerable. Therefore, by denying defendants the ability to discipline (expel) students for violation of the speech code, defendants' ability to express its message is not impaired because defendants retain numerous alternative means of expressing their views.

Defendants have not satisfied any of the legal prerequisites to claiming First Amendment protection under expressive associational rights. Plaintiffs argue that the case of *Pruneyard Shopping Center v. Robins* (1980) is directly on point. In *Pruneyard,* appellant private shopping center owner sought protection from Zionist picketers on precisely the same grounds on which defendants petition this Court—alleging that a private property owner has a First Amendment right of expressive association not to be forced by the State to use its property as a forum for the speech of others with whom it may disagree. In finding the California law constitutional, the Court distinguished expressly its prior ruling in *Wooley v. Maynard* (1977), in which it found unconstitutional a New Hampshire law requiring that all vehicles display the State motto, "Live Free or Die." In doing so, the Court distinguished between a State compelling a private actor to disseminate the State's ideology for the express purpose that it be read by the public—the *Wooley* issue—and a State compelling a private actor to allow speech of any content, irrespective of its conformity with State dogma—the *Pruneyard* issue.

More specifically, the Court distinguished *Pruneyard* on three grounds. First, the shopping center, by the owner's own choice, was not limited to the personal use of the appellant. The center was organized as an establishment open to the public to come and go as they please. Hence, the Court concluded that there was no likelihood that the views of the petitioner would be construed as those of the appellant. Second, no specific message was directed by the State. Accordingly, the fears of government viewpoint discrimination at issue in *Wooley* were nonexistent. Finally, the Court found that appellant could disavow any connection with the message proffered by petitioners by posting signs to that effect in the center.

Plaintiffs argue that the facts in this case are indistinguishable from *Pruneyard.* First, defendant Stanford University is not limited to the personal use of defendants, but rather opens up its campus and admissions process to the general public.[2] Furthermore, the public access and large size of the University confirm the assertion that the views expressed by any of its students will not be construed to represent those of the University. Additionally, defendants could easily disclaim any such wrongful attribution of a student's expressions for those of the University. Identical to the *Pruneyard* situation, plaintiffs validly argue that California does not dictate any specific message through the Leonard Law, a situation which eliminates any concerns over government-sponsored viewpoint discrimination.

In sum, therefore, the crucial inquiry in determining whether defendants' First Amendment rights are offended by the Leonard Law is whether there exists a nexus between the express purposes of the group and the activity which it seeks to continue (i.e., suppressing student speech rights). The determination includes analysis of various factors: whether there is a concern of State-sponsored viewpoint discrimination, whether observers are likely to construe the offensive speech as an endorsement by the University of such views, and whether the University has adequate means at its disposal by which to rebut or separate itself from the offensive message. As discussed above, in analyzing these factors, no sufficient nexus exists here which would affect defendants' rights of association. For these reasons, defendants' contention that the Leonard Law is unconstitutional since it infringes upon its First Amendment rights of association is unpersuasive.

III. *Conclusion*

In summary, based upon the above analysis, the following conclusion is reached: First, defendants' speech code does violate plaintiffs' First Amendment rights since the speech code proscribes more than just fighting words as defined in *Chaplinsky* and the later lines of case law. To this extent, therefore, defendants' speech code is overbroad. In addition, however, the speech code also targets the content of certain speech. Similar to the ordinance in *R.A.V.,* the speech code is an impermissible content-based regulation since it does not proscribe all fighting words, but only those which are based upon sex, race, color, and the like. Accordingly, the speech code is unconstitutional not only due to its overbreadth but also due to its content-based restrictions.

Second, since defendants are private parties, the only means by which the Court can have standing to take action against the defendants is through the enforcement of Education Code §94367 (the "Leonard Law"). In this case, Education Code §94367 does apply and proscribe defendants' speech code. For these reasons, plaintiffs' motion for a preliminary injunction should therefore be granted.

Endnotes

1. It must be noted that the *Chaplinsky* court originally set out a two-part definition for fighting words: (1) words which by their very utterance inflict injury; and (2) words which by their very utterance tend to inflict an immediate breach of the peace.

2. Additionally, it is important to note that a shopping center is located on the University campus. This, too, appears to be a location where the Code applies; the Stanford Shopping Center is a very similar forum to that in *Pruneyard.*

48. *Free Speech and Bias on College Campuses*

ACLU POLICY STATEMENT[1]

Preamble

The significant increase in reported incidents of racism and other forms of bias at colleges and universities is a matter of profound concern to the ACLU. Some have proposed that racism, sexism, homophobia, and other such biases on campus must be addressed in whole or in part by restrictions on speech. The alternative to such restrictions, it is said, is to permit such bias to go unremedied and to subject the targets of such bias to a loss of equal educational opportunity. The ACLU rejects both these alternatives and reaffirms its traditional and unequivocal commitment both to free speech and to equal opportunity.

Policy

1. Freedom of thought and expression are indispensable to the pursuit of knowledge and the dialogue and dispute that characterize meaningful education. All members of the academic community have the right to hold and to express views that others may find repugnant, offensive, or emotionally distressing. The ACLU opposes all campus regulations which interfere with the freedom of professors, students, and administrators to teach, learn, discuss, and debate or to express ideas, opinions, or feelings in classroom, public, or private discourse.[2]

2. The ACLU has opposed and will continue to oppose and challenge disciplinary codes that reach beyond permissible boundaries into the realm of protected speech, even when those codes are directed at the problem of bias on campus.[3]

3. This policy does not prohibit colleges and universities from enacting disciplinary codes aimed at restricting acts of harassment, intimidation, and invasion of privacy.[4] The fact that words may be used in connection with otherwise actionable conduct does not immunize such conduct from appropriate regulation.[5] As always, however, great care must be taken to avoid applying such provisions overbroadly to protected expression. The ACLU will continue to review such college codes and their application in specific situations on a case-by-case basis under the principles set forth in this policy and in Policy 72.[6]

4. All students have the right to participate fully in the educational process on a nondiscriminatory basis. Colleges and universities have an affirmative obligation to combat racism, sexism, homophobia, and other forms of bias, and a responsibility to provide equal opportunities through education. To address these responsibilities and obligations, the ACLU advocates the following actions by colleges and universities:

(a) to utilize every opportunity to communicate through its administrators, faculty, and students its commitment to the elimination of all forms of bigotry on campus;

(b) to develop comprehensive plans aimed at reducing prejudice, responding promptly to incidents of bigotry and discriminatory harassment, and protecting students from any such further incidents;

(c) to pursue vigorously efforts to attract enough minorities, women, and members of other historically disadvantaged groups as students, faculty members, and administrators to alleviate isolation and to ensure real integration and diversity in academic life;

(d) to offer and consider whether to require all students to take courses in the history and meaning of prejudice, including racism, sexism, and other forms of invidious discrimination;[7]

(e) to establish new-student orientation programs and continuing counseling programs that enable students of different races, sexes, religions, and sexual orientations to learn to live with each other outside the classroom;

(f) to review and, where appropriate, revise course offerings as well as extracurricular programs in order to recognize the contributions of those whose art, music, literature, and learning have been insufficiently reflected in the curriculum of many American colleges and universities;

(g) to address the question of *de facto* segregation in dormitories and other university facilities; and

(h) to take such other steps as are consistent with the goal of ensuring that all students have an equal opportunity to do their best work and to participate fully in campus life.

This policy is issued in connection with, and is intended as an interpretation and enhancement of, the binding resolution on racist speech adopted at the 1989 Biennial Conference. That resolution provides:

The ACLU should undertake educational activities to counter incidents of racist, sexist, anti-semitic, and homophobic behavior (including speech) on school campuses and should encourage school administrators to speak out vigorously against such incidents. At the same time the ACLU should undertake educational activities to counter efforts to limit or punish speech on university campuses.

Endnotes

1. Adopted by ACLU National Board of Directors, without dissent, on October 13, 1990.

2. See generally ACLU Policy Nos. 60, 63, 65, 71.

3. The ACLU to date has opposed overbroad student speech codes adopted by the University of Connecticut, University of Michigan, University of Wisconsin, and the University of California.

4. Although "harassment," "intimidation," and "invasion of privacy" are imprecise terms susceptible of impermissibly overbroad application, each term defines a type of conduct which is legally proscribed in many jurisdictions when directed at a specific individual or individuals and when intended to frighten, coerce, or unreasonably harry or intrude upon its target. Threatening telephone calls to a minority student's dormitory room, for example, would be proscribable conduct under the terms of this policy. Expressive behavior which has no other effect than to create an unpleasant learning environment, however, would not be the proper subject of regulation. See also Policy No. 316.

5. For example, intimidating phone calls, threats of attack, extortion, and blackmail are unprotected forms of conduct which include an element of verbal or written expression.

6. In determining whether a university disciplinary code impermissibly restricts protected speech, there must be a searching analysis both of the language of the code and the manner in which it is applied. Many factors, which are heavily fact-oriented, must be considered, including time, place, pattern of conduct and, where relevant, the existence of an authority relationship between speaker and target.

7. All courses and programs must be taught consistent with the principles prescribed in ACLU Policy 60.

Suggestions for Further Reading

Anthologies

Matsuda, Mari J., Lawrence, Charles R. III, and Delgado, Richard. *Words That Wound* (Westview, 1993).

Whillock, Rita Kirk, and Slayden, David. *Hate Speech* (London: Sage Publications, 1995).

Basic Concepts

Walker, S. *Hate Speech: The History of an American Controversy* (Lincoln: University of Nebraska Press, 1994).

Alternative Views

Fish, Stanley. *There's No Such Thing as Free Speech, and It's a Good Thing Too* (Oxford: Oxford University Press, 1994).

Hentoff, N. *Free Speech for Me—But Not For Thee* (New York: Harper Collins, 1992).

MacKinnon, Catharine. *Only Words* (Cambridge: Harvard University Press, 1993).

Rauch, J. *Kindly Inquisitors: New Attacks on Free Thought* (Chicago: University Press of Chicago, 1993).

Sunstein, Cass. *Democracy and the Problem of Free Speech* (New York: Free Press, 1993).

Gay and Lesbian Rights

Introduction

Basic Concepts

The prohibition of homosexuality has ancient roots, but its enforcement has usually been haphazard at best because acts between consenting adults make it hard to find a complainant. Even so, twenty-four states and the District of Columbia still have statutes prohibiting homosexual acts. Penalties range from three months in prison or one year's probation to life imprisonment.

Moreover, these statutes prohibit *sodomy*, which involves more than just homosexuals. For example, the Georgia statute whose constitutionality was upheld by the Supreme Court in *Bowers v. Hardwick* holds that "a person commits the offense of sodomy when he performs or submits to any sexual act involving the sex organs of one person and the mouth or anus of another." Sodomy is defined broadly here because the main complaint against homosexual acts—that they are unnatural—also applies to a range of other acts. More specifically, the complaint applies to oral and anal intercourse between heterosexuals, masturbation, and bestiality, as well as homosexual acts.

Now we must understand what is considered unnatural about these acts. One sense of *natural* refers to what is found in nature as contrasted with what is artificial or the product of human artifice. In this sense, homosexuality would seem natural: It is found in virtually every human society. But even if homosexuality is understood to be a product of a certain type of upbringing or socialization and hence artificial, that would hardly seem grounds for condemning it: Much human behavior has a similar origin.

Another sense of natural refers to what is common or statistically normal as contrasted with what is uncommon or statistically abnormal. In this sense, homosexuality would not be natural: Most people are not homosexuals, even though one study found that about half of all American males have engaged in homosexual acts at some time in their lives. But being unnatural in this sense could not be grounds for condemning homosexuality because many traits we most value in people are also statistically abnormal and, hence, unnatural in this sense.

Still another sense of natural refers to a thing's proper function; it is this sense of natural that is frequently used to condemn homosexuality. If we maintain that the proper function of human sexual organs is simply procreation, then any use of those organs for any other purpose would be unnatural. Thus, homosexuality, contraception, masturbation, and bestiality would all be unnatural. But clearly the proper function of human sexual organs is not limited to procreation. These organs are also used to express love and provide pleasure for oneself and others. Given that our sexual organs can be properly used for these other purposes, we would need to argue that every use of these organs must serve their procreative function if we are to be able to condemn homosexuality. No nontheologically based argument has succeeded in establishing this conclusion.* Moreover, once we grant that, for example, contraception and masturbation can be morally permissible, no ground seems to be left, based on the proper functioning of our sexual organs, for denying that homosexuality can be morally permissible as well.

Alternative Views

In Selection 49, John Finnis sets out the following argument against homosexuality:

---

1. In masturbating as in being masturbated or sodomized, one disintegrates oneself in two ways: (a) by treating one's body as an instrument for one's own gratification and (b) by making one's choosing self the quasi-slave of one's experiencing self.
2. By so doing one is not actualizing or experiencing a common good.
3. Marriage with its twofold goals of procreation and friendship is a common good.
4. Marriage is a common good that can be experienced in the orgasmic union of the reproductive organs of a man and a woman united in commitment to that good.
5. This common good makes husband and wife a biological and a personal unit.
6. The common good of friends who are not and cannot be married has nothing to do with procreation and hence their procreative organs cannot make them a biological and a personal unit.
7. Hence, homosexual acts cannot actualize the common good of friendship.
8. Nor is such conduct the participation in some intelligible good because it is not focused on the

---

exercise of a skill but rather on the satisfaction of a desire for one's own pleasure.
9. Such conduct is also deeply hostile to the self-understanding of those members of the community who are committed to real marriage with its shared responsibilities.
10. For this reason, a political community is justified in denying the validity of such conduct, and in taking appropriate steps to discourage it.

The thrust of Finnis's argument is directed not only at homosexual acts, but also at heterosexual masturbation and sodomy, bestiality, and contraception. For Finnis, all of these acts are wrong for the same reason. So, if we accept Finnis's argument, we cannot consistently allow for the moral permissibility of some of these acts but not of others; the moral permissibility of all of these acts must stand or fall together.

In Selection 50, Martha Nussbaum criticizes Finnis for assuming without argument that the purpose of homosexual acts is always the instrumental use of another person's body for one's own gratification. She contends that both the past and the present provide ample evidence against this assumption. Nussbaum also criticizes Finnis for assuming without argument that the only type of community that a sexual relationship can create is a procreative community. Again, she contends that both the past and the present provide ample evidence against this assumption.

In Selection 51, Richard D. Mohr surveys various ways in which homosexuals are discriminated against in our society. Mohr cites one study in which 90 percent of gays and lesbians report that they have been victimized because of their sexual orientation. Mohr argues that being gay or lesbian is not a matter of choice, making it difficult, if not impossible to change one's sexual orientation. Obviously, then, what sodomy statutes demand of homosexuals is that they not act as they are. A difficult charge indeed! Moreover, it is a charge that does not appear to be sup-

---

*Clearly if there is to be freedom of religion, a nontheologically based argument is needed here.

ported by a defensible account of what is wrong with homosexual behavior.

While opposing antisodomy laws, Carl Horowitz (Selection 52) contends that those who decide to live openly as homosexuals should accept the disapproval of those around them. He further contends that although the homosexual rights movement began as an acceptable demand for the state not to interfere with private homosexual behavior, it has evolved into an unacceptable demand for the state to act on behalf of public homosexual behavior. But it is not clear whether Horowitz endorses the same legal rights for homosexuals as for heterosexuals—for example, the right to marriage, the right to job opportunities, and the right to child custody and adoption. On the one hand, Horowitz does require that homosexuals have the same legal rights to noninterference as heterosexuals. On the other hand, he holds that homosexuals should not expect to be treated equally. But shouldn't the equal treatment that homosexuals expect be the same legal rights that heterosexuals enjoy?

Practical Applications

An important Supreme Court case dealing with homosexuality is *Bowers v. Hardwick* (1986). In this case, the issue before the Court was whether the Georgia sodomy statute violates the federal Constitution. In delivering the opinion of the court, Justice White argues that the statute does not because the Constitution does not confer a fundamental right on homosexuals to engage in sodomy. While in previous cases, the Constitution was interpreted to confer a right to decide whether or not to beget or bear a child and a right not to be convicted for possessing and reading obscene material in the privacy of one's home, White argues that the Constitution cannot analogously be interpreted to confer a fundamental right on homosexuals to engage in sodomy. Justice Burger concurs, stressing the ancient roots of

sodomy statutes. Justice Blackmun, joined by Justices Brennan and Marshall, argues that notwithstanding the ancient roots of prohibitions against homosexuality, a right to be let alone that is the underpinning of previous court decisions justifies in this case a right to engage in sodomy at least in the privacy of one's home.

In this case, the majority of the Supreme Court seemed to reach its conclusion by interpreting previous decisions in an excessively literal manner in much the same way that the majority of the court ruled in *Olmstead v. United States* (1928) that warrantless wiretapping did not violate Fourth Amendment prohibitions against search and seizure because the framers of the amendment were not explicitly prohibiting this method of obtaining incriminating evidence. Just as it later repudiated its ruling in *Olmstead*, the Supreme Court in *Romer v. Evans* (Selection 53) recently struck down Colorado's Amendment 2 for imposing a disability on homosexuals—a decision that appears to be at least a partial repudiation of *Bowers v. Hardwick*.

In Selection 54, Ken Corbett tries to explain the fear and hatred that was expressed regarding ending the ban against gays and lesbians in the military. He contends that the fear that some men express is the fear of being desired in the way most men feel only a woman should be desired—as a sexual object. Does this suggest that being desired as a sexual object is not so great after all?

It is also important to note that adherents of all three of our political ideals generally tend to favor granting homosexuals the same rights as heterosexuals. Libertarians favor this view because to do otherwise would deny homosexuals important basic liberties. Welfare liberals favor this view because to do otherwise would deny homosexuals fundamental fairness. Socialists favor this view because to do otherwise would deny homosexuals basic equality.

49. *Homosexual Conduct Is Wrong*

JOHN FINNIS

John Finnis argues against homosexuality on the grounds that it involves treating one's body as an instrument for one's own gratification rather than actualizing or experiencing a common good. He also argues that because homosexual conduct is deeply hostile to the self-understanding of those members of the community who are committed to real marriage with its shared responsibilities, a political community is justified in taking appropriate steps to discourage it.

The underlying thought is on the following lines. In masturbating, as in being masturbated or sodomized, one's body is treated as instrumental for the securing of the experiential satisfaction of the conscious self. Thus one disintegrates oneself in two ways, (1) by treating one's body as a mere instrument of the consciously operating self, and (2) by making one's choosing self the quasi-slave of the experiencing self which is demanding gratification. The worthlessness of the gratification, and the disintegration of oneself, are both the result of the fact that, in these sorts of behavior, one's conduct is not the actualizing and experiencing of a real common good. Marriage, with its double blessing—procreation and friendship—is a real common good. Moreover, it is a common good that can be both actualized and experienced in the orgasmic union of the reproductive organs of a man and a woman united in commitment to that good. Conjugal sexual activity, and—as Plato and Aristotle and Plutarch and Kant all argue—*only* conjugal activity is free from the shamefulness of instrumentalization that is found in masturbating and in being masturbated or sodomized.

At the very heart of the reflections of Plato, Xenophon, Aristotle, Musonius Rufus, and Plutarch on the homoerotic culture around them is the very deliberate and careful judgment that homosexual *conduct* (and indeed all extramarital sexual gratification) is radically incapable of participating in, or actualizing, the common good of friendship. Friends who engage in

such conduct are following a natural impulse and doubtless often wish their genital conduct to be an intimate expression of their mutual affection. But they are deceiving themselves. The attempt to express affection by orgasmic nonmarital sex is the pursuit of an illusion. The orgasmic union of the reproductive organs of husband and wife really unites them biologically (and their biological reality is part of, not merely an instrument of, their *personal* reality); that orgasmic union therefore can actualize and allow them to experience their real common good—their marriage with the two goods, children and friendship, which are the parts of its wholeness as an intelligible common good. But the common good of friends who are not and cannot be married (man and man, man and boy, woman and woman) has nothing to do with their having children by each other, and their reproductive organs cannot make them a biological (and therefore a personal) unit. So their genital acts together cannot do what they may hope and imagine.

In giving their considered judgment that homosexual conduct cannot actualize the good of friendship, Plato and the many philosophers who followed him intimate an answer to the questions why it should be considered shameful to use, or allow another to use, one's body to give pleasure, and why this use of one's body differs from one's bodily participation in countless other activities (e.g., games) in which one takes and/or gets pleasure. Their response is that pleasure is indeed a good, when it is the experienced aspect of one's participation in some intelligible good, such as a task going well, or a game or a dance or a meal or a reunion. Of course, the activation of sexual organs

Reprinted from the legal depositions from the trial in Colorado on the constitutionality of Amendment 2.

with a view to the pleasures of orgasm is sometimes spoken of as if it were a game. But it differs from real games in that its point is not the exercise of skill; rather, this activation of reproductive organs is focused upon the body precisely as a source of pleasure for one's consciousness. So this is a "use of the body" in a strongly different sense of "use." The body now is functioning not in the way one, as a bodily person, acts to instantiate some other intelligible good, but precisely as providing a service to one's consciousness, to satisfy one's desire for satisfaction.

This disintegrity is much more obvious when masturbation is solitary. Friends are tempted to think that pleasuring each other by some forms of mutual masturbation could be an instantiation or actualization or promotion of their friendship. But that line of thought overlooks the fact that if their friendship is not marital . . . activation of their reproductive organs cannot be, in reality, an instantiation or actualization of their friendship's common good. In reality, whatever the generous hopes and dreams with which the loving partners surround their use of their genitals, *that use* cannot express more than is expressed if two strangers engage in genital activity to give each other orgasm, or a prostitute pleasures a client, or a man pleasures himself. Hence, Plato's judgment, at the decisive moment of the *Gorgias,* that there is no important distinction in essential moral worthlessness between solitary masturbation, being sodomized as a prostitute and being sodomized for the pleasure of it. . . .

Societies such as classical Athens and contemporary England (and virtually every other) draw a distinction between behavior found merely (perhaps extremely) offensive (such as eating excrement) and behavior to be repudiated as destructive of human character and relationships. Copulation of humans with animals is repudiated because it treats human sexual activity and satisfaction as something appropriately sought in a manner that, like the coupling of animals, is divorced from the expressing of an intelligible common good—and so treats human bodily life, in one of its most intense activities, as merely animal. The deliberate genital coupling of persons of the same sex is repudiated for a very similar reason. It is not

simply that it is sterile and disposes the participants to an abdication of responsibility for the future of humankind. Nor is it simply that it cannot *really* actualize the mutual devotion that some homosexual persons hope to manifest and experience by it; nor merely that it harms the personalities of its participants by its disintegrative manipulation of different parts of their one personal reality. It is also that it treats human sexual capacities in a way that is deeply hostile to the self-understanding of those members of the community who are willing to commit themselves to real marriage [even one that happens to be sterile] in the understanding that its sexual joys are not mere instruments or accompaniments to, or mere compensation for, the accomplishments of marriage's responsibilities, but rather are the *actualizing and experiencing* of the intelligent commitment to share in those responsibilities. . . .

This pattern of judgment, both widespread and sound, concludes as follows. Homosexual orientation—the deliberate willingness to promote and engage in homosexual acts—is a standing denial of the intrinsic aptness of sexual intercourse to actualize and give expression to the exclusiveness and open-ended commitment of marriage as something good in itself. All who accept that homosexual acts can be a humanly appropriate use of sexual capacities must, if consistent, regard sexual capacities, organs, and acts as instruments to be put to whatever suits the purposes of the individual "self" who has them. Such an acceptance is commonly (and in my opinion rightly) judged to be an active threat to the stability of existing and future marriages; it makes nonsense, for example, of the view that adultery is per se (and not merely because it may involve deception), and in an important way, inconsistent with conjugal love. A political community that judges that the stability and educative generosity of family life is of fundamental importance to the community's present and future can rightly judge that it has a compelling interest in denying that homosexual conduct is a valid, humanly acceptable choice and form of life, and in doing whatever it properly can, as a community with uniquely wide but still subsidiary functions, to discourage such conduct.

50. *Homosexual Conduct Is Not Wrong*

MARTHA NUSSBAUM

Martha Nussbaum criticizes John Finnis for assuming without argument that the purpose of homosexual acts is always the instrumental use of another person's body for one's own gratification. Nussbaum also criticizes Finnis for assuming without argument that the only type of community that a sexual relationship can create is a procreative community.

Finnis's arguments against homosexuality set themselves in a tradition of "natural law" argumentation that derives from ancient Greek traditions. The term "law of nature" was first used by Plato in his *Gorgias.* The approach is further developed by Aristotle, and, above all, by the Greek and Roman Stoics, who are usually considered to be the founders of natural law argumentation in the modern legal tradition, through their influence on Roman law. This being so, it is worth looking to see whether those traditions did in fact use "natural law" arguments to rule homosexual conduct morally or legally substandard.

Plato's dialogues contain several extremely moving celebrations of male–male love, and judge this form of love to be, on the whole, superior to male–female love because of its potential for spirituality and friendship. The *Symposium* contains a series of speeches, each expressing conventional views about this subject that Plato depicts in an appealing light. The speech by Phaedrus points to the military advantages derived by including homosexual couples in a fighting force: Because of their intense love, each will fight better, wishing to show himself in the best light before his lover. The speech of Pausanias criticizes males who seek physical pleasure alone in their homosexual relationships, and praises those who seek in sex deeper spiritual communication. Pausanias mentions that tyrants will sometimes promulgate the view that same-sex relations are shameful in order to discourage the kind of community of dedication to political liberty that such relations foster. The speech of Aris-

tophanes holds that all human beings are divided halves of formerly whole beings, and that sexual desire is the pursuit of one's lost other half; he points out that the superior people in any society are those whose lost "other half" is of the same sex—especially the male–male pairs—since these are likely to be the strongest and most warlike and civically minded people. Finally, Socrates's speech recounts a process of religious-mystical education in which male–male love plays a central guiding role and is a primary source of insight and inspiration into the nature of the good and beautiful.

Plato's *Phaedrus* contains a closely related praise of the intellectual, political, and spiritual benefits of a life centered around male–male love. Plato says that the highest form of human life is one in which a male pursues "the love of a young man along with philosophy," and is transported by passionate desire. He describes the experience of falling in love with another male in moving terms, and defends relationships that are mutual and reciprocal over relationships that are one-sided. He depicts his pairs of lovers as spending their life together in the pursuit of intellectual and spiritual activities, combined with political participation. (Although no marriages for these lovers are mentioned, it was the view of the time that this form of life does not prevent its participants from having a wife at home, whom they saw only rarely and for procreative purposes.)

Aristotle speaks far less about sexual love than does Plato, but it is evident that he too finds in male–male relationships the potential for the highest form of friendship, a friendship based on mutual well-wishing and mutual awareness of good character and

Reprinted from the legal depositions from the trial in Colorado on the constitutionality of Amendment 2.

good aims. He does not find this potential in male–female relationships, since he holds that females are incapable of good character. Like Pausanias in Plato's *Symposium,* Aristotle is critical of relationships that are superficial and concerned only with bodily pleasure; but he finds in male–male relationships—including many that begin in this way—the potential for much richer developments.

The ideal city of the Greek Stoics was built around the idea of pairs of male lovers whose bonds gave the city rich sources of motivation for virtue. Although the Stoics wished their "wise man" to eliminate most passions from his life, they encouraged him to foster a type of erotic love that they defined as "the attempt to form a friendship inspired by the perceived beauty of young men in their prime." They held that this love, unlike other passions, was supportive of virtue and philosophical activity.

Furthermore, Finnis's argument . . . against homosexuality is a bad moral argument by any standard, secular or theological. First of all, it assumes that the purpose of a homosexual act is always or usually casual bodily pleasure and the instrumental use of another person for one's own gratification. But this is a false premise, easily disproved by the long historical tradition I have described and by the contemporary lives of real men and women. Finnis offers no evidence for this premise, or for the equally false idea that procreative relations cannot be selfish and manipulative. Second, having argued that a relationship is better if it seeks not casual pleasure but the creation of a community, he then assumes without argument that the only sort of community a sexual relationship can create is a "procreative community." This if, of course, plainly false. A sexual relationship may create, quite apart from the possibility of procreation, a community of love and friendship, which no religious tradition would deny to be important human goods. Indeed, in many moral traditions, including those of Plato and Aristotle, the procreative community is ranked beneath other communities created by sex, since it is thought that the procreative community will probably not be based on the best sort of friendship and the deepest spiritual concerns. That may not be true in a culture that values women more highly than ancient Greek culture did; but the possibility of love and friendship between individuals of the same sex has not been removed by these historical changes.

51. *Prejudice and Homosexuality*

RICHARD D. MOHR

Richard D. Mohr begins by noting that although gays are a significant percentage of the American population, they are characterized by stereotypes based on false generalizations. He cites one study in which 90 percent of gays and lesbians report that they have been victimized because of their sexual orientation. Mohr also questions whether a correct understanding of Christianity would condemn homosexuality, and he denies that any argument from nature supports such a condemnation. He further argues that if gays were socially accepted, society would be enriched and a step closer to its goal of "liberty and justice for all."

Who are gays anyway? A 1993 *New York Times*–CBS poll found that only one-fifth of Americans suppose that they have a friend or family member who is gay or lesbian. This finding is extraordinary given the number of practicing homosexuals in America. In 1948, Alfred Kinsey published a study of the sex lives of 12,000 white males. Its method was so rigorous that it set the standard for subsequent statistical research across the social sciences, but its results shocked the nation: Thirty-seven percent of the men had at least one homosexual experience to orgasm in their adult lives; an additional thirteen percent had homosexual fantasies to orgasm; four percent were exclusively homosexual in their practices; another five percent had virtually no heterosexual experience, and nearly one fifth had at least as many homosexual as heterosexual experiences. Kinsey's 1953 study of the sex lives of 8,000 women found the occurrence of homosexual behavior at about half the rates for men.

Every second family in the country has a member who is essentially homosexual and many more people regularly have homosexual experiences. Who are homosexuals? They are your friends, your minister, your teacher, your bank teller, your doctor, your mail carrier, your officemate, your roommate, your congressional representative, your sibling, parent, and spouse. They are we. We are everywhere, virtually all ordinary, virtually all unknown.

Ignorance about gays, however, has not stopped people from having strong opinions about them. The void which ignorance leaves has been filled with stereotypes. Society holds two oddly contradictory groups of antigay stereotypes. One revolves around an individual's allegedly confused gender identity: Lesbians are females who want to be, or at least look and act like, men—bull dykes, diesel dykes; while gay men are males who want to be, or at least look and act like, women—queens, fairies, nances, limp-wrists, nellies, sissies, aunties. These stereotypes of mismatches between biological sex and socially defined gender provide the materials through which lesbians and gay men become the butts of ethnic-like jokes. These stereotypes and jokes, though derisive, basically view gays as ridiculous: "How do you identify a bull dyke?" Answer: "She kick-starts her vibrator and rolls her own tampons." Or, "How many fags does it take to change a light bulb?" Answer: "Eight—one to replace it and seven to scream 'Faaaaabulous!'"

The other set of stereotypes revolves around gays as a pervasive sinister conspiratorial threat. The core stereotype here is that of the gay person—especially gay man—as child molester, and more generally as sex-crazed maniac. Homosexuality here is viewed as a vampire-like corruptive contagion. These stereotypes carry with them fears of the very destruction of family and civilization itself. Now, that which is essentially ridiculous can hardly have such a staggering effect. Something must be afoot.

Sense can be made of this incoherent amalgam if the nature of stereotypes is clarified. Stereotypes are not simply false generalizations from a skewed sample of cases examined. Admittedly, false generalizing plays some part in the stereotypes society holds about gays and other groups. If, for instance, one takes as one's sample gay men who are in psychiatric hospitals or prisons, as was done in nearly all early investigations, not surprisingly one will probably find them to be of a crazed or criminal cast. Such false generalizations, though, simply confirm beliefs already held on independent grounds, ones that likely led the investigator to the prison and psychiatric ward to begin with. Evelyn Hooker, who in the late 1950s carried out the first rigorous studies of nonclinical gay men, found that psychiatrists, when presented with case files including all the standard diagnostic psychological profiles—but omitting indications of sexual orientation—were unable to distinguish gay files from nongay ones, even though they believed gay men to be crazy and supposed themselves to be experts in detecting craziness. These studies proved a profound embarrassment to the psychiatric establishment, the financial well-being of which has been substantially enhanced by "curing" allegedly insane gays. The studies led the way to the American Psychiatric Association's finally, in 1973, dropping homosexuality from its registry of mental illnesses. Nevertheless, the stereotype of gays as sick continues apace in the mind of America.

False generalizations help maintain stereotypes, they do not form them. As the story of Hooker's discoveries shows, stereotypes have a life beyond facts; their origins lie in a culture's ideology—the general system of beliefs by which it lives—and they are sustained across generations by diverse cultural transmissions, hardly any of which, including slang and jokes, even purport to have a scientific basis. Stereotypes, then, are not the products of bad science, but reflections of society's conception of itself.

On this understanding, it is easy to see that stereotypes about gays as gender-confused reinforce still powerful gender roles in society. If, as these stereotypes presume and condemn, one is free to choose one's social roles independently of one's biological sex, many guiding social divisions, both domestic and commercial, might be threatened. Blurred would be the socially sex-linked distinctions between breadwinner and homemaker, boss and secretary, doctor and nurse, protector and protected, even God and His world. The accusations "fag" and "dyke" serve in significant part to keep women in their place and to prevent men from breaking ranks and ceding away theirs.

The stereotypes of gays as civilization destroyers function to displace (possibly irresolvable) social problems from their actual source to a remote and (society hopes) manageable one. For example, the stereotype of child molester functions to give the traditionally defined family unit a false sheen of innocence. It keeps the unit from being examined too closely for incest, child abuse, wife-battering, and the terrorizing of women and children by a father's constant threats. The stereotype teaches that the problems of the family are not internal to it, but external.

One can see these cultural forces at work in society's and the media's treatment of current reports of violence, especially domestic violence. When a husband kills his wife or a father rapes his daughter—regular Section B fare even in major urban papers—this is never taken by reporters, columnists, or pundits as evidence that there is something wrong with heterosexuality or with traditional families. These issues are not even raised. But when a homosexual child molestation is reported, it is taken as confirming evidence of the way homosexuals are. One never hears of "heterosexual murders," but one regularly hears of "homosexual" ones.

If this account of stereotypes holds, society has been profoundly immoral. For its treatment of gays is a grand-scale rationalization, a moral sleight-of-hand. The problem is not that society's usual standards of evidence and procedure in decision making have been misapplied to gays, rather when it comes to gays, the standards themselves have simply been ruled out of court and disregarded in favor of mechanisms that encourage unexamined fear and hatred.

Partly because lots of people suppose they don't know any gay people and partly through the maintaining of stereotypes, society at large is unaware of the many ways in which gays are subject to discrimination in consequence of widespread fear and hatred. Contributing to this social ignorance of discrimination is the difficulty for gay people, as an invisible minority, even to complain of discrimination. For if one is gay, to register a complaint would suddenly target oneself as a stigmatized person, and so, especially in the absence of any protection against discrimination, would simply invite additional discrimination. So, discrimination against gays, like rape, goes seriously underreported. Even so, known discrimination is massive.

Annual studies by the National Gay and Lesbian Task Force have consistently found that more than ninety percent of gay men and lesbians have been victims of violence or harassment in some form on the basis of their sexual orientation. Greater than one in five gay men and nearly one in ten lesbians have been punched, hit, or kicked; a quarter of all gays have had objects thrown at them; a third have been chased; a third have been sexually harassed, and fourteen percent have been spit on, all just for being perceived to be gay.

The most extreme form of antigay violence is queerbashing—where groups of young men target a person who they suppose is a gay man and beat and kick him unconscious and sometimes to death amid a torrent of taunts and slurs. Few such cases with gay victims reach the courts. Those that do are marked by inequitable procedures and results. Frequently judges will describe queerbashers as "just All-American Boys." A District of Columbia judge handed suspended sentences to queerbashers whose victim had been stalked, beaten, stripped at knife point, slashed, kicked, threatened with castration, and pissed on, because the judge thought the bashers were good boys at heart—they went to a religious prep school. In 1989, a judge in Dallas handed a sentence he acknowledged as light to the eighteen-year-old murderer of two gay men, because the murderer had killed them in a gay cruising zone, where the judge said they might be molesting children. The judge thereby justified a form of vigilantism that bears an eerie resemblance to the lynching of black men on the grounds that they might molest white women. Indeed, queerbashing has the same function that past lynchings of blacks had—to keep a whole stigmatized group in line. As with lynchings, society has routinely averted its eyes, giving its permission or even tacit approval to violence and harassment.

Police and juries will simply discount testimony from gays; they frequently construe assaults on and murders of gays as "justified" self-defense. The killer simply claims his act was an understandably panicked response to a sexual overture. Alternatively, when guilt seems patent, juries will accept highly implausible "diminished capacity" defenses, as in the case of Dan White's 1978 assassination of openly gay San Francisco city councilman Harvey Milk. Hostess Twinkies made him do it, or so the successful defense went. These inequitable procedures collectively show that the life and liberty of gays, like those of blacks, simply count for less than the life and liberty of members of the dominant culture.

The equitable rule of law is the heart of an orderly society. The collapse of the rule of law for gays shows that society is willing to perpetrate the worst possible injustices against them. As the ethnic and religious wars in the former Yugoslavia have made clear, there is only a difference in degree between the collapse of the rule of law and systematic extermination of members of a population simply for having some group status. In the Nazi concentration camps, gays were forced to wear pink triangles as identifying badges, just as Jews were forced to wear yellow stars. In remembrance of that collapse of the rule of law, the pink triangle has become the chief symbol of the gay rights movement.

Gays are also subject to widespread discrimination in employment. Governments are leading offenders here. They do a lot of discriminating themselves, require that others do it, and set precedents favoring discrimination in the private sector. Lesbians and gay men are barred from serving in the armed forces. The federal government has also denied gays employment in the CIA, FBI, National Security Agency, and the state department. The government refuses to give security clearances to gays and so forces the country's considerable private sector military and aerospace contractors to fire employees known to be gay and to avoid hiring those perceived to be gay. State and local

governments regularly fire gay teachers, policemen, firemen, social workers, and anyone else who has contact with the public. Further, state licensing laws (though frequently honored only in the breech) officially bar gays from a vast array of occupations and professions—everything from doctors, lawyers, accountants, and nurses to hairdressers, morticians, even used car dealers.

Gays are subject to discrimination in a wide variety of other ways, including private-sector employment, public accommodations, housing, insurance of all types, custody, adoption, and zoning regulations that bar "singles" or "nonrelated" couples from living together. A 1988 study by the congressional Office of Technology Assessment found that a third of America's insurance companies openly admit that they discriminate against lesbians and gay men. In nearly half the states, same-sex sexual behavior is illegal, so that the central role of sex to meaningful life is officially denied to lesbians and gay men.

Illegality, discrimination, and the absorption by gays of society's hatred of them all interact to impede and, for some, block altogether the ability of gay men and lesbians to create and maintain significant personal relations with loved ones. Every facet of life is affected by discrimination. Only the most compelling reasons could justify it.

Many people think society's treatment of gays is justified because they think gays are extremely immoral. To evaluate this claim, different senses of "moral" must be distinguished. Sometimes by "morality" is meant the values generally held by members of a society—its mores, norms, and customs. On this understanding, gays certainly are not moral: Lots of people hate them, and social customs are designed to register widespread disapproval of gays. The problem here is that this sense of morality is merely a descriptive one. On this understanding, every society has a morality—even Nazi society, which had racism and mob rule as central features of its "morality" understood in this sense. What is needed in order to use the notion of morality to praise or condemn behavior is a sense of morality that is prescriptive or normative.

As the Nazi example makes clear, that a belief or claim is descriptively moral does not entail that it is normatively moral. A lot of people in a society saying something is good, even over aeons, does not make it so. The rejection of the long history of socially approved and state-enforced slavery is another good example of this principle at work. Slavery would be wrong even if nearly everyone liked it. So consistency and fairness require that one abandon the belief that gays are immoral simply because most people dislike or disapprove of gays.

Furthermore, recent historical and anthropological research has shown that opinion about gays has been by no means universally negative. It has varied widely even within the larger part of the Christian era and even within the Church itself. There are even societies—current ones—where homosexual behavior is not only tolerated but is a universal compulsory part of male social maturation. Within the last thirty years, American society has undergone a grand turnabout from deeply ingrained, near total condemnation to near total acceptance on two emotionally charged "moral" or "family" issues—contraception and divorce. Society holds its current descriptive morality of gays not because it has to, but because it chooses to.

If popular opinion and custom are not enough to ground moral condemnation of homosexuality, perhaps religion can. Such arguments usually proceed along two lines. One claims that the condemnation is a direct revelation of God, usually through the Bible. The other claims to be able to detect condemnation in God's plan as manifested in nature; homosexuality (it is claimed) is "contrary to nature."

One of the more remarkable discoveries of recent gay research is that the Bible may not be as univocal in its condemnation of homosexuality as many have believed. Christ never mentions homosexuality. Recent interpreters of the Old Testament have pointed out that the story of Lot at Sodom is probably intended to condemn inhospitality rather than homosexuality. Further, some of the Old Testament condemnations of homosexuality seem simply to be ways of tarring those of the Israelites' opponents who happen to accept homosexual practices when the Israelites themselves did not. If so, the condemnation is merely a quirk of history and rhetoric rather than a moral precept.

What does seem clear is that those who regularly cite the Bible to condemn an activity like homosexuality do so by reading it selectively. Do ministers who

cite what they take to be condemnations of homosexuality in Leviticus maintain in their lives all the hygienic and dietary laws of Leviticus? If they cite the story of Lot at Sodom to condemn homosexuality, do they also cite the story of Lot in the Cave to praise incestuous rape? It seems then not that the Bible is being used to ground condemnations of homosexuality as much as society's dislike of homosexuality is being used to interpret the Bible.

Even if a consistent portrait of condemnation could be gleaned from the Bible, what social significance should it be given? One of the guiding principles of society, enshrined in the Constitution as a check against the government, is that decisions affecting social policy are not made on religious grounds. The Religious Right has been successful in stymieing sodomy-law reform, in defunding gay safe-sex literature and gay art, and in blocking the introduction of gay materials into school curriculums. If the real ground of the alleged immorality invoked by governments to discriminate against gays is religious (as it seems to be in these cases), then one of the major commitments of our nation is violated. Religious belief is a fine guide around which a person might organize his own life, but an awful instrument around which to organize someone else's life.

People also try to justify society's treatment of gays by saying they are unnatural. Though the accusation of unnaturalness looks whimsical, when applied to homosexuality, it is usually delivered with venom of forethought. It carries a high emotional charge, usually expressing disgust and evincing queasiness. Probably it is nothing but an emotional charge. For people get equally disgusted and queasy at all sorts of things that are perfectly natural, yet that could hardly be fit subjects for moral condemnation. Two typical examples in current American culture are some people's responses to mothers' suckling in public and to women who do not shave body hair. Similarly people fling the term "unnatural" against gays in the same breath and with the same force as when they call gays "sick" and "gross." When people have strong emotional reactions, as they do in these cases, without being able to give good reasons for them, they are thought of not as operating morally, but as being obsessed and manic. So the feelings of disgust that some people have toward gays will hardly ground a charge of immorality.

When "nature" is taken in technical rather than ordinary usages, it also cannot ground a charge of homosexual immorality. When unnatural means "by artifice" or "made by humans," it can be pointed out that virtually everything that is good about life is unnatural in this sense. The chief feature that distinguishes people from other animals is people's very ability to make over the world to meet their needs and desires. Indeed people's well-being depends on these departures from nature. On this understanding of human nature and the natural, homosexuality is perfectly unobjectionable; it is simply a means by which some people adapt nature to fulfill their desires and needs.

Another technical sense of natural is that something is natural and so, good, if it fulfills some function in nature. On this view, homosexuality is unnatural because it violates the function of genitals, which is to produce babies. One problem with this view is that lots of bodily parts have lots of functions and just because some one activity can be fulfilled by only one organ (say, the mouth for eating), this activity does not condemn other functions of the organ to immorality (say, the mouth for talking, licking stamps, blowing bubbles, or having sex). So the possible use of the genitals to produce children does not, without more, condemn the use of the genitals for other purposes, say, achieving ecstasy and intimacy.

The functional view of nature will only provide a morally condemnatory sense to the unnatural if a thing that might have many uses has but one proper function to the exclusion of other possible functions. But whether this is so cannot be established simply by looking at the thing. For what is seen is all its possible functions. The notion of function seemed like it might ground moral authority, but instead it turns out that moral authority is needed to define proper function.

Some people try to fill in this moral authority by appeal to the "design" or "order" of an organ, saying, for instance, that the genitals are designed for the purpose of procreation. But these people cheat intellectually if they do not make explicit who the designer and orderer is. If the "who" is God, we are back to square one—holding others accountable to one's own religious beliefs.

Further, ordinary moral attitudes about childbearing will not provide the needed supplement which would produce a positive obligation to use the genitals for procreation. Though there are local exceptions, society's general attitude toward a childless couple is that of pity not censure—even if the couple could have children. The pity may be an unsympathetic one, that is, not registering a course one would choose for oneself, but this does not make it a course one would require of others. The couple who discovers they cannot have children are viewed not as having thereby had a debt cancelled, but rather as having to forgo some of the richness of life, just as a quadriplegic is viewed not as absolved from some moral obligation to hop, skip, and jump, but as missing some of the richness of life. Consistency requires then that, at most, gays who do not or cannot have children are to be pitied rather than condemned. What *is* immoral is the willful preventing of people from achieving the richness of life. Immorality in this regard lies with those social customs, regulations, and statutes that prevent lesbians and gay men from establishing blood or adoptive families, not with gays themselves.

Many gays would like to raise or foster children—perhaps those alarming number of gay kids who have been beaten up and thrown out of their "families" for being gay. And indeed many lesbian and gay male couples are now raising robust, happy families where children are the blessings of adoption, artificial insemination, or surrogacy. The country is experiencing something approaching a gay and lesbian babyboom.

Sometimes people attempt to establish authority for a moral obligation to use bodily parts in a certain fashion simply by claiming that moral laws are natural laws and vice versa. On this account, inanimate objects and plants are good in that they follow natural laws by necessity, animals follow them by instinct, and persons follow them by a rational will. People are special in that they must first discover the laws that govern them. Now, even if one believes the view—dubious in the post-Newtonian, post-Darwinian world— that natural laws in the usual sense ($e = mc^2$, for instance) have some moral content, it is not at all clear how one is to discover the laws in nature that apply to people.

On the one hand, if one looks to people themselves for a model—and looks hard enough—one finds amazing variety, including homosexual relations as a social ideal (as in upper-class fifth-century Athens) and even as socially mandatory (as in some Melanesian initiation rites today). When one looks to people, one is simply unable to strip away the layers of social custom, history, and taboo in order to see what's really there to any degree more specific than that people are the creatures that make over their world and are capable of abstract thought. That this is so should raise doubts that neutral principles are to be found in human nature that will condemn homosexuality.

On the other hand, if one looks to nature apart from people for models, the possibilities are staggering. There are fish that change sex over their lifetimes: Should we "follow nature" and be operative transsexuals? Orangutans, genetically our next of kin, live completely solitary lives without social organization of any kind among adults: Ought we to "follow nature" and be hermits? There are many species where only two members per generation reproduce: Shall we be bees? The search in nature for people's purpose far from finding sure models for action is likely to leave one morally rudderless.

But (it might also be asked) aren't gays willfully the way they are? It is generally conceded that if sexual orientation is something over which an individual—for whatever reason—has virtually no control, then discrimination against gays is presumptively wrong, as it is against racial and ethnic classes.

Attempts to answer the question whether or not sexual orientation is something that is reasonably thought to be within one's own control usually appeal simply to various claims of the biological or "mental" sciences. But the ensuing debate over genes, hormones, hypothalamuses, twins, early childhood development, and the like is as unnecessary as it is currently inconclusive. All that is needed to answer the question is to look at the actual experience of lesbians and gay men in current society and it becomes fairly clear that sexual orientation is not likely a matter of choice.

On the one hand, the "choice" of the gender of a sexual partner does not seem to express a trivial desire which might as easily be fulfilled by a simple substitution of the desired object. Picking the gender of a sex partner is decidedly dissimilar, that is, to such activities as picking a flavor of ice cream. If an ice cream parlor is out of one's flavor, one simply picks another. And if people were persecuted, threatened with jail terms, shattered careers, loss of family and

housing and the like for eating, say, rocky road ice cream, no one would ever eat it. Everyone would pick another easily available flavor. That gay people abide in being gay even in the face of persecution suggests that being gay is not a matter of easy choice.

On the other hand, even if establishing a sexual orientation is not like making a relatively trivial choice, perhaps it is relevantly like making the central and serious life-choices by which individuals try to establish themselves as being of some type or having some occupation. Again, if one examines gay experience, this seems not to be the general case. For one virtually never sees anyone setting out to become a homosexual, in the way one does see people setting out to become doctors, lawyers, and bricklayers. One does not find gays-to-be picking some end—"At some point in the future, I want to become a homosexual"—and then setting about planning and acquiring the ways and means to that end, in the way one does see people deciding that they want to become lawyers, and then sees them plan what courses to take and what sort of temperaments, habits, and skills to develop in order to become lawyers. Typically gays-to-be simply find themselves having homosexual encounters and yet, at least initially, resisting quite strongly the identification of being homosexual. Such a person even very likely resists having such encounters, but ends up having them anyway. Only with time, luck, and great personal effort, but sometimes never, does the person gradually come to accept her or his orientation, to view it as a given material condition of life, coming as materials do with certain capacities and limitations. The person begins to act in accordance with his or her orientation and its capacities, seeing its actualization as a requisite for an integrated personality and as a central component of personal well-being. As a result, the experience of coming out to oneself has for gays the basic structure of a discovery, not the structure of a choice. And far from signaling immorality, coming out to others affords one of the few remaining opportunities in ever more bureaucratic, technological, and socialistic societies to *manifest* courage.

How would society at large be changed if gays were socially accepted? Suggestions to change social policy with regard to gays are invariably met with claims that to do so would invite the destruction of civilization itself: After all, isn't that what did Rome in? Actually, Rome's decay paralleled not the flourishing of homosexuality but its repression under the later Christianized emperors. Predictions of American civilization's imminent demise have been as premature as they have been frequent. Civilization has shown itself to be rather resilient here, in large part because of the country's traditional commitments to respect for privacy, to individual liberties, and especially to people minding their own business. These all give society an open texture and the flexibility to try out things to see what works. And because of this, one now need not speculate about what changes reforms in gay social policy might bring to society at large. For many reforms have already been tried.

Half the states have decriminalized lesbian and gay male sex acts. Can you guess which of the following states still have sodomy laws: Wisconsin, Minnesota; New Mexico, Arizona; Vermont, New Hampshire; Nebraska, Kansas? One from each pair does and one does not have sodomy laws. And yet one would be hard pressed to point out any substantial social differences between the members of each pair. (If you're interested: It's the second of each pair with them.) Empirical studies have shown that there is no increase in other crimes in states that have decriminalized.

Neither has the passage of legislation barring discrimination against gays ushered in the end of civilization. Nearly a hundred counties and municipalities, including some of the country's largest cities (like Chicago and New York City) have passed such statutes, as have eight states: Wisconsin, Connecticut, Massachusetts, Hawaii, New Jersey, Vermont, California, and Minnesota. Again, no more brimstone has fallen in these places than elsewhere. Staunchly anti-gay cities, like Miami and Houston, have not been spared the AIDS crisis.

Berkeley, California, followed by a couple dozen other cities including New York, has even passed "domestic partner" legislation giving gay couples at least some of the same rights to city benefits as are held by heterosexually married couples, and yet Berkeley has not become more weird than it already was. A number of major universities (like Stanford and the University of Chicago) and respected corporations (like Levi Strauss and Company, the Montefiore Medical Center of New York, and Apple Computer, Inc.) are also following Berkeley's lead.

Seemingly hysterical predictions that the American family would collapse if such reforms would pass proved false, just as the same dire predictions that the availability of divorce would lessen the ideal and desirability of marriage proved unfounded. Indeed if current discrimination, which drives gays into hiding and into anonymous relations, ended, far from seeing gays destroying American families, one would see gays forming them.

Virtually all gays express a desire to have a permanent lover. But currently society and its discriminatory impulse make gay coupling very difficult. It is difficult for people to live together as couples without having their sexual orientation perceived in the public realm and becoming targets for discrimination. Life in hiding is a pressure-cooker existence not easily shared with another. Members of nongay couples are asked to imagine what it would take to erase every trace of their own sexual orientation for even just one week.

Even against oppressive odds, gays have shown an amazing tendency to nest. And those gay couples who have survived the odds show that the structure of more usual couplings is not a matter of destiny, but of personal responsibility. The so-called basic unit of society turns out not to be a unique immutable atom, but can adopt different parts, be adapted to different needs, and even be improved. Gays might even have a thing or two to teach others about divisions of labor, the relation of sensuality and intimacy, and the stages of development in such relations.

If discrimination ceased, gay men and lesbians would enter the mainstream of the human community openly and with self-respect. The energies that the typical gay person wastes in the anxiety of leading a day-to-day existence of systematic disguise would be released for use in personal flourishing. From this release would be generated the many spin-off benefits that accrue to a society when its individual members thrive.

Society would be richer for acknowledging another aspect of human diversity. Families with gay members would develop relations based on truth and trust rather than lies and fear. And the heterosexual majority would be better off for knowing that they are no longer trampling their gay friends and neighbors.

Finally, and perhaps paradoxically, in extending to gays the rights and benefits reserved for its dominant culture, America would confirm its deeply held vision of itself as a morally progressing nation, a nation itself advancing and serving as a beacon for others—especially with regard to human rights. The words with which our national pledge ends—"with liberty and justice for all"—are not a description of the present, but a call for the future. America is a nation given to a prophetic political rhetoric that acknowl-edges that morality is not arbitrary and that justice is not merely the expression of the current collective will. It is this vision that led the black civil rights movement to its successes. Those senators and representatives who opposed that movement and its centerpiece, the 1964 Civil Rights Act, on obscurantist grounds, but who lived long enough and were noble enough came in time to express their heartfelt regret and shame at what they had done. It is to be hoped and someday to be expected that those who now grasp at anything to oppose the extension of that which is best about America to gays will one day feel the same.

---

52. *Homosexuality's Legal Revolution*

CARL F. HOROWITZ

While opposing antisodomy laws, Carl Horowitz contends that homosexuals who decide to live openly as homosexuals should accept the disapproval of those around them. He further contends that while the homosexual rights movement began as an acceptable demand for the state not to interfere with private homosexual behavior, it has evolved into an unacceptable demand for the state to interfere on behalf of public homosexual behavior.

Last April, a brief series of events occurred in a Madison, Wisconsin, restaurant that spoke volumes about the current character of the homosexual rights movement. An employee of the Espresso Royal Cafe asked two women—presumably lesbians—to refrain from passionately kissing as they sat at a window table. Madison's gay community was not amused. The very next day, about 125 homosexual demonstrators showed up on the premises, and conducted a "kiss-in" for several minutes. A spokeswoman for the protesters, Malvene Collins, demanded, "You say gays and lesbians cannot show affection here? Why not here but in every other restaurant in Madison?" The establishment's chastised owner, Donald Hanigan, assured the crowd, "I regret that this incident ever happened. I want all of you to come in here every day."[1]

In October, several dozen homosexual males, many dressed in women's clothing, openly hugged and kissed in a terminal of Seattle-Tacoma Airport, and handed out condoms and leaflets to travelers. Matt Nagel, spokesman for the Seattle chapter of a new homosexual organization, Queer Nation, seemed to sum up the feeling among militants in the local homosexual community. "We're going to homophobic bars, we're going to pack them, we're going to be openly affectionate, we're going to dance together and make it uncomfortable for all the straight people there."[2]

At the same time in Chicago, six homosexual couples staged a "kiss-in" at the cosmetics counter of a Bloomingdale's department store until they were escorted out by security guards. Far from being deterred, the couples shortly went down to the cafeteria of a nearby office building, where they resumed their public display of affection.[3]

Dr. Horowitz is a policy analyst at The Heritage Foundation in Washington, D.C. He formerly taught at Virginia Polytechnic Institute.

A B*id for L*egitimacy

After some two decades of confrontation, the homosexual rights movement is consolidating its bid for legitimacy. The phrase "Out of the closet, and into the streets" sounds quaint. That battle has already been won. Openly homosexual adults are certainly in the streets—and in stores, airports, and "homophobic" bars. Openly gay television characters, each with handsome, well-scrubbed looks, populate daytime and evening drama. Gay-oriented news programming is available on radio and television. Homosexual activists have all but completed their campaign to persuade the nation's educational establishment that homosexuality is normal "alternative" behavior, and thus any adverse reaction to it is akin to a phobia, such as fear of heights, or an ethnic prejudice, such as anti-Semitism.[4]

The movement now stands on the verge of fully realizing its use of law to create a separate homosexual society paralleling that of the larger society in every way, and to intimidate heterosexuals uncomfortable about coming into contact with it. Through aggressive lobbying by such gay organizations as the Human Rights Campaign Fund, the Lambda Legal Defense and Education Fund, and the National Gay and Lesbian Task Force, the first part of that mission has enjoyed enormous success. About 90 counties and municipalities now have ordinances banning discrimination on the basis of gender orientation. There are roughly 50 openly gay public officials, up from less than a half-dozen in 1980.[5]

Gay couples increasingly receive the full benefits of marriage, if not through state recognition of homosexual marriage ceremonies, then through enactment of domestic partnership laws.[6] The State of California recently took a big step toward legalization of such marriages: This December it announced that "nontraditional" families, including homosexual couples, could formally register their unions as "unincorporated nonprofit associations."[7] Divorced gay parents are receiving with increasing frequency the right to custody of natural children. Gay adults without children are increasingly receiving the right to adopt them. Aspiring homosexual clergy are demanding—and receiving—the right to be ordained. Openly gay teachers are teaching in public schools. Homosexual soldiers, aware that their sexual orientation is grounds for expulsion from the military, openly declare their proclivities.

A Federal gay rights bill is the ultimate prize, and homosexual activists are blunt and resolute in pursuing such legislation. For example, Jeff Levi, spokesman for the National Gay and Lesbian Task Force, remarked at a press conference coinciding with the national gay march on Washington in October 1987:

> . . . we are no longer seeking just a right to privacy and a protection from wrong. We also have a right—as heterosexual Americans already have—to see government and society affirm our lives. . . . Until our relationships are recognized in the law—through domestic partner legislation or the definition of beneficiaries, for example—until we are provided with the same financial incentives in tax law and government programs to affirm our family relationships, then we will not have achieved equality in American society.[8]

Yet homosexual activists know that this legal revolution will never succeed without the unpleasant task of coercing heterosexuals into masking their displeasure with homosexuality. It is thus not enough merely to break down all existing barriers to homosexual affection being expressed through marriage, child-rearing, or employment. The law must additionally be rewritten to make it as difficult as possible for heterosexuals to avoid contact with such displays, or to show discomfort toward them.

This two-edged approach would create a world in which stringent laws at all levels, aggressively enforced and strictly interpreted, force business owners to refuse to discriminate against the openly homosexual in patronage, leasing, and hiring. Removing overtly homosexual patrons from a bar, an airport, or any other public space would result in heavy fines and even jail sentences against property owners or their employees (or in lieu of these sanctions, mandatory purgation). Derogatory remarks directed at homosexuals, even with sexuality only incidental, would likewise result in criminal penalties.

1990: A Pivotal Year

The year 1990 was pivotal for the homosexual legal revolution. The states of Massachusetts and Wisconsin in the late 1980s had enacted laws forbidding discrimination against homosexuals. The victories would come quickly now, especially at the local level. In March, the City of Pittsburgh voted to include sexual orientation as a right protected under the City Code. In October, Stanford University allowed homosexual couples to qualify for university student housing. In November, voters in San Francisco, buoyed by a heavy turnout of that city's large gay population, produced a "lavender sweep," not only passing Proposition K, a city initiative to allow homosexuals to register as domestic partners at City Hall (a similar measure was defeated in 1989), but electing two openly lesbian candidates to the City Board of Supervisors, and an openly homosexual male candidate to the Board of Education.

Voters in Seattle refused to repeal an existing gender orientation ordinance. Congress did its part early in the year by overwhelmingly passing the Hate Crimes Statistics Act (or Hate Crimes Act), which requires the Justice Department to publish hate crime statistics according to classifications that include sexual orientation.[9]

This agenda would likely have been even further realized with Michael Dukakis as President. In 1988, his Presidential campaign organization placed an advertisement in a New York homosexual newspaper, pledging, "As President, I will fight for Federal legislation to add a prohibition against discrimination based on sexual orientation to the existing protections of the 1964 Civil Rights Act."[10] Rank-and-file pressure on even a centrist Democratic Presidential candidate would be difficult to fend off. Rule 5C of the National Democratic Party currently states: "With respect to groups such as . . . lesbians and gay men . . . each state party shall develop and submit party outreach programs for such groups identified in their plans, including recruitment, education and training, in order to receive full participation by such groups in the delegate-selection process and at all levels of party affairs."

For close to 20 years, old-time party regulars have been walking on eggshells on this issue, praying it would go away, yet never really having the stomach for open conflict. Now the day of reckoning looms. Democratic candidates and party officials opposing this recent requirement (none dare call it a quota) must be willing either silently to watch the slow disintegration of their party, or to speak out and face de facto expulsion. It is therefore not surprising that all candidates for the Democratic Party Presidential nomination in 1988, in response to a questionnaire circulated by the National Gay and Lesbian Task Force, promised to support a Federal gay rights bill.

Republicans offer only little more resistance. The few . . . who do speak out against the homosexual lobby—most notably, U.S. Representative William Dannemeyer of California—enjoy little support from their party.[11] One need only remember how reluctantly and belatedly Congress acted merely to reprimand U.S. Representative Barney Frank, Massachusetts Democrat, for aiding a male roommate in running a prostitution service from the basement of his Washington, D.C., townhouse. One need only remember also how quickly a Bush White House official, Doug Wead, who circulated a memorandum complaining of the high visibility of gay activists at the Hate Crimes Act signing ceremony, was fired from his post.

"Gay Civil Rights"

The homosexual lobby speaks of itself as struggling for "civil rights." "The gay community's goal is integration—just as it was with Martin Luther King," argues homosexual activist and San Francisco Board of Supervisors President Harry Britt.[12] Yet, underneath the surface, gay civil rights seems analogous to Black "civil rights" *after* Reverend King's death. Far from seeking integration with the heterosexual world, it vehemently avoids it. More important, the movement seeks to win sinecures through the state, and over any objections by "homophobic" opposition. With a cloud of a heavy fine or even a jail sentence hanging over a mortgage lender, a rental agent, or a job interviewer who might be discomforted by them, homosexuals under these laws can win employment, credit, housing, and other economic entitlements. Heterosexuals would have no right to discriminate against homosexuals, but apparently, not vice versa.

Libertarians as well as traditionalists ought to be troubled by this.

Consider a recent controversy in Madison, Wisconsin, as noted earlier, a national bastion of "enlightened" attitudes. Three single women had recently moved into the same apartment, and one announced that she was a lesbian. The other two, not unreasonably, asked her to move. The lesbian filed a grievance with the local Human Rights Board, and, predictably, won. The shock came in the punishment. The two heterosexual women had to pay $1,500 in "damages" to the lesbian, send her a public letter of apology, attend a two-hour "briefing' on homosexuality (conducted, needless to say, by homosexuals), and submit to having their living arrangements monitored for two years.[13]

With such laws in effect, this outcome would not be so much played out as simply avoided. Let one hypothetical example suffice, one that no doubt *has* been played out regularly, and that goes a long way in explaining why in any metropolitan area gays tend to cluster in a few neighborhoods.

A man enters an apartment rental office, inquiring about a vacancy. He openly indicates he is a homosexual, or at least implies as much through certain mannerisms. For good measure, he brings along his lover. The rental manager fudges, clears his throat, and says, "Well, er, several people are looking at the apartment. Call me later." An hour later, a second man, alone, walks in. He does not announce his sexuality. Who gets the apartment?

In the absence of gay protectionism, and assuming equal incomes, the manager (sighing with relief) would probably award the apartment to the second applicant. Gay militants would cry, "Discrimination!"—and miss the point. Discrimination based on sexual orientation is fundamentally different from that based on race. Homosexuality constitutes a behavioral, not a genetic trait. It is within the moral right of a landlord, job interviewer, banker, or anyone else performing a "gatekeeper" function to discourage economically risky behavior, sexual or otherwise. Libertarian columnist Doug Bandow articulates this:

> The point is, homosexuals have no right to force others to accept or support their lifestyle. Certainly government has no business discriminating against them: Antisodomy laws, for instance, are a vicious intrusion in the most intimate form of human conduct. And gays who pay taxes have as much right to government services and employment as anyone else.
>
> But someone who decides to live openly as a homosexual should accept the disapproval of those around him. For many Americans still believe that there is a fundamental, unchangeable moral code by which men are to live. . . .
>
> Using government to bludgeon homophobics into submission is even more intolerant than the original discrimination.[14]

Under normal circumstances, the rental manager would not want to lease to gays who, once moved in, might tell their friends that the neighborhood could have possibilities as a "gay" one. Word-of-mouth travels fast within their world. Beyond a certain "tipping-point," many heterosexual residents near and within the complex, rather than risk feeling stigmatized, would choose to move. Their places largely would be taken by overt homosexuals.

In fact this is exactly how neighborhoods such as Castro (San Francisco), West Hollywood (formerly part of Los Angeles, now separately incorporated largely due to gay pressure), the West Village (New York City), and Dupont Circle (Washington, D.C.) all rapidly developed reputations as "gay neighborhoods," and how large sections of Martha's Vineyard, Fire Island, and Rehoboth Beach became "gay resorts."[15] The tipping-point principle also applies to public facilities such as restaurants. At the Grapevine Cafe in Columbus, Ohio, for example, heterosexual customers stopped coming when the clientele became heavily gay.[16]

What would happen with a sexual orientation law in place? The rental manager knows that if he turns down an openly homosexual applicant, he risks prosecution. Any rejection can serve as proof of discriminatory intent, even with factors such as length of employment, income, and previous tenant record taken into account.[17] In response to such a fear, the manager, though reluctantly, is likely to award the apartment to the homosexual.

For gay activists, therein lies the payoff. By codifying into law "protection" of homosexual mannerisms, they can intimidate gatekeepers into providing job security and housing for the openly homosexual.

Thus, without necessarily mentioning anything about quotas or, for that matter, homosexuality, law in the United States is increasingly mandating *homosexual affirmative action*.[18] Such law has the same intent as the recently vetoed Kennedy–Hawkins Civil Rights Act.

Sexual Schism

If the homosexual rights movement is in large measure an affirmative action strategy, certain consequences should be evident, all of which already are on their way to being entrenched. Most obviously, American culture is experiencing a sexual schism as deep as any racial one. There are other damaging ramifications.

First, wherever such laws exist, they will attract homosexuals to the jurisdictions enacting them. Common sense dictates that any community laying out the welcome mat for homosexuality lays it for homosexuals, implicitly telling others to kindly step aside. Aside from legal protection, there is political strength in concentrated numbers. Most aspiring elected officials in San Francisco, for example, must now pay homage to the achievement of local gays, and show up at gay events. As Proposition K coordinator Jean Harris remarked following the November elections, "We've shocked the world and made history with this lavender sweep. . . . It's clear that if you don't get the support of the gay-lesbian community you're going to be in trouble."[19] While the homosexual voting bloc will never be a majority in any city, even San Francisco, it can wield enormous veto power over the objections of all other blocs.

Second, having learned the power of the gate-keeper role, many homosexuals will seek to become gatekeepers themselves. It takes no great stretch of imagination, for example, to understand that the growing number of college administrations severely punishing antigay harassment (even if such "harassment" takes no more sinister a form than a satirical campus newspaper editorial or cartoon) has much to do with the growing number of college administrators and faculty who are themselves homosexual (and possibly were hired on that very basis).[20] Nor does it take much imagination to understand that gay employers have more reason than ever to favor homosexuals in their hiring and promotion practices.

Third, these laws will create market bottlenecks. Heterosexuals and even "closeted" homosexuals will be at a competitive disadvantage for jobs and housing. For them, prices will be higher and wages lower than in the absence of such "safeguards." This is especially significant since gay culture is visible in high-cost cities such as New York and San Francisco.

Gays view economic victories to be won here, and few have been as resounding as the *Braschi* decision.[21] In July 1989, the New York State Court of Appeals ruled that a gay lover had the right to stay in his deceased partner's rent-controlled apartment because he qualified as a member of the partner's family, a decision recently upheld by the Appellate Division of the State Supreme Court. "We conclude that the term 'family,'" the lower court argued, "should not be rigidly restricted to those people who have formalized their relationship by obtaining, for instance, a marriage certificate or an adoption order. . . . A more realistic, and certainly equally valid, view of a family includes two adult lifetime partners whose relationship is long term and characterized by an emotional and financial commitment and interdependence."[22]

Gay activists understandably were elated at this imprimatur for homosexual marriage; they know household economics. Homosexual couples defined as "married" could reduce not only their housing costs, but also their income taxes (by filing jointly), pensions, and insurance premiums. They also would qualify for paid medical leave, spousal bereavement leave, and other employee benefits. At this writing, the San Francisco chapter of the American Civil Liberties Union is considering suing several locally based corporations that deny benefits to their homosexual employees' partners.[23]

Fourth, the new legalism will increase heterosexual anger—and even violence—toward homosexuals. Reports of "gay bashing" (the real kind) simultaneous with increased homosexual visibility cannot be a co-incidence. What economist Thomas Sowell[24] and psychologist Stephen Johnson[25] have each revealed about racial affirmative action can apply to sexual affirmative action as well; unprotected groups, lacking recourse through rule of law, may resort to violence against innocent members of protected groups. Those who make it their bailiwick to monitor every incident of petty harassment of gays are impervious to any possibility that when laws force heterosexuals to bottle up dialogue, their feelings may erupt in more destructive ways. *Gay bashing, then, is in some measure a product of the very laws designed to punish it.*

The Language of Victimhood

The radical homosexual movement seeks centralization of state power in the name of "civil rights." What began as a demand for the state not to interfere [with] private homosexual behavior has evolved into a demand for the state to intercede on behalf of public homosexual behavior. In so doing, the movement has advanced further into the same totalitarian netherworld that various Black and feminist movements also have come to occupy. In each case, activists proclaim "victim" status, malign the intentions of critics, and demand government entitlements that necessarily discriminate against others. "Once upon a time," syndicated columnist Paul Greenberg writes in *The Washington Times*, "civil rights were unifying and universal—a way to open society to the claims of individual merit. Now 'civil rights' becomes a code word for dividing society into competing, resentful groups."[26]

Gay militants know the cue-card language of victimhood. For example, Gara LaMarche and William B. Rubenstein write in *The Nation*, "The targets of the 1950s witch hunts were both Communists and other leftists, labeled 'subversives,' and homosexuals, labeled 'sexual perverts.' Today, as the cold war mentality collapses, enemies are again being found at home, but this time lesbians and gay men are leading the list."[27] With former President Ronald Reagan and Cardinal John O'Connor leading the list of personages in the "McCarthy" role, the authors can make believe this really is the 1950s.

Just as opposing current racial and ethnic civil rights orthodoxies inevitably invites being labelled "racist" and "ethnocentric," opposing the current homosexual orthodoxy almost guarantees being denounced as "homophobic." One is simply not free to not pay tribute to them. The few people willing to toe the line pay the consequences. Pete Hamill, hardly an ally of the hard Right, knows this too well. Having written a column in the August 1990 *Esquire* sharply critical of those aggressively politicizing their homosexuality (though with genuine warmth for his homosexual friends), he was subsequently subject to constant attack by ACT-UP (AIDS Coalition to Unleash Power) and other homosexual gendarmes.[28] When early in 1990, Martin Luther King III remarked in a speech in Poughkeepsie, New York, that "something must be wrong" with homosexuals, enraged gay leaders demanded (and got) an apology.

Heterosexuals need not even fire the first shot to invoke gay wrath. When a pair of Queer Nation activists disrupted the airing of the December 14, 1990, segment of *The Arsenio Hall Show*, they insisted that the host explain why so few of his guests were gay. Unappeased by Hall's assurance that many are, the activists continued their on-camera ranting for about 10 minutes. Hall, of course, must now bear the onus as a "homophobe."[29]

Gay activists may incessantly speak of their "rights," yet oddly care little for those of others. Articles in *Outweek*, a year-old tabloid dedicated to exposing homosexual liaisons (real or imagined) of public figures believed otherwise to be heterosexual, routinely call for removing freedom of speech from anyone alleged to be "homophobic."[30] A placard at a recent gay rights march in Washington read, "BAN HOMOPHOBIA, NOT HOMOSEXUALITY."[31] Radical homosexuals apparently do not reciprocate when it comes to the First Amendment.

The most shameful example of the gays' civil rights double standard . . . was their temporarily successful attempt to blackball Andy Rooney, long-time humorist of CBS's *60 Minutes* program. The details of the saga—Rooney's allegedly antigay comments on a CBS news special reviewing the events of 1989;[32] the subsequent storm of protest by gay militants; Rooney's explanation to them in the form of a letter to and an interview with a national gay newspaper, the *Advocate*; the anti-Black comments falsely attributed to Rooney in the interview; and his three-month suspension without pay from CBS—are well-known.[33]

[The] interview was a pure frame-up [and] homosexual militants routinely make hate-filled denunciations of "straights." More ominous is how quickly CBS moved to institute damage control, choosing to take the word of a gay cub reporter, lacking any tape of the interview, over that of Mr. Rooney, a loyal and popular CBS employee for some four decades. This is how CBS, which now hires a homosexual group to conduct "gay sensitivity seminars" for its news personnel, responded to its fear of a lawsuit or a boycott of network sponsors. The network's action was an indication of how readily small businesses might capitulate under a federal gay civil rights law.

Rooney . . . was reinstated on *60 Minutes* before the three months, but no thanks to any good graces from CBS top brass. Give the credit instead to Rooney's supportive *60 Minutes* colleagues and the show's falling Nielsen ratings. Yet Rooney, chastened, had to issue a public apology prior to reinstatement, one that virtually forfeited his right to say "offensive" things about gays in the future, ironic since his job requires being cantankerously peevish. Free speech lost.

Homosexual militants also have little use for the right to privacy save their own. They view any public figure's possible homosexual behavior as grist for voyeuristic public consumption. The mere existence of a spurious scandal sheet like *Outweek* ought to outrage the sensibilities of all individualists. The hypocrisy of it all begs a comparison. Suppose the *National Enquirer* or some other general circulation gossip magazine exposed as homosexuals the same celebrities that *Outweek* does. Homosexual activists would properly see this as character assassination. Yet . . . when a homosexual publication engages in the identical practice, it is creating "positive gay role models."[34]

"Now, the idea that one must be either in the closet or out of it is an invention of those who would politicize sex and abolish privacy," Thomas Short writes in *National Review.* "They wrongly make whatever is not publicly proclaimed seem secret, furtive. This dichotomy of being either in the closet or out of it should not exist. . . . We all have some secrets to keep."[35] Homosexual radicals do not keep sexual secrets. Since a homosexual act is political, even the most casual encounter by an otherwise heterosexual person must be made public, at whatever cost to that person. *Outweek*, and the mentality to which it caters, is more than indiscreet; it is totalitarian.

The Growing Threat of Violence

There is something about encountering homosexuality in its militant and pugnacious form that touches a deep, almost reflexive anger, even among most heterosexual liberals. That is why attempts at "mainstreaming" gay culture, even when holding an olive branch, are bound to fail. One of the saddest books to appear in recent years is *After the Ball: How America Will Conquer Its Fear and Hatred of Gays in the 90s.*[36] Authors Marshall Kirk and Hunter Madsen, both homosexual, advocate a national campaign to cheerfully "sell" gay culture. They suggest, for example, that gay organizations buy up advertising space in "straight" newspapers with pictures of historical figures such as Alexander the Great, asking, "Did you know he was gay?"

Kirk and Madsen, like their surlier compatriots, fail to grasp that public homosexuality strikes at both a heterosexual's fear of loss of sexual identity and sense of belonging to a family. For even in this age of artificial insemination, families are not sustainable without heterosexuality. No matter how much the homosexual activist naively protests, "Gays are people, too," such a plea will receive in return grudging respect, and little else.

In a summary piece for *Newsweek*'s March 12, 1990, cover story, "The Future of Gay America," Jonathan Alter revealed a rare understanding of this dynamic.[37] He notes, "'Acting gay' often involves more than sexual behavior itself. Much of the dislike for homosexuals centers not on who they are or what they do in private, but on so-called affectations—'swishiness' in men, the 'butch' look for women—not directly related to the more private sex act." Quite rightly so—one doubts if more than a tiny fraction of heterosexuals have even *inadvertently* witnessed a homosexual act. Alter then gets to the core of the issue. "Heterosexuals," he writes, "tend to argue that gays can downplay these characteristics and 'pass' more easily in the straight world than Blacks can in a white world. . . . This may be true, but it's also irrelevant. For most gays those traits aren't affectations but part of their identities; attacking their swishiness is the same as attacking *them.*"

Yet if gays, through their carefully practiced "gay" mannerisms, know fully well they are antagonizing many heterosexuals, then why do they display them? Is it not in part to make heterosexuals sweat?[38] By aggressively politicizing these traits, and demanding that those objecting must grin and bear it, they are in a sense restricting heterosexual freedom of speech.

Male and even female opposition to persons with these traits is slowly taking a nasty turn, moving from violence of language to violence of fists. And yet, given the emerging legal climate, one discovers within oneself a disquieting empathy with the inchoate rage behind such acts.

Most heterosexuals are reasonably libertarian; an October 1989 Gallup Poll indicated that by a 47-to-36 margin (with the remainder undecided), Americans prefer legalization of homosexual relations between consenting adults.[39] This is all to the good. Anti-sodomy laws serve no purpose but to intimidate people out of private, consensual acts. On the other hand, the brazen, *open* display of homosexuality—as if to taunt, to tease, to maliciously sow confusion into sexual identities—is something most heterosexuals do not handle gracefully. With an unofficial government mandate for preferential treatment, it is not difficult to imagine a backlash. When homosexual lawyer-artist William Dobbs plastered explicit homosexual artwork throughout the Yale University campus back in 1989, he was not simply making a homoerotic statement; he was daring "homophobes" to remove the art, and risk suspension or expulsion from the university.[40] Those having little to lose may accept his dare—and it may be people like Dobbs as well as such art that gets torn up.

Should a sober discussion of the possibilities for heterosexual violence be forbidden? Nobody in a *rational* state of mind would seek to emulate the exploits of "skinheads" or the late San Francisco Supervisor Dan White. Yet let readers here imagine themselves in that Madison restaurant or Seattle airport, being witness to mass displays of homosexual kissing, and feeling utterly helpless to evince the slightest disapproval. Wouldn't such a scenario provoke an impulse, however fleeting and irrational, to do bodily harm? Doesn't the knowledge that the law is now stacked against even nonviolent disapproval ("hate crimes") merely add to the likelihood of a conflagration?

The principal motive of the gay movement is coming into focus with each passing month: to bait heterosexuals' less morally sturdy side, goading them into verbal or (better) physical assaults against the openly homosexual. That way, cries of homosexual victimhood would carry even more self-fulfilling prophecy, so much the better to vilify heterosexuals.

Gay militants aren't hesitant about admitting to such motives. Some want nothing less than war in the streets. Homosexual playwright and ACT-UP founder Larry Kramer recently called upon a gay audience to take gun practice for use in eventual combat against police and gay-bashers. "They hate us anyway," he rationalized. A cover of a recent issue of *Outweek* displayed a lesbian pointing a gun at the reader, with the headline, "Taking Aim at Bashers," while another cover announced, "We Hate Straights."[41] Even "mainstream" gay leaders, such as Urvashi Vaid, executive director of the National Gay and Lesbian Task Force, endorse such tactics, whatever the loss of potential supporters.[42]

The crowning legacy of the new gay legalism may yet be widespread violence, a violence brought on by state inhibition of rational dialogue at the behest of gay radicals, and in the name of "sensitivity." That alone is enough reason to oppose it.

Endnotes

1. "Gay Rights Protesters Win Right to Kiss," *The Washington Times,* April 18, 1990.

2. Joyce Price, "Queer Nation Decides It's Time to Bash Back," *The Washington Times,* October 15, 1990.

3. Price, "Queer Nation."

4. One of the best arguments that homosexuality is not simply a statistical aberration, but a behavioral abnormality, can be found in Steven Goldberg, "Is Homosexuality Normal?" *Policy Review,* Summer 1982, pp. 119–38.

5. "The Future of Gay America," *Newsweek,* March 12, 1990, pp. 21–22.

6. "Gay Measure Stirs Florida," *The Washington Times,* August 24, 1990.

7. Tupper Hall, "Gay Couples Allowed to File as 'Nonprofit' Associations," *The Washington Times,* December 17, 1990.

8. Jeff Levi, speech to National Press Club, October 10, 1987.

9. The term "hate crime," in the hands of the homosexual lobby, is so vague that even an accidental epithet could qualify as an offense. For example, of the 462 antihomosexual "hate crimes" committed in Virginia in

1987, 423—over 90 percent—involved mere name calling. See Patrick Buchanan, "The Real Victims of Hate Crimes," *The Washington Times*, March 7, 1990. The National Gay and Lesbian Task Force (NGLTF), in its own estimate of hate crimes committed nationwide in 1988, admitted that 77 percent were verbal. In fact, the origin of the legislation lay in a 1985 NGLTF presentation before the National Institute of Justice. See Congressman William Dannemeyer, *Shadow in the Land: Homosexuality in America* (San Francisco: Ignatius Press, 1989), pp. 71–75. Congressman Dannemeyer's book is the best currently available on the homosexual lobby.

10. Advertisement in the *New York Native*, April 18, 1988.

11. See Dannemeyer, *Shadow in the Land*.

12. Quoted in *Newsweek*, "The Future of Gay America," p. 21.

13. Phyllis Schlafly, "A Choice, Not an Echo in California," *The Washington Times*, March 2, 1990.

14. Doug Bandow, "Government as God," in *The Politics of Plunder: Misgovernment in Washington* (New Brunswick, NJ: Transaction, 1990), pp. 18–20.

15. Even sympathetic observers of this process admit that public identification of a neighborhood as "gay" induces nongays to move out. See Manuel Castells and Karen Murphy, "Cultural Identity and Urban Structure: The Spatial Organization of San Francisco's Gay Community," in Norman I. and Susan S. Fainstein, eds., *Urban Policy Under Capitalism* (Beverly Hills, CA: Sage Publications, 1982), pp. 237–59. For a decidedly unsympathetic (and highly personal) account of how the process works in resort communities, see Midge Decter, "The Boys on the Beach," *Commentary*, September 1980, pp. 35–48.

16. James N. Baker and Shawn D. Lewis, "Lesbians: Portrait of a Community," *Newsweek*, March 12, 1990, p. 24.

17. For evidence of this, see Dannemeyer, *Shadow in the Land*, p. 70.

18. For example, gay activists have now convinced the courts that having AIDS qualifies as a condition covered by Federal handicap discrimination laws. *Shuttleworth v. Broward County*, 41 FEP Cases 406 (S.D. Fla. 1986); *Thomas v. Atascadero Unified School District*, 662 F. Supp. 376 (C.D. Cal. 1987).

19. Valerie Richardson, "Gay Voters Claim Biggest Victory in San Francisco," *The Washington Times*, November 9, 1990.

20. At Harvard University, for example, the administration quickly suspended a student who removed a sign from an empty table in a dining hall indicating that it was reserved for a campus homosexual organization. Leave aside the absurd notion that a lunch table ought to be reserved for any particular sexual group, and the absence of malice on the part of the student (who simply sought a vacant seat in an otherwise crowded room). This student's suspension could only have come about either because the administrators meting out the punishment were radical homosexuals or because they were heterosexual but feared crossing swords with campus homosexuals.

In a sad coda to this incident, the suspended student later committed suicide. See Thomas Sowell, "Call of the Woolly Pulpit," *The Washington Times*, December 7, 1990.

21. *Braschi v. Stahl Associates Co.*, 74 N.Y.2d 201.

22. Dennis Hevesi, "Court Extends 'Family' Rule to Rent-Stabilized Units," *The New York Times*, December 6, 1990.

23. Richardson, "Gay Voters Claim Biggest Victory."

24. Thomas Sowell, "Affirmative Action: A Worldwide Disaster," *Commentary*, December 1989, pp. 21–41; see also Sowell, *Preferential Policies, An International Perspective* (New York: William Morrow, 1990).

25. Stephen Johnson, "Reverse Discrimination and Aggressive Behavior," *Journal of Psychology*, January 1980, pp. 11–19; Johnson, "Consequences of Reverse Discrimination," *Psychological Reports*, December 1980, pp. 1035–1038.

26. Paul Greenberg, "Decline and Fall of Civil Rights," *The Washington Times*, November 8, 1990.

27. Gara LaMarche and William B. Rubenstein, "The Love That Dare Not Speak," *The Nation*, November 5, 1990, p. 524.

28. Pete Hamill, "Confessions of a Heterosexual," *Esquire*, August 1990, pp. 55–57.

29. "Gay Protesters Confront Arsenio Hall," *The Washington Times*, December 17, 1990.

30. Quoted in Andrew Sullivan, "Gay Life, Gay Death," *The New Republic*, December 27, 1990, p. 24. That Sullivan, an ally of the homosexual legal revolution, is alarmed over the totalitarianism inherent in such pronouncements should be taken seriously; he supports—on conservative grounds, no less—legalizing homosexual marriage. See Sullivan, "Here Comes the Groom," *The New Republic*, August 28, 1989, pp. 20–22.

31. David Rieff, "The Case Against Sensitivity," *Esquire*, November 1990, p. 124.

32. Here was Rooney's "antigay" remark: "Many of the ills which kill us are self-induced." They include, "too much alcohol, too much food, drugs, homosexual unions, and cigarettes." Given that at the time of that statement, over 50,000 persons already had died of AIDS, Rooney would hardly qualify as anything other than a bearer of unpleasant truth.

33. For good interpretations of this episode, see Eric Breindel, "The Andy Rooney Affair," *Commentary*, May

1990, pp. 56–57; Cal Thomas, "Silence from the Pluralism Corner," *The Washington Times*, March 12, 1990.

34. The evidence suggests that increased social tolerance of homosexuality does not necessarily lead to homosexuals themselves being happier. See Martin S. Weinberg and Colin J. Williams, *Male Homosexuals* (New York: Oxford University Press, 1974); Samuel McCracken, "Are Homosexuals Gay?" *Commentary*, January 1979, pp. 19–29.

35. Thomas Short, "Gay Rights or Closet Virtues?" *National Review*, September 17, 1990, pp. 43–44.

36. Marshall Kirk and Hunter Madsen, *After the Ball:*

How America Will Conquer Its Fear and Hatred of Gays in the 90s (Garden City, NY: Doubleday, 1989).

37. Jonathan Alter, "Degrees of Discomfort," *Newsweek*, March 12, 1990, p. 27.

38. This is the position taken in McCracken, "Are Homosexuals Gay?" pp. 27–28.

39. The Gallup Report, Report No. 289 (Princeton, NJ: The Gallup Poll, October 1989), p. 13.

40. "The Future of Gay America," pp. 22–23.

41. See Sullivan, "Gay Life, Gay Death," p. 25.

42. "The Future of Gay America," p. 23.

53. *Romer* v. *Evans*

SUPREME COURT OF THE UNITED STATES

The issue before the Supreme Court was whether Amendment 2 of the Colorado state constitution—which precluded all legislative, executive, or judicial action at any level of state or local government that was designed to protect the status of persons based on their "homosexual, lesbian, or bisexual orientation, conduct, practices, or relationship"—violated the Equal Protection Clause of the Fourteenth Amendment. Writing for the majority, Justice Kennedy held that it did because the amendment imposes a broad disability on homosexuals that is not rationally related to any legitimate government interest. In dissent, Justice Scalia, joined by Justices Rehnquist and Thomas, argued that the disability imposed by Amendment 2 is like other disabilities that are legitimately imposed on various groups. Specifically, it is like the disability that is imposed on polygamists by various state constitutions. In addition, Scalia argued that the amendment is a legitimate expression of the moral and cultural values of a democratic majority.

Justice *Kennedy* delivered the opinion of the Court, in which Justices *Stevens, O'Connor, Souter, Ginsburg,* and *Breyer* joined.

One century ago, the first Justice Harlan admonished this Court that the Constitution "neither knows nor tolerates classes among citizens." Unheeded then, those words now are understood to state a commitment to the law's neutrality where the rights of persons are at stake. The Equal Protection Clause enforces this principle and today requires us to hold invalid a provision of Colorado's Constitution.

The enactment challenged in this case is an amendment to the Constitution of the State of Colorado, adopted in a 1992 statewide referendum. The parties and the state courts refer to it as "Amendment 2," its

designation when submitted to the voters. The impetus for the amendment and the contentious campaign that preceded its adoption came in large part from ordinances that had been passed in various Colorado municipalities. For example, the cities of Aspen and Boulder and the City and County of Denver each had enacted ordinances which banned discrimination in many transactions and activities, including housing, employment, education, public accommodations, and health and welfare services. What gave rise to the statewide controversy was the protection the ordinances afforded to persons discriminated against by reason of their sexual orientation. Amendment 2 repeals these ordinances to the extent they prohibit discrimination on the basis of "homosexual, lesbian, or bisexual orientation, conduct, practices, or relationships." Yet Amendment 2, in explicit terms, does more than repeal or rescind these provisions. It prohibits all legislative, executive, or judicial action at any level of state or local government designed to protect the named class, a class we shall refer to as homosexual persons or gays and lesbians.

The State's principal argument in defense of Amendment 2 is that it puts gays and lesbians in the same position as all other persons. So, the State says, the measure does no more than deny homosexuals special rights. This reading of the amendment's language is implausible. We rely not upon our own interpretation of the amendment but upon the authoritative construction of Colorado's Supreme Court. The state court, deeming it unnecessary to determine the full extent of the amendment's reach, found it invalid even on a modest reading of its implications. The critical discussion of the amendment is as follows:

> The immediate objective of Amendment 2 is, at a minimum, to repeal existing statutes, regulations, ordinances, and policies of state and local entities that barred discrimination based on sexual orientation. The "ultimate effect" of Amendment 2 is to prohibit any governmental entity from adopting similar, or more protective statutes, regulations, ordinances, or policies in the future unless the state constitution is first amended to permit such measures.

Homosexuals, by state decree, are put in a solitary class with respect to transactions and relations in both the private and governmental spheres. The amendment withdraws from homosexuals, but no others, specific legal protection from the injuries caused by discrimination, and it forbids reinstatement of these laws and policies.

The change that Amendment 2 works in the legal status of gays and lesbians in the private sphere is far-reaching, both on its own terms and when considered in light of the structure and operation of modern anti-discrimination laws. That structure is well illustrated by contemporary statutes and ordinances prohibiting discrimination by providers of public accommodations. "At common law, innkeepers, smiths, and others who 'made profession of a public employment,' were prohibited from refusing, without good

reason, to serve a customer." The duty was a general one and did not specify protection for particular groups. The common law rules, however, proved insufficient in many instances, and it was settled early that the Fourteenth Amendment did not give Congress a general power to prohibit discrimination in public accommodations. In consequence, most States have chosen to counter discrimination by enacting detailed statutory schemes.

These statutes and ordinances also depart from the common law by enumerating the groups or persons within their ambit of protection. Enumeration is the essential device used to make the duty not to discriminate concrete and to provide guidance for those who must comply. In following this approach, Colorado's state and local governments have not limited anti-discrimination laws to groups that have so far been given the protection of heightened equal protection scrutiny under our cases. Rather, they set forth an extensive catalogue of traits which cannot be the basis for discrimination, including age, military status, marital status, pregnancy, parenthood, custody of a minor child, political affiliation, physical or mental disability of an individual or of his or her associates—and, in recent times, sexual orientation.

Amendment 2 bars homosexuals from securing protection against the injuries that these public-accommodations laws address. That in itself is a severe consequence, but there is more. Amendment 2, in addition, nullifies specific legal protections for this targeted class in all transactions in housing, sale of real estate, insurance, health and welfare services, private education, and employment.

[W]e cannot accept the view that Amendment 2's prohibition on specific legal protections does no more than deprive homosexuals of special rights. To the contrary, the amendment imposes a special disability upon those persons alone. Homosexuals are forbidden the safeguards that others enjoy or may seek without constraint. They can obtain specific protection against discrimination only by enlisting the citizenry of Colorado to amend the state constitution or perhaps, on the State's view, by trying to pass helpful laws of general applicability. This is so no matter how local or discrete the harm, no matter how public and widespread the injury. We find nothing special in the protections Amendment 2 withholds. These are protections taken for granted by most people either because they already have them or do not need them; these are protections against exclusion from an almost limitless number of transactions and endeavors that constitute ordinary civic life in a free society.

The Fourteenth Amendment's promise that no person shall be denied the equal protection of the laws must co-exist with the practical necessity that most legislation classifies for one purpose or another, with resulting disadvantage to various groups or persons. We have attempted to reconcile the principle with the reality by stating that, if a law neither burdens a fundamental right nor targets a suspect class, we will uphold the legislative classification so long as it bears a rational relation to some legitimate end.

Amendment 2 fails—indeed defies—even this conventional inquiry. First, the amendment has the peculiar property of imposing a broad and undifferentiated disability on a single named group, an exceptional and, as we shall explain, invalid form of legislation. Second, its sheer breadth is so discontinuous with the reasons offered for it that the amendment seems inexplicable by anything but animus toward the class that it affects; it lacks a rational relationship to legitimate state interests.

In the ordinary case, a law will be sustained if it can be said to advance a legitimate government interest, even if the law seems unwise or works to the disadvantage of a particular group, or if the rationale for it seems tenuous. See *New Orleans v. Dukes* (1976) (tourism benefits justified classification favoring pushcart vendors of certain longevity); *Williamson v. Lee Optical of Okla., Inc.* (1955) (assumed health concerns justified law favoring optometrists over opticians); *Railway Express Agency, Inc. v. New York* (1949) (potential traffic hazards justified exemption of vehicles advertising the owner's products from general advertising ban); *Kotch v. Board of River Port Pilot Comm'rs for Port of New Orleans* (1947) (licensing scheme that disfavored persons unrelated to current river boat pilots justified by possible efficiency and safety benefits of a closely knit pilotage system). The laws challenged in the cases just cited were narrow enough in scope and grounded in a sufficient factual context for us to ascertain that there existed some relation between the classification and the purpose it served. By requiring that the classification bear a ra-

tional relationship to an independent and legitimate legislative end, we ensure that classifications are not drawn for the purpose of disadvantaging the group burdened by the law.

Amendment 2 confounds this normal process of judicial review. It is at once too narrow and too broad. It identifies persons by a single trait and then denies them protection across the board. The resulting disqualification of a class of persons from the right to seek specific protection from the law is unprecedented in our jurisprudence. The absence of precedent for Amendment 2 is itself instructive; "[d]iscriminations of an unusual character especially suggest careful consideration to determine whether they are obnoxious to the constitutional provision."

It is not within our constitutional tradition to enact laws of this sort. Central both to the idea of the rule of law and to our own Constitution's guarantee of equal protection is the principle that government and each of its parts remain open on impartial terms to all who seek its assistance. "Equal protection of the laws is not achieved through indiscriminate imposition of inequalities" *Sweatt v. Painter* (1950). Respect for this principle explains why laws singling out a certain class of citizens for disfavored legal status or general hardships are rare. A law declaring that in general it shall be more difficult for one group of citizens than for all others to seek aid from the government is itself a denial of equal protection of the laws in the most literal sense.

Davis v. Beason (1890), not cited by the parties but relied upon by the dissent, is not evidence that Amendment 2 is within our constitutional tradition, and any reliance upon it as authority for sustaining the amendment is misplaced. In *Davis*, the Court approved an Idaho territorial statute denying Mormons, polygamists, and advocates of polygamy the right to vote and to hold office because, as the Court construed the statute, it "simply excludes from the privilege of voting, or of holding any office of honor, trust, or profit, those who have been convicted of certain offenses, and those who advocate a practical resistance to the laws of the Territory and justify and approve the commission of crimes forbidden by it." To the extent *Davis* held that persons advocating a certain practice may be denied the right to vote, it is no longer good law. To the extent it held that the groups designated in the statute may be deprived of the right to vote because of their status, its ruling could not stand without surviving strict scrutiny, a most doubtful outcome. To the extent *Davis* held that a convicted felon may be denied the right to vote, its holding is not implicated by our decision and is unexceptionable.

The primary rationale the State offers for Amendment 2 is respect for other citizens' freedom of association, and in particular the liberties of landlords or employers who have personal or religious objections to homosexuality. Colorado also cites its interest in conserving resources to fight discrimination against other groups. The breadth of the Amendment is so far removed from these particular justifications that we find it impossible to credit them. We cannot say that Amendment 2 is directed to any identifiable legitimate purpose or discrete objective. It is a status-based enactment divorced from any factual context from which we could discern a relationship to legitimate state interests; it is a classification of persons undertaken for its own sake, something the Equal Protection Clause does not permit.

We must conclude that Amendment 2 classifies homosexuals not to further a proper legislative end but to make them unequal to everyone else. This Colorado cannot do. A State cannot so deem a class of persons a stranger to its laws. Amendment 2 violates the Equal Protection Clause, and the judgment of the Supreme Court of Colorado is affirmed.

It is so ordered.

Justice *Scalia*, with whom [Chief Justice *Rehnquist*] and Justice *Thomas* join, dissenting.

The Court has mistaken a Kulturkampf for a fit of spite. The constitutional amendment before us here is not the manifestation of a "bare . . . desire to harm" homosexuals, but is rather a modest attempt by seemingly tolerant Coloradans to preserve traditional sexual mores against the efforts of a politically powerful minority to revise those mores through use of the laws. That objective, and the means chosen to achieve it, are not only unimpeachable under any constitutional doctrine hitherto pronounced (hence the opinion's heavy reliance upon principles of righteousness rather than judicial holdings); they have been specifically approved by the Congress of the United States and by this Court.

In holding that homosexuality cannot be singled out for disfavorable treatment, the Court contradicts a decision, unchallenged here, pronounced only ten years ago (see *Bowers v. Hardwick*, 1986), and places the prestige of this institution behind the proposition that opposition to homosexuality is as reprehensible as racial or religious bias. Whether it is or not is precisely the cultural debate that gave rise to the Colorado constitutional amendment (and to the preferential laws against which the amendment was directed). Since the Constitution of the United States says nothing about this subject, it is left to be resolved by normal democratic means, including the democratic adoption of provisions in state constitutions. This Court has no business imposing upon all Americans the resolution favored by the elite class from which the Members of this institution are selected, pronouncing that "animosity" toward homosexuality is evil.

The amendment prohibits special treatment of homosexuals, and nothing more. It would not affect, for example, a requirement of state law that pensions be paid to all retiring state employees with a certain length of service; homosexual employees, as well as others, would be entitled to that benefit. But it would prevent the State or any municipality from making death-benefit payments to the "life partner" of a homosexual when it does not make such payments to the long-time roommate of a nonhomosexual employee. Or again, it does not affect the requirement of the State's general insurance laws that customers be afforded coverage without discrimination unrelated to anticipated risk. Thus, homosexuals could not be denied coverage, or charged a greater premium, with respect to auto collision insurance; but neither the State nor any municipality could require that distinctive health insurance risks associated with homosexuality (if there are any) be ignored.

Despite all of its hand-wringing about the potential effect of Amendment 2 on general antidiscrimination laws, the Court's opinion ultimately does not dispute all this, but assumes it to be true. The only denial of equal treatment it contends homosexuals have suffered is this: They may not obtain preferential treatment without amending the state constitution. That is to say, the principle underlying the Court's opinion is that one who is accorded equal treatment under the laws, but cannot as readily as others obtain preferential treatment under the laws, has been denied equal protection of the laws. If merely stating this alleged "equal protection" violation does not suffice to refute it, our constitutional jurisprudence has achieved terminal silliness.

The central thesis of the Court's reasoning is that any group is denied equal protection when, to obtain advantage (or, presumably, to avoid disadvantage), it must have recourse to a more general and hence more difficult level of political decision making than others. The world has never heard of such a principle, which is why the Court's opinion is so long on emotive utterance and so short on relevant legal citation. And it seems to me most unlikely that any multilevel democracy can function under such a principle. For whenever a disadvantage is imposed, or conferral of a benefit is prohibited, at one of the higher levels of democratic decision making (i.e., by the state legislature rather than local government, or by the people at large in the state constitution rather than the legislature), the affected group has (under this theory) been denied equal protection. To take the simplest of examples, consider a state law prohibiting the award of municipal contracts to relatives of mayors or city councilmen. Once such a law is passed, the group composed of such relatives must, in order to get the benefit of city contracts, persuade the state legislature—unlike all other citizens, who need only persuade the municipality. It is ridiculous to consider this a denial of equal protection, which is why the Court's theory is unheard of.

I turn next to whether there was a legitimate rational basis for the substance of the constitutional amendment—for the prohibition of special protection for homosexuals. It is unsurprising that the Court avoids discussion of this question, since the answer is so obviously yes. The case most relevant to the issue before us today is not even mentioned in the Court's opinion: In *Bowers v. Hardwick* (1986), we held that the Constitution does not prohibit what virtually all States had done from the founding of the Republic until very recent years—making homosexual conduct a crime. That holding is unassailable, except by those who think that the Constitution changes to suit current fashions. But in any event it is a given in the present case: Respondents' briefs did not urge overruling

Bowers, and at oral argument respondents' counsel expressly disavowed any intent to seek such overruling. If it is constitutionally permissible for a State to make homosexual conduct criminal, surely it is constitutionally permissible for a State to enact other laws merely disfavoring homosexual conduct.

The foregoing suffices to establish what the Court's failure to cite any case remotely in point would lead one to suspect: No principle set forth in the Constitution, nor even any imagined by this Court in the past 200 years, prohibits what Colorado has done here. But the case for Colorado is much stronger than that. What it has done is not only unprohibited, but eminently reasonable, with close, congressionally approved precedent in earlier constitutional practice.

First, as to its eminent reasonableness. The Court's opinion contains grim, disapproving hints that Coloradans have been guilty of "animus" or "animosity" toward homosexuality, as [if] that has been established as un-American. Of course it is our moral heritage that one should not hate any human being or class of human beings. But . . . one could consider certain conduct reprehensible—murder, for example, or polygamy, or cruelty to animals—and could exhibit even "animus" toward such conduct. Surely that is the only sort of "animus" at issue here: moral disapproval of homosexual conduct, the same sort of moral disapproval that produced the centuries-old criminal laws that we held constitutional in Bowers. The Colorado amendment does not, to speak entirely precisely, prohibit giving favored status to people who are homosexuals; they can be favored for many reasons—for example, because they are senior citizens or members of racial minorities. But it prohibits giving them favored status because of their homosexual conduct—that is, it prohibits favored status for homosexuality.

But though Coloradans are, as I say, entitled to be hostile toward homosexual conduct, the fact is that the degree of hostility reflected by Amendment 2 is the smallest conceivable. The Court's portrayal of Coloradans as a society fallen victim to pointless, hate-filled "gay-bashing" is so false as to be comical. Colorado not only is one of the 25 States that have repealed their antisodomy laws, but was among the first to do so. But the society that eliminates criminal punishment for homosexual acts does not necessarily abandon the view that homosexuality is morally wrong and socially harmful; often, abolition simply reflects the view that enforcement of such criminal laws involves unseemly intrusion into the intimate lives of citizens.

There is a problem, however, that arises when criminal sanction of homosexuality is eliminated but moral and social disapprobation of homosexuality is meant to be retained. The Court cannot be unaware of that problem; it is evident in many cities of the country, and occasionally bubbles to the surface of the news, in heated political disputes over such matters as the introduction into local schools of books teaching that homosexuality is an optional and fully acceptable "alternate life style." The problem (a problem, that is, for those who wish to retain social disapprobation of homosexuality) is that, because those who engage in homosexual conduct tend to reside in disproportionate numbers in certain communities, and of course care about homosexual-rights issues much more ardently than the public at large, they possess political power much greater than their numbers, locally and statewide. Quite understandably, they devote this political power to achieving not merely a grudging social toleration, but full social acceptance, of homosexuality.

By the time Coloradans were asked to vote on Amendment 2, their exposure to homosexuals' quest for social endorsement was not limited to newspaper accounts of happenings in places such as New York, Los Angeles, San Francisco, and Key West. Three Colorado cities—Aspen, Boulder, and Denver—had enacted ordinances that listed "sexual orientation" as an impermissible ground for discrimination, equating the moral disapproval of homosexual conduct with racial and religious bigotry. The phenomenon had even appeared statewide: The Governor of Colorado had signed an executive order pronouncing that "we recognize the diversity in our pluralistic society and strive to bring an end to discrimination in any form," and directing state agency-heads to "ensure nondiscrimination" in hiring and promotion based on, among other things, "sexual orientation."

[What the Court said] is proved false every time a state law prohibiting or disfavoring certain conduct is passed, because such a law prevents the adversely affected group—whether drug addicts, or smokers, or gun owners, or motorcyclists—from changing the policy thus established in "each of [the] parts" of the State. What the Court says is even demonstrably false at the constitutional level. The Eighteenth Amendment to the Federal Constitution, for example, deprived those who drank alcohol not only of the power to alter the policy of prohibition locally or through state legislation, but even of the power to alter it through state constitutional amendment or federal legislation. The Establishment Clause of the First Amendment prevents theocrats from having their way by converting their fellow citizens at the local, state, or federal statutory level; as does the Republican Form of Government Clause prevent monarchists.

But there is a much closer analogy, one that involves precisely the effort by the majority of citizens to preserve its view of sexual morality statewide, against the efforts of a geographically concentrated and politically powerful minority to undermine it. The constitutions of the States of Arizona, Idaho, New Mexico, Oklahoma, and Utah to this day contain provisions stating that polygamy is "forever prohibited." Polygamists, and those who have a polygamous "orientation," have been "singled out" by these provisions for much more severe treatment than merely denial of favored status; and that treatment can only be changed by achieving amendment of the state constitutions. The Court's disposition today suggests that these provisions are unconstitutional, and that polygamy must be permitted in these States on a state-legislated, or perhaps even local-option, basis—unless, of course, polygamists for some reason have fewer constitutional rights than homosexuals.

To the extent, if any, that this opinion permits the imposition of adverse consequences upon mere abstract advocacy of polygamy, it has of course been overruled by later cases. But the proposition that polygamy can be criminalized, and those engaging in that crime deprived of the vote, remains good law.

It remains to be explained how the Idaho Revised Statutes was not an "impermissible targeting" of polygamists, but (the much more mild) Amendment 2 is an "impermissible targeting" of homosexuals. Has the Court concluded that the perceived social harm of polygamy is a "legitimate concern of government" and the perceived social harm of homosexuality is not?

When the Court takes sides in the culture wars, it tends to be with the knights rather than the villains—

and more specifically with the Templars, reflecting the views and values of the lawyer class from which the Court's Members are drawn. How that class feels about homosexuality will be evident to anyone who wishes to interview job applicants at virtually any of the Nation's law schools. The interviewer may refuse to offer a job because the applicant is a Republican; . . . he is an adulterer; . . . he went to the wrong prep school or belongs to the wrong country club; . . . he eats snails; . . . he is a womanizer; . . . she wears real-animal fur; or even because he hates the Chicago Cubs. But if the interviewer should wish not to be an associate or partner of an applicant because he disapproves of the applicant's homosexuality, then he will have violated the pledge that the Association of American Law Schools requires all its member schools to exact from job interviewers: "assurance of the employer's willingness" to hire homosexuals. This law-school view of what "prejudices" must be stamped

out may be contrasted with the more plebeian attitudes that apparently still prevail in the United States Congress, which has been unresponsive to repeated attempts to extend to homosexuals the protections of federal civil rights laws, and which took the pains to exclude them specifically from the Americans With Disabilities Act of 1990.

Today's opinion has no foundation in American constitutional law, and barely pretends to. The people of Colorado have adopted an entirely reasonable provision which does not even disfavor homosexuals in any substantive sense, but merely denies them preferential treatment. Amendment 2 is designed to prevent piecemeal deterioration of the sexual morality favored by a majority of Coloradans, and is not only an appropriate means to that legitimate end, but a means that Americans have employed before. Striking it down is an act, not of judicial judgment, but of political will. I dissent.

---

54. *Gays in the Military: Between Fear and Fantasy*

KEN CORBETT

Ken Corbett tries to explain the fear and hatred that was expressed regarding ending the ban against gays and lesbians in the military.

Military officials and Congressional leaders cite the possible threat of violence to homosexuals as a reason to continue discriminating against gays in the military. This raises the obvious question of whether we should be governed by threat. But we also are left to ask what fuels such aggression.

Throughout the debate, straight military men keep voicing concern that they will not be able to control

their aggression against gay men. Gay soldiers and sailors are threatened with the prospect of being beaten, even murdered. As if to prove the point, three marines beat a homosexual man outside a gay bar in Wilmington, N.C., Saturday morning while shouting, "Clinton must pay!"

Why is this aggression almost exclusively focused on gay men? Newspaper articles are full of the anger and concerns of male soldiers. Talk shows feature verbal slugfests between gay and straight military men. Women are almost never mentioned. This no doubt reflects military demographics, but it also reflects the manner in which the hatred of male homosexuality is founded on fears of femininity. The equation is simple: Male homosexuality equals femininity, which produces fear, which produces aggression.

More specifically, hatred of gay men is based on fear of the self, not of an alien other. This was expressed by Martin Jones, a 22-year-old airman quoted in this paper as saying he wouldn't be able to sleep at night if the ban were lifted because he would be "worried that some homosexual is going to sneak over and make a pass."

Seemingly unaware of the slippery slope between fear and fantasy, he conveyed a suspicion that gay men will not be able to control their sexual appetite, and rape will ensue. Leaving aside the fact that rape is largely a heterosexual phenomenon (and a prevalent heterosexual male fantasy), Airman Jones's concern smacks of the pernicious misconception that gay men and women have a devouring sexual appetite— that they are hungry sirens eager to bite.

More to the point, Mr. Jones imagines himself the object of a man's desire. He anxiously pictures himself wanted in a way that most men feel only a woman should be wanted. In so fantasizing, he must, if ever so briefly, put himself in the place of a man who desires another man.

But Mr. Jones quickly sheds this threatening desire: He and his like-minded colleagues turn the object of desire into a hated, threatening object. Mr. Jones creates a distinct border between "them" and "us." He is not one of them, he hates them.

Hatred thrives on rigid order. Armed with hatred and protected by institutional values, Mr. Jones does not have to take responsibility for his aggressive impulses. Mr. Jones, his commanders and many in Congress would have us believe this kind of phobic behavior should guide military policy. But what kind of policy is built on a phobic solution? What kind of law is built on hatred?

Apparently these are not questions that Mr. Jones is asking himself when he can't fall asleep. He thinks sneaky homosexuals cause his insomnia. But it is really his own fears and fantasies that keep him awake.

Suggestions for Further Reading

Anthologies

Baird, Robert, and Baird, Katherine. *Homosexuality: Debating the Issues.* Amherst: Prometheus Books, 1995.

Batchelor, E. *Homosexuality and Ethics.* New York: Pilgrim Press, 1980.

Dudley, William. *Homosexuality—Opposing Viewpoints.* San Diego: Greenhaven Press, 1993.

Basic Concepts

"Survey on the Constitutional Right to Privacy in the Context of Homosexual Activity." *Miami Law Review* (1986), pp. 521–657.

Alternative Views

du Mas, F. *Gay Is Not Good.* Nashville, Tenn.: Thomas Nelson Publishers, 1979.

Finnis, John. "Law, Morality, and 'Sexual Orientation,'" *Notre Dame Law Review,* 1994.

Friedman, R. *Male Homosexuality.* New Haven, Ct.: Yale University Press, 1988.

Harrigan, J. *Homosexuality: The Test Case for Christian Ethics.* Mahwah, N.J.: Paulist Press, 1988.

Hoagland, Sarah. *Lesbian Ethics.* Palo Alto: Institute of Lesbian Studies, 1988.

Malloy, E. *Homosexuality and the Christian Way of Life.* Lanham, Md.: University Press of America, 1981.

Mohr, R. *Gays/Justice.* New York: Columbia University Press, 1988.

Nussbaum, Martha. "Platonic Love and Colorado Law: The Relevance of Ancient Greek Norms to Modern Sexual Controversies," *Virginia Law Review,* 1994.

Ruse, Michael. *Homosexuality.* Oxford: Basil Blackwell, 1988.

Section X

Gun Control

Introduction

Basic Concepts

Americans own about 150–200 million firearms. Fifty percent of American households contain guns and half of these homes contain the estimated 70 million handguns currently in private hands. Each year, approximately 38,000 Americans are killed with firearms. Of this number, 19,000 are suicides, 18,000 are homicides, and the remaining 2,000 are gun accidents. By comparison, in 1990, twenty-two people were killed in Great Britain with handguns, thirteen in Sweden, ninety-one in Switzerland, eighty-seven in Japan, ten in Australia, and sixty-eight in Canada. In addition, 40,000 gun-related injuries, whether intentional or accidental, are inflicted upon Americans each year. Meanwhile in any given year, there are up to one million crimes committed involving guns. According to recent surveys, 68 percent of Americans believe that firearms laws should be stricter, 80 percent favor handgun registration, and 93 percent favor the seven-day waiting period for handgun purchases initially required by the Brady bill (see Selection 59). But public opinion has only minimally been reflected in legislation in the United States. The National Rifle Association has been particularly effective in defeating legislation that it opposes. But what is the right thing to do here? Does morality favor gun control or oppose it? This is the moral problem of gun control, and its resolution requires weighing the arguments for and against gun control set out in this section.

Alternative Views

In their study of King County, Washington, Arthur Kellerman and Donald Reay (Selection 55) found that there are forty-three suicides, criminal homicides, or accidental deaths involving guns kept at home for every case of a homicide for self-protection. In addition, they found that over 80 percent of the homicides occurred during arguments or altercations. In light of their findings, Kellerman and Reay raise the question of whether keeping firearms in the home increases a family's protection or places it at greater risk.

In Selection 56, the National Rifle Association defends each person's right to own and use arms in self-defense. The NRA cites figures from a study by Gary Kleck that indicates that there are about 645,000 defensive uses of handguns each year, excluding police and military uses. The NRA further notes that while handguns are used in domestic arguments, in many cases they are being used by women to shoot their husbands.

This implies, according to the NRA, that such uses are not really aggressive, and hence may in fact be justified. But this conclusion surely requires further argument. Finally, the NRA contends that the majority of the accidental deaths from firearms involve rifles, not handguns. But this is contradicted by the Kellerman study, which states that only one in twelve accidental deaths from firearms involved a rifle.

In another study (see Selection 57), Carl Bogus compares two cities, Seattle and Vancouver, which are similar in all the relevant respects except that Vancouver has a relatively strong gun control law whereas Seattle does not. The results are shown in the table below.

Notice that all the indicated differences between these two cities relate to firearms. There are more firearm assaults, and more firearm-related homicides and suicides in Seattle than in Vancouver. Furthermore, while there were presumably more defensive uses of guns in Seattle than in Vancouver, there were not more burglaries or homicides in Vancouver than in Seattle. In fact, there were fewer homicides in Vancouver than in Seattle. Bogus cites another study done in the District of Columbia, which found that there were 25 percent fewer homicides and 23 percent fewer suicides in the nine years following passage of a gun control law than in the nine years before passage. According to Bogus, the evidence from these two studies alone constitutes a strong case for gun control.

In making his case against gun control, Edward Leddy (Selection 58) cites the example of Morton Grove, Illinois, and Oak Park, Illinois, where laws banning handguns were followed by increased crime rates. He also cites the example of Highland Park, Michigan, where the police trained storekeepers in the use of guns and store robberies dropped from eighty in the previous four months to zero in the subsequent four months. What needs to be determined is how this evidence is to be evaluated against Bogus's Seattle/Vancouver study. Did something other than the presence of a ban on handguns cause the increase of crime in Morton Grove and Oak Park? Does something other than the absence of a ban on handguns explain the greater gun-related crime in Seattle than in Vancouver?

There is also the question of the burden of proof. Do supporters of gun control have to show that the lack of gun control is actually harmful overall or do opponents of gun control have to show that its absence is actually beneficial, or at least not harmful overall? Surely, at the very least, neither side should be comfortable with a tie. Thus, each side needs to show that the weight of all the available evidence favors its side of the debate over the other side. Perhaps the key question can be put as follows: Can we justifiably impose a greater risk of suicide, wrongful assault, and accidental injury on some with the aim of securing a more effective defense against wrongful attack for others?

	Seattle	Vancouver
Firearm assaults	8 times higher	8 times lower
Homicides	388	204
Households with guns	40 percent	12 percent
Burglary rate	Same	Same
Homicides from self-defense	4 percent	4 percent
Homicide rates for other weapons	Same	Same
Suicide rate	40 percent higher	40 percent lower
Firearm adolescent suicide rate	10 times higher	10 times lower

Practical Applications

In 1993 after much opposition, the Brady Bill was enacted into law. The bill was named for James S. Brady, who was shot by John Hinkley during an assassination attempt on President Ronald Reagan. Brady was seriously wounded and suffered permanent debilitating injuries. He and his wife have actively lobbied for gun control.

The Brady Bill requires a five-day waiting period. In a concession to the NRA, the bill stipulates that the law expires after five years, which gives states time to computerize their criminal records for instant checks of gun purchasers. Obviously, the key question here and elsewhere is how free should people be? In particular, should people be free to own and carry handguns for self-defense, and how is this freedom related to others that people have or should have?

55. Protection or Peril? An Analysis of Firearm-Related Deaths in the Home

ARTHUR L. KELLERMAN AND DONALD T. REAY

In their study of King County, Washington, Arthur Kellerman and Donald Reay found that there are forty-three suicides, criminal homicides, or accidental deaths involving guns kept at home for every case of a homicide for self-protection. In addition, they found that over 80 percent of the homicides occurred during arguments or altercations. In light of their findings, Kellerman and Reay raise the question of whether keeping firearms in the home increases a family's protection or places it at greater risk.

There are approximately 120 million guns in private hands in the United States. About half of all the homes in America contain one or more firearms. Although most persons who own guns keep them primarily for hunting or sport, three-quarters of gun owners keep them at least partly for protection. One-fifth of gun owners identify "self-defense at home" as their most important reason for having a gun.

Adapted from Arthur L. Kellerman and Donald T. Reay, "Protection or Peril? An Analysis of Firearm-Related Deaths in the Home." The complete article, with references and graphics, can be found in *The New England Journal of Medicine* 314 (24): 1557–60. Reprinted with permission.

Risks of Guns in the Home

Keeping firearms in the home carries associated risks. These include injury or death from unintentional gunshot wounds, homicide during domestic quarrels, and the ready availability of an immediate, highly lethal means of suicide. To understand better the epidemiology of firearm-related deaths in the home, we studied all the gunshot deaths that occurred in King County, Washington, between 1978 and 1983. We were especially interested in characterizing the gunshot deaths that occurred in the residence where the firearm involved was kept.

King County, Washington (1980 census population 1,270,000), contains the cities of Seattle (population 494,000) and Bellevue (population 74,000), as well as a number of smaller communities. The county population is predominantly urban (92 percent) and white (88.4 percent), with smaller Black (4.4 percent) and Asian (4.3 percent) minorities. All violent deaths in King County are investigated by the office of the medical examiner.

We systematically reviewed the medical examiner's case files to identify every firearm-related death that occurred in the county between January 1, 1978, and December 31, 1983. In addition to general demographic information, we obtained specific data regarding the manner of death, the scene of the incident, the circumstances, the relationship of the suspect to the victim, the type of firearm involved, and the blood alcohol level of the victim at the time of autopsy. When records were incomplete, corroborating information was obtained from police case files and direct interviews with the original investigating officers.

Types of Gunshot Deaths

Gunshot deaths involving the intentional shooting of one person by another were considered homicides. Self-protection homicides were considered "justifiable" if they involved the killing of a felon during the commission of a crime; they were considered "self-defense" if that was the determination of the investigating police department and the King County prosecutor's office. All homicides resulting in criminal charges and all unsolved homicides were considered criminal homicides.

The circumstances of all homicides were also noted. Homicides committed in association with another felony (e.g., robbery) were identified as "felony homicides." Homicides committed during an argument or fight were considered "altercation homicides." Those committed in the absence of either set of circumstances were termed "primary homicides."

Deaths from self-inflicted gunshot wounds were considered suicides if they were officially certified as such by Donald T. Reay, . . . the medical examiner. Unintentional self-inflicted gunshot wounds were classified as accidental. Although the medical exam-

iner's office considers deaths involving the unintentional shooting of one person by another as homicide, we classified these deaths as accidental for our analysis. Deaths [with uncertainties] about the circumstances or motive were identified as "undetermined."

Over the six-year interval, the medical examiner's office investigated 743 deaths from firearms (9.75 deaths per 100,000 person-years). This total represented 22.7 percent of all violent deaths occurring in King County during this period, excluding traffic deaths. Firearms were involved in 45 percent of all homicides and 49 percent of all suicides in King County—proportions lower than the national averages of 61 and 57 percent, respectively. Guns accounted for less than 1 percent of accidental deaths and 5.7 percent of deaths in which the circumstances were undetermined.

Of the 743 deaths from firearms noted during this six-year period, 473 (63.7 percent) occurred inside a house or dwelling, and 398 (53.6 percent) occurred in the home where the firearm involved was kept. Of these 398 firearm deaths, 333 (83.7 percent) were suicides,. 50 (12.6 percent) were homicides, and 12 (3 percent) were accidental gunshot deaths. The precise manner of death was undetermined in three additional cases involving self-inflicted gunshot wounds.

In 265 of the 333 cases of suicide (80 percent), the victim was male. A blood ethanol test was positive in 86 of the 245 suicide victims tested (35 percent) and showed a blood ethanol level of 100 mg per deciliter or more in 60 of the 245 (24.5 percent). Sixty-eight percent of the suicides involved handguns. In eight cases, the medical examiner's case files specifically noted that the victim had acquired the firearm within two days of committing suicide.

The victim was male in thirty of the fifty homicide deaths (60 percent). A blood ethanol test was positive in twenty-seven of forty-seven homicide victims tested (5 percent) and showed a blood ethanol level of 100 mg per deciliter or more in ten of the victims (21 percent). Handguns were involved in thirty-four of these deaths (68 percent).

Forty-two homicides (84 percent) occurred during altercations in the home, including seven that were later determined to have been committed in self-defense. Two additional homicides involving the shooting of burglars by residents were considered legally "justifiable." Forty-one homicides (82 percent) resulted in criminal charges against a resident of the house or apartment in which the shooting occurred.

Four of the twelve accidental deaths involved self-inflicted gunshot wounds. All twelve victims were male. A blood ethanol test in the victims was positive in only two cases. Eleven of these accidental deaths involved handguns.

Excluding firearm-related suicides, sixty-five deaths occurred in the house where the firearm involved was kept. In two of these cases, the victim was a stranger to the persons living in the house, whereas in twenty-four cases (37 percent), the victim was an acquaintance or friend. Thirty-six gunshot victims (55 percent) were residents of the house in which the shooting occurred, including twenty-nine who were victims of homicide. Residents were most often shot by a relative or family member (eleven cases), their spouse (nine cases), a roommate (six cases), or themselves (seven cases).

Household Members at Risk

Guns kept in King County homes were involved in the deaths of friends or acquaintances 12 times as often as in those of strangers. Even after the exclusion of firearm-related suicides, guns kept at home were involved in the death of a member of the household 18 times more often than in the death of a stranger. For every time a gun in the home was involved in a "self-protection" homicide, we noted 1.3 accidental gunshot deaths, 4.6 criminal homicides, and 37 firearm-related suicides.

We found the home to be a common location for deaths related to firearms. During our study period, almost two-thirds of the gunshot deaths in King County occurred inside a house or other dwelling. Over half these incidents occurred in the residence in which the firearm involved was kept. Few involved acts of self-protection.

Less than 2 percent of homicides nationally are considered legally justifiable. Although justifiable homicides do not include homicides committed in self-defense, the combined total of both in our study was still less than one-fourth the number of criminal homicides involving a gun kept in the home. A majority of these homicide victims were residents of the house or apartment in which the shooting occurred.

More than 80 percent of the homicides noted during our study occurred during arguments or altercations. Susan Baker has observed that in cases of assault, people tend to reach for the most lethal weapon readily available. Easy access to firearms may therefore be particularly dangerous in households prone to domestic violence.

Guns and Suicide

We found the most common form of firearm-related death in the home to be suicide. Although previous authors have correlated regional suicide rates with estimates of firearm density, the precise nature of the relation between gun availability and suicide is unclear. The choice of a gun for suicide may involve a combination of impulse and the close proximity of a firearm. Conversely, the choice of a gun may simply reflect the seriousness of a person's intent. If suicides involving firearms are more a product of the easy availability of weapons than of the strength of intent, limiting access to firearms will decrease the rate of suicide. If the opposite is true, suicidal persons will only work harder to acquire a gun or kill themselves by other means. For example, although the elimination of toxic coal gas from domestic gas supplies in Great Britain resulted in a decrease in successful suicide attempts, a similar measure in Australia was associated with increasing rates of suicide by other methods.

A study of thirty survivors of attempts to commit suicide with firearms suggests that many of them acted on impulse. Whether this observation applies to nonsurvivors as well is unknown. The recent acquisition of a firearm was noted in only eight of our cases, and we do not know how long before death any suicide victim planned his or her attempt. However, given the high case-fatality rate associated with suicide attempts involving firearms, it seems likely that easy access to guns increases the probability that an impulsive suicide attempt will end in death.

Detectable concentrations of ethanol were found in the blood of a substantial proportion of the victims tested. This suggests that ethanol may be an independent risk factor for gunshot death. Although this hypothesis is compatible with the known behavioral and physiologic effect of ethanol, the strength of this association remains to be defined.

There are many reasons [why] people own guns. Unfortunately, our files rarely identified why the firearm involved had been kept in the home. We cannot determine, therefore, whether guns kept for protection were more or less hazardous than guns kept for other reasons.

Self-Defense Handguns Outnumber Long Guns

We did note, however, that handguns were far more commonly involved in gunshot deaths in the home than shotguns or rifles. The single most common reason for keeping firearms given by owners of handguns, unlike owners of shoulder weapons, is "self-defense at home." About 45 percent of the gun-owning households nationally own handguns. If the proportion of homes containing handguns in King County is similar to this national average, then these weapons were 2.6 times more likely to be involved in a gunshot death in the home than were shotguns and rifles combined.

Several limitations of this type of analysis must be recognized. Our observations are based on a largely urban population and may not be applicable to more rural communities. Also, various rates of suicide and homicide have been noted in other metropolitan counties. These differences may reflect variations in social and demographic composition as well as different patterns of firearm ownership.

Mortality studies like ours do not include cases in which burglars or intruders are wounded or frightened away by a firearm's use or display. Cases in which would-be intruders may have purposely avoided a house known to be armed are also not identified. We did not report the total number or extent of nonlethal firearm injuries involving guns kept in the home. A complete determination of firearm risks versus benefits would require that these figures be known.

The home can be a dangerous place. We noted forty-three suicides, criminal homicides, or accidental gunshot deaths involving a gun kept in the home for every case of homicide for self-protection. In the light of these findings, it may reasonably be asked whether keeping firearms in the home increases a family's protection or places it in greater danger. Given the unique status of firearms in American society and the national toll of gunshot deaths, it is imperative that we answer this question.

56. *A Question of Self-Defense*

National Rifle Association
Institute for Legislative Action

The National Rifle Association defends each person's right to own and use arms in self-defense. The NRA cites figures from a study by Gary Kleck that indicates that there are about 645,000 defensive uses of handguns each year, excluding police and military uses. The NRA further contends that the majority of the accidental deaths from firearms involve rifles and not handguns.

On February 18, 1982, the Court of Appeals for the State of New York handed down a decision that chilled New York's subway passengers.

Two suits against the New York City Transit Authority charged the agency with negligence for not taking steps to correct conditions it, the Authority knew presented a clear danger to passengers. In one incident, a woman was raped in a subway station that was the scene of four separate rapes over a span of a few months. The second involved a retired school board official who was robbed and injured by knife-wielding thugs at a stop where thirteen separate robberies (eight with knives) occurred over a ten-month period.

The court dismissed both.

The court ruled that the Transit Authority was free from liability just as was any municipality or governmental agency. The Transit Authority had no responsibility *"to protect a person on its premises from assault by a third person"* nor did it have an obligation to increase police protection for well-documented high crime areas within the subway system, according to the court.

The cold, harsh legal facts are that by statute and court decree, local and state governments and "their agents," the police, have no obligation to provide protection for the individual.

Civilians Armed for Self-Defense

The concept of self-defense strikes at the heart of the debate, pro and con, over the private ownership of firearms.

Today . . . the focus of the controversy has been primarily on handguns. Each argument, each consideration seems to raise yet another question.

Government research indicates that the majority of firearms owned by Americans are owned for sport and recreational purposes rather than for self-protection, by a rate of three-to-one. The increase in gun sales seems to be among people who already own one or more guns rather than among non–gun-owning families. *However, among the 10 to 15 million women handgun owners, the figures favor self-protection as the main reason for owning a gun in urban areas.*

What thoughts run through a woman's mind, particularly after an assault or attempted assault, when she considers owning or using a gun for protection?

Do they differ from those of a male?

Does a handgun provide real or imagined security for the woman living alone . . . for the merchant in a high crime area . . . for families with small children?

Are handguns more of a danger to their owners than to criminals?

Are they "accidents waiting to happen"?

Protection: The Root of Gun Ownership

On the negative side is the notion that handguns should be banned to the average citizen. Proponents of this position may concede restricted use of handguns by on-duty military, police, and private security personnel, but handguns for protection would not be allowed.

Ironically, police and military views of handguns are 180 degrees opposite to the rhetoric of such prohibitionists. The official view by police and the military is that their on- and off-duty handguns are strictly "defensive" arms. Rifles and shotguns are considered "offensive" implements.

Unresolved, too, is an apparent contradiction in the prohibitionists' line of argument. On one hand, they argue that the handgun, particularly when used by a criminal or enraged family member, is the most lethal of instruments. On the other, they discount its protective value to the honest citizen because of what they describe as a handgun's "inherent inaccuracy."

Literally tens of millions of Americans disagree with the prohibitionist position. They see their handguns as critical tools that might spell the difference between becoming the victim of a crime or the victor in a confrontation with a criminal predator. Just what does the record show?

Protection of self, of one's loved ones, of one's home and community is the root of the American tradition of gun ownership. It is a concept cherished from the beginning of time and preserved most democratically within the English common law heritage where the defense of home, community, and kingdom rested upon an armed and ready populace. This was a distinct divergence from the continental practice of a disarmed peasantry "protected" by armed knights of the nobility.

Sir William Blackstone's "Commentaries"—on which the American legal system is based—described "the right of having and using arms for self-preservation and defense" as among the "Absolute Rights of Individuals."

Self-defense, said Sir William, was "justly called the primary law of nature, so it is not, neither can it be in fact, taken away by the laws of society."

What the Law Says

Gun ownership by convicted felons, drug addicts, and court-ruled mental defectives is currently forbidden by federal law. That law and more than 20,000 state and local laws not only forbid criminal purchase of, possession of, and use of all rifles, handguns, and shotguns by these people, but they also levy prison and/or monetary penalties against anyone misusing firearms in any manner. These laws are in addition to laws against murder, robbery, rape, etc.

Nevertheless, the push for yet more layers of federal, state, and local law continues. With virtually every imaginable criminal act covered by existing law, the new suggestions invariably focus on restricting the noncriminal acquisition, possession, and use of firearms—handguns in particular. Toward this end, the idea of handgun use for self-protection is continually dismissed.

Shortly after her husband left for work, a Waco, Texas, housewife heard the front door window break. A strange man reached in, unlocked the door, and entered the front room.

The housewife ran to the bedroom. She locked the door and grabbed a handgun kept beneath the mattress. The intruder kicked in the door. He saw the gun aimed at him. He left.

Twice a 51-year-old Los Angeles, California, woman had been raped by the same man. He had not yet been apprehended. After the second assault, she purchased a handgun. The man returned a third time. His criminal career came to an abrupt end.

Masquerading as a police officer, a man raped a Baltimore, Maryland, woman in front of her two children, ages one and two. When he threatened the older child, the woman lunged for a hidden revolver. It was the last thing the rapist saw.

When Phoenix, Arizona, authorities responded to a breaking-and-entering call, they found a 77-year-old woman gently rocking in her favorite chair. Her favorite .38 revolver was pointed at a man obediently lying half in and half out of her "pet door."

Those four incidents are not uncommon.

Based on several public opinion surveys, especially a Peter Hart survey commissioned by a handgun-ban organization, Florida State University Professor Gary Kleck has estimated that "there were about 645,000 defensive uses of handguns against persons per year, excluding police or military uses." Kleck also found that "guns of all types are used substantially more often defensively than criminally," and that "gun-wielding civilians in self-defense or some other legally justified cause" kill between 1,500 and 2,800 felons annually.

Since the night two decades ago when more than a score of neighbors watched as New York crime victim Kitty Genovese was slashed to death, headlines across the nation appear to be charting a new trend. Apathy and the attitude that the safety of neighbors and one's neighborhood is the job of the police and not of the community *together with the police* seems to be giving ground to a resurgence of community involvement. In fact, criminologists and police nationwide credit crime drops in the 1980s to increased community involvement.

In Baltimore, a 1979 *Evening Sun* headline ran: "Lady D.A. Outshoots Thugs." Chicago's *Tribune* chronicled one "Gunman Becomes The Victim" to an armed homeowner in 1982. Georgia's *Atlanta Constitution/Journal* ran the headline "Burglaries Fall in DeKalb (County) as Victims Take Aim" in 1982.

Esquire magazine ran two articles in defense of handgun ownership in 1981. And the trend toward citizens armed for defense was cover story material in *Woman's Day* (1983), *Boston Magazine* and Philadelphia's *Today Magazine* (1982), and *Savvy* (1981).

Television's popular talk show host Phil Donahue was surprised at the audience's reaction to his attempt to discount handguns as useful self-defense aids. He was hooted at by his largely female audience with taunts that he had "never been raped." Had Donahue read *Glamour* magazine's readership survey in May of 1981 he would have known that 65 percent of Glamour readers said they own guns; 66 percent of those owned guns primarily for self-defense. Sixty-eight percent opposed banning handguns.

Risk of Injury

The idea that a potential crime victim runs a greater risk of injury if he or she is armed has been proven groundless.

According to U.S. Justice Department victimization studies analyzed by Prof. Kleck, "for both robbery and assault, victims who used guns for protection were less likely either to be attacked or injured than victims who responded in any other way, including those who did not resist at all" and "victims who resisted robbers with guns . . . were less likely to lose their property. . . . When victims use guns to resist crimes, the crimes usually are disrupted and the victims are not injured."

A follow-up study of rape found that using a gun or knife for protection reduces the likelihood of a completed rape, and using a gun reduces the likelihood of injury to near zero. Such resistance also reduces the likelihood of psychological trauma.

More incidents of victims' successful use of guns would occur, and would be reported to the police, if there were fewer laws against carrying firearms.

Criminals face greater risk of injury from armed citizens than police, according to available Justice Department data.

One glaring statistic is that burglars who choose, either unintentionally or otherwise, to ply their trade in occupied homes are twice as likely to be shot or killed as they are to be caught, convicted, and imprisoned by the U.S. criminal justice system.

Armed citizens kill two to seven times the number of criminals killed each year by law enforcement. Additionally, Prof. Kleck estimates that annually "there were about 8,700–16,600 nonfatal, legally permissible woundings of criminals by gun-armed civilians," with no estimates available on the number held for authorities.

None of this has been lost on the typical criminal.

Research gathered by Professors James Wright and Peter Rossi, co-authors of the U.S. Justice Department's benchmark three-year study of weapons and criminal violence in America, points to the armed citizen or the threat of the armed citizen as possibly the most effective crime deterrent in the nation.

Criminals Fear Armed Citizens

Wright and Rossi questioned over 1,800 prisoners serving time in prisons across the nation. They found:

- 85 percent agreed that the "smart criminal" will attempt to find out if a potential victim is armed,
- 75 percent felt that burglars avoided occupied dwellings for fear of being shot,
- 60 percent felt that the typical criminal feared being shot by citizens more than he feared being shot by police,
- 80 percent of "handgun predators" had encountered armed citizens,
- 53 percent did not commit a specific crime for fear that the victim was armed, and
- 57 percent of "handgun predators" were scared off or shot at by armed victims.

The classic example of the threat of armed citizens to criminals and the corresponding effect on an area's crime rate remains Orlando, Florida.

In 1966, rape in that city skyrocketed from 12.8 per 100,000 citizens in 1965 to 35.9 per 100,000. The Orlando police organized a handgun-training program for women. The program ran from October 1966 through April 1967. The media gave extraordinary coverage to the fact that Orlando's female population was armed and more than willing to resist criminal attack. One year later, Orlando's rape rate plummeted to 4.1 per 100,000. Elsewhere in the state (excluding Orlando) rape rates increased that year.

Other areas that saw similar crime drops in armed robbery or rape after instituting well-publicized firearm training programs for merchants or women were Detroit and Highland Park, Michigan, and Montgomery, Alabama.

Fears that handguns are somehow home accident or "crime of passion" catalysts are unfounded in view of research into both areas.

Criminologist James Wright described the typical incident of family violence as "that mythical crime of passion" on a television documentary, "Gunfight, USA" aired over the Public Broadcasting System in 1983.

Wright denied that the typical "crime of passion" was an isolated incident by otherwise normally placid and loving individuals. Available research showed that it was in fact "the culminating event in a long history of interpersonal violence between the parties."

Wright further noted that handguns did not play the aggressive role most often attributed to them.

"The common pattern, the more common pattern, is for wives to shoot their husbands. Proportionately, men kill their women by other means, more brutal means, more degrading means. To deny that woman the right to own the firearms is in some sense to guarantee in perpetuity to her husband the right to beat her at will," said Wright.

It should be repeated that these men who kill their spouses are not "nice" folks.

Many of the homicides listed by the FBI as occurring between relatives, neighbors, and acquaintances are not simple domestic squabbles.

Inflated Homicide Statistics

Homicide by street gang members of rival gang members, homicide between drug traffickers, organized crime "hits," slayings of neighbors by a neighborhood criminal predator are listed as "nonfelony homicides." They are included in the "relative, friend, acquaintance, neighbor" categories that are used by handgun prohibitionists to inflate "crime of passion" statistics.

As "accidents waiting to happen" handguns once again appear to bear the brunt of unfair and unwarranted rhetoric.

The National Safety Council *does not* break down incidents of handgun versus rifle or shotgun-related accidental deaths. Research now underway at Florida State University suggests long guns are involved in a majority of the 1,800 accidental firearm-related deaths logged in the United States annually. That research also indicates that a sizeable number of those deaths are, in fact, not accidents but well-disguised homicides or suicides. Alcohol also seems to play a disproportionately large factor in the overall accidental death toll (50 percent).

Since Prohibition, the rate of firearm-related accidental deaths in the United States has been reduced by two-thirds according to the Centers for Disease Control (U.S. Public Health Service).

At its highest (during Prohibition) the rate was 2.5 per 100,000 citizens. It leveled out at 0.8 per 100,000 since 1978 before falling to 0.6 from 1987 to 1990.

The American public should be commended for its long record of safe firearms handling. Credit, too, should be given to training programs such as those offered by the National Rifle Association, an organization which has pioneered the field of safe firearms handling and training for more than a century.

The first hunter safety program was introduced by the NRA in 1949. The accidental hunting firearms death rate has dropped to 0.9 per 100,000 hunting licenses. Hunter safety is now taught by the fish and wildlife departments of all fifty states. The result of such training is evident.

The most recent program introduced by the NRA is the Personal Protection Program. This program, taught by NRA certified instructors nationwide, is aimed at individuals, women in particular, who feel they want a handgun for self-protection.

An Individual Choice

NRA instructors teach the principles of safe firearms handling and marksmanship excellence to hundreds of thousands of civilians and police each year.

It is not the intention of the NRA to suggest that handguns are the only means of self-defense. Nor is it the intention to suggest that handguns should be purchased for this purpose. The question of handgun ownership is one that is highly personal. It is a choice that should be made by the individual. It is a choice that should not be forbidden to the honest citizen by an overprotective government, particularly one that has no responsibility to provide real protection when one's life is threatened. It is a choice that should be approached with information and not emotion.

The purpose of the self-defense handgun is to preserve life and to discourage criminal violence. It may well prove to be the most immediate means of thwarting criminal activity. In that sense, it serves to provide security in a manner similar to health or life insurance. If ever there arises that time when it is needed, no substitute will do.

57. *The Strong Case for Gun Control*

CARL T. BOGUS

Carl Bogus compares two cities, Seattle and Vancouver, which are similar in all the relevant respects except that Vancouver has a relatively strong gun control law whereas Seattle does not. According to his study, there are more firearm assaults, and more firearm-related homicides and suicides in Seattle than in Vancouver. Furthermore, there were not more burglaries or homicides in Vancouver than in Seattle. In fact, there were fewer homicides in Vancouver than in Seattle. Bogus cites another study done in the District of Columbia, which found that there were 25 percent fewer homicides and 23 percent fewer suicides in the nine years following passage of a gun control law than in the nine years before passage. According to Bogus, the evidence from these two studies alone constitutes a strong case for gun control.

While abhorring violence, Americans generally believe that gun control cannot do much to reduce it. A majority of Americans questioned in a 1992 CBS–*New York Times* poll responded that banning handguns would only keep them away from law-abiding citizens rather than reduce the amount of violent crime. Many serious scholars have accepted the argument that the huge number of guns already in circulation would make any gun control laws ineffective. Until recently, it has been difficult to answer these objections. But in the past few years, new research has demonstrated that some gun control laws do work, dramatically reducing murder rates.

Gun violence is a plague of such major proportions that its destructive power is rivaled only by wars and epidemics. During the Vietnam War, more than twice as many Americans were shot to death in the United States as died in combat in Vietnam. Besides the 34,000 Americans killed by guns each year, more than 60,000 are injured—many seriously—and about a quarter of a million Americans are held up at gunpoint.

Measures that demonstrably reduce gun violence would gain wide public support. But that has been exactly the problem: A public that approves of gun control by wide margins also is skeptical about its effectiveness and . . . constitutionality. Both sources of doubt can now be put to rest.

A Tale of Two Cities

Perhaps the most dramatic findings about the efficacy of gun control laws come from a study comparing two cities that have followed different policies for regulating handguns: Seattle, Washington, and Vancouver, British Columbia.[1] Only 140 miles apart, the two cities are remarkably alike despite being located on opposite sides of an international border. They have populations nearly identical in size and, during the study period (1980–86), had similar socioeconomic profiles. Seattle, for example, had a 5.8 percent unemployment rate while Vancouver's was 6.0 percent. The median household income in Seattle was $16,254; in Vancouver, adjusted in U.S. dollars, it was $16,681. In racial and ethnic makeup, the two cities are also similar. Whites represent 79 percent of Seattle's inhabitants and 76 percent of Vancouver's. The principal racial difference is that Asians make up a larger share of Vancouver's population (22 percent versus 7 percent). The two cities share not only a common frontier history but a current culture as well. Most of the top ten television shows in one city, for example, also rank among the top ten in the other.

As one might expect from twin cities, burglary rates in Seattle and Vancouver were nearly identical. The aggravated assault rate was, however, slightly higher in Seattle. On examining the data more closely, the Sloan study found "a striking pattern." There

Reprinted by permission from *The American Prospect*, No. 10 (Summer 1992), pp. 19–28.

were almost identical rates of assaults with knives, clubs, and fists, but there was a far greater rate of assault with firearms in Seattle. Indeed, the firearm assault rate in Seattle was nearly eight times higher than in Vancouver.

The homicide rate was also markedly different in the two cities. During the seven years of the study, there were 204 homicides in Vancouver and 388 in Seattle—an enormous difference for two cities with comparable populations. Further analysis led to a startling finding: The entire difference was due to gun-related homicides. The murder rates with knives—and all other weapons excluding firearms—were virtually identical, but the rate of murders involving guns was five times greater in Seattle. That alone accounted for Seattle having nearly twice as many homicides as Vancouver.

People in Seattle may purchase a handgun for any reason after a five-day waiting period; 41 percent of all households have handguns. Vancouver, on the other hand, requires a permit for handgun purchases and issues them only to applicants who have a lawful reason to own a handgun and who, after a careful investigation, are found to have no criminal record and to be sane. Self-defense is not a valid reason to own a handgun, and recreational uses of handguns are strictly regulated. The penalty for illegal possession is severe—two years' imprisonment. Handguns are present in only 12 percent of Vancouver's homes.

The Seattle–Vancouver study provides strong evidence for the efficacy of gun control. Sloan and his colleagues concluded that the wider proliferation of handguns in Seattle was the sole cause of the higher rate of murders and assaults. The study answered other important questions as well.

- *Do handguns deter crime?* If handguns deter burglary, the burglary rate in Seattle—where so many more homes have handguns—should have been lower than the burglary rate in Vancouver. But it was not.
- *How often are handguns used for self-defense?* Less than 4 percent of the homicides in both cities resulted from acts of self-defense.
- Perhaps most important: *If handguns are unavailable, will people merely use other weapons instead?* The answer must be "no." Otherwise, the cities would

have had similar total murder rates and Vancouver would have had higher rates of homicide with other weapons.

A more recent study measured gun control legislation more directly.[2] In 1976 the District of Columbia enacted a new gun control law. Residents who lawfully owned firearms had sixty days to reregister them. After the sixty-day period, newly acquired handguns became illegal. Residents could continue to register rifles and shotguns, provided they purchased them from licensed dealers and complied with other regulations.

The researchers compared gun-related violence in the nine years prior to the law's enactment with the following nine years. They also compared the experience within the District with that of the immediately surrounding metropolitan area. The law was, of course, only in force within the boundaries of the District itself and not in contiguous areas of Maryland and Virginia that belong to the same metropolitan area, as the Census Bureau defines it.

The results of the study were surprising even to the most ardent gun control advocates. Within the District, gun-related homicides fell by more than 25 percent and gun-related suicides declined by 23 percent. Meanwhile, there was no statistically significant change in either gun-related homicides or suicides in the adjacent areas. Here again the data demonstrated that people did not switch to other weapons: Within the District there was no statistically significant change in either homicides or suicides with other weapons.

Perhaps most surprising of all was the suddenness of the change. Any decline in murders and suicides was expected to be gradual, as the number of weapons in the district slowly shrank. Yet homicides and suicides abruptly declined when the law went into effect. The D.C. law, therefore, had a significant and virtually immediate benefit.

The D.C. study demonstrates that gun control can work in the United States. Despite the similarities between Seattle and Vancouver, some critics of the Sloan study have suggested that Canada and the United States are sufficiently different to make extrapolations questionable. The D.C. study shows that even local gun control laws can be effective in the United States. Previously, the prevailing opinion was

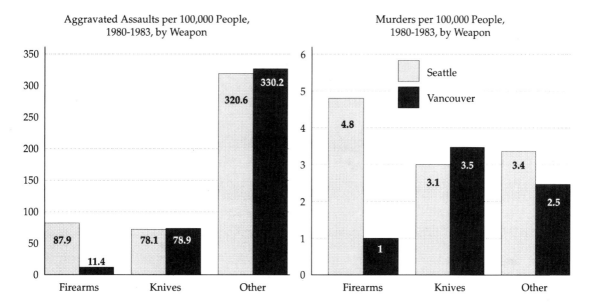

Aggravated Assaults per 100,000 People, 1980-1983, by Weapon

Murders per 100,000 People, 1980-1983, by Weapon

Source: John Henry Sloan et al., "Handgun Regulations, Crime, Assaults, and Homicide," *The New England Journal of Medicine*, Nov. 10, 1988, pp. 1256-1262.

that only national legislation could be effective. Critics said that if local laws blocked handgun purchases, buyers would simply import one from a nearby area. Many people probably do that, and there is little doubt that national legislation would be far more effective.

Washington D.C.'s gun control law has not transformed the city into a utopia. It has remained a violent city, and—along with many other large cities—its murder rate rose sharply in the last few years of the study (1986–88), when the use of "crack" cocaine was increasing. Yet the fact remains that for the full nine-year period after the gun control law was enacted, the mean D.C. murder rate was more than 25 percent lower and its mean suicide rate was 23 percent lower than in the preceding nine years. The effect of the law was not only immediate but sustained as well.

Why Gun Control Works

The gun lobby is fond of saying, "If guns are outlawed, only outlaws will have guns." What's wrong with this picture?

The National Rifle Association (NRA) slogan leads us to envision two groups—solid citizens and hard-

ened criminals—but the real world cannot be neatly divided into good guys and bad guys. Many people are law-abiding citizens until they become inflamed in a domestic dispute, a drunken argument in a bar, even a fender-bender on the highway. Murder is usually an act of rage; it is more often impulsive than premeditated. In fact, 80 percent of all murders occur during altercations and 71 percent involve acquaintances, including lovers, family members, and neighbors. Only 29 percent of those arrested for murder are previously convicted felons.

Rage can pass quickly, but if there is a gun available, even a few seconds may not be soon enough. Of course, enraged lovers and brawlers use other weapons, but it is better to be attacked with anything other than a gun. Guns are, by far, the most lethal weapons. The second deadliest is the knife, but knife attacks result in death only one-fifth as often as with guns.

For the same reason that it is better to face a knife than a gun in a lover's quarrel, it is better to be robbed at knifepoint rather than gunpoint. There are good reasons to believe that reducing the number of guns in the general population will reduce them in the hands of muggers and robbers. Prison inmates report that they acquired one-third of their guns by stealing them, typically in home burglaries. There are also people at the margin—not yet career criminals but drifting in that direction—who are more inclined to have guns if they are cheap and readily available. And since handguns are lawful almost everywhere, these people do not even have to cross a psychological Rubicon to get a gun.

Many of the people at the margin are youngsters. Nearly 70 percent of all serious crimes are committed by boys and young men, ages fourteen to twenty-four. Many of them are not yet career criminals. They are the children of despair, kids from dysfunctional families and impoverished communities who thirst for a feeling of importance. They are angry, immature, and unstable. In the 1950s, they carried switchblades, but since the early 1960s they have increasingly been carrying handguns. Packing a gun makes them feel like men, and it just takes a little alcohol or drugs, a buddy's dare, or a moment of bravado to propel them into their first mugging or holdup of a convenience store. Many juvenile robbers say that they did not intend to commit a robbery when they went out. The nation will be a less dangerous place if these kids go out without guns.

There is a frightening increase in the number of youngsters carrying guns. The National Adolescent Student Health Survey discovered that by 1987, nearly 2 percent of all eighth and tenth graders across the nation said they carried a gun to school within the past year. A third of them said they took a gun to school everyday—more than 100,000 students packing a pistol all the time. In just the first two months of 1992, more than a hundred firearms were confiscated in New York City schools.

And kids are not just carrying guns, they are using them. New York City was shaken earlier this year when, moments before Mayor David Dinkins was to give a speech to the students at Brooklyn's Thomas Jefferson High School, a fifteen-year-old pulled out a Smith & Wesson .38 and killed two other students. Had it not been for the mayor's presence at the school, the shootings might not have been front-page news.

It is somewhat disingenuous to be shocked about youths with handguns. Kids emulate adults. They live in a society that has not attached a sense of gravity to owning handguns. In half of the fifty states, handguns are completely unregulated; anyone may walk into a gun shop and buy a handgun just as easily as a quart of milk at a grocery. Most of the other states have only modest handgun regulations; four states, for example, have forty-eight hour waiting periods. Except in a very few locales, automobiles are regulated far more rigorously than handguns.

There are 35 million handguns in the United States; a quarter of all homes have at least one handgun in them. We can tell a teenage boy that he is really safer if he does not pack a gun. But why should he believe adults who keep handguns in their nightstand drawers, even though they have been told that a gun in the home is six times more likely to be used to shoot a family member than an intruder?

For more than a decade some observers, such as Charles Silberman, have noted a rising tide of savagery. Today, for example, my morning newspaper carries a report about a robbery at a local McDonald's restaurant. A man with a pistol demanded the restaurant's cash, which the manager immediately gave him. The robber then told the manager and two other employees to lie down, and proceeded to shoot two to death while one of the three ran away. Not long ago it would have been extremely rare for a robber—with the money in his hand—to kill his victims gratuitously; now it seems commonplace. We may wonder what impels someone to top off a robbery with a double murder, but whatever the motive, the handgun makes that act possible.

We are also witnessing a bewildering escalation in suicides. In 1960 there were about 19,000 suicides in the United States; now there are more than 30,000 each year. (This represents a rise in the suicide rate from 10.6 per 100,000 in 1960 to 12.4 per 100,000 in 1988.) Nearly two-thirds of all suicides in the United States are committed with firearms, more than 80 percent of those with handguns. The rising number of suicides is due almost completely to firearm suicides. While the number of suicides with other weapons has remained relatively stable (even slightly declining over the past two decades), the number of firearm suicides has more than doubled since 1960.

Why should that be so? If someone really wants to kill himself, is he not going to find a way to do so regardless of whether a handgun is available? This is something of a trick question. The rabbit in the hat is the phrase "really wants to kill himself" because suicide, like murder, is often an impulsive act, particularly among the 2,000 to 3,000 American teenagers who commit suicide each year. If an individual contemplating suicide can get through the moment of dark despair, he may reconsider. And if a gun is not available, many potential suicides will resort to a less lethal method, survive, and never attempt suicide again. Nothing is as quick and certain as a gun. The desire to die need only last as long as it takes to pull a trigger, and the decision is irrevocable.

In the Seattle–Vancouver study, the researchers found a 40 percent higher suicide rate among the fifteen- to twenty-five-year-olds in Seattle, a difference they discovered was due to a firearm suicide rate that is ten times higher among Seattle adolescents. Other research reveals that a potentially suicidal adolescent is *seventy-five times* as likely to kill himself when there is a gun in the house.[3]

This is the one area, however, where the type of gun may not matter. While more than 80 percent of all gun-related suicides are with handguns, research suggests that when handguns are not available, people attempting suicide may just as readily use long guns. But many homes only have a handgun, and reducing the number of homes with handguns will therefore reduce the number of suicides.

What Kind of Gun Control Works?

No one suggests that gun control legislation will be a panacea. Nevertheless, strong evidence suggests that the right kind of gun control legislation can reduce murders, suicides, and accidents substantially in the United States.

First and foremost, gun control means controlling handguns. Handguns account for only about one-third of all firearms in general circulation, but they are used in more than 75 percent of all gun-related homicides and more than 80 percent of all gun-related robberies. No other weapon is used nearly so often to murder. While handguns are used in half of all murders in America, knives are used in 18 percent, shotguns in 6 percent, rifles in 4 percent.

Two basic approaches are available to regulate handguns. One is to allow anyone to have a handgun,

except for individuals in certain prohibited categories such as convicted felons, the mentally ill, drunkards, and the like. This approach is fatally flawed. The vast majority of people who end up abusing handguns do not have records that place them in a high-risk category. Whenever someone commits a murder, we can in retrospect always say that the murderer was mentally unstable, but it is not easy to check potential handgun purchasers for signs of instability or smoldering rage. There is no test to give. Many mentally unstable individuals have no record of psychiatric treatment and, even if they do, their records are confidential. Because we want to encourage people who need psychological help to seek treatment, legislation that would open psychiatric records to the government or place them in some national data bank would be counterproductive. Moreover, even someone who clearly falls into a prohibited category, such as a convicted felon, can easily circumvent this system by sending a surrogate to purchase a handgun for him.

The second approach, known as a need-based or a restrictive permitting system, allows only people who fall within certain categories to own handguns. Handgun permits are, of course, issued to law enforcement personnel, but among the general population someone who wants a handgun permit must demonstrate a special need. Simply wanting a handgun for self-defense is not enough, but someone who can provide a sufficiently concrete reason to fear attack would be granted a handgun permit. Sportsmen can obtain special permits, but their handguns must be kept under lock and key at a gun club. It may inconvenience them, but when public safety is balanced against recreation, public safety must win out.

Many states have similar systems for permits to carry a concealed weapon in public, but in the United States only New Jersey and a few cities have true need-based permitting systems for handgun possession. Canada adopted this system nationally in 1978.

One of the most difficult aspects of a restrictive permitting system is the development of criteria for the granting of permits. Should a shopkeeper who has been held up at gunpoint three times get a handgun permit? What about a shopkeeper held up once? What about a woman who was beaten by an ex-boyfriend and fears it may happen again? What about a physician who has received death threats because he performs abortions? It is impossible to develop a list of criteria to address every individual instance; someone must have the discretion to make case-by-case decisions. But here disagreement arises. Gun control advocates want this discretionary power vested in the police, preferably the state police, while pro-gun groups favor the sheriffs, who . . . are elected and therefore reluctant to offend constituents.

A second dilemma of selective permitting concerns the inherent nature of discretion. Whenever there is a permit system of this type, pro-gun groups complain about a lack of uniformity. They are often right. No one will ever successfully draw a bright line between those who should, and should not, receive permits. There will always be an unsuccessful applicant who can argue that his or her situation is as compelling as that of someone who received a permit. Short of a system that grants permits either to everyone or no one, a certain amount of inconsistency is inevitable. To be effective, a restrictive permitting system must lean heavily toward the grant-no-one-a-permit end of the spectrum, allowing only a small number of exceptions in situations of clear need. Applicants should have a right to judicial review to ensure that authorities are exercising their discretion in good faith.

Handgun registration should be part of a restrictive permitting system. Owners should be required to register their handguns, and a permanent identification number should be engraved on every handgun. All transfers should be recorded. Everyone who has a driver's license or owns a car understands such a system, and even 78 percent of gun owners in America favor the registration of handguns, according to a 1991 Gallup poll.

With one exception, long guns do not present the same kind of threat to public safety as handguns. The exception, of course, is assault weapons. We remember how Patrick Purdy fired his AK-47 into a schoolyard in Stockton, California. In less than two minutes, he fired 106 rounds at children and teachers, killing five and wounding twenty-nine.

The NRA argues that it is impossible to differentiate an assault weapon from a standard hunting rifle—and to some extent it is right. Both hunting rifles and the assault weapons that are sold to the general public are semiautomatic. With a semiautomatic, firing repeat rounds requires pulling the trigger back for each one; with an automatic weapon, one must only pull the trigger back once and keep it depressed. This, however, is an inconsequential difference. A thirty-round magazine can be emptied in two seconds with a fully automatic weapon and in five seconds with a semiautomatic.

The way to regulate long guns, therefore, is to limit the size of magazines. Civilians should not be permitted to have magazines that hold more than five rounds. This simply means that after five rounds one must stop, remove the empty magazine, and either reload it or insert another full magazine. No hunter worth his salt blasts away at a deer as if he were storming the beach at Guadalcanal, and therefore this is no real inconvenience for hunters. But as Patrick Purdy demonstrated with his seventy-five-round magazine in Stockton, large-capacity magazines pose an unreasonable danger to public safety and should not be available to civilians.

The gun lobby urges that instead of regulating handguns (or assault weapons), severe and mandatory penalties should be imposed on persons who violate firearm laws. The weight of the evidence, however, suggests that these laws are not as effective. In 1987, for example, Detroit enacted an ordinance that imposed mandatory jail sentences on persons convicted of unlawfully concealing a handgun or carrying a firearm within the city. The strategy was to allow the general population to keep guns in their homes and offices but to reduce the number of people carrying guns on the streets. After evaluating the law, researchers concluded that, at best, "the ordinance had a relatively small preventive effect on the incidence of homicides in Detroit."[4] The researchers were, in fact, dubious that there was any effect. An analysis of the case histories of more than a thousand persons charged under the ordinance revealed that only 3 percent spent time in prison. With overcrowded jails, judges choose instead to incarcerate people convicted of more serious crimes. This is consistent with other studies of mandatory sentencing laws.[5]

Barriers to Change

The evidence is compelling: A restrictive permit system for handguns can significantly reduce the number of murders and suicides. If this type of legislation were no more effective on a national basis than it was in the District of Columbia, handgun murders and suicides would be cut by a quarter, which would mean saving more than 5,000 lives a year. Tens of thousands of others would be spared serious injury or the trauma of being assaulted at gunpoint. And many millions of dollars would be saved as well; the medical costs of handgun injuries exceed $800 million annually, 85 percent of which is paid for by public sources such as Medicaid and Medicare.

Public opinion clearly supports gun control legislation. According to a 1991 Gallup poll, 68 percent of Americans believe that firearm laws should be stricter, and 80 percent favor handgun registration. The will of the majority is clear, yet it has long been frustrated. As of this writing, gun control advocates have not even been able to get final congressional approval of a seven-day waiting period for handgun purchases—modest legislation favored by 93 percent of the public.

The nation would probably not tolerate the present level of gun violence if it had suddenly been thrust upon us. But like the proverbial frog who is put in an open pot of cold water on a hot stove and boils to death before realizing the water is getting hot, we have gradually become accustomed to the situation.

Guns have always been part of American culture. The colonists had guns to protect themselves in a hostile New World, and we have romantic images of pioneers such as Daniel Boone and Davy Crockett settling the frontier with the aid of their guns. But while early America was certainly a rough environment, crime was not one of its major problems. In the eighteenth century, Pennsylvania averaged only a single burglary a year and one murder every three years. There were no paid police and no need for them.

In the mid-nineteenth century, as the cities started to grow, they were frequently terrorized by mobs—bands of hoodlums in some instances, vigilantes in others. Police forces were formed, but they were often too small to confront the mobs, and city residents increasingly armed themselves for self-protection. Meanwhile, a technological innovation made mass production of guns possible: In about 1850, Samuel Colt developed a way to use machine tools to manufacture interchangeable parts for the revolver. Between 1865 and 1885, murders quadrupled and mug-

gings became common. America would never be the same.

This history leads, for many, to a sense of futility. Guns have always been with us, thus guns will always be with us. And the apparent ubiquity of guns in American life is intertwined with the belief that people have a constitutional right to own guns.

Engraved over the NRA's portals in Washington, D.C., is the following statement: "The right of the people to keep and bear arms shall not be infringed." Those words have a sacred ring. More than three quarters of the public believes that the Constitution guarantees an individual right to own weapons.

But the NRA has taken a pair of scissors and cut the Constitution's actual language in half. The Second Amendment actually says, "A well regulated Militia, being necessary to the security of a free state, the right of the people to keep and bear arms shall not be infringed." The courts have consistently held that this guarantees only a *collective* right, that is, it gives states the right to have armed militias, not individuals the right to own guns.

The U.S. Supreme Court has handed down three decisions touching on the Second Amendment. In the most recent—the 1939 case *United States v. Miller*—a man was convicted of transporting a double-barrel shotgun in interstate commerce, in violation of federal law. He argued that the legislation was invalid because it violated his rights under the Second Amendment. In affirming the conviction, the Court held that the Second Amendment must be interpreted and applied in the context of the government's organizing, arming, disciplining, or calling into service the militia.

In many court cases since 1939, the NRA has argued that the Supreme Court did not rule definitively on the Second Amendment in *United States v. Miller*, but time and again the courts have held otherwise. For example, a federal court of appeals specifically rejected the NRA's argument when it held that the Second Amendment did not prohibit the village of Morton Grove from banning handguns within its borders. On issuing an injunction ordering the Texas Emergency Reserve (the military arm of the KKK) to stop conducting paramilitary training and parading with firearms, a federal district court, citing *Miller*, held that the Second Amendment only guarantees that weapons can be kept and borne within the context of a militia organized and regulated by the state. These are but two of many such rulings, including decisions by the federal courts of appeals in the first, third, fourth, sixth, seventh, and eighth circuits. No contrary authority exists.

Seldom, if ever, has there been such a wide chasm between a popular myth of what the Constitution provides, on the one side, and what the Constitution actually says and how the courts have interpreted it, on the other. Both liberal and conservative lawyers, judges, and legal scholars are amazed at how thoroughly the phrase "right to bear arms" has been taken out of context and emblazoned upon the American consciousness. Former Chief Justice Warren E. Burger has said that the Second Amendment "has been the subject of one of the greatest pieces of fraud, and I repeat the word fraud, on the American public . . . that I have ever seen in my lifetime."

One might expect that Americans believe that the Constitution guarantees a right to bear arms because they favor such a guarantee, but that is not the case. While the overwhelming majority of Americans believes the Constitution *does* guarantee the right to own a gun, only 39 percent believe that it *should* guarantee that right.

The Gun Control Paradox

We thus have the makings of the gun control paradox: The majority would like to have gun control but they don't believe they can. They doubt it would work; they doubt it is constitutional. They want gun control in the same way that they would like to have the nation powered by solar energy—it is more a dream than a potential reality. This allows a committed minority to control the issue.

The shifting stances of two Pennsylvania politicians illustrate what this means in the political realm. In the late 1960s and early 1970s, Arlen Specter was the district attorney for Philadelphia and Richard L. Thornburgh was the U.S. attorney in Pittsburgh. Both of these bright young prosecutors knew something about crime, and both were ardent supporters of gun control legislation.

Thornburgh felt so strongly about it that he wrote an article for the *American Bar Association Journal*, in which he said that "the relatively unregulated handgun . . . constitutes the single biggest threat to the well-being of our police in the performance of their duties." Only those "who can affirmatively establish a legitimate need to do so" should be permitted to have handguns, said Thornburgh, adding that all handguns should be registered and all owners photographed and fingerprinted.

Subsequently both Specter and Thornburgh ran for statewide office—Specter for the U.S. Senate and Thornburgh for the governorship and later the Senate. Each took stock of the fact that [with hundreds of rural miles between Philadelphia and Pittsburgh] Pennsylvania has the second-largest NRA membership in the country (only California is larger). Each decided that gun control was not such a good idea after all.

Specter has consistently voted against gun control bills in the Senate, and when he was Governor, Thornburgh earned an "A" rating from the NRA for an unswerving opposition to gun control. Both have been amply rewarded. The NRA's political action committee spent $111,757 to support Specter's reelection to the Senate in 1986 and more than $50,000 to assist Thornburgh's Senate race in 1991. Thornburgh ultimately lost, but not because of his gun control stand; his opponent, Harris Wofford, also opposed gun control during the campaign.

Blame for the failure of gun control is generally laid at the feet of the NRA, but the problem is not so much a zealous minority as it is a quiescent majority. There has not been a sufficiently clear understanding of why the majority of Americans want gun control but do not want it enough to make it a priority in the voting booth. Much effort has been wasted describing the magnitude and horror of gun violence in America. The gun lobby has taken one broadside after another—from television network specials and newsweekly cover stories—all to no avail.

In talking about the horror of gun violence, however, the news media are preaching to the converted. Americans are aware of the level of gun violence, and they detest it. But news specials decrying gun violence may unwittingly have the same effect as the entertainment media's glorification of gun violence. They only reinforce a sense of hopelessness. If things could be different, Americans think, they would be. Otherwise, the carnage would not be tolerated.

The media portrayals may also have a numbing effect. Research shows that if people are frightened but believe there is no way to escape or to improve conditions, the fear becomes debilitating. Majority passivity is rooted in the belief that the status quo is immutable. It is this attitude that gun control advocates must try to change, by communicating the evidence that gun control laws do work. Americans know how bad gun violence is; they must now hear the evidence that reducing the violence is possible.

Endnotes

1. John Henry Sloan et al., "Handgun Regulations, Crime, Assaults, and Homicide," *The New England Journal of Medicine,* Nov. 10, 1988, pp. 1256–1262.

2. Colin Loftin et al., "Effects of Restrictive Licensing of Handguns on Homicide and Suicide in the District of Columbia," *The New England Journal of Medicine,* Dec. 5, 1991, pp. 1615–1649.

3. David A. Brent et al., "The Presence and Accessibility of Firearms in the Homes of Adolescent Suicides," *Journal of the American Medical Association,* Dec. 4, 1991, pp. 2989–2993.

4. Patrick W. O'Carroll, "Preventing Homicide: An Evaluation of the Efficacy of a Detroit Gun Ordinance," *American Journal of Public Health,* May 1991, pp. 576–581.

5. Alan Lizotte and Marjorie A. Zatz, "The Use and Abuse of Sentence Enhancement for Firearms Offenses in California," *Law and Contemporary Problems* (1986), pp. 199–221.

58. The Ownership and Carrying of Personal Firearms and Reduction of Crime Victimization

EDWARD F. LEDDY

To make his case against gun control, Edward Leddy cites the example of Morton Grove, Illinois, and Oak Park, Illinois, where laws banning handguns were followed by increased crime rates. He also cites the example of Highland Park, Michigan, where the police trained storekeepers in the use of guns and store robberies dropped from eighty in the previous four months to zero in the subsequent four months.

It is widely accepted that the ownership and carrying of pistols and revolvers by anyone except the police and those whom they choose to permit is a cause of

Excerpted from Edward F. Leddy, "The Ownership and Carrying of Personal Firearms and Reduction of Crime Victimization," in *The Gun Culture and Its Enemies,* William R. Tonso, ed. Copyright 1990 by the Second Amendment Foundation. Reprinted with permission.

violent crime. We know this without having to prove it, because it is so obviously reasonable to assume so. Indeed, until recently, in academic circles one would be accused of being radical or at least slightly eccentric to assert that this might not be true. Most of the governments of both Eastern and Western Europe have justified their laws and policies on this belief. Yet there is another side to the issue. . . .

A *Duty to Protect Oneself*

Historically, keeping the peace and suppressing rebellion were considered the duty of the state in most of Europe. There was little effort made in the past to track down criminals or to protect individuals. People were expected to protect themselves. Until the early decades of this century, the average citizen was permitted and often encouraged to own and carry guns freely. Travelers routinely went armed and in groups. [According to Colin Greenwood in *Firearms Control:*]

> . . . the Common Law right to keep arms and the tradition of owning arms for protection, was built up [in England] during a period when there was no effective police when the individual was compelled to see to his own protection.

Prohibiting the private ownership and carrying of guns is often justified by the assertion that the modern state is now able to provide all the protection a person can reasonably need. Armed self-protection is derided as vigilantism. However, as we all know, crime rates have risen in the last twenty years to the point that it is four times more likely that we shall be the victims of violence today than in 1963. Accordingly, this claim rings rather hollow. The ability of the state to protect us from personal violence is limited by resources, legal restraints, and personnel shortages.

Most of all, the state is usually unable to know that we need protection from attack until it is too late. By the time that the police can be notified and then arrive at the scene the violent criminal has ample opportunity to do you serious harm. I once waited twenty minutes for the New York City Police to respond to an "officer needs assistance" call which has their highest priority. On the other hand a gun provides immediate protection. Even where the police are prompt and efficient, the gun is speedier.

Handgun Ownership

In the United States, people in forty-four of the fifty states can legally own and purchase pistols without obtaining a police permit for ownership. Laws do prohibit possession of handguns by felons, and other undesirables. There has been much more research on the issue of handgun ownership than on carrying. There are extensive studies in this area which I will not touch on here except to note that it has not been established that crime is increased by widespread gun ownership. I wish to address the specific problem of legal gun carrying as a crime preventive program.

Carrying concealed weapons is much more regulated than ownership, requiring permits in most states. I find this rather odd because it would seem that if one has a gun there is little practical obstacle to prevent putting it on and carrying it. I found in many years of gun carrying when I was a Parole Officer that people do not notice.

However, there are many more laws regulating carrying than ownership. Many people who own pistols cannot legally carry them. Yet it is generally accepted that there is a need for *some* people to carry guns for protection. In almost all states, procedures are established to license selected people to legally carry concealed weapons. . . .

Because of its diverse laws, the United States can be regarded as a "vast sociological laboratory." In some parts of the nation, guns are almost banned by strict regulations. In others, gun possession in the home or business is not restricted except that persons with records of crime or insanity, minors, and certain other categories may not have guns. Carrying concealed weapons is regulated by both mandatory and discretionary permit systems.

One can compare the results of different gun law strategies because of the variety of laws. These, in effect, have been informal experiments in the use of guns by civilians. While they have not been formal controlled experiments, the results have been so dramatic that the relatively small experimental errors which may have occurred are probably of no real significance.

In Detroit, Michigan, grocery robberies declined 90 percent after a firearms training program for grocers was instituted by a grocers association.

Highland Park, Michigan, police trained storekeepers to shoot producing a dramatic decrease in store robberies from 80 in the previous four months to none in the subsequent four-month period.

In New Orleans, Louisiana, pharmacy robberies dropped from three per week to three in six months.

In Kennesaw, Georgia, all households have been required by law to keep a firearm since 1982. Serious crime dropped 74.4 percent in the year after the passage of the law and has remained low.

On the other hand the town of Morton Grove, Illinois, adopted a ban on handguns. Rates of armed crime increased dramatically in comparison with neighboring communities.

Nearby Oak Park, Illinois, passed a similar law in 1984. Burglary rose 35 percent in the following year.

According to a 1985 NBC News survey, about one in twenty (7,500,000) Americans carry a firearm for self-defense. If the fears of antigun advocates were of substance this would produce millions of gun murders instead of the total of about five thousand actually committed in the United States. Crimes of any kind committed by citizens having gun licenses are so rare that the police do not even bother to keep statistics. Few murders are committed by people without prior criminal records. Of course people with criminal histories should not be licensed.

What If Everyone Carried a Gun?

Opponents of allowing citizens to be armed often present this "what if?" argument. They imply that the removal of the discretionary restrictions that they believe in would result in catastrophe. Gun carrying would become universal and we would re-enter "the wild west" with everyone going armed. Aside from its historical inaccuracy, this is pure speculation. Where gun licensing is mandatory no such thing has happened. Instead researchers have found that when a mandatory permit system is implemented, only 3 to 8 percent (4 percent is the most frequent) of the population apply for a license. These are largely individuals who are in real danger from crime. Many of these people only carry guns on dangerous occasions, e.g., when they are carrying large sums of money or traveling in bad neighborhoods. Some others apply because they wish the convenience of a carry license to transport guns for sport without legal concerns. Far from becoming universal, gun carrying increases by only a few percentage points. The main difference is that many people without criminal records who were carrying illegally regularize their activity.

The 4 percent figure, however, would project nationwide to a potential carrying population of 8–10 million [out of 225,000,000], a figure higher than that for those who carry regularly now, but lower than that for those who carry handguns for protection some of the time. With regard to most of the population, widespread issuance of permits to carry to those who wish them, or allowing concealed carrying without a permit, would result in legalizing the technically unlawful activities of a few million Americans and in causing an additional percentage or two of the population to carry protective handguns.

The writer lived for six years in Laramie, Wyoming, where gun carrying openly is legal. I never saw anyone carry except during "Jubilee Days" when we were asked to dress "Western.". . .

The Criminal's View

In 1985, the U.S. Department of Justice conducted a study of criminal behavior. Convicted criminals were asked a series of questions on their behavior. Thirty-four percent reported that they had been scared off, shot at, wounded, or captured by an armed victim. Forty percent reported they had decided not to commit a crime because they thought the victim was armed:

> The first example in the sequence asked the sample to agree or disagree that "a criminal is not going to mess around with a victim he knows is armed with a gun." About three-fifths (56%) agreed. Another item read, "A smart criminal always tries to find out if a potential victim is armed." More than four-fifths agreed with that. Yet another item read, "Most criminals are more worried about meeting an armed victim than they are about running into the police." About three-fifths (57%) also agreed with that.

The actual frequency of gun use for self-protection varies widely depending on the local laws. (In the United States most gun laws are made by the fifty states. They differ widely in severity, from almost complete prohibition to easy availability.) Accordingly [as stated in *Attitudes of the American Electorate Toward Gun Control*, 1978], one can compare the results of different levels of control:

Use of guns in defense of person and property is most common where "controls" on guns are fewest. and having needed but not had a gun for self-defense is most common in big cities where "controls" on gun ownership are generally most stringent.

Rates of those crimes deterrable by guns vary with the strictness of gun laws. Robbery (theft by violence) is highest in those states with the lowest gun ownership. It is lowest where private citizens own many guns. This seems reasonable since robbery tends to be a crime committed by repeat offenders. As one Wyoming police official said, "Where citizens have no guns, robbers commit long strings of crimes before the police catch them. Here a storekeeper shoots them on the second or third robbery." This prevents future crimes and thus protects many who are unaware that they would otherwise have become victims.

The Extent of Self-Defense

Fourteen percent of the gun-owning households in the United States (about 14,000,000 people) report that they have used a gun for protection of person or property exclusive of military or police work. In 60 percent of these cases, the gun was not fired and was used only as a threat. In only 9 percent of the instances was anyone injured or killed. Only 31 percent of instances were reported to the police. Accordingly officials tend to be unaware of the extent of citizen self-defense. Armed citizens in the United States protect themselves from criminals at least 380,000 times a year. [According to Gary Kleck and David J. Bordua, in *Law and Policy Quarterly*, 1983:]

> Given the data on private citizens' use of firearms against criminals and evidence on the slight risks of legal punishment associated with most crimes, it is a perfectly plausible hypothesis that private gun ownership currently exerts as much or more deterrent effect on criminals as do the activities of the criminal justice system. The gun-owning citizenry is certainly more omnipresent than the police, and the potential severity of private justice is at least as severe as more formal legal justice, given the frequency of citizen shootings of criminals and the de facto near abolition of capital punishment by the federal judiciary.

While the value to the potential victim of a gun for self-protection may be admitted, officials might well be concerned about the danger that citizens would misuse their weapons injuring innocent people, committing crimes, and violating the laws on use of deadly force. Research in the United States [by David Conover, in *The American Rifleman*, September 1985] indicates that this problem is more theoretical than real. A comparison was made between errors made by the police and those made by private citizens:

> . . . police were successful in shooting or driving off criminals 68 percent of the time, private citizens were successful in 83 percent of their encounters. While 11 percent of the individuals involved in police shootings were later found to be innocents misidentified as criminals, only 2 percent of those in civilian shootings were so misidentified.
>
> Private citizens encounter and kill about three times as many criminals each year as do law enforcement officials.

It appears, from the writer's experience, that citizens commit fewer errors in the use of force than the police because the police often enter dangerous situations with little information. They arrive on a crime scene often not knowing who is the victim and who is the criminal. In contrast, the citizen almost always uses a weapon in response to attack. Thus the citizen can generally be sure of the criminal's identity.

The reason few crimes are committed by licensed citizens is that criminals tend to commit crimes and acquire records early in their lives. In a properly operating mandatory system, criminals cannot get licenses and seldom seek them. The chance that a citizen without any record will commit a crime is small. Giving him a gun license does not change this. . . .

Criminalization of the Victim

In New York City, which has had extremely strict gun laws for eighty years, there is widespread disregard for the law on the part of honest citizens. A perennial news story in that city is the honest citizen who is attacked by criminals, wards them off with a gun, and is then arrested for violation of the gun law. The internationally reported Bernard Goetz case is only a recent example. [Reported by David Conover, in *The American Rifleman*, September 1985:]

> In the City of New York alone, about 6 percent of the population admits to owning a firearm for protection. This figure represents about 450,000 gun owners in the Big Apple or seven times the number of citizens granted permits to legally own, carry or transport their personal firearms. In other words, about 85 percent of those people honest enough to admit owning a gun are technical criminals under the laws of New York. But these New Yorkers have made the choice. They would rather be "criminals" under a bad law than bodies in a police morgue.

According to a 1985 survey by NBC News, about one American in twenty (7,500,000) carries a gun for self-protection. (If such carrying was legal everywhere under a mandatory permit system the figure would probably rise to 8,800,000.) In many areas this carrying is illegal. This brings up the consideration that the vast majority of these "law breakers" are ordinary citizens without any record of criminal behavior. They are merely seeking to protect themselves from the violent criminals who prey on them. Discretionary licensing systems which refuse to grant licenses to these people are being disregarded. Instead they follow the old police maxim "It is better to be tried by twelve than carried by six."

Judge David J. Shields of Chicago, who tries many such illegal gun carrying cases, wrote:

> Probably the most striking experience that one takes away from Gun Court is awareness of the kinds of people who appear there as defendants. For most it is their first arrest; many are old people. Shopkeepers, persons who have been victims of violent crimes, and others who carry their guns because of a sincere belief in their need for protection—these constitute the greatest part of the call. . . .

The National Rifle Association of America has proposed and a number of American states have adopted a model law regulating carrying concealed weapons. This law contains the following principles:

1. A permit to carry concealed weapons is required.
2. A character investigation is conducted. The person must supply identifying information.
3. It is presumed that the person has a right to a license unless there is cause for denial. The license must be issued unless there is a record of past violent crimes, pending charges, narcotic use, alien or fugitive status. Commitment to a mental institution or drug/alcohol treatment center is also cause for denial unless a physician certifies that there is no danger to the public.
4. As in other American laws, there is a presumption of innocent intent. If the person is found suitable to carry a gun, evaluation of his or her reason for going armed is not considered the business of the state.

The most significant elements of this law are the refusal to allow police to arbitrarily deny licenses and restriction of their inquiry to clearly defined considerations of personal suitability. These are important limitations because they are designed to prevent personal prejudices from affecting the decision and to prevent social standing, race, wealth, or other extraneous factors from being considered.

A *Clear Deterrence*

Experience indicates that the ownership and carrying of guns by potential victims reduces victimization both for the individual and for other potential victims. The deterrence of such crimes as robbery, assault, rape, and home invasion (illegal entry into occupied dwellings) is clear and dramatic. The hazards of citizen use have been greatly exaggerated because of theoretical fears, not actual evidence. Therefore a revision of firearms laws in the direction of the mandatory model appears both prudent and desirable from the viewpoint of potential victims. This would benefit those who do not choose to carry guns as well as those who do so, since, when many people are armed, the criminal cannot be sure that any potential victim is unarmed. This measure would both provide protection to the potential victim and pose a significant threat to the violent criminal.

59. *The Brady Bill*

CONGRESS OF THE UNITED STATES

To provide for a waiting period before the purchase of a handgun, and for the establishment of a national instant criminal background check system to be contacted by firearms dealers before the transfer of any firearm.

Sec. 102. *Federal Firearms Licensee Required to Conduct Criminal Background Check Before Transfer of Firearm to Non-Licensee*

(a) INTERIM PROVISION.—

(1) IN GENERAL.—Section 922 of Title 18, U.S. Code, is amended by adding at the end the following:

(s) (1) Beginning on the date that is 90 days after the date of enactment of this subsection and ending on the day before the date that is 60 months after such date of enactment, it shall be unlawful for any licensed importer, licensed manufacturer, or licensed dealer to sell, deliver, or transfer a handgun to an individual who is not licensed under section 923, unless—

(A) after the most recent proposal of such transfer by the transferee—

(i) the transferor has—

(I) received from the transferee a statement of the transferee containing the information described in paragraph (3);

(II) verified the identity of the transferee by examining the identification document presented;

(III) within 1 day after the transferee furnishes the statement, provided notice of the contents of the statement to the chief law enforcement officer of the place of residence of the transferee; and

(IV) within 1 day after the transferee furnishes the statement, transmitted a copy of the statement to the chief law enforcement officer of the place of residence of the transferee; and

(ii) (I) 5 business days (meaning days on which State offices are open) have elapsed from the date the transferor furnished notice of the contents of the statement to the chief law enforcement officer, during which period the transferor has not received information from the chief law enforcement officer that receipt or possession of the handgun by the transferee would be in violation of Federal, State, or local law; or

(II) the transferor has received notice from the chief law enforcement officer that the officer has no information indicating that receipt or possession of the handgun by the transferee would violate Federal, State, or local law;

(B) the transferee has presented to the transferor a written statement, issued by the chief law enforcement officer of the place of residence of the transferee during the 10-day period ending on the date of the most recent proposal of such transfer by the transferee, stating that the transferee requires access to a handgun because of a threat to the life of the transferee or of any member of the household of the transferee;

(C) (i) the transferee has presented to the transferor a permit that—

    (I) allows the transferee to possess or acquire a handgun; and

    (II) was issued not more than 5 years earlier by the State in which the transfer is to take place; and

  (ii) the law of the State provides that such a permit is to be issued only after an authorized government official has verified that the information available to such official does not indicate that possession of a handgun by the transferee would be in violation of the law;

(D) the law of the State requires that, before any licensed importer, licensed manufacturer, or licensed dealer completes the transfer of a handgun to an individual who is not licensed under section 923, an authorized government official verify that the information available to such official does not indicate that possession of a handgun by the transferee would be in violation of law;

(E) the Secretary has approved the transfer under section 5812 of the Internal Revenue Code of 1986; or

(F) on application of the transferor, the Secretary has certified that compliance with subparagraph (A)(i)(III) is impracticable because—

  (i) the ratio of the number of law enforcement officers of the State in which the transfer is to occur to the number of square miles of land area of the State does not exceed 0.0025;

  (ii) the business premises of the transferor at which the transfer is to occur are extremely remote in relation to the chief law enforcement officer; and

  (iii) there is an absence of telecommunications facilities in the geographical area in which the business premises are located.

(2) A chief law enforcement officer to whom a transferor has provided notice pursuant to paragraph (1)(A)(i)(III) shall make a reasonable effort to ascertain within 5 business days whether receipt or possession would be in violation of the law, including research in whatever State and local record-keeping systems are available and in a national system designated by the Attorney General.

(3) The statement referred to in paragraph (l)(A)(i)(I) shall contain only—

(A) the name, address, and date of birth appearing on a valid identification document (as defined in section 1028(d)(l)) of the transferee containing a photograph of the transferee and a description of the identification used;

(B) a statement that the transferee—

  (i) is not under indictment for, and has not been convicted in any court of, a crime punishable by imprisonment for a term exceeding 1 year;

  (ii) is not a fugitive from justice;

  (iii) is not an unlawful user of or addicted to any controlled substance (as defined in section 102 of the Controlled Substances Act);

  (iv) has not been adjudicated as a mental defective or been committed to a mental institution;

  (v) is not an alien who is illegally or unlawfully in the United States;

  (vi) has not been discharged from the Armed Forces under dishonorable conditions; and

  (vii) is not a person who, having been a citizen of the United States, has renounced such citizenship;

(C) the date the statement is made; and

(D) notice that the transferee intends to obtain a handgun from the transferor.

(4) Any transferor of a handgun who, after such transfer, receives a report from a chief law enforcement officer containing information that receipt or possession of the handgun by the transferee violates Federal, State, or local law shall, within 1 business day after receipt of such request, communicate any information related to the transfer that the transferor has about the transfer and the transferee to—

(A) the chief law enforcement officer of the place of business of the transferor; and

(B) the chief law enforcement officer of the place of residence of the transferee.

(5) Any transferor who receives information, not otherwise available to the public, in a report under this subsection shall not disclose such informa-

tion except to the transferee, to law enforcement authorities, or pursuant to the direction of a court of law.

(6) (A) Any transferor who sells, delivers, or otherwise transfers a handgun to a transferee shall retain the copy of the statement of the transferee with respect to the handgun transaction, and shall retain evidence that the transferor has complied with subclauses (III) and (IV) of paragraph (1)(A)(i) with respect to the statement.

(B) Unless the chief law enforcement officer to whom a statement is transmitted under paragraph (l)(A)(i)(IV) determines that a transaction would violate Federal, State, or local law—

(i) the officer shall, within 20 business days after the date the transferee made the statement on the basis of which the notice was provided, destroy the statement, any record containing information derived from the statement, and any record created as a result of the notice required by paragraph (1)(A)(i)(III);

(ii) the information contained in the statement shall not be conveyed to any person except a person who has a need to know in order to carry out this subsection; and

(iii) the information contained in the statement shall not be used for any purpose other than to carry out this subsection.

(C) If a chief law enforcement officer determines that an individual is ineligible to receive a handgun and the individual requests the officer to provide the reason for such determination, the officer shall provide such reasons to the individual in writing within 20 business days after receipt of the request.

(7) A chief law enforcement officer or other person responsible for providing criminal history background information pursuant to this subsection shall not be liable in an action at law for damages—

(A) for failure to prevent the sale or transfer of a handgun to a person whose receipt or possession of the handgun is unlawful under this section; or

(B) for preventing such a sale or transfer to a person who may lawfully receive or possess a handgun.

(8) For purposes of this subsection, the term "chief law enforcement officer" means the chief of police, the sheriff, or an equivalent officer or the designee of any such individual.

(9) The Secretary shall take necessary actions to ensure that the provisions of this subsection are published and disseminated to licensed dealers, law enforcement officials, and the public.

(2) HANDGUN DEFINED.—Section 921(a) of title 18, United States Code, is amended by adding at the end the following: (29) The term "handgun" means—

(A) a firearm which has a short stock and is designed to be held and fired by the use of a single hand; and

(B) any combination of parts from which a firearm described in subparagraph (A) can be assembled.

(b) PERMANENT PROVISION.—Section 922 of title 18, United States Code, as amended by subsection (a)(1), is amended by adding at the end the following:

(t) (l) Beginning on the date that is 30 days after the Attorney General notifies licensees under section 103(d) of the Brady Handgun Violence Prevention Act that the national instant criminal background check system is established, a licensed importer, licensed manufacturer, or licensed dealer shall not transfer a firearm to any other person who is not licensed under this chapter, unless—

(A) before the completion of the transfer, the licensee contacts the national instant criminal background check system established under section 103 of that Act;

(B) (i) the system provides the licensee with a unique identification number; or

(ii) three business days (meaning a day on which State offices are open) have elapsed since the licensee contacted the system, and the system has not notified the licensee that the receipt of a firearm by such other person would violate subsection (g) or (n) of this section; and

(C) the transferor has verified the identity of the transferee by examining a valid identification document (as defined in section 1028(d)(l) of this title) of the transferee containing a photograph of the transferee.

(2) If receipt of a firearm would not violate section 922 (g) or (n) or State law, the system shall—

(A) assign a unique identification number to the transfer;

(B) provide the licensee with the number; and

(C) destroy all records of the system with respect to the call (other than the identifying number and the date the number was assigned) and all records of the system relating to the person or the transfer.

(3) Paragraph (1) shall not apply to a firearm transfer between a licensee and another person if—

(A)   (i) such other person has presented to the licensee a permit that—

(I) allows such other person to possess or acquire a firearm; and

(II) was issued not more than 5 years earlier by the State in which the transfer is to take place; and

(ii) the law of the State provides that such a permit is to be issued only after an authorized government official has verified that the information available to such official does not indicate that possession of a firearm by such other person would be in violation of law;

(B) the Secretary has approved the transfer under section 5812 of the Internal Revenue Code of 1986; or

(C) on application of the transferor, the Secretary has certified that compliance with paragraph (1)(A) is impracticable because—

(i) the ratio of the number of law enforcement officers of the State in which the transfer is to occur to the number of square miles of land area of the State does not exceed 0.0025;

(ii) the business premises of the licensee at which the transfer is to occur are extremely remote in relation to the chief law enforcement officer (as defined in subsection (s)(8)); and

(iii) there is an absence of telecommunications facilities in the geographical area in which the business premises are located.

(4) If the national instant criminal background check system notifies the licensee that the information available to the system does not demonstrate that the receipt of a firearm by such other person would violate subsection (g) or (n) or State law, and the licensee transfers a firearm to such other person, the licensee shall include in the record of the transfer the unique identification number provided by the system with respect to the transfer.

(5) If the licensee knowingly transfers a firearm to such other person and knowingly fails to comply with paragraph (1) of this subsection with respect to the transfer and, at the time such other person most recently proposed the transfer, the national instant criminal background check system was operating and information was available to the system demonstrating that receipt of a firearm by such other person would violate subsection (g) or (n) of this section or State law, the Secretary may, after notice and opportunity for a hearing, suspend for not more than 6 months or revoke any license issued to the licensee under section 923, and may impose on the licensee a civil fine of not more than $5,000.

(6) Neither a local government nor an employee of the Federal Government or of any State or local government, responsible for providing information to the national instant criminal background check system shall be liable in an action at law for damages—

(A) for failure to prevent the sale or transfer of a firearm to a person whose receipt or possession of the firearm is unlawful under this section; or

(B) for preventing such a sale or transfer to a person who may lawfully receive or possess a firearm.

(c) PENALTY.—Section 924(a) of title 18, United States Code, is amended—

(1) in paragraph (1), by striking "paragraph (2) or (3) of"; and

(2) by adding at the end the following:

"(5) Whoever knowingly violates subsection (s) or (t) of section 922 shall be fined not more than $1,000, imprisoned for not more than 1 year, or both."

Sec. 103. *National Instant Criminal Background Check System*

(a) DETERMINATION OF TIMETABLES.—Not later than 6 months after the date of enactment of this Act, the Attorney General shall—
  (1) determine the type of computer hardware and software that will be used to operate the national instant criminal background check system and the means by which State criminal records systems and the telephone or electronic device of licensees will communicate with the national system;
  (2) investigate the criminal records system of each State and determine for each State a timetable by which the State should be able to provide criminal records on an on-line capacity basis to the national system; and
  (3) notify each State of the determinations made pursuant to paragraphs (1) and (2).

(b) ESTABLISHMENT OF SYSTEM.—Not later than 60 months after the date of the enactment of this Act, the Attorney General shall establish a national instant criminal background check system that any licensee may contact, by telephone or by other electronic means in addition to the telephone, for information, to be supplied immediately, on whether receipt of a firearm by a prospective transferee would violate section 922 of title 18, United States Code, or State law.

Suggested Readings

Anthologies

Cozie, Charles. *Gun Control* (San Diego: Greenhaven Press, 1992).

Nisbet, Lee. *The Gun Control Debate* (Buffalo: Prometheus Books, 1990).

Alternative Views

Clark, Robert. *Deadly Force: The Lure of Violence* (Springfield: Charles C. Thomas, 1988).

Halbrook, Stephen. *That Every Man Be Armed* (Oakland: Independence Institute, 1990).

Kleck, Gary. *Point Blank: Guns and Violence in America* (New York: Aldine de Gruyter, 1991).

Prothrow-Stith, Deborah. *Deadly Consequences* (New York: HarperCollins, 1991).

Practical Applications

National Rifle Association of America (NRA)

Handgun Control Inc.

Animal Liberation and Environmental Justice

Introduction

Basic Concepts

The problem of animal liberation and environmental justice has begun to attract widespread public attention. Beginning with the 1973 publication of Peter Singer's article, "Animal Liberation," in the *New York Review of Books*, followed by the publication two years later of his book of the same title, people have become increasingly concerned with two of the most serious forms of exploitation: animal experimentation and factory farming.

Animal experimentation is a big business, involving 60 to 100 million animals a year. Two experiments alone—the rabbit-blinding Draize eye test and the LD50 toxicity test designed to find the lethal dose for 50 percent of a sample of animals—cause the deaths of more than 5 million animals per year in the United States alone. In factory farming, millions of animals are raised in such a way that their short lives are dominated by pain and suffering. Veal calves are put in narrow stalls and tethered with a chain so that they cannot turn around, lie down comfortably, or groom themselves. They are fed a totally liq-

uid diet to promote rapid weight gain, and they are given no water because thirsty animals eat more than those who drink water.

In recent years, environmental concern has focused on a myriad of problems from acid rain to the destruction of rainforests and the ozone layer. For example, the acidity of rainfall over the northeastern United States has quadrupled since 1900. Moreover, in 1995, some 12,350 square miles of Brazilian rainforest—an area larger than Belgium—was reduced to ashes, and over the past decade, ozone levels over Antarctica have diminished by 50 percent. In many cases, resolving these problems will require extensive programs and international cooperation. For example, in the Montreal protocol of 1987, dozens of nations agreed to cut their chlorofluorocarbon emissions (which are thought to be the major cause of ozone depletion) in half by the end of the century, and several countries and the major chlorofluorocarbon manufacturers have more recently announced their intentions to eliminate the chemicals by that deadline.

At the most general level, the problem of animal liberation and environmental concern raises the question of what should be our policies for treating animals and preserving the environment, or alternatively, what is the moral status of nonhuman living things. One possible answer is that nonhuman living things have no independent moral status at all; their moral status depends completely on the impact they have on human welfare. Another possible answer is that nonhuman living things have an independent moral status such that their welfare has to be weighed against, and at least sometimes outweigh, considerations of human welfare.

Obviously, supporters of animal liberation favor the view that animals have independent moral status, but they disagree as to the grounds for this independent moral status. Some claim that animals have independent moral status because taking their welfare into account would maximize overall utility. Others claim that the independent moral status of animals rests on a nonutilitarian foundation.

This conflict among supporters of animal liberation reflects a general conflict among utilitarians and nonutilitarians with respect to a wide range of practical problems (see the General Introduction to this anthology). However, with respect to this particular problem, supporters of animal liberation cannot rely on some form of a Kantian theory to reach an acceptable resolution because most animals are incapable of forming either an actual or hypothetical contract with human beings for the purpose of securing their common welfare. Kantian theory, however, is only a means to a goal, which is to achieve a fair resolution of morally relevant interests. Consequently, if nonhuman living things do have morally relevant interests, then to achieve that goal, some means other than Kantian theory will have to be employed.

This is not to say that Kantian theory is not useful for achieving a fair resolution of conflicts when only human interests pertain. In fact, it would seem that a fair resolution of conflicts among human and nonhuman interests would mirror a fair resolution of conflicts among purely human interests. For example, if a utilitarian (or a nonutilitarian) resolution were fair when only human interests are taken into account, a utilitarian (or a nonutilitarian) resolution would seem to be fair when both human and nonhuman interests are considered.

With respect to environmental concern, supporters do not agree that all nonhuman living things have independent moral status. Those who maintain that only sentient beings have independent moral status attempt to ground human concern for other living things on the impact they have on the welfare of sentient beings. Accordingly, to resolve the problem of animal liberation and environmental concern, we must determine which living beings have independent moral status and what sort of justification best accounts for that status.

Alternative Views

In Selection 60, R. D. Guthrie defends an anthropocentric environmental ethic in which nonhuman living things have no independent moral status. Instead their moral status depends entirely on the impact they have on the human community. Guthrie argues that it is both illogical and impractical to extend moral concern beyond the human community. Given that we already recognize the relationships of nonhuman organisms to each other and to ourselves to be nonmoral, Guthrie claims that it is illogical to think our relationship to nonhuman organisms was anything but nonmoral as well. Moreover, he argues that it would be impractical for us when making decisions as to what to do to have to weigh the effects our actions have on nonhuman organisms.

Yet although it is true that only moral agents like ourselves can recognize moral value, why should we think that we are the only ones to have moral value? Surely things can have moral value without being able to recognize it; in fact, some humans are like that. Of course, weighing the welfare of nonhuman organisms against our own will make our deliberations more complicated, but it need not render them impractical if we devise some reasonable weighing principles as James P. Sterba argues we can in Selection 63.

In Selection 61, Peter Singer argues for the independent moral status of animals by comparing the bias against animals, which he calls "speciesism," with biases against Blacks and women. According to Singer, the grounds we have for opposing racism and sexism are also grounds for opposing speciesism because all forms of discrimination run counter to the principle of equal consideration. Racists violate this principle by giving greater weight to the interests of members of their own race in cases of conflict; sexists violate this principle by favoring the interests of their own specific sex; and speciesists violate this principle by allowing the interests of their own species to override the greater interests of other species.

Animals have interests, Singer maintains, because they have a capacity for suffering and enjoyment. According to the principle of equal consideration, there is no justification for regarding the pain animals feel as less important than the same amount of pain (or pleasure) humans feel. As for the practical requirements of this view, Singer contends that we cannot go astray if we give the same respect to the lives of animals that we give to the lives of humans at a similar mental level. In the end, Singer thinks, this requires a utilitarian weighing of both human and animal interests.

Singer's view has been challenged on grounds that utilitarianism does not ultimately support a strong case for animal rights for several reasons. First of all, by Singer's own admission, it is permissible to eat farm animals, typically cattle and sheep, that are reared and killed without suffering. Second, Singer's objection to the suffering inflicted on animals in factory farms can be overcome by reforming the practices used on such

farms rather than by requiring that we become vegetarians. Third, a radical turn to vegetarianism would probably result in the elimination of most farm animals as we know them because they certainly cannot survive in the wild. This would seriously disrupt and/or eliminate many industries and social practices, resulting in significant disutility.

Responding to these criticisms in an article in the *New York Review of Books,* Singer makes two points. He first claims that adopting vegetarianism would improve people's general health, eliminate Third World poverty, and create new and beneficial industries and social practices. Second, Singer claims that in political campaigning, opposition to the current techniques of factory farming is not taken seriously unless one is also a committed vegetarian. According to Singer, only vegetarians can silence that invariable objection to reforming our treatment of animals: But don't you eat them?

Nevertheless, Singer's response turns on the political effectiveness of being a vegetarian and the effects vegetarianism would have on human welfare rather than its effects on animal welfare. However, it is in terms of animal welfare that the case for animal rights must ultimately be made.

In Selection 62, Paul W. Taylor argues that all living beings have independent moral status. He grounds his view on two central claims: (1) that each individual organism is a teleological center of life, pursuing its own good in its own way, and (2) that whether we are concerned with standards of merit or with the concept of inherent worth, there is no ground for believing that humans by their very nature are superior to other species. Taylor's argument for his second claim is similar to the argument used in the General Introduction to support morality against rational egoism. Both claim that their view represents a non-question-begging solution.

The main difficulty with Taylor's view is how we are to weigh human welfare against the good of other living beings if we were to grant that human beings are not superior to other species. In a later book that develops the argument of this essay, Taylor distinguishes between basic and nonbasic interests of living beings, but because he doesn't hold that the basic interests always have priority over nonbasic interests, it is difficult to know how decisions should be made when there is conflict between human and nonhuman interests.

In Selection 63, James P. Sterba seeks to resolve a central debate in contemporary environmental ethics between those who defend an anthropocentric ethics and those who defend a nonanthropocentric ethics by showing that when the most morally defensible versions of each of these perspectives are laid out, they do not lead to different practical recommendations. He develops a set of principles for weighing human against nonhuman welfare, contending that it should be acceptable to defenders of both anthropocentric and nonanthropocentric environmental ethics. Obviously, the crucial question is whether these principles do represent common ground between these opposing perspectives and whether they can be effectively applied.

In Selection 64, Karen Warren raises an important challenge to mainstream environmental ethics. The challenge is that such mainstream ethics have failed to recognize that the domination of nature is rooted in the domination of women, or at least has failed to recognize that both forms of domination are interconnected. To elucidate this connection, Warren claims that at least within the dominant Western culture, the following argument is sanctioned:

1. Women are identified with nature and the realm of the physical; men are identified with the "human" and the realm of the mental. (For example, naturist language describes women as cows, foxes, chicks, serpents, bitches, beavers, old bats, pussycats, cats, bird-brains, hare-brains. Sexist language feminizes and sexualizes Nature: Nature is raped, mastered, conquered, controlled, mined. Her "secrets" are "pene-

trated" and her "womb" is put into the services of the "man of science." "Virgin timber" is felled, cut down. "Fertile soil" is tilled and land that lies "fallow" is "barren," useless.)

2. Whatever is identified with nature and the realm of the physical is inferior to whatever is identified with the "human" and the realm of the mental; or, conversely, the latter is superior to the former.

3. Thus, women are inferior to men; or, conversely, men are superior to women.

4. For any X and Y, if X is superior to Y, then X is justified in subordinating Y.

5. Thus, men are justified in subordinating women.

Warren points out that there is a "logic of domination" to this argument. It begins with a *claim of difference.* It then moves from a claim of difference to a *claim of superiority* and then from a claim of superiority to a *claim of subordination* or *domination.* Warren contends that this same logic of domination is common to all forms of domination and so is used to support, for example, racism, classism, and ageism, as well as sexism and naturism (Warren's term for the domination of nature). If Warren is correct, it follows that if one is against any one of these forms of domination, one should be against them all.

Practical Applications

The next two selections come from the only federal law in the United States pertaining to the treatment of animals. The provisions of the Animal Welfare Act (Selection 65) pertain only to the transportation of animals and the treatment of animals for research and experimentation. The Act does not mention the treatment of animals in factory farms. The amendments to the Animal Welfare Act (Selection 66) passed in 1985 represent a considerable strengthening of the original Act. Specifically, the amendments call for a national data bank that will list the results of all animal experiments and thus prevent needless repetition. All laboratories using live animals are also required, under the amendments, to set up animal-care committees and submit to annual inspections. Facilities that house dogs must let them exercise, and those that house primates must provide for their "psychological well-being." Unfortunately, the implementation of these amendments is currently held up by the federal budget office.

In *Tennessee Valley Authority v. Hill* (Selection 67), the issue before the Supreme Court was whether the Endangered Species Act of 1973 prohibited the completion of a dam whose operation would destroy the habitat of the snail darter, an endangered species; the dam was virtually complete and Congress continued to appropriate large sums of money to the project even after the congressional appropriations committees were apprised of the project's apparent impact on the snail darter's survival. The Court held that the act did prohibit the dam's completion because its language and the debate that led to its passage required that its provisions be applied without exceptions. Immediately after this court decision, however, Congress amended the act to provide a "review" process that would relax the protection accorded endangered species in some circumstances. In the case of the snail darter, protection was relaxed because it was possible to transport snail darters to another river. Additional populations of snail darters were found in other rivers. An interesting sidelight to this case, however, was that an interim economic study found that the dam was a pork barrel construction project. Its benefits to the Tennessee economy could have been achieved in less costly ways while the natural state of the river was preserved.

Although there is no denying that existing federal laws that protect animals and the environment are quite limited in scope, it seems clear that any solution to the problem of animal liberation and environmental concern that gives independent moral status to all living beings, or even just to all sentient beings will, if implemented, have a significant impact on the way we live and work and, accordingly, on how we are able to solve the other practical problems discussed in this anthology.

---

60. *Anthropocentrism*

R. D. GUTHRIE

R. D. Guthrie argues that it is both illogical and impractical to extend moral concern beyond the human community. He argues that it is illogical to think that our relationship to nonhuman organisms is moral when we already recognize that the relationships of nonhuman organisms to each other and to ourselves are nonmoral. He argues that it is impractical for us to have to weigh the effect that our actions are having on nonhuman organisms when we are deciding what to do.

The nature of our responsibilities toward other organisms is certainly no new issue, but the controversy has been reignited recently by legislative action to regulate the care and maintenance of laboratory stock. Although this specific issue involves a decision of immediate concern to scientists, it also raises the even more basic question as to the general role that other organisms should occupy in our ethical system. It seems prudent that we should first examine the problem in its broadest context before further legislative action and the firm lines of political alignment are drawn.

An analysis of one aspect of our ethical system necessarily involves some dealings with the system as a whole. Unfortunately, the area of ethical theory can sometimes be an ideological quagmire from which few return enlightened. Much of the difficulty arises from our being drawn, by tradition, into thinking that our moral scaffolding is suspended from some outside agency. Rather, I would subscribe to the concept that moral principles, and the standards by which they are judged, are human constructs and thus can be evaluated on an empirical basis, even though the criteria are complex and the judgments sometimes difficult. Inherent in this position is the idea that our judgments are dependent upon generalizations from past experiences and may have to be altered as new situations are encountered. The only aprioristic element is the underlying assumption that man's rules of conduct are to be to his benefit. For the limited purposes of this essay, I will thus assume that the most desirable rules governing human behavior are those which, now and in the future, promote the welfare of the human population as an aggregate of individuals and contribute to the smooth functioning of its social machinery, while at the same time allowing for the greatest freedom of individual expression and fulfillment. Such a conceptual distillation necessarily includes academic deficiencies with which philosophers of ethical theory will quibble; but, by and large, this has become the gauge by which we evaluate political systems, economic policies, codes of sexual behavior, technological innovations, planned parenthood, and so forth. This assumption of the most desirable code of conduct forms the basis of the idea that I wish to present.

My thesis is that the inclusion of other organisms as primary participants in our ethical system is both logically unsound and operationally unfeasible. It is illogical because we cannot consider other organisms as moral bodies and amoral bodies simultaneously. By

From "The Ethical Relationship between Humans and Other Organisms." *Perspectives in Biology and Medicine.* Vol. II (1967–1968).

moral bodies I mean those entities ultimately to be considered in evaluating the action. As an example of this categorization, let us say that, as part of an experiment, a mineralogist wishes to dissolve a unique crystal. On what basis does he decide that the destruction will be worthwhile? The judgment has to be made on the effect of his action on living and future humans— the immediate benefits derived from the crystal's destruction weighed against the assets of its continued existence. The rare crystal is an amoral body, since our concern is with the ultimate effect on humans (the moral bodies which made this a moral question) and not with the welfare of the rock per se.

The relationships among nonhuman organisms are also not generally defined as moral or immoral. Most would agree that a wild wolf killing a wild deer is, in and of itself, not subject to moral analysis. We as humans may wish to keep the wolf from killing a game species, or the weeds from stunting the turnips, but we do not contend that the wolves and weeds are immoral for so doing. We wish to curtail the wolf and weed population, not ultimately for the sake of the deer and turnips, but for our own ends. In my categorization, then, rare crystals, wolves, deer, weeds, and turnips are all amoral bodies. Likewise, an act of another organism toward humans, say a mosquito bite, could also be classified as amoral. The mosquito is an amoral body, and we do not hold it morally responsible for having bitten us. Thus, at two bonds of a triangular relationship, we recognize the amoral nature of the nonhuman's act toward another nonhuman organism and, second, a nonhuman organism's act toward a human as being amoral. It is difficult not to conclude that the final bond—a human's act toward other organisms—is, in and of itself, an amoral one. It becomes a moral act only when humans are affected, because our moral codes are rules of human behavior, as I assumed in the beginning, and, as such, exclude other organisms as primary participants.

The fallacy of giving other organisms the status of moral bodies and amoral bodies simultaneously leads us into what we might refer to as "Schweitzer's dilemma." In his *reverence for life* philosophy, Schweitzer considered each organism as an individual whose suffering and death were to be avoided if at all possible. If one supports this philosophy—that it is the organism's discomfort, the welfare of the organism itself, that is our concern—he is confronted with the perplexing situation of having to regard pain that occurs "in the wild" as bad. Since it is an individual organism's discomfort that is emphasized and not the effect upon the human causing it, the pain will be just as real no matter what the origin. One is, as Schweitzer was, forced to regard predators as evil. However, predators avoid the pains of starvation and eventual death by causing pain and death to other organisms. This relationship is an inherent part of the community structure where energy is transferred from one trophic level to the next, ergo, the dilemma. Failure to have reverence for the predator's life is itself a contradiction of the basic tenet of Schweitzer's philosophy, yet to have reverence for the predator's life is to revere those processes which result in pain and death. Furthermore, if it is the organism's pain, in and of itself, that we wish to prevent, we incur responsibilities beyond our own species' actions. The Schweitzerian philosophy implies that the billions of nonhuman animals (and plants?) that are mutilated and killed in nature are the unattended wards of humankind.

Within our own species, if a fellow member becomes mentally or physically incapacitated to function within the moral code, we make corresponding adjustments by withholding some of those freedoms which are given to others (we confine him to a mental institution or hospital ward or require glasses while driving). To extend a similar sliding scale of conduct toward, or expected conduct from, other organisms is operationally unfeasible. First of all, we would have to formulate some sort of discriminatory system which would define the nature and extent of preferential moral treatment. Which organisms would we include in our moral system, and to what degree?

Some who apply our moral code to other organisms do so only to higher organisms. However, the concept of a "higher" organism is a rather nebulous affair. Which is "higher," a bee, apple tree, elephant, sailfish, or winter wheat? The ideas of "progressive," "advanced," or "higher" may be applied, with meaning, to a phylogenetic sequence—the older being more primitive—or with reference to one particular character—horses exhibiting a more advanced state of digit reduction than man. However, as a generalized concept, "higher" is interlaced with teleological overtones that are rejected by virtually all evolutionists.

The concept of phylogenetic proximity has also been suggested as a discriminatory basis for evaluating the behavior of other organisms. As well as having anthropocentric underwear, this idea also involves other problems; for example, sewer rats are probably just as close phylogenetically to humans as are cocker spaniels. Relying on something like the potential for learned behavior seems just as arbitrary and shallow. All organisms relying more on the equally successful "instinctive" behavior would be whimsically bypassed.

Not only do we face absurd decisions as to what organisms we are to apply the code among the different taxa, but the question can also be posed as to how individual variation within each species is to be regarded. There is even the problem of the fluctuation of our code through time. Does the evaluation of what constitutes "indecent exposure" also change for other organisms? These and many other questions arise. If, however, we are to consider our morality as an entirely human phenomenon, and apply it only to humans, many problems are eliminated, and the system is workable. We need not cringe in sin every time we bite into a pork chop, trim the hedge, or order the pooch to get the paper. The human ramifications of any deed are ponderous enough.

My contention that human acts committed toward other organisms can only be evaluated by their human effects should be interpreted in its broadest sense. One could even argue that a highly pathogenic species of bacteria should not be driven to extinction. It may be wise to maintain the species as a protected laboratory culture in the event that future development may be able to utilize the species as a valuable source of information or a unique research tool. Although hunting, fishing, butterfly collecting, and wildflower picking provide immediate recreation, these species must also be managed with regard to their recreational use by future generations of humans. The health of our livestock, both those in the private laboratory and those raised for commercial purposes, must necessarily have high priority because our health as consumers and the information that we as scientists derive from them depend upon their physical condition. In the management of livestock and game species, our concern is mainly with population parameters and not with specific individuals. This is not the case with pets. Since one of the chief functions of a pet is to provide companionship, the owner must be concerned about his pet as an individual—an organism from which he receives pleasure by exchanging affection—and should be able to expect that other people will treat his pet with this in mind. I do not wish to imply in the presentation of this philosophy of our relationships with other organisms that the owner should look upon his Rover without emotion or affection, for to do so would destroy the relationship from which the owner is receiving satisfaction. However, he should not deceive himself by thinking that he is giving the dog attention solely for the dog's sake. The motivation for domesticating and continuing to raise pets is not the improvement of these animals' welfare.

In general practice, we do not bring laboratory and domestic animals under the same moral consideration that we do other humans. We regulate their diet, decide on breeding time and specific mate, compel them to do tasks against their volition, eat them, and put them to death when they become senile. Only in rare instances have human slaves received similar treatment.

The basic distinction in the human interpretation of the two phenomena, slavery of other humans and slavery of other organisms, is rather revealing. We do not hesitate in our discrimination against those organisms who are not our own species. The categorization is discrete and operationally meaningful in its broadest application. Those times in the past when human slavery has been condoned, and those sentiments among us today that are sympathetic with human enslavement, can be tied to the idea that the subjugated are "other"—something else radically different from me and mine. A fairer criticism of the mistake of the *apartheid* attitude is not so much a breach of the moral code as it is bad taxonomy. The growing world pressure against racial discrimination is perhaps due to the increasing recognition that we are all one species with very little, if any, interpopulational variation in potential ability to accumulate information, to formulate ideas, and to experience the varied forms of social interaction.

Although it is but a small minority of humans that wish to extend such moral codes as "freedom from servitude" to other organisms, many rebel in revulsion when they witness other organisms experiencing pain. This, I believe, is because we have stronger emotions relating to the prevention of human pain than we do for preventing such things as freedom infringements, and have been more thorough in our anthropomorphic transference of these to other organisms. Yet, in the attempt to incorporate the pain experienced by other organisms directly into our moral judgments, we are courting the same logical and practical difficulties which we encounter in any consideration of them as moral bodies.

A current example will bring the question into better focus. Suppose society is faced with the decision whether to permit students the freedom to experiment with live laboratory animals, bred and maintained for that purpose, or to withhold this freedom by law on the basis that the animal's pain and ensuing death caused by the inexperienced hands of the student is not worth the information and experience that the student derives. It is difficult to imagine any basis of equivalency by which we could evaluate education in terms of some translatable value of rat pain. I contend that there is no common denominator. Even the problems that we face within our own moral system, in attempting to weigh the immediate discomforts of the varied forms of child discipline, and the dangers of testing a new drug, against their long-term advantages, border on being insurmountable. However, we still have a common foundation for our judgments—human welfare.

A recurrent thread in most discussions on the relationship of our ethics to other animals is the concept that none should be hurt or caused to die unnecessarily. Certainly all would agree with this in theory. However, we have no common basis to judge *necessity* in this context. One group contends that all vivisection is unnecessary; another feels that most is necessary. How does one judge if it is necessary to kill or cause other organisms pain for the aesthetic enjoyments of fishing, recovering from a mild parasitic infection, training a retriever dog, or having a mosquito-free back yard? What unresolvable quandaries we are led into! The act that is unnecessary to one is quite necessary to another, and we eventually return to the *effect upon humans* as the final basis of evaluation.

Also, if one wishes to assume the position that killing and causing other organisms pain is "justified when necessary for sustenance," but nevertheless immoral, then we must surely classify meat-eating societies, like the Eskimos, as more evil than some vegetarian agriculturists. Our own meat-eating habits would also have to be abandoned, for who among us would take the hypocritical position that we eat prime T-bone only for the necessary protein? We, by heritage and necessity, are organisms with heterotrophic habits and tastes and, therefore, are tethered to continued existence by the inexorable expenditure of the lives of other organisms. Our heterotrophic nature precludes any philosophy which would judge killing of other organisms as a sinful act against those organisms.

Throughout the evolution of social thought, man has not always visualized himself as separate from other organisms, just as he drew no distinct line between animate and inanimate objects. But the growing trend in the modern world to anthropomorphize the acts of other organisms arises from a rather different source. Early man had an intimate contact with other organisms, and his incorporation of these other species into his philosophy and religion no doubt was a result of this dependency upon and fear of other species. In the process of our self-domestication we have removed ourselves farther and farther from our contact with other species, and it is because of this lack of firsthand understanding and familiarity that we attribute human feelings and motivations to other organisms. Although science has enabled us to place ourselves in the proper phylogenetic scheme, it has also removed humanity as a whole from the firsthand contact with, and appreciation of, some basic ecological processes. We have seldom seen the organisms that we eat, when they were alive. It is not uncommon to meet people who are upset at the thought of eating the same lobster that they chose from the live-box earlier in the evening. Although perhaps small by comparison, the price that we pay for the benefits of modern society is the loss in breadth of experience gained from seeing ourselves "in the system," as direct participants in the life and death of other organisms somewhat similar to ourselves. Moreover, we can expect further increases in this price as society's relationship with other organisms becomes even more indirect. Perhaps the current boom and rising influence of animal suffrage groups exemplifies this trend.

One can identify the changes in attitude within this century as we grade from a rural to an urban society. On the farm there was a sharper line between humans and other organisms. The pigs were butchered and the peas canned. As urbanites, our contact with other organisms is usually with pets or even the more humanized cartoon characters. Children reared in our urban society may misread "roast duck" on the menu as roast Donald, and bears are those furry people who wear ranger hats in ads that tell you to use care with matches. Our increasingly limited experience with other organisms has caused us to extend further our moral code outside its sphere of applicability. What a black day for the nation if Alfred the alligator ended up in the last frame of Tuesday's Special chomping a half-skinned, intestines-dangling Pogo—but, of course, that is part of the real relationship between alligators and opossums.

We have generated a phobia of seeing viscera of other organisms and of seeing them killed. The idea that insides are repugnant, and our distaste for non-human death, probably originated as extensions of the fear of human death or witnessing human viscera. Relating emotionally to other organisms is no doubt a natural by-product of the breakdown of our sharp value delineation between humans and nonhumans, resulting from our increasing lack of contact with other organisms. However, this transference of our fears and concerns about humans to other species may detract from the welfare of our own species. If we are to sterilize our view of life by editing the realities of nature to suit our anthropomorphic attitudes, we can anticipate attendant limitations in our potential for understanding ourselves and the real world about us. To become involved in the births and deaths of other organisms in the laboratory or in the field, if it can be done without any recognizable loss to human welfare, may help us understand or at least feel more deeply the natural processes of life and death, of which we are a part. Also, witnessing the inner complexities of individual function surely contributes to our appreciation of the phenomenon of life. Denying ourselves these perspectives by letting our emotions completely humanize other organisms may be no trivial loss.

If we are to accept the idea that our moral system was designed by man for regulating the behavior of his own species and that it is improper to apply it to other organisms, we can then attempt to deal with a related issue—the nature of our moral obligation to other humans as it relates to our conduct toward other organisms. How must we behave if our treatment of a nonhuman organism offends others who empathize more than we do? In its extreme form, one pressure group attempts to legislate its tastes or emotional sensitivities on the minority group. Consider bullfighting and live pigeon shoots, both of which are illegal in the United States. Those who wish to outlaw these events have two alternative arguments, assuming that they themselves are not forced to experience or witness the event: They can take the position that it is detrimental either to the bull's welfare or to the welfare of those who are attending. In the case of the first position, one courts some of the problems that I have been reviewing. The basis of the second position has yet to be demonstrated. We are told by some who attend these events that they can be enjoyable and rewarding experiences, and in those countries where they occur now, we can but conclude that they are enjoyed by many people. Those who disagree take the position that an emphasis on the "humane" treatment of other organisms will further nurture those qualities in our relationship with other humans. In some situations this is probably true, but, unfortunately, blurring this difference also invites the other part of the association; and disposing of an intestinal parasite would be a poor analogy to our disposition toward a fellow human drawing unemployment compensation. I would rather take the other view, that it is the distinction between human welfare and the welfare of other things that will provide deeper meaning to the preciousness of the human individual. Debasing the value of human relationships by a loose analogy with our relationship to other organisms has affected, and no doubt could further affect, the esteem of human worth.

I refer again to the criteria for evaluating moral actions, stated in the beginning, that the rules governing human behavior should be constructed to regard the welfare of humans not only as a group but also as individuals. This necessitates maintaining the greatest possible latitude of individual behavior without markedly encroaching on the welfare of the unit as a whole. We must then make sure that to allow one

segment to perform an act does not, in consequence, detract materially from the freedom of another segment, and, if so, some mutual compromise will have to be made. Performing a physiology experiment with the exposed viscera of a live horse in the middle of a public park does not show moral regard for the individuals who, by witnessing it, would experience considerable discomfort. Even though the physiologist may feel that the squeamishness of the lady passerby is unjustified, he nevertheless has the responsibility to consider her emotional sensitivities. Likewise, the same lady must allow other segments of society to use other organisms in their education and enjoyment, so long as she is not personally forced to experience or witness those acts. This is, of course, the same principle that we use in other matters of individual taste (e.g., nudity, intoxication, and loud parties).

The classroom is a slightly different situation. The teacher has been given the responsibility to aid people in their education in the best way he knows. The teacher's judgment to require the student to work on living organisms (or to read *Catcher in the Rye*, for that matter) may be intended to give the student a more intimate contact with other perspectives that cannot be communicated by just reading a lab manual or a literary review. Thus a teacher has a less restricted license to expose his students to other ways of feeling and thinking than does one stranger to another. But certainly limitations remain. Interestingly enough, almost all of the opposition to vivisection in schools has been directed, not toward the question of the students' rights and discomforts, but of the animals'.

The error of extending moral judgment outside the system is widespread among scientists. Biologists are particularly susceptible. Most were attracted to their discipline because they were fascinated with animals in their youth, and in the modern world this fascination is generally on an individual basis with pets, cartoon characters, circus performers, and zoo inhabitants. We as biologists are hesitant to accord other organisms the same moral status as inorganic objects because of the striking kinship we share morphologically, physiologically, and behaviorally (those areas with which biologists are most familiar). And, of course, the philosophical tendency to include other organisms directly in human codes of behavior stems, indirectly, from these phylogenetic bonds. However, our ethical constructs apply to an entirely different level of organization, a level with which biologists typically do not deal professionally. Value judgments of human conduct are in the same realm as concepts such as citizenship and taxation where we categorize other animate objects in the same set with inorganic ones, and would consider as ludicrous the application of an idea such as proportional representation—"one individual, one vote"—to include gophers.

Although many other species have, like the human species, evolved their own codes of social behavior, they have only done so directly or indirectly to increase the welfare of the members of their own species. Not unexpectedly, these codes are not the same ones that we have constructed for ourselves.

The key theme of this essay is that the human species, or for that matter any species, is under no moral obligation to extend its own internal code of behavior to other species and that it can be a serious error to do so; however, it would be an equal or greater error to take the short-sighted view that a species' welfare is merely an intraspecific matter. Any species is a segment of the entire community, and its integrity and continued existence cannot be evaluated aside from the larger community unit. The quality of our future as humans depends on the quality of our management of the community of organisms of which we are an integral part. To impede this management by misunderstanding the nature of *either* our ecological or moral relationships can only be to [our] detriment.

61. *All Animals Are Equal*

PETER SINGER

Peter Singer begins his defense of animal liberation by comparing the bias against animals with biases against Blacks and women. According to Singer, all of these forms of discrimination violate the principle of equal consideration. According to this principle, there is no justification for regarding the pain that animals feel as less important than the same amount of pain (or pleasure) felt by humans.

"Animal Liberation" may sound more like a parody of other liberation movements than a serious objective. The idea of "The Rights of Animals" actually was once used to parody the case for women's rights. When Mary Wollstonecraft, a forerunner of today's feminists, published her *Vindication of the Rights of Women* in 1792, her views were widely regarded as absurd, and before long an anonymous publication appeared entitled *A Vindication of the Rights of Brutes*. The author of this satirical work (now known to have been Thomas Taylor, a distinguished Cambridge phi-

losopher) tried to refute Mary Wollstonecraft's arguments by showing that they could be carried one stage further. If the argument for equality was sound when applied to women, why should it not be applied to dogs, cats, and horses? The reasoning seemed to hold for these "brutes" too; yet to hold that brutes had rights was manifestly absurd; therefore the reasoning by which this conclusion had been reached must be unsound, and if unsound when applied to brutes, it must also be unsound when applied to women, since the very same arguments had been used in each case.

In order to explain the basis of the case for the equality of animals, it will be helpful to start with an examination of the case for the equality of women. Let

From *Animal Liberation* (New York: New York Review, 1975), pp. 1–22. Reprinted by permission of Peter Singer.

us assume that we wish to defend the case for women's rights against the attack by Thomas Taylor. How should we reply?

One way in which we might reply is by saying that the case for equality between men and women cannot validly be extended to nonhuman animals. Women have a right to vote, for instance, because they are just as capable of making rational decisions about the future as men are; dogs, on the other hand, are incapable of understanding the significance of voting, so they cannot have the right to vote. There are many other obvious ways in which men and women resemble each other closely, while humans and animals differ greatly. So, it might be said, men and women are similar beings and should have similar rights, while humans and nonhumans are different and should not have equal rights.

The reasoning behind this reply to Taylor's analogy is correct up to a point, but it does not go far enough. There *are* important differences between humans and other animals, and these differences must give rise to *some* differences in the rights that each have. Recognizing this obvious fact, however, is no barrier to the case for extending the basic principle of equality to nonhuman animals. The differences that exist between men and women are equally undeniable, and the supporters of Women's Liberation are aware that these differences may give rise to different rights. Many feminists hold that women have the right to an abortion on request. It does not follow that since these same feminists are campaigning for equality between men and women they must support the right of men to have abortions too. Since a man cannot have an abortion, it is meaningless to talk of his right to have one. Since a dog can't vote, it is meaningless to talk of its right to vote. There is no reason why either Women's Liberation or Animal Liberation should get involved in such nonsense. The extension of the basic principle of equality from one group to another does not imply that we must treat both groups in exactly the same way, or grant exactly the same rights to both groups. Whether we should do so will depend on the nature of the members of the two groups. The basic principle of equality does not require equal or identical *treatment;* it requires equal *consideration.* Equal consideration for different beings may lead to different treatment and different rights.

So there is a different way of replying to Taylor's attempt to parody the case for women's rights, a way that does not deny the obvious differences between humans and nonhumans but goes more deeply into the question of equality and concludes by finding nothing absurd in the idea that the basic principle of equality applies to so-called "brutes." At this point such a conclusion may appear odd; but if we examine more deeply the basis [for] our opposition to discrimination on grounds of race or sex ultimately, we will see that we would be on shaky ground if we were to demand equality for Blacks, women, and other groups of oppressed humans while denying equal consideration to nonhumans. To make this clear we need to see first exactly why racism and sexism are wrong.

When we say that all human beings, whatever their race, creed, or sex, are equal, what is it that we are asserting? Those who wish to defend hierarchical, inegalitarian societies have often pointed out that by whatever test we choose it simply is not true that all humans are equal. Like it or not we must face the fact that humans come in different shapes and sizes; they come with different moral capacities, different intellectual abilities, different amounts of benevolent feeling and sensitivity to the needs of others, different abilities to communicate effectively, and different capacities to experience pleasure and pain. In short, if the demand for equality were based on the actual equality of all human beings, we would have to stop demanding equality.

Still, one might cling to the view that the demand for equality among human beings is based on the actual equality of the different races and sexes. Although, it may be said, humans differ as individuals there are no differences between the races and sexes *as such.* From the mere fact that a person is Black or a woman we cannot infer anything about that person's intellectual or moral capacities. This, it may be said, is why racism and sexism are wrong. The white racist claims that whites are superior to Blacks, but this is false—although there are differences among individuals, some Blacks are superior to some whites in all of the capacities and abilities that could conceivably be relevant. The opponent of sexism would say the same: A person's sex is no guide to his or her abilities, and this is why it is unjustifiable to discriminate on the basis of sex.

The existence of individual variations that cut across the lines of race or sex, however, provides us with no defense at all against a more sophisticated opponent of equality, one who proposes that, say, the interests of all those with IQ scores below 100 be given less consideration than the interests of those with ratings over 100. Perhaps those scoring below the mark would, in this society, be made the slaves of those scoring higher. Would a hierarchical society of this sort really be so much better than one based on race or sex? I think not. But if we tie the moral principle of equality to the factual equality of the different races or sexes, taken as a whole, our opposition to racism and sexism does not provide us with any basis for objecting to this kind of inegalitarianism.

There is a second important reason why we ought not to base our opposition to racism and sexism on any kind of actual equality, even the limited kind that asserts that variations in capacities and abilities are spread evenly between the different races and sexes: We can have no absolute guarantee that these capacities and abilities really are distributed evenly, without regard to race or sex, among human beings. So far as actual abilities are concerned there do seem to be certain measurable differences between both races and sexes. These differences do not, of course, appear in each case, but only when averages are taken. More important still, we do not yet know how much of these differences is really due to the different genetic endowments of the different races and sexes, and how much is due to poor schools, poor housing, and other factors that are the result of past and continuing discrimination. Perhaps all of the important differences will eventually prove to be environmental rather than genetic. Anyone opposed to racism and sexism will certainly hope that this will be so, for it will make the task of ending discrimination a lot easier; nevertheless it would be dangerous to rest the case against racism and sexism on the belief that all significant differences are environmental in origin. The opponent of, say, racism who takes this line will be unable to avoid conceding that *if* differences in ability do after all prove to have some genetic connection with race, racism would in some way be defensible.

Fortunately there is no need to pin the case for equality to one particular outcome of a scientific investigation. The appropriate response to those who claim to have found evidence of genetically based differences in ability between the races or sexes is not to stick to the belief that the genetic explanation must be wrong, whatever evidence to the contrary may turn up: Instead we should make it quite clear that the claim to equality does not depend on intelligence, moral capacity, physical strength, or similar matters of fact. Equality is a moral idea, not an assertion of fact. There is no logically compelling reason for assuming that a factual difference in ability between two people justifies any difference in the amount of consideration we give to their needs and interests. *The principle of the equality of human beings is not a description of an alleged actual equality among humans: It is a prescription of how we should treat humans.*

Jeremy Bentham, the founder of the reforming utilitarian school of moral philosophy, incorporated the essential basis of moral equality into his system of ethics by means of the formula: "Each to count for one and none for more than one." In other words, the interests of every being affected by an action are to be taken into account and given the same weight as the like interests of any other being. A later utilitarian, Henry Sidgwick, put the point in this way: "The good of any one individual is of no more importance, from the point of view (if I may say so) of the Universe, than the good of any other." More recently leading figures in contemporary moral philosophy have shown a great deal of agreement in specifying as a fundamental presupposition of their moral theories some similar requirement which operates so as to give everyone's interests equal consideration—although these writers generally cannot agree on how this requirement is best formulated.[1]

It is an implication of this principle of equality that our concern for others and our readiness to consider their interests ought not depend on what they are like or on what abilities they may possess. Precisely what this concern or consideration requires us to do may vary according to the characteristics of those affected by what we do: Concern for the well-being of a child growing up in America would require that we teach him to read; concern for the well-being of a pig may require no more than that we leave him alone with other pigs in a place where there is adequate food and room to run freely. But the basic element—the taking into account of the interests of the being, whatever those interests may be —must, according to the principle of equality, be extended to all beings, Black or white, masculine or feminine, human or nonhuman.

Thomas Jefferson, who was responsible for writing the principle of the equality of men into the American Declaration of Independence, saw this point. It led him to oppose slavery even though he was unable to free himself fully from his slaveholding background. He wrote in a letter to the author of a book that emphasized the notable intellectual achievements of Negroes in order to refute the then common view that they had limited intellectual capacities:

> Be assured that no person living wishes more sincerely than I do, to see a complete refutation of the doubts I have myself entertained and expressed on the grade of understanding allotted to them by nature, and to find that they are on a par with ourselves . . . but whatever be their degree of talent it is no measure of their rights. Because Sir Isaac Newton was superior to others in understanding, he was not therefore lord of the property or person of others.[2]

Similarly when in the 1850s the call for women's rights was raised in the United States a remarkable Black feminist named Sojourner Truth made the same point in more robust terms at a feminist convention:

> . . . they talk about this thing in the head; what do they call it? ["Intellect," whispered someone near by.] That's it. What's that got to do with women's rights or Negroes' rights? If my cup won't hold but a pint and yours holds a quart, wouldn't you be mean not to let me have my little half-measure full?[3]

It is on this basis that the case against racism and the case against sexism must both ultimately rest; and it is in accordance with this principle that the attitude that we may call "speciesism," by analogy with racism, must also be condemned. Speciesism—the word is not an attractive one, but I can think of no better term—is a prejudice or attitude of bias toward the interests of members of one's own species and against those of members of other species. It should be obvious that the fundamental objections to racism and sexism made by Thomas Jefferson and Sojourner Truth apply equally to speciesism. If possessing a higher degree of intelligence does not entitle one human to use another for his own ends, how can it entitle humans to exploit nonhumans for the same purpose?[4]

Many philosophers and other writers have proposed the principle of equal consideration of interests, in some form or other, as a basic moral principle; but not many of them have recognized that this principle applies to members of other species as well as to our own. Jeremy Bentham was one of the few who did realize this. In a forward-looking passage written at a time when Black slaves had been freed by the French but in the British dominions were still being treated in the way we now treat animals, Bentham wrote:

> The day *may* come when the rest of the animal creation may acquire those rights which never could have been withholden from them but by the hand of tyranny. The French have already discovered that the blackness of the skin is no reason why a human being should be abandoned without redress to the caprice of a tormentor. It may one day come to be recognized that the number of the legs, the villosity of the skin, or the termination of the *os sacrum* are reasons equally insufficient for abandoning a sensitive being to the same fate. What else is it that should trace the insuperable line? Is it the faculty of reason, or perhaps the faculty of discourse? But a full-grown horse or dog is beyond comparison a more rational, as well as a more conversable animal, than an infant of a day or a week or even a month, old. But suppose they were otherwise, what would it avail? The question is not, Can they *reason?* nor Can they *talk?* but, *Can they suffer?*[5]

In this passage Bentham points to the capacity for suffering as the vital characteristic that gives a being the right to equal consideration. The capacity for suffering—or more strictly, for suffering and/or enjoyment or happiness—is not just another characteristic like the capacity for language or higher mathematics. Bentham is not saying that those who try to mark "the insuperable line" that determines whether the interests of a being should be considered happen to have chosen the wrong characteristic. By saying that we must consider the interests of all beings with the capacity for suffering or enjoyment Bentham does not arbitrarily exclude from consideration any interests at all—as those who draw the line with reference to the possession of reason or language do. The capacity for suffering and enjoyment is *a prerequisite for having interests at all,* a condition that must be satisfied before we can speak of interests in a meaningful way. It would be nonsense to say that it was not in the interests of a stone to be kicked along the road by a schoolboy. A stone does not have interests because it cannot suffer. Nothing that we can do to it could possibly make any difference to its welfare. A mouse, on the other hand, does have an interest in not being kicked along the road, because it will suffer if it is.

If a being suffers there can be no moral justification for refusing to take that suffering into consideration. No matter what the nature of the being, the principle of equality requires that its suffering be counted equally with the like suffering—in so far as rough comparisons can be made—of any other being. If a being is not capable of suffering, or of experiencing enjoyment or happiness, there is nothing to be taken into account. So the limit of sentience (using the term as a convenient if not strictly accurate shorthand for the capacity to suffer and/or experience enjoyment) is the only defensible boundary of concern for the interests of others. To mark this boundary by some other characteristic like intelligence or rationality would be to mark it in an arbitrary manner. Why not choose some other characteristic, like skin color?

The racist violates the principle of equality by giving greater weight to the interests of members of his own race when there is a clash between their interests and the interests of those of another race. The sexist violates the principle of equality by favoring the interests of his own sex. Similarly the speciesist allows the interests of his own species to override the greater interests of members of other species. The pattern is identical in each case.

Most human beings are speciesists. . . . Ordinary human beings—not a few exceptionally cruel or heartless humans, but the overwhelming majority of humans—take an active part in, acquiesce in, and allow their taxes to pay for practices that require the sacrifice of the most important interests of members of other species in order to promote the most trivial interests of our own species.

There is, however, one general defense of these practices . . . that needs to be disposed of. . . . It is a defense which, if true, would allow us to do anything at all to nonhumans for the slightest reason, or for no reason at all, without incurring any justifiable reproach. This defense claims that we are never guilty of neglecting the interests of other animals for one

breathtakingly simple reason: They have no interests. Nonhuman animals have no interests, according to this view, because they are not capable of suffering. By this is not meant merely that they are not capable of suffering in all the ways that humans are—for instance, that a calf is not capable of suffering from the knowledge that it will be killed in six months time. That modest claim is, no doubt, true; but it does not clear humans of the charge of speciesism, since it allows that animals may suffer in other ways—for instance, by being given electric shocks, or being kept in small, cramped cages. The defense I am about to discuss is the much more sweeping, although correspondingly less plausible, claim that animals are incapable of suffering in any way at all; that they are . . . unconscious automata, possessing neither thoughts nor feelings nor a mental life of any kind.

Although . . . the view that animals are automata was proposed by the seventeenth-century French philosopher René Descartes, to most people, then and now, it is obvious that if, for example, we stick a sharp knife into the stomach of an unanesthetized dog, the dog will feel pain. That this is so is assumed by the laws in most civilized countries which prohibit wanton cruelty to animals. Readers whose common sense tells them that animals do suffer may prefer to skip the next few paragraphs . . . since they do nothing but refute a position which they do not hold. Implausible as it is, though, for the sake of completeness this skeptical position must be discussed.

Do animals other than humans feel pain? How do we know? Well, how do we know if anyone, human or nonhuman, feels pain? We know that we ourselves can feel pain. We know this from the direct experiences of pain that we have when, for instance, somebody presses a lighted cigarette against the back of our hand. But how do we know that anyone else feels pain? We cannot directly experience anyone else's pain, whether that "anyone" is our best friend or a stray dog. Pain is a state of consciousness, a "mental event," and as such it can never be observed. Behavior like writhing, screaming, or drawing one's hand away from the lighted cigarette is not pain itself; nor are the recordings a neurologist might make of activity within the brain observations of pain itself. Pain is something that we feel, and we can only infer that others are feeling it from various external indications.

In theory, we *could* always be mistaken when we assume that other human beings feel pain. It is conceivable that our best friend is really a very cleverly constructed robot, controlled by a brilliant scientist so as to give all the signs of feeling pain, but really no more sensitive than any other machine. We can never know, with absolute certainty, that this is not the case. But while this might present a puzzle for philosophers, none of us has the slightest real doubt that our best friends feel pain just as we do. This is an inference, but a perfectly reasonable one, based on observations of their behavior in situations in which we would feel pain, and on the fact that we have every reason to assume that our friends are beings like us, with nervous systems like ours that can be assumed to function as ours do, and to produce similar feelings in similar circumstances.

If it is justifiable to assume that other humans feel pain as we do, is there any reason why a similar inference should be unjustifiable in the case of other animals?

Nearly all the external signs that lead us to infer pain in other humans can be seen in other species, especially [those] most closely related to us—other species of mammals, and birds. Behavioral signs— writhing, facial contortions, moaning, yelping or other forms of calling, attempts to avoid the source of pain, appearance of fear at the prospect of its repetition, and so on—are present. In addition, we know that these animals have nervous systems very like ours, which respond physiologically as ours do when the animal is in circumstances in which we would feel pain: an initial rise of blood pressure, dilated pupils, perspiration, an increased pulse rate, and, if the stimulus continues, a fall in blood pressure. Although humans have a more developed cerebral cortex than other animals, this part of the brain is concerned with thinking functions rather than with basic impulses, emotions, and feelings. These impulses, emotions, and feelings are located in the diencephalon, which is well developed in many other species of animals, especially mammals and birds.[6]

We also know that the nervous systems of other animals were not artificially constructed to mimic the pain behavior of humans, as a robot might be artificially constructed. The nervous systems of animals evolved as our own did, and in fact the evolutionary history of humans and other animals, especially mammals, did not diverge until the central features of our nervous systems were already in existence. A capacity to feel pain obviously enhances a species' prospects of survival, since it causes members of the species to avoid sources of injury. It is surely unreasonable to suppose that nervous systems which are virtually identical physiologically, have a common origin and a common evolutionary function, and result in similar forms of behavior in similar circumstances should actually operate in an entirely different manner on the level of subjective feelings.

It has long been accepted as sound policy in science to search for the simplest possible explanation of whatever it is we are trying to explain. Occasionally it has been claimed that it is for this reason "unscientific" to explain the behavior of animals by theories that refer to the animal's conscious feelings, desires, and so on—the idea being that if the behavior in question can be explained without invoking consciousness or feelings, that will be the simpler theory. Yet we can now see that such explanations, when placed in the overall context of the behavior of both human and nonhuman animals, are far more complex than their rivals. We know from our own experience that explanations of our own behavior that did not refer to consciousness and the feeling of pain would be incomplete; it is simpler to assume that the similar behavior of animals with similar nervous systems is to be explained in the same way than to try to invent some other explanation for the behavior of nonhuman animals as well as an explanation for the divergence between humans and nonhumans in this respect.

The overwhelming majority of scientists who have addressed themselves to this question agree. Lord Brain, one of the most eminent neurologists of our time, has said:

> I personally can see no reason for conceding mind to my fellow men and denying it to animals. . . . I at least cannot doubt that the interests and activities of animals are correlated with awareness and feeling in the same way as my own, and which may be, for aught I know, just as vivid.[7]

While the author of a recent book on pain writes:

> Every particle of factual evidence supports the contention that the higher mammalian vertebrates expe-

rience pain sensations at least as acute as our own. To say that they feel less because they are lower animals is an absurdity; it can easily be shown that many of their senses are far more acute than ours—visual acuity in certain birds, hearing in most wild animals, and touch in others; these animals depend more than we do today on the sharpest possible awareness of a hostile environment. Apart from the complexity of the cerebral cortex (which does not directly perceive pain) their nervous systems are almost identical to ours and their reactions to pain remarkably similar, though lacking (so far as we know) the philosophical and moral overtones. The emotional element is all too evident, mainly in the form of fear and anger.[8]

In Britain, three separate expert government committees on matters relating to animals have accepted the conclusion that animals feel pain. After noting the obvious behavioral evidence for this view, the Committee on Cruelty to Wild Animals said:

> . . . we believe that the physiological, and more particularly the anatomical, evidence fully justifies and reinforces the commonsense belief that animals feel pain.

And after discussing the evolutionary value of pain they concluded that pain is "of clear-cut biological usefulness" and this is "a third type of evidence that animals feel pain." They then went on to consider forms of suffering other than mere physical pain, and added that they were "satisfied that animals do suffer from acute fear and terror." In 1965, British government [reports] on experiments on animals, and on the welfare of animals under intensive farming methods, agreed with this view, concluding that animals are capable of suffering both from straightforward physical injuries and from fear, anxiety, stress, and so on.[9]

That might well be thought enough to settle the matter; but there is one more objection that needs to be considered. There is, after all, one behavioral sign that humans have when in pain which nonhumans do not have. This is a developed language. Other animals may communicate with each other, but not, it seems, in the complicated way we do. Some philosophers, including Descartes, have thought it important that while humans can tell each other about their experience of pain in great detail, other animals cannot.

(Interestingly, this once neat dividing line between humans and other species has now been threatened by the discovery that chimpanzees can be taught a language.)[10] But as Bentham pointed out long ago, the ability to use language is not relevant to the question of how a being ought to be treated—unless that ability can be linked to the capacity to suffer, so that the absence of a language casts doubt on the existence of this capacity.

This link may be attempted in two ways. First, there is a hazy line of philosophical thought, stemming perhaps from some doctrines associated with influential philosopher Ludwig Wittgenstein, that maintains we cannot meaningfully attribute states of consciousness to beings without language. This position seems to me very implausible. Language may be necessary for abstract thought, at some level anyway; but states like pain are more primitive, and have nothing to do with language.

The second and more easily understood way of linking language and the existence of pain is to say that the best evidence that we can have that another creature is in pain is when he tells us that he is. This is a distinct line of argument, for it is not being denied that a non-language-user conceivably *could* suffer, but only that we could ever have sufficient reason to *believe* that he is suffering. Still, this line of argument fails too. As Jane Goodall has pointed out in her study of chimpanzees, *In the Shadow of Man*, when it comes to the expressions of feelings and emotions language is less important than in other areas. We tend to fall back on nonlinguistic modes of communication such as a cheering pat on the back, an exuberant embrace, a clasp of the hands, and so on. The basic signals we use to convey pain, fear, anger, love, joy, surprise, sexual arousal, and many other emotional states are not specific to our own species.[11]

Charles Darwin made an extensive study of this subject, and the book he wrote about it, *The Expression of the Emotions in Man and Animals*, notes countless nonlinguistic modes of expression. The statement "I am in pain" may be one piece of evidence for the conclusion that the speaker is in pain, but it is not the only possible evidence, and since people sometimes tell lies, not even the best possible evidence.

Even if there were stronger grounds for refusing to attribute pain to those who do not have a language, the consequences of this refusal might lead us to reject the conclusion. Human infants and young children are unable to use language. Are we to deny that a year-old child can suffer? If not, language cannot be crucial. Of course, most parents understand the responses of their children better than they understand the responses of other animals; but this is just a fact about the relatively greater knowledge that we have of our own species, and the greater contact we have with infants, as compared to animals. Those who have studied the behavior of other animals, and those who have pet animals, soon learn to understand their responses as well as we understand those of an infant, and sometimes better. Jane Goodall's account of the chimpanzees she watched is one [example], but the same can be said of those who have observed species less closely related to our own. Two among many possible examples are Konrad Lorenz's observations of geese and jackdaws, and N. Tinbergen's extensive studies of herring gulls.[12] Just as we can understand infant human behavior in the light of adult human behavior, so we can understand the behavior of other species in the light of our own behavior—and sometimes we can understand our own behavior better in the light of the behavior of other species.

So to conclude: There are no good reasons, scientific or philosophical, for denying that animals feel pain. If we do not doubt that other humans feel pain we should not doubt that other animals do so too.

Animals can feel pain. As we saw earlier, there can be no moral justification for regarding the pain (or pleasure) that animals feel as less important than the same amount of pain (or pleasure) felt by humans. But what exactly does this mean, in practical terms? To prevent misunderstanding I shall spell out what I mean a little more fully.

If I give a horse a hard slap across its rump with my open hand, the horse may start, but it presumably feels little pain. Its skin is thick enough to protect it against a mere slap. If I slap a baby in the same way, however, the baby will cry and presumably does feel pain, for its skin is more sensitive. So it is worse to slap a baby than a horse, if both slaps are administered with equal force. But there must be some kind of blow . . . perhaps a blow with a heavy stick . . . that would cause the horse as much pain as we cause a baby by slapping it with our hand. That is what I mean by "the

same amount of pain" and if we consider it wrong to inflict that much pain on a baby for no good reason then we must, unless we are speciesists, consider it equally wrong to inflict the same amount of pain on a horse for no good reason.

There are other differences between humans and animals that cause other complications. Normal adult human beings have mental capacities which will, in certain circumstances, lead them to suffer more than animals would in the same circumstances. If, for instance, we decided to perform extremely painful or lethal scientific experiments on normal adult humans, kidnaped at random from public parks for this purpose, every adult who entered a park would become fearful that he would be kidnaped. The resultant terror would be a form of suffering additional to the pain of the experiment. The same experiments performed on nonhuman animals would cause less suffering since the animals would not have the anticipatory dread of being kidnaped and experimented upon. This does not mean, of course, that it would be right to perform the experiment on animals, but only that there is a reason, which is *not* speciesist, for preferring to use animals rather than normal adult humans, if the experiment is to be done at all. Note, however, that this same argument gives us a reason for preferring to use human infants—orphans perhaps—or retarded humans for experiments, rather than adults, since infants and retarded humans would also have no idea of what was going to happen to them. So far as this argument is concerned nonhuman animals and infants and retarded humans are in the same category; and if we use this argument to justify experiments on nonhuman animals we have to ask ourselves whether we are also prepared to allow experiments on human infants and retarded adults; and if we make a distinction between animals and these humans, on what basis can we do it, other than a barefaced—and morally indefensible—preference for members of our own species?

There are many areas in which the superior mental powers of normal adult humans make a difference: anticipation, more detailed memory, greater knowledge of what is happening, and so on. Yet these differences do not all point to greater suffering on the part of the normal human being. Sometimes an animal may suffer more because of his more limited understanding. If, for instance, we are taking prisoners in wartime we can explain to them that while they must submit to capture, search, and confinement they will not otherwise be harmed and will be set free at the conclusion of hostilities. If we capture a wild animal, however, we cannot explain that we are not threatening its life. A wild animal cannot distinguish an attempt to overpower and confine from an attempt to kill; the one causes as much terror as the other.

It may be objected that comparisons of the sufferings of different species are impossible to make, and that for this reason when the interests of animals and humans clash the principle of equality gives no guidance. It is probably true that comparisons of suffering between members of different species cannot be made precisely, but precision is not essential. Even if we were to prevent the infliction of suffering on animals only when it is quite certain that the interests of humans will not be affected to anything like the extent that animals are affected, we would be forced to make radical changes in our treatment of animals that would involve our diet, the farming methods we use, experimental procedures in many fields of science, our approach to wildlife and to hunting, trapping and the wearing of furs, and areas of entertainment like circuses, rodeos, and zoos. As a result, a vast amount of suffering would be avoided.

So far I have said a lot about the infliction of suffering on animals, but nothing about killing them. This omission has been deliberate. The application of the principle of equality to the infliction of suffering is, in theory at least, fairly straightforward. Pain and suffering are bad and should be prevented or minimized, irrespective of the race, sex, or species of the being that suffers. How bad a pain is depends on how intense it is and how long it lasts, but pains of the same intensity and duration are equally bad, whether felt by humans or animals.

The wrongness of killing a being is more complicated. I have kept, and shall continue to keep, the question of killing in the background because in the present state of human tyranny over other species the more simple, straightforward principle of equal consideration of pain or pleasure is a sufficient basis for identifying and protesting all the major abuses of animals that humans practice. Nevertheless, it is necessary to say something about killing.

Just as most humans are speciesists in their readiness to cause pain to animals when they would not cause a similar pain to humans for the same reason, so most humans are speciesists in their readiness to kill other animals when they would not kill humans. We need to proceed more cautiously here, however, because people hold widely differing views about when it is legitimate to kill humans, as the continuing debates over abortion and euthanasia attest. Nor have moral philosophers been able to agree on exactly what it is that makes it wrong to kill humans, and under what circumstances killing a human being may be justifiable.

Let us consider first the view that it is always wrong to take an innocent human life. We may call this the "sanctity of life" view. People who take this view oppose abortion and euthanasia. They do not usually, however, oppose the killing of nonhumans— so perhaps it would be more accurate to describe this view as the "sanctity of *human* life" view.

The belief that human life, and only human life, is sacrosanct is a form of speciesism. To see this, consider the following example.

Assume that, as sometimes happens, an infant has been born with massive and irreparable brain damage. The damage is so severe that the infant can never be any more than a "human vegetable," unable to talk, recognize other people, act independently of others, or develop a sense of self-awareness. The parents of the infant, realizing that they cannot hope for any improvement in their child's condition and being in any case unwilling to spend, or ask the state to spend, the thousands of dollars that would be needed annually for proper care of the infant, ask the doctor to kill the infant painlessly.

Should the doctor do what the parents ask? Legally, he should not, and in this respect the law reflects the sanctity of life view. The life of every human being is sacred. Yet people who would say this about the infant do not object to the killing of nonhuman animals. How can they justify their different judgments? Adult chimpanzees, dogs, pigs, and many other species far surpass the brain-damaged infant in their ability to relate to others, act independently, be self-aware, and any other capacity that could reasonably be said to give value to life. With the most intensive care possible, there are retarded infants who can never achieve the intelligence level of a dog. Nor can we appeal to the concern of the infant's parents, since they themselves, in this imaginary example (and in some actual cases), do not want the infant kept alive.

The only thing that distinguishes the infant from the animal, in the eyes of those who claim it has a "right to life," is that it is, biologically, a member of the species *Homo sapiens*, whereas chimpanzees, dogs, and pigs are not. But to use *this* difference as the basis for granting a right to life to the infant and not to the other animals is, of course, pure speciesism.* It is exactly the kind of arbitrary difference that the most crude and overt kind of racist uses in attempting to justify racial discrimination.

This does not mean that to avoid speciesism we must hold that it is as wrong to kill a dog as it is to kill a normal human being. The only position that is irredeemably speciesist is the one that tries to make the boundary of the right to life run exactly parallel to the boundary of our own species. Those who hold the sanctity of life view do this because while distinguishing sharply between humans and other animals they allow no distinctions to be made within our own species, objecting to the killing of the severely retarded and the hopelessly senile as strongly as they object to the killing of normal adults.

To avoid speciesism we must allow that beings which are similar in all relevant respects have a similar right to life—and mere membership in our own biological species cannot be a morally relevant criterion for this right. Within these limits we could still hold that, for instance, it is worse to kill a normal adult human, with a capacity for self-awareness, and the ability to plan for the future and have meaningful relations with others, than it is to kill a mouse, which

*I am here putting aside religious views, for example the doctrine that all and only humans have immortal souls, or are made in the image of God. Historically these views have been very important, and no doubt are partly responsible for the idea that human life has a special sanctity. Logically, however, these religious views are unsatisfactory, since a reasoned explanation of why it should be that all humans and no nonhumans have immortal souls is not offered. This belief too, therefore, comes under suspicion as a form of speciesism. In any case, defenders of the "sanctity of life" view are generally reluctant to base their position on purely religious doctrines, since these doctrines are no longer as widely accepted as they once were.

presumably does not share all of these characteristics; or we might appeal to the close family and other personal ties which humans have but mice do not have to the same degree; or we might think that it is the consequences for other humans, who will be put in fear of their own lives, that make the crucial difference; or we might think it is some combination of these factors, or other factors altogether.

Whatever criteria we choose, however, we will have to admit that they do not follow precisely the boundary of our own species. We may legitimately hold that there are some features of certain beings which make their lives more valuable than those of other beings; but there will surely be some nonhuman animals whose lives, by any standards, are more valuable than the lives of some humans. A chimpanzee, dog, or pig, for instance, will have a higher degree of self-awareness and a greater capacity for meaningful relations with others than a severely retarded infant or someone in a state of advanced senility. So if we base the right to life on these characteristics we must grant these animals a right to life as good as, or better than, such retarded or senile humans.

Now this argument cuts both ways. It could be taken as showing that chimpanzees, dogs, and pigs, along with some other species, have a right to life and we commit a grave moral offense whenever we kill them, even when they are old and suffering and our intention is to put them out of their misery. Alternatively one could take the argument as showing that the severely retarded and hopelessly senile have no right to life and may be killed for quite trivial reasons, as we now kill animals.

Since the focus of this book is on ethical questions concerning animals and not on the morality of euthanasia I shall not attempt to settle this issue finally. I think it is reasonably clear, though, that while both of the positions just described avoid speciesism, neither is entirely satisfactory. What we need is some middle position which would avoid speciesism but would not make the lives of the retarded and senile as cheap as the lives of pigs and dogs now are, nor make the lives of pigs and dogs so sacrosanct that we think it wrong to put them out of hopeless misery. What we must do is bring nonhuman animals within our sphere of moral concern and cease to treat their lives as expendable for whatever trivial purposes we may have. At the same time, once we realize that the fact that a being is a member of our own species is not in itself enough to make it always wrong to kill that being, we may come to reconsider our policy of preserving human lives at all costs, even when there is no prospect of a meaningful life or of existence without terrible pain.

I conclude, then, that a rejection of speciesism does not imply that all lives are of equal worth. While self-awareness, intelligence, the capacity for meaningful relations with others, and so on are not relevant to the question of inflicting pain—since pain is pain, whatever other capacities, beyond the capacity to feel pain, the being may have—these capacities may be relevant to the question of taking life. It is not arbitrary to hold that the life of a self-aware being, capable of abstract thought, of planning for the future, of complex acts of communication, and so on, is more valuable than the life of a being without these capacities. To see the difference between the issues of inflicting pain and taking life, consider how we would choose within our own species. If we had to choose to save the life of a normal human or a mentally defective human, we would probably choose to save the life of the normal human; but if we had to choose between preventing pain in the normal human or the mental defective—imagine that both have received painful but superficial injuries, and we only have enough painkiller for one of them—it is not nearly so clear how we ought to choose. The same is true when we consider other species. The evil of pain is, in itself, unaffected by the other characteristics of the being that feels the pain; the value of life is affected by these other characteristics.

Normally this will mean that if we have to choose between the life of a human being and the life of another animal we should choose to save the life of the human; but there may be special cases in which the reverse holds true, because the human being in question does not have the capacities of a normal human being. So this view is not speciesist, although it may appear to be at first glance. The preference, in normal cases, for saving a human life over the life of an animal when a choice *has* to be made is a preference based on the characteristics that normal humans have, and not on the mere fact that they are members of our own species. This is why when we consider members of our own species who lack the characteristics of normal humans we can no longer say their lives are always to be preferred to those of other animals. . . . In general, though, the question of when it is wrong to kill (painlessly) an animal is one to which we need give no precise answer. As long as we remember that we should give the same respect to the lives of animals as we give to the lives of those humans at a similar mental level, we shall not go far wrong.

Endnotes

1. For Bentham's moral philosophy, see his *Introduction to the Principles of Morals and Legislation*, and for Sidgwick's see *The Methods of Ethics* (the passage quoted is from the seventh edition, p. 382). As examples of leading contemporary moral philosophers who incorporate a requirement of equal consideration of interests, see R. M. Hare, *Freedom and Reason* (New York: Oxford University Press, 1963) and John Rawls, *A Theory of Justice* (Cambridge: Harvard University Press, Belknap Press, 1972). For a brief account of the essential agreement on this issue between these and other positions, see R. M. Hare, "Rules of War and Moral Reasoning," *Philosophy and Public Affairs*, vol. 1, no. 2 (1972).

2. Letter to Henri Gregoire, February 25, 1809.

3. Reminiscences by Francis D. Gage, from Susan B. Anthony, *The History of Woman Suffrage*, vol. 1; the passage is to be found in the extract in Leslie Tanner, ed., *Voices from Women's Liberation* (New York: Signet, 1970).

4. I owe the term "speciesism" to Richard Ryder.

5. *Introduction to the Principles of Morals and Legislation*, chapter 17.

6. Lord Brain, "Presidential Address," in C. A. Keele and R. Smith, eds., *The Assessment of Pain in Men and Animals* (London: Universities Federation for Animal Welfare, 1962).

7. Ibid., p. 11.

8. Richard Serjeant, *The Spectrum of Pain* (London: Hart-Davis, 1969), p. 72.

9. See the reports of the Committee on Cruelty to Wild Animals (Command Paper 8268, 1951), paragraphs 36–42; the Departmental Committee on Experiments on Animals (Command Paper 2641, 1965), paragraphs 179–182;

and the Technical Committee to Enquire into the Welfare of Animals Kept under Intensive Livestock Husbandry Systems (Command Paper 2836, 1965), paragraphs 26–28 (London: Her Majesty's Stationery Office).

10. One chimpanzee, Washoe, has been taught the sign language used by deaf people, and acquired a vocabulary of 350 signs. Another, Lana, communicates in structured sentences by pushing buttons on a special machine. For a brief account of Washoe's abilities, see Jane van Lawick-Goodall, *In the Shadow of Man* (Boston: Houghton Mifflin,

1971), pp. 252–254; and for Lana, see *Newsweek*, 7 January 1974, and *New York Times*, 4 December 1974.

11. *In the Shadow of Man*, p. 225; Michael Peters makes a similar point in "Nature and Culture," in Stanley and Roslind Godlovitch and John Harris, eds., *Animals, Men and Morals* (New York: Taplinger Publishing Co., 1972).

12. Konrad Lorenz, *King Solomon's Ring* (New York: T. Y. Crowell, 1952); N. Tinbergen, *The Herring Gull's World*, rev. ed. (New York: Basic Books, 1974).

---

62. *The Ethics of Respect for Nature*

Paul W. Taylor

According to Paul W. Taylor, the ethics of respect for nature is made up of three elements: a belief system, an ultimate moral attitude, and a set of rules of duty and standards of character. The belief system is said to justify the adoption of the attitude of respect for nature, which in turn requires a set of rules and standards of character. Two central elements of the belief system are (1) that each individual organism is a teleological center of life, pursuing its own good in its own way, and (2) that whether we are concerned with standards of merit or with the concept of inherent worth, the claim that humans by their very nature are superior to other species is groundless.

Human-Centered and Life-Centered Systems of Environmental Ethics

In this paper I show how the taking of a certain ultimate moral attitude toward nature, which I call "respect for nature," has a central place in the foundations of a life-centered system of environmental ethics. I hold that a set of moral norms (both standards of character and rules of conduct) governing human treatment of the natural world is a rationally grounded set if and only if, first, commitment to those norms is a practical entailment of adopting the attitude of

From "The Ethics of Respect for Nature," *Environmental Ethics* (1986), pp. 197–218. Reprinted by permission of the publisher. Notes renumbered.

respect for nature as an ultimate moral attitude, and second, the adopting of that attitude on the part of all rational agents can itself be justified. When the basic characteristics of the attitude of respect for nature are made clear, it will be seen that a life-centered system of environmental ethics need not be holistic or organicist in its conception of the kinds of entities that are deemed the appropriate objects of moral concern and consideration. Nor does such a system require that the concepts of ecological homeostasis, equilibrium, and integrity provide us with normative principles from which could be derived (with the addition of factual knowledge) our obligations with regard to natural ecosystems. The "balance of nature" is not itself a moral norm, however important may be the role it plays in our general outlook on the natural world that underlies the attitude of respect for nature. I argue that finally it is the good (well-being, welfare) of individual organisms, considered as entities having inherent worth, that determines our moral relations with the Earth's wild communities of life.

In designating the theory . . . as life-centered, I intend to contrast it with all anthropocentric views. According to the latter, human actions that affect the natural environment and its nonhuman inhabitants are right (or wrong) by either of two criteria: They have consequences that are favorable (or unfavorable) to human well-being, or they are consistent (or inconsistent) with the system of norms that protect and implement human rights. From this human-centered standpoint it is to humans and only to humans that all duties are ultimately owed. We may have responsibilities *with regard to* the natural ecosystems and biotic communities of our planet, but these responsibilities are in every case based on the contingent fact that our treatment of those ecosystems and communities of life can further the realization of human values and/or human rights. We have no obligation to promote or protect the good of nonhuman living things, independently of this contingent fact.

A life-centered system of environmental ethics is opposed to human-centered ones precisely on this point. From the perspective of a life-centered theory, we have prima facie moral obligations that are owed to wild plants and animals themselves as members of the Earth's biotic community. We are morally bound (other things being equal) to protect or promote their good for *their* sake. Our duties to respect the integrity of natural ecosystems, to preserve endangered species, and to avoid environmental pollution stem from the fact that these are ways in which we can help make it possible for wild species populations to achieve and maintain a healthy existence in a natural state. Such obligations are due those living things out of recognition of their inherent worth. They are entirely additional to and independent of the obligations we owe to our fellow humans. Although many of the actions that fulfill one set of obligations also fulfill the other, two different grounds of obligation are involved. Their well-being, as well as human well-being, is something to be realized *as an end in itself.*

If we were to accept a life-centered theory of environmental ethics, a profound reordering of our moral universe would take place. We would begin to look at the whole of the Earth's biosphere in a new light. Our duties with respect to the "world" of nature would be seen as making prima facie claims on us to be balanced against our duties with respect to the "world" of human civilization. We could no longer simply take the human point of view and consider the effects of our actions exclusively from the perspective of our own good.

The Good of a Being and the Concept of Inherent Worth

What would justify acceptance of a life-centered system of ethical principles? In order to answer this it is first necessary to make clear the fundamental moral attitude that underlies and makes intelligible the commitment to live by such a system. It is then necessary to examine the considerations that would justify any rational agent's adopting that moral attitude.

Two concepts are essential to the taking of a moral attitude of the sort in question. A being which does not "have" these concepts, that is, which is unable to grasp their meaning and conditions of applicability, cannot be said to have the attitude as part of its moral outlook. These concepts are, first, that of the good (well-being, welfare) of a living thing, and second, the idea of an entity possessing inherent worth. I examine each concept in turn.

(1) Every organism, species population, and community of life has a good of its own which moral agents can intentionally further or damage by their actions. To say that an entity has a good of its own is simply to say that, without reference to any *other* entity, it can be benefited or harmed. One can act in its overall interest or contrary to its overall interest, and environmental conditions can be good for it (advantageous to it) or bad for it (disadvantageous to it). What is good for an entity is what "does it good" in the sense of enhancing or preserving its life and well-being. What is bad for an entity is something that is detrimental to its life and well-being.[1]

We can think of the good of an individual nonhuman organism as consisting in the full development of its biological powers. Its good is realized to the extent that it is strong and healthy. It possesses whatever capacities it needs to successfully cope with its environment and so preserving its existence throughout the various stages of the normal life cycle of its species. The good of a population or community of such individuals consists in the population or community maintaining itself from generation to generation as a coherent system of genetically and ecologically related organisms whose average good is at an optimum level for the given environment. (Here *average good* means that the degree of realization of the good of *individual organisms* in the population or community is, on average, greater than would be the case under any other ecologically functioning order of interrelations among those species populations in the given ecosystem.)

The idea of a being having a good of its own . . . does not entail that the being must have interests or take an interest in what affects its life for better or for worse. We can act in a being's interest or contrary to its interest without its being interested in what we are doing to it in the sense of wanting or not wanting us to do it. It may, indeed, be wholly unaware that favorable and unfavorable events are taking place in its life. [Trees], for example, have no knowledge or desires or feelings. Yet it is undoubtedly the case that trees can be harmed or benefited by our actions. We can crush their roots by running a bulldozer too close to them. We can see to it that they get adequate nourishment and moisture by fertilizing and watering the soil around them. Thus we can help or hinder them in the realization of their good. It is the good of trees themselves that is thereby affected. We can similarly act so as to further the good of an entire tree population of a certain species (say, all the redwood trees in a California valley) or the good of a whole community of plant life in a given wilderness area, just as we can do harm to such a population or community.

When construed in this way, the concept of a being's good is not coextensive with sentience or the capacity for feeling pain. William Frankena has argued for a general theory of environmental ethics in which the ground of a creature's being worthy of moral consideration is its sentience. I have offered some criticisms of this view elsewhere, but the full refutation of such a position . . . finally depends on the positive reasons for accepting a life-centered theory of the kind I am defending in this essay.[2]

It should be noted further that I am leaving open the question of whether machines—in particular, those which are not only goal-directed, but also self-

regulating—can properly be said to have a good of their own.[3] Since I am concerned only with human treatment of wild organisms, species populations, and communities of life as they occur in our planet's natural ecosystems, it is to those entities alone that the concept "having a good of its own" will here be applied. I am not denying that other living things, whose genetic origin and environmental conditions have been produced, controlled, and manipulated by humans for human ends, do have a good of their own in the same sense as do wild plants and animals. It is not my purpose in this essay, however, to set out or defend the principles that should guide our conduct with regard to their good. It is only insofar as their production and use by humans have good or ill effects upon natural ecosystems and their wild inhabitants that the ethics of respect for nature comes into play.

(2) The second concept essential to the moral attitude of respect for nature is the idea of inherent worth. We take that attitude toward wild living things (individuals, species populations, or whole biotic communities) when and only when we regard them as entities possessing inherent worth. Indeed, it is only because they are conceived in this way that moral agents can think of themselves as having validly binding duties, obligations, and responsibilities that are *owed* to them as their *due*. I am not at this juncture arguing why they *should* be so regarded; I consider it at length below. But so regarding them is a presupposition of our taking the attitude of respect toward them and accordingly understanding ourselves as bearing certain moral relations to them. This can be shown as follows:

What does it mean to regard an entity that has a good of its own as possessing inherent worth? Two general principles are involved: the principle of moral consideration and the principle of intrinsic value.

According to the principle of moral consideration, wild living things are deserving of the concern and consideration of all moral agents simply in virtue of their being members of the Earth's community of life. From the moral point of view their good must be taken into account whenever it is affected for better or worse by the conduct of rational agents. This holds no matter what species the creature belongs to. The good of each is to be accorded some value and so acknowledged as having some weight in the deliberations of all rational agents. Of course, it may be necessary for such agents to act in ways contrary to the good of this or that particular organism or group of organisms in order to further the good of others, including the good of humans. But the principle of moral consideration prescribes that, with respect to each being an entity having its own good, every individual is deserving of consideration.

The principle of intrinsic value states that, regardless of what kind of entity it is in other respects, if it is a member of the Earth's community of life, the realization of its good is something *intrinsically* valuable. This means that its good is prima facie worthy of being preserved or promoted as an end in itself and for the sake of the entity whose good it is. Insofar as we regard any organism, species population, or life community as an entity with inherent worth, we believe that it must never be treated as if it were a mere object or thing whose entire value lies in being instrumental to the good of some other entity. The well-being of each is judged to have value in and of itself.

Combining these two principles, we can now define what it means for a living thing or group of living things to possess inherent worth. To say that it possesses inherent worth is to say that its good is deserving of the concern and consideration of all moral agents, and that the realization of its good has intrinsic value, to be pursued as an end in itself and for the sake of the entity whose good it is.

The duties owed to wild organisms, species populations, and communities of life in the Earth's natural ecosystems are grounded on their inherent worth. When rational, autonomous agents regard such entities as possessing inherent worth, they place intrinsic value on the realization of their good and so hold themselves responsible for performing actions that will have this effect and for refraining from actions having the contrary effect.

The Attitude of Respect for Nature

Why should moral agents regard wild living things in the natural world as possessing inherent worth? To answer this question we must first take into account the fact that, when rational, autonomous agents subscribe to the principles of moral consideration and intrinsic value and so conceive of wild living things as having that kind of worth, such agents are *adopting a certain ultimate moral attitude toward the natural world.* This is the attitude I call "respect for nature." It parallels the attitude of respect for persons in human ethics. When we adopt the attitude of respect for persons as the proper (fitting, appropriate) attitude to take toward all persons as persons, we consider the fulfillment of the basic interests of each individual to have intrinsic value. We thereby make a moral commitment to live a certain kind of life in relation to other persons. We place ourselves under the direction of a system of standards and rules that we consider validly binding on all moral agents as such.[4]

Similarly, when we adopt the attitude of respect for nature as an ultimate moral attitude we make a commitment to live by certain normative principles. These principles constitute the rules of conduct and standards of character that are to govern our treatment of the natural world. This is, first, an *ultimate* commitment because it is not derived from any higher norm. The attitude of respect for nature is not grounded on some other, more general, or more fundamental attitude. It sets the total framework for our responsibilities toward the natural world. It can be justified, as I show below, but its justification cannot consist in referring to a more general attitude or a more basic normative principle.

Second, the commitment is a *moral* one because it is understood to be a disinterested matter of principle. It is this feature that distinguishes the attitude of respect for nature from the set of feelings and dispositions that comprise the love of nature. The latter stems from one's personal interest in and response to the natural world. Like the affectionate feelings we have toward certain individual human beings, one's love of nature is nothing more than the particular way one feels about the natural environment and its wild inhabitants. And just as our love for an individual person differs from our respect for all persons as such (whether we happen to love them or not), so love of nature differs from respect for nature. Respect for nature is an attitude we believe all moral agents ought to have simply as moral agents, regardless of whether or not they also love nature. Indeed, we have not truly taken the attitude of respect for nature ourselves unless we believe this. To put it in a Kantian way, to adopt the attitude of respect for nature is to take a stance that one wills it to be a universal law for all rational beings. It is to hold that stance categorically, as being validly applicable to every moral agent without exception, irrespective of whatever personal feelings toward nature such an agent might have or might lack.

Although the attitude of respect for nature is, in this sense, a disinterested and universalizable attitude, anyone who does adopt it has certain steady, more or less permanent dispositions. These dispositions, which are themselves to be considered disinterested and universalizable, comprise three interlocking sets: dispositions to seek certain ends, dispositions to carry on one's practical reasoning and deliberation in a certain way, and dispositions to have certain feelings. We may accordingly analyze the attitude of respect for nature into the following components. (a) The disposition to aim at, and to take steps to bring about, as final and disinterested ends, the promoting and protecting of the good of organisms, species populations, and life communities in natural ecosystems. (These ends are "final" in not being pursued as means to further ends. They are "disinterested" in being independent of the self-interest of the agent.) (b) The disposition to consider actions that tend to realize those ends to be prima facie obligatory *because* they have that tendency. (c) The disposition to experience positive and negative feelings toward states of affairs in the world *because* they are favorable or unfavorable to the good of organisms, species populations, and life communities in natural ecosystems.

The logical connection between the attitude of respect for nature and the duties of a life-centered system of environmental ethics can now be made clear. Insofar as one sincerely takes that attitude and so has the three sets of dispositions, one will at the same time be disposed to comply with certain rules of duty (such as nonmaleficence and noninterference) and with standards of character (such as fairness and benevolence) that determine the obligations and virtues of moral agents with regard to the Earth's wild living things. We can say that the actions one performs and the character traits one develops in fulfilling these moral requirements are the way one *expresses* or *embodies* the attitude in one's conduct and character. In his famous essay, "Justice as Fairness," John Rawls describes the rules of the duties of human morality

(such as fidelity, gratitude, honesty, and justice) as "forms of conduct in which recognition of others as persons is manifested."[5] I hold that the rules of duty governing our treatment of the natural world and its inhabitants are forms of conduct in which the attitude of respect for nature is manifested.

The Justifiability of the Attitude of Respect for Nature

I return to the question posed earlier, which has not yet been answered: Why *should* moral agents regard wild living things as possessing inherent worth? I now argue that the only way we can answer this question is by showing how adopting the attitude of respect for nature is justified for all moral agents. Let us suppose that we were able to establish that there are good reasons for adopting the attitude, reasons which are intersubjectively valid for every rational agent. If there are such reasons, they would justify anyone's having the three sets of dispositions mentioned above as constituting what it means to have the attitude. Since these include the disposition to promote or protect the good of wild living things as a disinterested and ultimate end, as well as the disposition to perform actions for the reason that they tend to realize that end, we see that such dispositions commit a person to the principles of moral consideration and intrinsic value. To be disposed to further, as an end in itself, the good of any entity in nature just because it is that kind of entity, is to be disposed to give consideration to *every* such entity and to place intrinsic value on the realization of its good. Insofar as we subscribe to these two principles we regard living things as possessing inherent worth. Subscribing to the principles is what it *means* to so regard them. To justify the attitude of respect for nature, then, is to justify commitment to these principles and thereby to justify regarding wild creatures as possessing inherent worth.

We must keep in mind that inherent worth is not some mysterious sort of objective property belonging to living things that can be discovered by empirical observation or scientific investigation. To ascribe inherent worth to an entity is not to describe it by citing some feature discernible by sense perception or inferable by inductive reasoning. Nor is there a logically necessary connection between the concept of a being having a good of its own and the concept of inherent worth. We do not contradict ourselves by asserting that an entity that has a good of its own lacks inherent worth. In order to show that such an entity "has" inherent worth we must give good reasons for ascribing that kind of value to it (placing that kind of value upon it, conceiving of it to be valuable in that way). Although it is humans (persons, valuers) who must do the valuing, for the ethics of respect for nature, the value so ascribed is not a human value. That is to say, it is not a value derived from considerations regarding human well-being or human rights. It is a value that is ascribed to nonhuman animals and plants themselves, independently of their relationship to what humans judge to be conducive to their own good.

Whatever reasons, then, justify our taking the attitude of respect for nature as defined above are also reasons that show why we *should* regard the living things of the natural world as possessing inherent worth. We saw earlier that, since the attitude is an ultimate one, it cannot be derived from a more fundamental attitude nor shown to be a special case of a more general one. On what sort of grounds, then, can it be established?

The attitude we take toward living things in the natural world depends on the way we look at them, on what kind of beings we conceive them to be, and on how we understand the relations we bear to them. Underlying and supporting our attitude is a certain *belief system* that constitutes a particular world view or outlook on nature and the place of human life in it. To give good reasons for adopting the attitude of respect for nature, then, we must first articulate the belief system which underlies and supports that attitude. If it appears that the belief system is internally coherent and well ordered, and if, as far as we can now tell, it is consistent with all known scientific truths relevant to our knowledge of the object of the attitude (which in this case includes the whole set of the Earth's natural ecosystems and their communities of life), then there remains the task of indicating why scientifically informed and rational thinkers with a developed capacity of reality awareness can find it acceptable as a way of conceiving of the natural world and our place in it. To the extent we can do this we

provide at least a reasonable argument for accepting the belief system and the ultimate moral attitude it supports.

I do not hold that such a belief system can be *proven* to be true, either inductively or deductively. As we shall see, not all of its components can be stated in the form of empirically verifiable propositions. Nor is its internal order governed by purely logical relationships. But the system as a whole, I contend, constitutes a coherent, unified, and rationally acceptable "picture" or "map" of a total world. By examining each of its main components and seeing how they fit together, we obtain a scientifically informed and well-ordered conception of nature and the place of humans in it.

This belief system underlying the attitude of respect for nature I call (for want of a better name) "the biocentric outlook on nature." Since it is not wholly analyzable into empirically confirmable assertions, it should not be thought of as simply a compendium of the biological sciences concerning our planet's ecosystems. It might best be described as a philosophical world view, to distinguish it from a scientific theory or explanatory system. However, one of its major tenets is the great lesson we have learned from the science of ecology: the interdependence of all living things in an organically unified order whose balance and stability are necessary conditions for the realization of the good of its constituent biotic communities.

Before turning to an account of the main components of the biocentric outlook, it is convenient here to set forth the overall structure of my theory of environmental ethics as it has now emerged. The ethics of respect for nature is made up of three basic elements: a belief system, an ultimate moral attitude, and a set of rules of duty and standards of character. These elements are connected with each other in the following manner. The belief system provides a certain outlook on nature which supports and makes intelligible an autonomous agent's adopting, as an ultimate moral attitude, the attitude of respect for nature. It supports and makes intelligible the attitude in the sense that, when an autonomous agent understands its moral relations to the natural world in terms of this outlook, it recognizes the attitude of respect to be the only *suitable* or *fitting* attitude to take toward all wild forms of life in the Earth's biosphere. Living things are now viewed as *the appropriate objects of the attitude of respect* and are accordingly regarded as entities possessing inherent worth. One then places intrinsic value on the promotion and protection of their good. As a consequence of this, one makes a moral commitment to abide by a set of rules of duty and to fulfill (as far as one can by one's own efforts) certain standards of good character. Given one's adoption of the attitude of respect, one makes that moral commitment because one considers those rules and standards to be validly binding on all moral agents. They are seen as embodying forms of conduct and character structures in which the attitude of respect for nature is manifested.

This three-part complex which internally orders the ethics of respect for nature is symmetrical with a theory of human ethics grounded on respect for persons. Such a theory includes, first, a conception of oneself and others as persons, that is, as centers of autonomous choice. Second, there is the attitude of respect for persons as persons. When this is adopted as an ultimate moral attitude it involves the disposition to treat every person as having inherent worth or "human dignity." Every human being, just in virtue of her or his humanity, is understood to be worthy of moral consideration, and intrinsic value is placed on the autonomy and well-being of each. This is what Kant meant by conceiving of persons as ends in themselves. Third, there is an ethical system of duties which are acknowledged to be owed by everyone to everyone. These duties are forms of conduct in which public recognition is given to each individual's inherent worth as a person.

This structural framework for a theory of human ethics is meant to leave open the issue of consequentialism (utilitarianism) versus nonconsequentialism (deontology). That issue concerns the particular kind of system of rules defining the duties of moral agents toward persons. Similarly, I am leaving open [here] the question of what particular kind of system of rules defines our duties with respect to the natural world.

The Biocentric Outlook on Nature

The biocentric outlook on nature has four main components. (1) Humans are thought of as members of the Earth's community of life, holding that membership on the same terms as apply to all the nonhuman members. (2) The Earth's natural ecosystems as a totality are seen as a complex web of interconnected elements, with the sound biological functioning of each being dependent on the sound biological functioning of the others. (This is the component referred to above as the great lesson that the science of ecology has taught us.) (3) Each individual organism is conceived of as a teleological center of life, pursuing its own good in its own way. (4) Whether we are concerned with standards of merit or with the concept of inherent worth, the claim that humans by their very nature are superior to other species is a groundless claim and, in the light of elements (1), (2), and (3) above, must be rejected as nothing more than an irrational bias in our own favor. . . .

The Denial of Human Superiority

This fourth component of the biocentric outlook on nature is the single most important idea in establishing the justifiability of the attitude of respect for nature. Its central role is due to the special relationship it bears to the first three components of the outlook. This relationship will be brought out after the concept of human superiority is examined and analyzed.[6]

In what sense are humans alleged to be superior to other animals? We are different from them in having certain capacities that they lack. But why should these capacities be a mark of superiority? From what point of view are they judged to be signs of superiority and what sense of superiority is meant? After all, various nonhuman species have capacities that humans lack. There is the speed of a cheetah, the vision of an eagle, the agility of a monkey. Why should not these be taken as signs of *their* superiority over humans?

One answer . . . is that these capacities are not as *valuable* as the human capacities that are claimed to make us superior. Such uniquely human characteristics as rational thought, aesthetic creativity, autonomy and self-determination, and moral freedom, it might be held, have a higher value than the capacities found in other species. Yet we must ask: valuable to whom, and on what grounds?

The human characteristics mentioned are all valuable to humans. They are essential to the preservation and enrichment of our civilization and culture. Clearly it is from the human standpoint that they are being judged to be desirable and good. It is not difficult here to recognize a begging of the question. Humans are claiming human superiority from a strictly human point of view, that is, from a point of view in which the good of humans is taken as the standard of judgment. All we need to do is to look at the capacities of nonhuman animals (or plants, for that matter) from the standpoint of *their* good to find a contrary judgment of superiority. The speed of the cheetah, for example, is a sign of its superiority to humans when considered from the standpoint of the good of its species. If it were as slow a runner as a human, it would not be able to survive. And so for all the other abilities of nonhumans which further their good but which are lacking in humans. In each case the claim to human superiority would be rejected from a nonhuman standpoint.

When superiority assertions are interpreted in this way, they are based on judgments of *merit*. To judge the merits of a person or an organism one must apply grading or ranking standards to it. (As I show below, this distinguishes judgments of merit from judgments of inherent worth.) Empirical investigation then determines whether it has the "good-making properties" (merits) in virtue of which it fulfills the standards being applied. In the case of humans, merits may be either moral or nonmoral. We can judge one person to be better than (superior to) another from the moral point of view by applying certain standards to their character and conduct. Similarly, we can appeal to nonmoral criteria in judging someone to be an excellent piano player, a fair cook, a poor tennis player, and so on. Different social purposes and roles are implicit in the making of such judgments, providing the frame of reference for the choice of standards by which the nonmoral merits of people are determined. Ultimately such purposes and roles stem from a society's way of life as a whole. Now a society's way of life may be thought of as the cultural form given to the realization of human values. Whether moral or nonmoral standards are being applied, then, all judgments of people's merits finally depend on human values. All are made from an exclusively human standpoint.

The question that naturally arises at this juncture is: Why should standards that are based on human values be assumed to be the only valid criteria of merit and hence the only true signs of superiority? This question is especially pressing when humans are being judged superior in merit to nonhumans. [A] human being may be a better mathematician than a monkey, but the monkey may be a better tree climber than a human being. If we humans value mathematics more than tree climbing, that is because our conception of civilized life makes the development of mathematical ability more desirable than the ability to climb trees. But is it not unreasonable to judge nonhumans by the values of human civilization, rather than by values connected with what it is for a member of *that* species to live a good life? If all living things have a good of their own, it makes sense to judge the merits of nonhumans by standards derived from *their* good. To use only standards based on human values is already to commit oneself to holding that humans are superior to nonhumans, which is the point in question.

A further logical flaw arises in connection with the widely held conviction that humans are *morally* superior beings because they possess, while others lack, the capacities of a moral agent (free will, accountability, deliberation, judgment, practical reason). This view rests on a conceptual confusion. As far as moral standards are concerned, only beings that have the capacities of a moral agent can properly be judged to be *either* moral (morally good) *or* immoral (morally deficient). Moral standards are simply not applicable to beings that lack such capacities. Animals and plants cannot therefore be said to be morally inferior in merit to humans. Since the only beings that can have moral merits *or be deficient in such merits* are moral agents, it is conceptually incoherent to judge humans as superior to nonhumans on the ground that humans have moral capacities while nonhumans don't.

Up to this point I have been interpreting the claim that humans are superior to other living things as a grading or ranking judgment regarding their comparative merits. There is, however, another way of understanding the idea of human superiority. According to this interpretation, humans are superior to nonhumans not as regards their merits but as regards their inherent worth. Thus the claim of human superiority is to be understood as asserting that all humans, simply in virtue of their humanity, have *a greater inherent worth* than other living things.

The inherent worth of an entity does not depend on its merits.[7] To consider something as possessing inherent worth, we have seen, is to place intrinsic value on the realization of its good. This is done regardless of whatever particular merits it might have or might lack, as judged by a set of grading or ranking standards. In human affairs, we are all familiar with the principle that one's worth as a person does not vary with one's merits or lack of merits. The same can hold true of animals and plants. To regard such entities as possessing inherent worth entails disregarding their merits and deficiencies, whether they are being judged from a human standpoint or from the standpoint of their own species.

The idea of one entity having more merit than another, and so being superior to it in merit, makes perfectly good sense. Merit is a grading or ranking concept, and judgments of comparative merit are based on the different degrees to which things satisfy a given standard. But what can it mean to talk about one thing being superior to another in inherent worth? In order to get at what is being asserted in such a claim it is helpful first to look at the social origin of the concept of degrees of inherent worth.

The idea that humans can possess different degrees of inherent worth originated in societies having rigid class structures. Before the rise of modern democracies with their egalitarian outlook, one's membership in a hereditary class determined one's social status. People in the upper classes were looked up to, while those in the lower classes were looked down upon. In such a society one's social superiors and social inferiors were clearly defined and easily recognized.

Two aspects of these class-structured societies are especially relevant to the idea of degrees of inherent worth. First, those born into the upper classes were deemed more worthy of respect than those born into the lower orders. Second, the superior worth of upper class people had nothing to do with their merits nor did the inferior worth of those in the lower classes rest on their lack of merits. One's superiority or inferiority entirely derived from a social position one was born into. The modern concept of a meritocracy simply did not apply. One could not advance into a higher class by any sort of moral or nonmoral achievement. Similarly, an aristocrat held his title and all the privileges that went with it just because he was the eldest son of a titled nobleman. Unlike the bestowing of knighthood in contemporary Great Britain, one did not earn membership in the nobility by meritorious conduct.

We who live in modern democracies no longer believe in such hereditary social distinctions. Indeed, we would wholeheartedly condemn them on moral grounds as fundamentally unjust. We have come to think of class systems as a paradigm of social injustice, it being a central principle of the democratic way of life that among humans there are no superiors and no inferiors. Thus we have rejected the whole conceptual framework in which people are judged to have different degrees of inherent worth. That idea is incompatible with our notion of human equality based on the doctrine that all humans, simply in virtue of their humanity, have the same inherent worth. (The belief in universal human rights is one form that this egalitarianism takes.)

The vast majority of people in modern democracies, however, do not maintain an egalitarian outlook when it comes to comparing human beings with other living things. Most people consider our own species to be superior to all other species and this superiority is understood to be a matter of inherent worth, not merit. There may exist thoroughly vicious and depraved humans who lack all merit. Yet because they are human they are thought to belong to a higher class of entities than any plant or animal. That one is born into the species *Homo sapiens* entitles one to have lordship over those who are one's inferiors, namely, those born into other species. The parallel with hereditary social classes is very close. Implicit in this view is a hierarchical conception of nature according to which an organism has a position of superiority or inferiority in the Earth's community of life simply on the basis of its genetic background. The "lower" orders of life are looked down upon and it is considered perfectly proper that they serve the interests of those belonging to the highest order, namely humans. The intrinsic value we place on the well-being of our fellow humans reflects our recognition of their rightful position as our equals. No such intrinsic value is to be placed on the good of other animals, unless we choose to do so out of fondness or affection for them. But their well-being imposes no moral requirement on us. In this respect there is an absolute difference in moral status between ourselves and them.

This is the structure of concepts and beliefs that people are committed to insofar as they regard humans to be superior in inherent worth to all other species. I now wish to argue that this structure of concepts and beliefs is completely groundless. If we accept the first three components of the biocentric outlook and from that perspective look at the major philosophical traditions which have supported that structure, we find it to be at bottom nothing more than the expression of an irrational bias in our own favor. The philosophical traditions themselves rest on very questionable assumptions or else simply beg the question. I briefly consider three of the main traditions to substantiate the point. These are classical Greek humanism, Cartesian dualism, and the Judeo-Christian concept of the Great Chain of Being.

The inherent superiority of humans over other species was implicit in the Greek definition of man as a rational animal. Our animal nature was identified with "brute" desires that need the order and restraint of reason to rule them (just as reason is the special virtue of those who rule in the ideal state). Rationality was then seen to be the key to our superiority over animals. It enables us to live on a higher plane and endows us with a nobility and worth that other creatures lack. This familiar way of comparing humans with other species is deeply ingrained in our Western philosophical outlook. The point to consider here is that this view does not actually provide an argument *for* human superiority but rather makes explicit the framework of thought that is implicitly used by those who think of humans as inherently superior to nonhumans. The Greeks who held that humans, in virtue of their rational capacities, have a kind of worth greater than any nonrational being, never looked at rationality as but one capacity of living things among many others. But when we consider rationality from the standpoint of the first three elements of the ecological outlook, we see that its value lies in its importance for *human* life. Other creatures achieve their species-specific good without the need of rationality, although they often make use of capacities that humans lack. So the humanistic outlook of classical Greek thought does not give us a neutral (non–question-begging) ground on which to construct a scale of degrees of inherent worth possessed by different species of living things.

The second tradition, centering on the Cartesian dualism of soul and body, also fails to justify the claim to human superiority. That superiority is supposed to derive from the fact that we have souls while animals do not. Animals are mere automata and lack the divine element that makes us spiritual beings. I will not go into the now familiar criticisms of this two-substance view. I only add the point that, even if humans are composed of an immaterial, unextended soul and a material, extended body, this in itself is not a reason to deem them of greater worth than entities that are only bodies. Why is a soul substance a thing that adds value to its possessor? Unless theological reasoning is offered here (which many, including myself, would find unacceptable on epistemological grounds), no logical connection is evident. An immaterial something that thinks is better than a material something that doesn't think only if thinking itself has value, either intrinsically or instrumentally. Now it is intrinsically valuable to humans alone, who value it as an end in itself, and it is instrumentally valuable to those who benefit from it, namely humans.

For animals that neither enjoy thinking for its own sake nor need it for living the kind of life for which they are best adapted, it has no value. Even if "thinking" is broadened to include all forms of consciousness, there are still many living things that can do without it and yet live what is, for their species, a good life. The anthropocentricity underlying the claim to human superiority runs throughout Cartesian dualism.

A third major source of the idea of human superiority is the Judeo-Christian concept of the Great Chain of Being. Humans are superior to animals and plants because their Creator has given them a higher place on the chain. It begins with God at the top, and then moves to the angels, who are lower than God but higher than humans, then to humans, positioned between the angels and the beasts (partaking of the nature of both), and then on down to the lower levels occupied by nonhuman animals, plants, and finally inanimate objects. Humans, being "made in God's image," are inherently superior to animals and plants by virtue of their being closer (in their essential nature) to God.

The metaphysical and epistemological difficulties with this conception of a hierarchy of entities are, in my mind, insuperable. Without entering into this matter here, I point out that if we are unwilling to accept the metaphysics of traditional Judaism and Christianity, we are again left without good reasons for holding to the claim of inherent human superiority.

The foregoing considerations (and others like them) leave us with but one ground for the assertion that a human being, regardless of merit, is a higher kind of entity than any other living thing. This is the mere fact of the genetic makeup of the species *Homo sapiens*. But this is surely irrational and arbitrary. Why should the arrangement of genes of a certain type be a mark of superior value, especially when this fact about an organism is taken by itself, unrelated to any other aspect of its life? We might just as well refer to any other genetic makeup as a ground of superior value. Clearly we are confronted here with a wholly arbitrary claim that can only be explained as an irrational bias in our own favor.

That the claim is nothing more than a deep-seated prejudice is brought home to us when we look at our relation to other species in the light of the first three elements of the biocentric outlook. Those elements taken conjointly give us a certain overall view of the natural world and of the place of humans in it. When we take this view we come to understand other living things, their environmental conditions, and their ecological relationships in such a way as to awake in us a deep sense of our kinship with them as fellow members of the Earth's community of life. Humans and nonhumans alike are viewed together as integral parts of one unified whole in which all living things are functionally interrelated. Finally, when our awareness focuses on the individual lives of plants and animals, each is seen to share with us the characteristic of being a teleological center of life striving to realize its own good in its own unique way.

As this entire belief system becomes part of the conceptual framework by which we understand and perceive the world, we come to see ourselves as bearing a certain moral relation to nonhuman forms of life. Our ethical role in nature takes on a new significance. We begin to look at other species as we look at ourselves, seeing them as beings which have a good they are striving to realize just as we have a good we are striving to realize. We accordingly develop the disposition to view the world from the standpoint of their good as well as from the standpoint of our own good. Now if the groundlessness of the claim that humans are inherently superior to other species were brought clearly before our minds, we would not remain intellectually neutral toward that claim but would reject it as fundamentally at variance with our total world outlook. In the absence of any good reasons for holding it, the assertion of human superiority would then appear simply as the expression of an irrational and self-serving prejudice that favors one particular species over several million others.

Rejecting the notion of human superiority entails its positive counterpart: the doctrine of species impartiality. One who accepts that doctrine regards all living things as possessing inherent worth—the *same* inherent worth, since no one species has been shown to be either "higher" or "lower" than any other. Now we saw earlier that, insofar as one thinks of a living thing as possessing inherent worth, one considers it to be the appropriate object of the attitude of respect and believes that attitude to be the only fitting or suitable one for all moral agents to take toward it.

Here, then, is the key to understanding how the attitude of respect is rooted in the biocentric outlook on nature. The basic connection is made through the denial of human superiority. Once we reject the claim that humans are superior either in merit or in worth to other living things, we are ready to adopt the attitude of respect. The denial of human superiority is itself the result of taking the perspective on nature built into the first three elements of the biocentric outlook.

Now the first three elements of the biocentric outlook, it seems clear, would be found acceptable to any rational and scientifically informed thinker who is fully "open" to the reality of the lives of nonhuman organisms. Without denying our distinctively human characteristics, such a thinker can acknowledge the fundamental respects in which we are members of the Earth's community of life and in which the biological conditions necessary for the realization of our human values are inextricably linked with the whole system of nature. In addition, the conception of individual living things as teleological centers of life simply articulates how a scientifically informed thinker comes to understand them as the result of increasingly careful and detailed observations. Thus, the biocentric outlook recommends itself as an acceptable system of concepts and beliefs to anyone who is clear-minded, unbiased, and factually enlightened, and who has a developed capacity of reality awareness with regard to the lives of individual organisms. This is as good a reason for making the moral commitment involved in adopting the attitude of respect for nature as any theory of environmental ethics could possibly have.

Moral Rights and the Matter of Competing Claims

I have not asserted anywhere in the foregoing account that animals or plants have moral rights. This omission was deliberate. I do not think that the reference class of the concept, bearer of moral rights, should be extended to include nonhuman living things. My reasons for taking this position, however, go beyond the scope of this paper. I believe I have been able to accomplish many of the same ends which those who ascribe rights to animals or plants wish to accomplish. There is no reason, moreover, why plants and animals, including whole species populations and life communities, cannot be accorded *legal* rights under my the-

ory. To grant them legal protection could be interpreted as giving them legal entitlement to be protected, and this would be a means by which a society that subscribed to the ethics of respect for nature could give public recognition to their inherent worth.

There remains the problem of competing claims, even when wild plants and animals are not thought of as bearers of moral rights. If we accept the biocentric outlook and accordingly adopt the attitude of respect for nature as our ultimate moral attitude, how do we resolve conflicts that arise from our respect for persons in the domain of human ethics and our respect for nature in the domain of environmental ethics? This is a question that cannot adequately be dealt with here. My main purpose in this paper has been to try to establish a base point from which we can start working toward a solution to the problem. I have shown why we cannot just begin with an initial presumption in favor of the interests of our own species. It is after all within our power as moral beings to place limits on human population and technology with the deliberate intention of sharing the Earth's bounty with other species. That such sharing is an ideal difficult to realize even in an approximate way does not take away its claim to our deepest moral commitment.

Endnotes

1. The conceptual links between an entity *having* a good, something being good *for* it, and events doing good *to* it are examined by G.H. Von Wright in *The Varieties of Goodness* (New York: Humanities Press, 1963), chaps. 3 and 5.

2. See W. K. Frankena, "Ethics and the Environment," in K. E. Goodpaster and K. M. Sayre, eds., *Ethics and Problems of the 21st Century* (Notre Dame: University of Notre Dame Press, 1979), pp. 3–20. I critically examine Frankena's views in "Frankena on Environmental Ethics," *Monist* (1981): 237–243.

3. In the light of considerations set forth in Daniel Dennett's *Brainstorms: Philosophical Essays on Mind and Psychology* (Montgomery, Vt.: Bradford Books, 1978), it is advisable to leave this question unsettled at this time. When machines are developed that function in the way our brains do, we may well come to deem them proper subjects of moral consideration.

4. I have analyzed the nature of this commitment of human ethics in "On Taking the Moral Point of View,"

Midwest Studies in Philosophy, vol. 3, *Studies in Ethical Theory* (1978), pp. 35–61.

5. John Rawls, "Justice As Fairness," *Philosophical Review* 67 (1958): 183.

6. My criticisms of the dogma of human superiority gain independent support from a carefully reasoned essay by R. and V. Routley showing the many logical weaknesses in arguments for human-centered theories of environmental ethics. R. and V. Routley, "Against the Inevitability of Human Chauvinism," in K. E. Goodpaster and K. M. Sayre, eds., *Ethics and Problems of the 21st Century* (Notre Dame: University of Notre Dame Press, 1979), pp. 36–59.

7. For this way of distinguishing between merit and inherent worth, I am indebted to Gregory Vlastos, "Justice and Equality," in R. Brandt, ed., *Social Justice* (Englewood Cliffs, N.J.: Prentice-Hall, 1962), pp. 31–72.

63. *Environmental Justice*

JAMES P. STERBA

James P. Sterba seeks to resolve a central debate in contemporary environmental ethics between those who defend anthropocentric ethics and those who defend nonanthropocentric ethics by showing that when the most morally defensible versions of each of these perspectives are laid out, they do not lead to different practical recommendations. In this way he hopes to show how it is possible for defenders of anthropocentric and nonanthropocentric environmental ethics, despite their theoretical disagreement concerning whether humans are superior to members of other species, to agree on a common set of principles for achieving environmental justice.

A central debate, if not the most central debate, in contemporary environmental ethics is between those who defend anthropocentric ethics and those who defend nonanthropocentric ethics. This debate pits deep ecologists like George Sessions against reform or shallow ecologists like John Passmore.[1] It divides biocentric egalitarians like Paul Taylor from social ecologists like Murray Bookchin.[2] In this paper I propose to go some way toward resolving this debate by showing that when the most morally defensible versions of each of these perspectives are laid out, they do not lead to different practical requirements. In this way I hope to show how it is possible for defenders of anthropocentric and nonanthropocentric environmental ethics, despite their theoretical disagreement concerning whether humans are superior to members of other species, to agree on a common set of principles for achieving environmental justice.

Nonanthropocentric Environmental Ethics

Consider first the nonanthropocentric perspective. In support of this perspective it can be argued that we have no non–question-begging grounds for regarding the members of any living species as superior to the

From "Violence against Nature," in *Social Philosophy Today*, ed. Creighton Peden and Yeager Hudson (1993). Reprinted by permission.

members of any other. It allows that the members of species differ in a myriad of ways, but argues that these differences do not provide grounds for thinking that the members of any one species are superior to the members of any other. In particular, it denies that the differences between species provides grounds for thinking that humans are superior to the members of other species. Of course, the nonanthropocentric perspective recognizes that humans have distinctive traits that members of other species lack, like rationality and moral agency. It just points out that the members of nonhuman species also have distinctive traits that humans lack, like the homing ability of pigeons, the speed of the cheetah, and the ruminative ability of sheep and cattle.

Nor will it do to claim that the distinctive traits humans have are more valuable than the distinctive traits members of other species possess because there is no non–question-begging standpoint from which to justify that claim. From a human standpoint, rationality and moral agency are more valuable than any distinctive trait found in nonhuman species, since, as humans, we would not be better off if we were to trade in those traits for the distinctive traits found in nonhuman species. Yet the same holds true of nonhuman species. Pigeons, cheetahs, sheep, and cattle would not be better off if they were to trade in their distinctive traits for the distinctive traits of other species.

Of course, the members of some species might be better off if they could retain the distinctive traits of their species while acquiring one or another of the distinctive traits possessed by some other species. For example, we humans might be better off if we could retain our distinctive traits while acquiring the ruminative ability of sheep and cattle. But many of the distinctive traits of species cannot be even imaginatively added to the members of other species without substantially altering the original species. For example, in order for the cheetah to acquire the distinctive traits possessed by humans, presumably it would have to be so transformed that its paws became something like hands to accommodate its humanlike mental capabilities, thereby losing its distinctive speed, and ceasing to be a cheetah. So possessing distinctively human traits would not be good for the cheetah. And with the possible exception of our nearest evolutionary relatives, the same holds true for the members of other species: They would not be better off having distinctively human traits. Only in fairy tales and in the world of Disney can the members of nonhuman species enjoy a full array of distinctively human traits. So there would appear to be no non–question-begging perspective from which to judge that distinctively human traits are more valuable than the distinctive traits possessed by other species. Judged from a non–question-begging perspective, we would seemingly have to regard the members of all species as equals.[3]

Nevertheless, regarding the members of all species as equals still allows for human preference in the same way that regarding all humans as equals still allows for self-preference.

First of all, human preference can be justified on grounds of defense. Thus, we have

A Principle of Human Defense: Actions that defend oneself and other human beings against harmful aggression are permissible even when they necessitate killing or harming animals or plants.[4]

This principle is strictly analogous to the principle of self-defense that applies in human ethics and permits actions in defense of oneself or other human beings against harmful human aggression.[5] In the case of human aggression, however, it will sometimes be possible to effectively defend oneself and other human beings by first suffering the aggression and then securing adequate compensation later. Since in the case of nonhuman aggression, this is unlikely to obtain,

more harmful preventive actions such as killing a rabid dog or swatting a mosquito will be justified.

Second, human preference can also be justified on grounds of preservation. Accordingly, we have

A Principle of Human Preservation: Actions that are necessary for meeting one's basic needs or the basic needs of other human beings are permissible even when they require aggressing against the basic needs of animals and plants.

Now needs, in general, if not satisfied, lead to lacks or deficiencies with respect to various standards. The basic needs of humans, if not satisfied, lead to lacks or deficiencies with respect to a standard of a decent life. The basic needs of animals and plants, if not satisfied, lead to lacks or deficiencies with respect to a standard of a healthy life.[6]

In human ethics, there is no principle that is strictly analogous to this Principle of Human Preservation. There is a principle of self-preservation in human ethics that permits actions that are necessary for meeting one's own basic needs or the basic needs of other people, even if this requires *failing to meet* (through an act of omission) the basic needs of still other people. For example, we can use our resources to feed ourselves and our family, even if this necessitates failing to meet the basic needs of people in Third World countries. But, in general, we don't have a principle that allows us to aggress against (through an act of commission) the basic needs of some people in order to meet our own basic needs or the basic needs of other people to whom we are committed or happen to care about. Actually, the closest we come to permitting aggressing against the basic needs of other people in order to meet our own basic needs or the basic needs of people to whom we are committed or happen to care about is our acceptance of the outcome of life and death struggles in lifeboat cases, where no one has an antecedent right to the available resources. For example, if you had to fight off others in order to secure the last place in a lifeboat for yourself or for a member of your family, we might say that you justifiably aggressed against the basic needs of those whom you fought to meet your own basic needs or the basic needs of the member of your family.

Nevertheless, our survival requires a principle of preservation that permits aggressing against the basic needs of at least some other living things whenever this is necessary to meet our own basic needs or the basic needs of other human beings. Here there are two possibilities. The first is a principle of preservation that allows us to aggress against the basic needs of both humans and nonhumans whenever it would serve our own basic needs or the basic needs of other human beings. The second is the principle, given above, that allows us to aggress against the basic needs of only nonhumans whenever it would serve our own basic needs or the basic needs of other human beings. The first principle does not express any general preference for the members of the human species, and thus it permits even cannibalism provided that it serves to meet our own basic needs or the basic needs of other human beings. In contrast, the second principle does express a degree of preference for the members of the human species in cases where their basic needs are at stake. Happily, this degree of preference for our own species is still compatible with the equality of all species because favoring the members of one's own species to this extent is characteristic of the members of all the species with which we interact and is thereby legitimated. The reason it is legitimated is that we would be required to sacrifice the basic needs of members of the human species only if the members of other species were making similar sacrifices for the sake of the members of the human species. In addition, if we were to prefer consistently the basic needs of the members of other species whenever those needs conflicted with our own (or even if we do so half the time), given the characteristic behavior of the members of other species, we would soon be facing extinction, and, fortunately, we have no reason to think that we are morally required to bring about our own extinction. For these reasons, the degree of preference for our own species found in the above Principle of Human Preservation is justified, even if we were to adopt a nonanthropocentric perspective.

Nevertheless, preference for humans can go beyond bounds, and the bounds that are compatible with a nonanthropocentric perspective are expressed by the following:

A Principle of Disproportionality: Actions that meet nonbasic or luxury needs of humans are prohibited when they aggress against the basic needs of animals and plants.

This principle is strictly analogous to a principle in human ethics that prohibits meeting some people's nonbasic or luxury needs by aggressing against the basic needs of other people.[7]

Without a doubt, the adoption of such a principle with respect to nonhuman nature would significantly change the way we live our lives. Such a principle is required, however, if there is to be any substance to the claim that the members of all species are equal. We can no more consistently claim that the members of all species are equal and yet aggress against the basic needs of some animals or plants whenever this conflicts with our own nonbasic or luxury needs than we can consistently claim that all humans are equal and yet aggress against the basic needs of some other human beings whenever this conflicts with our nonbasic or luxury needs.[8] Consequently, if species equality is to mean anything, it must be that the basic needs of the members of nonhuman species trump the nonbasic needs of humans in these cases of conflict.

So while a nonanthropocentric perspective allows a degree of preference for the members of the human species, it also significantly limits that preference.

Nevertheless, animal liberationists may wonder about the further implications of this nonanthropocentric perspective for the treatment of animals. Obviously, a good deal of work has already been done on this topic. Initially, philosophers thought that humanism could be extended to include animal liberation and eventually environmental concern.[9] Then Baird Callicott argued that animal liberation and environmental concern were as opposed to each other as they were to humanism.[10] The resulting conflict Callicott called "a triangular affair." Agreeing with Callicott, Mark Sagoff contended that any attempt to link animal liberation and environmental concern would lead to "a bad marriage and a quick divorce."[11] Yet more recently, such philosophers as Mary Ann Warren have tended to play down the opposition between animal liberation and environmental concern, and even Callicott now thinks he can bring the two back together again.[12] There are good reasons for thinking that such a reconciliation is possible.

Right off, it would be good for the environment if people generally, especially people in the First World, adopted a more vegetarian diet of the sort that animal liberationists are recommending. This is because a good portion of livestock production today consumes grains that could be more effectively used for direct human consumption. For example, 90 percent of the protein, 99 percent of the carbohydrate, and 100 percent of the fiber value of grain is wasted by cycling it through livestock, and currently 64 percent of the U.S. grain crop is fed to livestock.[13] So by adopting a more vegetarian diet, people generally, and especially people in the First World, could significantly reduce the amount of farmland that has to be kept in production to feed the human population. This, in turn, could have beneficial effects on the whole biotic community by eliminating the amount of soil erosion and environmental pollutants that result from raising livestock. For example, it has been estimated that 85 percent of U.S. topsoil lost from cropland, pasture, range land, and forest land is directly associated with raising livestock.[14]

But even though a more vegetarian diet seems in order, it is not clear that the interests of farm animals would be well served if all of us became complete vegetarians. Sagoff assumes that in a completely vegetarian human world people would continue to feed farm animals as before.[15] But it is not clear that we would have any obligation to do so. Moreover, in a completely vegetarian human world, we would probably need about half of the grain we now feed livestock to meet people's nutritional needs, particularly in Second and Third World countries. There simply would not be enough grain to go around. And then there would be the need to conserve cropland for future generations. So in a completely vegetarian human world, it seems likely that the population of farm animals would be decimated, relegating many of the farm animals that remain to zoos. On this account, it would seem to be more in the interest of farm animals generally that they be maintained under healthy conditions, and then killed relatively painlessly and eaten, rather than that they not be maintained at all. So a completely vegetarian human world would not seem to serve the interest of farm animals.

Nor, it seems, would it be in the interest of wild species who no longer have their natural predators not to be hunted by humans. Of course, where possible, it may be preferable to reintroduce natural predators. But this may not always be possible because of the proximity of farm animals and human popula-

tions, and then if action is not taken to control the populations of wild species, disaster could result for the species and their environments. For example, deer, rabbits, squirrels, quails, and ducks reproduce rapidly, and in the absence of predators can quickly exceed the carrying capacity of their environments. So it is in the interest of certain wild species and their environments that humans intervene periodically to maintain a balance. Of course, there will be many natural environments where it is in the interest of the environment and the wild animals that inhabit it to be simply left alone. But here, too, animal liberation and environmental concern would not be in conflict. For these reasons, animal liberationists would have little reason to object to the proposed three principles for a nonanthropocentric environmental ethics.

Anthropocentric Environmental Ethics

But suppose we were to reject the central argument of the nonanthropocentric perspective and deny that the members of all species are equal. We might claim, for example, that humans are superior because, through culture, they "realize a greater range of values" than members of nonhuman species; or we might claim that humans are superior in virtue of their "unprecedented capacity to create ethical systems that impart worth to other life-forms."[16] Or we might offer some other grounds for human superiority.[17] Suppose, then, we adopt this anthropocentric perspective. What follows?

First of all, we will still need a principle of human defense. However, there is no need to adopt a different principle of human defense from the principle favored by a nonanthropocentric perspective. Whether we judge humans to be equal or superior to the members of other species, we will still want a principle that allows us to defend ourselves and other human beings from harmful aggression, even when this necessitates killing or harming animals or plants.

Second, we will also need a principle of human preservation. But here, too, there is no need to adopt a different principle from the principle of human preservation favored by a nonanthropocentric perspective. Whether we judge humans to be equal or superior to the members of other species, we will still want a principle that permits actions that are necessary for meeting our own basic needs or the basic needs of other human beings, even when this requires aggressing against the basic needs of animals and plants.

The crucial question is whether we will need a different principle of disproportionality. If we judged humans to be superior to the members of other species, will we still have grounds for preferring in this way the basic needs of animals and plants over the nonbasic or luxury needs of humans?

Here it is important to distinguish between two degrees of preference that we noted earlier. First, we could prefer the basic needs of animals and plants over the nonbasic or luxury needs of humans when to do otherwise would involve *aggressing against* (by an act of commission) the basic needs of animals and plants. Second, we could prefer the basic needs of animals and plants over the nonbasic or luxury needs of humans when to do otherwise would involve simply *failing to meet* (by an act of omission) the basic needs of animals and plants.

Now in human ethics when the basic needs of some people are in conflict with the nonbasic or luxury needs of others, the distinction between failing to meet and aggressing against basic needs seems to have little moral force. In such conflicting cases, both ways of not meeting basic needs are objectionable.[18]

But in environmental ethics, whether we adopt an anthropocentric or a nonanthropocentric perspective, we would seem to have grounds for morally distinguishing between the two cases, favoring the basic needs of animals and plants when to do otherwise would involve *aggressing against* those needs in order to meet our own nonbasic or luxury needs, but not when it would involve simply *failing to meet* those needs in order to meet our own nonbasic or luxury needs. This degree of preference for the members of the human species would be compatible with the equality of species insofar as members of nonhuman species also fail to meet the basic needs of members of the human species.

Even so, this theoretical distinction would have little practical force since most of the ways that we have of preferring our own nonbasic needs over the basic needs of animals and plants actually involve aggressing against their basic needs to meet our own nonbasic or luxury needs rather than simply failing to meet their basic needs.[19]

Yet even if most of the ways we have of preferring our own nonbasic or luxury needs do involve aggressing against the basic needs of animals and plants, wouldn't human superiority provide grounds for making such sacrifices? Or put another way, shouldn't human superiority have more theoretical and practical significance than I am allowing? Not, I claim, if we are looking for the most morally defensible position to take.

For consider: The claim that humans are superior to the members of other species, if it can be justified at all, is something like the claim that a person came in first in a race where others came in second, third, fourth, and so on. It would not imply that the members of other species are without intrinsic value. In fact, it would imply just the opposite—that the members of other species are also intrinsically valuable, although not as intrinsically valuable as humans, just as the claim that a person came in first in a race implies that the persons who came in second, third, fourth, and so on are also meritorious, although not as meritorious as the person who came in first.

This line of argument draws further support once we consider that many animals and plants are superior to humans in one respect or another—e.g., the sense of smell of the wolf, the acuity of sight of the eagle, or the photosynthetic power of plants. So any claim of human superiority must [recognize] excellences in nonhuman species, even for excellences that are superior to their corresponding human excellences. In fact, it demands that recognition.

Moreover, if the claim of human superiority is to have any moral force, it must rest on non–question-begging grounds. Accordingly, we must be able to give a non–question-begging response to the non-anthropocentric argument for the equality of species. Yet for any such argument to be successful, it would have to recognize the intrinsic value of the members of nonhuman species. Even if it could be established that human beings have greater intrinsic value, we would still have to recognize that nonhuman nature has intrinsic value as well. So the relevant question is: How are we going to recognize the presumably lesser intrinsic value of nonhuman nature?

Now if human needs, even nonbasic or luxury ones, are always preferred to even the basic needs of the members of nonhuman species, we would not be giving any recognition to the intrinsic value of nonhuman nature. But what if we allowed the nonbasic or luxury needs of humans to trump the basic needs of nonhuman nature half the time, and half the time we allowed the basic needs of nonhuman nature to trump the nonbasic or luxury needs of humans. Would that be enough? Certainly, it would be a significant advance over what we are presently doing. For what we are presently doing is meeting the basic needs of nonhuman nature, at best, only when it serves our own needs or the needs of those we are committed to or happen to care about, and that does not recognize the intrinsic value of nonhuman nature at all. A fifty-fifty arrangement would be an advance indeed. But it would not be enough.

The reason it would not be enough is that the claim that humans are superior to nonhuman nature no more supports the practice of aggressing against the basic needs of nonhuman nature to satisfy our own nonbasic or luxury needs than the claim that a person came in first in a race would support the practice of aggressing against the basic needs of those who came in second, third, fourth and so on to satisfy the nonbasic or luxury needs of the person who came in first. A higher degree of merit does not translate into a right of domination, and to claim a right to aggress against the basic needs of nonhuman nature in order to meet our own nonbasic or luxury needs is clearly to claim

a right of domination. All that we would be justified in doing, I have argued, is not meeting the basic needs of nonhuman nature when this conflicts with our nonbasic or luxury needs. What we are not justified in doing is aggressing against the basic needs of nonhuman nature when this conflicts with our nonbasic or luxury needs. But this is no more than is justified assuming the equality of species.

In sum, whether we endorse anthropocentric or nonanthropocentric environmental ethics, we should favor the very same principles: a Principle of Human Defense, a Principle of Human Preservation, and a Principle of Disproportionality as I have interpreted them. Taken together these three principles strike the right balance between concerns of human welfare and the welfare of nonhuman nature.

Of course, the practical implications of these three principles would include proposals for conserving existing resources, particularly nonrenewable ones, proposals for converting to renewable resources, proposals for redistributing resources to meet basic needs of both humans and nonhumans, and proposals for population control, all implemented principally by educational changes and by changes in the tax and incentive structures of our society. In the longer work from which this paper is drawn, I go on to discuss these practical proposals in more detail. In this paper, I have sought to provide the nonanthropocentric and anthropocentric grounding for such proposals in a common set of conflict resolution principles that are required for achieving environmental justice.

Endnotes

1. See John Passmore, *Man's Responsibility for Nature* (London: Charles Scribner's Sons, 1974) and George Sessions and Bill Devall, *Deep Ecology* (Salt Lake City: Glibb Smith, 1985).

2. See Paul Taylor, *Respect for Nature* (Princeton: Princeton University Press, 1987) and Murray Bookchin, *The Ecology of Freedom* (Montreal: Black Rose Books, 1991). It is also possible to view Passmore as pitted against Taylor and Bookchin as pitted against Sessions, but however one casts the debate, those who defend an anthropocentric ethics are still opposed to those who defend a nonanthropocentric ethics.

3. I am assuming here that either we treat humans as superior overall to other living things or we treat them as equal overall to other living things. Accordingly, if there is no self-evident or non–question-begging grounds for claiming that humans are superior overall to other living things, then, I claim that we should treat humans as equal overall to all other living things.

4. For the purposes of this paper, I will follow the convention of excluding humans from the class denoted by "animals."

5. Of course, one might contend that no principle of human defense applies in human ethics because either

"nonviolent pacifism" or "nonlethal pacifism" is the most morally defensible view. However, I have argued elsewhere that this is not the case, and that still other forms of pacifism more compatible with just war theory are also more morally defensible than either of these forms of pacifism. See Selection 75.

6. For further discussion of basic needs, see *How to Make People Just* (Totowa, N.J.: Rowman & Littlefield, 1988), pp. 45–50.

7. This principle is clearly acceptable to welfare liberals and socialists, and it can even be shown to be acceptable to libertarians. See Selection 4.

8. Of course, libertarians have claimed that we can recognize that people have equal basic rights while failing to meet, but not aggressing against, the basic needs of other human beings. However, I have argued that this claim is mistaken. See Selection 4.

9. Peter Singer's *Animal Liberation* (New York: New York Review, 1975) inspired this view.

10. Baird Callicott, "Animal Liberation: A Triangular Affair," *Environmental Ethics* (1980), 311–328.

11. Mark Sagoff, "Animal Liberation and Environmental Ethics: Bad Marriage, Quick Divorce," *Osgood Hall Law Journal* (1984), 297–307.

12. Mary Ann Warren, "The Rights of the Nonhuman World," in *Environmental Philosophy,* edited by Robert

Elliot and Arran Gare (London, 1983), 109–134, and Baird Callicott, *In Defense of the Land Ethic* (Albany: SUNY Press, 1989), chapter 3.

13. *Realities for the 90's* (Santa Cruz, 1991), p. 4.

14. Ibid., p. 5.

15. Mark Sagoff, op. cit., pp. 301–305.

16. Holmes Rolston, *Environmental Ethics* (Philadelphia: Temple University Press, 1988), pp. 66–68; Murray Bookchin., op. cit., p. xxxvi.

17. See the discussion of possible grounds of human superiority in Taylor, pp. 135–152 and in Byran Norton, *Why Preserve Natural Variety?* (Princeton: Princeton University Press, 1987), 135–150.

18. This is clearly true for welfare liberals and socialists, and it can even be shown to be true for libertarians because most failings to meet the basic needs of others really turn out to be acts of aggressing against the basic needs of others. See *How To Make People Just,* chapter 7.

19. The same holds true in human ethics where most of the ways that we have of preferring our own nonbasic needs over other humans actually involve aggressing against their needs to meet our own nonbasic or luxury needs rather than simply failing to meet them. See the previous note.

---

64. *The Power and the Promise of Ecological Feminism*

KAREN J. WARREN

Karen Warren challenges mainstream environmental ethics to recognize that the domination of nature is rooted in the domination of women, or at least has failed to recognize that both these forms of domination are interconnected. According to Warren, women are identified with nature and the realm of the physical, while men are identified with the "human" and the realm of the mental. On the basis of this identification, Warren argues that women are judged inferior to men and their subordination to men is taken to be thereby justified. She calls this argumentative move from a claim of difference to a claim of superiority to a claim of domination the "logic of domination."

Ecological feminism (ecofeminism) has begun to receive a fair amount of attention lately as an alternative feminism and environmental ethic. Since Francoise d'Eaubonne introduced the term *ecofeminisme* in 1974 to bring attention to women's potential for bringing about an ecological revolution, the term has been used in a variety of ways. As I use the term here, ecological feminism is the position that there are important connections—historical, experiential, symbolic, and theoretical—between the domination of women and the domination of nature, an understanding of which is crucial to both feminism and environmental ethics. I argue that the promise and power of ecological feminism is that *it provides a distinctive framework both for reconceiving feminism and for developing an environmental ethic which takes seriously connections between the domination of women and the domination of nature.* I do so by discussing the nature of a feminist ethic and the ways in which ecofeminism provides a feminist and environmental ethic. I conclude that any feminist theory *and* any environmental ethic which fails to take seriously the twin and interconnected dominations of women and nature is at best incomplete and at worst simply inadequate.

Feminism, Ecological Feminism, and Conceptual Frameworks

Whatever else it is, feminism is at least the movement to end sexist oppression. It involves the elimination of any and all factors that contribute to the continued and systematic domination or subordination of women. While feminists disagree about the nature of and solutions to the subordination of women, all feminists agree that sexist oppression exists, is wrong, and must be abolished.

A "feminist issue" is any issue that contributes in some way to understanding the oppression of women. Equal rights, comparable pay for comparable work, and food production are feminist issues whenever an understanding of them contributes to an understanding of the continued exploitation or subjugation of women. Carrying water and searching for firewood are feminist issues wherever and whenever women's primary responsibility for these tasks contributes to their lack of full participation in decision making, income producing, or high status positions

engaged in by men. What counts as a feminist issue, then, depends largely on context, particularly the historical and material conditions of women's lives.

Environmental degradation and exploitation are feminist issues because an understanding of them contributes to an understanding of the oppression of women. In India, for example, both deforestation and reforestation through the introduction of a monoculture species tree (e.g., eucalyptus) intended for commercial production are feminist issues because the loss of indigenous forests and multiple species of trees has drastically affected rural Indian women's ability to maintain a subsistence household. Indigenous forests provide a variety of trees for food, fuel, fodder, household utensils, dyes, medicines, and income-generating uses, while monoculture species forests do not. Although I do not argue for this claim here, a look at the global impact of environmental degradation on women's lives suggests important respects in which environmental degradation is a feminist issue.

Feminist philosophers claim that some of the most important feminist issues are *conceptual* ones: These issues concern how one conceptualizes such mainstay philosophical notions as reason and rationality, ethics, and what it is to be human. Ecofeminists extend this feminist philosophical concern to nature. They argue that, ultimately, some of the most important connections between the domination of women and the domination of nature are conceptual. To see this, consider the nature of conceptual frameworks.

A *conceptual framework* is a set of *basic* beliefs, values, attitudes, and assumptions which shape and reflect how one views oneself and one's world. It is a socially constructed lens through which we perceive ourselves and others. It is affected by such factors as gender, race, class, age, affectional orientation, nationality, and religious background.

Some conceptual frameworks are oppressive. An *oppressive conceptual framework* is one that explains, justifies, and maintains relationships of domination and subordination. When an oppressive conceptual framework is *patriarchal*, it explains, justifies, and maintains the subordination of women by men.

I have argued elsewhere that there are three significant features of oppressive conceptual frameworks: (1) value-hierarchical thinking, i.e., "up-down" thinking which places higher value, status, or prestige on

Reprinted from *Environmental Ethics* (1990) by permission of the author.

what is "up" rather than on what is "down"; (2) value dualisms, i.e., disjunctive pairs in which the disjuncts are seen as oppositional (rather than as complementary) and exclusive (rather than as inclusive), and which place higher value (status, prestige) on one disjunct rather than the other (e.g., dualisms which give higher value or status to that which has historically been identified as "mind," "reason," and "male" than to that which has historically been identified as "body," "emotion," and "female"); and (3) logic of domination, i.e., a structure of argumentation which leads to a justification of subordination.

The third feature of oppressive conceptual frameworks is the most significant. A logic of domination is not *just* a logical structure. It also involves a substantive value system, since an ethical premise is needed to permit or sanction the "just" subordination of that which is subordinate. This justification typically is given on grounds of some alleged characteristic (e.g., rationality) which the dominant (e.g., men) have and the subordinate (e.g., women) lack.

Contrary to what many feminists and ecofeminists have said or suggested, there may be nothing *inherently* problematic about "hierarchical thinking" or even "value-hierarchical thinking" in contexts other than contexts of oppression. Hierarchical thinking is important in daily living for classifying data, comparing information, and organizing material. Taxonomies (e.g., plant taxonomies) and biological nomenclature seem to require *some* form of "hierarchical thinking." Even "value-hierarchical thinking" may be quite acceptable in certain contexts. (The same may be said of "value dualisms" in nonoppressive contexts.) For example, suppose it is true that what is unique about humans is our conscious capacity to radically reshape our social environments (or "societies"), as Murray Bookchin suggests. Then one could truthfully say that humans are better equipped to radically reshape their environments than are rocks or plants—a "value-hierarchical" way of speaking.

The problem is not simply *that* value-hierarchical thinking and value dualisms are used, but *the way* in which each has been used *in oppressive conceptual frameworks* to establish inferiority and to justify subordination.[1] It is the logic of domination, *coupled* with value-hierarchical thinking and value dualisms, which "justifies" subordination. What is explanato-

rily basic, then, about the nature of oppressive conceptual frameworks is the logic of domination.

For ecofeminism, that a logic of domination is explanatorily basic is important for at least three reasons. First, without a logic of domination, a description of similarities and differences would be just that: a description of similarities and differences. Consider the claim, "Humans are different from plants and rocks in that humans can (and plants and rocks cannot) consciously and radically reshape the communities in which they live; humans are similar to plants and rocks in that they are both members of an ecological community." Even if humans are "better" than plants and rocks with respect to the conscious ability of humans to radically transform communities, one does not *thereby* get any *morally* relevant distinction between humans and nonhumans, or an argument for the domination of plants and rocks by humans. To get *those* conclusions one needs to add at least two powerful assumptions, viz., (A2) and (A4) in argument A below:

(A1) Humans do, and plants and rocks do not, have the capacity to consciously and radically change the community in which they live.

(A2) Whatever has the capacity to consciously and radically change the community in which it lives is morally superior to whatever lacks this capacity.

(A3) Thus, humans are morally superior to plants and rocks.

(A4) For any X and Y, if X is morally superior to Y, then X is morally justified in subordinating Y.

(A5) Thus, humans are morally justified in subordinating plants and rocks.

Without the two assumptions that *humans are morally superior* to (at least some) nonhumans, (A2), and that *superiority justifies subordination*, (A4), all one has is some difference between humans and some nonhumans. This is true *even if* that difference is given in terms of superiority. Thus, it is the logic of domination, (A4), which is the bottom line in ecofeminist discussions of oppression.

Second, ecofeminists argue that, at least in Western societies, the oppressive conceptual framework which sanctions the twin dominations of women and nature is a patriarchal one characterized by all three features of an oppressive conceptual framework. Many ecofeminists claim that, historically, within at least the dominant Western culture, a patriarchal conceptual framework has sanctioned the following argument B:

(B1) Women are identified with nature and the realm of the physical; men are identified with the "human" and the realm of the mental.

(B2) Whatever is identified with nature and the realm of the physical is inferior to ("below") whatever is identified with the "human" and the realm of the mental; or, conversely, the latter is superior to ("above") the former.

(B3) Thus, women are inferior to ("below") men; or, conversely, men are superior to ("above") women.

(B4) For any X and Y, if X is superior to Y, then X is justified in subordinating Y.

(B5) Thus, men are justified in subordinating women.

If sound, argument B establishes *patriarchy*, i.e., the conclusion given at (B5) that the systematic domination of women by men is justified. But according to ecofeminists, (B5) is justified by just those three features of an oppressive conceptual framework identified earlier: value-hierarchical thinking, the assumption at (B2); value dualisms, the assumed dualism of the mental and the physical at (B1) and the assumed inferiority of the physical vis-à-vis the mental at (B2); and a logic of domination, the assumption at (B4), the same as the previous premise (A4). Hence, according to ecofeminists, insofar as an oppressive patriarchal conceptual framework has functioned historically (within at least dominant Western culture) to sanction the twin dominations of women and nature (argument B), both argument B and the patriarchal conceptual framework, from whence it comes, ought to be rejected.

Of course, the preceding does not identify which premises of B are false. What is the status of premises (B1) and (B2)? Most, if not all, feminists claim that (B1), and many ecofeminists claim that (B2), have been assumed or asserted within the dominant Western philosophical and intellectual tradition.[2] As such, these feminists assert, as a matter of historical fact, that the dominant Western philosophical tradition has assumed the truth of (B1) and (B2). Ecofeminists,

however, either deny (B2) or do not affirm (B2). Furthermore, because some ecofeminists are anxious to deny any historical identification of women with nature, some ecofeminists deny (B1) when (B1) is used to support anything other than a strictly historical claim about what has been asserted or assumed to be true within patriarchal culture—e.g., when (B1) is used to assert that women properly are identified with the realm of nature and the physical.[3] Thus, from an ecofeminist perspective, (B1) and (B2) are properly viewed as problematic though historically sanctioned claims: They are problematic precisely because of the way they have functioned historically in a patriarchal conceptual framework and culture to sanction the dominations of women and nature.

What *all* ecofeminists agree about, then, is the way in which the *logic of domination* has functioned historically within patriarchy to sustain and justify the twin dominations of women and nature.[4] Since *all* feminists (and not just ecofeminists) oppose patriarchy, the conclusion given at (B5), all feminists (including ecofeminists) must oppose at least the logic of domination, premise (B4), on which argument B rests—whatever the truth-value status of (B1) and (B2) *outside* of a patriarchal context.

That *all* feminists must oppose the logic of domination shows the breadth and depth of the ecofeminist critique of B: It is a critique not only of the three assumptions on which this argument for the domination of women and nature rests, viz., the assumptions at (B1), (B2), and (B4); it is also a critique of patriarchal conceptual frameworks generally, i.e., of those oppressive conceptual frameworks which put men "up" and women "down," allege some way in which women are morally inferior to men, and use that alleged difference to justify the subordination of women by men. Therefore, ecofeminism is necessary to *any* feminist critique of patriarchy, and, hence, necessary to feminism (a point I discuss again later).

Third, ecofeminism clarifies why the logic of domination, and any conceptual framework which gives rise to it, must be abolished in order both to make possible a meaningful notion of difference which does not breed domination and to prevent feminism from becoming a "support" movement based primarily on shared experiences. In contemporary society, there is no one "woman's voice," no *woman* (or *human*) sim-

pliciter: Every woman (or human) is a woman (or human) of some race, class, age, affectional orientation, marital status, regional or national background, and so forth. Because there are no "monolithic experiences" that all women share, feminism must be a "solidarity movement" based on shared beliefs and interests rather than a "unity in sameness" movement based on shared experiences and shared victimization. In the words of Maria Lugones, "Unity—not to be confused with solidarity—is understood as conceptually tied to domination."

Ecofeminists insist that the sort of logic of domination used to justify the domination of humans by gender, racial or ethnic, or class status is also used to justify the domination of nature. Because eliminating a logic of domination is part of a feminist critique— whether a critique of patriarchy, white supremacist culture, or imperialism—ecofeminists insist that *naturism* is properly viewed as an integral part of any feminist solidarity movement to end sexist oppression and the logic of domination which conceptually grounds it.

Ecofeminism Reconceives Feminism

The discussion so far has focused on some of the oppressive conceptual features of patriarchy. As I use the phrase, the "logic of traditional feminism" refers to the location of the conceptual roots of sexist oppression, at least in Western societies, in an oppressive patriarchal conceptual framework characterized by a logic of domination. Insofar as other systems of oppression (e.g., racism, classism, ageism, heterosexism) are also conceptually maintained by a logic of domination, appeal to the logic of traditional feminism ultimately locates the basic conceptual interconnections among *all* systems of oppression in the logic of domination. It thereby explains at a *conceptual* level why the eradication of sexist oppression requires the eradication of the other forms of oppression. It is by clarifying this conceptual connection between systems of oppression that a movement to end sexist oppression—traditionally the special turf of feminist theory and practice—leads to a reconceiving of feminism as *a movement to end all forms of oppression.*

Suppose one agrees that the logic of traditional feminism requires the expansion of feminism to include other social systems of domination (e.g., racism and classism). What warrants the inclusion of nature in these "social systems of domination"? Why must the logic of traditional feminism include the abolition of "naturism" (i.e., the domination or oppression of nonhuman nature) among the "isms" feminism must confront? The conceptual justification for expanding feminism to include ecofeminism is twofold. One basis has already been suggested: By showing that the conceptual connections between the dual dominations of women and nature are located in an oppressive and, at least in Western societies, patriarchal conceptual framework characterized by a logic of domination, ecofeminism explains how and why feminism, conceived as a movement to end sexist oppression, must be expanded and reconceived as also a movement to end naturism. This is made explicit by the following argument C:

(C1) Feminism is a movement to end sexism.

(C2) But sexism is conceptually linked with naturism (through an oppressive conceptual framework characterized by a logic of domination).

(C3) Thus, Feminism is (also) a movement to end naturism.

Because, ultimately, these connections between sexism and naturism are conceptual—embedded in an oppressive conceptual framework—the logic of traditional feminism lends to the embrace of ecological feminism.

The other justification for reconceiving feminism to include ecofeminism has to do with the concepts of gender and nature. Just as conceptions of gender are socially constructed, so are conceptions of nature. Of course, the claim that women and nature are social constructions does not require anyone to deny that there are actual humans and actual trees, rivers, and plants. It simply implies that *how* women and nature are conceived is a matter of historical and social reality. These conceptions vary cross-culturally and by historical time period. As a result, any discussion of the "oppression or domination of nature" involves reference to historically specific forms of social domination of nonhuman nature by humans, just as discussion of the "domination of women" refers to historically specific forms of social domination of women by men. Although I do not argue for it here, an ecofeminist defense of the historical connections between the dominations of women and of nature, claims (B1) and (B2) in argument B, involves showing that within patriarchy the feminization of nature and the naturalization of women have been crucial to the historically successful subordinations of both.

If ecofeminism promises to reconceive traditional feminism in ways which include naturism as a legitimate feminist issue, does ecofeminism also promise to reconceive environmental ethics in ways which are feminist? I think so. This is the subject of the remainder of the paper.

Climbing from Ecofeminism to Environmental Ethics

Many feminists and some environmental ethicists have begun to explore the use of first-person narrative as a way of raising philosophically germane issues in ethics often lost or underplayed in mainstream philosophical ethics. Why is this so? What is it about narrative which makes it a significant resource for theory and practice in feminism and environmental ethics? Even if appeal to first-person narrative is a helpful literary device for describing ineffable experience or a legitimate social science methodology for documenting personal and social history, how is first-person narrative a valuable vehicle of argumentation for ethical decision making and theory building? One fruitful way to begin answering these questions is to ask them of a particular first-person narrative.

Consider the following first-person narrative about rock climbing:

> For my very first rock climbing experience, I chose a somewhat private spot, away from other climbers and on-lookers. After studying "the chimney," I focused all my energy on making it to the top. I climbed with intense determination, using whatever strength and skills I had to accomplish this challenging feat. By midway I was exhausted and anxious. I couldn't see what to do next—where to put my hands or feet. Growing increasingly more weary as I clung somewhat desperately to the rock,

I made a move. It didn't work. I fell. There I was, dangling midair above the rocky ground below, frightened but terribly relieved that the belay rope had held me. I knew I was safe. I took a look up at the climb that remained. I was determined to make it to the top. With renewed confidence and concentration, I finished the climb to the top.

> On my second day of climbing, I rappelled down about 200 feet from the top of the Palisades at Lake Superior to just a few feet above the water level. I could see no one—not my belayer, not the other climbers, no one. I unhooked slowly from the rappel rope and took a deep cleansing breath. I looked all around me—really looked—and listened. I heard a cacophony of voices—birds, trickles of water on the rock before me, waves lapping against the rocks below. I closed my eyes and began to feel the rock with my hands—the cracks and crannies, the raised lichen and mosses, the almost imperceptible nubs that might provide a resting place for my fingers and toes when I began to climb. At that moment I was bathed in serenity. I began to talk to the rock in an almost inaudible, child-like way, as if the rock were my friend. I felt an overwhelming sense of gratitude for what it offered me—a chance to know myself and the rock differently, to appreciate unforeseen miracles like the tiny flowers growing in the even tinier cracks in the rock's surface, and to come to know a sense of *being in relationship* with the natural environment. It felt as if the rock and I were silent conversational partners in a longstanding friendship. I realized then that I had come to care about this cliff which was so different from me, so unmovable and invincible, independent and seemingly indifferent to my presence. I wanted to be with the rock as I climbed. Gone was the determination to conquer the rock, to forcefully impose my will on it; I wanted simply to work respectfully with the rock as I climbed. And as I climbed, that is what I felt. I felt myself *caring* for this rock and feeling thankful that climbing provided the opportunity for me to know it and myself in this new way.

There are at least four reasons why use of such a first-person narrative is important to feminism and environmental ethics. First, such a narrative gives voice to a felt sensitivity often lacking in traditional analytical ethical discourse, viz., a sensitivity to conceiving of oneself as fundamentally "in relationship with" others, including the nonhuman environment. It is a modality which *takes relationships themselves seriously.* It thereby stands in contrast to a strictly reductionist modality that takes relationships seriously only or primarily because of the nature of the *relators* or parties to those relationships (e.g., relators conceived as moral agents, right holders, interest carriers, or sentient beings). In the rock-climbing narrative above, it is the climber's relationship with the rock she climbs which takes on special significance—which is itself a locus of value—in addition to whatever moral status or moral considerability she or the rock or any other parties to the relationship may also have.[5]

Second, such a first-person narrative gives expression to a variety of ethical attitudes and behaviors often overlooked or underplayed in mainstream Western ethics, e.g., the difference in attitudes and behaviors toward a rock when one is "making it to the top" and when one thinks of oneself as "friends with" or "caring about" the rock one climbs.[6] These different attitudes and behaviors suggest an ethically germane contrast between two different types of relationship humans or climbers may have toward a rock: an imposed conqueror-type relationship, and an emergent caring-type relationship. This contrast grows out of, and is faithful to, felt, lived experience.

The difference between conquering and caring attitudes and behaviors in relation to the natural environment provides a third reason why the use of first-person narrative is important to feminism and environmental ethics: It provides a way of conceiving of ethics and ethical meaning as *emerging out of* particular situations moral agents find themselves in, rather than as being *imposed on* those situations (e.g., as a derivation or instantiation of some predetermined abstract principle or rule). This emergent feature of narrative centralizes the importance of *voice.* When a multiplicity of cross-cultural *voices* are centralized, narrative is able to give expression to a range of attitudes, values, beliefs, and behaviors which may be overlooked or silenced by imposed ethical meaning and theory. As a reflection of and on felt, lived experiences, the use of narrative in ethics provides a stance from which ethical discourse can he held accountable to the historical, material, and social realities in which moral subjects find themselves.

Lastly, and for our purposes perhaps most importantly, the use of narrative has argumentative significance. Jim Cheney calls attention to this feature of narrative when he claims, "To contextualize ethical deliberation is, in some sense, to provide a narrative or story, from which the solution to the ethical dilemma emerges as the fitting conclusion." Narrative has argumentative force by suggesting *what counts* as an appropriate conclusion to an ethical situation. One ethical conclusion suggested by the climbing narrative is that what counts as a proper ethical attitude toward mountains and rocks is an attitude of respect and care (whatever that turns out to be or involve), not one of domination and conquest.

In an essay entitled "In and Out of Harm's Way: Arrogance and Love," feminist philosopher Marilyn Frye distinguishes between "arrogant" and "loving" perception as one way of getting at this difference in the ethical attitudes of care and conquest. Frye writes:

> The loving eye is a contrary of the arrogant eye.
> The loving eye knows the independence of the other. It is the eye of a seer who knows that nature is indifferent. It is the eye of one who knows that to know the seen, one must consult something other than one's own will and interests and fears and imagination. One must look at the thing. One must look and listen and check and question.
> The loving eye is one that pays a certain sort of attention. This attention can require a discipline but not a self-denial. The discipline is one of self-knowledge, knowledge of the scope and boundary of the self. . . . In particular, it is a matter of being able to tell one's own interests from those of others and of knowing where one's self leaves off and another begins. . . .
> The loving eye does not make the object of perception into something edible, does not try to assimilate it, does not reduce it to the size of the seer's desire, fear, and imagination, and hence does not have to simplify. It knows the complexity of the other as something which will forever present new things to be known. The science of the loving eye would favor The Complexity Theory of Truth [in contrast to The Simplicity Theory of Truth] and presuppose The Endless Interestingness of the Universe.

According to Frye, the loving eye is not an invasive, coercive eye which annexes others to itself, but one which "knows the complexity of the other as something which will forever present new things to be known."

When one climbs a rock as a conqueror, one climbs with an arrogant eye. When one climbs with a loving eye, one constantly "must look and listen and check and question." One recognizes the rock as something very different, something perhaps totally indifferent to one's own presence, and finds in that difference joyous occasion for celebration. One knows "the boundary of the self," where the self—the "I," the climber—leaves off and the rock begins. There is no fusion of two into one, but a complement of two entities *acknowledged* as separate, different, independent, yet *in relationship;* they are in relationship *if only* because the loving eye is perceiving it, responding to it, noticing it, attending to it.

An ecofeminist perspective about both women and nature involves this shift in attitude from "arrogant perception" to "loving perception" of the nonhuman world. Arrogant perception of nonhumans by humans presupposes and maintains *sameness* in such a way that it expands the moral community to those beings who are thought to resemble (be like, similar to, or the same as) humans in some morally significant way. Any environmental movement or ethic based on arrogant perception builds a moral hierarchy of beings and assumes some common denominator of moral considerability in virtue of which like beings deserve similar treatment or moral consideration and unlike beings do not. Such environmental ethics are or generate a "unity in sameness." In contrast, "loving perception" presupposes and maintains *difference*—a distinction between the self and other, between human and at least some nonhumans—in such a way that perception of the other as other is an expression of love for one who/which is recognized at the outset as independent, dissimilar, different. As Maria Lugones says, in loving perception, "Love is seen not as fusion and erasure of difference but as incompatible with them." "Unity in sameness" alone is an *erasure of difference.*

"Loving perception" of the nonhuman natural world is an attempt to understand what it means *for humans* to care about the nonhuman world, a world

acknowledged as being independent, different, perhaps even indifferent to humans. Humans are different from rocks in important ways, even if they are also both members of some ecological community. A moral community based on loving perception of oneself *in relationship with* a rock, or with the natural environment as a whole, is one which acknowledges and respects difference, whatever "sameness" also exists. The limits of loving perception are determined only by the limits of one's (e.g., a person's, a community's) ability to respond lovingly (or with appropriate care, trust, or friendship)—whether it is to other humans or to the nonhuman world and elements of it.

If what I have said so far is correct, then there are very different ways to climb a mountain, and *how* one climbs it and *how* one narrates the experience of climbing it matter ethically. If one climbs with "arrogant perception," with an attitude of "conquer and control," one keeps intact the very sorts of thinking that characterize a logic of domination and an oppressive conceptual framework. Since the oppressive conceptual framework which sanctions the domination of nature is a patriarchal one, one also thereby keeps intact, even if unwittingly, a patriarchal conceptual framework. Because the dismantling of patriarchal conceptual frameworks is a feminist issue, *how* one climbs a mountain and *how* one narrates—or tells the story—about the experience of climbing also are *feminist issues.* In this way, ecofeminism makes visible why, at a conceptual level, environmental ethics is a feminist issue.

Conclusion

I have argued in this paper that ecofeminism provides a framework for a distinctively feminist and environmental ethic. Ecofeminism grows out of the felt and theorized about connections between the domination of women and the domination of nature. As a contextualist ethic, ecofeminism refocuses environmental ethics on what nature might mean, morally speaking, *for* humans, and on how the relational attitudes of humans to others—humans as well as nonhumans—sculpt both what it is to be human and the nature and ground of human responsibilities to the nonhuman environment. Part of what this refocusing does is to take seriously the voices of women and other oppressed persons in the construction of that ethic.

A Sioux elder once told me a story about his son. He sent his seven-year-old son to live with the child's grandparents on a Sioux reservation so that he could "learn the Indian ways." Part of what the grandparents taught him was how to hunt the four-leggeds of the forest. As I heard the story, the boy was taught, "to shoot your four-legged brother in his hind area, slowing it down but not killing it. Then, take the four-legged's head in your hands, and look into his eyes. The eyes are where all the suffering is. Look into your brother's eyes and feel his pain. Then, take your knife and cut the four-legged under his chin, here, on his neck, so that he dies quickly. And as you do, ask your brother, the four-legged, for forgiveness for what you do. Offer also a prayer of thanks to your four-legged kin for offering his body to you just now, when you need food to eat and clothing to wear. And promise the four-legged that you will put yourself back into the earth when you die, to become nourishment for the earth, and for the sister flowers, and for the brother deer. It is appropriate that you should offer this blessing for the four-legged and, in due time, reciprocate in turn with your body in this way, as the four-legged gives life to you for your survival." As I reflect on that story, I am struck by the power of the environmental ethic that grows out of and takes seriously narrative, context, and such values and relational attitudes as care, loving perception, and appropriate reciprocity, and doing what is appropriate in a given situation—however that notion of appropriateness eventually gets filled out. I am also struck by what one is able to see, once one begins to explore some of the historical and conceptual connections between the dominations of women and of nature. A *re-conceiving* and *re-visioning* of both feminism and environmental ethics, is, I think, the power and promise of ecofeminism.

Endnotes

1. It may be that in contemporary Western society, which is so thoroughly structured by categories of gender, race, class, age, and affectional orientation, that there simply is no meaningful notion of "value-hierarchical thinking" which does not function in an oppressive context. For the purposes of this paper, I leave that question open.

2. Many feminists who argue for the historical point that claims (B1) and (B2) have been asserted or assumed to be true within the dominant Western philosophical tradition do so by discussion of that tradition's conceptions of reason, rationality, and science. For a sampling of the sorts of claims made within that context, see "Reason, Rationality, and Gender," ed. Nancy Tuana and Karen J. Warren, a special issue of the American Philosophical Association's *Newsletter on Feminism and Philosophy* 88, no. 2 (Match 1989): 17–71. Ecofeminists who claim that (B2) has been assumed to be true within the dominant Western philosophical tradition include: Gray, *Green Paradise Lost*; Griffin, *Woman and Nature: The Roaring Inside Her*; Merchant, *The Death of Nature*; Ruether, *New Woman/New Earth*. For a discussion of some of these ecofeminist historical accounts, see Plumwood, "Eco-feminism." While I agree that the historical connections between the domination of women and the domination of nature is a crucial one, I do not argue for that claim here.

3. Ecofeminists who deny (B1) when (B1) is offered as anything other than a true, descriptive, historical claim about patriarchal culture often do so on grounds that an objectionable sort of biological determinism, or at least harmful female sex-gender stereotypes, underlie (B1). For a discussion of this "split" among those ecofeminists ("nature feminists") who assert and those ecofeminists ("social feminists") who deny (B1) as anything other than a true historical claim about how women are described in patriarchal culture, see Griscom, "On Healing the Nature/History Split."

4. I make no attempt here to defend the historically sanctioned truth of these promises.

5. Suppose . . . that a necessary condition for the existence of a moral relationship is that at least one party to the relationship is a moral being (leaving open for our purposes what counts as a "moral being"). If this is so, then the Mona Lisa cannot properly be said to have or stand in a moral relationship with the wall on which she hangs, and a wolf cannot have or properly be said to have or stand in a moral relationship with a moose. Such a necessary-condition account leaves open the question whether *both* parties to the relationship must be moral beings. The point here is simply that however one resolves *that* question, recognition of the relationships themselves as a locus of value is a recognition of a source

of value that is different from and not reducible to the values of the "moral beings" in those relationships.

6. It is interesting to note that the image of being friends with the Earth is one which cytogeneticist Barbara McClintock uses when she describes the importance of having "a feeling for the organism," "listening to the material [in this case the corn plant]," in one's work as a scientist. See Evelyn Fox Keller, "Women, Science, and Popular Mythology," in *Machina Ex Dea: Feminist Perspectives on Technology*, ed. Joan Rothschild (New York: Pergamon Press, 1983), and Evelyn Fox Keller, *A Feeling For the Organism: The Life and Work of Barbara McClintock* (San Francisco: W. H. Freeman, 1983).

65. *From the Animal Welfare Act*

CONGRESS OF THE UNITED STATES

Sec. 13. The Secretary shall promulgate standards to govern the humane handling, care, treatment, and transportation of animals by dealers, research facilities, and exhibitors. Such standards shall include minimum requirements with respect to handling, housing, feeding, watering, sanitation, ventilation, shelter from extremes of weather and temperatures, adequate veterinary care, including the appropriate use of anesthetic, analgesic or tranquilizing drugs, when such use would be proper in the opinion of the attending veterinarian of such research facilities, and separation by species when the Secretary finds such separation necessary for the humane handling, care, or treatment of animals. In promulgating and enforcing standards established pursuant to this section, the Secretary is authorized and directed to consult experts, including outside consultants where indicated. Nothing in this Act shall be construed as authorizing the Secretary to promulgate rules, regulations, or orders with regard to design, outlines, guidelines, or performance of actual research or experimentation by a research facility as determined by such research facility: *Provided* That the Secretary shall require, at least annually, every research facility to show that professionally acceptable standards governing the care, treatment, and use of animals, including appropriate use of anesthetic, analgesic, and tranquilizing drugs, during experimentation are being followed by the research facility during actual research or experimentation.

66. *Amendments to the Animal Welfare Act*

CONGRESS OF THE UNITED STATES

The bill amends the Animal Welfare Act as follows:

1. Expands the definition of the term *research facility* to include each department, agency or instrumentality of the United States which uses animals for research or experimentation; defines the term *Federal agency* to mean any Executive agency from which a research facility has received or may receive Federal funds to support the conduct of research, experimentation, or testing involving the use of animals; and, makes it clear that the definition of "animal" is the same as that provided under the current Act.

2. Deletes the language stating that minimum requirements be applied to the standards promulgated by the Secretary of Agriculture to govern the humane handling, care, treatment, and transportation of animals by dealers, research facilities and exhibitors; adds exercise for dogs as a standard; and, allows the Secretary to make exceptions to the standards, but only when such exceptions are specified by the research protocol.

3. Requires the Secretary to promulgate standards for research facilities, including requirements for animal care, treatment, and practices in experimental procedures, to ensure that animal pain and distress are minimized. Requires each research facility, in its annual statement of compliance, to provide the Secretary of Agriculture with assurances that such standards are being followed. Also requires the research facility to provide annual training sessions for personnel involved with animal care and treatment.

4. Provides that any State (or political subdivision of that State) may promulgate standards in addition to those promulgated by the Secretary.

5. Mandates the establishment and makeup of an animal research committee of three or more members within each research facility. Makes it unlawful for any member of the committee to release trade secrets or confidential information. The committee must make inspections at least semiannually of all animal study areas of the research facility and file an inspection report which must remain on file at the research facility for three years. The committee must notify, in writing, the Animal and Plant Health Inspection Service (APHIS) of the Department of Agriculture and the funding Federal agency of any unacceptable conditions that are not corrected despite notification. Federal support for a particular project can be suspended or revoked for continued failure by a research facility to comply with the standards of animal care, treatment or practices; such suspension or revocation may be appealed.

6. The inspection results of the animal research committee must be available to the Department of Agriculture's inspectors for review during inspection. These inspectors must forward to APHIS and the funding Federal agency any inspection records of the committee which include reports of any deficient conditions of animal care or treatment and any deviations of research practices from the originally approved proposal that adversely affect animal welfare.

7. Prohibits the Secretary from promulgating rules, regulations, or orders that may require a research facility to disclose trade secrets or commercial or financial information which is privileged or confidential.

8. Mandates the establishment of an information service on improved methods of animal experimentation at the National Agricultural Library. . . .

67. Tennessee Valley Authority v. Hill

SUPREME COURT OF THE UNITED STATES

The issue before the Supreme Court was whether the Endangered Species Act of 1973 prohibited the completion of a dam whose operation would destroy the habitat of the snail darter, an endangered species. The dam was virtually completed, and Congress had continued to appropriate large sums of money to the project even after congressional appropriations committees were apprised of the apparent impact on the snail darter's survival. Chief Justice Burger, delivering the opinion of the Court, held that the Endangered Species Act did prohibit the completion of the dam because the language of the act and the history that led to its passage required that its provisions be applied without exceptions.

We begin with the premise that operation of the Tellico Dam will either eradicate the known population of snail darters or destroy their critical habitat. Petitioner does not now seriously dispute this fact. . . . The Secretary of the Interior is vested with exclusive authority to determine whether a species such as the snail darter is "endangered" or "threatened" and to ascertain the factors which have led to such a precarious existence. . . . Congress has authorized—indeed commanded—the Secretary to "issue such regulations as he deems necessary and advisable to provide for the conservation of such species." . . . As we have seen, the Secretary promulgated regulations which declared the snail darter an endangered species whose critical habitat would be destroyed by creation of the Tellico Dam. Doubtless petitioner would prefer not to have these regulations on the books, but there is no suggestion that the Secretary exceeded his authority or abused his discretion in issuing the regulations. Indeed, no judicial review of the Secretary's determinations has ever been sought and hence the validity of his actions are not open to review in this Court. . . .

[It is] curious . . . that the survival of a relatively small number of three-inch fish among all the countless millions of species extant would require the permanent halting of a virtually completed dam for which Congress has expended more than $100 million. The paradox is not minimized by the fact that Congress continued to appropriate large sums of public money for the project, even after congressional Appropriations Committees were apprised of its apparent impact on the survival of the snail darter. We conclude, however, that the explicit provisions of the Endangered Species Act require precisely that result. . . .

. . . By 1973, when Congress held hearings on what would later become the Endangered Species Act of 1973, it was informed that species were still being lost at the rate of about one per year, . . . and "the pace of disappearance of species" appeared to be "accelerating." Moreover, Congress was also told that the primary cause of this trend was something other than the normal process of natural selection:

> [M]an and his technology has [*sic*] continued at an ever-increasing rate to disrupt the natural ecosystem. This has resulted in a dramatic rise in the number and severity of the threats faced by the world's wildlife. The truth in this is apparent when one realizes that half of the recorded extinctions of mammals over the past 2,000 years have occurred in the most recent 50-year period. . . .

That Congress did not view these developments lightly was stressed by one commentator:

> The dominant theme pervading all Congressional discussion of the proposed [Endangered Species Act of 1973] was the overriding need *to devote whatever effort and resources were necessary* to avoid further diminution of national and worldwide wildlife resources. Much of the testimony at the hearings and much debate was devoted to the biological problem of extinction. Senators and Congressmen uniformly deplored the irreplaceable loss to aesthetics, science, ecology, and the national heritage should more species disappear. . . .

The legislative proceedings in 1973 are . . . replete with expressions of concern over the risk that might lie in the loss of *any* endangered species. Typifying these sentiments is the Report of the House Committee on Merchant Marine and Fisheries on . . . a bill that contained the essential features of the subsequently enacted Act of 1973; in explaining the need for the legislation, the Report stated:

> As we homogenize the habitats in which these plants and animals evolved, and as we increase the pressure for products that they are in a position to supply (usually unwillingly) we threaten their—and our own—genetic heritage.
>
> *The value of this genetic heritage is, quite literally, incalculable.*
>
> From the most narrow possible point of view, *it is in the best interests of mankind to minimize the losses of genetic variations.* The reason is simple: They are potential resources. They are keys to puzzles which we cannot solve, and may provide answers to questions which we have not yet learned to ask.
>
> To take a homely, but apt, example: One of the critical chemicals in the regulation of ovulations in humans was found in a common plant. Once discovered, and analyzed, humans could duplicate it synthetically, but had it never existed—or had it been driven out of existence before we knew its potentialities—we would never have tried to synthesize it in the first place.

Who knows, or can say, what potential cures for cancer or other scourges, present or future, may lie locked up in the structures of plants which may yet be undiscovered, much less analyzed? . . . Sheer self-interest impels us to be cautious. . . .

As the examples cited here demonstrate, Congress was concerned about the *unknown* uses that endangered species might have and about the *unforeseeable* place such creatures may have in the chain of life on this planet. . . .

. . . Representative Dingell provided an interpretation of what the Conference bill would require, making it clear that the mandatory provisions . . . were not casually or inadvertently included:

> . . . A recent article . . . illustrates the problem which might occur absent this new language in the bill. It appears that the whooping cranes of this country, perhaps the best known of our endangered species, are being threatened by Air Force bombing activities along the gulf coast of Texas. Under existing law, the Secretary of Defense has some discretion as to whether or not he will take the necessary action to see that this threat disappears. . . . [O]nce the bill is enacted, [the Secretary of Defense] *would be required to take the proper steps.* . . .
>
> Another example . . . [has] to do with the continental population of grizzly bears which may or may not be endangered, but which is surely threatened. . . . Once this bill is enacted, the appropriate Secretary, whether of Interior, Agriculture or whatever, *will have to take action* to see that this situation is not permitted to worsen, and that these bears are not driven to extinction. The purposes of the bill included the conservation of the species and of the ecosystems upon which they depend, and *every agency of government is committed* to see that those purposes are carried out. . . . [T]he agencies of Government can no longer plead that they can do nothing about it. *They can, and they must. The law is clear.* . . .

Notwithstanding Congress's expression of intent in 1973, we are urged to find that the continuing appropriations for Tellico Dam constitute an implied repeal of the 1973 Act, at least insofar as it applies to the Tellico Project. In support of this view, TVA points to the statements found in various House and Senate

Appropriations Committees' Reports. . . . Since we are unwilling to assume that these latter Committee statements constituted advice to ignore the provisions of a duly enacted law, we assume that these Committees believed that the Act simply was not applicable in this situation. But even under this interpretation of the Committees' actions, we are unable to conclude that the Act has been in any respect amended or repealed. . . .

. . . The starting point in this analysis must be the legislative proceedings leading to the 1977 appropriations since the earlier funding of the dam occurred prior to the listing of the snail darter as an endangered species. In all successive years, TVA confidently reported to the Appropriations Committees that efforts to transplant the snail darter appeared to be successful; this surely gave those Committees some basis for the impression that there was no direct conflict between the Tellico Project and the Endangered Species Act. Indeed, the special appropriation for 1978 of $2 million for transplantation of endangered species supports the view that the Committees saw such relocation as the means whereby collision between Tellico and the Endangered Species Act could be avoided. . . .

. . . Here we are urged to view the Endangered Species Act "reasonably," and hence shape a remedy "that accords with some modicum of common sense and the public weal." . . . But is that our function? We have no expert knowledge on the subject of endangered species, much less do we have a mandate from the people to strike a balance of equities on the side of the Tellico Dam. Congress has spoken in the plainest of words, making it abundantly clear that the balance has been struck in favor of affording endangered species the highest of priorities, thereby adopting a policy which it described as "institutionalized caution."

Our individual appraisal of the wisdom or unwisdom of a particular course consciously selected by the Congress is to be put aside in the process of interpreting a statute. Once the meaning of an enactment is discerned and its constitutionality determined, the judicial process comes to an end. We do not sit as a committee of review, nor are we vested with the power of veto. The lines ascribed to Sir Thomas More by Robert Bolt are not without relevance here:

The law, Roper, the law. I know what's legal, not what's right. And I'll stick to what's legal. . . . I'm *not* God. The currents and eddies of right and wrong, which you find such plain-sailing, I can't navigate, I'm no voyager. But in the thickets of the law, oh there I'm a forester. . . . What would you do? Cut a great road through the law to get after the Devil? . . . And when the last law was down, and the Devil turned round on you—where would you hide, Roper, the laws all being flat? . . . This country's planted thick with laws from coast to coast—Man's laws, not God's—and if you cut them down .

. . d'you really think you could stand upright in the winds that would blow then? . . . Yes, I'd give the Devil benefit of law, for my own safety's sake.
—R. Bolt, *A Man for All Seasons*

We agree with the Court of Appeals that . . . the commitment to the separation of powers is too fundamental for us to pre-empt congressional action by judicially decreeing what accords with "common sense and the public weal." Our Constitution vests such responsibilities in the political branches.

Suggestions for Further Reading

Anthologies

Armstrong, Susan, and Botzler, Richard. *Environmental Ethics*. New York: McGraw Hill, 1993.

Regan, T., and Singer, P. (eds.). *Animal Rights and Human Obligation*. Englewood Cliffs, N.J.: Prentice-Hall, 1976.

Sterba, James P. *Earth Ethics*. New York: Macmillan, 1993.

Alternative Views

Attfield, Robin. *Environmental Philosophy*. Aldershot: Avebury, 1994.

Carruthers, Peter. *The Animals Issue*. Cambridge: Cambridge University Press, 1992.

Dombrowski, D. *The Philosophy of Vegetarianism*. Amherst, MA: University of Massachusetts Press, 1984.

Frey, R. G. *Rights, Killing and Suffering*. Oxford, England: Basil Blackwell, 1983.

Hargrove, Eugene. *The Foundations of Environmental Ethics*. Englewood Cliffs, N.J.: Prentice-Hall, 1988.

Marrietta, Don. *For People and the Planet*. Philadelphia: Temple University Press, 1995.

Plumwood, Val. *Feminism and the Mastery of Nature*. London: Routledge, 1993.

Rachels, James. *Created from Animals*. Oxford: Oxford University Press, 1990.

Regan, T. *The Case for Animal Rights*. Berkeley: University of California Press, 1984.

Singer, P. *Animal Liberation* (rev. ed.). New York: New York Review, 1990.

Stone, C. *Earth and Other Ethics*. New York: Harper & Row, 1987.

Taylor, P. *Respect for Nature*. Princeton: Princeton University Press, 1988.

Practical Applications

Akers, K. *A Vegetarian Sourcebook*. New York: G. P. Putnam and Sons, 1983.

Boas, M., and Chain, S. *Big Mac: The Unauthorized Story of McDonald's*. New York: New American Library, 1976.

Gore, Al. *Earth in the Balance*. New York: Houghton Mifflin, 1992.

Swanson, W., and Schultz, G. *Prime Rip*. Englewood Cliffs, N.J.: Prentice-Hall, 1982.

Punishment and Responsibility

Introduction

Basic Concepts

The problem of punishment and responsibility is the problem of who should be punished and in what their punishment should consist. It is a problem of punishment *and* responsibility because determining who should be punished and what their punishment should consist of involves an assessment of responsibility. However, before discussing alternative justifications for assigning punishment, it is important to first clarify the concepts of punishment and responsibility.

Let us begin with the concept of punishment. Consider the following definition:

(a) Punishment is hardship inflicted on an offender by someone entitled to do so.

This definition certainly seems adequate for many standard cases of punishment. For example, suppose you pursue and capture a young man who has just robbed a drug store. The police then arrive and arrest the fellow. He is tried, convicted, and sentenced to two years in prison. Surely it would seem that a sentence of two years in prison in this case would constitute punishment, and obviously the sentence meets the conditions of (a).

But suppose we vary the example a bit. Suppose that, as before, you pursue the robber, but this time he gets away and in the process drops the money he took from the drug store, which you then retrieve. Suppose further that two eyewitnesses identify you as the robber, and you are arrested by the police, tried, and sentenced to two years in prison. Surely we would like to say that in this example it is you who is being punished, albeit unjustly; however, according to (a), this is not the case. For according to this definition, punishment can only be inflicted on offenders, and you are not an offender. But this simply shows that (a) is too narrow a definition of punishment. There clearly are cases, like our modified example, in which we can truly say that nonoffenders, that is, innocent people, are being punished. Accordingly, an acceptable definition of punishment should allow for such cases.

Let us consider, then, the following definition of punishment, which does allow for the possibility that nonoffenders can be punished:

(b) Punishment is hardship inflicted on a person by someone entitled to do so.

Although (b) clearly represents an advance over (a) in that it allows for the possibility that innocent people can be punished, serious difficulties remain. For according to (b), paying taxes is punishment, as is civil commitment of mentally ill persons who have not committed any offense. And even though we may have good reasons for opposing taxation and even good reasons for opposing civil commitment, it is usually not because we regard such impositions as punishments. Clearly, then, a definition of punishment that includes paying taxes and civil commitment as punishments is simply too broad; what is needed is a definition that is narrower than (b) but broader than (a).

Consider the following possibility:

(c)   Punishment is hardship inflicted on a person who is found guilty of an offense by someone entitled to do so.

This definition, like (b), allows that innocent people can be punished, because it is possible that a person can be found guilty by some procedure or other without really being guilty. Yet (c), unlike (b), does not allow that just any hardship imposed by someone entitled to do so is punishment. Rather, only a hardship imposed *for an offense* can be a punishment.

But is this definition adequate? It would seem not. According to (c), paying a $5 parking ticket or suffering a 15-yard penalty in a football game are both punishments. Yet in both cases the hardship imposed lacks the moral condemnation and denunciation that is characteristic of punishment. This suggests the following definition:

(d)   Punishment is hardship involving moral condemnation and denunciation inflicted on a person who is found guilty of an offense by someone entitled to do so.

Examples like the $5 parking ticket and the 15-yard penalty indicate that we need to distinguish between punishments proper, which satisfy the conditions of (d), and mere penalties, which only satisfy the conditions of (c). When we impose mere penalties, we are claiming that a person has done something wrong, perhaps

even something morally wrong, but, because of the insignificant nature of the offense, we don't attempt to determine whether the person is morally blameworthy for so acting. Because we do not make this determination, we do not go on to morally condemn and denounce those we penalize. By contrast, when we impose punishments proper, we do make such a determination and, as a consequence, we do condemn and denounce those we penalize.

Turning to the concept of responsibility, we find that this concept is employed in a variety of different but related ways. For example, in everyday usage, we say that people are responsible for their actions if they could have acted otherwise than they did. In making this claim, we usually assume that people could have acted otherwise than they did in two respects. First, we assume that they could have acted otherwise if they had the ability to do so; for example, as presumably most varsity athletes have even when they play badly. Second, we assume that people could have acted otherwise if they had the opportunity to do so; for example, as you or I might have, even if we lacked the relevant ability, when, by chance, we were substituted in some varsity game and performed miserably. Thus, we can say that people are responsible for their actions if they had the ability and opportunity to act otherwise than they did.

Lawyers, however, usually approach the concept of responsibility differently. They are typically concerned with determining whether people have "mens rea," which translated means "a guilty mind." When people are said to have *mens rea*, they are held responsible for their actions.

Mens rea is said to involve three conditions:

1. Knowledge of circumstances
2. Foresight of consequences
3. Voluntariness

The first condition of mens rea is said to be absent when, for example, you didn't know the gun was loaded, or you didn't know the person you shot breaking into your home was a plain-clothes police officer operating on a false lead. In such a case, lawyers would say you lacked mens rea because you lacked the knowledge of the relevant circumstances. The second condition of mens rea is said to be absent when, for example, you had no reason to suspect the person you shot would be wandering behind your target in a fenced-off range. In such a case, lawyers would say you lacked mens rea because you lacked foresight of the relevant consequences. The third condition of mens rea is said to be absent when, for example, you are having an epileptic fit or being attacked by a swarm of bees. This third condition is the least understood of the three conditions of mens rea.

But actually this weakness of the lawyer's mens rea notion of responsibility with respect to its third condition seems to be the strength of the everyday notion. This is because the everyday notion of responsibility is an unpacking of what it is for an action to be voluntary. Consequently, if we put the two notions together, we arrive at the following more adequate analysis.

People are responsible for their action if they have:

1. Knowledge of circumstances
2. Foresight of consequences
3. The ability and opportunity to act otherwise than they did.

Armed with a clearer understanding of the notions of punishment and responsibility, we should be in a better position to examine alternative justifications for assigning punishment in a society.

Forward-Looking and Backward-Looking Views

There are basically two kinds of justification for punishment: forward-looking and backward-looking. Forward-looking justifications maintain that punishment is justified because of its relationship to what *will occur*. Backward-looking justifications maintain that punishment is justified because of its relationship to what *has occurred*. An example of a forward-looking justification would be the claim that punishment is justified because it deters or reforms persons from crime. An example of a backward-looking justification would be the claim that punishment is justified because it fits or is proportionate to a crime or is applied to a person who is responsible for a crime. Those who adopt forward-looking justifications for punishment view punishment from the point of view of a social engineer seeking to produce certain good consequences in society. By contrast, those who adopt backward-looking justifications view punishment from the point of view of a stern balancer seeking to achieve a moral balance between punishment and the crime.

Karl Menninger provides us with a forceful example of a forward-looking justification for punishment—one that is directed at the reform of the offender (Selection 68). Menninger criticizes the existing criminal justice system as ineffective at preventing crime, grounded as it is on a theory of human motivation that fails to recognize the similarities between the motives of offenders and nonoffenders. In its place, Menninger advocates a therapeutic treatment program that would detain offenders, and possibly potential offenders, until they are reformed. Thus, Menninger would replace vengeful punishment—which he regards as itself a crime—with humanitarian reform.

One prerequisite for the justification of Menninger's system of humanitarian reform that is not generally recognized is that the opportunities open to offenders for leading a good life must be reasonably adequate, or at least arguably just and fair. If this is not the case, there would be little justification for asking criminal offenders to live their lives within the bounds of the legal system. Nor for that matter could we expect any attempt at implementing a system of reform like Menninger's to be generally effective in a society characterized by basic social and economic injustices. In such a society, criminal offenders who perceive these injustices will have a strong moral reason to resist any attempt to turn them into law-abiding citizens.

Richard B. Brandt (Selection 69), however, argues that a system of punishment similar to the actual systems found in the United States and Great Britain can be justified on utilitarian or forward-looking grounds. Such a system would be justified, Brandt claims, because it would secure the good consequences of both reform and deterrence. Yet C.S. Lewis (Selection 70) claims that the goals of both reform and deterrence are opposed to a fundamental requirement of justice: giving people what they deserve. Obviously, if Lewis's critique is sound, it presents a serious difficulty for both Menninger's and Brandt's views, as well as for any other forward-looking view.

Obviously, raising difficulties for forward-looking justifications for punishment is not the same as directly defending backward-looking justifications, thus the importance of the attempt by Edmund L. Pincoffs (Selection 71) to provide us with such a defense. Pincoffs begins by setting out the following three principles that he claims are characteristic of the traditional backward-looking justification for punishment:

1. The only acceptable reason for punishing a person is that he or she has committed a crime.
2. The only acceptable reason for punishing a person in a given manner and degree is that the punishment is equal to the crime.
3. Whoever commits a crime must be punished in accordance with his or her desert.

Pincoffs claims that the underlying rationale for these principles can be expressed as follows:

(a) A proper justification for punishment is one that justifies it to the criminal.
(b) Punishment is justified because the criminal has willed the punishment he or she now suffers.

But how can criminals be said to will their own punishment if they do not like or want to be punished? One possible answer, which seems consistent with Pincoffs's analysis, is that criminals, by deliberately violating the rights of others (e.g., by harming others in some way), imply that they think it is reasonable for them to do so. But if this were the case, it would be reasonable for anyone else in similar circumstances to do the same. As a result, criminals would be implicitly conceding that it is all right for others to violate their rights by punishing them, and in this sense they could be said to will their own punishment.

In response to such a defense of a backward-looking justification for punishment, supporters of the forward-looking view might claim that the above principles and their underlying rationale are only proximate answers to the question of why punishment is justified, the ultimate answer to which is still given by the forward-looking view. Since Pincoffs's principles and their underlying rationale do not seem to be compatible with Menninger's system of humanitarian reform, such a response does imply that the ultimate forward-looking justification for punishment is to be found more in general deterrence, as in Brandt's system, than in humanitarian reform. But even if this were the case, the ultimate justification for punishment would still be forward-looking.

To meet this response, supporters of a backward-looking view need to show why Pincoffs's principles and their underlying rationale cannot be subsumed under a forward-looking justification. This might be done by showing that Pincoffs's principles and their underlying rationale can be grounded in a social contract theory of corrective justice analogous to the social contract theory of distributive justice discussed in Section I. Because many philosophers believe that a social contract theory of distributive justice conflicts with forward-looking goals, it should be possible to argue that a social contract theory of corrective justice does the same.[1]

Practical Applications

Obviously, a crucial area for the application of forward-looking and backward-looking views is capital punishment. Ernest van den Haag (Selection 72) argues that although we don't know for sure whether capital punishment deters would-be offenders, the greater severity of capital punishment still gives us reason to expect more deterrence from it. Accordingly, van den Haag maintains that the burden of proof is on opponents of capital punishment to show why the greater severity of capital punishment does not lead to more deterrence. In Selection 73, Jeffrey Reiman attempts to meet van den Haag's challenge. He maintains that greater severity in and of itself does not mean more deterrence; a less severe punishment might suffice to deter a particular crime. Moreover, Reiman argues if greater severity were always justified on grounds of producing more deterrence, then torturing criminals to death would be justified because torturing criminals to death is clearly a more severe punishment than simply executing them. Since van den Haag presumably does not want to endorse torturing criminals to death, he must reject one or more of the premises on which his argument for capital punishment is based.

In 1976 the U.S. Supreme Court (Selection 74) examined the question of whether capital punishment violates the Eighth Amendment prohibition of cruel and unusual punishment. The majority of the Court held that it does not violate that prohibition. In support of its ruling, the majority maintained that capital punishment does not offend contemporary standards of decency as shown by recent legislation in this area. But with regard to the harder question of whether capital punishment is contrary to human dignity and so lacks either a forward-looking or a backward-looking justification, the Court simply deferred to state legislatures. That left the Court with the easier task of deciding whether the procedures for imposing capital punishment, as provided by the Georgia statute that was under review, were capricious and arbitrary. On this score the Court found no reason to fault the George statute.

In more recent cases, however, the Court has gone beyond this purely procedural issue and ruled that the imposition of capital punishment for rape (*Coker v. Georgia*) and on anyone who did not fire a fatal shot or intend the death of a victim (*Locket v. Ohio*) would be unconstitutional. Given that the Court has not seen fit to defer to the judgment of state legislatures in these matters, it is not clear why the Court should continue to defer to their judgment with regard to the question of whether capital punishment can be supported by an adequate forward-looking or backward-looking justification.

In any case, once you have faced that question yourself and worked out a theory of corrective justice, you will still not know exactly how to apply that theory unless you also know how just the distribution of goods and resources is in your society. This is because, regardless of whether you adopt an essentially forward- or backward-looking theory of corrective justice, you will need to know what economic crimes—that is, crimes against property— should be punished according to your theory; and in order to know that, you will need to know what demands are placed on the available goods and resources by solutions to the other problems discussed in this anthology. Of course, some crimes (e.g., many cases of murder and rape) are crimes against people rather than property. And presumably these crimes would be proscribed by your theory of corrective justice independent of the solutions to other contemporary moral problems. Nevertheless, because most crimes are crimes against property, the primary application of your theory will still depend on solutions to the other moral problems discussed in this anthology. In particular, you will need to know to what extent goods and resources can legitimately be expended for military purposes—which just happens to be the moral problem taken up in the next section of this anthology.

Endnote

1. James P. Sterba, "Retributive Justice," *Political Theory* (1977); "Social Contract Theory and Ordinary Justice," *Political Theory* (1981); "Is There a Rationale for Punishment?" *American Journal of Jurisprudence* (1984); "A Rational Choice Justification for Punishment," *Philosophical Topics* (1990).

68. *The Crime of Punishment*

KARL MENNINGER

Karl Menninger argues that the reason crime is so difficult to eradicate is that it serves the needs of offenders and nonoffenders alike. In fact, according to Menninger, the motives of offenders and nonoffenders are quite similar; what distinguishes serious offenders is simply a greater sense of helplessness and hopelessness in the pursuit of their goals. Menninger concludes that we must find better ways to enable people to realize their goals. Menninger also argues that punishment as a vengeful response to crime does not work because crime is an illness requiring treatment by psychiatrists and psychologists. Thus, Menninger finds vengeful punishment itself to be a crime.

Few words in our language arrest our attention as do "crime," "violence," "revenge," and "injustice." We abhor crime; we adore justice; we boast that we live by the rule of law. Violence and vengefulness we repudiate as unworthy of our civilization, and we assume this sentiment to be unanimous among all human beings.

Yet crime continues to be a national disgrace and a worldwide problem. It is threatening, alarming, wasteful, expensive, abundant, and apparently increasing! In actuality it is decreasing in frequency of occurrence, but it is certainly increasing in visibility and the reactions of the public to it.

Our system for controlling crime is ineffective, unjust, expensive. Prisons seem to operate with revolving doors—the same people going in and out and in and out. *Who cares?*

Our city jails and inhuman reformatories and wretched prisons are jammed. They are known to be unhealthy, dangerous, immoral, indecent, crime-breeding dens of iniquity. Not everyone has smelled them, as some of us have. Not many have heard the groans and the curses. Not everyone has seen the hate and despair in a thousand blank, hollow faces. But, in a way, we all know how miserable prisons are. *We want them to be that way.* And they are. *Who cares?*

Professional, big-time criminals prosper as never before. Gambling syndicates flourish. White-collar crime may even exceed all others but goes undetected in [most] cases. We are all being robbed and we know who the robbers are. They live nearby. *Who cares?*

The public filches millions of dollars worth of food and clothing from stores, towels and sheets from hotels, jewelry and knick-knacks from shops. The public steals, and the same public pays it back in higher prices. *Who cares?*

Time and time again somebody shouts about this state of affairs, just as I am shouting now. The magazines shout. The newspapers shout. The television and radio commentators shout (or at least they "deplore"). Psychologists, sociologists, leading jurists, wardens, and intelligent police chiefs join the chorus. Governors and mayors and Congressmen are sometimes heard. They shout that the situation is bad, bad, bad, and getting worse. Some suggest that we immediately replace obsolete procedures with scientific methods. A few shout contrary sentiments. Do the clear indications derived from scientific discovery for appropriate changes continue to fall on deaf ears? Why is the public so long-suffering, so apathetic and thereby so continuingly self-destructive? How many Presidents (and other citizens) do we have to lose before we do something?

The public behaves as a sick patient does when a dreaded treatment is proposed for his ailment. We all know how the aching tooth may suddenly quiet down in the dentist's office, or the abdominal pain disappear in the surgeon's examining room. Why should a sufferer seek relief and shun it? Is it merely the fear of pain of the treatment? Is it the fear of unknown complications? Is it distrust of the doctor's ability? All of these, no doubt.

But, as Freud made so incontestably clear, the sufferer is always somewhat deterred by a kind of subversive, internal opposition to the work of cure. He suffers on the one hand from the pains of his affliction

and yearns to get well. But he suffers at the same time from traitorous impulses that fight against the accomplishment of any change in himself, even recovery! Like Hamlet, he wonders whether it may be better after all to suffer the familiar pains and aches associated with the old method than to face the complications of a new and strange, even though possibly better way of handling things.

The inescapable conclusion is that society secretly *wants* crime, *needs* crime, and gains definite satisfactions from the present mishandling of it! We condemn crime; we punish offenders for it; but we need it. The crime and punishment ritual is a part of our lives. We need crimes to wonder at, to enjoy vicariously, to discuss and speculate about, and to publicly deplore. We need criminals to identify ourselves with, to envy secretly, and to punish stoutly. They do for us the forbidden, illegal things we *wish* to do and, like scapegoats of old, they bear the burdens of our displaced guilt and punishment—"the iniquities of us all."

We have to confess that there is something fascinating for us all about violence. That most crime is not violent we know but we forget, because crime is a breaking, a rupturing, a tearing—even when it is quietly done. To all of us crime seems like violence.

The very word "violence" has a disturbing, menacing quality. . . . In meaning it implies something dreaded, powerful, destructive, or eruptive. It is something we abhor—or do we? Its first effect is to startle, frighten—even to horrify us. But we do not always run away from it. For violence also intrigues us. It is exciting. It is dramatic. Observing it and sometimes even participating in it gives us acute pleasure.

The newspapers constantly supply us with tidbits of violence going on in the world. They exploit its dramatic essence often to the neglect of conservative reporting of more extensive but less violent damage—the flood disaster in Florence, Italy, for example. Such words as crash, explosion, wreck, assault, raid, murder, avalanche, rape, and seizure evoke pictures of eruptive devastation from which we cannot turn away. The headlines often impute violence metaphorically even to peaceful activities. Relations are "ruptured," a tie is "broken," arbitration "collapses," a proposal is "killed."

Meanwhile on the television and movie screens there constantly appear for our amusement scenes of fighting, slugging, beating, torturing, clubbing, shooting, and the like which surpass in effect anything that the newspapers can describe. Much of this violence is portrayed dishonestly; the scenes are only semirealistic; they are "faked" and romanticized.

Pain cannot be photographed; grimaces indicate but do not convey its intensity. And wounds—unlike violence—are rarely shown. This phony quality of television violence in its mentally unhealthy aspect encourages irrationality by giving the impression to the observer that being beaten, kicked, cut, and stomped, while very unpleasant, are not very painful or serious. For after being slugged and beaten the hero rolls over, opens his eyes, hops up, rubs his cheek, grins, and staggers on. The *suffering* of violence is a part both the TV and movie producers *and* their audience tend to repress.

Although most of us *say* we deplore cruelty and destructiveness, we are partially deceiving ourselves. We disown violence, ascribing the love of it to other people. But the facts speak for themselves. We do love violence, all of us, and we all feel secretly guilty for it, which is another clue to public resistance to crime-control reform.

The great sin by which we all are tempted is the wish to hurt others, and this sin must be avoided if we are to live and let live. If our destructive energies can be mastered, directed, and sublimated, we can survive. If we can love, we can live. Our destructive energies, if they cannot be controlled, may destroy our best friends, as in the case of Alexander the Great, or they may destroy supposed "enemies" or innocent strangers. Worst of all—from the standpoint of the individual—they may destroy us.

Over the centuries of man's existence, many devices have been employed in the effort to control these innate suicidal and criminal propensities. The earliest of these undoubtedly depended upon fear—fear of the unknown, fear of magical retribution, fear of social retaliation. These external devices were replaced gradually with the law and all its machinery, religion and its rituals, and the conventions of the social order.

The routine of life formerly required every individual to direct much of his aggressive energy against the environment. There were trees to cut down, wild animals to fend off, heavy obstacles to remove, great burdens to lift. But the machine has gradually changed

all of this. Today, the routine of life, for most people, requires no violence, no fighting, no killing, no life-risking, no sudden supreme exertion: occasionally, perhaps, a hard pull or a strong push, but no tearing, crushing, breaking, forcing.

And because violence no longer has legitimate and useful vents or purposes, it must *all* be controlled today. In earlier times, its expression was often a virtue; today, its control *is* the virtue. The control involves symbolic, vicarious expressions of violence—violence modified; "sublimated," as Freud called it; "neutralized," as Hartmann described it. Civilized substitutes for direct violence are the objects of daily search by all of us. The common law and the Ten Commandments, traffic signals and property deeds, fences and front doors, sermons and concerts, Christmas trees and jazz bands—these and a thousand other things exist today to help in the control of violence.

My colleague Bruno Bettelheim thinks we do not properly educate our youth to deal with their violent urges. He reminds us that nothing fascinated our forefathers more. The *Iliad* is a poem of violence. Much of the Bible is a record of violence. Our penal system and many methods of childrearing express violence— "violence to suppress violence." And, he concludes [in the article "Violence: A Neglected Mode of Behavior"]: "We shall not be able to deal intelligently with violence unless we are first ready to see it as a part of human nature, and then we shall come to realize the chances of discharging violent tendencies are now so severely curtailed that their regular and safe draining-off is not possible anymore."

Why aren't we all criminals? We all have the impulses; we all have the provocations. But becoming civilized, which is repeated ontologically in the process of social education, teaches us what we may do with impunity. What then evokes or permits the breakthrough? Why is it necessary for some to bribe their consciences and do what they do not approve of doing? Why does all sublimation sometimes fail and overt breakdown occur in the controlling and managing machinery of the personality? Why do we sometimes lose self-control? Why do we "go to pieces"? Why do we explode?

These questions point up a central problem in psychiatry. Why do some people do things they do not want to do? Or things we do not want them to do? Sometimes crimes are motivated by a desperate need to act, to do *something* to break out of a state of passivity, frustration, and helplessness too long endured, like a child who shoots a parent or a teacher after some apparently reasonable act. Granting the universal presence of violence within us all, controlled by will power, conscience, fear of punishment, and other devices, granting the tensions and the temptations that are also common to us all, why do the mechanisms of self-control fail so completely in some individuals? Is there not some pre-existing defect, some moral or cerebral weakness, some gross deficiency of common sense that lets some people tumble or kick or strike or explode, while the rest of us just stagger or sway?

When a psychiatrist examines many prisoners, writes [Seymour] Halleck [in *Psychiatry and the Dilemmas of Crime*], he soon discovers how important in the genesis of the criminal outbreak is the offender's previous *sense of helplessness or hopelessness*. All of us suffer more or less from infringement of our personal freedom. We fuss about it all the time; we strive to correct it, extend it, and free ourselves from various oppressive or retentive forces. We do not want others to push us around, to control us, to dominate us. We realize this is bound to happen to some extent in an interlocking, interrelated society such as ours. No one truly has complete freedom. But restriction irks us.

The offender feels this way, too. He does not want to be pushed around, controlled, or dominated. And because he often feels that he is thus oppressed (and actually is) and because he does lack facility in improving his situation without violence, he suffers more intensely from feelings of helplessness.

Violence and crime are often attempts to escape from madness; and there can be no doubt that some mental illness is a flight from the wish to do the violence or commit the act. Is it hard for the reader to believe that suicides are sometimes committed to forestall the committing of murder? There is no doubt of it. Nor is there any doubt that murder is sometimes committed to avert suicide.

Strange as it may sound, many murderers do not realize whom they are killing, or, to put it another way, that they are killing the wrong people. To be sure, killing anybody is reprehensible enough, but the worst of it is that the person who the killer thinks should die (and he has reasons) is not the person he attacks. Sometimes the victim himself is partly responsible for the crime committed against him. It is this unconscious (perhaps sometimes conscious) participation in the crime by the victim that has long held up the very humanitarian and progressive-sounding program of giving compensation to victims. The public often judges the victim as well as the attacker.

Rape and other sexual offenses are acts of violence so repulsive to our sense of decency and order that it is easy to think of rapists in general as raging, oversexed, ruthless brutes (unless they are conquering heroes). Some rapists are. But most sex crimes are committed by undersexed rather than oversexed individuals, often undersized rather than oversized, and impelled less by lust than by a need for reassurance regarding an impaired masculinity. The unconscious fear of women goads some men with a compulsive urge to conquer, humiliate, hurt, or render powerless some available sample of womanhood. Men who are violently afraid of their repressed but nearly emergent homosexual desires, and men who are afraid of the humiliation of impotence, often try to overcome these fears by violent demonstrations.

The need to deny something in oneself is frequently an underlying motive for certain odd behavior—even up to and including crime. Bravado crimes, often done with particular brutality and ruthlessness, seem to prove *to the doer* that "I am no weakling! I am no sissy! I am no coward. I am no homosexual! I am a tough man who fears nothing." The Nazi storm troopers, many of them mere boys, were systematically trained to stifle all tender emotions and force themselves to be heartlessly brutal.

Man perennially seeks to recover the magic of his childhood days—the control of the mighty by the meek. The flick of an electric light switch, the response of an automobile throttle, the click of a camera, the touch of a match to a skyrocket—these are keys to a sudden and magical display of great power induced by the merest gesture. Is anyone already so blasé that he is no longer thrilled at the opening of a door specially for him by a magic-eye signal? Yet for a few pennies one can purchase a far more deadly piece of magic—a stored explosive and missile encased within a shell which can be ejected from a machine at the touch of a finger so swiftly that no eye can follow. A thousand yards away something falls dead—a rabbit, a deer, a beautiful mountain sheep, a sleeping child, or the President of the United States. Magic! Magnified, projected power. "Look what I can do. I am the greatest!"

It must have come to every thoughtful person, at one time or another, in looking at the revolvers on the policemen's hips, or the guns soldiers and hunters carry so proudly, that these are instruments made for the express purpose of delivering death to someone. The easy availability of these engines of destruction, even to children, mentally disturbed people, professional criminals, gangsters, and even high school girls is something to give one pause. The National Rifle Association and its allies have been able to kill scores of bills that have been introduced into Congress and state legislatures for corrective gun control since the death of President Kennedy. Americans still spend about $2 billion on guns each year.

Fifty years ago, Winston Churchill declared that the mood and temper of the public in regard to crime and criminals is one of the unfailing tests of the civilization of any country. Judged by this standard, how civilized are we?

The chairman of the President's National Crime Commission, Nicholas Katzenbach, declared . . . that organized crime flourishes in the United States because enough of the public wants its services, and most citizens are apathetic about its impact. It will continue uncurbed as long as Americans accept it as inevitable and, in some instances, desirable.

Are there steps that we can take which will reduce the aggressive stabs and self-destructive lurches of our less well-managing fellow men? Are there ways to prevent and control the grosser violations, other than the clumsy traditional maneuvers which we have inherited? These depend basically upon intimidation and slow-motion torture. We call it punishment, and justify it with our "feeling." We know it doesn't work.

Yes, there *are* better ways. There are steps that could be taken; some *are* taken. But we move too slowly. Much better use . . . could be made of the members of my profession and other behavioral scientists than having them deliver courtroom pronunciamentos. The consistent use of a diagnostic clinic would enable trained workers to lay what they can

learn about an offender before the judge who would know best how to implement the recommendation.

This would no doubt lead to a transformation of prisons, if not to their total disappearance in their present form and function. Temporary and permanent detention will perhaps always be necessary for a few, especially the professionals, but this could be more effectively and economically performed with new types of "facility" (that strange, awkward word for institution).

I assume it to be a matter of common and general agreement that our object in all this is to protect the community from a repetition of the offense by the most economical method consonant with our other purposes. Our "other purposes" include the desire to prevent these offenses from occurring, to reclaim offenders for social usefulness, if possible, and to detain them in protective custody, if reclamation is *not* possible. But how?

The treatment of human failure or dereliction by the infliction of pain is still used and believed in by many nonmedical people. "Spare the rod and spoil the child" is still considered wise counsel by many.

Whipping is still used by many secondary schoolmasters in England, I am informed, to stimulate study, attention, and the love of learning. Whipping was long a traditional treatment for the "crime" of disobedience on the part of children, pupils, servants, apprentices, employees. And slaves were treated for centuries by flogging for such offenses as weariness, confusion, stupidity, exhaustion, fear, grief, and even overcheerfulness. It was assumed and stoutly defended that these "treatments" cured conditions for which they were administered.

Meanwhile, scientific medicine was acquiring many new healing methods and devices. Doctors can now transplant organs and limbs; they can remove brain tumors and cure incipient cancers; they can halt pneumonia, meningitis, and other infections; they can correct deformities and repair breaks and tears and scars. But these wonderful achievements are accomplished on *willing* subjects, people who voluntarily ask for help by even heroic measures. And the reader will be wondering, no doubt, whether doctors can do anything with or for people who *do not want* to be treated at all, in any way! Can doctors cure willful aberrant behavior? Are we to believe that crime is a *disease* that can be reached by scientific measures? Isn't it merely "natural meanness" that makes all of us do wrong things at times even when we "know better"? And are not self-control, moral stamina, and will power the things needed? Surely there is no medical treatment for the lack of those!

Let me answer this carefully, for much misunderstanding accumulates here. [With] the prevalent understanding of the words, crime is *not* a disease. Neither is it an illness, although I think it *should* be! It *should* be treated, and it could be; but it mostly isn't.

These enigmatic statements are simply explained. Diseases are undesired states of being which have been described and defined by doctors, usually given Greek or Latin appellations, and treated by long-established physical and pharmacological formulae. Illness, on the other hand, is best defined as a state of impaired functioning of such a nature that the public expects the sufferer to repair to the physician for help. The illness may prove to be a disease; more often it is only vague and nameless misery; but something which doctors, not lawyers, teachers, or preachers, are supposed to be able and willing to help.

When the community begins to look upon the expression of aggressive violence as the symptom of an illness or as indicative of illness, it will be because it believes doctors can do something to correct such a condition. At present, some better-informed individuals do believe and expect this. However angry at or sorry for the offender, they want him "treated" in an effective way so that he will cease to be a danger to them. And they know that the traditional punishment, "treatment-punishment," will not effect this.

What *will*? What effective treatment is there for such violence? It will surely have to begin with motivating or stimulating or arousing in a cornered individual the wish and hope and intention to change his methods of dealing with the realities of life. Can this be done by education, medication, counseling, training? I would answer *yes*. It can be done successfully in a majority of cases, if undertaken in time.

The present penal system and the existing legal philosophy do not stimulate or even expect such a change to take place in the criminal. Yet change is what medical science always aims for. The prisoner, like the doctor's other patients, should emerge from his treatment experience a different person, differ-

ently equipped, differently functioning, and headed in a different direction than when he began treatment.

It is natural for the public to doubt that this can be accomplished with criminals. But remember that the public *used* to doubt that change could be effected in the mentally ill. No one a hundred years ago believed mental illness to be curable. Today *all* people know (or should know) that *mental illness is curable* in the great majority of instances and that the prospects and rapidity of cure are directly related to the availability and intensity of proper treatment.

The forms and techniques of psychiatric treatment used today number in the hundreds. No one patient requires or receives all forms, but each patient is studied with respect to his particular needs, basic assets, interests, and special difficulties. A therapeutic team may embrace a dozen workers—as in a hospital setting—or it may narrow down to the doctor and the spouse. Clergymen, teachers, relatives, friends, and even fellow patients often participate informally but helpfully in the process of readaptation.

All of the participants in this effort to bring about a favorable change in the patient—i.e., in his vital balance and life program—are imbued with what we may call a *therapeutic attitude*. This is one in direct antithesis to attitudes of avoidance, ridicule, scorn, or punitiveness. Hostile feelings toward the subject, however justified by his unpleasant and even destructive behavior, are not in the curriculum of therapy or in the therapist. This does not mean that therapists approve of the offensive and obnoxious behavior of the patient; they distinctly disapprove of it. But they recognize it as symptomatic of continued imbalance and disorganization, which is what they are seeking to change. They distinguish between disapproval, penalty, price, and punishment.

Doctors charge fees; they impose certain "penalties" or prices, but they have long since put aside primitive attitudes of retaliation toward offensive patients. A patient may cough in the doctor's face or vomit on the office rug; a patient may curse or scream or even struggle in the extremity of his pain. But these acts are not "punished." Doctors and nurses have no time or thought for inflicting unnecessary pain even on patients who may be difficult, disagreeable, provocative, and even dangerous. It is their duty to care for them, to try to make them well, and to prevent them from doing themselves or others harm. This requires love, not hate. This is the deepest meaning of the therapeutic attitude. Every doctor knows it; every worker in a hospital or clinic knows it (or should).

There is another element in the therapeutic attitude. It is the quality of hopefulness. If no one believes that the patient can get well, if no one—not even the doctor—has any hope, there probably won't be any recovery. Hope is just as important as love in the therapeutic attitude.

"But you were talking about the mentally ill," readers may interject, "those poor, confused, bereft, frightened individuals who yearn for help from you doctors and nurses. Do you mean to imply that willfully perverse individuals, our criminals, can be similarly reached and rehabilitated? Do you really believe that effective treatment of the sort you visualize can be applied to people *who do not want any help,* who are so willfully vicious, so well aware of the wrongs they are doing, so lacking in penitence or even common decency that punishment seems the only thing left?"

Do I believe there is effective treatment for offenders, and that they *can* be changed? *Most certainly and definitely I do.* Not all cases, to be sure; there are also some physical afflictions which we cannot cure at the moment. Some provision has to be made for incurables—pending new knowledge—and these will include some offenders. But I believe the majority of them would prove to be curable. The willfullness and the viciousness of offenders are part of the thing for which they have to be treated. These must not thwart the therapeutic attitude.

It is simply not true that most of them are "fully aware" of what they are doing, nor is it true that they want no help from anyone, although some of them say so. Prisoners are individuals: Some want treatment, some do not. Some don't know what treatment is. Many are utterly despairing and hopeless. Where treatment is made available in institutions, many prisoners seek it even with the full knowledge that doing so will not lessen their sentences. In some prisons, seeking treatment by prisoners is frowned upon by the officials.

Various forms of treatment are even now being tried in some progressive courts and prisons over the country—educational, social, industrial, religious, recreational, and psychological treatments. Socially ac-

ceptable behavior, new work-play opportunities, new identity and companion patterns all help toward community reacceptance. Some parole officers and some wardens have been extremely ingenious in developing these modalities of rehabilitation and reconstruction—more than I could list here even if I knew them all. But some are trying. The secret of success in all programs, however, is the replacement of the punitive attitude with a therapeutic attitude.

Offenders with propensities for impulsive and predatory aggression should not be permitted to live among us unrestrained by some kind of social control. *But the great majority of offenders, even "criminals," should never become prisoners if we want to "cure" them.*

There are now throughout the country many citizens' action groups and programs for the prevention and control of crime and delinquency. With such attitudes of inquiry and concern, the public could acquire information (and incentive) leading to a change of feeling about crime and criminals. It will discover how unjust is much so-called "justice," how baffled and frustrated many judges are by the ossified rigidity of old-fashioned, obsolete laws and state constitutions which effectively prevent the introduction of sensible procedures to replace useless, harmful ones.

I want to proclaim to the public that things are not what it wishes them to be, and will only become so if it will take an interest in the matter and assume some responsibility for its own self-protection.

Will the public listen?

If the public does become interested, it will realize that we must have more facts, more trial projects, more checked results. It will share the dismay of the President's Commission in finding that no one knows much about even the incidence of crime with any definiteness or statistical accuracy.

The average citizen finds it difficult to see how any research would in any way change his mind about a man who brutally murders his children. But just such inconceivably awful acts most dramatically point up the need for research. Why should—how can—a man become so dreadful as that in our culture? How is such a man made? Is it comprehensible that he can be born to become so depraved?

There are thousands of questions regarding crime and public protection which deserve scientific study. What makes some individuals maintain their interior equilibrium by one kind of disturbance of the social structure rather than by another kind, one that would have landed him in a hospital? Why do some individuals specialize in certain types of crime? Why do so many young people reared in areas of delinquency and poverty and bad example never become habitual delinquents? (Perhaps this is a more important question than why some of them do.)

The public has a fascination for violence, and clings tenaciously to its yen for vengeance, blind and deaf to the expense, futility, and dangerousness of the resulting penal system. But we are bound to hope that this will yield in time to the persistent, penetrating light of intelligence and accumulating scientific knowledge. The public will grow increasingly ashamed of its cry for retaliation, its persistent demand to punish. This is its crime, *our* crime against criminals—and, incidentally, our crime against ourselves. For before we can

diminish our sufferings from the ill-controlled aggressive assaults of fellow citizens, we must renounce the philosophy of punishment, the obsolete, vengeful penal attitude. In its place we would seek a comprehensive constructive social attitude—therapeutic in some instances, restraining in some instances, but preventive in its total social impact.

In the last analysis this becomes a question of personal morals and values. No matter how glorified or how piously disguised, vengeance as a human motive must be personally repudiated by each and every one of us. This is the message of old religions and new psychiatries. Unless this message is heard, unless we, the people—the man on the street, the housewife in the home—can give up our delicious satisfactions in opportunities for vengeful retaliation on scapegoats, we cannot expect to preserve our peace, our public safety, or our mental health.

---

69. A Utilitarian Theory of Punishment

RICHARD B. BRANDT

Richard B. Brandt argues that a system of punishment similar to that found in the United States and Great Britain can be justified on utilitarian or forward-looking grounds. He rejects the view that a utilitarian theory cannot approve of any excuses for criminal liability. He also denies that a utilitarian theory must approve of occasionally punishing the innocent provided the theory is understood in an extended sense to require a principle of equal distribution.

The ethical foundations of the institution and principles of criminal justice require examination just as do the ethical foundations of systems of economic distribution. In fact, the two problems are so similar that it is helpful to view either one in the light of conclusions reached about the other. It is no accident that the two are spoken of as problems of "justice," for the institu-

tion of criminal justice is essentially a mode of allocating welfare (or "illfare," if we prefer). Also, just as economic return can be regarded as a reward for past services, the punishment of criminals can be regarded as punishment for past disservices. Moreover, just as a major reason for differences in economic reward is to provide motivation for promoting the public welfare by industrious effort, so a major reason for a system of punishment for criminals is to give motivation for not harming the public by crime. The two topics, then, are very similar; but they are also sufficiently different to require separate discussion. . . .

Abridged from *Ethical Theory* (1959), pp. 480, 489–495, 503–505. Reprinted by permission of Richard B. Brandt. Notes renumbered.

The broad questions to be kept in the forefront of discussion are the following: (1) What justifies anyone in inflicting pain or loss on an individual on account of his past acts? (2) Is there a valid general principle about the punishments proper for various acts? (Possibly there should be no close connection between offense and penalty; perhaps punishment should be suited to the individual needs of the criminal, and not to his crime.) (3) What kinds of defense should excuse from punishment? An answer to these questions would comprise prescriptions for the broad outlines of an ideal system of criminal justice. . . .

The Utilitarian Theory of Criminal Justice

. . . It is convenient to begin with the utilitarian theory. Since we have tentatively concluded that an "extended" rule-utilitarianism is the most tenable form of theory, we shall have this particular type of theory in mind. For present purposes, however, it would make no difference, except at two or three points where we shall make note of the fact, if we confined our attention to a straight rule-utilitarian principle. There is no harm in thinking of the matter in this way. . . .

The essence of the rule-utilitarian theory, we recall, is that our actions, whether legislative or otherwise, should be guided by a set of prescriptions, the conscientious following of which by all would have maximum net expectable utility. As a result, the utilitarian is not, just as such, committed to any particular view about how anti-social behavior should be treated by society—or even to the view that society should do anything at all about immoral conduct. It is only the utilitarian principle *combined* with statements about the kind of laws and practices which will maximize expectable utility that has such consequences. Therefore, utilitarians are free to differ from one another about the character of an ideal system of criminal justice; some utilitarians think that the system prevalent in Great Britain and the United States essentially corresponds to the ideal, but others think that the only system that can be justified is markedly different from the actual systems in these Western countries. We shall concentrate our discussion, however, on the more traditional line of utilitarian thought which holds that

roughly the actual system of criminal law, say in the United States, is morally justifiable, and we shall follow roughly the classic exposition of the reasoning given by Jeremy Bentham[1]—but modifying this freely when we feel amendment is called for. At the end of the chapter we shall look briefly at a different view.

Traditional utilitarian thinking about criminal justice has found the rationale of the practice, in the United States, for example, in three main facts. (Those who disagree think the first two of these "facts" happen not to be the case.) (1) People who are tempted to misbehave, to trample on the rights of others, to sacrifice public welfare for personal gain, can usually be deterred from misconduct by fear of punishment, such as death, imprisonment, or fine. (2) Imprisonment or fine will teach malefactors a lesson; their characters may be improved, and at any rate a personal experience of punishment will make them less likely to misbehave again. (3) Imprisonment will certainly have the result of physically preventing past malefactors from misbehaving, during the period of their incarceration.

In view of these suppositions, traditional utilitarian thinking has concluded that having laws forbidding certain kinds of behavior on pain of punishment, and having machinery for the fair enforcement of these laws, is justified by the fact that it maximizes expectable utility. Misconduct is not to be punished just for its own sake; malefactors must be punished for their past acts, according to law, as a way of maximizing expectable utility.

The utilitarian principle, of course, has implications for decisions about the severity of punishment to be administered. Punishment is itself an evil, and hence should be avoided where this is consistent with the public good. Punishment should have precisely such a degree of severity (not more or less) that the probable disutility of greater severity just balances the probable gain in utility (less crime because of the more serious threat). The cost, in other words, should be counted along with the value of what is bought; and we should buy protection up to the point where the cost is greater than the protection is worth. How severe will such punishment be? Jeremy Bentham had many sensible things to say about this. Punishment, he said, must be severe enough so that it is to no one's advantage to commit an offense even if he receives the punishment; a fine of $10 for bank robbery would give no security at all. Further, since many criminals will be undetected, we must make the penalty heavy enough in comparison with the prospective gain from crime that a prospective criminal will consider the risk hardly worth it, even [when] it is not certain he will be punished at all. Again, the more serious offenses should carry the heavier penalties, not only because the greater disutility justifies the use of heavier penalties . . . to prevent them, but also because criminals should be motivated to commit a less serious rather than a more serious offense. Bentham thought the prescribed penalties should allow for some variation at the discretion of the judge, so that the actual suffering caused should roughly be the same in all cases; thus, a heavier fine will be imposed on a rich man than on a poor man.

Bentham also argued that the goal of maximum utility requires that certain facts should *excuse* from culpability, for the reason that punishment in such cases "must be inefficacious." He listed as such (1) the fact that the relevant law was passed only after the act of the accused, (2) that the law had not been made public, (3) that the criminal was an infant, insane, or was intoxicated, (4) that the crime was done under physical compulsion, (5) that the agent was ignorant of the probable consequences of his act or was acting on the basis of an innocent misapprehension of the facts, such that the act the agent thought he was performing was a lawful one, and (6) that the motivation to commit the offense was so strong that no threat of law could prevent the crime. Bentham also thought that punishment should be remitted if the crime was a collective one and the number of the guilty so large that great suffering would be caused by its imposition, or if the offender held an important post and his services were important for the public, or if the public or foreign powers would be offended by the punishment; but we shall ignore this part of his view.

Bentham's account of the logic of legal "defenses" needs amendment. What he should have argued is that *not* punishing in certain types of cases (cases where such defenses as those just indicated can be offered) reduces the amount of suffering imposed by law and the insecurity of everybody, and that failure to impose punishment in these types of case will cause only a negligible increase in the incidence of crime.

How satisfactory is this theory of criminal justice? Does it have any implications that are far from being acceptable when compared with concrete justified convictions about what practices are morally right?[2]

Many criminologists . . . would argue that Bentham was mistaken in his facts: The deterrence value of [the] threat of punishment, they say, is much less than he imagined, and criminals are seldom reformed by spending time in prison. If these contentions are correct, then the ideal rules for society's treatment of malefactors are very different from what Bentham thought, and from what actual practice is today in the United States. To say all this, however, is not to show that the utilitarian *principle* is incorrect, for in view of these facts presumably the attitudes of a "qualified" person would not be favorable to criminal justice as practiced today. Utilitarian theory might still be correct, but its implications would be different from what Bentham thought—and they might coincide with justified ethical judgments. We shall return to this.

The whole utilitarian approach, however, has been criticized on the ground that it ought not in consistency to approve of *any* excuses from criminal liability.[3] Or at least, it should do so only after careful empirical inquiries. It is not obvious, it is argued, that we increase net expectable utility by permitting such defenses. At the least, the utilitarian is committed to defend the concept of "strict liability." Why? Because we could get a more strongly deterrent effect if everyone knew that *all behavior* of a certain sort would be punished, irrespective of mistaken supposals of fact, compulsion, and so on. The critics admit that knowledge that all behavior of a certain sort will be punished will hardly deter from crime the insane, persons acting under compulsion, persons acting under erroneous beliefs about facts, and others, but, as Professor Hart points out, it does not follow from this that general knowledge that certain acts will always be punished will not be salutary.

[But the] utilitarian has a solid defense against charges of this sort. We must bear in mind (as the critics do not) that the utilitarian principle, *taken by itself, implies nothing whatever* about whether a system of law should excuse persons on the basis of certain defenses. What the utilitarian does say is that, when we *combine* the principle of utilitarianism with *true* propositions about a certain thing or situation, then we shall come out with true statements about obligations. The utilitarian is certainly not committed to saying that one will derive true propositions about obligations if one starts with *false* propositions about fact or about what will maximize welfare, or with *no* such propositions at all. Therefore the criticism sometimes made (for example, by Hart), that utilitarian theory does not render it "obviously" or "necessarily" the case that the recognized excuses from criminal liability should be accepted as excusing from punishment, is beside the point. Moreover, in fact the utilitarian can properly claim that we do have excellent reason for believing that the general public would be no better motivated to avoid criminal offenses than it now is, if the insane and others were also punished along with intentional wrong-doers. Indeed, he may reasonably claim that the example of punishment of these individual could only have a hardening effect—like public executions. Furthermore, the utilitarian can point out that abolition of the standard exculpating excuses would lead to serious insecurity. Imagine the pleasure of driving an automobile if one knew one could be executed for running down a child whom it was absolutely impossible to avoid striking! One certainly does not maximize expectable utility by eliminating the traditional excuses. In general, then, the utilitarian theory is not threatened by its implications about exculpating excuses.

It might also be objected against utilitarianism that it cannot recognize the validity of *mitigating* excuses (which presumably have the support of "qualified" attitudes). Would not consequences be better if the distinction between premeditated and impulsive acts were abolished? The utilitarian can reply that people who commit impulsive crimes, in the heat of anger, do not give thought to legal penalties; they would not be deterred by a stricter law. Moreover, such a person is unlikely to repeat his crime, so that a mild sentence saves an essentially good man for society.[4] Something can also be said in support of the practice of judges in giving a milder sentence when a person's temptation is severe: At least the *extended* rule-utilitarian can say, in defense of the practice of punishing less severely the crime of a man who has had few opportunities in life, that a judge ought to do what he can to repair inequalities in life, and that a mild sentence to a man who has had few opportunities is one way of doing

this. There are, then, utilitarian supports for recognizing the mitigating excuses. . . .

Another popular objection to the utilitarian theory is that the utilitarian must approve of prosecutors or judges occasionally withholding evidence known to them, for the sake of convicting an innocent man, if the public welfare really is served by so doing. Critics of the theory would not deny that there *can* be circumstances where the dangers are so severe that such action is called for; they only say that utilitarianism calls for it all too frequently. Is this criticism justified? Clearly, the utilitarian is not committed to advocating that a provision should be written into the *law* so as to permit punishment of persons for crimes they did not commit if to do so would serve the public good. Any such provisions would be a shattering blow to public confidence and security. The question is only whether there should be an informal moral rule to the same effect, for the guidance of judges and prosecutors. Will the rule-utilitarian necessarily be committed to far too sweeping a moral rule on this point? We must recall that he is not in the position of the act-utilitarian, who must say that an innocent man must be punished if in *his particular case* the public welfare would be served by his punishment. The rule-utilitarian rather asserts only that an innocent man should be punished if he falls within a class of cases such that net expectable utility is maximized if *all* members of the class are punished, taking into account the possible disastrous effects on public confidence if it [knows] that judges and prosecutors are guided by such a rule. Moreover, the "extended" rule-utilitarian has a further reason for not punishing an innocent man unless he has had more than his equal share of the good things of life already; namely, that there is an obligation to promote equality of welfare, whereas severe punishment is heaping "illfare" on one individual person. When we take these considerations into account, it is *not* obvious that the rule-utilitarian (or the "extended" rule-utilitarian) is committed to action that we are justifiably convinced is immoral.[5] . . .

Utilitarianism and Reform

Some thinkers today believe that criminal justice in Great Britain and the United States is in need of substantial revision. If we agree with their proposals, we have even less reason for favoring the retributive principles; but we must also question the traditional utilitarian emphasis on deterrence as the primary function of the institution of criminal justice.

Their proposal, roughly, is that we should extend, to all criminal justice, the practices of juvenile courts and institutions for the reform of juvenile offenders. Here, retributive concepts have been largely discarded at least in theory, and psychiatric treatment and programs for the prevention of crime by means of slum clearance, the organization of boys' clubs, and so forth, have replaced even deterrence as guiding ideas for social action.

The extension of these practices to criminal justice as a whole would work somewhat as follows: First, the present court procedure would be used to determine whether an offense has actually been committed. Such procedure would necessarily include ordinary rules about the admission of evidence, trial by jury, and the exculpating justifications and excuses for offenses (such as wrong suppositions about the facts). Second, if an accused were adjudged guilty, decisions about his treatment would then be in the hands of the experts, who would determine what treatment was called for and when the individual was ready for return to normal social living. The trial court might, of course, set some maximum period during which such experts would have a right to control the treatment of the criminal. What the experts would do would be decided by the criminal's condition; it would be criminal-centered treatment, not crime-centered treatment.

One might object to this proposal that it overlooks the necessity of disagreeable penalties for crime, in order to deter prospective criminals effectively. But it is doubtful whether threats of punishment have as much deterrent value as is often supposed. Threats of punishment will have little effect on morons, or on persons to whom normal living offers few prospects of an interesting existence.[6] Moreover, persons from better economic or social circumstances will be de-

terred sufficiently by the prospect of conviction in a public trial and being at the disposal of a board for a period of years.

Such proposals have their difficulties. For instance, would the police be as safe as they are if criminals knew that killing a policeman would be no more serious in its consequences than the crime for which the policeman was trying to arrest them? However, there is much factual evidence for answering such questions, since systems of criminal justice along such lines are already in operation in some parts of the world, in particular among the Scandinavian countries. In fact, in some states the actual practice is closer to the projected system than one might expect from books on legal theory.

Another objection that many would raise is that psychiatry and criminology have not yet advanced far enough for such weighty decisions about the treatment of criminals to be placed in their hands. The treatment of criminals might vary drastically depending on the particular theoretical predilections of a given theorist, or on his personal likes and dislikes. One can probably say as much, or more, however, about the differences between judges in their policies for picking a particular sentence within the range permitted by law.

An institution of criminal justice operating on such basic principles would come closer to our views about how parents should treat their children, or teachers their students, than the more traditional practices of criminal justice today.

We should repeat that this view about the ideal form for an institution of criminal justice is not in conflict with utilitarianism; in fact, it is utilitarian in outlook. The motivation behind advocating it is the thought that such a system would do more good. It differs from the kind of institution traditionally advocated by utilitarians like Bentham only in making different factual assumptions, primarily about the deterrence value of threat of imprisonment, and the actual effect of imprisonment on the attitudes of the criminal.

Endnotes

1. In *Principles of Morals and Legislation.*

2. Act-utilitarians face special problems. For instance, if I am an act-utilitarian and serve on a jury, I shall work to get a verdict that will do the most good, irrespective of the charges of the judge, and of any oath I may have taken to give a reasonable answer to certain questions on the basis of the evidence presented—unless I think my doing so will have indirect effects on the institution of the jury, public confidence in it, and so on. This is certainly not what we think a juror should do. Of course, neither a juror nor a judge can escape his prima facie obligation to do what good he can; this obligation is present in some form in every theory. The act-utilitarian, however, makes this the whole of one's responsibility.

3. See H. L. A. Hart, "Legal Responsibility and Excuses," in Sidney Hook (ed.), *Determinism and Freedom* (New York: New York University Press, 1958), pp. 81–104; and David Braybrooke, "Professor Stevenson, Voltaire, and the Case of Admiral Byng," *Journal of Philosophy*, LIII (1956), 787–796.

4. The utilitarian must admit that the same thing is true for many deliberate murders; and probably he should also admit that some people who commit a crime in the heat of anger would have found time to think had they known that a grave penalty awaited them.

5. In any case, a tenable theory of punishment must approve of punishing persons who are *morally* blameless. Suppose someone commits treason for moral reasons. We may have to say that his deed is not reprehensible . . . and might even (considering the risk he took for his principles) be morally admirable. Yet we think such persons must be punished no matter what their motives; people cannot be permitted to take the law into their own hands.

6. It is said that picking pockets was once a capital offense in England, and hangings were public, in order to get the maximum deterrent effect. But hangings in public had to be abolished, because such crimes as picking pockets were so frequent during the spectacle! See N. F. Cantor, *Crime, Criminals, and Criminal Justice* (New York: Henry Holt & Company, Inc., 1932).

70. A Critique of the Humanitarian Theory of Punishment

C. S. LEWIS

C. S. Lewis argues that the humanitarian theory of punishment is not in the interests of the criminal. According to Lewis, this is because the theory is concerned with the goals of reform and deterrence and not the requirements of justice. Hence, it permits the violation of the criminal's rights as a way of promoting these goals. Moreover, Lewis claims, deciding what promotes reform and deterrence, unlike deciding what is required by justice, seems best left to experts. Yet these experts, Lewis argues, even with the best of intentions, may act "as cruelly and unjustly as the greatest tyrants."

From "The Humanitarian Theory of Punishment," *Res Judicatae* (1953), pp. 224-230. Reprinted by permission of the *Melbourne University Law Review* and the Trustee for the C. S. Lewis Estate.

In England we have lately had a controversy about Capital Punishment. I do not know whether a murderer is more likely to repent and make a good end on the gallows a few weeks after his trial or in the prison infirmary thirty years later. I do not know whether the fear of death is an indispensable deterrent. I need not [here] decide whether it is a morally permissible deterrent. Those are questions which I propose to leave untouched. My subject is not Capital Punishment in particular, but that theory of punishment in general which the controversy showed to be almost universal among my fellow countrymen. It may be called the Humanitarian theory. Those who hold it think that it is mild and merciful. In this I believe that they are seriously mistaken. I believe that the "Humanity" which it claims is a dangerous illusion and disguises the possibility of cruelty and injustice without end. I urge a return to the traditional or Retributive theory not solely, not even primarily, in the interests of society, but in the interests of the criminal.

According to the Humanitarian theory, to punish a man because he deserves it, and as much as he deserves, is mere revenge, and, therefore, barbarous and immoral. It is maintained that the only legitimate motives for punishing are the desire to deter others by example or to mend the criminal. When this theory is combined, as frequently happens, with the belief that all crime is more or less pathological, the idea of mending tails off into that of healing or curing and punishment becomes therapeutic. Thus it appears at first sight that we have passed from the harsh and self-righteous notion of giving the wicked their deserts to the charitable and enlightened one of tending the psychologically sick. What could be more amiable? One little point which is taken for granted in this theory needs, however, to be made explicit. The things done to the criminal, even if they are called cures, will be just as compulsory as they were in the old days when we called them punishments. If a tendency to steal can be cured by psychotherapy, the thief will no doubt be forced to undergo the treatment. Otherwise, society cannot continue.

[T]his doctrine, merciful though it appears, really means that each one of us, from the moment he breaks the law, is deprived of the rights of a human being.

The reason is this: The Humanitarian theory removes from Punishment the concept of Desert. But the concept of Desert is the only connecting link between punishment and justice. It is only as deserved or undeserved that a sentence can be just or unjust. I do not here contend that the question "Is it deserved?" is the only one we can reasonably ask about a punishment. We may very properly ask whether it is likely to deter others and to reform the criminal. But neither of these two last questions is a question about justice. There is no sense in talking about a "just deterrent" or a "just cure." We demand of a deterrent not whether it is just but whether it will deter. We demand of a cure not whether it is just but whether it succeeds. Thus when we cease to consider what the criminal deserves and consider only what will cure him or deter others, we have tacitly removed him from the sphere of justice altogether; instead of a person, a subject of rights, we now have a mere object, a patient, a "case."

The distinction will become clearer if we ask who will be qualified to determine sentences when sentences are no longer held to derive their propriety from the criminal's deservings. On the old view the problem of fixing the right sentence was a moral problem. Accordingly, the judge who did it was a person trained in jurisprudence: trained, that is, in a science which deals with rights and duties, and which, in origin at least, was consciously accepting guidance from the Law of Nature, and from Scripture. We must admit that in the actual penal code of most countries at most times these high originals were so much modified by local custom, class interests, and utilitarian concessions, as to be very imperfectly recognizable. But the code was never in principle, and not always in fact, beyond the control of the conscience of the society. And when (say, in eighteenth-century England) actual punishments conflicted too violently with the moral sense of the community, juries refused to convict and reform was finally brought about. This was possible because, so long as we are thinking in terms of Desert, the propriety of the penal code, being a moral question, is a question on which every man has the right to an opinion, not because he follows this or that profession, but because he is simply a man, a rational animal enjoying the Natural Light. But all this is changed when we drop the concept of Desert. The only two questions we may now ask about a punishment are whether it deters and whether it cures. But these are not questions on which anyone is entitled to have an opinion simply because he is a man. He is not entitled to an opinion even if, in addition to being a man, he should happen also to be a jurist, a Christian, and a moral theologian. For they are not questions about principle but about matter of fact; and for such *cuiquam in sua arte credendum*. Only the expert "penologist" (let barbarous things have barbarous names), in the light of previous experiment, can tell us what is likely to deter: Only the psychotherapist can tell us what is likely to cure. It will be in vain for the rest of us, speaking simply as men, to say, "but this punishment is hideously unjust, hideously disproportionate to the criminal's deserts." The experts with perfect logic will reply, "but nobody was talking about deserts. No one was talking about *punishment* in your archaic vindictive sense of the word. Here are the statistics proving that this treatment deters. Here are the statistics proving that this other treatment cures. What is your trouble?"

The Humanitarian theory, then, removes sentences from the hands of jurists whom the public . . . is entitled to criticize and places them in the hands of technical experts whose special sciences do not even [use] such categories as rights or justice. . . . [S]ince this transference results from an abandonment of the old idea of punishment, and, therefore, of all vindictive motives, it will be safe to leave our criminals in such hands. I will not . . . comment on the simple-minded view of fallen human nature which such a belief implies. Let us rather remember that the "cure" of criminals is to be compulsory; and let us then watch how the theory actually works in the mind of the Humanitarian. The immediate starting point of this article was a letter I read in [a leftist weekly]. The author [pleaded] that a certain sin, now treated by our laws as a crime, should henceforward be treated as a disease. And he complained that under the present system the offender, after a term in gaol, was simply let out to return to his original environment where he would probably relapse. What he complained of was not the shutting up but the letting out. On his remedial view of punishment the offender should . . . be detained until he was cured. And of course the official straighteners are the only people who can say when that is. The first result of the Humanitarian theory is, therefore, to substitute for a definite sentence (reflecting to some extent the community's moral judgment on the degree of ill-desert involved) an indefinite sentence terminable only by the word of those experts—and they are not experts in moral theology or . . . the Law of Nature—who inflict it. Which of us, if he stood in the dock, would not prefer to be tried by the old system?

It may be said that by the continued use of the word *punishment* and the use of the verb "inflict" I am misrepresenting Humanitarians. They are not punishing, not inflicting, only healing. But do not . . . be deceived by a name. To be taken without consent from my home and friends; to lose my liberty; to undergo all those assaults on my personality that modern psychotherapy knows how to deliver; to be remade after some pattern of "normality" hatched in a Viennese laboratory to which I never professed allegiance; to know that this process will never end until either my captors have succeeded or I have grown wise enough to cheat them with apparent success—who cares whether this is called Punishment or not? That it includes most of the elements for which any punishment is feared—shame, exile, bondage, and years eaten by the locust—is obvious. Only enormous ill-desert could justify it; but ill-desert is the very conception which the Humanitarian theory has thrown overboard.

If we turn from the curative to the deterrent justification of punishment we shall find the new theory even more alarming. When you punish a man *in terrorem*, make of him an "example" to others, you are admittedly using him as a means to an end; someone else's end. This, in itself, would be a very wicked thing to do. On the classical theory of Punishment it was of course justified on the ground that the man deserved it. That was assumed to be established before any question of "making him an example" arose. You then, as the saying is, killed two birds with one stone; in the process of giving him what he deserved you set an example to others. But take away desert and the whole morality of the punishment disappears. Why, in Heaven's name, am I to be sacrificed to the good of society in this way?—unless, of course, I deserve it.

But that is not the worst. If the justification of exemplary punishment is not to be based on desert but solely on its efficacy as a deterrent, it is not absolutely necessary that the man we punish should even have committed the crime. The deterrent effect demands that the public should draw the moral, "If we do such an act we shall suffer like that man." The punishment of a man actually guilty whom the public think innocent will not have the desired effect; the punishment of a man actually innocent will, provided the public think him guilty. But every modern State has powers which make it easy to fake a trial. When a victim is urgently needed for exemplary purposes and a guilty victim cannot be found, all the purposes of deterrence will be equally served by the punishment (call it "cure" if you prefer) of an innocent victim, provided that the public can be cheated into thinking him guilty. It is no use to ask me why I assume that our rulers will be so wicked. The punishment of an innocent, that is, an undeserving, man is wicked only if we grant the traditional view that righteous punishment means deserved punishment. Once we have abandoned that criterion, all punishments have to be justified, if at all, on other grounds that have nothing to do with desert. Where the punishment of the innocent can be justified on those grounds (and it could in some cases be justified as a deterrent) it will be no less moral than any other punishment. Any distaste for it on the part of a Humanitarian will be merely a hang-over from the Retributive theory.

It is, indeed, important to notice that my argument so far supposes no evil intentions on the part of the Humanitarian and considers only what is involved in the logic of his position. My contention is that good men (not bad men) consistently acting upon that position would act as cruelly and unjustly as the greatest tyrants. They might in some respects act even worse. Of all tyrannies a tyranny sincerely exercised for the good of its victims may be the most oppressive. It may be better to live under robber barons than under omnipotent moral busybodies. The robber baron's cruelty may sometimes sleep, his cupidity may at some point be satiated; but those who torment us for our own good will torment us without end for they do so with the approval of their own conscience. They may be more likely to go to Heaven yet at the same time likelier to make a Hell of earth. Their very kindness stings with intolerable insult. To be "cured" against one's will and cured of states which we may not regard as disease is to be put on a level with those who have not yet reached the age of reason or those who never will; to be classed with infants, imbeciles, and domestic animals. But to be punished, however severely, because we have deserved it, because we "ought to have known better," is to be treated as a human person made in God's image.

In reality, however, we must face the possibility of bad rulers armed with a Humanitarian theory of pun-

ishment. A great many popular blueprints for a Christian society are merely what the Elizabethans called "eggs in moonshine" because they assume that the whole society is Christian or that the Christians are in control. This is not so in most contemporary States. Even if it were, our rulers would still be fallen men, and, therefore, neither very wise nor very good. As it is, they will usually be unbelievers. And since wisdom and virtue are not the only or the commonest qualifications for a place in the government, they will not often be even the best unbelievers. The practical problem of Christian politics is not that of drawing up schemes for a Christian society, but that of living as innocently as we can with unbelieving fellow-subjects under unbelieving rulers who will never be perfectly wise and good and who will sometimes be very wicked and very foolish. And when they are wicked the Humanitarian theory of punishment will put in their hands a finer instrument of tyranny than wickedness ever had before. For if crime and disease are to be regarded as the same thing, it follows that any state of mind which our masters choose to call "disease" can be treated as crime and compulsorily cured. It will be vain to plead that states of mind which displease government need not always involve moral turpitude and do not therefore always deserve forfeiture of liberty. For our masters will not be using the concepts of Desert and Punishment but those of disease and cure. We know that one school of psychology already regards religion as a neurosis. When this particular neurosis becomes inconvenient to government, what is to hinder government from proceeding to "cure" it? Such "cure" will, of course, be compulsory; but under the Humanitarian theory it will not be called by the shocking name of Persecution. No one will blame us for being Christian, no one will hate us, no one will revile us. The new Nero will approach us with the silky manners of a doctor, and though all will be in fact as compulsory as the *tunica molesta* or Smithfield or Tyburn, all will go on within the unemotional therapeutic sphere where words like *right* and *wrong* or *freedom* and *slavery* are never heard. And thus when the command is given, every prominent Christian in the land may vanish overnight into Institutions for the Treatment of the Ideologically Unsound, and it will rest with the expert gaolers to say when (if ever) they are to reemerge. But it will not be persecution. Even if the treatment is painful, even if it is life-long, even if it is fatal, that will be only a regrettable accident; the intention was purely therapeutic. Even in ordinary medicine there were painful operations and fatal operations; so in this. But because they are "treatment," not punishment, they can be criticized only by fellow-experts and on technical grounds, never by men as men and on grounds of justice.

That is why I think it essential to oppose the Humanitarian theory of punishment, root and branch, wherever we encounter it. It carries on its front a semblance of mercy which is wholly false. That is how it can deceive men of good will. The error began, perhaps, with Shelley's statement that the distinction between mercy and justice was invented in the courts of tyrants. It sounds noble, and was indeed the error of a noble mind. But the distinction is essential. The older view was that mercy "tempered"justice, or (on the highest level of all) that mercy and justice had met and kissed. The essential act of mercy was to pardon; and pardon in its very essence involves the recognition of guilt, and ill-desert in the recipient. If crime is only a disease which needs cure, not sin which deserves punishment, it cannot be pardoned. How can you pardon a man for having a gumboil or a club foot? But the Humanitarian theory wants simply to abolish Justice and substitute Mercy for it. This means that you start being "kind" to people before you have considered their rights, and then force upon them supposed kindnesses which they in fact had a right to refuse, and finally kindnesses which no one but you will recognize as kindnesses and which the recipient will feel as abominable cruelties. You have overshot the mark. Mercy, detached from Justice, grows unmerciful. That is the important paradox. As there are plants which will flourish only in mountain soil, so it appears that Mercy will flower only when it grows in the crannies of the rock of Justice: Transplanted to the marshlands of mere Humanitarianism, it becomes a man-eating weed, all the more dangerous because it is still called by the same name as the mountain variety. But we ought long ago to have learned our lesson. We should be too old now to be deceived by those humane pretensions that have served to usher in every cruelty of the revolutionary period in which we live. These are the "precious balms" that will "break our heads."

There is a fine sentence in Bunyan: "It came burning hot into my mind, whatever he said, and however he flattered, when he got me home to his house, he would sell me for a slave." There is a fine couplet, too, in John Ball:

> *Be ware ere ye be woe*
> *Know your friend from your foe.*

One last word. You may ask why I sent this to an Australian periodical. The reason is simple . . . : I can get no hearing for it in England.

---

71. *Classical Retributivism*

EDMUND L. PINCOFFS

Edmund L. Pincoffs begins by setting out three principles that, he holds, express the essence of a Kantian retributive theory of punishment. He then claims that the underlying rationale for these principles is to provide a justification of the punishment to the criminal on the grounds that she has willed the punishment she now suffers. Pincoffs concludes by noting two difficulties for the retributive theory of punishment that he has not addressed: how to make punishment equal to the crime and how to distinguish punishment from revenge.

I.

The classification of Kant as a retributivist[1] is usually accompanied by a reference to some part of the following passage from the *Rechtslehre*, which is worth quoting at length.

> Juridical punishment can never be administered merely as a means for promoting another good either with regard to the criminal himself or to civil society, but must in all cases be imposed only because the individual on whom it is inflicted *has committed a crime*. For one man ought never to be dealt with merely as a means subservient to the purpose of another, nor be mixed up with the subjects of real right. Against such treatment his inborn personality has a right to protect him, even though he may be condemned to lose his civil personality. He must first be found guilty and *punishable* before there can be any thought of drawing from his punishment any benefit for himself or his fellow-citizens. The penal law is a categorical imperative; and woe to him who creeps through the serpent-windings of utilitarianism to discover some advantage that may discharge him from the justice of punishment, or even from the due measure of it, according to the Pharisaic maxim: "It is better that *one* man should die than the whole people should perish." For if justice and righteousness perish, human life would no longer have any value in the world. . . .
>
> But what is the mode and measure of punishment which public justice takes as its principle and standard? It is just the principle of equality, by which the pointer of the scale of justice is made to incline no more to the one side than the other. It may be rendered by saying that the undeserved evil which any one commits on another, is to be regarded as perpetrated on himself. Hence it may be said: "If you slander another, you slander yourself; if you steal from another, you steal from yourself; if you strike another, you strike yourself; if you kill another, you kill yourself." This is the Right of RETALIATION *(jus talionis)*; and properly understood, it is the only principle which in regulating a public

court, as distinguished from mere private judgment, can definitely assign both the quality and the quantity of a just penalty. All other standards are wavering and uncertain; and on account of other considerations involved in them, they contain no principle conformable to the sentence of pure and strict justice.[2]

Obviously we could mull over this passage for a long time. What, exactly, is the distinction between the Inborn and the Civil Personality? How is the Penal Law a Categorical Imperative: by derivation from one of the five formulations in the *Grundlegung*, or as a separate formulation? But we are on the trail of the traditional retributive theory of punishment and do not want to lose ourselves in niceties. There are two main points in this passage to which we should give particular attention:

i. The only acceptable reason for punishing a man is that he has committed a crime.

ii. The only acceptable reason for punishing a man in a given manner and degree is that the punishment is "equal" to the crime for which he is punished.

These propositions, I think it will be agreed, express the main points of the first and second paragraphs respectively. Before stopping over these points, let us go on to a third. It is brought out in the following passage from the *Rechtslehre*, which is also often referred to by writers on retributivism.

> Even if a civil society resolved to dissolve itself with the consent of all its members—as might be supposed in the case of a people inhabiting an island resolving to separate and scatter themselves throughout the whole world—the last murderer lying in prison ought to be executed before the resolution was carried out. This ought to be done [so] that everyone may realize the desert of his deeds, and that bloodguiltiness may not remain upon the people; for otherwise they will all be regarded as participators in the murder as a public violation of justice.[3]

It is apparent from this passage that, [as far] as the punishment of death for murder is concerned, the punishment awarded not only may but must be carried out. If it must be carried out "so that everyone may realize the desert of his deeds," then punishment

From *The Rationale of Legal Punishment* (1966), pp. 2–16. Reprinted by permission of Humanities Press, Inc., Atlantic Highlands, N.J., 07716.

for deeds other than murder must be carried out too. We will take it, then, that Kant holds that:

iii. Whoever commits a crime must be punished in accordance with his desert.

Whereas (i) tells us what kind of reason we must have *if* we punish, (iii) now tells us that we must punish *whenever* there is desert of punishment. Punishment, Kant tells us elsewhere, is "The *juridical* effect or consequence of a culpable act of Demerit."[4] Any crime is a culpable act of demerit, in that it is an "*intentional* transgression—that is, an act accompanied with the consciousness that it is a transgression."[5] This is an unusually narrow definition of crime, since crime is not ordinarily limited to intentional acts of transgression but may also include unintentional ones, such as acts done in ignorance of the law, and criminally negligent acts. However, Kant apparently leaves room for "culpable acts of demerit" outside of the category of crime. These he calls "faults," which are unintentional transgressions of duty; but "are nevertheless imputable to a person."[6] I can only suppose, though it is a difficulty in the interpretation of the *Rechtslehre*, that when Kant says that punishment must be inflicted "only because he has committed a crime," he is not including in "crime" what he would call a fault. Crime would, then, refer to any *intentional* imputable transgressions of duty and these are what must be punished as involving ill desert. The difficulties involved in the definition of crime as the transgression of duty, as opposed to the mere violation of a legal prohibition, will be taken up later.

Taking the three propositions we have isolated as expressing the essence of the Kantian retributivistic position, we must now ask a direct and obvious question. What makes Kant hold this position? Why does he think it apparent that consequences should have *nothing to do* with the decision whether, and how, and how much to punish? There are two directions an answer to this question might follow. One would lead us into an extensive excursus on the philosophical position of Kant, the relation of this to his ethical theory, and the relation of his general theory of ethics to his philosophy of law. It would, in short, take our question as one about the consistency of Kant's position concerning the justification of punishment with the whole of Kantian philosophy. This would involve

discussion of Kant's reasons for believing that moral laws must be universal and categorical in virtue of their form alone, and divorced from any empirical content; of his attempt to make out a moral decision-procedure based on an "empty" categorical imperative; and, above all, of the concept of freedom as a postulate of practical reason, and as the central concept of the philosophy of law. This kind of answer, however, we must forego here; for while it would have considerable interest in its own right, it would lead us astray from our purpose, which is to understand as well as we can the retributivist position, not as a part of this or that philosophical system but for its own sake. It is a position taken by philosophers with diverse philosophical systems; we want to take another direction, then, in our answer. Is there any *general* (nonspecial, nonsystematic) reason why Kant rejects consequences in the justification of punishment?

Kant believes that consequences have nothing to do with the justification of punishment partly because of his assumptions about the *direction* of justification; and these assumptions are . . . also to be found underlying the thought of Hegel and Bradley. Justification is not only *of* something, it is also *to* someone: It has an addressee. Now there are important confusions in Kant's and other traditional justifications of punishment turning on the question what the "punishment" *is* which is being justified. . . . But if we are to feel the force of the retributivist position, we can no longer put off the question of the addressee of justification.

To whom is the Kantian justification of punishment directed? The question may seem a difficult one to answer, since Kant does not consider it himself as a separate issue. Indeed, it is not the kind of question likely to occur to a philosopher of Kant's formalistic leanings. A Kantian justification or rationale stands, so to speak, on its own. It is a structure which can be examined, tested, probed by any rational being. Even to speak of the addressee of justification has an uncomfortably relativistic sound, as if only persuasion of A or B or C is possible, and proof impossible. Yet, in practice, Kant does not address his proffered justification of punishment so much to any rational being (which, to put it otherwise, is to address it not at all), as to the being most affected: the criminal himself.

It is the criminal who is cautioned not to creep through the serpent-windings of utilitarianism. It is the criminal's rights which are in question in the debate with Beccaria over capital punishment. It is the criminal we are warned not to mix up with property or things: the "subjects of Real Right." In the *Kritik der Praktischen Vernunst,* the intended direction of justification becomes especially clear.

> Now the notion of punishment, as such, cannot be united with that of becoming a partaker of happiness; for although he who inflicts the punishment may at the same time have the benevolent purpose of directing this punishment to this end, yet it must be justified in itself as punishment, that is, as mere harm, so that if it stopped there, and the person punished could get no glimpse of kindness hidden behind this harshness, he must yet admit that justice was done him, and that his reward was perfectly suitable to his conduct. In every punishment, as such, there must first be justice, and this constitutes the essence of the notion. Benevolence may, indeed, be united with it, but the man who has deserved punishment has not the least reason to reckon upon this.[7]

Since this matter of the direction of justification is central in our understanding of traditional retributivism, and not generally appreciated, it will be worth our while to pause over this paragraph. Kant holds here, as he later holds in the *Rechtslehre,* that once it has been decided that a given "mode and measure" of punishment is justified, then "he who inflicts punishment" may do so in such a way as to increase the long-term happiness of the criminal. This could be accomplished, for example, by using a prison term as an opportunity for reforming the criminal. But Kant's point is that reforming the criminal has nothing to do with justifying the infliction of punishment. It is not inflicted because it will give an opportunity for reform, but because it is merited. The passage does not need my gloss; it is transparently clear. Kant wants the justification of punishment to be such that the criminal "who could get no glimpse of kindness behind this harshness" would have to admit that punishment is warranted.

Suppose we tell the criminal, "We are punishing you for your own good." This is wrong because it is then open to him to raise the question whether he deserves punishment, and what you consider good to be. If he does not deserve punishment, we have no right to inflict it, especially in the name of some good of which the criminal may not approve. So long as we are to treat him as rational—a being with dignity—we cannot force our judgements of good upon him. This is what makes the appeal to supposedly good consequences "wavering and uncertain." They waver because the criminal has as much right as anyone to question them. They concern ends which he may reject, and means which he might rightly regard as unsuited to the ends.

In the "Supplementary Explanations of the Principles of Right" of the *Rechtslehre,* Kant distinguishes between "punitive justice *(justitia punitiva),* in which the ground of the penalty is moral *(quia peccatum est),*" and "punitive *expediency,* the foundation of which is merely pragmatic *(ne peccetur)* as being grounded on the experience of what operates most effectively to prevent crime." Punitive justice, says Kant, has an "entirely distinct place *(locus justi)* in the topical arrangement of the juridical conceptions." It does not seem reasonable to suppose that Kant makes this distinction merely to discard punitive expediency entirely, that he has no concern at all for the *ne peccetur.* But he does hold that there is no place for it in the justification of punishment proper: For this can only be to show the criminal that the punishment is just.

How is this to be done? The difficulty is that on the one hand the criminal must be treated as a rational being, an end in himself; but on the other hand the justification we offer him cannot be allowed to appear as the opening move in a rational discussion. It cannot turn on the criminal's acceptance of some premise which, as a rational being, he has a perfect right to question. If the end in question is the well-being of society, we are assuming that the criminal will not have a different view of what that well-being consists in, and we are telling him that he should sacrifice himself *to* that end. As a rational being, he can question whether any end we propose is a good end. And we have no right to demand that he sacrifice himself to the public well-being, even supposing he agrees with us on what that consists in. No man has a duty, on Kant's view, to be benevolent.[8]

The way out of the quandary is to show the criminal that we are not inflicting the punishment on him for some questionable purpose of our own choice, but that he, as a free agent, has exercised *his* choice in such a way as to make the punishment a necessary consequence. "His own evil deed draws the punishment upon himself."[9] "The undeserved evil which anyone commits on another, is to be regarded as perpetuated on himself."[10] But may not the criminal rationally question this asserted connection between crime and punishment? Suppose he wishes to regard the punishment *not* as "drawn upon himself" by his own "evil deed?" Suppose he argues that no good purpose will be served by punishing him? But this line of thought leads into the "serpent-windings of utilitarianism," for if it is good consequences that govern, then justice goes by the board. What may not be done to him in the name of good consequences? What proportion would remain between what he has done and what he suffers?[11]

But punishment is *inflicted.* To tell the criminal that he "draws it upon himself" is all very well, only how do we justify *to ourselves* the infliction of it? Kant's answer is found early in the *Rechtslehre.*[12] There he relates punishment to crime *via* freedom. Crime consists in compulsion or constraint of some kind: a hindrance of freedom.[13] If it is wrong that freedom should be hindered, it is right to block this hindrance. But to block the constraint of freedom it is necessary to apply constraint. Punishment is a "hindering of a hindrance of freedom." Compulsion of the criminal is, then, justified only to the extent that it hinders his compulsion of another.

But how are we to understand Kant here? Punishment comes after the crime. How can it hinder [it]? The reference cannot be to the hindrance of future crime, or Kant's doctrine reduces to a variety of utilitarianism. The picture of compulsion versus compulsion is clear enough, but how are we to apply it? Our answer must be somewhat speculative, since there is no direct answer to be found in the *Rechtslehre.* The answer must begin from yet another extension of the concept of a crime. For the crime cannot consist merely in an act. What is criminal is acting in accordance with a wrong maxim—a maxim which would, if made universal, destroy freedom. The adoption of the maxim is criminal. Should we regard punishment, then, as the hindrance of a wrong maxim? But how do we hinder a maxim? We show, exhibit, its wrongness by taking it at face value. If the criminal has adopted it, he is claiming that it can be universalized. But if it is

universalized it warrants the same treatment of the criminal as he has accorded to his victim. So if he murders he must be executed; if he steals we must "steal from" him.[14] What we do to him he willed, in willing to adopt his maxim as universalizable. To justify the punishment to the criminal is to show him that the compulsion we use on him proceeds according to the same rule by which he acts. This is how he "draws the punishment upon himself." In punishing, we are not adopting his maxim but demonstrating its logical consequences if universalized: We show the criminal *what* he has willed. This is the positive side of the Kantian rationale of punishment.

II.

Hegel's version of this rationale has attracted more attention, and disagreement, in recent literature. It is the Hegelian metaphysical terminology that is partly responsible for the disagreement and that has stood in the way of an understanding of the retributivist position. The difficulty turns around the notions of "annulment of crime" and punishment as the "right" of the criminal. Let us consider "annulment" first.

In the *Philosophie des Rechts*[15] Hegel tells us that

> Abstract right is a right to coerce, because the wrong which transgresses it is an exercise of force against the existence of my freedom in an external thing. The maintenance of this existent against the exercise of force therefore itself takes the form of an external act and an exercise of force annulling the force originally brought against it.[16]

Holmes complains that by the use of his logical apparatus, involving the negation of negations (or annulment), Hegel professes to establish what is only a mystic (though generally felt) bond between wrong and punishment.[17] Hastings Rashdall asks how any rational connection can be shown between the evil of the pain of punishment, and the twin evils of the suffering of the victim and the moral evil which "pollutes the offender's soul," unless appeal is made to the probable good consequences of punishment. The notion that the "guilt" of the offense must be, in some mysterious way, wiped out by the suffering of the offender does not seem to provide it.[18] Crime, which is an evil, is apparently to be "annulled" by the addition to it of punishment, which is another evil. How can two evils yield a good?[19]

But in fact Hegel is following the *Rechtslehre* quite closely here, and his doctrine is very near to Kant's. In the notes taken at Hegel's lectures,[20] we find Hegel quoted as follows:

> If crime and its annulment . . . are treated as if they were unqualified evils, it must, of course, seem quite unreasonable to will an evil merely because "another evil is there already." . . . But it is not merely a question of an evil or of this, that, or the other good; the precise point at issue is wrong, and the righting of it. . . . The various considerations which are relevant to punishment as a phenomenon and to the bearing it has on the particular consciousness, and which concern its effects (deterrent, reformative, etcetera) on the imagination, are an essential topic for examination in their place, especially in connection with modes of punishment, but all these considerations presuppose as their foundation the fact that punishment is inherently and actually just. In discussing this matter the only important things are, first, that crime is to be annulled, not because it is the producing of an evil, but because it is the infringing of the right as right, and secondly, the question of what that positive existence is which crime possesses and which must be annulled; it is this existence which is the real evil to be removed, and the essential point is the question of where it lies. So long as the concepts here at issue are not clearly apprehended, confusion must continue to reign in the theory of punishment.[21]

While this passage is not likely to dethrone confusion, it does bring us closer to the basically Kantian heart of Hegel's theory. To "annul crime" should be read "right wrong." Crime is a wrong which consists in an "infringement of the right as right."[22] It would be unjust, says Hegel, to allow crime, which is the invasion of a right, to go unrequited. For to allow this is to admit that the crime is "valid": that is, that it is not in conflict with justice. But this is what we do want to admit, and the only way of showing this is to pay back the deed to the agent: Coerce the coercer. For by intentionally violating his victim's rights, the criminal in effect claims that the rights of others are not binding on him; and this is to attack *das Recht* itself: the system

of justice in which there are rights which must be respected. Punishment not only keeps the system in balance, it vindicates the system itself.

Besides talking about punishment's "annulment" of crime, Hegel has argued that it is the "right of the criminal." The obvious reaction to this is that it is a strange justification of punishment which makes it someone's right, for it is at best a strange kind of right which no one would ever want to claim! McTaggart's explanation of this facet of Hegel's theory is epitomized in the following quotation:

> What, then, is Hegel's theory? It is, I think, briefly this: In sin, man rejects and defies the moral law. Punishment is pain inflicted on him because he has done this, and in order that he may, by the fact of his punishment, be forced into recognizing as valid the law which he rejected in sinning, and so repent of his sin—really repent, and not merely be frightened out of doing it again.[23]

If McTaggart is right, then we are obviously not going to find in Hegel anything relevant to the justification of legal punishment, where the notions of sin and repentance are out of place. And this is the conclusion McTaggart of course reaches. "Hegel's view of punishment," he insists, "cannot properly be applied in jurisprudence, and . . . his chief mistake regarding it lay in supposing that it could."[24]

But though McTaggart may be right in emphasizing the theological aspect of Hegel's doctrine of punishment, he is wrong in denying it a jurisprudential aspect. In fact, Hegel is only saying what Kant emphasized: That to justify punishment to the criminal is to show him that *he* has chosen to be treated as he is being treated.

> The injury (the penalty) which falls on the criminal is not merely *implicitly* just—as just, it is *eo ipso* his implicit will, an embodiment of his freedom, his right; on the contrary, it is also a right *established* within the criminal himself, that is, in his objectively embodied will, in his action. The reason for this is that his action is the action of a rational being and this implies that it is something universal and that by doing it the criminal has laid down a law which he has explicitly recognized in his action and under which in consequence he should be brought as under his right.[25]

To accept the retributivist position, then, is to accept a thesis about the burden of proof in the justification of punishment. Provided we make the punishment "equal" to the crime it is not up to us to justify it to the criminal, beyond pointing out to him that it is what he willed. It is not that he initiated a chain of events likely to result in his punishment, but that in willing the crime he willed that he himself should suffer in the same degree as his victim. But what if the criminal simply wanted to commit his crime and get away with it (break the window and run, take the funds and retire to Brazil, kill but live)? Suppose we explain to the criminal that *really* in willing to kill he willed to lose his life; and, unimpressed, he replies that *really* he wished to kill and save his skin. The retributivist answer is that to the extent that the criminal understands freedom and justice he will understand that his punishment was made inevitable by his own choice. No moral theory can hope to provide a justification of punishment which will seem such to the criminal merely as a nexus of passions and desires. The retributivist addresses him as a rational being, aware of the significance of his action. The burden of proof, the retributivist would argue, is on the theorist who would not start from this assumption. For to assume from the beginning that the criminal is not rational is to treat him, from the beginning, as merely a "harmful animal."

> What is involved in the action of the criminal is not only the concept of crime, the rational aspect present in crime as such whether the individual wills it or not, the aspect which the state has to vindicate, but also the abstract rationality of the individual's *volition.* Since that is so, punishment is regarded as containing the criminal's right and hence by being punished he is honored as a rational being. He does not receive this due of honor unless the concept and measure of his punishment are derived from his own act. Still less does he receive it if he is treated as a harmful animal who has to be made harmless, or with a view to deterring and reforming him.[26]

To address the criminal as a rational being aware of the significance of his action is to address him as a person who knows that he has not committed a "bare" act; to commit an act is to commit oneself to the universalization of the rule by which one acted. For a man to complain about the death sentence for murder is as absurd as for a man to complain that when he pushed down one tray of the scales, the other tray goes up; whereas the action, rightly considered, is of pushing down *and* up. "The criminal gives his consent already by his very act."[27] "The Eumenides sleep, but crime awakens them, and hence it is the very act of crime which vindicates itself."[28]

F. H. Bradley's contribution to the retributive theory of punishment adds heat but not much light. The central, and best-known, passage is the following:

> If there is any opinion to which the man of uncultivated morals is attached, it is the belief in the necessary connection of punishment and guilt. Punishment is punishment, only where it is deserved. We pay the penalty because we owe it, and for no other reason; and if punishment is inflicted for any other reason whatever than because it is merited by wrong, it is a gross immorality, a crying injustice, an abominable crime, and not what it pretends to be. We may have regard for whatever considerations we please—our own convenience, the good of society, the benefit of the offender; we are fools, and worse, if we fail to do so. Having once the right to punish, we may modify the punishment according to the useful and the pleasant; but these are external to the matter, they cannot give us a right to punish, and nothing can do that but criminal desert. This is not a subject to waste words over; if the fact of the vulgar view is not palpable to the reader, we have no hope, and no wish, to make it so.[29]

Bradley's sympathy with the "vulgar view" should be apparent. And there is at least a seeming variation between the position he expresses here and that we have attributed to Kant and Hegel. For Bradley can be read here as leaving an open field for utilitarian reasoning, when the question is how and how much to punish. Ewing interprets Bradley this way, and argues at some length that Bradley is involved in an inconsistency.[30] However, it is quite possible that Bradley did not mean to allow kind and quantity of punishment to be determined by utilitarian considerations. He could mean, as Kant meant, that once punishment is awarded, then "it" (what the criminal must suffer: time in jail, for example) may be made use of for utilitarian purposes. But, it should by this time go without saying, the retributivist would then wish to insist that we not argue backward from the likelihood of attaining these good purposes to the rightness of inflicting the punishment.

Bradley's language is beyond question loose when he speaks, in the passage quoted, of our "modifying" the punishment, "having once the right to punish." But when he says that "we pay the penalty because we owe it, and for no other reason," Bradley must surely be credited with the insight that we may owe more or less according to the gravity of the crime. The popular view, he says, is "that punishment is justice; that justice implies the giving what is due."[31] And "punishment is the complement of criminal desert; is justifiable only so far as deserved."[32] If Bradley accepts this popular view, then Ewing must be wrong in attributing to him the position that kind and degree of punishment may be determined by utilitarian considerations.[33]

III.

Let us sum up traditional retributivism, as we have found it expressed in the paradigmatic passage, we have examined. We have found no reason in Hegel or Bradley to take back or qualify importantly the *three propositions* we found central in Kant's retributivism:

i.   The only acceptable reason for punishing a man is that he has committed a crime.

ii. The only acceptable reason for punishing a man in a given manner and degree is that the punishment is "equal" to the crime.

iii. Whoever commits a crime must be punished in accordance with his desert.

To these propositions should be added *two underlying assumptions*:

i.   An assumption about the direction of justification: to the criminal.

ii. An assumption about the nature of justification: To show the criminal that it is he who has willed what he now suffers.

Though it may have been stated in forbidding metaphysical terms, traditional retributivism cannot be dismissed as unintelligible, or absurd, or implau-

sible.[34] There is no obvious contradiction in it; and there are no important disagreements among the philosophers we have studied over what it contends. Yet in spite of the importance of the theory, no one has yet done much more than sketch it in broad strokes. If, as I have surmised, it turns mainly on an assumption concerning the direction of justification, then this assumption should be explained and defended.

And the key concept of "desert" is intolerably vague. What does it mean to say that punishment must be proportionate to what a man *deserves?* This seems to imply, in the theory of the traditional retributivists, that there is some way of measuring desert, or at least of balancing punishment against it. How this measuring or balancing is supposed to be done, we will discuss later. What we must recognize here is that there are alternative criteria of "desert," and that it is not always clear which of these the traditional retributivist means to imply.

When we say of a man that he "deserves severe punishment" how, if at all, may we support our position by arguments? What kind of considerations tend to show what a man does or does not deserve? There are at least two general sorts: those which tend to show that what he has done is a member of a class of action which is especially heinous; and those which tend to show that his doing of this action was, in (or because of) the circumstances, particularly wicked. The argument that a man deserves punishment may rest on the first kind of appeal alone, or on both kinds. Retributivists who rely on the first sort of consideration alone would say that anyone who would do a certain sort of thing, no matter what the circumstances may have been, deserves punishment. Whether there are such retributivists I do not know. Kant, because of his insistence on *intention* as a necessary condition of committing a crime, clearly wishes to bring in considerations of the second sort as well. It is not, on his view, merely *what* was done, but the intention of the agent which must be taken into account. No matter what the intention, a man cannot commit a crime deserving punishment if his deed is not a transgression. But if he does commit a transgression, he must do so intentionally to commit a crime; and all crime is deserving of punishment. The desert of the crime is a factor both of the seriousness of the transgression, considered by itself, and the degree to which the intention to transgress was present. If, for Kant, the essence of morality consists in knowingly acting from duty, the essence of immorality consists in knowingly acting against duty.

The retributivist can perhaps avoid the question of how we decide that one crime is morally more heinous than another by hewing to his position that no such decision is necessary so long as we make the punishment "equal" to the crime. To accomplish this, he might argue, it is not necessary to argue to the *relative* wickedness of crimes. But at best this leaves us with the problem how we *do* make punishments equal to crimes, a problem which will not stop plaguing retributivists. And there is the problem *which* transgressions, intentionally committed, the retributivist is

to regard as crimes. Surely not every morally wrong action!

And how is the retributivist to fit in appeals to punitive expediency? None of our authors denies that such appeals may be made, but where and how do they tie into punitive justice? It will not do simply to say that justifying punishment to the criminal is one thing, and justifying it to society is another. Suppose we must justify in both directions at once? And who are "we" anyway—the players of which roles, at what stage of the game? And has the retributivist cleared himself of the charge, sure to arise, that the theory is but a cover for a much less commendable motive than respect for justice: elegant draping for naked revenge?

Endnotes

1. . . . [S]ince in our own time there are few defenders of retributivism, the position is most often referred to by writers who are opposed to it. This does not make for clarity. In the past few years, however, there has been an upsurge of interest, and some good articles have been written. Cf. esp. J. D: Mabbott, "Punishment," *Mind,* XLVIII (1939), pp. 152–167; C. S. Lewis, "The Humanitarian Theory of Punishment," *20th Century* (Australian), March, 1949; C. W. K. Mundle, "Punishment and Desert," *The Philosophical Quarterly,* IV (1954), pp. 216–228; A. S. Kaufman, "Anthony Quinton on Punishment," *Analysis,* October, 1959; and K. G. Armstrong, "The Retributivist Hits Back," *Mind,* LXX (1961), pp. 471–490.

2. *Rechtslehre.* Part Second, 49, E. Hastie translation, Edinburgh, 1887, pp. 195–197.

3. Ibid., p. 198. Cf. also the passage on p. 196 beginning "What, then, is to be said of such a proposal as to keep a Criminal alive who has been condemned to death. . . ."

4. Ibid., Prolegomena, General Divisions of the Metaphysic of Morals, IV. (Hastie, p. 38).

5. Ibid., p. 32.

6. Ibid., p. 32.

7. Book I, Ch. I, Sec. VIII, Theorem IV, Remark II (T. K. Abbott translation, 5th ed., revised, London, 1898, p. 127).

8. *Rechtslehre.*

9. "Supplementary Explanation of The Principles of Right," V.

10. Cf. long quote from the *Rechtslehre,* above.

11. How can the retributivist allow utilitarian considerations even in the administration of the sentence? Are we not then opportunistically imposing our conception

of good on the convicted man? How did we come by this right, which we did not have when he stood before the bar awaiting sentence? Kant would refer to the loss of his "Civil Personality"; but what rights remain with the "Inborn Personality," which is not lost? How is human dignity modified by conviction of crime?

12. Introduction to The Science of Right, General Definitions and Divisions, D. Right is Joined with the Title to Compel. (Hastie, p. 47).

13. This extends the definition of crime Kant has given earlier by specifying the nature of an imputable transgression of duty.

14. There are serious difficulties in the application of the "Principle of Equality" to the "mode and measure" of punishment. This will be considered. . . .

15. I shall use this short title for the work with the formidable double title of *Naturrecht und Stattswissenschaft in Grundrisse; Grundlinien der Philosophie des Rechts (Natural Law and Political Science in Outline: Elements of The Philosophy of Right.)* References will be to the T. M. Knox translation *(Hegel's Philosophy of Right,* Oxford, 1942).

16. *Philosophie des Rechts,* Sect. 93 (Knox, p. 67).

17. O.W. Holmes, Jr., *The Common Law, Boston,* 1881, p. 42.

18. Hastings Rashdall, *The Theory of Good and Evil,* 2nd. Edn., Oxford, 1924, vol. 1, pp. 285–286.

19. G.E. Moore holds that, consistently with his doctrine of organic wholes, they might; or at least they might yield that which is less evil than the sum of the constituent evils. This indicates for him a possible vindication of the Retributive theory of punishment. *(Principia Ethica,* Cambridge, 1903, pp. 213–214).

20. Included in the Knox translation.
21. Knox translation, pp. 69–70.
22. There is an unfortunate ambiguity in the German word *Recht,* here translated as "right." The word can mean either that which is a right or that which is in accordance with the law. So when Hegel speaks of "infringing the right as right" it is not certain whether he means a right as such or the law as such, or whether, in fact, he is aware of the ambiguity. But to say that the crime infringes the law is analytic, so we will take it that Hegel uses *Recht* here to refer to that which is right. But what the criminal does is not merely to infringe a right, but "the right (*das recht*) as right," that is, to challenge by his action the whole system of rights. (On *"Recht,"* Cf. J. Austin, *The Province of Jurisprudence Determined* (London, Library of Ideas Edition, 1954), Note 26, pp. 285–288 esp. pp. 287–288).
23. J. M. E. McTaggart, *Studies in The Hegelian Cosmology,* Cambridge, 1901, Ch. V, p. 133.
24. Ibid., p. 145.
25. Op Cit., Sect. 100 (Hastie, p. 70.)
26. Ibid., Lecture-notes on Sect. 100, Hastie, p. 71.

27. Ibid., Addition to Sect. 100, Hastie, p. 246.
28. Ibid., Addition to Sect. 101, Hastie, p. 247. There is something ineradicably *curious* about retributivism. We keep coming back to the metaphor of the balance scale. Why is the metaphor powerful and the same time strange? Why do we agree so readily that "the assassination" cannot "trammel up the consequence," that "evenhanded justice commends the ingredients of our poisoned chalice to our own lips?"
29. F. H. Bradley, *Ethical Studies,* Oxford, 1952, pp. 26–27.
30. A. C. Ewing, *The Morality of Punishment,* London, 1929, pp. 41–42.
31. Op. Cit., p. 29.
32. Ibid., p. 30.
33. Op. Cit., p. 41.
34. Or, more ingeniously, "merely logical," the "elucidation of the use of a word"; answering the question, "When (logically) *can* we punish?" as opposed to the question answered by the utilitarians, "When (morally) *may* or *ought* we to punish?" (Cf. A. M. Quinton, "On Punishment," *Analysis,* June, 1954, pp. 133–142).

72. *Deterrence and Uncertainty*

Ernest van den Haag

Ernest van den Haag argues that although we don't know for sure whether capital punishment deters would-be offenders, the greater severity of capital punishment still gives us reason to expect more deterrence from it. Accordingly, van den Haag maintains that the burden of proof is on opponents of capital punishment to show why the greater severity of capital punishment does not lead to more deterrence.

. . . If we do not know whether the death penalty will deter others [in a uniquely effective way], we are confronted with two uncertainties. If we impose the death penalty, and achieve no deterrent effect thereby, the life of a convicted murderer has been expended in vain (from a deterrent viewpoint). There is a net loss. If we impose the death sentence and thereby deter

Reprinted with permission of the publisher from the *Journal of Criminal Law, Criminology and Police Science,* vol. 60, no. 2 (1969).

some future murderers, we spared the lives of some future victims (the prospective murderers gain too; they are spared punishment because they were deterred). In this case, the death penalty has led to a net gain, unless the life of a convicted murderer is valued more highly than that of the unknown victim, or victims (and the nonimprisonment of the deterred nonmurderer).

The calculation can be turned around, of course. The absence of the death penalty may harm no one and therefore produce a gain—the life of the convicted murderer. Or it may kill future victims of murderers who could have been deterred, and thus produce a loss—their life.

To be sure, we must risk something certain—the death (or life) of the convicted man, for something uncertain—the death (or life) of the victims of murderers who may be deterred. This is in the nature of uncertainty—when we invest, or gamble, we risk the money we have for an uncertain gain. Many human actions, most commitments—including marriage and crime—share this characteristic with the deterrent purpose of any penalization, and with its rehabilitative purpose (and even with the protective).

More proof is demanded for the deterrent effect of the death penalty than is demanded for the deterrent effect of other penalties. This is not justified by the absence of other utilitarian purposes such as protection and rehabilitation; they involve no less uncertainty than deterrence.[1]

Irrevocability may support a demand for some reason to expect more deterrence than revocable penalties might produce, but not a demand for more proof of deterrence. . . . The reason for expecting more deterrence lies in the greater severity, the terrifying effect inherent in finality. Since it seems more important to spare victims than . . . murderers, the burden of proving that the greater severity inherent in irrevocability adds nothing to deterrence lies on those who oppose capital punishment. Proponents of the death penalty need show only that there is no more uncertainty about it than about greater severity in general.

The demand that the death penalty be proved more deterrent than alternatives cannot be satisfied any more than the demand that six years in prison be proved to be more deterrent than three. But the uncertainty that confronts us favors the death penalty as long as [it] might save future victims of murder. This effect is as plausible as the general idea that penalties have deterrent effects which increase with their severity. Though we have no proof of the positive deterrence of the penalty, we also have no proof of zero, or negative effectiveness. I believe we have no right to risk additional future victims of murder for the sake of sparing convicted murderers; on the contrary, our moral obligation is to risk the possible ineffectiveness of executions. However rationalized, the opposite view appears to be motivated by the simple fact that executions are more subjected to social control than murder. However, this applies to all penalties and does not argue for the abolition of any.

Endnote

1. Rehabilitation or protection are of minor importance in our actual penal system (though not in our theory). We confine many people who do not need rehabilitation and against whom we do not need protection (e.g., the exasperated husband who killed his wife); we release many unrehabilitated offenders against whom protection is needed. Certainly rehabilitation and protection are not, and deterrence is, the main actual function of legal punishment, if we disregard nonutilitarian purposes.

73. *Civilization, Safety, and Deterrence*

JEFFREY H. REIMAN

Jeffrey Reiman maintains that greater severity in and of itself does not mean more deterrence. Moreover, Reiman argues if greater severity were always justified on grounds of producing more deterrence, then torturing criminals to death would be justified because torturing criminals to death is clearly a more severe punishment than simply executing them.

. . . By placing execution alongside torture in the category of things we will not do to our fellow human beings even when they deserve them, we broadcast the message that totally subjugating a person to the power of others *and* confronting him with the advent of his own humanly administered demise is too horrible to be done by civilized human beings to their fellows even when they have earned it: too horrible to do, and too horrible to be capable of doing. And I contend that broadcasting this message loud and clear would in the long run contribute to the general detestation of murder and be, to the extent to which it worked itself into the hearts and minds of the populace, a deterrent. In short, refusing to execute murderers though they deserve it both reflects and continues the taming of the human species that we call civilization. Thus, I take it that the abolition of the death penalty, though it is a just punishment for murder, is part of the civilizing mission of modern states. . . .

. . . I said that judging a practice too horrible to do even to those who deserve it does not exclude the possibility that it could be justified if necessary to avoid even worse consequences. Thus, were the death penalty clearly proven a better deterrent to the murder of innocent people than life in prison, we might have to admit that we had not yet reached a level of civilization at which we could protect ourselves without imposing this horrible fate on murderers, and thus we might have to grant the necessity of instituting the death penalty. But this is far from proven. The available research by no means clearly indicates that the death penalty reduces the incidence of homicide more than life imprisonment does. . . .

Conceding that it has not been proven that the death penalty deters more murders than life imprisonment, van den Haag has argued that neither has it been proven that the death penalty does *not* deter more murders, and thus we must follow common sense which teaches that the higher the cost of something, the fewer people will choose it, and therefore at least some potential murderers who would not be

deterred by life imprisonment will be deterred by the death penalty. Van den Haag writes:

> . . . our experience shows that the greater the threatened penalty, the more it deters.
>
> . . . Life in prison is still life, however unpleasant. In contrast, the death penalty does not just threaten to make life unpleasant—it threatens to take life altogether. This difference is perceived by those affected. We find that when they have the choice between life in prison and execution, 99 percent of all prisoners under sentence of death prefer life in prison. . . .
>
> From this unquestioned fact a reasonable conclusion can be drawn in favor of the superior deterrent effect of the death penalty. Those who have the choice in practice . . . fear death more than they fear life in prison. . . . If they do, it follows that the threat of the death penalty, all other things equal, is likely to deter more than the threat of life in prison. One is most deterred by what one fears most. From which it follows that whatever statistics fail, or do not fail, to show, the death penalty is likely to be more deterrent than any other.[1]

Those of us who recognize how common sensical it was, and still is, to believe that the sun moves around the earth, will be less willing than Professor van den Haag to follow common sense here, especially when it comes to doing something awful to our fellows. Moreover, there are good reasons for doubting common sense on this matter. Here are four:

1. From the fact that one penalty is more feared than another, it does not follow that the more feared penalty will deter more than the less feared, unless we know that the less feared penalty is not fearful enough to deter everyone who can be deterred—and this is just what we don't know with regard to the death penalty. Though I fear the death penalty more than life in prison, I can't think of any act that the death penalty would deter me from that an equal likelihood of spending my life in prison wouldn't deter me from as well. Since it seems to me that whoever would be deterred by a given likelihood of death would be deterred by an *equal* likelihood of life behind bars, I suspect that the commonsense argument only seems plausible because we evaluate it unconsciously assuming that potential criminals will face larger likeli-

From Jeffrey H. Reiman, "Justice, Civilization, and the Death Penalty: Answering van den Haag." *Philosophy and Public Affairs,* vol. 14 (Spring 1985). Excerpt, pp. 141–147, reprinted with permission of Princeton University Press.

hoods of death sentences than of life sentences. If the likelihoods were equal, . . . where life imprisonment was improbable enough to make it too distant a possibility to worry much about, a similar low probability of death would have the same effect. After all, we are undeterred by small likelihoods of death every time we walk the streets. And if life imprisonment were sufficiently probable to pose a real deterrent threat, it would pose as much of a deterrent threat as death. And this is just what most of the research we have on the comparative deterrent impact of execution versus life imprisonment suggests.

2. In light of the fact that roughly 500 to 700 suspected felons are killed by the police in the line of duty every year, and the fact that the number of privately owned guns in [the United States] is substantially larger than the number of households . . . , it must be granted that anyone contemplating committing a crime *already* faces a substantial risk of ending up dead. . . . It's hard to see why anyone *who is not already deterred by this* would be deterred by the addition of the more distant risk of death after apprehension, conviction, and appeal. Indeed, this suggests that people consider risks in a much cruder way than van den Haag's appeal to common sense suggests—which should be evident to anyone who contemplates how few people use seatbelts (14 percent of drivers, on some estimates), when it is widely known that wearing them can spell the difference between life (outside prison) and death.

3. Van den Haag has maintained that deterrence does not work only by means of cost-benefit calculations made by potential criminals. It works also by the lesson about the wrongfulness of murder that is slowly learned in a society that subjects murderers to the ultimate punishment.[2] But if I am correct in claiming that the refusal to execute even those who deserve it has a civilizing effect, then the refusal to execute also teaches a lesson about the wrongfulness of murder. My claim here is admittedly speculative, but no more so than van den Haag's to the contrary. [My] view has the added virtue of accounting for the failure of research to show an increased deterrent effect from executions *without having to deny the plausibility of van den Haag's common sense argument that at least some additional potential murderers will be deterred by the pros-*

pect of the death penalty. If there is a deterrent effect from *not executing,* then . . . while executions will deter some murderers, this effect will be balanced by the weakening of the deterrent effect of not executing, such that no net reduction in murders will result. And this . . . also disposes of van den Haag's argument that, in the absence of knowledge one way or the other on the deterrent effect of executions, we should execute murderers rather than risk the lives of innocent people whose murders might have been deterred. . . . If there is a deterrent effect of not executing, it follows that we risk innocent lives either way. And if this is so, it seems that the only reasonable course of action is to refrain from imposing what we know is a horrible fate.

4. Those who still think that van den Haag's common-sense argument for executing murderers is valid will find that the argument proves more than they bargained for. Van den Haag maintains that, in the absence of conclusive evidence on the relative deterrent impact of the death penalty versus life imprisonment, we must follow common sense and assume that if one punishment is more fearful than another, it will deter some potential criminals not deterred by the less fearful punishment. Since people sentenced to death will almost universally try to get their sentences changed to life in prison, it follows that death is more fearful than life imprisonment, and thus . . . will deter some additional murderers. Consequently, we should institute the death penalty to save the lives these additional murderers would have taken. But, since people sentenced to be tortured to death would surely try to get their sentences changed to simple execution, the same argument proves that death-by-torture will deter still more potential murderers. Consequently, we should institute death-by-torture to save the lives these additional murderers would have taken. Anyone who accepts van den Haag's argument is then confronted with a dilemma: Until we have conclusive evidence that capital punishment is a greater deterrent to murder than life imprisonment, he must grant *either* that we should not follow common sense and not impose the death penalty; *or* we should follow common sense and torture murderers to death. In short, either we must abolish the electric chair or reinstitute the rack. Surely, this is the *reductio ad absurdum* of van den Haag's common sense argument.

Endnotes

1. Ernest van den Haag and John P. Conrad, *The Death Penalty: A Debate* (New York: Plenum Press, 1983), pp. 68–69.

2. Ibid., p. 63.

74. *Gregg v. Georgia*

SUPREME COURT OF THE UNITED STATES

The issue before the Supreme Court of the United States was whether capital punishment violates the Eighth Amendment's prohibition of cruel and unusual punishment. The majority of the Court held that it does not violate this prohibition because capital punishment (1) accords with contemporary standards of decency, (2) may serve some deterrent or retributive purpose that is not degrading to human dignity, and (3) is no longer arbitrarily applied in the case of the Georgia law under review. Dissenting Justice Brennan argued that (1) through (3) do not suffice to show that capital punishment is constitutional; it would further have to be shown that capital punishment is not degrading to human dignity. Dissenting Justice Marshall objected to the majority's decision on the grounds that capital punishment is not necessary for deterrence and that a retributive purpose for it is not consistent with human dignity. He also contended that contemporary standards of decency with respect to capital punishment are not based on informed opinion.

We address initially the basic contention that the punishment of death for the crime of murder is, under all circumstances, "cruel and unusual" in violation of the Eighth and Fourteenth Amendments of the Constitution. . . .

The Court on a number of occasions has both assumed and asserted the constitutionality of capital punishment. In several cases that assumption provided a necessary foundation for the decision, as the Court was asked to decide whether a particular method of carrying out a capital sentence would be allowed to stand under the Eighth Amendment. But until *Furman v. Georgia* (1972), the Court never confronted squarely the fundamental claim that the punishment of death always, regardless of the enormity of the offense or the procedure followed in imposing the sentence, is cruel and unusual punishment in violation of the Constitution. Although this issue was presented and addressed in *Furman*, it was not resolved. . . . Four Justices would have held that capital punishment is not unconstitutional *per se;* two Justices would have reached the opposite conclusion; and three Justices, while agreeing that the statutes then before the Court were invalid as applied, left open the question whether such punishment may ever be imposed. We now hold that the punishment of death does not invariably violate the Constitution. . . .

It is clear from the foregoing precedents that the Eighth Amendment has not been regarded as a static concept. As Mr. Chief Justice Warren said, in an oft-quoted phrase, "[t]he Amendment must draw its meaning from the evolving standards of decency that mark the progress of a maturing society." . . . Thus, an assessment of contemporary values concerning the infliction of a challenged sanction is relevant to the application of the Eighth Amendment. As we develop below more fully, this assessment does not call for a subjective judgment. It requires, rather, that we look to objective indicia that reflect the public attitude toward a given sanction.

But our cases also make clear that public perceptions of standards of decency with respect to criminal sanctions are not conclusive. A penalty also must accord with "the dignity of man," which is the "basic concept underlying the Eighth Amendment." This means, at least, that the punishment not be "excessive." When a form of punishment in the abstract (in this case, whether capital punishment may ever be imposed as a sanction for murder) rather than in the particular (the propriety of death as a penalty to be applied to a specific defendant for a specific crime) is under consideration, the inquiry into "excessiveness" has two aspects. First, the punishment must not involve the unnecessary and wanton infliction of pain. Second, the punishment must not be grossly out of proportion to the severity of the crime.

Of course, the requirements of the Eighth Amendment must be applied with an awareness of the limited role to be played by the courts. This does not mean that judges have no role to play, for the Eighth Amendment is a restraint upon the exercise of legislative power. . . .

But, while we have an obligation to insure that constitutional bounds are not overreached, we may not act as judges as we might as legislators.

> Courts are not representative bodies. They are not designed to be a good reflex of a democratic society. Their judgment is best informed, and therefore most dependable, within narrow limits. Their essential quality is detachment, founded on independence. History teaches that the independence of the judiciary is jeopardized when courts become embroiled in the passions of the day and assume primary responsibility in choosing between competing political, economic and social pressures. *Dennis v. United States* (1951)

Therefore, in assessing a punishment selected by a democratically elected legislature against the constitutional measure, we presume its validity. We may not require the legislature to select the least severe penalty possible so long as the penalty selected is not cruelly inhumane or disproportionate to the crime involved. And a heavy burden rests on those who would attack the judgment of the representatives of the people.

This is true in part because the constitutional test is intertwined with an assessment of contemporary standards and the legislative judgment weighs heavily in ascertaining such standards. "[I]n a democratic society legislatures, not courts, are constituted to respond to the will and consequently the moral values of the people." *Furman v. George.* The deference we owe to the decisions of the state legislatures under our federal system, is enhanced where the specification of punishments is concerned, for "these are peculiarly questions of legislative policy." *Gore v. United States.* . . . A decision that a given punishment is impermissible under the Eighth Amendment cannot be reversed short of a constitutional amendment. The ability of the people to express their preference through the normal democratic processes, as well as through ballot referenda, is shut off. Revisions cannot be made in the light of further experience.

. . . We now consider specifically whether . . . death for the crime of murder is a *per se* violation of the Eighth and Fourteenth Amendments to the Constitution. We note first that history and precedent strongly support a negative answer to this question.

The imposition of the death penalty for the crime of murder has a long history of acceptance both in the United States and in England. The common-law rule imposed a mandatory death sentence on all convicted murderers. And the penalty continued to be used into the twentieth century by most American States, although the breadth of the common-law rule was diminished, initially by narrowing the class of murders to be punished by death and subsequently by widespread adoption of laws expressly granting juries the discretion to recommend mercy.

It is apparent from the text of the Constitution itself that the existence of capital punishment was accepted by the Framers. At the time the Eighth Amendment was ratified, capital punishment was a common sanction in every State. Indeed, the First Congress of the United States enacted legislation providing death as the penalty for specific crimes. . . .

For nearly two centuries, this Court, repeatedly and often expressly, has recognized that capital punishment is not invalid *per se*. . . .

Four years ago, the petitioners in *Furman* and its companion cases predicated their argument primarily on the asserted proposition that standards of decency had evolved to the point where capital punishment no longer could be tolerated. The petitioners in those cases said, in effect, that the evolutionary process had come to an end, and that standards of decency required that the Eighth Amendment be construed finally as prohibiting capital punishment for any crime regardless of its depravity and impact on society. This view was accepted by two Justices. Three others were unwilling to go so far; focusing on the procedures by which convicted defendants were selected for the death penalty rather than on the actual punishment inflicted, they joined in the conclusion that the statutes before the Court were constitutionally invalid.

The petitioners . . . before the Court today renew the "standards of decency" argument, but developments . . . since *Furman* have undercut substantially the assumptions on which their argument rested. Despite the continuing debate, dating back to the nineteenth century, over the morality and utility of capital punishment, it is now evident that a large proportion of American society continues to regard it as an appropriate and necessary criminal sanction.

The most marked indication of society's endorsement of the death penalty for murder is the legislative response to *Furman*. The legislatures of at least thirty-five States have enacted new statutes that provide for the death penalty for at least some crimes that result in the death of another person. And the Congress of the United States, in 1974, enacted a statute providing the death penalty for aircraft piracy that results in death. These recently adopted statutes have attempted to address the concerns expressed by the Court in *Furman* primarily (i) by specifying the factors to be weighed and the procedures to be followed in deciding when to impose a capital sentence, or (ii) by making the death penalty mandatory for specified crimes. But all of the post-*Furman* statutes make clear that capital punishment itself has not been rejected by the elected representatives of the people. . . .

As we have seen, however, the Eighth Amendment demands more than that a challenged punishment be acceptable to contemporary society. The Court also must ask whether it comports with the basic concept of human dignity at the core of the Amendment. Although we cannot "invalidate a category of penalties because we deem less severe penalties adequate to serve the ends of penology," the sanction imposed cannot be so totally without penological justification that it results in the gratuitous infliction of suffering.

The death penalty is said to serve two principal social purposes: retribution and deterrence of capital crimes by prospective offenders.

In part, capital punishment is an expression of society's moral outrage at particularly offensive conduct. This function may be unappealing to many, but it is essential in an ordered society that asks its citizens to rely on legal processes rather than self-help to vindicate their wrongs.

> The instinct for retribution is part of the nature of man, and channeling that instinct in the administration of criminal justice serves an important purpose in promoting the stability of a society governed by law. When people begin to believe that organized society is unwilling or unable to impose upon criminal offenders the punishment they "deserve," then there are sown the seeds of anarchy—of self-help, vigilante justice, and lynch law. *Furman v. Georgia.*

"Retribution is no longer the dominant objective of the criminal law," but neither is it a forbidden objective nor one inconsistent with our respect for the dignity of men. Indeed, the decision that capital punishment may be the appropriate sanction in extreme cases is an expression of the community's belief that certain crimes are themselves so grievous an affront to humanity that the only adequate response may be the penalty of death.

Statistical attempts to evaluate the worth of the death penalty as a deterrent to crimes by potential offenders have occasioned a great deal of debate. The results simply have been inconclusive. As one opponent of capital punishment has said:

> [A]fter all possible inquiry, including the probing of all possible methods of inquiry, we do not know; and for systematic and easily visible reasons cannot know; what the truth about this "deterrent" effect may be. . . .
>
> The inescapable flaw is . . . that social conditions in any state are not constant through time, and that social conditions are not the same in any two states. If an effect were observed (and the observed effects, one way or another, are not large) then one could not at all tell whether any of this effect is attributable to the presence or absence of capital punishment. A "scientific"—that is to say, a soundly based—conclusion is simply impossible, and no

methodological path out of this tangle suggests itself. C. Black, *Capital Punishment: The Inevitability of Caprice and Mistake* 25–26 (1974).

Although some of the studies suggest that the death penalty may not function as a significantly greater deterrent than lesser penalties, there is no convincing empirical evidence either supporting or refuting this view. We may nevertheless assume safely that there are murderers, such as those who act in passion, for whom the threat of death has little or no deterrent effect. But for many others, the death penalty undoubtedly is a significant deterrent. There are carefully contemplated murders, such as murder for hire, where the possible penalty of death may well enter into the cold calculus that precedes the decision to act. And there are some categories of murder, such as murder by a life prisoner, where other sanctions may not be adequate.

The value of capital punishment as a deterrent of crime is a complex factual issue the resolution of which properly rests with the legislatures, which can evaluate the results of statistical studies in terms of their own local conditions and with a flexibility of approach that is not available to the courts. . . .

In sum, we cannot say that the judgment of the Georgia Legislature that capital punishment may be necessary in some cases is clearly wrong. Considerations of federalism, as well as respect for the ability of a legislature to evaluate, in terms of its particular State, the moral consensus concerning the death penalty and its social utility as a sanction, require us to conclude, in the absence of more convincing evidence, that the infliction of death as a punishment for murder is not without justification and thus is not unconstitutionally severe.

Finally, we must consider whether the punishment of death is disproportionate in relation to the crime for which it is imposed. There is no question that death as a punishment is unique in its severity and irrevocability. When a defendant's life is at stake, the Court has been particularly sensitive to insure that every safeguard is observed. But we are concerned here only with the imposition of capital punishment for the crime of murder, and when a life has been taken deliberately by the offender, we cannot say that the punishment is invariably disproportionate to the crime. It is an extreme sanction, suitable to the most extreme of crimes.

We hold that the death penalty is not a form of punishment that may never be imposed, regardless of the circumstances of the offense, regardless of the character of the offender, and regardless of the procedure followed in reaching the decision to impose it.

We now consider whether Georgia may impose the death penalty on the petitioner in this case. . . .

The basic concern of *Furman* centered on those defendants who were being condemned to death capriciously and arbitrarily. Under the procedures before the Court in that case, sentencing authorities were not directed to give attention to the nature or circumstances of the crime committed or the [defendant's] character or record. . . . Left unguided, juries imposed the death sentence in a way that could only be called freakish. The new Georgia sentencing procedures, by contrast, focus the jury's attention on the particularized nature of the crime and the particularized characteristics of the individual defendant. While the jury is permitted to consider any aggravating or mitigating circumstances, it must find and identify at least one statutory aggravating factor before it may impose a penalty of death. In this way the jury's discretion is channeled. No longer can a jury wantonly and freakishly impose the death sentence; it is always circumscribed by legislative guidelines. In addition, the review function of the Supreme Court of Georgia affords additional assurance that the concerns that prompted our decision in *Furman* are not present to any significant degree in the Georgia procedure applied here.

For the reasons expressed in this opinion, we hold that the statutory system under which Gregg was sentenced to death does not violate the Constitution. Accordingly, the judgment of the Georgia Supreme Court is affirmed. . . .

Mr. Justice *Brennan,* dissenting.*

The Cruel and Unusual Punishments Clause "must draw its meaning from the evolving standards of decency that mark the progress of a maturing society." The opinions of Mr. Justice Stewart, Mr. Justice Powell, and Mr. Justice Stevens today hold that "evolving

---

*[This opinion applies also to No. 75-5706, *Proffitt v. Florida, post,* p. 242, and No. 75-5394, *Jurek v. Texas, post,* p. 262.]

standards of decency" require focus not on the essence of the death penalty itself but primarily upon the procedures employed by the State to single out persons to suffer the penalty of death. Those opinions hold further that, so viewed, the Clause invalidates the mandatory infliction of the death penalty but not its infliction under sentencing procedures that Mr. Justice Stewart, Mr. Justice Powell, and Mr. Justice Stevens conclude adequately safeguard against the risk that the death penalty was imposed in an arbitrary and capricious manner.

In *Furman v. Georgia,* I read "evolving standards of decency" as requiring focus on the essence of the death penalty itself and not primarily or solely on the procedures under which the determination to inflict the penalty upon a particular person was made. . . .

This Court inescapably has the duty, as the ultimate arbiter of the meaning of our Constitution, to say whether, when individuals condemned to death stand before our Bar, "moral concepts" require us to hold that the law has progressed to the point where we should declare that the punishment of death, like punishments on the rack, the screw, and the wheel, is no longer morally tolerable in our civilized society. My opinion in *Furman v. Georgia* concluded that our civilization and the law had progressed to this point and that therefore the punishment of death, for whatever crime and under all circumstances, is "cruel and unusual" in violation of the Eighth and Fourteenth Amendments of the Constitution. I shall not again canvass the reasons that led to that conclusion. I emphasize only that foremost among the "moral concepts" recognized in our cases and inherent in the Clause is the primary moral principle that the State, even as it punishes, must treat its citizens in a manner consistent with their intrinsic worth as human beings—a punishment must not be so severe as to be degrading to human dignity. A judicial determination whether the punishment of death comports with human dignity is therefore not only permitted but compelled by the Clause.

. . . Death for whatever crime and under all circumstances "is truly an awesome punishment. The calculated killing of a human being by the State involves, by its very nature, a denial of the executed person's humanity. . . . An executed person has indeed 'lost the right to have rights.'" Death is not only an unusually severe punishment, unusual in its pain, in its finality, and in its enormity, but it serves no penal purpose more effectively than a less severe punishment; therefore the principle inherent in the Clause that prohibits pointless infliction of excessive punishment when less severe punishment can adequately achieve the same purposes invalidates the punishment. . . .

Mr. Justice *Marshall,* dissenting.

. . . My sole purposes here are to consider the suggestion that my conclusion in *Furman* has been undercut by developments since then, and briefly to evaluate the basis for my Brethren's holding that the extinction of life is a permissible form of punishment under the Cruel and Unusual Punishments Clause.

In *Furman* I concluded that the death penalty is constitutionally invalid for two reasons. First, the death penalty is excessive. And second, the American people, fully informed as to the purposes of the death penalty and its liabilities, would in my view reject it as morally unacceptable.

Since the decision in *Furman,* the legislatures of thirty-five States have enacted new statutes authorizing the imposition of the death sentence for certain crimes, and Congress has enacted a law providing the death penalty for air piracy resulting in death. I would be less than candid if I did not acknowledge that these developments have a significant bearing on a realistic assessment of the moral acceptability of the death penalty to the American people. But if the constitutionality of the death penalty turns, as I have urged, on the opinion of an *informed* citizenry, then even the enactment of new death statutes cannot be viewed as conclusive. In *Furman,* I observed that the American people are largely unaware of the information critical to a judgment on the morality of the death penalty, and concluded that if they were better informed they would consider it shocking, unjust, and unacceptable. A recent study, conducted after the enactment of the post-*Furman* statutes, has confirmed that the American people know little about the death penalty , and that the opinions of an informed public would differ significantly from those of a public unaware of the consequences and effects of the death penalty.

Even assuming, however, that the post-*Furman* enactment of statutes authorizing the death penalty renders the prediction of the views of an informed citizenry an uncertain basis for a constitutional decision, the enactment of those statutes has no bearing whatsoever on the conclusion that the death penalty is unconstitutional because it is excessive. An excessive penalty is invalid under the Cruel and Unusual Punishments Clause "even though popular sentiment may favor" it. The inquiry here, then, is simply whether the death penalty is necessary to accomplish the legitimate legislative purposes in punishment, or whether a less severe penalty—life imprisonment—would do as well.

The two purposes that sustain the death penalty as nonexcessive in the Court's view are general deterrence and retribution. In *Furman,* I canvassed the relevant data on the deterrent effect of capital punishment. The state of knowledge at that point, after literally centuries of debate, was summarized as follows by a United Nations Committee:

> It is generally agreed between the retentionists and abolitionists, whatever their opinions about the validity of comparative studies of deterrence, that the data which now exist show no correlation between the existence of capital punishment and lower rates of capital crime.

The available evidence, I concluded in *Furman,* was convincing that "capital punishment is not necessary as a deterrent to crime in our society."

The Solicitor General in his *amicus* brief in these cases relies heavily on a study by Isaac Ehrlich, reported a year after *Furman,* to support the contention that the death penalty does deter murder. . . .

. . . Ehrlich found a negative correlation between changes in the homicide rate and changes in execution risk. His tentative conclusion was that for the period from 1933 to 1967 each additional execution in the United States might have saved eight lives.

The methods and conclusions of the Ehrlich study have been severely criticized on a number of grounds. . . .

. . . Analysis of Ehrlich's data reveals that all empirical support for the deterrent effect of capital punishment disappears when the five most recent years are removed from his time series—that is to say, whether a decrease in the execution risk corresponds to an increase or a decrease in the murder rate depends on the ending point of the sample period. This

finding has cast severe doubts on the reliability of Ehrlich's tentative conclusions. . . .

The Ehrlich study, in short, is of little, if any, assistance in assessing the deterrent impact of the death penalty. The evidence I reviewed in *Furman* remains convincing, in my view, that "capital punishment is not necessary as a deterrent to crime in our society." The justification for the death penalty must be found elsewhere.

The other principal purpose said to be served by the death penalty is retribution. The notion that retribution can serve as a moral justification for the sanction of death finds credence in the opinion of my Brothers Stewart, Powell, and Stevens, and that of my Brother White in *Roberts* v. *Louisiana.* It is this notion that I find to be the most disturbing aspect of today's unfortunate decisions.

The concept of retribution is a multifaceted one, and any discussion of its role in the criminal law must be undertaken with caution. On one level, it can be said that the notion of retribution or reprobation is the basis of our insistence that only those who have broken the law be punished, and in this sense the notion is quite obviously central to a just system of criminal sanctions. But our recognition that retribution plays a crucial role in determining who may be punished by no means requires approval of retribution as a general justification for punishment. It is the question whether retribution can provide a moral justification for punishment—in particular, capital punishment—that we must consider. . . .

The . . . contentions—that society's expression of moral outrage through the imposition of the death penalty pre-empts the citizenry from taking the law into its own hands and reinforces moral values—are not retributive in the purest sense. They are essentially utilitarian in that they portray the death penalty as valuable because of its beneficial results. These justifications for the death penalty are inadequate because the penalty is, quite clearly I think, not necessary to the accomplishment of those results.

There remains for consideration, however, what might be termed the purely retributive justification for the death penalty—that the death penalty is appropriate, not because of its beneficial effect on society, but because the taking of the murderer's life is itself morally good. . . .

The mere fact that the community demands the murderer's life in return for the evil he has done cannot sustain the death penalty for . . . "The Eighth Amendment demands more than that a challenged punishment be acceptable to contemporary society." To be sustained under the Eighth Amendment, the death penalty must "compor[t] with the basic concept of human dignity at the core of the Amendment"; the objective in imposing it must be "[consistent] with our respect for the dignity of [other] men." Under these standards, the taking of life "because the wrongdoer deserves it" surely must fall, for such a punishment has at its very basis the total denial of the wrongdoer's dignity and worth.

The death penalty, unnecessary to promote the goal of deterrence or to further any legitimate notion of retribution, is an excessive penalty forbidden by the Eighth and Fourteenth Amendments. I respectfully dissent from the Court's judgment upholding the sentences of death imposed upon the petitioners in these cases.

Suggestions for Further Reading

Anthologies

Acton, H. B. *The Philosophy of Punishment*. London: Macmillan & Co., 1969.

Adams, David. *Philosophical Problems in the Law*. Belmont: Wadsworth Publishing Co., 1996.

Altman, Andrew. *Arguing About Law*. Belmont: Wadsworth Publishing Co., 1996.

Ezorsky, Gertrude. *Philosophical Perspectives on Punishment*. Albany: State University of New York Press, 1972.

Feinberg, Joel, and Gross, Hyman. *Philosophy of Law*. Belmont: Wadsworth Publishing Co., 1980.

Gorr, Michael, and Harwood, Sterling. *Crime and Punishment*. Boston: Jones and Bartlett, 1995.

Murphy, Jeffrie G. *Punishment and Rehabilitation*. Belmont: Wadsworth Publishing Co., 1984.

Basic Concepts

Golding, Martin P. *Philosophy of Law*. Englewood Cliffs: Prentice-Hall, 1975.

Richards, David A. J. *The Moral Criticism of Law*. Belmont: Dickenson Publishing Co., 1977.

The Forward-Looking and Backward-Looking Views

Andenaes, Johannes. *Punishment and Deterrence*. Ann Arbor: The University of Michigan Press, 1974.

Gross, Hyman. *A Theory of Criminal Justice*. New York: Oxford University Press, 1979.

Menninger, Karl. *The Crime of Punishment*. New York: The Viking Press, 1968.

Murphy, Jeffrie G. *Retribution, Justice and Therapy*. Boston: D. Reidel Publishing Co., 1979.

Packer, Herbert. *The Limits of the Criminal Sanction*. Stanford: Stanford University Press, 1968.

Von Hirsh, Andrew. *Doing Justice*. New York: Hill and Wang, 1976.

Practical Application

Bedau, Hugo. *The Death Penalty in America*. New York: Oxford University Press, 1996.

Black, Charles L., Jr. *Capital Punishment*. New York: W. W. Norton & Co., 1974.

———. "Reflections on Opposing the Penalty of Death." *St. Mary's Law Journal* (1978), pp. 1-12.

Van den Haag, Ernest. *Punishing Criminals*. New York: Basic Books, 1975.

War and Humanitarian Intervention

Introduction

Basic Concepts

The problem of war and humanitarian intervention is simply the problem of determining the moral limits of the international use of force. *Just war theories* attempt to specify what these moral limits are. Such theories have two components: a set of criteria that establishes a right to go to war *(jus ad bellum)*, and a set of criteria that determines legitimate conduct in war *(jus in bello)*. The first set of criteria can be grouped under the label "just cause," the second under "just means."

Consider the following specification of just cause:

1. There must be substantial aggression.
2. Nonbelligerent correctives must be either hopeless or too costly.
3. Belligerent correctives must be neither hopeless nor too costly.

This specification of just cause excludes the criterion of legitimate authority, which has had a prominent place in just war theories. This criterion is excluded because it has the character of a second-order requirement; it is a requirement that must be satisfied whenever there is a ques-tion of group action with respect to any moral problem whatsoever. For example, with respect to the problem of the distribution of goods and resources in a society, we can certainly ask who has the (morally legitimate) authority to distribute or redistribute goods and resources in a society. But before we ask such questions with respect to particular moral problems, it is important to understand first what are the morally defensible solutions to these problems because a standard way of identifying morally legitimate authorities is by their endorsement of such solutions. With respect to the problem of war and humanitarian intervention, we first need to determine the nature and existence of just causes before we try to identify morally legitimate authorities by their endorsement of such causes.

Assuming that there are just causes, just war theorists go on to specify just means. Consider the following specification of just means:

1. The harm inflicted on the aggressor must not be disproportionate to the aggression.
2. Harm to innocents should not be directly intended as an end or a means.

The first criterion is a widely accepted requirement of just means. The second criterion is also widely accepted and contains the main requirement of the doctrine of double effect (see the introduction to Section III). Many philosophers seem willing to endorse the application of the doctrine in this context given that those to whom the doctrine applies are generally recognized to be persons with full moral status.

To evaluate these requirements of just war theory, we need to determine to what degree they can be supported by the moral approaches to practical problems presented in the General Introduction. Of course, one or more of these approaches may ultimately favor the pacifist position, but assuming that these approaches favored some version of a just war theory, which version would that be?

Obviously, a utilitarian approach would have little difficulty accepting the requirement of just cause and requirement (1) on just means because these requirements can be interpreted as having a utilitarian backing. However, this approach would only accept requirement (2) on just means conditionally, because occasions would surely arise when violations of this requirement would maximize net utility.

Unlike a Utilitarian Approach, an Aristotelian Approach is relatively indeterminate in its requirements. All that is certain, as I have interpreted the approach, is that it would be absolutely committed to requirement (2) on just means.[1] Of course, the other requirements on just cause and just means would be required by particular versions of this approach.

A Kantian Approach is distinctive in that it seeks to combine and compromise both the concern of a Utilitarian Approach for maximal net utility and the concern of an Aristotelian Approach for the proper development of each individual.[2] In its hypothetical choice situation, persons would clearly favor the requirement of just cause and requirement (1) on just means, although they would not interpret them in a strictly utilitarian fashion.

Yet what about the requirement (2) on just means? Because persons behind a veil of ignorance would not be committed simply to whatever maximizes net utility, they would want to put a stricter limit on the harm that could be inflicted on innocents in defense of a just cause than could be justified on utilitarian grounds alone. This is because persons behind a veil of ignorance would be concerned not only with what maximizes net utility, but also with the distribution of utility to particular individuals. Persons imagining themselves to be ignorant of what position they are in would be particularly concerned that they might turn out to be in the position of those who are innocent, and, consequently, they would want strong safeguards against harming those who are innocent, such as requirement (2) on just means.

Yet even though persons behind a veil of ignorance would favor differential restriction on harm to innocents, they would not favor an absolute restriction on intentional harm to innocents. They would recognize as exceptions to such a restriction cases where intentional harm to innocents is either:

1. Trivial (e.g., stepping on someone's foot to get out of a crowded subway).
2. Easily reparable (e.g., lying to a temporarily depressed friend to keep her from committing suicide).
3. Sufficiently outweighed by the consequences of the action (e.g., shooting one of two hundred civilian hostages to prevent in the only way possible the execution of all two hundred).

Accordingly, while persons behind a veil of ignorance would favor requirement (2) on just means, their commitment to this requirement would also have to incorporate the above exceptions. Even so, these exceptions are far more limited than those that would be tolerated by an Utilitarian Approach.

In sum, a Kantian Approach would strongly endorse the requirement of just cause and requirements (1) and (2) on just means. Yet its commitment to requirement (2) on just means would fall short of the absolute commitment that is characteristic of an Aristotelian Approach to practical problems.

It is clear, therefore, that our three moral approaches to practical problems differ significantly with respect to their requirements for a just war theory. A Utilitarian Approach strongly endorses the requirement of just cause and requirement (1) on just means, but only conditionally endorses requirement (2) on just means. An Aristotelian Approach endorses requirement (2) on just means as an absolute requirement, but is indeterminate with respect to the other requirements of just war theory. Only a Kantian Approach strongly endorses all of the basic requirements of a traditional just war theory, although it does not regard requirement (2) on just means as an absolute requirement. Fortunately for traditional just war theory, there are good reasons for favoring a Kantian Approach over the other two moral approaches to practical problems.

One reason for favoring a Kantian over a Utilitarian Approach is that its requirements are derived from a veil of ignorance decision procedure that utilitarians and Kantians alike recognize to be fair. It is not surprising, therefore, to find such utilitarians as John Harsanyi and R. M. Hare simply endorsing this decision procedure and then trying to show that the resulting requirements would maximize utility.[3] Yet we have just seen how the concern of persons behind a veil of ignorance with the distribution of utility would lead them to impose a stricter limit on the harm that could be inflicted on innocents in defense of a just cause than could be justified on grounds of maximizing utility alone. At least with respect to just war theory, therefore, a Utilitarian Approach and a Kantian Approach differ significantly in their practical requirements.

Utilitarians who endorse this decision procedure are faced with a difficult choice: give up their commitment to this decision procedure or modify their commitment to utilitarian goals. Utilitarians cannot easily choose to give up their commitment to this decision procedure because the acceptability of utilitarianism as traditionally conceived has always depended on showing that fairness and utility rarely conflict, and that when they do, it is always plausible to think that the requirements of utility are morally overriding. Consequently, when a fair decision procedure significantly conflicts with utility—which it is not plausible to think can always be morally overridden by the requirements of utility—that procedure exposes the inadequacy of a Utilitarian Approach to practical problems.

These reasons for favoring a Kantian over a Utilitarian Approach to practical problems are also reasons for favoring an Aristotelian Approach, because an Aristotelian Approach is also concerned with fairness and the distribution of utility to particular individuals. Nevertheless, there are other reasons for favoring a Kantian Approach over an Aristotelian Approach.

One reason is that a Kantian Approach does not endorse any absolute requirements. In particular, a Kantian Approach does not endorse an absolute requirement not to intentionally harm innocents. A Kantian Approach recognizes that if the harm is trivial, easily reparable, or sufficiently outweighed by the consequences, such harm can be morally justified.

Another reason for favoring a Kantian Approach over an Aristotelian is that a Kantian Approach is determinate in its requirements; it actually leads to a wide range of practical recommendations. By contrast, an Aristotelian Approach lacks a deliberative procedure that can produce agreement with respect to practical requirements. This is evident because supporters of this approach tend to endorse radically different practical requirements. In this regard, the veil of ignorance decision procedure employed by a Kantian Approach appears to be just the sort of morally defensible device needed to achieve determinate requirements.

Finally, the particular requirements of just war theory endorsed by a Kantian Approach are further supported by the presence of analogous requirements for related areas of conduct. Thus, the strong legal prohibitions that exist against punishing the innocent provide support for the strong prohibition against harming innocents expressed by requirement (2) on just means. This is the type of correspondence we would expect from an adequate moral theory; requirements in one area of conduct would be analogous to those in related areas of conduct.

Alternative Views

In the first selection (Selection 75), James P. Sterba argues that when pacifism and just war theory are given their most morally defensible interpretations, they can be reconciled both in theory and practice. He argues that the most morally defensible form of pacifism is antiwar pacifism (which prohibits participation in all wars) rather than nonviolent pacifism (which prohibits any use of violence against other human beings) or nonlethal pacifism (which prohibits any use of lethal force against other human beings). He also argues that when just war theory is given its most morally defensible interpretation, it favors a strong just means prohibition against intentionally harming innocents and favors the use of belligerent means only when such means (1) minimize the loss and injury to innocent lives overall; (2) threaten innocent lives only to prevent the loss of innocent lives; and (3) threaten or take the lives of unjust aggressors when it is the only way to prevent serious injury to innocents. He contends that the few wars and large-scale conflicts that meet these stringent requirements of just war theory (e.g., India's military action against Pakistan in Bangladesh and the Tanzanian incursion into Uganda during the rule of Idi Amin) are the only wars and large-

scale conflicts to which antiwar pacifists cannot justifiably object. He calls the view that emerges from this reconciliation "just war pacifism."

In Selection 76, Michael Walzer argues in favor of humanitarian intervention whenever cruelty and suffering are extreme and no local forces are capable of putting an end to them. In such situations, Walzer maintains that anyone who can should intervene, but that wealthy and powerful states have an obligation to do so. Walzer notes that some of these interventions will allow one to enter a country, get the job done, and leave relatively quickly. But others will not allow this, and virtually all such interventions will require putting one's soldiers at risk.

By contrast, Barbara Conry argues in Selection 77 that a U.S. military intervention is generally not a viable solution to regional conflicts. In the first place, she argues, in the vast majority of cases such interventions do not work because the altruism of those intervening cannot usually outlast the nationalism or self-interest of the parties in the conflict. Secondly, she argues that it is virtually impossible for such interventions to be impartial; an intervening power almost always ends up siding with one or the other party in the conflict. Thirdly, she claims that such interventions give rise to anti-American sentiment based on the north–south conflict between the rich and the poor, and they constitute a drain on U.S. resources.

Thus, while Walzer thinks that interventions in regional conflicts motivated by altruism can and should be undertaken, Conry thinks that only those relatively few interventions that are also motivated by national interest can and should be undertaken.

Practical Applications

The readings in this section have already suggested a number of practical solutions to the problem of war and humanitarian intervention. However, a more sweeping solution is proposed by the final selection (Selection 78). In this selection, Robert S. McNamara argues that with the end of the Cold War, nations should move toward a system of collective security with conflict resolution and peacekeeping functions performed by multinational institutions. Agreeing with a recent proposal from President Yeltsin, McNamara also favors a return, insofar as practicable, to a nonnuclear world. Noting that the 1991 U.S. defense budget in constant dollars is still 40 percent higher than it was a decade ago, McNamara favors cutting military budgets throughout the world by 50 percent. It is significant that these recommendations come from the very person who was Secretary of Defense under Kennedy and Johnson and who presided over our increased military involvement in Vietnam.

Nevertheless, it is important to recognize that a solution to the problem of war and humanitarian intervention cannot stand alone; it requires solutions to the other practical problems discussed in this anthology as well. For example, a solution to the problem of the distribution of income and wealth may show that it is morally illegitimate to increase military security by sacrificing the basic needs of the less advantaged members of a society rather than by sacrificing the nonbasic needs of the more advantaged members of the society. Accordingly, it is impossible to reach a fully adequate solution to this or any other practical problem discussed in this anthology without solving the other practical problems as well.

Endnotes

1. See General Introduction.
2. See General Introduction.
3. See John Harsanyi, *Rational Behavior and Bargaining Equilibrium in Games and Social Situations* (Cambridge: Cambridge University Press, 1977), and R. M. Hare, "Justice and Equality," in *Justice: Alternative Political Perspectives*, ed. James P. Sterba (Belmont, Calif.: Wadsworth Publishing Co., 1991).

75. *Reconciling Pacifists and Just War Theorists*

JAMES P. STERBA

James P. Sterba argues that when pacifism and just war theory are given their most morally defensible interpretations, they can be reconciled both in theory and practice. He argues that the most morally defensible form of pacifism is antiwar pacifism rather than nonviolent pacifism or nonlethal pacifism. He also argues that when just war theory is given its most morally defensible interpretation, it favors a strong just means prohibition against intentionally harming innocents and favors the use of belligerent means only when such means (1) minimize the loss and injury to innocent lives overall, (2) threaten innocent lives only to prevent the loss of innocent lives, and (3) threaten or take the lives of unjust aggressors when it is the only way to prevent serious injury to innocents. He contends that the few wars and large-scale conflicts that meet these stringent requirements of just war theory are the only wars and large-scale conflicts to which antiwar pacifists cannot justifiably object.

Traditionally pacifism and just war theory have represented radically opposed responses to aggression. Pacifism has been interpreted to rule out any use of violence in response to aggression. Just war theory has been interpreted to permit a measured use of violence in response to aggression. It has been thought that the two views might sometimes agree in particular cases—for example, that pacifists and just war theorists might unconditionally oppose nuclear war, but beyond that it has been generally held that the two views lead to radically opposed recommendations. In this paper, I hope to show that this is not the case. I will argue that pacifism and just war theory, in their most morally defensible interpretations, can be substantially reconciled both in theory and practice.

In traditional just war theory there are two basic elements: an account of just cause and an account of just means. Just cause is usually specified as follows:

1. There must be substantial aggression;
2. Nonbelligerent correctives must be either hopeless or too costly; and
3. Belligerent correctives must be neither hopeless nor too costly.

Needless to say, the notion of substantial aggression is a bit fuzzy, but it is generally understood to be the type of aggression that violates people's most fundamental rights. To suggest some specific examples of what is and is not substantial aggression, usually the taking of hostages is regarded as substantial aggression while the nationalization of particular firms owned by foreigners is not so regarded. But even when substantial aggression occurs, frequently nonbelligerent correctives are neither hopeless nor too costly. And even when nonbelligerent correctives are either hopeless or too costly, in order for there to be a just cause, belligerent correctives must be neither hopeless nor too costly.

Traditional just war theory assumes, however, that there are just causes and goes on to specify just means as imposing two requirements:

1. Harm to innocents should not be directly intended as an end or a means.
2. The harm resulting from the belligerent means should not be disproportionate to the particular defensive objective to be attained.

While the just means conditions apply to each defensive action, the just cause conditions must be met by the conflict as a whole.

It is important to note that these requirements of just cause and just means are not essentially about war at all. Essentially, they constitute a theory of just defense that can apply to war but can also apply to a wide range of defensive actions short of war. Of course, what needs to be determined is whether these requirements can be justified. Since just war theory is usually opposed to pacifism, to secure a non–question-begging justification for the theory and its requirements we need to proceed as much as possible from premises that are common to pacifists and just war theorists alike. The difficulty here is that there is not just one form of pacifism but many. So we need to determine which form of pacifism is most morally defensible.

Now when most people think of pacifism they tend to identify it with a theory of nonviolence. We can call this view "nonviolent pacifism." It maintains that:

Any use of violence against other human beings is morally prohibited.

It has been plausibly argued, however, that this form of pacifism is incoherent. In a well-known article, Jan Narveson rejects nonviolent pacifism as incoherent because it recognizes a right to life yet rules out any use of force in defense of that right. The view is incoherent, Narveson claims, because having a right entails the legitimacy of using force in defense of that right at least on some occasions.

Given the cogency of objections of this sort, some have opted for a form of pacifism that does not rule out all violence but only lethal violence. We can call this view "nonlethal pacifism." It maintains that

Any lethal use of force against other human beings is morally prohibited.

In defense of nonlethal pacifism, Cheyney Ryan has argued that there is a substantial issue between the pacifist and the nonpacifist concerning whether we can or should create the necessary distance between ourselves and other human beings in order to make the act of killing possible. To illustrate, Ryan cites George Orwell's reluctance to shoot at an enemy soldier who jumped out of a trench and ran along the top of a parapet half-dressed and holding up his trousers with both hands. Ryan contends that what kept Orwell from shooting was that he couldn't think of the soldier as a thing rather than a fellow human being.

However, it is not clear that Orwell's encounter supports nonlethal pacifism. For it may be that what kept Orwell from shooting the enemy soldier was not his inability to think of the soldier as a thing rather than a fellow human being but rather his inability to think of the soldier who was holding up his trousers with both hands as a threat or a combatant. Under this interpretation, Orwell's decision not to shoot would accord well with the requirements of just war theory.

Let us suppose, however, that someone is attempting to take your life. Why does that permit you, the defender of nonlethal pacifism might ask, to kill the person making the attempt? The most cogent response, it seems to me, is that killing in such a case is not evil, or at least not morally evil, because anyone who is wrongfully engaged in an attempt upon your life has already forfeited his or her right to life by engaging in such aggression.[1] So, provided that you are reasonably certain that the aggressor is wrongfully engaged in an attempt upon your life, you would be morally justified in killing, assuming that it is the only way of saving your own life.

There is, however, a form a pacifism that remains untouched by the criticisms I have raised against both nonviolent pacifism and nonlethal pacifism. This form of pacifism neither prohibits all violence nor even all uses of lethal force. We can call the view "antiwar pacifism" because it holds that

Any participation in the massive use of lethal force in warfare is morally prohibited.[2]

In defense of antiwar pacifism, it is undeniable that wars have brought enormous amounts of death and destruction in their wake and that many of those who have perished in them are noncombatants or innocents. In fact, the tendency of modern wars has been to produce higher and higher proportions of noncombatant casualties, making it more and more difficult to justify participation in such wars. At the same time, strategies for nonbelligerent conflict resolution are rarely intensively developed and explored before nations choose to go to war, making it all but impossible to justify participation in such wars.

To determine whether the requirements of just war theory can be reconciled with those of antiwar pacifism, however, we must consider whether we should distinguish between harm intentionally inflicted on innocents and harm whose infliction on innocents is merely foreseen. On the one hand, we could favor a uniform restriction against the infliction of harm on innocents that ignores the intended/foreseen distinction. On the other hand, we could favor a differential restriction that is more severe against the intentional infliction of harm upon innocents but is less severe against the infliction of harm that is merely foreseen. What needs to be determined, therefore, is whether there is any rationale for favoring this differential restriction on harm over a uniform restriction. . . .

Let us first examine the question from the perspective of those suffering the harm. Initially, it might appear to matter little whether the harm would be intended or just foreseen by those who cause it. From the perspective of those suffering harm, it might appear that what matters is simply that the overall amount of harm be restricted irrespective of whether it is foreseen or intended. But consider—don't those who suffer harm have more reason to protest when the harm is done to them by agents who are directly engaged in causing harm to them than when the harm is done incidentally by agents whose ends and means are good? Don't we have more reason to protest when we are being used by others than when we are affected by them only incidentally?

Moreover, if we examine the question from the perspective of those causing harm, additional support for this line of reasoning can be found. For it would seem that we as agents have more reason to protest a restriction against foreseen harm than we have reason to protest a comparable restriction against intended harm. This is because a restriction against foreseen harm limits our actions when our ends and means are good whereas a restriction against intended harm only limits our actions when our ends or means are evil or harmful, and it would seem that we have greater grounds for acting when both our ends and means are good than when they are not. Consequently, because we have more reason to protest when we are being used by others than when we are being affected by them only incidentally, and because we have more reason to act when both our ends and means are good than when they are not, we should favor the foreseen/intended distinction that is incorporated into just means.

It might be objected, however, that at least sometimes we could produce greater good overall by violating the foreseen/intended distinction of just means and acting with the evil means of intentionally harming innocents. On this account, it might be argued that it should be permissible at least sometimes to intentionally harm innocents in order to achieve greater good overall.

Now it seems to me that this objection is well taken insofar as it is directed against an absolute restriction upon intentional harm to innocents. It seems clear that there are exceptions to such a restriction when intentional harm to innocents is:

1. Trivial (for example, as in the case of stepping on someone's foot to get out of a crowded subway);
2. Easily reparable (for example, as in the case of lying to a temporarily depressed friend to keep him from committing suicide); or
3. Greatly outweighed by the consequences of the action, especially to innocent people (for example, as in the case of shooting one of two hundred civilian hostages to prevent in the only way possible the execution of all two hundred).

Yet while we need to recognize these exceptions to an absolute restriction upon intentional harm to innocents, there is good reason not to permit simply maximizing good consequences overall because that would place unacceptable burdens upon particular individuals. More specifically, it would be an unacceptable burden on innocents to allow them to be intentionally harmed in cases other than the exceptions we have just enumerated. So allowing for these exceptions, we would have reason to favor a differential restriction against harming innocents that is more severe against the intentional infliction of harm upon innocents but is less severe against the infliction of harm upon innocents that is merely foreseen. Again, the main grounds for this preference is that we would have more reason to protest when we are being used by others than when we are being affected by them only incidentally, and more reason to act when both our ends and means are good than when they are not.

So far, I have argued that there are grounds for favoring a differential restriction on harm to innocents that is more severe against intended harm and less severe against foreseen harm. I have further argued that this restriction is not absolute so that when the evil intended is trivial, easily reparable, or greatly outweighed by the consequences, intentional harm to innocents can be justified. Moreover, there is no reason to think that antiwar pacifists would reject either of these conclusions. Antiwar pacifists are opposed to any participation in the massive use of lethal force in warfare, yet this need not conflict with the commitment of just war theorists to a differential but nonabsolute restriction on harm to innocents as a requirement of just means.[3] Where just war theory goes wrong, according to antiwar pacifists, is not in its restriction on harming innocents but rather in its failure to adequately determine when belligerent correctives are too costly to constitute a just cause or lacking in the proportionality required by just means. According to antiwar pacifists, just war theory provides insufficient restraint in both of these areas. Now to evaluate this criticism, we need to consider a wide range of cases where killing or inflicting serious harm on others in defense of oneself or others might be thought to be justified, beginning with the easiest cases to assess from the perspectives of antiwar pacifism and the just war theory and then moving on to cases that are more difficult to assess from these perspectives.

Case 1. Only the intentional or foreseen killing of an unjust aggressor would prevent one's own death.[4] This case clearly presents no problems. In the first place, antiwar pacifists adopted their view because they were convinced that there were instances of justified killing. And, in this case, the only person killed is an unjust aggressor. So surely antiwar pacifists would have to agree with just war theorists that one can justifiably kill an unjust aggressor if it is the only way to save one's life.

Case 2. Only the intentional or foreseen killing of an unjust aggressor and the foreseen killing of one innocent bystander would prevent one's own death and that of five other innocent people.[5] In this case, we have the foreseen killing of an innocent person as well as the killing of the unjust aggressor, but since it is the only way to save one's own life and the lives of five other innocent people, antiwar pacifists and just war theorists alike would have reason to judge it morally permissible. In this case, the intended life-saving benefits to six innocent people is judged to outweigh the foreseen death of one innocent person and the intended or foreseen death of the unjust aggressor.

Case 3. Only the intentional or foreseen killing of an unjust aggressor and the foreseen killing of one innocent bystander would prevent the death of five other innocent people. In this case, even though we lack the justification of self-defense, saving the lives of five innocent people in the only way possible still provides antiwar pacifists and just war theorists with sufficient grounds for granting the moral permissibility of killing an unjust aggressor, even when the killing of an innocent bystander is foreseen. Here the intended life-saving benefits to five innocent people would still outweigh the foreseen death of one innocent person and the intended or foreseen death of the unjust aggressor.

Case 4. Only the intentional or foreseen killing of an unjust aggressor and the foreseen killing of five innocent people would prevent the death of two innocent people. In this case, neither antiwar pacifists nor just war theorists would find the cost and proportionality requirements of just war theory to be met. Too many innocent people would have to be killed to save too few. Here the fact that the deaths of the innocents would be merely foreseen does not outweigh the fact that we would have to accept the deaths of five innocents and the death of the unjust aggressor in order to be able to save two innocents.

Notice that up to this point in interpreting these cases, we have simply been counting the number of innocent deaths involved in each case and opting for whichever solution minimized the loss of innocent lives that would result. Suppose, however, that an unjust aggressor is not threatening the lives of innocents but only their welfare or property. Would the taking of the unjust aggressor's life in defense of the welfare and property of innocents be judged proportionate? Consider the following case.

Case 5. Only the intentional or foreseen killing of an unjust aggressor would prevent serious injury to oneself and/or five other innocent people. Since in this case the intentional or foreseen killing of the unjust aggressor is the only way of preventing serious injury to oneself and five other innocent people, then, by analogy with Cases 1 through 3, both antiwar pacifists and just war theorists alike would have reason to affirm its moral permissibility. Of course, if there were any other way of stopping unjust aggressors in such cases short of killing them, that course of action would clearly be required. Yet if there is no alternative, the intentional or foreseen killing of the unjust aggressor to prevent serious injury to oneself and/or five other innocent people would be justified.

In such cases, the serious injury could be bodily injury, as when an aggressor threatens to break one's limbs, or it could be serious psychological injury, as when an aggressor threatens to inject mind-altering drugs, or it could be a serious threat to property. Of course, usually where serious injury is threatened, there will be ways of stopping aggressors short of killing them. Unfortunately, this is not always possible.

In still other kinds of cases, stopping an unjust aggressor would require indirectly inflicting serious harm, but not death, upon innocent bystanders. Consider the following cases.

Case 6. Only the intentional or foreseen infliction of serious harm upon an unjust aggressor and the foreseen infliction of serious harm upon one innocent bystander would prevent serious harm to oneself and five other innocent people.

Case 7. Only the intentional or foreseen infliction of serious harm upon an unjust aggressor and the foreseen infliction of serious harm upon one innocent bystander would prevent serious harm to five other innocent people.

In both of these cases, serious harm is indirectly inflicted upon one innocent bystander in order to prevent greater harm from being inflicted by an unjust aggressor upon other innocent people. In Case 6, we also have the justification of self-defense, which is lacking in Case 7. Nevertheless, with regard to both cases, antiwar pacifists and just war theorists should agree that preventing serious injury to five or six innocent people in the only way possible renders it morally permissible to inflict serious injury on an unjust aggressor, even when the serious injury of one innocent person is a foreseen consequence. In these cases, by analogy with Cases 2 and 3, the foreseen serious injury of one innocent person and the intended or foreseen injury of the unjust aggressor should be judged proportionate given the intended injury-preventing benefits to five or six other innocent people.

Up to this point there has been the basis for general agreement among antiwar pacifists and just war theorists as to how to interpret the proportionality requirement of just means, but in the following case this no longer obtains.

Case 8. Only the intentional or foreseen killing of an unjust aggressor and the foreseen killing of one innocent bystander would prevent serious injuries to the members of a much larger group of people.

The interpretation of this case is crucial. In this case, we are asked to sanction the loss of an innocent life to prevent serious injuries to the members of a much larger group of people. Unfortunately, neither antiwar pacifists nor just war theorists have explicitly considered this case. Both antiwar pacifists and just war theorists agree that we can inflict serious injury on an unjust aggressor and an innocent bystander to prevent greater injury to other innocent people, as in Cases 6 and 7, and that one can even intentionally or indirectly kill an unjust aggressor to prevent serious injury to oneself or other innocent people as in Case 5. Yet neither antiwar pacifists nor just war theorists have explicitly addressed the question of whether we can indirectly kill an innocent bystander in order to prevent serious injuries to the members of a much larger group of innocent people. Rather they have tended to confuse Case 8 with Case 5, where it is agreed that one can justifiably kill an unjust aggressor to prevent serious injury to oneself and/or five other innocent people. In Case 8, however, one is doing something quite different: One is killing an innocent bystander in order to prevent serious injury to the members of a much larger group of people.

Now this kind of trade-off is not accepted in standard police practice. Police officers are regularly instructed not to risk innocent lives simply to prevent serious injury to other innocents. Nor is there any reason to think that a trade-off that is unacceptable in standard police practice would be acceptable in larger scale conflicts. Thus, for example, even if the Baltic republics could have effectively freed themselves from the Soviet Union by infiltrating into Moscow several bands of saboteurs who would then attack several military and government installations in Moscow, causing an enormous loss of innocent lives, such trade-offs would not have been justified. Accordingly, it follows that if the proportionality requirement of just war theory is to be met, we must save more innocent lives than we cause to be lost, we must prevent more injuries than we bring about, and we must not kill innocents, even indirectly, simply to prevent serious injuries to ourselves and others. Moreover, even when our lives and the lives of others are being threatened, we must save more innocent lives than we cause to be lost.

Of course, sometimes our lives and well-being are threatened together. Or better, if we are unwilling to sacrifice our well-being then our lives are threatened as well. Nevertheless, if we are justified in our use of lethal force to defend ourselves in cases where we will indirectly kill innocents, it is because our lives are also threatened, not simply our well-being. And the same holds for when we are defending others.

What this shows is that the constraints imposed by just war theory on the use of belligerent correctives are actually much more severe than antiwar pacifists have tended to recognize. In determining when belligerent correctives are too costly to constitute a just cause or lacking in the proportionality required by just means, just war theory under its most morally defensible interpretation:

1. Allows the use of belligerent means against unjust aggressors only when such means minimize the loss and injury to innocent lives overall;

2. Allows the use of belligerent means against unjust aggressors to indirectly threaten innocent lives only to prevent the loss of innocent lives, not simply to prevent injury to innocents; and

3. Allows the use of belligerent means to directly or indirectly threaten or even take the lives of

unjust aggressors when it is the only way to prevent serious injury to innocents.

Now it might be objected that all that I have shown through the analysis of the above eight cases is that killing in defense of oneself or others is morally permissible, not that it is morally required or morally obligatory. That is true. I have not established any obligation to respond to aggression with lethal force in these cases, but only that it is morally permissible to do so. For one thing, it is difficult to ground an obligation to use lethal force on self-defense alone, as would be required in Case 1 or in one version of Case 5. Obligations to oneself appear to have an optional quality that is absent from obligations to others. In Cases 2, 3, and 5 through 7, however, the use of force would prevent serious harm or death to innocents, and here I contend it would be morally obligatory if either the proposed use of force required only a relatively small personal sacrifice from us or if we were fairly bound by convention or a mutual defense agreement to come to the aid of others. In such cases, I think we can justifiably speak of a moral obligation to kill or seriously harm in defense of others.

Another aspect of Cases 1 through 3 and 5 through 7 to which someone might object is that it is the wrongful actions of others that put us into situations where I am claiming that we are morally justified in seriously harming or killing others. But for the actions of unjust aggressors, we would not be in situations where I am claiming that we are morally permitted or required to seriously harm or kill.

Yet doesn't something like this happen in a wide range of cases when wrongful actions are performed? Suppose I am on the way to the bank to deposit money from a fundraiser, and someone accosts me and threatens to shoot if I don't hand over the money. If I do hand over the money, I would be forced to do something I don't want to do, something that involves a loss to myself and others. But surely it is morally permissible for me to hand over the money in this case. And it may even be morally required for me to do so if resistance would lead to the shooting of others in addition to myself. So it does seem that bad people, by altering the consequences of our actions, can alter our obligations as well. What our obligations are under nonideal conditions are different from what they would be under ideal conditions. If a group of thugs comes into this room and make it very clear that they intend to shoot me if each of you doesn't give them one dollar, I think, and I would hope that you would also think, that each of you now has an obligation to give the thugs one dollar when before you had no such obligation. Likewise, I think that the actions of unjust aggressors can put us into situations where it is morally permissible or even morally required for us to seriously harm or kill when before it was not.

Now it might be contended that antiwar pacifists would concede the moral permissibility of Cases 1–3 and 5–7 but still maintain that any participation in the massive use of lethal force in warfare is morally prohibited. The scale of the conflict, antiwar pacifists might contend, makes all the difference. Of course, if this simply means that many large-scale conflicts will have effects that bear no resemblance to Cases 1–3 or 5–7, this can hardly be denied. Still, it is possible for some large-scale conflicts to bear a proportionate resemblance to the above cases. For example, it can be argued plausibly that India's military action against Pakistan in Bangladesh and the Tanzanian incursion into Uganda during the rule of Idi Amin resemble Cases 3, 5, or 7 in their effects upon innocents.[6] What this shows is that antiwar pacifists are not justified in regarding every participation in the massive use of lethal force in warfare as morally prohibited. Instead, antiwar pacifists must allow that, at least in some real-life cases, wars and other large-scale military operations both have been and will be morally permissible.

This concession from antiwar pacifists, however, needs to be matched by a comparable concession from just war theorists themselves, because too frequently they have interpreted their theory in morally indefensible ways. When just war theory is given a morally defensible interpretation, I have argued that the theory favors a strong just means prohibition against intentionally harming innocents. I have also argued that the theory favors the use of belligerent means only when such means (1) minimize the loss and injury to innocent lives overall; (2) threaten innocent lives only to prevent the loss of innocent lives, not simply to prevent injury to innocents; and (3) threaten or even take the lives of unjust aggressors when it is the only way to prevent serious injury to innocents.

Obviously, just war theory, so understood, is going to place severe restrictions on the use of belligerent means in warfare. In fact, most of the actual uses of belligerent means in warfare that have occurred turn out to be unjustified. For example, the U.S. involvement in Nicaragua, El Salvador, and Panama; the Soviet Union's involvement in Afghanistan; and Israeli involvement in the West Bank and the Gaza Strip all violate the just cause and just means provisions of just war theory as I have defended them. Even the recent U.S.-led war against Iraq violated both the just cause and just means provisions of just war theory.[7] In fact, one strains to find examples of justified applications of just war theory in recent history. Two examples I have already referred to are India's military action against Pakistan in Bangladesh and the Tanzanian incursion into Uganda during the rule of Idi Amin. But after mentioning these two examples it is difficult to go on. What this shows is that when just war theory and antiwar pacifism are given their most morally defensible interpretations, both views can be reconciled. In this reconciliation, the few wars and large-scale conflicts that meet the stringent requirements of just war theory are the only wars and large-scale conflicts to which antiwar pacifists cannot justifiably object.[8] We can call the view that emerges from this reconciliation "just war pacifism." It is the view which claims that due to the stringent requirements of just war theory, only very rarely will participation in a massive use of lethal force in warfare be morally justified. It is the view on which I rest my case for the reconciliation of pacifism and just war theory.[9]

Endnotes

1. Alternatively, one might concede that even in this case killing is morally evil, but still contend that it is morally justified because it is the lesser of two evils.

2. For two challenging defenses of this view, see Duane L. Cady, *From Warism to Pacifism* (Philadelphia: Temple University Press, 1989), and Robert L. Holmes, *On War and Morality* (Princeton: Princeton University Press, 1989).

3. This is because the just means restrictions protect innocents quite well against the infliction of intentional harm.

4. By an "unjust aggressor" I mean someone who the defender is reasonably certain is wrongfully engaged in an attempt upon her life or the lives of other innocent people.

5. What is relevant in this case is that the foreseen deaths are a relatively small number (one in this case) compared to the number of innocents whose lives are saved (six in this case). The primary reason for using particular numbers in this case and those that follow is to make it clear that at this stage of the argument no attempt is being made to justify the large-scale killing that occurs in warfare.

6. Although there is a strong case for India's military action against Pakistan in Bangladesh and the Tanzanian incursion into Uganda during the rule of Idi Amin, there are questions that can be raised about the behavior of Indian troops in Bangladesh following the defeat of the Pakistanian forces and about the regime Tanzania put in power in Uganda.

7. The just cause provision was violated because the extremely effective economic sanctions were not given enough time to work. It was estimated that when compared to past economic blockades, the blockade against Iraq had a near 100 percent chance of success if given about a year to work. (See the *New York Times*, January 14, 1991.) The just means provision was violated because the number of combatant and noncombatant deaths was disproportionate. As many as 120,000 Iraqi soldiers were killed, according to U.S. intelligence sources.

8. Of course, antiwar pacifists are right to point out that virtually all wars that have been fought have led to unforeseen harms and have been fought with less and less discrimination as the wars progressed. Obviously, these are considerations that in just war theory must weigh heavily against going to war.

9. Of course, more needs to be done to specify the requirements of just war pacifism. One fruitful way to further specify these requirements is to appeal to a hypothetical social contract decision procedure as has been done with respect to other practical problems. Here I have simply tried to establish the defensibility of just war pacifism without appealing to any such procedure. Yet once the defensibility of just war pacifism has been established, such a decision procedure will prove quite useful in working out its particular requirements.

76. The Politics of Rescue

MICHAEL WALZER

Michael Walzer argues in favor of humanitarian intervention whenever cruelty and suffering are extreme and no local forces are capable of putting an end to them. In such situations, Walzer maintains that anyone who can should intervene, but that wealthy and powerful states also have an obligation to do so. Walzer notes that some of these interventions will allow one to enter a country, get the job done, and leave relatively quickly. But others will not allow this, and virtually all such interventions will require putting one's soldiers at risk.

To intervene or not?—this should always be a hard question. Even in the case of a brutal civil war or a politically induced famine or the massacre of a local minority, the use of force in other people's countries should always generate hesitation and anxiety. So it does today among small groups of concerned people, some of whom end up supporting, some resisting interventionist policies. But many governments and many more politicians seem increasingly inclined to find the question easy: The answer is *not!* Relatively small contingents of soldiers will be sent to help out in cases where it isn't expected that they will have to fight—thus the United States in Somalia, the Europeans in Bosnia, the French in Rwanda. The aim in all these countries (though we experimented briefly with something more in Mogadishu) is not to alter power relations on the ground, but only to ameliorate their consequences—to bring food and medical supplies to populations besieged and bombarded, for example, without interfering with the siege or bombardment.

This might be taken as a triumph for the old principle of nonintervention, except that the reasons on which the principle is based, which I will rehearse in a moment, do not appear to be the reasons that move governments and politicians today. They are not focused on the costs of intervention or, for that matter, of nonintervention to the men and women whose danger or suffering poses the question, but only on the costs to their own soldiers and to themselves, that

is, to their political standing at home. No doubt, governments must think about such things: Political leaders have to maintain their domestic support if they are to act effectively abroad. But they must also *act effectively abroad* when the occasion demands it, and they must be able to judge the urgency of the demand in the appropriate moral and political terms. The ideology of the cold war once provided a set of terms, not in fact always appropriate to the cases at hand, but capable of overriding domestic considerations. In the aftermath of the cold war, no comparable ideology has that capacity. The question "To intervene or not?" gets answered every day, but with no sign that the judgments it requires are actually being made.

What About "Humanitarian Intervention"?

I am going to focus on the arguments for and against "humanitarian intervention," for this is what is at issue in the former Yugoslavia, the Caucasus, parts of Asia, much of Africa. Massacre, rape, ethnic cleansing, state terrorism, contemporary versions of "bastard feudalism," complete with ruthless warlords and lawless bands of armed men: These are the acts and occasions that invite us, or require us, to override the presumption against moving armies across borders and using force inside countries that have not threatened or attacked their neighbors. There is no external aggression to worry about, only domestic brutality,

Reprinted from *Dissent* (Winter 1995) by permission of publisher and author.

civil war, political tyranny, ethnic or religious perse-cution. When should the world's agents and powers (the United Nations, the European Community, the Pan American Alliance, the Organization of African Unity, the United States) merely watch and protest? When should they protest and then intervene?

The presumption against intervention is strong; we (on the left especially) have reasons for it, which derive from our opposition to imperial politics and our com-mitment to self-determination, even when the process of self-determination is something less than peaceful and democratic. Ever since Roman times, empires have expanded by intervening in civil wars, replacing "anarchy" with law and order, overthrowing suppos-edly noxious regimes. Conceivably, this expansion has saved lives, but only by creating in the process a "prison-house of nations," whose subsequent history is a long tale of prison revolts, brutally repressed. So it seems best that people who have lived together in the past and will have to do so in the future should be allowed to work out their difficulties without imperial assistance, among themselves. The resolution won't be stable unless it is locally grounded; there is little chance that it will be consensual unless it is locally produced.

Still, nonintervention is not an absolute moral rule: Sometimes, what is going on locally cannot be toler-ated. Hence the practice of "humanitarian interven-tion"—much abused, no doubt, but morally neces-sary whenever cruelty and suffering are extreme and no local forces seem capable of putting an end to them. Humanitarian interventions are not justified for the sake of democracy or free enterprise or economic justice or voluntary association or any other of the social practices and arrangements that we might hope for or even call for in other people's countries. Their aim is profoundly negative in character: to put a stop to actions that, to use an old-fashioned but accurate phrase, "shock the conscience" of humankind. There are some useful, and to my mind justified, contempo-rary examples: India in East Pakistan, Tanzania in Uganda, Vietnam in Cambodia. Interventions of this sort are probably best carried out by neighbors, as in these three cases, since neighbors will have some understanding of the local culture. They may also, however, have old scores to settle or old (or new) ambitions to dominate the neighborhood. If we had more trust in the effectiveness of the United Nations

or the various regional associations, we could require international or at least multilateral endorsement, co-operation, and constraint. I will consider this possibil-ity later on. It might be a way of controlling the economically or politically self-aggrandizing inter-ventions of single states. For now, though, the agent-of-last-resort is anyone near enough and strong enough to stop what needs stopping.

But that's not always easy. On the standard view of humanitarian intervention (which I adopted when writing *Just and Unjust Wars* almost twenty years ago), the source of the inhumanity is conceived as somehow external and singular in character: a tyrant, a con-queror or usurper, or an alien power set over against a mass of victims. The intervention then has an aim that is simple as well as negative: Remove the tyrant (Pol Pot, Idi Amin), set the people free (Bangladesh), and then get out. Rescue the people in trouble from their troublers, and let them get on with their lives. Help them, and then leave them to manage as best they can by themselves. The test of a genuinely hu-manitarian intervention, on this view, is that the inter-vening forces are quickly in and out. They do not intervene and then stay put for reasons of their own, as the Vietnamese did in Cambodia.

But what if the trouble is internal, the inhumanity locally and widely rooted, a matter of political culture, social structures, historical memories, ethnic fear, re-sentment, and hatred? Or what if the trouble follows from state failure, the collapse of any effective govern-ment, with results closer to Hobbes's than to Kropot-kin's predictions—not quite a "war of all against all" but a widely dispersed, disorganized, and murderous war of some against some? No doubt, there are still identifiable evil-doers, but now, let's say, they have support at home, reserves, evil-doers in waiting: What then? And what if there are overlapping sets of victims and victimizers, like the Somalian clans and warlords or, perhaps, the religious/ethnic/national groupings in Bosnia? In all these cases, it may well happen that the quick departure of the intervening forces is followed immediately by the reappearance of the conditions that led to intervention in the first place. Give up the idea of an external and singular evil, and the "in and out" test is very hard to apply.

We are extraordinarily dependent on the vic-tim/victimizer, good guys/bad guys model. I am not sure that any very forceful intervention is politically possible without it. One of the reasons for the weakness of the United Nations in Bosnia has been that many of its representatives on the ground do not believe that the model fits the situation they have to confront. They are not quite apologists for the Serbs, who have (rightly) been condemned in many United Nations resolutions, but they do not regard the Serbs as wholly "bad guys" or as the only "bad guys" in the former Yugoslavia. And that has made it difficult for them to justify the measures that would be necessary to stop the killing and the ethnic cleansing. Imagine that they took those measures, as (in my view) they should have done: Wouldn't they also have been required to take collateral measures against the Croats and Bosnian Moslems? In cases like this one, the politics of rescue is certain to be complex and messy.

It is much easier to go into a place like Bosnia than to get out, and the likely costs to the intervening forces and the local population are much higher than in the classic humanitarian interventions of the recent past. That is why American politicians and military officers have insisted that there must be an exit strategy before there can be an intervention. But this demand is effectively an argument against intervening at all. Exit strategies can rarely be designed in advance, and a public commitment to exit within such and such a time would give the hostile forces a strong incentive to lie low and wait. Better to stay home than to intervene in a way that is sure to fail.

Where the policies and practices that need to be stopped are widely supported, sustained by local structures and cultures, any potentially successful intervention is not going to meet the "in and out" test. It is likely to require a much more sustained challenge to conventional sovereignty: a long-term military presence, social reconstruction, what used to be called "political trusteeship" (since few of the locals—at least, the locals with power—can be trusted), and along the way, making all this possible, the large-scale and reiterated use of force. Is anyone ready for this? The question is especially hard for people on the left who are appalled by what happened or is happening in Bosnia, say, or Rwanda, but who have long argued, most of us, that the best thing to do with an army is to keep it at home. Even those who supported humanitarian interventions in the past have emphasized

the moral necessity of a rapid withdrawal, leaving any ongoing use of force to indigenous soldiers.

Now this moral necessity seems to have become a practical, political necessity. Hence the general search for a quick fix, as in President Clinton's proposal (never very vigorously pursued) to "bomb the Serbs, arm the Bosnians." I would have supported both these policies, thinking that they might produce a local solution that, however bloody it turned out to be, could not be worse than what was happening anyway. But what if the quick fix failed, brought on an ever more brutal civil war, with no end in sight? Would we be ready then for a more direct and long-lasting military intervention—and if so, with what sort of an army? Under whose direction? With what weapons systems, what strategy and tactics, what willingness to take casualties and to impose them?

Putting Soldiers at Risk

This last question is probably the crucial one in making intervention increasingly difficult and unlikely. It is very hard these days, in the Western democracies, to put soldiers at risk. But humanitarian interventions and peacekeeping operations are first of all military acts directed against people who are already using force, breaking the peace. They will be ineffective unless there is a willingness to accept the risks that naturally attach to military acts—to shed blood, to lose soldiers. In much of the world, bloodless intervention, peaceful peacekeeping is a contradiction in terms: If it were possible, it wouldn't be necessary. Insofar as it is necessary, we have to acknowledge the real status and function of the men and women whom we send to do the job. Soldiers are not like Peace Corps volunteers or Fulbright scholars or USIA musicians and lecturers—who should not, indeed, be sent overseas to dangerous places. Soldiers are destined for dangerous places, and they should know that (if they don't, they should be told).

This is not to say that soldiers should be sent recklessly into danger. But acknowledging their status and function poses the question that must be answered before they are sent anywhere, at the moment their mission is being defined: Is this a cause for which we are prepared to see American soldiers die? If this question gets an affirmative, then we cannot panic when the first soldier or the first significant number of soldiers, like the eighteen infantrymen in Somalia, are killed in a firefight. The Europeans in Bosnia, it has to be said, didn't even wait to panic: They made it clear from the beginning that the soldiers they sent to open roads and transport supplies were not to be regarded as *soldiers* in any usual sense; these were grown-up Boy Scouts doing good deeds. But this is a formula for failure. The soldiers who were not soldiers became, in effect, hostages of the Serbian forces that controlled the roads, subject to attack if anyone challenged that control. And the European governments became in turn the opponents of any such challenge.

Should we put soldiers at risk in faraway places when our own country is not under attack or threatened with attack (not Maine or Georgia or Oregon) and when national interests, narrowly understood, are not at stake? I am strongly inclined, sometimes, to give a positive answer to this question (whether volunteers or conscripts should bear these risks is too complicated to take up here). The reason is simple enough: All states have an interest in global stability and even in global humanity, and in the case of wealthy and powerful states like ours, this interest is seconded by obligation. No doubt, the "civilized" world is capable of living with grossly uncivilized behavior in places like East Timor, say—offstage and out of sight. But behavior of that kind, unchallenged, tends to spread, to be imitated or reiterated. Pay the moral price of silence and callousness, and you will soon have to pay the political price of turmoil and lawlessness nearer home.

[T]hese successive payments are not inevitable, but they come in sequence often enough. We see the sequence most clearly in Hannah Arendt's description of how European brutality in the colonies was eventually carried back to Europe itself. But the process can work in other ways too, as when terrorist regimes in the Third World imitate one another (often with help from the First World), and waves of desperate refugees flee to countries where powerful political forces, not yet ascendant, want only to drive them back. How long will decency survive *here*, if there is no decency *there*? Now obligation is seconded by interest.

As already acknowledged, interest and obligation together have often provided an ideology for imperial

expansion or cold war advance. So it's the political right that has defended both, while the left has acquired the habit of criticism and rejection. But in this postimperial and post–cold war age, these positions are likely to be reversed or, at least, confused. Many people on the right see no point in intervention today when there is no material or, for that matter, ideological advantage to be gained. "What's Bosnia to them or they to Bosnia/that they should weep for her?" And a small but growing number of people on the left now favor intervening, here or there, driven by an internationalist ethic. They are right to feel driven. Internationalism has always been understood to require support for, and even participation in, popular struggles. Liberation should always be a local initiative. In the face of human disaster, however, internationalism has a more urgent meaning. It's not possible to wait; anyone who can take the initiative should do so. Active opposition to massacre and massive deportation is morally necessary; its risks must be accepted.

Enduring the Intervention

Even the risk of a blocked exit and a long stay. These days, for reasons we should probably celebrate, countries in trouble are no longer viewed as imperial opportunities. Instead, the metaphors are ominous: They are "bogs" and "quagmires." Intervening armies won't be defeated in these sticky settings, but they will suffer a slow attrition—and show no quick or obvious benefits. How did the old empires ever get soldiers to go to such places, to sit in beleaguered encampments, to fight an endless round of small, wearying, unrecorded battles? Today, when every death is televised, democratic citizens (the soldiers themselves or their parents) are unlikely to support or endure interventions of this kind. And yet, sometimes, they ought to be supported and endured. Consider: If some powerful state or regional alliance had rushed troops into Rwanda when the massacres first began or as soon as their scope was apparent, the terrible exodus and the cholera plague might have been avoided. But the troops would still be there, probably, and no one would know what had not happened.

Two forms of long-lasting intervention, both associated in the past with imperial politics, now warrant reconsideration. The first is a kind of trusteeship, where the intervening power actually rules the country it has "rescued," acting in trust for the inhabitants, seeking to establish a stable and more or less consensual politics. The second is a kind of protectorate, where the intervention brings some local group or coalition of groups to power and is then sustained only defensively to ensure that there is no return of the defeated regime or the old lawlessness and that minority rights are respected. Rwanda might have been a candidate for trusteeship; Bosnia for a protectorate.

These are arrangements that are hard to recommend and that would, no doubt, be hard to justify in today's political climate. The lives they saved would be speculative and statistical, not actual lives; only disasters that *might have* occurred (but how can we be sure?) would be avoided. This is rescue-in-advance, and it will be resisted by those local elites who believe that the need for rescue will never arise if they are allowed to take charge—or who are prepared to take charge at any cost. The very idea of a "failed state" will seem patronizing and arrogant to a group like, say, the Rwandan Patriotic Front, which hasn't yet had a chance to succeed. Nor is the history of trusteeships and protectorates particularly encouraging: The contemporary horror of the Sudanese civil war, for example, is no reason to forget the oppressiveness of the old "Anglo-Egyptian Sudan." Nonetheless, given what is now going on in Southeast Europe and Central Africa, morally serious people have to think again about the human costs and benefits of what we might call "standing interventions." Haiti today [October 1994] might provide a test case, since the U.S.-led, multinational force serves as the protector of the restored Aristide government—and that role is likely to be an extended one.

Which States Should Intervene?

Who will, who should, do the "standing" and pay the price of the possible but often invisible victories? This is no doubt the hardest question, but it isn't, curiously, the one that has attracted the most attention. The public debate has had a different focus—as if there were (as perhaps there once were) a large number of states eager to intervene. So the question is: Who can

authorize and constrain these interventions, set the ground rules and the time frame, worry about their strategies and tactics? The standard answer on the left, and probably more widely, is that the best authority is international, multilateral—the U.N. is the obvious example. Behind this preference is an argument something like Rousseau's argument for the general will: In the course of a democratic decision procedure, Rousseau claimed, the particular interests of the different parties will cancel each other out, leaving a general interest untainted by particularity. As with individuals in domestic society, so with states in international society: If all of them are consulted, each will veto the self-aggrandizing proposals of the others.

But this isn't a wholly attractive idea, for its result is very likely to be stalemate and inaction, which cannot always be the general will of international society. It is possible, of course, that some coalition of states, cooperating for the sake of shared (particular) interests, will have its way; or that stalemate will free the U.N.'s bureaucracy to pursue a program of its own. Multilateralism is no guarantee of anything. It may still be better than the unilateral initiative of a single powerful state—though in the examples with which I began, India, Vietnam, and Tanzania, local powers, did not do entirely badly; none of their interventions, with the possible exception of the last, would have been authorized by the U.N. In practice, we should probably look for some concurrence of multilateral authorization and unilateral initiative—the first for the sake of moral legitimacy, the second for the sake of political effectiveness—but it's the initiative that is essential.

Can we assume that there are states ready to take the initiative and sustain it? In Somalia, the United States made the undertaking but was unprepared for the long haul (perhaps the long haul was not called for in this case—no one is reporting today on conditions in the Somalian countryside, so we don't know). Bosnia provides a classic example of a serial rejection of the undertaking: Everyone deplored the war and the ethnic cleansing; no one was prepared to stop them—and no one is prepared now to reverse their effects. Similarly, the African states and the Western powers stood by and watched the Rwandan massacres. (Remember the Biblical injunction: "Do not stand idly by the blood of thy neighbor." The Rwandans, it turned out, had no local or global neighbors until they were dying by the thousands on foreign soil and on television.)

It seems futile to say what is also obvious: that some states should be prepared to intervene in some cases. It is probably equally futile to name the states and the cases, though that is what I mean to do, on the principle that even futility is improved when it is made less abstract. The European Community or, at least, the French and British together (the Germans were disqualified by their aggression in World War II) ought to have intervened early on in Bosnia. The Organization of African Unity, with the financial help of Europeans and Americans, should have intervened early on in Rwanda. (I concede that the Nigerian-led intervention in Liberia is not an entirely happy precedent, though it has probably slowed the killing.) The United States should have intervened in Haiti months before it did, though the probably necessary protectorate would best have been undertaken by a coalition of Central American and Caribbean states. It is harder to say who should have stopped the killing in southern Sudan or East Timor: There isn't always an obvious candidate or a clear responsibility. It is also hard to say how responsibility passes on, when the obvious candidates refuse its burdens. Should the United States, as the world's only or greatest "great power," be nominated agent-of-last-resort? With the transportation technology at our command, we are probably near enough, and we are certainly strong enough, to stop what needs stopping in most of the cases I have been discussing (though not in all of them at once).

But no one really wants the United States to become the world's policeman, even of-last-resort, as we would quickly see were we to undertake the role. Morally and politically, a division of labor is better, and the best use of American power will often be to press other countries to do their share of the work. Still, we will, and we should be, more widely involved than other countries with fewer resources. Sometimes, the United States should take the initiative; sometimes we should help pay for and even add soldiers to an intervention initiated by somebody else. In many cases, nothing at all will be done unless we are prepared to play one or the other of these parts— either the political lead or a combination of financial backer and supporting player. Old and well-earned

suspicions of American power must give way now to a wary recognition of its necessity. (A friend comments: You would stress the wariness more if there were a Republican president. Probably so.)

Many people on the left will long for a time when this necessary American role is made unnecessary by the creation of an international military force. But this time, though it will obviously come before the much heralded leap from the realm of necessity to the realm of freedom, is still a long way off. Nor would a U.N. army with its own officers, capable of acting independently in the field, always find itself in the right fields (that is, the killing fields). Its presence or absence would depend on decisions of a Security Council likely to be as divided and uncertain as today, still subject to great-power veto and severe budgetary constraints. The useful role played by the U.N. in Cambodia (organizing and supervising elections) suggests the importance of strengthening its hand. But it wasn't the U.N. that overthrew Pol Pot and stopped the Khmer Rouge massacres. And so long as we can't be sure of its ability and readiness to do that, we will have to look for and live with unilateral interventions. It is a good thing, again, when these are undertaken by local powers like Vietnam; most often, however, they will depend on global powers like the United States and (we can hope) the European Community.

Despite all that I have said so far, I don't mean to abandon the principle of nonintervention—only to honor its exceptions. It is true that right now there are a lot of exceptions. One reads the newspaper these days shaking. The vast numbers of murdered people; the men, women, and children dying of disease and famine willfully caused or easily preventable; the masses of desperate refugees—none of these are served by reciting high-minded principles. Yes, the norm is not to intervene in other people's countries; the norm is self-determination. But not for *these* people, the victims of tyranny, ideological zeal, ethnic hatred, who are not determining anything for themselves, who urgently need help from outside.

And it isn't enough to wait until the tyrants, the zealots, and the bigots have done their filthy work and then rush food and medicine to the ragged survivors. Whenever the filthy work can be stopped, it should be stopped. And if not by us, the supposedly decent people of this world, then by whom?

77. The Futility of U.S. Intervention in Regional Conflicts

BARBARA CONRY

Barbara Conry argues that U.S. military intervention is generally not a viable solution to regional conflicts. In the first place, she argues, in the vast majority of cases such interventions do not work because the altruism of those intervening cannot usually outlast the nationalism or self-interest of the parties in the conflict. Secondly, she argues that it is virtually impossible for such interventions to be impartial. Thirdly, she claims that such interventions give rise to anti-American sentiment based on the north–south conflict between the rich and the poor, and they constitute a drain on U.S. resources.

The threat of tensions escalating into superpower confrontations helped stifle regional conflicts for many years, but age-old disputes across the globe have exploded since the end of the Cold War, and regional conflicts are on the rise. The "World Military and Social Expenditures" report counted an unprecedented twenty-nine "major" wars in 1992. ("Major" meant a war that involved one or more governments and killed at least 1,000 people in the year.) An informal *Time* magazine study a number of years ago revealed that approximately twenty wars were likely to be under way at any given time, but a [February 7] 1993 *New York Times* study identified forty-eight wars in progress (defined as two organized sides fighting and causing casualties). Although such precise numbers are not often cited, there is widespread agreement that regional conflicts, driven by religion, nationalism, and political and economic disputes, are rising dramatically and will continue to do so.

American Desire to Intervene

"Regional conflict" is difficult to define precisely, and experts use the term in a variety of ways. For the

Abridged from Barbara Conry, "The Futility of U.S. Intervention in Regional Conflicts," *Cato Institute Policy Analysis*, May 19, 1994. Reprinted by permission of the Cato Institute, Washington, D.C.

purpose of this analysis, the term will mean all armed upheaval, either cross-border or internecine, that affects a limited area but has little direct impact on the security of the rest of the world. The definition is necessarily broad, applicable to wars between established sovereign states, such as the Iran-Iraq conflict in the 1980s; internal strife in the absence of a functioning government, as in Somalia; a dispute between a sovereign government and an armed group within its borders, as in Sudan; or a conflict that involves both sovereign states and external nonstate parties, as in the former Yugoslavia.

In the age of mass communication, the entire world often witnesses the human tragedy associated with regional wars. Americans who are accustomed to basic human rights, relative stability, and freedom are often moved by distressing media images of remote war-torn regions. Those tragedies inspire in many Americans a sincere desire—even a sense that it is the duty of the United States—to alleviate the suffering. There is also widespread conviction that we have the means to do so. Since the American triumph in the Cold War and the successful expulsion of the world's fourth largest army [Iraq's] from Kuwait with so few allied casualties, Americans and foreigners alike have tended to assume that the U.S. military is capable of managing regional conflagrations whenever it chooses to do so.

In reality, U.S. military intervention is generally not a viable solution to regional conflicts and should not be undertaken except in the rare instances in which American national security is at stake. In most cases regional conflicts cannot be helped—and may well be exacerbated—by the intervention of outside parties. U.S. intervention can be especially counterproductive, since it often intensifies smaller, less powerful countries' (the very nations most likely to be involved in regional conflicts) fears of America's hegemonic intentions. Militarily, too, the United States is ill suited to suppress regional conflicts, in which warring forces frequently rely on guerrilla warfare, street fighting, and other tactics that are not easily met by America's high-tech war machine. Retired British diplomat Jonathan Clarke has pointed out that

> America's adversaries know full well that they are uncompetitive on a "First World" battlefield. Their response, like that of the Massachusetts Minuteman confronting that British Redcoat, is to lower the threshold of war to prevent the full range of American advanced weaponry and electronic wizardry from operating. The result is that Americans enter today's messy Third World battles not as odds-on favorites but on level terms.

Indeed, it was precisely that type of warfare that prevented the United States from achieving its objectives in both Vietnam and Somalia—proving that the most powerful military in the world is far from invincible.

Not only does inappropriate military intervention fail to reconcile regional conflicts, it also has negative consequences for the United States. There can be significant political costs, ranging from diminished American credibility as the result of an unsuccessful mission to resentment on the part of foreign governments and populations of Washington's meddling in their affairs. More serious, injudicious military intervention can create threats to national security where none previously existed, stoking the fires of anti-Americanism, jeopardizing the lives of U.S. troops, and ultimately undermining our ability to protect vital national interests in the event of a direct threat. . . .

Idealism in Intervention

In the absence of a clear and defensible strategic rationale for intervention in regional conflicts, a smattering of idealistic justifications has emerged. In the past, idealism sometimes served as a fig leaf for more mundane motives. During the Gulf War, for instance, President Bush invoked such notions as the preservation of the new world order, protection of sovereignty, and a stance against "naked aggression" to obscure the harsher truth that he was deploying U.S. troops primarily to protect economic interests—American access to gulf oil. The idealistic arguments were essential to gain the support of those who are uncomfortable with the notion of war for self-interest yet accept war as a tragic but necessary sacrifice for the sake of altruistic objectives. For some people, humanitarian reasons or the advancement of various moral principles are in themselves adequate justification for U.S. military involvement in regional wars.

Democracy, human rights, national self-determination, and humanitarian assistance are the most common rationales for military intervention where no threat to national security exists. All are admirable ideals. Yet military interventions based on such ideals are even more problematic than those that are at least rhetorically rooted in national security, and intervention is usually an ineffective way to advance ideals. If anything, coercion tends to make a mockery of the very principle it was intended to defend. As Paul W. Schroeder of the United States Institute of Peace argued in the *Washington Quarterly,* "The more the lesson desired is inflicted by external armed force, the less the experience of defeat and failure is likely to be internalized in a useful way and lead to the kind of durable change desired."

Military intervention for reasons unrelated to American security also forces the United States to embrace inherently hypocritical policies. Because it is impossible for the United States to intervene in every instance in which American principles are offended, the necessary selection process inevitably gives priority to some conflicts while marginalizing others. As Robert Oakley, President Clinton's special envoy to Somalia, said, "The international community is not disposed to deploying 20, 40, 60,000 military forces each time there is an internal crisis in a failed state." To take action in some cases and not others does not make for consistent policy.

If the United States were to declare genocide in Bosnia sufficient grounds for American military intervention, for example, it would be blatantly hypocritical to ignore the (clearer and considerably more severe) genocide in Sudan. Similarly capricious was Washington's determination that the breakdown of the Somali government merited U.S. intervention, while officials ignored the crisis in Rwanda after the apparent assassination of President Habyarimana on April 6, 1994 (100,000 were said to have been killed in the first two weeks of fighting alone) except to evacuate Americans from the area. Likewise, demands that U.S. troops protect democracy in Haiti are incongruous in light of Washington's quiet indifference toward the suspension of democracy in Algeria when Muslim extremists were poised to win elections in 1992. The inconsistency and hypocrisy of those policies are evidence of the weakness of intervention on the basis of nebulous principles.

A History of Failure

The United States should also avoid military intervention in regional conflicts because, in the vast majority of cases, it does not work. In fact, it usually aggravates the situation. Even if a consensus were to develop that global stability or any other objective should be pursued by all viable means, military intervention would remain an unwise course in most cases. It rarely achieves its purpose and often has the perverse effect of obstructing, rather than advancing, what it seeks to achieve. (American peacekeepers in Lebanon in 1983, for example, were an aggravating rather than a stabilizing force.) Intervention usually harms American interests as well. The most compelling arguments against American intervention are its ineffectiveness and the harm it causes all parties involved.

The ability of military action to achieve political objectives in the modern era is very limited. "Beware of the facile assumption that wars are fightable and winnable again. Beware of the illusion that there is a military solution to every geopolitical problem," warns journalist Theo Sommer. Many deeply rooted political and economic problems are impervious to military solutions.

Lack of Endurance

Intervening powers are at a disadvantage because their stake in the outcome is usually far smaller than that of the primary combatants. In the former Yugoslavia, for example, Bosnian Muslims, Croats, and Serbs are fighting out of nationalism, which they perceive as closely related to their very existence as states (or as distinct cultures). Nationalism in that case is an ideal for which many people are prepared to kill and die. Outside parties that become involved for essentially altruistic reasons are not prepared to fight with the same intensity or endurance. Altruism and nationalism simply do not inspire equal determination.

Moreover, the American public is renowned for its unwillingness to sustain heavy casualties in remote regional wars. American support for military action abroad tends to decline dramatically at the prospect of an extended occupation that will entail significant U.S. casualties. The erosion of public support usually leads to the erosion of congressional support, resulting in serious divisions within the government that is supposed to be directing the intervention. With leadership divided, there is little chance for success. The military, already operating under handicaps inherent to intervention, is virtually assured of failure. As political scientist Richard Falk has commented, "It is not that intervention can *never* work but that it will almost never succeed unless a costly, prolonged occupation is an ingredient of the commitment."

The failure of interventionism is not merely a post–Cold War phenomenon. During the Cold War it may have been easier to "sell" an intervention because Soviet influence in a regional conflict was always a potential, if indirect, threat to American security. Nevertheless, in the instances in which Washington deemed the threat sufficient to warrant intervention, the track record was poor. The pinnacle of failed Cold War intervention—at immense cost to the United States—may have been Vietnam, but it certainly was not the only failure. In Korea there were 137,000 American casualties in a war that ended in stalemate; there were a number of other, smaller but equally ineffectual interventions in conflicts in Africa and Central America during the Cold War as well. In all instances Americans bore significant human and economic costs, yet their sacrifices brought no lasting substantive gain and made little sense, even when rivalry with the Soviet Union was a factor. Similar sacrifices would make even less sense today in the absence of a superpower challenger.

The Vietnam disaster greatly diminished Washington's enthusiasm for military involvement overseas. Ronald Reagan tentatively resumed foreign adventurism, most notably by sending U.S. Marines to Beirut, Lebanon, as "impartial" peacekeepers in the Lebanese civil war. American interests in the outcome of the Lebanese war were remote at best, and Reagan's foray into the conflict was unproductive. The costs, however, were great—especially to the 241 Marines killed in their barracks by a suicide bomber, who clearly did not consider American involvement impartial.

The Impossibility of Impartiality

Indeed, U.S. involvement was not impartial. The presence of U.S. troops strengthened the position of the Christian-dominated regime of President Amin Geymayel at the expense of the other factions. The Lebanon debacle underscores a larger problem. It is exceedingly difficult for any outside party, acting alone or in concert with others, to remain impartial during an armed conflict, no matter how sincere the intention. That point was painfully proven once again in Mogadishu [Somalia] ten years after Beirut.

When President Bush sent U.S. troops to Somalia in 1992, he cited a humanitarian reason: to feed the starving Somali population. Civil order had broken down, and warring factions were using starvation as a weapon against innocent people. Despite the simple and narrow focus of the mission, the United States eventually found itself party to the civil war. Under the auspices of the United Nations, American troops were engaged for several months in a manhunt for "warlord" Mohammad Farah Aideed, culminating in a ferocious firefight on October 3, 1993, that cost the lives of eighteen Army Rangers. The search for Aideed was futile and, in the end, abandoned. In an ironic twist of events, a U.S. military plane carried "political leader" Aideed to a peace conference in Ethiopia only weeks after U.S. troops gave up their search.

Nothing substantial was accomplished. While it is true that Somalis were no longer starving, the worst of the famine was over before American troops arrived. According to many sources, some regions of Somalia were actually producing an agricultural surplus at the time the United States intervened. "Mission creep" transformed the objective from easing starvation to "nation building," and no substantive progress was made toward that goal. Street fighting diminished for a time, but even before the American withdrawal in March 1994 it began to resume. Again, the costs have been tremendous: American, U.N., and Somali lives; scarce economic resources ($1.3 billion for the United States alone); and American credibility were all squandered in the unsuccessful mission. . . .

Yankee Go Home

Another cost of military intervention is a rise in anti-American sentiment, which was evident throughout the Cold War in Africa and Latin America and more recently in Somalia. When U.S. Marines made their dramatic landing in Mogadishu in December 1992, the Somalis greeted them with cheers. Less than a year later, on October 3, 1993, eighteen Americans died in a single day at the hands of Somalis. Hatred of the United States was unmistakable, particularly in the gruesome and widely published photograph of smiling Somalis dragging the corpse of an American soldier through the streets. Despite the apparent goodwill at the beginning of the mission, American involvement was violently resented once the United States became part of the war.

Similar ill will greeted U.S. soldiers when they attempted to land in Haiti as part of a U.N. force assisting the implementation of the Governors Island accord. Given the long history of U.S. interference in Haitian domestic affairs, the resistance should not have been surprising. The United States has meddled so much there—American troops occupied Haiti for nearly twenty years beginning in 1915, and Washington has frequently granted or withheld financial assistance in crude attempts to influence Haiti's domestic affairs—that U.N. secretary-general Boutros Boutros-Ghali initially rejected American participation in the peacekeeping force. Only after President

Clinton threatened to withdraw American support for the agreement did the United Nations reluctantly accept a U.S. contingent. Faced with violent opposition to the American presence, which occurred soon after the massacre of U.S. troops in Mogadishu, the Clinton administration ordered the ships not to land. (The most powerful country in the world's lack of will to confront opposition described as a few hundred "thugs" also did significant damage to American credibility.)

Anti-Americanism in Haiti and Somalia should not be dismissed lightly. The Pentagon has identified north–south conflict—the "haves" versus the "have-nots"—as a serious future problem for the United States. In a study entitled "Terrorism Futures," religious, ethnic, and regional conflicts were cited as probable sources of terrorism in the next decade. At the beginning of the study in late 1991, researchers anticipated that religious extremism would be the gravest threat. The unexpected conclusion, though, was that an "us versus them" mentality would be a more alarming threat, pitting "fanatics from impoverished countries" against wealthier nations.

In view of the likelihood that the Third World, or the south, will be the site of many future conflicts, American intervention could provide the impetus for an era of divisive north–south confrontation. An interventionist policy could also make the United States a high-priority target for terrorists and other disgruntled factions. The flaring of hostility toward American military personnel in Somalia may be an omen of that danger.

Creating New Problems

Interventionism also jeopardizes U.S. vital interests in other ways. The most obvious threat is to the lives of American soldiers sent into the conflict. Once troops have been deployed, it becomes a vital interest to ensure their security. If they are in danger or if troops have been taken hostage, the United States has a responsibility to protect them. It was for that reason that President Clinton announced March 31, 1994, as the date for withdrawal from Somalia and, at the same time, took what appeared to be the contradictory action of sending several thousand additional troops

to Mogadishu. To guarantee the security of the troops already there, additional forces had to be deployed. The intervention had created a threat to U.S. interests where there had previously been none.

Other, more abstract, threats arise from interventionism as well. The argument has been made that American credibility, like American soldiers, constitutes a vital interest that must be protected at all costs. Owen Harries, editor of the *National Interest,* made this argument with reference to American interests in Bosnia:

> At the beginning of the Bosnian crisis there was, in my opinion, no significant American interest at stake. . . . But that was then. In the meantime, the Clinton administration has managed to create a serious national interest in Bosnia where none before existed: an interest, that is, in the preservation of this country's prestige and credibility.

Harries goes on to say that American credibility is not merely a matter of national self-respect or patriotism. It is a vital interest with implications for national security. "For the greater one's prestige, the less necessary it is to resort to force and other forms of coercion in order for one's will to be effective—and vice versa," he says.

Intervention in regional wars is a distraction and a drain on resources. Diverting time, money, and manpower from areas that have a significant impact on national security to peripheral nonsecurity interests is never desirable. But in the event of a crisis that affects U.S. vital interests, it is downright dangerous. It is difficult for the United States to be well prepared to protect national security when its military resources are diffused all over the globe and are configured to participate in nebulous peacekeeping or peace enforcement operations.

Unnecessary interventions also waste another very important and readily depleted resource: public support for U.S. military operations. Failed military missions engender tremendous public skepticism about future operations. Although that caution may serve a useful purpose in keeping troops out of other regional conflicts, it may be dangerous in the event of a genuine threat to national security. The American people's support is essential to the success of military operations. Lack of public support when vital interests are at stake could weaken U.S. resolve—and therefore jeopardize our ability—to protect those interests. . . .

The United States should avoid regional intervention except in cases in which there is a direct and substantial threat to national security or American vital interests. No matter how superficially appealing the rationale, military intervention in regional con-

flicts generally does not work and often creates threats to U.S. security where none previously existed. In this era of proliferating regional wars, the United States must resist the impulse to intervene. To do otherwise is to invite further tragedy, increasing the suffering not only of the combatants but of the American people as well.

---

78. A *New* World Security Order

ROBERT S. MCNAMARA

Robert S. McNamara argues that with the end of the Cold War, nations have been slow to revise their foreign and defense policies. He argues that we should move toward a system of collective security with conflict resolution and peacekeeping functions performed by multinational institutions. He also favors a return, insofar as practicable, to a nonnuclear world and cutting military budgets throughout the world by 50 percent.

Although there has been clear evidence for several years that the Cold War was ending, nations across the globe have been slow to revise their foreign and defense policies, and slow to strengthen regional and international security organizations, to reflect that fact. This has been true of the United States.

In the United States, for example, in 1991, defense expenditures totaled $300 billion. In constant dollars that was 40 percent more than a decade ago, only 7 percent less than at the height of the Vietnam War. Moreover, the President's five-year defense program, presented to Congress in early 1992, projects that expenditures will decline only gradually from the 1991 levels. Defense outlays in 1997, in constant dollars, are estimated to be about 15 percent higher than 21 years earlier, under President Nixon, in the midst of the Cold War.

Such a defense program is not consistent with my view of the post–Cold War world.

From "A Vision of a 'New World Security Order,'" *The Joan B. Kroc Institute for International Peace Studies Report* (1992). Reprinted by permission.

Before we can respond to the changes in Soviet policy that ended the Cold War, we need a vision of a world no longer dominated by the East–West rivalry which for more than 40 years shaped the foreign policies and defense programs of Western nations.

As the Iraqi action demonstrated, the world of the future will not be a world without conflict, conflict among disparate groups within nations and conflict extending across national borders. Racial and ethnic differences will remain. Political revolutions will erupt as societies advance. Historical disputes over political boundaries will continue. Economic differentials among nations, as the technological revolution of the twenty-first century spreads unevenly across the globe, will increase.

In the past 45 years, 125 wars, leading to 40 million deaths, have taken place in the Third World. Third World military expenditures now approximate $200 billion per year. They have quintupled in constant dollars since 1960, increasing at an annual rate two to three times that of the industrialized countries. They are now only slightly less than the total amount the developing countries spend on health and education.

It is often suggested that the Third World was turned into an ideological battleground by the Cold War and the rivalries of the Great Powers. That rivalry was a contributing factor, but the underlying causes for Third World conflict existed before the origin of the Cold War and will almost certainly continue even though it has ended.

Thus, in those respects the world of the future will not be different from the world of the past—conflicts within and among nations will not disappear.

But it is also clear that in the twenty-first century relations among nations will differ dramatically from those of the postwar decades. In the postwar years the United States had the power—and to a considerable degree it exercised that power—to shape the world as it chose. In the next century that will not be possible. While remaining the world's strongest nation, the United States will live in a multipolar world and its foreign policy and defense programs must be adjusted to that reality.

Japan is destined to play a larger and larger role on the world scene, exercising greater political power and, hopefully, assuming greater political and economic responsibility. The same can be said of Western Europe, which will take a giant step toward economic integration by the end of this year. From that is bound to follow greater political unity which will strengthen Europe's power in world politics.

And by the middle of the next century several of what we think of as Third World countries—in particular, China—will have so increased in size and economic power as to be major participants in decisions affecting relations among nations. India is likely to have a population of 1.6 billion, Nigeria 400 million, Brazil 300 million. If China achieves its economic goals for 2000 and then moves forward during the next fifty years at satisfactory but not spectacular growth rates, the income per capita of its approximately 1.6 billion people in 2050 may be roughly equal to that of the British in 1965. China's total gross national product would approximate that of the United States, Western Europe, or Japan, and likely would substantially exceed Russia's. These figures, are, of course, highly speculative. I point to them simply to emphasize the magnitude of the changes that lie ahead and the need to begin now to adjust our goals, our policies, and our institutions to take account of them.

In such a multipolar world, there clearly is need for developing new relationships both among the Great Powers and between the Great Powers and Third World nations. I believe that, at a minimum, the new order should accomplish four objectives. It should

- Provide to all states guarantees against external aggression;
- Establish a mechanism for resolution of regional conflicts without unilateral action by the Great Powers;
- Commit the Great Powers to ending their military involvement in military conflicts among and within Third World nations;
- Increase the flow of both technical and financial assistance to the developing countries to help them accelerate their rates of social and economic advance.

In sum, we should strive to move toward a world in which relations among nations would be based on the rule of law, supported by a system of collective security, with conflict resolution and peace-keeping functions performed by multilateral institutions—a reorganized and strengthened United Nations and new and expanded regional organizations.

That is my vision of the post–Cold War world.

In contrast to my vision, many political theorists predict a return to the power politics of the nineteenth century. They claim that as ideological competition between East and West is reduced, there will be a reversion to more traditional relationships. They say that major powers will be guided by basic territorial and economic imperatives: that the United States, Russia, China, India, Japan, and Western Europe will seek to assert themselves in their own regions while competing for dominance in other areas of the world where conditions are fluid.

This view has been expressed, for example, by Michael J. Sandel, a political theorist at Harvard, and it underlies the recently leaked Defense Department conception of the post–Cold War world.

Professor Sandel has said: "The end of the Cold War does not mean an end of global competition between the Great Powers. Once the ideological dimension fades, what you are left with is not peace and harmony, but old-fashioned global politics based on dominant powers competing for influence and pursuing their internal interests."

Professor Sandel's conception of relations among nations in the post–Cold War world is historically well founded, but I would argue it is not consistent with the increasingly interdependent world—interdependent economically, environmentally, and in terms of security—into which we are now moving. In that interdependent world, I do not believe any nation will be able to stand alone. The U.N. Charter offers a far more appropriate framework for relations among nations in such a world than does the doctrine of power politics.

Such a world will, of course, need leaders. The leadership role may shift among nations depending on the issue at hand. Often it will be fulfilled by the United States. However, in such a system of collective security, whenever the United States plays a leadership role it must accept collective decision making. Correspondingly, other nations—and that includes both Germany and Japan—should accept a sharing of the risks and the costs: the political risks, the financial costs, and the risk of casualties and bloodshed.

Had the United States and the other major powers made clear their conception of and support for such a system of collective security, and had they committed themselves both to pursuing their own interests without the use of force and to protecting Third World nations from external attack, the Iraqi action might well have been deterred.

While steps are being taken to establish a worldwide system of collective security, the arms reduction actions that have been under way should be expanded rapidly in scope and accelerated in time.

In recent days, there has been much discussion of reductions in nuclear forces. But the fact is that there are today approximately 50,000 nuclear warheads in the world, with a destructive power equivalent to well over one million times that of the Hiroshima bomb. Even assuming that the reductions called for by the START treaties and by the unilateral proposals of Bush, Gorbachev, and Yeltsin are implemented, the stock of nuclear weapons will remain in the tens of thousands. The danger of nuclear war—the risk of destruction of our societies—will have been lowered but not eliminated. Can we go further? Surely the answer must be Yes.

More and more political and military leaders are accepting that basic changes in the world's approach to nuclear weapons are required. A few weeks ago, President Yeltsin went so far as to state that the long-term objective should be complete elimination of such weapons.

That is a very controversial proposition: Leading Western security experts—both military and civilian—continue to believe that the threat of the use of nuclear weapons prevents war. And Zbigniew Brzezinski, President Carter's National Security Advisor, has said with reference to a proposal for eliminating nuclear weapons: "It is a plan for making the world safe for conventional warfare. I am therefore not enthusiastic about it." However, even if one accepts that argument, it must be recognized that the nuclear deterrent to conventional-force aggression carries a very high long-term cost: the risk of a nuclear exchange. Should we not begin immediately, therefore, to debate the merits of alternative long-term objectives for nuclear forces of existing nuclear powers, choosing, for example, from among three basic options:

- A continuation of the present strategy of "extended deterrence"—as recommended in a . . . report to the Secretary of Defense—but with each side limited to approximately 5,000 warheads; or
- A minimum deterrent force—as recommended by a committee of the National Academy of Sciences—with each side retaining perhaps 1,000 warheads; or
- As I myself would prefer, a return, insofar as practicable, to a nonnuclear world.

And, should we not debate as well how best to deal with the proliferation of weapons of mass destruction and with the export of arms to the Third World? If we truly wish to stop proliferation and limit arms exports, I see no alternative to some form of collective, coercive action by order of the Security Council.

As we move toward a system providing for collective action against military aggression wherever it may occur, military budgets throughout the world—in both developed and developing countries—can be reduced substantially. They have totaled almost $1 trillion per year. I would say that amount could be cut in half. The huge savings—some $500 billion per year—could be used to address the pressing human and physical infrastructure needs across the globe.

That is my vision of a "New World Security Order" and it is an agenda I set before you for the twenty-first century.

It is not an agenda that any single nation can carry out by itself. But if together we are bold—if East and West and North and South dare break out of the mind-sets of the past four decades—we can reshape international institutions, as well as relations among nations, in ways that will lead to a far more peaceful world and a far more prosperous world for all the peoples of our interdependent globe.

It is the first time in my adult life we have had such an opportunity. Pray God we seize it.

Suggestions for Further Reading

Anthologies

Sterba, James P. *The Ethics of War and Nuclear Deterrence.* Belmont: Wadsworth, 1985.

Wakin, Malham. *War, Morality and the Military Profession.* Boulder: Westview Press, 1979.

Winters, Paul. *Interventionism.* San Diego: Greenhaven Press, 1995.

Basic Concepts

Cady, Duane. *From Warism to Pacifism.* Philadelphia: Temple University Press, 1989.

Holmes, Robert. *On War and Morality.* Princeton: Princeton University Press, 1989.

Walters, LeRoy. *Five Classic Just-War Theories.* Ann Arbor: University Microfilms, 1971.

Walzer, Michael. *Just and Unjust Wars.* New York: Basic Books, 1994.

Alternative Views

Adelman, Howard. "The Ethics of Humanitarian Intervention." *Public Affairs Quarterly* (1992): 61–87.

Brzezinski, Zbigniew. "Selective Global Commitment." *Foreign Affairs* (1992): 1–20.

Falk, Richard. "Recycling Interventionism." *Journal of Peace Research* (1992): 129–134.

Hehir, Bryan. "Intervention: From Theories to Cases." *Ethics and International Affairs* (1995): 1–14.

Laberge, Pierre. "Humanitarian Intervention: Three Ethical Positions." *Ethics and International Affairs* (1995): 14–36.

Luper-Foy, Steven. "Intervention and Refugees." *Public Affairs Quarterly* (1992): 45–60.

Phillips, Robert, and Cady, Duane. *Humanitarian Intervention: Just War vs. Pacifism.* Lanham: Rowman and Littlefield, 1995.

Pogge, Thomas. "An Institutional Approach to Humanitarian Intervention." *Public Affairs Quarterly* (1992): 89–103.

Powell, Colin. "U.S. Forces: Challenges Ahead." *Foreign Affairs* (1992): 32–45.